THE OXFORD HANDBOOK OF

QUR'ANIC STUDIES

Traditionally revered as the literal word of God, the Qur'an serves as Islam's sacred book of revelation. Accordingly, its statements and pronouncements rest at the core of the beliefs and teachings that have inexorably defined expressions of the Islamic faith. Indeed, over the centuries, engaging with and poring over the contents of the Qur'an inspired an impressive range of traditional scholarship. Notwithstanding its religious pre-eminence, the Qur'an is also considered to be the matchless masterpiece of the Arabic language and its impact as a text can be discerned in all aspects of the Arabic literary tradition. Presenting contributions from leading experts in the field, *The Oxford Handbook of Qur'anic Studies* offers an authoritative collection of chapters that guide readers through the gamut of themes, subjects, and debates that have dominated the academic study of the Qur'an and its literary heritage. These range from chapters that explore the text's language, vocabulary, style, and structure, to detailed surveys of its contents, concepts, transmission, literary influence, historical significance, commentary tradition, and even the scholarship devoted to translations. With the aim of serving as an indispensable reference resource, the *Handbook* assesses the implications of research discourses and discussions shaping the study of the Qur'an today. There exists no single volume devoted to such a broad review of the scholarship on the Qur'an and its rich commentary tradition.

THE OXFORD HANDBOOK OF

QUR'ANIC STUDIES

Edited by

MUSTAFA SHAH

and

MUHAMMAD ABDEL HALEEM

OXFORD
UNIVERSITY PRESS

OXFORD
UNIVERSITY PRESS

Great Clarendon Street, Oxford, OX2 6DP,
United Kingdom

Oxford University Press is a department of the University of Oxford.
It furthers the University's objective of excellence in research, scholarship,
and education by publishing worldwide. Oxford is a registered trade mark of
Oxford University Press in the UK and in certain other countries

First published 2020
First published in paperback 2023

Published in the United States of America by Oxford University Press
198 Madison Avenue, New York, NY 10016, United States of America

British Library Cataloguing in Publication Data
Data available

Library of Congress Cataloging in Publication Data

Data available

ISBN 978-0-19-969864-6 (Hbk.)
ISBN 978-0-19-889620-3 (Pbk.)

Acknowledgements

The editors would like to express their profound appreciation to Tom Perridge for proposing this volume for the Handbook series some years back and for all his encouragement throughout the intervening periods. The support offered by Karen Raith has been exceptional and we should also like to express our gratitude to her. For help in securing permissions for the use of images, we would like to thank the British Library; the Chester Beatty Library and its trustees; the New York Metropolitan Museum of Art; the Austrian National Library; the Nasser D. Khalili Collection of Islamic Art, London and the Khalili Family Trust; the Asiatic Press in St Petersburg; and Sinéad Ward, Sheila S. Blair, Jonathan M. Bloom, and Efim Rezvan. The editors also wish to thank Valerie Joy Turner for all her work.

Table of Contents

List of Illustrations xiii
List of Contributors xv

Introduction 1
Mustafa Shah

PART I THE STATE OF QUR'ANIC STUDIES

1. Academic Scholarship and the Qur'an 27
Andrew Rippin

2. Modern Developments in Qur'anic Studies 39
Oliver Leaman

3. Islamic Origins and the Qur'an 51
Herbert Berg

4. Qur'anic Studies: Bibliographical Survey 64
Anna Akasoy

PART II THE HISTORICAL SETTING OF THE QUR'AN

5. Late Antique Near Eastern Context: Some Social and Religious Aspects 81
Muntasir F. Al-Hamad and John F. Healey

6. The Arabian Context of the Qur'an: History and the Text 97
Harry Munt

7. The Linguistic Landscape of pre-Islamic Arabia: Context for the Qur'an 111
Ahmad Al-Jallad

8. Qur'anic Exempla and Late Antique Narratives 128
MARIANNA KLAR

9. The Qur'an and Judaism 140
REUVEN FIRESTONE

10. The Qur'an and Christianity 152
NEAL ROBINSON

PART III THE QUR'AN: TEXTUAL TRANSMISSION, CODIFICATION, MANUSCRIPTS, INSCRIPTIONS, AND PRINTED EDITIONS

11. The Manuscript and Archaeological Traditions: Physical Evidence 167
FRANÇOIS DÉROCHE

12. The Form of the Qur'an: Historical Contours 182
YASIN DUTTON

13. The Corpus of Qur'anic Readings (*qirāʾāt*): History, Synthesis, and Authentication 194
MUSTAFA SHAH

14. Glorifying God's Word: Manuscripts of the Qur'an 217
SHEILA S. BLAIR

15. Inscribing God's Word: Qur'anic Texts on Architecture, Objects, and Other Solid Supports 239
SHEILA S. BLAIR

16. A History of Printed Editions of the Qur'an 255
EFIM A. REZVAN

PART IV STRUCTURAL AND LITERARY DIMENSIONS OF THE QUR'AN

17. Language of the Qur'an 277
A. H. MATHIAS ZAHNISER

18. Vocabulary of the Qur'an: Meaning in Context 294
MUSTAFA SHAH

19. Qur'anic Syntax 315
MICHEL CUYPERS

20. Rhetorical Devices and Stylistic Features of Qur'anic Grammar 327
MUHAMMAD ABDEL HALEEM

21. Inner-Qur'anic Chronology 346
NICOLAI SINAI

22. The Structure of the Qur'an: The Inner Dynamic of the Sura 362
MUSTANSIR MIR

23. Discussions of Qur'anic Inimitability: The Theological Nexus 374
AYMAN A. EL-DESOUKY

24. The Qur'an and the Arabic Medieval Literary Tradition 388
GEERT JAN VAN GELDER

25. The Qur'an and Arabic Poetry 401
STEFAN SPERL

PART V TOPICS AND THEMES OF THE QUR'AN

26. Revelation and Prophecy in the Qur'an 419
ULRIKA MÅRTENSSON

27. Doctrine and Dogma in the Qur'an 430
STEPHEN R. BURGE

28. Law and the Qur'an 445
JOSEPH E. LOWRY

29. Qur'anic Ethics 464
EBRAHIM MOOSA

30. Eschatology and the Qur'an 472
SEBASTIAN GÜNTHER

31. Prophets and Personalities of the Qur'an 488
ANTHONY H. JOHNS

32. Politics and the Qur'an 502
STEFAN WILD

33. Jihad and the Qur'an: Classical and Modern Interpretations 512
ASMA AFSARUDDIN

34. Women and the Qur'an 527
ASMA AFSARUDDIN

PART VI THE QUR'AN IN CONTEXT: TRANSLATION AND CULTURE

35. Translations of the Qur'an: Western Languages 541
ZIAD ELMARSAFY

36. Translations of the Qur'an: Islamicate Languages 552
M. BRETT WILSON

37. Presenting the Qur'an Out of Context 565
MUHAMMAD ABDEL HALEEM

38. Popular Culture and the Qur'an: Classical and Modern Contexts 578
BRUCE LAWRENCE

39. The Western Literary Tradition and the Qur'an: An Overview 592
JEFFREY EINBODEN

PART VII QUR'ANIC INTERPRETATION: SCHOLARSHIP AND LITERATURE OF EARLY, CLASSICAL, AND MODERN EXEGESIS

40. Early Qur'anic Commentaries 607
ANDREW RIPPIN

41. Exegetical Designs of the *Sīra*: *Tafsīr* and *Sīra* 620
MAHER JARRAR

42. Early Qur'anic Exegesis: From Textual Interpretation to Linguistic Analysis 634
KEES VERSTEEGH

43. Early Medieval *Tafsīr* (Third/Ninth to the Fifth/Eleventh Century) 651
ULRIKA MÅRTENSSON

44. Medieval Exegesis: The Golden Age of *Tafsīr* 666
Walid A. Saleh

45. The Corpora of *Isrāʾīliyyāt* 682
Roberto Tottoli

46. Contemporary *Tafsīr*: The Rise of Scriptural Theology 693
Walid A. Saleh

PART VIII QUR'ANIC EXEGESIS: DISCOURSES, FORMATS, AND HERMENEUTICS

47. Twelver Shīʿī Exegesis 707
Sajjad Rizvi

48. Ismāʿīlī Scholarship on *Tafsīr* 721
Ismail Poonawala

49. Ibāḍī *Tafsīr* Literature 734
Valerie J. Hoffman and Sulaiman bin Ali bin Ameir al-Shueili

50. Sufi Commentary: Formative and Later Periods 746
Alexander Knysh

51. Theological Commentaries 766
Tariq Jaffer

52. Philosophical Commentaries 780
Jules Janssens

53. Aesthetically Oriented Interpretations of the Qur'an 794
Kamal Abu-Deeb

54. *Tafsīr* and Science 806
Robert Morrison

55. Classical Qur'anic Hermeneutics 818
Johanna Pink

56. Sunnī Hermeneutical Literature 832
Martin Nguyen

57. Modern Qur'anic Hermeneutics: Strategies and Development 848
Massimo Campanini

List of Illustrations

7.1 Ancient South Arabian (ASA) script chart. © Peter Stein. Used by permission. 112

7.2 Distribution of the scripts and languages of pre-Islamic Arabia. © A. Al-Jallad. 116

13.1 A folio from the British Library's oldest manuscript of the Qur'an, Or. 2165, featuring verses from Q. 18:57–68 (The Cave). The manuscript comprises 121 folios containing over two-thirds of the complete text. © British Library Board. 195

14.1 Verso of a detached palimpsest folio from an early Qur'an manuscript copied on parchment in *Ḥijāzī* script with a non-ʿUthmānic recension beneath another copy of the text. Copenhagen, David Collection, inv. no. 86/2003. Photo by: Pernille Klemp. 223

14.2 Opening text folio from the Qur'an manuscript copied on paper and signed by ʿAlī ibn Hilāl known as Ibn al-Bawwāb at Baghdad in 391/1000–1. Dublin, Chester Beatty Library, ms 1431, fol. 9b © The Trustees of the Chester Beatty Library, Dublin. 227

14.3 Colophon detached from *juzʾ* 28 of a 30-volume Qur'an manuscript copied by Aḥmad al-Suhrawardī and illuminated by Muḥammad ibn Aybak ibn ʿAbd Allāh between 701 and 708 (1301–8). New York, Metropolitan Museum of Art, www.metmuseum.org, Rogers Fund 55.44. 230

14.4 Double-page spread from a manuscript made for the Ottomans in 1204/1789–90 in the *tevâfuklu* style, a rubrication of congruence in which sections of identical text were written in red on facing pages. London, Khalili Collection, ms QUR33, fols. 189b–190a. The Nasser D. Khalili Collection of Islamic Art ms QUR33, fols. 189b–190a; courtesy of the Khalili Family Trust. 234

15.1 Interior of the Dome of the Rock in Jerusalem, 72/691–2, showing the mosaic inscription at the top of the west section of the arcade with Q. 4:171–2. Photo: Sheila S. Blair and Jonathan M. Bloom. 242

15.2 Roundel with Q. 33:33 on the façade of the Aqmar Mosque erected under the Fatimids in Cairo in 519/1125. Photo: Sheila S. Blair and Jonathan M. Bloom. 246

15.3 Foundation inscription around the portal of the Masjid-i ʿAlī in Isfahan rebuilt during the reign of the Safavid Shāh Ismāʿīl with twelve Qurʾanic verses containing the name Ismāʿīl. Photo: Sheila S. Blair and Jonathan M. Bloom. 249

15.4 Minaret of Jām erected by the Ghurid Sultan Ghiyāth al-Dīn on 570/1174–5, with the entire text of *Sūrat Maryam* (Q.19:1–98) inscribed around the lower shaft. Photo: David Thomas, MJAP2005. 251

16.1 The title page of Theodor Bibliander and Philip Melanchthon (eds.) *Machumetis Saracenorum principis, eiusque successorum vitae doctrina ac, ipse Alcoran*... Basel: Ioannes Oporinus, 1543. The Austrian National Library (19.B.40). Courtesy of the Library. 257

16.2 Bifolio from Ludovico Marracci, *Alcorani textus universus:ex correctioribus Arabum exemplaribus summa fide, atque pulcherrimis characteribus descriptus*. Patavii: Ex Typographia Seminarii, 1698. The Austrian National Library (14.L.36). Courtesy of the Library. 259

16.3 Page 2 of the standard 'Kazan Qur'an' which reproduced the Saint Petersburg edition published, following the 1787 decree of Catherine II, at the privately owned 'Asiatic Press' in St. Petersburg. 262

16.4 Bifolio from the full-size traced facsimile of 'Samarqand Kūfic Qur'an', which was published in St. Petersburg. 264

19.1 The composition of *Sūrat al-Fātiḥa's* according to Semitic Rhetoric. 323

19.2 Mirror composition of *Sūrat Yūsuf.* 324

19.3 Ring composition of *Sūrat al-Takwīr*, verses 19–25. 325

21.1 The suras ordered by increasing MVL, part 1. 353

21.2 The suras ordered by increasing MVL, part 2. 353

21.3 MVL and 95 per cent confidence intervals, part 1. 353

21.4 MVL and 95 per cent confidence intervals, part 2. 354

21.5 The correlation of MVL and characteristic introductory elements. 355

21.6 MVL correlated with three important Qur'anic terms. 355

21.7 MVL correlated with formulaic density. 356

List of Contributors

Muhammad Abdel Haleem is King Fahd Professor of Islamic Studies at SOAS. He is Director of the Centre of Islamic Studies at SOAS and Editor in Chief of the *Journal of Qur'anic Studies*. Among his published works are *The Qur'an: English Translation with Parallel Arabic Text* (Oxford University Press, 2010), *The Qur'an: A New Translation* (Oxford University Press, 2016), *Understanding the Qur'an: Themes and Style* (I. B. Tauris, 2010), and *Exploring the Qur'an: Context and Impact* (I. B. Tauris, 2017). He also wrote, with Elsaid Badawi, *An Arabic-English Dictionary of Qur'anic Usage* (Brill, 2007).

Kamal Abu-Deeb is Emeritus Professor of Arabic in the University of London, where he held the Chair of Arabic 1992–2007. He was awarded the prestigious al-Owais Prize for Literary Studies and Criticism for the 2014–15 session. He has published numerous books and articles, including *al-Jurjānī's Theory of Poetic Imagery* (Aris & Phillips Ltd, 1979). He has taught and lectured at a number of universities including Oxford, Columbia, Berkeley, Princeton, Pennsylvania, Dartmouth, Yarmouk, and Sanaa. He has been Visiting Professor at the Institute of Ismaili Studies, the Agha Khan University, London, since 2015.

Asma Afsaruddin is Professor of Near Eastern Languages and Cultures in the Hamilton Lugar School of Global and International Studies at Indiana University, Bloomington, USA. Her publications include *Jihad: What Everyone Needs to Know* (forthcoming from Oxford University Press), *Contemporary Issues in Islam* (Edinburgh University Press, 2015), *Striving in the Path of God: Jihad and Martyrdom in Islamic Thought* (Oxford University Press, 2013), and *The First Muslims: History and Memory* (Oneworld Publications, 2008).

Anna Akasoy is Professor of Islamic Intellectual History at the Graduate Center, City University of New York. Her areas of expertise include the intellectual culture of Muslim Spain and contacts between the Islamic world and other cultures. Her publications include *Philosophie und Mystik in der späten Almohadenzeit: Die Sizilianischen Fragen des Ibn Sabʿīn* (Brill, 2006), *Islam and Tibet: Interactions along the Musk Routes* (Routledge, 2011), and *Renaissance Averroism and Its Aftermath: Arabic Philosophy in Early Modern Europe* (Springer, 2012).

Muntasir F. Al-Hamad is Associate Professor of Arabic for Non-Native Speakers at Qatar University. He specializes in comparative syntax in the Semitic languages. He is a Fellow of the UK's Higher Education Academy. He has recently edited *Lisān al-ʿArab:*

Studies in Contemporary Arabic Dialects (LIT Verlag, 2017), co-edited *Near Eastern and Arabian Essays: Studies on Arabia in Honour of John F. Healey* (Oxford University Press, 2019), and is the author of *Non-Verbal Communication in Qatari Culture* (in Arabic) (Qatar University Press, in press).

Ahmad Al-Jallad is the Sofia Chair of Arabic at Ohio State University, USA. His work focuses on the languages and writing systems of pre-Islamic Arabia and the ancient Near East. He has authored and edited books and articles on the early history of Arabic, language classification, North Arabian and Arabic epigraphy, and historical Semitic linguistics, including *An Outline of the Grammar of the Safaitic Inscriptions* (Brill, 2015), *A Dictionary of the Safaitic Inscriptions* (W. K. Jaworska, 2019), and *The Damascus Psalm Fragment: Middle Arabic and the Legacy of Old Ḥigāzī* (Oriental Institute, 2019).

Sulaiman bin Ali bin Ameir Al-Shueili is Associate Professor and Head of the Department of Islamic Sciences at Sultan Qaboos University. He received his BA in *Uṣūl al-Dīn* at Sultan Qaboos University, his MA in Quranic Sciences from the University of Jordan, and his Ph.D. in Islamic Studies from the University of Edinburgh.

Herbert Berg is Professor of Religion in the Department of Philosophy and Religion at the University of North Carolina Wilmington. His research focuses on the formation of Islam (particularly on Ibn ʿAbbās) and the formation of African American forms of Islam (particularly on Elijah Muhammad). His publications include *The Development of Exegesis in Early Islam* (Routledge, 2000), *Method and Theory in the Study of Islamic Origins* (Brill, 2003), *Elijah Muhammad and Islam* (NYU Press, 2009) and he recently edited the *Routledge Handbook on Early Islam* (Routledge, 2017).

Sheila S. Blair recently retired from the Norma Jean Calderwood University Professorship of Islamic and Asian Art at Boston College and the Hamad bin Khalifa Endowed Chair in Islamic Art at Virginia Commonwealth University, positions she shared with her husband and colleague Jonathan Bloom. She has written, co-written, or edited two dozen books and hundreds of articles on all aspects of Islamic art, but her special interests are the uses of writing and the arts of the Mongol period. She is the author of *Text and Image in Medieval Persian Art* (Edinburgh University Press, 2014).

Stephen R. Burge is Senior Research Associate at the Institute of Ismaili Studies, London. He is the author of *Angels in Islam: Jalāl al-Dīn al-Suyūṭī's* al-Ḥabāʾik fī akhbār al-malāʾik (Routledge 2012), and editor of *The Meaning of the Word: Lexicology and Qur'anic Exegesis* (Oxford University Press, 2015). His main research interests are Qur'anic Studies, the works of Jalāl al-Dīn al-Suyūṭī, *ḥadīth* studies, *tafsīr* and angelology.

Massimo Campanini was previously Associate Professor of Islamic Studies at Trent University. He has translated the literary works of many Muslim philosophers into Italian (al-Ghāzalī, al-Fārabī, Averroes) and published several monographs on medieval and contemporary issues alike, among which are *The Qur'an: Modern Muslim Interpretations*

(Routledge, 2011), *The Qur'an the Basics* (Routledge, 2016) and *al-Ghazālī and the Divine* (Routledge, 2018).

Michel Cuypers Doctor of Persian Literature (University of Teheran, 1983), is a member of the Dominican Institute for Oriental Studies (Cairo), specializing in the exegesis of the Qur'an and the text's composition according to the theory of Semitic rhetoric. His publications include *The Banquet: A Reading of the Fifth Sura of the Qur'an* (Convivium Press, 2009), and *The Composition of the Qur'an* (Bloomsbury, 2015), and *A Qur'ānic Apocalypse: A Reading of the Thirty-Three Last Sūrahs of the Qur'ān* (International Qur'ānic Studies Association, 2018).

François Déroche is Professor of the History of the Qur'an: Text and Transmission at the Collège de France in Paris. Among his many publications are: *The Abbasid Tradition: Qur'ans of the 8th to 10th Centuries* (Nour Foundation,1992); *Islamic Codicology: An Introduction to the Study of Manuscripts in Arabic Script* (Al-Furqan Islamic Heritage Foundation, 2006); *La transmission écrite du Coran dans les débuts de l'islam: Le codex Parisino-petropolitanus* (E. J. Brill, 2009); *Qur'āns of the Umayyads: A First Overview.* (Brill, 2014); and he has edited along with Christian Robin and Michel Zink the recently published *Les origines du Coran, le Coran des origins* (Académie des Inscriptions et Belles-Lettres, 2015).

Yasin Dutton is Emeritus Professor of Arabic Studies in the University of Cape Town. He is the author of *The Origins of Islamic Law: The Qur'an, the Muwatta' and Madīnan 'Amal* (Curzon Press, 1999) and *Original Islam: Mālik and the Madhhab of Madīna* (Routledge, 2007), as well as numerous articles on early Islamic law, early Qur'anic manuscripts, and the application of Islamic law in the modern world, particularly in relation to economic and environmental issues.

Jeffrey Einboden is a Presidential Research, Scholarship and Artistry Professor at Northern Illinois University, and author of *Nineteenth-Century U.S. Literature in Middle Eastern Languages* (Edinburgh University Press, 2013), *Islam and Romanticism: Muslim Currents from Goethe to Emerson* (Oneworld, 2014), and *The Islamic Lineage of American Literary Culture: Muslim Sources from the Revolution to Reconstruction* (Oxford University Press, 2016).

Ayman A. El-Desouky is Chair of Comparative Literature at the Doha Institute for Graduate Studies. He studied comparative literature, literary theory and modern philosophy at the University of Texas at Austin and taught at Johns Hopkins and Harvard before relocating to the UK in 2002. Among his publications are: 'A Life in Quotes: Notes on Frye's Theory of Typology and the Discontinuous Temporalities of Qur'anic Revelations' (forthcoming, 2019); 'Between Hermeneutic Provenance and Textuality: The Qur'an and the Question of Method in Approaches to World Literature' (*Journal of Qur'anic Studies*, 2014); 'Naẓm, Iʿjāz, Discontinuous Kerygma: Approaching Qur'anic Voice on the Other Side of the Poetic' (*Journal of Qur'anic Studies*, 2013); and '*Ego eimi*: Kerygma or Existential Metaphor? Frye, Bultmann and the Problem of Demythologizing" (*Canadian Review*, 2007). He is currently preparing a short monograph on *Questions of Untranslatability: Toward a Comparative Critical Method.*

Ziad Elmarsafy is Professor of Comparative Literature at King's College London. He has published in a number of areas, including the literature and culture of early modern France, the Enlightenment, and modern Arabic literature. He is the author of *The Enlightenment Qur'an* (Oneworld, 2015), *Sufism in the Contemporary Arabic Novel* (Edinburgh University Press, 2012), and he is co-editor of *What Postcolonial Theory Doesn't Say* (Routledge, 2015).

Reuven Firestone is the Regenstein Professor of Medieval Judaism and Islam at Hebrew Union College, Los Angeles. His published works include *Holy War in Judaism: The Fall and Rise of a Controversial Idea* (Oxford University Press, 2012) and *Learned Ignorance: Intellectual Humility among Jews, Christians and Muslims* (Oxford University Press, 2011). He is also the author of the *Journeys in Holy Lands: The Evolution of the Abraham-Ishmael Legends in Islamic Exegesis.* Albany: State University of New York Press, 1990. And *Jihad: The Origin of Holy War in Islam.* NY: Oxford University Press, 1999.

Geert Jan van Gelder was formerly Lecturer in Arabic, University of Groningen from 1975 to 1998 and Laudian Professor of Arabic at the University of Oxford from 1998 to 2012. His books include *Beyond the Line: Classical Arabic Literary Critics on the Coherence and Unity of the Poem* (Brill, 1982), *Close Relationships: Incest and Inbreeding in Classical Arabic Literature* (I. B. Tauris, 2005), and *Sound and Sense in Classical Arabic Poetry* (Harrassowitz, 2012).

Sebastian Günther is Professor and Chair of Arabic and Islamic Studies at the University of Göttingen, Germany. He is co-editor of the *Islamic History and Civilization* series (Brill), and a Past President of the Union Européenne des Arabisants et Islamisants. Günther's recent publications include the co-edited volumes *Roads to Paradise: Eschatology and Concepts of the Hereafter in Islam* with Todd Lawson (Brill, 2017) and *Die Geheimnisse der oberen und der unteren Welt: Magie im Islam zwischen Glaube und Wissenschaft* with Dorothee Pielow (Brill, 2018).

John F. Healey is Professor Emeritus of Semitic Studies at the University of Manchester, and has worked primarily on the pre-Islamic Middle East. He has published extensively, including *The Nabataean Tomb Inscriptions of Mada'in Salih* (Oxford University Press, 1993), *The Religion of the Nabataeans* (Brill, 2001), and *Aramaic Inscriptions and Documents of the Roman Period* (Oxford University Press, 2009).

Valerie J. Hoffman is Professor and Head of the Department of Religion at the University of Illinois at Urbana-Champaign. She is the author of *Sufism, Mystics and Saints in Modern Egypt* (University of South Carolina Press, 1995) and *The Essentials of Ibāḍī Islam* (Syracuse University Press, 2012), is editor of *Making the New Middle East: Politics, Culture, and Human Rights* (Syracuse University Press, 2019), and has published numerous articles on Sufism, Islamic gender ideology, Ibāḍī Islam, human rights, and contemporary Islamic movements.

Tariq Jaffer is Associate Professor of Religion at Amherst College in Massachusetts. He studied at the universities of McGill and Yale, where he completed his Ph.D. in Religious Studies. While at Yale, he studied the Qur'an and Qur'anic commentaries, Islamic philosophy and theology, Aristotle and Neoplatonism, medieval philosophy, classical Arabic poetry, Ancient Greek, Persian (Middle and Modern), and Islamic Mysticism. He is the author of *Razi: Master of Quranic Interpretation and Theological Reasoning* (Oxford University Press, 2015).

Jules Janssens is Collaborator of the De Wulf-Mansioncentrum, KU Leuven and Associate Researcher of the CNRS (UMR 8230, Centre Jean Pépin). His current research concerns mainly Ibn Sīnā and the reception of the latter's thought in both the Islamic world and the West. His publications include *An Annotated Bibliography on Ibn Sīnā* (Leuven University Press, 1991; First Supplement, Brepols, 1999; Second Supplement, Arizona University Press, 2017) and *Ibn Sīnā and his Influence on the Arabic and Latin World* (Routledge, 2006). Among his many papers, a few deal with the specific use of the Qur'an in classical *falsafa* (al-Kindī, Ibn Sīnā).

Maher Jarrar is Professor in the Civilization Studies Program and in the Department of Arabic at the American University of Beirut. He is also Director of the Center for Arts and Humanities. He has published numerous books and articles in the field of Arabic and Islamic Literature. Among his recent articles are, 'Ibn Abī Yaḥyā: A Controversial Medinan Akhbārī of the 2nd/8th Century' in Nicolet Boekhoff-van der Voort, Kees Versteegh, and Joas Wagemakers (eds.). *The Transmission and Dynamics of the Textual Sources of Islam: Essays in Honour of Harald Motzki* (Brill, 2011) and 'Strategies of Paradise: Paradise Virgins and Utopia' in Sebastian Günther and Todd Lawson (eds.). *Roads to Paradise: Eschatology and Concepts of the Hereafter in Islam* (Brill, 2017).

Anthony H. Johns is Visiting Fellow at the Department of Political and Social Change at the Australian National University of which he is Emeritus Professor. He is also Adjunct Professor at the Australian Catholic University. He has carried out research on the transmission and fecundation of Islamic learning in Southeast Asia, with emphasis on *tafsīr* and *taṣawwuf*. Prompted by an engagement with Fakhr al-Dīn al-Rāzī's *al-Tafsīr al-Kabīr*, he has published a number of significant papers in the *Journal of Qur'anic Studies*, and the *Mélanges* of the *Institut Dominicain d'Études Orientales du Caire* on the Qur'anic presentation of figures known also in the Bible.

Marianna Klar is currently Post-Doctoral Researcher at Oxford University, Senior Research Associate at Pembroke College, Oxford, and Research Associate at the Centre of Islamic Studies, SOAS, University of London. Her most recent publications focus on the Qur'an's structure, its narratives, and its literary context. She has also worked extensively on tales of the prophets within the medieval Islamic historiographical tradition and on Qur'anic exegesis. Her monograph on al-Thaʿlabī's *Tales of the Prophets* was published in 2009. An edited volume, *Structural Dividers in the Qur'an*, is currently under review.

Alexander Knysh is Professor of Islamic Studies at the University of Michigan and Principal Investigator of a research project on Islamic studies at the St. Petersburg State University, Russia. His research interests include Islamic mysticism, Qur'anic studies, the history of Muslim theological, philosophical, and juridical thought, as well as Islamic movements in comparative perspective. He has numerous academic publications on these subjects, including ten books. Since 2005, he has served as section editor for 'Sufism' on the Editorial Board of the *Encyclopaedia of Islam*, 3rd edition (E. J. Brill) and is currently Executive Editor of the Brill series Handbooks of Sufi Studies.

Bruce Lawrence is Marcus Family Professor of Religion Emeritus at Duke University and adjunct Professor at Fatih Sultan Mehmet Vakf University, Istanbul. He is currently Visiting Al-Qasimi Professor in Islamic Studies at Exeter University. His most recent monograph, *The Koran in English: A Biography*, was published by Princeton University Press (2017). He is also co-editor, with Vincent Cornell, of *The Wiley-Blackwell Companion to Islamic Spirituality* (forthcoming, 2019), and with Rafey Habib, he is working to complete *The Qur'an: A Verse Translation* (W. W. Norton, forthcoming 2020). In addition, he has drafted a manifesto on *Islamicate Cosmopolitan* (Wiley-Blackwell, forthcoming 2021).

Oliver Leaman is Professor of Philosophy at the University of Kentucky. He is the author and editor of books on Islamic, Jewish, and Asian Philosophy and Theology. His publications include *Controversies in Contemporary Islam* (Routledge, 2013) and *The Qur'an: A Philosophical Guide* (Bloomsbury, 2016). He is the editor of *The Qur'an: An Encyclopedia* (Routledge, 2006) and has co-written *Islam: The Key Concepts* with Kecia Ali (Routledge, 2008). His latest book is *Islam and Morality* (Bloomsbury, 2019).

Joseph E. Lowry is Associate Professor of Arabic and Islamic Studies at the University of Pennsylvania. His interests include Islamic legal thought, Arabic literature and the Qur'an. He is the author of *Early Islamic Legal Theory* (Brill, 2007) and has edited and translated the *Risāla* of al-Shāfiʿī for the Library of Arabic Literature (NYU Press, 2013).

Ulrika Mårtensson is Professor of Religious Studies in the Department of Philosophy and Religious Studies at the Norwegian University of Science and Technology. Her research includes the Qur'an and *tafsīr*; early Islamic historiography; and contemporary Islam, especially in Scandinavian contexts. Areas of interest concern epistemic and methodological challenges in the study of religion and Islam, regarding how religious concepts are understood as expressing norms for constitutional and institutional order. She jointly edited *Islamic Myths and Memories: Mediators of Globalization* (Ashgate, 2014) with Itzchak Weismann and Mark Sedgwick.

Mustansir Mir teaches Islamic studies at Youngstown State University in Youngstown, Ohio. His main research interests are Qur'anic studies and Iqbal studies. He is the author of *Dictionary of Qurʾānic Terms and Concepts* (Garland, 1987), *Coherence in the Qurʾān: A Study of Iṣlāḥī's Concept of Naẓm in Tadabbur-i Qurʾān* (American Trust

Publications, 1986), *Verbal Idioms of the Qur'an, Understanding the Islamic Scripture,* and *Iqbal* (University of Michigan Library, 2011).

Ebrahim Moosa is Professor of Islamic Studies at the University of Notre Dame's Keough School of Global Affairs and the Department of History. He co-directs the Contending Modernities programme, a global research initiative devoted to generating new knowledge and greater understanding of the ways that religious and secular forces interact in the modern world. Moosa's interests span both classical and modern Islamic thought with a focus on Islamic law, ethics, and theology. He is the author of *Ghazālī and the Poetics of Imagination* (University of North Carolina Press, 2006) and *What is a Madrasa?* (University of North Carolina Press, 2015).

Robert Morrison is George Lincoln Skolfield, Jr. Professor of Religion at Bowdoin College. He is the author of *Islam and Science: The Intellectual Career of Niẓām al-Dīn al-Nīsābūrī* (Routledge, 2007) and *The Light of the World: Astronomy in al-Andalus* (University of California Press, 2016).

Harry Munt is Lecturer in Medieval History at the University of York. He is the author of several articles on the history of early Islamic Arabia as well as *The Holy City of Medina: Sacred Space in Early Islamic Arabia* (Cambridge University Press, 2014).

Martin Nguyen is Associate Professor of Religious Studies, Director of Islamic World Studies, and Faculty Chair for Inclusive Excellence at Fairfield University. His areas of research include the Qur'an and its exegesis, theology, Sufism, and Islamic history. He is the author of *Sufi Master and Qur'an Scholar:Abū'l-Qāsim al-Qushayrī and the Laṭā'if al-Ishārāt* (Oxford University Press, 2012) and *Modern Muslim Theology: Engaging God and the World with Faith and Imagination* (Rowman & Littlefield, 2019).

Johanna Pink is Professor of Islamic Studies at the Albert Ludwigs University of Freiburg, Germany. Her publications include *Sunni Tafsir in the Modern Islamic World: Academic Traditions, Popularisation, and Nation-State Interests* (Brill, 2011, in German) and *Muslim Qur'ānic Interpretation Today: Media, Genealogies and Interpretive Communities* (Equinox, 2019) as well as numerous articles on *tafsīr* and Qur'an translation.

Ismail Poonawala is Emeritus Professor of Arabic and Islamic Studies at the University of California, Los Angeles, where he has taught since 1974. He also lectured at McGill and Harvard universities. A specialist in Ismaili history and doctrines, he is the author of *Biobibliography of Ismāʿīlī Literature* (UCLA, 1977), which is a comprehensive survey of Ismaili authors and their writings including manuscript holdings in public and private libraries. He has edited several important early Ismaili texts, written numerous articles and contributed to various encyclopaedias. He has also translated with annotations, volume 9 of Ṭabarī's history, entitled *The Last Years of the Prophet* (State University of New York Press, 1990) and *The Pillars of Islam, Volume I: Acts of Devotion and Religious Observances* (Oxford University Press, 2002); *Volume II: Laws Pertaining to Human Intercourse* (2004), by the distinguished Ismaili jurist al-Qāḍī al-Nuʿmān.

Recently, he edited *Turks in the Indian Subcontinent, Central and West Asia: The Turkish Presence in the Islamic World* (Oxford University Press, 2016).

Efim A. Rezvan is Editor-in-Chief of 'Manuscripta Orientalia, International Journal for Oriental MSS Research', Deputy Director of Peter the Great Museum of Anthropology and Ethnography at Kunstkamera, Russian Academy of Sciences. Professor at UNESCO Chair in Comparative Studies of Spiritual Traditions, Their Specific Cultures and Interreligious Dialogue. His main scientific achievements are connected with the study of archival and manuscript collections of St. Petersburg.

The late **Andrew Rippin** was Professor of Islamic History at the University of Victoria, Canada. His research into the formative period of Islamic thought as well as the history of the Qur'an and its interpretation has resulted in numerous publications. Among his published works are *Muslims: Their Religious Beliefs and Practices*, first published in 1990 and 1993 and now in its 4th edition (Routledge, 2012). He also edited a number of significant works, including *Approaches to the History of the Interpretation of the Qur'an* (Oxford University Press, 1988), *The Qurʾan: Formative Interpretation* (Ashgate, 1999), *The Qur'an: Style and Contents* (Ashgate, 2001), and *The Islamic World* (Routledge, 2008). He published numerous articles on *tafsīr*, many of which appeared in *The Qur'an and its Interpretative Tradition* (Variorum, 2001).

Sajjad Rizvi is Associate Professor of Islamic Intellectual History and Director of the Centre for the Study of Islam at the University of Exeter. An intellectual historian who specializes in the study of philosophy in the Mughal-Safavid sphere, his other primary research interest lies in exegesis. Among his published works are *Mulla Sadra and Metaphysics: Modulation of Being* (Routledge, 2009) and *The Spirit and the Letter: Esoteric Approaches to the Interpretation of the Quran* (Oxford, 2016), which he jointly edited with Annabel Keeler. He is currently completing a monograph on philosophy in eighteenth-century Iran and North India.

Neal Robinson is an independent researcher based in Brussels, and was formerly Visiting Professor in Astana and a semester in Kazan. He has written extensively on the Qur'an and Muslim perceptions of Jesus. His publications include *Christian in Islam and Christianity: The Representation of Jesus in the Qur'an and the Classical Muslim Commentaries* (Macmillan, 1991) and *Discovering the Qur'an: A Contemporary Approach to a Veiled Text* (Georgetown University Press, 2004).

Walid A. Saleh is Professor of Religion at the University of Toronto. He specializes in Qur'anic Studies, *tafsīr*, Islamic Arabic literature, and Islamic apocalyptic literature. He is the author of *The Formation of the Classical Tafsir Tradition: The Qur'ān Commentary of al-Thaʿlabī* (d. 427/1035) (Brill, 2004) and *In Defence of the Bible* (Brill 2008). Saleh has published an extensive number of articles on the history of *tafsīr* and the Qur'an.

Mustafa Shah is Senior Lecturer in the School of Languages, Cultures and Linguistics at SOAS. His research focuses on *qirāʾāt* literature, hadith scholarship, classical theology, and the early Arabic linguistic tradition. He has edited a collection of articles on *The Ḥadīth* (Routledge, 2010) and a further work on exegesis, *Tafsīr: Interpreting the Qurʾān* (Routledge, 2013). He is currently editing the *Oxford Handbook of Ḥadīth Studies.*

Nicolai Sinai is Professor of Islamic Studies at the University of Oxford and a Fellow of Pembroke College. His published research deals with the literary and historical-critical study of the Qur'an against the background of earlier Jewish, Christian, and Arabian traditions; with Islamic scriptural interpretation; and with the history of philosophical and theological thought in the Islamic world. His most recent book is *The Qurʾan: A Historical-Critical Introduction* (Edinburgh University Pres, 2017) and he is about to publish the edited volume *Unlocking the Medinan Qurʾan.*

Stefan Sperl is Emeritus Professor of Arabic and Middle Eastern Studies at SOAS, University of London. His publications include *Mannerism in Arabic Poetry: A Structural Analysis of Selected Texts* (Cambridge University Press, 1989), *The Kurds: A Contemporary Overview* (with Philip Kreyenbroek, Routledge, 1991), *Qasida Poetry in Islamic Asia and Africa* (with Christopher Shackle, 2 vols., Brill, 1996), *The Cosmic Script: Sacred Geometry and the Science of Arabic Penmanship* (with Ahmed Moustafa, 2 vols., Thames & Hudson, 2014), as well as numerous articles on Arabic, Islamic, and Refugee Studies.

Roberto Tottoli teaches Islamic studies at the University of Naples L'Orientale. He is the editor of *Routledge Handbook of Islam in the West* (Routledge, 2014) and *Books and Written Culture of the Islamic World* (with Andrew Rippin; Brill, 2014). His authored works include *Biblical Prophets in the Qurʾan and Muslim Literature* (Routledge, 2009). He recently published with Reinhold F. Glei, *Ludovico Marracci at Work: The Evolution of his Latin Translation of the Qurʾān in the Light of his Newly Discovered Manuscripts. With an Edition and a Comparative Linguistic Analysis of Sura 18* (Harrassowitz, 2016).

Kees Versteegh is Emeritus Professor of Arabic and Islam at the University of Nijmegen, the Netherlands. He specializes in historical linguistics and the history of linguistics, focusing on processes of language change and language contact. His books include *The Arabic Language* (revised edition; Edinburgh University Press, 2014), *The Foundations of Arabic Linguistics II* (Brill, 2015), *Arabic Grammar and Qurʾānic Exegesis in Early Islam* (Brill, 1993), *The Arabic Linguistic Tradition* (Routledge, 1997), and *The Arabic Language* (revised edition Edinburgh University Press, 2014). He co-edited the *Handbuch für die Geschichte der Sprach- und Kommunikationswissenschaft* (De Gruyter, 2000–5) and was the editor-in-chief of the *Encyclopedia of Arabic Language and Linguistics* (Brill, 2006–9).

Stefan Wild is Emeritus Professor of Semitic Philology and Islamic Studies at the University of Bonn, Germany. In addition to the political aspects of modern Arab history, his research interests include the Qur'an, classical Arabic literature and lexicography, as well as modern Arabic literature. A long-time editor of *Die Welt des Islams* (Leiden), his publications include *The Qurʾan as Text* (Brill, 1996), *Mensch, Prophet und Gott im Koran* (Rhema, 2001), and *Self-Referentiality in the Qurʾan* (Harrassowitz, 2006).

M. Brett Wilson is Associate Professor of History at Central European University. He is the author of *Translating the Qur'an in an Age of Nationalism: Print Culture and Modern Islam in Turkey* (Oxford University Press, 2014). Additionally, his work has appeared in the *International Journal of Middle Eastern Studies, Die Welt des Islams, Comparative Islamic Studies*, the *Journal of Qur'anic Studies*, and the *Encyclopedia of Women & Islamic Cultures*.

A. H. Mathias Zahniser, Ph.D. 1973, a student of Georg Krotkoff, completed his dissertation on al-Jāḥiẓ's *Kitāb al-ʿUthmāniyya*, and has taught at Central Michigan University, Asbury Seminary, and Greenville University, where he is now Scholar-in-Residence. He demonstrated a coherent architecture in four Medinan suras: 'Major Transitions and Thematic Borders in Two Long Sūras: *al-Baqara* and *al-Nisāʾ*', in Issa J. Boullata (ed.). *Literary Structures of Religious Meaning in the Qurʾān* (Curzon, 2000). He also published 'Sūra as Guidance and Exhortation: The Composition of *Sūrat al-Nisāʾ*', in Asma Afsaruddin and A. H. Mathias Zahniser (eds.). *Humanism, Culture, and Language in the Near East* (Eisenbrauns, 1997). He is the author of *The Mission and Death of Jesus in Islam and Christianity* (Orbis Books, 2009).

INTRODUCTION

MUSTAFA SHAH

In terms of achievements, it is often lamented that the academic field of Qur'anic Studies lags significantly behind the extended range of scholarship that the Bible has attracted. As one scholar astutely observed 'modern biblical scholarship fills a library many times the size of that devoted to the Qur'an' and that 'by contrast, it is still possible to point to individual works in the history of the study of the Qur'an and declare them pivotal texts that provide the foundation for all later studies' (Rippin 2004: iv). Bearing in mind the historical background of the development of Qur'anic Studies, this contrast in accomplishments is unsurprising. It was only in the mid-nineteenth century that concerted efforts materialised to engage critically with the Qur'an. Previously, in Early Modern Europe the scholarly engagement with the Qur'an principally gained traction within two separate contexts: firstly, this occurred through the production of translations of the Qur'an; and secondly, through the framework of supporting studies in biblical theology and philology.[1] With regards to the latter, having been nominated as the first professor of Arabic at Leiden in 1613, Thomas Erpenius (1584–1624), who had initially studied Arabic under the supervision of the English Arabist William Bedwell (1563–1632), prepared an oration on the prestige and dignity of Arabic in which he emphasized the importance of the language not only for the acquisition of knowledge, but also for aiding scholarship in biblical philology. Displaying remarkable insight, he explained that key aspects of the Hebrew language, in terms of figures of speech, meaning, and etymology could be illuminated by reference to Arabic, and even authored a book expounding upon the subject (Jones 1986: 20). Pursuing this approach with even greater vigour, in his 1706 thesis entitled *Dissertatio theologico-philologica de utilitate linguae Arabicae in interpretenda sacra lingua*, Albert Schultens (1686–1750), Professor of Oriental Languages at Leiden, set out an elaborate synthesis of how Arabic could assist in the clarification of the meaning of Hebrew words. Based on linguistic affinities between the languages and their common origin, the assumption was that over the passage of time Arabic had

[1] Knowledge of Arabic was considered requisite for the study of the Islamic tradition's contribution to the preservation and synthesis of the Greeks' philosophical and scientific literary heritage; in addition, missionary, political, and economic considerations played a key role in fostering interest in the study of Islam and Arabic (Bevilacqua 2018: 13 and 26; cf. Dannenfeldt 1955: 96).

preserved more of the lost primeval language of Hebrew (Burnett 2008: 792–3).To this end, the Qur'an was considered one of the essential texts which enabled students to 'acquire an adequate knowledge of the language' (Loop 2017: 232). In the visionary words of Joseph Scaliger (1540–1609), who was an inspiration to Erpenius and his mentor at Leiden, 'You can no more master Arabic without the Qur'an than Hebrew without the Bible' (Hamilton 1985: 84).[2]

Designed to promote the study of the language, Arabic grammatical works and lexicons, of which many were written over the course of the seventeenth, eighteenth, and nineteenth centuries, sought to make effective use of classical literary sources, including materials from the Qur'an. Erpenius, who authored the *Grammatica arabica*, which for centuries served as the authoritative reference text in Europe, published his *Historia Iosephi Patriarchae ex Alcorano* in 1617. It was an Arabic edition of the twelfth sura of the Qur'an featuring his own Latin rendition of the chapter together with explanatory notes and citations from other translations (Hamilton 2017: 221–3). Jacobus Golius (1596–1667), Erpenius' student and successor at Leiden and the author of the renowned *Arabico-Latinum* lexicon, produced an edition of Erpenius' grammar in which he included a chrestomathy of Qur'anic materials. Golius, who possessed impeccable scholarly talents having excelled in the study of medicine, mathematics, and astronomy, supplemented his own select Latin translations of the Qur'an with discussions in which he adduced materials gleaned from the classical Qur'an commentaries of cynosures such as al-Zamakhsharī (d. 538/1144), al-Bayḍāwī (d. *c*.719/1319), and al-Suyūṭī (d. 911/1505); and he included an essay on the history of the Qur'an. While the works of Erpenius and Golius were aimed at scrupulously mining Arabic literary sources, including the Qur'an, for their linguistic value, their preliminary contributions were to prove portentous for later developments within the study of Arabic philology. They tenaciously set in motion the preliminary processes which would pave the way for the study of Arabic primary sources.[3]

Informed by an undercurrent of polemical influences, the scholarship devoted to translating the Qur'an possesses even greater historical depth, revealing both the sustained level of interest in the text and the formidable linguistic challenges faced by its translators. Peter the Venerable's pioneering project to translate Islamic texts in the twelfth century, for which Robert of Ketton (*fl.* 1136–57), an accomplished translator of Arabic scientific texts, produced the first complete Latin translation of the Qur'an, was followed over the centuries by a phenomenal number of translations and refutations of the text (Burman 2007: 60).[4] Making ample use of Ketton's translation, in his *Cribratio*

[2] This observation is preserved in Scaliger's correspondence with Isaac Casaubon in 1603, the *Epistolae omnes* (Hamilton 1985: 151 for the Latin text). The creation of chairs for the study of Hebrew, Chaldean, Arabic, and Greek at the universities of Paris, Oxford, Bologna, and Salamanca was first approved in 1311–12 by the Ecumenical Council of Vienne.

[3] Materials from the collection of manuscripts acquired by Erpenius are housed in Cambridge as they were purchased by the Duke of Buckingham in 1625 and passed by his widow to the university; while manuscripts from Golius' collection are kept at the Bodleian Library at Oxford.

[4] For example: Mark of Toledo (*fl.* 1193–1216); Johannes Zechendorff (1580–1662); Dominicus Germanus of Silesia (d. 1670); André du Ryer' (1580–1660); Claude-Etienne Savary; and Friedrich Rückert (1788–1866). A Hebrew translation of the Qur'an was authored in 1857 by Hermann Reckendorf (1825–75), an expert in Semitic languages; his son Hermann Solomon Reckendorf (1863–1923) went on to write several texts on Arabic syntax.

Alcorani, which was intended to serve as a refutation of the Qur'an, Nicholas of Cusa (1401–64), collated its teachings on Christian doctrine. While insisting that the text had actively appropriated biblical materials, Cusa floated the idea that in doing so it had misconstrued basic Christian teachings (Monfasani 2018: 104–6). With the objective of making a corpus of sources available for the confutation of Islam and the Qur'an, Theodor Bibliander (d. 1564) included the *Cribratio* in the anthology of materials he collated in his *Machumetis saracenorum principis*, which also featured a Greek version of Riccoldo da Monte di Croce's refutation of the Qur'an (Miller 2013: 250). Despite these earlier efforts, it has been observed that by the late seventeenth century no one had yet published a scholarly treatment of the Qur'an, particularly in terms of presenting a systematic examination of its contents and features (Bevilacqua 2018: 47). However, it should be borne in mind that during these formative periods the philological, grammatical, and exegetical study of the primary Arabic sources, which would have been vital to the pursuit of such scholarship, was still in its nascent phases of development.

One work which surpassed all other efforts in the realm of translations was the complete Latin rendition of the Qur'an authored by Ludovico Marracci (1612–1700).[5] Originally conceived with the aim of unmasking 'Islam as a heresy', the *Alcorani textus universus* (1698) featured the complete bilingual Arabic-Latin text of the Qur'an, a lavish commentary, and a refutation of the Qur'an which Marracci had originally published some years earlier in 1691 (Bevilacqua 2018: 50; cf. Hamilton 2018: 175).[6] Securing a copy of the Qur'an was fraught with difficulties: the text had been added to the list of prohibited books (*Index Librorum Prohibitorum*) and the Holy Congregation of Roman Censors had issued a decree banning 'its publication in any form', which meant that Marracci had to apply for permission to get access to a copy (Bevilacqua 2013: 98). Marracci, who spent decades working on the project, held the chair of Arabic at the University of Rome, and was eventually able to draw from coveted classical exegetical sources, including materials housed in the Vatican library, among which were primary texts such as the commentaries of Ibn Abī Zamanīn (d. *c*.399–1008), al-Thaʿlabī (d. 427/1035), al-Zamakhsharī, al-Bayḍāwī, and al-Suyūṭī (Glei and Tottoli 2016).[7] Commended for its philological insights and range of coverage, his work furnished the template for subsequent translations in other European languages and brought together a valuable repository of philological material on the Qur'an. Criticisms were made of Marracci's Latin style and even his deferential reliance on the commentary literature, although the texts he used represented only a fraction of the vast library of materials composed over the centuries within the classical exegetical tradition. In 1734, George

[5] Adriaan Reland (1676–1718) was the author of the *De religione Mohammedica libri duo*, which eschewed a polemical approach to the exploration of Islam. Marracci's mentor, Filippo Guadagnoli (1596–1656), a scholar of Arabic and Syriac, had already authored the *Apologia pro Christiana religione*, a polemical critique of Islam.

[6] The Sacra Congregatio de Propaganda Fide was set up in 1622 by Pope Gregory XV to facilitate missionary work using Arabic materials. To mark the Ottoman's failed Siege of Vienna in 1683, Marracci later dedicated the work to the Emperor Leopold I.

[7] The earliest printed edition of the Qur'an produced in Venice (*c*.1537–8) was published by the Italian Paganino de Paganini (d. *c*. 1450–1538) and was discovered in a monastery in Venice by Angela Nuovo.

Sale (*c*.1696–1736), the author of the first English translation of the Qur'an, spoke of Marracci's effort as generally being 'very exact', although he also raised the objection that it 'adheres to the Arabic idiom too literally to be easily understood'. Sale even described Marracci's refutations as 'being often unsatisfactory, and sometimes impertinent' (Sale 1734: viii; Bevilacqua 2013: 94).[8] Nonetheless, sealing its historical legacy, the 'pivotal' texts which ultimately defined the scholarly study of the Qur'an in the nineteenth and twentieth centuries made copious use of Marracci's work (Hamilton 2018: 183; Rippin 2004: iv).

With regards to the fortunes of Arabic philology and grammar, it was through the meticulous industry of individuals such as Johann Jakob Reiske (1716–74), a former student of Schultens, and Heinrich Fleischer (1801–88) that a more independent approach to the study of Arabic was cultivated. The aim was to steer it towards the evaluation of 'Arabic as a language and culture in its own right' (Jankowsky 2007: 185). Such a shift in emphasis was in no way meant to temper the intuitive use of Arabic in biblical philology, as attested by the work of Fleischer, but it simultaneously raised the profile of a wider range of Arabic literary texts, inevitably creating new perspectives from which they could be examined. While Reiske had earlier worked on an edition of the historical chronicle, *al-Mukhtaṣar fī akhbār al-bashar*, authored by Abū'l-Fidāʾ (d. 732/1331), the Syrian historian, Fleischer published the first complete printed critical edition of a classical commentary on the Qur'an, al-Bayḍāwī's *Anwār al-tanzīl* (1846–8), which served students of comparative Semitics and Arabic philology; and he dutifully included in the text a dedication to the memory of Reiske.[9] Having been a student of biblical theology and oriental languages, Fleischer had studied with the French Arabist Antoine-Isaac Silvestre de Sacy (1758–1838), author of the renowned *Grammaire arabe*. The influence of Fleischer was profound: he consolidated the study of Arabic philology and inspired a generation of Arabic and Islamic specialists, including David Heinrich Müller (1846–1912), Albert Socin (1844–99), Hartwig Derenbourg (1844–1908), and Carl Caspari (1814–92). He was also one of the main mentors of the Hungarian scholar Ignaz Goldziher (1850–1921), whose *Die Richtungen der islamischen Koranauslegung* (1920), a work based on a set of lectures that he had planned to deliver at the University of Uppsala in 1913, offered one of the first historical surveys of the Qur'anic commentary tradition.

During the course of the nineteenth century significant strides were made in the analysis of the Qur'an with the appearance of specialized studies produced with 'modern scholarly aspirations' in mind (Rippin 2001: xi; Rippin 2006: 235). Such

[8] Johann David Michaelis voiced strident criticisms of Marracci's translation due to its reliance on *tafsīr* (Hamilton 2018: 183; Burman 2007: 36f.). Recognizing that prevailing perceptions of the Islamic faith were far too simplistic, and following his encounter with the Andalusian scholar Aḥmad ibn Qāsim al-Ḥajarī (d. *c*.1052/1642), Erpenius wrote to Isaac Casaubon intimating that 'the errors of the Muslims are not [as]easy to refute as many like to think' (Vrolijk 2017: 27).

[9] Fleischer published the first parts of Abū'l-Fidāʾ's *al-Mukhtaṣar fī taʾrīkh al-bashr* with the Latin translation. Reiske also published excerpts from Abū'l-Fidāʾ's *Taqwīm al-buldān*. Interestingly, Scaliger and Erpenius pioneered the publication of a critical edition of Abū ʿUbayd's *Kitāb al-Amthāl*.

developments in the scholarship were not redolent of a fundamental break with previous scholarly conventions and paradigms applied in the quest to explore the Arabic literary sources of Islam, but rather represented a subtle progression and augmentation of the scholarship. Indeed, confirming the intersections which defined biblical scholarship and the study of the Qur'an, scholars who authored these seminal works were trained in biblical philology and the oriental languages by luminaries who were renowned for their contributions to learning in those established fields. In these studies selected themes such as the identification of biblical influences in the Qur'an, theories about the chronology of its contents, and, most significantly, the question of its textual transmission were brought to the fore. Tackling the subject of influence, the first of these efforts was the prizewinning Latin essay by Abraham Geiger (1810–74) which was later published in German under the title *Was hat Mohammed aus dem Judenthume aufgenommen?* (1833).[10] The text sought to identify and shed light on substrate Jewish and rabbinical traces within the narratives and exempla of the Qur'an. In the context of the age in which he was writing, the frame of reference used by Geiger to broach the study of the Qur'an was considered pioneering, reflecting a qualified move away from polemical treatments which the text had hitherto attracted. In the preface to his work Geiger referred to the generous support provided by Georg Wilhelm Freytag (1788–1861), who held the position of Professor of Oriental Languages at the University of Bonn and with whom he had also studied Arabic. It is worth noting that having read theology and philology at the University of Göttingen, Freytag studied Arabic with de Sacy in Paris and later compiled the influential *Lexicon Arabico-Latinum*, configured around Golius' original lexicon. Further advances in the publication of studies of the Qur'an were marked by the works of Gustav Weil (1808–89), who was a student of Friedrich Wilhelm Umbreit (1795–1860), the Professor of Old Testament Studies and Philology at the University of Heidelberg.[11] Addressing the theme of the chronology of the Qur'an, Weil authored the *Historisch-kritische Einleitung in den Koran* (1844) and a connected study covering the subject of biblical legends in the Qur'an, *Biblische Legenden der Muselmänner* (1845). Among his other influential writings were a biography of the Prophet; several historical surveys; and he worked on a German translation of the *One Thousand and One Nights*.

The works of Geiger and Weil forged key precedents that helped shape the scholarly treatment of the Qur'an in the nineteenth century and the themes and topics analysed in their writing were subjected to further resolution in Theodor Nöldeke's *Geschichte des Qorâns* (1860) which, in the words of one scholar, set 'the agenda for subsequent generations of Qur'anic scholarship' (Rippin 2004: x). The text itself has a fascinating history: based

[10] His essay was originally submitted to a contest in 1832 held by the University of Bonn and he was later awarded a doctorate for it by the University of Marburg. The theme of Jewish influences on the Qur'an had been explored as early as the sixteenth century: see the discussion of the Latin works of D. Mill and H. Lyth in (Heschel 1998: 258 (fn. 36)).

[11] Umbreit had studied with the Austrian Arabist Joseph von Hammer-Purgstall (1774–1856) and with Johann Gottfried Eichhorn (1752–1827), Professor of Oriental Languages at Jena University. Hammer-Purgstall established the periodical, *Fundgruben des Orients*, and in one of its editions he published his own German translation of forty chapters of the Qur'an which sought to replicate the text's rhyme.

on an original dissertation in Latin, it was submitted to a competition held in Paris by the Académie des Inscriptions et Belles-Lettres in 1856 along with essays authored by Aloys Sprenger and Michele Amari, whose chosen subject was early Qur'an manuscripts. Nöldeke's essay won the prize and was later published in an expanded German edition in 1860. Introducing new areas of enquiry such as the Qur'an's textual transmission, Nöldeke's training in the classical disciplines was critical: he was a student of Heinrich Ewald (1803–75), a renowned authority on biblical criticism, theology and oriental languages and to whom he included a dedication in the 1860 edition of the text.[12] The revisions to the *Geschichte* prepared by Nöldeke's student and friend Friedrich Schwally in 1909 and 1919 and the lengthy supplements by Gotthelf Bergsträsser (1886–1933) and Otto Pretzl (1893–1941) enhanced the text's cachet. Schwally, Bergsträsser, and Pretzl were all accomplished scholars in areas of biblical studies and Semitic philology.

Encouraged by scholars such as Fleischer it was also during the course of the nineteenth century that avid attention was eventually turned towards the publication of critical editions of original Arabic sources, permitting scholars to have at their disposal a broader selection of primary Islamic literary texts. In the introduction to the German edition of his work Geiger recounts his having had so few materials available to him for the original essay: he mentions having used a printed edition of the Qur'an prepared by Abraham Hinckelmann (1652–95), a German Protestant theologian who composed a polemical critique of the Qur'an in his foreword to the text; the translation of the Qur'an by Günther Wahl (1760–1834); and transcripts comprising passages from the second and third suras in al-Bayḍāwī's *tafsīr*, which were supplied by his mentor Freytag.[13] Geiger also refers to having recourse to his own profound knowledge of Judaism and its literature. Turning the issue of the lack of primary source materials to his advantage, he stated that he wished to avoid broaching the Qur'an through the lens of later Qur'an commentators and their contrived perceptions and explanations of its narratives (Geiger 1833: iii).[14] Commenting on his preparation of the German edition of his essay, Geiger explained that he was able to draw from a number of additional works, including the historical treatises of Abū'l-Fidāʾ; the works of Edward Pococke (1604–91), who had produced critical editions, translations, and notes on the historical writings of the Syriac Orthodox Prelate Gregory Bar Hebraeus (1226–86); the *Bibliothèque orientale* of Barthélemy

[12] In addition to writing grammars on Hebrew and texts on biblical criticism, Ewald composed a number of Arabic reference texts and a work on Arabic prosody, *De metris carminum Arabicorum* (1825). And Ewald's mentor, Thomas Christian Tychsen (1758–1834), authored a grammatical primer. Freytag compiled a grammatical primer and works on poetry. In his encyclopaedic work, *Promtuarium sive Bibliotheca Orientalis*, the Swiss scholar, Johann Heinrich Hottinger (1620–67) devoted the second chapter, *De Bibliotheca Arabica*, to a discussion of Arabic manuscript sources that he consulted, many of which he copied from Golius' collection at Leiden. Among the books he mentions are al-Zamakhsharī's *al-Kashshāf* and al-Bayḍāwī's *Anwār al-tanzīl wa-asrār al-taʾwīl* (Loop 2013: 138f.).

[13] In his foreword Hinckelmann discusses the exegetical utility of Arabic for the study of the Hebrew scriptures.

[14] The point made by Geiger about the disjunction between early *tafsīr* and the Qur'an has become a standard refrain in studies of the commentary tradition.

d'Herbelot de Molainville (1625–95); and Marracci's Latin translation of the Qur'an and his refutation, a text he describes as being extremely valuable (Geiger 1833: iv).[15] He also refers to his consulting al-Bayḍāwī's commentary on sura 10 and the seminal *Maᶜālim al-tanzīl*, composed by al-Baghawī (d. 516/1122).[16] Discussing his use of sources, in the introduction to the *Geschichte* Nöldeke rues the fact that he was unable to utilize al-Ṭabarī's seminal commentary on the Qur'an nor the bibliographical reference work of Ibn al-Nadīm, *al-Fihrist*, which would have afforded him valuable information on the textual transmission of the text and variant readings (1860: vii).[17] Nöldeke's original work and its lengthy supplements were primarily concerned with the study of themes such as the chronology and transmission of the text and not its stylistic or rhetorical features, which were areas that had yet to be explored. Nonetheless, guided by their philological knowledge and the insights afforded to them by their training in biblical and classical studies, Geiger, Weil, and Nöldeke fostered new approaches to the study of the Qur'an and their works became landmark publications. Although in many ways they were profoundly indebted to the legacy of scholarship refined by individuals such as Erpenius, Golius, Marracci, Reiske, de Sacy, Freytag, Umbreit, Ewald, and Fleischer, in terms of coverage, their work therefore marked a decisive phase in the history of the academic study of the Qur'an.

In a survey which assessed not only the historical significance of the achievements of Geiger, Weil, Nöldeke, and later generations of scholars influenced by their legacy, but also debates within recent scholarship on the Qur'an, Fred Donner voiced concerns that Qur'anic Studies appears to be in 'a state of disarray' and 'lacks consensus'. Mentioning his dissatisfaction with the state of the field, Donner was particularly critical of the fact that scholars had adopted a view of the Qur'an and its origins that 'followed in most of its details the view presented by the Islamic tradition' (Donner 2008: 29–50). Donner insists that those 'who study Islam's origins have to admit collectively that we simply do not know some very basic things about the Qur'an—things so basic that the knowledge of them is usually taken for granted by scholars dealing with other texts'. Separately, the point had been made that 'Qur'anic Studies is not informed by the methods of religious studies as currently practised internationally, but still follows a limited and selective set of methods which tend to

[15] The *Bibliothèque* was published in 1697 and comprised over 8,000 alphabetical entries on a range of Islamic historical and cultural topics. One of its main sources was Kātib Çelebi's *Kashf al-ẓunūn ᶜan asāmī al-kutub wa'l-funūn*, the bibliographical compendium.

[16] Al-Baghawī was ostensibly known by his sobriquet al-Farrāʾ which was rendered as 'Elpherar' in Europe. The manuscript began from sura 7 and was purchased in Cairo in 1807 by the German explorer Ulrich Seetzen (1767–1811) (Hamilton 2014: 206, fn. 239; and Shah 2013: 37).

[17] Nöldeke deferred to a Persian translation of al-Ṭabarī's work. He did make use of the commentaries of al-Baghawī, al-Bayḍāwī, and al-Zamakhsharī; and Gustav Flügel's study of the *Fihrist* which had been published in the *Zeitschrift der Deutschen Morgenländischen Gesellschaft* (Nöldeke 1860: xi–xii). Flügel's edition of the *Fihrist* was published posthumously in 1871–2. Johann Heinrich Hottinger had access to a partial copy of the *Fihrist* owned by Jacobus Golius from which he copied materials (Loop 2013: 181 and 206).

be essentialist in their attitude towards the Qur'an' (Neuwirth 2007: 115–27).[18] Some scholars have also referred to the 'lacunae of the field' which are 'impossible to overlook when confronted with the impressive list of what has been achieved in biblical or classical studies'. However, one does need to bear in mind the context of the historical genesis of scholarly treatments of the Qur'an and the fact that they belatedly emerged from the matrix of a thriving tradition of biblical studies and translations of the text; this very fact goes some way towards explaining the gap in achievements between the two disciplines.[19] To this end, the suggestion that there has been a tendency to follow the 'view presented by the Islamic tradition' seemingly overlooks the reality that scholars are actually some way from attaining a critical understanding of the nuances and dynamics which shape this 'view'.[20] Over recent decades, the panoply of academic discourses and discussions the field of Qur'anic Studies has successfully garnered is reflected in the flurry of publications devoted to the text. These range from treatments of the Qur'an's language, aesthetics, style, structure, literary influence, textual transmission, preservation, manuscript tradition and calligraphy, to analyses of its contents, concepts, historical contexts, the commentary tradition and even the sphere of translations, all of which indicate that the prospects for the field are promising. Introducing subjects, themes, and issues which feature in the examination of the Qur'an, this volume sets out to provide a percipient gauging of the burgeoning field of scholarship devoted to the text and its commentary tradition. With a concern for historical context and relevance, it aims to serve as a reference work and resource, broaching the range of debates and discussions which have defined the academic study of the Qur'an.

The Contents

Part I. The State of Qur'anic Studies

Discussions and themes which have loomed large in the academic study of the Qur'an, ranging from disciplinary challenges to methodological questions, are examined in the first part of the Handbook. Commencing with a survey which considers what is meant

[18] Also, see the statement 'Qur'anic Studies today is most strikingly characterised not by impressive scholarly achievements of the field itself, but by the large-scale interest of the media that the Qur'an's origin and interpretation have solicited during the last decade or so' (Neuwirth, Sinai, and Marx 2010: 1).

[19] It is worth noting that there are only two dedicated academic journals devoted to Qur'anic Studies: Muhammad Abdel Haleem established the *Journal of Qur'anic Studies* in 1999, a triannual bilingual publication; and the *Journal of the International Qur'anic Studies Association*, which appeared in 2016. On the question of resources, in the preface to the *Encyclopaedia of the Qur'ān* Jane McAuliffe states that the 'number of reference works for the Qur'an that are accessible in European languages remains quite small' (McAuliffe 2001: x).

[20] For example, current views on the historical synthesis of variant readings and their transmission principally refer to Ibn Mujāhid's *Kitāb al-Sabʿa* as an analogue for establishing a timeline of the movements towards the establishment of a fixed text. Yet, it remains one of a profusion of texts on variants composed in these formative periods. (Shah 2004: 72–3).

by 'academic scholarship' on the Qur'an, the chapter by Andrew Rippin sets out in lucid detail some of the difficulties and challenges inherent in defining this scholarship. Assessing the historical impact of the work of scholars such as Geiger, Weil, and Nöldeke, he explains why their efforts have 'proven to be of lasting significance'. Rippin also proffers the observation that while the goals and achievements of the academic engagement with the Qur'an are often hotly disputed, they 'remain fully embedded in the academy of today and remain key to fostering an appreciation of the Qur'an's role in history and in Muslim life'.[21] Focusing on the modern study of the Qur'an and developments therein, Oliver Leaman explores the ways in which Muslim scholarship has tackled issues in the text and the intersection with recent academic discourses germane to its study (Campanini 2016; Taji-Farouki 2015).

The question of the reliability of the early Islamic literary sources has been at the forefront of debates about the historical emergence of the Qur'an. Questioning the tendency to link the issue of Islamic origins with the Qur'an and vice versa, Herbert Berg pores over the range of theoretical problems which impinge upon the analysis and contextualization of these literary sources. His view is that the text needs to be approached independently of perceptions about its relevance to debates about origins and influences. In her bibliographical survey Anna Akasoy presents a broad selection of publications covering the various areas of scholarship connected to the study of the Qur'an and the commentary tradition. Observing that 'the number of books concerned with the Qur'an which have been published in the twenty-first century in English alone is staggering', she also considers the reasons for the rise of academic interest in the Qur'an.

Part II. The Historical Setting of the Qur'an

Attempts to locate the Qur'an within the historical context of the world of Late Antiquity are viewed as being essential to cultivating an appreciation of its contents. Highlighting the significance of the milieu in which Islam emerged, in their contribution Muntasir Al-Hamad and John Healey deal with the nature of its relationship with pre-Islamic social and religious traditions. The chapter examines how the Qur'an was able to articulate these traditions in ways which were both novel and creative; it also discusses the text's achievement in establishing its unique 'web of significance' on what it inherited (Neuwirth 2019; Fisher 2015). Studies of the late antique context of the Qur'an have played an important role in shaping deliberations on the value of the Qur'an as a source of history and this issue is probed in the chapter by Harry Munt. Taking into account the Qur'an's own perceptions of history and their broader context, Munt assesses the implications of developments made in the study of the text as a literary source. The use of epigraphic

[21] Andrew Rippin had been planning to work on a monograph covering the subject of this chapter before his death in late 2016. His contribution to the academic study of the Islamic commentary tradition and Qur'anic studies is immense; he leaves behind him a wealth of publications and completed projects. See Majid Daneshgar and Walid A. Saleh (eds.). *Islamic Studies Today: Essays in Honor of Andrew Rippin*, Leiden; Boston: Brill, 2017.

evidence, including ancient inscriptions from North and South Arabia, has created a whole new framework for the linguistic exploration of the Qur'an and the recent scholarship on this area is presented in Ahmad Al-Jallad's chapter. Mediating the historical significance of issues germane to writing and the emergence of the Arabic script, the chapter offers an assessment of how debates about literacy in the pre-Islamic context have advanced attempts to circumscribe the historical context of the Qur'an. Al-Jallad affirms that recent discoveries of inscriptions are helping to fill in many of the previous gaps in our knowledge of the development of the language.

With the aim of shedding further light on the historical context of the Qur'an, the relationship between Qur'anic exempla and late antique narratives is tackled in Marianna Klar's contribution. She explains that while it was previously common to seek to place the narratives and themes of the Qur'an within the vector of the influence of literary materials from the Judaeo-Christian traditions, as evidenced by the work of scholars such as Weil, Hartwig Hirschfeld, William St. Clair Tisdall, Heinrich Speyer, Tor Andrae, and Karl Ahrens, recent scholarship has sought a revision of the arguments apropos the Qur'an's contextual framework and the question of antecedents. Within this context, it is posited that a greater sophistication and coordination rest at the heart of the Qur'an's narratives; indeed, as Klar observes, while reading the text through reference to this larger body of material may prove beneficial, the internal literary integrity and dynamic of the Qur'an's synthesis of exempla must be taken into account in any final assessments, as in her estimation 'the identification of possible parallels is really just the starting point for any discussion of the likelihood of lexical or thematic transfer'.

Staying with the topic of relationships and interactions, the Qur'an's discourses on Jewish and Christian traditions and practices are evaluated in two separate chapters. In the first of these, the Qur'an and Judaism, which is divided into two parts, Reuven Firestone initially deals with the historical-phenomenological relationship discussing various theses used to explain the dynamic of the links between the two faiths: these include the Thesis of Borrowing; the Thesis of Cultural Diffusion; and finally the Semitic Civilization Thesis. In the second part of the chapter (the Qur'an on Judaism), Firestone investigates Qur'anic references to Jewish practices, doctrines, and perspectives, seeking to 'explain their striking similarities and equally glaring differences'. Probing the various Qur'anic references to Christianity and Christians, Neal Robinson highlights some of the methodological difficulties and shortcomings concerning notions of normativeness which are prevalent in the study of the relationship between Islam and Christianity. Adopting a new framework of analysis, Robinson submits a re-evaluation of the significance of several Qur'anic dicta referring to Christian doctrine and themes.[22] Among the tentative findings presented by Robinson are that the opening chapter of the Qur'an, *al-Fātiḥa*, was intended to replace the Lord's Prayer and that sura 112 symbolizes an instinctive monotheistic response to the Christology of the Nicene-Constantinopolitan Creed.

[22] Fred Donner described some of the earlier work on the Qur'an and its relationship with Judaism and Christianity as being 'crassly reductionist' (Donner 2006: 35).

Part III. The Qur'an: Textual Transmission, Codification, Manuscripts, Inscriptions, and Printed Editions

The study of early Qur'anic manuscript materials has a distinguished history and in the chapter by François Déroche a summary is presented of the pioneering work of scholars such as Jacob Georg Christian Adler, Michele Amari, Adolf Grohmann, and Nabia Abbott. Commending the technical advances in the field, Déroche also acknowledges the positive contribution made to the study of early Qur'an manuscripts by disciplinary scholarship in palaeography, epigraphy, codicology, numismatics, art history, and papyrology. He predicts that such advances in the scholarship will play an important role in the resolution of questions such as the chronology of the textual transmission of the Qur'an (Déroche 2019). It is the historical trajectories of the transmission of the Qur'an from its origins until its final presentation as a fixed text which are traced in the contribution by Yasin Dutton. Probing the elaborate nature of the relationship between pre-revelation and post-revelation phases of the text's spoken and written Qur'an form, Dutton discusses the historical steps which led to the standardization of the corpus of Qur'anic readings. The ground-breaking study of Qur'anic variants was pioneered by scholars such as Theodor Nöldeke, Gotthelf Bergsträsser, Otto Pretzl, and Arthur Jeffery. In his chapter Mustafa Shah presents a survey of their work and its impact. He contends that, hitherto, treatments of *qirāʾāt* have been broached through a confined pool of materials which obscure the context of their history. He estimates that the wider availability of critical editions of manuscripts on *qirāʾāt* and early Qur'an manuscripts should help achieve a profounder understanding of approaches to their authentication and synthesis within classical Islamic scholarship.

The illustrious way in which the text of the Qur'an was transcribed, embellished, and preserved is addressed in two chapters by Sheila Blair. In the first of these Blair investigates how an oral revelation was transformed into a written document and how the form of that document changed to meet the varying needs of the expanding Muslim community. The conclusions reached by Blair are significant for she explains that Qur'anic materials are not only vital sources for artistic expression, but they also furnish key windows into the social and cultural history of the Islamic tradition. In her second contribution Blair explores some of the latest research findings on the inscriptions of Qur'anic texts on architecture, physical objects, and other solid materials. Blair's summation of the importance of these inscriptions draws critical attention to the precision of layout, technique, and style employed in their use on buildings and objects in ways which enrich aspects of the Qur'an's message. In her chapter apposite consideration is given to the application of methodologies for the study of inscriptions. Efim Rezvan's chapter reviews the production of printed editions of the Qur'an and the role of technological innovations.With a concern for identifying key phases in their production, Rezvan explains the elaborate history which lay behind the appearance of these editions, highlighting materials produced by means of movable type and lithography; he also discusses the appearance of facsimile editions of the Qur'an.

Part IV. Structural and Literary Dimensions of the Qur'an

The study of the literary elements of the Qur'an has attracted considerable attention in recent years. In this part of the Handbook research germane to the text's language, vocabulary, composition, style, chronology, structure, inimitability, influence, and its relationship with other literary forms is discussed. The chapter by Mathias Zahniser assesses the debates surrounding the question of the language of the Qur'an and notions of a formal literary koine. Stressing the fact that scholarship has yet to form a consensus as to the 'exact language of the Qur'an as uttered by Muḥammad and received by the Muslim community during his lifetime', Zahniser compares the various theories adduced to explain the characteristics of the original Qur'anic dialect. He begins with a discussion of the thesis advocated by Karl Vollers (d. 1909) in his *Volkssprache und Schriftsprache im alten Arabien* (1906) in which it is maintained that the original Arabic of the Qur'an did not exhibit grammatical inflection and moves on to assess the work of Jan Retsö, who postulates that *ʿarabiyya* was 'a medium for messages from the non-human world'.

It was the Australian scholar Arthur Jeffery who in his work on the foreign vocabulary of the Qur'an commented that 'Little further advance can be made in our interpretation of the Qur'an or of the life of Muḥammad until an exhaustive study has been made of the vocabulary of the Qur'an' (Jeffery 1938: vii). Showing that much of the early scholarship devoted to the vocabulary of the Qur'an fell within the contours of the attempts to shed light on the Qur'an's perceived substrate influences, Mustafa Shah probes key contributions produced over the years. Moving on from the vocabulary of the Qur'an to its composition, Michel Cuypers's chapter provides an investigation into the question of the thematic unity and coherency of elements of the Qur'an's narratives and pericopes. Based on the theories of the biblical scholar Roland Meynet, who explored rhetorical paradigms and patterns in ancient Semitic materials, Cuypers's work on the Qur'an's composition seeks to expound upon the manner by which suras 'are connected' and how they 'compose coherent sets with semantic unity'. Cuypers claims that his work demonstrates that 'we can no longer endorse what Voltaire wrote in his *Dictionnaire philosophique*: "The Qur'an is a rhapsody without connections, without order, without art"' (Cuypers 2015: 181–2).

Rhetorical dimensions of the Qur'an are previewed in Muhammad Abdel Haleem's contribution. Underscoring the importance of rhetoric to understanding Qur'anic narratives and discourse, Haleem maintains that although the study of the language and style of the Qur'an has attracted more attention in recent Western academic scholarship, the relevance of *balāgha* (normally translated as 'rhetoric') has been imprudently overlooked in such treatments (Haleem 2017). Propounding the view that a solid grasp of the aesthetic features of the Qur'an is essential to achieving a profounder understanding of the nuances of meaning in the text, Haleem explains that they are incontrovertibly interrelated in their functions.

The structure of the Qur'an with reference to its inner-Qur'anic chronology is examined in the chapter by Nicolai Sinai. Briefly taking stock of some of the early scholarship on chronology, he explains that the chronological sequencing of the chapters and passages of the Qur'an was initially developed by Weil in his *Historisch-kritische*, where he subdivided chapters into four consecutive periods, three of which were identified as being Meccan and one Medinan. The classification was complemented by Nöldeke, who refined the boundaries of these broad periods of revelation; in his era such was the influence of Nöldeke's classification of the later suras that John Rodwell commented that Nöldeke's theory 'is based upon a searching criticism and minute analysis of the component verses of each, and may be safely taken as a standard, which ought not to be departed from without weighty reasons' (Rodwell 1909: 3). It is proposed that a perceptive understanding of the complexities of the internal chronology of the Qur'an can help shed light on its concepts, themes, and narratives. Dismissing criticisms made against a diachronic approach to the analysis of the text's inner structure, Sinai states that it is also possible to discern 'relationships of temporal priority and posteriority between different suras or passages', which in turn demonstrate that the Qur'anic corpus displays a striking 'convergence of style (including verse length and rhyme), literary structure, terminology, and content' (Sinai 2017 and 2010). A conspectus of the impressive body of research devoted to the subject of inner-sura structure is set out in the chapter by Mustansir Mir. Explaining the advantages of a synchronic approach to the analysis of structure, he points out that analyses of topics such as intertextuality, contextual effects, discourse markers, verbal echoes and correspondences, scriptural authority, and the proportionate length of a sura's sections are adequately effective in revealing the constructional unity of suras. Mir's work has been influential in drawing attention to the theme of Qur'anic coherence as formulated through the pioneering work of Farāhī and Amīn Aḥsan Iṣlāḥī. This is predicted on a theory of *naẓm* (composition) which theorizes that each Qur'anic sura has a distinctive central theme or *ʿamūd* which cohesively binds the chapter (Mir 1986).

The doctrine of the Qur'an's inimitability (*iʿjāz al-Qurʾān*) posed all sorts of theoretical challenges which were expounded upon in classical theological, exegetical, and literary texts, including seminal works such as al-Bāqillānī's *Iʿjāz al-Qurʾān*, al-Qāḍī ʿAbd al-Jabbār's *Iʿjāz al-Qurʾān*, and al-Jurjānī's *Dalāʾil al-iʿjāz*. Ayman El-Desouki's chapter offers a synopsis of the discussions on the concept of *iʿjāz*, indicating that certain modern attempts to develop a critical theoretical language with which to approach the singularity of a text have faced similar challenges. The imposing debates about the complexities of *iʿjāz* illustrate the scale of the Qur'an's literary influence and this is reviewed in Geert Jan van Gelder's chapter. He posits that although one should not underestimate the 'influence of the Qur'an on all aspects of medieval Islamic culture, including the Arabic literary tradition', this influence was chiefly manifested in interactions with the text and its ideas as opposed to ambitious attempts to emulate its style.[23] A further aspect of the Qur'an's literary influence is reflected in the interface between the Qur'an and Arabic poetry and this is appraised in the contribution by Stefan Sperl. One of the striking features of the Qur'an's references to poetry is the fact that the text is at pains to distance itself from the claim by the Prophet's adversaries that he himself was a poet or that the Qur'an constituted poetry. Commenting on the complex nature of the relationship between the Qur'an and Arabic poetry, Sperl makes the potent point that poetry has

[23] For a range of related studies on the relationship between *adab* and the Qur'an see Sha'ar 2017.

long been avidly engaged in an inter-textual dialogue with the Qur'an which has taken numerous forms, subject to changing historical and cultural circumstances. A cursory glance at classical grammatical and exegetical literature brings to light the extent to which poetry was enthusiastically used for the purposes of linguistic justification and exemplification in classical studies of the language of the Qur'an.

Part V. Topics and Themes of the Qur'an

The attempt within recent scholarship to isolate and detach the Qur'an from its later exegetical treatments and expositions has led to the gauging of the text's topics and themes from a variegated range of perspectives. In her chapter Ulrika Mårtensson examines the Qur'anic notion of revelation (*waḥī* or *ilhām*), discussing its conceptual relevance and link to the more specific doctrines of prophecy. Adopting a comparative approach, Mårtensson contends that there is persuasive evidence which corroborates the existence of parallels between biblical and Qur'anic concepts of divine-to-human communication. She also looks at how these share similarities with the classical Greek theory of oracle communication. Exploring the core theological proclamations and doctrines of the Qur'an, Stephen Burge's chapter examines the context in which they are articulated in the text. These include the central belief in the oneness of God (*tawḥīd*); the theme of God as the Creator of the universe; and doctrines relating to the supernatural world.

Shifting focus to the topic of law and the Qur'an, Joseph Lowry scrutinizes the distinctive range of legislative passages and legal-ethico discussions which are found in the text. He observes that although the epistemological primacy of the Qur'an is taken as a given in later legal discourses, the question of its historical basis has divided opinions. Lowry presses home the point that 'specific rules of conduct and larger ideas about law constitute important features of the Qur'anic text'. Turning attention to the moral framework of the Qur'an, the subject of ethics is discussed in Ebrahim Moosa's chapter in which he sets out to trace the confluence of ethical themes and ideas in the Qur'an and their place within the history of Islamic moral thought. Referring to the fact that considerable research has been devoted to the analysis of the moral vision of the Qur'an, Moosa explains that while Muslim ethicists would 'insist that the Qur'an forms the basis of their ethical deliberations', the fact remains that a conjunction of factors shaped ethical discourses. Accordingly, Moosa points out that the quest to find an exclusively Qur'an-based ethics remains 'a work-in-progress'.

In the chapter by Sebastian Günther a survey is presented of the eschatological doctrines of the Qur'an. These include the Qur'anic conception of the apocalyptic cessation of this world; the end of life on earth; the resurrection and judgement of the dead; and their attendant reward or punishment in the afterlife. Günther focuses on the symbolism and imagery which the Qur'an imposingly employs in its treatment of such themes. The expressive imagery associated with Islamic eschatological teachings has for centuries played a critical role in shaping perceptions of the faith and Günther's chapter imparts some sense of the requisite context in which such teachings need to be understood.

Confirming the fact that the Qur'an is carried by a large cast of dramatis personae, the majority of whom have counterparts in the Bible, Anthony Johns reflects on the portrayal of these figures and individuals in its exempla and narratives. Johns does take the opportunity to explain that for many years the Qur'an was regarded as 'an epigone that appeared without antecedents in 7th century Arabia, lacking internal coherence, and the roles played by its characters of minor interest'. Dismissing such interpretations as being impressionistic and disingenuous, Johns affirms that the eloquence and vividness with which personalities and characters are depicted substantiate the status of the Qur'an as a worthy participant in the discourses of Late Antiquity.

Switching to the subject of politics and the Qur'an, Stefan Wild investigates the connection between the Qur'an as a receptacle of political ideas in the formative years of the Islamic tradition and the relevance of its political constructs within modern contexts. Wild defines 'Politics' as the question of legitimate versus illegitimate Muslim rule. Also focusing on the issue of constructs, it is the Qur'anic conception of jihad which is subjected to critical review in the chapter by Asma Afsaruddin. Offering an overview of the discussions and debates concerning its import in both classical and modern contexts, Afsaruddin reaches the conclusion that there existed distinctions between its historical bases in the Qur'an and its representation as a conceptualized construct in later exegetical and juridical literature. In a second contribution Afsaruddin reflects on contested interpretations of key verses in the Qur'an that relate to women and gendered roles in society, presenting their critique by modern Muslim feminist exegetes; in such critiques interpretations are historicized and construed as being 'specific products of their time and milieu'. Her conclusion is that in the framework of the current debates about modernity and reform in Islamic thought, it is possible to retrieve 'a more faithful, non-patriarchal understanding of Qur'anic injunctions concerning women'; this proceeds from the premise that an egalitarian ethic serves as the desideratum of Qur'anic teachings and legislation.

Part VI. The Qur'an in Context: Translation and Culture

Over the centuries the determined efforts to translate the text of the Qur'an led to the accumulation of a fecund body of literary materials. In the first of three chapters devoted to reviewing the material and ideas associated with the translation of the Qur'an, Ziad Elmarsafy chronicles the history of key translations of the Qur'an into Western languages (mainly English, French, German, and Latin) from the Middle Ages to the present day. In the chapter Elmarsafy discusses the production and reception of these translations and he considers the translation of the text with reference to the growth of Arabic and Islamic Studies as an academic discipline. Drawing attention to the translation of the Qur'an into non-European languages including Swahili, Persian, Turkish, Mandarin Chinese, and Malay, Brett Wilson examines the combination of factors which had a bearing on efforts to translate the text; and he assesses the historical context of vernacular commentaries.[24] Wilson concludes that crucial advances in print technology, the activities of missionaries, and even the discourses of reform contributed to the intensification of activity in the sphere of translations. In a related study, the role that context plays in determining the meaning of words and sentences in the translation of the Qur'an is considered by Muhammad Abdel Haleem. Identifying linguistic features which can cause difficulties in determining meaning, and referring to a selection of examples from translations of the Qur'an, *tafsīr* literature, and Qur'anic Studies, Haleem rehearses what contextual clues are given in the Qur'an to elucidate the semantic compass of words.[25]

From the techniques and challenges of translating the text to aspects of its impact, the dynamic role of the Qur'an as a vehicle and transformer of popular culture forms the central theme of the chapter by Bruce Lawrence. Referring to a selection of examples from magic and popular music, Lawrence shows how interactions with the text assertively expanded the temporal and spatial boundaries of the Qur'an. Pursuing the question of external literary influences, Jeffrey Einboden studies the Qur'an's discernible impact on Western literatures. This is traced not only in terms of 'oppositions and overlaps', but also with regard to topical 'subjects and stylistic techniques'. Referring to an arresting range of literary texts and materials, Einboden argues that this formal influence is evident in the work of Western poets and prose writers from the Middle Ages to postmodernity.

Part VII. Qur'anic Interpretation: Scholarship and Literature of Early, Classical, and Modern Exegesis

The discipline of *tafsīr* has occupied a prominent place within the academic study of the Qur'an and this section of the Handbook presents forms of Qur'anic exegesis and their frameworks of analysis across a range of historical periods and contexts. Andrew Rippin's opening chapter follows the historical rise of the commentary tradition, reflecting upon the significance of the early exegetical treatises attributed to Maʿmar ibn Rāshid (d. 154/770), Ibn Jurayj (d. 150/767), Muqātil ibn Sulaymān (d. 150/767), Muḥammad ibn al-Sāʾib al-Kalbī (d. 146/763), Sufyān al-Thawrī (d. 161/787), and Yaḥyā ibn Sallām (d. 200/815). Indicating that 'the examination of early *tafsīr* inevitably involves difficult historiographical questions that are common to many facets of the study of the rise of Islam', he weighs up the historical importance of the debates about the authenticity and design of these early texts. The literary analysis of early exegetical treatises led John Wansbrough to question the traditional accounts of the historical emergence of the Qur'an and in this regard he attached particular importance to the

24 The sensitivities and controversies surrounding the issue of translating the text even in the modern context can be gauged from Wilson's account of Marmaduke Pickthall's attempts to persuade Egyptian Azhari scholars of the benefits of such an edition (Wilson 2014: 196–204).

25 An extended version of this chapter appeared as 'The Role of Context in Interpreting and Translating the Qur'an', *Journal of Qur'anic Studies* 20/1 (2018), 44–66.

connection between commentaries and the biography of the Prophet (*tafsīr* and *sīra*). It is this topic which forms the subject of Maher Jarrar's chapter. Presenting a digest of the academic propositions regarding the exegetical designs of the *sīra*, Jarrar advances the view that the *sīra* does not represent a scheme of salvation history, but rather a communal cultural memory which was preserved by interlocking processes of oral and written transmission. (Rippin 1985: 151; Wansbrough 1977: 121–8).

It is widely recognized that the early grammarian contribution to activity in the field of *tafsīr* is colossal. With specific reference to the works of the grammarians, in his chapter Kees Versteegh considers the importance of the types of exegesis found in the earliest grammatical commentaries on the Qur'an. The chapter advances the view that grammar emerged from the matrices of the exegetical sciences as a corollary of the decision by early scholars to confine their attention to the analysis of the structural edifices of the Qur'an's language. Trends and developments in classical exegesis during the period 800–1000 are studied in Ulrika Mårtensson's chapter. Mårtensson is particularly interested in assessing the impact that the systematization of the classical Islamic sciences and transformations in the discourses of linguistics and legal hermeneutics had upon the genre of *tafsīr*. Taking this process of systematization as her cue, she assesses the achievements of seminal commentaries produced in the early medieval periods.[26]

With its focus on the development of medieval *tafsīr* scholarship, Walid Saleh's chapter discusses the extent to which regional and ideological factors seemingly shaped the discourses of exegesis. The chapter also gives due consideration to the historical significance of the works produced between the appearance of al-Ṭabarī's renowned *tafsīr* and the commentaries of al-Zamakhsharī, al-Bayḍāwī, and al-Qūnawī (d. 673/1274). Deliberating the question of impact, Saleh appraises the nature of the Ottoman contribution to the field and draws attention to the dynamic role that its libraries played in preserving *tafsīr*'s abundant literary heritage. He also points out that although the number of published commentaries available is unquestionably immense, there remains a vast number of unpublished materials. For this reason, Saleh makes the assertion that our understanding of the discipline is still evolving. Within exegetical literature, the attestation of materials from the corpus of literary materials comprising biblical stories and Jewish and Christian sacred history, *isrāʾīliyyāt*, is a salient feature of its narratives. Explaining the importance of this corpus of material and its edifying function, Roberto Tottoli compares changing attitudes within the early and classical exegetical tradition towards its utilization. Although in the early historical periods *isrāʾīliyyāt* materials were frequently adduced in *tafsīr* works, Tottoli explains that a pronounced hostility towards their employment crystallized in the medieval periods and resurfaced in the modern era. Noting the methodological problems inherent in defining this body of materials, Tottoli introduces the growing body of research devoted to its study and also highlights the importance of understanding later medieval attempts to augment and embellish these narratives.

Within the context of the contemporary periods, in his second contribution Walid Saleh charts the meteoric rise of interest in *tafsīr*. He attributes the popularity of *tafsīr* to

[26] For translations of texts and accompanying analysis see Hamza, Rizvi, with Mayer 2008.

a number of factors: firstly, the role of the internet in facilitating access to sources; and, secondly, the prominence of *tafsīr* in Islamicate languages. The discerning point is made that the politics of scriptural theology also had an acute impact upon the promotion and dissemination of specific genres within the field of *tafsīr*. It was Norman Calder who made the compelling assertion that 'in the hands of a skilled and sensitive exegete any Qur'anic verse might be found to have implications ranging across the scholastic disciplines' (Calder 1993: 101).

Part VIII. Qur'anic Exegesis: Discourses, Formats, and Hermeneutics

The genre of exegesis supplies a unique forum for the expression of ideological, doctrinal, and literary constructs and various forms of scholarship produced in these contexts are presented in the ensuing selection of chapters. Focusing on historical developments, the chapter by Sajjad Rizvi investigates normative approaches to exegesis from a Twelver Shīʿī standpoint. Rizvi discloses that in its early expressions the exegesis of the Qur'an tended to be confined to selective glosses attributed to the Imams, who were considered inviolate authorities. However, the countenance of the approach to *tafsīr* within Twelver Shīʿī thought dramatically changed with the appearance of works by scholars such as Abū Jaʿfar al-Ṭūsī (d. 460/1067), author of the *al-Tibyān fī tafsīr al-Qurʾān* and Shaykh al-Faḍl al-Ṭabrisī (d. 548/1154), who compiled the *Majmaʿ al-bayān fī tafsīr al-Qurʾān*. As Rizvi observes, these were texts which covered discussions and debates germane to language, law, philosophy, and theology, including mystical treatments of the Qur'an. Remaining with Imāmī approaches to *tafsīr*, Ismāʿīlī interpretive strategies are examined in the chapter by Ismail Poonawala. It should be noted that the normative and conventional forms of exegesis which were in vogue in Sunnī, Shīʿī, and Zaydī circles were considered to be peripheral to Ismāʿīlī *taʾwīl*, which was concerned principally with the decipherment of the esoteric meaning of the text and its hidden truths (*ḥaqāʾiq*). Poonawala contends that despite the fact that Ismāʿīlīs did not cultivate the science of *tafsīr* in terms of compiling standard Qur'anic commentaries, their literature is replete with instances of the esoteric and allegorical interpretation of Qur'anic verses, for which they devised complex principles and elaborate frameworks.

The chapter by Valerie J. Hoffman and Sulaiman al-Shueili surveys the exegetical activities of one of the last surviving offshoots of the Khārijī movement, the Ibāḍīs. Their survey shows that while the Ibāḍīs were prolific and skilled writers in the area of philology, rhetoric, theology, and even the sciences of Qur'an interpretation, their own *tafsīr* efforts were interwoven and amassed with Sunnī materials, and used apposite junctures in the various commentaries to proclaim their own teachings. As the authors demonstrate, this was certainly true for the earliest extant Ibāḍī *tafsīr* by the Berber scholar Hūd ibn Muḥakkam al-Hawwārī (d. *c.*290/903), which was 'an abridged and doctrinally adapted version of the *tafsīr* of the Basran scholar Yaḥyā ibn Sallām'.

The exponential growth of the Muslim ascetic-mystical (Sufi) exegetical tradition from its inception in the eighth century CE, through its 'classical period' in the tenth–eleventh centuries, to its evolution in the late Middle Ages is examined in the chapter by Alexander Knysh. Covering a monumental range of commentaries and treatises, Knysh discusses the originality and calibre of the accomplishments of mystical exegesis. The chapter also dissects the intricacies of the hermeneutical techniques that Sufis adopted in order to reveal the allegorical-esoteric aspects of the Qur'an, intimating why they sought to demonstrate the unassailable superiority of their inspired exegesis (*taʾwīl*) over the exoteric, historical-philological, and legal commentary (*tafsīr*) of non-Sufi scholars. From the numinous commentaries of the Sufis to speculative theological discourses, Tariq Jaffer's chapter reviews a range of dogmatic discussions in *tafsīr* literature. Examining the import and design of theological statements attributed to Ibn ʿAbbās (d. *c.*68/687) and Mujāhid (d. 104/722), together with related discussions which permeate the works of al-Ṭabarī, al-Māturīdī (d. 333/944), and Fakhr al-Dīn al-Rāzī (d. 606/1210), the chapter also defines the theoretical basis of theological tendencies in the writings of select Muʿtazilī and Shīʿī luminaries. Turning to the subject of philosophical exegesis, the chapter by Jules Janssens gives a systematic overview of the ways in which philosophers such as al-Kindī (d. *c.*256/870), Ibn Sīnā (d. 427/1037), and Ibn Rushd (d. 595/1198) sought to use the forum of *tafsīr* to elaborate on affinities and confluences between doctrinal statements found in the Qur'an and their own conceptual standpoints on a range of philosophical issues. These included views on the absolute transcendence of God and His immateriality; the doctrine of emanation; and the legitimacy of philosophy as a discipline. Janssens also describes how individuals such as al-Suhrawardī (d. 587/1191), Ibn ʿArabī (d. 638/1240), and Mullā Ṣadrā (d. 1050/1640) skilfully used their own schema of philosophical and mystical thought as an explicatory guiding framework for the interpretation of the Qur'an.

Focusing on aesthetic treatments of the Qur'an, in the chapter by Kamal Abu-Deeb an analytical study is provided of three of the arguably finest commentaries which were renowned for their commanding exposition of the stylistic and rhetorical virtues of the Qur'an: al-Zamakhsharī's *al-Kashshāf*, Ibn ʿArabī's *al-Futūḥāt al-Makkiyya*, and Abū Ḥayyān's *al-Baḥr al-muḥīṭ*. Explaining that the tradition of Qur'anic interpretation forms one of the richest aspects of cultural production in Arabic, Abu-Deeb points to the promise offered by aesthetic approaches to the explication of the text. His view is that they allow the text to be appreciated in evocative ways. The connection between science and *tafsīr* is considered in the chapter by Robert Morrison. Applauding the ingenuity with which the epistemological claims of science were absorbed into the body of *tafsīr* literature, Morrison also flags the use of scientific material in exegesis with reference to the modern periods. The aforementioned forms and types of commentary confirm that the inference that classical exegesis was driven by the vapid and derivative treatment of previously transmitted materials and thought is mistaken and belied by the sophisticated range of discourses assiduously cultivated within the confines of *tafsīr*.

Scholarship on classical and modern approaches to defining theoretical tools, paradigms, and procedures for the explication of the Qur'an (processes often equated with hermeneutics) provides the background for the final selection of chapters. Making the point that the manner by which preliminary theoretical frameworks regulated and informed the pursuit of *tafsīr* remains a moot point, Johanna Pink discusses the significance of applied hermeneutics as evidenced in classical Qur'anic commentaries. The chapter also looks at how external factors influenced the formulation of exegetical strategies. Expanding the discussions on approaches to exegesis, the voluminous body of literature associated with the 'classical sciences of the Qur'an' is surveyed in the chapter by Martin Nguyen. Assessing the historical importance of treatises composed by Abū'l-Qāsim Ibn Ḥabīb (d. 406/1016), al-Zarkashī (d. 794/1392), and al-Suyūṭī, Nguyen also details the main features and contents of these works. From classical discussions of hermeneutics to modern conceptions of the subject, the final chapter in this volume by Massimo Campanini discusses the possibility of deriving a philosophical hermeneutics from the Qur'an's commentary tradition. Grappling with the essential character of this hermeneutics and its tenor, he also highlights the relevance of the concept of *aletheia* or disclosure (in Heidegger's terms) with reference to the Qur'an. Campanini comments that the aggregation of new methods and frameworks of *taʾwīl* has the potential to contribute constructively to the discourses of reform in Islamic thought.

Bibliography

Abdel Haleem, Muhammad. *Exploring the Qur'an: Context and Impact*. London and New York: I. B. Tauris, 2017.

Afsaruddin, Asma. *Contemporary Issues in Islam*. Edinburgh: Edinburgh University Press, 2015.

Bakhos, Carol and Michael Cook (eds.). *Islam and Its Past: Jahiliyya, Late Antiquity, and the Qur'an*. Corby: Oxford University Press, 2017.

Bevilacqua, Alexander. 'The Qur'an Translations of Marracci and Sale', *Journal of the Warburg and Courtauld Institutes* 76 (2013), 93–130.

Bevilacqua, Alexander. *The Republic of Arabic Letters: Islam and the European Enlightenment*. Cambridge, MA: The Belknap Press of Harvard University Press, 2018.

Blair, Sheila and Jonathan Bloom. *By the Pen and What They Write: Writing in Islamic Art and Culture*. New Haven and London: Yale University Press, 2017.

Burge, Stephen (ed.). *The Meaning of the Word: Lexicology and Qur'anic Exegesis*. Oxford: Oxford University Press, in association with the Institute of Ismaili Studies, 2015.

Burman, Thomas E. *Reading the Qurʾān in Latin Christendom, 1140–1560*. Philadelphia: University of Pennsylvania Press, 2007.

Burnett, Stephen C. 'Later Christian Hebraists'. In: Magna Sæbø (eds.). *Hebrew Bible/Old Testament: The History of its Interpretation, II: From the Renaissance to the Enlightenment*, pp. 785–801. Göttingen: Vandenhoeck & Ruprecht, 2008.

Calder, Norman. '*Tafsīr* from Ṭabarī to Ibn Kathīr: Problems in the Description of a Genre, Illustrated with Reference to the Story of Abraham'. In: Gerald R. Hawting and Abdul-Kader A. Shareef (eds.). *Approaches to the Qurʾān*, pp. 101–40. New York: Routledge, 1993.

Campanini, Massimo. *Philosophical Perspectives on Modern Qurʾānic Exegesis: Key Paradigms and Concepts*. Sheffield: Equinox Publishing Ltd, 2016.

Cuypers, Michel. *The Composition of the Qur'an: Rhetorical Analysis*. London: Bloomsbury, 2015.

Cuypers, Michel. *A Qurʾānic Apocalypse: A Reading of the Thirty-Three Last Sūrahs of the Qurʾān*. Atlanta, GA: Lockwood Press, 2018.

Dannenfeldt, K. H. 'The Renaissance Humanists and the Knowledge of Arabic', *Studies in the Renaissance* 2 (1955), 96–117.

Déroche, François. *Le Coran, une histoire plurielle: Essai sur la formation du texte coranique*. Paris: Le Seuil, 2019.

Donner, Fred. 'The Historical Context'. In: Jane Dammen McAuliffe (ed.). *Cambridge Companion to the Qurʾān*, pp. 23–39. Cambridge: Cambridge University Press, 2006.

Donner, Fred. 'The Qur'ān in Recent Scholarship: Challenges and Desiderata'. In: Gabriel Reynolds (ed.). *The Qurʾān in its Historical Context*, pp. 29–50. London: Routledge, 2008.

Fisher, Greg (ed.). *Arabs and Empires Before Islam*. Oxford: Oxford University Press, 2015.

Fleischer, H. *Beidhawii Commentarius in Coranum*. Lipsiae: Sumptibus F. C. G. Vogelii, 1846–48.

Flügel, Gustav. 'Ueber Muḥammad bin Isḥâḳ's *Fihrist al-ʿulûm*'. *Zeitschrift der Deutschen Morgenländischen Gesellschaft* 13/4 (1859), 559–650.

Fück, Johann. *Die arabischen Studien in Europa bis in den Anfang des 20 Jahrhunderts*. Leipzig: Otto Harrassowitz, 1955.

Geiger, Abraham. *Was hat Mohammed aus dem Judenthume aufgenommen*? Bonn: F. Baaden, 1833. Translated as *Judaism and Islam*, trans. F. M. Young (Madras, M.D.C.S.P.C.K. Press, 1898).

Glei, Reinhold F. and Roberto Tottoli. *Ludovico Marracci at Work: The Evolution of his Latin Translation of the Qur'ān in the Light of his Newly Discovered Manuscripts. With an Edition and a Comparative Linguistic Analysis of Sura 18*. Wiesbaden: Harrassowitz, 2016.

Görke, Andreas and Johanna Pink (eds.). *Tafsīr and Islamic Intellectual History: Exploring the Boundaries of a Genre*. Oxford: Oxford University Press in association with the Institute of Ismaili Studies, 2014.

Hamilton, Alistair. *William Bedwell, the Arabist, 1563–1632*. Leiden: E. J. Brill/Leiden University Press, 1985.

Hamilton, Alastair. 'To Rescue the Honour of the Germans: Qurʾan Translations by Eighteenth- and Early Nineteenth-Century German Protestants', *Journal of the Warburg and Courtauld Institutes* 77 (2014), 173–209.

Hamilton, Alastair. 'The Qur'an as Chrestomathy in Early Modern Europe'. In: Jan Loop, Alastair Hamilton, and Charles Burnett (eds.). *The Teaching and Learning of Arabic in Early Modern Europe*, pp. 213–29. Leiden and Boston: Brill, 2017.

Hamilton, Alastair. 'After Marracci: The Reception of Ludovico Marracci's Edition of the Qur'an in Northern Europe from the Late Seventeenth to the Early Nineteenth Centuries', *Journal of Qur'anic Studies* 20/3 (2018), 175–92.

Hamza, Feras, Sajjad Rizvi (eds.). with Farhana Mayer. *The Anthology of Qurʾānic Commentaries: On the Nature of the Divine*. Oxford: Oxford University Press in association with the Institute of Ismaili Studies, 2008.

Hawting, Gerald R. *The Idea of Idolatry and the Emergence of Islam: From Polemic to History*. Cambridge: Cambridge University Press, 1999.

Hawting, G. R. and Abdul-Kader A. Shareef (eds.). *Approaches to the Qurʾān*, New York: Routledge, 1993.

Heschel, Susannah. *Abraham Geiger and the Jewish Jesus*. Chicago: University of Chicago, 1998.

Hilali, Asma. *The Sanaa Palimpsest: The Transmission of the Qur'an in the First Centuries* AH. London and Oxford: Oxford University Press, in association with the Institute of Ismaili Studies, 2016.

Jankowsky, Kurt R. 'Johann Jacob Reiske (1716–1774): Leading Force in the Establishment of Oriental and Classical Scholarship in Germany'. In: Eduardo Guimarães and Diana Luz Pessoa de Barros (eds.). *History of Linguistics*, pp. 183–96. Philadelphia: J. Benjamins Pub. Co., 2007.

Jeffery, Arthur. *The Foreign Vocabulary of the* Qurʾān. Baroda: Oriental Institute,1938.

Jones, Robert. 'On the Value of the Arabic Language' by Thomas Erpenius. Translated from the Latin. *Manuscripts of the Middle East* 1 (1986), 15–25.

Loop, Jan. *Johann Heinrich Hottinger: Arabic and Islamic Studies in the Seventeenth Century.* Oxford: Oxford University Press, 2013.

Loop, Jan. 'Arabic Poetry as Teaching Material in Early Modern Grammars and Textbooks'. In Jan Loop et al. (eds.). *The Teaching and Learning of Arabic in Early Modern Europe*, pp. 230–71. Leiden and Boston: Brill, 2017.

Loop, Jan, Alastair Hamilton, and Charles Burnett (eds.). *The Teaching and Learning of Arabic in Early Modern Europe*. Leiden; Boston: Brill, 2017.

McAuliffe, Jane (ed.). *Encyclopaedia of the Qurʾān*. (6 vols., including index) Leiden: E. J. Brill, 2001–6.

McAuliffe, Jane Dammen (ed.). *Cambridge Companion to the Qurʾān*. Cambridge: Cambridge University Press, 2006.

McAuliffe, Jane Dammen, Barry D. Walfish, and Joseph W. Goering (eds.). *With Reverence for the Word: Medieval Scriptural Exegesis in Judaism, Christianity, and Islam*. Oxford and New York: Oxford University Press, 2003.

Marracci, Ludovico. *Prodromus ad refutationem Alcorani*. 4 vols. Rome, 1691.

Marracci, Ludovico. *Alcorani Textus Universus: ex Correctioribus Arabum Exemplaribus Summa Fide, atque Pulcherrimis Characteribus Descriptus*... 2 vols. Padua: Ex Typographia Seminarii, 1698.

Miller, Gregory J. 'Theodor Bibliander's Machumetis saracenorum principis eiusque successorum vitae, doctrina ac ipse alcoran (1543) as the Sixteenth-Century "Encyclopedia" of Islam', *Islam and Christian–Muslim Relations* 24/2 (2013), 241–54.

Monfasani, John. 'Cusanus, the Greeks, and Islam'. In: Thomas M. Izbicki, J. Aleksander, and D. Duclow (eds.). *Nicholas of Cusa and Times of Transition*, pp. 96–112. Leiden: Brill, 2018.

Neuwirth, Angelika. 'Orientalism in Oriental Studies: Qurʾānic Studies as a Case in Point', *Journal of Qur'anic Studies* 9/2 (2007), 115–27.

Neuwirth, Angelika. *The Qur'an and Late Antiquity: A Shared Heritage*. New York: Oxford University Press, 2019. (Translation of *Der Koran als Text* by Samuel Wilder).

Neuwirth, Angelika, Nicolai Sinai, and Michael Marx (eds.). *The Qurʾān in Context: Historical and Literary Investigations into the Qurʾānic Milieu*, pp. 1–15. Leiden: E. J. Brill, 2010.

Nöldeke, Theodor. *Geschichte des Qorâns*. Göttingen, 1860. Revised by Friedrich Schwally and supplemented by Gotthelf Bergsträsser and Otto Pretzl. Leipzig: Dieterich'sche Verlagsbuchhandlung, 1909–38.

Reynolds, Gabriel (ed.). *The Qurʾān in its Historical Context*. London: Routledge, 2008.

Reynolds, Gabriel. *The Qurʾān and its Biblical Subtext*. London: Routledge, 2010.

Reynolds, Gabriel (ed.). *New Perspectives on the Qurʾān: the Qurʾān in its Historical Context II*. London: Routledge, 2011.

Rippin, Andrew (ed.). *The Qur'an: Formative Interpretation*. Aldershot: Ashgate Publishing, 1999.

Rippin, Andrew (ed.). *The Qur'an: Style and Contents*. Aldershot: Ashgate Publishing, 2001.

Rippin, Andrew. 'Western Scholarship and the Qur'an'. In: Jane McAuliffe (ed.). *Companion to the Qurʾān*, pp. 236–51. Cambridge: Cambridge University Press, 2006.

Rippin, Andrew (ed.). *The Blackwell Companion to the Qur'an*. Oxford; Malden: Blackwell, 2006 (2nd edn. 2017).

Rodwell, J. M. *The Koran*. Translated from the Arabic. Introduction by Revd G. Margoliouth. London, Dent & Sons, 1909.

Sale, George. *AlCoran of Mohammed With Explanatory Notes; Various Readings from Savary's Version of the Koran; And a Preliminary Discourse on the Religious and Political Condition of the Arabs Before the Days of Mohammed*. London: William Tegg and Co., 1877 (1st edn. 1734).

Sha'ar, Nuha (ed.). *The Qur'an and Adab: the Shaping of Literary Traditions in Classical Islam*. London: Oxford University Press in association with the Institute of Ismaili Studies, 2017.

Shah, Mustafa. 'The Early Arabic Grammarians' Contributions to the Collection and Authentication of Qurʾānic Readings: The Prelude to Ibn Mujāhid's *Kitāb al-Sabʿa*', *Journal of Qur'anic Studies* 6 (2004), 72–102.

Shah, Mustafa (ed.). *Tafsīr: Interpreting the Qurʾān*, Critical Concepts in Islamic Studies. 4 vols. London: Routledge, 2013.

Sinai, Nicolai. *The Qur'an: A Historical-Critical Introduction*. New Edinburgh Islamic Surveys. Edinburgh: Edinburgh University Press, 2017.

Taji-Farouki, Suha (ed.). *The Qur'an and its Readers Worldwide: Contemporary Commentaries and Translations*. Oxford: Oxford University Press in association with the Institute of Ismaili Studies, 2015.

Toomer, G. J. *Eastern Wisedome and Learning: The Study of Arabic in Seventeenth-Century England*. Oxford: Clarendon Press, 1996.

Tottoli, Roberto. 'The Latin Translation of the Qurʾān by Johann Zechendorff (1580–1662) Discovered in Cairo Dar al-Kutub: A Preliminary Description', *Oriente Moderno* 95 (2015), 5–31.

Vrolijk, Arnoud. 'The Prince of Arabists and his Many Errors: Thomas Erpenius's Image of Joseph Scaliger and the Edition of the "Proverbia Arabica" (1614)', *Journal of the Warburg and Courtauld Institutes* 73 (2010), 297–325.

Vrolijk, Arnoud. 'Arabic Studies in the Netherlands and the Prerequisite of Social Impact: A Survey'. In: Jan Loop, Alastair Hamilton, and Charles Burnett (eds.). *The Teaching and Learning of Arabic in Early Modern Europe*, pp. 13–32. Leiden, Boston: Brill, 2017.

Vrolijk, Arnoud and Richard van Leeuwen (eds.). *Arabic Studies in the Netherlands: A Short History in Portraits, 1580–1950*. Leiden; Boston: Brill, 2013.

Wansbrough, John. *Quranic Studies: Sources and Methods of Scriptural Interpretation, Foreword, Translations and Expanded Notes* by Andrew Rippin. Amherst, NY: Prometheus Books, 2004. (Originally published in 1977.)

Watt, Montgomery. *Bell's Introduction to the Qur'an, completely revised and enlarged by* W. Montgomery Watt. Edinburgh: Edinburgh University Press, 1997. (First published 1970.)

Wilson, Brett. *Translating the Qur'an in an Age of Nationalism: Print Culture and Modern Islam in Turkey*. Oxford: Oxford University Press in association with the Institute of Ismaili Studies, 2014.

PART I

THE STATE OF QUR'ANIC STUDIES

CHAPTER 1

ACADEMIC SCHOLARSHIP AND THE QUR'AN

ANDREW RIPPIN

On the surface of it, the topic of academic scholarship and the Qur'an appears to call for a straightforward recounting of the emergence of some of the highlights of European-language works that compose what scholars might consider the 'canon' of books and essays devoted to the study of the Qur'an in its various aspects. There are, however, some fundamental definitional questions that need to be posed first, because the answers to those questions will help lead us to an appreciation of the contribution of academic scholarship on the Qur'an in the fullness of its expression, approaches, and attitudes over its relatively short history.

The key question here must be to ask what we mean by academic scholarship. Probably most people in the discipline have an intuitive sense of what this means and take the approach of saying that, like art and obscenity, 'I know it when I see it'. That, however, can hardly suffice as a reasonable means of defining the discipline or in understanding the issues that are stake.

One approach to the matter might be to focus on the word 'academic' and associate that with the academy, as we know it today in the university. That seems simple enough. However, this does raise the issue of the relationship of the university to the seminary. Certainly, academic work would generally be agreed to happen in Jewish and Christian seminary contexts; there is no immediate reason to suggest that it cannot occur in Muslim settings as well, and, indeed, many would point to some excellent critical work that emerges from Turkish theological schools, for example. The development of Islamic Theology degree programmes in some German universities also signals the merging of academic and reflective religious research. It does then becomes apparent, however, that not all work in seminaries is 'academic' in the sense that word is generally used because it is readily seen to hold to values that constrain its perceptions. That can work in both negative and positive ways, resulting in polemic or theology. However, the invocation of values likewise does not solve the issue of how to distinguish academic scholarship from academic theology: most scholars have long since given up on naive notions of objectivity (in the sense of freedom from values) as being the hallmark of their work, having had their faith in such a perspective shaken by general philosophical tendencies and, finally in the field of Islamic studies in general, by Edward Said's *Orientalism* (1978).

Certainly academic scholarship must be free of religious dogma; on that all would agree. It must be free from the tendency to make absolute truth claims. It does not accept anything as 'obvious'. The freedom to ask questions of all kinds of texts is central; that freedom is unconstrained by tradition or dogma, and, within the academic setting, it is upheld by the tradition of tenure. This does also imply that the text cannot be taken as an arbiter of truth when it comes to analysing the text itself. In the study of the Qur'an this issue seems often to emerge in epistemological terms: because the text 'says' that it is revelation from God does not demand that this be the perspective from which the text must be examined. A typical case stems from the declaration made in classical times that the Qur'an has no words in it derived from languages other than Arabic because the Qur'an says of itself that it is *ʿarabī mubīn*, 'clear Arabic'. The logic of that statement cannot be defended as a valid deduction for academic scholarship. Fundamentally, the study of the Qur'an, like all academic study of religion, is not concerned with religious truths: it is 'a cognitive undertaking rather than a religious quest' (Wiebe 2000: 363). I will return to the nature and structure of that cognition below.

The word 'critical' is often used as a substitute for 'academic' in understanding the nature of scholarship. This can be helpful but here, too, definitions are important. The term 'critical' often seems to create confusion; a tendency especially notable among aspiring undergraduate students is that of conflating 'critical' and 'criticism'. That distinction, too, has become something of a flash point for some, especially to be noted in the backlash against Islam driven by polemicists who like to put forth the charge that scholars are afraid to 'criticize' Islam. Criticism in that sense means making a value judgement, of declaring something 'wrong'. That is something quite different, scholars would say, from not taking what religious people say at face value and employing critical inquiry as the starting point for analysis of any religion (Lincoln 2012: 2–3—thesis 12). The most important aspect that might be isolated here in understanding what it means to be 'critical' in scholarship is the idea of maintaining a personal distance from the subject. Put directly, the goal of academic scholarship on the Qur'an is clearly not to determine what 'true' Islam is. At the same time, scholars also need to recognize and accept the impact on the audience of their work in terms of the way in which the Qur'an is perceived and analysed; again, we do not have the alibi of absolute objectivity to fall back on.[1] The need to understand that the questions we ask and the issues we raise have

[1] Here it is important that we recognize the significance of the work of Mohammed Arkoun.

an impact upon the very broad context in which we work is acute. Some caution is also needed to not consider critique as the defining element of the modern but to recognize that supposedly 'pre-critical' readers 'were surprisingly audacious in dramatising recoil and alienation even as they performed obedience and devotion' (Sherwood 2012: 87), an observation made in the context of biblical studies but just as applicable to the study of the Qur'an in its historical manifestations.

Following on those considerations, it is also necessary to reflect upon our roles as writers of academic scholarship. Such work occurs in certain contexts and it is important to separate the role of the 'scholar' from the other roles that an academic plays within his or her job.[2] Most people involved in academic scholarship are also teachers and members of broader communities. In each of those settings there are different goals in the communication of our scholarship because there are different audiences. What precise difference that might make need not detain us here but it should serve to remind us that academic scholarship is not what one reads in the newspaper or in popular magazines; nor is it what might hear in a public forum (such as an open presentation at a neighbourhood library or seniors' group); nor is it usually what would fall under the banner of input to public policy. Such differentiation is, of course, one of the major challenges of the modern university as it tangles with the expectation of 'mobilization of knowledge' in a context where publicly funded institutions experience the demand for accountability and access.

In the end, all of these aspects come together in one further consideration about the nature of academic scholarship. This returns us to a consideration of the nature of the university as an institution of higher learning and its fundamental existence as a community of people who share a common discourse and epistemology. The history of the university itself is critical to understanding scholarship because that sets the context for what we mean by academic discourse. The study of the Qur'an in Europe had its beginnings within a church-oriented context. Leaving aside polemical interests and the use of the Qur'an in intra-Christian disputes (see Elmarsafy 2009), interest in the Islamic world increased significantly in the sixteenth and seventeenth centuries with a special focus on the study of Arabic. This was driven to a large extent by political and economic factors: the ability to engage the Islamic world through language and culture was recognized early on. Language was also central to certain aspects of self-interest on the part of Europeans: Arabic was thought of as a key to understanding the Bible. Both of those factors led to the development of Arabic studies at the emerging major universities in Europe. The discourse of these early studies was fully dominated by traditional Christian attitudes but that started to taper off especially in the nineteenth century as curiosity about the Islamic world increased due to travel and commerce, and as other aspects of that we tend to refer to as 'modernity' truly took hold. This was a gradual transition, in which certain figures (e.g. Antoine-Isaac Silvestre de Sacy (1758–1838) and his student

[2] See the issue of *Method and Theory in the Study of Religion* 24/4–5 (2012) on the state of Islamic studies in the study of religion and especially the essay of Herbert Berg therein, 'The Essence of Essentializing: A Critical Discourse on "Critical Discourse in the Study of Islam"', pp. 337–56.

Georg Freytag (1788–1861)) stand out as significant in creating a firm base for scholarly work (see Lassner 2012: chapter 1).

That appeal to modernity, of course, then requires its own set of definitions in order to understand the character of scholarly work of the era. On one level, the concerns are intertwined: the seventeenth/eighteenth-century rise of the university is one of the defining characteristics of the modern age, itself best thought of as a period of intense economic, political, social, and cultural change that has produced complex, interlinked communities. The very shift of the study of religion from a religious setting to the university likewise marks this transition since the modern era is characterized by the rejection and critique of the authority of traditional religious structures (Wiebe 2000: 354–5). That critique was based upon scientific thought, the idea that the world could be known independently of a religious perspective in which knowledge involves 'virtue' and 'the good' (Wiebe 2000: 358–9, discussing the work of Robert Hoopes), and the separation of 'truth' from 'The Truth'. It was the university that became the home for this search for knowledge. In that context, the development of the study of religion (a contested subject in definitional terms, potentially to be viewed as an academic construction in itself) was a markedly modern development. Religion was no longer to be considered in its isolated cultural form but to be examined as a cross-cultural phenomenon, a study that would find its eventual home in departments of religious studies (Wilson 1987: 17). While studies of the Qur'an are by no means limited to that academic administrative setting, the perspective lying underneath that development is the context in which academic scholarship on the Qur'an takes place.

In terms of attempting to formulate a positive definition, then, we might say that academic scholarship may best be viewed as an ideal that is an agreed-upon perspective among a group of people who study in the context of higher education a given subject at a given time. That agreed-upon perspective itself is not an absolute over time nor is it singular at any given time; it is also unenunciated for the most part. The grouping in which academic scholarship takes place is, in that sense, a 'community'. Stanley Fish (1982) can help us here: he argues that communication takes place only on the basis of certain shared assumptions, creating 'interpretive communities'.

In saying this we can then also come to terms with various problems that seem to emerge in how the discipline of Qur'anic studies as an academic approach is to be conceptualized. Hava Lazarus-Yafeh (1992) has argued that there is a case to be made for an intellectual heritage of biblical criticism (especially in raising questions of authorship) as coming from Muslims such as Ibn Ḥazm (d. 456/1064), passing through the Jewish Ibn Ezra (d. *c.*1167) to Spinoza (d. 1677) and onward to nineteenth-century Germanic scholarship. Certainly such medieval writers can be acknowledged as critical scholars in their own right even if, judging by their perspectives, they do not fit within our modern sense of 'academic' scholarship as the canon of such works is thought to exist. Their intellectual world was a different one; they worked in a discourse not marked by the characteristics of modernity with its orientation to history and philology. But, as remarked earlier, that does not mean that they did not use the attitude of critique.

Working within this perspective on academic scholarship can help overcome some of the stumbling blocks (that are primarily linguistic) in trying to define what we mean by academic scholarship. Terms such as 'non-Muslim' or 'Western' are no longer sufficient to provide a workable definition. Muslims, along with confessing members of other religions and those who proclaim no religious affiliation at all, are all full participants in contemporary academic scholarship. Neither is the physical place of academic scholarship limited to 'Euro-American' universities. Those observations are the sociological facts of the academic world today.

Thus, to reiterate the basic perspective, what is meant by academic scholarship is an agreed-upon (if unenunciated) discourse and epistemology that takes place in the context of institutions of higher learning. Understanding this can make it easier to appreciate the significance (and continuing worth) of works written several generations ago that still stand, in the eyes of the academic community, as significant contributions and disciplinary milestones and yet may be jarring in their perspective by contemporary standards. The most obvious examples of academic critical practices are seen in nineteenth- and twentieth-century works of the foundational figures in Qur'anic studies, people such as Abraham Geiger (1810–74), Theodor Nöldeke (1836–1930), Richard Bell (1876–1952), Régis Blachère (1900–73), and Rudi Paret (1901–83). While each of these authors worked within the frame of reference and employed the tone of the language of his times, the critical basis of the work has proven to be of lasting significance. When compared to works of today, however, there are certain aspects which display a shift in the perspective that marks what the notion of 'critical practice' evokes today. The attitude to issues such as the authorial composition of the Qur'an, the relationship to Jewish and Christian antecedents, and the structural and literary attributes of the Qur'anic text shows striking contrasts in the manner in which they are dealt with in these foundational works when compared to that of today's research. This is inevitable. Academic scholarship is an evolving concept that reflects the mood, ideology, and knowledge of the era in which it is written. A glance at the bibliography of Qur'anic studies—available in a published form composed of almost 9,000 items (Karimi-Nia 2012)—will show the diversity and development of the discipline as it has explored the various aspects of the Qur'an that capture of the attention of academics.

The dominance of the historical model of examining the Qur'an, both in relationship to the sources of the text and in the text's own internal progression, may be seen in the foundational scholarly works in the discipline and continues down until today. To many scholars, the historical approach is the hallmark of academic scholarship; however, critics have pointed out that the framework in which such scholars conduct their analyses of the Qur'an is essentially one derived from, or at least coherent with, the data provided by Muslim tradition. An issue arises then of the extent to which it is possible to assert these historical ideas with evidence that is independent of the tradition itself and thus uphold the ultimate approach of academic scholarship in its posing of questions that get to the core of adherents' assumptions (Lincoln 2012: 1—'destabilizing and irreverent questions', thesis 4).

Central within the various views on how to approach the historical formation of the Qur'an is what is usually referred to as Nöldeke's refinement of the traditional Meccan-Medinan division of suras. The initial credit for elaborating on this fundamental Muslim categorization is normally given to Gustav Weil, whose *Historisch-kritische Einleitung in den Koran* was published in 1844 (Stefanidis 2008). His approach noted a sense of progression in the Meccan grouping, referring to this as the first, second, and third Meccan periods. Thematic and literary characteristics were used to separate out the groupings as well as ideas about Muḥammad's prophetic career and the development of the Muslim community. Noldeke's *Geschichte des Qorâns* published in 1860 (and which started off as a Latin dissertation in 1856) continued to refine Weil's insights through a careful assessment of the historical sources as well the themes and styles found in the Qur'an. While some of the precise details of Nöldeke's chronology have been refined by subsequent generations of scholars, the basic framework continues to dominate discussions. One partial challenge came from Richard Bell (1937) who, while agreeing with the overall approach of Nöldeke, felt that the Qur'an's composition was more fractured than Nöldeke assumed when he treated each sura of the text as a whole unit (with a few exceptions). Bell picked up on a notion in the Muslim tradition that the Qur'an was initially written on palm leaves, rocks, and 'the hearts of men'; he suggested that these vehicles for transmission only allowed for the preservation of short fragments which were then put together in a relatively arbitrary manner. Bell's approach has increasingly been rejected by those who see a structural unity within each sura and thus Nöldeke's framework remains largely intact for most historically based academic studies.

More contemporary studies, especially those associated with Angelika Neuwirth, have continued to add refinement to the chronological criteria especially in their literary aspects. Neuwirth's particular contributions have been multiple. Her 1981 work, *Studien zur Komposition der mekkanischen Suren*, argued for the structural unity of the suras of the Meccan period, based around observations of rhyme, verse and paragraph structure (generally seeing a tripartite arrangement emerge), and semantic elements. In later work, Neuwirth (2010, 2011) has concentrated on the historical process of the Qur'an's formation during the lifetime of Muḥammad in a process she refers to (inspired by the ideas of Jan Assmann) as 'canonization from below' rather than the 'canonization from above' that was imposed by communal authorities after the death of Muḥammad. Neuwirth observes a process of inner-Qur'anic interpretation, with passages of the text referring back to historically earlier sections and elaborating or commenting on them in light of a new communal setting (sometimes within debates with Jewish and Christian audiences, for example). She urges a perspective on the Qur'an in which attention is paid to it as a 'work in progress' as the text develops during the lifetime of Muḥammad.

The reaction against this sense of history in the text is primarily associated with the 1977 work of John Wansbrough who argued that analysis of literary attributes of the text do not allow for historical conclusions about its composition. No evidence from different literary forms (such as short verses as compared to long verses) can demonstrate the historical fact of a change from Mecca to Medina, he suggested. There is no necessary correlation between form and history. In fact, Wansbrough argued, the themes and style of the Qur'an suggested a much longer compositional framework than the traditional biography of Muḥammad would allow; such a period could stretch from the centuries before Muḥammad to the generations after him, the text itself coalescing into a canon under the pressures of the community's need for an established liturgical and legal reference point. Wansbrough's arguments certainly have not convinced many scholars of the Qur'an and some—noticeably in Neuwirth, Sinai, and Marx (2010)—have lamented the impact that the implication that viewing the Qur'an historically is not possible has had on the progress of academic scholarship, forcing it, as has indeed been the case, to pay primary attention to post-canonical concerns both surrounding the message of the text and the Muslim reception of it.

The controversies that the historical approach evoke also have their ramifications in the ways in which the matter of the 'background' to the text is assessed. The work of Abraham Geiger, *Was hat Mohammed aus dem Judenthume aufgenommen?*, written as a prize-winning essay in Latin and published in German in 1833, is frequently hailed as the beginnings of academic scholarship on the Qur'an for its attention to understanding the relationship between Judaism and the origins of Islam: not only the question of 'what' continued on from one religion to the next, but also the questions of 'how' and 'in what way were they different' were tackled for the first time by Geiger. Geiger situated the text of the Qur'an in its historical context (although not tracing in any detail a sense of historical progression in the text) and he was careful to avoid back-projection of later sources both for the details of Judaism (thus in citing sources he tended to concentrate on the Hebrew Bible and the Talmud) and for the interpretation of the Qur'an itself. Geiger's main accomplishment was to recognize that the differences between the stories found in Jewish sources and their Qur'anic retellings were likely intentional and not based, as earlier polemically inclined writers tended to suggest, on misunderstandings; rather, it would have been the circumstances of Muḥammad's context that demanded the changes in those stories that historical scholarship could now observe. The key to discovering these shifts and their significance is to be found through philological means, especially as demonstrated by tracing the meaning of significant religious words found in the Qur'an to their Hebrew and Aramaic origins. Overall, Geiger's scholarly accomplishment conveys that Muḥammad is not to be viewed as an imposter or a heretic but as a genuine religious leader with a message specifically tailored to his own people and his own time.

This tendency to trace the sources of the Qur'an's ideas, vocabulary, and imagery to earlier religions has continued to be a major theme of Qur'anic studies, with other efforts to document in detail both Jewish and Christian sources and to weigh the relative value of those different contexts. The current mood of Qur'anic studies tends towards the Syriac Christian side, often with some sense of an undetermined (and misleadingly labelled) Jewish-Christian confessional group positioned as the likely context in which Qur'anic expression developed. The area has become a focus of considerable controversy as a result of the appearance of works by Günter Lüling (2003) and the pseudonymous Christoph Luxenberg (2000/2007) that argue that Islam developed by suppressing this Christian connection in a process that involved some sort of 'conspiracy', or that Islam emerged out of sheer ignorance of the original versions of the Jewish-Christian religious texts (and thus this conclusion entails a non-academic moral valuation of the historical process). More carefully enunciated work by scholars such as Gabriel Reynolds (2010) which delve into the details of Christian texts as a context for Qur'anic echoes are proving more influential.

One problem this approach to the background of the Qur'an creates is fitting the Jewish-Christian context into an understanding of the Meccan-Medinan historical progression. The ability to understand this interaction with Syriac Christianity as developing in the isolated context of Mecca seems limited and demands other postulates: that hitherto unrecognized and undocumented (Jewish-) Christian groups existed in the Ḥijāz at the time of Muḥammad, that the Qur'an did not emerge in the Ḥijāz at all but further north in closer proximity to Syriac Christian communities, or that all hope of reconstructing the history of the development of the Qur'an is beyond reach and is simply an imposition of the Muslim framework on the text. These avenues of research are still being explored.

Partially as a response to this situation, an entirely different way of conceiving the text has emerged, apparent especially in the work of Gerald Hawting (1999) and Patricia Crone (2010, 2012–13). By raising the question of who is being attacked dogmatically as unbelievers or polytheists in the text of the Qur'an, both authors see the need to conceive the historical context in a far more nuanced manner than Muslim tradition has suggested or than has been adopted in most academic approaches. Crone, for example, points out that the issues that the 'disbelievers' who are mentioned in the Qur'an raise with reference to notions of resurrection and the afterlife are best contextualized within a monotheist environment because of the nature of the objections suggested and the perspectives put forth.

There are other ways of approaching the Qur'an within the context of academic scholarship that do not privilege history as a framework within which to develop an analysis. Wansbrough's approach has already been mentioned for its critique of the presuppositions of historical treatments. His own analysis of the text elicits a number of themes that he argues are the basic framework of the monotheist perspective (retribution, sign, exile, covenant, prophethood). Other modes of analysis that downplay the sense of chronology in the Qur'an have also proven successful. The employment of a rigorous semantic methodology by Toshihiko Izutsu (1964, 1966), while deeply embedded in the dualism of structuralism that finds less favour in many circles today, has managed to illuminate many themes and arguments in the Qur'an.

The critique of approaches such as those of Izutsu tends to focus on the lack of history that it entails: Izutsu and others who take such an approach accept the existence of the completed canon of the Qur'an as the work upon which to reflect. Such has been suggested to be a 'theological' approach rather than a critical one (Ernst 2011: 10). One might reply to this objection by saying that it also depends upon how one is conceiving the goal of one's study and that, while the study of religion is deeply and fundamentally historical, that history can and should extend beyond the period of 'origins' and reflect upon the Qur'an as a source of data for the Muslim community. As previously mentioned, Neuwirth's approach is one that attempts to walk a path between these two by arguing for a process of historical development within the text. Thus, she argues, we can see the community interact with the canon in the process of its formation in the text itself. However, overall, the claim that the academic task should be confined to the search for the 'original context' or the 'meaning to the first hearers' does tend to dominate academic work in the field; that this is a distinctly modern approach that, regardless of its secularist claims, tends to maintain 'a certain sovereignty [for the text of the Qur'an]...through acts of annotation, supplementation and contextualization' (Sherwood 2012: 84) in common with the religious devotee is a fact that is not always recognized or grappled with.

A more recent trend that needs to be considered within a discussion of academic scholarship is the impact of that scholarship on polemical and apologetic works, a phenomenon usefully framed as Christian appropriation and Muslim reaction. The internet abounds with discussions in which academic insights are cited in the attempt either to demolish Muslim presuppositions or to expose the mendacity of scholarship (often pictured as a crypto-Christian attack on Islam). Such approaches are also found within published works such as those edited by Ibn Warraq (1998, 2002, 2011), who argues for the irrationality of religious belief and, in the other direction, in the book by Muḥammad al-Aʿẓamī (2003) who argues for the textual superiority of the Qur'an over the biblical record. The volumes that Ibn Warraq has assembled provide an illustration of the historical development of Qur'anic studies; the transplantation of nineteenth-century academic language—in which Muḥammad is spoken of as the author of the Qur'an (as though that was a certain historical fact)—into the twenty-first century context illustrates the difficulties of defining academic scholarship that the opening paragraphs of this chapter have tried to broach. Similarly, within this polemical context the examination of the background to the Qur'an, an essential part of any reading of the text, is viewed through the lens of errors, misunderstandings, and corruption (a reversal of the perspective of Geiger, for example).

It also needs to be emphasized that the history of the academic discipline of Qur'anic studies is composed of several additional areas of interest that both feed into the discussions already mapped out in this chapter and add more aspects to the mix. Detailed textual and manuscript studies, led today by François Déroche (2009), proceed on the basis of the work of earlier generations (e.g. G. Bergsträsser and O. Pretzl in the third part of the second edition of Nöldeke 1909–38; Jeffery 1937) and necessarily underpin the fundamental approaches to the Qur'an: academic work needs a firm textual basis on which to proceed. The ongoing project in Berlin known as Corpus Coranicum aims to document the history of the text of the Qur'an as fully as possible, down to its minute details on the basis of manuscript evidence especially. This is an area of considerable controversy because of traditional Muslims' views about the integrity of the text of scripture; outside the academic arena, the entire exercise may well be deemed redundant (if not offensive to certain religious sensibilities), yet this is an area of academic scholarship that requires considerable expertise and recovers an otherwise lost history.

The history of the academic study of Muslim exegesis (*tafsīr*) is similar to that of detailed textual studies. Early attention to this area which may be first seen in the works of Ignaz Goldziher (1920/2006) and Friedrich Schwally (in his revisions to Nöldeke's work in the second edition 1909–38) has likewise provided a vehicle into the world of the Qur'an as well as being an independent stream of investigation that demands an academic perspective. The academic study of *tafsīr* is not based around a search for the 'true' meaning of the Qur'an but rather centres on understanding how (and why) Muslim writers through the centuries went about constructing their own arguments for the meaning of the text of scripture. Wansbrough (1977) was instrumental in drawing attention to the existing body of exegetical texts from the early Muslim centuries that were devoted to defining and elaborating the text of the Qur'an; work has continued on the analysis of the early texts of *tafsīr* (e.g. Rippin 2001) in order to understand 'the process by means of which revelation became scripture' (Wansbrough 1977: 288). More recent work by scholars such as Walid Saleh (2004) and Bruce Fudge (2011) exemplify an approach to Muslim exegesis that extends the period of interest into later centuries and evidences the centrality of the exegetical enterprise to Muslim scholastic endeavours. Such studies also tend to explore related disciplines such as law, theology, and grammar in order to determine the place of the Qur'an in the broader spectrum of Muslim thought (see e.g. Schwarb 2007).

Finally, studies utilizing methods from anthropology and sociology have been employed to consider the role of the Qur'an in Muslim life, especially in the context of ritual. Such approaches have become an important part of Qur'anic studies as a whole but they have been, in general, the result of more recent initiatives. Recitation has been a particular area of interest, again seeing its origins in the work of Bergsträsser (1932, 1933) primarily on a textual basis but today being manifested in works that pay detailed attention to the performative aspects that evidence the Qur'an as a living text in the community (Nelson 1985; Rasmussen 2010). Also as evidence of this emerging tendency in Qur'anic studies and worthy of special attention are the studies of the Qur'an in material culture, both as decoration and as an object of art in itself (Suleman 2007).

All the evidence points to a complex history of the academic study of the Qur'an as well as to a vibrant future for the discipline. The scholarly study of the Qur'an is fully embedded in the academy of today; while its methods and goals are, at times, hotly debated it remains an essential element of Islamic studies and a fundamental force in coming to an appreciation of the Qur'an's role in history and in Muslim life.

Bibliography

Al-Aʿẓamī, Muḥammad Muṣṭafā. *The History of the Qurʾānic Text from Revelation to Compilation: A Comparative Study with the Old and New Testaments.* Leicester: UK Islamic Academy, 2003.

Bell, Richard. *The Qurʾān, Translated, with a Critical Re-arrangement of the Surahs.* 2 vols. Edinburgh: T. & T. Clark, 1937.

Bergsträsser, Gotthelf. 'Koranlesung in Kairo', *Der Islam* 20 (1932), 1–42; 21 (1933), 110–40.

Blachère, Régis. *Le Coran: Traduction selon un essai de reclassement des sourates.* 2 vols. Paris: Maissoneuve et Larose, 1949–50.

Crone, Patricia. 'The Religion of the Qur'ānic Pagans: God and the Lesser Dieties', *Arabica* 57 (2010), 151–200.
Crone, Patricia. 'The Quranic *Mushrikūn* and the Resurrection', *Bulletin of the School of Oriental and African Studies* 75 (2012), 445–72; 76 (2013), 1–20.
Déroche, François. *La transmission écrite du Coran dans les débuts de l'Islam*. Leiden: Brill, 2009.
Elmarsafy, Ziad. *The Enlightenment Qur'an: The Politics of Translation and the Construction of Islam*. Oxford: Oneworld, 2009.
Ernst, Carl. *How to Read the Qur'an: A New Guide, with Select Translations*. Edinburgh: Edinburgh University Press, 2011.
Fish, Stanley. *Is There a Text in This Class? The Authority of Interpretive Communities*. Cambridge, MA: Harvard University Press, 1982.
Fudge, Bruce. *Qur'ānic Hermeneutics: Al-Ṭabrisī and the Craft of Commentary*. London: Routledge, 2011.
Geiger, Abraham. *Judaism and Islam*. Trans. F. M. Young. Delhi; SPCK, 1898 (German original 1833).
Goldziher, Ignaz. *Schools of Koranic Commentators with an Introduction on Goldziher and Hadith from 'Geschichte des Arabischen Schrifttums' by Fuat Sezgin*. Trans. Wolfgang H. Behn. Wiesbaden: Harrassowitz Verlag, 2006 (German original Leiden, 1920).
Hawting, G. R. *The Idea of Idolatry and the Emergence of Islam: From Polemic to History*. Cambridge: Cambridge University Press, 1999.
Ibn Warraq (ed.). *The Origins of the Koran: Classic Essays on Islam's Holy Book*. Amherst NY: Prometheus Press, 1998.
Ibn Warraq (ed.). *What the Koran Really Says: Language, Text, and Commentary*. Amherst NY: Prometheus Press, 2002.
Ibn Warraq (ed.). *Which Koran? Variants, Manuscripts, Linguistics*. Amherst NY: Prometheus Press, 2011.
Izutsu, Toshihiko. *God and Man in the Koran: Semantics of the Koranic Weltanschauung*. Tokyo: The Keio Institute of Cultural and Linguistic Studies, 1964.
Izutsu, Toshihiko. *Ethico-religious Concepts in the Qur'ān*. Montreal: McGill University Press, 1966.
Jeffery, Arthur. *Materials for the History of the Text of the Qur'ān*. Leiden: Brill, 1937.
Karimi-Nia, Morteza. *Bibliography of Qur'ānic Studies in European Languages*. Qum: The Centre for Translation of the Holy Qur'ān, 2012.
Lassner, Jacob. *Jews, Christians, and the Abode of Islam: Modern Scholarship, Medieval Realities*. Chicago: University of Chicago Press, 2012.
Lazarus-Yafeh, Hava. *Intertwined Worlds: Medieval Islam and Bible Criticism*. Princeton: Princeton University Press, 1992.
Lincoln, Bruce. 'Theses on Method'. In: Bruce Lincoln (ed.). *God and Demons, Priests and Scholars: Critical Explorations in the History of Religions*, pp. 1–3. Chicago: University of Chicago Press, 2012.
Lüling, Gunter. *A Challenge to Islam for Reformation: The Rediscovery and Reliable Reconstruction of a Comprehensive Pre-Islamic Christian Hymnal Hidden in the Koran under Earliest Islamic Reinterpretation*. Delhi: Motital Banarsidass, 2003 (revised from German editions of 1974 and 1993).
Luxenberg, Christoph. *The Syro-Aramaic Reading of the Koran: A Contribution to the Decoding of the Language of the Koran*. Berlin: Hans Schiler, 2007 (German original 2000).

Nelson, Kristina. *The Art of Reciting the Qur'an*. Austin: University of Texas Press, 1985.
Neuwirth, Angelika. *Studien zur Komposition der mekkanischen Suren*. Berlin: Walter de Gruyter, 1981.
Neuwirth, Angelika. *Der Koran als Text der Spänantike: Ein europäischer Zugang*. Berlin: Verlag der Weltreligionen, 2010.
Neuwirth, Angelika. *Der Koran: Band I: Frühmekkanische Suren*. Berlin: Verlag der Weltreligionen, 2011.
Neuwirth, Angelika, Nicolai Sinai, and Michael Marx (eds.). *The Qurʾān in Context: Historical and Literary Investigations into the Qurʾānic Milieu*. Leiden: Brill, 2010.
Nöldeke, Theodor. *Geschichte des Qorāns*. 2nd rev. edn. Ed. F. Schwally (vols. 1 and 2), G. Bergsträsser, O. Pretzl (vol. 3). Leipzig: Dieterichsche, 1909–38 (1st edn. 1860).
Paret, Rudi. *Der Koran: Übersetzung*. Stuttgart: W. Kohlhammer, 1962.
Rasmussen, Anne K. *Women, the Recited Qur'an, and Islamic Music in Indonesia*. Berkeley: University of California Press, 2010.
Reynolds, Gabriel. *The Qurʾān and its Biblical Subtext*. London: Routledge, 2010.
Rippin, Andrew. *The Qurʾān and its Interpretative Tradition*. Aldershot: Variorum, 2001.
Said, Edward. *Orientalism*. New York: Pantheon Books, 1978.
Saleh, Walid. *The Formation of the Classical* Tafsīr *Tradition: The Qurʾān Commentary of al-Thaʿlabī (d. 427/1035)*. Leiden: Brill, 2004.
Schwarb, Gregor. 'Capturing the Meanings of God's Speech: The Relevance of *uṣūl al-fiqh* to an Understanding of *uṣūl al-tafsīr* in Jewish and Muslim *kalām*'. In: Meir M. Bar-Asher, Simon Hopkins, Sarah Stroumsa, and Bruno Chiesa (eds.). *A Word Fitly Spoken: Studies in Medieval Exegesis of the Hebrew Bible and the Qurʾān presented to Haggai Ben-Shammai*, pp. 111–56. Jerusalem: Ben Zvi Institute for the History of the Jewish Communities of the East Yad Izhak Ben Zvi and the Hebrew University of Jerusalem, 2007.
Sherwood, Yvonne. *Biblical Blaspheming: Trials of the Sacred for a Secular Age*. Cambridge: Cambridge University Press, 2012.
Suleman, Fahmida (ed.). *Word of God, Art of Man. The Qurʾān and its Creative Expressions*. Oxford: Oxford University Press, 2007.
Stefanidis, Emmanuelle. 'The Qur'an Made Linear: A Study of the Geschichte des Qorâns' Chronological Reordering', *Journal of Quranic Studies* 10/2 (2008), 1–22.
Wansbrough, John. *Quranic Studies: Sources and Methods of Scriptural Interpretation*. Oxford: Oxford University Press, 1977.
Weil, Gustav. *Historisch-kritische Einleitung in den Koran*. Bielefeld: Velhagen & Klasing, 1844.
Wiebe, Donald. 'Modernism'. In: Willi Braun and Russell T. McCutcheon (eds.). *Guide to the Study of Religion*, pp. 351–64. London: Cassell, 2000.
Wilson, John F. 'Modernity and Religion: A Problem of Perspective'. In: William Nicholls (ed.). *Modernity and Religion*, pp. 9–18. Waterloo: Canadian Corporation for the Study of Religion/Wilfrid Laurier University Press, 1987.

CHAPTER 2

MODERN DEVELOPMENTS IN QUR'ANIC STUDIES

OLIVER LEAMAN

MODERN interpretations of the Qur'an are linked with earlier interpretations, and often repeat or imitate traditional approaches to the Book. For many Muslims the need for interpretation is limited since they find the verses and meaning of the text perfectly clear and evident. They find them appropriate as a system of guidance for their lives and beliefs. In some ways casting around for a hermeneutic strategy may seem to be impious given the way in which the Qur'an describes itself. However it is often argued that any text is capable of a variety of interpretations, especially writing from a long time ago, even divinely inspired writing. The Qur'an does indeed often represent itself as clear and so exemplary as a work of guidance. Not only is it fit for purpose, it is often held to be miraculously so. There are many attempted proofs both today and in the past of its miraculous status, both in terms of what it says and how it is presented.

There is a tendency to contrast writing on the Qur'an with that on other major books of religion especially the Hebrew Bible and the Christian New Testament. Those works have been subjected to radical examination, reorganization, and reinterpretation. These intellectual efforts represent the influence of what is often called 'modernity', a cultural movement which is taken not to have had much of an effect on the Islamic world, especially where scriptural criticism is concerned. But this is of course a vast oversimplification. Like all religions, Islam has been full of thinkers taking radical views of traditional religious texts and their meanings, and this is even more true in modern times. On the other hand, a very large number of commentators have stuck to the traditional interpretations but have framed them and expressed them in rather novel ways. This is a general way of characterizing many of the commentators who could be called the popularizers, those thinkers whose efforts are directed more to the traditional activity of reviving Islam, through instilling a renewed enthusiasm for its Book, rather than producing any very radical reinterpretation of it.

The Popularizers

Two of the Turkish popularizers are Said Nursi (1878–1960) and his follower Fethullah Gülen (b. 1941), both of whom are Sunnī and lived much of their lives within the context of a Turkey that was decidedly secular in orientation. The role they saw themselves playing was to rescue Islam from being regarded as old-fashioned, out of date, and irrelevant in the modern age. One way of doing this is to present lively and well composed responses to the sorts of challenges that come from the forces of secularism, which in the case of Nursi and Gülen often are a matter of reiterating in colourfully vivid language traditional understandings of the Qur'an. Although both thinkers and their organizations have sought to reach out to the wider Islamic world, they have on the whole been restricted to the Turkish cultural sphere, and indeed much of the rest of the Islamic world has not felt the need to defend itself from the sort of secularism as presented by the Kemalist governments of the twentieth century. Nursi presented an exciting and moving commentary on the Qur'an which is designed to reflect, to the extent that this is possible when written by a human being, its inimitable style and force. There is also a considerable sophistication in his ideas, employing concepts taken from both Sufi and Ishrāqī philosophy, and because he wrote a good deal when he was effectively in exile or on the run, there is a directness and fluency to his approach that is very attractive. For example, many of his explanations of parts of the Qur'an combine his personal emotional reaction to the particular verses, like a Sufi, with the idea that the light of conviction comes to the reader or hearer, like an Ishrāqī (self-awareness or presence). Many of the same ideas are produced by Gülen. Both thinkers have large groups of followers among the public, for whom both Nursi and Gülen are significant guides to the ultimate guide, the Qur'an. Like the other popularizers, neither thinker has really had any impact on the serious academic study of the Qur'an, even in Turkey.

The same could be said of two Sunnī popularizers from the Arab world, Yūsuf al-Qaraḍāwī (b. 1926) and ʿAmr Khāled (b. 1967). Al-Qaraḍāwī was based for a long time in Qatar, when his differences with the Egyptian government made life in Egypt difficult. He presents a straightforward approach to understanding the Qur'an and its relevance to modern life. His skill at using modern media has established his role as a religious authority to millions of Muslims and means that he is constantly called on to present legal judgements in various contexts, and this has led to a certain lack of sophistication in his views given the necessity to find a practical formula in the Qur'an, and of course the other sources of Islamic law such as the hadith, Arabic grammar, local custom, and the links that exist between them. For him Islam presents an easy to understand approach to how we should live and what we should believe, and his approach to the Qur'an is similarly direct, which no doubt is one of the factors attracting such a large TV audience. It would be wrong to see him as entirely simplistic in his views, however. For example, although he defends the accounts of *ḥadd* punishment that occur in the Qur'an, and their literal interpretation, he suggests that they only become valid in an Islamic state. An Islamic state is not a state that calls itself Islamic, there are plenty of those around, but one which is really Islamic and which totally embodies the ideals and practices advocated in the Qur'an. There are of course no such states in existence yet, according to him, and so the implementation of what are often regarded as the rather harsh *ḥudūd* punishments such as execution for offences against Islam, and the removal of limbs for theft, is not acceptable at the moment. ʿAmr Khāled is not as sophisticated as al-Qaraḍāwī but is also a considerable TV presence, and both commentators see themselves as having the task of presenting the Qur'an as a work of continuing relevance to the modern age when so many other cultural forces are pulling in the other direction.

An apparently more sophisticated representative of the same school is Tariq Ramadan (b. 1962), who has more of a European presence, and who also takes the Qur'an to be a fairly clear guide to how modern people are supposed to live, without however being prepared to say anything original or challenging about the text. He has carried out much the same role as al-Qaraḍāwī and ʿAmr Khālid when addressing the non-Islamic intellectual world, representing the Qur'an as a clear guide to how human beings are to live. Since Ramadan does not have to operate as a legal authority he can be more vague in his views on what the practical legal implications/requirements of the Book are, an approach which resonates well with his European audience. One feature of the work of all these thinkers which contrasts notably from the tradition of Islamic theology is that they are not constrained by any legal tradition in attaining their conclusions. They make it up on an ad hoc basis, seeking Qur'anic passages and hadith which they find relevant, a very different process of working with the Qur'an than persisted for much of the past. They appear to be traditional while eschewing the traditional ways of assessing Islamic sources of authority, which gives them a freedom to interpret texts in ways that resonate with the public. Hence their popularity, but this also leads to their not being taken very seriously by those involved in the academic study of Islam in modern times.

The 'Modernizers'

It is worth spending some time on those called here the popularizers since of course for many people they represent Islam and what the Qur'an means. The popularizers see no problem with the Qur'an, it is the divine message and is as relevant today as it was in the past. By contrast, the thinkers to whom I refer here as 'modernizers' do see that there is a problem in combining the Qur'an and modernity. For the Qur'an to be seen as relevant in modern times, some theoretical work needs to be undertaken which will explain how it would retain its authority in modern times. Fazlur Rahman (1919–88) is the outstanding representative of this movement. An approach that many modernizers follow is that one has to pay close attention to the context in which the Qur'an was produced, and once that has been done, all sorts of interesting hermeneutic issues arise. For example, the Qur'an was revealed many years ago in Arabia and one wonders how far local conditions shaped what it says and how far we should take very different local conditions to be relevant today in understanding it. A group of theologians in Turkey has come to be labelled the Ankara School (Körner 2006) because their views are based on those of the Theology Department at the University of Ankara and they try to balance viewing the Qur'an as a historical text with seeing it as not only a historical text, something they think follows trends in Protestant Christianity. They are convinced though that what is required is a new reading and thinking about the Qur'an to make it germane to modern society.

Naṣr Abū Zayd (d. 2010) puts the issue most clearly. This is why, perhaps, he attracted so much religious hostility in his native Egypt. He sharply distinguishes between Islam and the Qur'an, between the former as a human institution and the latter as the eternal word of God. On the other hand, he implies sometimes that the Qur'an was a collaborative effort between Muḥammad and divine inspiration, rather a radical idea in that it implies that part at least of the text might be more human than divine, or a mixture. Abū Zayd points out that the understandings of the Book have varied from place to place since Islam itself varies, and this is because when the early Arab invaders took over in the various countries they conquered they embedded the new religion in the old culture, and so the former was shaped by the latter. The Qur'an needs to be reinterpreted for today if it is to be relevant, and relying on old and fixed Ḥijāzī models of human behaviour just because it was first revealed in the Ḥijāz is limiting. A fresh approach is required if the language of the Qur'an is to be part of dynamic modern culture.

Some of the 'modernizers' develop this strategy by distinguishing sharply between the Meccan and the Medinan suras, which is of course not dissimilar from the traditional line. The latter are more concerned with law and administration, since when he was in Medina the Prophet was leading a community of believers who needed to be organized and defended against their enemies. The Meccan suras by contrast are often more spiritual in direction and abstract and reflect an earlier time when the Prophet was having problems attracting local support. The Indonesian thinker Nurcholish Madjid (1939–2005) argues that many Medinan verses tend to represent a time of pluralism, cohesion, and tolerance which the Islamic world ought to try to recapture. By contrast, Maḥmūd Ṭāhā (1909–85) suggests that these verses are to be related to the time at which they were revealed and are only relevant to that time. So the *ḥadd* punishments they prescribe, for example, are no longer relevant today, and he implies would not have arisen during the earlier period while the Prophet was in Mecca either. Mouhanad Khorchide points out that of the 6,236 verses in the Qur'an only 80 deal with punishment, and he also makes a strong distinction between the Meccan and Medinan verses, between the Prophet as a political and as a spiritual leader. If we can distinguish between those verses on the basis of their context then it might appear that there is nothing universal and eternal about them, although the Qur'an itself can be regarded as universal and eternal. On the other hand, it is not much of a move from arguing that parts of the Qur'an are only relevant for a particular place and time to coming to a similar conclusion about the whole of the Qur'an. The Sharīʿa is generally regarded as immutable, while *fiqh* as the body of legal opinions which are the result of human reasoning and experience is not. God is by definition perfect and infallible, but human beings may err in their understanding of what God reveals.

Ḥasan Ḥanafī (b. 1935) argues that the Qur'an needs to be regarded as existing on different levels. As a divine product it is an object of mystery, but at another level it clearly sets out to have a certain relationship with the other and earlier works of revelation (Campanini 2011). The Iranian thinker Abdolkarim Soroush puts the point in a similar way, pointing out that the level of debate about religion is inevitably social since it is based on language, and we can accept the point of disagreement here about the meaning of the Qur'an while maintaining the objectivity of what the language actually refers to, the Book itself. He argues that the Muʿtazilī notion of the createdness of the Qur'an which became established in Shīʿī thought, though largely rejected among the Sunnī makes it easier for the Shīʿa to take a historical view of the text than for the Sunnīs. He also goes a bit further and suggests that the Prophet is in some ways the author of the Qur'an, and that prophecy is not restricted to particular individuals. This approach has often led to strenuous criticism from within the Muslim community itself, while being enthusiastically taken up by those outside the community and keen on finding and sometimes funding insiders who are in favour of a historical approach to the Qur'an. This brings us to an issue which will be the point of much discussion here, when to contextualize is to demythologize, when to stress the power of historical features is to limit the force of the Book to precisely those features.

Among the 'modernizers' who deserve special mention, are those who argue that the Qur'an is a work of liberation theology (Farid Esack and Ali Shariati), and feminists who argue that it is based on the equality of men and women (Barlas and Wadud). There are some excellent ideas in all these works of interpretation, but they fail to do justice to the nuances of the Book, refusing to acknowledge that what is significant to the interpreter might be different from that of the divine author in his final revelation. It is all too easy to take any religious text and interpret it in any way one wants, and the demands of modernity often urge a progressive interpretation. These thinkers argue correctly that it is possible to interpret the text in a variety of different ways than has been established as the norm in the past by the *ʿulamāʾ*. They are also surely right in thinking that many of the previous modes of interpretation have been narrow and heavily reliant on patriarchal systems of power and privilege, which ultimately is reflected in the interpretation. Yet it is a slippery slope to argue from the fact that the Qur'an can be given a progressive interpretation to the conclusion that it should be. Perhaps a problem with the modernizing project as a whole is that the enthusiasm of the interpreters runs away with them. They fail to offer an account of the Qur'an which is nuanced enough to reflect a balance between tradition and modernity, and surely any plausible system of interpretation has to respect the idea of such a balance.

The 'Scientists' or 'Academics'

This brings us to the group of thinkers who are called here those who follow a 'scientific' or academic approach to the text, in the sense that they have no commitment to any particular interpretation of the Qur'an beyond that available through studying the text.

They are not usually Muslims and the point of their work is to present the evidence for the nature and meaning of the Qur'an entirely historically. Often they come up with some very challenging and surprising conclusions about the Qur'an, and this is part of that general movement in European thought to examine anew central religious documents. The 'scientific' approach takes a slightly different attitude to context than that of the modernizers, although for both context is the crucial explanatory concept. For the modernizers context explains why there are theological issues in interpretations of the Qur'an that resist an easy solution. Context explains why its permanent and universal meaning can appear to vary on occasion, since context changes from time to time and place to place. On the scientific approach, there is no presumption of a transcendental meaning, and a sharp distinction is made between history and sacred history.

This understanding of context is often very different from the sorts of context that are accepted by most Muslims. The traditional history of the Prophet, the timing and dating of the various revelations and their placement, and the additional material such as the hadith literature often do not survive strict 'scientific' inspection. It is not that these phenomena need to be accepted only on the basis of faith, since they are within themselves perfectly rational ways of exploring the meaning of the Qur'an. For example, the hadith are organized in terms of reliability and chains of transmission, and although many of them appear to be weak to almost everyone, some may well have stronger claims for acceptance than those regarded as *ṣaḥīḥ*. The important principle in operation here is perhaps that it is not a matter of what one would like to be genuine, but the issue is one of assessing the evidence. We may suspect that some are tempted to accept as genuine hadith those with which they personally approve, but this is not the official criterion of acceptance. There is a chapter in this volume looking at the various historical approaches taken to the Qur'an and there is no need to repeat the issues that have arisen here. It is worth mentioning that what many Muslims take to be history, and in particular the history of the Prophet and the redaction of the Qur'an, has been understood quite differently by others outside the Muslim community. The sacred history of a religion is precisely that, part of its self-explanation and justification and may not be universally accepted.

There have been a number of approaches to central religious texts which treat with scepticism the traditions embodied in those texts. The religion itself often produces its own methods of how to achieve an accurate understanding of the text and its original context. Religions tend also to like to use their own methods to decide what the canonical version of their scriptures are. Such approaches are often found in Islam, where Muslim and non-Muslim scholars tend to take very different strategies on how to understand the Qur'an and what its definitive structure is. The largest research project of this century is that overseen by Angelika Neuwirth (b. 1943) and presented in *Der Koran als Text der Spätantike: Ein europäischer Zugang* (Neuwirth 2010).

The main objective of the project is to document all the instances that can be found of the Qur'an as a written document, and an important and novel aspect of this is the use of photographs of old manuscripts by Bergsträsser and Pretzl from before the Second

World War. There is a rather exciting aspect to this since they were thought to have been destroyed in the bombing of the war yet were apparently concealed and now are again available for study and analysis. The main point of the project, something its organizers frequently say, is that the Qur'an did not appear in a vacuum, and by this is meant that we must pay attention to the context within which the *muṣḥaf* was redacted and codified. The project will link the manuscripts and orally transmitted readings of the text. The Qur'an will also be linked with a range of other texts, including those that came before it and also those which were contemporary. Finally, and probably most crucially, a very detailed commentary will be produced, a sort of supercommentary that will deal with a whole range of views on the meaning of the text. This quite rightly will not be limited to the traditional commentaries and their ways of understanding the Qur'an, but will encapsulate these within a broader interpretive approach, and the result will be a perspicuous grasp of the whole Qur'anic enterprise. The Corpus Coranicum project has become a significant media event in Germany, with its results often being flagged as though they produce radical new ideas about the Qur'an.

It might seem that this is a general issue that affects all religions, at least all religions that to a degree rest on historical facts. There has been in contemporary scholarship a general demythologizing strategy in the analysis of religion, and it would be interesting to speculate whether there are any particular reasons why such an approach is likely to be more, or less, effective when dealing with Islam as compared with other religions. The Corpus Coranicum project basically argues in favour of the creation of a *Wissenschaft des Islams* in line with previous attempts by theologians to distinguish sharply between the claims that religions make about themselves, and what they are entitled to say. At the same time, the project suggests that we do not have to accept the idea of such a dichotomy between aligning with a tradition and accepting a scientific approach.

The methodologies of Qur'anic and biblical studies are often contrasted, to the detriment of the former. For a considerable period now very strenuous moves have been adopted to understand the Bible, both Jewish and Christian, using a wide range of hermeneutic principles, in order to determine the nature and significance of this issue of context. Different authors have been identified speculatively, and for the Gospels themselves of course different authors are actually self-announced. A vast literature has grown up explaining the various parts of the Bibles and often this is very challenging to the ways in which both Jews and Christians have traditionally seen their Bibles. A *Wissenschaft des Judentums* and a higher criticism have both called for a new understanding of the basic Jewish and Christian texts. The Corpus Coranicum project sets out to avoid taking this sort of approach to the Qur'an, while at the same time freeing the Qur'an from the *tafsīr* tradition in Islam. It even tries to establish a link with Europe by arguing that the sorts of debates that were current in the Arabian Peninsula during the seventh century were similar to those taking place in the Mediterranean region, and so ultimately to European issues. It is a very enervated and insipid argument which ends up by saying, nevertheless correctly that the Qur'an is indeed linked with late antiquity but uses this to argue that it is also part of the contribution that late antiquity made to Europe.

According to Neuwirth, before the Qur'an was regarded as the definitive text of Islam, the Qur'an originated as a reflection on discussions within a community which responded to issues thrown up by late antiquity, before eventually taking the form of the canonical text of Islam. She argues that the Book should not be seen as the work of just one author, who seeks to define the Islamic community once and for all, but rather as the result of a cooperative effort in which a variety of voices are to be heard. It is clear that she is following rather closely the approach of Nöldeke who fostered a powerful tradition of analyzing the Qur'an in terms of its style, the audience it was seeking, how it tried to foster and indeed create community, and finally its attempt to establish some religious rules. Neuwirth has little time for traditional Islamic Qur'an interpretation, since it does not provide in her view an acceptable account of the 'context' of the text. So we have here two huge claims, one that the Qur'an is a sort of compilation built up over time and not by one author, and also that the vast category of traditional Muslim commentary is really besides the point in understanding the Book. These are far from being new claims, they are commonplace in European and particularly German approaches to the Qur'an, and many think they are both plausible and highly productive of research on the text.

Neuwirth does characterize well the difference between traditional Muslim approaches to the Book and the sorts of secular approaches that have become popular in what is often called 'the West'. The secularization of the Qur'an seems inevitable if it is to be treated historically in this way, since it is often represented as a reorganization, and a pretty confused one, of original biblical material. The style and structure of the Qur'an are investigated and compared with older religious texts to which references are apparently made in the Book, and the Book is then grounded in a historical religious context rather than in anything transcendental. Islamic scholars, the *ʿulamāʾ*, by contrast, often choose as the appropriate context aspects of the Prophet's life to explain the revelation. Neuwirth argues that these two apparently distinct approaches can be brought together and that they can be regarded as complementary.

The Qur'an's Audience

This project fits perfectly with what might be called the traditional 'untraditional' approach to the study of the Qur'an followed by the 'modernizers'. It is quite easy to sum up the argument which has for a long time been applied to the Qur'an. Understanding a text means understanding and identifying its context, and this is the inhabitants of the Arabian Peninsula and their cultural background. This is a point often made, and energetically in modern times by Gabriel Said Reynolds. A good source of information on how to interpret the Qur'an is not then to be found in the work of the *mufassirūn*, the commentators and theologians who are the traditional people to explain the text, since these were later writers and so did not appreciate the appropriate historical context. By contrast, in Reynolds's view we should see the audience of the Qur'an to be the People of the Book, and so it is the bibles of the Jews and Christians that need to be borne in mind when examining the Qur'an. Reynolds is a good representative of this approach, and considers a variety of examples dealing with the devil, Adam, Abraham, Jonah, Mary, Hāmān, and of course the Prophet, and what he does in each case is produce a Qur'anic passage which he says is puzzling. Then he considers the traditional Muslim commentators' views of the passage and says why they are unsatisfactory. Finally, he refers to what he calls the Bible, and by this he means not just the Jewish and Christian bibles, but also the wealth of commentatorial and less canonical literature that exists within the broader Jewish and Christian traditions. He goes on to argue that this context makes far better sense of the text than the Muslim commentators. The conclusion is that the implied original audience of the Qur'an is the People of the Book, and this vaguely biblical context is the one we should have in mind when reading the Book itself.

This is a tempting line to take, and reinforces the idea that the Qur'an is a derivative work. But when it is examined in detail problems appear. Take for instance the reference in Q. 11:71 to the laughter of Sarah, who is not identified by name, just before she hears that she will have a child. At least in the Qur'an, it precedes this news, although Reynolds argues this is related to the need for a certain rhyme. What is the source of this reading? According to Reynolds (2010: 92–7), it is the Jewish Bible and its reference to Sarah laughing when she is given the news. And there is also the lexical link in Hebrew, but not in Arabic, between the word for laughter and the name Isaac (Isḥāq).

Now, there are obviously some differences between the passage in the Bible and in the Qur'an. For example, in the Qur'an, it is evident that the messengers did not eat, while in the Bible they did eat. This is not a problem for the thesis, though, since there is an account in the wider Jewish literature in accordance with which the messengers did not eat, and since they might well have been angels, could not have eaten. So here is the argument. The reference to laughter in 11:71 then is to a Jewish source where Abraham is visited by messengers from God who tell him that he and Sarah are going to have a child, and her laughter is a reference to her reaction in the Jewish Bible. But Christian sources are not ignored here either, since Sarah is compared with Mary and her perfection, linked to a degree with her virginity, and this is brought out in the Qur'an by the reference not only to Isaac but to Jacob also which hints at those who are to follow on later, such as Mary herself and of course Jesus (ʿĪsā), and according to Reynolds makes a certain kind of rhyme possible as an added bonus.

Appealing to the need to establish a certain rhyme really will not work, since it is not that difficult to form rhymes in a whole variety of ways and not disrupt the accurate account of the order of events in time. It is not as though the composer of the text is strictly limited by the lexical resources that are within the sura in its present form, the sura could have been otherwise designed had it been necessary. So the argument from rhyme is weak. Were the composer of the Book to have made free and easy with the content to ensure a smoother literary structure, this would be to go against the idea of the text as primarily religious and presumably true. It may have been done, but we really need some evidence that it was impossible to use the Arabic of the time to produce a verse that rhymed and was accurate. This is not like the argument of the miraculousness of the Qur'an that tries to show that a particular formulation of a point could not have been made better. There exists a whole variety of ways of rhyming in Arabic and the idea that the author of the Qur'an was limited in going in only one direction seems implausible, especially if that way involves inaccuracy.

The argument for similarities between the Qur'anic text and Jewish and Christian sources is also questionable, since those sources are immense, and it is not difficult to find somewhere at least in those sources a reference which will fit in both with whatever one wants to find, and its contrary. When talking about Sarah laughing, for instance, Reynolds brings in Josephus and the Targum, which may indeed have been part of the local Jewish culture at the time of the Prophet, yet he is making huge assumptions about the general knowledge of the audience at the time. Even if the audience was familiar with this vast variety of interpretations and commentaries and historical accounts, these do not constitute a fixed corpus of accepted Jewish explanations of the Bible, but rather a variety of views, and the fact that the Qur'an is in line with at least some of these views does nothing to show it was influenced by them. We should not think of the Jewish literature as consisting of a body of agreement, the opposite is true, it is made up of arguments, speculations, assumptions, stories, and so on that put forward a variety of comments on the text.

The major problem then is that the biblical literature in the wide sense that is being used here is so vast and diverse that if one is looking for something to relate to a passage in the Qur'an it is almost too easy to find. There will always be something, and usually more than one thing, that fits in nicely. 'Scientific' approaches will really need to be more nuanced if they are to throw light on the Qur'an.

Negative Views

There is a range of hostile accounts of the Qur'an in modern times. Ibn Warraq says he is a former Muslim from Pakistan and presents a broad assault on the Qur'an, as does Robert Spencer who directs his attention particularly at the lack of historical evidence for anything to do with it and early Islamic history. Christoph Luxenberg, another pseudonym, wrote a remarkable book on how the Qur'an is wrongly linked with Arabic but in fact should be read as though it were originally written in Aramaic, which indeed hardly surprisingly produces different interpretations of the text. What is remarkable about these approaches is that none of them comes near to being scientific apart from Luxenberg, which is well argued but unfortunately based on an entirely false premise about the languages then current in the Ḥijāz. Much biblical criticism also takes that form, it starts with a weird premise and uses it to argue quite logically for an entirely new interpretation of either or both bibles. A variety of other writers attack the Qur'an along with Islam especially for its treatment of women but again there is no subtlety in any of these approaches, no capacity to distinguish between the Qur'an and how it has come to be understood in a variety of cultural contexts, and basically no attempt at treating the Qur'an as worthy of any respect at all. Although these books are greeted with great enthusiasm by those hostile to Islam, they are so narrow and limited in their approach to the topic that they really cannot be said to have taken the debate over how to interpret the Qur'an any further.

Bibliography

Abū Zayd, Naṣr. *Reformation of Islamic Thought.* Amsterdam: Amsterdam University Press, 2006.

Barazangi, Nimat Hafez. *Woman's Identity and the Qur'an: A New Reading.* Gainesville, FL: University Press of Florida, 2004.

Barlas, Asma. 'Women's Readings of the Qur'an'. In: Jane McAuliffe (ed.). *The Cambridge Companion to the Qur'an*, pp. 255–72. Cambridge: Cambridge University Press, 2006.

Campanini, Massimo. *The Qur'an: Modern Muslim Interpretations.* Trans. Caroline Higgitt. London: Routledge, 2011.

Esack, Farid. *Qur'an, Liberation and Pluralism: An Islamic Perspective of the Interreligious Solidarity against Oppression.* Oxford: Oneworld, 1997.

Gülen, F. *Questions and Answers about Islam* 1. Somerset, NJ: Light Inc., 2010.

Ibn Warraq. *What the Qur'an Really Says.* Amherst, NY: Prometheus, 2002.

Karimi-Nịa, M. *Bibliography of Qur'anic Studies in European Languages.* Qum: The Centre for Translation of the Holy Qur'an, 2012.

Khorchide, Mouhanad. *Islam ist Barmherzigkeit: Grundzüge einer modernen Religion*, Freiburg: Verlag Herder, 2012.

Körner, Felix. *Alter Text—neuer Kontext: Koranhermeneutik in der Türkei heute. Ausgewählte Texte übersetzt und kommentiert.* Freiburg: Herder, 2006.

Leaman, Oliver. 'Does Islam need an Enlightenment?', *Islamic Philosophy* (2009), 191–210.

Leaman, Oliver. *Islamic Philosophy*, Oxford: Polity, 2009.

Leaman, Oliver. *Controversies in Contemporary Islam.* London: Routledge, 2013.

Luxenberg, Christoph. *Die Syro-Aramäische Lesart des Koran: Ein Beitrag zur Entschlüsselung der Koransprache.* Berlin: Verlag Hans Schiler, 2000.

Mahmood, Saba. 'Secularism, Hermeneutics, and Empire: The Politics of Islamic Reformation', *Public Interest* 18/2 (2006), 323–47.

Neuwirth, Angelika. *Der Koran als Text der Spätantike: Ein europäischer Zugang.* Berlin: Verlag der Weltreligionen, 2010.

Nöldeke, Theodor. *Geschichte des Qorâns.* Göttingen: Verlag der Dieterichschen Buchhandlung, 1860.

Nursi, Said. *The Rays.* Trans. S. Vahide. Istanbul: Sözler, 1998.

Nursi, Said. *The Twenty-Fifth Word: The Miraculous Qur'an.* Trans. Ali Ünal. Clifton, NJ: Light Publishing, 2006.

al-Qaraḍāwī, Yūsuf. *al-Ḥalāl wa'l-ḥarām fi'l-Islām* (The Lawful and the Prohibited in Islam). Casablanca: Dār al-Maʿrifa, 1975.

Rahman, Fazlur. *Major Themes of the Qur'an* 2. Edited by Ebrahim Moosa. Chicago: University of Chicago Press, 2009.

Ramadan, Tariq. *What I Believe.* Oxford: Oxford University Press, 2009.

Reynolds, Gabriel Said. *The Qur'ān and its Biblical Subtext*. London: Routledge, 2010.
Soroush, Abdolkarim. *Reason, Freedom and Democracy in Islam: Essential Writings of Adbolkarim Soroush*. Trans. and ed. with a critical introduction by M. Sadri and A. Sadri. Oxford: Oxford University Press, 2000.
Ṭāhā, Maḥmūd Muḥammad. *The Second Message of Islam*. Trans. A. A. Na'im, Syracuse, NY: Syracuse University Press, 1987.
Wadud, Amina. *Qur'an and Woman: Rereading the Sacred Text from a Woman's Perspective*. Oxford: Oxford University Press, 1999.
Wild, Stefan (ed.). *The Qur'an as Text*. Leiden: Brill, 1996.

CHAPTER 3

ISLAMIC ORIGINS AND THE QUR'AN

HERBERT BERG

INTRODUCTION

AT first glance, the fixation of scholars of Islamic origins on the Qur'an seems natural. Most Muslims believe that the Qur'an is eternal and that the religion of Islam is as old as humanity and its first prophet, Adam, but the religion as it is practised by over a billion Muslims today is also believed to have begun with the last prophet, Muḥammad. His status as messenger, and so Islam, began with the '*iqraʾ*' of the first revelation of the Qur'an on Mount Ḥirāʾ. The Qur'an, however, is also critical to the study of Islamic origins for historiographical reasons, not just theological ones. The authenticity of other literatures that speak of the formative period of Islam, the Sunna and the *sīra*, have both been called into question. Muslim scholars themselves doubted the veracity of many individual hadiths. Even al-Bukhārī and Muslim trusted only a few thousand of the hundreds of thousands of hadiths that they collected. These two *Ṣaḥīḥ*s have achieved a canonical status within Sunnī Islam, yet even classical Sunnī scholars such as al-Dāraquṭnī criticized the inclusion of many hadiths (Brown 2007: 117–20). Many non-Muslim scholars go much farther by suggesting that so many hadiths were fabricated or redacted in transmission that it is best to assume inauthenticity. These doubts were raised most notably by Ignaz Goldziher and then by Joseph Schacht. The former argued that hadiths could 'not serve as a document for the history of the infancy of Islam, but rather as a reflection of the tendencies which appear in the community during the mature stages of its development' (Goldziher 1971: 2:19). The latter was even more sceptical: 'every legal tradition from the Prophet, until the contrary is proved, must be taken not as authentic or essentially authentic, ... but is the fictitious expression of a legal doctrine formulated at a later date' (Schacht 1959: 149). Some faith has been restored in hadiths by Harald Motzki, for example, in his work on ʿAbd al-Razzāq's *Muṣannaf* (Motzki 1991: 1–21) and his use of his *isnād-cum-matn* technique, in which the providence of a report may be determined by comparing the *isnāds* and the *matns* of a substantial number of related hadiths (Motzki et al. 2010).

But when this technique is applied to historical hadiths, even later ones (such as those about the conquest of Damascus), the historicity is less than reassuring (Scheiner 2010). Moreover, the hadiths that comprise the *sīra* did not even undergo the rigorous evaluation to which al-Bukhārī and Muslim subjected their hadiths. Consequently, many modern scholars only feel confident in the historical accuracy of those parts of the *sīra* that can be confirmed by an external source: the Qur'an. Only recently has the earliest biography of Muḥammad, those materials ascribed to ʿUrwa ibn al-Zubayr, undergone vigorous critical evaluation, particularly by Gregor Schoeler and Andreas Görke. They are unfortunately limited to those events that have multiple lines of transmission. Even so, they conclude:

> The material that can be securely ascribed to ʿUrwa was collected some 30 to 60 years after Muḥammad's death. It partly goes back to eye witnesses and to persons in close contact to Muḥammad. It may therefore be assumed that these reports reflect the general outline of the events correctly. (Görke and Schoeler 2008: 294)

Elsewhere, they recognize that one cannot be certain that these reconstructed texts say anything definitive about the historical Muḥammad (Görke, Motzki, and Schoeler 2012: 55). Regardless of whether one accepts their technique, what remains striking is how few of the events within the *sīra* can be 'verified' as likely authentic by this method: the *hijra*, the slander against ʿĀʾisha, and the treaty of al-Ḥudaybiya and the subsequent conquest of Mecca. It is notable that Schoeler's methodology suggests that story of the initial revelation of the Qur'an on Mt. Ḥirāʾ is a product of a story teller (Schoeler 1996: 59–117; see also Görke, Motzki, and Schoeler 2012: 22–33) Moreover, even if the events listed above were part of ʿUrwa's *sīra* traditions and so within a few decades of the events they purport to describe, one may doubt their assumption that chronological proximity implies historicity. The examples of the canonical Christian Gospels and particularly the gospel of Q (the reconstructed sayings source for Matthew and Luke) and the letters of Paul caution us from treating such texts' perspectives as historical rather than theological (Berg and Rollens 2008: 271–92). An excellent example of this comes from David S. Powers, who demonstrates that several significant episodes usually accepted as historical seem to be almost entirely the product of theological and political aims (Powers 2009).

This situation therefore suggests to some scholars that the Qur'an is the only wholly reliable source for reconstructing the origins of Islam. Before turning to the specific, often (crypto-) theological, problems associated with three main methodological approaches to the study of Islamic origins (based on how much trust one puts in the historicity of the Qur'an and *sīra*)—one must be aware of the far more fundamental theoretical problem of a fixation on origins and the genetic fallacy of the identifying origins with authenticity.

Theoretical Issues: Origin(s), Islamic and Otherwise

The use of 'Islamic origins' by scholars of early Islam is modelled on the use of 'Christian origins' by scholars of texts that later came to be adopted by a movement known as Christianity. As William E. Arnal points out, the term 'Christian origins' was meant to replace the confessional, anachronistic, and misleading 'New Testament Studies'. Yet, as he points out, the scholarship remains centred on the canonical writings of the New Testament,

> and that as such they serve as sources for, and stand in social, historical, and/or conceptual unity with, the ecclesiastical structures and ideologies of the second century and later. In some respects, the language of 'Christian Origins' actually exacerbates the problem, since in two words it manages to impute both an originary status to the New Testament writings, and to claim for those writings a specifically *Christian* identity. (Arnal 2011: 194)

Islamic origins is not replacing an earlier problematic term 'Qur'an Studies'. Rather, 'Islamic origins' is a convenient term for those of us who focus on the formative period of Islam (1) to convey to our colleagues in Religious Studies departments what it is that we do, and (2) to unite into one enterprise the disparate but overlapping activities of scholars of the Qur'an and early Islamic history, law, Sunna, exegesis, and grammar. Yet, each term, 'Islamic' and 'origins' is just as problematic, but the latter in two related ways.

First, as Tomoko Masuzawa points out, if one means 'origin' in the strong sense, in the sense of absolute beginning, 'it eradicates any possibility of precedent, preexisting condition or prototype—in fact, anything other than itself—that might in any way account for later developments'. Origin thus understood 'is an essentially theological idea' (Masuzawa 2000: 209). Nietzsche notes that the focus on origin is a focus on essence and authenticity when he stated, ' "In the Beginning". To glorify the origin—that is the metaphysical aftershoot that breaks out when we meditate on history and makes us believe that what stands at the beginning of all things is also what is most valuable and essential' (Nietzsche 1996: 302). Michel Foucault elaborates:

> Why does Nietzsche challenge the pursuit of origin (*Ursprung*)...? First, because it is an attempt to capture the exact essence of things, the purist possibilities, and their carefully protected identities.... We tend to think that this is the moment of greatest perfection, when they emerged dazzling from the hands of a creator...
>
> (Foucault 1977: 142–3)

One would have to be incredibly naive to think that somehow the study of Islamic origins is immune to these tacitly theological concerns with essence, truth, identity, and authenticity. For the Qur'an to claim 'When he wants something, He says to it, "Be!" and it is!' (Q. 36:82) is not problematic. For a historian to employ such *ex nihilo* explanations is to cease to be a historian.

> Social theory requires us to explain individuals rather than simply posit them as the ground of our explanations. To posit self-causing monads, even out of apparent respect for individuals, is to turn social theory into liberal ideology or, worse, theology—for what is more theological than self-causing agents, which escape causal fields yet make effects in the world? (Martin unpublished)

Closely related is a second problem: the genetic fallacy. This is most obvious in the rhetoric of Salafis, who maintain that Islam was perfect and complete during the days of Muḥammad and his Companions. This perspective is also evident in others with an overtly theological agenda. Christian polemicists and the secular polemicists such as the New Atheists' Christopher Hitchens in his chapter 'The Koran is Borrowed from Both Jewish and Christian Myths' (Hitchens 2009: 211–37) look to the Qur'an and Muḥammad to find a negative essence of Islam. Scholars who study Islamic origins do not normally share the same positive or negative theologies, but they can share a remarkably similar approach. Fred Donner recently argued that based on the Qur'an the movement that became Islam was originally a movement of ecumenical believers that included Jews and Christians. It is a depiction that is remarkably compatible with our modern Western theology of religious pluralism, and certainly seems to imply that this is the authentic form of Islam. Moreover, to fall prey to the genetic fallacy is to say that to truly understand Rābiʿa al-ʿAdawiyya, Malcolm X, or the Muslim student in my classroom, all I really need to do is understand the first fifty years or so of the authentic or real Islam. Likewise, the genetic fallacy leads one to suggest that the Islam of an illiterate Indonesian woman living in a hut is the same as that of a twentieth-century Saudi prince living in Mecca, is the same as a fourteenth-century jurist living in Cordoba, is the same as a seventeenth-century African just sold in the United States as a slave, is the same as the Islam of Ibn ʿAbbās in the seventh-century Medina. Their experiences and understandings of the Qur'an and Islam are as equally authentic as they are completely different. To assume that there is some essence that connects all these people who call themselves Muslims is once again to adopt a theological position.

As for the 'Islamic' in Islamic origins, it is also problematic in two ways. First, it encourages us to project later understandings of classical Islam back onto the data, obscuring what really happened, just as the use of 'Christian' in Christian origins. Second, if one sees Islam as rooted almost solely in the Qur'an and/or Muḥammad, one cannot help but recapitulate in an academic voice the basic position of Muslims—what I call crypto-theology. Nevertheless, Muslims themselves focus very much on this early period. The Qur'an (presumably), the *sīra*, and the Sunna all harken back to this early period. It is not surprising that scholarly interest continues in how the movement that came to be known as Islam was formulated. It is a valid, and I would say intriguing, avenue for scholarly exploration. But without an awareness of the often tacitly theological perspective at the heart of such explorations it is not surprising that the methodologies used to investigate Islamic origins are problematic in much the same way.

Methodological Issues: The Nature of The Sources

Despite the theological motivations or, hopefully, merely the underlying theological legacy of our fixation on origins, we scholars of Islamic origins continue our investigations apace. There seem to be three broad approaches, or rather three clusters of approaches on a continuum of scepticism about the trustworthiness of the sources: the Qur'an and the *sīra* are historically accurate, the Qur'an at least is historically accurate, and, not even the Qur'an is historical. Each is methodologically problematic.

Both the Qur'an and *Sīra* are Reliable

The first position is that of most Muslims who, generally speaking, consider the historical references in the Qur'an as obviously accurate and maintain that the *sīra* confirms this. So together they provide a reasonably accurate depiction of the origins of Islam. The latter is not thought of as inspired in the way some Christians view the Gospels, so that it is possible that some material within the *sīra* is inaccurate, especially where Ibn Isḥāq, Ibn Hishām, al-Wāqidī, al-Ṭabarī, and various *mufassirūn* and *muḥaddithūn* record conflicting variations of events. Some non-Muslim scholars share this perspective, most notably W. Montgomery Watt. He maintains that the basic facts in the *sīra* are accurate. Following Theodor Nöldeke, he suggests that there has been 'tendential shaping' usually by distorting motives of actors. 'The traditional accounts are in general to be accepted, are to be received with care and as far as possible corrected where "tendential shaping" is suspected, and are only to be rejected outright where there is internal contradiction' (Watt 1953: xiv). It is not too surprising, therefore, that Watt's biography of Muḥammad more or less reproduces what the Islamic tradition says about its own origins, and so he has provoked little criticism.

Of course Watt is not suspending disbelief in hopes of avoiding criticism; Watt believed the Qur'an was inspired by 'God': 'I believe that the Qur'an came from God, that it is Divinely inspired. Muhammad could not have caused the great upsurge in religion that he did without God's blessing' (Watt 2000: 10). He is not crypto-theological, but blatantly theological. He states that he writes 'as a professing monotheist' (Watt 1953: xi), though in considering neither the Bible nor the Qur'an infallibly true, he is hardly orthodox.

Only the Qur'an is Reliable

Whether because of the questions raised about the hadiths or the legendary and contradictory material sprinkled throughout the *sīra*, may other scholars prefer to rely on the Qur'an as the only sure historical source for the origins of Islam. Alford T. Welch argues that 'the Qurʾān is a historical document that reflects the prophetic career of Muḥammad and responds constantly to the specific needs and problems of the emerging Muslim community. It abounds in references and allusions to historical events that occurred during the last twenty or so years of Muḥammad's lifetime...' (Welch 1980: 626). Maxime Rodinson said much the same a decade earlier: one cannot be certain that anything in the *sīra* dates back to Muḥammad, but 'we can start with the text of the Koran, which is a firm and authentic base' (Rodinson 1971: xi–xii). Richard Bell also shared a similar view so perhaps Watt had his mentor in mind when he wrote, 'What in fact Western scholars have done is to assume the truth of the broad outlines of the picture *of the Meccan period* given by the *Sīrah*, and to use this as a framework into which to fit as much Qurʾanic material as possible' (Watt 1953: xv; italics added). Remove the italicized qualification and Watt's characterization contains a still poignant critique of this methodological approach. Scholars who claim to use only the Qur'an as a sole historical source either tacitly assume the background supplied by the *sīra* or use the Qur'an to justify employing it. The net result is to describe an Islamic origins that differs little from those of Watt.

More recently Donner tries to reconstruct the earliest Islam or proto-Islam. He recognizes that the miracle stories, contradictions, and so forth limit the historian's ability to trust traditional Muslim accounts of Muḥammad's life, but the 'traditional narratives do seem to contain some very early material' about his life—though they should be used cautiously (Donner 2010: 52). Donner thus concurs with Rodinson and Welch: 'The Qurʾān text, as we now have it, must be an artifact of the earliest historical phase of the community of Believers, and so can be used with some confidence to understand the values and beliefs of that community' (Donner 1998: 61). So his guide is the Qur'an alone and he argues that Muḥammad's original movement was a 'strongly monotheistic, intensely pietistic, and ecumenical or confessionally open religious movement that enjoined people who were not already monotheists to recognize God's oneness and enjoined all monotheists to live in strict observance of the law that God had repeatedly revealed to mankind—whether in the form of the Torah, the Gospels, or the Qur'an' (Donner 2010: 75; see also Shoemaker 2012: 199–218). In other words, these ecumenical Believers included (non-trinitarian) Christians, Jews, or 'Qurʾanic monotheists'. The theological implications of this conclusion have already been noted, but it also highlights the greater fluidity of interpretation once the *sīra* is (selectively) jettisoned. These possibilities become only more liquid if one also begins to question the historicity of the Qur'an.

The Qur'an Is Not Historical Either

Those scholars who are willing to unmoor the Qur'an and thus Islamic origins from Muḥammad or even the Hijāz are often referred to as revisionists. And chief among them was John Wansbrough. He seemingly decoupled the Qur'an and *sīra* from each other by arguing that the prophetic *logia* that make up the Qur'an existed independently of the prophetic *evangelium* that make up the *sīra*. (He actually recoupled them by suggesting that the *sīra* was a form of narrative exegesis on the Qur'an.) This argument has been challenged on a number of fronts, but most convincingly on the *sīra* by those working with the *isnād-cum-matn* technique. Wansbrough suggested that the Qur'an was 'the product of an organic development from originally independent traditions during a long period of transmission', and so the material may have existed in some form, but the *ne varietur* text was fixed only 'towards the end of the second century' (Wansbrough 1977: 47 and 44). Moreover, this development took place within a Judaeo-Christian sectarian milieu. The significance of that is that it does not see the tradition as a unique, singular origin (as Martin cautioned above).

He is not alone in seeing an alternate origin for Islam. Günter Lüling argued that some suras were revisions of pre-Islamic, originally Christian hymns (Lüling 1974). In a similar vein, Christoph Luxenberg hopes to demonstrate that the Arabic Qur'an was excerpted from a Syriac canonical and/or proto-scriptural *urtext*. Luxenberg then argues that Mecca was an Aramean settlement in which an Aramaic-Arabic hybrid was spoken. Later, Arabic speaking exegetes and philologists were unfamiliar with the hybrid language and the initially defective script of the Qur'an, which was standardized only in the second half of the eighth century (Luxenberg 2000). Most scholars of Islam, if they do not ignore Luxenberg, critique his methodology sharply. An exception might be Claude Gilliot, who entertains the possibility of a pre-Qur'anic lectionary because of the close interacting with the nearby Aramaic, Jewish, and Christian cultures (Gilliot 2010: 164). More recently, Gabriel S. Reynolds has also insisted that the Qur'an be read using biblical and post-biblical traditions since both traditional *tafsīr* and the *sīra* are removed from the period of Islamic origins (Reynolds 2010: 22).

David Powers's recent study is in many ways just as provocative, for it shows how complex the questions of authenticity can be. He questions both the Qur'an and the *sīra*, yet relies on both. By examining the Qur'anic and *sīra* accounts of Zayd ibn Ḥāritha, Muḥammad's one-time adopted son whose ex-wife Zaynab he married, Powers argues that Q. 4:23 and 33:6 were revised and Q. 33:36–40 were added. By examining Manuscript BNF 328a, Powers concludes that Q. 4:12 was altered to deal with the political issue of succession, which in turn required the addition of Q. 4:176. The Qur'an therefore remained open and fluid for three-quarters of a century between the death of the Prophet and the caliphate of ʿAbd al-Malik (Powers 2009: 227). These were not merely minor variations or misreadings of the ambiguous consonantal text, but theologically and politically motivated additions and revisions. All of the events of Zayd's biography as given in the *sīra* were likewise motivated and based on Jewish and Christian biblical models. His arguments for the additions and revisions of the Qur'an seem to lend strong support to the Marwanid hypothesis put forward by Paul Casanova (1911: 103–42), but revived by Alfred-Louis de Prémare (2002: 278–306 and 2010: 189–221; see also Shoemaker 2012: 146–58). Michael Cook concurs by pointing out that numismatic evidence, Qur'anic 'quotations' (by al-Ḥasan al-Baṣrī, for example), and the claims that al-Ḥajjāj, the governor of Iraq who died in 95/714, made a series of changes to the text of the Qur'an. He concludes, 'in the period after ʿUthmān, things were more complicated than the story of his establishment of the canonical text would suggest' (Cook 2000: 122–3). Chase Robinson in his study of ʿAbd al-Malik questions how in a single generation the Qur'an could have moved 'from individual lines scribbled on camel shoulder blades and rocks to complete, single, fixed and authoritative text on papyrus or vellum' and how the rudimentary polity could have the authority to canonize a text. ʿAbd al-Malik, on the other hand, had the motivation and means to impose such standardization (Robinson 2005: 102). Omar Hamdan, however, has argued that al-Ḥajjāj's project, though an act of canonization, was not so radical; it mainly sought to propagate an official codex with a standardized and improved script (Hamdan 2010: 825).

Attempts to find earlier manuscripts especially of the Qur'an (Sadeghi and Bergmann 2010: 343–436); to reconstruct them (as Schoeler and Görke do); to defend the *isnād* system (as Motzki and Schoeler do); or to defend the reports about the collection of the Qur'an as credible using 'common sense' and what we know of the use of writing in early Islam (Schoeler 2010); all support the first two approaches against that of the revisionists. It does seem, as Cook noted, 'Instead of data serving to determine our general notions, it is our general notions which determine the way in which we interpret the data. We know how to *maintain* rival theories; but we can do little to decide *between* them' (Cook 1981: 155).

An 'Orientalist' Conclusion

As I have argued, any exploration into the origins of a religion is in danger of being theological by the very nature of the enterprise: the kinds of assumptions made, data employed, or questions asked. Some of the methodological approaches increase the propensity to reproduce (often crypto-theologically) traditional Muslim understanding of the origins of Islam. But even revisionists are not immune; they have been *accused* of having a theological agenda and certainly their conclusions have been deployed by those with one (Hitchens 2009: 211–37). But what of the elephant in the room? A constant in *all* of the examples that I have used, even that of Watt, is the assumption of significant Jewish and Christian influences on early Islam. Bell put it bluntly: 'To any student of the Qur'an the presence in it of Jewish and Christian elements is evident almost at the first glance,' though there may have been no direct contact (Bell 1926: 66–7). G. R. Hawting concurs: 'That Islam is a monotheistic religion related to Judaism and Christianity is a generally accepted commonplace'; to believe otherwise is to dissociate 'Islam from the historical development of the monotheist stream of religion as a whole. Islam is shown to be the result of an act of divine revelation made to an Arab prophet who was born and lived most of his life in a town (Mecca) beyond the borders of the then monotheistic world' (Hawting 1997: 24). That this influence on Islamic origins is 'evident' and 'accepted' is illustrated in some of the most noteworthy books in the field, from older works such as Abraham Geiger's *Was hat Mohammed aus dem Judenthume aufgenommen?* and Bell's *The Origin of Islam in its Christian Environment*, to newer ones such as

Wansbrough's *The* [Judaeo-Christian] *Sectarian Milieu*, Patricia Crone and Michael Cook's *Hagarism* (which emphasizes the supposed role of Samaritans and Babylonian Jews in the early formation of Islam) (Crone and Cook 1977), Luxenberg's *Die syro-aramäische Lesart des Koran*, and Reynolds's *The Qur'ān and its Biblical Subtext*. The various hypotheses they present are largely mutually exclusive, though all have been accused in various ways of being orientalist efforts to rob Islam, Muḥammad, and the Qur'an of its originality by giving it Jews and Christians. Bell himself pointed out, 'it is no means easy to determine what elements came through Jewish channels and what through Christian. Scholars are apt to stress the influence of each according to their own predilections'—an ironic statement given his emphasis on the 'Christian environment' (Bell 1926: 66–7). The revisionists, of course, have been most castigated far more for their suggestion of a Judaeo-Christian sectarian milieu. For example, R. B. Serjeant castigates Wansbrough's *Quranic Studies* as 'a thoroughly reactionary stand in reverting to the over-emphasis of the Hebrew element in Islam... [and] a disguised polemic seeking to strip Islam and the Prophet of all but the minimum of originality', which ignores 'the vital Arabian element (about which he appears ill- or uninformed)'. As for Cook and Crone, he berates *Hagarism* even more harshly as 'foaled in the same stable, though lacking the depth of Dr. Wansbrough's undisputed learning, is not only bitterly anti-Islamic in tone but anti-Arabian' (Serjeant 1978: 76–8). And more mildly, G. H. A. Juynboll states, 'I am always annoyed by those who do not dare to ascribe any originality to the Arabs and constantly look for Jewish and Christian models which the community of Muḥammad might have borrowed' (Juynboll 1979: 294). Either way, the message is clear: stop noting the elephant's existence. A more recent version of this position is advocated by Reynolds who sees in the Qur'an references to biblical and post-biblical lore current among the pre-Islamic Arabs who were familiar with Jewish and Christian mythology and less pagan than is usually assumed (Reynolds 2012). Far more subtle but no less provocative than the revisionists are Donner's proto-Muslim believers who included Jews and Christians and Powers' compelling case for the use of biblical models for the construction of Zayd's biography. As they demonstrate, if one is to seriously engage in the study of Islamic origins, be it called a 'Believers movement', 'Semitic monotheism', 'Judaeo-Christian sectarian milieu', etc., there is no avoiding this issue.

To attempt to avoid it, one must take the route of Watt. For him, speaking of influences and development was permitted, though not on Muḥammad or the Qur'an, just on the Arabian environment and development of his community's outlook. Muḥammad's messages, after all, come to him from (the Judaeo-Christian-Islamic) 'God' (Watt 1953: 18). As my scare quotes around the word God here and above suggest, he advocates a particular theological position. That is, the Jewish, Christian, and Muslim gods are all the same God—an eirenic and pluralistic position for Jews, Christians, and Muslims to take, but not a critical one for the scholar to advocate. (And if one accepts the claim(s) of Christian scripture about the Jewish god, and those of Muslim scripture about the Christian god, then why not those of Baha'i and Sikh scriptures about the Muslim god or even of Scientology's Eighth Dynamic?) But Watt's more narrowly defined monotheism meant that those concepts, morality, figures, and rituals in the

Qur'an that are also found within Christianity and Judaism are to be expected—they have the same source.

But what if one wishes to prioritize critical scholarship rather than this kind of pluralist theology or eirenic agenda? As Bruce Lincoln eloquently puts it: 'Reverence is a religious, and not a scholarly virtue. When good manners and good conscience cannot be reconciled, the demands of the latter ought to prevail.' And,

> When one permits those whom one studies to define the terms in which they will be understood... or fails to distinguish between 'truths', 'truth-claims', and 'regimes of truth', one has ceased to function as historian or scholar. In that moment, a variety of roles are available: some perfectly respectable (amanuensis, collector, friend and advocate), and some less appealing (cheerleader, voyeur, retailer of import goods). None, however, should be confused with scholarship. (Lincoln 1996: 225–7)

Yet in so doing, scholars of religion are likely to be accused of reductionism and other scholars of orientalism (Berg 2012: 112–28).

Islamic origins is not alone in this challenge. Its namesake, Christian origins, requires the study of the Graeco-Roman world, its social organizations, political ideologies, systems of cultural values, and the various Judaisms it contained. And it is not radical to suggest that Christianity was a second-century invention or even to question the Christian-ness of its foundational texts including canonical Gospels. It is a theological Jesus and his symbolic currency—not the historical Jesus—that is central to the texts of Christian origins. To attempt to isolate the origins of Islam from the culture that generated it inhibits our understanding. Islam was not an isolated cult, as the Qur'an itself testifies. Yet even here the spectre of theology appears. The use of 'monotheistic' or 'Judaeo-Christian sectarian', for example, to describe its milieu imbues the term with theological overtones.

The threat of a theological taint is strong in the study of Islamic origins because not only is the very enterprise of origin studies genealogically rooted in a theological perspective, but also, regardless of one's view of the historical value of the Qur'an and the *sīra*, they are undoubtedly theological texts first. As movements from Salafīs to the New Atheists, and scholars from Watt to myself demonstrate, one's own beliefs affect how one sees the data. It seems more than a coincidence that Bell saw the influence of Christianity and Geiger that of Judaism. The study of Islamic origins will no doubt forge ahead even though the threat cannot be eliminated. What is needed is a little more theoretical and methodological sophistication including a healthy dose of self-reflexivity when using the Qur'an in hopes of discerning Islamic origins.

Bibliography

Arnal, William E. 'The Collection and Synthesis of "Tradition" and the Second-Century Invention of Christianity', *Method and Theory in the Study of Religion* 23 (2011), 193–215.

Bell, Richard. *The Origin of Islam in its Christian Environment: The Gunning Lectures, Edinburgh University 1925*. London: Macmillan and Co., 1926.

Bell, Richard. *The Qur'ān: Translated, with a Critical Re-arrangement of the Surahs*. 2 vols. Edinburgh: T. & T. Clark, 1937–9.

Berg, Herbert (2012). 'Failures (of Nerve?) in the Study of Islamic Origins'. In: William E. Arnal, Willi Braun, and Russell T. McCutcheon (eds.). *Failure and Nerve in the Study of Religion: Working with Donald Wiebe*, pp. 112–28. London: Equinox.

Berg, Herbert and Sarah Rollens. 'The Historical Muhammad and the Historical Jesus: A Comparison of Scholarly Reinventions and Reinterpretations', *Studies in Religion/Sciences Religieuses* 32 (2008), 271–92.

Brown, Jonathan. *The Canonization of al-Bukhārī and Muslim: The Formation and Function of the Sunnī Ḥadīth Canon*. Leiden: Brill, 2007.

Casanova, Paul. *Mohammed et la fin du monde: étude critique sure l'Islam primitive*. Paris: P. Gauthier, 1911–24.

Cook, Michael. *Early Muslim Dogma: A Source-Critical Study*. Cambridge: Cambridge University Press, 1981.

Cook, Michael. *The Koran: A Very Short Introduction*. Oxford: Oxford University Press, 2000.

Crone, Patricia and Michael Cook. *Hagarism: The Making of the Islamic World*. Cambridge: Cambridge University Press, 1977.

Donner, Fred M. *Narratives of Islamic Origins: The Beginnings of Islamic Historical Writing*. Princeton: The Darwin Press, 1998.

Donner, Fred M. *Muhammad and the Believers at the Origins of Islam*. Cambridge: Belknap Press of Harvard University Press, 2010.

Foucault, Michel. 'Nietzsche, Genealogy, History'. In: *Language Counter-Memory, Practice: Selected Essays and Interviews*. Ed. Donald Bouchard, trans. Donald Bouchard and Sherry Simon, pp. 139–64. Ithaca, NY: Cornell University Press, 1977.

Geiger, Abraham. *Was hat Mohammed aus dem Judenthume aufgenommen?* Bonn: F. Baaden, 1833.

Gilliot, Claude. 'On the Origins of the Informants of the Prophet'. In: Karl-Heinz Ohlig and Gerd-R. Puin (eds.) *The Hidden Origins of Islam*, pp. 153–87. Amherst, NY: Prometheus Books, 2010.

Goldziher, Ignaz. *Muslim Studies (Muhammedanische Studien)*. ed. S. M. Stern, trans. C. R. Barber and S. M. Stern. 2 vols. London: George Allen and Unwin, 1971.

Görke, Andreas, Harald Motzki, and Gregor Schoeler. 'First Century Sources for the Life of Muḥammad? A Debate', *Der Islam* 89/2 (2012), 2–59.

Görke, Andreas and Gregor Schoeler. *Die Ältesten Berichte über Muhammads: Das Korpus 'Urwa ibn az-Zubair*. Princeton: Darwin Press, 2008.

Hamdan, Omar. 'The Second *Maṣāḥif* Project: A Step towards the Canonization of the Qur'anic Text.' In: Angelika Neuwirth, Nicolai Sinai, and Michael Marx (eds.). *The Qur'ān in Context: Historical and Literary Investigations into the Qur'ānic Milieu*, pp. 795–835. Leiden: Brill, 2010.

Hawting, G. R. 'John Wansbrough, Islam, and Monotheism', *Method & Theory in the Study of Religion* 9/1 (1997), 23–38.

Hitchens, Christopher. *God is not Great: How Religion Poisons Everything*. New York: Twelve, 2009.

Juynboll, G. H. A. 'Review of *Quranic Studies: Sources and Methods of Scriptural Interpretation* by John Wansbrough', *Journal of Semitic Studies* 24 (1979), 293–6.

Lincoln, Bruce. 'Theses on Method', *Method & Theory in the Study of Religion* 8/3 (1996), 225–7.

Lüling, Günter. *Über den Ur-Quran: Ansätze z. Rekonstruktion vorislam, christl. Strophenlieder Quran*. Erlangen: Lüling, 1974.
Luxenberg, Christoph. *Die syro-aramäische Lesart des Koran: Ein Beitrag zur Entschlüsselung des Koransprache*. Berlin: Das Arabische Buch, 2000.
Martin, Craig. '"Individuality is Zero": Freedom and Ethnocentrism in *The Division of Labor*'. Unpublished.
Masuzawa, Tomoko. 'Origin'. In: Willi Braun and Russell T. McCutcheon (eds.). *Guide to the Study of Religion*, pp. 209–24. London: Cassell, 2000.
Motzki, Harald. 'The *Muṣannaf* of ʿAbd al-Razzāq al-Ṣanʿānī as a Source of Authentic *aḥādīth* of the First Century A.H.', *Journal of Near Eastern Studies* 50 (1991), 1–21.
Motzki, Harald, Nicolet Boekhoff-van der Voort, and Sean W. Anthony. *Analysing Muslim Tradition: Studies in Legal, Exegetical and Maghāzī Ḥadīth*. Leiden: Brill, 2010.
Nietzsche, Friedrich. *Human, All Too Human*. Trans. R. J. Hollingdale. Cambridge: Cambridge University Press, 1996.
Powers, David S. *Muhammad is Not the Father of Any of Your Men: The Making of the Last Prophet*. Philadelphia: University of Pennsylvania, 2009.
de Prémare, Alfred-Louis. *Les fondations del'Islam: entre écriture et histoire*. Paris: Éditions du Seuil, 2002.
de Prémare, Alfred-Louis. 'ʿAbd al-Malik b. Marwān and the Processes of the Qurʾān's Composition'. In: Karl-Heinz Ohlig and Gerd-R. Puin (eds.). *The Hidden Origins of Islam*, pp. 189–221. Amherst, NY: Prometheus Books, 2010.
Reynolds, Gabriel S. *The Qurʾān and its Biblical Subtext*. London: Routledge, 2010.
Reynolds, Gabriel S. *The Emergence of Islam: Classical Traditions in Contemporary Perspective*. Minneapolis: Fortress Press, 2012.
Robinson, Chase F. *ʿAbd al-Malik*. Oxford: Oneworld, 2005.
Rodinson, Maxime. *Muhammad*. Trans. Anne Carter. New York: Pantheon Books, 1971.
Sadeghi, Behnam and Uwe Bergmann. 'The Codex of a Companion of the Prophet and the Qurʾān of the Prophet', *Arabica* 57 (2010), 343–436.
Schacht, Joseph. *The Origins of Muhammadan Jurisprudence*. 3rd rev. edn. Oxford: Clarendon Press, 1959.
Schiener, Jens J. *Die Eroberung von Damaskus: Quellenkritische Untersuchung zur Historiographie in klassisch-islamischer Zeit*. Leiden: Brill, 2010.
Schoeler, Gregor. *Charakter und Authentie der muslimischen Überlieferung über das Leben Mohammeds*. Berlin: Walter de Gruyter, 1996.
Schoeler, Gregor. 'The Codification of the Qurʾān: A Comment on the Hypotheses of Burton and Wansbrough'. In: Angelika Neuwirth, Nicolai Sinai, and Michael Marx (eds.). *The Qurʾān in Context: Historical and Literary Investigations into the Qurʾānic Milieu*, pp. 779–94. Leiden: Brill, 2010.
Serjeant, R. B. 'Review of *Quranic Studies: Sources and Methods of Scriptural Interpretation* by John Wansbrough and *Hagarism: The Making of the Islamic World* by Patricia Crone and Michael Cook', *Journal of the Royal Asiatic Society* n.v. (1978), 76–8.
Shoemaker, Stephen J. *The Death of a Prophet: The End of Muhammad's Life and the Beginnings of Islam*. Philadelphia: University of Pennsylvania Press, 2012.
Wansbrough, John. *Quranic Studies: Sources and Methods of Scriptural Interpretation*. Oxford: Oxford University Press, 1977.
Wansbrough, John. *The Sectarian Milieu: Content and Composition of Islamic Salvation History*. Oxford: Oxford University Press, 1978.

Watt, W. Montgomery. *Muhammad at Mecca*. Oxford: Oxford University Press, 1953.
Watt, W. '"The whole house of Islam, and we Christians with them…": An Interview with "the Last Orientalist" by Bashir Maan & Alastair Mclntosh', *Coracle* 3/151 (August 2000), 8–11.
Watt, W. Montgomery and Richard Bell. *Introduction to the Qur'ān*. Edinburgh: Edinburgh University Press, 1970.
Welch, Alford T. 'Introduction: Qur'ānic Studies Problems and Prospects', *Journal of the American Academy of Religion* 47 (1980), 620–34.

CHAPTER 4

QUR'ANIC STUDIES

Bibliographical Survey

ANNA AKASOY

In issue 64 of *The Muslim World*, published in 1974, Willem A. Bijlefeld published in three instalments (79–102, 172–9, 259–74) 'Some Recent Contributions to Qurʾānic Studies: Selected Publications in English, French, and German, 1964–1973'. In the first part, he discussed select translations of the Qur'an, in the second part introductions and in the third part studies on topics such as revelation, God and humans, Abraham and Jesus, death and eternal life, and ethics. While Bijlefeld was able to offer a survey with comments in some detail, the number of books concerned with the Qur'an which have been published in the twenty-first century in English alone is staggering and does not allow for a similar presentation in such limited space. Numerous articles have appeared in edited volumes and periodicals and, since 1999, the Centre for Islamic Studies at SOAS has been publishing a specialized *Journal of Qur'anic Studies*.

The reasons for the rise of academic interest in the Qur'an are manifold. Some areas in the study of Islam, the Middle East, and Islamicate languages have proved to be particularly dynamic. Our view of early Islamic history, for example, has been fundamentally transformed over the last three decades. To a large extent, however, the growth of scholarship on the Qur'an is owed to the sheer number of scholars interested in this and related areas. Areas which have long been underrepresented (such as contemporary Muslim interpretations of the Qur'an) are now receiving attention, long-neglected primary sources (such as commentaries from different periods of history and different parts of the Islamic world) are being made available, and the expansion of disciplinary connections has led to a diversification of scholarship on the Qur'an as well. The text is nowadays explored from philological, historical, sociological, theological, philosophical, literary, and political angles.

The purpose of the following survey is to provide an introduction to some of the most important areas of Qur'anic research. While the selection of publications is mostly limited to monographs and edited volumes published within the last fifteen years in the English language, a small number of articles, earlier publications, and publications in other Western European languages have been included as well.

More complete bibliographies are Morteza Karimi-Nia's *Bibliography of Qurʾānic Studies in European Languages* (Qum: The Centre for Translation of the Holy Qurʾān, 2012), the introductions to the volumes *The Qur'an: Formative Interpretation* (Aldershot: Ashgate, 1999) and *The Qur'an: Style and Contents* (Aldershot: Ashgate, 2001), both edited by Andrew Rippin, and Rippin's 'Qur'an' in *Oxford Bibliographies Online*. These should also be consulted for twentieth-century publications.

See also chapters 1 ('Academic Scholarship and the Qur'an: An Historical Overview') and 2 ('Modern Developments in Qur'anic Studies').

Surveys and Introductions

Varying in focus and selection of material, introductions to the Qur'an published within the last fifteen years usually provide outlines of the historical and religious context of the emergence of Islam, discuss major theological and literary themes of the Qur'an, questions of transmission and translation, the significance of the Qur'an in Muslim scholarship and religious practices, and historical and modern interpretations in both the Muslim and non-Muslim world. Originally published in 1953, Richard Bell's *Introduction to the Qur'ān*, updated by W. Montgomery Watt (Edinburgh: Edinburgh University Press, 1970) remains worth reading, in particular for the inner structure of the Qur'an. Michael Cook's *The Koran: A Very Short Introduction* (Oxford: Oxford University Press, 2000) includes an account of issues of transmission with helpful examples. Bruce Lawrence's *The Qur'an: A Biography* (New York: Atlantic Monthly Press, 2007) offers diverse insights into the reception of the Qur'an. Other single-authored introductions include Abdullah Saeed, *The Qur'an: An Introduction* (Abingdon: Routledge, 2008); Farid Esack, *The Qur'an: A Short Introduction* (Oxford: Oneworld, 2002); a greater focus on select aspects distinguishes Muhammad Abdel Haleem, *Understanding the Qur'an: Themes and Style* (London: IB Tauris, 2010) and his *Exploring the Qur'an: Context and Impact* (London: IB Tauris, 2017); also Ingrid Mattson, *The Story of the Qur'an: Its History and Place in Muslim Life* (Oxford: Blackwell, 2008). Several monographs such as Mustansir Mir, *Understanding the Islamic Scripture: A Study of Selected Passages from the Qurʾān* (New York: Pearson Longman, 2007) and Carl W. Ernst, *How to Read the Qur'an: A New Guide*, with new translations (Chapel Hill, NC: University of North Carolina Press, 2011) are concerned with ways of understanding the Qur'an and serve also as introductions to the text. Nicolai Sinai, *The Qur'an: A Historical-critical Introduction* (Edinburgh: Edinburgh University Press, 2017) examines the text with reference to the historical contexts of its origins and its structure. Neal Robinson, *Discovering the Qur'an: A Contemporary Approach to a Veiled Text* (London: SCM Press, 1996), also includes balanced accounts of previous scholarship. Michael Sells offers his own translations and literary analyses of suras 1; 53:1–18; 81–114 in *Approaching the Qur'án: The Early Revelations*, 2nd edition (Ashland, OR: White Cloud Press, 2006) Angelika Neuwirth and Michael Anthony Sells (eds.), *Qurʾānic Studies Today* (New York: Routledge, 2016), offers a selection of studies covering specific passages and themes of the Qur'an; it also discusses the state of the field. A similar range of materials is presented in Michael Cook and Carol Bakhos (eds.), *Islam and Its Past. Jahiliyya, Late Antiquity, and the Qur'an* (Corby: Oxford University Press, 2017).

The Blackwell Companion to the Qurʾān, edited by Andrew Rippin (Oxford: Blackwell, 2006 (2nd edition 2017)) with 32 chapters and *The Cambridge Companion to the Qurʾān*, edited by Jane Dammen McAuliffe (Cambridge: Cambridge University Press, 2006) with 14 chapters cover similar topics in more detail and reflect the diversity of perspectives inherent in multi-authored works. Among reference works, the *Encyclopaedia of the Qurʾān*, edited by Jane Dammen McAuliffe in six volumes (Leiden: Brill, 2001–6) encapsulates best the substantial advances in scholarship and contains authoritative articles on a number of subjects. A smaller selection of topics is covered in Oliver Leaman (ed.), *The Qur'an: An Encyclopedia* (London: Routledge, 2006).

Important reprinted examples of earlier scholarship are included in the four volumes edited by Colin Turner, *The Koran: Critical Concepts in Islamic Studies* (London: Routledge, 2004) and the two volumes edited by Andrew Rippin: *The Qur'an: Style and Contents* and *The Qur'an: Formative Interpretation.*

Critical surveys and discussions of Western scholarship can be found in Andrew Rippin, 'Western Scholarship and the Qurʾān', in Jane Dammen McAuliffe (ed.), *The Cambridge Companion to the Qurʾān* (Cambridge: Cambridge University Press, 2006), 235–51; Parvez Manzoor, 'Method against Truth: Orientalism and Qurʾānic Studies', *Muslim World Book Review* 7/4 (1987), 33–49. (Reprint in Rippin (ed.), *The Qur'an: Style and Contents*); and Daniel Madigan, 'Reflections on Some Current Directions in Qurʾānic Studies', *The Muslim World* 85 (1995), 345–62.

The Qur'an and Its Historical Environment

See also chapters 3, 5, 6, 7, and 8 in this volume.

The flourishing of scholarship on the emergence of Islam since the late 1970s has inspired a number of studies concerning the nature of the Qur'an and its historical context. Likewise, the Qur'an is frequently used as a source for the earliest days of Islamic history. A trend often referred to as revisionism is defined by the reassessment of the sources on which conventional views of the emergence of Islam are based. Dismissing *sīra* and hadith as well as other sources about late sixth- and early seventh-century western Arabia as tendentious and anachronistic, revisionist scholars explain the emergence of Islam within a sectarian milieu of monotheists, rather than a monotheistic revolution within a polytheistic environment, or suggest other major revisions of the traditional narrative of Islamic origins. Introductions to the Qur'an tend to include this scholarship, although not all authors agree with the conclusions.

John Wansbrough is a crucial figure in this reevaluation. His *Quranic Studies: Sources and Methods of Scriptural Interpretation* (Oxford: Oxford University Press, 1977) has been published with a foreword, translations, and expanded notes by Andrew Rippin (Amherst NY: Prometheus, 2004). Patricia Crone explored individual elements in a series of articles including 'The Religion of the Qur'ānic Pagans: God and the Lesser Deities', *Arabica* 57 (2010), 151–200, and the two-part 'The Quranic *Mushrikūn* and the Resurrection', *Bulletin of the School of Oriental and African Studies* 75 (2012), 445–72, and 76 (2013), 1–20.

Two scholars writing in German have made a case for Christian texts underlying Muslim scripture. Both are available in English translation: Christoph Luxenberg, *The Syro-Aramaic Reading of the Koran: A Contribution to the Decoding of the Language of the Koran* (Berlin: Hans Schiler, 2007; Amherst, NY: Prometheus, 2009) and Günter Lüling, *A Challenge to Islam for Reformation: The Rediscovery and Reliable Reconstruction of a Comprehensive Pre-Islamic Christian Hymnal Hidden in the Koran under Earliest Islamic Reinterpretation* (Delhi: Motilal Banarsidars Publishers, 2003). Examples of earlier revisionist scholarship in English translation are also included in Ibn Warraq (ed.), *The Origins of the Koran: Classical Essays on Islam's Holy Book* (Amherst NY: Prometheus, 1998).

Other volumes include contributions which are marked by a critical approach to the Islamic tradition, but less committed to a rival account of the origins of Islam. Noteworthy examples of this scholarship are the volumes edited by Gabriel Said Reynolds, *The Qur'ān in its Historical Context* (London: Routledge, 2008) and *New Perspectives on the Qur'ān: The Qur'ān in its Historical Context 2* (London: Routledge, 2011), and by Angelika Neuwirth, Nicolai Sinai and Michael Marx, *The Qur'ān in Context: Historical and Literary Investigations into the Qur'ānic Milieu* (Leiden: Brill, 2010).

Angelika Neuwirth, founder of the Berlin-based project Corpus Coranicum which assembles manuscripts and oral material of and around the Qur'an, surveyed some of these academic trends critically in her 'Qur'ān and History—A Disputed Relationship: Some Reflections on Qur'ānic History and History in the Qur'ān', *Journal of Qur'anic Studies* 5 (2003), 1–18 and 'Orientalism in Oriental Studies? Qur'anic Studies as a Case in Point', *Journal of Qur'ānic Studies* 9 (2007), 115–27. Like many of her revisionist peers, she situates the Qur'an in a late antique environment, for example in her *Der Koran als Text der Spätantike: Ein europäischer Zugang* (Berlin: Insel Verlag, 2010). Her *Scripture, Poetry, and the Making of a Community. Reading the Qur'an as a Literary Text* (Oxford: Oxford University Press, 2014) offers previously published articles.

Relationship Between Bible and Qur'an

The relationship between the Qur'an and monotheistic sacred literature has inspired comparative work and has been of particular interest to historians who seek to reconstruct the origins of Islam. In *The Qur'ān and its Biblical Subtext* (London: Routledge, 2010),

Gabriel Said Reynolds argues that the audience of the Qur'an would have been familiar with the biblical counterparts of common Qur'anic references. Emran El-Badawi, *The Qurʾān and the Aramaic Gospel Tradition* (New York: Routledge, 2013) interprets the Qur'an against the backdrop of disputes in Aramaic-speaking Christian communities. A wider range of aspects is covered by the contributors to John C. Reeves (ed.), *Bible and Qur'an: Essays in Scriptural Intertextuality* (Atlanta: Society of Biblical Literature, 2003). Stefan Sperl draws broader comparisons in 'The Literary Form of Prayer: Qurʾān Sura One, the Lord's Prayer and a Babylonian Prayer to the Moon God', *Bulletin of the School of Oriental and African Studies* 57 (1994), 213–27.

Historical and Material Development

See also chapters 11, 12, 14, 15, and 16 in this volume.

Scholarship concerned with the early history of the Qur'an has paid particular attention to theories of compilation and material evidence. In *Discovering the Qur'an*, Neal Robinson surveys different views. Harald Motzki challenges revisionist views in 'The Collection of the Qurʾān: A Reconsideration of Western Views in Light of Recent Methodological Developments', *Der Islam* 78 (2001), 1–34.

Yasin Dutton analysed aspects of early manuscripts in a number of articles, including 'Red Dots, Green Dots, Yellow Dots and Blue: Some Reflections on the Vocalization of Early Qurʾānic Manuscripts', *Journal of Qur'anic Studies* 1/1 (1999), 115–40 and 2/1 (2000), 1–24; 'An Early *Muṣḥaf* according to the Reading of Ibn ʿĀmir', *Journal of Qur'anic Studies* 3/1 (2001), 71–89. 'An Umayyad Fragment of the Qurʾān and its Dating', *Journal of Qur'anic Studies* 9/2 (2007), 57–87. Behnam Sadeghi explored related questions of the early development in 'The Codex of the Prophet and the Qurʾān of the Prophet', *Arabica* 57/4 (2010), 343–436 (with Uwe Bergmann); 'The Chronology of the Qurʾān: A Stylometric Research Program', *Arabica* 58/3–4 (2011), 210–99; 'Ṣanʿāʾ 1 and the Origins of the Qurʾān', *Der Islam* 87/1–2 (2012), 1–129 (with Mohsen Goudarzi). Sadeghi focuses on editorial problems in 'Criteria for Emending the Text of the Qur'ān', in Michael Cook et al. (eds.), *Law and Tradition in Classical Islamic Thought: Studies in Honor of Professor Hossein Modarressi* (New York: Palgrave Macmillan, 2013), 21–41. Keith E. Small discusses similar issues in *Textual Criticism and Qurʾān Manuscripts* (Lanham, MD: Lexington Books, 2012), while a survey of the Ṣanʿāʾ manuscripts is offered by Asma Hilali in *The Sanaa Palimpsest: The Transmission of the Qur'an in the First Centuries A. H.* (London: Oxford University Press, in association with the Institute of Ismaili Studies, 2016).

François Déroche discussed Qur'an manuscripts of early Islamic periods in *La Transmission écrite du Coran dans les débuts de l'islam: le codex Parisino-petropolitanus* (Leiden: Brill, 2009), *Qur'ans of the Umayyads: A Preliminary Overview* (Leiden: Brill, 2014) and the richly illustrated volume with examples from the Nasser D. Khalili Collection of Islamic Art, *The Abbasid Tradition: Qurʾāns of the 8th to the 10th Centuries* AD (London: Oxford University Press, 1992). Other related studies include Éléonore

Cellard's *Codex Amrensis 1* (Leiden: Brill, 2018). Later Qur'an manuscripts are presented in two volumes by David James, *The Master Scribes: Qur'āns from the 10th to 14th Centuries* AD (London: Nour Foundation et al., 1992) and *After Timur: Qur'āns of the 15th and 16th Centuries* (London: Nour Foundation et al., 1992) and Manijeh Bayani, Anna Contadini, and Tim Stanley, *The Decorated Word: Qur'ans of the 17th to 19th Centuries* (London: Nour Foundation et al., Part One 1999; Part Two 2009).

David J. Roxburgh explores the development of calligraphic traditions in *Writing the Word of God: Calligraphy and the Qur'an* (New Haven: Yale University Press, 2008). Art historical aspects of Qur'anic representations are the subject of Fahmida Suleman (ed.), *Word of God, Art of Man: The Qur'an and its Creative Expressions* (Oxford: Oxford University Press, 2012). Comics as a more recent medium are the subject of a chapter in Allen Douglas and Fedwa Malti-Douglas, *Arab Comic Strips: Politics of an Emerging Mass Culture* (Bloomington, 1994), 83–109, in which the authors explore Youssef Seddik's series *Si le Coran m'était conté* which contains several volumes on select parts of the Qur'an.

Articles which deal with the use of the material Qur'an in later periods of Islamic history include Amira K. Bennison, 'The Almohads and the Qur'ān of Uthmān: The Legacy of the Umayyads of Cordoba in the Twelfth Century Maghrib', *Al-Masāq* 19/2 (2007), 131–54, and Travis Zadeh, 'Touching and Ingesting: Early Debates over the Material Qur'an', *The Journal of the American Oriental Society* 129/3 (2009), 443–66.

Formal Aspects

See also chapter 13 in this volume.

Apart from matters of compilation, material evidence has been exploited to reconstruct the development of canonical readings (*qirā'āt*) of the Qur'an. Christopher Melchert has explored the issue in 'Ibn Mujāhid and the Establishment of Seven Qur'ānic Readings', *Studia Islamica* 91 (2000), 5–22, and 'The Relation of the Ten Readings to One Another', *Journal of Qur'ānic Studies* 10 (2008), 73–87; Mustafa Shah in 'The Early Arabic Grammarians' Contributions to the Collection and Authentication of Qur'ānic Readings: The Prelude to Ibn Mujāhid's *Kitāb al-Sabʿa*', *Journal of Qur'anic Studies* 6 (2004), 72–102; Intisar A. Rabb in 'Non-Canonical Readings of the Qur'an: Recognition and Authenticity' (The Ḥimṣī Reading)', *Journal of Qur'anic Studies* 8/2 (2006), 84–127; and Yasin Dutton in 'Orality, Literacy, and the Seven *ḥurūf*', *Journal of Islamic Studies* 23 (2012), 1–49. Shady Hekmat Nasser traces the changing position towards the authentication of readings in the disciplines of early Islamic scholarship, *fiqh* and hadith, in *The Transmission of the Variant Readings of the Qur'ān: The Problem of Tawātur and the Emergence of Shawādhdh* (Leiden: Brill, 2012). Ahmad ʿAli al-Imam presents a traditional Islamic view in *Variant Readings of the Qur'ān: A Critical Study of their Historical and Linguistic Origins* (Herndon, VA: International Institute of Islamic Thought, 2nd edition 2006).

Etan Kohlberg and Mohammad Ali Amir-Moezzi have made one of the earliest Shīʿī texts on variant readings, which also discusses claims of falsification, available in a critical edition, accompanied by an introduction and notes: *Revelation and Falsification: The Kitāb al-qirāʾāt of Aḥmad b. Muḥammad al-Sayyārī* (Leiden: Brill, 2009). Christiane Gruber has studied the significance of the Shīʿī view of the Qur'an's compilation in later centuries in 'The "Restored" Shīʿī *muṣḥaf* as Divine Guide? The Practice of *fāl-i Qurʾān* in the Ṣafavid Period', *Journal of Qur'anic Studies* 13/2 (2011), 29–55.

Religious Themes and Motifs in the Qur'an

See also chapters 9, 10, 23, 26, 27, 29, 30, 31, 33, and 34 in this volume.

A number of publications survey the major themes of the Qur'an or focus on one of them. The 1980 monograph by the influential modernist Fazlur Rahman, *Major Themes of the Qur'an*, has been republished with a new foreword by Ebrahim Moosa (Chicago: University of Chicago Press, 2009). The themes covered include God, man as individual, man in society, nature, prophethood and revelation, eschatology, Satan and evil, and the emergence of the Muslim community, with two appendices devoted to the religious situation of the Muslim community in Mecca and to the People of the Book and diversity of religions. Surveys of the most prominent topics in the Qur'an in other publications often display similar selections.

The topics also reflect some of the most important areas of scholarship which frequently encompasses exegetical material as well. Some authors have focused on Qur'anic prophets with varying degrees of attention paid to the biblical counterparts. Jacques Jomier, *The Great Themes of the Qur'an* (London: SCM Press, 1997), has an introductory character and pays particular attention to topics familiar to Christians. Broad studies include Roberto Tottoli's *Biblical Prophets in the Qurʾān and Muslim Literature* (Richmond: Curzon, 2002) and Brannon M. Wheeler's *Prophets in the Quran: An Introduction to the Quran and Muslim Exegesis* (London: Continuum, 2002). More specific studies are Hosn Abboud's *Mary in the Qur'an: A Literary Reading* (London: Routledge, 2014), Brannon Wheeler's *Moses in the Quran and Islamic Exegesis* (London: Routledge, 2002), and Todd Lawson, *The Crucifixion and the Qur'an: A Study in the History of Muslim Thought* (Oxford: Oneworld, 2009).

Some studies deal with Qur'anic references to other religious communities, these include Jane Dammen McAuliffe, *Qurʾānic Christians: An Analysis of Classical and Modern Exegesis* (Cambridge: Cambridge University Press, 1991). Likewise, Uri Rubin considers the Qur'an and the wider tradition in his *Between Bible and Qur'ān: The Children of Israel and the Islamic Self-Image* (Princeton: Darwin Press, 1999). David Marshall explores the relationship between Muḥammad and his audience in *God, Muhammad and the Unbelievers: A Qur'anic Study* (Richmond: Curzon, 1999).

Toshihiko Izutsu's classic studies of semantic analysis, *God and Man in the Koran: Semantics of the Koranic Weltanschauung* (originally published Tokyo: The Keio Institute of Cultural and Linguistic Studies, 1964) and *Ethico-Religious Concepts in the Qur'ān* (Montreal: McGill University Press, 1966) remain relevant and have been reprinted several times. Rosalind W. Gwynne explores formal aspects of Qur'anic speech in *Logic, Rhetoric, and Legal Reasoning in the Qur'ān: God's Arguments* (London: Routledge Curzon, 2004).

John W. Bowker addresses 'The Problem of Suffering in the Qur'ān', *Religious Studies* 4 (1969), 183–202, while Robert Morrison writes about the Qur'anic statement that God placed a seal over the hearts of the unbelievers in 'Science and Theodicy in Qur'ān 2:6/7', in Jitse M. van der Meer and Scott Mandelbrote (eds.), *Nature and Scripture in the Abrahamic Religions: Up to 1700*, vol. 1 (Leiden: Brill, 2008), 249–72. Morrison explores related issues in 'The Portrayal of Nature in a Medieval Qur'ān Commentary', *Studia Islamica* 94 (2002), 115–38 and 'Reasons for a Scientific Portrayal of Nature in Medieval Qur'ān Commentaries', *Arabica* 52 (2005), 182–202.

Some topics have recently attracted a lot of attention outside the academy, in particular religious diversity, violence, and gender issues. Relevant publications include Barbara Freyer Stowasser, *Women in the Qur'an, Traditions, and Interpretation* (Oxford: Oxford University Press, 1996); Karen Bauer, *Gender Hierarchy in the Qur'ān: Medieval Interpretations, Modern Responses* (New York: Cambridge University Press, 2015); Reuven Firestone, *Jihad: The Origin of Holy War in Islam* (New York: Oxford University Press, 1999). In his 'Disparity and Resolution in the Qur'ānic Teachings on War: A Reevaluation of a Traditional Problem', *Journal of Near Eastern Studies* 56 (1997), 1–19, Firestone also touches on problems related to the historical composition of the Qur'an as well as to the development of exegetical traditions.

Literary Aspects

See also chapters 17, 18, 19, 20, 21, 22, 24, 25, and 53 in this volume.

While many publications take matters of literary tropes, structure, and style into consideration, some assign a particularly high priority to the Qur'an as a piece of literature.

A number of studies analyse the language of the Qur'an on a lexicographical level. Some have the character of handbooks and reference works: Mustansir Mir, *Verbal Idioms of the Qur'ān* (Ann Arbor: University of Michigan, Center for Near Eastern and North African Studies, 1989); Martin R. Zammit, *A Comparative Lexical Study of Qur'ānic Arabic* (Leiden: Brill, 2002); Elsaid M. Badawi and Muhammad Abdel Haleem, *Arabic-English Dictionary of Qur'anic Usage* (Leiden: Brill. 2008). Stephen Burge edited *The Meaning of the Word: Lexicology and Qur'anic Exegesis* (Oxford: Oxford University Press, 2015).

The volume *The Qur'ān as Text*, edited by Stefan Wild (Leiden: Brill, 1996), unites a variety of contributions, some more concerned with historical questions, others more with matters of language and interpretation, which seek to study the Qur'an 'as a text', which implies the same analytical principles which a scholar would apply to any text. In the eyes of the editor, the title also signals a shift away from problems of the milieu in which Islam emerged. The volume edited by Issa J. Boullata, *Literary Structures of Religious Meaning in the Qurʾān* (Richmond: Curzon, 2000), is marked by a greater focus on literary features of the text. The literary impact of the Qur'an and its interpretive tradition is examined in Nuha Sha'ar (ed.), *The Qur'an and Adab: The Shaping of Literary Traditions in Classical Islam* (Oxford; London: Oxford University Press in association with the Institute of Ismaili Studies, 2017). Michel Cuypers analysed several formal aspects in *The Composition of the Qur'an: Rhetorical Analysis* (London: Bloomsbury Academic, 2015). For more on aesthetics see Sarah bin Tyeer, *The Qur'an and the Aesthetics of Premodern Arabic Prose* (London: Palgrave, 2016).

An important voice from the Muslim world in favour of an approach to the Qur'an as a text or as literature is that of Naṣr Ḥāmid Abū Zayd (d. 2010), whose views have stirred controversy in his native Egypt. For his views see 'The Dilemma of the Literary Approach to the Qurʾān', *Alif: Journal of Comparative Poetics* 23 (2003), 8–47 and *Rethinking the Qur'ān: Towards a Humanistic Hermeneutics* (Amsterdam: Humanistics University Press, 2004). For an interpretation see Sukidi, 'Naṣr Ḥāmid Abū Zayd and the Quest for a Humanistic Hermeneutics of the Qurʾān', *Die Welt des Islams* 49 (2009), 181–211. Navid Kermani, one of the scholars who have made Abū Zayd's work public to a broader Western readership, has published his own study of the Qur'an's aesthetic qualities in *God is Beautiful: The Aesthetic Experience of the Quran* (Cambridge: Polity Press, 2014).

Daniel A. Madigan explores the important feature of Qur'anic self-referentiality in his *The Qurʾān's Self-Image: Writing and Authority in Islam's Scripture* (Princeton: Princeton University Press, 2001), a subject also explored by the contributors to Stefan Wild (ed.), *Self-Referentiality in the Qurʾān* (Wiesbaden: Harrassowitz, 2006). The Qur'anic distinction between unambiguous verses (*muḥkamāt*) and those in need of interpretation (*mutashābihāt*) is the subject of Stefan Wild, 'The Self-Referentiality of the Qurʾān: Sura 3:7 as an Exegetical Challenge', in Jane Dammen McAuliffe, Barry D. Walfish, and Joseph W. Goering (eds.), *With Reverence for the Word: Medieval Scriptural Exegesis in Judaism, Christianity, and Islam* (Oxford, 2003), 422–36. The common exegetical tendency to select short passages from the Qur'an for interpretation can distract from consideration of the unity of longer passages and the sura as a unit. Mustansir Mir has addressed such matters in a range of publications, including *Coherence in the Qurʾān: A Study of Iṣlāḥī's Concept of Naẓm in Tadabbur-i Qur'ān* (Indianapolis: American Trust Publications, 1986); 'The *Sūra* as a Unity: A Twentieth Century Development in Qur'ān Exegesis', in G. R. Hawting and Abdul Kader A. Shareef (eds.), *Approaches to the Qurʾān* (New York: Routledge, 1993), 211–24.

Given the prominence of poetry at the time Islam emerged, the close connections between the style of pre-Islamic poetry and some parts of the Qur'an (see Sells, *Approaching the Qur'án*), as well as the speaker's insistence that the prophet is not a poet, the relationship between the Qur'an and poetry has attracted some attention. Michael Zwettler explores such issues in 'A Mantic Manifesto: The Sūra of "the Poets" and the Qurʾānic Foundations of Prophetic Authority', in James L. Kugel (ed.), *Poetry and Prophecy: The Beginnings of a Literary Tradition* (Ithaca, NY: Cornell University Press, 1999), 75–119. Thomas Hoffmann analyses poetic techniques of the text in his *The Poetic Qurʾān: Studies on Qurʾānic Poeticity* (Wiesbaden: Harrassowitz, 2007).

Qur'anic storytelling has been analysed in particular in the case of the prophet Joseph. Studies include Mustansir Mir, 'The Qurʾānic Story of Joseph: Plot, Themes and Characters', *Muslim World* 76 (1986), 1–15 and A. Johns, 'The Quranic Presentation of the Joseph Story: Naturalistic or Formulaic Language?', in Gerald R. Hawting and A. A. Shareef (eds.), *Approaches to the Qurʾān* (London, 1993), 39–70. Georges Tamer explores 'The Qur'ān and Humor', in Georges Tamer (ed.), *Humor in der arabischen Kultur* (Berlin: Walter de Gruyter, 2009), 3–28.

Exegesis (*Tafsīr*) and Practical Application

See also chapters 28, 32, 36, 38, 40, 41, 42, 43, 44, 45, 47, 48, 49, 50, 51, 52, 54, 55, and 56 in this volume.

In Islamic scholarly practice, hermeneutical problems encapsulated in exegetical traditions loom large in Islamic law, theology, and philosophy (for which see the relevant chapters in the surveys). In religious practice, recitation enjoys an important place, but also talismanic uses.

Ignaz Goldziher's original 1920 monograph, available in English translation as *Schools of Koranic Commentators with an Introduction on Goldziher and Hadith from* Geschichte des Arabischen Schrifttums *by Fuat Sezgin*, edited and translated by Wolfgang Behn (Wiesbaden: Harrassowitz, 2006) still commands authority. Andreas Görke and Johanna Pink edited *Tafsīr and Islamic Intellectual History: Exploring the Boundaries of a Genre* (Oxford: Oxford University Press, 2015). Several contributions in *With Reverence for the Word: Medieval Scriptural Exegesis in Judaism, Christianity, and Islam*, edited by Jane Dammen McAuliffe, Barry D. Walfish, and Joseph W. Goering (Oxford: Oxford University Press, 2010) concern Islamic and Qur'anic exegesis. Bruce Fudge reviews the position of *tafsīr* in the West in 'Qurʾānic Exegesis in Medieval Islam and Modern Orientalism', *Die Welt des Islam* 46 (2006), 115–47, and Walid Saleh offers 'Preliminary Remarks on the Historiography of Tafsīr in Arabic: A History of the Book Approach', *Journal of Qur'anic Studies* 12 (2010), 6–40. Mustafa Shah has compiled four volumes of reprinted articles under the title *Tafsīr: Interpreting the Qur'ān* (London: Routledge, 2013).

Anthologies of Qur'an commentaries, both premodern and modern, allow for comparative insights. Mahmoud Ayoub published *The Qur'an and its Interpreters* (Albany: State University of New York Press), the first volume of which (1984) offers impressions of medieval and modern interpretations from suras *al-Fātiḥa* and *al-Baqara* and the second (1992) from *Āl ʿImrān*. Feras Hamza, Sajjad Rizvi, and Farhana Mayer assembled *An Anthology of Qur'anic Commentaries*, vol. 1 ('On the Nature of the Divine') (Oxford: Oxford University Press, 2010). Detailed interpretive material is included in Seyyed Hossein Nasr (editor in chief), with Caner K. Dagli, Maria Massi Dakake, Joseph E. B. Lumbard, general editors; Mohammed Rustom, assistant editor. *The Study Quran: A New Translation and Commentary* (New York, NY: HarperOne, 2015).

Aims, Methods and Contexts of Qur'anic Exegesis (2nd/8th—9th/15th Centuries), edited by Karen Bauer (Oxford: Oxford University Press, 2014), covers a range of historical Qur'an commentaries. Other works focus on a particular historical context or author. Examples include Mustafa Shah, 'Al-Ṭabarī and the Dynamics of *Tafsīr*: Theological Dimensions of a Legacy', *Journal of Qur'anic Studies* 15 (2013), 83–139; Walid A. Saleh, *The Formation of the Classical Tafsīr Tradition: The Qurʾān Commentary of al-Thaʿlabī (d. 427/1035)* (Leiden: Brill, 2004); Andrew J. Lane, *A Traditional Muʿtazilite Qurʾān Commentary: The Kashshāf of Jār Allāh al-Zamakhsharī (d. 538/1144)* (Leiden: Brill, 2006); *Keys to the Arcana: Shahrastānī's Esoteric Commentary on the Qur'an*, trans. Toby Mayer (London: Institute of Ismaili Studies in association with Oxford University Press, 2009); Bruce Fudge, *Qur'ānic Hermeneutics: Al-Ṭabrisī and the Craft of Commentary* (London: Routledge, 2011) about the exegetical work of the twelfth-century Shīʿī scholar al-Ṭabrisī; Walid A. Saleh, 'Ibn Taymiyya and the Rise of Radical Hermeneutics: An Analysis of *An Introduction to the Foundations of Qur'ānic Exegesis*', in Yossef Rapoport and Shahab Ahmed (eds.), *Ibn Taymiyya and His Times* (Oxford: Oxford University Press, 2010), 123–62, and Shuruq Naguib, 'Guiding the Sound Mind: Ebu's-Suʿūd's Tafsir and Rhetorical Interpretation of the Qurʾān in the Post-Classical Period', *The Journal of Ottoman Studies* 42 (2013), 1–52. Issues germane to approaches are explored in Alexander Key's *Language between God and the Poets: Ma'ná in the Eleventh Century* (California: University of California Press, 2018).

Some publications deal with the matter of translations into languages of Muslim-majority communities, an issue intricately connected with exegesis. See Travis Zadeh, *The Vernacular Qurʾān: Translation and the Rise of Persian Exegesis* (Oxford: Oxford University Press, 2012) and Raphael Israeli, 'Translation as Exegesis: The Opening Sura of the Quran in Chinese', in Peter G. Riddell and Tony Street (eds.), *Islam: Essays on Scripture, Thought and Society* (Leiden, 1997), 81–103.

Ṣūfī Commentaries on the Qurʾān in Classical Islam by Kristin Zahra Sands (London: Routledge, 2006) can serve as an introduction to Sufi exegesis. Some publications focus on passages of the Qur'an particularly popular among Sufis. Examples include Gerhard Böwering, 'The Light Verse: Qurʾānic Text and Ṣūfī Interpretation', *Oriens* 36 (2001), 113–44, and Hugh Talat Halman, *Where the Two Seas Meet: The Qurʾānic Story of al-Khidr and Moses in Sufi Commentaries as a Model for Spiritual Guidance* (Louisville, KY: Fons Vitae, 2013). Among the publications included in the series devoted by Fons Vitae to Qur'anic commentaries are Farhana Mayer, *Spiritual Gems: The Mystical Qur'ān Commentary Ascribed to Jaʿfar al-Ṣādiq as Contained in Sulamī's* Ḥaqāʾiq al-Tafsīr *from the Text of Paul Nwyia* (Louisville, KY: Fons Vitae, 2011) which covers an early tradition as preserved in the work by al-Sulamī (d. 412/1021), and *Tafsīr al-Tustarī by Sahl b. ʿAbd Allāh al-Tustarī*, translated and annotated with an introduction by Annabel Keeler and Ali Keeler (Louisville, KY: Fons Vitae, 2011) which offers the work of the ninth-century mystic. Martin Nguyen, *Sufi Master and Qur'an Scholar: Abū'l-Qāsim al-Qushayrī and the Laṭā'if al-Ishārāt* (Oxford: Oxford University Press, 2012) discusses a fifth-/eleventh-century writer. Annabel Keeler, *Sufi Hermeneutics: The Qur'ān Commentary of Rashīd al-Dīn Maybudī* (Oxford: Oxford University Press in association with the Institute of Ismaili Studies, 2006) presents a twelfth-century Persian interpretation. *The Immense Ocean: Al-Baḥr al-Madid. A Thirteenth/Eighteenth Century Qur'ānic Commentary on the Chapters of the All-Merciful, the Event, and Iron* (Louisville, KY: Fons Vitae, 2009), translated by Mohamed Fouad Aresmouk and Michael Abdurrahman Fitzgerald, covers the work of the eighteenth-century North African Sufi Aḥmad ibn Aḥmad.

A number of studies analyse interpretations of and approaches to the Qur'an in specific Muslim societies. Vanessa De Gifis, for example, studies an early example of the significance of the Qur'an in Abbasid rhetoric in *Shaping a Qur'ānic Worldview: Scriptural Hermeneutics and the Rhetoric of Moral Reform in the Caliphate of al-Ma'mūn* (Abingdon: Routledge, 2014). Susan Gunasti discusses 'Political Patronage and the Writing of Qur'ān Commentaries among the Ottoman Turks', *Journal of Islamic Studies* 24 (2013), 335–57.

Case studies of the modern world include Anna M. Gade, *Perfection Makes Practice: Learning, Emotion and the Recited Qur'ān in Indonesia* (Honolulu: University of Hawai'i Press, 2004); Abdullah Saeed (ed.), *Approaches to the Qur'ān in Contemporary Indonesia* (Oxford: Oxford University Press, 2005); Helen N. Boyle, *Quranic Schools: Agents of Preservation and Change* (New York: Routledge, 2004) which features case studies from Yemen, Morocco, and Nigeria; Anne K. Rasmussen, *Women, the Recited Qur'ān, and Islamic Music in Indonesia* (Berkeley: University of California Press, 2010). For the Qur'an in popular culture see also Ehab Galal, 'Magic Spells and Recitation Contests: The Quran as Entertainment on Arab Satellite Television', *Northern Lights: First & Media Studies Yearbook* 6/1 (2008), 165–79.

Modern Muslim Reception

See also chapters 46 and 57 in this volume.

The volume edited by Suha Taji-Farouki, *Modern Muslim Intellectuals and the Qur'an* (Oxford: Oxford University Press, 2006), serves as an introduction to modern Muslim views of the Qur'an (see also the Naṣr Ḥāmid Abū Zayd literature listed above), as does Massimo Campanini's *The Qur'an: Modern Muslim Interpretations* (London: Routledge, 2010) and his *Philosophical Perspectives on Modern Qur'ānic Exegesis: Key Paradigms and Concepts* (Sheffield: Equinox Publishing Ltd, 2016). A short overview is Erik Ohlander, 'Modern Qur'ānic Hermeneutics', *Religion Compass* 3 (2009), 620–36.

Modern liberal Muslim readers of the Qur'an frequently discuss hermeneutical strategies allowing for a contemporary reading of the text, which distils a universal and unchanging normative message and separates it from historically contingent and descriptive elements. An example is the Britain-based author of Pakistani origin, Ziauddin Sardar, who presents his own views in *Reading the Qur'an: The Contemporary Relevance of the Sacred Text of Islam* (Oxford: Oxford University Press, 2011). Amina Wadud, a North American scholar and religious leader, represents a prominent trend in modernist interpretations of the Qur'an with her interest in the position of women in the text's reception. She discusses her approach in *Qur'an and Woman: Re-reading the Sacred Text from a Woman's Perspective* (Oxford: Oxford University Press, 1999). Asma Barlas made a similar effort in *Believing Women in Islam: Unreading Patriarchal Interpretations of the Qur'an* (Austin: University of Texas Press, 2002). Karen Bauer explores interpretations of Qur'anic passages related to women in '"Traditional" Exegeses of Q4:34', *Comparative Islamic Studies* 2/2 (2006), 129–42 and '*The Male Is Not Like the Female* (Q 3:36): The Question of Gender Egalitarianism in the Qur'ān', *Religion Compass* 3 (2009), 637–54. The issue of how key hermeneutical concepts in classical Qur'anic exegesis (*tafsīr*) are gendered is examined in Aisha Geissinger, *Gender and Muslim Construction of Exegetical Authority: A Rereading of the Classical Genre of Qurʾān Commentary* (Leiden: Brill, 2015).

While Western publishing houses tend to focus on examples and studies of modern Muslim exegesis of a liberal bent, rather different tendencies are the subject of Adis Duderija's 'Neo-traditional Salafi Qurʾān-Sunnah Hermeneutic and the Construction of a Normative Muslimah Image', *Hawwa* 5 (2007), 289–323.

The reconciliation of Qur'anic worldview and modern science is addressed by many Muslim authors, among them Nidhal Guessoum, *Islam's Quantum Question: Reconciling Muslim Tradition and Modern Science* (London: I. B. Tauris, 2010). Isra Yazicioglu analyses related problems in hermeneutics concerning miracles in her *Understanding the Qurʾānic Miracle Stories in the Modern Age* (University Park: Penn State University Press, 2013).

Non-Muslim Reception

See also chapters 35, 37, and 39 in this volume.

Over the last years, scholars have been shedding increasing light on the Western reception of the Qur'an. Thomas E. Burman has studied the medieval Latin reception, including translations and their underlying hermeneutics. Results of his analysis are published in 'Polemic, Philology, and Ambivalence: Reading the Qurʾān in Latin Christendom', *Journal of Islamic Studies* 15/2 (2004), 181–209, as well as *Reading the Qurʾān in Latin Christendom, 1140–1560* (Philadelphia: University of Pennsylvania Press, 2007). Hartmut Bobzin explored the Qur'an in the age of Reformation and the emerging academic traditions around the study of Arabic and Islam in *Der Koran im Zeitalter der Reformation: Studien zur Frühgeschichte der Arabistik und Islamkunde in Europa* (Stuttgart: Franz Steiner, 1995). Ziad Elmarsafy covers a later period in *The Enlightenment Qur'an: The Politics of Translation and the Construction of Islam* (Oxford: Oneworld, 2009). The significance of the sources utilized by Ludovico Marracci (1612–1700) in his landmark translation is examined in Reinhold F. Glei and Roberto Tottoli, *Ludovico Marracci at Work: The Evolution of his Latin Translation of the Qurʾān in the Light of his Newly Discovered Manuscripts. With an Edition and a Comparative Linguistic Analysis of Sura 18* (Wiesbaden: Harrassowitz Verlag, 2016). Alexander Bevilacqua covers European responses to Qur'an translations in his *The Republic of Arabic Letters: Islam and the European Enlightenment* (Cambridge, MA: Belknap Press of Harvard University Press, 2018). An impressive range of vernacular traditions of translation is reviewed in Suha Taji-Farouki (ed.), *The Qur'an and its Readers Worldwide: Contemporary Commentaries and Translations* (Oxford: Oxford University Press, 2015). Andrew Rippin offers a survey of more recent material in 'The Reception of Euro-American Scholarship on the Qurʾān and *tafsīr*: An Overview', *Journal of Qurʾānic Studies* 14 (2012), 1–8.

PART II

THE HISTORICAL SETTING OF THE QUR'AN

CHAPTER 5

LATE ANTIQUE NEAR EASTERN CONTEXT

Some Social and Religious Aspects

MUNTASIR F. AL-HAMAD
AND JOHN F. HEALEY

Historical Background

The most significant event leading to the emergence of Middle Eastern society on the eve of Islam was the conquest of the region by Alexander the Great (crossing the Hellespont in 334 BCE). Books on the 'Ancient Near East' frequently stop at the point of Alexander's arrival and imply that the Ancient Near East came to an abrupt end, to be succeeded by a fundamentally different cultural phase, that of Hellenization and the later Roman and Byzantine empires. In fact the Ancient Near East did *not* simply come to an end: Ancient Near Eastern languages like Aramaic and religious traditions such as those of Babylon continued well into the Hellenistic-Roman period. But Alexander and the political entities which emerged after his death in 323 BCE did have a profound impact. Greek became the prestige language of the whole region, pushing Aramaic into second place, and Greek culture became pervasive. Henceforth any native of the western part of the Middle East who wanted to get on in the world had to be educated in the Greek tradition and worship the Greek gods. Perhaps most obviously, architecture and town planning were henceforth Greek in style, as surviving monuments testify.

The Roman Empire inherited this legacy, with Greek (rather than Latin) as the normal language of administration and culture in the eastern part of the Empire. The elite of society in cities like Jerusalem and Antioch, even if they had family roots in the Middle East, became standard-bearers of Hellenistic culture. In Jerusalem, Josephus (37–*c.*100 CE), a pious Jew, was educated in the Roman way and wrote in Greek, eventually (after some hesitation) throwing in his lot with the imperial power. In Palmyra of the second and third centuries CE prominent merchants and officials adopted Roman personal names, combining them with native Palmyrene names and becoming Romanized.

It is noteworthy, however, that in both of these examples we can see a certain ambiguity. Hellenized and Romanized Jews retained their link to their religious traditions expressed through the medium of Hebrew and Aramaic, and nationalist insurgency eventually led to the destruction of the Temple, which had been rebuilt in grand Hellenistic style. In Palmyra public administration was primarily conducted in Greek and the temple of Bēl was regarded as a temple of Zeus, but in the private sphere, that of burials and tomb property, and to a large extent in the less visible aspects of religion, Aramaic retained its primacy. And again there were undercurrents of local identity and ambition, which led in the case of Palmyra to the destruction of the city by the Romans in the 270s CE after the anti-Roman revolt of Odainat and Zenobia (Smith 2013: 175–81).

In 330 CE the emperor Constantine shifted the focus of the Roman Empire eastwards, to Byzantium on the Bosphorus, renamed Constantinople. This significant change was accompanied by another, even more dramatic shift, the legalization of Christianity through the 'Edict of Milan' (313 CE) and eventually its recognition under Theodosius I (who ruled 379–95 CE) as the official religion of the newly emergent Byzantine Empire, whose vast domains covered most of the territory the Romans had ruled in the Middle East and North Africa (King 1961).

Christianity had already spread before the time of Constantine to various major cities of the Roman Middle East. Antioch (a Greek foundation which became the capital of the Roman Province of Syria) is recorded already in the New Testament as one of the early centres of proselytization (see Acts 11:19–26; 13:14–50; Zetterholm 2003). But Christianity had spread also into Aramaic-speaking areas such as Edessa (capital of Osrhoene) and Mesopotamia. In these regions a distinctive version of Christianity had taken root which did not use Greek as its primary linguistic medium, though it was later heavily influenced by Greek ideas (see recently Tannous 2013; King 2013).

Although it was founded in Palestine on the life and teaching of a pious Aramaic-speaking Jew, Christianity came into its recognizable form as a 'world' religion under the influence of St. Paul, a thoroughly Hellenized Jew who was a Roman citizen and who wrote in Greek. Much of its earliest theologizing was conducted in Antioch, Alexandria, and Rome in a Westernized cultural context. Under Constantine and his successors the association of the Church with the Byzantine state effectively created Christian 'orthodoxy', which was worked out in Greek philosophical terms and expressed in decisions by church councils which conducted their business in Greek and in creeds formulated in Greek. The creedal statement still used almost universally by Western Christians is the Creed of Nicaea of 325 CE (later revised at the Council of Constantinople in 381; Kelly 1972: 205–62).

It was this Greek orthodoxy and creed and subsequent elaborations of it that Byzantine emperors tried to impose on the non-Greek Christians of the Middle East and Egypt (though a few, like Anastasius I (d. 518), showed support for non-orthodox positions). This led to resistance on some issues of theology—both wording and substance—and ultimately to the fracturing of the Middle Eastern Church in the pre-Islamic period.

Much of the contentious debate concerned the person of Jesus (the Christological controversy). All could agree on the statements of the New Testament itself, such as the claim that Jesus was the son of God (e.g. Luke 1:32, 35; Matt 3:16–17 and 16:15–17; and especially John's Gospel, e.g. 5:17–23), but the more technical definition of precisely what that meant proved to be contentious. Broadly, Syrian and Egyptian bishops wanted to emphasize the divinity of Christ. The 'catchphrase' which embodied this emphasis was the title 'Mother of God' applied to Mary: Jesus was divine, Mary was his mother, therefore Mary was the Mother of God (Greek *theotókos*). Other theologians, notably Theodore of Mopsuestia (*c.*350–428) and Nestorius (Patriarch of Constantinople 428–31), whose views were supported by the Christians of Mesopotamia, spoke rather of the *two* aspects of Jesus, the Divine *and* the Human. This approach was not in itself unorthodox, but there was considerable difficulty in explaining in a way that would satisfy all factions how Jesus' divinity and humanity were linked to each other. Fundamentally, how could Jesus Christ be *both* divine and human? Nestorius was in the end declared a heretic and deposed, but he had a number of supporters who became disaffected.

The Byzantine Church, in the meetings of a succession of church councils from 325 to 451 CE, failed to find a formula which would ultimately satisfy either the Syrian/Egyptian faction or the Mesopotamian faction, so both effectively went their own way and this led gradually to the formation of two additional church communities alongside the Byzantine or 'Greek Orthodox' Church of Constantinople.

In Syria and Egypt, especially under the organizational influence of Jacob Baradaeus (Bishop of Edessa 543–78) and with some support from sympathizers in Constantinople (especially Theodora, the wife of Justinian, emperor 527–65), the 'Syrian Orthodox Church' and the 'Coptic Orthodox Church' came into existence, with their own bishops and structures and their own Patriarchs (Atiya 1968: 69–91, 169–92; Hage 1987; Chaillot 1998: 21–8; van Rompay 2005). In Mesopotamia (with the focus on Seleukia-Ctesiphon to the south of the later Baghdad) a series of church synods from 410 onwards gradually gave formal approval to the teachings of Theodore and Nestorius. Mesopotamia was not in fact inside the Byzantine Empire, but part of the Sasanian Empire, an aspect of *Realpolitik* which encouraged the growing independence of this Church, now known as the 'Church of the East' (though Western sources long referred to it as the 'Nestorian Church', a tendentious title now avoided) (Baum and Winkler 2003; Brock 1996).

The northern Arabs came into contact with these newly formed Middle Eastern Churches and many were converted to the particular form of Christianity which they represented (Trimingham 1979; Shahid 1984). In Syria the Ghassanids and others became Syrian Orthodox, with their own bishops. In the Byzantine-Persian wars they allied themselves with the Byzantine Empire (despite the doctrinal differences). In Mesopotamia the Lakhmids and others became members of the Church of the East and naturally allied themselves with the Sasanians against Byzantium. This contact with Christians in the Levant is reflected in the well-known story of the Prophet Muḥammad travelling as a boy with his uncle for trade in the Levant. In Buṣrā he met a monk, Baḥīrā, who recognized that the young man would be a great prophet (Ibn Isḥāq, *Sīrā*, 79–81), though the authenticity of the report is questioned by some.

There were also outreaches of these Churches beyond the Middle East. The Church of the East in particular developed a strong missionary tradition, sending missionaries along the Silk Route to China and along the western coast of India. It established Christian communities wherever trade and Sasanian power were extended: the Gulf (al-Baḥrayn), Oman, Yemen (including Socotra) (Fiey 1979; Baum and Winkler 2003: 42–83).

Yemen in fact became the strongest centre of Christianity in the Arabian Peninsula during the fifth and sixth centuries, largely as a result of missionary activity by Ethiopian Christians (whose Christology was aligned with that of the Copts and Syrians). Ethiopian missions in Yemen were, however, linked with imperial ambition and this led to the well-known events of the early sixth century, the persecution of Christians by Dhū Nuwās and the martyrdom of Christians at Najrān in 523 (Beaucamp et al. 1999–2000; Hoyland 2001: 50–5; Gajda 2009: 82–102; Beaucamp et al. 2010). This latter event became notorious throughout the Christian/Byzantine world and it led to the overthrow of the Himyarite kingdom by a combination of Ethiopian and Byzantine power (though subsequently, in the late sixth century, Yemen was colonized by the Sasanians).

This, then, is the religious and cultural situation of Christian Late Antiquity on the eve of the Islamic period. Perhaps the most significant feature, which undoubtedly had some impact on the way Islam spread so quickly, is the lack of religious unity among the Christians. Islam did not confront Christianity; it confronted at least three Christianities (Greek Orthodox, Syrian Orthodox, Church of the East) and most Middle Eastern Christians were at odds with the Byzantine and Sasanian authorities.

Arabia itself, which contained only small settlement centres, retained its pagan traditions, though there were also Jewish communities and Jewish tribes, such as the Banū Thaʿlaba, Banū Qurayẓa, Banū Qaynuqāʿ and the people of Khaybar. The origins of these communities are disputed. Some trace their origins to migration from Palestine as a result of oppression at the hands of Romans in the first and second centuries CE, while others claim they were Arab converts (Lammens 1928: 51–99; Newby 1988: especially 49–77; Noja 1979; Gil 1984; Robin 2004: 862–7).

For south Arabia, approximating to modern Yemen, we have an abundance of epigraphic evidence stretching back into the early Iron Age and intensifying in the first centuries CE, right down to the period of Dhū Nuwās and the final collapse of the Mārib dam *c.*600 (Q. 34: 15–17). Because of the abundance of epigraphic evidence we can document a gradual shift in Yemen from full polytheism (with astral deities taking a leading role, e.g. at the great Maḥram Bilqīs temple of the god Almaqah in Mārib), to a modified polytheism in which certain deities were privileged and treated as of a higher order ('henotheism') and finally to the disappearance of the polytheistic formulae in favour of monotheism, the cult of Raḥmānān, 'the Merciful One'. This cult is, on present evidence, best understood as a form of Jewish monotheism, though distinct from Rabbinic Judaism as such (Gajda 2009; Robin 2003; 2004: 862–7).

The pagan traditions are those we hear much about in the Qur'an itself, but also in the *sīra* of the Prophet and later Islamic sources such as Ibn al-Kalbī's *Kitāb al-Aṣnām*. Such sources do not, of course, give us a clear and coherent account of what must have been a very diverse set of traditions and some revisionist historians have treated them very critically (see Hawting 1999). They certainly do not lack religious bias: we would not expect Islamic sources to show much sympathy for the pagan past which had just been overthrown. We can, however, use epigraphic evidence to supplement the information provided by these sources, along with archaeology. And there are some non-Islamic sources, Byzantine and Syriac, which give us a different perspective on practices and beliefs in Arabia before Islam.

We can also, with caution, use more direct earlier pagan sources of information. For example a number of the deities mentioned by Muslim authors are also known to us from Nabataean and Palmyrene inscriptions. Palmyra might be regarded as too remote and too Romanized to be much of a guide, but that is not true of the Nabataean sources (Healey 2001). The Nabataean inscriptions extend from Syria to Sinai and deep into northern Arabia (Ḥegrā/Madāʾin Ṣāliḥ) and date from the first century BCE to the fourth CE. A little further south beyond Ḥegrā was the kingdom of Liḥyān, also well represented epigraphically. Further east there is evidence from Taymāʾ and al-Jawf (Dūmat al-Jandal). In inner Arabia there are sporadic materials, such as those from Qaryat al-Fāw (al-Ansary 1982).

The Fertile Crescent was in the late pre-Islamic period in a completely different situation. There were minority religious groups, such as Jews, and also some other communities which had their roots either in Judaism or in a combination of Judaism with pagan ideologies going back to ancient Mesopotamia. Well-known examples include the Manichaeans, followers of the prophet Mani (215–75 CE), who led a prophetic movement similar in many ways to early Christianity, but emphasizing dualistic ideas derived partly from Zoroastrianism and partly from Judaism (Lieu 1992). Zoroastrianism itself had become the state religion of the Sasanians. It too has deep historical roots, but with a clear cosmological view (sacred elements of fire, water, earth, air) and a dualistic monotheism (Boyce 1979).

The Mandaeans of southern Iraq and Iran existed already in this pre-Islamic period. They have roots in the ancient Near Eastern world but emerged as a baptist movement living beside the rivers of Mesopotamia and southern Iran. Purification rituals are their most obvious characteristic. Their claim to monotheism is clear, though their literature is full of subordinate heavenly beings and it is not easy to characterize theologically. This community was always recognized by Islam as one of the 'peoples of the book' and given protected status on the basis of the reference to the *ṣābiʾūn* in the Qurʾan (2:62; 5:69; 22:17), though it is not absolutely clear that the Mandaeans were being referred to (Gündüz 1994; Lupieri 2002; Buckley 2002).

Some Themes in Pre-Islamic Religion

There is considerable methodological difficulty in trying to say anything in summary form about the diverse material on religion which is spread over many centuries and numerous geographical regions. The temptation lies in trying to give coherence to what was probably incoherent: there is no justification, for example, in assuming that Nabataean religious beliefs in the first century CE have any coherence with beliefs and practices reflected in Ibn al-Kalbī (English translation Faris 1952). One cannot, however, ignore the fact that there are some common themes which can be detected even on the basis of the limited evidence. And some practices appear to have persisted into the Islamic period.

Deities Worshipped

Particular deities are mentioned in the Qur'an itself. Islamic tradition regards these as imports into Arabia which led to the corruption of true religion, though it is more likely that the polytheism of Arabia was extremely ancient. According to Ibn al-Kalbī, ʿAmr ibn Rabīʿa ibn Luḥayy was the first person to bring the idols to the Arabian Peninsula, having experienced their worship in the Levant and brought some to the Kaʿba (Ibn al-Kalbī, *Kitāb al-Aṣnām*, 8). The best-known idols found there were mentioned in the Qur'an: 'Have you seen al-Lāt, and al-ʿUzzā and al-Manāt—the third one! . . . ' (Q. 53:19–20). '. . . they [the polytheists] said: Do not forsake your gods! nor forsake Wadd, nor Suwāʿ, nor Yaghūth, Yaʿūq and Nasr. They have misled greatly' (Q. 71:23).

Different tribes adopted different idols. The Hudhayl adopted Suwāʿ, Kalb adopted Wadd, and Madhḥij adopted Yaghūth, while Manāt, one of the longest established idols of the Arabs, was situated between Mecca and Medina and received the attention of pilgrims. Al-Fals was linked with Ṭayyʾ and al-Lāt with al-Ṭāʾif (Ibn al-Kalbī, *Kitāb al-Aṣnām*, 9, 10, 16–17, 59, 62). The latest addition to the idols worshipped in Arabia was said to be al-ʿUzzā, but the greatest idol of the Quraysh was Hubal, made in human form of red garnet, with one of his hands replaced with a golden hand (Ibn al-Kalbī 1924: 27–8). In line with the earliest Ancient Near Eastern tradition, personal names reflected religious affiliation, names such as: 'Abdullāt ('Servant of Lāt'), Saʿdullāt ('Joy of Lāt') and ʿAbdmanāt ('Servant of Manāt') (Ibn al-Kalbī, *Kitāb al-Aṣnām*, 13, 17–18).

Al-anṣāb ('the idols') were stones the Arabs worshipped on the move or in the courtyard of the Kaʿba (Ibn al-Kalbī, *Kitāb al-Aṣnām*, 33, 42). They also sanctified trees such as the trunk of the palm tree which Khālid ibn al-Walīd cut down, and sacred spaces like Suqām (near Mecca), which was protected by the Quraysh (Ibn al-Kalbī, *Kitāb al-Aṣnām*, 19).

It has long been noted that many of the deities worshipped in Arabia in pre-Islamic times were fundamentally astral in character, even if we eschew the exaggeration which would claim that *all* Arabian (or even all Semitic) religion was astral in origin (cf. Henninger 1981: 11–12). The raising of stars and planets to the status of deities is not really surprising in cultures where they dominate a large part of daily life in a way which is less true in cloudy regions where little is normally visible beyond the sun and the moon. The moon also had significance in ancient Arabia (and Syria and Mesopotamia) in relation to the calendar and the cycle of recurrent events such as trade fairs and pilgrimages. Astral deities are prominent also in South Arabian religion (i.e. in Saba and Ḥimyar, as well as the other south Arabian states): Almaqah, Sin, ʿAthtar and Dhāt Ḥimyam, though identifications with particular celestial bodies are not certain. (For further details on individual deities see Ibn al-Kalbī and modern works such as those by Wellhausen (1897), Höfner (1965), Fahd (1968: 37–201), ʿAlī (1968–72), Healey (2001) and also the *Encyclopaedia of Islam*.)

Aniconism

Another discernible theme, at least in the north-west of Arabia, is that of aniconism (Lammens 1928: 101–79; Mettinger 1995, especially 69–79; Healey 2001: 185–9). The term aniconism is used for a number of different religious phenomena and they are not peculiarly Arabian. Thus Mettinger distinguished programmatic and non-programmatic aniconism. In the former there is a theological prohibition or at least reluctance to make images of the deity. It is easily exemplified in the monotheistic context of Judaism and Islam, though the ways in which these aniconisms are expressed, essentially through what Mettinger calls 'empty-space aniconism', is quite different from the worship of uncarved or geometrically carved stones, which is what is normally meant by aniconism. (The prohibition of images of the divine does not really apply in Christianity, or not in the same way: the orthodox Christian view was to treat Jesus as the visible presence of God (John 14:8–9; Col. 1:15): but images of God the Father in heaven were generally avoided.)

In the pagan context of ancient Arabia and Syria, what we find is a non-programmatic aniconism, that is, a *tendency* to represent or worship deities not in human form, but in the form of stone blocks, minimally carved stelae, etc. This habit of worshipping stone blocks is particularly evident also among the Nabataeans (Healey 2001: 188–9). These blocks still 'represented' the deity, as is evident from accompanying inscriptions and sometimes the addition of facial markings. In some other cases the stones being worshipped were completely uncarved boulders, as appears to be the case at Emesa (modern Ḥomṣ in Syria). Al-Ṣabbāgh refers to the multiplicity of stone images in pre-Islamic Arabia as reflecting an 'aniconistic' stage in the emergence of the later prohibition of images, and an attempt to represent the mysterious aspect of unexplained natural phenomena (1998: 12–18; see also Lammens 1928: 101–79).

Mettinger's studies (1995, 1997) have shown, however, that aniconism was a widespread phenomenon. In the Atargatis temple at Manbij in Syria the images of the sun and moon deities were notable for their absence (Lightfoot 2003: 270–1, 449–55 on §34). In Phoenicia there is evidence of the directing of worship towards an empty chair on which the invisible deity was believed to sit. But also in the Greek world, Pausanias in particular describes numerous cults in which only a rough-hewn stone was worshipped (Gaifman 2012: 47–75).

We have little clue as to what the theological significance of such cults was. They are not necessarily monotheistic and they do not necessarily reflect a belief that it would be impious or impossible to depict the deity in the form of a statue. Such cults could arise from belief in the intrinsic potency of stones and especially stones which appear to have an unusual origin, such as meteorites. In Greece and in the Near East they existed alongside cults involving figural representations of gods.

Pilgrimage

There is evidence that the pre-Islamic Arabs practised rituals of pilgrimage focused on sacred sites associated with particular deities. Ibn al-Kalbī tells us about numerous such cult centres.

Pilgrimage is linked to the month of pilgrimage, Dhū'l-Ḥijja, the eleventh month of the lunar year, one of the sacred months, though some have thought that the pilgrimage was more tied to the seasons, whether it was held in spring or autumn (Wensinck in Wensinck and Lewis 1971: 31–2). Pilgrimage was not exclusively directed to Mecca, but it is claimed that all went to the Sacred House of the Kaᶜba in Mecca when they had a very significant matter to pray for. They would wear special necklaces to alert everyone to the fact that they were going to perform the pilgrimage and some Arabs had their own rituals which were different from those of others (ᶜAlī 1968–72: 6:349, 390).

Local people competed to offer services to pilgrims and pilgrimage was directly linked to trade and seasonal commercial markets. Since participation was almost obligatory to all the tribes, especially in the western part of the Arabian Peninsula, it was ideal to have the pilgrimage occurring in the sacred months when fighting, looting, etc. were prohibited and socially unacceptable. Some tribes, however, could not wait for the season of pilgrimage to finish and therefore started to play tricks with the calendar, switching some lunar months with others or prolonging the year. These stratagems were allowed provided that notice was given, though they were condemned under Islam (Q. 9:37; ʿAlī 1968–72: 8:488–509).

Some regular pilgrimages linked religious zeal with the demands of trade. We can assume that trade fairs took place at places like Medina and perhaps Mecca and that this brought an annual (or more frequent) influx of semi-nomadic peoples. Seasonal markets were also held at such places as Dūmat al-Jandal, ᶜUkāẓ, al-Mushaqqar, Dhū al-Majāz, and Majanna. Some were linked to religious seasons, while others were also used for cultural exchanges. The attendees competed with each other in poetry and oratory. It was in these markets that they formulated treaties and alliances and they were also the place for missionaries to go to spread their message (al-Ṣabbāgh 1998: 76–8).

Temples and Sacrifices

Sacred houses or temples and various *kaᶜbas* similar to the very popular one in Mecca, called 'the House of God', were scattered around the peninsula, as we can see from Ibn al-Kalbī (see details in Fahd 1968: 203–47). Thus there was the *kaᶜba* of the Banū al-Ḥārith in Najrān and the *kaᶜba* of the Iyād in Sindād (Ibn al-Kalbī, *Kitāb al-Aṣnām*, 44–46).

The Arabs also built other temples, the most famous of which were al-Qalīs in Sanaa, built by Abraha al-Ashram (Ibn al-Kalbī, *Kitāb al-Aṣnām*, 46–47), Riʾām in Ḥimyar (11) and Bayt al-Lāt in al-Ṭāʾif (16).

Offerings were made to the idols in the Meccan *kaʿba* and it is unsurprising that animal sacrifice played an important role in the cults of the various temples. We know this from limited Nabataean evidence, but there is also the evidence of Ibn al-Kalbī and others.

The ritual of circumambulation of the holy place in the sanctuary existed before Islam (Wellhausen 1897: 109–12). Circumambulation (*ṭawāf*) of the Meccan *kaʿba* was accompanied in pre-Islamic times by whistling and the clapping of hands (Ibn al-Kalbī, *Kitāb al-Aṣnām*, 33, 42). 'And their prayer at the sacred house was not but whistling and clapping' (Q. 8:35). The pre-Islamic Arabs also circled around the tombs of their elites and their fathers (Ibn al-Kalbī, *Kitāb al-Aṣnām*, 51–53). Some Arabs carried out the circumambulation naked as a symbol of the casting aside of sin (Muslim 1998: 486). This practice remained until it was abolished in the ninth year after the *hijra* (630–1 CE).

On temple personnel we do not have a great deal of information, but the *sādin* (plur. *sadana*) was the guardian of a sanctuary and of its idols (also when they were moved from place to place) (Lammens 1928: 106–10). He was responsible for access to the idols and kept the keys to sacred buildings. The *kāhin* was a priest or seer or revealer of the divine will, who regulated worship and interpreted omens. The word is etymologically linked with the Hebrew word for 'priest', *kōhēn* (root k-h-n, 'predict, tell the future'; see Fahd 1966: 91–120 on cultic personnel).

Divination

Perhaps a more distinctively Arabian phenomenon is that of divination, seeking the will of heaven by means of mantic practices. Such practices are frequently mentioned by Arab and non-Arab authors as being particularly common in Arabia, though they are not, of course, uniquely confined to Arabian or Semitic religion (Fahd 1966). The flight of birds was regarded as being significant in this respect (Fahd 1966: 431–50), the way that arrows fell, etc. Such 'random' phenomena are similarly the basis of mantic practices elsewhere: they require the services of an interpreter, a specialist who knows the meaning of the apparently random phenomena, the *kāhin* (above). Some of these practices may have very ancient roots (see recently Crone and Silverstein 2010 on lot-casting).

The Arabs associated bad luck with cosmic phenomena such as eclipses, meteor showers, the direction of the wind, and specific types of animals such as crows and owls, and also other birds if they flew in a particular way. They were superstitious about some involuntary human actions—such as sneezing—and about people with disabilities and diseases, as well as about Wednesdays if they coincided with certain days of the month (Fahd 1966: 483–8). Islam, of course, forbade such superstition, though these practices persisted for a long time.

Monotheism and Monotheistic Tendencies

One of the most controversial aspects of religion in the pre-Islamic Middle East, touched on above, involves the question of emergent monotheism.

This is a separate question from that of the *existence* of monotheistic religions in the pre-Islamic era. So far as such religions are concerned, there is clear evidence in the case of Judaism and slightly more complicated evidence in the case of Christianity. The doctrine of the Trinity obscures, at least for the outside observer, the monotheism of orthodox Christianity. However, there is no doubt that Christians have always regarded themselves as monotheists and the Trinitarian theology of Father, Son, and Holy Spirit is universally understood as a theological construct explaining the operation of the single Godhead.

Apart from the Jews and Christians there were other groups before Islam who would have regarded themselves as monotheists, even if they would not have used such a term. Dualism, with the concession of power to an evil power alongside the good god, can be regarded as a nuanced form of monotheism, just as can some ancient Jewish cults in which the one god was regarded as having a spouse (Hadley 2000; Dever 2005). These are not true polytheisms, but complex monotheisms. The Mandaeans could be placed in this sort of category, as could the Yezidis of northern Iraq.

Some controversy arises over the *process* whereby polytheistic cults, especially in Yemen, appear to have been replaced by monotheistic cults. Beeston (1984) took Himyarite monotheism to be an independent development, not to be attributed to Jewish or Christian influence, though this view is not widely accepted. Rather, the impact of Judaism in south Arabia is now seen in such a way that one would be justified in speaking of Himyarite monotheism as reflecting *judaization* (see especially Robin 2004: 867–9).

Long before Christianity (and without Jewish influence) there were, however, monotheizing tendencies in both Mesopotamian and Greek religion. The process involved is often connected with philosophical reflection or modes of scientific thought. In Greece and Rome philosophy played a role (Athanassiadi and Frede 1999; Mitchell and van Nuffelen 2010), while in Mesopotamia it may have been a result of scientific systematizing, partly related to the incorporation of varied cults into major temples (Lambert 1975; Parpola 2000).

In the immediate chronological and geographic context it has been argued that there is evidence of monotheizing both in Nabataea and Palmyra (Teixidor 1977: 161). In the former case the evidence is circumstantial rather than direct and consists in the fact that one deity, Dushara, came to have such a dominant role (Healey 2001: 189–91). Other deities did not cease to be worshipped, so the term 'monotheism' would not be appropriate. Nineteenth-century scholarship coined the word 'henotheism' for this kind of cult: one god is regarded as being far more important for the particular community, even if the existence of the other gods is not actually denied. (The term was first used in this context by Max Müller: Versnel 2000: 87 n. 21).

In Palmyra there is the added feature of a layer of abstract theologizing. Here we find frequent reference to the unnamed god described as 'Blessed be his name forever' (Teixidor 1977: 122–6). In fact we have no real understanding of what is meant by this divine title or to whom it refers, but it does suggest a level of theological sophistication, of the kind that we find in the Jewish tradition, in avoiding the proper name of the deity. Also at Palmyra there is a tendency to associate Bēl and Baalshamin with divine epithets which again indicate a level of abstraction and sophistication. The deity can be called 'the one who gives reward', 'the kindly god', 'the merciful one'. In fact divine titles of this kind go back a long way in the ancient Near East (Healey 1998). The epithet 'Merciful One', as we have seen earlier, is also found in south Arabia, precisely at the same time as there is the decline in polytheistic cults in favour of concentration on a single god. Above all there is a real question of Jewish and, perhaps, Christian influence.

There is not enough evidence here to argue for a general trend towards monotheism in the Greek and Near Eastern worlds in antiquity, but there is sufficient evidence to suggest that Judaism, which was widely known for its insistence on monotheism, proved to be very persuasive in terms of conversion and association. The royal family of Adiabene in northern Mesopotamia was converted to Judaism in the first century CE (Josephus, *Antiquities* XX.2), in the Roman world so-called 'god-fearers' associated themselves with Jewish communities even if they did not convert completely (Reynolds and Tannenbaum 1987; Mitchell 1999), and a series of Jewish kings ruled Yemen between 380 and 520 (Robin 2004; 2008). The wide and quick spread of Christianity and then of Islam may in part be explained by the fact the polytheistic cults had to some extent become discredited and lost their attraction.

None of this is to suggest that there was any automatic process at work. Polytheism might have survived in the Middle East and might have become more popular again. It did have its defenders in Ḥarrān (Green 1992; Gündüz 1994). The case can be made, however, for the view that Islam arrived on the scene at a fortuitous moment of religious history, at a time when monotheism was in the ascendant and the main existing form of monotheism, Christianity, was in a parlous state theologically and politically.

Apart from the phenomenon of monotheizing cults in the Fertile Crescent and in South Arabia, we also have the Islamic evidence of the presence of *ḥunafāʾ* (singular *ḥanīf*) in north-west Arabia (al-Ṣabbāgh 1998; Rubin 1990; de Blois 2002, 2010). These appear to be monotheists who are distinct from Jews (and Christians), and indeed from Muslims, though belonging to the Abrahamic tradition of true Muslims before the preaching of the Prophet. What their precise origin was is unknown: the (Christian) Syriac word for 'pagan' is *ḥanpā*. It is used disapprovingly of pagans, while in Islamic tradition *ḥanīf* is used approvingly of non-Muslims of the pre-Islamic and early Islamic period. The *ḥunafāʾ* did not form communities, but held their beliefs as individuals. Ibn Isḥāq reports (*Sīra*, 99) that Zayd ibn ʿAmr ibn Nawfal of the Quraysh did not like the way his people worshipped, he criticized it, ridiculed it, even mocked it at times, but he stopped short of accepting Judaism or Christianity even though he abandoned the religion of his people. He kept away from idols, forbade the infanticide of girls, refrained from consuming the flesh of animals which had died naturally and blood, and never sacrificed to idols.

Another *ḥanīf* was the gifted orator Quss ibn Sāʿida. The Prophet admired him and liked one of his speeches and even said of him: 'He will be raised and judged as a whole nation by himself on the Day of Judgement' (Muslim, *Ṣaḥīḥ*, 88). Another was Waraqa ibn Nawfal, who was the cousin of Khadīja (555–619) (Ibn Isḥāq, *Sīra*, 83).

These traditions acknowledge monotheism before Islam, though there is an opinion which sees these individuals as Christians (see Ibn Isḥāq, *Sīrat*, 99 on Waraqa and others as Christians). Almost all Muslim scholars agree that the Prophet himself was a *ḥanīf* before Islam, since he habitually performed meditation in the cave of Ḥirāʾ to ponder on the creation of God and had never prostrated himself to an idol (Ibn Isḥāq, *Sīra*, 105). Some of the *ḥunafāʾ* worshipped Raḥmān, 'The Merciful One' (al-Ṣabbāgh 1998: 42), whose title we have referred to above in relation to Palmyrene and South Arabian religion.

Conclusions

It is tempting from the above survey to emphasize the continuities which link the pre-Islamic to the Islamic period. Researchers have frequently been struck by the presence in Arabia before Islam of monotheistic ideas, aniconic cults, and particular rituals found later also in Islam. The significance of these individual details is, however, easy to exaggerate, since other common pre-Islamic features were disavowed by Islam (superstitions and divination, multiplicity of gods and temples).

On the other hand it is not surprising from a History of Religions perspective, that a newly founded religious tradition should inherit some fundamental attitudes and features from earlier times. One could only be surprised if one were to assume that the uniqueness of a religious tradition has to be measured in terms of its being radically different in *all* respects from what went before. This kind of assumption is certainly not today applied either by believers or non-believers to either Judaism or Christianity. Christianity is the easy case: it is a derivative of Judaism and wherever it has spread Christianity has assimilated pre-existent local religious traditions. Christmas is a Christian version of the annual worship of the returning sun-deity at the winter solstice. Easter (with its pagan Easter eggs and rabbits!) is celebrated in part as a festival of the spring and the renewal of nature. In Judaism, partly because of layers of antique theologizing in the Old Testament, it is less easy to trace pre-Torah roots, but the Passover, for example, is obviously connected with spring rituals celebrated by shepherds and was then linked theologically with the 'Exodus' from Egypt, while other festivals are linked to the agricultural year (which existed before Moses).

The uniqueness of a religion does not lie in the uniqueness of its every detail. It lies in the 'web of significance' which links these details together to form a religious narrative or whole (Geertz 1993). For Christians Christmas means more than the winter solstice because it forms part of the narrative of the life of Jesus and celebrates the doctrine of the Incarnation and the beginning of the Christian era.

In the case of Islam, even the earliest Islamic tradition emphasizes the idea that the Prophet *purified* the worship which had come to disfigure the Kaʿba. His campaign was against the association of other gods with Allāh. It was a kind of purification of religion, in European terms a 'Reformation' (Peters 1994: 28–9; Healey 2001: 84–6).

The conducting of pilgrimage was not in itself bad, but it had to be directed towards the purpose revealed by God. So it is not surprising that pilgrimage and some aspects of ritual (aniconism, sacrifice, circumambulation of sanctuaries) had pagan precedents. But all of these things were given new significance by Islam, which imposed its own 'web of significance' on what it inherited.

Bibliography

ʿAlī, Jawād. *al-Mufaṣṣal fī tārīkh al-ʿArab qabla al-Islām*. Beirut: Dār al-ʿIlm, 1968–72.

al-Ansary, A. R. *Qaryat al-Fau: A Portrait of Pre-Islamic Civilisation in Saudi Arabia*. London: Croom Helm, 1982.

Athanassiadi, P. and M. Frede (eds.). *Pagan Monotheism in Late Antiquity*. Oxford: Oxford University Press, 1999.

Atiya, A. S. *A History of Eastern Christianity*. London: Methuen, 1968; reprint 1991.

Baum, W. and D. W. Winkler. *The Church of the East: A Concise History*. London/New York: RoutledgeCurzon, 2003.

Beaucamp, J., F. Briquel-Chatonnet and Ch. J. Robin. 'La Persécution des chrétiens de Nagrān et la chronologie ḥimyarite', *Aram* 11–12 (1999–2000), 15–83.

Beaucamp, J., F. Briquel-Chatonnet and Ch. J. Robin (eds.). *Juifs et chrétiens en Arabie aux Vᵉ et VIᵉ siècles: regards croisés sur les sources* (actes du colloque de novembre 2008) (Le massacre de Najrân 2). Paris: Association des amis du Centre d'histoire et civilisation de Byzance, 2010.

Beeston, A. F. L. 'Himyarite Monotheism'. In: A. T. al-Ansary et al. (eds.) *Studies in the History of Arabia II: Pre-Islamic Arabia*, pp. 149–54. Riyadh: King Saud University Press, 1984.

Boyce, M. *Zoroastrians: Their Religious Beliefs and Practices*. London/New York: Routledge and Kegan Paul, 1979.

Brock, S. P. 'The "Nestorian" Church: A Lamentable Misnomer', *BJRL* 78 (1996), 23–35.

Buckley, J. J. *The Mandaeans: Ancient Texts and Modern People* (American Academy of Religion; Religions Series). Oxford: Oxford Unversity Press, 2002.

Chaillot, Ch. *The Syrian Orthodox Church of Antioch and All the East: Introduction to its Life and Spirituality*. Geneva: Inter-Orthodox Dialogue, 1998.

Crone, P. and A. Silverstein. 'The Ancient Near East and Islam: The Case of Lot-Casting.' *JSS* 55 (2010), 423–50.

de Blois, F. '*Naṣrānī* (*Ναζωραῖος*) and *ḥanīf* (*ἐθνικός*): Studies on the Religious Vocabulary of Christianity and of Islam', *Bulletin of the School of Oriental and African Studies* 65 (2002), 1–30.

de Blois, F. 'Islam in its Arabian Context'. In: Angelika Neuwirth, Nicolai Sinai, and Michael Marx (eds.) *The Qurʾān in Context: Historical and Literary Investigations into the Qurʾānic Milieu*, pp. 615–24. Leiden: E. J. Brill, 2010.

Dever, W. G. *Did God Have a Wife? Archaeology and Folk Religion in Ancient Israel*. Grand Rapids, MI/Cambridge: W. B. Eerdmans, 2005.

Fahd, T. *La Divination arabe: études religieuses, sociologiques et folkloriques sur le mileu natif de l'Islam*. Strasbourg: Université de Strasbourg, 1966.

Fahd, T. *Le Panthéon de l'arabie centrale à la veille de l'Hégire* (B.A.H. 88). Paris: P. Geuthner, 1968.

Faris, N. A. (trans.). *Ibn al-Kalbi: The Book of Idols*. Princeton, NJ: Princeton University Press, 1952.

Fiey, J. M. *Communautés syriaques en Iran et Irak des origines à 1552* (Variorum Collected Studies 106). London: Variorum Reprints, 1979.

Gaifman, M. *Aniconism in Greek Antiquity* (Oxford Studies in Ancient Culture and Representation). Oxford: Oxford University Press, 2012.

Gajda, I. *Le Royaume de Ḥimyar à l'époque monothéiste* (Mémoires de l'Académie des inscriptions et belles-lettres 40). Paris: AIBL, 2009.

Geertz, C. 'Religion as a Cultural System'. In: *The Interpretation of Cultures: Selected Essays*, pp. 87–125. London: Fontana Press, 1993 (original 1966).

Gil, M. 'The Origin of the Jews of Yathrib', *JSAI* 4 (1984), 203–24.

Green, T. M. *The City of the Moon God: Religious Traditions of Harran* (Religions in the Graeco-Roman World 114). Leiden: E. J. Brill, 1992.

Gündüz, Ş. *The Knowledge of Life: The Origins and Early History of the Mandaeans and their Relation to the Sabians of the Qur'ān and to the Harranians* (Journal of Semitic Studies Supplement 3). Oxford: Oxford University Press, 1994.

Hadley, J. M. *The Cult of Asherah in Ancient Israel and Judah: Evidence for a Hebrew Goddess*. Cambridge: Cambridge University Press, 2000.

Hage, W. 'Jakobitische Kirche'. In: *Theologische Realenzylopädie* 16:474–85. Berlin/New York: de Gruyter, 1987.

Hawting, G. R. *The Idea of Idolatry and the Emergence of Islam: From Polemic to History* (Cambridge Studies in Islamic Civilization). Cambridge: Cambridge University Press, 1999.

Healey, J. F. 'The Kindly and Merciful God: On Some Semitic Divine Epithets'. In: M. Dietrich and I. Kottsieper (eds.). *'Und Mose schrieb dieses Lied auf': Studien zum Alten Testament und zum Alten Orient. Festschrift für Oswald Loretz*, pp. 349–56. Münster: Ugarit-Verlag, 1998.

Healey, J. F. *The Religion of the Nabataeans: A Conspectus* (Religions in the Graeco-Roman World 136). Leiden: E. J. Brill, 2001.

Henninger, J. 'Pre-Islamic Bedouin Religion'. In: M. L. Swartz (ed. and trans.). *Studies on Islam*, pp. 3–22. New York: Oxford University Press, 1981.

Höfner, M. 'Die Stammesgruppen Nord-und Zentralarabiens in vorislamischer Zeit; Sübarabien'. In: H. W. Haussig (ed.). *Götter und Mythen im vorderen Orient: Wörterbuch der Mythologie* I/1, pp. 407–552. Stuttgart: E. Klett, 1965.

Hoyland, R. G. *Arabia and the Arabs from the Bronze Age to the Coming of Islam*. London/New York: Routledge, 2001.

Ibn Isḥāq (Ibn Hishām). *The Life of Muhammad (Sīrat Rasūl Allāh)*. Trans. A. Guillaume. Oxford: Oxford University Press, 1955.

Ibn al-Kalbī. *Kitāb al-Aṣnām: le livre des idoles*. 2nd edn. Ed. Ahmed Zeki Pacha. Cairo: Imprimerie Bibliothèque Egyptienne, 1924.

Kelly, J. N. D. *Early Christian Creeds*. 3rd edn. London: Longman, 1972.

King, D. 'Why Were the Syrians Interested in Greek Philosophy?' In: P. Wood (ed.). *History and Identity in the Late Antique Near East*, pp. 61–81. Oxford: Oxford University Press, 2013).

King, N. Q. *The Emperor Theodosius and the Establishment of Christianity* (Library of History and Doctrine). London: SCM, 1961.
Lambert, W. G. 'The Historical Development of the Mesopotamian Pantheon: A Study in Sophisticated Polytheism'. In: H. Goedicke and J. J. M. Roberts (eds.). *Unity and Diversity*, pp. 191–200. Baltimore/London: Johns Hopkins University Press, 1975.
Lammens, H. *L'Arabie occidentale avant l'hégire*. Beirut: Imprimerie catholique, 1928.
Lieu, S. N. C. *Manichaeism in the Later Roman Empire and Medieval China: A Historical Survey*. 2nd edn. Tübingen: Mohr-Siebeck, 1992.
Lightfoot, J. L. *Lucian On the Syrian Goddess: Edited with Introduction, Translation and Commentary*. Oxford: Oxford University Press, 2003.
Lupieri, E. *The Mandaeans: The Last Gnostics*. Grand Rapids, MI/Cambridge: W. B. Eerdmans, 2002.
Mettinger, T. N. D. *No Graven Image? Israelite Aniconism in its Ancient Near Eastern Context*. Stockholm: Almqvist & Wiksell International: Collectanea Biblica, OT Series 42, 1995.
Mettinger, T. N. D. 'Israelite Aniconism: Development and Origins'. In: K. van der Toorn (ed.). *The Image and the Book: Iconic Cults, Aniconism, and the Rise of Book Religion in Israel and the Ancient Near East*, pp. 173–204. Leuven: Peeters, 1997.
Mitchell, S. 'The Cult of Theos Hypsistos between Pagans, Jews, and Christians'. In: P. Athanassiadi and M. Frede (eds.). *Pagan Monotheism in Late Antiquity*, pp. 81–148. Oxford: Oxford University Press, 1999.
Mitchell, S. and P. van Nuffelen. *One God: Pagan Monotheism in the Roman Empire*. Cambridge: Cambridge University Press, 2010.
Muslim, Ibn al-Ḥajjāj. *Ṣaḥīḥ Muslim*. Riyadh: Bayt al-Afkār al-Dawliyya, 1998.
Newby, G. D. *A History of the Jews of Arabia from Ancient Times to their Eclipse under Islam*. Columbia: University of South Carolina Press, 1988.
Noja, S. 'Testimonianze epigrafiche di giudei nell'arabia settentrionale', *Bibbia e Oriente* (Brescia) 21 (1979), 283–316.
Parpola, S. 'Monotheism in Ancient Assyria'. In: B. N. Porter (ed.). *One God or Many? Concepts of Divinity in the Ancient World* (Transactions of the Casco Bay Assyriological Institute 1), pp. 165–209. Casco Bay, ME: Assyriological Institute, 2000.
Peters, F. E. *The Hajj: The Muslim Pilgrimage to Mecca and the Holy Places*. Princeton: Princeton University Press, 1994.
Reynolds, J. and R. Tannenbaum. *Jews and Godfearers at Aphrodisias* (Cambridge Philological Society Supplementary Vol. 12). Cambridge: Cambridge Philological Society, 1987.
Robin, Ch. J. 'Le Judaïsme de Ḥimyar', *Arabia (Revue de Sabéologie)* 1 (2003), 97–172.
Robin, Ch. J. 'Ḥimyar et Israël', *Comptes rendus des séances de l'Académie des Inscriptions et Belles-Lettres* 148/2 (2004), 831–908.
Robin, Ch. J. 'Joseph, dernier roi de Ḥimyar (de 522 à 525, ou une des années suivantes)', *JSAI* 34 (2008), 1–124.
Rompay, L. van. 'Society and Community in the Christian East'. In: M. Maas (ed.). *Cambridge Companion to the Age of Justinian*, pp. 240–66. Cambridge: Cambridge University Press, 2005.
Rubin, U. '*Ḥanīfiyya* and Kaᶜba: An Inquiry into the Arabian Pre-Islamic Background of *Dīn Ibrāhīm*', *JSAI* 13 (1990), 85–112.
al-Ṣabbāgh, ᶜA. *al-Aḥnāf: dirāsa fi'l-fikr al-dīnī al-tawḥīdī fi'l-manṭiqa al-ʿarabiyya qabl al-Islām*. Damascus: Dār al-Ḥaṣād, 1998.
Shahid, I. *Byzantium and the Arabs in the Fourth Century*. Washington, DC: Dumbarton Oaks Research Library and Collection, 1984.

Smith, A. M. *Roman Palmyra: Identity, Community, and State Formation*. New York: Oxford University Press, 2013.

Tannous, J. 'You Are What You Read: Qenneshre and the Miaphysite Church in the Seventh Century'. In: P. Wood (ed.). *History and Identity in the Late Antique Near East*, pp. 83–102. Oxford: Oxford University Press, 2013.

Teixidor, J. *The Pagan God: Popular Religion in the Greco-Roman Near East*. Princeton, NJ: Princeton University Press, 1977.

Trimingham, J. S. *Christianity among the Arabs in Pre-Islamic Times* (Arab Background Series). London/New York: Longman/Libairie du Liban, 1979.

Versnel, H. S. 'Thrice One: Three Greek Experiments in *The* Oneness'. In: B. N. Porter (ed.). *One God or Many? Concepts of Divinity in the Ancient World* (Transactions of the Casco Bay Assyriological Institute 1), pp. 79–163. Casco Bay: Assyriological Institute, 2000.

Wellhausen, J. *Reste arabischen Heidentums gesammelt und erläutert*. 2nd edn. Berlin: G. Reimer, 1897.

Wensinck, A. J. and B. Lewis. 'Ḥadjdj'. In: *Encyclopaedia of Islam* 2nd edn. 3:31–8. Leiden: E. J. Brill, 1971.

Zetterholm, M. *The Formation of Christianity in Antioch: A Social-Scientific Approach to the Separation between Judaism and Christianity* (Routledge Early Church Monographs). London/New York: Routledge, 2003.

CHAPTER 6

THE ARABIAN CONTEXT OF THE QUR'AN

History and the Text

HARRY MUNT

FROM the very beginnings of historical-critical study of the Qur'an in the early nineteenth century, much European scholarship has tended to seek to account for the clear and obvious intertextual parallels between a number of Qur'anic verses and material in various Jewish and Christian scriptural and exegetical traditions. (An oft-cited classic is Geiger 1833/1902; an overview of much of this scholarship can be found in Reynolds 2010: 3–22.) Such research was generally based on the acceptance of two important assumptions: firstly, that an adequate historical context for the Qur'an's promulgation was to be found in the extra-Qur'anic Arabic sources for Muḥammad's life and times, principally ʿAbd al-Malik ibn Hishām's (d. 213/828–9 or 218/833) redaction of Muḥammad ibn Isḥāq's (d. *c*.150/767) biography (*sīra*) of the Prophet, which was first edited by Ferdinand Wüstenfeld and published in 1860, the same year in which the great German Orientalist Theodor Nöldeke published the first edition of his magisterial *Geschichte des Qorâns*. Secondly, that the Qur'an itself was primarily a source for the life and thought of Muḥammad: Nöldeke, even before the publication of his *Geschichte des Qorâns*, described the Qur'an as: 'The only unadulterated, thoroughly reliable witness to Muḥammad and his teaching' (Nöldeke 1858: 700; see also Nöldeke 1860: 2 [= Nöldeke et al. 1909–38: 1:3/Nöldeke et al. 2013: 2]; there is an interesting discussion of this assumption in Sinai 2008).

This approach—the consideration of the Qur'an as the best primary witness to Muḥammad's life and message as well as the Arabian historical context in which he operated, but a realization that it could only be meaningfully interpreted in light of the more extensive narrative material provided by later Arabic sources—continued to dominate scholarship on the historical background of the Qur'anic revelations for more than a century after Nöldeke's work (e.g. Paret 1961). This approach was famously challenged in the late 1970s by a handful of studies (most notably Wansbrough 1977; Wansbrough 1978;

Crone and Cook 1977), in which it was forcefully argued that many of the later Arabic extra-Qur'anic sources did not provide independent testimony for the history of the early first-/seventh-century Ḥijāz; rather, so it was made clear, the narratives which these sources provide are themselves often exercises in Qur'anic exegesis. Ibn Isḥāq's narrative of the first revelation to Muḥammad was not, as it has come down to us, an independently transmitted memory, but rather an intricate attempt to explain some of the obscurities of Q. 96; likewise his account of the South Arabian ruler Abraha's assault on the Kaʿba of Mecca is to a large extent an exegesis of Q. 105. The older methodology did not die away immediately (see e.g. Watt 1988), but there was an ever greater shift away from any thoughts that we can assume to know much at all about the historical context of the Qur'an. Shortly after the appearance of John Wansbrough's works, for example, Alford Welch published a study that already sought to investigate Muḥammad's understanding of himself on the basis of data in the Qur'an itself, removed to some degree—although by no means totally—from the background provided by the later Arabic material (Welch 1983). Only seventeen years later, however, Welch's attempt was condemned by Andrew Rippin: 'To me, it does seem that in no sense can the Qur'an be assumed to be a primary document in constructing the life of Muḥammad. The text is far too opaque when it comes to history; its shifting referents leave the text in a conceptual muddle for historical purposes' (Rippin 2000: 307). There is even a long history of questioning whether we can actually understand the '*muḥammad*' of four verses in the Qur'an (Q. 3:144, 33:40, 47:2 and 48:29; he is also referred to as '*aḥmad*' in Q. 61:6) as its Messenger's name, an issue which seems to be attracting increasing attention again (overview in Reynolds 2010: 185–99).

The same period has seen a challenge to historians' attempts to envisage a late sixth- and early seventh-century CE Ḥijāzī context against which the text of the Qur'an might be evaluated. Even if we set aside those arguments against viewing the material within the Qur'an at least as having originated in a western Arabian environment—some of my arguments in favour of the Ḥijāzī setting will be offered later—many scholars remain unsure of how to reconstruct that contemporary Arabian backdrop. Post-first-/seventh-century Arabic narratives about pre-Islamic Arabia have come under the same sustained critiques as biographies of Muḥammad (see especially Crone 1987: 203–30; Hawting 1999; also now Rippin 2013), and modern scholars have begun to talk of a land without a context, an 'empty Ḥijāz' (Wansbrough 1987/2003; Montgomery 2006) and, thus, of the Qur'an as a 'text without context' (Peters 1991: 300). As a result, while some scholars do continue to use the later Arabic sources alongside the Qur'anic text to understand the religious history of the late antique Ḥijāz (e.g. Gilliot 1996; Gilliot 2005; Gilliot 2008; al-Azmeh 2014), other historians have tended to widen the search for a historical context, some looking elsewhere in the Arabian Peninsula (many studies by Christian Robin could be cited here, but, for examples with direct relevance for the interpretation of Qur'anic passages, see Robin 2000; Robin 2015a), others going even further afield. (See the many articles collected together in Reynolds 2008; Reynolds 2011; Neuwirth et al. 2010; Neuwirth 2010 is a particularly impressive and expansive attempt to understand the Qur'an's late antique Near Eastern context.)

With some important exceptions, to be discussed later in this chapter, the study of material in the Qur'an as a way of ascertaining something of its own Arabian context is not very popular any more, at least not in modern European and North American scholarship. This is something of a pity, since although certainly not an Arabian—let alone a Ḥijāzī—'local history', the Qur'an is an extremely rare source much of whose material is increasingly accepted again by modern scholars as having at least its origins in the early-to-mid seventh-century CE Ḥijāz. However difficult a source it may be to interpret, it does thus offer us our most detailed contemporary material on western Arabia at the time of the emergence of Islam. In the remainder of this chapter, I will outline some of the ways in which historians have tried over the past decade or so to use the Qur'an as a source for its own context without carrying over assumptions based on the later Arabic exegetical and biographical material, and then make some suggestions how this line of research might profitably be carried forward.

History in the Qur'an

As has frequently been noted, the Qur'an certainly does not provide a historical narrative of western Arabia or any other neighbouring region. Very broadly speaking, four different types of Qur'anic material are easily apparent: eschatology; legal injunctions; debates with other religious groups; and stories of prophets sent by God before the Qur'anic Messenger. Most of the clearest narrative material which the Qur'an does contain is of the latter type; Q. 12, containing the story of Joseph, is a good example, as are Q. 18—with its stories about the 'Companions of the Cave' (*aṣḥāb al-kahf*), Moses and Dhū'l-Qarnayn—and Q. 20:9–99, which offers narratives about Moses. The only sections of the Qur'an which could, just perhaps, be considered 'Arabian' historical narratives are those which offer accounts of the prophets Hūd, Ṣāliḥ, and Shuʿayb (e.g. within Q. 7:65–102, and 11:58–68, 84–95; further discussion in Bosworth 1984; Tottoli 2002: 45–50), although by many modern definitions such narratives offer legend and myth rather than history; it is possible that such narratives were among those parts of the Qur'an's message which some of its opponents criticized as mere 'stories of the ancients' (*asāṭīr al-awwalīn*; see Q. 6:25, 8:31, 16:24, 23:83, 25:5, 27:68, 46:17, 68:15, 83:13). They do, however, at least give us some indication of the stories that developed around Arabian tribes such as ʿĀd and Thamūd (Hūd's and Ṣāliḥ's peoples respectively), even if they have presumably been reworked as they appear in the Qur'an to fit the latter's particular view of humankind's past and future (Neuwirth 2010: 228–9).

That view is generally understood to have been largely ahistorical: 'The very concept of history is fundamentally irrelevant to the Qur'an's concerns, because all people have been, and will be, confronted with the same eternal moral choice—the choice between good and evil, with the guidance of the revelation and of the prophets as the criteria provided by God for choosing. Since the moral choice is presented as eternal, the question of historical change is of no importance to the Qur'an.' (For general discussions of the

Qur'an on history, see Donner 1998: 75–85 (quotation here from p. 80); Neuwirth 2003: 14–16; Neuwirth 2010: esp. 182–234.) The stories of earlier prophets and their peoples certainly emphasize this; they are moralizing narratives of divine retribution—Horovitz (1926: 10–32) called them *Straflegenden*; Wansbrough (1977: 2–5) preferred 'retribution pericopes'—which describe how God destroyed earlier communities because they failed to heed His Message as delivered by one of His Messengers. (Q. 91 offers a good and explicit example of the message expected to be derived from these stories; further discussion in Neuwirth 2010: 226–30.) They present a rather cyclical view of the world's history, with one eradicated community followed by another (the Qur'an is rarely explicit about the order in which these communities arose). This cyclical progression is then promised to come to an end with the seemingly imminent advent of the Hour and the period that Angelika Neuwirth terms 'heilsgeschichtliche Zeit' (2010: 214–15). There also does seem to be an indication in at least one instance (Q. 33:33) of the Qur'anic usage of the term '*al-jāhiliyya*'—which came to be used as a common term for the pre-Islamic period of Arabia's history—of an idea of a distinct phase of history before the current revelation brought by that text. There are a handful of references in the Qur'an to occurrences which are seemingly loosely contemporary (for examples, see Neuwirth 2010: 232–34, 513–15; Robin 2015a), but, although Muslim exegetes came to understand them as attached to specific events preceding and during the lifetime of Muḥammad, such attachments are rarely mandated by the Qur'anic text alone.

So the Qur'an has some historical material—in the sense that it offers narratives about a past—but it is certainly not a historiographical text. What then can modern historians do with the text? Historians, especially of pre-modern times, are well used to dealing with texts possessing relatively poorly understood contexts, although the Qur'an does provide more formidable challenges than most. One of these challenges is ascertaining its material's original geographical context. For reasons I can only go into briefly here, in spite of a range of modern scholarship challenging the Ḥijāzī provenance of the Qur'an (see e.g. Shoemaker 2003; and the more general comments in Shoemaker 2012), I do consider it to comprise material at least originally circulating in the early seventh-century CE Ḥijāz, albeit this material may have been collected and codified in other regions and at other times. (For other arguments in this direction, see Donner 1998: 35–63; Rubin 2009; Sinai 2017: 59–65.) It has often been noted that the Qur'an 'has little concern with the proper names of its own place and time' (Reynolds 2010: 198; see also Robin 2015a: 27–8), which, I think, makes it all the more significant that it does mention a handful of Ḥijāzī toponyms, including Badr (Q. 3:123), Ḥunayn (Q. 9:25), Yathrib (Q. 33:13), and Mecca (Q. 48:24)—this last notably in close conjunction with *al-masjid al-ḥarām*, 'the sacred place of worship', which appears in the following verse—as well as the tribe of Quraysh (Q. 106:1). Furthermore, the so-called 'Constitution of Medina', which is widely accepted as a genuinely early (i.e. start of the first-/seventh-century) document preserved in two third-/ninth-century Arabic works, does place a 'Prophet' (*nabī*) and a 'Messenger of God' (*rasūl Allāh*) called Muḥammad in a place called Yathrib (Lecker 2004). It is for these reasons that in what follows I will generally assume the original geographical context of much of the material in the Qur'an to be the early seventh-century CE Ḥijāz, although by no means necessarily the Mecca and Medina as described in Arabic sources of the second/eighth century and later.

Even if we take for granted the likelihood of the Qur'an's origins in the Ḥijāz, there remain the problems of the time and place of its collection, codification, and canonization, not to mention the chronology of the emergence of the various verses and chapters it contains. (These issues are discussed frequently; e.g. in de Prémare 2004 and Sinai 2009.) The fact that the Qur'an's own internal chronology has, in spite of many admirable and determined efforts, not yet been fixed to general scholarly consensus is a serious hindrance to historical research using the text. (Much of Angelika Neuwirth's research—her 2010 book is a good example—shows what is possible if you do accept a proposed chronological sequence of the suras, as does Welch 1979.) There is also the often raised fact of the Qur'an's rather allusive exposition, which led Wansbrough (1977: 1) to characterize its style as 'distinctly referential' (further discussion in Rippin 1985: 159–61).

Nonetheless, the Qur'an is ultimately a sizeable enough work, comprising a collection of fascinating material, and it would be a great shame if historians were led by the existence of the problems raised above into ignoring it completely. After all, whatever your views on all of the complications outlined above, it did not come into existence in a vacuum and presumably, therefore, carries some kind of social logic as a text. (I allude here, of course, to Spiegel 1990.) The Qur'an itself seems appropriately aware of this, for example in Q. 59:21—'We coined those parables (*amthāl*) for the people so perhaps they will ponder [them]'—as well as several passages in which it is asserted that the Qur'an has specifically been revealed in Arabic, a language that its audience can comprehend (Wild 2006; cf. in part now Webb 2016: 115–26). We have to assume that the Qur'an was engaging directly with audiences for whom it was hoped its message would be intelligible. The ways in which it speaks to those audiences, therefore, offer important clues as to its context. On a very blunt level, for example, we can learn from the Qur'an that a considerable number of late antique biblical and extra-biblical ideas, philosophies, legends, and more besides were accessible in some form to some residents of western Arabia. They may have had to travel outside the Ḥijāz to access them—we simply do not know—but they could access them (see recently Hoyland 2018). (It is worth highlighting here, however, that there is very little evidence for the existence of a pre-Islamic Arabic version of any text of the Bible; see Griffith 2013: 7–53, although cf. Kashouh 2012.) This is not to argue, as many have before, that we can learn how the Qur'an was simply 'influenced by' or 'based upon' earlier Jewish and Christian literature (for a critique of such arguments, see Pregill 2007), but rather to show that we can see clear evidence in the Qur'an for the extent of western Arabia's integration into a number of late antique intellectual trends, as well as the ways in which its inhabitants creatively interacted with (can we even say 'deconstructed'?) them. (There are some examples of this in Hughes 2003 and Neuwirth 2008; Neuwirth 2010: 215–23.) Reynolds (2010: 230–58) has even recently restated a somewhat controversial argument that much of the Qur'an might appropriately be understood as biblical homily, a genre well known from the lands to the north of the Ḥijāz.

One of the historians who has done the most over the past decade or so to investigate the Qur'an's audiences by paying careful attention to the ways in which it addresses some of them—without assuming any context offered by other sources—is Patricia Crone. In one article (Crone 2005), she analysed the data contained within the Qur'an relating to the occupations of its audiences, both those who supported the new kerygma and those who opposed it. The results are significant for two reasons. Firstly, it is worth highlighting that Crone was actually able to find a considerable amount of information concerning the livelihoods of those towards whom the Qur'anic message was addressed. Secondly, it is quite difficult to fit the occupations described in the Qur'an with many of the exegetical narratives later provided to explain that text. Loosely speaking, the Qur'an assumes an audience of agriculturalists which also contained a number of traders, and seems to suggest that its message was more successful among the traders. It is, as she makes clear, difficult to reconcile this picture with the exegetes' Meccan setting for many of the Qur'anic revelations; agricultural activity is easy enough to fit with Medina's environment, or indeed that of al-Ṭāʾif (*c.*40 miles south-east of Mecca) or other Ḥijāzī oases, but not Mecca. Even al-Ṭāʾif, Medina, and the other cultivable oases of the Ḥijāz pose some problems, since olives are mentioned as produce on at least one occasion (Q. 6:99) and they are apparently extremely difficult to cultivate properly in most areas of the Ḥijāz (Crone 2005: 393–4).

In another group of articles (Crone 2010; Crone 2012; Crone 2013), Patricia Crone has investigated the religious beliefs of one of the audiences who opposed the Qur'anic message. In the first of these, she demonstrated that the Qur'anic *mushrikūn*, long assumed to have been polytheistic idol worshippers, actually frequently 'come across as Bible-based monotheists' (Crone 2010: 191). They worshipped the same God as the Qur'anic believers, but they also accepted other beings—sometimes called gods, sometimes angels—as intermediaries between themselves and God. They do not seem to have worshipped these beings in place of God; idols are also rarely mentioned outside biblical contexts. Crone then compares these beliefs which the Qur'an accuses its opponents of holding with other Near Eastern religious traditions, although the conclusions are tentative: 'It is hard to avoid the impression that both Jews and Judaising pagans are involved, but this is as far as one can go' (Crone 2010: 200). In the other, two-part article, Crone focuses on the evident dispute in the Qur'an between its Messenger and his community on the one hand, who held to the resurrection and judgement of the dead, and some of their opponents, who were either unconcerned by this, doubted it, or denied it entirely. The results of this more recent investigation largely confirm the conclusions of the earlier 2010 article, that many of the opponents were biblical monotheists with strong Jewish roots. (For another brief overview of much of the same material, but drawing some rather different conclusions, see Sinai 2017: 65–72. The paucity of references to pagan idol-worship and cultic practices in the Qur'an has long been recognized, with Hawting 1999 being a particularly important analysis.)

The significance of the results of studies such as Patricia Crone's for historians of late antique and early Islamic Arabia should not be denied. It has long been known that wherever the Qur'an was propagated—somewhere in the Ḥijāz being most likely—it was a region that knew of notable biblically aware communities of Christians and Jews;

we are now coming ever closer to counting the *mushrikūn* among them. In this sense, much material in the Qur'an—when interpreted unencumbered by later exegeses—can lead us an enormous distance away from the *Heilsgeschichte* of the pre-Islamic Ḥijāz as imagined by Muslim biographers of the Prophet, Qur'anic commentators, and historians of the second/eighth century and beyond. The Qur'an came into existence in an environment thoroughly acquainted with (perhaps several) biblical monotheistic trends; that environment may also have been filled with idols and their shrines, attendants, and worshippers (see especially now al-Azmeh 2014), but if so the Qur'an is not particularly interested in them.

This research and its conclusions are exciting, but the possibilities do have limits. It does not look as though the Qur'an will ever help us to understand the chronology and events of Muḥammad's lifetime. I have already mentioned the frequent impossibility for modern historians of doing much with the all-too-vague references to contemporary events in the Qur'an. When Q. 48:18, to give just one example, declares that 'God was certainly pleased with the believers when they pledged oaths of allegiance to you under the tree', what are we to do? We have absolutely no way of knowing the original event to which this verse refers. There is also the problem that even if we assume the Qur'an to carry a certain social logic, we frequently cannot know what that logic was. There may be no reason to assume, for example, that much of the commercial vocabulary used in the Qur'an reflects an actual historical economic situation; rather it might reflect an observable trend in monotheistic traditions more broadly to use the vocabulary of everyday worldly affairs in eschatological symbolism (as suggested by Rippin 1996; see also Neuwirth 2008: 160–1). Where Crone then sees the inclusion of olives as agricultural produce in the Qur'an as posing something of a problem for the traditional geographical identification of that verse (Q. 6:99) as Meccan, others would interpret it as evidence of the Qur'an's participation in a world in which common eschatological tropes were shared between believers of different faiths. (The significance of the Qur'an's eschatological material has recently been re-emphasized in Shoemaker 2018a: 116–45.)

Finally, there are occasions where it is unclear if a Qur'anic pronouncement is describing a current practice to which it offers either support or objection, or alternatively if it is issuing a new command. Such is the case with Q. 5:90, which declares, 'O those who believe! Wine, [the game] *maysir*, stones for sacrifice (*anṣāb*) and divining arrows are filth, one of Satan's doings. Shun them and perhaps you will be successful.' We cannot tell from this whether society in the region had always disapproved of such activities, albeit that they may have been around anyway, or if they had been widely acceptable prior to the Qur'an's pronouncement on the issue.

History Outside the Qur'an

Problems along these lines are one of the main reasons why more research nowadays, at least in Europe and North America, is more interested in seeking to provide a 'late antique' context of one sort or another, for either the Qur'an as a whole (e.g. Neuwirth 2010) or particular parts of it (see especially the essays collected in Reynolds 2008; Reynolds 2011; Neuwirth et al. 2010), or even to reject the idea of any search for a historical context. Gabriel Said Reynolds declared in a recent book that: 'In the present work my study of the Qurʾān is not based at all on a historical context, whether pagan, Jewish or Christian' (Reynolds 2010: 35). Ultimately, of course, even only if taken to a rather extreme level, Reynolds's position is untenable; intertextual (or, indeed subtextual) comparisons should be supported by historical contextualization. Reynolds's own work, on a very broad level, assumes a historical context in which the promulgator(s) of the Qur'anic material could be aware, on some level, of precedents in biblical and extra-biblical late antique literature.

One can see to a degree, however, how a position that the Qur'an should be studied without thinking of its context has arisen as a legitimate reaction to some modern scholarship, not only that which has interpreted the Qur'an in light of later Islamic exegetical sources or sought to see it as almost entirely derivative from earlier Jewish and Christian literature, but also a number of essays which have sought to suggest certain late antique contexts for select Qur'anic ideas and which, it has to be said, stretch the available evidence beyond its limit. One example of this has been the various efforts to see in the biblical monotheists engaged in the Qur'an a specific community of 'Jewish Christians', a community perhaps known from some other parts of the late antique world at some point in time, but whom no evidence has ever placed anywhere near the Ḥijāz at any time close to the appearance of the Qur'an. The identification of 'Jewish Christians' among the Qur'an's interlocutors has long been suggested, including recently by Patricia Crone in two articles in which she takes the conclusions of her earlier studies of the beliefs of the *mushrikūn* even further (Crone 2015; Crone 2016, both with reference to much earlier scholarship; this conclusion was already hinted at in Crone 2013: 19). That there are parallels between certain Qur'anic doctrines and ideas credited by late antique authors to 'Jewish Christian' groups seems clear enough (see also Zellentin 2013; Stroumsa 2015: 139–58), but, as many recent studies have argued, this is not enough to locate a specific, identifiable 'Jewish Christian' community in Muḥammad's Ḥijāz (e.g. Griffith 2011; Dye 2018; Hoyland 2018; Shoemaker 2018b: esp. 107–8; Tannous 2018: 247–53).

Nonetheless, that some conclusions drawn overstep the available evidence should not be allowed to detract from the ultimate importance of using the relevant materials from the pre-Islamic Near East, which should be considered alongside a careful reading of the Qur'an in its own right, to help contextualize that text and, at the same time, to use the Qur'an as a source for the history of the communities for whom it was propagated. This is certainly a more promising avenue for future research than the more traditional method of providing a historical context for the Qur'an through the material in later Arabic narratives. After all, the Qur'an presumably did share much in common with religious attitudes and texts contemporary with its own production, much more so than with those exegeses composed after the political, social, cultural, and religious map of the Near East had been dramatically altered.

The potential of combining a close reading of the Qur'an in its own right with an investigation of the pertinent late antique Near Eastern literary and documentary sources has been thoroughly demonstrated by Patricia Crone's articles, discussed in the section 'History in the Qur'an'. As she states: 'One point I do hope to have established in this article is that reading the Qur'an in light of the Qur'an itself, without reference to the exegetical literature, makes sense; and relating the result to the earlier religious literature produced in the Near East is illuminating' (Crone 2010: 200; on the significance of finding *appropriate* late antique sources for contextualization, see also Rippin 2013: 175). Where then are we to find appropriate sources for contextualization and how might we use them together with an investigation of the Qur'an's own material?

Assuming the geographical context of the Qur'an to be the early seventh-century CE Ḥijāz, obviously we would like as much of our contextualizing material as possible to come from western Arabia in particular, but that from the Arabian Peninsula more broadly is also potentially useful. As is well known, there is very little such material from the Ḥijāz itself, so most of the exciting recent advances in our understanding of the Qur'an's context have come through the use of sources written within the late Roman and, to a lesser extent, Sasanian empires. Although there are more sources from the Arabian Peninsula outside the Ḥijāz, especially South Arabia, which can be used to understand something of the increasingly biblically monotheist religious milieu on the eve if Islam in these areas, only some offer relevant parallels to Qur'anic material (Hoyland 2001 remains a useful overview; see also now, for example, many articles by Christian Robin, the conclusions of several of which are surveyed in Robin 2012; the relevant chapters in Fisher 2015 and Robin 2015b; and other contributions in this *Handbook*). We should not use the relevant material which remains to offer unsound contextualization (for the potential pitfalls, see e.g. Rippin 1991 and Saleh 2010), but there is still so much useful work which can be done. Pre-Islamic Arabic poetry, for example, provides a number of interesting parallels to stories and exhortations in the Qur'an. (A classic study is Horovitz 1923/1975, but see also more recently Bauer 2010; Neuwirth 2010: 220–3, 225; Sinai 2011; and Horn 2017.) These parallels further emphasize the point that the Qur'anic milieu knew of local western Arabian cultural traditions that carried sufficient capital to help forge an extremely successful and novel kerygma. Frédéric Imbert's work on very early Islamic (first-century AH) Arabic graffiti from the Ḥijāz demonstrates the very ready willingness displayed by the Qur'an's audience to adopt its pious formulae and invocations (Imbert 2000; Imbert 2011). In a book on early Islamic Medina, I have argued that by considering the Qur'an's understanding of sacred spaces alongside those provided by pre-Islamic Arabian inscriptions and Arabic poetry, together with more limited reference to the testimony of non-Arabian ancient and late antique references to Arabia, we can appreciably improve our knowledge of the particular forms of enclosed and protected space in the late antique Ḥijāz known as *ḥaram* and *ḥimā* (Munt 2014: 16–41). We are gradually moving away from F. E. Peters's assertion as recently as 1991 that: 'Quite simply, there is no appropriate commentary and contopological setting against which to read the Qurʾan' (Peters 1991: 292).

The Qur'an is an enigmatic, but all the more fascinating for that, source for the history of western Arabia in the early-to-mid seventh century CE. Recent research into the late antique context of the Qur'an has done a great deal to mitigate the enigma, but much more remains to be done, especially both with the Arabian contextualizing material and with the text of the Qur'an itself, read carefully and sympathetically in its own context.

Bibliography

al-Azmeh, Aziz. *The Emergence of Islam in Late Antiquity: Allāh and His People*. Cambridge: Cambridge University Press, 2014.

Bauer, Thomas. 'The Relevance of Early Arabic Poetry for Qurʾānic Studies Including Observations on *Kull* and on Q. 22:27, 26:225, and 52:31'. In: Angelika Neuwirth, Nicolai Sinai, and Michael Marx (eds.). *The Qurʾān in Context: Historical and Literary Investigations into the Qurʾānic Milieu*, pp. 699–732. Leiden: Brill, 2010.

Bosworth, Clifford Edmund. 'Madyan Shuʿayb in Pre-Islamic and Early Islamic Lore and History', *Journal of Semitic Studies* 29/1 (1984), 53–64.

Crone, Patricia. *Meccan Trade and the Rise of Islam*. Oxford: Blackwell, 1987.

Crone, Patricia. 'How Did the Quranic Pagans Make a Living?' *Bulletin of the School of Oriental and African Studies* 68/3 (2005), 387–99.

Crone, Patricia. 'The Religion of the Qurʾānic Pagans: God and the Lesser Deities', *Arabica* 57/2–3 (2010), 151–200.

Crone, Patricia. 'The Quranic *Mushrikūn* and the Resurrection (Part I)', *Bulletin of the School of Oriental and African Studies* 75/3 (2012), 445–72.

Crone, Patricia. 'The Quranic *Mushrikūn* and the Resurrection (Part II)', *Bulletin of the School of Oriental and African Studies* 76/1 (2013), 1–20.

Crone, Patricia. 'Jewish Christianity and the Qurʾān (Part One)', *Journal of Near Eastern Studies* 74/2 (2015), 225–53.

Crone, Patricia. 'Jewish Christianity and the Qurʾān (Part Two)', *Journal of Near Eastern Studies* 75/1 (2016), 1–21.

Crone, Patricia, and Michael Cook. *Hagarism: The Making of the Islamic World*. Cambridge: Cambridge University Press, 1977.

Donner, Fred M. *Narratives of Islamic Origins: The Beginnings of Islamic Historical Writing*. Princeton: Darwin Press, 1998.

Dye, Guillaume. 'Jewish Christianity, the Qurʾān, and Early Islam: Some Methodological Caveats'. In: Francisco del Río Sánchez (ed.). *Jewish Christianity and the Origins of Islam*, pp. 11–29. Turnhout: Brepols, 2018.

Fisher, Greg (ed.) *Arabs and Empires before Islam*. Oxford: Oxford University Press, 2015.

Geiger, Abraham. *Was hat Mohammed aus dem Judenthume aufgenommen*. Bonn: Baaden, 1833; 2nd edn. Leipzig: Kaufman, 1902.

Gilliot, Claude. 'Muḥammad, le Coran et les "contraintes de l'histoire"'. In: Stefan Wild (ed.). *The Qurʾān as Text*, pp. 3–26. Leiden: Brill, 1996.

Gilliot, Claude. 'Zur Herkunft der Gewährsmänner des Propheten'. In: Karl-Heinz Ohlig and Gerd-R. Puin (ed.). *Die dunklen Anfänge: Neue Forschungen zur Entstehung und frühen Geschichte des Islam*, pp. 148–78. Berlin: Hans Schiler, 2005.

Gilliot, Claude. 'Reconsidering the Authorship of the Qurʾān: Is the Qurʾān Partly the Fruit if a Progressive and Collective Work?' In: Gabriel Said Reynolds (ed.). *The Qurʾān in Its Historical Context*, pp. 88–108. London: Routledge, 2008.

Griffith, Sidney. '*al-Naṣārā* in the Qurʾān: A Hermeneutical Reflection'. In: Gabriel Said Reynolds (ed.). *New Perspectives on the Qurʾān: The Qurʾān in its Historical Context 2*, pp. 301–22. London: Routledge, 2011.

Griffith, Sidney. *The Bible in Arabic: The Scriptures of the 'People of the Book' in the Language of Islam*. Princeton: Princeton University Press, 2013.

Hawting, Gerald R. *The Idea of Idolatry and the Emergence of Islam: From Polemic to History*. Cambridge: Cambridge University Press, 1999.

Horn, Cornelia. 'Tracing the Reception of the Protoevangelium of James in Late Antique Arabia: The Case of the Poetry of Umayya ibn Abī aṣ-Ṣalt and Its Intersection with the Quran'. In: Kirill Dmitriev and Isabel Toral-Niehoff (eds.). *Religious Culture in Late Antique Arabia: Selected Studies on the Late Antique Religious Mind*, pp. 123–46. Piscataway, NJ: Gorgias Press, 2017.

Horovitz, Josef. 'Das koranische Paradies', *Scripta Universitatis atque Bibliothecae Hierosolymitanarum* 1 (1923), no. VI. Reprinted in *Der Koran*. Ed. Rudi Paret, pp. 53–73. Darmstadt: Wissenschaftliche Buchgesellschaft, 1975.

Horovitz, Josef. *Koranische Untersuchungen*. Berlin and Leipzig: Walter de Gruyter, 1926.

Hoyland, Robert G. *Arabia and the Arabs: From the Bronze Age to the Coming of Islam*. London: Routledge, 2001.

Hoyland, Robert G. 'The Jewish and/or Christian Audience of the Qurʾān and the Arabic Bible'. In: Francisco del Río Sánchez (ed.). *Jewish Christianity and the Origins of Islam*, pp. 31–40. Turnhout: Brepols, 2018.

Hughes, Aaron. 'The Stranger at the Sea: Mythopoesis in the Qurʾân and early Tafsîr', *Studies in Religion* 32/3 (2003), 261–79.

Ibn Hishām, Abū Muḥammad ʿAbd al-Malik. *al-Sīra al-nabawiyya*. Ed. Ferdinand Wüstenfeld. Göttingen: Dieterichsche Universitäts-Buchhandlung, 1860.

Imbert, Frédéric. 'Le Coran dans les graffiti des deux premiers siècles de l'hégire', *Arabica* 47/3 (2000), 381–90.

Imbert, Frédéric. 'L'Islam des pierres: l'expression de la foi dans les graffiti arabes des premiers siècles'. In: Antoine Borrut (ed.). *Écriture de l'histoire et processus de canonisation dans les premiers siècles de l'islam: hommage à Alfred-Louis de Prémare*, pp. 57–78. Aix-en-Provence: Presses Universitaires de Provence, 2011. [= *Revue du monde musulman et de la Méditerranée* 129 (2011).]

Kashouh, Hikmat. *The Arabic Versions of the Gospels: The Manuscripts and Their Families*. Berlin: De Gruyter, 2012.

Lecker, Michael. *The 'Constitution of Medina': Muḥammad's First Legal Document*. Princeton, NJ: Darwin Press, 2004.

Montgomery, James E. 'The Empty Ḥijāz'. In: James E. Montgomery (ed.). *Arabic Theology, Arabic Philosophy, from the Many to the One: Essays in Celebration of Richard M. Frank*, pp. 37–97. Leuven: Peeters, 2006.

Munt, Harry. *The Holy City of Medina: Sacred Space in Early Islamic Arabia*. Cambridge: Cambridge University Press, 2014.

Neuwirth, Angelika. 'Qurʾān and History—a Disputed Relationship: Some Reflections on Qurʾānic History and History in the Qurʾān', *Journal of Qurʾanic Studies* 5/1 (2003), 1–18.

Neuwirth, Angelika. 'Psalmen—Im Koran neu gelesen (Ps 104 und 136)'. In: Dirk Hartwig, Walter Homolka, Michael J. Marx, and Angelika Neuwirth (eds.). *'Im vollen Licht der Geschichte': Die Wissenschaft des Judentums und die Anfänge der kritischen Koranforschung*, pp. 157–89. Würzburg: Ergon, 2008.

Neuwirth, Angelika. *Der Koran als Text der Spätantike: Ein europäischer Zugang*. Berlin: Verlag der Weltreligionen, 2010.

Neuwirth, Angelika, Nicolai Sinai, and Michael Marx (eds.). *The Qurʾān in Context: Historical and Literary Investigations into the Qurʾānic Milieu*. Leiden: Brill, 2010.

Nöldeke, Theodor. 'Hatte Muḥammad christliche Lehrer?' *Zeitschrift der deutschen morgenländischen Gesellschaft* 12 (1858), 699–708.

Nöldeke, Theodor. *Geschichte des Qorâns*. Göttingen: Verlag der Dieterichschen Buchhandlung, 1860.

Nöldeke, Theodor, Friedrich Schwally, Gotthelf Bergsträßer, and Otto Pretzl. *Geschichte des Qorāns*. 2nd edn., 3 vols. Leipzig: Dieterich'sche Verlagsbuchhandlung, 1909–38.

Nöldeke, Theodor, Friedrich Schwally, Gotthelf Bergsträßer, and Otto Pretzl. *The History of the Qurʾān*. (ed.) and trans. Wolfgang H. Behn. Leiden: Brill, 2013.

Paret, Rudi. 'Der Koran als Geschichtsquelle', *Der Islam* 37 (1961), 24–42.

Peters, Francis E. 'The Quest of the Historical Muhammad', *International Journal of Middle East Studies* 23/3 (1991), 291–315.

Pregill, Michael E. 'The Hebrew Bible and the Quran: The Problem of the Jewish "Influence" on Islam', *Religion Compass* 1/6 (2007), 643–59.

Prémare, Alfred-Louis de. *Aux origines du Coran: questions d'hier, approches d'aujourd'hui*. Paris: Téraèdre, 2004.

Reynolds, Gabriel Said (ed.). *The Qurʾān in its Historical Context*. London: Routledge, 2008.

Reynolds, Gabriel Said. *The Qurʾān and its Biblical Subtext*. London: Routledge, 2010.

Reynolds, Gabriel Said (ed.). *New Perspectives on the Qurʾān: The Qurʾān in its Historical Context 2*. London: Routledge, 2011.

Rippin, Andrew. 'Literary Analysis of *Qurʾān*, *Tafsīr*, and *Sīra*: The Methodologies of John Wansbrough'. In: Richard C. Martin (ed.). *Approaches to Islam in Religious Studies*, pp. 151–63. Tucson: University of Arizona Press, 1985.

Rippin, Andrew. 'RḤMNN and the Ḥanīfs'. In: Wael B. Hallaq and Donald P. Little (eds.). *Islamic Studies Presented to Charles J. Adams*, pp. 153–68. Leiden: Brill, 1991.

Rippin, Andrew. 'The Commerce of Eschatology'. In: Stefan Wild (ed.). *The Qur'an as Text*, pp. 125–35. Leiden: Brill, 1996.

Rippin, Andrew. 'Muḥammad in the Qurʾān: Reading Scripture in the 21st Century'. In: Harald Motzki (ed.). *The Biography of Muḥammad: The Issue of the Sources*, pp. 298–309. Leiden: Brill, 2000.

Rippin, Andrew. 'The Construction of the Arabian Historical Context in Muslim Interpretation of the Qurʾān'. In: Karen Bauer (ed.). *Aims, Methods and Contexts of Qurʾānic Exegesis (2nd/8th–9th/15th c.)*, pp. 173–98. Oxford: Oxford University Press, 2013.

Robin, Christian Julien. 'Les "Filles de Dieu" de Sabaʾ à la Mecque: réflexions sur l'agencement des panthéons dans l'Arabie ancienne', *Semitica* 50 (2000), 113–92.

Robin, Christian Julien. 'Arabia and Ethiopia'. In: Scott Fitzgerald Johnson (ed.). *The Oxford Handbook of Late Antiquity*, pp. 247–332. Oxford: Oxford University Press, 2012.

Robin, Christian Julien. 'L'Arabie dans le Coran: réexamen de quelques termes à la lumière des inscriptions préislamiques'. In François Déroche, Christian Julien Robin, and Michel Zink (eds.). *Les origines du Coran, le Coran des origines*, pp. 27–74. Paris: Académie des Inscriptions et Belles-Lettres, 2015a.

Robin, Christian Julien (ed.). *Le Judaïsme de l'Arabie antique*. Turnhout: Brepols, 2015b.

Rubin, Uri. 'On the Arabian Origins of the Qurʾān: The Case of *al-Furqān*', *Journal of Semitic Studies* 54/2 (2009), 421–33.

Saleh, Walid A. 'The Etymological Fallacy and Qurʾānic Studies: Muhammad, Paradise, and Late Antiquity.' In: Angelika Neuwirth, Nicolai Sinai, and Michael Marx (eds.). *The Qurʾān in Context: Historical and Literary Investigations into the Qurʾānic Milieu*, pp. 649–98. Leiden: Brill, 2010.

Shoemaker, Stephen J. 'Christmas in the Qurʾān: The Qurʾānic Account of Jesus' Nativity and Palestinian Local Tradition', *Jerusalem Studies in Arabic and Islam* 28 (2003), 11–39.

Shoemaker, Stephen J. 'Muḥammad and the Qurʾān'. In: Scott Fitzgerald Johnson (ed.). *The Oxford Handbook of Late Antiquity*, pp. 1078–1108. Oxford: Oxford University Press, 2012.

Shoemaker, Stephen J. *The Apocalypse of Empire: Imperial Eschatology in Late Antiquity and Early Islam*. Philadelphia: University of Pennsylvania Press, 2018a.

Shoemaker, Stephen J. 'Jewish Christianity, Non-Trinitarianism and the Beginnings of Islam'. In: Francisco del Río Sánchez (ed.). *Jewish Christianity and the Origins of Islam*, pp. 105–16. Turnhout: Brepols, 2018b.

Sinai, Nicolai. 'Orientalism, Authorship, and the Onset of Revelation: Abraham Geiger and Theodor Nöldeke on Muḥammad and the Qurʾān.' In: Dirk Hartwig, Walter Homolka, Michael J. Marx, and Angelika Neuwirth (eds.). *'Im vollen Licht der Geschichte': Die Wissenschaft des Judentums und die Anfänge der kritischen Koranforschung*, pp. 145–54. Würzburg: Ergon, 2008.

Sinai, Nicolai. *Fortschreibung und Auslegung: Studien zur frühen Koraninterpretation*. Wiesbaden: Harrassowitz, 2009.

Sinai, Nicolai. 'Religious Poetry from the Quranic Milieu: Umayya b. Abī al-Ṣalt on the Fate of Thamūd', *Bulletin of the School of Oriental and African Studies* 74/3 (2011), 397–416.

Sinai, Nicolai. *The Qurʾan: A Historical-Critical Introduction*. Edinburgh: Edinburgh University Press, 2017.

Spiegel, Gabrielle M. 'History, Historicism, and the Social Logic of the Text in the Middle Ages', *Speculum* 65/1 (1990), 59–86.

Stroumsa, Guy G. *The Making of the Abrahamic Religions in Late Antiquity*. Oxford: Oxford University Press, 2015.

Tannous, Jack. *The Making of the Medieval Middle East: Religion, Society, and Simple Believers*. Princeton: Princeton University Press, 2018.

Tottoli, Roberto. *Biblical Prophets in the Qurʾān and Muslim Literature*. Richmond: Curzon, 2002.

Wansbrough, John. *Quranic Studies: Sources and Methods of Scriptural Interpretation*. Oxford: Oxford University Press, 1977.

Wansbrough, John. *The Sectarian Milieu: Content and Composition of Islamic Salvation History*. Oxford: Oxford University Press, 1978.

Wansbrough, John. *Res ipsa loquitur: History and Mimesis*. Jerusalem: The Israel Academy of Science and Humanities, 1987. Reprinted in *Method and Theory in the Study of Islamic Origins*. (ed.). Herbert Berg, pp. 3–19. Leiden: Brill, 2003.

Watt, W. Montgomery. *Muḥammad's Mecca: History in the Qurʾān*. Edinburgh: Edinburgh University Press, 1988.

Webb, Peter. *Imagining the Arabs: Arab Identity and the Rise of Islam*. Edinburgh: Edinburgh University Press, 2016.

Welch, Alford T. 'Allāh and Other Supernatural Beings: The Emergence of the Qurʾānic Doctrine of *Tawḥīd*', *Journal of the American Academy of Religion* 47 (1979), 733–58.

Welch, Alford T. 'Muhammad's Understanding of Himself: The Koranic Data'. In: Richard G. Hovannisian and Speros Vryonis Jr. (eds.). *Islam's Understanding of Itself*, pp. 15–52. Malibu, CA: Undena, 1983.
Wild, Stefan. 'An Arabic Recitation: The Meta-Linguistics of Qurʾānic Revelation'. In: Stefan Wild (ed.). *Self-Referentiality in the Qurʾān*, pp. 135–57. Wiesbaden: Harrassowitz, 2006.
Zellentin, Holger Michael. *The Qurʾān's Legal Culture: The* Didascalia Apostolorum *as a Point of Departure*. Tübingen: Mohr Siebeck, 2013.

CHAPTER 7

THE LINGUISTIC LANDSCAPE OF PRE-ISLAMIC ARABIA

Context for the Qur'an

AHMAD AL-JALLAD

THE twenty-first century has witnessed an unprecedented interest in the use of primary source materials in the quest for the origins of Islam and its primary text, the Qur'an. Indeed, two recent edited volumes on the subject contain the word 'context' in their titles.[1] While scholars have made great strides in balancing the later Islamic traditions with the ever-sharpening picture of a multicultural late antique Near East, the literary works and materials of the Arabic grammarians from the eighth and ninth centuries continue to be the primary source for the Arabic of the pre-Islamic period and its linguistic context.[2] The growing corpus of epigraphic evidence from all parts of the Peninsula, however, suggests that these writers were largely unaware of Arabia's linguistic diversity and cosmopolitanism in the centuries preceding the rise of Islam. This chapter will outline the linguistic map of pre-Islamic Arabia and discuss issues such as the development of the Arabic script, literacy, and multilingualism in this context. I conclude with a discussion on the stylistic parallels to the Qur'an found in the inscriptions.

[1] These are *Qurʾān in Context*, edited by Neuwirth, Sinai, and Marx (2010) and *The Qurʾān in its Historical Context*, edited by G. S. Reynolds (2008).

[2] For example, see al-Sharkawi's contribution 'Pre-Islamic Arabic' to the *Encyclopedia of Arabic Language and Linguistics*.

The Linguistic Landscape of Arabia

The Arabian Alphabets

Arabia was home to an indigenous alphabetic tradition which scholars have conventionally labelled the 'South Semitic' script. The common ancestor of the South Semitic scripts descended from the original proto-Sinaitic alphabet sometime in the second millennium BCE and is therefore a sister script of the West Semitic alphabet, from which the Phoenician script and ultimately the Latin script derive. While the West Semitic script, as applied to languages like Old Aramaic and Hebrew, contained several polyphonic glyphs, the South Semitic alphabets represented each phoneme with a single glyph. The earliest example of the South Semitic script is the Ancient South Arabian alphabet, which contains twenty-nine glyphs all signifying consonants.

Macdonald (2000) established two main divisions in the South Semitic script family: Ancient South Arabian (ASA) (Figure 7.1), which expressed the four principal languages of Ancient Yemen—Sabaic, Minaic, Qatabanic, and Ḥaḍramitic—and Ancient North Arabian (ANA), which covers all of the remaining South Semitic scripts of Arabia and the southern Levant. The ASA script is known in two basic varieties—the monumental script, used for texts carved on hard surfaces such as rock or bronze, and the miniscule hand, employed to carve texts on perishable materials such as palm-bark and sticks. The latter was used primarily for the composition of day-to-day documents. The inscriptional record of ASA spans more than 1,500 years, from the tenth century BCE to the rise of Islam, and possibly as late as the third/ninth century (Drewes et al. 2013).

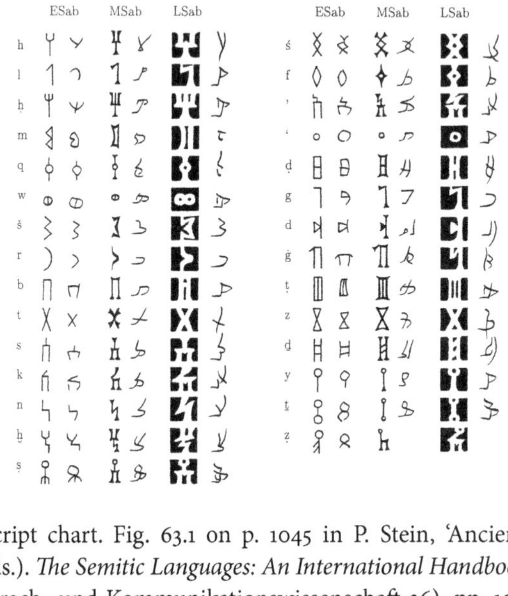

FIGURE 7.1 ASA script chart. Fig. 63.1 on p. 1045 in P. Stein, 'Ancient South Arabian', in: S. Weninger et al. (eds.). *The Semitic Languages: An International Handbook*, Berlin/Boston 2011 (Handbücher zur Sprach- und Kommunikationswissenschaft 36), pp. 1042–73. © Peter Stein. Used by permission.

Unlike the ASA script, ANA does not constitute a unity in any sense, but reflects several distinct scripts which express a myriad of languages and dialects, the interrelationships of which remain to be worked out. ANA comprises four established script categories, Safaitic, Hismaic, Taymanitic, and Dadanitic, and one pending category into which all of the unclassified inscriptions are placed, Thamudic (no relation to the ancient tribe of Thamud). It is impossible to date when the production of the ANA inscriptions began or ended. The earliest datable texts are in the Taymanitic and Thamudic B scripts, produced in the early to mid-first millennium BCE based on their contents, while the latest dated text is part of a polyglot inscription from Ḥegrā dated to 267 CE (JSNab 17; this text is dealt with in detail in the section on 'Multilingualism'). Many scholars have assumed that the inscriptions cease in the fourth century CE based on the absence of references to Christianity—which is thought to have spread among the nomads in the fourth century CE—or events from the Byzantine period. While this reason is most certainly unsatisfactory, it would, moreover, only apply to the Safaitic inscriptions, since they constitute the only corpus in which occasional references to events beyond the desert can be found. The production of texts in the Taymanitic and Dadanitic scripts seems to have ended much earlier. There is no way to chronologically delimit most of the Thamudic inscriptions based on their contents, since they consist primarily of personal names and short prayers.

The Languages of Pre-Islamic Arabia

South Arabia

The languages expressed by these scripts are equally diverse. The four attested ASA languages are not considered varieties of early Arabic, but rather constitute an independent branch of Central Semitic, also called Ancient South Arabian. Some of the common grammatical features include a post-positive definite article -*(h)n* and *m*-endings (mimation) on singular and broken plural nouns which are not in the construct state, analogous to nunation (*tanwīn*) in Arabic. It is unclear when these languages were replaced by Arabic, but they may have continued to be spoken as late as the ninth century CE. Arabic writers from that period noted the existence of non-Arabic languages in Yemen which they called Himyaritic. While the examples of Himyaritic these writers recorded share some features in common with the languages of the inscriptions, the hallmark isoglosses of ASA—such as post-positive definite marking and mimation—are absent. This phenomenon has been the subject of multiple interpretations (see Stein 2008 and Robin 2001).

The Languages of Central and North Arabia: Old Arabic and Ancient North Arabian

Among epigraphists, the term Old Arabic is used to refer to the corpus of material composed in the Arabic language in the pre-Islamic period, and excludes texts attributed to the pre-Islamic period from later times, such as the Jāhilī poetry. This strict definition is meant to exclude oral texts which could have been edited during the process of transmission. Nevertheless, most scholars assumed that the linguistic character of the Arabic of the latter sources reached far into the pre-Islamic past. The failure then to encounter the Classical language in the inscriptional record gave rise to the belief that 'Arabic' was either rarely or never written prior to the sixth century CE. The focus on the differences between the forms of Arabic known from the Islamic period and the languages of the pre-Islamic epigraphy of North Arabia and Syria led to the formulation of two mutually exclusive branches: Arabic, as defined by the Qur'an, poetry, the Arabic grammarians, etc., and Ancient North Arabian, the epigraphic varieties written in the ANA alphabets. This division was largely justified by the shape of the definite article, *h(n)* in the ANA epigraphy and *ʾ(l)* in the Arabic of the Islamic age (Beeston 1981). However, a closer examination of the evidence proves that such a classification is not maintainable. Variation between *ʾl* and *h(n)* articles is found throughout the ANA corpus, and Hismaic lacks a definite article altogether. From a linguistic point of view, the entire focus on the definite article as a diagnostic feature is misguided. Semiticists have recognized that it is a late feature which spread among the Central Semitic languages through contact or as the result of parallel development (Huehnergard and Rubin 2011: 269–70), and therefore is an unsuitable feature for linguistic diagnosis, especially its phonological shape (Al-Jallad 2018: 11–16).

If we shift our focus away from differences between the Arabic of the Islamic age and the ANA inscriptional material towards shared developments in grammar, another picture emerges. Many of the grammatical innovations which are unique to Arabic are widely attested in the Safaitic corpus, such as *t*-demonstratives (Safaitic: *t h-snt* 'this year'), negation with the particle *mā* and *lam* (Safaitic: *m hnʾ* 'he was not pleased' and *lm yʿd* 'he did not return'), the *mafʿūl* passive (Safaitic: *mqtl* 'killed), a subjunctive in *-a* and its syntax (Safaitic: *f nḥyy* 'so that we may live'), in addition to the occasional use of the *ʾ(l)* article (for a full list of features, see Al-Jallad 2015; 2019). The Hismaic inscriptions also share important grammatical developments with Arabic, although their brevity masks the extent of these similarities. The language of two of the longest texts composed in this script is clearly a form of Arabic (see Graf and Zwettler 2004). These facts argue against the existence of a separate Ancient North Arabian language. Instead, Old Arabic should be viewed as a continuum of dialects stretching from southern Syria into Jordan, the Negev, Sinai, and the northern Ḥijāz, encompassing the dialects composed in the Safaitic, Hismaic, occasionally in the Nabataean, and finally in the early Arabic scripts (Al-Jallad 2018). This material is complemented by copious transcriptions in Greek from the second century CE onwards, which provide an unequalled view of Old Arabic vocalism (see Al-Jallad 2017 for a comprehensive treatment of this material).

The Non-Arabic Languages Inscribed in Ancient North Arabian Alphabets

As we move deeper into the Arabian Peninsula, the inscriptions become more enigmatic, and their linguistic character more remote from Arabic. The two major oases of North

Arabia, Taymāʾ and Dadān, are each home to a unique script and language. Both of these corpora were produced in the mid-first millennium BCE, but it is impossible to know when the first or last inscriptions were carved.

Taymanitic is in some ways closer to Hebrew and Aramaic than the languages of the other ANA corpora. Most of these texts are short graffiti containing prayers to the oasis' primary deity, *Ṣlm*, or the recordings of participation in the wars of the oasis against its rivals. As such, only a very incomplete picture of its grammar can be formed. Among its characteristic features are the sound change of *w* > *y* in word initial position, e.g. *yrḫ* 'month' and *ydʿ* 'he knew', the assimilation of *n* and *l* in unstressed position, e.g. *b* for *bin 'son of' and *ṣm* for *ṣlm* in personal names, and the merger of s^3 and *ṯ*, as opposed to the merger of s^3 and s^1 in Arabic, the merger of *z* and *ḏ*, and the merger of *ẓ* and *ṣ* (Kootstra 2016).

Dadanitic is the only ANA script attested in both monumental inscriptions and graffiti. The largest genre of texts records the performance of a ritual called *ẓll*—the nature and purpose of which remain unclear—for the patron deity of Dadān, *dhu ghabt*. The Dadanitic inscriptions exhibit considerable internal diversity, exemplified by the verb 'to perform the *ẓll* ritual' which is found in four forms, all in identical contexts: *ʾẓll*, *hẓll*, *ʾẓl*, and *hẓl* (Sima 1999: 93). Both definite articles *h(n)* and *ʾl* are attested (Al-Jallad 2018: 23–4). A few other features attested in this corpus suggest that the dialects of this oasis were closely related to, but not forms of, Arabic (see Al-Jallad 2018: §4).

The town of Qaryat al-Fāw has yielded a so far unique text which nearly all authors have considered an example of Old Arabic—the Rbbl bn Hfʿm epitaph (see Beeston 1979; Macdonald 2000:50). Recently, however, I have subjected the text to a close linguistic examination and concluded that it is probably a transitional dialect between some North Arabian variety and ASA (Al-Jallad 2014; Al-Jallad 2018: §7).

The graffiti carved by the nomads of North and Central Arabia, the so-called Thamudic inscriptions, are rather brief, but they are clearly distinct from languages of the oasis towns. Most inscriptions are short and enigmatic, and even the most basic introductory formulae elude interpretation. Nevertheless, some of these texts lend themselves to straightforward interpretations, such as SESP.U 31 *h rḍw hb l- yd -n nt{n} m ḫṭb* 'O Rḍw (name of a deity), grant into our hands as a gift that which was requested', while others continue to defy satisfactory decipherment, e.g. Esk 204: *wdd f sw// tʾlsswʾ//wdd*. Currently, it is impossible to say how many languages are covered by the rubric Thamudic and no internal chronology is possible. The challenge they pose to decipherment alone demonstrates that Arabic was not the language of all the Arabian nomads in the earliest periods.

Unlike the western two-thirds of the Peninsula, the inhabitants of the eastern third, along the Persian Gulf, seem only occasionally to have employed writing, and no indigenous scripts from this area have been discovered. Several scattered texts in Cuneiform, Greek, and Aramaic, however, have been found. The ASA script was also used to inscribe the texts on a corpus of tombstones from the region of al-Ḥaṣā in north-eastern Saudi Arabia to the Oman Peninsula. These are highly formulaic so it is difficult to say much about their grammar, but their non-Arabic character is clear. Sima has identified the presence of a post-positive definite article -ʾ, as in Aramaic, a feature unknown in the Arabian languages of the western half of the Peninsula (2002: 193–4; Stien 2017).

Writing and Literacy

The abundance of written records in Arabia suggests that writing was widespread among both settled people and nomads (Figure 7.2); however, its function among both groups was quite different. Macdonald (2009: vol. 1; 2010) established an important distinction between literate societies and non-literate societies based on the role of writing for the functioning of society. Ancient South Arabia exemplifies a literate society. Its officials set up thousands of public inscriptions, recording their deeds, dedications to deities, legal decrees, and so on. The existence of public inscriptions, however, cannot stand as witness to widespread literacy among the general population, as they reflect the work of professional scribes and highly skilled masons. As Stein has pointed out, the wording of even the most personal letters suggests that the sender did not compose

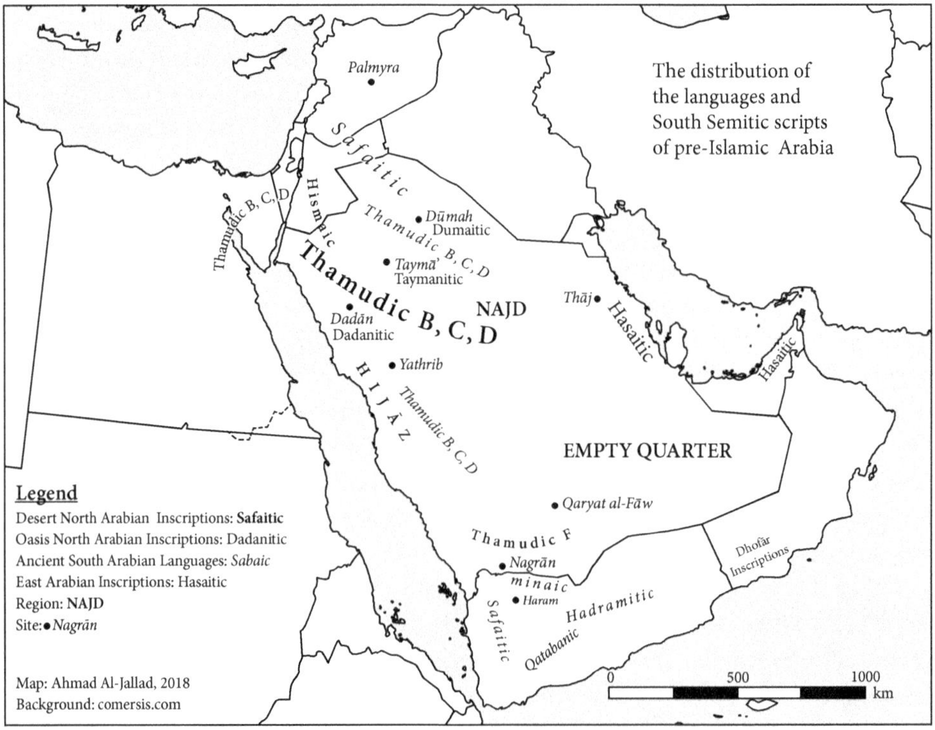

FIGURE 7.2 Distribution of the scripts and languages of pre-Islamic Arabia. © A. Al-Jallad.

the text himself, and that recipients were not expected to read them. To explain this, he hypothesized the existence of scribal centres where documents were composed on the behalf of their authors (2005: 148–50). On the other hand, Macdonald (2010: 8) draws our attention to another category of inscriptions in South Arabia that intimates widespread knowledge of reading and writing: *graffiti*. Unlike commissioned inscriptions, graffiti are informal works of individual expression, and, as such, must be carved by the author. The existence of thousands of graffiti in South Arabia, always composed in the monumental and only rarely the miniscule script, suggests that a sizable segment of the population could employ writing for informal purposes. The use of the monumental script rather than the day-to-day script of the wooden sticks could have been symptomatic of the medium and need not imply that knowledge of the miniscule hand was more restricted.

The evidence for the major oasis towns of North and West Arabia is not as plentiful. Nevertheless, after a close and skilful analysis of the material, focusing mainly on the appearance of informal letter forms and ligatures in the inscriptions, Macdonald concluded that the settled populations of these areas also belonged to literate societies, and, as in South Arabia, large segments of the population knew how to write, and presumably, read (2010: 9–15).

The nomadic societies of Arabia and the southern Levant, on the other hand, cannot be considered literate according to Macdonald's definition. They would have had no need to compose administrative or legal texts, and perishable materials were hard to come by. The tens of thousands of rock graffiti scattered throughout the deserts of Arabia and the southern Levant, however, indicate that a large number of nomads were able to read and write. Macdonald hypothesized that nomads simply learned writing from the inhabitants of the oasis towns out of curiosity, and used it to pass the hours in the desert as they watched over their herds (2009: 1: 78–82). Nevertheless, most of the inscriptions they composed follow strict stylistic and thematic conventions. These conventions, moreover, differ from corpus to corpus, suggesting that distinct writing traditions, as it were, were associated with the various ANA scripts. Research into the ideological conditions under which these texts were produced will no doubt shed light as to the intentions of their authors and their purpose.

Development of the Arabic Script

Like Ancient South Arabia, the Nabataean kingdom of north-west Arabia was also a literate society. However, an important difference distinguished the two. Stein argued convincingly that the language of written documents in South Arabia, whether on stone or on the sticks, must have been rather close to the vernacular, while in the Classical Nabataean period, a form of Achaemenid Official Aramaic was used for inscriptions and administration, even though it is unlikely that it was used as a spoken language among its population. It is difficult to determine from this chronological distance how diverse Nabataea was linguistically, but we can be sure that a large segment of its population spoke some form(s) of Arabic, perhaps alongside dialects of western Aramaic. The substratal influence of Arabic on the syntax—such as the optative use of the suffix conjugation—of Nabataean Aramaic is obvious throughout the corpus. The Nabataean legal papyri from the Dead Sea have yielded dozens of Arabic technical terms, which Macdonald suggested could point towards the use of Arabic orally in Nabataean legal proceedings (2010: 19). Arabic loanwords occasionally enter the inscriptions of North Arabia and the Sinai, but a skilled scribe could have easily avoided these and so they cannot, in and of themselves, delimit the geographic distribution of Arabic as a vernacular. Macdonald reconstructs a situation in which Nabataea, or at least its southern parts, was inherently bilingual. Arabic was used for spoken communication, religious liturgies, oral literary works, and face-to-face political administrative and legal activity, while Aramaic expressed these functions in written form (2010: 20). The finding of a long Arabic-language inscription in Madaba in the Hismaic script (Graf and Zwettler 2004) and the distribution of Arabic vocabulary and onomastica in Greek transcription (Al-Jallad 2017), however, suggest that Arabic was much more widely spoken in the central and perhaps northern parts of the kingdom as well.

The use of Nabataean Aramaic for inscriptions, both public and graffiti, continued even after Rome's annexation of the kingdom in the early second century CE, but became more and more restricted to the southern areas of the kingdom, while Greek replaced Aramaic in the north. This period saw the gradual increase in the cursive character of the Nabataean script and the more extensive use of ligatures. The inscriptions exhibiting a more cursive character are termed 'Nabataeo-Arabic' by Laila Nehmé (2010), the leading scholar working on this material. These texts lie in terms of development between 'Classical Nabataean', namely, the script employed in monuments at Ḥegrā (modern Madāʾin Ṣāliḥ) and Petra, and the early Arabic script. While rock inscriptions constitute our only evidence for the transitional script, the cursive developments which characterize it likely took place on perishable materials, rather than through the vehicle of graffiti, as cursive forms develop to economize writing with a pen and ink (Macdonald 2010: 52).

The appearance of this transitional script on stone strongly suggests that scribes continued to write extensively in the Nabataean script on perishable materials following the second century CE, and that the classical calligraphic script, typically used to produce rock inscriptions, began to give way to the book-hand. We can only guess as to the language and the content of the post-classical Nabataean writings. It seems safe to assume that administrative and legal texts made up the bulk of this material, but whether writing was extended to other domains is impossible to determine. It is also important to remember that not all Arabic speech communities made use of the Nabataeo-Arabic script. Many Arabic speakers in the north simply used Greek for administration, as evidenced by the Petra Papyri (sixth century CE). The concentration of inscriptions in the Nabataeo-Arabic script in north-west Arabia suggests that it developed at the chancelleries of the principalities in this area, who then brought it to Syria in the late fifth or early sixth century CE (Nehmé 2013:14). In the past decade, the corpus of Arabic-script inscriptions has grown steadily, and now includes new texts from across Arabia, Najrān

(Robin et al. 2014),[3] Dūmat al-Jandal (Nehmé 2017), and the Ḥijāz (unpublished). These join the well-known inscriptions from Syria—Zebed, Ḥarrān, and Usays (see Macdonald's contribution to Fiema et al. 2015 for an outline of these texts and further bibliography).[4]

In addition to the intrusions of cursive forms from the day-to-day script, the later inscriptions are also characterized by a growing presence of Arabic lexical and grammatical features. The increase in the appearance of Arabic forms does not necessitate a decline in the knowledge of Aramaic, but signals a growing trend in the use of the vernacular for written expression. Indeed, perfectly fine Aramaic inscriptions are produced in Arabia as late as the fourth and fifth centuries CE. Thus, the growing body of pre-Islamic evidence strongly indicates that the use of Arabic for administration in the early Islamic period does not reflect an ad hoc invention, but the continuation of an established tradition of administration in Arabic which must have its origins in North Arabian and Syrian scribal practices.

Multilingualism

The Nabataean inscriptions not only illustrate the gradual emergence of the Arabic script, but they also bear witness to centuries of Arabic-Aramaic language contact and bilingualism. One of the earliest examples of this is two lines of an Arabic prayer set within a Nabataean Aramaic votive text, which contextually pre-dates 150 CE, the so-called ʿĒn ʿAvdat inscription (for the *editio princeps*, see Negev 1986; for further bibliography, see Macdonald 2008). Authors of Nabataean graffiti from the Sinai, which usually begin with the passive participle of √*ḏkr* 'may he be remembered', occasionally substitute Arabic *mdkwr* for Aramaic *dkyr*. Since *dkyr* is one of the most commonly used words in Nabataean inscriptional formulae, it is unlikely that these authors were unaware of the Aramaic form, but rather made a conscious choice to use Arabic.

One of the best examples of Arabic-Aramaic contact is the epitaph of *Raqōš bint ʿabd manōtō* (JSNab 17, 267 CE).[5] The text exhibits a mix of Arabic and Aramaic vocabulary and grammar, and has been the subject of widely differing interpretations. Blau (1977: 11), for instance, called the inscription 'almost pure Arabic', implying that the intention was to compose an Arabic inscription, and the Aramaicisms were intrusions, while others have attributed the presence of Arabic to the author's poor grasp of Aramaic.

[3] These nine short texts were discovered by the Franco-Saudi epigraphic survey mission near Bīr Ḥimà, north of Najrān. They appear to have been produced by travellers from the north, as the two dated ones use the era of the Roman Province of Arabia.

[4] Recently, nine short texts on a trade route near Najrān in the transitional script have been discovered, one dated to the late fifth century according to the era of the Roman Province of Arabia. This would suggest that those who inscribed these texts were travellers from the North.

[5] For the latest edition, see Macdonald's contribution to Fiema et al. 2015.

If we, however, look at the distribution of the two languages, another scenario seems more likely.

JSNab 17 (Aramaic is bolded)

1. ***dnh*** *qbrw ṣnʿ-h* kʿbw ***br***
2. ḥrtt l-rqš ***brt***
3. ʿbdmnwtw *ʾm-h w hy*
4. *hlkt py ʾl-ḥgrw*
5. šnt ***mʾh w štyn***
6. ***w tryn b-yrḥ tmwz*** *w lʿn*
7. ***mry ʿlmʾ*** *mn yšnʿ ʾl-qbrw*
8. *d[ʾ] w mn yptḥ-h ḥšy (w)*
9. *wld -h w lʿn mn yqbr w {y}ʿly mn -h*

'(1) **This** is the tomb which Kaʿbō **son** of Ḥāreṯah built (2) for Rqwš **daughter** (3) of ʿbdmnwtw his mother, and she (4) died in ʾal-Ḥegrō (= Ḥegrā) (5) in the year **one hundred and sixty** (6) **two in the month of Tammūz** so may (7) Mry-ʿlmʾ (lit. lord of eternity) curse whosoever alters[6] this tomb (8) or opens it except (9) his children and may he curse whosoever buries or removes from it [a body].'

The distribution of the Arabic makes it unlikely that the author was filling in gaps of his knowledge of Aramaic. Surely, the Aramaic name of Ḥegrā, *ḥgrʾ*, was still known, and the author could have easily used the preposition *b-* instead of Arabic *py*[7] in line 4, as line 6 clearly shows its function was known to him. Aramaic is used for patronymics, introductory and dating formulae, and the divine epithet *mry ʿlmʾ*. The remaining content is Arabic. I would therefore suggest that this distribution points towards code-switching between Arabic and Aramaic, and may reflect the balance between the two languages at Ḥegrā, and perhaps elsewhere in Nabataea. Dating formulae and divine epithets belong to the class of vocabulary usually expressed by Aramaic, while the prose was composed in Arabic, similar to the way in which Moroccan speakers of Arabic might switch to French to express certain concepts.

Another interesting source for Arabic-Aramaic bilingualism comes from the Greek papyri of Petra (sixth century CE). This corpus contains the private documents dealing with matters such as property disputes, inheritance, and tax records. The documents include names of the plots of land, houses, and slaves, most of which are of Semitic extraction. The micro-toponymy provides interesting evidence for language contact. Two plots of land in P. Petra 17 are derived from the Semitic root q-ṣ-b, but one of them carries the Arabic definite article *Αλκεσεβ* /al-qeṣeb/while the other has the Aramaic suffixed article ā, *Κισβα* /qiṣbā/. Likewise, P. Petra 17 *Αλνασβα* /al-naṣbah/'the farm'

[6] The sense of the root š-nʿ 'to alter' is found in Aramaic but is not known in Classical Arabic, but it is uncertain if the word had this sense in Old Arabic as well, so I have not bolded it.

[7] The Aramaic *p* glyph is used to represent Arabic *f*. Moreover, it is unclear how this sound was pronounced in Old Arabic, and [p] is certainly a possibility (see Al-Jallad 2017).

appears to be the Arabic equivalent of Aramaic *Νασβαθα* /naṣbatā/in 98v.[8] Aramaic loans into the local Arabic dialect also preserve their Aramaic morphology. The word *Χαφφαθ* /kaffat/, perhaps the equivalent of Greek *θημοβολών* 'grain depository', seems to be of Aramaic origin and forms an Aramaic plural, *Χαφφι* /kaffī/(Al-Jallad et al. 2013: 38–9). All three cases reflect an awareness of Aramaic grammar on the part of the Arabic-speaking population of Petra.

Arabic-Greek contact is more difficult to assess in the pre-Islamic period. Two of the three pre-Islamic inscriptions in the Arabic script from Syria accompany a Greek text. A few important bilingual Greek-Safaitic inscriptions also indicate that at least some members of the nomadic communities of the Syro-Arabian desert had a command of Greek:[9]

l nṣrʾl bn ʿlw	'by Naṣrʾel son of ʿAlw'
Μνησθῇ Νασρηλος Αλουου	'may Naṣrʾel son of ʿAlw be remembered'

The Inscriptions and the Literary Background of the Qur'an

Poetry, it seems, was not often put into writing in South Arabia, and so our examples of this genre of oral literature are limited. The few poetic texts discovered so far exhibit striking structural parallels with the Qur'an, especially the shorter, mystical suras which are assumed to be of an earlier provenance. The South Arabian Hymn of Qāniya, which was produced at the end of the first century CE, in the Middle Sabaic period, addresses the goddess S^2ms^1 (*Shams*) and consists of twenty-seven lines, each containing roughly four words, ending in the rhyme *ḥk*. While most rhyme sequences in the Qur'an are based on a single vowel-consonant sequence, consonant-vowel-consonant rhymes also exist, for example 75:21–5 in *rah*, but never spanning an entire sura. Even though the exact meaning of this hymn continues to elude scholars, its structural similarity to some of the Meccan suras, such as Q. 87, which consists of nineteen lines of a similar length all ending in *y*, is striking (Beeston 1994).

South Arabian Hymn of Qāniya	Quran 75:21–5
3. *w-krnw s²ʿd b-qs¹d qs¹**ḥk***	21. *wa taḏarūna l-ʾāḫi**rah***
4. *(w-ḫb) ʿlhn ḏ-yhr fq**ḥk***	22. *wuǧūhun yawmaʾiḏin nāḍi**rah***
5. *(w-yṯ)lt ʾ(ʾ)db ṣlʿ fḏ**ḥk***	23. *ʾilā rabbihā nāẓi**rah***
6. *(w- my)n ms²qr hn-bḥr wṣ**ḥk***	24. *wuǧūhun yawmʾiḏin bāsi**rah***

[8] Inventory 98 will appear in volume 5 of the Petra Papyri.

[9] This text was published with a photograph in Macdonald (2009: 1: 76–7).

The votive inscription ZI 11 resembles even more closely Qur'anic style.[10] The inscription contains an introductory formula and six strophes of four verses, each unified by a single rhyme letter, *l*, *k*, *l*, *ḥ*, *m*, *q*. This text is comparable to Meccan suras, such as Q. 75 and Q.84, in which the verses are typically composed of three to six words, and have six changes of rhyme throughout the composition. (See Stein (2008) for a discussion on the language of these texts and bibliography.)

South Arabian ZI 11	Quran 84:16-23
b-khl k-bgw ṯwn khl	16. *fa-lā ʾuqsimu biš-šafaq*
w-kl ʾḍrr-k ḥs^{3}*l*	17. *wal-layli wa mā wasaq*
ḫms^{1}*-k mrʾ-n ḏll*	18. *wal-qamari ʾiḏā ttasaq*
kl ḏ-ʿly w-s^{1}*fl*	19. *la-tarkabunna ṭabaqan ʿan ṭabaq*
b-khl bḥt ḏ- whn ḏrḥ	20. *fa-mā lahum lā yuʾminūn*
hrd ḏ-mlwb w?- rzḥ	21. *wa ʾiḏa quriʾa ʿalayhimu l-qurʾānu lā yasǧudūn*
ʾlmq ḏ-hs^{1}*kr ʾrmḥ*	22. *bali llaḏina kafarū yukaḏḏibūn*
tḥt-k ʾḫms^{1} *rḍḥ*	23. *wallāhu ʾaʿlamu bimā yūʿūn*

Other poems bear a closer resemblance to Arabic metrical poetry. The inscription VL 24 = Ja 2353 (see Stein 2008) contains ten lines which can be split into half-verses rhyming in *r*, although lines four and six terminate in *n*. Not only is *r* one of the most frequent rhyme letters of the Qur'an, but Qur'anic style also permits a rhyme with the liquids *l* and *n*. Whether such compositions acted as a proto-type for the Qur'anic stylistic conventions is at the moment unclear, but further research into the stylistic connections between the Qur'an and such inscriptions will no doubt prove to be a fruitful endeavour.

In addition to style, the ASA inscriptions contain many parallels in content. By the fourth century CE, references to the pagan gods disappear almost entirely from the inscriptions, ushering in what scholars have termed the 'monotheistic period'. In their place, a new, single god is venerated, *Rḥmnn*, literally 'the merciful', which finds a direct Arabic equivalent in *al-raḥmān*, who is equated with Allāh in the Qur'an (Q. 17:110). Other literary phrases common to monotheistic South Arabian inscriptions, specifically the Jewish ones, and the Qur'an are found. An epithet of Rḥmnn, *mrʾ s*^{1}*myn w- ʾrḍn* 'lord of the heavens and the earth', has a transparent Qur'anic equivalent: *rabbu s-samāwāti wa'l-arḍi*. In another Jewish inscription, the following is attested: *[b]rk w tbrk s*^{1}*m rḥmnn* 'may the name of Rḥmnn bless and be blessed', which is essentially equivalent to Q. 55:78 *tabāraka smu rabbika* 'blessed is the name of your lord'.[11] While religious terms such as 'prayer' *ṣlt* = Qur'an *ṣlwh*, voweled *ṣalāh*, and 'aid/assistance' *zkt = Qur'anic zkwh*, voweled *zakāh*, are also attested in Jewish South Arabian inscriptions, their spellings in the Qur'an preclude a South Arabian origin (see Jeffery 2007).

[10] For a partial translation of this text, see al-Iryāni (2005). See Stein (2008) for a refutation of the Himyaritic hypothesis for which these texts have been used to advance.

[11] See Robin (2004: appendix 1) for the inscriptions and bibliography.

A remarkable graffito recently published in the miniscule South Arabian script (Al-Hajj and Faqʿas 2018) attests a late pre-Islamic variant of the *basmala* and a prayer to God in vocabulary and style strikingly similar to the Qur'an, and later Islamic phraseology, but not identical to it.[12]

bsmlh rḥmn rḥmn rb smwt
'In the name of Allāh, Raḥmān; Raḥmān lord of the heavens'
rzq-n m-fḍl-k w-ʾṯr-n mḫ-h śkmt ʾymn
'Bless us from your favor and grant us the best of it: the gift of faith'

The inscriptions of the nomads also yield valuable points of comparison. The seeking of refuge, Qur'an 2:67, *ʾaʿūḏu bi-llāhi* 'I seek refuge in Allāh' is comparable to Safaitic WH 390 *ʿwḏ b- Rḍy* 'he sought refuge in (the god) Rḍy', or WH 3923 *ʿw{ḏ} b- {h}- {ʾ}lh* 'he sought refuge in God (lit. the god). The *qasam* 'oath' (cf. Q. 70:40) is attested in SIJ 293 *ʾqsm b-ʾlh ḥy* 'he swore by ʾlh (ʾallāh or ʾilāh) who is living'. Divine qualities associated with the monotheistic deity are also attributed to the pre-Islamic gods. They are *ḥ y* 'living' (SIJ 293; cf. Q. 2:225 *al-ḥayyu*) and 'merciful' *rḥm* (C 4341; Q. *ar-raḥīm passim*); they grant life *ḥyy* (C 4803; cf. Q. 2:28 *yuḥyī*), cause death *ymyt* (C 4341; cf. Q. 2:28 *yumītu*). They 'curse' wrong-doers *lʿn* (LP 360; cf. Q. 33:64 *laʿana*) and bless the faithful *w yh brk* (AWS 218; cf. 7:131 *bāraknā*). God, as the knower of the unseen, Qur'an *ʿālimu l-ġayb*, is also paralleled in a divine name in Safaitic (KRS 3074) *ʾlt ʾ-ġb* 'goddess of the unseen'. The deity as 'owner' or 'sovereign' of heaven *h mlk h-s¹my* 'O sovereign of the sky/heaven' (KRS 1944) offers a close parallel to the common Qur'anic phrase *lillāhi mulku s-samāwāti waʾl-arḍị* 'For Allāh is the dominion of the heavens and the earth'. The use of natural phenomenon as a symbol of divine power is also attested, Safaitic (KRS 2453) *mykn ḫlf lyly-h w ʾwm-h* 'established is the alternation of his nights and days', compare with Qur'an 23:80 'and his is the alternation of night and day'.

The inscriptions also offer us a small view of religion and ritual among the pre-Islamic nomads. One writer records that he performed a ritual ablution *rḥd* before embarking on a pilgrimage *ḥg* (WH 3053). Other rituals include animal sacrifice *ḏbḥ* (C 853), building cairns over the dead *rgm* (WH 234), erecting sacred stones *nṣb* (C 527) as representations of deities, and giving burnt offerings *ʾṣly* (SIJ 293). Perhaps most interesting is the religious/ritualistic role of writing and reading. Authors often invoke a god to bestow blessings upon those who read their inscriptions aloud, and to curse those who efface them—HaNSB 307 *dʿy ʾl [l]t ʿl mn yḫbl-h* 'he called upon (dʿy) Lt against whosoever would efface it (the inscription)'. Texts such as these also indicate that the Aramaic terms *qrʾ* 'to read' and *ktb* 'to write' had entered Arabic, presumably through Nabataean Aramaic, at a very early period, and were not the result of the spread of Christianity in Arabia.

[12] The reading and interpretation provided is my own. The *editio princeps* offers two different understandings of the text, differing in minor points of grammar.

C 4803: *ʿwr {l}- ḏ y ʿwr h-s*^{1}*fr w ḥyy l- ḏ* **yqr**ʾ *h-ktb*
'may he who would efface this writing go blind and may he who would read this writing aloud have long life'

MNM b 6: *ḏkrt lt mḥrs*^{1} *bn ḫlflh bn whbn w kll ʿs*^{2}*r ṣdq w kll mn* **yqry** *wqʿ-n ḏh*
'may Lt be mindful of Mḥrs^1 son of Ḫlflh son of Whbn and all true kinsmen and all who read this inscription of ours'

Several of the deities mentioned in the Qur'an are encountered in the inscriptions. The three goddesses mentioned in Q. 53:19–22, al-Lāt, al-ʿUzzā, and al-Manāt, were worshipped in Nabataea, and with varying degrees of popularity in north-west Arabia. Al-Lāt was the most popular deity in North Arabia, invoked in almost all of the epigraphic corpora, and was probably the most ancient; she is found in theophoric names dating back to the early first millennium BCE. Al-ʿUzzā is also encountered in the inscriptions, but her worship was more restricted. She is limited to theophoric names in the Safaitic and Hismaic inscriptions, but was especially popular among the Nabataeans (Healey 2001: 114ff.), and is found in theophoric names at Dadān with the *hn* article, that is, *hn-ʿzy*.

After a meticulous study of the distribution of *Lt* and *ʾlʿzy/ʾ* in the Nabataean inscriptions, Healey suggests that the latter was an epithet of al-Lāt, meaning 'the mightiest' (Healey 2001: 114). There is also some evidence to suggest that *Lt* was a mother goddess, if Healey's interpretation of the inscription on an altar of Lt (CIS II, 185) as *ʾm ʾlhy dy mʾrnʾ rbʾl* 'the mother of the gods of our lord, Rabbel' is correct (Healey 2001: 109–10). In Safaitic, al-Lāt was regarded as the daughter of Rḍw/y, deified 'satisfaction' (AWS 283, 291).

The third member of the Qur'anic trinity, *mnwh*, also makes an appearance in the inscriptions, but is not as common in the North Arabian and Nabataean inscriptions as *Lt* and *ʿzy*. She frequently appears in conjunction with Dusares, the principal Nabataean deity, in the inscriptions of Ḥegrā (Healey 2001: 132–3). An important clue regarding the pronunciation of this deity's name comes from a Latin inscription in Hungary (CIL III, 7954), dedicated by a Palmyrene, in which her name is spelled MANAVAT, suggesting an original pronunciation, *manawat-*. In Arabia, it seems that the sequence *awa* monophthongized to /ō/, as suggested by Nabataean spellings *mnwtw* =/manōtō/, Safaitic and Hismaic *ʾs*^{1}*mnt*, Dadanitic *zdmnt*, and even South Arabian *ʿbdmntm*. The Qur'anic *mnwh* probably signals the pronunciation *manōh*, suggesting the following sound changes: *manawat* > *manawah* > *manōh*. *Mnwtw* seems to be a deification of fate, which is depicted as dooming the living in the common Safaitic epitaph, *rġm mny* 'struck down by Fate'.

Interestingly, no inscriptions mention all three goddesses together as we find in Q. 53:19–20 'have you considered ʾlt (vocalized, *allāt*) and *ʾlʿzy* (vocalized *al-ʿuzzā*)? and Mnwh (vocalized *manāt*) the third and last one?' or imply that they were daughters of the principal deity, as in Q. 53:21 'is the male for you and for him the female?'

Concluding Remark

The historical-critical study of the Qur'an based on the growing body of documentary evidence from the pre-Islamic period is in its infancy. The proper utilization of this material has the potential to transform our understanding of the composition and language of the text. Many desiderata remain, perhaps most importantly an independent linguistic study of the consonantal skeleton of the Qur'an in light of the pre-Islamic epigraphy and a lexical study of Qur'anic vocabulary in light of the North Arabian inscriptions.

Sigla

AWS	Safaitic inscriptions in Alolow 1996
C	Safaitic inscriptions in *Corpus Inscriptionum Semiticarum. Pars V.* Paris, 1950–1
ESK	Thamudic inscriptions in Eskoubi 1999
HaNSB	Safaitic Inscriptions in Ḥarāḥišah 2010
SIJ	Safaitic inscriptions in Winnett 1957
SESP.U	Thamudic Inscription in Macdonald et al. 1996
WH	Safaitic inscriptions in Winnett and Harding 1978
WTay	Taymanitic inscriptions in Winnett and Reed 1970
WTI	Dumaitic, Hismaic, and Thamudic B, C, and D inscriptions in Winnett and Reed 1970

Bibliography

Al-Jallad, A. 'On the Genetic Background of the ʿIgl bn Hfʿm Grave Inscription at Qaryat al-Faw', *Bulletin of the School of Oriental and African Studies* 77/3 (2014), 445–65.
Al-Jallad, A. *An Outline of the Grammar of the Safaitic Inscriptions.* Leiden: Brill, 2015.
Al-Jallad, A. 'Graeco-Arabica I: the Southern Levant'. In: A. Al-Jallad (ed.). *Arabic in Context: Celebrating 400 Years of Arabic at Leiden University*, pp. 99–186. Leiden: Brill, 2017.
Al-Jallad, A. 'What is Ancient North Arabian'. In: N. Pat-El and D. Birnstiel (eds.). *Re-engaging Comparative Semitic and Arabic Studies*, pp. 1–45. Wiesbaden: Harrassowitz, 2018.
Al-Jallad, A. 'Safaitic'. In: N. Pat-El and J. Huehnergard (eds.). *The Semitic Languages, second edition.* pp. 342–66. London: Routledge, 2019.
Al-Jallad, A., R. Daniel, and O. Al-Ghul. 'The Arabic Toponyms and Oikonyms in 17'. In: L. Koenen, M. Kaimo, and R. Daniel (eds.). *The Petra Papyri II*, pp. 23–48. Amman: ACOR.
Alolow, Ġ. *Dirāsat nuqūš ṣafawiyyah ǧadīdah min Wādī as-Sūʿ ǧanūb Sūriyā.* Masters Thesis. Irbid, Institute of Archaeology and Anthropology, Yarmouk University, 1996.
Beeston, A. F. L. 'Nemara and Faw', *BSOAS* 42 (1979), 1–6.
Beeston, A. F. L. 'Languages of Pre-Islamic Arabia', *Arabica* (numéro special double: Études de linguistique arabe) (1981), pp. 178–86.
Beeston, F. 'Antecedents of Classical Arabic Verse?' In: W. Heinrichs and G. Schoeler (eds.). *Festschrift Ewald Wagner zum 65. Geburtstag. Bd. 1. Semitische Studien unter besonderer*

Berücksichtigung der Südsemitistik (Beiruter Texte und Studien 54), pp. 234–43. Beirut: Franz Steiner Verlag Stuttgart, 1994.

Blau, J. 'The Beginnings of the Arabic Diglossia: A Study in the Origins of Neo-Arabic', *Afro-Asiatic Linguistics* 4/4 (1977), 1–28.

Drewes, A. J., T. F. G. Higham, M. C. A. Macdonald, and C. B. Ramsey. 'Some Absolute Dates for the Development of the Ancient South Arabian Minuscule Script', *Arabian Archaeology and Epigraphy* 24 (2013), 196–207.

Eskoubi, Ḫ. M. *Dirāsah taḥlīliyyah muqāranah li-nuqūš min minṭaqat (rum) ǧanūb ġarb taymāʾ*. [English title: *An Analytical and Comparative Study of Inscriptions from 'Rum' region, South West of Taymai*]. Riyadh: Wizārat al-Maʿārif, Wakālat al-Āṯār wa-l-Matāḥif, 1999.

Farès-Drappeau, S. *Dédān et Liḥyān: histoire des Arabes aux confins des pouvoirs perse et hellénistique (IVe—Iie avant l'ère chrétienne)* (Travaux de la maison de l'orient et de la Méditerranée 42). Lyon: Maison de l'Orient et de la Méditerranée, 2005.

Fiema, Zbigniew T., Ahmad Al-Jallad, Michael C. A. Macdonald, and Laïla Nehmé. 'Provincia Arabia: Nabataea, the Emergence of Arabic as a Written Language, and Graeco-Arabica'. In: G. Fisher (ed.). *Arabs and Empires before Islam*, pp. 373–433. Oxford: Oxford University Press, 2015.

Graf, D. F. and M. J. Zwettler. 'The North Arabian "Thamudic E" Inscriptions from Urayniba West', *Bulletin of the American Schools of Oriental Research* 55 (2004), 53–89.

Al-Hajj, M. A. and A. A. Faqʿas. 'Naqš ǧabal ḏubūb: naqš ǧadīd bi-ḫaṭṭ al-zabūr al-yamānī fī al-ʾistiʿānah biʾllāh wa-taqwiyyat al-ʾīmān', *al-ʿIbar Journal* (2018), 12–43.

Ḥarāḥišah, R. *Nuqūš Ṣafāʾiyyah Mina 'l-Bādiyah al-ʾUrduniyyah*. Amman: Ward Books, 2010.

Healey, J. F. *The Religions of the Nabataeans: A Conspectus*. Leiden: Brill, 2001.

Huehnergard, J. and A. Rubin. 'Phyla and Waves: Models of Classification of the Semitic Languages'. In: S. Weninger, G. Khan, M. Streck, and J. Watson (Eds.) *The Semitic Languages: An International Handbook* (Handbücher zur Sprach- und Kommunikationswissenschaft 36), pp. 259–78. Boston/Berlin: De Gruyter Mouton, 2011.

Al-Iryāni, M. 'Unšūdah min Maḥram Bilqīs', *Aṯ-ṯawābit* 41 (July–Sept. 2005), 64–106.

Jeffery, A. *The Foreign Vocabulary of the Qur'ān*. Leiden: Brill, 2007.

Kootstra, F. 'The Language of the Taymanitic Inscriptions and its Classification', *Arabian Epigraphic Notes* 2 (2016), 67–140.

Macdonald, M. C. A. 'Reflections on the Linguistic Map of pre-Islamic Arabia', *Arabian Archaeology and Epigraphy* 11 (2000), 28–79.

Macdonald, M. C. A. *Literacy and Identity in Pre-Islamic Arabia*. Surrey: Ashgate, 2009.

Macdonald, M. C. A. 'Arabia and the Written Word'. In: M. C. A. Macdonald (ed.). *The Development of Arabic as a Written Language: Papers from the Special Session of the Seminar for Arabian Studies Held on 24 July, 2009* (Supplement to the Proceedings of the Seminar for Arabian Studies, 40), pp. 103–12. Oxford: Archaeopress, 2010.

Macdonald, M. C. A. 'Goddesses, Dancing Girls or Cheerleaders? Perceptions of the Divine and the Female Form in the Rock Art of Pre-Islamic North Arabia'. In: Isabelle Sachet and Christian Robin (eds.). *Dieux et déesses d'Arabie Images et representations: actes de la table ronde tenue au Collège de France (Paris) les 1er et 2 octobre 2007*. Paris: De Boccard, 2012.

Macdonald, M. C. A. and G. M. H. King. 'Thamudic'. In: *Encyclopaedia of Islam*, second edition, 10:436–8 Leiden: Brill, 2000.

Macdonald, M. C. A., M. al-Muʾazzin, and L. Nehmé, 'Les Inscriptions safaïtiques de Syrie, cent quarante ans après leur découverte', *Comptes rendus des séances de l'Académie des Inscriptions & Belles-Lettres*, 140/1 (1996), 435–94.

Müller, W. W. 'Das Frühnordarabische'. In: W. Fischer (ed.). *Grundriß der arabischen Philologie*, vol. 1: *Sprachwissenschaft*, pp. 17–29. Wiesbaden: Reichert, 1982.

Nehmé, L. 'A Glimpse of the Development of the Nabataean Script into Arabic Based on Old and New Epigraphic Material. In: M. C. A. Macdonald (ed.) *The Development of Arabic as a Written Language: Papers from the Special Session of the Seminar for Arabian Studies held on 24 July, 2009*. (Supplement to the Proceedings of the Seminar for Arabian Studies, 40), pp. 47–88. Oxford: Archaeopress, 2010.

Nehmé, L. *Epigraphy on the Edges of the Roman Empire: A Study of the Nabataean Inscriptions and Related Material from the Darb al-Bakrah, Saudi Arabia, 1st–5th century* AD. Mémoire scientifique d'Habilitation à Diriger des recherches, Paris: École Pratique des Hautes Études, 2013.

Nehmé, L. 'New Dated Inscriptions (Nabataean and Pre-Islamic Arabic) from a Site near al-Jawf, Ancient Dūmah, Saudi Arabia', *Arabian Epigraphic Notes* 3 (2017), 121–64.

Negev, A., J. Naveh, and S. Shaked. 'Obodas the God', *Israel Exploration Journal* 36 (1986), 56–60.

Neuwirth, Angelika, Nicolai Sinai, and Michael Marx (eds.). *The Qurʾān in Context: Historical and Literary Investigations into the Qurʾānic Milieu*. Leiden: Brill, 2010.

Robin, Ch. 'Himyar et Israël', Comptes rendus des séances de l'Académie des Inscriptions et Belles-Lettres 148 (2004), 831–908.

Robin, Ch., A. I. al-Ghabbān, and S. F. al-Saʿīd. 'Inscriptions antiques de la région de Najrān (Arabie séoudite méridionale): nouveaux jalons pour l'histoire de l'écriture, de la langue et du calendrier arabe', *Comptes rendus des séances de l'Académie des Inscriptions & Belles-Lettres* (2014), 1033–128.

Sachet, I. and C. Robin (eds.). *Dieux et déesses d'Arabie: images et representations. Actes de la table ronde tenue au Collège de France (Paris) les 1er et 2 octobre 2007*. Paris: De Boccard, 2012.

Sima, A. *Die liḥyanischen Inschriften aus al-ʿUḏayb (Nordwestarabien)*. (Epigraphische Forschungen auf der Arabischen Halbinsel 1). Rahden/Westf.: Verlag Marie Leidorf, 1999.

Sima, A. 'Die hasaitischen Inschriften'. In: N. Nebes (ed.). *Neue Beiträge zur Semitistik: Erstes Arbeitstreffen der Arbeitsgemeinschaft Semitistik in der Deutschen Morgenländischen Gesellschaft von 11. bis 13. September 2000 an der Friedrich- Schiller-Universität Jena* (Jenaer Beiträge zum Vorderen Orient 5), pp. 167–200. Wiesbaden: Harrassowitz, 2002.

Stein, P. 'The "Ḥimyaritic" Language in pre-Islamic Yemen: A Critical Re-evaluation', *Semitica et Classica* 1 (2008), 203–12.

Stein, P. 'Ancient South Arabian'. In: S. Weninger, G. Khan, M. Streck, and J. Watson (eds.). *The Semitic Languages: An International Handbook* (Handbücher zur Sprach- und Kommunikationswissenschaft 36), pp. 1042–72. Boston/Berlin: De Gruyter Mouton, 2011.

Stein, P. 'South Arabian Zabūr Script in the Gulf: Some Recent Discoveries from Mleiha (Sharjah, UAE)', *Arabian Archaeology and Epigraphy* 28 (2017), 110–23.

Winnett, F. *Safaitic Inscriptions from Jordan* (Near and Middle East Series 2). Toronto: University of Toronto Press, 1957.

Winnett, F. and G. Harding. *Inscriptions from Fifty Safaitic Cairns* (Near and Middle East Series 9). Toronto: University of Toronto Press, 1978.

Winnett, F. V. and W. L. Reed. *Ancient Records from North Arabia* (Near and Middle East Series 6). Toronto: University of Toronto, 1970.

CHAPTER 8

QUR'ANIC EXEMPLA AND LATE ANTIQUE NARRATIVES

MARIANNA KLAR

INTRODUCTION

THE Qur'anic corpus is characterized by a pervasive technique of deploying narratives as exempla relevant to its own addressees. Minimal or more expanded references to biblical figures such as Noah and Moses are utilized in order to illustrate key exhortatory themes in a large number of suras, a feature that has struck readers of the Qur'an from ancient times to the present. Recent scholarship has replaced a search for straightforward parallels in narratives from the Judaeo-Christian tradition with a growing trend for a re-evaluation of the Qur'an's contextual framework, and a rethinking of the references to other literatures and religious traditions included therein. This has necessitated the methodological acceptance of cultural sophistication for the Qur'anic text and its literary environment. The focus is to remain firmly on the Qur'an: a discrete rhetorical system that comments on itself as well as on other religious traditions. The emphasis is to be placed not on influence but on dialogue, within a general ethos (it is variously argued) of polemic, critique, neutralization, or persuasion. This represents a deliberate rethinking of nineteenth/early twentieth-century scholarship on the Qur'an, and can be seen to reflect a similar refinement of the positioning of the Hebrew Bible tradition within its Sumerian, Hurrian, Babylonian, and Ugaritic contexts.

TEXTUAL EXAMPLES

Much of the most recent contextual Qur'anic scholarship has focused on wordplay with the apocryphal and liturgical texts of Syriac Christianity: attempts to connect specific terms within Ethiopic Christianity to a narrative or rhetorical context remain rudimentary, with difficulties in establishing philological evidence for the pre-Qur'anic Ethiopic Bible tradition substantially complicating this issue. The significance of the rabbinical interface with the Qur'an has similarly been the subject of very little dedicated scholarly attention in recent years. The 1833 treatment by Abraham Geiger (*Was hat Mohammed aus dem Judenthume aufgenommen*), and Heinrich Speyer's *Die biblischen Erzählungen im Qoran* (first published between 1937 and 1939) remain in need of reconsideration and updating.

One article that does draw on the Jewish heritage of the period is Adam Silverstein's 2011 study of the Qur'anic Pharaoh, which utilizes a fleeting reference to the Near Eastern story of Aḥīqār the Sage in the midrashic *Book of Tobit* to identify the Hāmān of the Qur'anic Pharaoh story (Q. 28:38 and Q. 40:36–7) with Aḥīqār's nephew Nādān/Hāmān. This episode, and, more specifically, the mention of (typically Mesopotamian) baked bricks within the (typically Egyptian) Pharaoh pericope at Q. 28:38, led scholars such as Neal Robinson and Brannon Wheeler to assume that the Qur'an was here conflating two narratives: that of Pharaoh and that of the Tower of Babel. As Silverstein points out, however, 'the Bible itself refers to baked bricks with reference to Pharaoh's Egypt on more than one occasion' (Silverstein 2011: 472). Within the *Tale of Aḥīqār the Sage*, meanwhile, a narrative that is widely attested in the Near East from the Achaemenid era onwards, the Assyrian ruler Esarhaddon is challenged by the Egyptian Pharaoh to build for him a tower that bridges heaven and earth. Aḥīqār's nephew Nādān is nominated to accept this challenge, even though the task itself is eventually completed by Aḥiqār himself. In the variant recorded in the *Book of Tobit*, the name Nādān is replaced by the orthographically similar Hāmān, the term we find in the Qur'an. Silverstein then carries this Near Eastern typology into his reading of the *ṣarḥ* through which Solomon convinces the Queen of Sheba of the truth of his faith in Q. 27:44. As he points out, 'the relationship between Wisdom and building towers—or craftsmanship in general—is a feature of ancient Near Eastern culture' (Silverstein 2011: 476). It should come as no surprise, then, that Solomon (and Aḥīqār) should succeed where Pharaoh is destined to fail. The refined late antique context serves to augment and clarify both Qur'anic pericopes.

The work of Sidney Griffith is particularly influential in the field of contextual Qur'anic scholarship.[1] While Griffith's work has tended to focus on a discussion of Christian theological terms, in a 2008 article Griffith offers a reading of the Companions of the Cave narrative in Q. 18 (*al-Kahf*) in the light of a liturgical homily (*mêmrā*) by Jacob of Serugh (d. 521). Among other observations, Griffith posits an interpretation of *al-raqīm* in Q. 18:9 ('Do you find the Companions in the Cave and *al-raqīm* so wondrous, among all Our other signs?')[2] as an allusion to the 'tablets of lead' of Jacob of Serugh (Griffith 2008: 126). The passage in the *mêmrā* describes how, when the pagan Emperor Decius declared his intention to seal the sleepers in the cave, two sophists who happened to be present transcribed the sleepers' names and the reason for their entombment on tablets of lead, which they then placed beside them. Many years later, these tablets serve

[1] This is especially true of the methodological safeguards he recommends, which are widely adduced by other contemporary scholars.

[2] Qur'an translations are taken, with minor modifications, from Abdel Haleem 2010.

to inform the Christian Emperor Theodosius II of what has transpired. In this respect Griffith is correcting Bellamy's 1991 proposal that *al-raqīm* is a misreading of *al-ruqūd*. It should be noted, of course, that 'inscribed tablet' is one of several options offered in explanation of this term by the medieval exegetical tradition, a fact that is acknowledged by Griffith. The sleeping dog of Q. 18:18 Griffith reads, meanwhile, in the context of the Syriac text's 'guardian of their limbs': an angel posted at the entrance of the *mêmrā*'s cave (Griffith 2008: 128).

The identity of the 'protector' and 'partner' the Qur'an refers to in Q. 18:26 ('they have no one to protect them other than Him; He does not allow anyone to share His rule') is similarly a topic for scholarly discussion. Griffith comments of this verse: 'the true meaning of the Christian story corrects what the Qur'an considers to be one of the major errors of the Christian understanding. Namely, the doctrine that God has a son and that he is Jesus, the Messiah' (Griffith 2008: 118). Whitney Bodman, however, identifies the disputed source of protection in Q. 18:26 as the Companions themselves, who, far from being the 'proto-Muslims' identified by Ian Netton in his 2000 article, are there to be criticized for their 'waking confusion' in Q. 18:19 (Bodman 2011: 118).

Bodman builds his case, in part, on the mention of a *masjid* ('place of worship') to be built over the Companions' bodies in Q. 18:21. He observes: 'This last element would raise... concerns about partnership with God' (Bodman 2011: 118). Gabriel Said Reynolds also notices this verse, and comments (Reynolds 2010: 184; cf. Griffith 2008: 129):

> The *Ecclesiastical History* of Zacharias of Mitylene (d. 536) relates that 'a great sanctuary has been built over the cave for honor's sake, and for a house of worship (*bayt ṣlūtā*) and for liturgy (*teshmeshtā*) over their bodies.'

This Reynolds takes as a reason to dispute the exegetical interpretation of this passage (Reynolds 2010: 184):

> It is thus rather unnerving to encounter the opinion of Ibn Kathīr, who argues that the building of this *masjid* was an act of infidelity, with reference to the prophetic *ḥadīth*: 'May God curse the Jews and the Christians for making the graves of their prophets and holy people into places of prayer.'

Yet the *mêmrā* of Jacob of Serugh could be argued to corroborate Ibn Kathīr's reading of this passage. There the appropriateness of the erection of a commemorative building is similarly questioned. The relevant passage tells us that 'Theodosius tried to persuade the youths to return to Ephesus where he would build a temple (*hayklā*) over their bodies, but they refused'. It would appear that the same incident was alluded to in the words of Gregorius Turonensis (d. 594), as reflected in the later Latin of Jacobus de Voragine (d. 1298): 'When the Emperor Theodosius wanted to construct a tomb out of gold (*sepulchra ex auro*) for them, he was forbidden through a vision from doing it.' An understanding of Q. 18:21 as suggesting that Christian attempts to commemorate these events were rebuffed is in keeping with the Qur'an's declaration that the Christians would have fled in terror had they actually witnessed these events (Q. 18:18). Similarly, the Qur'an informs the reader that it is only God who knows the true length of the Companions' sleep or their actual number (Q. 18:22), leading, ultimately, to the statement 'they have no one to protect them other than Him; He does not allow anyone to share His rule' (Q. 18:26). It therefore seems unlikely that the 'protector' of Q. 18:26 refers to the Companions themselves; a more general criticism of Christian doctrine and leadership would appear to be at play here.

A number of recent articles investigate the relevance of Patristic sources to our understanding of the figure of Mary in the Qur'an. These are drawn upon by Michael Marx in his 2009 essay focusing on the 'surplus meaning' that is created by the existence of differences between the Qur'anic portrayal of Mary and other late antique sources.[3] Marx, who is consciously building upon Suleiman Mourad's (2002) and Samir Khalil Samir's (2008) studies of the Qur'anic Mary, observes that the Mary story is explicitly located at the Temple (*miḥrāb*) in both *Sūrat Maryam* and *Sūrat Āl ʿImrān*. The reference to an 'Eastern place' in Q. 19:16 Marx reads (more tenuously) as a further reference to the Temple, on the strength of Patristic images of the virginity of Mary as representing the locked gate of the Temple (Marx cites an example from a Syriac liturgical manuscript of uncertain date).

Marx then argues for a rethinking of the significance of Mary's Aaronid genealogy (Q. 19:28, 3:35, and 66:12). He disputes Samir's assumption that the term *Āl ʿImrān*, read in the light of the five covenants of Patristic literature, conflates the figures of Moses and Jesus (Samir 2008: 143). In contrast, Marx highlights the absence of Moses from all of the Medinan lists of the chosen men of God, and concludes that 'the intention appears to be to revive memories of the Temple tradition founded by Aaron rather than to recall memories of the Mosaic covenant' (Marx 2009: 547). Similarly weighty in Marx's view is the Qur'anic reference, in stark contrast to the Christian covenant texts which explicitly name Adam, Noah, *Abraham*, Moses and *Christ* (Samir 2008: 143–4; emphasis mine), to the *descendants* of Abraham and of ʿImrān; this is read by Marx as a conscious allusion to the Qur'an's contemporary communities of, respectively, Jews and Christians, with the religious-political purpose of equalizing the perceived prestige of the two groups.[4]

A religious-political agenda is likewise adduced in the parallels Joseph Witztum perceives between Abraham's raising of the foundations of the House in Q. 2:127, and Syriac descriptions of Isaac's participation in preparations for the Abrahamic sacrifice at Genesis 22. That the Qur'anic passage does most probably refer to the rebuilding of the Kaʿba Witztum defends through the repeated lexical item *bayt* in both Q. 2:127 and in Q. 5:97, where the meaning 'Kaʿba' is directly specified (Witztum 2009: 27). Witztum nonetheless connects the Qur'anic and biblical traditions on the strength of several post-biblical Christian sources, in which Isaac and Abraham are described as building

[3] A similar methodological stance is professed in Bauer 2009: 704–6, who terms this 'negative intertextuality', and Sinai 2011.

[4] For this and the preceding argument see also various of the publications of Angelika Neuwirth as listed in Marx's bibliography.

the altar upon which Isaac is to be sacrificed *together*, just as Abraham and Ismāʿīl build the House together in the Qur'anic account. Witztum further argues his case via specific vocabulary that occurs with reference to the sacrifice of Isaac in Jacob of Serugh's *mêmrā* (Witztum 2009: 30–2): Abraham, 'the master-builder' (*ardeklā*), is here similarly said to have 'extended the foundation' (*ngad dumsā*) in order to build a 'house' (*baytā*).

Witztum pursues his case for the association of the Qur'anic exemplum with traditions pertaining to Gen. 22 by observing that Q. 2:124, which arguably serves to introduce this pericope, describes Abraham as being 'tested' (*ibtalā*), a term used with reference to the Abrahamic sacrifice in Q. 37:106, where the Qur'an states 'it was a test (*al-balāʾ*) to prove [their true characters]'. The prayer in Q. 2:127–9, meanwhile, makes mention of favour being granted to Abraham's descendants; God states in Gen. 22:15–18, 'I will make your offspring as numerous as the stars of heaven and as the sand that is on the seashore. And your offspring shall possess the gate of their enemies, and by your offspring shall all the nations of the earth gain blessing for themselves' (Witztum 2009: 33). Finally, recalling that Gen. 22 'serves as an etiology for the worship at the temple in Jerusalem', Witztum concludes that 'the scene in the Qur'an may be understood as an appropriation of the foundation story of the Jerusalem temple, adapting it to the founding of the Kaʿba' (Witztum 2009: 38).

In contrast to this emphasis on the Judaeo-Christian textual tradition, Walid Saleh makes an argument for widening our contextual approach to encompass 'the by-then universal mythological heritage of the late antique world' (Saleh 2009: 689). He posits the pagan horizon as a major interface for the Qur'anic portrayal of Paradise, with *wildān* likened to Ganymede (Saleh 2009: 689) and the *ḥūr ʿīn* to Hera (Saleh 2009: 690–1): 'The whole joyful hedonistic atmosphere of the Qur'anic paradise is more akin to the lives of the gods of Olympus than to the asceticism and sensibilities of late antique Christianity' (Saleh 2009: 689). Suleiman Mourad likewise takes recourse to the myth of Leto giving birth to Apollo in his treatment of the birth of Jesus at Q. 19:22–6 (Mourad 2002).[5] Kevin van Bladel cites examples of physical or spiritual ascents to heaven in Magian and Zoroastrian, as well as Judaeo-Christian, traditions in support of an understanding of the *asbāb* of the Dhū'l-Qarnayn narrative (Q. 18:85 *et passim*) as 'heavenly sky-cords' (van Bladel 2007).

Pre- or early Islamic poetry is convincingly drawn upon as an appropriate foil by Nicolai Sinai, who suggests that the Thamūd poetry of Umayya ibn Abī'l-Ṣalt indicates the existence of several versions of the Thamūd narrative circulating in pre-Islamic Arabia. Sinai then utilizes Umayya's poetry in order to highlight some of the narrative features that are specific to the Qur'anic portrayal of the Thamūd exemplum at Q. 91. Prominent among these are the Qur'anic introduction of a messenger figure, entirely absent from the poetic narrative, and the consequent downplaying of the importance of Umayya's Aḥmar character, who is the actual slayer of the camel in the poetic account. Indeed, many of the dramatic details that make up the poetic version of events are removed for

[5] Cf. Stephen Shoemaker 2003 for a rival thesis, invoking the *Protevangelium of James* and local Palestinian traditions about the Dormition of Mary.

the Qur'anic narrative: 'the Quran reorganizes existing narrative lore in order to harness it for the expression of its own prophetology' (Sinai 2011: 411). Thomas Bauer meanwhile posits a reading of the Qur'anic *mubīn* as a comment on the deliberate stylistic obfuscity of pre-Islamic poetry. He also argues that terms such as *yahīmūn* at Q. 26:225 ('to die of thirst', as attested in the poems of Labīd and ʿĀmir ibn al-Ṭufayl), and *rayb al-manūn* at Q. 52:30 ('a lament in poetry of mourning'; Bauer 2009: 724), are deliberate poetic references used to emphasize the mendacity of the poet: 'this is exactly what the poets, as members of a wealthy and aristocratic upper class, did not do: "die from thirst" in the desert' (Bauer 2009: 727). This influences our understanding of the accusations of madness, poetry, soothsaying, and magic at Q. 37:35–7, 38:4, 52:29 *et passim*, and corrects earlier readings of these passages as intended more literally.

Potential Difficulties

In order for studies such as those illustrated above to convince, they require a broad-based specialization, and any argument for the contextual repositioning of a particular lexical item, theological concept, or narrative motif included within a Qur'anic exemplum must be built on a sound historical, textual, and rhetorical basis if it is to present a plausible thesis. There are substantial pitfalls inherent in a methodology that requires the positing of hypothetical oral traditions, a widely held position (see, *inter alia*, Bodman 2011: 43; Griffith 2007: 89; Griffith 2008: 116; Griffith 2013: 91–2; Neuwirth 2009: 501; Pregill 2007; Zellentin 2013: 20 *et passim*). Furthermore, the question of the directionality of this dialogue remains in need of constant reappraisal. Thus, there is evidence of two-way transfer in the usage of late antique theological terms. Sean Anthony remarks, with regard to *ṣibghat Allāh* in Q. 2:138: 'even with the evidence of the (Christian) usage of *ṣibgha* as baptism in one text by the ninth century CE, the importance of this text for interpreting Qurʾān 2:138 is severely attenuated by the likelihood that this Christian usage of *ṣibgha* for "baptism" arises from the influences of Quranic diction and/or the Quranic exegetical tradition on Christian Arabic rather than from autochthonous Christian usage' (Anthony 2014: 124, building upon Swanson 1998). The authenticity of the proposed point of contact between the Qur'an's rhetoric and the theological or cultural entity for which interaction is being posited must also be carefully established. As François de Blois observes, 'It is one thing to notice similarities between the teachings of two religious traditions, and another to construct a plausible historical model to account for the influence of one upon the other' (de Blois 2002); such assessments by their nature remain highly subjective.

Some of these problems can be illustrated via Kevin van Bladel's 2008 essay on the Qur'anic account of Dhū'l-Qarnayn at Q. 18:83–102, which uses the *Alexander Legend* (*Neṣḥānā dileh d-Aleksandros*), in a quasi-exegetical fashion to 'make sense of the cryptic Qurʾānic story' (van Bladel 2008: 179, see also Tesei 2014). Building on Reinink 2003, who dates the *Neṣḥānā* to between 629 and 630 on the strength of historical allusions contained therein, van Bladel justifies his initial assumption that the Qur'an might feasibly postdate the *Neṣḥānā* by fixing a relatively late date of between 632 and 656 for the passage in *Sūrat al-Kahf*, based upon traditional reports of the final compilation of the Qur'anic codex. This methodology, however, puts to one side the probable existence of oral versions both of the account in *Sūrat al-Kahf* prior to the creation of a written codex, and of the specifically narrative elements of the *Neṣḥānā*, whose pedigree is not addressed in Reinink's study. While Tommaso Tesei, in his 2014 refinement of van Bladel's argument, is more thorough in his analysis of a number of Alexander *topoi*, like van Bladel he concludes from this that 'the size and precision of these common elements [between the two texts] can be explained only by identifying the *Neṣḥānā* as the source of the Qurʾānic passage' (Tesei 2014: 274). That 'authors made the same choices independently of one another' is dismissed by Tesei as improbable (Tesei 2014: 279); the only model considered by Tesei is one in which written works serve as predecessors for other written works, as is evident in his conclusion that 'the author of the *Neṣḥānā* appears as the most plausible actor for the process of pasting together and cutting out episodes within and from the narration' (Tesei 2014: 287, see also 280–1).

In order to prove a direct derivative relationship between the two traditions, both van Bladel and Tesei emphasize the similarities and gloss over the disparities between the Qur'an and its supposed contextual foil. The Qur'anic exemplum is highly allusive, and makes no reference to vast tracts of the narrative line attested in the *Neṣḥānā*. Where the two sources would appear to utilize the same motif, there are substantial differences to the way these motifs are framed. These differences are sometimes so significant as to suggest that the motifs might not, in fact, be comparable at all.

To cite an initial example, the *Neṣḥānā* describes how Alexander declares his intention to discover what surrounds the edges of the earth, and prays to God for power over the entire earth. Van Bladel states that 'This in essence matches Q 18:83–84 ... where God gives the two-horned one power over the entire earth' (van Bladel 2008: 179). The precise wording of the Qur'anic passage is, however, 'We established him in the earth' (or 'land': *arḍ*), and a very similar statement is made of Joseph in Q. 12:21 and 12:56, of previous generations destroyed for their misdeeds at Q. 6:6, of the disbelievers at Q. 7:10, of the righteous at Q. 22:41, and of the Israelites at Q. 28:6. The Qur'anic expression does not appear to mean 'power over the *entire* earth' (emphasis mine) and it is not used exclusively for Dhū'l-Qarnayn or even for kings or political figures. This *could* be a translation of the wording of the *Neṣḥānā* into Qur'anic terms. It could equally well, however, refer to something else entirely.

More substantively, the Qur'an narrates how Dhū'l-Qarnayn travels by heavenly skycord to the place of the setting of the sun. There Dhū'l-Qarnayn comes across a people; he is given the choice between punishing them or showing them kindness (Q. 18:86). The *Neṣḥānâ*, in contrast, describes how Alexander sails for four months and twelve days to a distant land encircled by a fetid sea. Upon his arrival, Alexander asks to be given prisoners condemned to death so that he can send them into the sea to test the proverbial deadliness of the water. They all die, and Alexander abandons his attempt to cross the sea. Van Bladel sees this as a 'precise correspondence' to Q. 18:86–8 (van Bladel 2008: 180), a view corroborated by Tesei (Tesei 2014: 277). Tesei adds to this an observation that the fetid sea is, in other parts of the corpus of Alexander legends, described as a barrier which prevents Alexander from crossing into Paradise. Indeed, Tesei sees this reflected in the *Neṣḥānā*'s own description of the four rivers of Paradise: 'As for Paradise, He surrounded it with seas, rivers, and the ocean, the Fetid Sea, so that men cannot get close to it, nor can they see where the rivers have their source' (cited in Tesei 2014: 278). This sea is, therefore, an integral and important part of the Alexander legend as reflected in the *Neṣḥānā*. The journey to the setting of the sun, meanwhile, does occur within the *Neṣḥānā* narrative, but, as we shall see, independently of the fetid sea motif.

The discrepancies within the alleged parallels here are manifold. There are, for instance, significant differences in the nature of the water that is being referred to: in the Qur'anic account we have a localized pool, in the Syriac a ring of pus that encircles the earth. The water in the Arabic account is usually read as *ḥamiʾatin* and linked to the mud God uses to create Adam in Q. 15:26, 28, and 33. It is also however widely read in accordance with the Kufan variant *ḥāmiyatin*, which indicates scalding hot and is associated with hell at Q. 9:35 ('On the Day it is **heated up** in Hellfire'), Q. 88:4 ('as they enter the **blazing** fire') and Q. 101:11 ('a **blazing** fire'). In order for the Syriac and the Qur'anic texts to be read as equivalent, we must assume that the Syriac ring of pus-like sea is transformed into a boiling-hot (or murky) pool in order to reflect its new Qur'anic context, but the shift from a ring of presumably cold pus that prevents men from travelling beyond the bounds of the earth into a murky (or boiling hot) pool into which the sun sets, where Dhū'l-Qarnayn can have limited access to the tools of God's punishment, is by no means negligible.

Moreover, the Qur'anic punishment passage itself reads (Q. 18:86–8):

> We said, 'Dhū'l-Qarnayn, you may choose [which of them] to punish or show kindness to.' He said, 'We shall punish those who have done evil, and when they are returned to their Lord He will punish them [even more] severely, while those who believed and did good deeds will have the best of rewards: we shall command them to do what is easy for them.'

Van Bladel writes, 'When Alexander came to the people in the west, he tested the efficacy of the deadly, fetid waters with the lives of convicts. This passage helps to explain the option given, for no apparent reason, by God to Dhū'l-Qarnayn in the Qur'ān' (van Bladel 2008: 181). The transmutation of this punishment motif into Qur'anic terms does not, however, read like the blind transference of a motif from one context into another, and the either/or scenario of the Qur'anic exemplum is, in fact, reflected more closely in the *Neṣḥānā*'s preceding description of the brass and iron workers collected by Alexander on his travels. These are to be given the choice between remaining abroad, or returning to Egypt once their task is done (Budge 2003: 147):

> 'Give me seven thousand smiths, workers in brass and iron, to go with me; and when I come from the countries whither I am going, if they wish [to return] hither,

> I will send them, and if they wish [to stay in] one of the countries under my sovereign rule, I will grant it them, and they shall not give tribute to the king, but they shall give...to us.'

Both van Bladel and Tesei emphasize that the Qur'an and the *Neṣḥānā* reproduce the same narrative motifs in the same order (van Bladel 2008: 181; Tesei 2014: 274), but the parallels between the two sources are by no means clear-cut, and the suggestion that there is a *Neṣḥānā* 'punishment' intertext at play here would appear to obscure rather than clarify the Dhū'l-Qarnayn narrative.

To further confuse matters, in the Syriac legend these events do not occur at the place where the sun sets, as we see in the Qur'an ('when he came to the setting of the sun', Q. 18:86). Rather Alexander *travels* from the fetid sea to the place where the sun sets. The curiosities of the sun's path are mentioned independently to the details of Alexander's journey, but there is indeed mention of a people who must needs take refuge from the sun's rising by submerging themselves in the sea. This van Bladel sees as parallel to the Qur'anic allusion to 'people for whom We had provided no shelter' at the point of sunrise (Q. 18:90). However, the omission of any reference in the Qur'an to those who live in the mountains that line the sun's path is disquieting. The *Neṣḥānā* speaks of people who 'hide in the caves, for rocks are rent by [the sun's] burning heat and fall down, and whether they be men or beasts, as soon as the stones touch them they are consumed' (Budge 2003: 148). The transformation of the motif of shelter provided by sea or caves into one of 'no shelter' (*sitr*, Q. 18:90, cf. Q. 17:45, 41:22) is deserving of note. Although van Bladel states that 'Alexander's journeys west and east match Q 18:85–91...exactly in many specific details' (van Bladel 2008: 179), if the *Neṣḥānā* were indeed the 'source' of the Qur'anic exemplum, the extent to which the Qur'an would here be modifying its raw materials is worthy of significant attention.

Particularly disconcerting is the motif of the devastating wars described in the *Neṣḥānā* for when the wall constructed by Alexander is breached. This supposedly 'corresponds closely with Q. 18:99–102', a description of the end times which van Bladel includes as 'the fifth and last part of the story of Dhū'l-Qarnayn' (van Bladel 2008: 180). In the Qur'an, the reference to the barrier's future destruction at God's hands (Q. 18:98) does indeed occur adjacent to an eschatological section, running from the mention of the Last Day at Q. 18:99; there is some disagreement on where this section ends. Van Bladel sees a precise correspondence between the Qur'anic expression 'We shall let them surge against each other like waves' (Q. 18:99) and the Syriac 'kingdoms will fall upon each other'. In view of other Qur'anic eschatological passages (see e.g. the variety of scenarios depicted in Q. 27:87, 36:51, 39:68, 69:13–16, 78:18) such a direct connection seems unlikely: his declaration that 'relating Dhū'l-Qarnayn's first prophecy is...the very purpose of the story in the Qur'ān' (van Bladel 2008: 189) and 'God's judgment will come in a time of wars between great armies' (van Bladel 2008: 191) is somewhat overstated.

Furthermore, in the *Neṣḥānā*, the barriers erected by Alexander the Great will be breached by the Huns, who will then subjugate the earth for 114 years until the last Christian emperor appears. At this point God will bring about the end of the world. Van

Bladel sees the absence of such explicit Christian propaganda in *Sūrat al-Kahf* as evidence of its *removal* from the Qur'anic account. This final section of the *Neṣḥānā*, which transparently alludes, through the precision of its dates, to Heraclius' successes against the Persians in 628–30 CE, is however cited by van Bladel as a propagandist modification of the accounts of Gog and Magog in the New Testament Apocalypse of St John 20:7 and Ezekiel 38–9, among others (van Bladel 2008: 181); Tesei adduces the precise Caucasian geographical data included in this part of the *Neṣḥānā* in order to suggest that 'the version of the story of Alexander's wall that the Syriac author included in the *Neṣḥānā* probably originated in that geographical area' (Tesei 2014: 277). It seems more likely, therefore, that it is the *Neṣḥānā* that is the anomalous source here, and the Qur'an simply does not depart from an already established theme.

The cumulative instances of mismatch between the Qur'anic exemplum and the *Neṣḥānā* cast doubt on the accuracy of Tesei's conclusion that 'the Syriac text is the direct source of the Qur'anic pericope' (Tesei 2014: 283, see also 287), and a directly derivative relationship between the two traditions has been assumed rather than established. Without a contextualized discussion of the rhetorical benefit that might stem from such a deliberate rearrangement of supposedly pre-existing material, such studies remain, ultimately, incomplete.

Concluding Remarks

The enhanced understanding that the late antique context has added to our reading of *al-raqīm* (Griffith), *ṣarḥ* (Silverstein), *sabab* (van Bladel), *ṣibgha* (Anthony), *bayt* (Witztum), and many other Qur'anic terms, is testament to the potential value of this area of research. It is however evident from the above that there are a number of general, methodological stumbling blocks that require careful thought before any comparative study is undertaken. The insights that are provided by late antique narrative contexts rarely sit in total isolation to the medieval exegetical tradition: Griffith's reading of 'inscribed tablet' for *al-raqīm* is attested in countless Islamic sources, as he himself acknowledges. It is also clear that there remains a relative paucity of dedicated modern studies on the interface between Qur'anic narrative and rabbinic Judaism, while very few comparative studies engage with Ethiopic Christianity and the pre-Islamic Arab heritage beyond the identification of isolated words and themes.

The crucial importance of the Qur'anic context to any study of this type is stressed by a number of scholars. As Nicolai Sinai declares, 'not only must one read a given surah in the light of its contemporary historical context, but one must also carefully explore the possibility that it might stand in an interpretive relationship to some of the previous surahs' (Sinai 2009: 430). Walid Saleh asserts that 'a proper approach... is first and foremost an analysis of... the Qur'ān' (Saleh 2009: 659). Michael Marx declares that 'to retrace the real situation behind the text, we first have to read the verse in the context of the surah' (Marx 2009: 548). Sidney Griffith emphasizes the importance of our awareness of 'the literary, or scriptural, integrity of the Qur'an' (Griffith 2011: 321). Indeed, I would argue that the greatest unresolved weak point in the positing of a late antique context for Qur'anic exempla resides in attempts to expand factually condensed Qur'anic material through the wider narrative lens of late antique sources, without paying due diligence to the precise wording of the Qur'anic text. The identification of possible parallels is really just the starting point for any discussion of the likelihood of lexical or thematic transfer.

Bibliography

Abdel Haleem, M. A. S. *The Qur'an: A New Translation*. Oxford: Oxford University Press, 2010.

Anthony, Sean W. 'Further Notes on the Word *ṣibgha* in Qurʾān 2:138', *Journal of Semitic Studies* 59/1 (Spring 2014), 117–29.

Bauer, Thomas. 'The Relevance of Early Arabic Poetry for Qurʾānic Studies including Observations on *kull* and on Q. 22:27, 26:225, and 52:31'. In: A. Neuwirth, N. Sinai, and M. Marx (eds.). *The Qurʾān in Context: Historical and Literary Investigations into the Qurʾānic Milieu*, pp. 699–732. Leiden and Boston: Brill, 2009.

Bellamy, James A. 'Al-Raqīm or al-Ruqūd? A Note on Sūrah 18:9', *Journal of the American Oriental Society* 111/ 1 (1991), 115–17.

Bodman, Whitney. *The Poetics of Iblīs: Narrative Theology in the Qur'ān*. Cambridge, MA: Harvard University Press, 2011.

Budge, Ernest A. Wallis. *The History of Alexander the Great, Being the Syriac Version of the Pseudo Callisthenes. Edited from Five Manuscripts, with an English Translation and Notes.* Reprint. Piscataway, NJ: Gorgias Press, 2003.

De Blois, Francois. '*Naṣrānī* (Ναζωραῖος) and *Ḥanīf* (ἐθνικός): Studies on the Religious Vocabulary of Christianity and Islam', *Bulletin of the School of Oriental and African Studies* 65/1 (2002), 1–30.

Griffith, Sidney. 'Syriacisms in the "Arabic Qur'ān": Who were those who said "Allāh is third of three" according to *al-Mā'idah* 73?' In: Meir M. Bar-Asher et al. (eds.). *A Word Fitly Spoken: Studies in Mediaeval Exegesis of the Hebrew Bible and the Qurʾān; presented to Haggai Ben-Shammai*, pp. 83–110. Jerusalem: The Ben-Zvi Institute, 2007.

Griffith, Sidney. 'Christian Lore and the Arabic Qurʾān: The "Companions of the Cave" in Sūrat al-Kahf and in Syriac Christian Tradition'. In: Gabriel Said Reynolds (ed.). *The Qurʾān in its Historical Context*, pp. 109–37. London and New York: Routledge, 2008.

Griffith, Sidney. '*Al-Naṣāra* in the Qurʾān: A Hermeneutical Reflection'. In: Gabriel Said Reynolds (eds.). *New Perspectives on the Qurʾān: The Qurʾān in its Historical Context 2*, pp. 301–22. London and New York: Routledge, 2011.

Griffith, Sidney. *The Bible in Arabic: The Scriptures of the 'People of the Book' in the Language of Islam*. Princeton: Princeton University Press, 2013.

Marx, Michael. 'Glimpses of a Mariology in the Qurʾān: From Hagiography to Theology via Religious-Political Debate'. In: A. Neuwirth, N. Sinai, and M. Marx (eds.). *The Qurʾān in Context: Historical and Literary Investigations into the Qurʾānic Milieu*, pp. 533–63. Leiden and Boston: Brill, 2009.

Mourad, Sulaiman A. 'From Hellenism to Christianity and Islam: The Origin of the Palm Tree Story concerning Mary and Jesus in the Gospel of Pseudo-Matthew and the Qurʾān', *Oriens Christianus* 86 (2002), 205–19.

Netton, Ian Richard. 'Towards a Modern *tafsīr* of *Sūrat al-Kahf*: Structure and Semiotics', *Journal of Qurʾānic Studies* 2/1 (2000), 67–87.

Neuwirth, Angelika. 'The House of Abraham and the House of Amram: Genealogy, Patriarchal Authority, and Exegetical Professionalism'. In: A. Neuwirth, N. Sinai, and M. Marx (eds.). *The Qurʾān in Context: Historical and Literary Investigations into the Qurʾānic Milieu*, pp. 499–531. Leiden and Boston: Brill, 2009.

Pregill, Michael E. 'The Hebrew Bible and the Quran: The Problem of the Jewish "Influence" on Islam', *Religion Compass* 1/6 (2007), 643–59.

Reinink, G. J. 'Alexander the Great in Seventh-Century Syriac "Apocalyptic" Texts', *Byzantinorossica* 2 (2003), 150–78.

Reynolds, Gabriel Said. *The Qurʾān and its Biblical Subtext*. London and New York: Routledge, 2010.

Saleh, Walid, A. 'The Etymological Fallacy and Qurʾānic Studies: Muhammad, Paradise and Late Antiquity'. In: A. Neuwirth, N. Sinai, and M. Marx (eds.). *The Qurʾān in Context: Historical and Literary Investigations into the Qurʾānic Milieu*, pp. 649–98. Leiden and Boston: Brill, 2009.

Samir, Samir Khalil. 'The Theological Christian Influence on the Qurʾān: A Reflection'. In: Gabriel Said Reynolds (ed.). *The Qurʾān in its Historical Context*, pp. 141–62. London and New York: Routledge, 2008.

Shoemaker, Stephen J. 'Christmas in the Qurʾān: The Qurʾānic Account of Jesus' Nativity and Palestinian Local Tradition', *Jerusalem Studies in Arabic and Islam* 28 (2003), 11–39.

Silverstein, Adam. 'The Qurʾānic Pharaoh'. In: Gabriel Said Reynolds (ed.). *New Perspectives on the Qurʾān: The Qurʾān in its Historical Context* 2, pp. 467–77. London and New York: Routledge, 2011.

Sinai, Nicolai. 'The Qurʾān as Process'. In: A. Neuwirth, N. Sinai, and M. Marx (eds.). *The Qurʾān in Context: Historical and Literary Investigations into the Qurʾānic Milieu*, pp. 407–39. Leiden and Boston: Brill, 2009.

Sinai, Nicolai. 'Religious Poetry from the Qurʾānic Milieu: Umayya b. Abī l-Ṣalt on the Fate of the Thamūd', *Bulletin of the School of Oriental and African Studies* 74/3 (2011), 397–416.

Swanson, Mark. 'Beyond Prooftexting: Approaches to the Qur'an in Some Early Arabic Apologies', *Muslim World* 88 (1998), 305–7.

Tesei, Tommaso. 'The Prophecy of Ḏū-l-Qarnayn (Q 18:83–102) and the Origins of the Qurʾānic Corpus', *Miscellanea Arabica 2013–2014* (2014), 273–90.

van Bladel, Kevin. 'Heavenly Cords and Prophetic Authority in the Quran and its Late Antique Context', *Bulletin of the School of Oriental and African Studies* 70/2 (2007), 223–46.

van Bladel, Kevin. 'The *Alexander Legend* in the Qurʾān 18:83–102'. In: Gabriel Said Reynolds (ed.). *The Qurʾān in its Historical Context*, pp. 175–203. London and New York: Routledge, 2008.

Witztum, Joseph. 'The Foundations of the House (Q. 2:127)', *Bulletin of the School of Oriental and African Studies* 72/1 (2009), 25–40.

Zellentin, Holger. *The Qurʾān's Legal Culture: The* Didascalia Apostolorum *as a Point of Departure*. Tübingen: Mohr Siebeck, 2013.

CHAPTER 9

THE QUR'AN AND JUDAISM

REUVEN FIRESTONE

The Qur'an and Judaism

The Qur'an includes many characters and narratives, laws, notions, and even language that are familiar from the Bible, but they appear differently in their Qur'an contexts. Moreover, episodes from biblical stories may not appear in Qur'anic renderings, or Qur'anic stories may include material that does not appear in biblical renderings. So too, similar laws are often immediately recognizable but distinctive in each scriptural context. The remarkable likeness unsurprisingly raises the question of relationship. How does the Qur'an fit into the history of monotheist tradition and the relationship between monotheist expressions? How does one explain their striking similarities and equally glaring differences?

The Qur'an itself seems to reflect a consciousness of association with Jewish and Christian scripture, thought, and practice. The Qur'anic awareness also conveys a certain level of anxiety: 'Surely it [the Qur'an] is a communication sent down from the Lord of the worlds, which the trustworthy spirit has brought down on your heart [Muḥammad] so you will be one of the warners in a clear Arabic tongue. It is most certainly in the scriptures of the ancients. Is it not a sign for them that the learned among the Children of Israel know it?' (Q. 26:192–7). These verses raise a number of interesting issues. They argue that the Qur'an is authentic, which of course suggests that there were at least some among its audience who questioned its authenticity. They provide a source for the revelation and a mode for its transmission, justify its particular discourse in the Arabic language, and authorize the role of a new prophet. Moreover, the verses claim that it (the Qur'an, the revelation, the words, or at least the message) can be found also in the scriptures that are already known and claimed by other religious communities. It can even be asserted that the 'it' which 'the learned among the Children of Israel know' includes the entire discourse of the verses in question, including the claim for the authenticity of the new warner-messenger. The passage asserts outright that Jewish scholars already know about it.

These and many other verses express something of the natural tension inherent in and around the process of religious genesis. There is no neutral context for the birth of religion, for religions are always born into a world in which some already exist. And those established religions predictably resent the appearance of competition. The scripture and beliefs of a new religion are always scrutinized by contemporary observers in relation to prior scripture and religion, and the burden rests on the new faith to demonstrate to a mixed public of potential joiners and sceptics that it embodies authentic representations of the divine will.

New scripture must demonstrate its legitimacy specifically in relation to prior scripture and religious practice—or tradition in the event that established religion is not scriptural, as in the case of the ancient Near East. Proving authenticity and validity is typically accomplished through a process combining the condemnation of certain aspects of former scripture and religious practices or notions, and the appropriation of others (Deut. 6:14; Psalms 135:15–21; Gal. 3:6–14; Heb. 8:6–13). This is no less the case with the Qur'an, which also moves to correct problematic aspects of previously recognized scripture. The statement that God does not tire in Q. 50:38, for example, can be read to correct the suggestion in the Hebrew Bible that God felt the need to rest after Creation (Exod. 20:11, 31:17), and Q. 5:72–5 corrects the New Testament articulation of what has been understood as the divine nature of Jesus (Col. 1:14–20).

The Qur'an similarly considers and critiques Jewish law and practice as articulated in Jewish scripture and tradition. In Q. 16:114–18, for example, we observe a consideration of dietary law articulated in reference to the eating practices of Jews. 'Eat from what God has provided you that is lawful (*ḥalāl*) and wholesome, and give thanks for the favor of God, if it is Him you serve. God has forbidden you only dead things (*al-mayta*) and blood (*al-dam*) and the flesh of pigs (*laḥm al-khinzīr*), and anything offered up to something other than God... But do not assert a falsehood with your tongues, saying "this is permissible and this is forbidden," to invent a lie against God. Those who invent a lie against God will not thrive... We forbade for the Jews what We have told you before. We did not oppress them; rather, they oppressed themselves' (see also Q. 3:93–4, and Cf. Lev. 11, Deut. 14:3–21).

Three Theses of Relationship

These and many more cases reflect a complex intertextual relationship between the new revelation of the Qur'an as the word of God and prior revelations of God's word. Modern scholars have reflected on this connection and have suggested a variety of propositions to account for it. These can be broken down, roughly, into three groups.

The 'Borrowing Thesis'

Those holding this approach generally presume that Muḥammad wrote the Qur'an and that parallels between it and prior scripture result from his having learned much of his information from Jews or Christians. The borrowing thesis reflects an old argument found in both Jewish and Christian pre-modern polemics, namely, that Muḥammad was not a prophet and that the Qur'an which he brought was not a divine revelation. The fact that the borrowing thesis is addressed and rejected by the Qur'an itself is a demonstration of the pertinence of the proposition: '... They say "you are a forger." No! Most of them do not know [anything]. Say, "The holy spirit [*rūḥ al-qudus*] has brought it down from your Lord in truth..." We know that they say, "But a human teaches him." [But] the language that they wrongly attribute to him is foreign, while this language is clear Arabic' (Q. 16:101–3).

The assumption of Qur'anic borrowing is articulated in its classic modern Jewish form by Abraham Geiger (d. 1874), one of the earliest modern comparative scholars of the Qur'an (*Was hat Mohammed aus dem Judenthume aufgenommen?* 1833). Geiger, however, along with most Jewish scholars, took an approach that differed both from the pre-modern articulations and also from most of their Christian colleagues engaged in the same endeavour, in that the Jewish analysis tended to be less politically charged (Pregill 2007: 650; Lassner 1999).

Geiger, unlike many of his Jewish and Christian colleagues engaged in study of the Qur'an, considered Muḥammad a sincere religious enthusiast and not a pretender seeking political or material gain by inventing a new religion. He held that because Muḥammad was unlearned and wished to validate what he believed to be the genuine heavenly status of the Qur'an, he sought to use material known to derive from prior scripture. Jews were greatly esteemed as an ancient monotheist community during Muḥammad's lifetime, so it would have been natural to incorporate Jewish wisdom in order to strengthen his belief that he was taught by direct revelation from God. According to Geiger, Muḥammad had abundant opportunity to learn from local Jews, but because the Jews of Arabia possessed no written scripture, his knowledge of Judaism and Bible derived from an oral tradition. It is the fluidity and exegetical nature of oral tradition that explains the disparity between Qur'anic and biblical material.

Geiger's general approach was taken up by subsequent scholars such as Charles Cutler Torrey (1933) and Irwin Rosenthal (1961). Meanwhile, Christian scholars often held the view that Muḥammad borrowed his ideas from Christians (Wellhausen 1887; Smith 1897; and to a certain extent Bell 1926), while some suggested that he borrowed equally from both (Margoliouth 1905).

The 'Cultural Diffusion Thesis'

Geiger and other Western scholars of the Qur'an prior to the late nineteenth and early twentieth centuries pre-dated the development of modern anthropological and literary studies in cultural diffusion, orality, and the transmission of tradition, and modern and postmodern literary theories of composition and literary assimilation. These developments have had a profound impact on Qur'an scholarship ever since, though some lesser informed investigators continue to work with the pre-twentieth-century assumptions. Certainly since the mid-twentieth century, the major approach to comparative studies of Qur'an and Bible assumes processes of cultural diffusion through which non-indigenous notions and themes entered into local cultures, a perspective developed in a different context by Leo Frobenius (1898). According to the 'cultural diffusion thesis', the Qur'an naturally reflects a great deal of Jewish as well as Christian and other traditions and ideas through one or more processes of transmission across the porous boundaries of culture.

According to one articulation of this perspective, biblical and religious ideas deriving from Judaism and Christianity came to Arabia with the migration of Jews and Christians who brought their religious notions, practices, and stories of biblical characters with them. As the religious newcomers integrated into Arabian culture and societies, their religious *realia* became integrated into Arabian culture as well, so it was natural for the Qur'an to reflect these along with all the other cultural and intellectual material through which its message is articulated (Firestone 1990). An advantage of this approach is that it allows for a wider range of possibilities to explain the origin of the Qur'an. Not only could it have developed as a human product that reflects the contemporary literary *realia* of its culture, it could have developed as a divine message articulated via the language and culture, images and metaphors current among the receiving population.

The 'Semitic Civilization Thesis'

A somewhat different perspective is found in the work of Michel Cuypers, who takes a structure analysis approach (also called 'rhetorical analysis', Cuypers 2009: 30). Cuypers argues that both Western and traditional Muslim analyses of Qur'anic intertextuality with the Bible have been limited by the overwhelming intellectual appeal of Greek rhetorical analysis, which by its very nature, is unable to appreciate the particulars of the Semitic rhetorical style that governs the structure of the Qur'an. By engaging in a more culturally appropriate approach, one can discern the deep cultural and literary continuity with prior Semitic traditions. According to Cuypers, the Qur'an, similar to the Bible, 're-appropriates earlier writings, reusing them and turning them to a new perspective which makes revelation advance' (31). This approach assumes the continuous presence of what is commonly understood as 'biblical' themes in Semitic cultures external to the particular cultural and literary environment of the Bible. Arabia, like the Land of Israel, contained its own particular versions of a common library of ancient Near Eastern literatures, which existed in particular dialectical form wherever it was found. So-called 'biblical' material found in the Qur'an, therefore, was not inherently biblical. It was neither borrowed by a prophet nor deposited by visitors from outside, but existed as a basic part of Arabian civilization, just as it existed as a basic part of West Semitic or Mesopotamian civilization, available to be shaped by the particularities of history. A similar proposal has been suggested by others (Firestone 2000). One significant advantage of this approach is its neutral perspective, which places Qur'an and Bible on an equal footing in their unique formulation and creative treatment of common themes.

Both the 'borrowing' and 'cultural diffusion' approaches have been criticized as reflecting Western Orientalist perspectives, though they are no less sympathetic to the Qur'an than they are to the Bible. Nevertheless, they also evoke older, pre-modern polemical arguments used by members of established religions to delegitimize the Qur'an. These polemics began quite early. The Byzantine monk and historian, Theophanes the Confessor (d. 818), for example, claimed that Jews were persuaded to join the false-prophet Muḥammad until they learned that he was not the messiah they were expecting. Some remained with him out of fear and managed to prejudice him against Christianity by telling him lies that were presumably preserved in the text of the Qur'an (Theophanes, *Chronicle*, Annus Mundi 6122 [p. 464]). Some pre-modern Jewish texts from as early as the tenth to eleventh centuries found in the Cairo Geniza, a repository of ancient manuscripts from the ninth to nineteenth centuries discovered in the storage room of an ancient Cairo synagogue, claim that Jews infiltrated Muḥammad's entourage and actually wrote the Qur'an for him as a recognizable but flawed Jewish text, and embedded codes to prove that it is not the record of a truly divine revelation (Firestone 2014). These perspectives reflect the generally hostile environment that has typified the intellectual as well as political relations between the monotheistic traditions (Firestone 2011). That polemical environment is reflected in the Qur'anic perspective toward Jews and Judaism as well.

The Qur'an on Judaism

Common Arabic terms for Judaism, *al-yahūdiyya* and *diyānat al-yahūd*, do not occur in the Qur'an, even though Judaism was known in seventh-century Arabia (Rubin 2003). Al-Bukhārī includes references attributed to Muḥammad about conversion to Judaism with the word *hawwada* (*Janāʾiz* 440, 4401), and the Qur'an itself uses an idiom for Judaizing, *al-ladhīna hādū*, to refer to 'those who have Judaized' or 'those who have become Jews', though this expression may have been understood as a reference to 'those who are/have been Jews' (Q. 2:62; 4:46, 160; 5:44, etc.). Despite the lack of a specific referent for the religion or religious civilization of Judaism, the Qur'an refers frequently to Jews and occasionally also to Jewish practices.

Contemporary Arabian Jews as Reflected in the Qur'an

The Qur'an uses a wide variety of terms to refer to Jews. The most common is 'Children of Israel' (*banū isrāʾīl*) which appears forty-three times, and often refers to the ancient Israelites in narrations of stories with clear parallels from the Hebrew Bible. The term can also refer to Jews contemporary to the Qur'an, but in these cases it is evocative of their biblical origins and especially indicative of the biblical stories about Israelite opposition and even rebellion against God and Moses. Paralleled to this appellation are such terms as 'the people of Moses' (*qawm mūsā*) or in reference to Moses, 'his people' (*qawmihi*). 'Those who have Judaized' (*al-ladhīna hādū*) occurs ten times, 'Jews' (*al-yahūd*) eight times, and 'Jew' or 'Jewish' (*yahūdī*) once, these three latter terms referring to Jews living within the period of the Qur'an's emergence.

Another common locution is various forms of 'People of the Book' (*ahl al-kitāb*), which occurs thirty-three times: '[those] who have been given the Book' (*al-ladhīna ūtū al-kitāb*) nineteen times, '[those] whom We have given the Book' (*al-ladhīna ātaynā al-kitāb*) six times, [those] who have been given a portion of the Book (*al-ladhīna ūtū naṣīb*[an] *min al-kitāb*) three times, and occasionally other locutions such as '[those] who read/recite the Book' (*al-ladhīna yaqra'ūna al-kitāb*) or 'successors who have inherited the Book' (*khalfun warithu al-kitāb*), and People of the Reminder (*ahl al-dhikr*) twice, in which Reminder (*dhikr*) becomes a synonym (also elsewhere) for divine writ. These designations refer in general to people who are in possession of pre-Qur'anic scripture, meaning both Jews and Christians. While the terms may refer only to Jews, only to Christians or to both simultaneously, the contexts in which they appear most often reflect reference specifically to Jews. The distinctive language of the references is sometimes purposeful, such as the locution 'those who were given a portion of the Book', which suggests that the previous scriptures are not the only legitimate divine revelations (Rubin 2003).

The Qur'an uses still other terms, such as '[those] who have been given the Knowledge beforehand' (*al-ladhīna ūtū al-ʿilm min qablihi*, Q. 17:107), and the collective 'one who has knowledge of the Book' (*man ʿindahu ʿilmu al-kitāb*, Q. 13:43) which probably refers not only to Jews and Christians but also to followers of the Prophet. Other appellations include 'People of Abraham' (*āl ibrāhīm*, Q. 4:54), who were given 'the Book and the wisdom and... a great kingdom,' and 'the tribes' (*al-asbāṭ*) which always (four times) occur in the expression, 'Abraham, Ishmael, Isaac, Jacob and the tribes'.

The Qur'an also refers to two additional categories within the community of Jews. One refers to rabbis (*rabbāniyūn*, Q. 3:79; 5:44, 63) and perhaps Q. 3:14 (*rabbiyyūn*), and the other to scholar-colleagues (*aḥbār*, Q. 5:44, 63; 9:34), the latter category known in the Talmud as learned Jews who are slightly less accomplished than rabbis (Jastrow 1903: 421–2; Sokoloff 2002: 428).

The large number and variety of references to Jews, and as we shall observe below also Jewish practice, show how Jews and Judaism were significant to the emergence of the Qur'an. The Qur'an calls on sceptics to consult with the 'People of the Reminder' to learn the truth about revelation and scripture (Q. 16:43–4), and even instructs the Prophet to consult '[those who] have been reciting the Book before you' if he has any doubt the revelation he himself received (Q. 10:94). The hadith also mentions both directly and indirectly how Jews were a respected community of monotheists in the pre- and earliest Islamic periods (Bukhārī, *anbiyā'* 50; Kister 1972). The recognized status of Jews in the Arabian communities in which they lived seems to have persuaded many people considering new claims to divine revelation to take Jewish ideas, practices, and opinions into account. Because established religions inevitably oppose the emergence of new religions, and because Jews represented one important established monotheist community that resisted the advancement of a new expression of monotheism, it is natural for Jewish opinions and practices to appear in the Qur'an. In most but not all cases, the Jewish opinions, practices, and behaviours found in the Qur'an are critiqued in polemical contexts.

Torah and Covenant

The Torah (*tawrāt*) appears by name eighteen times in the Qur'an, and it is referred to by other names such as the Book (*al-kitāb*), the Remembrance (or the Reminder, *al-dhikr*), and the Redemption (or Deliverance, *al-furqān*), these last three terms being used also for the Qur'an. Sometimes, the Qur'an associates *tawrāt* with the law in the first five books of the Hebrew Bible (Q. 3:93), which are also known in Jewish religious parlance as *Torah*. In other contexts, *tawrāt* refers to a larger corpus of Hebrew Bible literatures (Q. 5:43–6). Other terms referring to a portion of the Hebrew Bible are *zabūr*, perhaps referring to Psalms (Q. 4:163) and *ṣuḥuf*, referring to sheets or scrolls associated with Moses and/or Abraham (Q. 87:19). 'Tablets' (*alwāḥ*) refers to what God gave to Moses (Q. 7:150). God gave Moses the Book as a guidance (*hudan*) for the Israelites (Q. 17:2) and made with them a covenant (Q. 2:83) (Adang 2003).

The Torah is the record of a true divine revelation (Q. 5:44), confirmed both by Jesus (Q. 3:50) and the Prophet (Q. 3:3). The giving of revelation is associated with the divine covenant God gave to Israel at the mountain (Q. 4:154, that is Sinai through association with Q. 23:20, 95:2), and which God will not break (Q. 2:80). The Torah contains the judgement of God, guidance, and light (Q. 5:43–4). The Jews, however, broke their covenant (Q. 4:155; 5:13)—or, some Jews broke their covenant (Q. 13:25) and perverted their scripture either by distorting the text (Q. 5:13) or by twisting the meaning of the words (Q. 4:46). The Torah and the Gospel teach about the coming of the new Prophet (Q. 3:81; 7:157; 61:6), but the People of the Book conceal the truth that they know from their own scripture (Q. 2:146).

The Torah contains divine laws, but some of the laws therein are punishments inflicted upon the Jews for taking usury, oppressing the poor, and turning people away from God (Q. 4:160–1). Jews accepted the scripture revealed directly to them, but they refused to accept subsequent divine revelations including the Qur'an, for which God is extremely angry with them (Q. 2:87–91). Some did not even accept their own Torah (Q. 62:5). Prophecies of the coming of Prophet Muḥammad are given in the Torah (Q. 3:81; 7:157), but they were concealed by Jews (Q. 2:146, 3:71). Israelites/Jews disbelieved the divine signs, disobeyed God, and killed their own prophets (Q. 2:61). They did not accept God's revelation given through Jesus (Q. 3:52) nor the new revelation given through Muḥammad (Q. 4:153). Because of their refusal, most Jews are not true believers (Q. 3:110; 26:67).

This elaborate position regarding prior revelation and those who claim to follow it reflects the complexity of relationship between emergent monotheism and established monotheism. A similar position is found in the New Testament in relation to the Hebrew Bible. In fact, the very reference to the Hebrew Bible as the 'Old Testament' in Christian parlance conveys the ambivalence of the relationship. On the one hand, it is true revelation. On the other, its history and promise are incomplete and unfulfilled as long as its completion in the New Testament (or testimony) of God is not accepted. 'By speaking of a new one [referring to the covenant or testament—*diathéké*—in Heb. 8:8], he has pronounced the first one old; and anything that is growing old and aging will shortly disappear' (Heb. 8:13). Establishment monotheisms are not inherently or entirely wrong, according to newly emergent monotheisms, but neither are they practised correctly or carried out according to the true will of God.

The Qur'an represents itself as a continuation or expression of the same message found in the Torah (and Gospel) tradition (Q. 3:3–4). Given that the Jews did not follow the divine message given specifically to them, it should not be surprising that they resist or even oppose the message given through a new prophet (Q. 3:184; 6:91–3).

On the other hand, some People of the Book are indeed believers, believing in God and what was revealed to the new community of believers as well as their own community (Q. 3:199), though those among adherents of prior religions who actually carry out God's will represent a minority (Q. 3:113–14). The Qur'an also contains material that seems to reflect positively on Jews in general—not simply on a minority that goes against the grain of normative Jewish practice or belief. These verses refer to Jews along with believers, Christians, and Sabeans (an unidentified religious community) as people 'who believe in God, the Last Day, and do righteousness'. They need not fear, for they will be rewarded by God (Q. 2:62; 5:69). They believe in the Book given to them prior to the revelation of the Qur'an, and 'when [that prior Book] is recited to them they say, "We believe in it, for it is the truth from our Lord. We have certainly submitted ourselves [to God] beforehand"' (Q. 28:52–3). It appears, therefore, that at least in some Qur'anic layers, People of the Book who remain Jews or Christians may hold the same status as believers, meaning followers of the new prophet and revelation (Donner 2002–3). Some interpreters of Q. 2:62 and Q. 5:69, however, understand the description of the religiosity among these groups to be a limiting qualifier, meaning that these verses refer only to those among the aforementioned groups who do indeed believe in God, the Last Day, and do righteousness—not Jews and Christians in general.

Qur'an Supportive of Jewish Ritual Practice and Piety

The Qur'an allows believers to eat the food and marry the virtuous women of those who have been given the Book (Q. 5:5). Likewise, the requirement for fasting is introduced as a requirement upon the believers just as it was required for those—presumably Jews—before them (Q. 2:183). Synagogues as well as churches, mosques, and other places 'in which the name of God is mentioned often' are to be respected and protected (Q. 22:40). Some of the People of the Book are very pious. 'They recite the verses of God during the hours of the night and prostrate themselves' (Q. 3:113). In a reference to the revelation of the Qur'an is found a comparative note that 'those who have been given the Knowledge beforehand, when it is recited to them they fall down on their faces [lit. "chins"] in prostration and say, "Glory to our Lord! Surely the promise of our Lord has been fulfilled!"' (Q. 17:107–8). Elsewhere, '[those] to whom We have given the Book' are doubly rewarded because 'they have endured, they drive off evil with good, and contribute from what We have provided them. When they hear idle talk they turn away and say, "We keep our behaviors and you keep your behaviors. Peace be upon you. We are not interested in the ignorant"' (Q. 28:54–5).

Jewish Practices and Beliefs Reflected in the Qur'an

The Qur'an occasionally refers innocently to normative Jewish practice, such as the Jewish legal obligation (*halakhah*) to ransom Jewish captives (Q. 2:85). It also notes that there are People of the Book (perhaps sectarians?) whom it perceives as worshipping idols (Q. 5:64), a common problem of the ancient Israelites critiqued frequently in the Hebrew Bible. Elsewhere the Qur'an criticizes Jews for saying ʿUzayr is the son of God' in parallel with the complaint that Christians say, 'Al-Masīḥ is the son of God' (Q. 9:30), and that both revere their religious leaders and teachers as lords (Q. 9:31—perhaps a play on the Hebrew word *rabbi*, which is linguistically equivalent to the Qur'anic term, 'my Lord', *rabbī*). As noted, fasting and Sabbath observance are mentioned in the Qur'an and not criticized as false behaviours, though the Qur'an criticizes some Jews for not observing the Sabbath properly as commanded in the Torah (Q. 2:63–6; 4:47, 54; 7:163).

Qur'an Condemning of Jewish Behaviour

More often than not, the Qur'an is more condemning than admiring or even neutral regarding Jewish behaviour, and this is articulated in a manner that is reminiscent of the attacks upon Jews found in the New Testament (Reynolds 2010; Rubin 2003: 23). Some Jews believe in the divine message brought by the new emissary of God's word, but most are condemned for criticizing or worse, denouncing both the messenger and the message of God. They hinder believers from joining the new religion (Matt. 23:13–14/Q. 2:109; 3:99) and stir up the locals against the new messenger (Acts 14:2/Q. 3:181; 6:147). They do not keep the very revelation that they were personally given by

God (Acts 7:53/Q. 2:89), and they believe wrongly that they are God's only chosen people (Rom. 4:29, 11:7/Q. 2:94; 62:6). Jews [Children of Israel] committed the horrendous sin of killing their own prophets long before the advent of the new revelation and its messenger (Matt. 23:30–1/Q. 2:61; 3:183).

Additionally, the Jews were covenanted with God to teach their Scripture to the people at large, but they ignored it and considered it of no value (Q. 3:187), and they even concealed it (Q. 2:159, 2:174). They disbelieve the signs of God (or God's verses of revelation—*ayāt Allāh*—Q. 3:70, 3:98). They failed to observe the Sabbath as required by the covenant and were cursed as a result (Q. 2:63–6; 4:154–5). They turned many away from the path of God, unlawfully took usury, and falsely consumed the resources of the people, for which they were punished with severe legal strictures (Q. 4:160–1). They are arrogant in their claim, along with Christians, that they are the children of God (Q. 5:18). Jews (or perhaps Zoroastrians?) claim that they are purer than others (the subjects are not identified—Q. 4:49). Jews, like idolaters, are the most hostile toward the believers (Q. 5:82).

Caution not to be Influenced by People of the Book

People of the Book are depicted in the Qur'an as actively discouraging people from appreciating the new revelation and religion. 'Neither the Jews nor the Christians will ever be pleased with you until you follow their creed (*milla*)' (Q. 2:120, see also Q. 2:135, 2:142). 'O you who believe, do not take as associates those who were given the Book before you or disbelievers who take your religion in mockery and jest' (Q. 5:57, see also 5:51, 42:15, 45:18). Abraham and other foundational figures were not Jews or Christians, but represented a primordial monotheism that preceded the religions practised at the time of Qur'anic revelation by Jews and Christians (Q. 2:140, 2:135; 3:65, 3:67–8). People should therefore resist the attempt of Jews and Christians to malign the new message brought by the Prophet and the practices of the new community of Believers.

Conclusion: The Qur'an in a Phenomenology of Emergent Religions

The Qur'an represents Jews, along with Christians, as devotees of established monotheistic religions that were challenged by the emergence of a new and threatening expression of monotheism. The Jews as a community rejected the new prophet and the revelation that he brought (Q. 2:89–90, 2:105; 4:153), though some individuals and perhaps small groups joined the new community of Believers (Q. 3:199).

The tension between established and newly emergent religions continues to influence religionists long after as the consequential polemics become embedded in religious civilization. Those who remain identified with established religions naturally incline toward the critique employed by their forebears against once emergent religions, and those who identify with the emergent religion tend to engage the kinds of perspectives that their religious ancestors engaged during the time of their religions' genesis. These unintentional predispositions affect nearly everybody, sometimes including scholarly researchers.

Current methodologies influenced by postmodern, post-colonial, and gender studies have sensitized researchers to the complexity of identity construction and the impact that has on one's perspectives and overall worldview. As scholars continue to develop analytical and self-analytical tools, we will observe continued development in the approach and results of research on the elusive relationship between the Qur'an and prior religions and their sacred scriptures.

Bibliography

Adang, Camilla. 'Torah', In: Jane Dammen McAuliffe (ed.). *Encyclopaedia of the Qur'ān*. 6 vols., 5:300–11 Leiden: Brill, 2001–6.

Bell, Richard. *The Origin of Islam in its Christian Environment*. London: Frank Cass, 1926.

Cuypers, Michel. *The Banquet: A Reading of the Fifth Sura of the Qur'an*. Miami: Convivium Press, 2009.

Donner, Fred. 'From Believers to Muslims: Confessional Self-Identity in the Early Muslim Community', *al-Abhath* 50–1 (2002–3), 9–53.

Firestone, Reuven. *Journeys in Holy Lands: The Evolution of the Abraham-Ishmael Legends in Islamic Exegesis*. Albany: State University of New York Press, 1990.

Firestone, Reuven. 'Comparative Studies in Bible and Qur'an: A Fresh Look at Genesis 22 in Light of Surah 37'. In: Benjamin Hary, John Hayes, and Fred Astren (eds.). *Judaism and Islam: Boundaries, Communication and Interaction: Essays in Honor of William M. Brinner*, pp. 169–84. Leiden: Brill, 2000.

Firestone, Reuven. 'The Qur'an and the Bible: Some Modern Studies of their Relationship'. In: John C. Reeves (ed.). *Bible and Qur'an: Essays in Scriptural Intertextuality*, pp. 1–22. Atlanta: Society of Biblical Literature, 2003.

Firestone, Reuven. 'Chosenness and the Exclusivity of Truth'. In: Reuven Firestone, James Heft, and Omid Safi (eds.). *Learned Ignorance: An Investigation into Humility in Interreligious Dialogue between Christians, Muslims and Jews*, pp. 107–28. Oxford: Oxford University Press, 2011.

Firestone, Reuven. 'Muhammad in Pre-modern Jewish Literatures'. In: Christiane Gruber and Avinoam Shalom (eds.). *The Image of the Prophet between Ideal and Ideology*, pp. 27–44. Berlin: De Gruyter, 2014.

Frobenius, Leo. *Der westafrikanische Kulturkreis*. Gotha: Justus Perthes, 1898.

Geiger, Abraham. *Was hat Mohammed aus dem Judenthume aufgenommen*? Bonn, 1833; Eng. trans. *Judaism and Islam*. Madras, 1874 (repr. New York: Ktav, 1970).

Jastrow, Marcus. *A Dictionary of the Targumim, the Talmud Babli and Yerushalmi, and the Midrashic Literature*. London: Luzac, 1903.

Kister, M. J. '*Ḥaddithū 'an banī isrā'īla wa-lā ḥaraja*: A Study of an Early Tradition', *Israel Oriental Studies* 2 (1972), 215–39.

Lassner, Jacob. 'Abraham Geiger: A Nineteenth-Century Jewish Reformer on the Origins of Islam', pp. 103–35. In: Martin Kramer (ed.). *The Jewish Discovery of Islam*. Tel Aviv: Tel Aviv University, 1999.

Margoliouth, David Samuel. *Mohammed and the Rise of Islam*. New York & London: G. P. Putnam's Sons, 1905.

Pregill, Michael. 'The Hebrew Bible and the Qurʾān: The Problem of the Jewish "Influence" on Islam', *Religion Compass* 1/6 (2007), 643–59.

Reynolds, Gabriel. 'On the Qurʾānic Accusation of Scriptural Falsification (*taḥrīf*) and Christian Anti-Jewish Polemic', *Journal of the American Oriental Society* 130 (2010), 1–14.

Rosenthal, Erwin. *Judaism and Islam*. London: Yoseloff, 1961.

Rubin, Uri. 'Jews and Judaism', In: Jane Dammen McAuliffe (ed.). *Encyclopaedia of the Qurʾān*. 6 vols., 3:21–34. Leiden: Brill, 2001–6.

Smith, Henry P. *The Bible and Islam: The Influence of the Old and New Testaments on the Religion of Mohammed*. New York: Charles Scribner's Sons, 1897.

Sokoloff, Michael. *A Dictionary of Jewish Babylonian Aramaic*. Ramat Gan: Bar Ilan University Press, 2002.

Stroumsa, Sarah. 'Jewish Polemics against Islam and Christianity in Light of Judaeo-Arabic Texts'. In: N. Golb (ed.). *Judeo-Arabic Studies: Proceedings of Founding Conference*, pp. 241–50. Amsterdam: Harwood Academic, 1997.

Stroumsa, Sarah. 'Islam in the Historical Consciousness of Jewish Thinkers of the Arab Middle Ages'. In: N. Ilan (ed.). *The Intertwined Worlds of Islam: Essays in Memory of Hava Lazarus-Yafeh* (Hebrew), pp. 443–58. Jerusalem: Ben Zvi Institute, 2002.

Theophanes the Confessor. *The Chronicle of Theophanes Confessor (Byzantine and Near Eastern History* AD *284–813)*. Trans. with introduction and commentary by Cyril Mango and Roger Scott, with the assistance of Geoffrey Greatrex. Oxford: Oxford University Press, 1997.

Torrey, Charles Cutler. *The Jewish Foundation of Islam*. New York: Bloch, 1933.

Wellhausen, Julius. *Reste arabischen Heidentums*. Berlin: Georg Reimer, 1887.

CHAPTER 10

THE QUR'AN AND CHRISTIANITY

NEAL ROBINSON

Issues in Methodology

The Problem of Normative Christianity

The main denominations (the Roman Catholic, Orthodox, Anglican, and the various Protestant Churches) have the same canon of 27 New Testament writings. They also all acknowledge the authority of the creedal statements and definitions of faith issued by the fourth- and fifth-century ecumenical councils of Nicaea, Constantinople, Ephesus, and Chalcedon. Not surprisingly therefore, scholars from within those Churches often assume that they are heirs to the non-negotiable common core of authentic Christianity.

This state of affairs is the result of the vicissitudes of history. Jesus' disciples were Aramaic-speaking Torah-observant Palestinian Jews who revered him as a teacher and miracle-worker. After the crucifixion, they experienced visions that convinced them that he was the Messiah and that he had been raised into God's presence, from whence he would shortly return in glory. But that did not alter the fact that for them he was essentially human. However, the Jewish rebellion against Rome, which resulted in the destruction of the temple in 70 CE, led in turn to the increasing marginalization of the original Palestinian Jesus movement and the prevalence of the Gentile-orientated Churches in Greece, Asia Minor, and Rome, that had been founded by Paul or were influenced by his theology. Christians in these Churches worshipped Jesus as the pre-existent Son of God whose sacrificial death established a new covenant that superseded the old covenant with Israel based on the Torah.

The conversion of Constantine in 312 CE was the second major turning point in the history of dogma. It initiated a period of consolidation, in which the canon of the Greek

New Testament was fixed, and successive Byzantine emperors summoned councils of bishops to define Christian doctrine and condemn heresies. The canon marks the triumph of Pauline Christianity. The four Gospels record Jesus' putative teaching in Greek, rather than Aramaic, and they set it in a narrative framework that foregrounds the crucifixion, the central focus of Paul's theology. Seven of the New Testament letters were written by Paul himself; a further six were attributed to him pseudonymously; and many of the other writings, including the quasi-historical Acts of the Apostles, were written by his posthumous followers or admirers. In this period too, works of second- and third-century authors who saw themselves as guardians of the apostolic tradition were copied and circulated, whereas those of their 'heretical' opponents generally fell out of favour. This led to a distorted image of pre-Constantinian Christianity as essentially proto-orthodox. Despite persecution, however, so-called 'heresies' thrived among the linguistic minorities at the margins of the empire as well as in neighbouring Persia. Unless one subscribes to the view that might is right, or believes that the triumph of the Nicene-Chalcedonian faith was providential, there is no cogent reason for regarding some of these less well-known forms of Christianity as deviant or inferior.

The Problem of Normative Islamic Tradition

At first sight, the early history of Islam seems very different. The Qur'an is written in Arabic, the language of the Prophet and his Companions. Islam became the state religion in Medina during the Prophet's lifetime, and the standard edition of the Qur'an was promulgated by ʿUthmān within twenty years of the Prophet's death. To be sure, there are major differences between Sunnī and Shīʿa, with the latter preferring traditions transmitted by the imams and their followers to those traced to the Prophet via the Companions. Nevertheless, there is a consensus that the revelations were memorized from the very first and that the ʿUthmānic text accords with the uninterrupted oral transmission from the Prophet.

From the standpoint of critical historiography however, the picture is less clear. In the formative period of Islam there were several momentous politico-religious developments. In 637, when the Arabs conquered Jerusalem, ʿUmar restored religious sanctity to the Temple Mount after centuries of Christian disrespect for Judaism's holiest site. In 661, with the triumph of the Umayyads, the centre of power shifted from Medina, a desert oasis with a sizeable Jewish minority, to Damascus, an ancient centre of Graeco-Roman civilization and Christian orthodoxy. It shifted again in 762 when the Abbasids founded Baghdad near the ruins of Ctesiphon, the former Persian capital, not far from the renowned Jewish academies that produced the Babylonian Talmud. The *Sīra* of Ibn Hishām (d. 213/828–9 or 218/833) and the standard hadith collections were all compiled after this last date. To be sure the editors worked with earlier sources, some of them originating in Medina, but they inevitably included material that read later beliefs and practices back into the lifetime of the Prophet. Yet if the Islamic tradition is discounted, the internal evidence of the Qur'an is scarcely sufficient even to anchor the revelations in time and space. Nor can we be certain when the consonantal text was finalized. We do not know whether the earliest extant manuscripts of the text attributed to ʿUthmān, such as the *scriptio superior* of the Ṣanʿāʾ palimpsest, are pre-Umayyad or early Umayyad (Déroche 2014).

The Problem of Revisionist Historians of Early Islam

Since the 1970s, a number of non-Muslim scholars have proposed radical reconstructions of the rise of Islam. Their accounts differ considerably. Günter Lüling claims that many of the Meccan suras were reworkings of Christian hymns composed in strophic vernacular Arabic but that Muḥammad subsequently turned away from 'Hellenistic Trinitarian Christianity' towards the tribal religion of Arabia. Luxenberg and Sawma likewise posit a Christian origin for much of the material in the Qur'an. However, they assume that it was composed in Syro-Aramaic and that this has been obscured by the artificial vocalization of the text. John Wansbrough thought that Muḥammad was a member of a Judaeo-Christian sect; that the Qur'an went through a long period of unchecked oral tradition; and that the written text reflects the scribal practices of the Talmudists. Crone and Cook (1977) alleged that Muḥammad and his followers were Hagarenes (*muhājirūn*)—Arab monotheists who claimed descent from Abraham and Hagar (Hajār), and who stressed the importance of the *hijra*—not an emigration from Mecca to Medina but a mass movement spear-headed from Medina, in which Arabs combined forces with Jews in a successful bid to reconquer Palestine. After Jerusalem had been taken, the political aspirations of Jewish messianism became an embarrassment to the Hagarenes who consequently broke with the Jews and adopted the non-political Messiah of Christianity, albeit retaining their hostility to the crucifixion and Trinitarian theology. Hawting, another member of Wansbrough's circle, argues (1999) that the Qur'anic polemic against 'associators' (*mushrikūn*) was originally aimed at Christians whose beliefs compromised true monotheism, but that it was misinterpreted in Islamic tradition as an attack on Arab polytheism. Bonnet-Eymard frequently explains the vocabulary of the Qur'an by reference to biblical Hebrew. He thinks that Muḥammad was an Arab influenced by Judaism and Arian Christianity. Like Crone and Cook, he maintains that he was still alive when Jerusalem was taken. Gallez (2005) is convinced that Islam originated in Syro-Palestine and that the Dead Sea Scrolls are evidence for the existence of an extensive messianic movement which was not confined to Qumran. He coined the term *judéonazaréens* to denote members of the movement who acknowledged Jesus as the Messiah born of a virgin. In his view it is misleading to call them Jewish Christians for they were really proto-Muslims. They expected the Messiah to return for the eschatological conflict in which believers would annihilate God's enemies, and their goal was to reconquer 'the Land' and inaugurate the final temple. Nevo and Koren (2003) likewise posit a Syro-Palestinian origin for Islam. On the basis of popular Arabic inscriptions on the desert rocks, they argue that as late as the beginning of the Umayyad period the prevailing religion was still an 'indeterminate monotheism' in which God was invoked as 'Allāh' and 'the Lord of Moses and Jesus'. Muḥammad is not mentioned in these inscriptions and is not, in their view, a historical figure. He makes his first public appearances on an Arab-Sassanian coin struck in Damascus in 690–1 and in the Dome of the Rock inscription in Jerusalem a year later.

Several of the above-mentioned authors assume that the current vocalization of the Qur'an is incorrect. If this were the case, there would be a precedent with the Hebrew Bible, which was vocalized in the seventh century by the Jews of the Masoretic school in Tiberius. We know from transliterations in other scripts, such as Greek, that the system adopted by the Masoretes differed from the ordinary pronunciation. It was an artificial form more suitable for public reading and it probably altered the grammatical structure of the language. We can also deduce from the Septuagint, the Greek translation produced by the Jews of Alexandria in pre-Christian times, that the Masoretes sometimes imposed a particular pronunciation for doctrinal reasons. For instance, in the Masoretic Text of I Kings 10:19, the back of Solomon's throne is described as 'rounded' whereas according to the Septuagint it depicted the heads of calves. The Alexandrine translators presumably read *'gl* correctly as *'ēgel* ('calf') but the Masoretes, for whom this smacked of idolatry, chose to vocalize the word as *'āgōl* ('rounded'). Unfortunately there are no early transliterations or translations of the Qur'an and if one adopts the extreme position that the current vocalization is totally unreliable the scope for emendation is almost limitless, witness the rival claims that the original language was vernacular Arabic, Syro-Aramaic, or Arabic with a Hebrew substrate. There almost certainly are some loan words that have been misunderstood and wrongly vocalized. There may also be places where the vocalization of the Arabic text has been modified for dogmatic reasons. However, proposed emendations, even when supported by detailed discussion (which is rarely the case) can never be more than conjectures.

Another common denominator of most of the revisionist histories is their reliance on Christian anti-Muslim polemic, which has long attributed the rise of Islam to the influence of Christian heretics. Two of the authors mentioned are Levantine Christians now living in the West, and at least three others are European Christians with extensive experience of living in Syria or the Lebanon. However, Nevo and Koren, who are Israelis, quote John of Damascus with evident approval. More surprisingly still, Crone and Cook, who boast that their book was 'written by infidels for infidels', take statements from a number of polemical works at face value.

Despite these caveats, the revisionist histories repay careful study. Collectively they signal a widespread dissatisfaction with the traditional account of the rise of Islam. However, in view of their failure to reach a consensus it is clear that it is too early to speak of a paradigm shift.

The Qur'anic Corpus

The *Fātiḥa*

The opening sura of the Qur'an is approximately the same length as the prayer which Christians attribute to Jesus (Matt. 6:9–14). It also has a comparable role in the life of Muslims. In addition there are structural similarities: both are couched in the first person plural, and both comprise praise followed by petition. The similarities in vocabulary may be due to the fact that they both echo Jewish liturgical usage. Note, however, the reference to God's 'name', the allusion to His royalty (reading *maliki yawmi 'l-dīn*, 'Sovereign on the Day of Judgement') and to the 'worlds' or 'ages' (*rabb al-ʿālamīn* is normally translated 'Lord of the worlds' whereas *eis tous aiōnas* means 'unto the ages'. However, the Hebrew *'ôlāmîm* can have both meanings and probably lies behind the Arabic and the Greek). All in all, it seems likely that the *fātiḥa* was intended as a substitute for the Lord's Prayer. God is not addressed as 'Our Father', because elsewhere in the Qur'an Christians are criticized for claiming that they are God's sons (Q. 5:18), but there are no other obvious correctives to Christian theology. Traditional exegesis identifies 'those who have erred' as the Christians. However, in the light of sura 2, this expression probably denotes the Jews of Arabia (Q. 2:16 and 2:175) and the Arab polytheists (Q. 2:198).

Sura 112

This short sura near the end of the corpus is recited frequently, for the obvious reason that it stresses the unity of God. The early commentators disagreed, however, as to whether it was revealed in Mecca in response to Arab polytheists or in Medina in reply to the Jews. The first *āya* clearly echoes the *Shema*, the central creed of Judaism, which begins 'Hear O Israel, the Lord is our God, the Lord is one' (Deut. 6:4). However, the *Shema* is also cherished by Christians because of the tradition that Jesus quoted it when asked which commandment was the greatest (Mark 12:29). Despite this, the Nicene-Constantinopolitan Creed, which begins with the assertion 'We believe in One God', additionally affirms belief in 'One Lord Jesus Christ, the only-begotten Son of God, begotten of the Father before all worlds, light from light, true God from true God, begotten not made, consubstantial with the Father'. It is probably in deliberate contrast to this that sura 112 asserts that God is *al-Ṣamad* ('impenetrable substance'?), that he 'does not beget and is not begotten', and that equal to him there is not one.

Why 114 Suras?

Apart from the Qur'an, the only extant pre-Islamic religious writing that is divided into 114 sections is the *Gospel of Thomas*. Unlike the New Testament Gospels, this work lacks a narrative framework. It comprises 114 sayings attributed to Jesus, sometimes embedded in short dialogues. They are allegedly his secret teaching recorded in writing by the apostle Thomas. Hippolytus of Rome, a third-century proto-orthodox Christian author, attributed the Gospel of Thomas to a gnostic sect called the Naassenes. Be that as it may, before it was officially excluded from the canon it was probably widely read. It is part of the 'Nag Hammadi Library', a cache of banned books hidden in the fourth century by 'orthodox' monks from the monastery of St Pachomius in order to save them from destruction. Several Church Fathers stated that this gospel was favoured by Mani, the founder of Manichaeism, an eclectic religion which drew heavily on Christianity. Mani taught that Jesus was a prophet but denied that he was crucified. He also claimed to be the Paraclete promised by Jesus, a role which the Qur'an implicitly ascribes to Muḥammad.

Q. 61:6b and Q. 7:157: Medinan Verses or Later Additions?

There is a consensus that sura 61 is Medinan. However, some Western scholars suspect that the middle section of v. 6 is a later gloss. They give four reasons. First, whereas the received text has Jesus 'announcing a messenger who will come after me, whose name is Aḥmad', Ubayy allegedly read, 'I announce to you a Prophet whose community will be the last community and by whom God will set the seal on the prophets and messengers.' The two readings are incompatible, which raises the possibility that both are later additions. Second, if this part of the verse were omitted, the sura would still be coherent. It would then be concerned solely with the mission of Moses and Jesus. On this view the 'associators' in v. 9 are Trinitarian Christians rather than Arab polytheists; the 'Messenger' in v. 9 is Jesus as in v. 6; and the final statement in v. 6—'And when he came to them with clear signs, they said this is sheer magic!'—refers to Jesus (as in Q. 5:110) rather than Aḥmad. Third, the name Aḥmad ('most praiseworthy', 'renowned') is derived from an ingenious interpretation of a passage in the New Testament which would have required knowledge of Greek. Jesus foretold the mission of another *paraklētos* ('advocate', 'comforter') who would guide the disciples into all truth (John 14:16–17, cf. 14:23–6, 15:26, 16:7–14). Unlike Semitic languages, Greek is not written without the vowels. However, if it were, the consonantal text *prklts* could also be read *periklutos* ('heard of all round', 'famous', 'renowned' 'glorious'). Fourth, in the *Sīra*, Muḥammad is never called Aḥmad although he is identified with the *munaḥḥemana* ('the life-giver'), the word used in the Palestinian Syriac Lectionary to translate *paraklētos*.

Sura 7 is generally considered Meccan, although most Western scholars regard v. 157 as part of a Medinan addition, and some attribute it to a later editor. The clause that concerns us is the reference to the *ummī* prophet 'mentioned in the Torah and Gospel'. Regardless of the meaning of *ummī* ('belonging to the community' or 'unlettered'?), the scriptural passages envisaged are almost certainly Deuteronomy 18:15–19, where God promises to raise up a prophet like Moses, and the references to the Paraclete in John. Critics who attribute the verse to a later editor point out that it sits oddly in its context (where God is addressing Moses) and that as with 61:6b it involves subtle scriptural exegesis. They fail to understand the ancient mind-set. Writing to Christians in first-century Rome, Paul said of the Jewish scriptures, 'For everything that was written long ago was written to instruct us' (Rom. 15:4). Had he lived in the seventh century, he would not have found the reference to 'the Gospel' in Q. 7:157 anachronistic. Those, like him, who are convinced that their religious history is foretold in the Scriptures, are prone to take liberty with the text. There are many examples of this in both the Dead Sea Scrolls and the New Testament. For instance, parts of the book of Isaiah were uttered in the sixth century BCE when Cyrus offered the Jewish exiles in Babylon the possibility of returning to Palestine. The anonymous prophet depicts this as a new Exodus and mentions

> The voice of one crying out, 'Prepare the way of the Lord in the wilderness. Make his paths straight'. (Isa. 40:3)

Five and a half centuries later, Mark read this verse as a prophecy of the coming of John the Baptist and construed it as

> The voice of one crying out in the wilderness, 'Prepare the way of the Lord. Make his paths straight'. (Mark 1:3)

The alteration in punctuation, for which there is a precedent in the Septuagint, makes the text fit the new historical context. This is a relatively simple example; anyone who has wrestled with Paul's more abstruse exegesis is unlikely to be perturbed by the Qur'an's identification of the Messenger of Allah with the Prophet like Moses and Paraclete. In short, although there are grounds for suspecting that Q. 61:6b may have been added by an editor, the case against the authenticity of Q. 7:157 is weak; it is probably Medinan.

The Dynamics of the Qur'anic Discourse

Irrespective of whether Q. 61:6b and 7:157 are secondary, the biblical teaching about the prophet like Moses and the Paraclete are of fundamental importance for understanding the Qur'an. There are numerous Qur'anic passages of we-thou discourse in which the implied Magisterial Speaker, God, addresses the Messenger personally and entrusts him with revelation that he is to convey to a wider audience. In one instance, the Messenger is instructed not to move his tongue to speed up the process of revelation (Q. 75:16–18) and in another, God informs the auditors that if the Messenger had fabricated false revelations, 'we would have seized him by the right hand and cut off his main artery' (Q. 69:44–6). The Messenger is thus a mere channel of communication, in the manner of the awaited 'Prophet like Moses' and Paraclete. Of the former God says, 'I will put my words in his mouth' and adds that the prophet who speaks presumptuously will die (Deut. 18:18–20). Jesus says of the Paraclete, 'He will not speak from himself but he will speak only what he hears' (John 16:13). There are also precedents in the Torah and Gospel for the Magisterial Speaker's employment of 'we', 'us', and 'our' to refer to himself. In the opening chapter of the Torah, God says 'Let us make man in our own image' (Gen. 1:26) and in one of the Paraclete passages Jesus says, 'If a man love me he will keep my word and my father will love him and we will come to him' (John 14:23). The presence of the divine 'we' in the Qur'an thus signifies the resumption of scriptural revelation, and the irruption of we-thou discourse signals that the Messenger of Allah is indeed the promised Paraclete.

Jesus' Name al-Masīḥ ʿĪsā ibn Maryam

Ibn Maryam

The earliest reference to Mary (*Maryam*) is in Q. 19:16–33. In this brief account of the annunciation, birth, and infancy of her child, which Nöldeke ascribes to the second Meccan period, the child himself is not named. This is probably why in Q. 43:57 and Q. 23:50, which are slightly later, he is simply called 'Mary's son' (ibn Maryam). However, in the other twenty-one occurrences of this expression, which are all Medinan, it is immediately preceded by 'Jesus' (ʿĪsā), 'the Messiah' (*al-Masīḥ*) or 'the Messiah Jesus' (al-Masīḥ ʿĪsā). In these passages it is part of a name and should be rendered 'Son of Mary'. The context is polemical: calling him 'Son of Mary' served as a tacit reminder that he was not 'Son of God' as Christians alleged.

ʿĪsā

The name ʿĪsā (Jesus) is attested once in the second Meccan period (Q. 43:63); twice in the third Meccan period (Q. 42:13 and 6:85); and twenty-two times in the Medinan period (counting Q. 19:34 as a Medinan addition to a Meccan sura). The spelling has given rise to much discussion because it differs from any now favoured by Christians. The earliest extant references to Jesus are in the Greek New Testament, where he is always called Iēsous. However, according to tradition his original Hebrew name was Yēshūaʿ, which was popularly understood to mean 'God saves' (see Matt. 1:21). Consequently, when the New Testament was translated into Syriac, Iēsous was rendered Yeshūʿ, and when the Syriac was in turn translated into Arabic he came to be known as Yasūʿ.

It is sometimes alleged that the Jews duped the Prophet into calling Jesus ʿĪsā because they identified him with the hated figure of Esau (Arabic ʿIsaw). However, although the Talmud refers to Christians as the 'offspring of Esau' it calls Jesus Yesu. It is more likely therefore that the Qur'anic form of Jesus' name is derived from a dialectical variant used in circles where he was respected. Syriac-speaking Nestorian Christians and Manichees pronounced his name Ishoʿ, and in the Syriac translation of the Gospel of Marcion he was called Isu, but there may have been other variations. The final long vowel of ʿĪsā could have resulted from assimilation to Mūsā and Yaḥyā (Moses and John) with whom he is paired in the third Meccan period. This minor adaptation might in turn account for the transposition of the ʿayn from the end of the name to the beginning. Nevertheless, it should be noted that unlike the Hebrew Yēshūaʿ, the name ʿĪsā lacks salvific connotations.

al-Masīḥ

The expression al-Masīḥ ('The Messiah') is attested eleven times but only in Medinan suras. The earliest occurrence is at Q. 3:45 where the angels tell Maryam, 'God gives you news of a word from him, whose name will be al-Masīḥ ʿĪsā Ibn Maryam'. The full name is repeated in Q. 4:157 and Q. 4:171. It is subsequently shortened to al-Masīḥ Ibn Maryam in Q. 5:17 (twice), Q. 5:72a, Q. 5:75, and Q. 9:31. In the three remaining instances—Q. 4:172, Q. 5:72b, and Q. 9:30—al-Masīḥ is used in isolation but it is obvious from the context that it denotes the same individual.

The Arabic lexicographers regarded al-Masīḥ as a nickname (*laqab*) and indicated a variety of possible interpretations. Most, however, were of the opinion that it was derived from the Arabic verb masaḥa which elsewhere in the Qur'an means 'wipe' or 'stroke', but which can also mean 'anoint'. On this view, Jesus was called al-Masīḥ, because he laid hands on the sick or because he himself was anointed with God's blessing or with oil like previous prophets.

This last suggestion comes closest to the correct solution for there can be little doubt that al-Masīḥ is a loanword derived ultimately from the Hebrew Māshīaḥ, which originally meant 'anointed'. In the Hebrew Bible it is used with reference to kings, priests, and prophets who were consecrated with anointing oil. By the first century however, it was in widespread use as the title of a future deliverer. The Jews held various opinions about the identity of this 'Messiah' but the belief which is reflected in the New Testament is that he would be a descendant of David who would re-establish the Davidic monarchy and institute a reign of peace. In the canonical gospels, Jesus is depicted as fulfilling these expectations while eschewing their militaristic overtones.

In the Greek New Testament, Christos ('Christ'), the Greek word for anointed, occurs more than 550 times, whereas Messias, the Hellenized transliteration of Māshīaḥ, is attested only twice (John 1:21, 4:25). However, in the Syriac translation of the New Testament, Christos is invariably re-Semitized as Mshīḥ, which probably accounts for the Qur'anic version of the word.

Although, in the New Testament, 'Christ' is frequently treated as a name ('Jesus Christ', 'Christ Jesus', or simply 'Christ'), nevertheless the four Gospels, Romans, 2 Timothy, and Revelation all emphasize descent from David. In the Qur'an, on the other hand, Jesus' link with David is extremely tenuous (Q. 5:78).

The Designation of Christians as Naṣārā

Introduction

Although the Qur'an calls Jesus *al-masīḥ*, it never refers to his followers as *masīḥiyyūn*, which is the usual Arabic word for Christians. Instead, in the Medinan revelations they are called *naṣārā*. The plural is attested fourteen times in Q. 2:62, 111, 113 twice, 120, 135, 140; Q. 5:14, 18, 51, 69, 82; Q. 9:30; and Q. 22:17. The singular, *naṣrānī*, occurs only at Q. 3:67. In the Abbasid period Muslims used this word as a blanket term to cover Melkites (Chalcedonian Orthodox), Jacobites (Monophysites), and Nestorians. In those days most Christians accepted this label because of the benefits accruing from classification as 'People of the Book'. However, it would be anachronistic to project this state of affairs back onto the Qur'an. There the situation is subtly different. The Qur'an gives qualified approval to those who call themselves *naṣārā* (Q. 5:14 and 82) and it employs the term to designate all Christians. Regardless of the ultimate origin of the word, in its Qur'anic context it has semantic links with the verb *naṣara* ('to help') and its derivatives. The true vocation of the *naṣārā* is not to be followers of Christ—Christians—but to be helpers, *anṣār*, in God's cause, like Christ's first disciples (Q. 3:52; Q. 61:14). In return they are assured of God's help, *naṣr*, in their struggle with their enemies (Q. 61:13–14, cf. 110:1 etc.).

Christians and Nazoreans in the New Testament

According to Acts 11:26 'the disciples were first called Christians (*christianoi*) at Antioch'. This is the only occurrence of the plural form in the New Testament. Judging by the two instances of the singular *christianos* (Acts 26:28, 1 Pet. 4:16) it was probably a designation for Gentile Christians. Jews who accepted Jesus as the Messiah were apparently known as followers of the 'Way' (Acts 9:2, 22:4)—a term also found in the Qumran Scrolls—and 'Nazoreans' (Acts 24:5).

Jesus himself was called a 'Nazorean' (Greek *Nazoraios*, 12 times in Matthew, John, Luke, and Acts) or a 'Nazarene' (*Nazarenos*, 6 times in Mark and Luke), ostensibly because he came from a village in Galilee named 'Nazareth' (6 times in Matthew, Luke and Acts), 'Nazaret' (4 times in Matthew, Mark and John) or 'Nazara' (twice in Matthew and Luke). On the way to Damascus with a mandate from the high priest to round up followers of 'the Way', Paul, who had never met Jesus during his earthly life, is said to have seen a blinding light and heard the words, 'I am Jesus the Nazorean whom you are persecuting' (Acts 22:8). As a result, he experienced a dramatic reversal and was subsequently accused by his fellow Jews of being 'a ring-leader of the sect of Nazoreans' (Acts 24:5—the only occurrence of the plural).

It is generally assumed that the variations in spelling merely reflect the difficulty of transliterating Semitic words. All the same, the New Testament data remain puzzling.

Matthew's linking of Nazarene with Nazaret is laboured and his scriptural derivation of the former cryptic (Matt. 2:23). The alleged stigma attached to Jesus' village (John 1:46) hardly explains why his nickname was included in the placard stating the reason for his execution (John 19:19). And it is unlikely that a Jewish high priest would have risked the ire of the Roman authorities by sanctioning Paul's persecution of heretics in another province of the empire (Acts 22:5). Jesus and Paul may in fact have had links with pre-Christian Jewish Messianists labelled Nazoreans because of the description of the Davidic Messiah as a 'branch' (Isa. 11:1, Hebrew *nētzer*). In which case Paul's 'Damascus' was probably not the Syrian capital but a settlement in northern Judaea which was given that sobriquet in the *Damascus Document* from Qumran. There are two further pointers in this direction. First, the three years that he spent there after his conversion (Gal. 1:17–18) corresponds to the Essene probationary period (Josephus, *Jewish War*, 2:137–8). Second, his account of his escape (2 Cor. 11:32–3) appears to have been edited by someone who attempted to eliminate the ambiguity by clumsily glossing 'Damascus' as 'the city of the Damascenes'.

Subsequent Pre-Islamic References to Nazaoreans

At the beginning of the third century, Tertullian stated that the Jews called Christians Nazarenes. A hundred and thirty years or so later, Eusebius said that 'in ancient times' this was what all Christians were called. Both these theologians may have derived their information principally from the New Testament. From the second half of the fourth century onwards, however, Christian authors reserved the term Nazarenes for Jewish Christians who practised circumcision and observed the Sabbath. The earliest extant evidence for this is a compendium of heresies compiled by Epiphanius in 377 CE. He acknowledged that all Christians were once called Nazarenes but alleged that the name was subsequently appropriated by heretics who believed that Jesus was the Messiah and observed the Jewish Law. He also mentions that they read the Gospel of Matthew in Hebrew and in Hebrew letters. In his view they were 'Jews and nothing else' although he adds that the Jews hated them and cursed them three times a day in their synagogues. The references to Jewish Christians in the works of Epiphanius and other heresiographers are inconsistent and should be treated with caution. It is often unclear whether they concern Gentile converts to Christian sects that adopted Jewish practices or Jews who maintained the traditions of the original Palestinian Jesus movement. However, Jewish hatred of Jewish Christians is borne out by manuscripts in the Cairo Geniza that indicate that in the earlier version of the *ʿamīda* prayer there was a curse on the *nōṣrīm* aimed at excluding them from the synagogue.

Bibliography

Ap-Thomas, D. R., *A Primer of Old Testament Text Criticism*. 2nd edn. Oxford: Blackwell, 1965.

Ayoub, M. M. *The Qurʾān and its Interpreters*. Vol. 1. Albany: State University of New York Press, 1984.

Bell, R. *The Origin of Islam in its Christian Environment.* London: Macmillan, 1926.
Bonnet-Eymard, B. *Le Coran: traduction et commentaire systématique* I–III (Saint-Parres-Lès-Vaudes: Le Contre-Réforme Catholique, 1988, 1990, 1997.
Crone, P. and M. Cook. *Hagarism.* Cambridge: Cambridge University Press, 1977.
De Blois, F. '*Naṣrānī* (*Ναζωραῖος*) and *ḥanīf* (*ἐθνικός*) Studies on the Religious Vocabulary of Christianity and Islam', *Bulletin of the School of Oriental and African Studies* 65/1 (2002), 1–30.
Déroche, François. *Qur'āns of the Umayyads: A First Overview.* Leiden and Boston: Brill, 2014.
Gallez, Edouard-Marie. *Le Messie et son prophète* I—I. Versailles: Editions de Paris, 2005.
Guillaume, A. *The Life of Muhammad: A Translation of Ibn Isḥāq's Sīrat Rasūl Allāh.* Oxford: Oxford University Press, 1955.
Hawting, G. R. *The Idea of Idolatry and the Emergence of Islam.* Cambridge: Cambridge University Press, 1999.
Hoyland, R. 'Epigraphy and the Linguistic Background to the Qur'ān'. In: G. Reynolds (ed.). *The Qur'ān in its Historical Context*, pp. 51–69. London: Routledge, 2008.
Lawson, T. *The Crucifixion and the Qur'ān.* Oxford: Oneworld, 2009.
Lüling, G. *Über den Ur-Qur'ān.* Erlangen: Verlangsbuchhdlg H. Lüling, 1974.
Lüling, G. *A Challenge to Islam for Reformation.* Delhi: Motilal Banarsidass, 2003.
Luxenberg, C. *The Syro-Aramaic Reading of the Koran.* Berlin: Verlag Hans Schiler, 2007.
McAuliffe, Jane Dammen. *Qur'ānic Christians: An Analysis of Classical and Modern Exegesis.* Cambridge: Cambridge University Press, 1991.
Nevo, Y. D. and J. Koren. *Crossroads to Islam.* New York: Prometheus, 2003.
Parrinder, G. *Jesus in the Qur'ān.* London: Faber and Faber, 1965.
Risse, Günter. *'Gott ist Christus, der Sohn der Maria': Eine Studie zum Christusbild im Koran.* Bonn: Borengässer, 1989.
Robinson, Neal. *Christ in Islam and Christianity: The Representation of Jesus in the Qur'an and the Classical Muslim Commentaries.* Basingstoke: Macmillan, 1991.
Robinson, Neal. *Discovering the Qur'an: A Contemporary Approach to a Veiled Text.* London: SCM, 1996; 2nd edn. 2003.
Robinson, Neal. 'Sectarian and Ideological Bias in English Translations of the Qur'an by Muslims', *Islam and Christian-Muslim Relations* 8/3 (1997), 261–78.
Robinson, Neal. 'The Structure and Interpretation of *Sūrat al-muʿminūn*', *Journal of Qur'ānic Studies* 2/1 (2000), 89–106.
Robinson, Neal. 'Antichrist'. In: Jane Dammen McAuliffe (ed.). *Encyclopaedia of the Qur'ān.* 6 vols., 1:107–11. Leiden: Brill, 2001–6.
Robinson, Neal. 'Clay'. In: Jane Dammen McAuliffe (ed.). *Encyclopaedia of the Qur'ān.* 6 vols., 1:339–41. Leiden: Brill, 2001–6.
Robinson, Neal. 'Crucifixion'. In: Jane Dammen McAuliffe (ed.). *Encyclopaedia of the Qur'ān.* 6 vols., 1:487–89. Leiden: Brill, 2001–6.
Robinson, Neal. 'Hands Outstretched: Towards a Re-reading of Sūrat al-Mā'ida', *Journal of Qur'ānic Studies* 3/1 (2001), 1–19.
Robinson, Neal. 'Sayyid Qutb and Christianity: Qutb's Treatment of Surah 9:29–35 in *fī zilâl al-qur'ān*'. In: L. Ridgeon (ed.). *Islamic Interpretations of Christianity*, pp. 159–78. Richmond: Curzon, 2001.
Robinson, Neal. 'Jesus'. In: J. D. McAuliffe (ed.). *The Encyclopaedia of the Qur'an*, 3:7–21. Leiden: Brill, 2003.
Robinson, Neal. 'Surah Al 'Imrān and Those with the Greatest Claim to Abraham', *Journal of Qur'ānic Studies* 6/2 (2004), 1–21.

Robinson, Neal. 'The Quranic Jesus, the Jesus of History, and the Myth of God Incarnate'. In: R. S. Sugirtharaja (ed.). *Wilderness: Essays in Honour of Frances Young*, pp. 186–97. London: T. & T. Clark International, 2005.

Robinson, Neal. 'Which Islam? Which Jesus?' In: G. Barker (ed.). *Jesus in the World's Faiths*, pp. 132–41. New York: Orbis, 2005.

Robinson, Neal. 'The Dynamics of Surah *āl 'Imrān*'. In: Pak Tae-Shik (ed.). *Saramui Jonggyo, Jonggyoui Saram*, pp. 425–86. Seoul: Baobooks, 2008.

Robinson, Neal. 'Apostle'. In: J. Nawas (ed.). *The Encyclopaedia of Islam*. 3rd edn. Part 2009–3, pp. 104–5. Leiden: Brill, 2009.

Robinson, Neal. Review of 'Gordon Nickel. Narratives of Tampering in the Earliest Commentaries on the Qur'ān', *Zeitschrift der Deutschen Morgenländischen Gesellschaft* 165/2 (2013), 541–4.

Robinson, Neal. 'The Dynamics of the Quranic Discourse: Tradition and Redaction'. In: B. Broeckaert, S. Van Den Branden, and J.-J. Pérennès (eds.). *Perspectives on Islamic Culture: Essays in Honour of Emilio G. Platti*, pp. 8–18. Leuven: Peeters, 2013.

Sawma, G. *The Qur'ān Misinterpreted and Misread.* Plainsboro, NJ: Adibooks.com: 2006.

Trimingham, J. Spencer. *Christianity among the Arabs in Pre-Islamic Times.* London and Beirut: Longman and Libraire du Liban, 1979.

Wansbrough, J. *Quranic Studies.* Oxford: Oxford University Press, 1977.

Wansbrough, J. *The Sectarian Milieu.* Oxford: Oxford University Press, 1978.

PART III

THE QUR'AN: TEXTUAL TRANSMISSION, CODIFICATION, MANUSCRIPTS, INSCRIPTIONS, AND PRINTED EDITIONS

CHAPTER 11

THE MANUSCRIPT AND ARCHAEOLOGICAL TRADITIONS

Physical Evidence

FRANÇOIS DÉROCHE

RESEARCH on the material evidence of Qur'anic written transmission started at the end of the eighteenth century with J. C. G. Adler (Adler 1780), but faced the problem of identifying and dating the Qur'anic manuscripts and fragments which could belong to the earliest period, that is, the first/seventh century. The advances made in this field during the nineteenth century, for instance by M. Amari (Amari 1910), remained confidential or faced harsh criticism. For a long time, the early handwritten transmission remained largely confined to studies on palaeography and was approached chiefly from a chronological perspective (Abbott 1939; Grohmann 1958). However, a growing interest in this material and new discoveries recently spurred scholars to look more closely at it. On the other hand, the development of Arabic epigraphy, numismatics, and papyrology during the nineteenth century led to the discovery of another kind of textual witnesses, Qur'anic 'quotations' which provide other information about the text. This written material, especially the manuscripts, are now seen as important witnesses for the history of the text.

Sources provide some information about the use of written records of the revelations during Muḥammad's lifetime and the accounts about the compilation of the Qur'an allude to a variety of supports used previously (pieces of papyrus, flat stones, palm ribs, shoulder-blades, etc.). However, these meagre data fail to provide precise information and their reliability has been questioned. To this date, no trace of this pre-ʿUthmānic material has been found. On the other hand, the writing down of the Qur'an as we know it today during Muḥammad's lifetime was technically difficult to combine with the closed structure of a codex as the text, according to the data transmitted by the tradition, is not organized in a chronologically linear way, with the last revelation coming after the previous one. The sequence of the suras and the reports about the insertion of a newly revealed passage within a unit of older material imply that the writing support was versatile enough to adapt to these changes. Richard Bell actually developed a theory about what he called 'scraps of paper' which were used during a first stage of the writing down (Watt and Bell 1977: 101–5). It cannot be excluded that notations on provisional materials as well as partial compilations in codex shape have existed.

Traditional Arabic sources insist on the fact that the Qur'an was transcribed before the middle of the first century of Islam. The multiplication of the codices after Muḥammad's death, if we accept the information from the sources, mirrors both the wish to preserve the Revelation and the possibility to have it in the shape of a codex. The accounts about the writing down of the Qur'an as the result of a decision taken by Abū Bakr, the first caliph, then by ʿUthmān, are well known (Schwally 1919) and find to some extent a confirmation in some sources about copyists of the Qur'anic text active at an early date (Whelan 1998). Harald Motzki, using critical methods, was able to show that reports about the copies produced under the third caliph's reign were circulating by the extreme end of the seventh or early eighth century CE (Motzki 2001: 1–34). According to him,

> the two traditions which tell the history of the *muṣḥaf* and are widely adopted in Muslim scholarship were both brought into circulation by Ibn Shihāb [al-Zuhrī] and can be dated to the first quarter of the 2nd century AH. The date of al-Zuhri's death [124/742] is the *terminus post quem*. (Motzki 2001: 29)

Do we have extant copies contemporary with ʿUthmān's reign—or even with his predecessors? Seen from a palaeographical and codicological point of view, the possibility cannot be discarded, although the methods of dating the earliest copies of the Qur'an do not reach—at least for the moment—a level of accuracy which would allow one to pinpoint a fragment or copy to this precise period. And, of course, unless an authentic colophon substantiates any claim, a manuscript cannot be attributed to any individual.

Copies Attributed to ʿUthmān

The Islamic scholarly tradition devoted much attention to the canonical text which was established under the reign of ʿUthmān, but it does not seem to have been much interested in the Qur'anic copies which were said to be the caliph's manuscript(s) and are mentioned in various sources—some of them being still preserved. There is actually some ambiguity about what covered this concept: were these copies written by the caliph, or sent by him to the various cities of the empire, or were they the copy he was reading when he was murdered? The Tashkent manuscript for instance contained stains which were supposed to be from the caliph's own blood (Shebunin 1891: 76–7). However, already in the second/eighth century, an unimpeachable Medinese authority, Mālik ibn Anas, when asked about the fate of ʿUthmān's own copy, answered flatly that it had disappeared (Jahdani 2006: 274).

In addition to the manuscripts attributed to ʿUthmān which are known through sources to have been preserved in various places in pre-modern times (Quatremère 1838: 41–5; Mouton 1993: 247–54; Buresi 2008: 273–80; Rezvan 2000 and 2004), a few actual manuscripts are today said to be the caliph's own copy (see e.g. the list in Munajjid 1972: 50–60). In some cases, a colophon substantiates these claims, but in other instances, like the Tashkent copy, we are just dealing with a word-of-mouth attribution. Ṣalāḥ al-Dīn al-Munajjid examined them and came to the conclusion that, in spite of their age, the various copies were not linked to ʿUthmān (Munajjid 1972: 50–60). More recently, Tayyar Altıkulaç published a facsimile of three such copies, one kept in Cairo (Altıkulaç 2009), and two in Istanbul, one in the Topkapı Sarayı Library, the other in the Turkish and Islamic Arts Museum (Altıkulaç 2007). The latter contains a colophon stating that ʿUthmān ibn ʿAffān had completed the copy in 30/650–1. Using the information collected by medieval Muslim scholars in treatises devoted to the *rasm ʿuthmānī*, Altıkulaç reached the same conclusion as Munajjid that these copies were not related to the caliph. A look at the Turkish and Islamic Arts Museum copy shows that it is actually a gross forgery: a fourth/tenth-century illuminated folio has been manipulated in order to have the 'colophon', written in a clumsy imitation of the third/ninth-century script of the rest of the manuscript, awkwardly glued in its centre. The case of the copies attributed to other prominent figures of the same period, like ʿAlī ibn Abī Ṭālib or his son, Ḥusayn, is similar.

Criteria of Identification

The evidence related to the early handwritten transmission of the Qur'an has been principally retrieved from deposits containing discarded fragments of varying size and located in Damascus, al-Fusṭāṭ, Sanaa, and to a lesser extent Qayrawan. They have been identified on the basis of a set of criteria—some information derived from Arabic sources, internal evidence provided by the manuscripts and modern techniques of datation.

Some historical accounts may sometimes provide elements more directly usable for the identification of the earliest copies of the Qur'an. A short description found in Ibn al-Nadīm's *Fihrist* has proven crucial in the definition of the first script to have been used, the *Ḥijāzī* style:

> The first of the Arab scripts was the script of Makkah, the next of al-Madīnah, then of al-Basrah, and then of al-Kūfah. For the *alifs* of the scripts of Makkah and al-Madīnah there is a turning of the hand to the right and lengthening of the strokes, one form having a slight slant... Scripts of copies of the Qurʾān. Those of Makkah, the people of al-Madīnah, the *Nīm*, the *Muthallath*, and the *Mudawwar*. Also those of al-Kūfah and al-Basrah, and the *Mashq*, the *Tajāwīd*, the *Sitawatī*, the *Masnāʿ*, the *Munābadh*.... (al-Nadīm 1971: 9; Dodge 1970: 10)

Meagre as it is, this text has been used by palaeographers as a starting point for the identification of the earliest copies of the Qur'an. By the mid-nineteenth century,

Michele Amari had been able to link it with actual fragments in the Bibliothèque nationale de France collection and to suggest subsuming the scripts of Mecca and Medina under the geographically broader concept of *Ḥijāzī*, after the name of the region where both cities are located. He also noted the relationship of these scripts with that of contemporaneous papyri (Amari 1910: 16).

Codicology can also be of some help in the identification of early Qur'anic copies (Déroche et al. 2005). At the beginning of Islam, the codex had already become the dominant format of book in the Mediterranean area, although the volumen remained in use in the Jewish tradition for the Torah. At this moment, parchment and papyrus were the materials commonly used in the production of books. Some variations existed in the way of transforming the sheet of parchment into quires: in some copies, the hair sides face systematically the hair sides (and conversely for the flesh sides), in others we find the sequence which is later dominant in Islamic manuscripts in parchment, namely all the rectos in the first half of the quire being of the same nature. The commonly found description of the *muṣḥaf* 'between two boards' (*lawḥayn*) may refer to the wooden structure of the binding, using wood for the boards. To this day, no binding from this period has been found.

The identification of copies of the Qur'an in *Ḥijāzī* style on this basis led to the observation by Amari of their orthographic peculiarities, above all a deficiency in noting the vowel /ā/ in the *rasm*, usually characterized as *scriptio defectiva*, by contrast with the *scriptio plena* (Amari 1910: 20). This results for instance in the homographic writing of *qāla* and *qul* (*qāf* + *lām*). These features began to be used more systematically in recent studies. The analysis of an important handwritten witness of this stage, the *Codex Parisino-petropolitanus* (pl. 1; Déroche 2009), led to the observation of orthographic discrepancies between the five copyists cooperating in the transcription of the text, but also of a process of orthographic enhancement of the *rasm*. In many copies in *scriptio defectiva* the orthography was modified by later readers who added for instance the *alif* after the *qāf* in *qāla*, thus indicating that the evolution was in favour of the *scriptio plena*. However, these changes cannot be expected to follow a regularly progressive evolution. The copyists are not always entirely coherent and many manuscripts exhibit cases where the *scriptio plena* did not completely supersede the *scriptio defectiva*. The manuscript Dublin, CBL Is 1615 also demonstrates that some readers clung at least partially to the 'old' orthography (Arberry 1967: 15; James 1980: 14). In this case, the copyist(s) had written *shayʾ* in the 'modern' way (*shīn* + *yā*ʾ), leaving in a few cases only the early form with an *alif* (*shīn* + *alif* + *yā*ʾ). A reader corrected the text and added an *alif* in most of the cases, but also and conversely *qāla* and *qālū* when the copyist(s) had used the *scriptio defectiva*. As a rule, the copies in *scriptio plena* can be expected to have been produced at a later date and the orthography can therefore be used in association with other elements in order to appreciate the chronological position of a manuscript.

Art history can also contribute to the dating of early Qur'anic manuscripts, although this approach only applies to the copies which include ornaments—which constitute a minority of the material during the period under consideration. The results can however be extended to copies without illumination which are related by their script to the illuminated ones. C 14 (Radiocarbon dating) analyses of the parchment have also begun to play an increasing role, although results have to be taken with caution. Their accuracy is still disputed and cannot be relied upon to provide a chronology of the manuscripts, but C14 is helpful as a first indication of the age of a copy and should be used along with other data.

The *Ḥijāzī* Evidence

The '*Ḥijāzī* corpus' thus constituted has been subjected to increasingly focused studies over the last decade, a development which has been benefiting from the publication of facsimiles giving access to this material to a wider audience. To this date, no manuscript which could be dated to the first/seventh century and containing the entire text of the Qur'an as we know it today has been found.

The *Codex Parisino-petropolitanus* (Déroche 2009) is representative of the copies in *Ḥijāzī* style (pl. 1; facsimile published by Déroche and Noja 1998). This quarto manuscript in vertical format (33 × 25 cm) has been written on parchment, like most of the early material which has been preserved. Being a codex, it is constituted of quaternions, that is to say quires made with four sheets folded in two by their middle and sewn together with other quires, with the hair sides facing the hair sides and the flesh sides facing the flesh sides. Its ninety-eight folios contain about 50 per cent of the ʿUthmānic text, distributed in fourteen sequences of variable length separated by lacunae, starting with 2:275 and ending at 72:2. Its analysis suggests that the transcription was largely a matter of personal choice as far as the script, the orthography and, to some extent, the division into verses are concerned. The *Codex*, like other Qur'anic manuscripts from this period, is the result of team work: five copyists were involved and the individual hands can be easily recognized, ranging from the clumsy to the professional (Déroche 2009: 31–43).

The text is written on the pages according to the rules of the *scriptio continua* of Late Antiquity applied to the Arabic script (Diem 1983: 386–7). As a consequence, a word can be cut at the end of a line when it includes at least one letter which does not connect to the next one and the place available is not sufficient to have it written on the end of the line. Similarly, the script is distributed evenly on the page, spaces of similar length appearing between the words and within those which contain one or more letters which do not connect to the next one. Another feature of the manuscripts of this period is the lack of real outer margins: the text reaches the edge of the page. They are also devoid of any ornamentation between the suras.

The diacritics are scarce, but present in the copies. According to the sources, the diacritics were introduced into the script at the time of al-Ḥajjāj's '*maṣāḥif* project' (Hamdan 2006: 141). However, early documents, like the Ahnas papyrus dated 22/643, already include diacritics to distinguish homographs, which supports an attribution of Qur'anic copies with diacritics to a period prior to al-Ḥajjāj's time. The '*Ḥijāzī* corpus' shows that the copyists of *maṣāḥif* were also aware of their use, but rarely added them to the text or added them sometimes on letters which do not seem to require them for proper identification, for instance final *nūn*. In addition, each copyist added them according to his own views. In the *Codex Parisino-petropolitanus*, each of the five hands punctuated differently, one of them (E) using no diacritics at all, C dotting four letters over 16 folios. B put a dot below *bāʾ* and A did not. Conversely, A singled out *khāʾ*, *ḍād*, *ẓāʾ*, and *ghayn* but B did not mark these letters (Déroche 2009: 44–5). Neither the short vowels nor the orthoepic signs are indicated.

As in most of the Qur'anic manuscripts of this period, the division into verses is carefully indicated, but it does not accord with any of the systems defined by the various schools (Spitaler 1935; Rabb 2006: 108; Déroche 2009: 79–94). In a similar way, the copyists do not agree between them on the status of the *basmala*, some of them indicating a verse ending after it, others not, thus leaving open the possibility that they were not following the same recitation. On the other hand, the lack of signs for the short vowels or for the *shadda* and *hamza* prevents one from drawing conclusions on this aspect. In a few cases, a canonical verse is divided into two verses in the manuscript, the second being short and often formulaic.[1] As the latter also contains the element rhyming with the adjoining verses, it has been hypothesized that it was a trace of an editorial work on the Qur'anic text (Déroche 2009: 138–41).

The copyists did not content themselves with a mere transcription of an original; they enhanced the *rasm* and eliminated some ambiguities. In this copy, the Hand B corrected for instance what he had written first in 7:146 and 148, thus revealing an almost live process of orthographic enhancement which was probably a common procedure at that time when the transcription was based on some older and more defective exemplar (Déroche 2009: 153).

This copy has been attributed to the third quarter of the first/seventh century: some scribal mistakes show that it has been transcribed from an older exemplar and the script of hand D heralds the style which is associated with manuscripts produced under ʿAbd al-Malik's reign (from 65/685 to 86/705, see Déroche 2009: 157).

Another important manuscript from this group is BL Or. 2165 (pl. 2; facsimile, see Déroche and Noja 2001). With 130 folios, it covers a larger extent of the Qur'anic text. Its script seems more developed than the *Codex Parisino-petropolitanus*, with a larger number of homographs identified by a diacritical mark and a slightly increased use of the *scriptio plena*. The script is also more homogeneous from a copyist to the next one.

A copy has aroused a special interest since its discovery in 1972. It is a palimpsest kept for its most part in Sanaa (pl. 3; Codex Ṣanʿāʾ I, see Sadeghi and Goudarzi 2010; also Fedeli 2007; Ḥamdūn 2004; Puin 2008, 2009, and 2010),[2] that is to say a copy on parchment which has been subjected to a thorough erasure in order to eliminate the script (*scriptio inferior*) before a new text (*scriptio superior*) was written over it. Both texts are Qur'anic. To this day 80 folios have been found, although only half of them have started to be properly investigated. A first C 14 dating of the parchment concluded with 95 per cent possibility that it was produced between 578 CE and 669 CE and with 68 per cent

[1] This refers to a verse which is divided in the same way in the various traditions recorded by Spitaler.

[2] Another palimpsest has been known for some time, see Mingana and Lewis 1914.

possibility between 614 and 656 CE (Sadeghi and Bergman 2010: 348–54). The size of the folios (36.5 × 28.5 cm) is close to that of copies like the *Codex Parisino-petropolitanus*. The later text (*scriptio superior*) is a copy of the Qur'an which accords with the ʿUthmānic *rasm*—in spite of some orthographic peculiarities like *ʿalā* with an *alif mamdūda* (*lām-alif*) instead of *alif maqṣūra* (*yāʾ*). The *scriptio inferior* in *Ḥijāzī* style differs from the canonical text by the sequence of the suras and textual variants of varying importance. The suras are separated by crude ornaments and a final formula; and the title of the preceding sura can be observed. *Qāla* is sometimes written with an *alif*, as is the case for *ʿadhāb*. The sequence of the suras differs from the ʿUthmānic text: we find 11→8, 9→19, 12→18, 15→25, 34→13 and 63→62→89.

The textual variants cover a variety of situations: transpositions, synonyms of various kinds, verbal forms, omissions and additions (Puin 2010: 262–75). Elizabeth Puin, Behnam Sadeghi, and Mohsen Goudarzi reached the conclusion that the *scriptio inferior* of the Ṣanʿāʾ palimpsest is 'another Qur'an' (Puin 2010: 235; Sadeghi and Goudarzi 2010: 17). The state of the orthography and the use of ornaments between the suras suggest that this copy could have been produced in the second half of the first/seventh century.

Within the '*Ḥijāzī* corpus' (as defined on the basis of Ibn al-Nadīm's description and the criteria set forth above), two groups could be differentiated on the basis of a formal feature. Some manuscripts, like the *Codex Parisino-petropolitanus* (pl. 1), have no real margin around the writing area whereas others include this element in their page setting. In addition, the use of end of line fillers and the more regular appearance of the script in this second group of copies represent a clear change. Actually, various manuscripts exhibit the same script, to such an extent that it can be defined as a coherent palaeographic group (B Ia, see Déroche 1983: 37 and pl. IX; Déroche 1992: 35 and 38). The study of the orthography of these copies, like Saint Petersburg, NLR Marcel 18/2 or 9, reveals that their copyists were using more extensively the *scriptio plena* than those of the copies which have been discussed previously. In addition, some copies include crude decorations between the suras. These elements as well as the comparison with other early copies, which will be discussed below, suggest that this group may be of a later date. They also underscore the lack of information about the milieux in which these manuscripts were prepared as well as their place of production. Four geniza-like deposits of early Qur'anic manuscripts are known (Damascus, al-Fusṭāṭ, Sanaa, and to a lesser degree Qayrawan), but this does not mean that the codices they contained were produced locally.

The material which can be termed *Ḥijāzī* on the basis of Ibn al-Nadīm's description covers a variety of situations. A group which can be assembled around the *Codex Parisino-petropolitanus*, disregarding the format of the copies, vertical or oblong, corresponds to the earliest period of the manuscript tradition and would probably pre-date the last quarter of the first century (before *c.*695), under the reign of ʿAbd al-Malik. However, copyists trained in this style may have remained active beyond this moment. One of the features of this group is the diversity of the hands found on manuscripts, even when they are the result of a team work. As far as can be seen with the fragmentary state of the material, the copies seem to have been a one-volume edition.

The Later Umayyad *Muṣḥaf*

The earliest group of extant Qur'anic manuscripts and fragments can be dated with more precision thanks to the next stage in the development of the written transmission of the text. Two manuscripts, also in vertical format, the Umayyad codex of al-Fusṭāṭ (pl. 4; mainly Saint Petersburg, NLR Marcel 13; Déroche 2004) and the Umayyad codex of Damascus (Istanbul, TIEM ŞE 321; Déroche 2002: 629–34; Déroche 2014: 76–94) are particularly important for the periodization of manuscript production, notably because their illuminations indicate clearly a resemblance with the decoration of the Dome of the Rock and of other contemporary Umayyad buildings. Their script has some connections with the *Ḥijāzī* style, as exemplified by the H and D of the *Codex Parisino-petropolitanus* or by the copyists of BL Or. 2165 (pl. 2). The latter on the one hand as well as both the Damascus and al-Fusṭāṭ codices on the other hand intimates, however, a completely new phenomenon: the same style of writing can be used by various copyists because they have been specifically trained (Déroche, 2014: 100).

This has been confirmed by the discovery of a fair number of copies written in a style (O I) similar to that of the Damascus and al-Fusṭāṭ codices. It seems actually that a distinction should be made between an earlier version (O Ia), associated with a slightly more defective orthography, and that illustrated by the Damascus and al-Fusṭāṭ codices (O Ib). The probable swiftness of these developments may however have allowed for some overlap. Their formats vary mainly from a folio (a fragment of 41.2 × 36 cm) to an octavo size (about 25 × 19 cm), with a group of fair quarto volumes like the al-Fusṭāṭ codex (ranging from 32.5 × 28.5 cm to 37 × 31 cm). Copies of smaller size may have also existed. This diversity contrasts starkly with the fairly constant module of those scripts (between 10 and 12.7 mm in height). Some copies with the same characteristics are in horizontal format (Déroche 2014: 97–101).

The emergence of the O I script is probably related to the change which occurred at the end of the first/seventh century, under the reign of caliph ʿAbd al-Malik, when Arabic, both language and script, became the official medium of the administration (al-Jahshiyari 1938: 37; Latz 1958: 85–6). The relationship between the milestone script of ʿAbd al-Malik and that of contemporaneous *maṣāḥif* suggests that the latter were involved in this transformation which concurred with reforms involving the Qur'anic text. The use of the same script for a large number of copies stressed visually the fact that the text found on these manuscripts was identical. As part of the effort to control more precisely the text, the notation of the short vowels with red dots was introduced at that moment.

The page setting of the Damascus and al-Fusṭāṭ codices also exhibits new features: margins are found in both cases, although they are more conspicuously employed in the al-Fusṭāṭ copy than in the Damascus codex, and thus closer to the earlier *Ḥijāzī* tradition. Line-end fillers are introduced by the copyists after the last word of a line when a blank space was left before reaching the edge of the justification (Déroche 2014: 82). As Or. 2165, although palaeographically close to both manuscripts, does not include these features, we can conclude that they were introduced slightly afterwards and began to influence the copies which have been described above as a later development of the *Ḥijāzī* material.

The B Ia script which we have seen related to the later development of the *Ḥijāzī* style *muṣḥaf* could be a parallel and contemporaneous evolution—in another milieu and/or in another region. The consistent size and lay out of the largest copies can be the result of an official patronage—which the sources actually mention (e.g. al-Nadīm 1971: 9). It is tempting to deduce from the account of al-Nadīm about calligraphy in Umayyad times that there was even a structure where the transcription was performed. However, the diversity of the fragments in O I which have been preserved, ranging from the elegant al-Fusṭāṭ codex to more common copies, indicates that this style had some success and that its diffusion was not restricted to the elite or to official patronage.

Inscriptions and Coins

The evidence provided by the early epigraphy or by the coins struck under Umayyad rule is obviously of a more fragmented nature, but it has the enormous advantage of being possibly exactly dated in contrast to the contemporary manuscripts. Under the reign of ʿAbd al-Malik, in the 70s/690s, Qur'anic quotations appeared on the coinage: the combination of 48:29 and 9:33 on the obverse and Q. 112 (complete on the dirhams only) on the reverse remained unchanged until the fall of the Umayyad caliphate. The epigraphy reflects a more varied selection of texts (Dodd and Khairallah 1981). The most famous inscription is that of the mosaic inscription of the Dome of the Rock which draws from a selection of Qur'anic passages, with some subtle amendment aiming at adapting the quotation to the composition, conveying a message to ʿAbd al-Malik's Christian subjects (Kessler 1970). Closer to popular piety, the graffiti strewn on rocks or walls in the Near East are increasingly being investigated, although much remains to be done. More than half of a corpus of 200 texts collected in Northern Jordan are invocations, but less than 10 per cent contain elements which can be identified as Qur'anic verses, with suras 2, 3, 19, 26, and 42 most often quoted (Imbert 2000: 384 and 387). Variants are said to be rather numerous, but their nature has still to be analysed. It has been suggested that the authors of these texts were working from memory, hence the discrepancies, but the changes seem in many cases to meet personal requirements.

The Canon and the Manuscripts

The manuscripts of the first *Ḥijāzī* group are the most early direct evidence about the text involving extensive passages. Their study is still at its beginning, but they already raise a number of issues. They contain for instance small variations from the ʿUthmānic *rasm*. Most of the variants found in the *Codex Parisino-petropolitanus* or in Paris,

BnF Arabe 328 c and Arabe 6140, in addition to the canonical ones (also present in these manuscripts), are typologically close to those which account for a quarter of the variants said by the tradition to be characteristic of the *maṣāḥif al-amṣār*, for instance the Syrian reading *qālū* instead of *wa-qālū* (2:116) or the Medinan and Syrian *alladhīna* instead of *wa-lladhīna* (9:107). In the manuscripts mentioned, we find for instance *law* instead of *wa-law* or *alladhīna* instead of *wa-lladhīna* (Déroche 2009: 144). In other cases, the variants may be explained as scribal mistakes or as genuine variants, although not recorded in the literature. The *scriptio inferior* of the Ṣanʿāʾ palimpsest indicates that Qur'anic text(s) different from the ʿUthmānic *rasm* as well as from the concurrent recensions—like those of Ibn Masʿūd or Ubayy—have been circulating although no record about them has been preserved.

The distinction between what can be a genuine variant and a mistake is especially difficult in the Codex Ṣanʿāʾ I (Sadeghi and Goudarzi 2010: 49, 51, 64 etc.) since there is no other witness of this textual tradition available to provide a comparison. In contrast, the case of a fragment kept in the Turkish and Islamic art museum in Istanbul, ŞE 13316-1, seems in this respect relatively clear: it is a copy of the ʿUthmānic *rasm* fraught with copyist mistakes. However, it raises like the Ṣanʿāʾ palimpsest the issue of possible handwritten transmission outside of the mainstream (Déroche, 2014: 48–56).

The handwritten transmission of the Qur'an involved material features (like the parchment, the ink, etc.) as well as 'intellectual' tools (like philology, techniques of text control, etc.). The technique of collation plays an important role in this process. The systematic comparison of the copy with the exemplar helps detecting the scribal errors and maintaining the integrity of the text. According to the Islamic tradition, it has been applied since the beginning: as a last step in the writing down of the Qur'an under ʿUthmān, Zayd ibn Thābit compared the text he had compiled with Ḥafṣa's *ṣaḥīfa* (*fa-ʿaraḍa al-muṣḥaf ʿalayhā*) (Tabari 2005: 1: 81; Jeffery 1937: 156–7; Gacek 2006: 240). Viviane Comerro notes that the insistence on the conformity of the canon with a text miraculously kept or found again is a topos encountered in religious literature dealing with the passage from oral to written transmission (Comerro 2012: 59). The still somewhat fluid state of the text as found in the earliest manuscripts and the variants of the *rasm* attributed to the *maṣāḥif al-amṣār* are hardly compatible with a collation procedure. Theodor Nöldeke for instance did not take into account the couple *qāla/qul*—involving a difference which would not escape the attention of the collators when the text was read aloud—in his list of the *rasm* variants (Nöldeke 1860: 240–1). The early copies of the Qur'an which have been examined indicate clearly that the graphic distinction between the two verbal forms began only in a systematic way by the end of the first/seventh century. The *Codex Parisino-petropolitanus*, although transmitting a text which is certainly not Kufan, has in places like Q. 23:112 and Q. 23:114, *qāf+lām* which can be read both ways, *qāla* (as in all the traditions except a Kufan one) or *qul* (which is the Kufan reading). At that moment, neither the Kufan variant nor the majority reading could be effectively recognized in the *rasm*, although it has been argued that the ambiguous orthography left open the possibility of reading either form. This is not the case for the couple *Allāh/li-Llāh* (Q. 23:87 and 23:89) which cannot remain unnoticed during the collation process and is not interchangeable.

Actually, the correction by the copyists of the *Codex Parisino-petropolitanus* of *Allāh* into *li-Llāh* in at least two places (Q. 3:129 and 62:6) indicates that confusing the two forms is difficult (Déroche 2009: 152).

The traditional account about Zayd's collation is hardly compatible with the presence of variants in the copies produced immediately after this operation or with the state of the text as found in the manuscripts. The etiologic account of the origins of the canonical *rasm* variants provided a justification for the actual state of the ʿUthmānic text, probably as a consequence of the detection of discrepancies in the copies at a slightly later date, when the graphic accuracy had made headway and the transmission techniques developed. Collation was incorporated anachronistically into the account about the collection of the Qur'an itself in order to stress the fidelity of the text to its source and its stability (Déroche 2014: 138).

With the important exception of the Codex Ṣanʿāʾ I, the *rasm* found in the handwritten witnesses of that period which have been examined so far corresponds basically to the ʿUthmānic vulgate if we admit that, in spite of the orthographic peculiarities (i.e., the lack of most of the required diacritics and vowel and orthoepic signs), the text the copyists had in mind coincided to a large extent with the canonical version as we know it today. At the moment of the written transmission, it reflected an archaic state that still included traces of the history of the revelations. The comparison of the various witnesses in *Ḥijāzī* style suggests that the corpus was not completely closed and that the 'ʿUthmānic' transmission was still running along parallel tracks. By the beginning of the Umayyad period, the relative lack of concern about the use of diacritics evidenced by the manuscripts can be taken as an argument against the historicity of the worries expressed in the traditional account of the origins of ʿUthmān's decision. Moreover, other reports about al-Ḥajjāj's '*maṣāḥif* project'—to adopt Omar Hamdan's phrase (Hamdan 2006: 135)—show that their 'introduction' was a move seen as crucial for the clarity and reliability of the text. The later account by al-Dānī about the dotting of initial *yāʾ* and *tāʾ* in verbal forms, although probably being a later rationalization of the early *maṣāḥif* evolution, also goes in the same direction (al-Dānī, *al-Muḥkam*, 2 and 17; Hamdan 2006: 147). However, the manuscripts tell us another story. Although the copyists were familiar with the diacritics and started using them before al-Ḥajjāj's time, they did not use them coherently, for instance in places where they could have helped eliminating ambiguities. The accounts transmitted by traditional scholars about the increasing accuracy of the text reflect later reconstructions of this history rather than actual developments (Déroche 2014: 72).

Similar anachronisms can also be found in the two traditions which are the basis of the accounts of the writing down of the Qur'an during ʿUthmān's reign. Harald Motzki has demonstrated that they were probably circulating by the extreme end of the seventh or early eighth century CE and could at any rate be dated to the first quarter of the second/eighth century (Motzki 2001: 30–1). A comparison between the proclaimed aims of the caliph and the state of the written transmission of the text at that moment shows the anachronistic nature of the most 'technical' part of the account. The caliph's role may thus have been less far-reaching than the tradition reports imply, since in the early Umayyad period the manuscripts were unable to safeguard the text and non-canonical variants were still circulating (not to speak of different texts like that of the Codex Ṣanʿāʾ I which were in principle eliminated). The caliph may have been involved in the diffusion of a visual identity for the text he supported, eventually supporting the production and diffusion of copies—a move that was essential to safeguard the vulgate. The writing down of the Qur'an was an important undertaking and the Muslim tradition, although it may disagree on some points, is unanimous in providing the same strong argument in favour of recording the Revelation in written form (Watt and Bell 1977: 40–2 for instance; Comerro 2012: 32–6). In spite of the later position, which gives the recited Qur'an primacy in both accounts—the first one about Abū Bakr, the second one about ʿUthmān—the point is clear: the written text is the basis of a safe preservation of the revelation. The later science of the *qirāʾāt* did actually recognize, albeit in a subdued tone, the importance of the written version of the Qur'an: one of the three basic requirements for the acknowledgement of a reading is its conformity with the ʿUthmānic *rasm*.

The more precise chronology of the handwritten transmission undermines the hypothesis supporting a later dating of the text (Wansbrough 1977) or a cramming of events into a short period preceding the date of the earliest witnesses, although the lack of complete copies until the second/eighth century leaves the door open to speculations. The textual variants found in the manuscripts and the text of the Codex Ṣanʿāʾ I are slowly becoming part of a new approach to the history of the Qur'anic canon. They are to some extent paralleled by the study of the division of verses. These divisions have shown, on the basis of the analysis of specific copies, that they offer a variety of divergences from the canonical schools. In a further development, a comprehensive study of the complex relationship between the written text, as it appears on the copies from Umayyad times, and the *qirāʾāt* may help us understand the exponential multiplication of the latter during the second/eighth century (Nasser 2013: 229). Some points would require more research: the geography of the handwritten production and its possible links to various environments, social or religious, still elude us. However, as a whole, the conditions of the transmission of the Qur'anic text, both recited and written, will certainly benefit from a thorough knowledge of the material, a large part of which is still awaiting publication.

Bibliography

Primary Sources

al-Dānī. *Muḥkam fī naqṭ al-maṣāḥif*. Ed. ʿI. Ḥasan. Damas: Wizārat al-Thaqāfah wa'l-Irshād al-Qawmī, 1379/1960.

al-Jahshiyārī. *Kitāb al-Wuzarāʾ wa'l-kuttāb*. Ed. M. al-Saqqā, I. al-Abyārī, and ʿA. Shalabī. Cairo: Musṭafá al-Bābī al-Ḥalabī, 1938.

al-Jahshiyārī. *Das Buch der Wezire und Staatssekretäre von Ibn ʿAbdūs Al-Ğahsiyārī. Anfänge und Umaiyadenzeit*. Trans. J. Latz (Beiträge zur Sprach- und Kulturgeschichte des Orients, 11). Walldorf-Hessen, 1958.

al-Nadīm. K. *al-Fihrist*. Ed. R. Tajaddud. Tehran, 1971.

al-Nadīm. *The Fihrist of al-Nadîm: A Tenth-Century Survey of Muslim Culture* I. Trans. B. Dodge. New York/London, 1970.

al-Ṭabarī. *Jāmiʿ al-bayān ʿan taʾwīl āy al-Qurʾān*. Ed. M. M. Shākir and A. M. Shākir. Cairo-Alexandria: Dār al-Maʿārif, 2005.

Secondary Sources

Abbott, N. *The Rise of the North Arabic Script and its Kur'ānic Development*. Chicago: Oriental Institute Publications, 1939.

Adler, J. C. G. *Descriptio codicum quorumdam cuficorum partes Corani exhibentium in Bibliotheca regia hafniensi et ex iisdem de scriptura Arabum observationes novæ, Præmittitur disquisitio generalis de arte scribendi apud Arabes ex ipsis auctoribus arabicis adhuc ineditis sumta*. Altona, NY, 1780.

Altıkulaç, T. (ed.). *Al-muṣḥaf al-šarīf* (in Arabic). *Al-muṣḥaf al-sharīf attributed to ʿUthmān bin ʿAffān (The copy at the Topkapı Palace Museum)*. Istanbul: Istanbul Research Center For Islamic History, Art and Culture, 1428/2007.

Altıkulaç, T. (ed.). *al-Muṣḥaf al-Sharif attributed to ʿUthmān ibn ʿAffān (the copy at Mashhad Imam Husaini in Cairo)*. 1st edn. Istanbul: Research Center For Islamic History, Art and Culture, 1430/2009.

Amari, M. 'Bibliographie primitive du Coran... Extrait de son mémoire inédit sur la chronologie et l'ancienne bibliographie du Coran, publié et annoté par Hartwig Derenbourg'. In: *Centenario della nascita di Michele Amari* I, pp. 1–22. Palermo: Palermo Stab. tip. Virzì, 1910.

Arberry, Arthur. J. *The Koran Illuminated: A Handlist of the Korans in the Chester Beatty Library*. Dublin: Hodges Figgis & Co. Ltd., 1967.

Bergsträsser, G. and O. Pretzl. *Geschichte des Qorâns von Theodor Nöldeke*. 2nd edn. *III: Geschichte des Koranstext*. Leipzig: Martinus Nijhoff, 1938.

Buresi, P. 'Une relique almohade: l'utilisation du coran (attribué à ʿUthmān b. ʿAffān (644–656)) de la grande mosquée de Cordoue'. In: *Lieux de cultes: aires votives, temples, églises, mosquées. IXe colloque international sur l'histoire et l'archéologie de l'Afrique du Nord antique et médiévale. Tripoli, 19–25 février 2005*, pp. 273–80. (Etudes d'Antiquités africaines). Paris: Éditions du Centre National de la Recherche Scientifique, 2008.

Comerro, V. *Les Traditions sur la constitution du* muṣḥaf *de ʿUthmān*. (Beiruter Texte und Studien 134). Beirut: Erlon Verlag, 2012.

Cook, M. 'The Stemma of the Regional Codices of the Koran'. In: G. K. Livadas (ed.). *Festschrift in Honour of V. Christides, Graeco-arabica* 9–10 (2004), 89–104.

Déroche, F. *Les Manuscrits du Coran: aux origines de la calligraphie coranique* (Bibliothèque Nationale, Catalogue des manuscrits arabes, 2ᵉ partie, Manuscrits musulmans, I/1). Paris, 1983.

Déroche, F. *The Abbasid tradition, Qur'ans of the 8th to the 10th Centuries* (The Nasser D. Khalili collection of Islamic art, I). London: Nour Foundation in association with Azmimuth and Oxford University Press, 1992.

Déroche, F. 'New Evidence about Umayyad Book Hands'. In: *Essays in honour of Ṣalāḥ al-Dīn al-Munajjid* (al-Furqān publication, n° 70), pp. 611–42. London: Al-Furqan Islamic Heritage Foundation, 2002.

Déroche, F. 'Colonnes, vases et rinceaux: sur quelques enluminures d'époque omeyyade', *Académie des inscriptions et belles-lettres, Comptes rendus des séances de l'année 2004* (2006), 227–64.

Déroche, F. *La transmission écrite du Coran dans les débuts de l'islam: le codex Parisino-petropolitanus* (Texts and studies on the Qurʾān 5). Leiden-Boston: Brill, 2009.
Déroche, F. *Qur'ans of the Umayyads: A First Overview* (Leiden Studies in Islam & Society 1). Leiden: Brill, 2014.
Déroche, F., and S. Noja Noseda. *Le manuscrit Arabe 328 (a) de la Bibliothèque nationale de France* (Sources de la transmission manuscrite du texte coranique I, Les manuscrits de style ḥijāzī, 1). Lesa: Fondazione Ferni Noja Noseda, 1998.
Déroche, F. and S. Noja Noseda *(Le manuscrit Or. 2165 (f. 1 à 61) de la British Library* (Sources de la transmission manuscrite du texte coranique, I: Les manuscrits de style higâzî). Lesa: Fondazione Ferni Noja Noseda, 2001.
Déroche, F. et al. *Islamic Codicology: An Introduction to the Study of Manuscripts in Arabic Script*. London: Al-Furqan Islamic Heritage Foundation, 2005.
Diem, W. 'Untersuchungen zur frühen Geschichte der arabischen Orthographie. IV: Die Schreibung der zusammenhängenden Rede. Zusammenfassung', *Orientalia* NS 52 (1983), 357–404.
Dodd, E. C. and Khairallah, S. *The Image of the Word: A Study of Quranic Verses in Islamic Architecture*, 2 vols. Beirut: American University of Beirut, 1981.
Fedeli, A. 'Early Evidences of Variant Readings in Qurʾānic Manuscripts'. In: K.-H. Ohlig and G.-R. Puin (eds.). *Die dunklen Anfänge: Neue Forschungen zur Entstehung und frühen Geschichte des Islam*, pp. 293–316. Berlin: Hans Schiler Verlag, 2007.
Gacek, A. 'The Copying and Handling of Qurʾāns: Some Observations on the *Kitāb al-maṣāḥif* by Ibn Abī Dā'ūd al-Sijistānī', *Mélange de l'Université Saint-Joseph* 59 (2006) (Actes de la conférence internationale sur les manuscrits du Coran (Bologne, 26–8 septembre 2002)), pp. 229–51.
Grohmann, A. 'The Problem of Dating Early Qurʾāns', *Der Islam* 33 (1958), 213–31.
Hamdan, O. *Studien zur Kanonisierung des Korantextes: Al-Ḥasan al-Baṣrī's Beiträge zur Geschichte des Korans*. Wiesbaden: Harrassowitz, 2006.
Ḥamdūn, R. Gh. *'al-Makhṭūṭāt al-Qurʾāniyya fī Ṣanʿāʾ mundhu al-qarn al-awwal al-hijrī'*. Unpublished masters thesis, Sanaa, 2004.
Ibn Abī Dāwūd. *Kitāb al-maṣāḥif* = A. Jeffery, *Materials for the History of the Text of the Qur'ân*. Leiden: E. J. Brill, 1937.
Imbert, F. 'Le Coran dans les graffiti des deux premiers siècles de l'Hégire', *Arabica* 47 (2000), 384–90.
Jahdani, A. 'Du *fiqh* à la codicologie: quelques opinions de Mālik (m. 179/796) sur le Coran-codex', *Mélanges de l'Université Saint-Joseph* 56 (2006) (Actes de la conférence internationale sur les manuscrits du Coran (Bologne, 26–8 septembre 2002)), 269–79.
James, D. *Qur'ans and Bindings from the Chester Beatty Library*. London: World of Islam Festival Trust, 1980.
Jeffery, A. *Materials for the History of the Text of the Qur'ân*. Leiden: Brill, 1937.
Kessler, C. 'Abd al-Malik's Inscription in the Dome of the Rock: A Reconsideration', *Journal of the Royal Asiatic Society* (1970), 2–14.
Mingana, Alphonse and Agnes Smith Lewis. *Leaves from Three Ancient Qurâns Possibly Pre-'Othmânic: With a List of Their Variants*. Cambridge: Cambridge University Press, 1914.
Motzki, H. 'The Collection of the Qurʾān: A Reconsideration of Western Views in Light of Recent Methodological Developments', *Der Islam* 78 (2001), 1–34.
Mouton, J. M. 'De quelques reliques conservées à Damas au Moyen Age: stratégie politique et religiosité populaire sous les Bourides', *Annales islamologiques* 27 (1993), 247–54.

Al-Munajjid, Ṣ. *Dirāsāt fī tārīkh al-khaṭṭ al-ʿarabī mundhu bidāyatihi ilā nihāyat al-ʿaṣr al-umawī—études de paléographie arabe*. Beirut: Brill, 1972.

Nasser, Sh. H. *The Transmission of the Variant Readings of the Qurʾān: The Problem of* tawātur *and the Emergence of* shawādhdh' (Text and Studies on the Qurʾān 9). Leiden/Boston: Brill, 2013.

Nöldeke, T. *Geschichte des Qorâns*. Göttingen: Dieterich, 1860.

Puin, G.-R. 'Observations on Early Qurʾān Manuscripts in Ṣanʿā'. In: S. Wild (ed.). *The Qur'an as text*, pp. 107–11. Leiden/New York/Cologne: Brill, 1996.

Puin, E. 'Ein früher Koranpalimpsest aus Ṣanʿā' (DAM 01–27.1)'. In: M. Groß and K.-H. Ohlig (eds.). *Schlaglichter: Die beiden ersten islamischen Jahrhunderte* (Inârah. Schriften zur frühen Islamgeschichte und zum Koran, vol. 3), pp. 461–93. Berlin: Verlag Hans Schiler, 2008.

Puin, E. 'Ein früher Koranpalimpsest aus Ṣanʿā' (DAM 01–27.1)—Teil II'. In: M. Groß and K.-H. Ohlig (eds.). *Vom Koran zum Islam* (Inârah. Schriften zur frühen Islamgeschichte und zum Koran, vol. 4), pp. 523–81. Berlin: Schiler, 2009.

Puin, E. 'Ein früher Koranpalimpsest aus Ṣanʿā' (DAM 01–27.1)—Teil III: Ein nicht-ʿuṯmānischer Koran'. In: M. Groß and K.-H. Ohlig (eds.). *Die Entstehung einer Weltreligion I: Von der koranischen Bewegung zum Frühislam* (Inârah. Schriften zur frühen Islamgeschichte und zum Koran, vol. 5), pp. 233–305. Berlin: Schiler, 2010.

Quatremère, E. 'Sur le goût des livres chez les Orientaux', *Journal Asiatique* series 3, vol. 6 (1838), 35–78.

Rabb, I. 'Non-Canonical Readings of the Qur'ān: Recognition and Authenticity (The Ḥimsī Reading)', *Journal of Qurʾanic Studies* 8/2 (2006), 84–127.

Rezvan, E. 'Yet another "ʿUthmānic Qurʾān"' (on the history of manuscript E 20 from the St. Petersburg branch of the Institute of Oriental Studies), *Manuscripta Orientalia* 6/1 (March 2000), 49–68.

Rezvan, E. 'New Folios from the "ʿUthmānic Qurʾān"' I. (Library for administration of Muslim Affairs of the Republic of Uzbekistan), *Manuscripta Orientalia* 10/1 (March 2004), 32–41.

Sadeghi, B. and U. Bergmann. 'The Codex of a Companion of the Prophet and the Qur'an of the Prophet', *Arabica* 57 (2010), 343–436.

Sadeghi, B., and M. Goudarzi. 'Ṣanʿā' 1 and the Origins of the Qurʾān', *Der Islam* 87 (2010), 2–129.

Schwally, F. *Geschichte des Qorâns von Theodor Nöldeke*. 2nd edn. *II. Die Sammlung des Qorans*. Leipzig: Dieterich, 1919.

Shebunin, A. N. 'Kuficheskij Koran Imperatorskoj Sankt-Petersburgskoj publichnoj biblioteki', *Zapiski Vostochnogo Otdelenija imperatorskogo russkogo arkheologicheskogo obshchestva* 6 (1891), 69–133.

Spitaler, A. *Die Verszählung des Koran nach islamischer Überlieferung* (Sitzungsberichte der Bayerischen Akademie der Wissenschaften, Phil.-historische Abteilung. Jahrgang 1935, Heft 11). Munich: Verlag der Bayerischen Akademie der Wissenschaften, 1935.

Wansbrough, J. *Quranic Studies: Sources and Methods of Scriptural Interpretation* (London Oriental series, 31). Oxford: Oxford University Press, 1977.

Watt, W. M., and R. Bell, *Introduction to the Qur'an*. Edinburgh: Edinburgh University Press, 1977.

Whelan, E. 'Evidence for the Early Codification of the Qur'an', *Journal of the American Oriental Society* 118 (1998), 1–14.

CHAPTER 12

THE FORM OF THE QUR'AN

Historical Contours

YASIN DUTTON

THE Qur'an as we know it today reflects a text that has remained remarkably fixed, in written as well as spoken form, for well over 1,000 years. Indeed, the commonly received traditional picture is that it was fixed from the very beginning, over 1,400 years ago, and that it has been transmitted faithfully, at first orally and then in writing as well, since that very beginning. At the same time, however, our traditional sources indicate that, on a micro-level at least, there was initially a fair amount of variation in the text, particularly in the period before the decision of the caliph ʿUthmān, in or around the year 30/650, to unify the community on a single textual skeleton (*rasm*), but also—although to a much more limited extent—for the next 300 years or so as this text became more and more standardized into the form of 'readings', that is, preferred routes through a limited, but nevertheless existent, set of possibilities of how to 'read' the text. It is this first 300 years or so that we consider in the present chapter, with a special focus on ongoing research questions and, in particular, how to understand the idea of a 'fixed' text which nevertheless allows a degree of ongoing 'looseness' despite increasing standardization over the years.

The text as we know it today is effectively that endorsed by Ibn Mujāhid (d. 324/936) in his *Kitāb al-Sabʿa fī-l-qirāʾāt* ('The Book of the Seven with regard to Readings'), where he covers the readings, or textual variant choices, of seven main Readers. Since that time these 'Seven Readings' have gained the acceptance of all Muslim scholars, and thus the Muslim community, as acceptable presentations of the Qur'anic text.

It is important to recognize, firstly, that Ibn Mujāhid was the first to isolate 'seven readings'—*awwal man sabbaʿa al-sabʿa* ('the first to make the Seven into a group'), to use Ibn al-Jazarī's (d. 833/1429) phrase (Ibn al-Jazarī, *Ghāya*, 1:139)—thus implying that this was only a choice, and that other readings were possible. Indeed, we know of books both before and after his time that covered from five up to fifty readings. The concept of Ten Readings in particular, while not so frequently referred to as that of

Seven Readings, is nevertheless also considered perfectly acceptable in mainstream Muslim scholastic circles.

A first question to ask then is, what is the nature of the variation between these, say, Seven, or Ten, Readings? Briefly, one can say that the variants cover the usual spectrum of variants to be found in a textual tradition deriving from an oral source. There are variants in short vowels (unmarked in the consonantal 'skeleton' of the text), variants in long vowels (often, but not always, unmarked in the consonantal skeleton), variants in the pointing of homographic consonants (often unmarked in our earliest manuscripts), and variants in the reading of certain individual consonants (involving slight differences in the consonantal outline). In no instance, however, do these differences involve any significant change of meaning.

Beyond these Seven, or Ten, Readings, there is plenty of reference in the sources to other variants, referred to as *shādhdh* ('irregular', 'non-standard'), which, in addition to the above possibilities, also involve variations in individual words, or in the word-order, or in the inclusion or omission of individual words or phrases, or, occasionally, more substantial amounts of text.

A second question to ask is, how did these Readings, or, we could say, this level of variation, come about? Put more theologically, how should we understand all this material in the context of a book that is claimed to be a faithful reproduction of a heavenly original that has been subject to neither change nor alteration since its first promulgation on the tongue of the Prophet Muḥammad?

There are at least two ways to approach this question. The first, that of the so-called historico-critical approach adopted in particular by biblical scholars, is to say that the Qur'an has, like any other scriptural text, been subject to human editorial activity, thus, by clear implication, saying that it is *not* a faithful reproduction of a heavenly original and that it *has* been subject to change and alteration.

A second approach, and the one that is suggested here, is to take the tradition at face value and, rather than deny or seek to explain away seeming inconsistencies in the picture presented, to seek instead to understand the whole as a whole.

To start with, we note that the 'book' that we are talking about, conveniently referred to as 'the Qur'an', is initially a non-spatial, non-temporal, entity, although it does then come into space and time. That is to say, there is a stage envisaged where there is a 'book', but it has not yet become a *qurʾān* ('recitation'). As several scholars have noted (e.g. Madigan 2001; Jones 2003a; Jones 2003b), the word for 'book', *kitāb*, as used in the Qur'an, seems to refer most frequently not to a solid, physical document, but to a more metaphorical meaning. Thus, to take but one example, Q. 41:3 refers to the Qur'an as being a 'book' (*kitāb*) whose 'signs' (*āyāt* = 'verses') have been demarcated (or 'clarified') in the form of a *qurʾān*, thus positing a 'book' that then becomes revelation in a recited form. Other verses refer to a 'book' in which what has been divinely ordained has been 'written', e.g. Q. 17:58, 'That is written in the Book'. Such references are glossed by the commentators as referring to the 'Preserved Tablet' (*al-lawḥ al-maḥfūẓ*), echoing the verse which describes the Qur'an as being 'on a preserved tablet', or, in another reading from among the Seven, 'preserved on a tablet' (Q. 85:22).

This Preserved Tablet is understood to be referred to elsewhere in the Qur'an. For example, Q. 80:11–16 reads: 'Nay, it is a reminder—and whoever wishes will remember it—on honoured pages, exalted, purified, in the hands of noble and virtuous scribes.' Here the 'noble and virtuous scribes' are understood to be the angels in charge of the Preserved Tablet. This in turn allows an 'angelic' interpretation of a second passage where we are told that 'It is a noble Qur'an, in a protected book, touched only by the purified' (Q. 56:77–9), where the phrase 'touched only by the purified' is taken to refer to the angels. These verses are often equated with the command to be in a state of ritual purity when touching the Qur'an, but Imam Mālik, for instance, while accepting this judgement, bases it rather on the directive of the Prophet in his letter to ʿAmr ibn Ḥazm that only someone who is ritually pure should touch the Qur'an, and prefers to understand the meaning of the verses in the 'angelic' sense mentioned above (Mālik, *Muwaṭṭaʾ*, 1:158). Either way, the Qur'an is described as 'noble' and 'honoured', and being ritually pure before touching it is considered the most appropriate way of honouring it.

We also note that, in the traditional description, the material in this Preserved Tablet is transmitted to the 'noble recording angels'—and angels are made of light—and then to the Angel Gabriel, who then transmits it to the heart of the Prophet, who then recites it out to people. As it says in the Qur'an: 'The Trustworthy Spirit brought it down onto your heart in order for you to be a warner, in a clear Arabic tongue' (Q. 26:193–5).

There is thus a non-spatial, non-temporal source of the Qur'an that is described as a book, but which, by definition, is not like the physical books that we are familiar with.

We mention all this is in order to highlight the fact that what is 'preserved on a [heavenly] tablet' is not a 'book' in the normal everyday sense of the term, and this difference must be taken into account when trying to understand its 'preservation'. It is, in its own terms, a revelation (*tanzīl*), and our understanding of this will necessarily colour our understanding not only of the content of this 'book', but also—and perhaps most especially—its form.

Once this revelation has happened, it then—given its importance to the community—needs to be passed on. Linguistically speaking, this can happen in two obvious ways: by speech and by writing. In the case of the Qur'an, it is assumed *a priori* that the text was only *spoken* by the Prophet, so the first stage is spoken transmission, or *qurʾān*, which is, quite literally, something that is read, or recited, out loud. Indeed, the tradition is unanimous on the fact that the Prophet was 'unlettered' (*ummī*), that is, could not read or write. He did, however, have parts, possibly even most, of the Qur'an written down by others, thus initiating the process of written transmission alongside the spoken form. It is at this point that we find ourselves dealing with the beginnings of a 'book' in the more normal sense of the word.

Tradition tells us that the Prophet would have new revelations written down for him and that there were a number of Companions that he used for this purpose. At the same time, however, there is no clear indication that the whole of the Qur'an was ever written down during the lifetime of the Prophet. On the contrary, the picture of the Qur'an's 'collection' in written form after the death of the Prophet quite overtly refers to 'the hearts of men' as being one of the main sources of Qur'anic material (alongside palm-branches, stones, etc.). Indeed, given the limited surface area of these other materials, it would seem at least possible that, at the death of the Prophet, large portions of the Qur'an were still in 'the hearts of men' rather than being in a solid, written, form.

Recording an initially oral document, however—that is, making a *kitāb*, in the later non-metaphorical sense, out of a *qur'ān*—is not such a straightforward exercise as it may seem. As has been demonstrated in, for example, the case of Homer and early Greek poetry, but also increasingly in many other oral traditions, oral 'literature' allows for a level of variation that is hard to replicate in written form, but still remains true to an overall form and meaning. Thus scholars have seen fit to talk of multiformity—as opposed to uniformity—which indicates the nature of a 'text' before it gets written down, when every performance of it may generate, or be characterized by, slightly different expressions of the same word or phrase or idea (see e.g. Lord 1960). The same can be seen in the case of the Qur'an, where recent studies (e.g. Dutton 2012) have suggested this multiformity as the best way of understanding the various readings that have come down to us, both as ongoing systems of recitation (the Seven/Ten Readings), and as preserved more widely in the literature as memories of significant formal variations—which nevertheless maintain the same content—between what are referred to as 'the written copies (*maṣāḥif*) of the Companions'.

In aiming to understand this multiformity, it is essential to recognize the existence of 'seven *ḥarfs*' (*ḥarf* = lit. 'edge') both at the time of the Prophet and immediately after him during the time of the first three Rightly Guided Caliphs. This phenomenon is encapsulated in the well-known hadith about the Qur'an having been sent down 'on seven edges (*ʿalā sabʿat aḥruf*)':

> ʿUmar ibn al-Khaṭṭāb said, I heard Hishām ibn Ḥakīm ibn Ḥizām reciting *Sūrat al-Furqān* [Q. 23] differently to the way I recited it, and it was the Prophet, may Allāh bless him and grant him peace, who had taught me it. I was about to rush up to him, but I allowed him time to finish [his prayer]. Then I grabbed him by his cloak and took him to the Messenger of Allāh, may Allāh bless him and grant him peace, and said, 'Messenger of Allāh, I heard this man reciting *Sūrat al-Furqān* differently to the way you taught me.' The Messenger of Allāh, may Allāh bless him and grant him peace, said, 'Let him go.' He then said, 'Recite, Hishām,' and Hishām recited in the same way that he had done before. The Messenger of Allāh, may Allāh bless him and grant him peace, said, 'It was sent down like that. This Qur'an was sent down on seven edges (*ʿalā sabʿat aḥruf*), so recite whatever of it is easy for you.'
>
> (Mālik, *Muwaṭṭaʾ*, 1:159–60)

This hadith—or rather the phenomenon recorded in this hadith and especially what is implied by the word *ḥarf*—needs to be studied further, but it is immediately apparent that (a) there was significant variation at the level of detail in the form in the Qur'an (such that two renditions of one sura could be perceived as 'different'), and (b) that, although frequently encountered, the explanation that the 'seven *ḥarfs*' refer to seven dialects—if 'dialect' is taken as referring to regional variation in speech—is untenable: the two protagonists in the hadith were both members of the same tribe and would have spoken the same dialect.

This hadith, along with several other similar references in the hadith literature, indicates that there was Prophetic authority for these differences. Some scholars, however (e.g. Sadeghi and Bergmann 2010; Sadeghi and Goudarzi 2011), have suggested that, rather than suggesting multiformity, these 'Companion-*maṣāḥif*' variations are in fact 'deviations' (in a statistical sense) from a single, effectively uniform, text (a 'Prophetic prototype'). The arguments for and against this understanding need to be clearly marshalled.

Whatever the case may be, it is clear from the literature that the Companions in many instances had their own *muṣḥaf*s, or written copies of the Qur'an, which differed on a level of detail from each other. Thus, for example, there is good evidence that Ibn Masʿūd's *muṣḥaf*—one of these early *muṣḥaf*s—contained the phrase 'Say to those who disbelieve (*qul li-lladhīna kafarū*)' rather than what was to become the normal 'Say "O you who disbelieve (*qul yā-ayyuhā l-kāfirūn*)"' (Q. 109:1) (see e.g. al-Shaybānī, *Kitāb al-Āthār*, 72), which illustrates a purely grammatical reformulation of exactly the same meaning. Reference to Ibn Masʿūd's—and other Companions'—readings can be found scattered throughout the relevant literature on *tafsīr* ('commentary') and *qirāʾāt* ('readings') in particular. It is therefore important that researchers do not seek to explain away or ignore this aspect but rather seek to understand it as the norm before ʿUthmān's promulgation to unify the community on one agreed *muṣḥaf* in the sense of one agreed textual skeleton.

A major research question, then, is to ascertain to what extent 'the Qur'an' was limited by ʿUthmān's decision, meaning, effectively, what were the options allowed before ʿUthmān's promulgation, which were then prohibited by him, with the consensus of the Companions?

This question depends on an understanding of the 'seven *ḥarf*s' question above. If, as seems most likely, the 'seven *ḥarf*s' represent an acceptable level of variation at an oral level, then the fixing of the skeletal form of the text necessarily limited that level of variation. It did not, however, extinguish it. Indeed, there are variants that seem to depend on two different ways of not only reading, but of dividing up, the consonantal text once it has been established. Thus, for example, within the Seven Readings we find the two possibilities of *idhā dabara* and *idh adbara* (Q. 74:33) which depend on whether the *alif* in the middle of the phrase is taken as belonging to the end of the first word or the beginning of the second. The same applies to *anṣāran li-llāh* and *anṣārallāh* (Q. 61:14). (In both instances it should be remembered that, in early Arabic orthography, the gap between the final form of any letter and the next letter is the same whether it is in the middle of a word or at the end of one.)

What is important to recognize, though, in all these instances—indeed in the phenomenon of the readings as a whole—is that they only ever represent one dominant meaning. We find this reflected in the comment of the Younger Successor Ibn Shihāb al-Zuhrī (d. 124/742), who is recorded as saying, 'I have heard that these seven *ḥarf*s all relate to where there is a single meaning, without there being any difference with regard to what is permitted and what is forbidden' (Muslim, *Ṣaḥīḥ*, 2:202).

Once an initially oral phenomenon is reduced to writing, other issues immediately arise. In the case of the Arabic of the Qur'an, two particular issues become apparent: whether or not to point the consonants that can be pointed, and whether or not to spell out long vowels, especially those involving *alif*. Thus we find that our earliest Qur'anic fragments—and as yet the earliest period is only represented by fragments, albeit in some cases extensive ones, rather than complete copies of the Qur'an—tend to have very few pointed consonants and are often lacking many of the *alif*s that are later included. Some work has been done on the nature and frequency of this pointing (e.g. Jones 1998; Dutton 2007: 61–2, 66–8, 71–4; Puin 2008: esp. 466–8) but as yet there remains much to be done on this aspect of the Qur'an's orthography.

Two particular instances of the varying presence or absence of *alif* occur in the words *shay'*, where an extra *alif* is often present, and *qāla*, where the *alif* is often absent. These and other similar spellings have been noted by scholars (e.g. Puin 1996: 108–9; Dutton 2004: 64; Dutton 2007: 62–3, 68, 74; Déroche 2009: 51–75; Puin 2011; Déroche 2014: 21–6, 38, 42–3, 45–8, 51, 57–61, 68) but so far such changes of usage have not been sufficiently well analysed, beyond the obvious point that certain patterns, such as *qāla* without an *alif* and *shayʾun/shayʾin* with an *alif*, are frequently encountered in what seem to be our earliest fragments. It is to be hoped that further study will throw further light on this aspect.

Some of our earliest manuscripts also exhibit a certain fluidity and/or inconsistency in verse numbering. That is to say, the verses marked do not always correspond with the verse endings referred to in later texts on the subject, nor do the five- and ten-verse markers occur consistently at five- and ten-verse intervals (see Puin 1996: 109–110; Dutton 2001: 74–84; Dutton 2004: 48–65; Rabb 2006: 91–100; Dutton 2007: 64–5; Puin 2008: 466, 470–5; Déroche 2009: 77–102; Déroche 2014: 26–9). Exactly what these anomalies do represent, though, is a subject needing further research, especially those instances where full verse-ending markers are used to indicate what are considered by later authors on the subject, such as Ibn al-Anbārī (d. 328/939) in his *Kitāb al-Waqf wa'l-ibtidāʾ*, to be simply acceptable stopping places (*waqafāt ḥasana*) rather than full verse-endings (*waqafāt tāmma*).

Presenting the whole Qur'an in written form also necessitated another choice, namely, the order of the suras. The traditional view, as indicated, for example, by Ibn ʿAṭiyya (d. 546/1151) in his *Tafsīr*, is that the order of the suras was fixed at the time when ʿUthmān had the skeletal text standardized, rather than earlier, although certain sub-groups, such as the suras beginning with the letters *ḥā-mīm*, may have already been grouped in that way. This flexibility, or difference of order, is indicated by reports in, for example, al-Suyūṭī's (d. 911/1505) *al-Itqān* about the different order of suras in the *muṣḥaf*s of Ibn Masʿūd and Ubayy (al-Suyūṭī, *al-Itqān*, 1:181–3). Some rare examples of differences from the standard order occur in a few early manuscripts found in the Yemen (see Puin 1996: 110–11), but, to the best of my knowledge, these have yet to be systematically studied.

The Role of al-Ḥajjāj Ibn Yūsuf

One particular problem which needs further elucidation is the role of al-Ḥajjāj ibn Yūsuf (d. 95/714) in the further standardization of the ʿUthmānic skeletal text. It seems clear that certain orthographical reforms were made at his instigation while he was governor of Iraq (75–95/694–714). This activity, termed the 'second *maṣāḥif* project' by Omar Hamdan (Hamdan 2010: 795), and dated by him to *c.*84–5/703–4 (Hamdan 2010: 801), was carried out by a number of Basran specialists—special mention is made of al-Ḥasan al-Baṣrī, Yaḥyā ibn Yaʿmur, and Naṣr ibn ʿĀṣim, but there were others with them—and seems to have involved both the addition of diacritical points to distinguish between consonants of the same form, and also larger, coloured dots to indicate vowels. This team also seem to have concerned themselves with certain general matters of presentation, such as leaving a dividing line between suras, using groups of dots (or dashes) to mark the end of verses, and indicating groups of five and ten verses with special markers and/or rosettes. It is to be hoped that further study of early manuscripts, especially those with a likely dating to the Umayyad period, will provide clarification and/or corroboration of what the literary sources tell us, and thus help us to ascertain al-Ḥajjāj's role in this project and, indeed, what the project actually involved.

One thing is clear from the sources, though, and that is that al-Ḥajjāj was adamant in his opposition to the use of any of the earlier readings that were not in accord with the ʿUthmānic text. In Iraq, and especially in Kufa, this meant in particular the reading of Ibn Masʿūd, which must have still been in use to a limited extent there, despite ʿUthmān's earlier instructions to have any non-conforming *muṣḥaf*s destroyed. We are told that al-Ḥajjāj sent out a team to destroy such *muṣḥaf*s and, as a further act, sent copies of his new version to all the major cities. What is not clear, though, is the extent to which this 'new' version was in fact new, in the sense of different, or, as seems *a priori* more likely—given the absence of any objection to al-Ḥajjāj's activity with regard to the Qur'an, and, indeed, his being praised for it by the 'fifth' Rightly Guided Caliph, ʿUmar ibn ʿAbd al-ʿAzīz (r. 99–101/717–20), despite his severe censure of him otherwise (see Ibn ʿAsākir, *Mukhtaṣar Tārīkh Dimashq*, 6:231)—that it was merely a more standardized version in terms of orthography and verse-marking.

The Period of *Ikhtiyār*

At the same time as this 'second *maṣāḥif* project', we are told that a book was written—presumably also under the auspices of al-Ḥajjāj—which contained the different readings recorded from people that were in accord with the skeletal form (*rasm*) of the *muṣḥaf*; this, we are told, was used by people for a long time until Ibn Mujāhid (d. 324/936) wrote his book on the Seven Readings (see Ibn ʿAṭiyya, *Tafsīr*, 1:35). This period, from al-Ḥajjāj's second *maṣāḥif* project until the compiling of Ibn Mujāhid's book, is characterized by a certain freedom of choice (*ikhtiyār*) between readings based on the accepted skeleton (*rasm*) of the text. Thus we hear of a number of readers having an *ikhtiyār* attributed to them (*lahu ikhtiyār fī'l-qirā'a yunsabu ilayhi*), such as Ṭalḥa ibn Muṣarrif (d. 112/730) and Yazīd al-Sakūnī (*fl.* early second/eighth century?) (Ibn al-Jazarī, *Ghāya*, 1:343, 2:382), sometimes with the additional comment that this 'choice' included readings outside the commonly accepted readings of the community (*shādhdh ʿan al-ʿāmma/shadhdha fīhi*) such as the readings of Abū'l-Sammāl (*fl.* second/eighth century?) and Ibn al-Samayfaʿ (d. early second/eighth century?) (Ibn al-Jazarī, *Ghāya*, 2:27, 161). This suggests that for a considerable period of time there was indeed a degree of choice in how the text was read but that there was also a norm against which this choice could be measured. Since we know that the 'choices' of Seven, Eight, Ten Readings, etc., were later limitations—or circumscriptions—of an originally wider set of possibilities, this reference to a period of *ikhtiyār* suggests a critical period in the history of the Qur'anic text when, even with a fixed skeletal text, considerably more possibilities were entertained than was later the case (although always within a limited framework). Since we have manuscript copies almost certainly dating from this period, and since many of these early copies frequently indicate readings outside the Seven/Ten Readings, etc., this is an area where we can expect major breakthroughs into understanding the formation of the 'standard' readings as we know them today. Initial investigations (e.g. Dutton 1999 and 2000) show that in such early manuscripts there is frequently a non-alignment of actual vocalizations with the expectations engendered by the later *qirā'āt* literature, although, at the same time, there are early manuscripts whose readings exactly fit these later expectations. The same applies to verse-numbering: while general alignments often seem apparent in our early manuscripts, the frequent anomalies that occur suggest that this area, too, of Qur'anic presentation took some considerable time to become standardized into the systems—Medinan, Meccan, Syrian, Basran, Kufan, etc.—that are familiar to us from the literature today. This is another area where, as indicated earlier, much useful research can and should be done working on early manuscripts in conjunction with the literature describing the later systematizations of both readings and verse-numbering systems.

We have suggested above that the existence of a 'period of *ikhtiyār*' indicates (a) that there was some amount of choice between readings that *was* acceptable, even if, perhaps, it may have been a little idiosyncratic, and (b) that there was nevertheless a norm, or norms, that had developed that were generally accepted by most readers. Indeed, the scholars and/or readers to whom such a 'choice' of readings is attributed were generally active in the second century AH, which is precisely the same period of time to which the Seven/Ten Readers belong. It therefore seems that two processes were going on at the same time—the *shādhdh* becoming *shādhdh* and the reading of the generality (*qirā'āt al-ʿāmma*) becoming general—as the possibilities of *ikhtiyār*, or personal choice, became more and more limited by the rise of what can be called regional schools, i.e. those of Medina, Mecca, Syria, Basra, Kufa, etc. An important area of research, therefore, is to examine this *ikhtiyār*—again, using early manuscripts along with literary sources—to ascertain its limits and arrive at an estimation of its exact nature and extent.

As just indicated, the 'period of *ikhtiyār*' was also the period when the main regional schools and traditions were being established. Ibn Mujāhid was the first to choose seven of these, in his *Kitāb al-Sabʿa*, as representative of the complete tradition. These seven were:

1. Nāfiʿ (d. 169/785) in Medina
2. Ibn Kathīr (d. 120/738) in Mecca
3. Abū ʿAmr (d. *c.*154–6/770–2) in Basra
4. Ibn ʿĀmir (d. 118/736) in Damascus
5. ʿĀṣim (d. 127/745), in Kufa
6. Ḥamza (d. 156/773), also in Kufa
7. al-Kisāʾī (d. 189/804), also in Kufa.

In all cases, by the time Ibn Mujāhid was writing his book, these Seven Readers were known in the form of transmissions (*riwāyāt*, sing. *riwāya*) of particular students, typically two. Thus, for example, the reading of Nāfiʿ is known through the transmissions of Warsh (d. 197/812) and Qālūn (d. 220/835), and the reading of ʿĀṣim through the transmissions of Ḥafṣ (d. 180/796) and Shuʿba (d. 193/809), and so on for the other readers among the Seven.

We should reiterate, however, that 'seven' was only one man's choice. Perhaps as a reaction to this limitation of possibilities, we find other books soon being compiled which contain other readings, such as Ibn Ghalbūn's (d. 399/1008) *Tadhkira* on Eight Readings (including the reading of Yaʿqūb (d. 205/821), the imam of the Great Mosque in Basra), and Ibn Mihrān's (d. 381/991) *Mabsūṭ* on Ten Readings (including, as well as Yaʿqūb, the readings of Abū Jaʿfar (d. 130/747), the main Qur'an reciter in Medina in the generation before Nāfiʿ, and Khalaf (d. 229/844), one of the transmitters from Ḥamza, in Kufa). The addition of the Kufan al-Aʿmash (d. 148/765) made up Eleven Readings, as in, for example, the *Rawḍa* of Abū ʿAlī al-Ḥasan ibn Muḥammad al-Mālikī (d. 438/1047). In later years, three more readers were added alongside al-Aʿmash—the Makkan Ibn Muḥayṣin (d. 123/741), and the two Basrans al-Ḥasan al-Baṣrī (d. 110/728) and al-Yazīdī (d. 202/817–18)—to make up Fourteen Readers, as in al-Bannāʾ's (d. 1117/1705) *Itḥāf* (although collections of Twelve, Thirteen, Fifteen, and even Fifty Readers also appeared; see e.g. Ibn al-Jazarī, *Nashr*, 1:58–98, esp.83–84, 91, 97; Brockelmann, *Geschichte*, S 1:727). However, whereas the Ten Readings are generally considered *mutawātir*—that is, transmitted by multiple authorities from multiple authorities, back to the source, such that they could not have agreed on an error—these last four readings among the Fourteen are generally considered *shādhdh*. The distinction between *mutawātir* and *shādhdh* is another area that needs further research, perhaps along the lines suggested in Shady Nasser's study of this topic (Nasser 2013: esp. 231–2).

It should also be noted that, although all of these Fourteen Readings are described as having secondary transmitters, in eight out of the Fourteen the secondary transmitters are from a period significantly later than that of the original reader. It is important, therefore, that research is done on the chains of transmission—again, through manuscripts and literary sources—in order to ascertain how these readings and transmissions became 'chosen', and by whom, perhaps along the lines already taken by Intisar Rabb in her work on the Ḥimṣī Reading (Rabb 2006: 100–9) and Shady Nasser in his work on the chains of transmission of the Seven, particularly Ibn Kathīr, Nāfiᶜ, Ibn ᶜĀmir, and Abū ᶜAmr (Nasser 2013: 129–60).

As indicated, at the same time as the Seven and Ten Readings were becoming formalized, the flip-side was happening, in that anything outside this general formulation became considered as *shādhdh*, or irregular. Again, this finds expression in literary form, with books being written specifically on these *shādhdh* readings. Thus we have, amongst others, the *Mukhtaṣar fī'l-shawādhdh* of Ibn Khālawayhi (d. 370/980) one of Ibn Mujāhid's students; Ibn Jinnī's (d. 392/1002) *Kitāb al-Muḥtasab*; and, later, al-ᶜUkbarī's (d. 616/1219) *Iᶜrāb al-qirā'āt al-shawādhdh*. Indeed, Ibn Mujāhid himself is said to have written a book on the *shawādhdh* (Ibn Mujāhid, *Sabᶜa*, 20–2), although no copy of it is known to have survived until today.

More especially, this gradual curtailment of possibilities took an overtly political form in the years 322/934 and 323/935, when Ibn Mujāhid was involved in the trials of Ibn Miqsam (d. 354/965) and Ibn Shanabūdh (d. 328/939) respectively. Ibn Miqsam effectively allowed readings based on the *rasm* of the *muṣḥaf*, but without any chain of authority (*sanad*), as long as they were in good Arabic, while Ibn Shanabūdh held that it was permissible to recite using the *shādhdh* readings recorded from the Companions. Both were forced to retract their views and to accept that the only valid readings were those that had the backing of the overwhelming majority of the *ᶜulamā'* and readers of the Qur'an.

Thus by the mid-fourth/tenth century, and in particular, it seems, through these judgements of Ibn Mujāhid and the publication of his *Kitāb al-Sabᶜa*, the early possibilities suggested by the seven *aḥruf* hadith had been almost completely curtailed, and from then on the ongoing tradition is one of Seven, or sometimes Ten, acknowledged Readings for actual use in recitation, with all other readings being limited to references in the specialist books of *qirā'āt* (readings) and *tafsīr* (Qur'anic commentary).

In his *Muwaṭṭa'*, Mālik (d. 179/795) records the following statement from Ibn Masᶜūd (d. 32/652):

> You are in a time when men of understanding (*fuqahā'*) are many and Qur'an reciters (*qurrā'*) are few, when the limits of behaviour (*ḥudūd*) defined in the Qur'an are guarded and its letters (*ḥurūf*) are lost, when few people ask and many give, when they make the prayer long and the *khuṭba* short, and put their actions before their desires. A time will come upon people when their men of understanding are few but their Qur'an reciters are many, when the letters of the Qur'an are guarded but its limits are lost, when many ask but few give, when they make the *khuṭba* long but the prayer short, and put their desires before their actions. (Mālik, *Muwaṭṭa'*, 1:143–4)

Whatever else it tells us, this report indicates at least two things: (i) the initial variety of possibilities was reduced over time; and (ii) it is the meaning of the Qur'an, and its being acted upon, that dominates over its formal aspect. It seems entirely appropriate to end this survey with this last point, which is as relevant today as it was in the time of both Ibn Masʿūd and Mālik.

Bibliography

Brockelmann, Carl. *Geschichte der Arabischen Litteratur*. 2nd edn. 2 vols. Leiden: E. J. Brill, 1943–9; Supplements. 3 vols. Leiden: E. J. Brill, 1937–42.

Déroche, François. *La Transmission écrite du Coran dans les débuts de l'islam: le codex Parisino-petropolitanus*. Leiden and Boston: Brill, 2009.

Déroche, François. *Qurʾans of the Umayyads: A First Overview*. Leiden and Boston: Brill, 2014.

Dutton, Yasin. 'Red Dots, Green Dots, Yellow Dots and Blue: Some Reflections on the Vocalisation of Early Qur'anic Manuscripts—Parts I and II', *Journal of Qur'anic Studies* 1/1 (1999), 115–40 (Part I); 2/1 (2000), 1–24 (Part II).

Dutton, Yasin. 'An Early *Muṣḥaf* According to the Reading of Ibn ʿĀmir', *Journal of Qur'anic Studies* 3/1 (2001), 71–89.

Dutton, Yasin. 'Some Notes on the British Library's "Oldest Qur'an Manuscript" (Or. 2165)', *Journal of Qur'anic Studies* 6/1 (2004), 43–71.

Dutton, Yasin. 'An Umayyad Fragment of the Qur'an and its Dating', *Journal of Qur'anic Studies* 9/2 (2007), 57–87.

Dutton, Yasin. 'Orality, Literacy and the "Seven *Aḥruf*" *Hadith*', *Journal of Islamic Studies* 23/1 (2012), 1–49. (doi :10.1093/jis/etr092)

Hamdan, Omar. 'The Second *Maṣāḥif* Project: A Step Towards the Canonization of the Qurʾanic Text'. In: A. Neuwirth, N. Sinai, and M. Marx (eds.). *The Qurʾān in Context: Historical and Literary Investigations into the Qurʾānic Milieu*, pp. 795–835. Leiden and Boston: Brill, 2010.

Ibn al-Jazarī, *Ghāyat al-nihāya fī ṭabaqāt al-qurrāʾ*. 2 vols. Ed. G. Bergsträsser. Beirut: Dār al-Kutub al-ʿIlmiyya, 1301–2/1932–3.

Ibn al-Jazarī, *Kitāb al-Nashr fī ʾl-qirāʾāt al-ʿashr*. 2 vols. Ed. ʿAlī Muḥammad al-Ḍabbāʿ. Beirut: Dār al-Fikr, n.d.

Ibn ʿAsākir, *Mukhtaṣar Tārīkh Dimashq*. 29 vols. Ed. Muḥammad Muṭīʿ al-Ḥāfiẓ et al. Beirut: Dār al-Fikr, 1404/1984.

Ibn ʿAṭiyya, *Tafsīr* [= *al-Muḥarrar al-wajīz fī tafsīr al-kitāb al-ʿazīz*]. 16 vols. Mohammedia: Wizārat al-Awqāf wa-l-Shuʾūn al-Islāmiyya, 1395–1411/1975–91.

Ibn Mujāhid, *Kitāb al-Sabʿa fī-l-qirāʾāt*. Ed. Shawqī Ḍayf. 2nd edn. Cairo: Dār al-Maʿārif, *c*.1401/1980.

Jones, Alan. 'The Dotting of a Script and the Dating of an Era: The Strange Neglect of PERF 558', *Islamic Culture* 72/4 (1998), 95–103.

Jones, Alan. 'Orality and Writing in Arabia'. In: Jane Dammen McAuliffe (ed.). *Encyclopaedia of the Qurʾān*. 6 vols., 3:587–93. Leiden: Brill, 2001–6. [= Jones, 2003a]

Jones, Alan. 'The Word Made Visible: Arabic Script and the Committing of the Qurʾan to Writing'. In: Chase F. Robinson (ed.). *Texts, Documents and Artefacts: Islamic Studies in Honour of D. S. Richards*, pp. 1–16. Leiden and Boston: Brill, 2003. [= Jones, 2003b]

Lord, Albert. *The Singer of Tales*. Cambridge, MA: Harvard University Press, 1960.

Madigan, Daniel. *The Qur'ān's Self-Image*. Princeton: Princeton University Press, 2001.

Mālik, *al-Muwaṭṭaʾ*. 2 vols. Cairo: Maṭbaʿat al-Ḥalabī wa-Awlādih, 1349/1930.

Muslim, *Ṣaḥīḥ*. 8 vols. Ed. Muḥammad Shukrī ibn Ḥasan al-Anqarawī et al. Istanbul: al-Maṭbaʿa al-ʿĀmira, 1334/1916. [Republished: Beirut: Dār al-Fikr, no date.]

Nasser, Shady Hekmat. *The Transmission of the Variant Readings of the Qurʾān: The Problem of* Tawātur *and the Emergence of* Shawādhdh. Leiden and Boston: Brill, 2013.

Puin, Elisabeth. 'Ein früher Koranpalimpsest aus Ṣanʿāʾ (DAM 01–27.1)'. In: M. Gross and K.-H. Ohlig (eds.). *Schlaglichter: Die beiden ersten islamischen Jahrhunderte*, pp. 461–93. Berlin: Verlag Hans Schiler, 2008.

Puin, Gerd-Rüdiger. 'Observations on Early Qurʾān Manuscripts in Ṣanʿāʾ'. In: Stefan Wild (ed.). *The Qur'an as Text*, pp. 107–11. Leiden, New York, and Cologne: E. J. Brill, 1996.

Puin, Gerd-Rüdiger. 'Vowel Letters and Ortho-epic Writing in the Qurʾān'. In: Gabriel Said Reynolds (ed.). *New Perspectives on the Qurʾān: The Qurʾān in its Historical Context 2*, pp. 147–90. London and New York: Routledge, 2011.

Rabb, Intisar. 'Non-Canonical Readings of the Qur'an: Recognition and Authenticity (The Ḥimṣī Reading)', *Journal of Qur'anic Studies* 8/2 (2006), 84–127.

Sadeghi, Behnam and Uwe Bergmann. 'The Codex of a Companion of the Prophet and the Qurʾān of the Prophet', *Arabica* 57 (2010), 343–436.

Sadeghi, Behnam and Mohsen Goudarzi. 'Ṣanʿāʾ 1 and the Origins of the Qurʾān', *Der Islam* 87 (2011), 1–129.

al-Shaybānī, Muḥammad ibn al-Ḥasan. *The Kitāb al-āthār of Imam Abū Ḥanīfah: The Narration of Imam Muḥammad ibn al-Ḥasan ash-Shaybānī*. Arabic text, with translation by Abdassamad Clarke. London: Turath Publishing, 2006.

al-Suyūṭī, *al-Itqān fī ʿulūm al-Qurʾān*. 4 vols. Ed. Muḥammad Abū'l-Faḍl Ibrāhīm. Cairo: Dār al-Turāth, n.d.

CHAPTER 13

THE CORPUS OF QUR'ANIC READINGS (*QIRĀ'ĀT*)

History, Synthesis, and Authentication

MUSTAFA SHAH

According to traditional Islamic narratives, when the third caliph ʿUthmān ibn ʿAffān (d. 35/656) appointed a committee to prepare a standardized version of the Qur'an, the codices that were finally approved provided a skeletal outline (*rasm*) of the Qur'anic text (Figure 13.1). Constellated around the skeletal trace of these codices, the *qirā'āt* or variant readings constitute the wide range of vocalic and consonantal variants which were associated with the recitation of the sacred text. Over later historical periods, when transmitting the text of the Qur'an, expert readers from garrison towns and cities formulated amalgamated selections and sets (*ikhtiyārāt*) of readings which preserved and systematized the various manifestations of the ways in which the text of the Qur'an was vocalized and transmitted. A rich corpus of materials was amassed as a result of these processes of selection. Although classical Islamic sources maintain that over the centuries the *qirā'āt* were preserved with remarkable fidelity by a combination of oral and written means, the question of their historical genesis, preservation, and synthesis has been widely debated in studies of the textual transmission of the Qur'an and its codification. Examinations of the material of variant readings have also been critical to helping scholars understand key developments in early legal, exegetical, and linguistic discourses, underlining their value as a literary source.

Inspired by previous endeavours in the field, a catalogue of the most widely circulated readings listing the specific vocalization preferences of seven readers was compiled by Ibn Mujāhid (d. 324/936) in the distinctively titled *Kitāb al-Sabʿa* (the Book of Seven). In the text's insightful introduction it is explained that the book's vaunted aim was to provide

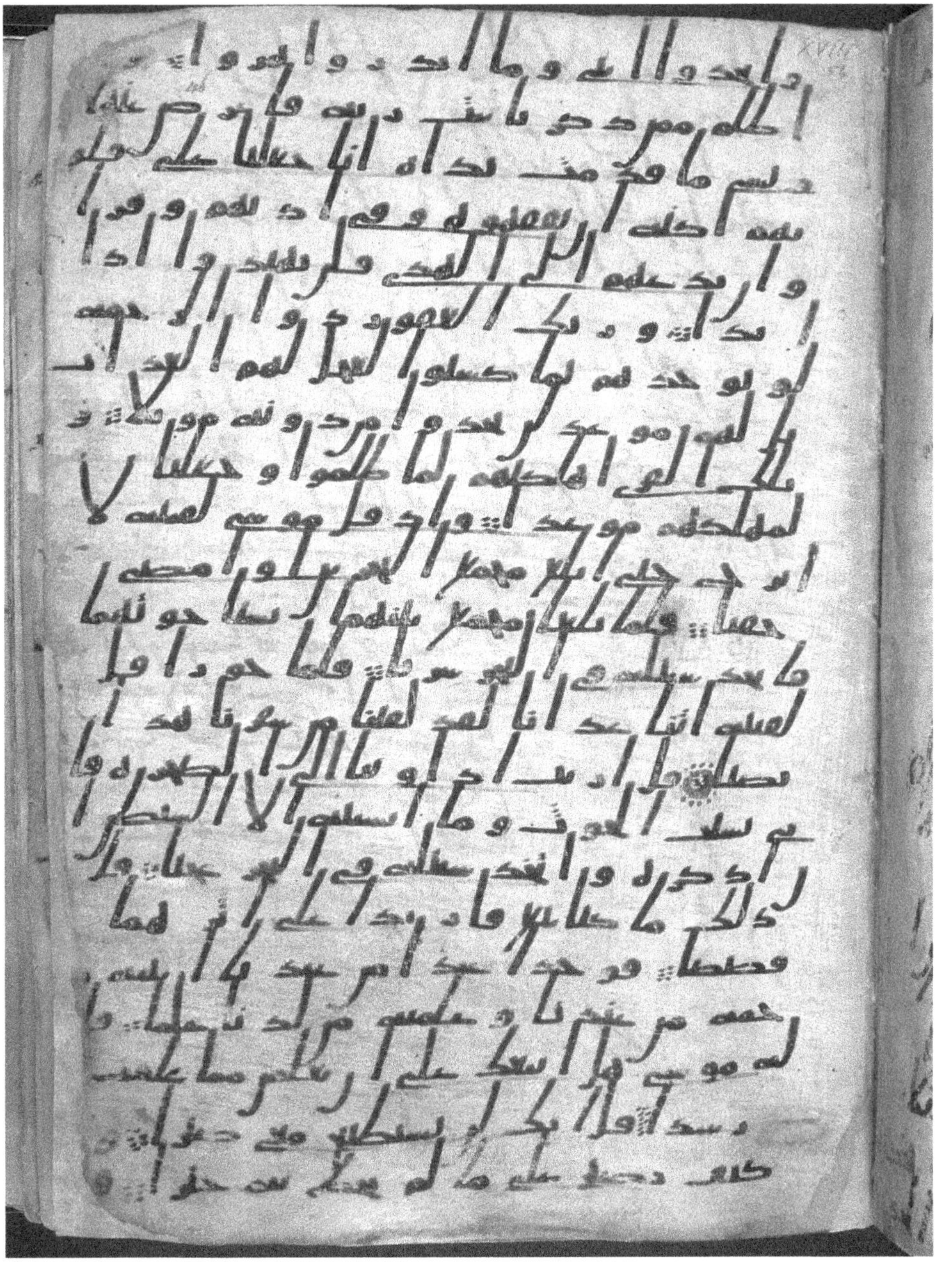

FIGURE 13.1 A folio from the British Library's oldest manuscript of the Qur'an, Or. 2165, featuring verses from Q. 18:57–68 (The Cave). The manuscript comprises 121 folios containing over two-thirds of the complete text. © British Library Board.

a register of readings (*qirāʾāt* or *ḥurūf*) which had acquired prominence in Ḥijāz, Iraq, and Syria (the Levant), citing their chief transmitters (Ibn Mujāhid, *Kitāb al-Sabʿa*, 45). With its impressive marshalling of the sources, works such as the *Kitāb al-Sabʿa* were effectively isolating instances of differences and points of agreement among readers, which were often confined to single lexical items within a verse of the Qur'an. The implication is that there existed a consensus among readers regarding the vocalization of the remaining segments of lexical items in such verses. In later years scholars developed criteria for dividing variants into canonical and non-canonical categories. Generally, variations among canonical readings tend to be confined to vocalic and consonantal variants and include instances of differences over the use of suffixation, prefixation, and conjunctions. Non-canonical categories of variants included not only vocalic, consonantal, and orthographical peculiarities, but also featured evident departures from the standard skeletal text and acute forms of exegetical interpolation. The importance attached to the circumscription of subtle variations among *qirāʾāt* would appear to underpin the significance of the Qur'an as a devotional text. The fact that a specific reading was classed as being canonical meant that it was valid for ritual use in acts of worship and formal recitation; despite this, even non-canonical *variae lectiones* were frequently adduced by scholars in their writings to illustrate legal, exegetical, and grammatical arguments and perspectives.

In the Islamic world today the most popular standard version of the text is vocalized and recited in accordance with the corpus of readings selected by ʿĀṣim ibn Abī al-Najūd (d. 127/745) and transmitted by Ḥafṣ ibn Sulaymān (d. 180/796). It was used as the basis for the standard Egyptian edition of the Qur'an which appeared in 1924. In North and West Africa the reading of Nāfiʿ ibn Abī al-Nuʿāym (d. 169/785) as transmitted by Warsh (d. 197/812) enjoys pre-eminence (Brockett 1988).[1] However, these readings constitute just two of the seven sets of readings collated in Ibn Mujāhid's book, intimating that the tradition of canonical readings was never viewed as being confined to one specific set of readings, but rather encompassed a distinctly larger corpus of materials. The other five canonical readings included those *lectiones* transmitted on the authority of the Damascene Ibn ʿĀmir (d. 118/736); the Meccan Ibn Kathīr (d. 120/738); the Basran Abū ʿAmr ibn al-ʿAlāʾ (d. c.154–6/770–2); and the two Kufans Ḥamza ibn Ḥabīb (d. 156/773 or 158/775) and al-Kisāʾī (d. 189/804). In the modern Islamic world traditional scholarship devoted to the study and transmission of the wider corpus of variants is still a revered endeavour. In the medieval context exegetes, jurists, and grammarians were fully aware of the extensive corpus of *qirāʾāt*, including non-canonical *lectiones*, coordinating the citation of these materials in their works. Among these scholars, the axiomatic view was that they embodied inimitable elements of the Qur'an's literary countenance.

[1] Recounting the biography of Abū ʿAmr ibn al-ʿAlāʾ in his *Ghāyat al-nihāya*, Ibn al-Jazarī stated that during his lifetime (ninth/fifteenth century), Abū ʿAmr's corpus of readings was prevalent in al-Shām, al-Ḥijāz, Yemen, and Egypt. He explains that Ibn ʿĀmir's readings were in widespread use in al-Shām until the fourth/tenth century. Abū ʿAmr's two famed narrators were al-Dūrī and al-Sūsī (Jeffery 1946).

EARLY ACADEMIC SCHOLARSHIP: ANALYSIS OF THE *QIRĀʾĀT*

A distinctive phase in the study of the textual history of the Qur'an and the corpus of *qirāʾāt* was inaugurated by the publication of Theodor Nöldeke's *Geschichte des Qorâns* (1860), which was revised and expanded by his student and friend Friedrich Schwally (1863–1919); editions of the text appeared in 1909 and 1919.[2] Supplements to the work were completed by Gotthelf Bergsträsser (1886–1933) during 1926 and 1929 and then by Otto Pretzl in (1893–1941), who published them all in his 1938 edition of the work. The 1860 and 1909 editions of the *Geschichte* included sections on the structural framework of the contents of the Qur'an; the significance of its collection; chronology; the question of biblical influences; traditional accounts of the synthesis of variants; orthography; the transmission of the text; and 'sectarian' criticisms of the ʿUthmānic collection (Schwally 1909: 234ff.).

The supplements of Bergsträsser and Pretzl brought the subject of variant readings and the classical scholarship on *qirāʾāt* into even sharper focus. Underscoring their interest in variants, Bergsträsser and Pretzl had already published a number of critical editions of manuscripts and studies of readings. Bergsträsser had begun work on editing part of Ibn Jinnī's *Kitāb al-Muḥtasab* and Ibn Khālawayhi's *Mukhtaṣar fī shawādhdh al-Qurʾān*, both of which were composed in the fourth/tenth century and provided inventories of non-canonical variant readings (*qirāʾāt shādhdha*) (Bergsträsser 1933b). He also edited the *Ghāyat al-nihāya fī ṭabaqāt al-qurrāʾ*, a biographical survey of expert reciters of the Qur'an which straddles early and classical historical periods. It was compiled by Ibn al-Jazarī (d. 833/1429), who was the author of the seminal *al-Nashr fīʾl-qirāʾāt al-ʿashr*, a work which collated ten sets of readings and featured an expanded introduction teeming with information on variants and classical literature devoted to their study. In 1930 Pretzl published the *Kitāb al-Taysīr*, a short didactic treatise on the seven canonical readings selected by Ibn Mujāhid and in 1932 the *Kitāb al-Muqniʿ fi rasm al-maṣāḥif*, which presented records of orthographical features of the ʿUthmānic codices; both texts were composed by the Andalusian expert on readings Abū ʿAmr al-Dānī (d. 444/1053) (George 2015). Many of the earlier literary sources which preserve materials on readings, including exegetical works by grammarians, had yet to be discovered, let alone published. Earlier, Nöldeke had at his disposal manuscripts of the works of al-Dānī, Ibn al-Jazarī, al-Suyūṭī (d. 911/1505); select exegetical texts such as the Qur'an commentaries of al-Baghawī (d. 516/1122), al-Zamakhsharī (d. 538/1144), and al-Bayḍāwī (d. *c*.719/1319); he also had access to various Qur'anic fragments held in Berlin (Nöldeke 1860: xi–xii). Among the subjects covered in the third part of the revised edition of the *Geschichte* were the orthography and synthesis of variant readings; key concepts and theories used in the

[2] Schwally died in 1919 having completed most of the work on the first two volumes of the revised *Geschichte*. See the Introduction to this edition for a discussion of the historical background of Nöldeke's work.

classification and transmission of *qirāʾāt*; non-canonical readings; a review of personal codices attributed to leading Companions; Qur'anic palimpsests; processes of canonization; systems of recitation in the medieval periods; genres associated with the study of *qirāʾāt*; and a summary of the state of research on manuscripts of the Qur'an. Steered by their philological expertise and training, Bergsträsser and Pretzl had aimed at developing an elaborately detailed overview of the extensive corpus of materials that they hoped would contribute to the development of an '*apparatus criticus*' and thereby assist the process of circumscribing crucial historical phases in the textual transmission of the Qur'an (Bergsträsser 1930).

Focusing on the early historical periods, Bergsträsser commenced his study of the corpus of *variae lectiones* with a discussion of the various anecdotes which mention the existence of linguistic inconsistencies and irregularities in the codices commissioned by ʿUthmān. One of these intimates that when the final copies of the edited codices were presented to the third caliph he stated: 'There are errors in these which the Arabs will put right' (al-Farrāʾ, *Maʿānī*, 2:293–4). Sensing that such dicta were intentionally designed to provide justification for the correction of errors in the official codices, Bergsträsser made the case that such prevailing attitudes led to the proliferation of variants as expert early readers readily adopted an untrammelled approach towards emendation based on the view that such errors did not impinge upon the quality of the original composition of the text, but were an indictment of those responsible for its transcription. His assessment presupposes that a considerable proportion of the body of *qirāʾāt* was generated following the imposition of the ʿUthmānic codices (Bergsträsser 1938: 2–4; and 104). Classical literary sources differ concerning the number of codices dispatched by ʿUthmān to key cities and garrison towns: some accounts mention that copies were sent to Kufa, Basra, Damascus, and Medina; other anecdotes record his dispatching seven codices (al-Dānī, *al-Muqniʿ*, 9; cf. Cook 2004; Hamdan 2010; Comerro 2012; Sinai 2014; Van Putten 2019). In addition to the *imām muṣḥaf ʿUthmān* (the primary codex), the early literary sources regularly refer to the *maṣāḥif al-amṣār* (the metropolitan codices) and the class of personal codices identified with revered figures among the Companions (*maṣāḥif al-ṣaḥāba*) such as the codices of Ibn Masʿūd (d. 32/652) and Ubayy ibn Kaʿb (d. 29/649 or 35/656) (Beck 1947). Following a different ordering of chapters, these personal codices incorporated a wide range of vocalic and consonantal variants, exegetical glosses, orthographical variants, and often featured changes in the sequence of the word order of verses (Ibn al-Nadīm, *Fihrist*, 29–30).

Recognizing the importance attached to transmission, Bergsträsser did accept that individual cities preserved and disseminated their local variants with remarkable acuity (Bergsträsser 1938: 8–9). He also held that linguistic considerations influenced the synthesis of readings, deducing that this led to an exponential growth of material which percolated through to supplement an already burgeoning body of variant readings (Bergsträsser 1938: 2–4). In his discussion of variants which he touched upon in his study of the exegetical tradition, it was Ignaz Goldziher (1850–1921) who drew a correlation between the genesis of variants and the embryonic nature of the Arabic script (Goldziher 1920: 4–5). The early codices were transcribed in a *scriptio defectiva*: namely, the orthography lacked a fully developed system for the annotation of long or short vowels;

in addition, the use of diacritics to distinguish specific consonants was applied in a somewhat erratic fashion (Blair 2006: 119). Goldziher too made the case that the exigencies of dogma led to the modification of the vocalization of a number of *variae lectiones*. Referring to the influence of exegetical factors in the growth of readings, he reasoned that the corpus of *qirāʾāt* was generated in the post-ʿUthmānic period (Goldziher 1920: 4–30).

Despite their relevance to discussions about variants, Bergsträsser did not address in detail the views of Karl Vollers, who, referring to specific remnants of non-canonical *qirāʾāt*, theorized that the dialect of the early Meccans was not consistent with the Arabs' formal literary diction in so far as it did not utilize a system of grammatical inflection; according to his thesis, the early grammarians assiduously worked at reconciling the language of the original revelations with the formal language (Vollers 1906). Vollers's theory was defended by Paul Kahle who questioned whether the classical Arabic diction was originally used for the recitation of the text (Kahle 1949). Kahle did go on to challenge some of the suppositions of Bergsträsser and Pretzl concerning the actual origin of *qirāʾāt*. In a more recent context Günter Lüling developed the thesis that the text of the Qur'an and its associated *variae lectiones* were formally superimposed onto an *urtext* which comprised pre-Islamic Christian strophic hymns. Luling's contention rested on the view that the original skeleton was reconfigured and animated by the addition of diacritical and related markings to ensure it supported the Arabic diction; within such a thesis, traditional *variae lectiones* were assumed to be spurious constructions and additions. Christoph Luxenberg, seemingly inspired by the work of Alphonse Mingana, who had referred to Syriac influences on the Qur'an, maintained that the underlying meaning of the lexical and syntactic structures of the Qur'an had to be sought in 'Syro-Aramaic', which he suggested was a branch of Aramaic used in the Near East. Referring to the unpointed and unvowelled script of the original text, and seemingly following the line of argument taken by Lüling, he too asserted that later variant readings were contrived by Islamic scholars as they adapted the original text through the calculated addition of diacritical markings (Luxenberg 2007: 22–32).

On the subject of the variants attributed to the Companions Ibn Masʿūd and Ubayy ibn Kaʿb, Bergsträsser emphasized that they provide only a glimpse of the vast store of non-canonical variants that existed in these early periods. For these reasons, he postulated that the ʿUthmānic recension was able to attain greater authority only once the liberal approach to the treatment of the text was gradually relinquished (Bergsträsser 1938: 103–5 and 149; cf. Beck 1939 and 1950). Maintaining that the existence of records and traces of the non-ʿUthmānic materials intimated that the process of the standardization of the text was a gradual one, Bergsträsser concluded that it was near completion when Ibn Mujāhid authored his famous *Kitāb al-Sabʿa*, a work in which the principle of support for readings promulgated by the majority prevailed. In his estimation Ibn Mujāhid had successfully relegated the study and dissemination of isolate and independent variants; and he was instrumental in insisting that readings which had high levels of transmission should be the focus of attention. Bergsträsser inferred that Ibn Mujāhid's project was the embodiment of 'a restrictive traditionalism' (Bergsträsser 1938: 138 and 152). On the historical importance of non-canonical variants, Bergsträsser contended that it was only later within the reading tradition that the term *shādhdh* evolved to connote those readings which were considered non-canonical (Bergsträsser 1938:155; cf. Hamdan 2006a). Still, it should be noted that the study of these *shādhdh* materials was considered an integral element of classical *qirāʾāt* scholarship and an enthusiastic interest in them is to be found in classical grammatical texts; moreover, it is important to bear in mind distinctions regarding the import of this term in the context of *qirāʾāt* scholarship and its use as a *terminus technicus* in hadith literature. (Shah 2016: 307). Bergsträsser died in a tragic mountaineering accident in August 1933, before he could complete the final sections of his supplement to the *Geschichte*. The main parts of his supplement had already been published during 1926 and 1929, after which he spent some time poring over the wealth of sources he scrupulously assembled for the final sections. Relying upon notes and manuscript materials left by his colleague, Pretzl went on to finalize the work. Indeed, in the introduction to the 1938 edition of the *Geschichte* he alluded to his faithfully following the general contours of the scheme for the work which he had previously discussed with Bergsträsser, who had requested that he concentrate his efforts on examining variants in the manuscript sources. Among the *Geschichte*'s contributors, Pretzl was the only figure to witness the actual publication of the completed edition of the revised work; in 1941 he was killed in an aircraft crash during the course of the Second World War.[3]

Towards the Creation of an Archive

With the aim of creating an archive of materials for the study of the textual transmission of the Qur'an, Bergsträsser and Pretzl had over the years been busily engaged in the task of collating various unpublished *qirāʾāt* manuscripts and copies of codices. Motivated by the appeal of acquiring early materials, they made excursions to the Middle East to photograph images of ancient Qur'an manuscripts using the newly invented Leica camera. In their endeavours they were assisted by Helmut Ritter (1892–1971), who was previously the Chair of Oriental Languages at the University of Hamburg, but who had taken up a position in Istanbul in 1926 and was able to gain access to the vast collections of Arabic and Islamic manuscripts haphazardly dispersed across the various libraries in the capital and other cities. At the behest of Bergsträsser, the Bavarian Academy of Sciences set up a 'Korankomission' to support the task; in later years following the death of Bergsträsser, Pretzl set about organizing the Academy's archive of materials. Prior to his death, Bergsträsser had been preparing the aforementioned critical edition of Ibn Khālawayhi's *Mukhtaṣar fī shawādhdh al-Qurʾān*. Arthur Jeffery, an Australian philologist with an enthusiastic interest in the materials of *variae lectiones*, was already assisting with the Cairo end of the publication and had previously agreed with Bergsträsser to prepare for him an appendix which compared citations in Ibn Khālawayhi's text with materials found in other sources. Upon Bergsträsser's death, Jeffery was invited to write the

[3] Pretzl supervised Edmund Beck's dissertation on the *qirāʾāt* which are cited in Sībawayhi's *Kitāb*. Beck was the author of a number of seminal studies on *variae lectiones*.

foreword for the work in which he mentioned that it was decided to publish the work without his appendix, producing only the materials prepared by Bergsträsser. In fact, since 1926, Jeffery had also been closely collaborating with Bergsträsser and Pretzl on their archive project for which he was in the process of producing a critical edition of Ibn Abī Dāwūd's *Kitāb al-Māṣāḥif*, a text published some years later in a volume entitled *Materials for the History of the Text of the Qur'an: The Old Codices* (Ibn Khālawayhi: *Mukhtaṣar*: foreword). In the text he included excerpts and passages citing Qur'anic non-canonical variants attributed to the personal codices of the Companions; these he had 'gathered from the commentaries, lexica, *qirā'āt* books and such sources' (Jeffery 1937: vii).

Commencing his edition of the *Kitāb al-Māṣāḥif* by stating that it was offered to students as 'a contribution to the problem of the history of the Qur'an text', Jeffery stated that eventually he hoped to be in a position to produce a critical edition of the Qur'an. Jeffery had, like Bergsträsser and Pretzl before him, subscribed to the view that within traditional narratives, the historical significance of the non-canonical *variae lectiones* linked to pre-ʿUthmānic codices had been obscured for ideological reasons. He held that in the later Islamic tradition the study of non-canonical variants (*shādhdha* or *shawādh*) had gravitated towards becoming a restricted enterprise and was somewhat frowned upon and discouraged, although, in fact, the material continued to be engaged with and analysed across a range of classical contexts and discourses, including law, theology, exegesis, and grammar. Jeffery averred that works produced within the genre of *maṣāḥif* literature, such as Ibn Abī Dāwūd's book on codices, demonstrated that the text canonized by the caliph ʿUthmān 'was just one out of many rival texts'; indeed, much of Jeffery's work was dedicated to the discovery and reconstruction of this non-canonical archive and related pre-ʿUthmānic substrate texts (Jeffery 1937: 10). He went on to state that 'we have only such readings as were useful for purposes of *tafsīr* and were considered to be sufficiently near orthodoxy to be allowed to survive' (Jeffery 1937: 10). Connected to the archive project was Jeffery's publication on *The Foreign Vocabulary of the Qur'ān*. In the *Geschichte* Pretzl did point out that Jeffery had been working on the establishment of an *apparatus criticus* based on an overview of Ḥafṣ's version (Pretzl 1938: 273). In a 1946 lecture Jeffery himself explained that his aim was to produce a 'consonantal text in the Kufic script, based on the oldest MSS available to us, with a critically edited Ḥafṣ text facing it on the opposite pages and with a complete collection of all known variant readings given at the foot of the page' (Jeffery 1946).

In later studies Jeffery did elaborate upon what he believed to be the principal stages of the standardization of the text of the Qur'an, observing that it was initially defined by the imposition of ʿUthmān's *textus receptus*, which was produced at a time when many non-ʿUthmānic texts were in circulation. Reflecting upon the proliferation of variants, Jeffery commented that although ʿUthmān had ordered the destruction of all codices which conflicted with his official version, the copy produced by him was 'a bare consonantal text, with no punctuation, no points to distinguish similar consonants, and no vowel or other orthographic signs', which led to 'considerable liberty of interpretation' (Jeffery 1948: 1). Jeffery explained that following the first attempts by the Umayyad caliph ʿAbd al-Malik (ruled 65–86/685–705) and his governor al-Ḥajjāj ibn Yūsuf (d. 95/714) to settle 'some of these difficulties', eventually 'the tradition as to pointing the *ḥurūf*, and as to the *qirāʾa*, or vowelling of them, naturally tended to crystallize under a succession of great teachers, whose systems would be transmitted by their pupils, until in 322 A.H., these traditions came to be fixed in the well-known Seven Systems by a decision of the Wazīrs Ibn Muqla (d. 328/940) and Ibn ʿĪsā (d. 335/946), acting under the guidance of the great savant Ibn Mujāhid' (Jeffery 1948: 1). He concluded that during these periods there had emerged a general consensus concerning the legal status of the liturgical validity of *variae lectiones* which prescribed three conditions for the acceptance of readings: they had to be consistent with the skeletal outline of the official codices; to conform with the diction of Arabic; and be supported by broad consensus (*ijmāʿ*). Although some of these criteria were applied much earlier within the tradition as evidenced by early grammatical commentaries such as al-Farrāʾ's *Maʿānī al-Qurʾān*, Jeffery's insistence is that the imposition of seven canonical readings by Ibn Mujāhid was prefigured by arguments about the legitimacy of *ikhtiyār*: namely, the regimented practice of synthesizing or amalgamating variant readings. The concept was flagged in Bergsträsser's supplement to the *Geschichte* in which it was noted that *ikhtiyār* was the process by which a reader, who principally adhered to a selection of *variae lectiones* acquired from an earlier authority, differed with him in a limited number of instances, favouring his own synthesis of the material (Bergsträsser 1938: 134). Yet for Jeffery, *ikhtiyār* inventively turned on the application of 'mental judgement on how the skeleton consonantal text should be pointed and vowelled for correct recitation'; and he highlighted the trials of two famous readers Ibn Shanabūdh (d. 328/939) and Ibn Miqsam (d. 354/965), who separately adopted speculative techniques in the amalgamation of *lectiones* which brought them into conflict with the ruling authorities; both figures were compelled to disavow and retract such approaches, despite protesting that they were following the conventions of their reader peers (Shah 2004: 78–9). Jeffery felt that at stake was the validity of the continued practice of *ikhtiyār* by readers and that the industrious efforts of Ibn Mujāhid were designed to curb the resort to this procedure (Jeffery 1948: 2).

The work of Nöldeke, Bergsträsser, Pretzl, and Jeffery constitutes a milestone in the study of the corpus of *variae lectiones*. They introduced a whole range of manuscript sources and materials germane to their study, providing intriguing insights into the early and classical traditions of learning devoted to readings; moreover, the sections of the *Geschichte* dealing with the late medieval tradition of *qirāʾāt* and the fecund body of literature produced in these periods remain indispensable resources for the study of variants. Ultimately, their efforts laid the foundations for later endeavour in the field and the archive of materials initially created by Bergsträsser and Pretzl served as the inspiration for the 2007 Corpus Coranicum project supported by the Berlin-Brandenburg Academy of Sciences and Humanities which has made use of their archival sources along with early Qur'an manuscript materials collated from around the world. The fate of the original archive was the subject of much speculation as Otto Pretzl's student, Anton Spitaler, was seemingly vague about rumours that it was destroyed when the Bavarian Academy of Science was bombed towards the end of the Second World War in 1944, although even

Jeffery lamented in a 1946 lecture that the whole of the archive 'was destroyed by bomb action and by fire'. However, the archive had survived, and remained in the possession of Spitaler throughout his lifetime. Accounts of the loss and discovery of the archives, and even the events surrounding the deaths of Bergsträsser and Pretzl, have been sensationalized to imply that the archive contains materials which were likely to be considered controversial and thereby potentially destabilize normative views of the history of the text; the inference is that Spitaler deliberately concealed the existence of the archive. However, it has been pointed out that material entered into the databases of the Corpus Coranicum project from Bergsträsser's archive does not reveal a skeletal text which differs from the range of early Qur'anic manuscripts and fragments that are currently available to scholars; for this reason, it has even been claimed that a mythology has been allowed to develop concerning the content of the archive and the academic work conducted by the project team (Marx 2009).[4]

Interpreting the Significance of *Variae Lectiones*: Approaches and Perspectives

Distinctive turning points in the study of *variae lectiones* were marked by the work of John Wansbrough and John Burton who separately set out to expound upon the connection between *variae lectiones* and the historical consolidation of the Qur'an's status as a fixed text (*textus receptus*). Wansbrough argued that the Qur'an probably evolved as a stable text around the turn of the third/ninth century. Employing sophisticated arguments about the typology and style of early Islamic literary texts, and gauging attitudes towards the corpus of *variae lectiones* within these materials to underpin his arguments, he concluded that material from these early periods did not presuppose the existence of a standardized Qur'an. Wansbrough placed existing forms of exegesis within several categories: the focus on *variae lectiones* was identified as one of the elements of masoretic exegesis, which included lexical explanation and grammatical analysis; he reckoned that specific types of variants were the product of exegetical activity which was not attested before the third/ninth century. Nöldeke and Schwally suggested that the accomplishment of a fixed text was achieved in the short span of a generation from the time of the Prophet as specified by the traditional sources. Although Wansbrough did not dismiss the possibility that elements of Qur'anic canon may have existed prior to the periods when intense literary activity took place, he questioned the putative existence of an early ʿUthmānic recension of the text

[4] See the website: <https://corpuscoranicum.de>. It introduces early Qur'anic manuscripts and presents records of a wide range of recorded variants. Other relevant sites include <https://cudl.lib.cam.ac.uk/collections/islamic/4>.

(Wansbrough 1977: 44–5 and 202f.). Wansbrough cited circumstantial evidence that he believed corroborated his arguments: firstly, he maintained that the study of codices and 'classical *maṣāḥif* literature (*variae lectiones*)' did not appear until the third/ninth century (Wansbrough 1977: 44–5). In this regard he was relying on Jeffery's provisional musings about the origins of classical works devoted to the study of codices and variants; however, it is important to bear in mind that such scholarship featured in the *maʿānī al-Qurʾān* genre of texts in which *variae lectiones* were grammatically analysed (Shah 2003a: 48 and 58; cf. Spitaler and Pretzl 1935). Secondly, he explained that Joseph Schacht's research had concluded that 'with very few exceptions, that Muslim jurisprudence was not derived from the contents of the Qur'an'; and thirdly, he observed that references to the Qur'an were conspicuously absent from a number of early theological treatises, all of which undermined the traditional narrative that a fixed text had been established (Wansbrough 1977: 44). He judged that it was 'impossible that canonization should have preceded, not succeeded, recognition of the authority of scripture within the Muslim community' (Wansbrough 1977: 202).

Referring to the vast corpus of *qirāʾāt* materials amassed by Bergsträsser, Pretzl, and especially Jeffery, Wansbrough commented that it 'could well be asked to what extent any of the variants, or variant codices (?), may be said to represent traditions genuinely independent of the ʿUthmānic recension' (Wansbrough 1977: 44–5). He reasoned that lexical differences among these so-called variants were 'infinitesimal' in countenance and were sanctioned by the prophetic tradition which spoke of the Qur'an being revealed in seven aspects or modes (*aḥruf*), supposedly permitting readers ample latitude and choice in their synthesis and selection of *qirāʾāt*. Wansbrough pointed to the fact that 'a special category of variant codex, the metropolitan codices (*maṣāḥif al-amṣār*), do not display the 'differences either among themselves or from the ʿUthmānic recension which are alleged to have provoked the editorial measures attributed to the third caliph' (Wansbrough 1977: 45). When referring to the *maṣāḥif al-amṣār*, Wansbrough was nominally following Jeffery's designation of those early materials which 'had been digested into codices in the great Metropolitan centres of Madina, Mecca, Basra, Kufa and Damascus' and were superseded by the ʿUthmānic version of the canonized Medinan codex (Jeffery 1937: 8; Beck 1950). Wansbrough was convinced that the so-called regional codices, and indeed even Companion codices, were purely fictive constructions. He went on to comment that 'either the suppression of substantial deviations was so instantly and universally successful that no trace of serious opposition remained, or that the story was a fiction designed to serve another purpose' (Wansbrough 1977: 45). Wansbrough's work fostered a new range of approaches to the study of the Qur'an and the early Islamic literary tradition, although the discovery and examination of early Qur'anic manuscript evidence undermined one of its key claims concerning the belated timeline for the emergence of the Qur'an as a fixed text (Déroche 2014: 14).

Adopting a series of equally sophisticated arguments, John Burton's study of the corpus of *variae lectiones* reached an entirely different set of conclusions about the standardization of the Qur'an and the origin of these readings. Burton was particularly interested in charting the relationship between the accounts of the collection of the Qur'an and their role in the elaboration of theoretical legal discourses. Burton was to argue that many unique forms of *qirāʾāt*, particularly those connected with twofold or concomitant readings which led to semantic shifts in the meaning of Qur'anic verses, were not the vestiges of a corpus of materials that expert readers had managed to preserve over the centuries with 'textual fidelity', but rather they revealed structural traces of the historical layers of arguments devised to defend legal doctrines by jurists in the early Islamic tradition. Although large numbers of canonical variants tend to be univocal, Burton was referring to verses such as Q. 5:6, which states 'Oh you who do believe, whenever you want to pray, then ***wash*** your faces and your hands up to the elbows; and ***wipe*** your heads; and (***"wipe" or "wash"***) your **feet** up to the ankles'. There existed two separate *lectiones* (or concomitant readings) of the term feet in the verse (*arjulikum* or *arjulakum*), one of which was adduced to support the practice of 'wiping' the feet when performing ritual ablution; while, the second was cited in support of 'washing' the feet (Nöldeke 1938: 3:141; Shah 2016: 307–10). Maintaining that classical scholars were seeking to place '*fiqh* views under the aegis of the Qur'an' by promoting changes to the text of the Qur'an, Burton estimated that such readings were generated to circumvent inconsistencies in the legal doctrines of the Qur'an (Burton 1977: 30–2). He explained that 'the Qur'an was flexible only within exiguous limits' so scholars were 'driven to seek the liberties they craved in varying vocalic data', allowing certain *qirāʾāt* to be manipulated to assume a counter-Sunna function (Burton 1977: 186; cf. Burton 1984). According to Burton, these complicated processes led to the resourceful inception of concomitant readings and interpretive glosses such as those which feature in the Companion codices of Ibn Masʿūd and Ubayy. On the subject of the ʿUthmānic codices and the accounts of their collection, Burton held that the reports of the collection of the Qur'an represented 'a mass of confusions, contradictions, and inconsistencies', claiming that they were formulated through a 'lengthy process of evolution' (Burton 1977: 225). One of the core contentions of Burton's study was his assertion that Qur'anic manuscripts actually exhibit the ʿUthmānic text and if one were to remove the collection reports as 'never having occurred', then there is every indication that the final recension of the Qur'an was evidently the work of the Prophet (Burton 1977: 227).

In a review of the role that concomitant (or twofold) readings played in the synthesis of law, Mustafa Shah has suggested that the attestation of variants had a subordinate function within the matrix of classical legal discourses. He claimed that concomitant readings which supported semantic variances tended to be confined, noting that had 'these materials been the products of inter-*madhhab* polemics, one would have expected their production to have been exponentially more prolific' (Shah 2016: 308). Shah also highlighted the significance of the use of non-canonical readings (*qirāʾāt shādhdha*) within classical legal discussions, confirming their continued relevance as sources.

The point has been made that while it seems undeniable that 'the consonantal outline of the Qur'an (*rasm*) appears to have been preserved with almost complete certainty from the first/seventh century' the diacritical marks and (vocalic values) which 'accompany that outline owe something to human reason and ingenuity' in that readers were not slavishly 'reproducing just what different Companions recited in the seventh century' (Melchert 2008: 82). However, the impression promoted by the imposing statements which feature in the introduction to Ibn Mujāhid's *Kitāb al-Sabʿa* intimates that cynosures of the reading tradition believed that they were faithfully adhering to established precedents (Sunna) in their synthesis of *qirāʾāt*. Similarly, classical grammatical and exegetical literature is replete with statements and assertions of loyalty to 'the Sunna' of recitation defined by the earliest generations of readers.

A text which has been hailed as being of 'major importance' for the history of the redaction of the Qur'an' and even doctrinal developments in Shīʿī thought is the *Kitāb al-Qirāʾāt*, a manuscript on *lectiones* attributed to Muḥammad al-Sayyārī (d. *c.* third/ninth century) (Kohlberg and Moezzi 2009: 23). It features a full-range of Qur'anic variants, many of which are designed to promote 'an Imāmī message' (Kohlberg 2009: 41). Despite the convoluted history of the original manuscript, it is presented as one of the earliest surviving Imāmī Shīʿī literary texts devoted to *variae lectiones*, although it evinces more about the development of the concept of *taḥrīf*, the allegation by some Shīʿī groups that the Qur'an was corrupted by the caliph ʿUthmān to suppress the rights of the imams, than it does about historical attitudes to the status of the ʿUthmānic codices (Kohlberg 2009: 46). If one were to place aside the polemical design of al-Sayyārī's text and the readings it includes which are of a sectarian countenance, one is left with a body of *qirāʾāt* which are typically consistent with the cluster of *variae lectiones* found in the traditional *qirāʾāt* literature; likewise, in their works prominent Shīʿī luminaries tended to defer to *variae lectiones* canonized in the traditional *qirāʾāt* sources (Kohlberg 2009: 27; Bar Asher 1993).

Qirāʾāt and the Relevance of Manuscript Evidence

Archival evidence is playing an increasingly important role in the study of the significance of the formation of *variae lectiones* in the early tradition. In his examination of the *Parisino-petropolitanus* codex, a codex probably emanating from the first two decades of Umayyad rule and discovered in the ʿAmr ibn al-ʿĀṣ mosque in Egypt, François Déroche maintained that while such texts are based on the ʿUthmānic consonantal outline, the fact that they originally had 'very few diacritics, no short vowels or orthoepic marks, simply could not have provided the solution which the caliph is said to have been seeking'. He proposes that ʿUthmān's efforts may have been conceived with the aim of providing a basic 'visual identity for the text he supported' (Déroche 2009: 178). Déroche argued that non-canonical variants which are present in the *Parisino petropolitanus*, and other contemporary fragments, appear to predate later compilations of variants by scholars in the second/eighth and early third/ninth centuries (Déroche 2009: 176–8 cf. Déroche 2014: 31). These points were revisited in his later study of Umayyad

Qur'ans in which he concluded that there is 'no certainty that the *qirāʾāt* of the Umayyad period were similar to those which we know'. However, he does concede that even the *Parisino-petropolitanus codex*, which displays textual and divisional peculiarities, remains 'consistent with the ʿUthmānic *rasm*' (Déroche 2014: 14; 31, 37, and 136). This is also confirmed for one of the oldest Qur'an manuscripts in the British Library (Or. 2165; see Fig. 13.1), which was the subject of separate studies by Yasin Dutton and Intisar Rabb, who concluded that the manuscript exhibits a distinct measure of fluidity in its synthesis of variants and its division of verses (Rabb 2006).[5] Déroche had worked with the late Sergio Noja Noseda on this manuscript (Déroche and Noseda 2001). On the subject of the ʿUthmānic collection, Déroche cautioned that 'the possibility that some of the fragments date back to the decade that elapsed between the murder of ʿUthmān or even before—and the beginning of Umayyad rule can in no way be excluded, but we do not have strong arguments—material or textual—to attribute precisely to this period any of the manuscripts or fragments which are currently known to us' (Déroche 2014: 136). He was to conclude that evidence from the early Qur'anic manuscript tradition indicates that a flexibility governed approaches to the early transmission of the Qur'an (Déroche 2019).

Surveys of early archival sources do attach particular importance to the fact that early Qur'an manuscripts frequently preserve non-canonical variants which are not documented or acknowledged in the later traditional sources; this is also the case for the system of verse counts and divisions which differ from conventions adhered to and set out in later classical sources.[6] Notwithstanding the work of Spitaler, a comprehensive study of the system of verse counts and divisions remains a desideratum. Similar observations feature in the debates about the 'Ṣanʿāʾ' codex, a palimpsest consisting of a cache of folios which were first discovered among fragments in the roof of the Great Mosque of Sanaa in 1972, along with further materials later found in the mosque's library (Puin 1996: 109; cf. Déroche 2014). In their study of the material Behnam Sadeghi and Mohsen Goudarzi confirmed the non-standard format of the *scriptio inferior*: namely, the underlying script which was erased to make way for the fresher canonical text (Sadeghi and Goudarzi 2012: 9). They argued that the palimpsest, which they designated as Ṣanʿāʾ I, offered direct evidence of the historical reality of the existence of non-ʿUthmānic texts such as the Companion codices of Ibn Masʿūd, Ubayy ibn Kaʿb and indeed others (Sadeghi and Goudarzi 2012: 19; cf. Puin 2008). They maintained that its unique constitution indicated that it was a 'distinct Companion codex'. The forms of variants in the codex include instances of 'additions, omissions, transpositions, and substitutions of entire words and sub-elements (morphemes)'. They observed that a large number of these variants involved 'suffixes, prefixes, prepositions and pronouns' and the ordering of the codex's chapters was closer to those of the codices of Ibn Masʿūd and Ubayy, than it was to the ʿUthmānic text (Sadeghi and Goudarzi 2012: 21 and 25).

[5] The manuscript Or. 2165 has been digitized: <http://www.bl.uk/manuscripts/FullDisplay.aspx?ref=Or_2165>.

[6] An analysis of the recitation of the Qur'an and the traditionally applied conventions for the division of verses features in Spitaler (1935).

Arguments about the dating of the *scriptio inferior* do have a bearing upon discussions about the synthesis of *qirāʾāt* within the early tradition. Sadeghi and Goudarzi estimated that that the upper text was probably written sometime 'during the seventh or the first half of the eighth century AD', estimating that the *scriptio inferior* had its origins in the seventh century and not beyond that. Déroche cautiously proposed the view that Ṣanʿāʾ I 'was written during the second-half of the first/seventh century', suggesting that it was still in use at the end of that century. He concluded that the later tradition of *qirāʾāt* scholarship perhaps discarded or did not take into account the specific variants which it preserved (Déroche 2014: 54 and 137). Sadeghi and Goudarzi claimed that the survival of such a variant codex showed that the transcription of personal codices, including those ascribed to Ibn Masʿūd and Ubayy, was permitted even in these later periods, although ultimately, they concluded that the attempts by ʿUthmān to establish a fixed text were 'fairly effective'.

In her examination of the material Asma Hilali cautioned against the reliance upon medieval theories about Qur'anic variants to broach the interpretation of material in the Ṣanʿāʾ codex, positing that these materials were 'produced much later' and were not 'a faithful mirror of the early material' (Hilali 2014: 13; Hilali 2016: 21–2). In a study of folios from the Ṣanʿāʾ codex, Alba Fedeli questioned whether non-standard variants had a pre-ʿUthmānic provenance, speculating that it was only in the fourth/tenth century when Ibn Mujāhid promoted variants consistent with a 'fairly uniform consonantal text' (Fedeli 2012: 315). However, Fedeli's view appears to overlook not only the objective of Ibn Mujāhid's efforts, but also the fact that his selection of readings was determined by the regnant status of specific sets of *lectiones* already widely in circulation. Indeed, the readings preserved in Ibn Mujāhid's text can be traced to much earlier sources such as the *maʿānī al-Qurʾān* genre of writings which include texts composed by al-Farrāʾ, al-Akhfash al-Awsaṭ (d. 215/830) and Abū ʿUbayda (d. 209/824–5) (Shah 2003a and 2003b; Versteegh 1993). Certainly, the study of the archival material of early Qur'anic manuscripts has progressed in recent years as evidenced by the publication of Éléonore Cellard's Codex Amrensis 1, which preserves four sets of fragments discovered within the ʿAmr ibn al-ʿĀṣ mosque in old Cairo (al-Fusṭāṭ) (Cellard 2018). It is evident that a profounder appreciation of the nature of *qirāʾāt* and attitudes to their synthesis within the early and classical tradition will be crucial to the efforts to unravel the significance of the manuscript data.

Separately, referring to the Egyptian edition of the Qur'an, Déroche commented that 'When the al-Azhar specialists convened to produce a reliable edition of the Qur'an towards 1920s, they never thought of looking for the earliest written witnesses, had they known to identify them, but used in the course of their work the specialized literature on the *qirāʾāt* or the orthography' (Déroche 2014: 14). It is important to bear in mind not only the purpose of the Cairo edition, but also the historical background to its production: the aim was to produce a copy which was based on the *lectio* of ʿĀṣim as transmitted by Ḥafṣ as preserved in the classical *qirāʾāt* literature and, in so doing, address the shortcomings of earlier attempts to produce a printed edition. The production of this edition did not represent an encroachment upon traditional scholarship germane to the transmission and teaching of the larger corpus of *qirāʾāt* which continued to thrive in religious seminaries and institutions. Pretzl noted the remarkable thoroughness with which the Egyptian edition was produced, although he stated that it tentatively obscured the fact that a manifold body of *lectiones* was connected with the text of the Qur'an (Pretzl 1938: 273). Jeffery criticized the fact that the editors of the Egyptian version relied on late authorities for Ḥafṣ's recension and that they had 'not quite succeeded in producing a pure type of Ḥafṣ text', but he spoke of the version being 'better than anything else available, and very much superior to the Flügel text' (Jeffery 1946). The edition of the Qur'an published by Gustav Flügel in Leipzig appeared in 1834 and had hitherto been relied upon in academic circles.

Ibn Mujāhid and the Moves Towards the Standardization of Readings

The standardization of seven sets of *variae lectiones* is conventionally identified as being one of the grand accomplishments of Ibn Mujāhid's *Kitāb al-Sabʿa*, an achievement repeatedly lauded in medieval biographical sources. Bergsträsser, Pretzl, and Jeffery all acknowledged the impact of his efforts and the importance of his legacy as did later scholars, although observations about the importance of his work were evidently informed by references to the text in later literary sources such as Ibn al-Jazarī's *al-Nashr*. Discussing Ibn Mujāhid's efforts in his essay on the Qur'an, Alford Welch maintained that he aimed to 'restrict the number of acceptable readings' by selecting seven well-known readers, even assuming, like Pretzl before him, that this was inspired by the Prophetic hadith which spoke of the Qur'an being revealed in seven *ḥurūf* or modes (*EI2* 408; Pretzl 1938: 3:184; cf. Watt 1970: 48). Curiously, classical sources record that Ibn Mujāhid was censured for basing his book on seven readings due to the fact this number could be confused with the aforementioned prophetic tradition which speaks of the Qur'an being revealed in seven modes (Shah 2004: 84). Other scholars also identified a paradigm of limitation inherent in Ibn Mujāhid's endeavour including Estelle Whelan who referred to Ibn Mujāhid's succeeding in 'reducing the number of acceptable readings to the seven that were predominant in the main Muslim centres of the time' (Whelan 1998: 1); Efim Rezvan pronounced that Ibn Mujāhid restricted not only the 'number of systems of variant vowellings of the text to seven', but he also proscribed 'the use of other variants (*al-ikhtiyār*)' (Rezvan 1998: 17). Despite the wealth of literary evidence from early grammatical texts, it has even been asserted that the 'set patterns of diacritics' and the 'precise vocalization of the short vowels' were not fixed until 'Ibn Mujāhid legitimized the Seven readings systems' (Small 2011: 183). Deliberating the historical significance of his work, Christopher Melchert argued that Ibn Mujāhid's promotion of seven readings presented a means to end 'the multiplication of readings, hence limiting the burden of Qur'anic scholarship' (Melchert 2000: 18). He signalled that the establishment of seven readings did 'restrain growing complexity', commenting that 'their recognition, however halting and incomplete, did mark a widely observable turn in the tenth century towards limited agreement and manageability' (Melchert 2000: 18–19).

In his study of the *Kitāb al-Sabʿa*, Shah maintained that it was never the intention of Ibn Mujāhid to curb the traditionally based practice of *ikhtiyār*, provided it was regulated by the pursuit of authenticated precedents defined within the reading tradition. His assessment was that Ibn Mujāhid specifically inveighed against the hypothetical projection of *lectiones* based on grammatical analogues, which he deemed an egregious practice, but that the imposition of seven sets of readings was not the intended objective of his work; indeed, there were occasions where he even criticized readings included in his work. For these reasons, he held that Ibn Mujāhid had simply selected sets of readings which were already widely accepted as being authoritative within the reading tradition (Shah 2004: 78). Explaining the prominence of the *Kitāb al-Sabʿa*, Shah claimed that this can be attributed to the fact that the work was the subject of several popular grammatical proof texts composed by luminaries such as Ibn al-Sarrāj (d. 316/928), Abū ʿAlī al-Fārisī (d. 377/987) and Ibn Khālawayhi (Shah 2004: 94). He also concluded that the forensic probing of linguistic variances among *lectiones* played an influential role in the development of grammatical discourses (Shah 2003a and 2003b).

More recently, Shady Nasser has weighed in with some enhanced arguments about approaches to variants in Ibn Mujāhid's era. He hypothesized that the latitude and flexibility which marked approaches to the adoption of legal rulings (*aḥkām*) were also a feature of approaches to the synthesis of variant readings. Nasser reasoned that Ibn Mujāhid, and indeed his peer, al-Ṭabarī (d. 310/923), never considered these variants to be of 'divine and absolute value' (Nasser 2013: 77 and 230; cf. Nasser 2016). On the issue of transmission, Nasser held that over subsequent centuries the authentication of readings was broached through the lens of hadith scholarship which witnessed the theory of multiple transmission (or *tawātur*) being retrospectively invoked to substantiate their historical dissemination. He too accepted that a construct of restriction lies at the heart of Ibn Mujāhid's endeavour and he described him as being 'the first to forcefully canonize his collection' (Nasser 2013: 41). Nasser deplored the fact that the larger corpus of variant Qur'anic readings is ominously overlooked in studies of the textual transmission of the Qur'an.

In his copious supplements to the *Geschichte* Bergsträsser had remarked that the introduction to Ibn al-Jazarī's *al-Nashr fī'l-qirāʾāt al-ʿashr* was a prized source on account of the fact that its extended introduction preserved a profusion of references and quotations derived from earlier literature on *qirāʾāt* (Bergsträsser 1938: 116–17). A number of earlier works cited in *al-Nashr* have been published and they confirm that vigorous activity in the authorship of collections of readings continued before and after the composition of Ibn Mujāhid's *Kitāb al-Sabʿa*. While many of these works were set around the consolidation of the seven canonical readings, others avidly supplemented them with additional documented *lectiones*. Although these compilations were often reiterating equivalent data about *qirāʾāt* preserved in earlier literary endeavours, their originality often turned on the imaginative presentation and organization of the data. Among them are works such as *al-Irshād fī'l-qirā'āt ʿan al-a'imma al-sabʿa* composed by Abū'l-Ṭayyib Ibn Ghalbūn (d. 389/998) and *al-Tadhkira fī'l-qirā'āt al-thamān*, collated by his son Ṭāhir ibn Ghalbūn (d. 399/1008), which brought together eight readings, adding the *lectiones* of Yaʿqūb al-Ḥaḍramī (d. 205/820) to the seven. The selection of al-Ḥaḍramī was not arbitrary but based on the unassailable fact that classical scholars considered his reading to be as equally valued as each of the seven. In the same periods Ibn Mihrān (d. 381/991) composed a work which collated ten sets of readings, *al-Mabsūṭ fī'l-qirā'āt al-ʿashr* and he put together two other collections: *al-Shāmil* and *al-Ghāya*. Similar trends persisted in the fifth/eleventh century: al-Dānī authored both the *Jāmiʿ al-bayān fī'l-qirā'āt al-sabʿa al-mashhūra* and the brief didactic treatise *al-Taysīr*, which was edited by Pretzl. Makkī ibn Abī Ṭālib (d. 437/1045), who had studied with Ibn Ghalbūn and his son, composed the *Kitāb al-Kashf ʿan wujūh al-qirā'āt al-sabʿ*, which set out a detailed exposition of the seven readings, and the *Tabṣira*, which was intended to serve as a primer for students. Renowned for his expertise in readings and his avowed traditionalism, al-Ahwāzī (d. 446/1055) composed a commentary on 'the eight readings of the five cities', the *Kitāb al-Wajīz*; complementing this text was a separate work he compiled on non-canonical readings, entitled *Kitāb al-Iqnā'*. He was also the author of separate treatises which listed variants associated with one specific reader from the early tradition (Hamdan 2006). Underpinning the intense levels of interest in such materials, a number of other scholars authored collections which collated canonical and non-canonical materials. This was a feature of the *Kitāb al-Kāmil* of al-Hudhalī (d. 465/1072), a book which boasts of covering fifty *lectiones*, and indeed the *Kitāb al-Mubhij* authored by Sibṭ al-Khayyāṭ (d. 541/1146). Focusing on the grammatical analysis of anomalous readings, Abū'l-Baqā' al-ʿUkbarī (d. 616/1219) wrote the commentary entitled *Iʿrāb al-qirā'āt al-shawādhdh*. When al-Dimyāṭī (d. 1117/1705) presented his collection of fourteen readings, *Itḥāf fuḍalā' al-bashar*, in which he nominally added four readings to the ten, he was in essence engaged in the gleaning and reorganization of the prodigious body of materials that had already been preserved, authenticated, and classified in the earlier literature.

It is perhaps fitting to return to al-Dānī's *al-Taysīr*: it provided the template for a versified commentary composed by the Andalusian scholar al-Qāsim ibn Firruh al-Shāṭibī (d. 590/1193), which appeared under the title *Ḥirz al-amānī wa-wajh al-tahānī*, and is referred to as the *Shāṭibiyya* in honour of its author (Pretzl 1938: 215–19). Numerous commentaries were composed on the *Shāṭibiyya*, consolidating its status as the coveted text for the teaching of the seven canonical readings in Qur'anic seminaries across the Islamic world. Among its most celebrated commentaries are Abū Shāma al-Dimashqī's *Ibrāz al-maʿānī min ḥirz al-amānī* and al-Jaʿbarī's *Kanz al-maʿānī fī sharḥ ḥirz al-amānī*. Concerning the *Shāṭibiyya*, Ibn al-Jazarī spoke of the unparalleled esteem in which the work was held in the Islamic tradition; the *Geschichte* acknowledged the importance of both the *Taysīr* and the *Shāṭibiyya* (Nöldeke 1860: 342 and 358 Pretzl 1938: 222). However, although these treatises remain the principal texts for the teaching of readings in the Islamic world, they constitute only a small proportion of the profuse range of materials and scholarship the discipline of *qirā'āt* preserved over the centuries.

Conclusions

The corpus of *qirā'āt* together with the traditions of learning which are associated with the scrutiny of these materials offers a sophisticated, rich range of literary sources. Historically, the treatment of *qirā'āt* has been broached through a pool of materials which provide only a partial context to the intricate processes of their history and synthesis. Building upon the foundations of the work by scholars such as Nöldeke, Bergsträsser, Pretzl, and Jeffery, and boosted by the availability of a broader range of critical editions of manuscripts on readings, including evidence from early Qur'anic manuscripts, a circumspect examination of this larger body of sources will facilitate a profounder appreciation of their importance to understanding not only the history of the textual transmission of the Qur'an, but also the subtle intricacies of classical *qirā'āt* scholarship across the centuries.

Bibliography

Primary Sources

Al-Ahwāzī, al-Ḥasan ibn ʿAlī. *al-Wajīz fī sharḥ qirā'āt al-qirā'a al-thamāniyya a'immat al-amṣār al-khamsa*. Ed. Durayd Ḥasan Aḥmad. Beirut: Dār al-Gharb al-Islāmī, 2002.

Al-Dānī, Abū ʿAmr ʿUthmān ibn Saʿīd. *al-Muḥkam fī naqṭ al-maṣāḥif*. Ed. ʿIzzat Ḥasan. 2nd edn. Damascus: Dār al-Fikr, 1986.

Al-Dānī, Abū ʿAmr ʿUthmān ibn Saʿīd. *Kitāb al-Taysīr fi'l-qirā'āt al-sabʿ*. Ed. Otto Pretzl. Istanbul: Matḅaʿat al-Dawla, 1930.

Al-Dānī, Abū ʿAmr ʿUthmān ibn Saʿīd. *Kitāb al-Muqniʿ fī rasm maṣāḥif al-amṣār maʿa Kitāb al-Naqṭ*. Ed. Otto Pretzl. Istanbul: Matḅaʿat al-Dawla, 1932.

Al-Dimyāṭī, Aḥmad ibn Muḥammad. *Itḥāf fuḍālā' al-bashr bi'l-qirā'āt al-arbaʿat ʿashar*. Ed. ʿAbd al-Raḥim al-Tarhūnī. 2 vols. Cairo: Dār al-Ḥadīth, 2009.

Al-Fārisī, al-Ḥasan ibn Aḥmad Abū ʿAlī. *al-Ḥujja fī ʿilal al-qirā'āt al-sabʿ*. 2 vols. Ed. Shalabī, Nāṣīf, Najjār & Najjāt. Cairo: al-Hay'at al-Miṣriyya, 1983.

Al-Farrā', Abū Zakariyyā', Yaḥyā ibn Ziyād. *Maʿānī al-Qur'ān*. 3 vols. Ed. Aḥmad Yūsuf Najātī and Muḥammad ʿAlī al-Najjār. Cairo: Dār al-Kutub al-Miṣriyya, 1955–72.

Ibn Ghalbūn, Ṭāhir ibn ʿAbd al-Munʿim, *Al-Tadhkira fi'l-qirā'āt al-thamān*. Ed. Saʿīd Ṣāliḥ Zaʿīma. Alexandria: Dār Ibn Khaldūn, 2001.

Ibn al-Jazarī, Muḥammad ibn Muḥammad. *al-Nashr fi'l-qirā'āt al-ʿashr*. 2 vols. Ed. ʿAlī Muḥammad al-Ḍabbāʿ. Beirut: Dār al-Kutub al-ʿIlmiyya, n.d.

Ibn al-Jazarī, Muḥammad ibn Muḥammad. *Ghāyat al-nihāya fī ṭabaqāt al-qurrā.'* 2 vols. Ed. Gotthelf Bergsträsser and Otto Pretzl. Cairo: Maṭbaʿat al-Saʿāda, 1935.

Ibn Khālawayhi, Abū ʿAbd Allāh al-Ḥusayn ibn Aḥmad. *al-Ḥujja fi'l-qirā'āt al-sabʿ*. Ed. ʿAbd al-ʿĀl Sālim Makram. Beirut: Dār al-Shurūq, 1971.

Ibn Khālawayhi, Abū ʿAbd Allāh al-Ḥusayn ibn Aḥmad. *Mukhtaṣar fī shawādhdh al-Qur'ān min Kitāb al-Badīʿ*. Ed. Gotthelf Bergsträsser with an introduction by Arthur Jeffery. Cairo: al-Maṭbaʿa al-Raḥmāniyya, 1934.

Ibn Jinnī, Abū'l-Fatḥ ʿUthmān. *al-Muḥtasab fī tabyīn wujūh shawādhdh al-qirāʾāt wa'l-īḍāḥ ʿanhā*. Ed. ʿAlī al-Najdī Nāṣif, ʿAbd al-Ḥālīm al-Najjār, ʿAbd al-Fattāḥ Shalabī. 2 vols. Cairo: Lajnat Iḥyāʾ al-Turāth al-ʿArabī, AH 1387.
Ibn al-Nadīm, Muḥammad. *al-Fihrist*. Ed. R. Tajaddud. 3rd edn. Beirut: Dār al-Masīra, 1988.
Ibn Mujāhid. *Kitāb al-Sabʿa fī'l-qirāʾāt*. Ed. Shawqī Ḍayf. 2nd edn. Cairo: Dār al-Maʿārif, *c*.1401/1980.
Makkī ibn Abī Ṭālib. *Kitāb al-Kashf ʿan wujūh al-qirāʾāt al-sabʿ wa-ʿilalihā wa-ḥujajihā*. Ed. M. Ramaḍān. Beirut: Muʾassasat al-Risāla, 1981.
Makkī ibn Abī Ṭālib, Abū Muḥammad. *Kitāb al-Tabṣira fī'l-qirāʾāt*. Ed. M. Ramaḍān. Kuwait: Manshūrāt Maʿhad al-Makhṭūṭāt al-ʿArabiyya, 1985.
al-Qasṭallānī, Shihāb al-Dīn. *Laṭāʾif al-ishārāt li-funūn al-qirāʾāt*. Ed. ʿAbd al-Ṣabūr Shāhīn and ʿĀmir al-Sayyid ʿUthmān. Cairo: Lajnat Iḥyāʾ al-Turāth al-Islāmī, 1972.
al-ʿUkbarī, Abū'l-Baqāʾ. *Iʿrāb al-qirāʾāt al-shawādhdh*. 2 vols. Beirut: ʿĀlam al-Kutub, 1996.

Secondary Sources

Bar-Asher, Meir. 'Variant Readings and Additions of the Imamī Shīʿite to the Qur'an', *Israel Oriental Studies* 13 (1993), 39–74.
Beck, Edmund. *Die Koranzitate bei Sībawaih*. Munich: 1939. (Diss. Published in 1959).
Beck, Edmund. 'Die Kodizesvarianten der Amsâr', *Orientalia* 16/3 (1947), 353–76.
Beck, Edmund. 'Studien zur Geschichte der kufischen Koranlesung in den beiden ersten Jahrhunderten', *Orientalia* 17/3 (1948), 326–55; 19/3 (1950), 328–50; 20/3 (1951), 316–28; 22/1 (1953), 59–78.
Bergsträsser, Gotthelf. 'Die Koranlesung des Ḥasan von Basra', *Islamica* 2 (1926), 11–57.
Bergsträsser, Gotthelf. 'Plan eines Apparatus Criticus zum Koran', *Sitzungsberichte der philosophisch-philologischen Klass der Bayerischen Akademie der Wissenschaften*, 7 (1930), 3–11.
Bergsträsser, Gotthelf. 'Koranlesung in Kairo', *Der Islam* 20/1 (1932), 1–42; and *Der Islam* 21 (1933a), 110–40.
Bergsträsser, Gotthelf, *Nichtkanonische Koranlesarten im Muḥtasab des ibn Ginnī*. Munich: Sitzungsberichte der Bayerischen Akademie der Wissenschaften, 1933b.
Blair, Sheila. *Islamic Calligraphy*. Edinburgh: Edinburgh University Press, 2006.
Brockett, Adrian. 'The Value of Ḥafṣ and Warsh Transmissions for the Textual History of the Qurʾān'. In: Andrew Rippin (eds.). *Approaches to the History of the Interpretation of the* Qurʾān, pp. 31–45. Oxford: Oxford University Press, 1988.
Burton, John. *The Collection of the Qurʾān*. Cambridge: Cambridge University Press, 1977.
Burton, John. 'The Vowelling of Q. 65:1', *Journal of Semitic Studies* 29/2 (1984), 267–83.
Cellard, Éléonore. *Codex Amrensis 1*. Leiden: Brill, 2018.
Comerro, Viviane. *Les Traditions sur la constitution du muṣḥaf de ʿUthmān*. Würzburg: Ergon-Verlag; Beirut: Orient-Institut, 2012.
Cook, Michael. 'The Stemma of the Regional Codices of the Koran', *Graeco-Arabica* 9–10 (2004), 89–104.
Déroche, François and Sergio Noja Noseda. *Le Manuscrit Or. 2165 (f.1 à 61) de la British Library*. Lesa and London: Fondazione Ferni Noja Noseda and British Library, 2001.
Déroche, François. *La transmission écrite du Coran dans les débuts de l'islam: le codex Parisino-petropolitanus*. Leiden and Boston: Brill, 2009.
Déroche, François. *Qur'ans of the Umayyads: A First Overview*. Leiden and Boston: Brill, 2014.

Déroche, François. *Le Coran, une histoire plurielle: Essai sur la formation du texte coranique.* Paris: Le Seuil, 2019.
Dutton, Yasin. 'Some Notes on the British Library's "Oldest Qur'an Manuscript" (Or. 2165)', *Journal of Qur'anic Studies* 6/1 (2004), 43–71.
Fedeli, Alba. 'Variants and Substantiated *qirāʾāt*: A Few Notes Exploring their Fluidity in the Oldest Qurʾānic Manuscripts'. In: Markus Gross and Karl-Heinz Ohlig (eds.). *Die Entstehung einer Weltreligion*, 2:403–40. Berlin: Verlag Hans Schiler, 2012.
George, Alain. 'Coloured Dots and the Question of Regional Origins in Early Qur'ans: Part I', Journal of Qur'anic Studies, 17/1(2015), 1–44.
Goldziher, Ignaz. *Die Richtungen der islamischen Koranauslegung*. Buchhandlung und Druckerei, Leiden: E. J. Brill, 1920.
Hamdan, Omar. *Studien zur Kanonisierung des Korantextes: al-Ḥasan al-Baṣrī's Beiträge zur Geschichte des Korans*. Wiesbaden: Harrassowitz, 2006a.
Hamdan, Omar. *Mufradat al-Ḥasan al-Baṣrī*. Abū ʿAlī al-Ḥasan ibn ʿAlī ibn Ibrahīm al-Ahwāzī. ʿUmar Ḥamdan (ed.). ʿAmmān: Dār Ibn Kathīr, 1427/2006b.
Hamdan, Omar. 'The Second *Maṣāḥif* Project: A Step Towards the Canonization of the Qurʾanic Text'. In: Angelika Neuwirth, Nicolai Sinai, and Michael Marx (eds.). *The Qurʾān in Context: Historical and Literary Investigations into the Qurʾānic Milieu*, pp. 795–835. Leiden; Boston: Brill, 2010.
Hilali, Asma. 'Was the Ṣanʿāʾ Qur'an Palimpsest a Work in Progress?' In: David Hollenberg, Christoph Rauch, and Sabine Schmidtke (eds.). *The Yemeni Manuscript Tradition*, pp. 12–27. Leiden: Brill, 2014.
Hilali, Asma. *The Sanaa Palimpsest: The Transmission of the Qur'an in the First Centuries A. H.* London: Oxford University Press in association with the Institute of Ismaili Studies, 2016.
Jeffery, Arthur. *Materials for the History of the Text of the Qur'an: The Old Codices*. Leiden: E. J. Brill, 1937.
Jeffery, Arthur. 'Textual History of the Qur'ān'. Lecture delivered in 1946 at the Middle East Society of Jerusalem.
Jeffery, Arthur. 'The Qurʾān Readings of Ibn Miqsam'. In: Samuel Löwinger and Joseph Somogyi (eds.). *Ignace Goldziher Memorial Volume*. 2 vols., pp. 1–38. Budapest: Globus, 1948–58.
Kahle, Paul. 'The Arabic Readers of the Koran', *Journal of Near Eastern Studies* 8/2 (1949), 65–71.
Kohlberg, Etan and Mohammed Ali Amir-Moezzi. *Revelation and Falsification: The Kitāb al-qirāʾāt* of Aḥmad b. Muḥammad al-Sayyārī. Critical Edition with an Introduction and Notes. Leiden and Boston: Brill, 2009.
Lier Thomas. 'Hellmut Ritter in Istanbul 1926–1949', *Die Welt des Islams* 38/3 (1998), 334–85.
Luxenberg, Christoph. *The Syro-Aramaic Reading of the Koran: A Contribution to the Decoding of the Language of the Koran*. Berlin: Verlag Hans Schiler, 2007 (German original 2000).
Marx, Michael. 'The Lost Archive, the Myth of Philology, and the Study of the Qur'an'. Published online, 19/01/2009. Accessed May 2018 at <https://edoc.bbaw.de/frontdoor/index/index/docId/799>.
Melchert, Christopher. 'Ibn Mujāhid and the Establishment of Seven Qur'anic Readings', *Studia Islamica* 91 (2000), 5–22.
Melchert, Christopher. 'The Relation of the Ten Readings to One Another', *Journal of Qur'anic Studies* 10/2 (2008), 73–87.

Nasser, Shady. *The Transmission of the Variant Readings of the Qurʾān: The Problem of* Tawātur *and the Emergence of* Shawādhdh. Leiden and Boston: Brill, 2013.

Nasser, Shady. 'The Two-Rāwī Canon Before and After ad-Dānī (d. 444/1052–3): The Role of Abū ṭ-Ṭayyib ibn Ghalbūn (d. 389/998) and the Qayrawān/Andalus School in Creating the Two Rāwī Canon', *Oriens* 41 (2013), 41–75.

Nasser, Shady. '(Q. 12:2) We have sent it down as an Arabic Qurʾan: Praying behind the Lisper', *Islamic Law and Society* 23 (2016), 23–51.

Nöldeke, Theodor. *Geschichte des Qorâns* (Göttingen, 1860). Revised by Friedrich Schwally and supplemented by Gotthelf Bergsträsser and Otto Pretzl. Leipzig: Dieterich'sche Verlagsbuchhandlung, 1909–38. See the translation: *The History of the Qurʾān*, Theodor Nöldeke, Friedrich Schwally, Gotthelf Bergsträsser, and Otto Pretzl. Ed. and trans. Wolfgang H. Behn. Leiden and Boston: Brill, 2013.

Pretzl, Otto. 'Die Wissenschaft der Koranlesung', *Islamica* 6 (1934), 1–47; 230–46; and 290–331.

Puin, Gerd. 'Observations on Early Qur'an Manuscripts in Ṣanʿāʾ'. In: Stefan Wild (ed.). *The Qur'an as Text*, pp. 107–11. Leiden: E. J. Brill, 1996.

Puin, Elisabeth. 'Ein früher Koranpalimpsest aus Ṣanʿāʾ (DAM 01–27.1)'. In: M. Gross and K.-H. Ohlig (eds.). *Schlaglichter: Die beiden ersten islamischen Jahrhunderte*, pp. 461–93. Berlin: Hans Schiler, 2008.

Rabb, Intisar. 'Non-Canonical Readings of the Qur'an: Recognition and Authenticity (The Ḥimṣī Reading)', *Journal of Qur'anic Studies* 8/2 (2006), 84–127.

Rezvan, Efim. 'The Qur'an and its World: VI. Emergence of the Canon: The Struggle for Uniformity', *Manuscripta Orientalia* 4/2 (1998), 13–54.

Sadeghi, Behnam and Mohsen Goudarzi. 'Ṣanʿāʾ 1 and the Origins of the Qurʾān', *Der Islam* 87 (2012), 1–129.

Shah Mustafa. 'Exploring the Genesis of Early Arabic Linguistic Thought: Qur'anic Readers and Grammarians of the Kūfan Tradition' (Part I), *Journal of Qur'anic Studies* 5/1 (2003a), 47–78.

Shah, Mustafa. 'Exploring the Genesis of Early Arabic Linguistic Thought: Qur'anic Readers and Grammarians of the Baṣran Tradition' (Part II), *Journal of Qur'anic Studies* 5/2 (2003b), 1–47.

Shah, Mustafa. 'The Early Arabic Grammarians' Contributions to the Collection and Authentication of Qur'anic Readings: The Prelude to Ibn Mujāhid's *Kitāb al-Sabʿa*', *Journal of Qur'anic Studies* 6/1 (2004), 72–102.

Shah, Mustafa. 'The Case of *variae lectiones* in Classical Islamic Jurisprudence: Grammar and the Interpretation of Law', *International Journal for the Semiotics of Law* (*Revue internationale de sémiotique juridique*) 29/2 (2016), 285–311.

Sinai, Nicolai. 'When Did the Consonantal Skeleton of the Quran Reach Closure?', *Bulletin of the School of Oriental and African Studies* 77 (2014), 273–92 (Part One) and 509–21 (Part Two).

Small, Keith. *Textual Criticism and Qurʾān Manuscripts*. Lanham, MD: Lexington Books, 2011.

Spitaler, Anton and Otto Pretzl. *Die Verszählung des Koran nach islamischer Überlieferung*. Munich: Verlag der Bayerischen Akademie der Wissenschaften, 1935.

Van Putten, Marijn.' "The Grace of God" as Evidence for a Written Uthmanic Archetype: the Importance of Shared Orthographic Idiosyncrasies', *Bulletin of the School of Oriental and African Studies*. 82 (2019), 271–288.

Versteegh, Kees. *Arabic Grammar and Qur'anic Exegesis in Early Islam*. Leiden: E. J. Brill, 1993.
Vollers, Karl. *Volkssprache und Schriftsprache im Alten Arabien*. Strasbourg: Verlag von Karl J. Trübner, 1906.
Wansbrough, John. *Quranic Studies: Sources and Methods of Scriptural Interpretation*. Oxford: Oxford University Press, 1977.
Watt, Montgomery. *Bell's Introduction to the Qur'an, completely revised and enlarged by W. Montgomery Watt*. Edinburgh: Edinburgh University Press, 1997 (first published 1970).
Welch, Alford. T. 'al-Kur'ān'. In: C. E. Bosworth, E van Donzel, B. Lewis, and Ch. Pellat (eds.). *The Encyclopaedia of Islam*, second edition, 5:400–29. Leiden: Brill, 1986.
Whelan, Estelle, 'Forgotten Witness: Evidence for the Early Codification of the Qur'an', *Journal of the American Oriental Society* 118/1 (1998), 1–14.

CHAPTER 14

GLORIFYING GOD'S WORD

Manuscripts of the Qur'an

SHEILA S. BLAIR

This chapter addresses the topic of how an oral revelation was transformed into a written document and how the form of that written document changed over time to meet the varying needs of the expanding Muslim community, in the same way that the revelation of the Qur'an evolved over time to meet the differing needs of the nascent community of believers (*EQ* 2:245f.; Ernst 2011). The chapter also considers the different methodologies appropriate to study these diverse documents, the different questions raised by them, and the different ways that this information has been and can be used. It opens with some general considerations about scope, methodology, and the like. Given the vast nature of the material, the many changes to it over time, and the goal of placing these physical changes in their historical and social contexts, the chapter then adopts a chronological framework, dividing the past millennium and a half of production into four major blocks. Details about many of these and other types of manuscripts along with further illustrations and extensive bibliographies can be found in works such as Déroche's long article on manuscripts in the *Encyclopaedia of the Qurʾān* (*EQ* 3:254–75), Blair's 2006 survey of Islamic calligraphy, George's 2010 monograph on early Arabic calligraphy, Déroche's 2014 overview of production during the Umayyad period, and the glossy catalogues to several recent exhibitions (e.g. *1400. Yilinda Kur'an-i Kerim* 2010; Farhad and Rettig 2016).

Perspectives, Practicalities, and Problems

This chapter covers writing on supple supports such as parchment and paper, in contrast to Chapter 15 in this volume, which treats writing on solid supports, although there is occasional overlap between the two. This chapter also concentrates on transcriptions of the entire revelation, whereas Chapter 15 on inscriptions deals mainly with individual verses or occasionally chapters from the full text. In terms of format, the discussion in this chapter basically concerns codices in the sense of books with leaves, although it also includes a few scrolls intended to be displayed vertically and some portfolios of loose sheets. These manuscripts are typically handwritten and thus can profitably be contrasted with the printed editions discussed in Chapter 16 of this volume.

Most research has concentrated on the finest manuscripts. Transcribed on expensive materials, they were often elaborately decorated to underscore the sacredness and importance of the text. This decoration served to divide the text into manageable units, enhance readability, and enliven the visual qualities of the page (*EQ* 3:593f.). Like the Jewish Torah but unlike the Christian Bible, Qur'an manuscripts were never illustrated with pictures of people. Hence in discussing manuscripts, historians of Islamic art make a careful distinction between illumination (non-figural decoration, typically geometric and vegetal) and illustration (pictures of people). In the study of Western medieval manuscripts, by contrast, the term illumination covers both figural and non-figural decoration. Muslims can therefore be said to be aniconic, in the sense that they avoided naturalistic representation in sacred texts, rather than iconoclastic, meaning that they destroyed images (*EQ* 2:473f. and 475f., respectively).

Indeed, the desire to avoid figural imagery in decorating God's word has meant that Muslims did not usually depict architecture in Qur'an manuscripts. The one exception—the large double-page frontispiece to an early parchment manuscript found in Sanaa (Dār al-Makhṭūṭāt, Ṣanʿāʾ, inv. no. 20-33.1; Bothmer 1987; Piotrovsky 2000: no. 36; George 2010: pls. 53–4)—stands out by its rarity, which complicates—and one might even argue vitiates—attempts to explain its unusual iconography, whether as two views of a specific building such as the Mosque of Damascus, two mosques, or a generic type of mosque. Works by modern painters such as the Los Angeles artist Sandow Birk, who transcribes the Qur'an and illustrates it with scenes from contemporary American life, stand outside the mainstream and to many Muslims may even seem blasphemous.

These finely produced copies of God's word carry inherent sacredness (*baraka*). Many were donated to mosques and shrines, and the endowment notices (*waqfiyya*) on them are important sources for dating and localizing production. The value of these copies, both spiritual and material, is also evident from the notes added to some of them, including reports ascribing their transcription to the earliest heroes of Islam such as ʿUmar or ʿAlī ibn Abī Ṭālib, and from the elaborate boxes made to store these manuscripts.

The sacredness and cost of this material present several challenges to research. Scholars have generally skirted the question of what was made versus what has survived. Manuscripts that were read repeatedly or used for teaching or instruction may have been damaged or worn out, whereas those donated to mosques and shrines have been preserved in better condition. Hence, what we study may (or may not) be representative of what was originally produced. Furthermore, coverage of all periods has not been uniform. Although more recent copies have been preserved in greater quantity, they are generally less studied, and much recent scholarship has focused on early manuscripts, which are particularly difficult of access because of their revered status.

One of the largest collections of early manuscripts, some 14,000 fragments from more than 950 Qur'an manuscripts, was discovered in 1972 when heavy rains caused the roof of the Great Mosque in Sanaa to collapse. Although occasionally exhibited (*Maṣāḥif Ṣanʿāʾ* 1985; Piotrovsky 2000: nos. 35–53) or partially illustrated (Dreibholz 2003; George 2010, *passim*), they have never been fully published and are best known from the UNESCO website and its CD-Rom 'The Sanaʿa Manuscripts'. Even more fragments from the Great Mosque of Damascus (some 200,000) are preserved in Istanbul. Removed after the disastrous fire at the end of the thirteenth/nineteenth century, they were sent from Damascus to Istanbul, capital of the Ottomans who ruled Syria at the time. The finest went to the Topkapı Palace, the rest to the Evkaf Museum, later renamed the Türk ve Islam Eserleri Müzesi (Déroche 2016). These fragments too lack complete documentation, although the catalogue to the 2010 exhibition *1400. Yilinda Kurʾan-i Kerim* provides excellent photographs of some specimens, Déroche's 2014 overview of Umayyad production illustrates some, and Farhad and Rettig's 2016 exhibition catalogue shows others. The fragments and manuscripts in the Dār al-Kutub in Cairo remain inaccessible to most scholars, as do many Iranian collections, notably those in the shrines at Mashhad and Qum.

This difficulty of access is compounded by the lack of adequate physical documentation. We do not have high-resolution photographs, let alone measurements and other basic information, of many examples. On-line catalogues, such as those of the Ṣanʿāʾ fragments or one of early folios and manuscripts now being compiled as part of the Corpus Coranicum project in Germany, may help to resolve these problems, but in most cases the images presently available are not of sufficient quality to allow close study, let alone reproduction. The catalogues of the Qur'an manuscripts in the Bibliothèque Nationale de France (Déroche 1983 and 1985) set a model for description, especially for early manuscripts in which the author pioneered a new method of palaeographic analysis, but these volumes too include limited illustrations, although the growing on-line catalogue of the library at gallica.bnf.fr, with zoomable images, is helping to alleviate the problem. The Chester Beatty Library in Dublin holds one of the largest collections of Qur'an manuscripts outside the Muslim world and is therefore more accessible to non-Muslims. Although there is an old handlist (Arberry 1967) as well as several exhibition catalogues (e.g. James 1981) and illustrated volumes (e.g Wright 2009), we lack a complete catalogue with pictures, and the museum's website provides only the most limited information. The finest recent publications of Qur'an manuscripts such as those of the folios acquired at auction for the Khalili Collection in London (Déroche 1992; James 1992a and 1992b; Bayani, Contadini, and Stanley 1999; Bayani, Rogers, and Stanley 2009) have excellent descriptions and photographs, but such quality comes at a price, and the high cost of these publications puts them beyond the reach of all but the most exclusive libraries and researchers. The same is true for facsimiles of some early manuscripts (e.g. Déroche and Noja Noseda 1998 and 2001 or the Club du Livre's facsimile of the manuscript copied by Ibn al-Bawwāb with the accompanying monograph by D. S. Rice, along with a French translation of the text by Jean Grosjean illustrated with silkscreens by the Iranian-born artist Charles Zenderoudi; *Le Coran* 1972).

This lack of basic information has in turn skewed the discussion, and so far it has been difficult to analyse the manuscripts as physical objects and discuss them in terms of the materials consumed, although new studies are moving in this direction. Déroche (2014: 111–16) showed, for example, that the large manuscript with the architectural frontispiece in Sanaa (Dār al-Makhṭūṭāt inv. no. 20–33.1), dubbed by him 'the Umayyad Qur'an of Ṣanʿāʾ required about 90 square metres of parchment, whereas another early manuscript known as the Tashkent Qur'an required four times as much: 362 square metres (Déroche 2013). Knowing such information, one can then consider the manuscripts, as is done with Western ones such as the Codex Amiatinus, in terms of the numbers of animals consumed (in the case of the Qur'an manuscripts, usually sheep). Such data gives us a basic way to compare the relative costs of various copies. Such comparative analysis could be extended to other materials, poorly studied as well. For example, we are similarly ill informed about the basic method of applying gold decoration, whether as ink or as leaf on glair, although the former adds quantitatively to the expense of production.

The rising price of folios from early or famous Qur'an manuscripts further hinders access. Folios from manuscripts that date to the first century of Islam command exceptionally high prices. For example, one badly damaged folio sold at Sotheby's in London on 22 April 2015 for £245,000. The Blue Qur'an is equally in demand: one folio sold for £365,000 at the same Sotheby's sale. Individual folios of the Blue Qur'an may well have been surreptitiously removed from the original codex, most of which is still in Tunisia (latest list of folios in Bloom 2015). Such thefts put the caretakers of manuscripts under further pressure to withhold their treasures from outsiders, as not only might the manuscripts be defiled but some folios might also be purloined.

Parchment Manuscripts From the First Centuries of Islam

The large group of fragments from parchment Qur'an manuscripts made in the first centuries of Islam has been the focus of an extraordinarily productive outburst of research in the last several decades, spurred in part by the debate over the date of the compilation of the text itself. While references from texts have added some snippets of information, by far the most informative area of investigation has been analysis of the folios themselves, alongside comparison to dated works of art and architecture. Not a single one of these many remaining fragments is dated or signed by the calligrapher, and the major question is how to date and localize them. Recent scholarship (e.g. Déroche 2002 and 2014; George 2010) has allowed scholars to distinguish several major groups of early manuscripts, although the names and dates of these groups remain somewhat flexible.

One large group of such early Qur'an fragments is done in the so-called *Ḥijāzī* style (Dutton 2001 and 2004; Rabb 2006; Déroche 2014: 37–73). The group includes Bibliothèque nationale de France 328a and British Library Or. 2165 (Déroche and Noja Noseda 1998 and 2001) as well as the so-called *Codex Parisino-petropolitanus* (Déroche 2009 and 2014: 17–35)—a large fragment containing almost half of the complete text that was taken from the ʿAmr ibn al-Āṣ Mosque in al-Fusṭāṭ, mainly to Paris (Bibliothèque nationale de France, ms arabe 328a and 328b) and St. Petersburg (National Library of Russia, Marcel 18), and one whose dispersal illustrates the need to track down and collate individual folios and the usefulness of coining a moniker to refer to all the dispersed folios. Often executed on vertical-format sheets of parchment, the text in these manuscripts in *Ḥijāzī* style is typically transcribed in dark brownish, tannin-based ink with an average of twenty-five lines to the page in a distinctive elongated script that slants to the right and is similar to that used on some early papyri, often administrative documents that are dated. Some Qur'an fragments contain one of the seven canonical readings (Kufa, Basra, Damascus, Hims, Mecca, and two from Medina) of the so-called ʿUthmānic recension, but others (e.g. the *Codex Parisino-petropolitanus*) do not.

Qur'an manuscripts in the *Ḥijāzī* style are usually assigned to the first/seventh century. Several methods have been used to determine this early date, although many of these approaches carry their own intrinsic problems. First, these manuscripts display non-uniform practice. A single copy sometimes shows multiple hands, with no attempt to make them look similar. The individual scribes also varied the number of lines per page and differed in their use of diacritical marks, their orthographic conventions (for example, whether or not to write long *alif*, as in *qāla*, an example of *scriptio defectiva*), and their verse counts (notably whether to include the *basmala*, or invocation to God, as a verse). Although the scribes typically indicated individual verses with groups of slashes, they did not distinguish the spaces between letters and words, which are typically divided at the end of a line of writing that extends to the very edge of the sheet. These manuscripts represent a time before codification of the text and standardization of practice.

Second, the parchment on which these manuscripts are transcribed can be dated using radiocarbon analysis. An evolving technique that is becoming more precise, this procedure nevertheless involves destruction of the page, albeit an increasingly miniscule part. The test, furthermore, yields a date for the production of the parchment, with the unspoken assumption that the skin was turned into a manuscript immediately following the slaughter of the animal, something that seems to be confirmed when testing dated manuscripts but is not necessarily valid in all cases. Scholars also differ markedly about the accuracy of this type of radiocarbon testing. Déroche is somewhat sceptical (2014: 11–13), whereas others (e.g. Sadeghi and Bergmann 2010; Sadeghi and Goudarzi 2011) are more accepting. In some cases, the results produced by such testing are totally implausible (e.g. a range of 388–535 CE at 68 per cent probability for a palimpsest manuscript dubbed Ṣanʿāʾ 1; Robin 2015: 65) and must be discarded as the result of contamination when cleaning the parchment for testing. In addition, various laboratories can produce slightly different dates. The optimum would be to test each sample at several sites with proven records of testing, as was done with the Shroud of Turin, which was tested in laboratories at Oxford, Zurich, and Tucson. Furthermore, as Sadeghi and others have repeatedly noted, it is inaccurate to present the results from radiocarbon testing as a specific date. Rather, the results indicate a range at a certain degree of probability.

A third method of establishing groups, the one set out by Déroche, involves the study of palaeographic differences in letter shapes (see Chapter 11 in this volume). A fourth method uses techniques of textual criticism by establishing stemmatics (families of manuscripts), a method pioneered by Michael Cook (2004), followed by many of his students (e.g. Sadeghi and Bergmann 2010), and often using textual comparison of recensions (e.g. Rabb 2006).

One manuscript within the group in *Ḥijāzī* style that is exceptional in being a palimpsest with a transcription of the Qur'anic text on top of another in a similar script has been the subject of particularly heated discussion. At least thirty-two leaves from this manuscript were among the cache of specimens found in the Great Mosque at Sanaa. Four more leaves were sold in London between 1992 and 2007 (Figure 14.1), including one auctioned at Christie's in London on 8 April 2008, lot 20, for £2,484,500, the highest price paid to date for a Qur'an leaf (Sadeghi and Bergmann 2010; Sadeghi and Goudarzi 2012). In 2012, forty more folios were discovered in the Maktaba al-Sharqiyya of the Great Mosque of Sanaa, bringing the total number of leaves close to that surviving from the *Codex Parisino-petropolitanus* (Déroche 2014: 48–56). The manuscript is a very rare example with two versions of the Qur'anic text. Most other palimpsests including the Mingana palimpsest in Cambridge (George 2011) have a Christian Arab text written over a Qur'anic one. In the Ṣanʿāʾ palimpsest the lower, and therefore earlier, text contains a different ordering of the suras, dividers (in this case, footers) between them, and dots for some short vowels. Features such as chapter dividers and pointing have generally been assumed to be a later stage in the transcription of the text, but this palimpsest shows that the addition of ornamentation such as verse counts, ten markers, chapter divisions, etc. to the consonantal skeleton of the text (*rasm*) was not a simple matter of linear chronological progression. Rather, different areas or communities, perhaps heterodox ones, may have followed different practices of production.

A gradual standardization of practice seems to have occurred under the Marwanid branch of the Umayyads at the end of the first/seventh century (Déroche 2002 and 2014: 75–105; Dutton 2007; George 2010). Still written on large, vertical sheets of parchment, these manuscripts are typically squarer with a more uniform, more vertical, and heavier rectilinear script that was calculated to look monumental. The script has traditionally been called kufic, though the name should not be taken to indicate that all manuscripts were produced in the city of Kufa, and it remains to distinguish variants of it, whether characteristic of a particular scribe or group of scribes, a place or region, or an evolution in time. Other signs of standardization within this group of manuscripts include a uniform style of script used throughout the text, which shows a fuller evolution toward *scriptio plena* with more frequent *alifs*, even lines with justified edges, a standard number of lines per page (often twenty), markers for five and ten verses, separators between chapters, wider margins around the text, and—most notably—extensive illumination in different colours with a range of decorative devices.

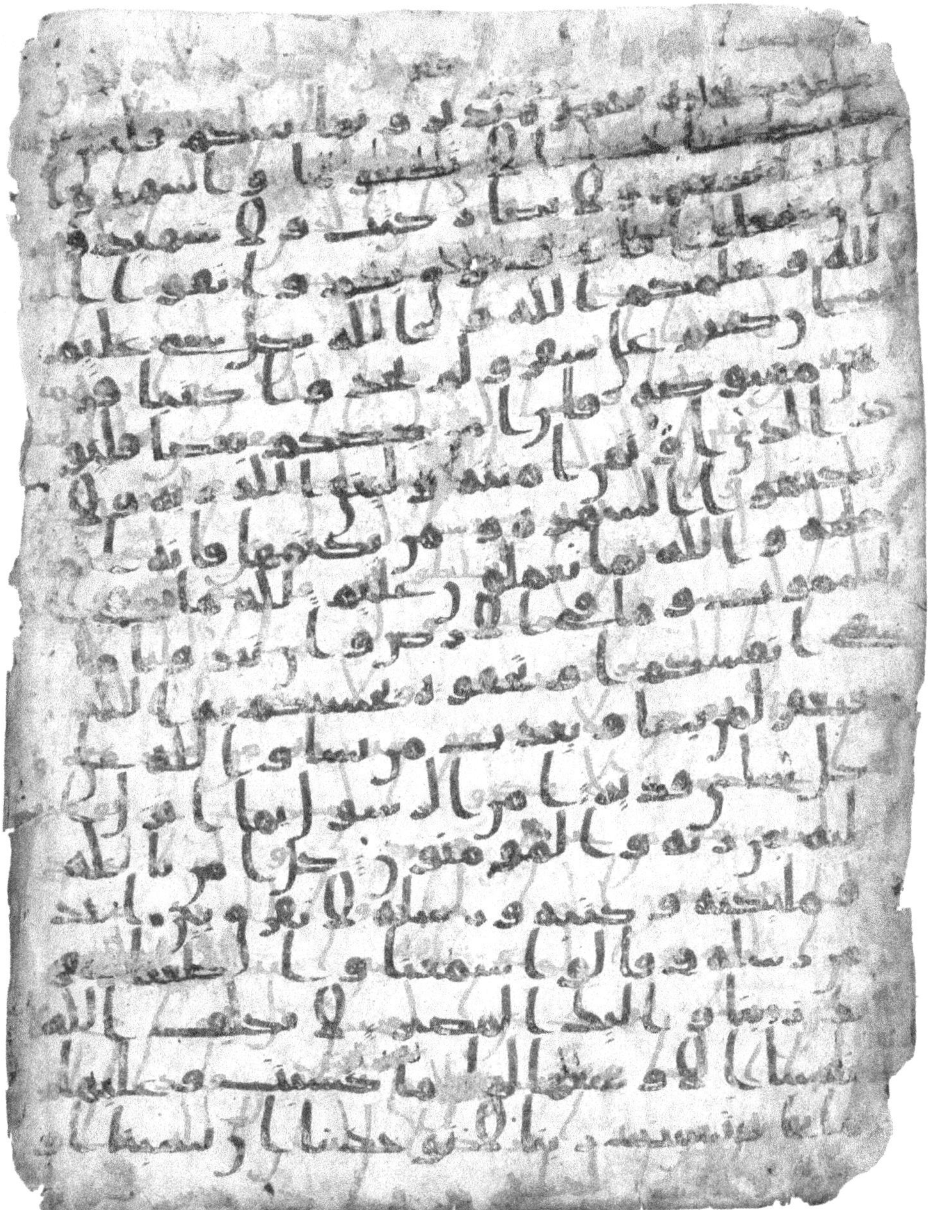

FIGURE 14.1 Verso of a detached palimpsest folio from an early Qur'an manuscript copied on parchment in *Ḥijāzī* script with a non-ʿUthmānic recension beneath another copy of the text. Copenhagen, David Collection, inv. no. 86/2003. Photo by: Pernille Klemp.

Two fragmentary manuscripts exemplify this change to a more professional, specifically Qur'anic script: one with 78 folios dubbed the 'Damascus Umayyad Qur'an' because it was removed from Damascus to Istanbul (Turk ve Islam Eserleri Müzesi, ŞE 321) and another with 73 folios dubbed the 'Umayyad codex of al-Fusṭāṭ' because it was taken from the ʿAmr Mosque there to Europe in the early thirteenth/nineteenth century and is now divided between St. Petersburg (National Library of Russia, Marcel 11, 13, and 15) and Paris (Bibliothèque nationale de France, Arabe 330c; for both codices, see most recently Déroche 2014: 75–98). These manuscripts presage the establishment of imperial scriptoria, exemplified by even larger (47 × 35 cm) manuscripts such as the one in Sanaa with the unique architectural frontispiece (Dār al-Makhṭūṭāt inv. no. 20–33.1) and another in Dublin (Chester Beatty Library, Is. 1404; see Whelan 1990; Déroche 2014: 107–11).

Many, if not most, of these Umayyad manuscripts seem to have been presentation copies designed for display and for reading by those who had already memorized the text. The script used in them can be compared to that in the mosaic inscription ringing the interior arcade of the Dome of Rock in Jerusalem, dated by inscription to 72/691–2 and some of the earliest dated evidence for the transcription of the Qur'an (see Chapter 15 and Figure 15.1). The illumination can also be compared to that used on other Umayyad buildings such as the Mosque of Damascus built under ʿAbd al-Malik's successor al-Walīd (r. 86–96/705–15). These manuscripts reflect a new concern for the beauty of the book, undoubtedly taken up as a challenge to the contemporary production of luxury Bibles such as the Codex Amiatinus. This group of Qur'an manuscripts also fits within the projection of a dynastic image pursued under the later Umayyads, a process seen in the reform of the chancery and coinage under ʿAbd al-Malik and other contemporary construction and architecture, such as the milestones erected around Damascus and Jerusalem and the standardization of the large hypostyle mosque under al-Walīd, but the precise dissemination of this style of Qur'anic manuscript remains to be established.

Sometime in the late second/eighth or third/ninth century, a new format became popular for transcribing the Qur'an. Manuscripts in this new style assumed a horizontal shape, adopted perhaps to distinguish Qur'an manuscripts from the Torah (always a roll) and the Bible (typically a codex in vertical format with columns of text). These Qur'an manuscripts are often multi-volume codices with a few (typically three, five, or seven) lines to the page; dots for vocalization; frontispieces and finispieces with geometric ornament, and leather covers stamped with many of the same designs. The illuminated pages, which functioned like the carpet pages in the Book of Kells and other Hibernian manuscripts as symbolic guardians of the sacred text, have often been detached for sale to collectors. While the codex format was typical, the same script and decoration was also used for a few hanging scrolls with selections from the Qur'an, such as one brought to Istanbul from the Great Mosque of Damascus (Ory 1965; *1400. Yilinda Kur'an-i Kerim* 2010, no. 9).

This new codex format is accompanied by a new type of evidence for dating: endowment notices (*waqfiyyāt*), such as those on two volumes of a dispersed copy indicating that Amājūr, governor of Damascus, donated it to an unidentified mosque in Tyre in 262/872 (Déroche 1987–9 and 1990–1). Such endowment notices probably existed earlier, but these are the first to survive. The date provides only a *terminus ante quem*, and using it as the date of the manuscript assumes that the donor bequeathed something he had just commissioned. Possible, and even likely, this assumption remains to be proven. Nevertheless, the emergence of this new style seems to coincide with the spread of an Abbasid artistic style throughout the caliphate, as seen for example in the proliferation of large hypostyle mosques with a wider central aisle and facing minaret or the development of the so-called 'beveled style' of stucco carving.

We are only beginning to identify regional variants within this new style of Qur'an manuscripts, and hence many manuscripts or leaves from them are generically identified as 'Near East or North Africa' or 'Abbasid' (although this rubric suggests that the dynasty had something to do with production). Scholars have followed several avenues to investigate the question of regionalization. One is the identification of markers for various recensions, such as different colours of dots for vocalization. The use of yellowish orange dots for *hamza* follows a Medinan convention that was taken up in the Maghrib, a feature mentioned as typical of the region by the local Maliki lawyer and Qur'an reader, Abū ʿAmr al-Dānī who died in 444/1053 (Dutton 1999 and 2000; George 2015). By contrast, a manuscript vocalized with red dots seems typical of the east (Syria, Iraq, and Iran). Pigment analysis here might be of some help as well, and it is essential to verify whether these dots could have been added or corrected at a much later time. A second avenue of investigation is palaeography, with features such as the exaggerated swooping tail of final *nūn*, the hair-thin tail of *mīm*, and hair-like lines used for pointing also identified with the Maghrib. A third is illumination, as the pyramid of six balls used to mark individual verses can also be found later in Maghribi manuscripts. The choice of sura titles and recension may also be indicative of different regional traditions. But overall what this research suggests is that localizing groups of Qur'an manuscripts requires the combined expertise of a variety of scholars, from textual specialists to conservators, curators, and art historians.

The popularity of a new style by the third/ninth century did not displace all other production, and a collection of outliers can also be identified within these early parchment manuscripts. Such manuscripts may have been produced later to emulate earlier models, and their singular visual aspects require specific historical explanations. One such copy is the large single-volume manuscript known as the Tashkent Qur'an. Déroche (2013) has suggested it may have been done during the reign of the third Abbasid caliph al-Mahdī (r. 158–69/775–85) in a retardataire style deliberately cultivated to imitate the distribution of manuscripts by the Umayyad governor al-Ḥajjāj, itself an emulation of the dissemination of copies by the Rightly-Guided caliph ʿUthmān (r. 23–35/644–56).

A second famous outlier is the so-called Blue Qur'an, a seven-volume manuscript, most of which is still in Tunisia, but with many single pages elsewhere. Its visual distinctiveness, which undoubtedly contributes to its collectability and high price, has provoked a range of attributions from Abbasid Baghdad to Fatimid Tunisia and Umayyad Iberia (George 2009). Yet basic technical questions about it remain to be clarified. The latest research (Bloom 2015; Porter 2018) suggests, for example, that, contrary to earlier claims, the sheepskin was coloured blue (and not dyed) and that the gold was applied as leaf over glair (and not as shell gold in the form of gold ink), a technique that necessitated the outlining of the letters to regularize their shape (hence showing that the outlining must have been contemporary with the original production). Furthermore, any explanation of the original provenance of this unusual manuscript should take into account why so much of it is now in Tunisia.

The Shift to Paper Codices in the Early Medieval Period (Third/Ninth–Seventh/Thirteenth Centuries)

Sometime in the third/ninth century, the physical nature of Qur'an production began to shift markedly, as paper manuscripts increasingly replaced parchment copies. The new support was a material that had been used in the Islamic lands for at least a century to transcribe other texts (Bloom 2001), and its slow adoption for scripture confirms the conservatism of the Qur'anic tradition. The use of paper meant that Qur'an manuscripts were cheaper and more easily transportable, a feature enhanced by the generally smaller format of most of these manuscripts in a single volume with many lines of text per page. Along with the new support came a new type of carbon-based ink that did not eat into the support, as tannin-based ink had done to parchment. These two new materials were accompanied by, and perhaps engendered, the canonization of a set of rounded, proportioned scripts known as the Six Pens (Arabic: *al-aqlām al-sitta*; Persian: *shīsh qalam*), often grouped in majuscule/miniscule pairs: *muḥaqqāq/rayḥān*; *thuluth/naskh*, and *tawqīʿ/riqāʿ*. The first of these pairs, *muḥaqqāq/rayḥān*, was most commonly used for Qur'an transcription.

Calligraphers adopted various features to enhance readability in these Qur'an manuscripts on paper. One was the reversion to the vertical format, chosen perhaps to make the line shorter and hence more easily readable. Other devices for enhanced readability include wider spaces between words, no division of words at the end of lines, and the introduction of *muhmila* characters to mark undotted variants of homographs such as *ḥāʾ*, *rāʾ*, *sīn*, and *ṣād* and distinguish them from *jīm/khāʾ*, *zāʾ*, *shīn*, and *ḍād*. Multiple frontis- and finispieces at the beginning and end of the volume contain such information as the recension used and the number of verses, words, and even individual letters in the manuscript (Tabbaa 1991).

The earliest surviving example of this new type of paper Qur'an manuscript seems to be a dispersed copy signed by ʿAlī ibn Shādhān al-Rāzī and dated 361/972 (Blair 2006: fig. 5.3). The most famous (Figure 14.2) is the one signed by ʿAlī ibn Hilāl known as Ibn

FIGURE 14.2 Opening text folio from the Qur'an manuscript copied on paper and signed by ʿAlī ibn Hilāl known as Ibn al-Bawwāb at Baghdad in 391/1000–1. Dublin, Chester Beatty Library, ms 1431, fol. 9b © The Trustees of the Chester Beatty Library, Dublin.

al-Bawwāb at Baghdad in 391/1000–1 (Dublin, Chester Beatty Library, ms 1431). As many of these paper manuscripts are signed and dated, the most pressing question about them is no longer provenance but rather the need to explain the underlying reasons for this dramatic shift in materials and format. The various explanations for this change, which are not necessarily mutually exclusive, depend in part on the training and interests of the scholars who have proposed them. Bloom (2001) looked to a change in materials, notably the introduction of paper. Historically, this shift corresponds to the period when society had become predominantly Muslim (Bulliet 1979) and a time when chancery secretaries assumed enhanced roles as copyists (Whelan 1990). This innovation seems to have begun in the eastern Islamic lands, and Tabbaa (1994) suggested that the new scripts were adopted for sectarian reasons, as part of the Sunnī revival. These round scripts, however, were not exclusive to Qur'an manuscripts, but—unlike the earlier kufic—were used for a wide variety of texts whose diverse subject matter from Sufi manuals to poetry and Arab-Christian treatises has little to do with official theology. A recent and promising line of investigation is the connection of this material shift to the intellectual change from oral to written and aural to read (Schoeler 2006 and 2009): whereas the earlier parchment manuscripts had been aide-mémoires, these paper copies were written to be read and represent a graphic revolution. Portable and personal, most of these paper manuscripts are quite different from the ceremonial or presentation copies on parchment and were intended for use by people who wanted to read, not recite, the text. Further work also remains to be done about the reasons why these paper manuscripts are so frequently signed by calligraphers, as well as their status, the identity of the patrons, and the role of the market in this burgeoning production.

Some Qur'an manuscripts produced at this time performed other functions and addressed other audiences. A few manuscripts continued the earlier type of large parchment volumes made for mosques, as in the four-volume paper set copied at Isfahan in Ramadan 383/October–November 993 (Istanbul, Turk ve Islam Eserleri Müzesi 453–6 and elsewhere; *1400. Yilinda Kur'an-i Kerim* 2010, no. 35) that is notable for its horizontal format, large and distinctive script, and rich illumination. Bilingual manuscripts with translation into other languages, particularly Persian and eastern Turkish, must have been used in proselytism and conversion. Such manuscripts may well have been produced from the fourth/tenth century, although the earliest surviving example seems to be one dated 416/1025 in the National Library of Iran (ms 3610; Karimi-Nia 2006). Some manuscripts also include commentaries, such as a very large four-volume copy copied by Muḥammad ibn ʿAlī al-Nīsābūrī in 584/1188–9 for the Ghurid amir Ghiyāth al-Dīn Muḥammad ibn Sām, with interlinear Persian translation and commentary at the end of each sura by Abū Bakr ʿAtīq al-Surābādī (d. *c.*495/1101), a leading scholar of the heterodox Karrāmiyya sect in Nishapur (Tehran, National Museum 3496, 3499, 3500, and 3507). The manuscript, in turn, was later endowed to the shrine for the Sufi shaykh Aḥmad Jām at Turbat-i Shaykh Jām in eastern Iran. These manuscripts are thus important documents to chart sectarianism and religious differences in the period.

These changes to Qur'an manuscript production seem to have been introduced in the eastern lands, where the vertical codex transcribed in round scripts remained standard for the next millennium, but the exact process of change needs to be documented more clearly, as do the reasons why this region was so distinct. The geographical distinction is clear when we consider that while this revolution in production was underway in the eastern and central Islamic lands, production in the Maghrib proceeded very differently. There, parchment continued to be the main support until the eighth/fourteenth century, and manuscripts typically assumed a more squarish format. On at least one occasion, a dispersed manuscript with three lines of text per page (Déroche 1992: no. 58; Blair 2006: fig. 4.8; see also George 2015: 15, Table 1), the text was also written with different pointing (e.g. *qāf* marked by one dot above and *fāʾ* by one dot below) and vocalization (e.g. an orange/yellow dot for *hamzat al-qaṭʿ* and a green dot for *hamzat al-waṣl*) in a visually distinctive script with strokes of uniform thickness, distinctive ways of penning individual letters (e.g. *alif* with a spur on the bottom left and *ṣād* with smooth horizontal bars) and exaggerated loopy descenders to rounded letters. The nib of the pen used was probably trimmed in a different way.

One of the earliest dated examples, the final page with colophon to a thirty-volume manuscript completed on Rajab 398/March–April 1008 (Istanbul, Türk ve Islam Eserleri Müzesi, ŞE 13216), shows that this Maghribi style was firmly established by the turn of the fourth/tenth century. A well-known manuscript dated to the end of Jumada II 703/early February 1304 (Paris, Bibliothèque nationale de France, arabe 385; Déroche 1985, no. 296) shows that the style remained current for at least three centuries. Again, we need to explain why this region developed a separate tradition and why it remained so steadfast.

The Development of Luxury Multi-Part Presentation Copies in the Late Medieval Period (Seventh/Thirteenth–Tenth/Sixteenth Centuries)

The most notable change following the Mongol upheavals of the early seventh/thirteenth century was the popularization of deluxe Qur'an manuscripts signed by famous calligraphers and designed for endowment to funerary complexes and other religious foundations. These copies are transcribed on standardized sizes of fine white paper in variants of the Six Pens. The first manuscripts made for the Ilkhanid sultans and their courtiers are copied with a mere five lines per page and hence divided into thirty volumes

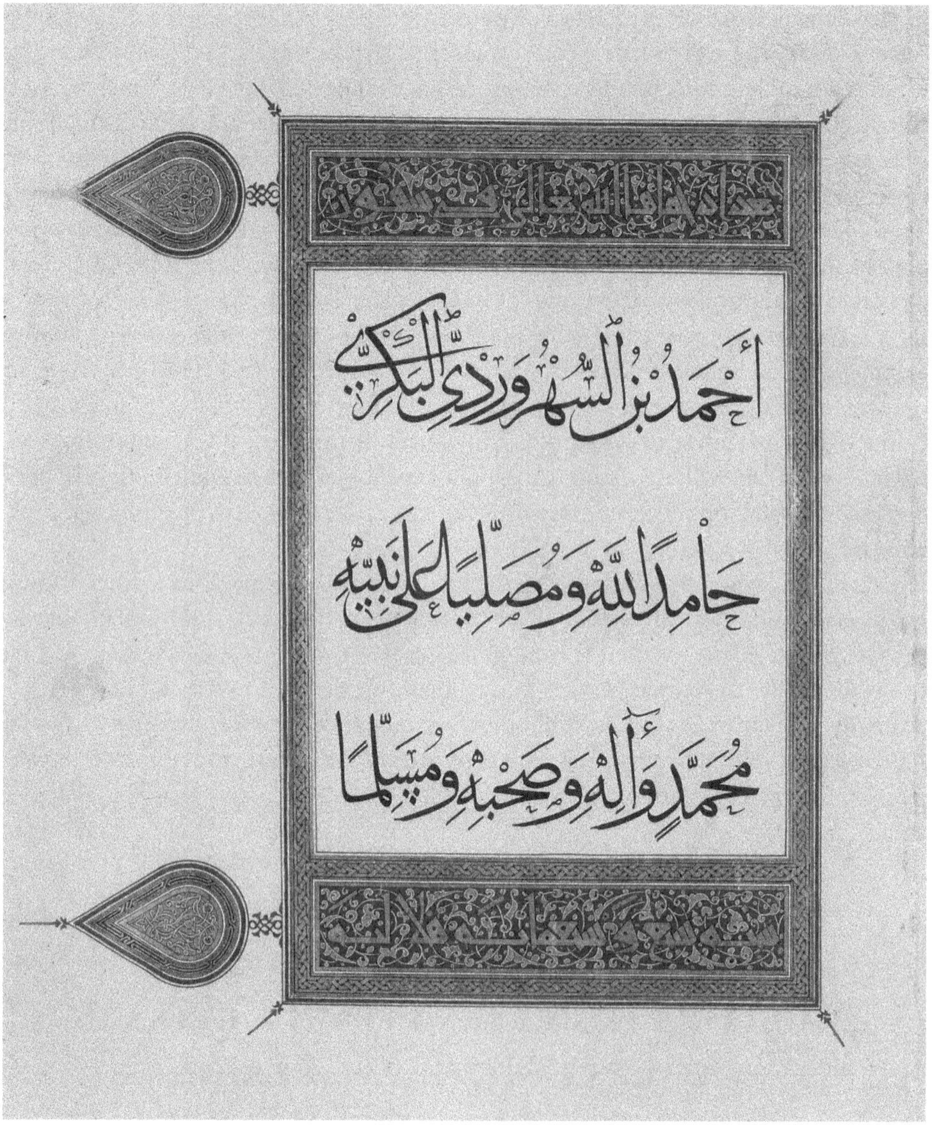

FIGURE 14.3 Colophon detached from *juzʾ* 28 of a 30-volume Qurʾan manuscript copied by Aḥmad al-Suhrawardī and illuminated by Muḥammad ibn Aybak ibn ʿAbd Allāh between 701 and 708 (1301–8). New York, Metropolitan Museum of Art, www.metmuseum.org, Rogers Fund 55.44.

(Figure 14.3). The most costly was the one made for the tomb of the Ilkhanid Sultan Uljaytū at Sultaniyya on full-*baghdādī* sheets measuring c. 70 × 100 cm with three lines of gold outlined in black alternating with two lines of black outlined in gold (James 1988: no. 40; Blair 2014: chapter 4; Blair forthcoming). Large copies were later produced for the Mamluk sultans of Egypt, following the same format but with more lines per page (typically 11 or 13) and hence compressed into one or two volumes (James 1988/1999).

These deluxe manuscripts produced over the course of the eighth/fourteenth century exemplify the desire to glorify the role of famous calligraphers such as Yāqūt and his followers (Blair 2003), but they also show some of the problems and modern biases in the field. The best survey of them is the monograph by David James (1988/1999). The title of the first edition, *Qur'āns of the Mamlūks*, is a misnomer as the volume covers manuscripts produced in the eighth/fourteenth century (hence only in the first half of the Mamluk period) and deals with production not just in Egypt and Syria, but also in Baghdad and the Ilkhanid realm and then its subsequent spread to the Mamluks. The title and even the organization of the volume, which begins with the Mamluks but then moves back slightly in time to Iran and the Ilkhanids, seems to be reflect the interests of the author and perhaps the underwriters of his publication, Mobil Oil, who held major investments in Saudi Arabia and elsewhere in the Gulf. In 1999 when the King Faisal Centre for Research and Islamic Studies reissued the book with slight corrections, the title was adjusted to read *Manuscripts of the Holy Qur'ān from the Mamlūk Era* to reflect the broader geographical coverage, though without correcting the chronological mismatch and regional bias.

The deluxe manuscripts made in the late medieval period reflect a sea change in the nature of production. Ibn al-Bawwāb both penned and illuminated his paper copy made at Baghdad in 391/1000–1; the copyist ʿUthmān ibn Muḥammad worked with the illuminator ʿAlī ibn ʿAbd al-Raḥmān on a paper manuscript made at Bust in Afghanistan in 505/1111–12 (Paris, Bibliothèque nationale de France, ms Arabe 6041; Déroche 1985: no. 522; Blair 2006: fig. 6.6), but these large and deluxe copies of the post-Mongol era required teams of artists working in ateliers. Named calligraphers were typically paired with named illuminators, who themselves became increasingly specialized in outlining and other tasks. Such manuscripts were extraordinarily time-consuming to produce: the multiple signatures and dates in the various volumes suggest that the huge Ilkhanid copies took six or seven years to complete. They fit with the Mongols' love of gold and their desire for the large and splashy, and art historians have looked into the connection between these manuscripts and the emergence of the illustrated book as a major feature of artistic production from this time and the role of paper in the dissemination of a new visual language. Many of the designs used on these magnificent (and dated) Qur'an manuscripts, for example, also occur in architectural decoration. But the exact ways that these styles moved, whether by the transfer of manuscripts or of artists, from capital to province (Blair 2015), and from Iran and environs to other regions such as India and then to China and later Indonesia, remain to be fully explored.

Book artists in this period devised various ways to monumentalize God's word. One was simply by size, a quest that culminated at the turn of the ninth/fifteenth century in the largest Qur'an manuscript known: the behemoth copy that Tīmūr commissioned for his congregational mosque at Samarqand whose elephantine leaves are estimated to have originally measured 2.5 × 1.5 metres, taller than a person (Blair and Bloom 2006). The leaves were so large that they required a new technique of manufacture using floating moulds that produced paper suitable for writing only on one side and necessitated an enormous stone Qur'an stand to display the loose-leaf sheets. Such a manuscript shows how the method of production dramatically affected transcription and presentation.

The quest for large, smooth, and perhaps cheaper sheets of paper also caused calligraphers to look beyond local products. An unusual Qur'an manuscript in the Khalili collection, attributed to mid eighth-/fourteenth-century Iraq or the Jazira, is transcribed on Italian paper with a European watermark (James 1992a: no. 34). Such a manuscript documents the trade beyond religious boundaries, but these commercial activities also raised their own problems, and some Muslims found the presence of such watermarks troubling, especially if they contained overtly Christian iconography such as a cross. One Maghribi jurist, Ibn Marzūq al-Ḥafīd, issued a fatwa in 812/1409 declaring that using such foreign (he called it *rūmī*) paper was acceptable as the copying of the sacred text and the writing of God's name would destroy the efficacy of the image (Halevi 2008). The physical composition of these manuscripts thus provides information for a range of scholars, from historians to theologians, who should be encouraged to exploit it further.

Another way of adding showiness to these deluxe Qur'an manuscripts was through colour, and some of the finest ninth/fifteenth century copies are transcribed on tinted and gold-flecked paper. One large manuscript in the Detroit Institute of Arts (30.323) datable to the mid-ninth/fifteenth century, for example, includes leaves in a rainbow of bright colours, including blue, green, purple, and pink, all lavishly sprinkled with gold. The relationship to Chinese paper is striking (Blair 2000), but the exact connection of imported and local products and the use of such bright papers for both secular and sacred manuscripts remain topics open for further investigation.

A third method of monumentalization was by pairing or juxtaposing different sizes of script on the same page. Such a layout, with three lines of large script sandwiching two blocks with more lines of a smaller script, had been used in the previous period, as in a large manuscript copied by ʿAbd al-Raḥmān ibn Abī Bakr ibn ʿAbd al-Raḥīm, the royal scribe (*al-kātib al-malikī*) known as Golden Pen (*zarīn qalam*) and finished on 15 Jumāda I 582/3 August 1186 (Dublin, Chester Beatty Library 1438; Blair 2006: fig. 6.13), but it became particularly popular in Iran and surrounding regions during this period. Bindings also became increasingly fancy, with gold filigree and stamping, coloured and cut leathers, and even lacquer. Each of these techniques is worthy of independent study, but their collective information is useful to scholars beyond the fields of codicology and art history. Other subjects worthy of exploration include the increased volume of commercial production and the exact role of the individual artist, whether as individual practitioner or head of an atelier.

This period also saw an increasing interest in the preservation and sacredness of earlier copies for talismanic reasons. Rulers commissioned elaborate boxes to store early parchment manuscripts, such as the container of wood plated with brass and inlaid with silver made for the Mamluk Sultan al-Nāṣir Muḥammad in 722/1322–3 and now in the library of al-Azhar mosque in Cairo (Blair and Bloom 1994: fig. 130). The attention to earlier artefacts documents the increasing attention to the past and the use, and in some cases even the invention, of tradition.

The Age of Empires (Tenth/Sixteenth–Thirteenth/Nineteenth Centuries)

Production of Qur'an manuscripts blossomed in the pre-modern period, but while more manuscripts survive, paradoxically they are less studied, perhaps because they are so plentiful. Rulers and their courtiers still commissioned luxury copies, but the market for Qur'an manuscripts was much broader, reflecting a wider readership and new functions. Ateliers worked to balance the sometimes-conflicting goals of beauty and efficiency. Calligraphers in this period experimented with other scripts, notably in Iran, where they occasionally used the hanging *nastaʿlīq* that had been devised for transcribing Persian poetry, but methods for reducing costs seem more prevalent. Commercial workshops like that of Rūzbihān Muḥammad al-Shīrāzī made large and fancy copies similar to those produced for royal patrons, but with less expensive, though still costly, materials (Wright 2018).

Another alternative was to produce selections from the full text. Some contained an individual thirtieth (*juzʾ*). The last thirtieth containing suras 78–114, for example, was popular under the Ottomans. Other selections had an individual chapter or two. Suras 6 (*Anʿām*), 36 (*Yāsīn*), 55 (*al-Raḥmān*), and 67 (*al-Mulk*) were common in the Ottoman lands, whereas readers in Iran and India preferred a different set with suras 36 (*Yāsīn*), 48 (*al-Fatḥ*), 56 (*al-Wāqiʿa*), 67 (*al-Mulk*), and 78 (*al-Nabāʾ*). Moriscos in Almonacid de la Sierra near Saragossa in the northern Iberian Peninsula commissioned small codices that contained about 12 per cent of the full text that including chapters 1, 36, 67, and 78–114 (the thirtieth *juzʾ*) as well as a handful of other verses in addition to prayers and invocations of the Prophet (Martínez de Castilla Muñoz 2014). It remains to sort out the reasons for these different preferences, whether they were used in different ways or recited at different times, and the connection of these selections to architectural inscriptions, such as the extraordinarily beautiful Qur'anic texts ringing the Taj Mahal in Agra (Begley 1978–9).

Calligraphers in the Ottoman provinces, notably the Ḥijāz, developed another method of standardization known as *āyat bar kinār* ('with freestanding verses'), in which the text is divided into 30 fascicules, each fascicule containing 20 pages, each with 15 lines of text and a discrete number of complete verses. Such a layout tests the mettle of the calligraphers, who had to stretch out the text on some pages but compact it on others. This format seems to have been adopted to aid in visual memorization, suggesting that these copies, like the early parchment manuscripts, were designed as *aide-mémoires* for recitation rather than reading. Such a template also allowed a reciter to use any of several manuscripts, as the same words would appear in roughly the same place on every copy (Stanley in Bayani, Rogers, and Stanley 2009: 188–90). In a way this standardization parallels the uniformity of printing, and the connection between the two might be profitably explored. One variant of this technique, the so-called *tevâfuklu* style (Figure 14.4), included another visual clue for memorization, a rubrication of congruence, in

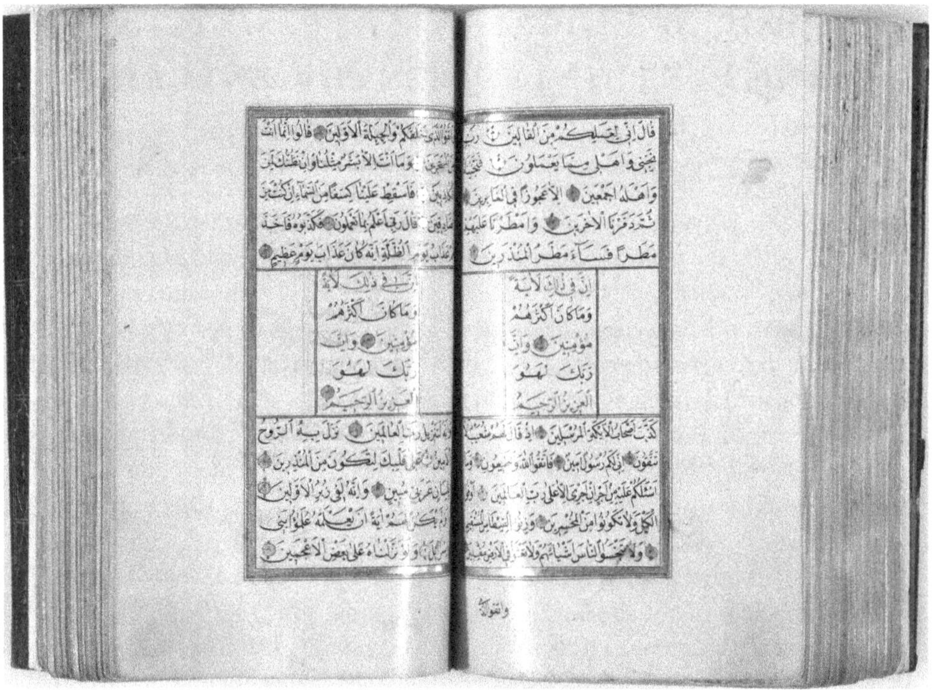

FIGURE 14.4 Double-page spread from a manuscript made for the Ottomans in 1204/1789–90 in the *tevâfuklu* style, a rubrication of congruence in which sections of identical text were written in red on facing pages. London, Khalili Collection, ms QUR33, fols. 189b–190a. The Nasser D. Khalili Collection of Islamic Art ms QUR33, fols. 189b–190a; courtesy of the Khalili Family Trust.

which sections of identical text were written in red in the same place on facing pages (Bayani, Contadini, and Stanley 1999: no. 40). Such innovations speak to some of the diverse uses of Qur'an manuscripts in later centuries and raise questions of audience and instruction.

The many uses of Qur'an manuscripts in the pre-modern period are also clear from the additional texts that were incorporated in them. Some include a type of text known as a *fālnāma* (book of divination) at the beginning or end; they may have been used for divination and bibliomancy. Other manuscripts have commentaries in the margins or prayers to be read after 'sealing' the Qur'an; they were used to swear oaths, mark births and deaths, and validate treaties, functions all underscoring the inherent sacredness of the text and its role in daily life. Still other copies have indices or traditions about the various chapters and their efficacy in various situations, including remedies for illness. These manuscripts therefore provide useful data for social and intellectual history.

This period also saw a continued interest in the preservation and sacredness of earlier copies, as rulers, notably the Ottomans, regularly commissioned elaborate boxes to store early parchment manuscripts for endowment to their tombs. Fancy Qur'an manuscripts were also used for presentation. The Safavids, for example, added the name of ʿAlī ibn Abī Ṭālib to early parchment manuscripts that they endowed to the shrines at Mashhad and Qum or presented as diplomatic gifts to their rivals, the Ottomans (e.g. Komaroff 2011: no. 148). Such manuscripts thus became part of the sectarian rivalry and gamesmanship between the so-called Gunpowder Empires.

Still other copies were designed for more popular and prophylactic functions. Some forms may well have been made in earlier times, but have survived mainly from this period. These include long talismanic rolls often carried in small amulet cases that were hung around the neck, tucked into armbands, or even carried on battle standards.

In this later period Qur'an production also spread to new areas such as South-East Asia and central Africa. The court at Terengganu in the north-west Malay Peninsula, for example, became the centre for production of a group of distinctly illuminated Qur'an manuscripts, including one on paper watermarked with a moon face in a shield that was probably produced at Pordenone near Venice between 1865 and 1885 (London, British Library, Or. 15227). It was one of the first Qur'an manuscripts in the library to be fully digitized on-line (<www.bl.uk>), with all the folios as double-page spreads, the binding, and the endpapers, all with zoomable access, thereby making it an invaluable resource for both scholars and students. These Qur'an manuscripts are important in documenting the interaction of imported materials with local traditions, whether with the brush in China or textile designs in Africa. As many manuscripts from this period are dated or datable, they in turn serve as convenient milestones to date other arts.

This period also saw a new and increased role of women as both calligraphers and users. The fifth/eleventh-century historian Ibn al-Fayyād had mentioned 170 women copying Qur'an manuscripts in kufic script in just one eastern quarter of Cordoba (George 2015: 88–9). None of their work has been identified, and we cannot tell whether the description reflects reality or hyperbole. Women certainly endowed Qur'an manuscripts in earlier periods, as with the famous Nurse's Qur'an, given by the nurse (*al-ḥāḍina*) of the Zirid prince al-Muʿizz ibn Badīs to the Great Mosque of Qayrawan in Ramadan 410/January 1020, but only from the age of empires do we have many surviving Qur'an manuscripts transcribed by women, both royal and from clerical families. The slowness of female participation points once again to the conservatism of the Qur'anic tradition, but more work is needed to ascertain where and when exceptions to this rule existed and how it impacted local society.

To sum up: Qur'an manuscripts have always been a vital source for artistic expression within the Muslim community, but they are also important social and historical documents whose value we are only beginning to exploit.

Bibliography

Arberry, A. J. *The Koran Illuminated: A Handlist of the Korans in the Chester Beatty Library.* Dublin: Hodges, Figgis, 1967.

Bayani, Manijeh, Anna Contadini, and Tim Stanley. *The Decorated Word: Qur'ans of the 17th to 19th Centuries.* Nasser D. Khalili Collection of Islamic Art 4, part 1. London: The Nour Foundation in association with Azimuth Editions and Oxford University Press, 1999.

Bayani, Manijeh, J. M. Rogers, and Tim Stanley. *The Decorated Word: Qur'ans of the 17th to 19th Centuries.* Nasser D. Khalili Collection of Islamic Art 4, part 2. London: Nour Foundation in association with Azimuth Editions, 2009.

Begley, Wayne. 'Amānat Khān and the Calligraphy on the Tāj Maḥal', *Kunst des Orients* 12 (1978–9), 5–60.
Blair, Sheila S. 'Color and Gold: The Decorated Papers Used in Manuscripts in Later Islamic Times', *Muqarnas* 17 (2000), 24–36.
Blair, Sheila S. 'Yaqut and his Followers', *Manuscripta Orientalia* 9/3 (2003), 39–47.
Blair, Sheila S. *Islamic Calligraphy*. Edinburgh: Edinburgh University Press, 2006.
Blair, Sheila S. *Text and Image in Medieval Persian Art*. Edinburgh: Edinburgh University Press, 2014.
Blair, Sheila S. 'The Ilkhanid Qurʾan: An Example from Maragha', *Journal of Islamic Manuscripts* 6/2–3 (2015), 174–95.
Blair, Sheila S. 'Sultan Öljeitü's Baghdad Qurʾan: A Life Story'. In: Massumeh Farhad and Simon Rettig (eds.). *The Word Illuminated: Form and Function of Qurʾanic Manuscripts*. Washington, DC: Smithsonian Scholarly Press, forthcoming.
Blair, Sheila S. and Jonathan M. Bloom. *The Art and Architecture of Islam 1250–1800*. Yale University Press Pelican History of Art. New Haven and London: Yale University Press, 1994.
Blair, Sheila S. and Jonathan M. Bloom. 'Timur's Koran: A Reappraisal'. In: Barbara Brend and Patricia Baker (eds.). *Sifting Sands, Reading Signs: Studies in Honour of Géza Fehérvári*, pp. 15–24. Bristol: Furnace Publication, 2006.
Bloom, Jonathan. *Paper before Print: The History and Impact of Paper in the Islamic World*. New Haven: Yale University Press, 2001.
Bloom, Jonathan. 'The Blue Koran Revisited', *Journal of Islamic Manuscripts* 6/2-3 (2015), 196–218.
Bothmer, H. C. Graf von. 'Architekturbilder im Koran: Eine Prachthandschrift der Umayyadenzeit aus dem Yemen', *Pantheon* 45 (1987), 4–20.
Bulliet, Richard. *Conversion to Islam in the Medieval Period: An Essay in Quantitative History*. Cambridge, MA: Harvard University Press, 1979.
Cook, Michael. 'The Stemma of the Regional Codices of the Koran', *Graeco-Arabica* 9/10 (2004), 89–104.
Le Coran. Paris: Club du Livre, 1972.
Déroche, François. *Les Manuscrits du coran, aux origines de la calligraphie coranique*. Paris: Bibliothèque nationale, 1983.
Déroche, François. *Les Manuscrits du coran, du Maghrib à l'Insulinde*. Paris: Bibliothèque nationale, 1985.
Déroche, François. 'Les Manuscrits arabes datés du IIIe/IXe siècle', *Revue des études islamiques* 55–7 (1987–9), 343–79.
Déroche, François. 'The Qurʾān of Amāǧūr', *Manuscripts of the Middle East* 5 (1990–1), 59–66.
Déroche, François. *The Abbasid Tradition: Qurʾans of the 8th to the 10th Centuries* AD. The Nasser D. Khalili Collection of Islamic Art 1. London: Nour Foundation in association with Azimuth Editions and Oxford University Press, 1992.
Déroche, François. 'New Evidence about Umayyad Book Hands'. In: *Essays in Honour of Ṣalāḥ al-Dīn al-Munajjid*, pp. 611–42. London: Al-Furqān Islamic Heritage Foundation, 1423/2002.
Déroche, François. *La Transmission écrite du Coran dans les début de l'islam: le Codex Parisino-petropolitanus*. Leiden and Boston: Brill, 2009.
Déroche, François. 'Twenty Leaves from the Tashkent Qurʾan'. In: Sheila Blair and Jonathan Bloom (eds.). *God is Beautiful and Loves Beauty: The Object in Islamic Art and Culture*, pp. 57–78. New Haven and London: Yale University Press in association with the Qatar

Foundation, Virginia Commonwealth University, and Virginia Commonwealth University School of the Arts in Qatar, 2013.

Déroche, François. *Qur'ans of the Umayyads: A First Overview*. Leiden: Brill. 2014.

Déroche, François. 'In the Beginning: Early Qur'ans from Damascus'. In: Massumeh Farhad and Simon Rettig (eds.). *The Art of the Qur'an: Treasures from the Museum of Turkish and Islamic Arts*, pp. 61–71. Washington, DC: Arthur M. Sackler Gallery, 2016.

Déroche, François and Sergio Noja Noseda (eds.). *Sources de la transmission manuscrite du texte coranique. I. Les Manusrits de style ḥijāzī. Volume 1: Le Manuscrit arabe 328(a) de la Bibliothèque nationale de France*. Leda: Fondazione Ferni Noja Noseda and Paris: Bibliothèque nationale de France, 1998.

Déroche, François and Sergio Noja Noseda (eds.). *Sources de la transmission manuscrite du texte coranique. I. Les Manusrits de style ḥijāzī. Volume 2, tome 1: Le Manuscrit Or. 2165 (f. 1 à 61) de la British Library*. Leda: Fondazione Ferni Noja Noseda and London: British Library. 2001.

Dreibholz, Ursula. *Frühe Koranfragmente aus der Grossen Moschee in Sanaa/Early Quran Fragments from the Great Mosque in Sanaa*. Hefte Zur Kulturgeschichte Des Jemen, 2. Sanʿa: Deutsches Archäologisches Institut Orient-Abteilung Aussenstelle Sanaʿa, 2003.

Dutton, Yasin. 'Red Dots, Green Dots, Yellow Dots & Blue: Some Reflections on the Vocalisation of Early Qur'anic Manuscripts—Part I', *Journal of Qur'anic Studies* 1/2 (1999), 115–40.

Dutton, Yasin. 'Red Dots, Green Dots, Yellow Dots and Blue: Some Reflections on the Vocalisation of Early Qur'anic Manuscripts (Part II)'. *Journal of Quranic Studies* 2/1 (2000), 1–24.

Dutton, Yasin. 'An Early *Muṣḥaf* According to the Reading of Ibn ʿAmīr', *Journal of Qur'anic Studies* 3/1 (2001), 71–9.

Dutton, Yasin. 'Some Notes on the British Library's "Oldest Qur'an Manuscript" (Or. 2165)', *Journal of Qur'anic Studies* 6/2 (2004), 43–71.

Dutton, Yasin. 'An Umayyad Fragment of the Qur'an and its Dating', *Journal of Qur'anic Studies* 9/2 (2007), 57–87.

Ernst, Carl. *How to Read the Qur'an*. Chapel Hill, NC: University of North Carolina Press, 2011.

Farhad, Massumeh and Simon Rettig, *The Art of the Qur'an: Treasures from the Museum of Turkish and Islamic Arts*. Washington, DC: Arthur M. Sackler Gallery, 2016.

George, Alain. 'Calligraphy, Colour and Light in the Blue Qur'an', *Journal of Qur'anic Studies* 11 (2009), 75–125.

George, Alain. *The Rise of Arabic Calligraphy*. London: Saqi Books, 2010.

George, Alain. 'Le Palimpseste Lewis-Mingana de Cambridge, témoin ancien de l'histoire du Coran', *Comptes-Rendus des Séances de l'Académie des Inscriptions et Belles Lettres* (March 2011), 377–429; reprinted in *Les Origines du Coran, le Coran des Origins*. Edited by François Déroche, Christian Julien Robin, and Michel Zink, 219–70. Paris: Académie des Inscriptions et Belles-Lettres, 2015.

George, Alain. 'Coloured Dots and the Question of Regional Origins in Early Qur'ans: Parts I and II', *Journal of Qur'anic Studies* 17/1 (2015), 1–44 and 17/2 (2015), 75–102.

Halevi, Leor. 'Christian Impurity vs. Economic Necessity: A Fifteenth-Century Fatwa on European Paper', *Speculum* 83/4 (2008), 917–45.

James, David. *Islamic Masterpieces of the Chester Beatty Library*. London: World of Islam Festival Trust, 1981.

James, David. *Qur'āns of the Mamlūks*. London: Alexandria Press: Thames and Hudson, 1988. Republished as *Manuscripts of the Holy Qur'ān from the Mamlūk Era*. Riyadh: King Faisal Centre for Research and Islamic Studies, 1999.

James, David. *The Master Scribes: Qurans of the 10th to 14th Centuries* AD. Nasser D. Khalili Collection of Islamic Art 2. New York: Nour Foundation in association with Azimuth Editions and Oxford University Press, 1992a.

James, David. *After Timur: Qurans of the 15th and 16th Centuries*. Nasser D. Khalili Collection of Islamic Art. New York: Nour Foundation in association with Azimuth Editions and Oxford University Press, 1992b.

Karimi-Nia, Morteza. 'Iranian Kufic Qurʾan Manuscripts: A Brief Survey', *Journal of Qurʾanic Studies* 8/2 (2006), 157–63.

Komaroff, Linda. *Gifts of the Sultan: The Arts of Giving at the Islamic Courts*. New Haven and London: Yale University Press, 2011.

Martínez de Castilla Muñoz, Nuria. 'Qurʾanic Manuscripts from Late Muslim Spain: The Collection of Almonacid de la Sierra', *Journal of Qurʾanic Studies* 16/2 (2014), 89–138.

Maṣāḥif Ṣanʿāʾ. Kuwait: Dār al-Āthār al-Islamiyya, 1985.

Ory, Solange. 'Un nouveau type de muṣḥaf: inventaire des Corans en rouleaux de provenance damascaine, conservés à Istanbul', *Revue des etudes islamiques* 33 (1965), 87–114.

Piotrovsky, Mikhail. *Heavenly Art; Earthly Beauty: Art of Islam*. London: Lund Humphries, 2000.

Porter, Cheryl. 'The Materiality of the Blue Qur'an: A Physical and Technological Study'. In: Glaire Anderson, Corisande Fenwick, and Mariam Rosser-Owen (Eds.) *The Aghlabids and their Neighbours: Art and Material Culture in Ninth-Century North Africa*, pp. 575–86. Leiden: Brill, 2018.

Rabb, Intisar. 'Non-Canonical Readings of the Qurʾan: Recognition and Authenticity (The Ḥimṣī Reading)', *Journal of Qurʾanic Studies* 8/2 (2006), 84–127.

Robin, Christian Julien. 'L'Arabie dans Le Coran'. In: François Déroche, Christian Julien Robin, and Michel Zink (eds.). *Les Origines du Coran, le Coran des Origins*, pp. 27–74. Paris: Académie des Inscriptions et Belles-Lettres, 2015.

Sadeghi, Behnam and Uwe Bergmann. 'The Codex of a Companion of the Prophet and the Qurʾān of the Prophet', *Arabica* 57 (2010), 342–436.

Sadeghi, Behnam and Mohsen Goudarzi. 'Ṣanʿāʾ I and the Origins of the Qurʾan', *Der Islam* 87 (2012), 1–129.

Schoeler, Gregor. *The Oral and the Written in Early Islam*. Abingdon: Routledge, 2006.

Schoeler, Gregor. *The Genesis of Literature in Islam: From the Aural to the Read*. Edinburgh: Edinburgh University Press, 2009.

Tabbaa, Yasser. 'The Transformation of Arabic Writing: Part 1 Qurʾānic Calligraphy', *Ars Orientalis* 21 (1991), 119–48.

Tabbaa, Yasser. 'The Transformation of Arabic Writing: Part 2, The Public Text', *Ars Orientalis* 24 (1994), 119–47.

Whelan, Estelle. 'Writing the Word of God: Some Early Qurʾān Manuscripts and their Milieux, Part I', *Ars Orientalis* 20 (1990), 113–48.

Wright, Elaine. 2009. *Understanding Islam: Faith, Art, Culture: Manuscripts of the Chester Beatty Library*. London: Scala.

Wright, Elaine. *Lapis and Gold: Exploring Chester Beatty's Ruzbihan Qurʾan*. Dublin: Ad Ilissum, 2018.

1400. yilinda Kur'an-i Kerim/The 1400th Anniversary of the Qurʾan. Istanbul: Antik A.S. Kültür Yayinlari/Antik A.S. Cultural Publications, 2010.

CHAPTER 15

INSCRIBING GOD'S WORD

Qur'anic Texts on Architecture, Objects, and Other Solid Supports

SHEILA S. BLAIR

SINCE the first century of Islam, Muslims have inscribed whole Qur'anic verses and phrases from them on buildings and other objects made for a wide range of purposes. This chapter addresses these inscriptions, all of which might be termed public texts (Bierman 1998). An introductory section lays out the scope and limitations of this study, the historiography of the subject, and some of the directions research has taken and might take. A second section surveys some of the ways that these Qur'anic texts have been used, discussing the evidence they offer in showing both how Muslims considered the revelation and how they cited it. A third section deals with considerations of layout, technique, and style, investigating how these formal features enhanced the message. Along the way, the chapter also points out directions in which such Qur'anic inscriptions might be profitably studied in these and other ways.

PERSPECTIVES, PRACTICALITIES, AND PROBLEMS

This chapter addresses the use of Qur'anic texts on solid supports, what one might call epigraphy, as opposed to calligraphy, writing on supple supports such as parchment and paper, a subject covered in Chapter 14. In general, the inscriptions contain short excerpts from the Qur'an, typically verses or phrases but occasionally full chapters. Inscriptions thus differ from manuscripts, whether codices or rolls, which usually contain the full text of the revelation or large parts of it.

These inscriptions are often placed on buildings or objects associated with the practice of the faith. Thus, we should not be surprised to find them frequently on mosques, madrasas, and tombs, places where the Qur'an was regularly recited and/or read. These texts are also common on the fittings associated with these religious buildings, objects such as minbars, mosque lamps, and prayer rugs, but Qur'anic inscriptions also occur in more secular settings. From the late first/seventh century, they became the main decoration on coins, objects that were exchanged and handled by both Muslims and others. These texts are also found on domestic buildings, ranging from houses to palaces as well as their fittings. For example, an early inscription inked in Rajab 117/August 735 on the walls of a ruined house in the village of Madina on the right bank of the Nile between Minya and Manfalus in Upper Egypt (van Berchem 1894–1903 = *MCIA Egypte 1*, no. 513; Combe, Sauvaget, and Wiet 1931ff. = *RCEA*, no. 30) contains several verses about the ḥajj (Q. 3:95–7), perhaps inscribed to commemorate the pilgrimage to the holy city of Mecca by the writer, one Mālik ibn Kathīr. Nevertheless, Qur'anic inscriptions were rarely if ever used on day-to-day objects intended for mundane purposes lest food or drink sully the sacred word. Instead, inscriptions with good wishes, texts from the hadith, and poems are more common there.

Qur'anic inscriptions are thus ubiquitous, and part of the difficulty in studying them lies in the very fact of their popularity. There is no single database listing all recorded examples. Indeed the only general volume (Dodd and Khairallah 1981), while a valiant pioneering effect, is hard to find and incomplete (Blair 1984). The compilation of such a database of Qur'anic inscriptions, preferably on-line so that it can be readily updated, is a major desideratum and one whose usefulness cannot be overstated in the field of Qur'anic studies.

The historiography of the study of Qur'anic inscriptions and the ways in which the data were compiled have compounded the problem. The Swiss scholar Max van Berchem (1894–1903) initiated the study of Arabic inscriptions on buildings and other works of art. Given how unfamiliar much of the basic chronology of Islamic history was at that time, he and other early scholars were understandably interested mainly in the historical information contained in the inscriptions. Hence, many Western scholars devoted most of their study to the historical parts of the texts. Some scholars even went so far as to label the Qur'anic sections 'banal', despite the fact that such Qur'anic citations were often longer than and integrated into the historical parts. Even when these scholars did include information about the Qur'anic texts, they did so numerically, citing only the numbers of sura and verse. This is typically the case in the major compendia of Arabic inscriptions, the various volumes in the *Matériaux pour un Corpus Inscriptionum Arabicarum*, generally abbreviated as *MCIA* (van Berchem 1894–1903 and 1920–2; Wiet 1929–30; Herzfeld 1954–5, etc.; for details about the various volumes by different authors, see Blair 1998: 207–9) and the *Répertoire Chronologique d'Épigraphie Arabe* (often abbreviated as *RCEA*; Combe, Sauvaget, and Wiet 1937ff.). One might contrast this approach to the one adopted in publications from the Muslim lands, such as Hunarfar's classic study of the inscriptions in the central Iranian city of Isfahan (1350/1978), where the text is written out in full in Arabic script, with a footnote identifying the number of the Qur'anic sura and verse.

A further snag results from the fact that these basic research tools, the *MCIA* and the *RCEA*, use the numbering system of the Qur'an that had been adopted by Gustav Flügel in his edition of the Qur'an and was widely used by Western scholars in the thirteenth/nineteenth and early fourteenth/twentieth centuries before the adoption of the Standard Egyptian edition, published in 1924 and the most common system used today. In many cases, it is easy to rectify the difference between the two numbering systems. The well-known Throne Verse (*Āyat al-kursī*), for example, is Q. 2:256 in the edition used by Flügel, but Q. 2:255 in the Standard Egyptian system. In some cases, especially when dealing with less common verses from longer suras, it is more difficult to identify which verses were used.

Without checking, scholars sometimes confuse the two and can be led astray by taking the numerical reference from an older source and applying it to the Standard Egyptian system. For example, the two verses about the Kaʿba in Mecca and pilgrimage to it as a duty incumbent on Muslims (Q. 3:96–7 in the Standard Egyptian system, but Q. 3:91–2 in the numbering system used by Flügel and others), cited on the portal to the Jamʿa Mosque in Delhi, have been mistakenly taken as referring to earlier verses now numbered Q. 3:85–6 in the Standard Egyptian system that refer to polytheists and disbelievers and then wrongly interpreted as references to the spolia from temples used to construct the mosque (Blair 2013: note 41). A further problem is that when citing by number, it is easy to mistype or drop a digit, something that also happened with this same citation, which then became truncated to Q. 3:91–9 in another article. Such mistakes were even more frequent when Roman numerals were used for sura numbers. Knowing when and where a citation was first recorded can give a researcher a hint of which numbering system was used, but it is essential to check pictures of the inscription to verify the text.

The lack of such a comprehensive database of Qur'anic inscriptions makes it difficult to distinguish the specific, and presumably meaningful, from the routine or generic. The problem is aggravated when all time periods are lumped together; for different verses can be and were interpreted in different ways by different groups in different places. Furthermore, early scholars were often interested in the rise of Islam, concentrating their work on inscriptions from the early period. Yet interpretations of the meaning of particular verses are easier to document in later times, when the *ʿulamāʾ* assumed a more important role and even composed treatises explaining their reasoning about the implications of individual verses. In her study of the Qur'anic inscriptions on the imperial Ottoman mosques designed by the court architect Sinan, Gülru Necipoğlu (2007: 79) pointed out that the Süleymaniye complex in Istanbul had five theological seminaries and that the audience for the elaborate programme of inscriptions included not only the resident professors and their students, but also visitors who may have read the inscriptions with the assistance of imams, muezzins, and salaried Qur'an reciters acting like tour guides.

Despite the early lack of interest in Qur'anic inscriptions, several features indicate the importance of these texts. The content of the text can do so. For example, some of these inscriptions, not only those from the early period (*EQ*: 2:25–53) but also those from

Ottoman times (Bacqué-Grammont, Lacquer, and Vatin 1990), invoke blessing on the person who reads the Qur'anic text and then says amen, thus showing that the text was meant not only to be read but also to be efficacious.

Physical position also underscores the importance of these Qur'anic texts inscribed on buildings and other objects. They are often set prominently on façades or walls or atop minarets and written in bold scripts, sometimes highlighted with colour. Although these inscriptions are sometimes difficult to decipher, especially before the invention of the telephoto lens, their position, technique, and style show their importance to the patron or sponsor, as they literally sat atop the monument, metaphorically proclaiming their message.

One example will suffice to prove the point that such inscriptions are not only important to scholars today, but already made an impact on viewers in medieval times: the mosaic band (Figure 15.1) that crowns both sides of the interior arcade in the Dome of the Rock in Jerusalem (van Berchem 1920–2 = *MCIA Jerusalem* II: nos. 215–16; Combe, Sauvaget, and Wiet 1931ff. = *RCEA*, nos. 9–10). The long (238 metre/780 ft) band is preserved in its entirety except near the end where the Abbasid caliph al-Maʾmūn (r. 189–218/813–33)

FIGURE 15.1 Interior of the Dome of the Rock in Jerusalem, 72/691–2, showing the mosaic inscription at the top of the west section of the arcade with Q. 4:171–2. Photo: Sheila S. Blair and Jonathan M. Bloom.

had his own name substituted for that of the original patron, the Umayyad caliph ʿAbd al-Malik. Al-Maʾmūn retained, nevertheless, the original date of 72/691–2. The main body of the text consists of a series of brief invocations and prayers combined with a series of passages from the Qur'an, many dealing with the theme of challenging Christian dogma in the main pilgrimage city for Christians. The text preserves some of the earliest dated evidence for the writing down of the Qur'an and is particularly interesting as it conflates parts of several verses (e.g. Q. 64:1 and 57:2) and sometimes changes the voice so that the text flows smoothly.

The material, placement, and style of the mosaic inscription in the Dome of the Rock did not pass unnoticed in medieval times. When the Fatimid caliph al-Ẓāhir had the mosaics in the drum repaired in 418/1027–8, the restoration was commemorated in a two-line band at the top (van Berchem 1920–2 = *MCIA Jerusalem*, II: no. 223; Combe, Sauvaget, and Wiet 1931ff. = *RCEA*, no. 2359). The text is again composed in a squat kufic script with gold letters against a green ground, the same style and technique used three centuries earlier, despite the fact that new styles of floriated script had become common by the fifth/eleventh century when the restoration text was executed. And after the same caliph had the nearby Aqsa Mosque restored a few years later (the work was completed on the last day of Dhu'l-Qaʿda 426/6 October 1035), a similar mosaic inscription was installed at the top of the triumphal arch (van Berchem 1920–2 = *MCIA Jerusalem* II, no. 275; Combe, Sauvaget, and Wiet, 1931ff. = *RCEA* 2410). The band, again written like its Umayyad predecessor in gold on green in the rectangular kufic script typical of early times, opens with the first verse of *Sūrat al-Isrāʾ* (Q. 17:1). The text, which mentions the Prophet's Night Journey, is the first epigraphic evidence to associate Jerusalem's mosque with the Qur'anic phrase *al-masjid al-aqṣā*. Such examples show that both the content and the style of Qur'anic inscriptions mattered to viewers in their own time.

Contemporary chroniclers rarely give the reasons for choosing a particular text on a specific building or object. One exception is the Nilometer in Cairo (Wiet 1929–30 = *MCIA Egypte* 2, no. 19). The Damascene scholar Ibn Khallikān (608–81/1211–82) did so in a story that he appended to the biography of the building's administrator Abū'l-Raddād. According to the report, Aḥmad ibn Muḥammad, the engineer in charge of renovations under the Abbasid caliph al-Mutawakkil in 247/861–2, searched the Qur'an for the most appropriate texts, selecting four verses of equal length that were inscribed in letters a finger thick so that they could be read from afar. The texts that Ibn Khallikān mentions (Q. 50:9, the last clause in Q. 22:5, Q. 22:63, and Q. 42:28) are indeed inscribed on marble plaques over the arches on the interior, although they are carved in relief and not made of lapis lazuli letters inset in the marble as carefully described by the chronicler. Both they and other Qur'anic inscriptions on the building (Q. 14:37; Q. 32:27; Q. 16:10–11; Q. 22:63; and Q. 25:50) aptly fit the structure's function, describing God's gift of water and the fecundity it brings. Nonetheless this medieval description, like the building itself, is singular, and Ibn Khallikān, writing four centuries after the event, may have felt compelled to explain its uniqueness. Virtually no other such examples are known, perhaps because medieval chroniclers deemed the reasons behind the choices of specific Qur'anic texts so obvious.

Lacking information from chronicles, we are left to deduce the principles that governed the choice and composition of individual texts by examining the corpus of Qur'anic inscriptions themselves. Some principles are evident, but others may become clearer after more study. One such principle was synecdoche, in which the part substitutes for the whole. A good example is the long wooden frieze with Qur'anic text encircling the ceiling of the prayer hall in the mosque of Ibn Ṭūlūn in Cairo, founded in 265/879. Measuring two kilometres (over one mile) in length, the frieze represents a wealth of timber in a forest-less land. The inscription is often said to contain the entire Qur'an. In fact, it contains only sura 2, the longest chapter in the Qur'an, but one that is often said to represent the entire revelation.

Another principle used for selection of Qur'anic texts in inscriptions was bracketing. For example, by using the first and last suras, themselves short and easily fitted into many tight spaces, one can be said to have encapsulated the Qur'an. Such a principle may explain the common use of these short suras on lustre tiles and other objects that were made in multiples.

Visual recognition may well have played an important role as well in the selection of appropriate Qur'anic texts. Certain words or phrases, such as *fatḥ*^{an}*mubīn*^{an} (clear triumph), are immediately recognizable because of the shapes of their letters. If readers could identify a word or phrase from such a well-known text, then they could supply the rest of the inscription, as with the opening phrase from the *Sūrat al-Fatḥ* (Q. 48:1). Indeed, the easiest way to read particularly ornate inscriptions in elaborate or unpointed scripts is to anticipate what that text might be.

At times, designers may even have exploited the complexity of the writing, transforming decipherment into a sort of intellectual game that caused viewers to reflect and ponder on the epigraphic content in the same way that early kufic scripts were deliberately intended to slow down reading and enhance aural retention. At the very least, such hard-to-read inscriptions functioned as symbolic affirmation, a useful term coined decades ago by Richard Ettinghausen (1974) to indicate the rhetorical significance of such texts in spite of their visual complexity.

Uses

Scholars have exploited this large, if still disparate, body of Qur'anic inscriptions, in several different ways. A few researchers have recently begun to use these inscriptions as evidence, often dated or datable, of how Muslims viewed the revelation. For example, Robert Hoyland (*EQ* 2:26–7) has looked at these Qur'anic inscriptions in the context of evolving scholarship on the text as *kitāb* or book (*EQ* 1:242–51). The term first occurs epigraphically in the mosaic inscription on the Dome of the Rock dated 72/691–2. The interior section contains two Qur'anic passages referring to the book (*al-kitāb*): Q. 4:171 on the south-east side invoking 'O People of the Book' (*ahl al-kitāb*), and Q. 3:19 on the south-west side referring to those who have been given the book. The term soon became more common. The inscription that the first Abbasid caliph al-Saffāḥ (r. 132–6/749–54) added to the Mosque of Prophet in Medina to announce his dynasty's succession to the Umayyads, a text that has been called a political profession of faith, refers twice to the Qur'an as God's book (*kitāb allāh*; Combe, Sauvaget, and Wiet 1931ff. = *RCEA* 38).

This identification of the revelation as book shows up on a more popular level as well. A graffito from northern Arabia datable to the second/eighth century (cited in *EQ* 2:26) refers to the 'book He has sent down', and the epitaph on an Egyptian tombstone dated 195/810 (Combe, Sauvaget, and Wiet 1931ff. = *RCEA* no. 89) says that the deceased testifies that the book is truth, which God sent down with His knowledge, followed by Q. 41:42, that it is a revelation sent down from the Wise One, Worthy of All Praise.

Similarly, inscriptions can be used to document theological debates within the Muslim community about the status of the Qur'an. For example, in an epitaph on an arch-shaped alabaster plaque set in the ʿUmariyya Mosque in Mosul and datable *c*.200/815, the author testifies to his faith in the uncreated Qur'an (Combe, Sauvaget, and Wiet 1931ff. = *RCEA*, no. 117), a reference reflecting the ongoing theological debate often associated with the heterodox theological school of the Muʿtazila about the createdness of the Qur'an. As François Déroche noted (2003: 604 and note 26), such an expression about the uncreated Qur'an was frequent used in Maghribi epigraphy between the late third/ninth century and the beginning of the fifth/eleventh, found in an inscription on the mihrab of the Great Mosque of Qayrawan (Zbiss 1955, no. 3) and five other places in the region (*Thesaurus d'épigraphie islamique*, nos. 294, 301, 398, 530, and 12918).

Such theological debates resonated in contemporary Qur'anic manuscripts and their illumination. The frontispiece to a splendid copy written in gold letters in Palermo, Sicily in 372/982–3 contains Q. 56:77–80 'that this is truly a noble Qur'an, in a protected Record that only the purified can touch, sent down from the Lord of all being' (Déroche 2001; Johns 2018). These verses are often found at the beginning of Qur'an manuscripts (see Chapter 14), but this seems to be the first dated occurrence, and here it takes on an unusual significance when read with the marginal palmette on the facing folio that contains the profession of faith (*shahāda*) followed by the statement that the Qur'an is the Word of God and was not created. This avenue of investigation using Qur'anic epigraphy to track theology is also relatively new, and given the growing interest in the historical context of Qur'an hermeneutics, it is one that will probably continue to and justifiably should expand, particularly with the publication of more texts, especially graffiti from the early period.

The more traditional avenue of investigation into Qur'anic epigraphy centres on why and how Muslims inscribed the text, and this study too has become more nuanced in recent years. While some Qur'anic inscriptions may be seen as a general affirmation of the faith, close study shows that we can often suggest more precise reasons for the particular choice at any particular time. Reasons can range from justification of sectarian allegiances and references to the object's function to plays-on-words and popular taste, and several factors in combination may have affected the choice of appropriate verse. Knowing the typical context of such texts can throw into relief unusual cases that deserve further investigation.

FIGURE 15.2 Roundel with Q. 33:33 on the façade of the Aqmar Mosque erected under the Fatimids in Cairo in 519/1125. Photo: Sheila S. Blair and Jonathan M. Bloom.

Certain Qur'anic verses reverberate with Shīʿī groups, particularly those that can be interpreted to justify their claims to the imamate of ʿAlī and his descendants. For example, Q. 33:33 containing the phrase *ahl al-bayt*, the people of the [Prophet's] House, was popular in inscriptions on religious buildings patronized by the Fatimids in their new capital of Cairo. The text is found in a roundel on the façade of the Aqmar Mosque erected on the main street in 519/1125 (Figure 15.2) and in many contemporary mausolea such as those for Sayyida Nafīsa and Sayyida Ruqayya (Williams 1983 and 1985). Similarly, the Fatimids and other Shīʿī rulers often cited Q. 5:55 (numbered 5:60 in the Flügel system), which contains the word *walīyyukum* [your true allies], taking it as a reference to the Prophet's cousin and son-in-law ʿAlī. It is found, for example, on the mausoleum of Sayyida Ruqqaya in Cairo and the Haram at Mashhad. But the use of this verse elsewhere needs further explanation, as, for example, why it was emblazoned atop the fourth story of the minaret added to the congregational mosque of Aleppo in 483/1090–91 during the reign of the Saljuq Sultan Malikshāh, along with praises of ʿAlī (Herzfeld 1954–5 = *MCIA Alep*, no. 76).

Recent work also shows the need for close contextualization of an individual choice. Fatimid coins continue to display the Qur'anic verse that had been standard since Umayyad times, the so-called Prophetic Mission (Q. 9:33), saying that Muḥammad is the Prophet of God, who sent him with the religion of truth to prevail over all others. The Fatimids, however, interpreted these verses differently. According to the theologian al-Nuʿmān, chief *qāḍī* under al-Muʿizz li-Dīn Allāh (r. 341–65/953–75), these verses related to the *qāʾim* (the Righteous Imam who ended a cycle) and the triumph of Ismāʿīlism (Bierman 1998:67).

Fatimid coins show furthermore that the Qur'anic texts on individual issues could send different messages. A hoard of coins minted in the name of al-Mahdī at the turn of the fourth/tenth century in the Yemen contains a different set of Qur'anic verses: Q. 17:81, that truth has come; Q. 30:3–4, about defeat turning into victory; and Q. 22:41, about those who command what is good and forbid what is wrong (Merchant 2007). They seem to reflect the specific political moment when the Fatimid mission (*daʿwa*) had suffered a setback in the Yemen, but was advancing in North Africa. The particular interpretation of individual Qur'anic verses thus needs to be tied to specific historical circumstances, and we need more such precisely focused studies.

Coins are a suitable place for such study, as they are typically dated and issued in the name of an individual ruler. They represent the official state view, one that might well be contrasted with views found on humbler types of objects that reflect more popular tastes and practices, subjects that are not always treated in written texts. One example is the inscriptions chosen for amulets and talismans, which can be prophylactic in warding off evil, malefic in destroying one's enemies, or propitiatory in securing comfort, happiness, and wealth. Block-printed amulets (*ṭarsh*) or even sura titles or ten-verse markers torn from manuscripts may have served such functions. These amulets were usually carried in small cases, themselves often marked with Qur'anic phrases. In the eastern Islamic lands, these popular objects were used as armbands and are hence known as *bāzūband* (armlet or armband). The choice of verse on them can help us to understand the desired end. For example, arm amulets inscribed with Q. 3:14 stating that 'The love of desirable things is made alluring for men—women, children, gold and silver treasures piled up high, horses with fine markings, livestock, and farmland—these may be the joys of this life, but God has the best place to return to' may be considered propitiatory, whereas others asking for God's victory (Q. 61:13 or 48:1) might have been intended to secure military victory (Maddison and Savage-Smith 1997: 1:132). We need more publications that include these kinds of small mundane objects and their Qur'anic inscriptions, for they provide a rare window into daily life in medieval times.

Qur'anic verses were also used to allude to the function of a particular building or object. The types of object most commonly studied are, quite naturally, those associated with the practice of the faith. The most common expression on mosques, for example, is Q. 9:18, containing the phrase *masājid allāh* referring to 'God's mosques' (Hillenbrand 1986). Similarly, mihrabs are often inscribed with Q. 17:78–9, verses referring to prayer. Windows often had the Light Verse (*āyat al-nūr*; Q. 24:35), referring to God as the light of the heavens and the earth, whereas doors might be inscribed with Q. 17:80, a verse referring to a truthful ingoing and outgoing, both used, for example, on the northern minaret added to the Fatimid mosque of al-Ḥākim in Cairo in 393/1003 (Bloom 1983:19).

But again, these general statements need more nuanced interpretations, and looking more closely can show why these verses were preferable to others that include some of the same words. Q. 9:18, for example, is not only one of the rare verses to mention mosques in the plural, but more importantly, one of the few to describe the duties of Muslims in them. Using that verse therefore emphasizes not the physical structure but the space within it and the practices of Muslims in that space. Similarly, Q. 17:78–9 are some of the many verses about ritual prayer, but they are the most suitable choice for mihrabs, as they again mention the role of the believer, specifically in actively reciting prayers (Blair 2007). The verses about light too had special meaning for Ismāʿīlīs, who saw God's light as transmitted to the successive ʿAlid imams and used such verses frequently on their mosques and mausoleums (Williams 1983 and 1985). These (and many other) examples show the necessity of in-depth investigation of the context that made individual words and phrases within suitable verses relevant in particular times and places.

Words and verses also need to be studied within the context of the entire inscription or programme of inscriptions. Plays-on-words are frequent, and several Qur'anic texts could be cited together to drive home the message. The stupendous Kutubiyya Minbar, made in Cordoba beginning on 1 Muharram 532/19 September 1137 and shipped nearly 1,000 kilometres (600 miles) to the Almoravid Mosque in Marrakesh, has two Qur'anic texts on opposite sides that play on different words for throne, including the Throne Verse (Q. 2:255), in which God's throne (*kursī*) is described as extending over the heavens and the earth, and Q. 7:54–61, in which God, having created the heavens and the earth in six days, then establishes himself on His throne (*ʿarsh*). The two texts were meant to be read together with the physical object, a very tall stepped pulpit from which the imam delivered the sermon in the mosque.

Other verses were chosen because they contained words that played on the patron's name, invoking qualities associated with God or the names of the prophets. The superb wooden mihrab that the Zangid ruler Nūr al-Dīn, whose honorific literally means 'Light of the Faith', had installed in the lower *maqām* constructed in the citadel of Aleppo in 563/1167–8, was inscribed with four friezes of Qur'anic texts (Herzfeld 1954–5 = *MCIA Alep*, I:1: 120). The first was the Light Verse or *Āyat al-nūr* (Q. 24:35), doubly appropriate as a pun on the patron's name and as a reference to the light that God brings. The Ottoman sultan Selim II (r. 974–82/1566–74), had the phrase from Q. 26:89 about a devoted heart (*qalb salīm*, the Arabic form from which Selim is derived) inscribed in mihrabs in the Selimiye Mosque in Edirne and elsewhere (Necipoğlu 2007: 85–7). Given the sultan's hedonistic lifestyle (his nickname was 'Selim the Sot'), such a citation might not only pun on the patron's name, but also reflect the supplicatory voice of the repentant sultan or the wishful thinking of the legal scholar who drew up the text.

These Qur'anic references to the patrons' names could be quite complex in later times. One extreme example is the upper gold inscription on the façade of the Masjid-i ʿAlī (completed 929/1522–3) in Isfahan (Figure 15.3), which include snippets from the twelve Qur'anic verses containing the name Ismāʿīl (Q. 2:125, 2:127, 2:133, 2:136, 2:140, 3:84, 4:123, 6:86, 14:39, 19:54, 21:85, and 36:48; Honarfar 1350: 371; Blair 2014: 19). The Qur'anic text

FIGURE 15.3 Foundation inscription around the portal of the Masjid-i ʿAlī in Isfahan rebuilt during the reign of the Safavid Shāh Ismāʿīl with twelve Qurʾanic verses containing the name Ismāʿīl. Photo: Sheila S. Blair and Jonathan M. Bloom.

must be read in conjunction with the rhyming foundation text below in white saying the mosque was rebuilt during the reign of the Safavid Shāh Ismāʿīl (r. 907–30/1501–24), who is lauded as 'the one on whom descends the grace of having his name repeated in the Qur'an as many times as there are Imams', a subtle reference to the ruler's instigation of Twelver Shīʿism as state religion in Iran and to the twelve instances of that name in the revelation. Such Qur'anic texts must thus be examined carefully in light of contemporary contexts, both political and personal.

A recent study of funerary inscriptions shows some of problems of interpreting Qur'anic texts over broad expanses of time and space (Diem and Schöller 2004). This exhaustive three-volume study of epitaphs culled from both preserved examples and texts attempts to reconstruct 'the place, impact and importance of epitaphs—i.e. funerary inscriptions—and relative funerary structures within the culture, society, and intellectual and religious history of the Islamic lands' (1:vii). Volume 1 treats the epitaphs themselves; volume 2 covers the social and material aspects of burial sites and funerary monuments. Volume 3 contains numerous indices, including one with more than 250 different Qur'anic excerpts. As the authors state in the introduction (1:xi), the role of the Qur'an in funerary discourse cannot be overestimated, from the point of view of eschatology, form, and style. Yet, they conclude that 'Qur'anic quotations in general tend often to become so conventional that they do not convey specific messages any longer'. The problem here is generalizing from the specific, for in many cases the individual text needs to be analysed in its own particular context.

Layout, Technique, and Style

Another area of increasing interest in the study of Qur'anic epigraphy considers not just what these inscriptions say but also where and how they are written. The ability to manipulate the text by stretching it out at the top of a building or wrapping it around an object was, of course, easier when the text was longer, but such manipulation seems to have taken place from the earliest times onward.

The deliberate shaping of the Qur'anic text to fit the space available occurred already in the Umayyad mosaic inscription on the Dome of the Rock. Some letters are stretched out and others cramped together so that different parts of the text fit the different spaces. The part of the inscription on the south or *qibla* side of the building, for example, contains complete texts with similar meanings on both interior and exterior faces: the interior has a conflation of Q. 64:1 with Q. 57:2, flanked by the *basmala* and a phrase about Muḥammad's role as messenger; the exterior has Q. 112, also flanked by the *basmala* and a phrase about Muḥammad's role as messenger. The inscription on the interior arcade has also been set to highlight the text. The cubes that compose the letters are the most expensive type of tesserae, made by sandwiching gold leaf between pieces of glass. Furthermore, these cubes are set at a 30° angle to reflect the light, a technique that required more time and hence demanded more money. Both materials and technique thus highlight the importance of the Qur'anic text on this very early monument.

In later centuries artisans grew more sophisticated in manipulating the layout, technique, and style of Qur'anic texts to enhance the meaning. Probably the most spectacular example of a Qur'anic inscription on a building occurs on the stunning minaret constructed by the Ghurid Sultan Ghiyāth al-Dīn Muḥammad ibn Sām at Jām in central Afghanistan in 570/1174–5 (Figure 15.4). The minaret, which soars an extraordinary 65 metres (215 ft), is set on an octagonal base that supports three superposed tapering shafts separated by *muqarnas* cornices, the top one crowned by a lantern. The interlacing band enveloping the lowest story contains the complete text of *Sūrat Maryam* (Q. 19:1–98). The inscription is remarkable for both its length and its intricate layout, and scholars have long debated why it was chosen. Finbarr Flood (2009:98–101) recently put forth the most convincing explanation to date, arguing that the text reflected the Ghurids' adherence to the Karrāmiyya, a Sunnī pietistic sect dominant in the region of Ghur in the second half of the sixth/twefth century. He noted that the one contemporary object made for the same patron—a large four-volume Qur'an manuscript with interlinear Persian translation completed on 8 Rabīʿ al-Akhīr 584/6 June 1188—contains a commentary (*tafsīr*) at the end of each chapter by Abū Bakr ʿAtīq ibn Muḥammad al-Surābādī (d. *c*.495/1101), a leading Karrāmiyya scholar from Nishapur. Flood's analysis points up the usefulness of studying Qur'anic epigraphy together with contemporary Qur'anic manuscripts and other texts.

Flood suggested further that the Qur'anic text on the minaret at Jām was laid out deliberately so that the phrase from from 19:35, *kun fayakūn* (Be! And it is) would fall on the

FIGURE 15.4 Minaret of Jām erected by the Ghurid Sultan Ghiyāth al-Dīn on 570/1174–5, with the entire text of *Sūrat Maryam* (Q.19:1–98) inscribed around the lower shaft. Photo: David Thomas, MJAP2005.

east face, the side that worshippers faced when praying toward the *qibla*, just at the intersection of the bottom two panels shaped like a niche and a star, symbolizing a mihrab and lamp. These words, which occur seven other times in the Qur'an, occupied a central position in the Karrāmiyya's attempts to distinguish between God's eternal attributes and His temporal acts. The hypothesis is an ingenious attempt to explain a puzzling choice of text and intricate layout, although one would have to say that the selection and layout were important more for designer than audience, as little would have been actually readable to worshippers on the ground some 10 metres (33 ft) below. The text would therefore have been less about communication and more about symbolic or rhetorical affirmation.

Decorators could manipulate Qur'anic texts on objects as well. This is clearly the case with mosque lamps made of enamelled glass. The typical lamp has a wide and flaring neck, bulbous body with six applied handles, and prominent foot. A small glass container for water and oil with a floating wick was inserted in the lamp, and the lamp itself was suspended by chains from the ceiling. Both neck and body of these glass lamps were typically decorated with bold inscriptions painted in different colours of enamel or written in reserve by decorating the ground around the letters. The decorators could—and did—modify technique and colour to enhance the Qur'anic texts.

For example, the neck of a lamp made *c.*730/1330 for Sayf al-Dīn Qawṣūn, cupbearer to the Mamluk Sultan al-Nāṣir Muḥammad is inscribed with the most popular Qur'anic text used on these lamps, the well-known Light Verse (Q. 24:35), usually translated as that 'God is the Light of the Heavens and the Earth. His Light is like this: there is a niche (*mishkāt*), and in it a lamp (*miṣbāḥ*), the lamp inside a glass (*zujāja*), a glass like a glittering star.' The text can be read as a literal description of the glass lamp, with the wickholder (*mishkāt*) providing flickering light in the glass container (*miṣbāḥ*) inside the glass lamp (*zujāja*). On this particular lamp made for Amir Qawṣūn, the Qur'anic inscription is written in reverse around the neck by outlining the letters in red and filling the background in dark blue. When the lamp was lit, the Qur'anic text would have glowed, a stunning visual realization of the Qur'anic metaphor inscribed on it.

That the decorator was deliberately playing with technique to enhance the meaning is clear because other decorators manipulated different texts differently on other lamps. Another lamp made slightly earlier for the *khānaqāh* (hospice) and tomb of the Mamluk Sultan Baybars II al-Jāshnakīr (r. 708–9/1309–10) has the name of the patron painted around the body in blue, the most expensive pigment (London, V&A, no. C322–1900). The neck is inscribed in yellow with a different and unusual set of Qur'anic verses: Q. 83:22 and Q. 83:24–5, saying that 'The truly good will live in bliss. You will recognize on their faces the radiance of bliss.' The verses must have been deliberately chosen, as the inscription fits the neck exactly, skipping verse 23, which mentions that they are seated on couches, gazing around. By painting the Qur'anic text in yellow, the decorator underscored the radiant bliss on the faces of those promised Paradise.

Enamelled mosques lamps thus provide a good example of how artists could manipulate layout and technique to underscore the meaning of Qur'anic verses on objects made for a sacred setting. These are useful as they present a relatively small set of high-class objects made for the Mamluk court in Egypt and Syria during a restricted period of time from the late seventh/thirteenth century to the mid-ninth/fifteenth. These two examples were chosen somewhat at random, but a more comprehensive study of this and similar groups of objects with Qur'anic inscriptions might show how changes occurred over time or for different settings. One might investigate, for example, the Qur'anic inscriptions on lustre tiles made by a few families of potters at Kashan in central Iran from the end of the sixth/twelfth century to the middle of the eighth/fourteenth. Such studies are becoming increasingly easy as more and better colour photographs are available of many of these objects, particularly from databases of museum collections.

Scholars are also devoting attention to the styles of script used for these Qur'anic inscriptions. Some styles are characteristic of particular times and places. Floriated kufic, for example, is characteristic of the Fatimid period, and a thick round *naskh* is associated with the Ayyubids. Some scholars have therefore questioned whether particular styles of script carried specific religious meaning for various groups. Floriated kufic, for example, has been connected with the duality of the exoteric (*ẓāhir*) and esoteric (*bāṭin*) aspects of Shīʿism (Bierman 1998) and *naskh* with the Sunnī revival (Tabbaa 2001). To my mind, these hypotheses are not convincing, as one can easily find cases where these scripts were used beyond their dynastic rubrics, as with the fine floriated kufic used already in the foundation inscription for the Biʾr al-Waṭāwiṭ in Cairo by the Ikhshidid vizier Ibn al-Furāt in 355/966 (Wiet 1929–30 = *MCIA Egypte* 2, no. 570). Styles of script became typical of certain times and places, but it remains to establish any inherent religious iconography that remained constant over time.

In sum, the study of Qur'anic texts on buildings and objects is a rich field whose furrows we are only beginning to plough.

Bibliography

Bacqué-Grammont, Jean-Louis, Hans-Peter Laqueur, and Nicolas Vatin. *Stelae Turcicae II: cimetières de la mosquée de Sokollu Meḥmed Paşa à Kadirga Limani, de Bostanci Ali et du türbe de Sokollu Meḥmed Paşa à Eyüb*. Deutsches Archaologisches Institut, Abteilung Istanbul. Istanbul Mitteilungen 36. Tübingen: Ernst Wasmuth Verlag, 1990.

Berchem, Max van. *Matériaux pour un Corpus Inscriptionum Arabicarum*, part I, *Égypte 1*. 4 vols. Paris: Leroux and Cairo: Institut français d'Archéologie orientale du Caire, 1894–1903.

Berchem, Max van. *Matériaux pour un Corpus Inscriptionum Arabicarum*, part II, *Syrie du Sud*, vol. 1: *Jerusalem*. 3 vols. Cairo: Institut Français d'archéologie orientale du Caire, 1920–2.

Bierman, Irene A. *Writing Signs: The Fatimid Public Text*. Berkeley and Los Angeles: University of California Press, 1998.

Blair, Sheila S. Review of Erica Dodd and Shereen Khairallah, *The Image of the Word: A Study of Quranic Verses in Islamic Architecture*. Arabica 31/3 (November 1984), 337–42.

Blair, Sheila S. *Islamic Inscriptions*. Edinburgh: Edinburgh University Press, 1998.

Blair, Sheila S. 'Written, Spoken, Envisioned: The Many Facets of the Qur'an in Art'. In: Fahmida Suleman (ed.). *Word of God, Art of Man: The Qur'an and its Creative Expression*, pp. 271–84. Oxford: Oxford University Press in association with the Institute of Ismaili Studies, 2007.

Blair, Sheila S. 'Inscribing the Hajj'. In: Venetia Porter and Liana Saif (eds.). *The Hajj: Collected Essays*, pp. 157–65. London: British Museum Publications, 2013.

Blair, Sheila S. 'Inscribing the Square: The Inscriptions on the Maidan-i Shah in Isfahan'. In: Mohammad Gharipour and Irvin Cemil Schick (eds.). *Calligraphy in Islamic Architecture Space, Form and Function*, pp. 13–28. Edinburgh: Edinburgh University Press, 2014.

Blair, Sheila S. and Jonathan Bloom. 'Inscriptions in Art and Architecture'. In: Jane McAuliffe (ed.). *The Cambridge Companion to the Qur'ān*, pp. 163–78. Cambridge: Cambridge University Press, 2006.

Bloom, Jonathan M. 'The Mosque of al-Ḥākim in Cairo', *Muqarnas* 1 (1983), 15–36.

Combe, Étienne, Jean Sauvaget, and Gaston Wiet (eds.). *Répertoire chronologique d'épigraphie arabe*. Cairo: Institut français d'archéologie orientale, 1931ff.

Déroche, François. 'Cercles et entrelaces: formats et décor des corans Maghrébins médiévaux', *Académie des Inscriptions & Belles-Lettres: Comptes Rendus* (2001), 593–620.

Diem, Werner and Marco Schöller. *The Living and the Dead in Islam: Studies in Arabic Epitaphs*. 3 vols. Wiesbaden: Harrassowitz, 2004.

Dodd, Erica Cruikshank and Shereen Khairallah. *The Image of the Word: A Study of Quranic Verses in Islamic Architecture*. 2 vols. Beirut: American University in Beirut Press, 1981.

Ettinghausen, Richard. 'Arabic Epigraphy: Communication or Symbolic Affirmation'. In: Dickran Kouymjian (ed.). *Near Eastern Numismatics, Iconography, Epigraphy and History: Studies in Honor of George C. Miles*, pp. 297–317. Beirut: American University of Beirut Press, 1974.

Flood, Finbarr B. *Objects of Translation: Material Culture and Medieval 'Hindu-Muslim' Encounter*. Princeton: Princeton University Press, 2009.

Herzfeld, Ernst. *Matériaux pour un corpus inscriptionum arabicarum*, part II, *Syrie du Nord: Inscriptions et Monuments d'Alep*. 3 vols. Cairo: Institut Français d'archéologie orientale du Caire, 1954–5.

Hillenbrand, Robert. 'Qur'anic Epigraphy in Medieval Islamic Architecture', *Revue des Études Islamiques* 54 (Mélanges offerts au Professeur Dominique Sourdel) (1986), 171–87.

Hunarfar, Luṭfallah. *Ganjīna-yi āthār-i tārīkhī-yi iṣfahān*. Tehran, 1350/1978.

Johns, Jeremy. 'The Palermo Quran (AH 372/982–3 CE) and its Historical Context', In: Glaire Anderson, Corisande Fenwick, and Mariam Rosser-Owen (eds.). *The Aghlabids and their Neighbours: Art and Material Culture in Ninth-Century North Africa*, pp. 587–610. Leiden: Brill, 2018.

Kahil, Abdallah. 'The Delight and Amiability of Light in Mamluk Architecture'. In Jonathan M. Bloom and Sheila S. Balir (eds.). *God is the Light of the Heavens and the Earth: Light in Islamic Art and Culture*, Proceedings of the Fifth Biennial Hamad bin Khalifa Symposium on Islamic Art, pp. 231–55. London: Yale University Press, 2015.

Maddison, Francis and Emilie Savage-Smith. *Science, Tools & Magic*. 2 vols. Nasser D. Khalili Collection of Islamic Art V. Oxford: Nour Foundation in association with Azimuth Editions and Oxford University Press, 1997.

Merchant, Alnoor Jehangir. '"And the word of your Lord has been fulfilled in truthfulness and righteousness": Qur'ānic Inscriptions on Fatimid Coinage, AH 296–488/AD 909–1095'. In: Fahmida Suleman (ed.). *Word of God, Art of Man: The Qur'an and its Creative Expressions*, pp. 105–21. Oxford: Oxford University Press in association with the Institute of Ismaili Studies, 2007.

Necipoğlu, Gülru. 'Qur'ānic Inscriptions on Sinan's Imperial Mosques: A Comparison with their Safavid and Mughal Counterparts'. In: Fahmida Suleman (ed.). *Word of God, Art of Man: The Qur'an and its Creative Expressions*, pp. 69–104. Oxford: Oxford University Press in association with the Institute of Ismaili Studies, 2007.

Tabbaa, Yasser. 2001. *The Transformation of Islamic Art during the Sunni Revival*. Seattle and London: University of Washington Press.

Thesaurus d'épigraphie islamique. Directed by Ludvik Kalus and elaborated by Frédérique Soudan. Available on-line by subscription at <www.epigraphie-islamique.org>.

Wiet, Gaston. *Matériaux pour un Corpus Inscriptionum Arabicarum*, part I, *Égypte 2*. Cairo: Institut Français d'archéologie orientale du Caire, 1929–30.

Williams, Caroline. 'The Cult of ʿAlid Saints in the Fatimid Monuments of Cairo', *Muqarnas* 1 (1983), 37–52 and 3 (1985), 39–60.

Word of God, Art of Man: The Qur'an and its Creative Expressions. (ed.). Fahmida Suleman. Oxford: Oxford University Press in association with the Institute of Ismaili Studies, 2007.

Zbiss, Slimane Mostafa. *Corpus des Inscriptions arabes de Tunisie*. Tunis: Institut national d'archéologie et arts, 1955.

CHAPTER 16

A HISTORY OF PRINTED EDITIONS OF THE QUR'AN

EFIM A. REZVAN

THE Qur'an is a text which occupies the central place in a religious-philosophical system and has for many centuries played an important role in human history. This is one of the most published and widely read books in the world. Its total circulation accounts for many millions of copies. Centuries have passed since the appearance of the very first Qur'anic printed edition and mankind has endured a multitude of ideological shifts and cultural revolutions. Indeed, mass political and religious movements have followed one after the other; philosophical conceptions and schools have become popular only to be forgotten; and cultural orientations and priorities have changed. In one fashion or another, the history of manuscripts, editions, translations of the Qur'anic text has found its expression in major events, affecting the world.

In a short review it is impossible even to summarize the history of the Qur'anic text publications. I will try to present here the *key editions* that influenced the history of the publication of the sacred text and will concentrate on the *complete* Arabic Qur'an produced by means of *movable type or lithography* as well as on certain facsimile editions of prime importance. It was Levi Della Vida who around seventy years ago for the first time examined at length the phenomenon of the Muslim block print (Levi Della Vida 1944: 473–4). Quite recently Geoffrey Roper (2002) and Karl Schaefer (2006) have shown that since the tenth century Muslim block print was widely used to produce texts for mass distribution, such as Qur'anic extracts, the 'beautiful names' of God, incantations, etc. (Kresier 2001).

WESTERN EUROPE

The fifteenth–seventeenth centuries witnessed the bloody wars between Christendom and the Ottoman Empire, which by the first half of the sixteenth century had succeeded in expanding its territorial gains in Europe to their maximum extent. The siege of Vienna was a shock to the Europeans, almost as profound as was the fall of Constantinople in 1453. The image of the Saracen was replaced by the image of the Turk, whose religious fanaticism seemed even more menacing. In this connection it is striking to note that the first printed editions of the Arabic text and translation of the Qur'an in Europe appeared respectively only fourteen and twenty-seven years after the first printed edition of the Greek text of the New Testament. The latter was produced by Erasmus, and also in Basel, in 1516 (see Rezvan 1998b: 41–51).

In the period of Catholic counter-reformation, which was gaining an ever greater hold on Italy, the first European edition of the Arabic text of the Qur'an appeared in 1530 in Venice, the European gate to the Muslim world (see Carboni 2007). It was carried out by Paganini Brixiensis (Paganino de Bresla) (Lange and Ludwig 1703; Rossi 1806), and was destroyed almost as soon as it appeared. At first glance this act seems to be only one in a series of similar incidents which culminated in 1557, when the *Index Librorum Prohibitorum* ('Index of Forbidden books') was sent out by the papal curia. The 'Index' included the most significant works of Renaissance writers. Earlier fear of the growth and spread of heresies also led to repeated bans (four in the thirteenth century alone) on the reading of the Vulgate. The fears of the Holy See are more easily understood if one recalls the interest of Renaissance thinkers in the cultural achievements of the Islamic world, and the heretical Unitarian movement (Bobzin 2002: 151–76).

A copy of Paganini's work, which was thought to have been completely destroyed, was discovered in 1986 by Professor Angela Nuovo in the library of an Italian monastery close to Venice (Nuovo 1987: 237–71; see also Nuovo 2013). Her study shows that the cause of the destruction of the printed copy, intended for distribution among the Muslims, was mostly not censorship or bans, but the incompetence of the publishers. Errors in the sacred text made its sale impossible (Nallino 1965–6: 1–12; Borrmans 1990: 3–12; Nuovo 1987: 237–71; Rezvan 2001: 360–1): for instance, orthographically it fails to distinguish between *kasra* and *fatḥa*: both are placed above the text and look identical.

The very ideological atmosphere of the period was dominated by the fact that the initiative in polemics with Islam, as well as the study of Muslim faith, passed to Protestant theologians and publicists. Theodor Buchman (Bibliander) (1504–64) published almost the entire *Corpus Toletanum* (or *Collectio Toletana*), including the translation of the Qur'an, an entire series of anti-Islamic polemical treatises (among them the *Cribratio Alcorani* by Nicholas of Cusa (1401–64), and historical and geographical works on Turkey (Figure 16.1). This unusual encyclopaedia on Islam and Ottoman Turkey appeared in 1543 in Basel, which was permeated by an atmosphere of religious and cultural tolerance (Bibliander and Melanchthon 1543). The publication was made possible, however, only after the personal intervention of Martin Luther (Bobzin 1995; see Rezvan 2001: 362–3). The appendices in the work included an epistle of Pope Pius II (1405–64) to the Ottoman Sultan Mehmet II (r. 1451–81), which invited the latter to adopt Christianity, as well as an appeal from Luther and Philip Melanchthon (1497–1560).

Despite the polemical intent of Bibliander's edition, he himself noted Islam's role in the great mission of spreading monotheism among the pagans. He was also the

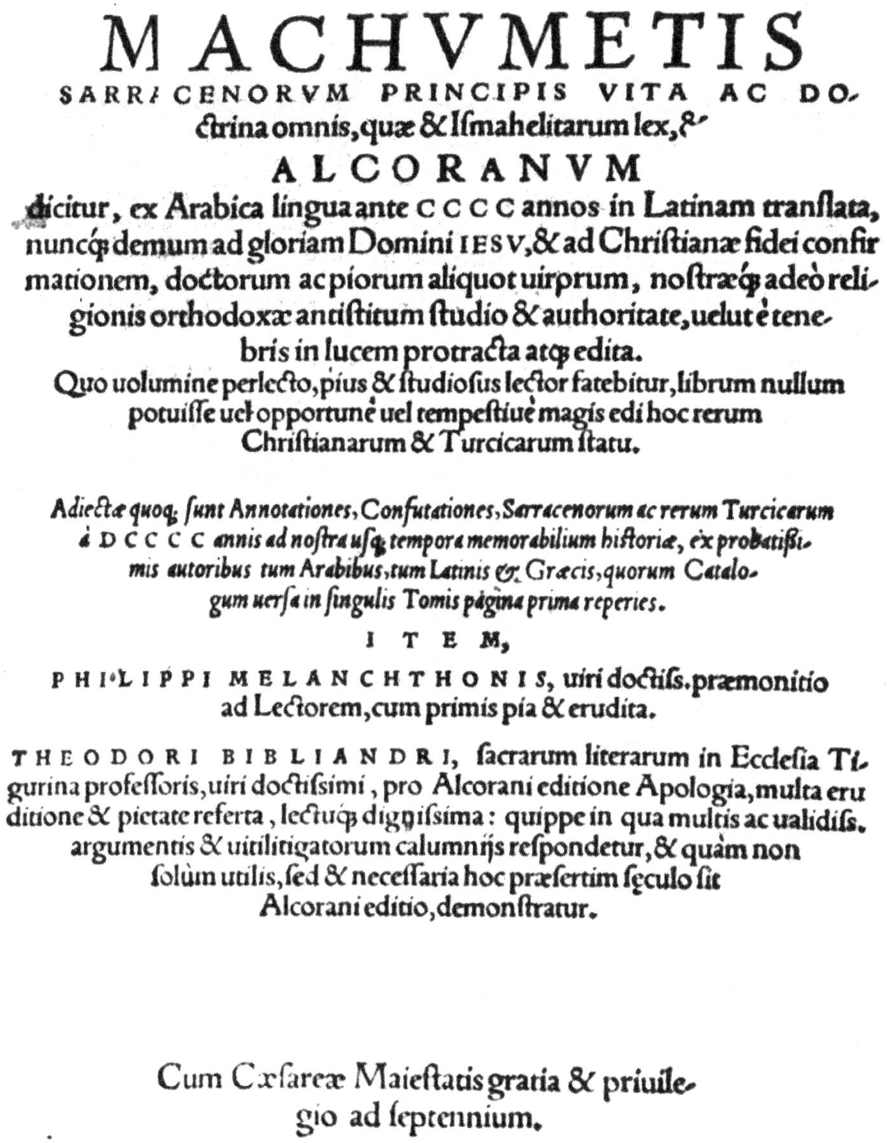

MACHVMETIS
SARRACENORVM PRINCIPIS VITA AC DOctrina omnis, quae & Ismahelitarum lex, &
ALCORANVM
dicitur, ex Arabica lingua ante CCCC annos in Latinam translata, nuncque demum ad gloriam Domini IESV, & ad Christianae fidei confirmationem, doctorum ac piorum aliquot uirprum, nostraeque adeò religionis orthodoxae antistitum studio & authoritate, uelut è tenebris in lucem protracta atque edita.
Quo uolumine perlecto, pius & studiosus lector fatebitur, librum nullum potuisse uel opportunè uel tempestiuè magis edi hoc rerum Christianarum & Turcicarum statu.

Adiectae quoque sunt Annotationes, Confutationes, Sarracenorum ac rerum Turcicarum à DCCCC annis ad nostra usque tempora memorabilium historiae, ex probatissimis autoribus tum Arabibus, tum Latinis & Graecis, quorum Catalogum uersa in singulis Tomis pagina prima reperies.

ITEM,

PHILIPPI MELANCHTHONIS, uiri doctiss. praemonitio ad Lectorem, cum primis pia & erudita.

THEODORI BIBLIANDRI, sacrarum literarum in Ecclesia Tigurina professoris, uiri doctissimi, pro Alcorani editione Apologia, multa eruditione & pietate referta, lectuque dignissima: quippe in qua multis ac ualidiss. argumentis & uitilitigatorum calumnijs respondetur, & quàm non solùm utilis, sed & necessaria hoc praesertim seculo sit Alcorani editio, demonstratur.

Cum Caesareae Maiestatis gratia & priuilegio ad septennium.

FIGURE 16.1 The title page of Theodor Bibliander and Philip Melanchthon (eds.). *Machumetis Saracenorum principis, eiusque successorum vitae doctrina ac, ipse Alcoran*... Basel: Ioannes Oporinus, 1543. The Austrian National Library (19.B.40). Courtesy of the Library.

author of a work in which he addresses all Christians, Jews, and Muslims with a greeting and wishes of peace and prosperity 'in the name of God, our Lord' (Bergmann 1980: 29–30). Such views were quite widespread in the period. Sometimes the distinction between Islam and monotheistic religions was regarded as not so significant. Luther, for example, considered Islam as a form of Judaism, while Erasmus (1469–1536) and Guillaume Postel (1510–81) viewed Muslims as half-Christian.

Although Bibliander did not know Arabic well enough to correct the Toledo translation, he had at his disposal several manuscripts of the Qur'an, including that with noted *qirāʾāt* (readings) in the margins. (It has survived at Basel, Ms. A III 19, see Bobzin 1996: 161.)

The Vatican's response under Pope Alexander VII (1599–1667) was to decree by a council of Roman censors a ban on the publication and translation of the Qur'an. (Alexander VII's actions led to the decline of the Collège de la Propagation which was founded in Rome in 1627 by Pope Urban VIII (1623–44). It had become one of the most important European centres of Oriental studies.) However, after the Arabic text of the book was published in 1694 by the Protestant theologian and Orientalist Abraham Hinckelmann the Vatican finally realized the uselessness of a ban which granted the Protestants the upper hand in anti-Islamic propaganda (Hinckelmann 1694, see Braun 1959: 149–66; Aboussouan 1982: 135–6; see Albin *EQ* 4:264f fig. i, p. 615).

In Padua in 1698, Ludovico Marracci (1612–1700), confessor of Pope Innocent XI (1611–89), published a Latin translation and Arabic text of the Qur'an based on the collation of several manuscripts (Figure 16.2). The Arabic text was arbitrarily divided into small fragments and followed by a translation equipped with commentaries and excerpts from Arabic *tafsīrs* both in the original and in Latin translation, and then by a refutation (Marracci 1698; see Levi Della Vida 1959: 193–210; Denison Ross 1921–3: 117–23). The quality of this translation was incomparably higher than those which had come to light before, but the form of the edition prevented it from gaining widespread popularity. The appearance of such a fine translation in Italy was no accident, as Italy had long enjoyed the most highly developed commercial and cultural contacts with the Muslim East. Italy, with her rich libraries, boasted a superb scholarly tradition encumbered only by ideological prohibitions. However, with the appearance of the Marracci edition, it seemed that the Holy See had regained its position of leadership in the study and refutation of Islam. But Christian Reineccius (1668–1752), a German Protestant, recovered the initiative for Protestant scholars by releasing a convenient edition which included only the text of the Marracci translation and an aptly composed introduction (Marracci 1721; for reproduction of the folios from Marracci edition, see Rezvan 2001: 367 and Albin *EQ* 4:264f. fig. ii, p. 616). Marracci's work ushered in an entire series of new translations of the Qur'an into European languages.

Russia

A new period in the history of the publication of the Qur'an was connected with Russia and the activities of Catherine II (1729–1796). A number of victorious wars against Ottoman

8

سورة البقرة مكية مايتان وست وثمانون آية

SURA II.

VACCA.

MECCANA COMMATUM CCLXXXVI.

بسم الله الرحمن الرحيم

Refutationes in Suram II. Alcorani. 9

In Nomine Dei Miseratoris Misericordis.

1. A. L. M. 2. Iste Liber, non est dubium de eo, *quin sit à Deo*: directio timentibus *eum*. 3. Qui credunt in Arcanum, & stare faciunt orationem (*idest observant tempora ejus:*) & ex eo quod in sustentaculum præbuimus illis, erogant *in eleemosynam*. 4. Et qui credunt in id, quod demissum est ad te (*idest Alcoranum*,) & *in id*, quod demissum fuit ante te (*idest Pentateuchum*, *Psalterium*, & *Evangelium*:) & in novissimum sæculum ipsi firmiter credunt. 5. Hi erunt super directionem (*idest dirigentur*) à Domino suo; & hi erunt felices. 6. Porrò qui infideles sunt; æquale *erit* super eos (*idest unum atque idem erit illis*) sive prædicaveris eis, sive non prædicaveris eis: non credent. 7. Sigillum impressit Deus super corda eorum, & super auditum eorum: & super [a] aspectus eorum *est* cooperimentum: & ipsis *erit* pœna magna. 8. Et ex hominibus aliquis dicit: Credidimus in Deum, & in diem novissimum: & non ipsi cum credentibus (*idest & tamen non credunt.*) [a] *oculos.*

9. Deceptoriè agunt, cum Deo, & *cum iis* qui crediderant, & non decipiunt nisi animas suas, & non sentiunt *hoc*. 10. In cordibus eorum *est* morbus: auxitque illis Deus morbum: & ipsis *erit* pœna discrucians pro eo quod mentiti sunt. 11. Et cùm dictum fuerit eis: Ne corrumpatis in terra; respondebunt: Certè quod nos *sumus* [b] redintegrantes. 12. An non certè ipsi sunt corruptores? Verumtamen non sentiunt *se esse tales*. 13. Et cùm dictum fuerit eis: Credite, sicut crediderunt homines: respon- [b] *resarcientes.*

FIGURE 16.2 Bifolio from Ludovico Marracci, *Alcorani textus universus:ex correctioribus Arabum exemplaribus summa fide, atque pulcherrimis characteribus descriptus*. Patavii: Ex Typographia Seminarii, 1698. The Austrian National Library (14.L.36). Courtesy of the Library.

Turkey and the subsequent annexation of the Crimea, in 1783, and other regions with a Muslim population demanded urgent measures in the organization of their administration and in the pacification of the new subjects. All this led to the appearance in the 1775 Manifesto entitled 'On Favours Royally Granted to Certain Estates on the Occasion of Peace Concluded with the Ottoman Porte', and especially in the 1785 edict on religious tolerance, of a number of articles guaranteeing and regulating the rights of Muslims within the Russian state.

In 1782 a *muftiyat* was founded in the Russian fortress of Ufa. Within six years, the Orenburg Mohammedan Religious Council was created and Muslim clerics for the first time received the official status of a religious estate (similar to the Orthodox Church). Mosques began to be built, including one in Moscow (1782), and Muslim religious schools were opened at that time too. Many Tatar *mūrzās* and Bashkir elders were accepted into the nobility (*dvorianstvo*) (1784), and Muslim merchants were granted privileges to trade with Turkestan, Iran, India, and China.

By the 1787 decree of Catherine II, the full Arabic text of the Qur'an was printed for the first time in Russia at the privately owned 'Asiatic Press' in St. Petersburg. It was intended for free distribution to the 'Kirghiz'. (The St. Petersburg edition consists of 447 pages plus a one-page list of *errata*). Thirteen corrections are given; the errors involve diacritics, not letters. The *errata* are given in Tatar (See also *Russkiy gosudarstvenniy istoricheskiy arkhiv* The Russian State Historical Archive; henceforth, RGIA). At the same time, the 'prayer from a part of the Alkuran' was apparently published in an edition of 10,000 copies (RGIA, fund 1329, inventory 4, file 296, fols. 3–4 (1 July 1797). Simultaneously an order was issued to construct mosques at the state's expense. In Catherine's own words, these measures were undertaken 'not to introduce Mohammedism, but as bait to lure [the Kirghiz]'. The Qur'an was published at state expense, partly to assuage Tatar complaints about the high cost of the books they acquired abroad. The Qur'an was printed with a typeface cast especially for this purpose. According to Friedrich Theodor Rink, Mullā ʿUthmān Ismāʿīl, the best expert in the field Russian authorities could find, provided the publisher, J. K. Schnoor, with the most beautiful and exact copies of the letters, from which, under his supervision, or rather, correction, the new Arabic typesetting was created (Rink 1809: 129–41). The new typeface surpassed all Arabic typefaces then in use in European printing-presses (see Catherine II, Empress of Russia 1803: 137). The edition also differed fundamentally from previous European printings in its Muslim character: the text was prepared for publication and equipped with a detailed marginal commentary by the same Mullā ʿUthmān Ismāʿīl. Between 1789 and 1798, this Qur'an went through five editions (various sources indicate that the run was either 1,200 or 3,600 copies). Later, the state treasury earned a tidy profit on the sale of Qur'ans. According to one of the documents, the production cost of the edition was 9,292 rubles, 25 kopecks. Profits from sales came to 12,000 rubles at a single-copy cost of six rubles, five kopecks. Two factors determined the commercial success of this and subsequent 'Kazan Qur'an' editions (Figure 16.3): their Muslim character and high-quality printing.

(For reproduction of the folios from Kazan editions, see Rezvan 1999: figs. 6–7 and Albin *EQ* 4:264f. fig. iii, pp. 617–18.).

The Qur'an's publication in Russia was actively exploited by Catherine in her foreign policy, especially during the war with Turkey, which gave the Empress an opportunity to present herself as a patron of Islam (see e.g. Catherine II, Empress of Russia 1803: 124–5). Catherine's initiatives encountered opposition from missionary circles, where the Qur'an continued to be viewed primarily as a 'harmful false teaching' which contradicted the Christian faith. Catherine was accused of strengthening the hold of Islam on the Tatars by publishing the Qur'an. On the whole, however, the Empress kept on with her policy of aiding the noticeable growth of central power in the outlying Muslim regions of the Empire. Merchants of Russian Muslim origin acted as liaisons between Russia and its Muslim neighbours, significantly aiding the former's penetration into Asia. Muslims began to serve in large numbers in the Russian army and navy, where the special positions of *mullā*, *ākhūnd*, and *mūʾadhdhin* were created for their spiritual significance.

By the decree of 15 December 1800, restrictions on the publication of Islamic religious literature were lifted in Russia. In 1801–2, the Arabic typeface of the St. Petersburg press was transferred to Kazan, where one year earlier, at the request of the Kazan Tatars, the Asiatic Press had been established at the Kazan gymnasium. In 1861, the Minister of Education deemed it advantageous for Muslims to print the Qur'an exclusively at the university press. The Ministry of Internal Affairs disagreed, citing a statute approved by the Council of Ministers on 25 October 1849 which permitted the printing of Qur'ans in privately owned presses. An edition of the Qur'an, marked with the year 1801 and closely resembling the St. Petersburg Qur'an, was published there. Copies of this edition, published 'at the expense of Yunusov' and, somewhat later, 'at the expense of Amir-Khanov' (16 February 1859), including later reprints, were generally termed Kazan Qur'ans. In 1829, the press was united with the university press; until nearly 1840 it was in fact the only press with the right to publish Muslim religious literature.

These editions, which earned high praise from European Orientalists, went through many print runs and, in essence, supplemented previous European editions of the Qur'an. The so-called 'Kazan Qur'ans', seen as the first Muslim edition of its type, became widespread in the East and were reproduced many times (manuscript copies have also been attested). In the opinion of Régis Blachère, they may have played a decisive role in the centuries-long process of establishing a unified text of the Qur'an (Blachère 1977: 133; on the 'Kazan Qur'ans' see Khalīdūf 2008; Schnurrer 1811: 418–20; Röhling 1977: 205–10). One of the publisher's achievements was the inclusion of Qur'anic variants (*al-qirāʾāt*) which featured the tradition of the 'seven readings' in the edition of 1857 alongside the basic text of the Ḥafṣ version. This was a unique attempt to draw closer to a critical edition; the attempt was subsequently repeated in a number of Eastern reprints (for details see Rezvan 1999: 32–51).

Catherine the Great's project, conceived as an openly colonial endeavour, was continued as the result of a special confluence of historical circumstances. By the mid-nineteenth

٢

سورة فاتحة الكتاب

بسم الله الرحمن الرحيم
الحمد لله رب العالمين ۞ الرحمن الرحيم ۞
مالك يوم الدين ۞ اياك نعبد واياك نستعين ۞
اهدنا الصراط المستقيم ۞ صراط الذين انعمت
عليهم ۞ غير المغضوب عليهم ولا الضالين ۞

العز يز سبع ايات مكية

سورة فاتحة الكتاب العز يز
سبع ايات اختلف العلماء فى
نزولها على قولين احدها
انها مكية والثانى انها مدنية
وتسمى ام القران وام الكتاب
والسبع المثانى والبسملة عند
الامام الشافعى رحمه الله وكلا
مها مائة وعشرون كلمة وحرو
فها مائة وثلث وعشرون حرفا

قرا عاصم والكساى مالك يوم
الدين بالالف وقرا الباقون
بغير الف ملك يوم الدين

قرا قنبل السراط فى جميع
القران بالسين واخلف بالزا
ى الزراط والاشمام وخلاد
انها هنا خاصة فى الاول والبا
قون بالصاد خالصة
قراءة عليهم بضم الهاء وابن
كثير وقالون بضم الميم التى
للجمع وبصلا نها بواو مع الهمز
ة وغيرها والباقون بكسر
الهاء عليهم

FIGURE 16.3 Page 2 of the standard 'Kazan Qur'an' which reproduced the Saint Petersburg edition published, following the 1787 decree of Catherine II, at the privately owned 'Asiatic Press' in St. Petersburg.

century, Kazan, the main centre of Russian Muslim life, had become one of the major intellectual capitals of Islam, and in a number of areas could compete with such cities as Istanbul, Cairo, and Beirut. This process was aided by the educational sophistication of the indigenous population and the ideas of religious and political rebirth which had engulfed not only the upper levels of the Muslim intelligentsia but the broad masses as well. The expansion of Russia into Central Asia was accompanied by the active penetration of the region by Tatar merchants and commercial capital. The products of Kazan printing presses were among the main goods on the book markets of Bukhara, Samarqand, and Tashkent. One could easily find Qur'ans printed in Kazan in Iran, Afghanistan, and India. Russian pilgrims brought them along to the Ḥijāz and they were used in the houses built with Russian money in Mecca for Russian Muslims. They dominated markets in spite of the growing competition from the British-Indian publications (compare: Roper 1985: 12–32; Roper 1989: 226–33; see also Wilson 2014). The first publication of the Arabic Qur'an in London (1833) was followed by Lucknow (first dated by 1850), Bombay (first dated by 1852), and Calcutta (first appeared in 1856) editions. Several of these editions included the *tafsīr* by al-Zamakhsharī (d. 538/1144) or Persian interlinear translations (Sarkīs 1928).

Yet there was a moment when the fate of the Kazan Qur'ans hung by a thread. In 1849, the procurator of the Holy Synod appealed to Tsar Nicholas I (1796–1855) with a request that the printing of Qur'ans in Kazan be halted, as they led to the exit of baptized Tatars from the Orthodox Church. The appeal stated that in the course of one year a single private press in Kazan had published 200,000 Qur'ans. The Tsar's resolution ran: 'The printing of the Qur'ans and other Muslim spiritual books can be banned.' While the matter was referred to the Committee of Ministers for review (*RGIA*, fund 1263, inventory 1, file 2033 (11 October 1849), fols. 12–19), the Kazan military governor reported that actually, between 1841 and 1846, only 26,000 copies of the full text of the Qur'an and its parts had been printed in two private Kazan presses. The number of other Muslim books of a religious character came to 45,000. The same figures for the Kazan University Press for the period 1841–9 came to 33,000 and 36,000. It was also acknowledged that both the Qur'an and the religious books were printed in a language that the great majority of Tatars did not know. Furthermore, the bulk of the editions was dispatched beyond the bounds of the Volga basin and made up a significant portion of Russia's trade with the states of Central Asia, where high-quality Russian editions had captured the market. To stop the printing of Muslim books in Kazan would, in the opinion of the Committee of Ministers, hand the initiative in the sale of such books to the English and lead to contraband within Russia. The ban would make obtaining the Qur'an even more important to Muslims and also result in their common animosity against Christianity. No direct connection was noticed between the rise in Muslim book printing and the readoption of Islam by baptized Tatars. The printing of the Qur'ans and other books on Islam was continued, although censorship became more strict, so that published books would not contain 'any harmful interpretations or ruminations against the government or Orthodox Christianity' (*RGIA*, fund 1263, inventory 1, file 2033

(11 October 1849), fol. 18). It was the Great Game (1813–1907), strategic rivalry between the British and the Russian Empires for supremacy in Central Asia, which gathered its strength, and the extremely successful project of 'Kazan Qur'ans' served as an important context in the conflict.

In 1869, Russian Turkestan Governor-General K. P. von Kaufmann (1818–82) handed over to the Public Library in St. Petersburg the so-called ʿUthmānic Qur'an, or the 'Samarqand Kufic Qur'an', which had belonged to the Khwāja Akhrār Mosque in Samarqand. It is no doubt one of the most outstanding copies of the Qur'an in the world. A. F. Shebunin (1867–?), Russian scholar and diplomat, described and analysed the copy in detail. He established its indubitable Near Eastern origins (presumably Iraq) and time of compilation (second century). Shebunin's work in many ways presaged the later ideas of G. Bergsträsser and A. Jeffery on the necessity of developing a project for the classification of early Qur'anic manuscripts.

In 1905, a traced facsimile of this manuscript was published in St. Petersburg by S. I. Pisarev in the form of a gigantic, full-size folio (on this edition and other copies of the 'Uthmānic Qur'an, see Rezvan 1998a: 47) (Figure 16.4). Only a small part of the print run of fifty copies made its way onto the book market. For many years the edition was a popular diplomatic gift presented by the Russian government to promote relations with countries in the Muslim East. In 1942, A. Jeffery and I. Mendelsohn, with reference to S. I. Pisarev's edition, conducted a detailed analysis of the copy in accordance with new scholarly standards (Jeffery and Mendelsohn 1942: 175–94). They had at their disposal the Cairo edition of the Qur'an, while A. F. Shebunin studied the orthography of the copy in comparison with the Flügel edition, the most authoritative edition of its time. This explains the fact that the number of variant readings revealed by Jeffery and Mendelsohn is significantly fewer than noted by Shebunin.

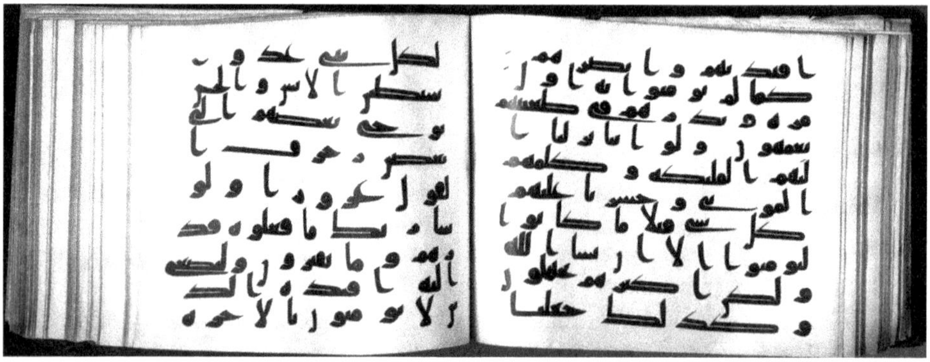

FIGURE 16.4 Bifolio from the full-size traced facsimile of 'Samarqand Kūfic Qur'an', which was published in St. Petersburg.

The so-called 'Qur'ans of ʿUthmān' remained symbols of power over centuries (Rezvan 2008: 21–7). In 2011 at the 4th Biennial Ḥamad bin Khalīfa symposium on Islamic art held in Qatar, François Déroche presented a detailed and useful description of the twenty folios from the Samarqand copy preserved now in Doha (Déroche 2013: 59–77). Unfortunately, he paid no attention to the recent studies of the history of the manuscript. In 1243, the Egyptian *sultan* Baybars sent the *khān* of the Golden Horde Berke a letter of 'accession to citizenship and subjugation'. Soon the Egyptian ambassadors brought presents to the Horde: clothes of honour, a throne incrusted with ebony, ivory, and silver and the 'Qur'an of 'Uthmān'. In April of 1391 in the battle at the river Kondurcha Tīmūr defeated the army of the Golden Horde. His warriors ransacked the whole Lower Volga region and Sarāy-Bātū, capital of the Golden Horde, and obtained vast loot. We have every reason to believe that Tīmūr brought to Samarqand the sacred copy once delivered to the Golden Horde from Egypt. It embodied the power of Mamluk Sultans of the Bahrid dynasty, that of Golden Horde rulers and Timurids who passed it to Naqshbandiyya brotherhood. The manuscript played an important role in the rise of authority of Naqshbandiyya led by Khwāja Aḥrār.

Undoubtedly, bringing the Samarqand relic to St. Petersburg also had symbolic significance. This was confirmed by the relocation to Russia of supreme power over Turkestan. The governor-general of Turkestan at the time, von Kaufmann, saw to this personally. It was also planned to send a giant stone stand (*lawḥ*) to the capital of the Empire. The *lawḥ* stood in the courtyard of the Bībī Khānum mosque and was once used as a pedestal for another Qur'an symbolizing power that was created by order of Tīmūr. In 1918, by order of Lenin, the manuscript was handed over to the regional Muslim congress. It was delivered to Ufa, and later to Tashkent. The handing over of the manuscript to Muslims was also a symbolic gesture. This meant the handing over of part of power in exchange for participation in the 'revolutionary project'. In 1921 the Scientific Association of Russian Orientalists declared 'Moscow is the new Mecca; it is the Medina of all repressed peoples'. In reality, the manuscript only reached Muslims (the Religious Administration of Muslims in Tashkent) after Uzbekistan gained independence.

A great success was the acquisition in 1937 by the Leningrad Institute of Oriental Studies of a significant fragment of the Qur'an (approximately 40 per cent of the text) in Ḥijāzī script. It appeared to be another copy of the ʿUthmānic Qur'an and the symbol of power. The studied part of its history was also connected with the struggle for power, first of all between Shaybanids and Timurids (see Rezvan 2004). Finally, before the Russian president Putin's visit to Saudi Arabia (February 2007), the manuscript was made in Russia on thin gold plates costing 'tens of millions of roubles'. Fourteen kilograms of triple-nine gold was used in the manufacture of the 'book' (163 gold pages around 14 cm high and around 10 cm wide) at the Russian Mint. The Golden Qur'an was meant to symbolize the fact that Russia is a world power with a Muslim population of many millions, whose relics and traditions are genuinely respected and honoured (Rezvan 2008: 26).

The Idea of a Critical Edition

The emergence in Germany in the second half of the eighteenth century of classical philology had a huge impact on scholarship. In conjunction with the successes of German biblical studies, it led to the pre-eminence of German scholars in the study of the Qur'an, a trend established in the nineteenth century. First, Gustav Flügel published a new, correlated text of the Qur'an (1834) and then a concordance to it (1842); they retained their value until the mid-twentieth century. A number of publications were edited by G. Redslob (1837, 1855, 1867), who continued the work of Flügel (Flügel and Redslob 1867; Flügel 1842; see also Smitskamp 1410/1995: 533–5). Such scholarship also served political purposes, although the German contribution to the study of the Qur'an was colossal.

In 1927, G. Bergsträsser and A. Jeffery together developed a plan for a critical edition of the Qur'an, since the Flügel edition of the Qur'anic text had revealed the complex character of the textological problems in this area. The text published by Flügel did not contain an *apparatus criticus* and the scholar did not follow any single Muslim tradition of textual transmission. The principles he employed in preparing his publication have remained unclear up to the present day. The plan for a critical edition developed by G. Bergsträsser and A. Jeffery included (i) excerpting from various sources Qur'anic variants; (ii) finding and publishing manuscripts of basic works by Muslim authors on the problems of Qur'anic readings (*al-qirāʾāt*); and (iii) creating a photo archive of the oldest copies of the Qur'an and their study. The scholars intended to base their text on that of Ḥafṣ (which also served as the basis for the Egyptian edition), but to take into account the characteristics of *sajʿ* in publishing it. They also planned to number the *āyāt* in accordance with both the Muslim tradition and Flügel. The text was to contain pausal signs and, in the margins, references to 'parallel passages'. The *apparatus criticus* was to have been located at the bottom of the page and consist of references to hundreds of variants of the text with a three-tiered chronological indication of their source: earlier than the tradition of the 'seven readings', belonging to that tradition, or later. They also hoped to indicate the school (or schools) to which 'readings' belonged.

The scholars planned also to release in a separate volume an 'Introduction' which would replace the '*Geschichte des Qorāns*' by T. Nöldeke, F. Schwally, G. Bergsträsser, and O. Pretzl. A third volume would have contained an extensive commentary on the *apparatus criticus*. Certainly, the authors understood the impossibility of taking into account all existing variants, but they planned to work with the main sources on the issue. A fourth volume would have provided a dictionary to the Qur'an. Although an enormous amount of preparatory work was done, for a variety of reasons the authors were unable to bring their project to completion (see Rezvan 1998a: 27; Jeffery 1935: 4–16; Jeffery 1937; Jeffery 1947: 35–49; Jeffery 1950: 41–55). In this regard, experts increasingly began to turn to the oldest existing copies of the sacred text.

Research and findings in the 1970s and 1980s convincingly demonstrate that the works of medieval Muslim authorities, as well as texts based on them by European scholars of the late nineteenth century and first half of the twentieth century, reveal only a part of a significantly more diverse and contradictory history of the sacred text's fixation. A discussion of J. Wansbrough's *Quranic Studies: Sources and Methods of Scriptural Interpretation*' showed that research based on the Muslim tradition is no longer capable at present of providing unambiguous answers to questions connected with the early history of the Qur'anic text (Rippin 1985: 228). The main problem was the fact that the study of the Muslim tradition took place in isolation from the description and study of actual Qur'anic manuscripts. This gap led, in large part, to the methodological crisis which Qur'anic studies experienced in the late 1970s and early 1980s.

A substantial number of the Qur'anic fragments which have reached us contain unique information on the initial period of the sacred text's existence. They preserved for us the most important elements of the authentic history of the establishment of the text. It was Professor Sergio Noja Noseda who at the very end of the 1990s initiated a realization of the bold and ambitious project entitled 'Sources de la transmission manuscrite du texte coranique', which aimed to publish the most important early Qur'anic manuscripts (see Déroche and Noseda 1998 and 2001). After the publication of the second volume Professor Noseda decided to change the title of the project to 'Early Qurʾāns: The Era of the Prophet, the Rightly-Guided Caliphs and the Umayyades' and continued it mostly alone. A new series should have started with the volume 'Fragments'. It included the fragments scattered in various libraries (Vaticana, Leiden, Philadelphia, Cairo, Chicago, Vienna, Berlin). The volume was ready to be printed; Professor Noseda finished the introduction to it, but on 31 January 2008, he died following a car accident in Italy. Following the death of Professor Noseda, Dr Keith Small continued the preparation of this volume. Another goal of Professor Noseda was the publication of the existing papyri fragments. This volume also remained half finished. Professor Noseda was also working on the famous palimpsest of Ṣanʿāʾ, and the other two early codices which were photographed by his team in October 2007 (Palimpsest 01-27.1 + MS 01-25.1 + MS 01-29.1). The entire Yemeni project was continued by Professor Christian Robin after Professor Noseda's death. The work continues now in cooperation between the French and the German ('Corpus Coranicum') sides. The publication of the Ṣanʿāʾ palimpsest and British Library volumes was announced in 2012 by Brill as a part of the new series 'Documenta Coranica'. A closely related project was started at the same time in the Soviet Union, but the collapse of the country put the brakes on its realization. (The goal was to publish early Qur'anic manuscripts mostly from Leningrad and Tashkent collections, see Rezvan 2004. The second part of the task was realized by F. Déroche, see Déroche 2009).

The publication of a Qur'anic text which differs from the *rasm ʿUthmānī* seems at present unproductive, in the first place because the entire complex of Muslim religious disciplines is based on that very edition. Such a text would become a 'second Flügel Qur'an'; it would never be recognized by the Muslim tradition. The reconstruction of some original form of the text is today of lesser interest; more important for our studies is the history of the text's consolidation and the evolution of its interpretation in various eras and areas of the Muslim world.

Muslim Orient

Block-printing techniques for the reproduction of text, graphics, and images were known and widely used in the Islamic world, primarily for the manufacture of amulets (e.g. bronze matrix for amulet printing (Iran, eighteenth to nineteenth centuries). However, these technologies made no further progress and the development of the medieval Islamic manuscript tradition was completed only in the nineteenth century. Under the influence of centuries-old tradition, movable type printing did not become popular immediately. It was lithography which served as a transition stage to typography. The rise of lithography was closely connected with the interests of a very large army of craftsmen connected with handwritten books, mostly scribes, who began to execute new orders and played an active role in the production of lithographs. The first lithographic Qur'ans appeared in the Muslim world (Ottoman Turkey, Egypt, Iran) around the 1820s. Reforms of Muḥammad ʿAlī in Egypt caused the first attempts to publish the Qur'an by means of metal type as early as 1833, but in reality the Muslim world became familiar with the considerable printings of the Qur'an only after the 1860s (Gdoura 1985; Albin *EQ* 4:267–72; see the works of Roper cited in the bibliography).

The final stage of work on the unification of the Qur'anic text is connected with the appearance in Cairo in 1919, 1923, and 1928 of a new edition of the text, completed under the patronage of the Egyptian King Fuʾād I (1868–1936) (for details see ʿAbd al-Fattāḥ al-Qāḍī 1968). The edition, which represents at present the final step in canonizing the orthography, structure of the text, and rules of reading, was drawn up by a special collegium of Muslim scholars. Work on this edition was preceded by a complete loss of interest in Qur'anic 'variants' (*al-qirāʾāt*) by Egyptian modernists. The edition was based on one of the 'seven readings', the most popular in the Muslim world at that time, namely, the Ḥafṣ ʿan ʿĀṣim 'reading'. The members of the collegium relied in their work not on an analysis of early manuscripts, but on contemporary Muslim works on the issue of 'readings' (*al-qirāʾāt*). This undoubtedly narrows the significance of the work. Nonetheless, the Egyptian edition, today accepted throughout the Muslim world as well as by European scholars, represented a significant step forward in the study of the text (Bergsträsser 1932: 1–42; Bergsträsser 1933: 110–40; see also Milo 2009: 492–521).

As had been the case earlier, the work of Muslim authorities on the Qur'anic text was not isolated from processes and changes then taking place in the Islamic world. The activities of Muslim reformers, who strove to renew Islam by reviving the great Islamic traditions, were then at a peak. In this connection, the creation of a canonical text of the Qur'an seemed a pressing matter of primary importance in establishing the unity of the Muslim world. It was then that the dissolution of the Sultanate in Turkey (1922) first separated the office of the caliphate from secular power and later abolished it (1924), events seen by many Muslims as a catastrophe. The publication of the Qur'an in Latin script, undertaken nearly at the same time in Turkey in the framework of the 'Turkization' and the politics of modernization, became a real challenge to tradition (see also Albin *EQ* 4:275, for a further effort to produce the Qur'anic text in romanized form published in 1973 in Jakarta).

In extending his patronage to the new edition of the Qur'an, Fuʾād I, who had become the leader of the largest Muslim state, manifested ambitious designs. Furthermore, successful work on the Qur'anic text was intended to demonstrate the priority of Muslim scholars over Western Orientalists in this field of such overwhelming importance to the Islamic world.

Since then Cairo continues to be one of the most important centres of Qur'an printing. In 1977 al-Azhar established a special press for printing the Qur'an and religious works. Eight years later the King Fahd Holy Qur'an Printing Complex, one of the world's largest printing complexes with a production capacity of ten million copies per year, was established near Medina. The years of 1984–5 were largely a milestone for the kingdom: because the Afghan war and the ability to influence the world with oil prices dramatically increased its importance in international affairs. The diplomatic representatives of foreign countries were transferred from Jeddah to Riyadh, the capital; a citizen of Saudi Arabia for the first time became the President of 'Aramco'; Saudi Prince Salmān Āl Saʿūd became the first Arab astronaut. Construction of the huge printing house was intended to mark the new role of the kingdom in the Islamic world. Free copies of the Qur'an were distributed among pilgrims and sent to mosques and other Islamic institutions worldwide, underlining the kingdom's worldwide ambitions.

Still, the appearance of the Egyptian edition, which has become the most widely distributed edition in the Muslim world, did not signify the complete disappearance of other traditions of textual transmission. In the west of the Muslim world and in Zaydite Yemen, traditions were preserved which go back to a different transmitter of the text—Warsh (d. 197/812). Today, publications of the Qur'an in this transmission appear not only in North Africa, but in Cairo and Saudi Arabia. Meanwhile, the Qur'an was published in Tunisia in a redaction which goes back to Ḥafṣ (Brockett 1988: 31–45).

New Information Technologies

Modern European innovations in Qur'an printing are primarily connected with the new information technologies that can help to develop fonts based on the manuscript tradition. Thomas Milo (Decotype, the Netherlands) is now the leader in the field. He was the first to realize that, on the graphical side, conventional Arabic computer typography does not handle traditional Arabic styles. He suggested that to design historically accurate Arabic typefaces, fundamental research into style-dependent contextual behaviour is a prerequisite. According to him, the resulting analysis will be a script grammar—the resulting font a script synthesis. Each major classic Islamic style needs to be described in this manner.

On the logistic side, the Arabic script as encoded by the Unicode Consortium only reflects the modern situation where letters consist of a skeleton base plus a disambiguating diacritic. However, the first generation Qur'an text is written in an earlier form of Arabic script where the disambiguation marks behave like independent characters, added to the text by different people in different moments of time, often with different colours. To reproduce the state of historical Qur'an texts accurately in the Unicode standard no independent dot diacritics are available as marks for combining with ambiguous *rasm* letters. As a result it is impossible to reproduce digitally passages where the same base letters are marked with one or more alternative, mutually exclusive disambiguation marks. Moreover, later Qur'anic orthography introduces a series of corrective (e.g. *hamza* on chair) and suppletive (e.g. *hamza* without its chair) diacritics to complete the original primary text. The category of suppletive diacritic is not on the radar of scholars, not known to the Unicode Consortium, and consequently not supported by any font technology. As a result of the combined defects observed above, logically integral and correctly shaped Qur'an text in any modern or historic orthography for information interchange and research is presently impossible. Instead existing text encoding uses multiple, incompatible *ad hoc* solutions that preclude text search or quotation at the web level. The current aim is to address the shortcomings of encoding and to create typefaces based on handwriting to be used for production of 'historical' editions of the Qur'an based on the script grammar and form system of the earliest Kūfī and Ḥijāzī fragments (see Milo 2005: 494–515; Milo 2012: 249–92).

Located in Medina, the King Fahd Holy Qur'an Printing Complex, mentioned above, seeks to use in the work all the best that is available in publishing today. 'Muṣḥaf al-Madina', the original copy of which was created by ʿUthmān Ṭāhā, is now the most widespread in the world. Since 1985 the Complex has produced over 200 million copies of the Qur'an, adding about 10 million copies per year. It has published also 55 different translations of the Qur'an in 39 languages. Its website (<http://www.qurancomplex.org/>; <http://www.youtube.com/watch?v=VY4Eg8_smEs>) presents material of a different kind, including: 'Font Computing Collection', 'Muṣḥaf Al Madinah for Printing', 'Muṣḥaf Al Madinah for desktop publishing', 'Digital Research Center', 'Muṣḥaf Al Madinah for Qurʾānic Services', 'Publication Images', 'Symposium of printing and publishing the Holy Qurʾān', 'Qurʾān Education with voice guidance', 'Forum for World Renowned Qurʾān Calligraphers', 'Interpretation of Qurʾānic Meaning in sign language', 'Audio Library', as well as the *Journal of Research and Qurʾānic Studies*. It presents itself as a specialized social network, a meeting place for all those who are interested in the Qur'an.

Bibliography

ʿAbd al-Fattāḥ al-Qāḍī. *al-Muṣḥaf fī dawr al-ṭibāʿa*. In: *Al-Muṣḥaf al-Sharīf: Abḥāth fī tarīkhihi*. Cairo: al-Majlis al-Aʿlā li'l-Ṣhuʾūn al-Islāmiyya, 1968.

Abdulrazak, Fawzi. *The Kingdom of the Book: The History of Printing as an Agency of Change in Morocco between 1865 and 1912*. Ph.D. diss. Boston University, 1990.

Aboussouan, Camille. 'Le Coran: l'édition printes de Hambourg'. In: *Le Livre et le Liban jusqu'a 1900 (Exposition)*, pp. 135–6. Paris: UNESCO, 1982.

Albin, Michael W. 'Printing of the Qur'ān'. In: J. D. McAuliffe (ed.). *Encyclopaedia of the Qur'ān*, 4:264–76. Leiden and Boston: Brill, 2004.

Bergmann, Gerhard. *Die Herausforderung des Islam*. Stuttgart: Hänssler, 1980.

Bergsträsser, Gotthelf. 'Koranlesung in Kairo', *Der Islam* 20 (1932), 1–42.

Bergsträsser, Gotthelf. 'Koranlesung in Kairo', *Der Islam* 21 (1933), 110–30.

Bibliander, Theodor and Philip Melanchthon (eds.). *Mahumetis Saracenorum principis, eiusque successorum vitae doctrina ac, ipse Alcoran*... Basel: Ioannes Oporinus, 1543.

Blachère, Régis. *Introduction au Coran*. Paris: G.-P. Maisonneuve et Larose, 1977.

Bloom, Jonathan M. *Paper before Print: The History and Impact of Paper on the Islamic World*. New Haven: Yale University Press, 2001.

Bobzin, Hartmut. *Der Koran im Zeitalter der Reformation: Studien zur Frühgeschichte der Arabistik und Islamkunde in Europa*. Beirut and Wiesbaden: Franz Steiner, 1995.

Bobzin, Hartmut. 'A Treasury of Heresies: Christian Polemics against the Koran'. In: S. Wild (eds.). *The Quran As Text*, pp. 157–75. Leiden, New York, and Cologne: E. J. Brill, 1996.

Bobzin, Hartmut. 'From Venice to Cairo: On the History of Arabic Editions of the Koran (16th–Early 20th Century)'. In G. Roper, E.-M. Hanebutt-Benz, D. Glaß, and Th. Svets (eds.). *Middle Eastern Languages and the Print Revolution: A Cross-Cultural Encounter: A Catalogue and Companion to the Exhibition*. Gutenberg Museum Mainz, Internationale Gutenberg-Gesellschaft, pp. 151–76. Westhofen: WVA-Verlag Skulima, 2002.

Borrmans, Maurice. 'Observations à propos de la premièr edition imprimée du Coran', *Quaderni di studi arabi* 8 (1990), 3–12.

Braun, Helmut. 'Der Hamburger Koran von 1694'. In: Ch. Voigt and E. Zimmermann (eds.). *Libris et litteris: Festschrift für H. Tiemann*, pp. 149–66. Stuttgart: Maximilian-Gesellschaft, 1959.

Brockett, Adrian. 'The Value of the Ḥafṣ and Warsh Transmissions for the Textual History of the Qur'ān'. In: A. Rippin (ed.). *Approaches to the History of the Interpretation of the Qur'ān*, pp. 31–45. Oxford: Clarendon Press, 1988.

Brockway, Duncan. 'The Second Edition of Volume 1 of Marracci's Alcorani Textus Universus', *Muslim World* 64/2 (1974), 141–4.

Carboni, Stefano (ed.). *Venezia e l'Islam: 828-1797. Catalogue of Exhibition Held in Venice, Palazzo Ducale 28 July–25 November 2007*. Venice: Marsilio, 2007.

Catherine II, Empress of Russia. *Filosofskaia i politicheskaia perepiska imperatritsy Ekateriny II s doktorom Zimmermanom s 1785 po 1792 god [The Philosophical and Political Correspondence of Empress Catherine II with Dr Zimmermann Between 1785 and 1792]*. St Petersburg: Imperatorskaia tipografiia, 1803.

Denison Ross, Edward. 'Ludovico Marracci', *Bulletin of the School of Oriental and African Studies* 2 (1921–3), 117–23.

Déroche, François. *La Transmission écrite du Coran dans le début de L'Islam: le Codex Parisino-petropolitanus*. Leiden and Boston: Brill, 2009.

Déroche, François. 'Twenty Leaves from the Tashkent Koran'. In: Sh. S. Blair and J. M. Bloom (eds.). *God Is Beautiful and Loves Beauty: The Object in Islamic Art and Culture*, pp. 59–77. New Haven and London: Yale University Press, 2013.

Déroche, François and Sergio Noja Noseda (eds.). *Sources de la transmission manuscrite du texte coranique. I. Les manuscrits de style hijazi. Volume I. Le manuscrit arabe 328a (a) de la Bibliothèque Nationale de France*. Lesa: Fondazione Ferni Noja Noseda and Paris: Bibliothèque Nationale de Paris, 1998.

Déroche, François and Sergio Noja Noseda (eds.). *Sources de la transmission manuscrite du texte coranique. I. Les manuscrits de style hijazi. Volume 2. Tome I. Le manuscrit Or. 2165 (f. 1 à 61) de la British Library*. Lesa: Fondazione Ferni Noja Noseda & London: British Library, 2001.

Flügel, Gustav. *Concordantiae Corani Arabicae*. Leipzig: Tauchnitz, 1842.

Flügel, Gustav and Gustav Moritz Redslob. *Coranus arabice: recensionis Flügelianae textum recognitum iterum exprimi curavit Gustavus Mauritius Redslob*. Leipzig: Sumptibus E. Bredtti, 1867.

Gdoura, Wahid. *Le Début de l'imprimerie arabe à Istanbul et en Syrie*. Tunis: ISD.

Hinckelmann, Abraham. *Alcoranus Muhammadis ad optimorum Codicum fidem edita*. Hamburg: Ex officina Schultzio-Schilleriana, 1694.

Jeffery, Arthur. 'Progress in the Study of the Qurʾān Text', *Muslim World* 25 (1935), 4–16.

Jeffery, Arthur. *Materials for the History of the Text of the Qurʾān*. Leiden: E. J. Brill, 1937.

Jeffery, Arthur. 'The Textual History of the Qurʾān', *Journal of Middle East Society*, 1/2 (1947), 35–49.

Jeffery, Arthur. 'The Qurʾān as Scripture', *Muslim World* 40/1 (1950), 41–55.

Jeffery, Arthur and Isaac Mendelsohn. 'The Orthography of the Samarqand Qurʾān Codex', *Journal of American Oriental Society* 3 (1942), 175–94.

Khalīdūf, Anās. *Al-kutub al-ʿarabiyya allati ṭubiʿat fī Rusiya: 1787–1917* [*Arabic Books Printed in Russia: 1787–1917*]. Dubai: Juma Al Majid Heritage and Culture Center, 2008.

Krasnenkova, Elena (ed.). *Vo dvortsakh i v shatrakh: Islamskii mir ot Kitaia do Evropy. Katalog vystavki* [*In Palaces and Tents: Islamic World from China to Europe*. Exhibition catalogue]. St Petersburg: Izdatel'stvo Gosudarstvennogo Ermitazha, 2008.

Kresier, Klaus (ed.). *The Beginnings of Printing in the Near and Middle East: Jews, Christians and Muslims*. Hg. Universität Bamberg. Katalog Bamberg. Wiesbaden: Harrassowitz, 2001.

Lange, Johann Michael and Michael Conrad Ludwig. *Dissertatio Historico-Philologico-Theologica De Alcorani Prima Inter Evropaeos Editione Arabica: ante sesqviseculum et qvod excurrit, in Italia per Paganinvm Brixiensem facta, sed jussu Pontificis Romani penitus abolita*. Altdorfi: Meyer, 1703.

Levi Della Vida, Giorgio. 'An Arabic Block Print', *Scientific Monthly* 59 (1944), 473–4.

Levi Della Vida, Giorgio. *Aneddoti e svaghi arabi e non arabi*. Milan and Naples: R. Ricciardi, 1959.

Marracci, Ludovico. *Alcorani textus universus:ex correctioribus Arabum exemplaribus summa fide, atque pulcherrimis characteribus descriptus*. Patavii: Ex Typographia Seminarii, 1698.

Marracci, Ludovico and Christian Reineccius (eds.). *Muhammedis Filii Abdallae Pseudo-Prophetae Fides Islamitica, i.e. Al-Coranus ex idiomate Arabico*. Leipzig: Sumtibus Lanckisianis, 1721.

Milo, Thomas. 'Computing and the Qurʾān, Some Caveats'. In: M. Groß and K.-H. Ohlig (eds.). *Schlaglichter: Die beiden ersten islamischen Jahrhunderte*, pp. 494–515. Berlin: Hans Schiler, 2005.

Milo, Thomas. 'Arabic Amphibious Characters: Phonetics, Phonology, Orthography, Calligraphy and Typography'. In: M. Groß and K.-H. Ohlig (eds.). *Vom Koran zum Islam: Schriften zur frühen Islamgeschichte und zum Koran*, pp. 492–521. Berlin: Hans Schiler, 2009.

Milo, Thomas. 'Towards Arabic Historical Script Grammar, through Contrastive Analysis of Qurʾān Manuscripts'. In: R. M. Kerr and T. Milo (eds.). *Writings and Writing, from Another World an Another Era: Investigations in Islamic Text and Script in Honour of Dr Januarius Justus Witkam*, pp. 249–92. Cambridge: Archetype, 2012.

Nallino, Carlo Alfonso. 'Le fonti arabe manoscritte dell' opera di Ludovico Marracci sul Corano', *Rendiconti della Reale Accademia dei Lincei* 6–7 (1931), 303–49.

Nallino, Maria. 'Una cinquecentesca edizione del Corano stampata a Venezia', *Atti dell'Istituto Veneto di Scienzie, Lettere ed Arti. Classe di scienzie morali, lettere ed arti* 124 (1965–6), 1–12.

Nuovo, Angela. 'Il Corano arabo ritrovato (Venezia, Paganino e Alessandro Paganini, tra l'agosto 1537 e l'agosto 1538)', *La Bibliofilia* 89 (1987), 237–71.

Nuovo, Angela. *The Book Trade in the Italian Renaissance*. Trans. L. G. Cochrane. Leiden and Boston: Brill, 2013.

Redslob, Gustav. *Coranus arabice: recensionis Flügelianae textum recognitum iterum exprimi curavit Gustavus Mauritius Redslob* (Leipzig: Ernest Bredt 1837, 1855, 1867).

Rezvan, Efim. 'The Qurʾān and its World: VI. Emergence of the Canon. The Struggle for Uniformity', *Manuscripta Orientalia* 4/2 (1998a), 13–54.

Rezvan, Efim. 'The Qurʾān and its World: VIII/1. Contra legem Saracenorum: The Qurʾān in Western Europe', *Manuscripta Orientalia* 4/4 (1998b), 41–51. Available at: <http://www.kunstkamera.ru/lib/978-5-88431-178-7/>.

Rezvan, Efim. 'The Qurʾān and its World: VIII/2. West-Östlichen Divans: The Qurʾān in Russia', *Manuscripta Orientalia* 5/1 (1999), 32–62. Available at: <http://www.kunstkamera.ru/files/lib/978-5-88431-178-7/978-5-88431-178-7_08.pdf>.

Rezvan, Efim. *Koran i ego mir [The Qurʾān and its World]*. St. Petersburg: Peterburgskoe vostokovedenie, 2001. Available at: <http://www.kunstkamera.ru/files/lib/978-5-85803-183-3/978-5-85803-183-3_10.pdf>.

Rezvan, Efim. *'The Qurʾān of ʿUthmān' (St Petersburg, Katta-Langar, Bukhara, Tashkent)*. St Petersburg: Peterburgskoe vostokovedenie, 2004.

Rezvan, Efim. 'The Qurʾān and Power in Russia. I: Manuscript', *Manuscripta Orientalia* 14/2 (2008), 21–7.

Rink, Friedrich Theodor. 'Was steht von der Kritik für den Koran zu erwarten?' In: *Fundgruben des Orients*, 1:129–41. Vienna: Gedruckt bei Anton Schmidt, K. K. privil. Buchdrucker, 1809.

Rippin, Andrew. 'Literary Analysis of Qurʾān, Tafsīr, and Sīra: The Methodologies of John Wansbrough'. In: R. Martin (ed.). *Approaches to Islam in Religious Studies*, pp. 151–63. Tucson: University of Arizona Press, 1985.

Röhling, Horst. 'Koranausgaben im russischen Buchdruck des 18. Jahrhunderts'. In: A. Ruppel (Ed.). *Gutenberg Jahrbuch*, pp. 205–10. Mainz: Gutenberg-Gesellschaft, 1977.

Roper, Geoffrey. 'Arabic Printing: Its History and Significance', *Ur* 1 (1982), 23–30.

Roper, Geoffrey. 'Arabic Printing and Publishing in England before 1820', *British Society for Middle Eastern Studies Bulletin* 12 (1985), 12–32. Available at <http://www.ghazali.org/articles/bsmes-12-1-85-gr.pdf>.

Roper, Geoffrey. 'The Export of Arabic Books from Europe to the Middle East in the 18th Century'. In: *BRISMES: British Society for Middle Eastern Studies (in association with AFEMAM): Proceedings of the 1989 International Conference on Europe and the Middle East*, pp. 226–33. Oxford: British Society for Middle Eastern Studies, 1989.

Roper, Geoffrey. 'The Beginnings of Arabic Printing by the ABCFM, 1822–1841', *Harvard Library Bulletin* 9/1 (1998), 50–68.

Roper, Geoffrey. 'The Printing Press and Change in the Arab World'. In S. A. Baron, E. N. Lindquist, and E. F. Shevlin (eds.). *Agent of Change: Print Cultural Studies after Elizabeth Eisenstein*, pp. 250–67. Amherst and Boston: University of Massachusetts Press, in association with the Center for the Book, Library of Congress, Washington, DC, 2007.

Roper, Geoffrey. *The History of the Book in the Middle East*. Farnham: Ashgate, 2013.

Roper, Geoffrey. *Historical Aspects of Printing and Publishing in Languages of the Middle East: Papers from the Third Symposium on the History of Printing and Publishing in the Languages and Countries of the Middle East, University of Leipzig, September 2008*. Leiden and Boston: Brill, 2014.

Roper, Geoffrey. 'Missionary Typography in Arabic Religious Texts and its Relationship with Orthodox and Muslim Sacred Printing in the 19th Century'. In: N. al-Bagdādī and M. Ḥasan (eds.). *Sacred Texts and Print Culture: The Case of the Qur'an and the Bible of the Eastern Churches, 18th and 19th Centuries* forthcoming.

Roper, Geoffrey, Eva-Maria Hanebutt-Benz, Dagmar Glaß, and Theo Svets (eds.). *Middle Eastern Languages and the Print Revolution: A Cross-cultural Encounter. A Catalogue and Companion to the Exhibition*. Gutenberg Museum Mainz, Internationale Gutenberg-Gesellschaft. Westhofen: WVA-Verlag Skulima, 2002.

Rossi, Giovanni Bernardo de. *De Corano Arabico Venetiis Paganini typis impresso sub in. sec. XVI dissertatio*. Parmae: Ex Imperiali Typographeo, 1806.

Sarkīs, Yūsuf Ilyān. *Muʿjam al-maṭbūʿāt al-ʿarabiyya wa'l-muʿarraba*. Cairo: Maṭbaʿat Sarkīs, 1928.

Schaefer, Karl. *Enigmatic Charms: Medieval Arabic Block Printed Amulets in American and European Libraries and Museums*. Boston and Leiden: Brill, 2006.

Schnurrer, Christian Friedrich. *Bibliotheca Arabica*. Halae ad Salam: Handel, 1811.

Smitskamp, Rijk. 'Flügel's Koran Edition', *ʿĀlam al-kutub* 15 (1410/1995), 533–5.

Wilson, Michael Brett. *Translating the Qurʾān in an Age of Nationalism: Print Culture and Modern Islam in Turkey*. Oxford: Oxford University Press in association with the Institute of Ismaili Studies, 2014.

PART IV

STRUCTURAL AND LITERARY DIMENSIONS OF THE QUR'AN

CHAPTER 17

LANGUAGE OF THE QUR'AN

A. H. MATHIAS ZAHNISER

In spite of the appearance of a plethora of new materials in the first decade of the twenty-first century, no consensus yet exists on the topic of this chapter: the language of the Qur'an as uttered by Muḥammad and received by the Muslim community during his lifetime, called here 'the original Qur'an'. The exploration of this issue will require first a consideration of two major proposals for the language of the original Qur'an: an 'esteemed literary koine' and a dialect of Old Arabic. After an introduction to the traditional Muslim position, the views of Theodor Nöldeke (d. 1930) and Karl Vollers (d. 1909) that divided the early post-Enlightenment research require attention. An examination of the various trajectories of existing research into the nature of the original Qur'an will follow, moving from the twentieth century to the twenty-first century. A final section suggests avenues of research likely to bear fruit in the future: discovering new materials and rereading old materials; mastering recitation systems; extending dialect studies; returning to the study of the Qur'anic text itself; and rethinking the Qur'an's uniqueness.

The Language of the Original Qur'an: A Dialect or an Esteemed Literary Koine?

An Esteemed Literary Koine

Muslim scholars have traditionally held that both the language of today's published Qur'an and the language of the original Qur'an equal the everyday speech of the Quraysh, Muḥammad's own tribe (Versteegh 2001: 102). According to Soha Abboud-Haggar, however, most scholars agree that 'Arab tribes spoke... colloquial linguistic varieties, which... differed from the variety used in poetry and the Qur'ān and also from one another' (*EALL* 1:614). They also appear to agree that the language of both the poetry and the Qur'an was a supra-tribal and supra-regional special language 'that had to be acquired like a foreign idiom' (*EALL* 1:617). The esteemed literary koine of this chapter's title refers to this special language. Since it is used mainly by poets and the Qur'an, it could also be termed *Liedersprache* or 'lyric discourse' (Neuwirth 2007: 330). And when compared with the consistent formal discourse of Classical Arabic codified by the grammarians, the esteemed literary koine obviously shares in the diverse features of its sister corpora of Old Arabic: poetry and the dialects.

Dialects of Old Arabic

Chaim Rabin, in 'The Beginnings of Classical Arabic', insists that the relation of the pre-Islamic Arabic dialects to Classical Arabic 'provides the key to the question' of the nature of the original Qur'an (1955: 23). But earlier, in *Ancient West-Arabian*, still the most comprehensive treatise on the subject, Rabin also admits, 'Owing mainly to our scanty knowledge of the ancient dialects, all views on the relations between them and Classical Arabic are guesses or working hypotheses' (1951: 17). That this is still true follows from Rafael Talmon's remark: 'Modern scholarship on the relations between the dialects of old Arabia and their relation to Qur'anic language reached its peak in the 1940s with the studies of Hans Koffler... and Chaim Rabin.... A revision of their findings is a desideratum....' (*EQ* 1:530–1). Michael C. A. Macdonald provides three consistent features as evidence for the continuity of Arabic from the first century BCE to the formal Arabic of modern times: the definite article *ʾl-* (Classical Arabic *al-*), the feminine singular relative pronoun *ʾlt* (Classical Arabic *allatī*), and the third person singular of weak verbs with final long/*ā*/, such as *banā*, *yabnī* (2000: 312). The Qur'an manifests all three. But the Qur'anic recitation systems (*qirāʾāt)* also share lexical and grammatical features with a variety of particular ancient dialects. For example, *al-arāʾik*, plural of *arīka*, a word from the Arabic dialect of Yemen, occurs in the recitation system represented by the most common published Qur'an. Al-Ḥasan [al-Baṣrī] (d. 110/728) reported, 'We did not know the meaning of *arāʾika* [Q. 18:31] until we met a man from the people of Yemen who informed us that *al-arīka* among them means *al-ḥajala* [a curtained alcove]' (al-Suyūṭī 1967: 2:89). Was the Qur'an, then, originally in the dialect of Muḥammad?

The Original Qur'an: Historical and Contemporary Views

The Traditional Muslim View

As stated above, the classic Muslim answer to this question is, Yes. The Qur'an was revealed in the language of the Quraysh, the tribe of Muḥammad, the purest, most accurate, and most elegant of varieties of Arabic (al-Sharkawi 2010: 30; Versteegh 2001: 38–9).

Setting the Stage: Theodor Nöldeke and Karl Vollers

Theodor Nöldeke held that

> it is very unlikely that Muḥammad in the Qurʾān employed a form of the language quite different from that customary in Mecca, and especially unlikely that he should have painstakingly inserted case and mood endings (*iʿrāb*) if his local people did not use them. And so I assume that the poems of that period represent the language the Bedouin at that time spoke and still—pretty long since—speak.
>
> (1904: 2, author's translation)

Other European linguists followed Nöldeke in this conviction (Versteegh 2001: 40–52). They deviated from the traditional Muslim majority, however, in allowing for some differences between the Meccan dialect and the Bedouin dialects (Abboud-Haggar, *EALL* 1:614–15). With this quote Nöldeke was responding to an early form of Karl Vollers's revisionist claim that Classical Arabic was the language variety of the poets and of the Bedouins of Nejd and Yamama, but not of the Quraysh (Vollers 1906: 169, 184). The Qur'an, he contended, originated in the colloquial dialect of the Quraysh without the usual diction of the poets, particularly without any of the distinctive word-end markers of case and mood (*iʿrāb*). According to him, later philologists rewrote the original tribal dialect of the Qur'an in Classical style, eliminating all trace of its colloquial dialect (Rabin 1955: 23–4; Talmon, *EQ* 2:346). Nöldeke ascertained that had Vollers's position been correct, 'the tradition supporting it would not have disappeared without a trace (*spurlos*)' (1910: 2). Against Nöldeke's contention that no evidence existed for Vollers's uninflected Qur'an, Paul E. Kahle (d. 1964) charged that Nöldeke had not known the supporting evidence. Kahle found traditions on Qur'anic recitation that promised a reward for reading the Qur'an with *iʿrāb* of four times the reward for reading it without *iʿrāb*. Clearly recitation of the Holy Book went on legitimately *sans iʿrāb* (1949: 67–71). In spite of Kahle's support, almost no one now holds that a vernacular Qur'an was upgraded at a later time to an inflected formal and literary language, especially when an inter-tribal esteemed literary discourse was at hand. Nevertheless, epigraphy admits no clear evidence for or against *iʿrāb* (Versteegh 2001: 47), a key issue in scholarly discussion. But Vollers's and Kahle's work helped enable the conviction, now widely held, that at the time the original Qur'an emerged, a diglossia prevailed in Arabia between an inter-tribal poetic koine and the tribal varieties of Arabic at the time of Muḥammad. The diglossia in the modern Arab world between regional dialects and Modern Standard Arabic resembles this Old Arabic diglossia (Rabin 1955: 24; Versteegh 2001: 41, 189–208). With few exceptions, European scholars until the mid-twentieth century accepted the broad outlines Muslim scholarship provided for the history of the Arabic of the Qur'an from its first recitations in Mecca to its codification in the tenth century. This consensus was challenged in the second half of the twentieth century.

The 1970s: A Decade of Challenges

John Wansbrough: Arabic Language as Evidence of Prophethood

The late British scholar John Wansbrough (d. 2002) in publications of the late 1970s analysed Qur'anic formulas and narrative conventions according to literary types familiar to biblical scholarship (1977). Because his analysis led to an abundance of formulas characteristic of biblical prophetic literature (1977: 12–20), Wansbrough held that in such passages as this, 'We have never sent a messenger who did not use his own people's language to make things clear for them' (Q. 14:4), the Qur'an was certifying Muḥammad as a genuine prophet. It was not necessarily touting Qur'anic language as a clear and accessible medium for communicating divine truth to Muḥammad's own people (1977: 98–9). Furthermore, Wansbrough's analysis led to the conviction that the Qur'an's elaborate array of material was too great to have been produced by one man in as short a time as the Muslim biography-of-Muḥammad tradition (*sīra*) allowed. Wansbrough speculated that the Qur'an had appeared in Mesopotamia in Abbasid times where and when it represented an Arabic and Arabian monotheistic scripture alongside those of the Jews and the Christians in the conquered territories of the Arab conquests (1977: 50, 83). The time required for this process allowed for the Arabic of the Qur'an to evolve from the simpler 'business Arabic' of the chancery papyri (1977: 91) to the elaborate *Kunstprosa* required by the Muslim doctrines of Qur'anic inimitability (*iʿjāz*) and 'the rhetorical potential of the Arabic language' (1977: 92). This time period corresponds to the two or three centuries required for the separate processes of Arabicization and Islamization to take place (Wansbrough 1977: 88–9, 92).

Wansbrough's position still finds adherents among competent scholars, for example Gilliot and Larcher (*EQ* 3:113–15) and Retsö (2003: 41). Other evaluations include Schoeler (2010: 789); Sinai and Neuwirth (2010: 7–11).

Günter Lüling and the Primitive Qur'an

Günter Lüling in another 1970s publication, *Über den Ur-Koran* (Now entitled *A Challenge to Islam for Reformation* 2003), argued for a number of pre-Islamic Christian texts which, stemming from a 'Christian Arabic *koine*' (Luxenberg 2007: 18–19) and altered in accordance with Muslim dogma, served as a basis for about a third of the Qur'an's discourse. The other two-thirds consist of pure Islamic texts. A fourth text type results from further editing by Muslims after the Prophet's time (Lüling 2003: 11–12). Lüling's work has not received the scholarly attention it deserves. Yet, Claude Gilliot and Pierre Larcher summarize Lüling's argument and refer to his book as 'an important study' (*EQ* 3:129–30).

Federico C. Corriente and Old Arabic Koine

In this same decade Federico C. Corriente published a series of articles dealing with the original Qur'an (1971; 1975; 1976). They concluded that the Qur'an appeared in what he called 'Old Arabic koine', an 'intertribal, poetic and rhetorical language used by all Arabs, but native to none and therefore learned with more or less ease depending on the degree of kinship with each vernacular' (1975: 41). Corriente especially draws attention to the difference between Arabic and such Indo-European languages as Sanskrit, Greek, and Latin at the point of their synthetic, or inflected, characteristics. Scholars tacitly assumed at the time of Nöldeke and Vollers—even at the time of Corriente's writing—that '*Iʿrāb*-Arabic indeed belonged to a highly synthetic linguistic structure, while *Iʿrāb*-less Middle Arabic and younger forms... had a rather analytical structure' (1971: 24). Suspicious of this, Corriente analysed six different short corpora of *ʿarabiyya* for the significance of their *iʿrāb* in conveying meaning: Imruʾ al-Qays's *Muʿallaqa*; Q. 12:1–30; parts of ʿUmar ibn Abī Rabīʿa's *Diwān*; the story of the lion and the jackal from *Kalīla wa-Dimna*; and selections from modern poet Aḥmad Shawqī; and from modern novelist Naguib Maḥfūẓ (1971: 35). He concluded that word-end *iʿrāb*, so precious to the identity of the *ʿArabiyya* actually had 'a negligible functional yield' (1971: 25), that is, the same discourse if transmitted without case endings would lose very little meaning (1971: 25–9). It turned out that Q. 12:1–30 was the least synthetic of all six sets of material with a functional yield of zero. Sensing it could be just a random phenomenon, Corriente further analysed Q. 5:1–30. There he found some examples of *iʿrāb* with a measure of functional yield, such as the first part of Q. 5:7, given here with key *iʿrāb* vowels superscripted to help illustrate functional yield: *wa-udhkurū niʿmat*^{a} *llāh*^{i} *wa-mithāq*^{a}*hu lladhī wāthaq*^{a}*kum bihi*. The *iʿrāb*-superscripted/*a*/vowel in *mithāq*^{a}*hu* ('his pledge') marks *mithāq* as the second object of the imperative *udhkurū*, yielding the translation, 'And remember God's favor and his pledge to you'. If *mithāq*^{a}*hu* had the superscripted *iʿrāb* vowel changed from /*a*/ to /*u*/, making it the subject of a circumstantial clause beginning with /*wa-*/(*wāw al-ḥāl*), the meaning would become, 'And remember God's favour, his promise being what he had pledged to you' (1971: 37, n. 26). In this not very common case, removal of the *iʿrāb* renders the sentence ambiguous.

On the basis of his research, Corriente concluded that the slightly greater role that *iʿrāb* may have played in pre-Islamic poetry suggests a more significant functional yield for *iʿrāb* in Arabic's pre-historical stages, than its functional yield for the Qur'an and subsequent prose. The 'almost impeccable, application' of *iʿrāb* in these historical forms of formal discourse does not alter noun-*iʿrāb*'s almost negligible functional yield in them (1971: 38). Evidently *iʿrāb* adds an esteem or 'prestige' quality to them that is 'indispensable for rhetorical purposes of high style', yet with decreasing functional yield. This increasing erosion—at least in urban dialects—by the sixth century CE could account for 'the faults in the Qur'an itself' (1971: 38). Furthermore, the greater functional yield of *iʿrāb* in the poetry examined can be attributed to an 'almost servile imitation of ancient models' (1971: 40). Finally, even though Corriente's data suggests 'the almost complete grammatical irrelevance of the *iʿrāb* in Arabic since Muhammad's time', when it was all dropped for 'other than rhetorical and didactic' purposes remains a mystery (1971: 40).

Corriente's work supplies further evidence for Owens's (2006) contention (discussed below) that the case dimension of even Qur'anic Arabic had a weak functional yield. Corriente's 1975 study of al-Iṣfahānī's (d. after 360/970–1) *Kitāb al-Aghānī* revealed abundant evidence of deviations from the standards of the Classical Arabic of the grammarians. For example, the poetry made use of a dual that did not change form in its genitive, accusative, and nominative grammatical positions (1975: 52). Instances of the mixing up of cases also occurred in poetry (1975: 57). Of particular significance in light of all Corriente's functional-yield analysis is his suggestion that the *lisān mubīn* (understandable language) of the original Qur'an may have been the idiolect of Muḥammad, learned among the Bedouin of his childhood, a 'lowest-yield *iʿrab*-Arabic, understandable and clear to all speakers regardless of their vernacular features, and yet formal enough to befit a heavenly message' (1975: 42–3).

Michael Zwettler and the Poetic Koine

The year 1978 saw the appearance of the late Michael Zwettler's (d. 2010) detailed scholarly contribution, *The Oral Tradition of Classical Arabic Poetry*. Zwettler examined this oral poetic tradition of principally pre-Islamic poetry in light of Milman Parry's (1971) and Albert Lord's (1965) '"oral formulaic" theory of poetic composition' (1978: ix). Particularly, but not exclusively, the works that have turned up in textual traditions—whether biblical, Homeric, or Arab—started out in some oral form, preserved by the prodigious memories of primarily illiterate people (Zwettler 1978: 4). The approach of Lord and Parry entails a scenario in which the earliest written form of an originally oral creation may be a transcript of 'a single performance by a singer, poet, or narrator who was, at the same time, not reciting from memory, but rather composing the work so taken down' (Zwettler 1978: 4). In other words, the poet or narrator was essentially a performer. Another scenario would be that the performer when dictating at the request of a scribe or scribes learns to perform more slowly and without the stimulation of 'music, tempo, or audience rapport' (1978: 5). Parry added the concept of 'oral formula': a group of words used regularly, employing a consistent metrical pattern to convey a particular idea (Zwettler 1978: 6). Readers familiar with the Qur'an will see immediately the relevance of this dimension of Zwettler's working theory. Indeed virtually everyone writing on the topic of this chapter of the *Handbook* cites Zwettler's long chapter, 'The Classical ʿArabīya', at some point (1978: 97–188).

Gregor Schoeler, submitting Zwettler's book to a thorough critical analysis (2006: 87–110), presents a number of reasons why the Parry/Lord criteria of oral poetry do not apply to ancient Arabic poetry (2006: 88–90). Schoeler also reports that American and European literary criticism has lost interest in oral poetry theory due to its zealous application of the Parry/Lord theory (2006: 105). Be that as it may, Zwettler's discussion of the topic of Classical Arabic (1978: 97–188) has endured. After extensive interaction with other linguists, Zwettler concludes that the Qur'an was at its outset a special, inter-tribal, and fully inflected *ʿarabiyya* like that of the pre- and early Islamic poetry and unlike any of the dialects of the time (1978: 145–7). In other words, only the poetry and the Qur'an featured *iʿrāb* at the time of Muḥammad (1978: 128–9).

Qur'an in Context: A Twenty-First-Century Response

The first decade of the twenty-first century and the new millennium has provided Qur'anic studies with a rich new crop of publications: two new major reference works, *The Encyclopaedia of the Qurʾān* (6 vols. 2001–6) and *The Encyclopedia of Arabic Language and Linguistics* (5 vols. 2006–9); and two anthologies that explore the Qur'an in context: Reynolds (2008) and Neuwirth, Sinai, and Marx (2010). Studies of an archive of very early Qur'anic manuscripts found in Yemen in the 1970s have appeared: Puin (1996), Sadeghi and Goudarzi (2012). A broad consensus exists today that, at the time the Qur'an emerged, Arab tribes, both settled and nomadic, spoke distinct dialects of Arabic, each differing from the variety of Arabic exhibited by the ancient poetry and the Qur'an as currently known. Nevertheless, this century also absorbed its revisionist shock.

Christoph Luxenberg and the Syro-Aramaic Ur-Qur'an

Christoph Luxenberg's *The Syro-Aramaic Reading of the Koran* (2007) brought the Syriac theme to prominence again in the new millennium. Mass media drew attention to Luxenberg's interpretation of the Qur'an's 'virgins of paradise' (*ḥūr ʿīn*) (Q. 44:54; 52:20; 56:22) as 'white, crystal (-clear) grapes' (2007: 250–1). Luxenberg offers a key methodology for unlocking the meaning of Qur'anic expressions that Western translators deem obscure. In essence he examines a classic commentary such as al-Ṭabarī's (d. 310/923) and a dictionary such as Ibn Manẓūr's (d. 711/1311) and different recitation systems (*qirāʾāt*) to discover words or meanings translators may have missed that improve the passage's sense. Then he checks to see if a change in the diacritical points added to the *scriptio defectiva rasm* (see Chapter 11 in this volume) based on a Syriac root provides the expression with more sense within its context (Luxenberg 2007: 23–7). Luxenberg's method omits a thorough search of traditional Muslim Qur'an scholarship, considering it 'fundamentally based on the erroneous historical-linguistic conceptions of Arabic exegesis' (2007: 11). Evaluations of Luxenberg's work include Gilliot and Larcher (*EQ* 3:129–32) and Neuwirth (2003; 2007: 13–18).

Angelika Neuwirth and a Return to the Qur'an Itself

Angelika Neuwirth bucked much of the revisionist tide of the 1970s with a myriad of treatises, including *Studien zur Komposition der mekkanischen Suren* (now in a second edition 2007), a detailed analysis of the broadly acknowledged Meccan suras of the Qur'an. She faults current scholarship for studying only the complete, fully canonical Qur'an as a codex—while neglecting its actual details. She proposes and engages in a micro-study of the Qur'an in a way that makes use of the Qur'an's distinctive self-revelation of its process of canonization. She demonstrates her pre-canonical micro-study method by examining themes from Genesis 3 as they occur progressively in seven suras (2000a and 2000b). She distinguishes between the liturgical role in community formation of the revelation as *qur'ān*, 'recitation', within the context of its being identified as *kitāb*, 'scripture', alongside other monotheistic holy books (2000a: 26–7, 37; 2007: 24–54). Neuwirth further contextualizes her proposals in Qur'anic Studies in a 54-page introduction to *Studien* (2007: 1–54), examining the history of Qur'anic Studies, and charting a return to the Qur'an itself as a focus for understanding its provenance and process of development. She views the original Qur'an, along with pre-Islamic poetry, as *Liedersprache*, 'lyric discourse' (2007: 330), the esteemed literary koine of this chapter.

Ernest Axel Knauf and Old Arabic Triglossia

Ernest Axel Knauf (2010) rejects both the traditional Muslim view of one inflected language unifying Bedouin dialects and lyrical poetry and Vollers's simple diglossia of *Volkssprache und Schriftsprache* (1906). Knauf favours a triglossial context for the two centuries just prior to the time of the revelation of the Qur'an. According to him, Nabataean Old Arabic had become 'some sort of standard Arabic as early as the second century BCE' (2010: 229). At first it was an unwritten language of Arabian traders and shippers. But sometime between the third and the fourth centuries BCE, as revealed by post-Nabataean texts, it became a written language (2010: 229). This 'inter-tribal lingua-franca' (Knauf's equivalent of a koine?) developed in spite of the absence of any political or religious unity among the Arabs (2010: 228). Knauf believes this 'trilingual situation' of the supra-regional 'Early Standard Arabic' lingua franca of the merchants, the literary language of poets and divines, and the tribal and regional dialects 'requires a reassessment of the language of the Qur'an' (2010: 247). The Prophet, in order to produce written scripture, employed the 'only written form of Arabic' available and formed it 'as close to the Poetic Old Arabic as possible' (2010: 247). Knauf's findings regarding both a trade lingua franca and a common literary discourse, reaching back into the pre-Islamic period, support Corriente's trade koine (1975: 38–9, n. 1). Al-Sharkawi's speculation that along trade routes from Lebanon through the Ḥijāz down to Yemen an inter-tribal trade koine may have been in play (2010: 57, 110) fits Knauf's scenario also. Jonathan Owens's thesis of two forms of pre-diasporic Arabic—one with word-end inflection and one without (2006)—seems compatible with Knauf's triglossia as well.

Kees Versteegh and the Force of an Absent Pseudo-correction

For Kees Versteegh, in common with most of the scholars surveyed, *lisān ʿarabiyy*, 'an Arabic tongue' (Q. 16:103), indicates a supra-tribal unity, a language that served as the binding factor for all those who lived in the Arabian Peninsula, as opposed to the ʿAjam, the non-Arabs who lived outside it and spoke different languages. In pre-Islamic poetry the term ʿArab indicates an ethno-cultural group (2001: 37).

But Versteegh's view of *lisān ʿarabiyy* does not necessarily mean that it contrasted starkly with the everyday language of Muḥammad. Against the koine consensus, he points out, stands the certainty of the complete absence of pseudo-correction in the pre-Islamic poetry. Pseudo-correction refers to people being *too* correct. For example, an Arab's mother tongue offers him *mā katabū*, *mā*, a negative particle, plus *past* tense 'they did not write'. He wants to write it in the formal written high language and knows that it can negate with *lam* plus the present tense of the verb. So he writes *lam yaktubūna*, forgetting that the high language requires the present *subjunctive* tense *yaktubū* in this context. Versteegh asks whether if the system of *iʿrāb* were limited to the poetic or Qur'anic high language and all mother-tongue Arabic lacked it, would pseudo-correction not have been more common (2001: 51, 115–20)? He then gives evidence that Bedouin really did provide the standard for Arabic up until the end of the fourth/tenth century (2001: 64). Since, according to Versteegh, no existing explanation for the emergence of new dialects proves satisfactory, more must be known about how language in general changes over time and about the sociological context of the early expansion of Islam in each particular area (2001: 112). Owens has plenty to say about the history of Arabic (2006), and al-Sharkawi about the social contexts or ecologies of Arabic acquisition during the expansion of the Arab Empire (2010).

Jonathan Owens and a Caseless Variety of Old Arabic

Owens uses comparative linguistics to identify characteristics of pre-diasporic Arabic, a task relevant to discovering the nature of the Qur'an's original language. He defines pre-diasporic Arabic as the Arabic from the beginning of the Arab expansion (10/630) to about 174/790, the time soon after the publication of the *Kitāb* of Sībawayhi (d. *c*.180/796), the grammarian who recorded 'eye witness' reports of pre-diasporic varieties of Arabic. Owens's comparative method involves examining the colloquial varieties of Arabic that now exist and can be analysed in detail in order to describe the probable common language variety from which they stemmed before being carried to widely diverse areas by the Arab expansion. Pre-diasporic Arabic consists then of 'a variety based on the results of a reconstruction of modern dialects' (2006: 3) 'through a set of linguistic rules' (2006: 8). For example, except for creoles and pidgins, all of the modern varieties studied 'minimally mark the first person singular of the perfect verb with -t': Egyptian, *katab-t*; Iraqi, (*qultu*) *katab-tu*; Najdī, *kitab-t*. Thus, their mother variety must have done so (2006: 13). Qur'anic variant readings (*qirāʾāt*) and the linguist Sībawayhi's observations and interpretations support Owens's comparative method. First on the question of case endings, Owens shows that both Nöldeke and Vollers misrepresented 'the entire concept of the variant readings' (2006: 121). Each assumed that his model of the original Qur'anic language variety, the one flowing from the mouth of Muḥammad, represented the language of the Imām Codex (see Chapter 11 in this volume) that was distinguished from an array of variant recitation systems compatible with it. Rather, the history of the recitation systems (*qirāʾāt*) entails that *all of them*—as decentralized, locally defined alternative readings of the Qur'an—have equal claim to being original. Any reading from among 'The Seven' is 'as old as any other' (2006: 120). Ibn Mujāhid's *Sabʿa* (see Chapter 13 in this volume) makes this very point. In other words, the uninflected Qur'an of Vollers and the fully inflected Qur'an of Nöldeke could both have been viable reading systems.

Owens in fact finds support from the *qirāʾāt* for the results of his comparative approach. In the reading (*qirāʾa*) of Abū ʿAmr ibn al-ʿAlāʾ (d. *c.*154–6/770–2), one of 'The Seven', Owens finds evidence of a recitation system in which 'a short final vowel was of negligible functional status' (2006: 129). The *qirāʾāt* literature singles out Abū ʿAmr's system for 'major assimilation' (*al-idghām al-kabīr*), its assimilation of two consonants not separated by a vowel (2006: 124). The absence of the final short vowels of word-end inflection (*iʿrāb*) entails major assimilation. Abū ʿAmr's reading was established before case and mood endings became so important for grammarians (2006: 122). With Sībawayhi's help, Owens shows that the bound object pronouns of forty-nine modern dialects cannot have sheltered the remnants of pre-diasporic case vowels. If an uninflected Arabic dialect had descended from an inflected variety, one would expect to find in the uninflected descendant fossil traces of the mood-vowel inflections that had once been bound between a verb and its object pronoun in the inflected ancestor, for example, *yusāʿid-u-ka*, 'he helps you'. But Owens found that in the forty-nine contemporary dialects that he surveyed all suspected bound object pronoun vowels could be accounted for as epenthetic vowels required by Arabic phonological laws. They were not fossils of mood-indicating inflection bound between a verb and its suffix (2006: 257–9). An instance of how this works can be summarized as follows: Sībawayhi reports that when a nominative *-u* or a genitive *-i* occurs before an object suffix, such as in *yaḍrib-u-hu*, 'he hits him', and in *min maʾman-i-ka*, 'from your place of safety', the contrast in the two vowels is neutralized, both becoming *-ə*: *yaḍrib-ə-hā* and *maʾman-ə-ka*. The epenthetic vowel *-ə* represents a barely audible sound (2006: 60). The Arabic grammatical tradition terms this short, centralized pronunciation of short high vowels (*-i-* and *-u-*) *ikhtilās*, 'furtiveness' (2006: 306). The Qur'anic *qirāʾāt* tradition calls it *takhfīf*, 'pronouncing lightly' (2006: 308; Sībawayhi, *Kitāb*. 2.324, referring to the reading of Abū ʿAmr). Obviously, 'the phonemic functionality of *-i-* and *-u-*, was severely curtailed' by *ikhtilās/takhfīf*, a feature 'very well established in Old Arabic' (2006: 61). Owens defends the theses that both a case and a caseless variety of the Old Arabic existed in pre-diasporic times, and that the modern dialects descend from the caseless variety (2006: 115).

Muhammad al-Sharkawi and the Ecology of Arabic Acquisition

As Versteegh advised, much more needs to be learned about the social context of Arabic in its various historical stages (2001: 112). Al-Sharkawi steps up to that challenge with a study of 'the Arabicisation process of the Middle East in the seventh century', according to the ecological factors that 'facilitated the process and shaped its results' (al-Sharkawi 2010: 1). 'Ecology' refers to the whole environment, external and internal, of the acquisition of Arabic in the garrison towns of the Arab conquests. For example, the majority population in such garrison towns as Fusṭāt in Egypt were native speakers of Arabic. Their workers came from the non-Arabic speaking, conquered people. The ecology of that situation included that learning Arabic informally was a desideratum of both majority Arabs and minority non-Arabs. The ecology of the mix of Arab and non-Arabs enabled the emergence of simplified true Arabic dialects, rather than creole or pidgin varieties. Such an ecology also accounts for the striking similarities among the modern colloquial varieties (2010: 141–3, 159–73). Al-Sharkawi gives significant attention to varieties of Arabic at the time the original Qur'an appeared (2010: 29–86). The Qur'an's own *al-ʿarabī al-mubīn*, 'clearly understandable Arabic' (Q. 16:103; 26:195), refers to 'the tongue of all the Arabs' and became the inclusive and ideal model for written and recited discourse (2010: 32, citing Versteegh 2001:37). Yet variation from the standard Arabic of the grammarians shows up again and again in Qur'anic and poetic discourse, suggesting a diglossia of tribal and regional dialects, on the one hand, and an inter-tribal 'poetic rendition' (2010: 31), on the other. Given the testimony that trade and socializing travelled between the urban centres of the Ḥijāz and Yemen (2010: 54) and that language innovation moves along such trade routes, al-Sharkawi speculates that a process of koineization may have been in play 'long before the succession of conquests' (2010: 57).

Jan Retsö: Who were the Arabs of the *ʿarabiyya*?

Jan Retsö argues that the name 'Arab' designates 'a group of initiates of a fellowship of sanctified warriors or guards around a divinity' (2003: 596) with many locations whose language, the *ʿarabiyya*, 'had an authority as a medium for messages from the non-human world' (2003: 52). Along with Wansbrough, Retsö rejects the traditional interpretation of Q. 14:4, 'We have sent no messenger except with (*bi*) the language of his people (*qawm*) to make clear' (Retsö's translation), in favour of seeing the verse as undergirding 'the authority of the message' (2003: 46–7). The verse addresses this closed circle of sanctified warriors (2003: 48). According to Retsö, *lisān ʿarabī* (Q. 16:103; 41:44) 'is not contrasted with Hebrew, Aramaic and Greek... but with [*lisān*] *aʿjamī*... probably a form of the language we today would call Arabic' (2003: 47). Several languages of these Arabs existed in Arabia before Islam, according to Retsö. They all contained archaic features and were for special—not everyday—use; the diviners (*kuhhān*) and the poets (*shuʿarāʾ*) lived among the Arabs and used them (2003: 595, 624). Retsö defines the *qurrāʾ*—usually understood to mean 'reciters' of the Qur'an—as *ahl al-qurā*, 'people of the villages' (Q. 7:96; the word *qurrāʾ* does not occur in the Qur'an). He then finds mention of *qurā ʿarabiyya*, 'Arab villages', in geographical dictionaries. This designation he believes refers to these guardian villages in Iraq's countryside (2003: 48–51, 61). For a thorough, fair, and constructively critical treatment of this issue with extensive bibliography, see Mustafa Shah (2005).

Five Fruitful Avenues for Further Research

Readers of the *Handbook* can readily see that the language of the original Qur'an offers a fascinating field for further research. At least five research traditions promise scholars ongoing and long-lasting opportunities for productivity, service, and satisfaction.

Discovering New Materials and Rereading of Old Materials

Recent analysis of early Qur'an manuscripts found in Yemen deserves special mention (Puin 1996). Although their discovery in a mosque in Sanaa occurred in the 1970s, their careful analysis awaited the twenty-first century. Nicolai Sinai maintains that the analysis of one palimpsest manuscript Ṣanʿāʾ 1 (Sadeghi and Goudarzi 2012) 'rules out the assumption that the Koranic corpus was produced any later than the middle of the seventh century' (2012: 27). Wansbrough's (1977) dating of the Qur'an's appearance considerably later, as mentioned above, must be modified in the light of these manuscripts.

Such new discoveries are not alone in their promise for scholarship, however. The variety and the abundance of long-standing early Muslim scholarship represent a rich vein deserving attention. It will be wise not to ignore this scholarship. For example, there is telling evidence in Sībawayhi's discussion of Q. 12:31, *mā hādha, basharan*, 'this is no human' (*Kitāb*. 1: 20, 13f.) that he knew ʿUthmān's (r. 23–35/644–56) Codex. The Qur'an, like the *Ḥijāzī* dialect, uses the negative *mā* here like *laysa* to put its object, *basharan*, in the accusative case. Sībawayhi reports that the Tamīmīs using their tribal dialect read it *basharun* in the nominative case, a rule congruent with Classical Arabic norms. Then he adds, *illā man ʿarafa kayfa hiya fī'l-muṣḥaf*, 'except the one who knows how it is in the Codex [of ʿUthmān]'. The Codex even in its *scriptio defectiva* original form marks the indefinite masculine accusative unambiguously with *alif ṭawīla* (سرا). Thus Schoeler observes that Sībawayhi 'quotes ʿUthmān's codex precisely as it exists today, without any variations at all' (2010: 789). Schoeler himself practices a sophisticated sifting of historical narratives as well as their chains of authority, with attention to the mixture of both oral and written transmission, illustrating the much needed critical use of the rich treasure of traditional Muslim scholarship (2006). This *rereading* mentality will more and more characterize successful investigation into the nature of the original Qur'an. Shah's use of such material in response to Retsö's interpretation of *qurrāʾ* requires mention here as well (2005).

Mastering Recitation Systems

Among these old materials the canonical and non-canonical *qirāʾāt*, 'readings' or 'recitation systems', frequently mentioned in this chapter, offer a rich linguistic clue to the nature of the original Qur'an. They have played a major role in the work of such scholars as Corriente (1976: 64–5), and Owens (2006: 120–5), and Shah (2005).

Extending Dialect Studies

The prolific activity of M. C. A. Macdonald and others working in a comprehensive way on the varieties of Old Arabic will continue. The variety of Old Arabic without word-end inflection that Owens projected by comparing modern dialects of Arabic (2006) appears congruent with the commercial or trade koine posited by Corriente (1971: 27, n. 9; 1975: 38, n. 1) and Knauf (2010: 227–31). Given the plethora of modern dialects acknowledged as strikingly similar, Owens's method foretokens a fruitful future for dialect studies (2006).

Return to the Study of the Qur'an's Text

Angelika Neuwirth exemplifies a recovery of attention to the text of the Qur'an itself (2007). While admiring much of Wansbrough's *Quranic Studies* (1977), she challenges his conviction that the Qur'an's composition consists of 'logia of the Prophet, framed by excerpts from later polemico-apologetical debates' (1996: 73–74; 2003: 5). She takes a more phenomenological approach to what the Qur'an reveals about itself, especially in its earliest suras, as an interactive engagement of a 'charismatic leader with his community' (2003: 5). Neuwirth shows that Qur'anic suras do not correspond to Wansbrough's 'concept of logia, isolated sayings, at all' (2003: 5–6). This conviction flows from her detailed inductive study of the Qur'anic text itself in numerous publications (e.g. 2007).

A community of scholars under her leadership has affirmed and complemented her project in *The Qurʾān in Context: Historical and Literary Investigations into the Qurʾānic Milieu* (Neuwirth, Sinai, and Marx 2010), an 864-page volume with twenty-eight papers, including two by Neuwirth dealing with the text of the Qur'an itself (2010: 499–531; 733–78).

In another return to the text of the Qur'an, treated elsewhere in this *Handbook* (Chapter 19), Michel Cuypers, using a method known as Semitic rhetorical analysis, demonstrates a holistic and consistent compositional form for the many spans of text he has analysed, especially his lengthy commentary on *Sūrat al-Māʾida*, Q. 5 (2009).

Nuancing the Qur'an's Uniqeness

Finally, more attention can profitably be focused on the Qur'an's unique diction termed in this chapter 'esteemed literary koine'. Did the Qur'an feature a basic trade koine (Corriente 1975: 41) with its literary esteem enhanced by the word-end case and mood markers, but its meaning not limited by them (Corriente 1976: 64–5)? Was its powerful *Liedersprache* (Neuwirth 2007:330) different from classical Arabic poetry in a way more indigenous to its audience? Sprinkled with lexical and syntactic features from Old Arabic dialects was the Qur'an even more relevant in its impact?

Corriente's expression of the inimitability (*iʿjāz*) of the Qur'an beckons in the direction of such a research project suggesting that Muḥammad's idiolect, nurtured among Bedouin, may have offered him more than did his Ḥijāzī dialect alone. Corriente sees the Qur'an as a clever linguistic compromise in the form of lowest-yield *iʿrāb* Arabic, understandable and clear to all speakers regardless of their vernacular features, and yet formal enough to befit a heavenly message (1975: 43).

One may hopefully be excused for referring to 'a heavenly message' as 'clever'; but one should likewise not experience surprise when the original language of a holy book of prophetic discourse in 'esteemed literary koine' turns out to be outstanding in its ability 'to make things clear' (Q. 14:4)!

Bibliography

Primary Sources

Ibn Manẓūr, Muḥammad ibn Makarram. *Lisān al-ʿArab*. 15 vols. Beirut: Dār Ṣādir, 1955.

Ibn Mujāhid, Aḥmad ibn Mūsā. *Kitāb al-Sabʿa fi'l-qirāʾāt*. Ed. Shawqī Ḍayf. Cairo: Dār al-Maʿārif, 1979.

al-Iṣfahānī, Abū'l-Faraj. *Kitāb al-Aghānī*. 31 vols. Ed. Ibrāhīm al-Ibyārī. Cairo: Dār al-Shaʿb, 1969–79.

Sībawayhi, Abū Bishr ʿAmr ibn ʿUthmān. *al-Kitāb*. Sībawayhi. *Le Livre de Sîbawaihi: Traité de grammaire arabe*. Texte arabe publié par Hartwig Derenbourg. 2 vols. Hildesheim and New York: Georg Olms Verlag, 1970.

al-Suyūṭī, Jalāl al-Dīn ʿAbd al-Raḥmān. *Al-Itqān fī ʿulūm al-Qurʾān*. Ed. Muḥammad Abū'l-Faḍl Ibrāhīm. 4 vols. in 2. Cairo: Maktabat wa-Maṭbaʿat al-Mashhad al-Ḥusaynī, 1967.

al-Ṭabarī, Abū Jaʿfar Muḥammad ibn Jarīr. *Jāmiʿ al-bayān ʿan taʾwīl ayy al-Qurʾān*. Ed. Bashshār ʿAwwād Maʿrūf, and ʿIṣām Fāris al-Ḥarastānī. 7 vols. Beirut: Muʾassasat al-Risāla, 1994.

Secondary Sources

Abboud-Haggar, Soha. 'Dialects: Genesis'. In: Kees Versteegh, Mushira Eid, et al. (eds.). *Encyclopedia of Arabic Language and Linguistics*. 5 vols., 1:613–22. Leiden: E. J. Brill, 2006–9.

Beeston, Alfred F. L. 'Nemara and Faw', *Bulletin of the School of Oriental and African Studies* 42/1 (1979), 1–6.

Corriente, Federico C. 'On the Functional Yield of Some Synthetic Devices in Arabic and Semitic Morphology', *The Jewish Quarterly Review*, NS 62/1 (1971), 20–50.

Corriente, Federico C. 'Marginalia on Arabic Diglossia and Evidence thereof in the *Kitab al-Aghani*', *Journal of Semitic Studies* 20/1 (1975), 38–61.

Corriente, Federico C. 'From Old Arabic to Classical Arabic through the Pre-Islamic Koine: Some Notes on the Native Grammarians' Sources, Attitudes and Goals', *Journal of Semitic Studies* 21/1 (1976), 62–98.

Cuypers, Michel. *The Banquet: A Reading of the Fifth Sura of the Qurʾān*. Series Rhetoria Semitica. Miami: Convivium Press, 2009.

Gilliot, Claude and Pierre Larcher. 'Language and Style of the Qurʾan'. In: Jane Dammen McAuliffe (ed.). *Encyclopaedia of the Qurʾān*. 6 vols., 3:109–35. Leiden and Boston: E. J. Brill, 2001–6.

Ibn Warraq (a pseudonym), editor and translater. *What the Koran Really Says*. Amherst, NY: Prometheus Books, 2002.

Kahle, Paul E. 'The Arabic Readers of the Qurʿān', *Journal of Near Eastern Studies* 8/1 (1949), 65–71. Reprinted in *What the Koran Really Says*. (ed.) with translations by Ibn Warraq, pp. 201–10. Amherst, NY: Prometheus Books, 2002.

Knauf, Ernest Axel. 'Arabo-Aramaic and ʿArabiyya: From Ancient Arabic to Early Standard Arabic'. In: Angelika Neuwirth, Nicolai Sinai, and Michael Marx (eds.). *The Qur'ān in Context: Historical and Literary Investigations into the Qur'ānic Milieu*, pp. 197–254. Leiden: E. J. Brill, 2010.

Lord, Albert. *The Singer of Tales*. New York: Atheneum, 1965.

Lüling, Günter. *A Challenge to Islam for Reformation: The Rediscovery and Reliable Reconstruction of a Comprehensive pre-Islamic Christian Hymnal Hidden in the Koran under Earliest Islamic Reinterpretations*. Delhi: Motilal Banarsidass Publishers, 2003.

Luxenberg, Christoph. *The Syro-Aramaic Reading of the Koran: A Contribution to the Decoding of the Language of the Koran*. Revised and enlarged edition of *Die syro-aramäische Lesart des Koran*, 2000. Berlin: Verlag Hans Schiler, 2007.

McAuliffe, Jane Dammen (ed.). *Encyclopaedia of the Qurʾān*. 6 vols. Leiden and Boston: E. J. Brill, 2001–6.

Macdonald, Michael C. A. *Literacy and Identity in pre-Islamic Arabia*. Variorum. Collected Studies, 906. Farnham: Ashgate, 2009.

Macdonald, Michael C. A. 'Reflections on the Linguistic Map of Pre-Islamic Arabia', *Arabian Archeology and Epigraphy*' 11 (2000), 28–79. Reprinted in Macdonald 2009.

Neuwirth, Angelika. 'Vom Rezitationstext über die Liturgie zum Kanon: Zu Entstehung und Wiederauflösung der Surenkomposition im Verlauf der Entwicklung eines islamischen Kultus'. In: Stefan Wild (ed.). *The Qur'an as Text*, pp. 69–105. Leiden: E. J. Brill, 1996.
Neuwirth, Angelika. 'Negotiating Justice: A Pre-Canonical Reading of the Qur'anic Creation Accounts. Part 1', *Journal of Qur'anic Studies* 2/1 (2000a), 25–41.
Neuwirth, Angelika. 'Negotiating Justice: A Pre-Canonical Reading of the Qur'anic Creation Accounts. Part 2', *Journal of Qur'anic Studies* 2/2 (2000b), 1–18.
Neuwirth, Angelika. 'Qur'an and History—a Disputed Relationship: Some Reflections on Qur'anic History and History in the Qur'an', *Journal of Qur'anic Studies* 5/1 (2003), 1–18.
Neuwirth, Angelika. *Studien zur Komposition der mekkanischen Suren: Die literarische Form des Koran—ein Zeugnis seiner Historizität?* 2nd edn. The first edition (1981) expanded by a historical introduction to Koranic studies. Berlin: De Gruyter, 2007.
Neuwirth, Angelika, Nicolai Sinai, and Michael Marx (eds.). *The Qur'ān in Context: Historical and Literary Investigations into the Qur'ānic Milieu*. Leiden: E. J. Brill, 2010.
Nöldeke, Theodor. *Beiträge zur semitishen Sprachwissenschaft*. 1904. In: *Beiträge und neue Beiträge: Achtzehn Aufsätze und Studien, teilweise in zweiter verbesserte und vermehrter Auflage min einem Nekrolog von Christiaan Snouck Hurgronje*. Amsterdam: APA—Philo Press, 1982.
Nöldeke, Theodor. *Neue Beiträge zur semitishen Sprachwissenschaft*. 1910. In: *Beiträge und neue Beiträge: Achtzehn Aufsätze und Studien, teilweise in zweiter verbesserte und vermehrter Auflage min einem Nekrolog von Christiaan Snouck Hurgronje*. Amsterdam: APA—Philo Press, 1982.
Owens, Jonathan. *A Linguistic History of Arabic*. Oxford and New York: Oxford University Press, 2006.
Parry, Milman. 'Studies in the Epic Technique of Oral Verse-Making, I. Homer and Homeric Style'. In: A. Parry (ed.). *The Making of Homeric Verses: The Collected Papers of Milman Parry*, pp. 251–65. Oxford: Clarendon Press, 1971.
Puin, Gerd-R. 'Observations on Early Qurʾan Manuscripts in Ṣanʿāʾ'. In: Stefan Wild (ed.). *The Qur'an as Text*, pp. 107–11. Leiden and New York: E. J. Brill, 1996.
Rabin, Chaim. *Ancient West-Arabian*. London: Taylor's Foreign Press, 1951.
Rabin, Chaim. 'The Beginning of Classical Arabic', *Studia Islamica* 4/1 (1955), 19–37.
Retsö, Jan. *The Arabs in Antiquity*. London: Kegan Paul, 2003.
Reynolds, Gabriel Said (ed.). *The Qur'ān in its Historical Context*. Routledge Studies in the Qurʿān. London: Routledge, 2008.
Sadeghi, Behnam and Mohsen Goudarzi, 'Sanʿāʾ 1 and the Origins of the Qur'ān', *Der Islam* 87 (2012), 1–129.
Schoeler, Gregor. 'The Codification of the Qurʾan: A Comment on the Hypotheses of Burton'. In: Angelika Neuwirth, Nicolai Sinai, and Michael Marx (eds.). *The Qur'ān in Context: Historical and Literary Investigations into the Qur'ānic Milieu*, pp. 779–94. Leiden: E. J. Brill, 2010.
Schoeler, Gregor. *The Oral and the Written in Early Islam*. Routledge Studies in Middle Eastern Literature, 13. London and New York: Routledge, 2006.
Shah, Mustafa. 'The Quest for the Origins of the *qurrāʾ* in the Classical Islamic Tradition', *Journal of Qur'anic Studies* 7/1 (2005), 1–35.
al-Sharkawi, Muhammad. *The Ecology of Arabic: A Study of Arabicization*. Boston, Leiden: E. J. Brill, 2010.
Sinai, Nicolai. *Die heilige Schrift des Islams: Die wichtigsten Fakten zum Koran*. Freiberg, Basel, Vienna: Herder, 2012.

Sinai, Nicolai and Angelika Neuwirth. 'Introduction'. In: Angelika Neuwirth, Nicolai Sinai, and Michael Marx (eds.). *The Qur'ān in Context: Historical and Literary Investigations into the Qur'ānic Milieu*, pp. 1–21. Leiden: E. J. Brill, 2010.
Talmon, Rafael. 'Dialects'. In: Jane Dammen McAuliffe (ed.). *Encyclopaedia of the Qurʾān*. 6 vols., 1:529–31. Leiden and Boston: E. J. Brill, 2001–6.
Talmon, Rafael. 'Grammar and the Qurʾān'. In: Jane Dammen McAuliffe (ed.). *Encyclopaedia of the Qurʾān*. 6 vols., 2:345–69. Leiden and Boston: E. J. Brill, 2001–6.
Versteegh, Kees. *The Arabic Language*. Reprint. Edinburgh: Edinburgh University Press, 2001.
Versteegh, Kees, Mushira Eid, et al. (eds.). *Encyclopedia of Arabic Language and Linguistics*. 5 vols. Leiden: E. J. Brill, 2006–9.
Vollers, Karl. *Volkssprache und Schriftsprache im alten Arabien*. Strassburgh: Trübner, 1906.
Wansbrough, John. *Quranic Studies*. School of Oriental and African Studies, University of London, London Oriental Series, 31. London: Oxford University Press, 1977.
Wild, Stefan (ed.). *The Qur'an as Text*. Leiden, New York, and Cologne: Brill, 1996.
Zwettler, Michael. *The Oral Tradition of Classical Arabic Poetry: Its Character and Implications*. Columbus: Ohio State University Press, 1978.

CHAPTER 18

VOCABULARY OF THE QUR'AN

Meaning in Context

MUSTAFA SHAH

It has been appositely observed that the study of the vocabulary of the Qur'an, particularly the detailed analysis of words which are presumed to possess a foreign provenance, has tended to be at the forefront of academic discussions about Islamic origins. Indeed, a not insignificant proportion of the early scholarship on the vocabulary of the Qur'an was subsumed under attempts to shed light on the text's perceived substrate influences. The expectation was that the attentive focus on areas such as etymology and the history of the usage of words would intimate the extent to which the Qur'an had drawn from and been inspired by biblical and other literary sources. It was also felt that such an approach would assist in the resolution of questions relating to the broader context of the narratives of the Qur'an thereby shedding light on the strategies adopted by classical exegetes in their explication of the text. Noting the historical connection between biblical philology and the study of the language of the Qur'an, this chapter reviews the various discussions, debates, and arguments which have defined the scholarship devoted to the vocabulary of the text.

The assumption that the narratives, themes, and exempla of the Qur'an were distilled from various traditional and apocryphal biblical sources has formed an axial theme in early studies of the text. Some of the early scholarship sought to draw attention to traceable Jewish sources and influences, including Abraham Geiger's original Latin essay, which was later published in German under the title *Was hat Mohammed aus dem Judenthume aufgenommen* (1833). The question of Jewish influences was also fleshed out in the work of Hartwig Hirschfeld, who authored a number of related studies, including *Jüdische Elemente im Korân: ein Beitrag zur Korânforschung* (1878), *Beiträge zur Erklärung des Korân* (1886), and *New Researches into the Composition and Exegesis of the Qoran* (1902), a text in which he emphatically declared that the 'Qoran, the text-book of Islam, is in reality nothing but a counterfeit of the Bible' and that 'its chaotic condition is in some way indicative of its contents' (Hirschfeld 1902: ii). Theodor Nöldeke's seminal work, *Geschichte des Qorâns* (1860) dedicates the opening chapter to a discussion of Jewish traces within the text; and this theme of influence was pursued with pronounced vigour in works such as William Clair Tisdall's *The Original Sources of the Qur'an* (1905); Wilhelm Rudolph's *Die Abhängigkeit des Qorans von Judentum und Christentum* (1922), which theorized about the Qur'an's dependence on Judaism and Christianity; and Heinrich Speyer's *Die biblischen Erzählungen im Qoran* (1931), which sought to identify biblical narrations in the Qur'an. The search for specific Christian themes and influences in the Qur'an was likewise a defining feature of a number of studies, including Richard Bell's *The Origin of Islam in its Christian Environment* (1925); Tor Andrae's *Der Ursprung des Islams und das Christentum* (1926), which looked at the connections between Islam and Christianity, and Karl Ahrens' 'Christliches im Qoran' (1930). Even the subject of Syriac stylistic influences within the Qur'an was tentatively probed in a study by Alphonse Mingana (1927).

Within the context of searching for remnants of biblical influences, it was the analysis of specific items of vocabulary from the Qur'an which became focal points of attention. Among prominent studies from these periods were Aloys Sprenger's 'Foreign Words Occurring in the Qoran' (1852); Rudolf Dvořák's *Über die Fremdwörter im Koran* (1884) and his *Ein Beitrag zur Frage über die Fremdwörter im Koran* (1884). Siegmund Fraenkel's *De Vocabulis in antiquis Arabum carminibus et in Corano peregrinis* (1880) examined the vocabulary of ancient Arabic poetry and lexical items in the Qur'an; and his *Die aramäischen Fremdwörter im Arabischen* (1886) traced Aramaic loanwords in Arabic. Key works on South Arabian studies, epigraphy, Semitic philology, and etymology also emerged during these periods. Among these were David Heinrich Müller's *Südarabische Studien* (1877) and his *Epigraphische Denkmäler aus Arabien* (1883); Ignazio Guidi's *Delia sede primitiva dei popoli semitici* (1879); Jacob Barth's *Sprachwissenschaftliche Untersuchungen zum Semitischen* and his *Etymologiscke Studien zum Semitischen* (1907–11); and Nöldeke's *Neue Beiträge zur semitischen Sprachwissenschaft* (1910), which presented fresh perspectives on the study of the Semitic languages, including sections devoted to identifying foreign words in the Qur'an (Nöldeke 1912: 23–30 and 31–66). Nöldeke's pupil Carl Brockelmann was the author of the monumental *Grundriss der vergleichenden Grammatik der semitischen Sprachen* (1908–13), an authoritative source for the comparative grammar of the Semitic languages. Other valuable work included Hubert Grimme's study of South Arabian loanwords in the Qur'an, 'Über einige Klassen südarabischer Lehnwörter im Koran' (1912). Grimme wrote an influential study of the life of Prophet in which he used examples from the vocabulary of the Qur'an to highlight putative instances of borrowing. Josef Horovitz took a different approach to the study of words in his 'Jewish Proper Names and Derivatives in the Qur'an' (1925) and his *Koranische Untersuchungen* (1926: 79ff). Referring to synergies of influence, Horovitz stressed the originality of the agency through which the Qur'an presented its materials. There also existed treatments of specific types of words in the Qur'an such as Charles Torrey's *The Commercial-Theological Terms in the Koran* (1892); he later authored *The Jewish Foundation of Islam* (1933) in which he ostensibly argued that the Prophet probably received all his information about biblical materials exclusively from Jewish sources and contacts. Although the works of scholars such as Hirschfeld, Torrey, and Bell were markedly polemical in tone, they were reflective of the general attitude towards the Islamic tradition prevalent at the time. Moreover, the views put forward in their writing ensured that the theme of influence would predominate studies of the Qur'an. It is a subject which continues to generate much interest (Zellentin 2017: 67; cf. Hoyland 2018).

Historically, in Early Modern Europe the study of Arabic was linked to supporting scholarship in biblical philology and it was this activity which provided an initial context for much of the aforementioned scholarship on the Qur'an. The importance attached to Arabic and its literary sources stemmed from the hypothesis that it retained more of the primeval language from which Hebrew and other cognate languages were also descended; scholars used shared affinities among these languages to hypothesize about the history of the usage of words. In this respect, in the seventeenth century among the earliest works to be published in Europe were Arabic lexicons.[1] Franciscus Raphelengius (1539–97), who taught Hebrew at Leiden, compiled a Latin dictionary, the *Lexicon Arabicum*, which appeared after his death in 1613 and Antonio Giggei (d. 1632) edited the *Thesaurus Linguae Arabicae* (4 vols.), a work based on the translation of primary Arabic sources, including the famous *al-Qāmūs al-muḥīṭ* compiled by al-Fīrūzābādī (d. 817/1414). In England the Arabist William Bedwell (1563–1632) had been in the process of compiling a lexicon which was never published; he did complete his *Arabian Trudgman*, which was meant to serve as a concise dictionary of Arabic terms to which he appended an index listing the chapters of the Qur'an (Hamilton 1985:66). It was in 1669 that Edmund Castell's masterpiece, the *Lexicon Heptaglotton*, appeared, representing a lifetime of scholarship. It was compiled to support biblical scholarship via the study of the oriental languages (Hamilton 1985: 93–4; and Hamilton 2017: 224).

The work which came to serve as the principal lexicon for the study of Arabic was Jacobus Golius' *Lexicon Arabico-Latinum* (1653), a text that drew from an eclectic range of primary Arabic sources, including the *Tāj al-lugha wa'l-ṣaḥāḥ*, the seminal work of al-Jawharī (d. *c.*400/1010) (Loop 2017: 10; cf. Toomer 1996: 48–9). Golius, an enthusiastic collector of Arabic manuscripts who spent extended periods in the Islamic world, had been a distinguished student of the celebrated Dutch scholar of Arabic Thomas van Erpen, or Erpenius (1584–1624), who was the first professor of Arabic at Leiden (Vrolijk and Leeuwen 2014; Bevilacqua 2018: 14). Golius' lexicon, with its unique arrangement of lexical data, was immensely influential as it provided the template for Georg Freytag's *Lexicon Arabico-Latinum*, which appeared between 1830 and 1837 and drew from an even wider selection of original sources. In the preface to his *Arabic English Lexicon* (1863–93), Edward William Lane ambitiously stated that he wanted to go beyond 'what Golius and others had already done in Latin' by drawing from 'the most copious Eastern sources'. His compilation was largely based on a translation of the lexicon, *Tāj al-ʿarūs*, authored by al-Zabīdī (d. 1205/1790), although he was also keen to trace the principal lexicographical sources from which it drew. Other important lexicons

[1] Encompassing forty years of scholarship, Ludovico Marracci's *Alcorani textus universus* appeared in 1698.

and concordances which furnished sources for the study of Arabic and the Qur'an were Reinhart Dozy's *Supplément aux dictionnaires arabes* (1881), C. H. Nallino's *Chrestomathia Qorani Arabica* (1893), and Friedrich Dieterici's *Arabisch-deutsches Handwörterbuch zum Koran* (1894). It was earlier in 1842 that Gustav Flügel (1802–70) published in Latin his *Concordantiae Corani arabicae*. Confirming the influence of Flügel's concordance, John Penrice, the author of the *Dictionary and Glossary of the Koran*, stated that it served as the 'sheet anchor' for his dictionary; Penrice also made extensive use of Heinrich Fleischer's edition of al-Bayḍāwī's Qur'an commentary (1846–8) and Georg Freytag's *Lexicon Arabico-Latinum* (Penrice 1873).

In the area of Arabic grammar, which provided an auxiliary framework for the study of Qur'anic vocabulary, for centuries the key Latin reference work had been Erpenius' *Grammatica arabica* (1611). In 1810 Antoine-Isaac Silvestre de Sacy published his *Grammaire arabe* and later in 1823 Thomas Christian Tychsen (1758–1834) compiled his *Grammatik der arabischen Schriftsprache*. The field was complemented by texts such as Carl Caspari's *Grammatica arabica* (1844–8), which William Wright translated from the Latin into English. Other relevant publications included Hartwig Derenbourg's edition of Sībawayhi's grammatical treatise, *al-Kitāb* (1881). Derenbourg had studied with scholars such as Joseph Toussaint Reinaud (1795–1867) and Fleischer, both of whom had been students of de Sacy.[2] The fecund body of scholarship produced over the centuries, together with the availability of primary texts and fragments acquired from the Islamic world, furnished materials and data which were used to lay the foundations for scholarship devoted to the study of the vocabulary of the Qur'an.

Vestiges of Influence

One work which drew substantially from the body of earlier scholarship was Arthur Jeffery's text on the foreign vocabulary of the Qur'an. Observing that debates about the question of Islamic origins had 'tended to run to a discussion of vocabulary' and with the intended aim of exploring the original literary environment of the text, Jeffery maintained that an examination of the vocabulary should form the basis for understanding not only the text of the Qur'an, but also the very life of the Prophet (Jeffery 1938: vii). He held that the religion of the Arabs was enhanced through its 'contact with higher religion and higher civilization' and that this led to their 'borrowing religious and cultural terms' (Jeffery 1938: vii). Commenting that Arabia at the time of the Arabs was 'not isolated from the rest of the world' and that its people were in full and constant contact with the surrounding peoples of Syria, Persia and Abyssinia', Jeffery suggested that this state of affairs brought about an exchange of vocabulary and ideas to the extent that the Qur'anic worldview along with the language of the Arabs was redolent of such

[2] Some sense of the scale of Fleischer's legacy is provided by the miscellany of shorter philological and grammatical studies preserved in his *Kleinere Schriften* (1885–8).

influences. Dismissive of the Qur'an's originality as a text, Jeffery even confidently claimed that the Jewish and Christian origin of words was obvious to the Western student, explaining that the greater part of the Qur'an's religious and cultural vocabulary 'is of a non-Arabic origin' (Jeffery 1938: 1–2). He proposed that by tracing words back to their original source languages, their true semantic bearing in the Qur'an would become more evident. Referring to the 'limitations of his own philological equipment for the task', he remarked that 'a work of this nature could have been adequately treated only by a Nöldeke, whose intimate acquaintance with the literatures of the Oriental languages involved, none of us in this generation can emulate' (Jeffery 1938: ix). Indeed, he pursued many of the lines of enquiry postulated in Nöldeke's *Neue Beiträge*. Referring to the achievements of previous scholarship on the vocabulary of the Qur'an, Jeffery indicated that for his own work he had sifted through a huge range of studies 'scattered in many periodicals in many languages', augmenting the data with his own analysis and comments.

Jeffery emphasized that attempts to explain complex lexical data in the Qur'an reveal more about later use of language and developments in exegesis than they do about the original import of such lexical data in the age of the Prophet (Jeffery 1938: vii; cf. Reynolds 2010: 19–20). Highlighting what he believed was the propensity of classical commentators to proffer a bewildering divergence of opinions as to the meaning of various lexical items, he held that the semantic compass of these words and phrases must have been lost on them. To illustrate this point he highlighted exegetical deliberations on the meaning of the term Ṣābiʾūn, for which he stated that there existed a plethora of conflicting opinions presented by classical exegetes. Jeffery bemoaned the fact that if classical exegetes were unable to recollect the correct identity of a group who at the time of the Prophet had been granted special recognition and favour in the Qur'an as a protected community, how could they be relied upon to preserve accurately explanations for lexical data considered to be relatively trivial in comparison? (Jeffery 1938; 4; cf. Wansbrough 1977: xxi). Speculating that classical scholars would have been patently aware of the presence of foreign vocabulary in the text, Jeffery concluded that theological strictures led them to temper their views on the subject and devise ingenious stratagems to explain away the idea that the Qur'an included foreign vocabulary (Jeffery 1938: 4–5; cf. Rippin 2003; Shah 1999: 34). He even espoused the view that the doctrine of the eternity of the Qur'an militated against scholars accepting the idea of the foreignness of words in the Qur'an, although a sophisticated range of factors coalesced to shape theological discussions on this issue.

In his introduction Jeffery mentions his starting on the collection back in 1926, recording that the book had been 'roughly four times the size of the present volume'; although in order to curtail production costs the final version was truncated. In fact he had intended to include in the original work's appendix a critical edition of Jalāl al-Dīn al-Suyūṭī's (d. 911/1505) *al-Muhadhdhab fī mā waqaʿa fī'l-Qurʾān min al-muʿarrab*, a work on foreign words in the Qur'an, which he edited from two manuscripts held in the Royal Library at Cairo, but which he omitted in the final 1938 edition (Jeffery 1938: viii). Jeffery did discuss the importance of a second tractate on the same subject by al-Suyūṭī, entitled *al-Mutawakkilī*. The text sets out a classification of the various languages from which foreign terms in the Qur'an supposedly originated, including languages such as Ethiopic, Persian, Greek, Indian, Syriac, Hebrew, Nabataean, and Coptic. Describing al-Suyūṭī's classification as the 'most complete that has come down to us', Jeffery's view was that much of the work was languidly based on 'mere guesswork' and that philologists quoted by al-Suyūṭī had very little conception of the meaning of the linguistic terms they used (Jeffery 1938: 12; Rippin 2003; cf. Hayajneh 2011).

In his own brief study on the subject of the foreign vocabulary of the Qur'an Michael Carter did describe Jeffery's account of the Islamic tradition's approach to the foreignness of words in the Qur'an as being 'somewhat patronizing', noting that 'his secondary sources even more so', although such approaches were often a corollary of the tendency to reduce the study of vocabulary to a search for origins. (Carter 2006: 121; Bevilacqua 2018: 75f.). Staying within the vector of the rigorous search for etymological evidence in the study of Qur'anic vocabulary, Catherine Pennacchio has cogently argued that advances in the study of the history of Arabic in its pre-Islamic context and the Semitic languages necessitate a circumspect review of some of the entries in Jeffery's work (Pennacchio 2011 and 2014). The impact of Jeffery's work was profound: he augmented and revised previous discussions, shaping the academic agenda for the study of the Qur'an's vocabulary.[3]

In traditional Islamic philological scholarship the analysis of specific Qur'anic words and expressions which were identified as being rare, abstruse, and even peculiar was reviewed within the genre of works referred to as *gharīb al-Qur'ān*. In these texts words were supplied with straightforward lexical equivalents (Rippin 1988: 158–9). The authorship of such treatises was popular among early generations of Kufan and Basran philologists, although the historical genesis of the genre together with the origin of the methodology employed within *gharīb* works, including their use of poetic citation, has been the subject of much debate (Wansbrough 1977: 216–18 cf. Rippin 1981 and 1983). The attestation of poetry for the purposes of linguistic clarification was initially challenged, although individuals such as Ibn al-Anbārī (d. 328/939) defended its use, dismissing theological objections that such practices granted poetry epistemological primacy over the language of the sacred text (Ibn al-Anbārī, *al-Waqf*, 1.99–102; cf. Burge 2015). Religious sensitivities are also cited to explain the manifestation of hostility to the practice of *tafsīr*, which encompassed the authorship of *gharīb* works, although the historicity of the debates about opposition has been questioned (Wansbrough 1977: 158; and Shah 2013: 72). The sophistication of the *gharīb* genre is demonstrated by the uniqueness of approaches and formats achieved in the works of scholars such as Ibn Qutayba (d. 276/889), al-Rāghib al-Iṣfahānī (d. early fifth/eleventh century), Ibn al-Jawzī (d. 597/1200), and Abū Ḥayyān (d. 745/1344). Moreover, the accomplishments of these philological endeavours were skillfully utilized in works such as the *ʿUmdat al-ḥuffāẓ fī tafsīr ashraf al-alfāẓ* authored by al-Samīn al-Ḥalabī (d. 756/1355). Alongside the study of dialectal materials, Arabic words perceived to have a foreign origin were explored in works entitled *lughāt*

[3] A brief supplement to Jeffery's work was compiled by David Margoliouth in 1939.

al-Qurʾān. Indeed, underlining the importance of earlier scholarship, when al-Jawāliqī (d. 539/1144) compiled his seminal treatise on loanwords, *Kitāb al-Muʿarrab min al-kalām al-aʿjamī ʿalā ḥurūf al-muʿjam*, he was heavily reliant on the lexical data collated by Kufan and Basran philologists (Rippin 2003: 228).

There did exist an impressive range of treatises and tracts composed on miscellaneous philological topics in which vocabulary from the Qur'an was adduced to illustrate key concepts and traits of Arabic. These included works on antonyms (*aḍdād*); synonyms (*tarāduf*); aspects of polysemy (*al-wujūh wa'l-naẓāʾir*); etymology (*ishtiqāq*); and even homonyms (*ishtirāk*). Scholars working in the nineteenth century recognized the effective importance of these specialized treatises for the study of Arabic: al-Jawāliqī's *Kitāb al-Muʿarrab* was published by Eduard Sachau (1845–1930) in 1867; and in 1881 Martinus Theodorus Houtsma (1851–1943) prepared a critical edition of Ibn al-Anbārī's *Kitāb al-Aḍdād*.[4] A conflated edition of a number of classical tracts on *al-aḍdād* was edited by August Haffner (1869–1941); and Nöldeke included a section devoted to *al-aḍdād* in his *Neue Beiträge* (Nöldeke 1910: 67f.; cf. Blachère 1967). Even in a text such as *Laysā fī kalām al-ʿArab*, authored by the reader specialist Ibn Khālawayhi (d. 370/980), discussions about idiosyncratic features of the Qur'an's vocabulary were occasionally introduced to exemplify the text's linguistic inimitability. A similar schema was adopted by Abū'l-Barakāt ibn al-Anbārī (d. 577/1181) in his *Asrār al-ʿarabiyya*, a text first edited in 1886 by Christian Friedrich Seybold (1859–1921) and in which select examples from the Qur'anic vocabulary were used to acclaim the linguistic profundities of Arabic. Arguments about the nature of the relationship between words and their meanings with reference to the Qur'an dominated discussions about the origin of language and debates about the existence of metaphors in the language of Arabic (Shah 2011; Rippin 2014). These were themes taken up with alacrity in specialized classical works on rhetoric and law and even in disquisitions on the inimitability of the Qur'an; materials from the aforementioned texts and tracts were meticulously assimilated into larger exegetical and lexicographical compilations, although a broad study of the significance of this material has yet to be ventured (Key 2018).

Philological Criticism in Context

Questions raised in Jeffery's study about the reliability of the traditional interpretation of the Qur'an were revisited in a seminal essay by Franz Rosenthal in which he set out to justify subjecting traditional Qur'anic interpretation to 'all the known rules of philological criticism' (Rosenthal 1953: 67). Rosenthal had commented that similar queries about the Bible had constituted the starting point of biblical criticism; indeed, he himself was an accomplished Semiticist who, in 1935, completed his Ph.D. on the subject of Palmyrenian inscriptions. Pointing to differences among classical commentators

[4] A partial manuscript of the *Kitāb al-Muʿarrab* was published by Sachau in Leipzig, 1867. Wilhelm Spitta, famed for his study of al-Ashʿarī, complemented the publication using a different manuscript. Haffner edited philological treatises by al-Aṣmaʿī and Ibn al-Sikkīt.

regarding the import of specific words, Rosenthal sensed that there were many instances where the meaning of foreign vocabulary in the Qur'an seemed to elude them, suggesting to him the 'possible fallibility of the traditional interpretation of the Qur'an'. His essay focused on the study of 'three well known problems in the Qur'an'. These included the meaning of the phrase '*jizya ʿan yadin*', which occurs in Q. 9:29 and discusses the payment of poll-tax and had 'so far completely defied interpretation'; the *hapax legomenon*, *al-Ṣamad* (Q. 112:2), which was traditionally explained in terms of God's not being 'hollow', to his being 'the enduring one'; and, the word *al-rajīm*, in the phrase *al-shayṭān al-rajīm*, which exegetes interpreted as being 'stoned' or pelted, but which was etymologically linked by Semiticists with the Ethiopic verb 'to curse'. Rosenthal accepted that the Prophet probably understood that the term *rajīm* connoted being 'stoned', concluding that classical exegetes had faithfully replicated his understanding of the word (Rosenthal 1953; cf. Jeffery 1938: 138–9; Silverstein 2013).

In his chapter Rosenthal did set out to isolate factors which he felt would help explain the existence of gaps in the knowledge of exegetes. Among these was guarded opposition to specific aspects of the pursuit of *tafsīr* during the time of the Prophet and even his supposed aversion to being questioned about certain aspects of the interpretation of the Qur'an. Rosenthal assumed that this may have led to a discontinuity of sorts between the Prophet's understanding of the vocabulary of the Qur'an and the levels of appreciation of those around him. In some of the subsequent scholarship on early *tafsīr*, such an approach would have been considered far too accepting of the reliability of the traditional accounts (Wansbrough 1977). Nonetheless, stating that the authorship of the Qur'an was 'a uniform one', he also explained that the changing milieu of post-Islamic Arabia in which pagan traditions were suppressed led to the genuine context of words being lost and that classical exegetes were not acquainted with the confluence of nuances and shifts in the idiomatic usage of words. While earlier scholarship on the vocabulary of the Qur'an provided the conceptual structures within which Rosenthal could locate his arguments, his own contributions were crucial for they invigorated discussions about the salutary importance of biblical and Semitic philology to the study of Qur'anic words. The etymological approach to the study of vocabulary did have its critics, but the profusion of further studies devoted to treatments of the lexical items featured in Rosenthal's study serves as testimony to the enduring influence of Rosenthal's work.

Suggesting that 'textual criticism' could be used to settle some of the arguments concerning the lexical ambiguities of certain items of Qur'anic vocabulary, it was a student of Rosenthal, James Bellamy, who authored a number of studies in which he presented a series of emendations to words in specific Qur'anic verses. Intriguingly, Bellamy mentions having discussed his interest in the area of emendation with Rosenthal, who advised him that he should not make his 'emendations too drastic, since they would not be accepted if they were too far out of line' (Bellamy 2006: 118; cf. Bellamy 1996). Bellamy contended that disagreements among classical commentators on the meaning of words or phrases in the Qur'an were probably 'a result of a mistake in the text than that the text is correct and some commentators got it right and others did not'. His studies sought to identify these 'errors', which he attributed to scribes, and propose plausible corrections. Bellamy remonstrated against modern scholarship's tendency to resort to the invoking of etymological arguments, rather than relying upon emendation. Despite describing his efforts as being reasonable, he does not seem to have heeded the counsel of Rosenthal as many of his examples of emendation are quite drastic ones guided by his assessment as to whether the 'text makes sense'; evidence from the early Qur'an manuscript tradition is not cited. The unintended consequences of such an approach have been brought to light by Shawkat Toorawa (Toorawa 2011: 240; cf. Ambros and Procházka 2004: 19).

In an earlier study Bellamy had developed a theory of the origin of the mysterious letters of the Qur'an (*al-ḥurūf al-muqaṭṭaʿa* or *fawātiḥ al-suwar*), propounding the view that these enigmatic letters, which appear in various combinations and groupings at the beginning of twenty-nine chapters of the Qur'an, were in effect old abbreviations of the invocation formula, the *basmala* (Bellamy 1973; cf. Paret 1971: 12). Suggesting they posed 'the most tantalising problem in Kor'anic studies', he maintained that the *basmala* was never an integral part of the Qur'an in the early Meccan years, but that it was used by later scribes to introduce verses of revelation. Bellamy reasoned that as the revealed chapters became longer in length, the use of the *basmala* increased, to the extent that scribes were now employing the convention of using abbreviations (Bellamy 1973: 270 and 284). He went on to claim that copyists in the post-ʿUthmānic period had forgotten that the letters were actually abbreviations of the *basmala*. Bellamy's theory was set out in the early seventies but even in later studies authored in the nineties, he continued to assert that he was 'more than ever convinced that the *fawātiḥ* are indeed old abbreviations of the *basmala* that suffered corruption at the hands of copyists' (Bellamy 1993: 573).

The idea of seeking an 'editorial' nexus for their origin was not novel: Nöldeke had initially subscribed to the view that these letters or logograms actually indicated the ownership of manuscripts used by the Prophet's scribe Zayd ibn Thābit (d. 42 or 57/662 or 676) when he collated the standard edition of the Qur'an; he suggested that these initials were carelessly retained in the final version. In his revised edition of the *Geschichte* Friedrich Schwally explained that there was an arbitrariness about the notion that the logograms were markers of possession, objecting that some of the combinations of letters could not be explained by such a theory; he also dismissed the idea that these were negligently left in the final copy by Zayd (Nöldeke 1919: 73). Schwally reported that Nöldeke eventually relinquished his views on the back of detailed criticisms by Otto Loth who set forth his account of these letters in a study devoted to al-Ṭabarī's commentary, ridiculing the notion that the initials of scribes could have been carelessly retained in the final version of the text. Reviewing Loth's views, Schwally referred to his claim that there existed an evident link between these letters and the statements that follow them, which convinced him of their original Qur'anic status. In his estimation Jewish influences in the form of cabbalistic ciphers could be discerned in their formulation (Nöldeke 1919: 2:75; cf. Jones 1962). Nöldeke went on to identify the letters as being a mystical allusion to an archetypal text in heaven and, like Loth, accepted that they were intended to form part of the original text. Although Nöldeke abandoned his original theory, it was ardently defended by Hirschfeld (Hirschfeld 1902: 141–3).

In subsequent years Eduard Goossens, a student of Hubert Grimme, propounded the view that the letters were abbreviations of disused titles of chapters; Goosens speculated that there originally existed a much greater variety of titles for chapters of the Qur'an. He even set about reorganizing the contents of chapters and verses to support his thesis. Some years later Goossens's theory was positively endorsed in a study by Jeffery, who described it as 'the biggest advance yet made toward the solution of the problem' (Jeffery 1924: 260). Jeffery also summarized a number of contemporary treatments of the topic, including studies by Aloys Sprenger and Franz Buhl. It was Bellamy who assuredly pronounced that many of the theories which preceded his work suffer from two principal defects: firstly, they isolate these letters from the textual history of the Qur'an; and, secondly, they overlook pre-ʿUthmānic variants. He spoke of his own theory attempting to take these into account while also grappling with the perplexing issue of why did the earliest commentators of the Qur'an have no recollection of their meaning. Debates about the significance of the letters continue: Keith Massey developed his version of the Nöldeke-Hirschfeld theory, linking the letters to markers of ownership and a process of ranking sources (Massey 1996: 300); Islam Dayeh's study of the *ḥawāmīm* chapters uses the literary character, cohesion, and unity of the chapters in which these clusters of letters feature to gauge their import (Dayeh 2010: 494). Referring to literary parallels, Devin Stewart raises the example of Greek and Babylonian oracular texts to highlight the symbolism of these letters (Stewart 2011: 333). In Alford Welch's summary of the scholarship on the mysterious letters, he concluded that the letters probably represented emblematic references to the Arabic alphabet, a view that was expressed in the commentary of al-Zamakhsharī (d. 538/1144), *al-Kashshāf ʿan ḥaqāʾiq ghawāmiḍ al-tanzīl wa-ʿuyūn al-aqāwīl fī wujūh al-taʾwīl*. It is not insignificant that it was Golius who auspiciously presented discussions about the meaning of these letters in the new edition of Erpenius' grammar that he published in 1656 (Hamilton 2017: 221).

Developments and Strategies

Following in the wake of Rosenthal's work, the term *ʿan yadin* was the subject of a number of studies, including papers by Claude Cahen (1962), M. J. Kister (1964), Meïr Bravmann (1966), Rudi Paret (1971), Uri Rubin (1993 and 2006), and more recently Muhammad Abdel Haleem (2012). It was Rubin who concluded that classical interpretations of the meaning of *ʿan yadin* were essentially reflections of views developed by later jurists, noting that 'rather than preserve the original meaning of Koranic legal injunctions, Muslim *tafsīr* reads into the Koran legal procedures that developed much later'. He posited that the true meaning of the term had to be sought in non-exegetical material, where it is used in reference to taxation and the possession of property, although a number of his conclusions were qualified in a subsequent study which referred to further evidence from poetry (Rubin 2006; cf. Abdel Haleem 2012). The word *Ṣamad* has been the subject of numerous appraisals, ranging from studies which focus on the intersection of exegetical and historical approaches such as that of Uri Rubin (1984), Arne Ambros (1986), Wesley Williams (2009), and Christos Simelidis (2011), to those which probe its theological and philosophical import, including the respective studies of Josef van Ess (1988) and Daniel De Smet–Maryem Sebti (2009).

One term which is often cited alongside *ʿan yadin* and *Ṣamad* in discussions about exegetical gaps in the knowledge of the classical commentators is the word *kalāla* (Q. 4:12 and 4:176). In a series of studies David Powers claimed that although the meaning of the word was eventually identified by classical scholars as representing the share of wealth awarded to collateral descendants, it originally connoted a 'daughter-in-law', but this meaning was insidiously suppressed for political reasons. Powers held that initially the verse granted a man the right to designate an heir. Implying that this original meaning was known to a select number of Companions, the evidence cited by Powers drew on some provisional arguments about peculiar etymological links between the Arabic term *kalāla* and a similar term in Akkadian, *kalla* (k-l-l), which refers to an adopted 'daughter in law' (Powers 1982: 82). In a number of later studies Powers cited further evidence which he felt corroborated his arguments, explaining that one of the earliest known manuscripts of the Qur'an held at the Bibliothèque nationale de France (328a) included folios which upon close analysis betray an amendment of the reading from *kalla* to *kalāla* (Powers 2009: 170–5). The classical works on variants, including non-canonical materials, preserve no such *lectio*. Central to Powers's argument is the view that the term *kalāla*, which replaced *kalla*, was contrived in the sense that it was not in vogue at the time of the Prophet. Powers contended that the purported aim of this process was to emphasize the finality of the Prophet's mission by the elimination of the symbolic importance of the Prophet's adopted son Zayd. Taking a different line of argument, in his treatment of the term Agostino Cilardo suggests that sinuous semantic shifts in its interpretation can be attributed to innovative legal strategies employed by jurists to augment the scope of Qur'anic legislation (Cilardo 2005). In two related studies Pavel Pavlovitch assessed the arguments of Powers and Cilardo using references to *isnād*s and *matn*s to explain shifts in the meaning of the term (Pavlovitch 2012 and 2015). Significantly, in Powers's study the allegedly foreign origin of the term *kalla*, the theme of suppression, and the hesitancy shown by classical exegetes when attempting to explain its meaning, are collectively cited to support his thesis.

Focusing on the Qur'anic use of the term *furqān*, a word that is connected with connotations of 'redemption', 'salvation', and 'distinction', Fred Donner used arguments about the transmission of the Qur'an to explain the term's etymology and its interpretation by classical exegetes. Confirming that its semantic range varied in the Qur'an, he claimed that the word *furqān* represented a conflation of two separate Aramaic/Syriac words: '*purqānā*' (salvation) and '*puqdānā*' (commandment), which he alleged were confused by later copyists when the Qur'an was transcribed. Jeffery had maintained that the 'vocabulary of the Aramaic-speaking Christians' was probably the source of the borrowing for the term (Jeffery 1938 226–8.) Notwithstanding Donner's claim that the materials must have been derived from Syriac sources when the Qur'an was compiled and that classical exegetes were not aware of all the nuances of the word, he stated that confusion among copyists concerning its meaning indicates that the text of the Qur'an must have been committed to writing from an early date. He contended that an oral tradition of transmission was not in place to prevent such confusion from occurring as scholars attempted 'to vocalize a text that was conveyed in purely written form'. Donner did claim that the explanations proffered by classical exegetes to explain the term were contrived and ponderous, particularly the idea that at a number of junctures in the Qur'an the term meant 'to separate and distinguish' (Donner 2007: 299–300). Citing an extensive range of philological dicta, Uri Rubin challenged the validity of a number of the main arguments presented in Donner's study. His view was that there was ample evidence to confirm that classical exegetes were not only acutely aware of the Targumic import of the Qur'an's use of *furqān*, but that it was not an exclusively non-Arabic loanword and actually had ancient Arabian roots. Rubin did conclude that explanations preserved by classical exegetes were wholly consistent with those meanings that the word had acquired within its Arabian context (Rubin 2009). Interestingly, it was concerns about the reliability of traditional explanations that triggered Donner's study.

The connection between disputes about the meaning of Qur'anic vocabulary and the historical timeline of the transmission of the Qur'an was invoked in a study by Patricia Crone. Discussing 'two legal problems' in the Qur'an, she argued that gaps in the knowledge of exegetes together with evidence concerning the discontinuity between Qur'anic legislation and subsequent expressions of Islamic law could be used to propose a review of the establishment of the Qur'an as a fixed text. The first of the two legal problems Crone examined relates to traditional explanations of the meaning of the term *kitāb* and its cognates in Q. 24:33. In the classical exegetical commentaries and legal literature (and even in a number of recent translations) the term was equated with a contract of manumission. Crone took exception to this, insisting that this interpretation was patently incorrect, as in the verse concerned, the term *kitāb* connoted a contract of marriage. She asserted that even if certain exegetes had forgotten the original meaning of *kitāb* in this verse, they could easily have deduced it from the context, yet 'they never tried', but rather persisted in the association of the term with the act of manumission (Crone 1994: 6). One could argue that classical commentators followed that line of interpretation because the 'marriage' of slaves is already mentioned and encouraged at the beginning of the sequence of Qur'anic verses which feature in this passage, but for Crone the explanations of the verse reveal the existence of gaps in the knowledge of exegetes and her study is an attempt to account for them. The second legal problem addressed in Crone's study related not to an item of vocabulary, but rather a pre-classical legal notion: namely, the law of succession and rules concerning the property of freedmen and freedwomen, the application of which, in her view, showed evident discontinuity between Qur'anic legislation and subsequent expressions of law.[5] Crone cautiously granted that although Rosenthal's attempts to explain the existence of exegetical gaps in the knowledge of early commentators go some way towards explaining their failure to grasp the meaning of terms such as *al-Ṣamad* and *al-rajīm*, they do not fully clarify why in other instances explanations were seemingly replete with inconsistencies. Her own explanation invoked the historical timeline of the standardization of the Qur'an with reference to the work of John Burton and John Wansbrough (Crone 1994: 21). Assessing the merits

[5] This she abbreviated, referring to it as the DAEP rule: namely, *dhawū 'l-arḥām* exclude patrons.

and disadvantages of both scholars' theories, in so far as they could be invoked to explain shortcomings in the interpretations offered by exegetes, Crone stated that although it can be contested, 'a theory of belated codification and canonization' as advocated by Wansbrough, 'works very well in the present context', adding that it would 'allow us to explain all the examples so far known of exegetical ignorance of, and juristic lack of attention to, the import of Qurʾānic passages' (Crone 1994: 21). Her rationale is that the 'belated canonization of the book would give us a period in between, in which a variety of religious works, including proto-Qurʾānic materials, were in circulation without having coalesced as an Arab scripture'. The assumption is that such a text would not yet have been endowed with 'overriding authority' and that in the absence of such an authoritative text, the early tradition of Qur'anic commentary in the Ḥijāz would not have existed (Crone 1994: 37). The fact that it is now accepted that the establishment of a fixed text precedes the periods posited by Wansbrough suggests that a different explanation for the existence of 'exegetical gaps' needs to identified.

The use of chronological criteria to determine the semantic compass of Qur'anic vocabulary has been adopted in a number of key studies. For example, applying internal chronological criteria relative to the Qur'an's narratives, Jacques Jomier's 1957 examination of the divine attribute *al-Raḥmān* isolates subtle semantic shifts in the technical compass of single words across different Qur'anic narratives and pericopes. A similar internal chronological approach is employed in William Graham's analysis of the term *qurʾān* with reference to its Syriac cognate (Graham 1984). Proposing that there were loci in the Qur'an where the word originally connoted the physical act of recitation, he explains that these were later glossed to reflect scripture in a more composite sense. It is in Fred Leemhuis's study of the etymology of the Qur'anic term *sijjīl* (baked clay or stone) that an attempt is made to use the Aramaic origins of the term to chart the chronological trajectories of its historical dissemination in the Arabic language (Leemhuis 1982; cf. Bellamy 1993). Accepting the traditional chronology for the establishment of the Qur'an, the semanticist Toshihiko Izutsu developed an approach to the study of the vocabulary of the Qur'an in which he argued that the context of a word's usage must be awarded primacy over any etymological considerations (Izutsu 1964 and 1966). Arguing that there were inherent shortcomings in comparing the meaning of words across different religious traditions and cultures, Izutsu insisted that the worldview of the Qur'an was also a factor which had to be considered when attempting to explain the meaning of its vocabulary (See Chapter 37). Arguments about the limits of the actual range and frequency of Qur'anic vocabulary prompted Robert Brunschvig to suggest that a rigorous investigation of words omitted by the Qur'an remained a desideratum (Brunschvig 1956). Separately, it is in the work of Holger Zellentin that attempts are also made to understand the vocabulary and discourse of the Qur'an through the literature of the communities with which the text interacts (Zellentin 2016). In these and other studies of the Qur'an's vocabulary, the fact that such radically different interpretations, approaches, and findings exist confirms the complexity of the relevant data and the rich vein of scholarship the vocabulary of the Qur'an has inspired over the years. Moreover, a circumspect review of the discussions featured in many of the aforementioned studies underlines not only the relevance of Jeffery's observation concerning the inextricable link between discourses on Islamic origins and the Qur'an's vocabulary, but also the fact that very slight differences in the respective weighting of arguments about textual transmission, emendation, etymology, and philological evidence, can lead to such strikingly divergent findings when it comes to defining the semantic compass of words in the Qur'an.

Outlooks and Prospects

In an essay which characterized studies devoted to the foreign vocabulary of the Qur'an as being irredeemably 'unruly', Walid Saleh questioned the foundational premise of these studies. The premise to which he was referring states that 'for every word in the Qur'an for which the native philological tradition fails to give a solitary explanation and instead offers multiple meanings, modern scholars have to presume that they are dealing with a foreign word' (Saleh 2010: 649). Notwithstanding his criticism of the defects inherent in this premise, the explanations provided by the resort to etymological arguments were considered by Saleh to be implausible. The implication is that the burden of proof for the study of such material should be placed not on a word's supposed foreign provenance, but rather its semantic bearing within the literary and contextual contours of the Qur'an; as Saleh notes, it was James Barr in his work on the Hebrew Bible who made the telling observation that the history of a word is by no means an 'infallible guide to its present meaning' (Saleh 2010: 658; Barr 1961: 107). Andrzej Zaborski had too expressed reservations concerning whether it was prudent to elevate the significance of etymological arguments over context when probing the meaning of words (Zaborski 2004: 143; cf. Amsler 1989). The concern here is that steered and cajoled by arguments about etymology, a Procrustean approach to defining select items of Qur'anic vocabulary was being adopted. Saleh insisted it was important to bear in mind that classical exegetes adopted an anthological approach when collating lexical data which led to an unseemly accumulation of conflicting material; accordingly, it was erroneous to postulate about the probable foreign origins of lexical items in the Qur'an using the musings of classical exegetes as a basis for initiating such enquiries. He also questioned the value of classical lexicons, highlighting that they slavishly reproduce linguistic analyses favoured by exegetes (Saleh 2010: 650–2). Alleging that the work of exegetes was a 'keenly crafted attempt to circumvent philology', Saleh suggested that within classical scholarship theological considerations weighed heavily upon the interpretation of words in so far as their import was often taken out of context to support ideologically driven perspectives (Saleh 2010: 652). Saleh's assessment predicates that a substantial element of exegetical activity was aimed at subverting the meaning of words and that, primarily, theological objectives were driving every aspect of scholarly discourses. It also presupposes that classical Islamic disciplines such as philology lacked an independent edge. Such views suffer from being too generalized, although Lothar Kopf deemed critical the impact that theological strictures and constraints had upon the development of philology (Kopf 1956: 33).

Nonetheless, it has been shown that a strong spirit of resourcefulness was a mark of the endeavours of early linguists which is evident from the inventive range of philological theories and concepts they developed (Shah 1999 and 2000). The attempts to attenuate the significance of classical Islamic philological scholarship deprive the study of early exegetical strategies of an important context.

With reference to his criticism of etymological arguments and the premises which informed them, Saleh adduces two examples to justify his views. The first of these was Rosenthal's study of the *hapax legomenon*, *al-Ṣamad*, in which it was hypothesized that the word was 'a survival of an ancient Northwestern Semitic religious term that may not have been properly understood by Muḥammad himself nor by the old poets' (Rosenthal 1953: 83; Saleh 2010: 654). Rosenthal noted that in Ugaritic the term (*ṣmd*) was used to connote 'a stick or club that is wielded by Baʿl'. In this instance Saleh argued that judgements surrounding the meaning of the term were not informed by an appreciation of the primary literary context in which the word was used in the Qur'an, but by the notion that disagreements about the term's import among exegetes intimated that the word possessed a foreign origin. He states that scholars took no interest in the word *al-Ṣamad* before 'it was pronounced foreign' (Saleh 2010: 656). Contrasting the findings of Rosenthal with Rubin's study of the same term, Saleh commented that the latter's work marked a gratifying departure from previous efforts as it extensively engaged with classical exegetical discussions with a concern for understanding their theological and philological contexts; within this approach, the search for a foreign element is only countenanced once all the internal evidence has been scrutinized. Rubin concluded that the term *al-Ṣamad* was a divine epithet and a genuine Arabic term which was in vogue in Arabia at the time of the Prophet.

In his second example Saleh concentrated on the protracted discussions concerning the Qur'anic usage of the word *ḥanīf*. Scholars had been struck by the fact that in the languages of Aramaic and Syriac the term possessed a pejorative connotation and was used to describe a heathen (*ḥanpā*); yet, in the Qur'an it evinces a positive meaning (Jeffery 1938: 115). Having discussed the opinions of Bell, David Margoliouth, Horovitz, Grimme, and Nöldeke, Jeffery had inclined to the view that it was probably a Syriac term, explaining that pre-Islamic Arabs might have been aware of its usage by Christians who used it to refer to those 'who were neither Jews or of their own faith' (Jeffery 1938: 115). Saleh cited a study of the term *ḥanīf* by Rippin, who commented that no other word had been so extensively examined within the academic tradition. Largely dismissive of the etymological solutions proffered to explain the meaning of *ḥanīf*, Rippin confirmed that in its Qur'anic context the term signified 'a notion of basic religious impulse in humanity towards dedication to the one God'. Saleh commended the fact that Rippin's study had shown that arguments about the word's putative foreign roots were 'not necessary for achieving a proper understanding of the term in the Qur'an' (Saleh 2010: 660). Despite this conclusion, even Rippin professed to being perplexed as to how 'the word transformed from a term of rebuke to one of eminent spiritual development'. Saleh suggests that such a statement betrays the baleful influence of the debates about etymology

(Rippin 1991: 167; cf. Saleh 2010: 660). On a more general point, Rippin did state that when faced with difficulties, classical exegetes would expediently resort to speaking of the foreignness of a word, but he also acknowledged the assured skill with which exegetes were able to find solutions to exegetical quandaries (Rippin 2003: 438). In a recent study of the terms *ḥanīf* and *naṣārā* François De Blois proposed that their usage had to be understood in the context of the Qur'an's discourse with 'Jewish Christianity' (early Christian groups), within which the connotation of the words was not deemed negative (De Blois 2002; cf. Stroumsa 2014). Given that Saleh's study represents an unswerving attempt to question the efficacy of awarding primacy to arguments about etymology in the study of the vocabulary of the Qur'an, it is not surprising that he reserves a substantial part of his essay for a detailed critique of Christoph Luxenberg's theory which postulated that the entire text of the Qur'an was a reformulation of an essentially Syro-Aramaic urtext; in Luxenberg's work, numerous items of Qur'anic vocabulary are reviewed in light of his theory (Luxenberg 2000). Saleh posits that the stubborn preoccupation with the issue of the foreignness of the Qur'an's vocabulary has incontrovertibly hindered the development of an approach to the analysis of the Qur'an in which its literary character is fully appreciated (Saleh 2010: 694).

Suggesting that the quest for historical truth in studies of the vocabulary of the Qur'an was fraught with hermeneutical difficulties, Rippin did remark that 'scholars will never become a seventh-century Arabian townsperson, but will remain forever a twentieth-century historian or theologian' (Rippin 1988: 3; cf. Neuwirth and Sells 2016: 3). He was adamant that the focus on traditional historical-philological methods of the analysis of the Qur'an could yield only approximate and speculative values of the original meaning of the text. Rippin's simple contention is that the study of 'reactions' to the text across the course of history, separating the text of scripture from its interpretation, offered a much more constructive way of understanding the relative importance of meanings. His comments provoked a mild rebuke from Patricia Crone who stated that while the effort to grasp the original meaning of the Qur'an should not deter other forms of investigation, the quest to uncover 'original' meanings must remain the principal concern of the historian of Islam (Crone 1994: 1; cf. Donner 2011: 36; Burge 2015: introd.). The attempt to unearth 'original meanings' has certainly been a mark of some of the recent scholarship in the field as demonstrated by the critical array of vocabulary-based studies which feature in the volumes edited by Gabriel Reynolds and other key works (Reynolds 2008 and 2011; cf. Neuwirth 2010 and Neuwirth and Sells 2016; Zellentin 2019). Such efforts confirm the intense level of interest the field of Qur'anic vocabulary continues to garner. Commenting on the publication of Qur'an dictionaries, Rippin commended the fact that they enriched lexicographical sources for the study of the Qur'an (Rippin 2011: 38f.). However, he went on to state that scholars were still in need of a work which provided 'specific studies of each word, considering the basis upon which the meaning is established' (Rippin 2011: 46). Such sentiments would appear to confirm the fact that the study of the vocabulary of the Qur'an will remain at the vanguard of attempts to engage with the Qur'an and its narratives.

Conclusions

Scholarship in biblical philology and Semitics profoundly influenced the development of early academic approaches to the study of the Qur'an's vocabulary. Within this framework, arguments about the history of the usage of words and etymology frequently served as an arterial route to exploring the semantic compass of selected words in the Qur'an. Although these arguments retain their pertinence, developments in the field have seen a complementary array of factors also being taken into consideration in the effort to resolve questions regarding the Qur'an's vocabulary. These broader based approaches are likely to contribute to attempts to gain a profounder understanding of the text.

Bibliography

Primary Sources

Ibn al-Anbārī, Abū Bakr Muḥammad ibn al-Qāsim. *Kitāb al-Aḍdād*. Ed. by Muḥammad Abū'l-Faḍl Ibrāhīm. Beirut, Sidon: al-Maktabat al-ʿAṣriyya, 1987.

Ibn al-Anbārī, Abū Bakr Muḥammad ibn al-Qāsim. *Kitāb Īḍāḥ al-waqf wa'l-ibtidāʾ*. Ed. by Muḥyī al-Dīn ʿAbd al-Raḥmān Ramaḍān. 2 vols. Damascus: Majmaʿ al-Lugha al-ʿArabiyya, 1971.

Ibn al-Jawzī. *Tadhkirat al-arīb fī tafsīr al-gharīb*. Ed. Ṭāriq Fatḥī Sayyid. Beirut: Dār al-Kutub al-ʿIlmiyya, 2004.

Ibn al-Mulaqqin, *Tafsīr gharīb al-Qurʾān*. Ed. Samīr al-Majdhūb. Beirut: ʿĀlam al-Kutub, 1987.

Ibn Qutayba. *Kitāb Tafsīr gharīb al-Qurʾān*. Ed. Aḥmad Ṣaqr. Beirut: Dār al-Kutub al-ʿIlmiyya, 1978.

Al-Jawālīqī. *al-Muʿarrab min kalām al-aʿjamī ʿalā ḥurūf al-muʿjam*. Ed. Aḥmad Muḥammad Shākir. Cairo: Maṭbaʿat Dār al-Kutub al-Miṣriyya, n.d.

al-Rāghib al-Iṣfahānī. *Muʿjam mufradāt alfāẓ al-Qurʾān*. Ed. Nadīm Marʿashlī. Beirut: Dār al-Kātib al-ʿArabī, 1972.

Al-Zamakhsharī. *Al-Kashshāf ʿan ḥaqāʾiq ghawāmiḍ al-tanzīl wa-ʿuyūn al-taʾwīl*. 4 vols. Beirut: Dār al-Fikr, 1977.

Secondary Sources

Abdel Haleem, Muhammad. 'The *jizya* Verse (Q. 9:29): Tax Enforcement on Non-Muslims in the First Muslim State', *Journal of Qur'anic Studies* 14/2 (2012), 72–89.

Ambros, Arne Amadeus. 'Die Analyse von Sure 112: Kritiken, Synthesen, neue Ansätze', *Der Islam* 63 (1986), 219–47.

Ambros, Arne Amadeus and Stephan Procházka. *A Concise Dictionary of Koranic Arabic*. Wiesbaden: Reichert, 2004.

Amsler, M. *Etymology and Grammatical Discourse in Late Antiquity and the Early Middle Ages*. Amsterdam: John Benjamins Publishing Company, 1989.

Baalbaki, Ramzi. *The Arabic Lexicographical Tradition: From the 2nd/8th to the 12th/18th Century*. Leiden: Brill, 2014.

Badawi, Elsaid and Muhammad Abdel Haleem. *Arabic–English Dictionary of Qurʾānic Usage*. Leiden: Brill, 2008.

Barr, James. *The Semantics of Biblical Language*. Oxford University Press, 1961.
Barr, James. *Comparative Philology and the Text of the Old Testament*. Oxford: Clarendon Press, 1968.
Bellamy, James. 'The Mysterious Letters of the Koran: Old Abbreviations of the *Basmalah*', *Journal of the American Oriental Society* 93/3 (1973), 267–85.
Bellamy, James. 'Some Proposed Emendations to the Text of the Qurʾān', *Journal of the American Oriental Society* 113/4 (1993), 562–73.
Bellamy, James. 'More Proposed Emendations to the Text of the Qurʾān', *Journal of the American Oriental Society* 116/2 (1996), 116–204.
Bellamy, James. 'Ten Qur'anic Emendations', *Jerusalem Studies in Arabic and Islam* 31 (2006), 118–38.
Bevilacqua, Alexander. *The Republic of Arabic Letters: Islam and the European Enlightenment*. Cambridge, MA: The Belknap Press of Harvard University Press, 2018.
Blachère, Régis. 'Origine de la théorie des *aḍdād*'. In: Jacques Berque and Jean-Paul Charney (eds.). *L'Ambivalence dans la culture arabe*, pp. 397–403. Paris: Éditions Anthropos, 1967.
Bravmann, Meïr. 'The Ancient Background of the Qurʾanic Concept *al-ǧizyatu ʿan yadīn*', *Arabica* 13 (1966), 307–14.
Brunschvig, Robert. 'Simples remarques negatives sur le vocabulaire du Coran', *Studia Islamica* 5 (1956), 19–32.
Burman, Thomas. 'Polemic, Philology, and Ambivalence: Reading the Qurʾān in Latin Christendom', *Journal of Islamic Studies* 15/2 (2004), 181–209.
Burge, Stephen (ed.). *The Meaning of the Word: Lexicology and Qurʾānic Exegesis*. Oxford: Oxford University Press, in association with the Institute of Ismaili Studies, 2015.
Cahen, Claude. 'Coran IX.29: Ḥatta yuʿṭu'l-jizyā ʿan yadin wa-hum sāghirūn', *Arabica* 9 (1962), 76–9.
Carter, Michael. 'Foreign Vocabulary'. In: Andrew Rippin (ed.). *The Blackwell Companion to the Qurʾān*, pp. 120–39. Oxford: Blackwell, 2006.
Cilardo, Agostino. *The Qurʾānic Term Kalāla: Studies in Arabic Language and Poetry, Ḥadīṯ, Tafsīr and Fiqh: Notes on the Origins of Islamic Law*. Edinburgh: Edinburgh University Press, 2005.
Crone, Patricia. 'Two Legal Problems Bearing on the Early History of the Qurʾān', *Jerusalem Studies in Arabic and Islam* 18 (1994), 1–37.
Dayeh Islam. '*Al-Ḥawāmīm*: Intertextuality and Coherence in Meccan *surahs*'. In: Angelika Neuwirth, Nicolai Sinai, and Michael Marx (eds.). *The Qurʾān in Context: Historical and Literary Investigations into the Qurʾānic Milieu*, pp. 461–98. Leiden: Brill, 2010.
De Blois, François. '*Naṣrānī* (*Ναζωραῖος*) and *Ḥanīf* (*ἐθνικός*): Studies on the Religious Vocabulary of Christianity and of Islam', *Bulletin of the School of Oriental and African Studies* 65 (2002), 1–30.
De Smet, Daniel and Maryem Sebti. 'Avicenna's Philosophical Approach to the Qur'an in the Light of his *Tafsīr Sūrat al-Ikhlāṣ*', *Journal of Qur'anic Studies* 11/2 (2009), 134–48.
Donner, Fred. 'Qurʾānic *Furqān*', *Journal of Semitic Studies* 52/2 (2007), 279–300.
Donner, Fred. 'The Historian, the Believer and the Qurʾān'. In: Gabriel Reynolds (ed.). *New Perspectives on the Qurʾān: The Qurʾān in its Historical Context II*, pp. 25–37. London: Routledge, 2011.
Fück, Johann. *Die arabischen Studien in Europa bis in den Anfang des 20. Jahrhunderts*. Leipzig: Otto Harrassowitz, 1955.
Goossens, Eduard. 'Ursprung und Bedeutung der koranischen Siglen', *Der Islam* 13 (1923), 191–226.

Graham, William. 'The Earliest Meaning of 'Qurʾān', *Die Welt des Islams* 23/24 (1984), 361–77.
Hamilton. Alistair. *William Bedwell, the Arabist, 1563–1632*. Leiden: Published for the Sir Thomas Browne Institute [by] E. J. Brill/Leiden University Press, 1985.
Hayajneh, Hani. 'The Usage of Ancient South Arabian and Other Arabian Languages as an Etymological Source for Qur'anic Vocabulary'. In: Gabriel Reynolds (ed.). *New Perspectives on the Qurʾān: The Qurʾān in its Historical Context II*, pp. 117–46. London: Routledge, 2011.
Hirschfeld, H. *New Researches into the Composition and Exegesis of the Qoran*. London: Royal Asiatic Society, 1902.
Hoyland, Robert. 'The Jewish and/or Christian Audience of the Qur'an and the Arabic Bible'. In Francisco del Río Sánchez (ed.). *Jewish Christianity and the Origins of Islam*, pp. 31–40. Turnhout: Brepols, 2018.
Izutsu, Toshihiko. *God and Man in the* Qurʾān*: Semantics of the Qurʾānic Weltanschauung*. Tokyo: The Keio Institute of Cultural and Linguistic Studies, 1964.
Izutsu, Toshihiko. *Ethico-Religious Concepts in the Qurʾān*. Montreal: McGill University Press, 1966.
Jeffery, Arthur. 'The Mystic Letters of the Koran', *Muslim World* 14 (1924), 247–60.
Jeffery, Arthur. *The Foreign Vocabulary of the Qurʾān*. Baroda: Oriental Institute, 1938.
Jomier, Jacques. 'Le nom divin "al-Raḥmān" dans le Coran'. In *Mélanges Louis Massignon*, 3 vols., 2:361–81. Damascus: Institut Français de Damas, 1957.
Jones, Alan. 'The Mystical Letters of the Qur'an', *Studia Islamica* 16 (1962), 5–11.
Key, Alexander. *Language between God and the Poets: Maʿnā in the Eleventh Century*. Oakland, California: University of California Press, 2018.
Kister, M. J. '"*ʿAn Yadin*" (Qurʾān IX.29). An Attempt at Interpretation', *Arabica* 11 (1964), 272–8.
Kopf, Lothar. 'Religious Influences on Medieval Arabic Philology', *Studia Islamica* 5 (1956), 33–59.
Leemhuis, Fred. 'Qurʾānic *Siǧǧīl* and Aramaic *SGYL*', *Journal of Semitic Studies* 27/1 (1982), 47–56.
Loop, Jan, Alastair Hamilton, and Charles Burnett (eds.). *The Teaching and Learning of Arabic in Early Modern Europe*. Leiden and Boston: Brill, 2017.
Luxenberg, Christoph. *Die syro-aramäische Lesart des Koran: Ein Beitrag zur Entschlüsselung der Koransprache*. Berlin: Verlag Hans Schiler, 2000.
Margoliouth, David. 'Some Additions to Professor Jeffery's *Foreign Vocabulary of the Qurʾān*', *Journal of the Royal Asiatic Society* 71 (1939), 53–61.
Massey, Kevin. 'A New Investigation into the "Mystery Letters" of the Qur'an', *Arabica* 43 (1996), 497–501.
Mingana, Alphonse. 'Syriac Influence on the Style of the Ḳurʾān', *Bulletin of the John Rylands Library* 11 (1927), 77–98.
Mir, Mustansir. *Dictionary of Qurʾānic Terms and Concepts*. New York: Garland, 1987.
Neuwirth, Angelika. *The Qurʾān in Context: Historical and Literary Investigations into the Qurʾānic Milieu*. Angelika Neuwirth, Nicolai Sinai, and Michael Marx (eds.). Leiden: Brill, 2010.
Neuwirth, Angelika and Michael Sells. *Qurʾānic Studies Today*. New York: Routledge, 2016.
Nöldeke, Theodor. *Geschichte des Qorâns*. Göttingen, 1860. Revised by Friedrich Schwally and supplemented by Gotthelf Bergsträsser and Otto Pretzl. Leipzig: Dieterich'sche Verlagsbuchhandlung, 1909, 1919, and 1938.
Nöldeke, Theodor. *Neue Beiträge zur semitischen Sprachwissenschaft*. Strasbourg: Verlag von Karl J. Trübner, 1910.
Paret, Rudi. *Der Koran: Kommentar und Konkordanz*. Stuttgart: Verlag W. Kohlhammer, 1971.
Pavlovitch, Pavel. 'Some Sunnī *Ḥadīth* on the Qurʾānic Term *Kalāla*: An Attempt at Historical Reconstruction'. *Islamic Law and Society* 19/1/2 (2012), 86–159.

Pavlovitch, Pavel. *The Formation of the Islamic Understanding of Kalāla in the Second Century AH (718–816 CE)*. Leiden: Brill, 2015.
Pennacchio, Catherine. 'Les emprunts lexicaux dans le Coran: les problèmes de la liste d'Arthur Jeffery'. *Bulletin du Centre de recherche français à Jérusalem* 22 (2011), 1–19.
Pennacchio, Catherine. *Les emprunts à l'hébreu et au judéo-araméen dans le Coran, Avant-propos de Moshe Bar-Asher*. Paris: Librairie d'Amérique et d'Orient, J. Maisonneuve: 2014.
Penrice, John. *A Dictionary and Glossary of the Koran, with Copious Grammatical References and Explanations of the Text*. London: Henry S. King, 1873; repr. Mineola, NY: Dover Publications, 2004.
Powers, David. 'The Islamic Law of Inheritance Reconsidered: A New Reading of Q. 4:12B', *Studia Islamica* 55 (1982), 33–53.
Powers, David. *Muḥammad Is Not the Father of Any of your Men: The Making of the Last Prophet*. Philadelphia: University of Pennsylvania, 2009.
Reynolds, Gabriel. (ed.). *The Qur'ān in its Historical Context*. London: Routledge, 2008.
Reynolds, Gabriel. *The Qur'ān and its Biblical Subtext*. London: Routledge, 2010.
Reynolds, Gabriel. (ed.). *New Perspectives on the Qur'ān: The Qur'ān in its Historical Context II*. London: Routledge, 2011.
Rippin, Andrew. 'Ibn ʿAbbās's *al-Lughāt fi'l-Qur'ān*'. *Bulletin of the School of Oriental and African Studies* 44 (1981), 15–25.
Rippin, Andrew. 'Ibn ʿAbbās's *Gharīb al-Qur'ān*'. *Bulletin of the School of Oriental and African Studies* 46 (1983), 332–3.
Rippin, Andrew. 'Lexicographical Texts and the Qur'ān'. In: *Approaches to the History of the Interpretation of the Qur'ān*, pp. 158–74. Oxford: Clarendon Oxford University Press, 1988.
Rippin, Andrew. 'RḤMNN and the ḤANĪFS'. In: W. B. Hallaq and P. D. Little (eds.). *Islamic Studies Presented to Charles J. Adams*, pp. 153–68. Leiden: Brill, 1991.
Rippin, Andrew. 'The Designation of "Foreign" Languages in the Exegesis of the Qur'ān'. In: Jane Dammen McAuliffe, Barry D. Walfish, and Joseph W. Goering (eds.). *With Reverence for the Word: Medieval Scriptural Exegesis in Judaism, Christianity, and Islam*, pp. 437–44. Oxford and New York: Oxford University Press, 2003.
Rippin, Andrew. 'Foreign Vocabulary'. In: J. D. McAuliffe (ed.). *Encyclopaedia of the Qur'ān*. 6 vols., including index 2:226–37. Leiden: Brill, 2001–6.
Rippin, Andrew. 'Studies in Qur'ānic Vocabulary: The Problem of the Dictionary'. In: Gabriel Reynolds (ed.). *New Perspectives on the Qur'ān: The Qur'ān in its Historical Context II*, pp. 38–46. London: Routledge, 2011.
Rippin, Andrew. 'Al-Mubarrad (d. 285/898) and Polysemy in the Qur'ān'. In: Andrew Rippin and Roberto Tottoli (eds.). *Studies Presented to Claude Gilliot on the Occasion of his 75th Birthday*, pp. 56–69. Leiden: Brill, 2014.
Rosenthal, Franz. 'Some Minor Problems in the Qur'ān'. In: *The Joshua Starr Memorial Volume*, pp. 67–84. New York: Conference on Jewish Relations, 1953.
Rubin, Uri. '*Al-Ṣamad* and the High God: An Interpretation of *sūra* CXII', *Der Islam* 61/2 (1984), 197–217.
Rubin, Uri. 'Qur'an and *tafsīr*: The Case of *ʿan yadin*', *Der Islam* 70/1 (1993), 133–44.
Rubin, Uri. 'Qur'an and Poetry: More Data Concerning the Qur'ānic Jizya Verse (*ʿAn Yadin*)', *Jerusalem Studies in Arabic and Islam* 31 (2006), 139–46.
Rubin, Uri. 'On the Arabic Origins of the Qur'ān: The Case of *al-Furqān*', *Journal of Semitic Studies* 54/2 (2009), 421–33.
Saleh, Walid. 'The Etymological Fallacy and Qur'ānic Studies: Muḥammad, Paradise, and Late Antiquity'. In: Angelika Neuwirth, Nicolai Sinai, and Michael Marx (eds.). *The Qur'ān*

in Context: Historical and Literary Investigations into the Qurʾānic Milieu, pp. 649–98. Leiden: Brill, 2010.

Shah, Mustafa. 'The Philological Endeavours of the Early Arabic Linguists: Theological Implications of the *tawqīf-iṣṭilāḥ* Antithesis and the *majāz* Controversy', (Parts I and II) *Journal of Qurʾānic Studies* 1 (1999), 27–46; 2 (2000), 44–66.

Shah, Mustafa. 'Classical Islamic Discourse on the Origins of Language: Cultural Memory and the Defense of Orthodoxy', *Numen: International Review for the History of Religions* 58/2–3 (2011), 314–43.

Shah, Mustafa (ed.). *Tafsīr: Interpreting the Qurʾān*. 4 vols. London; New York: Routledge, 2013.

Silverstein, Adam. 'On the Original Meaning of the Qur'anic Term *al-Shayṭān al-Rajīm*', *Journal of the American Oriental Society* 133/1 (2013), 21–33.

Simelidis, Christos. 'The Byzantine Understanding of the Qur'anic Term "*al-Ṣamad*" and the Greek Translation of the Qur'an', *Speculum* 86/4 (2011), 887–913.

Stewart, Devin J. 'The Mysterious Letters and other Formal Features of the Qurʾān in Light of Greek and Babylonian Oracular Texts'. In: Gabriel Reynolds (ed.). New Perspectives on the Qurʾān: The Qurʾān in its Historical Context II, pp. 323–48. London: Routledge, 2011.

Stroumsa, Guy. 'Jewish Christianity and Islamic Origins'. In: Behnam Sadeghi et al. (eds.). *Islamic Cultures, Islamic Contexts: Essays in Honor of Professor Patricia Crone*, pp. 72–96. Leiden: Brill, 2014.

Toomer, G. J. *Eastern Wisedome and Learning: The Study of Arabic in Seventeenth-Century England*. New York and Oxford: Clarendon Press of Oxford University Press, 1996.

Toorawa, Shawkat. 'Hapaxes in the Qurʾān: Identifying and Cataloguing Lone Words (and Loanwords)'. In: Gabriel Reynolds (ed.). *New Perspectives on the Qurʾān: The Qurʾān in its Historical Context II*, pp. 193–246. London: Routledge, 2011.

Van Ess, Josef. *The Youthful God: Anthropomorphism in Early Islam*. [Pamphlet] Arizona State University, 1988.

Vrolijk, Arnoud, and Richard van Leeuwen. *Arabic Studies in the Netherlands: A Short History in Portraits, 1580–1950*. Leiden; Boston: Brill, 2014.

Wansbrough, John. *Quranic Studies: Sources and Methods of Scriptural Interpretation. Foreword, Translations and Expanded Notes* by Andrew Rippin. Amherst, NY: Prometheus Books, 2004 (repr. of 1977).

Welch, A. T. 'al-Kur'ān'. In: C. E Bosworth, E van Donzel, B. Lewis, and Ch. Pellat (eds.). *The Encyclopaedia of Islam*, 5:400–29. Second edn. Leiden: Brill, 1986.

Williams, Wesley. 'A Body Unlike Bodies: Transcendent Anthropomorphism in Ancient Semitic Tradition and Early Islam', *Journal of the American Oriental Society* 129/1 (2009), 19–44.

Zaborski, Andrzej. 'Etymology, Etymological Fallacy and the Pitfalls of Literal Translation of Some Arabic and Islamic Terms'. In: R. Arnzen and J. Thielmann (eds.). *Words, Texts and Concepts Cruising the Mediterranean Sea*, pp. 143–8. Leuven: Peeters Publishers, 2004.

Zammit, Martin. *A Comparative Lexical Study of Qurʾānic Arabic*. Leiden: Brill, 2002.

Zellentin, Holger. '*Aḥbār* and *Ruhbān*: Religious Leaders in the Qur'an in Dialogue with Christian and Rabbinic Literature'. In: Angelika Neuwirth and Michael Anthony Sells (eds.). *Qurʾānic Studies Today*, pp. 262–93. New York: Routledge, 2016.

Zellentin, Holger, 'Trialogical Anthropology: The Qurʾān on Adam and Iblīs in View of Rabbinic and Christian Discourse'. In: Rüdiger Braun and Hüseyin Çiçek (eds.). *The Quest for Humanity: Contemporary Approaches to Human Dignity in the Context of the Qurʾānic Anthropology*, pp. 54–125. Cambridge: Cambridge Scholars Press, 2017.

Zellentin, Holger (ed). *The Qur'an's Reformation of Judaism and Christianity: Return to the Origins*. London: Routledge, 2019.

CHAPTER 19

QUR'ANIC SYNTAX

MICHEL CUYPERS

In the present study, 'syntax' will be understood as the way the diverse parts of a sura or diverse suras are connected between each other to compose coherent sets with semantic unity. The classical Islamic tradition has partially studied it under the titles of *naẓm*, 'composition (of the text)', and *ʿilm al-munāsaba*, 'the science of correlation (between verses or suras)'. This topic can be somehow related to the *dispositio* of the Graeco-Roman classical rhetoric, that is, the arrangement of the discourse into its specific parts, like exordium, narration, proposition, proof, refutation, and peroration, in judicial speech. But the way the Qur'anic text achieves the arrangement of its parts is totally different from Graeco-Roman rhetorical structures. Moreover, in the Islamic cultural tradition, the *ʿilm al-munāsaba* is not considered as part of rhetoric (*balāgha*), but as a specific 'Qur'anic science' developed in exegesis (*tafsīr*). It has had, however, a rather marginal position in the exegetical tradition, applied only by a few commentators. It was not until the 1980s that it really attracted attention in the field of Qur'anic studies, whether from Muslim or non-Muslim scholars. As for the *naẓm*, in the classical period, it did consider only the syntax of minimal elements of the text, like sentence or verse, and has been studied in this part of the *balāgha* known as *ʿilm al-maʿānī* ('semantics'). It is only in the twentieth century that the study of *naẓm* has been extended to the other textual levels (order of the verses in a sura, relationship between the suras or groups of suras), thus including an enlarged perspective of the ancient *ʿilm al-munāsaba* in a discipline studying the composition of the text at all levels.

The Question of the Discontinuity of the Qur'anic Text

The coherence of the Qur'anic text has always been questioned. According to the Qur'an, it would have arisen even during the lifetime of the Prophet: 'The disbelievers also say: "Why was the Qurʾān not sent down to him all at once"?' (25:32). In reply, the Qur'an recognizes its discontinuous character, while justifying it at the same time: 'We sent it in this way to strengthen your heart [Prophet]; We gave it to you in gradual revelation' (25:32). Or again: 'It is a recitation that We have revealed in parts, so that you can recite it to people at intervals; We have sent it down little by little' (17:106). The discontinuity of the text is thus attested by the Qur'an. This however does not mean that the Book is nothing but a collection of fragments set in a row without any logical order during the establishment of the *muṣḥaf*, as was long believed by Western orientalists, and is still believed by some of them.

The Order of the Suras in the Qur'an

At the level of the Book, the Qur'an certainly follows a global quantitative classification, starting from the longest suras (after the short introduction of the *Fātiḥa*) and ending with the shortest. This corresponds at the same time to a general inverted chronological order, the short suras dating from the beginning of revelation in Mecca, the longest dating from the end of the revelation, in Medina. A certain thematic classification corresponds to it: the short suras of the end of the Qur'an have, for the greater part, an eschatological character, while the first long suras deal with multiple subjects (laws, narratives, exhortations, etc.). The chronological classification in the Meccan and Medinan suras however is not rigorous: Medinan suras indeed appear among Meccan suras. The quantitative decreasing order of the suras is also far from being strict. A. T. Welch reorganizes the first thirty suras, according to their exact lengths in the following order: 2, 4, 3, 7, 6, 5, 9, 11, 16, 10, 12, 17, 18, 26, 28, 20, 24, 33, 22, 8, 21, 40, 39, 27, 23, 37, 19, 25, 43 and 34 (*EI*[2], art. '*Ḳurʾān*'). One can surmise that the disturbance of the decreasing lengths of the suras would be due to the interference of another, perhaps more important, order. But what could this order be?

The Coherence of the Text According To the Classical Tradition: *Naẓm* and *ʿIlm al-Munāsaba*

Several scholars of the third/ninth and fourth/tenth centuries undertook an examination of the structure of the text of the suras, in a series of works carrying the title of *Naẓm al-Qurʾān* (Composition of the Qurʾān). These books are unfortunately lost, but we know something of their content from other works which succeeded them, and dealt with the inimitability of the Qur'an (*iʿjāz al-Qurʾān*). These latest books try to answer certain criticisms concerning the lack of coherence in the Qur'anic text. The first book of this kind is the *Bayān iʿjāz al-Qurʾān* (Proof of the inimitability of the Qur'an) by al-Khaṭṭābī

(d. 388/998). His answers to the apparent lack of coherence of the text are still very partial and limited, concerning only small textual units, words, phrases, or verses, and not the correlation of verses or suras between them (i.e. the 'syntax of the text'). The same is true for other later theorists of rhetoric, such as al-Bāqillānī (d. 403/1013) and ʿAbd al-Qāhir al-Jurjānī (d. 471/1078), or the exegete al-Zamakhsharī (d. 538/1144). Their point of view is the one developed in the *ʿilm al-maʿānī* of Arabic rhetoric *(balāgha)*, and not that employed in the *ʿilm al-munāsaba* which developed later.

According to al-Zarkashī (d. 794/1392), in his encyclopaedia of the Qur'anic sciences, *al-Burhān fī ʿulūm al-Qurʾān* (Demonstration in the sciences of the Qur'an), the first scholar to have approached the Qur'anic text from the perspective of the relations between verses and suras would have been the Shāfiʿī jurist Abū Bakr al-Nīsābūrī (d. 324/936) (al-Zarkashī, *al-Burhān*, 1:49). In a sermon delivered in Baghdad, he was asked: 'Why was such a verse placed next to another one? According to what logic, was such a sura put next to another one?' He criticized the scholars of Baghdad for their ignorance in what he called the *ʿilm al-munāsaba*, 'the science of the correlation (between verses and suras)'.

As for the suras, we notice, says al-Zarkashī, that the beginning of every sura agrees perfectly with the end of the previous sura. As an example, he quotes the end of sura 56 which invites praises: 'Glorify the name of your Lord, the Supreme' (56:96), while sura 57 begins exactly with a praise: 'Everything in heavens and the earth glorifies God' (57:1). The beginning of sura 2: 'This is the Scripture in which there is no doubt, containing guidance for those who are mindful of God' matches the verse of the *Fātiḥa*: 'Guide us to the straight path'. As if the question: 'What is this straight path?' was answered: 'Well, the Scripture provides guidance to the straight path.'

In another chapter of his book (al-Zarkashī, *al-Burhān*, 1:184–5), al-Zarkashī explains that the arrangement (*tartīb*) of the suras does not always consist of thematic correspondence between the end of a sura and the beginning of the next, as we have already seen; it can be simply an assonance, like the end of sura 111 (its last word is *masad*), and the beginning of sura 112 (its first verse ends with the paronomasia *Ṣamad*), or a similar content in the overall contiguous suras such as suras 2 to 5, which contain a large number of laws.

Among the few scholars who were interested in correlations, in addition to Abū Bakr al-Nīsābūrī already mentioned, al-Zarkashī mentions Abū Jaʿfar ibn al-Zubayr (d. 708/1308), author of a book entitled *al-Burhān fī tartīb suwar al-Qurʾān* (Demonstration regarding consonance in the order of the Qur'an) and Fakhr al-Dīn al-Rāzī (d. 606/1210), who saw 'the greatest subtleties of the Qurʾān in its arrangements (*tartībāt*) and correlations (*rawābiṭ*)' (al-Zarkashī, *al-Burhān*, 1:48–9). And if only a few scholars are found to be interested in that aspect of the Qur'an, it is due, says al-Zarkashī, to its difficulty and subtlety.

A century after al-Zarkashī, Burhān al-Dīn al-Biqāʿī (d. 885/1480) explicitly applies 'the science of appositeness and correlations between verses and suras' in his commentary on the Qur'an, as announced in the title: *Naẓm al-durar fī tanāsub al-āyāt wa'l-suwar* (The order of the pearls: Correlation of the verses and the suras)—let us note the technical term *naẓm*.

Al-Suyūṭī (d. 911/1505) also devotes a chapter of his encyclopaedia of Qur'anic sciences (*al-Itqān fī ʿulūm al-Qurʾān*) to 'correlations between the verses and suras' (al-Suyūṭī, *Itqān*, 3:322–38). He essentially repeats al-Zarkashī, without adding anything very new. He distinguishes the following three types of relationships between the verses: (1) similar to similar (or relation of synonymy), (2) antithesis, (3) digression by association of ideas (*al-Itqān*, 3:324–7). He also emphasizes the correspondence between the beginning and the end of a sura, and between the end of one sura and the beginning of the next.

As other commentators who have been interested in the connections between verses and suras we can mention al-Khaṭīb al-Shirbīnī (d. 977/1569), Abū'l-Suʿūd (d. 982/1574), and al-Ālūsī (d. 1270/1854).

Despite these isolated attempts, the importance attached by al-Rāzī, al-Zarkashī, and al-Biqāʿī to the correlations between verses and suras and their coherence has not succeeded in establishing itself as a basic principle of exegesis. This is probably due to the fact that their attention was mainly focused on the relationship between successive verses: they adhered to an 'atomistic' treatment of the text, attempting only to put these atoms in conjunction. Mustansir Mir describes their method as 'linear-atomistic' (Mir 1993: 212) verse 1 of a sura is put in connection with verse 2, verse 2 with verse 3, and so on until the end of the sura. It looks more like a concatenation of the verses than a real organic structure of the text.

The Unity of the Text by Modern Muslim Commentators

According to Mustansir Mir, a profound change has taken place during the twentieth century. Many scholars consider the sura in its unity and affirm its coherence. Among them, he cites Ashraf ʿAlī Thanavī (d. 1943), Ḥamīd al-Dīn Farāhī (d. 1930), and Amīn Aḥsan Iṣlāḥī (d. 1997) in India-Pakistan, Muḥammad ʿIzzat Darwaza (d. 1984) and Sayyid Quṭb (d. 1966) in Egypt, Muḥammad Ḥusayn al-Ṭabāṭabāʾī (d. 1404/1981) in Iran (Mir 1993: 217–19). The common feature of these modern commentators is their 'organic-holistic' approach to the text, replacing the previous 'linear-atomistic' approach (Mir 1993: 219).

Among those commentators, it is certainly Iṣlāḥī who prompted further research on the coherence of the suras. He took the idea of his master, Farāhī, whereby each sura has a major theme, or 'pillar' (*ʿamūd*) of the sura, to which other verses cling logically. In his commentary in Urdu entitled *Taddabur-i Qurʾān* (Reflection on the Qur'an), completed in 1980, Iṣlāḥī scrutinizes every sura from this point of view (for a study of this commentary, see Mir 1986). This leads him to identify the major divisions of the suras and to analyse them in detail. Mir summarizes his analysis of sura 2 ('The Cow') as follows: an introduction (verses 1–39) and conclusion (284–6) frame four sections, (1) an address to the Israelites (40–121); (2) the Abrahamic Legacy (122–62); (3) the Sharīʿa or Law

(163–242); (4) the liberation of the Kaᶜba (243–83) (Mir 1993: 215–16). Within each of these sections, the link is shown between the different parts. Iṣlāḥī has also raised the issue of the link between the suras, which led him to the conclusion that most of the suras, if not all (the *Fātiḥa* would be an exception), would form complementary pairs. There are several types of complementarities, primarily: brevity and detail, principle and illustration, different types of evidence, difference in emphasis, premise and conclusion, unity of opposites (Mir 1986: 77–8). According to Iṣlāḥī, it is also possible to divide the entire text of the Qur'an into seven major thematic groups of suras: 1–5, 6–9, 10–24, 25–33, 34–49, 50–66, and 67–114 (Mir 1986: 85–98). One could say that with Iṣlāḥī we are dealing with a real study of the Qur'an from the perspective of the structure of the text, but a structure essentially established by the identification of thematic/logic connections between parts of the text, with the risk of a certain amount of subjectivity on the part of the interpreter.

While Iṣlāḥī was just finishing his commentary, the Syrian shaykh Saᶜīd Ḥawwā (d. 1989) started in the 1980s to write an extensive commentary entitled *al-Asās fī l-tafsīr* (Foundations of exegesis), in which he tries to show the composition of the text of the suras by dividing the text into four levels, in descending order: the part (*qism*), the piece (*maqṭaᶜ*), the paragraph (*faqra*), the group (*majmūᶜa*) (Ḥawwā 2003: 30–1). Its divisions follow the thematic of the text, but also correspondences of remote terms defining the literary units. Although still summary, the method already anticipates what would be a real analysis of the composition of the Qur'anic text.

'The real test of the sūra-as-a-unity thesis, then', argues Mir, 'is whether it gives rise to a new method for the study of the Qur'ān. Is the thesis capable, on the one hand, of generating techniques that will help establish plausible links between the verses and passages of the Qur'ān, and, on the other, of generating meaning that cannot otherwise be generated?' (Mir 1993: 219). The danger, of course, in the new approach to the text is appealing only to the intuition of the exegete to establish correlations between verses and suras. To avoid subjectivity, we need to rely on data provided by the text itself, in all objectivity. The question then arises as follows: does the Qur'anic text furnish indices of composition that allow the establishment of its structure and, consequently, its meaning?

The Structure of the Qur'anic Text, According to Recent Research

Two books were published in 1981, marking a milestone in the modern study of the Qur'an, hitherto dominated by the historical-critical approach: *Le Coran: aux sources de la parole oraculaire, structures rythmiques des sourates mecquoises* (At the sources of oracular speech, rhythmic structures of Meccan suras) by Pierre Crapon de Caprona, and *Studien zur Komposition der mekkanischen Suren* (Studies on the composition of the meccan suras), by Angelika Neuwirth. Both studies, assuming the textual unity of the suras, shared a similar approach to the Qur'anic text from a synthetic point of view instead of the diachronic point of view of historical criticism. They proposed to highlight the structure of the Meccan suras: Crapon de Caprona proposed doing this according to the rhythm of the text, while Neuwirth suggested that this be referenced to various indices, such as rhyme, rhythm, variations of themes, and genres. The research of P. Crapon de Caprona, who died before the publication of his work, has not been followed up so far. However, the thesis of Neuwirth was the beginning of a successful quest, continued in several books and articles and summarized in her article 'Form and Structure' in the *Encyclopaedia of the Qur'ān*.

Neuwirth stresses the importance of rhyme and groups of rhythmic units in structuring Meccan suras. 'Most Meccan suras display fixed sequences of formally and thematically defined verse groups distinctly separated by a change of rhyme or other clearly discernible, sometimes formulaic markers of caesurae' (Neuwirth 2002: 252). Verses can thus combine two, three, four, and up to ten verses or more. Apart from the shortest chapter, suras constitute a balanced set of these groups. These can be classified into various types: oaths, eschatological passages, the 'signs' (in nature or history), debates (polemics or apologetics), regulations, and the evocation of contemporary events (in Medinan suras), etc. The oldest Meccan suras are made up of one, two, or three parts. Later Meccan suras are characterized by the presence of a frame: in an introduction they refer to the Book, or take up a discursive section (apologetic, polemic, exhortation), and they end with a corresponding section, usually an affirmation of the revelation. In the middle appears a section evoking a biblical narrative. This tripartite division of the chapter tends to be blurred in the late Meccan period. 'In Medina, however, suras have not only given up their tripartite scheme, but they display much less sophistication in the patterns of their composition' (Neuwirth 2002: 264). Neuwirth's studies have the merit of being based on a careful analysis of the text. They also provide an abundant harvest of observations. But they are practically limited to Meccan suras. Long Medinan suras seem inaccessible to their methods of investigation. This is probably due to the dominating idea of Neuwirth's research, namely the liturgical nature of communication of the suras. This aspect of the Qur'anic text, evident in the Meccan suras, fades in the Medinan suras.

Salwa El-Awa published in 2006 a study entitled *Textual Relations in the Qur'ān: Relevance, Coherence and Structure*. Starting from modern linguistic theories of communication (coherence theory and relevance theory) and going on to explore textual relations, she addressed the issue of the structural unity of longer multi-thematic suras, whether Meccan or Medinan (she studied in detail the Meccan sura 75, *al-Qiyāma*, and the Medinan sura 33, *al-Aḥzāb*). She subdivides the text into thematic paragraphs using markers such as speech initials (like *bal, kallā*), introductory particles (*inna*), reopening particles (*waw*), vocatives (*yā ayyuhā*), pronoun shifts, or shifts of speaker and addressees. Paragraphs are divided into sections and subsections by minor markers such as *wa, idh, laqad, wa*, and *yā*. Whatever the relevance of linguistic theories used for this study, compositional markers (already well known to the ancient grammarians) can decompose a multi-thematic sura into its component parts, and then recompose it into a unified architecture, in which different topics appear interconnected, each constituting a meaningful context for the others. Repetition plays a particularly important role as an indicator of relationships between paragraphs.

Mathias Zahniser and Neal Robinson have analysed the structure of some long suras: *Sūrat al-Nisāʾ* (4) (Zahniser 1997: 71–85), *Sūrat al-Baqara* (2) (Zahniser 2000: 26–55; Robinson 2003: 201–23) and *Sūrat al-Māʾida* (5) (Robinson 2001: 1–19). In this latter study, Robinson's method is primarily (but not exclusively) to identify repetitions, at distances, of words, syntagmas, or whole identical or similar sentences, acting as indicators of the composition of the text. This method leads Robinson to various findings: the beginning and the end of a section or the second verse and the penultimate of a section are often similar; a section is often characterized by repetition of a word or key phrase while they are absent in the sections that frame it; theological stereotypical formulas often mark the end of a section. Here and there, Robinson distinguishes subsections within a section. It is not only the vocabulary that marks the transition from one section to another, it can also be a change of literary genre, of theme, a rhymed clausula, a change in the person to whom the speech is addressed, the change in time. Robinson also identifies certain processes linking sections together, including 'hook words' and 'parallel introductions'. Finally, he notes the importance of chiasmus structure at sentence level but also in larger sets.

Hussein Abdul-Raof has suggested a theory for Robinson's findings (Abdul-Raof 2003: 72–94). He distinguishes, various types of textual and conceptual chaining, at the micro-level, between the verses and the various parts of a sura, or at the macro-level, between consecutive suras: 'chaining between the beginning and the end of a Qurʾānic sura', 'chaining between the end of a sura and the beginning of the following sura', 'chaining between the beginning of two consecutive suras', 'chaining between two consecutive suras where the latter provides elaboration for matters raised in the former' (Abdul-Raof 2003: 81).

These recent analyses are certainly a great step towards discovery of the syntax of the Qur'anic text. Nevertheless, they still lack a general theory that brings together all these features (and all those that we have gleaned before in the history of Qur'anic exegesis and Qur'anic sciences) into a real system applicable to the composition of the entire text of the Qur'an, on all its levels. In fact, such a system exists. Although it was born and gradually developed in the field of biblical studies, for two and a half centuries, it appears now to be perfectly suited for the analysis of the structure of the Qur'anic text, as shown by several studies by Michel Cuypers (see bibliography).

Semitic Rhetoric and Rhetorical Analysis

The discontinuity of many texts of the Bible has indeed raised the same issue of coherence as that raised by the text of the Qur'an. Developed gradually, from the discovery of parallelism of the parts of the Psalms and the prophetic books, by the English biblical scholar Robert Lowth (1710–87), then developed by two more Englishmen, John Jebb (1775–1833) and Thomas Boys (1792–1880), at the beginning of the nineteenth century, this theory has now been fully systematized by Roland Meynet, in his *Treatise on Biblical Rhetoric* (2002). This theory appears to be the rediscovery, from a careful study of texts, of a Semitic rhetoric different from Greek rhetoric, and apparently used in all the ancient Middle East, as seems to be confirmed by various studies on Akkadian, Ugaritic, and Pharaonic texts. As text, the Qur'an belongs to the same cultural universe. It is thus not surprising that this general theory of composing texts proves suitable for studying the Qur'an, whatever the date, style, or genre of the suras.

While for the composition of speech Greek rhetoric proceeds in a linear and continuous manner, from an introduction, followed by a development, to end with a conclusion (introduction, narrative, discussion, summing up), Semitic rhetoric for its part proceeds by way of semantic correspondences, in a complex game of symmetries. This system has neither the simplicity nor the stiffness of a poetic form, but the sophistication of a large set of features or 'laws' with which the text plays to coalesce into a coherent whole. Two general characteristics distinguish Semitic rhetoric: parataxis and binarity. Parataxis, in grammar, means the juxtaposition of two sentences, with or without a coordinating conjunction. Very often, the Qur'anic text juxtaposes phrases, verses, or groups of verses, without conjunction, or it simply connects them with the conjunction *wa*, without any indication of a logical shade of cause, consequence, opposition, or other (see Mir 2006: 99–100). We can include in this phenomenon of parataxis the well-known Qur'anic feature of *iltifāt* or sudden change from one grammatical person to another. The overall use of parataxis in the Qur'an is one of the causes of apparent incoherence left by the Qur'anic text (other causes will be quoted below).

Binarity, the second general characteristic of Semitic rhetoric, consists in the fact that two linguistic or conceptual elements, close together or not, are set intentionally in relationship in the text. The most important binary feature is symmetry, which is the basic principle of the structure of the text, according to Semitic rhetoric. 'Rhetorical analysis' will essentially pinpoint the various forms of symmetry which make up the text, defining the relationships which they have with one another, and the textual divisions which they determine.

The main features of Semitic rhetoric will be described below, from the clear and simple example of the *Fātiḥa*. It goes without saying that most of the suras have a more complex form. But it is always the same structural principles that are at work, be it a sura of a few lines or of 286 verses like *Sūrat al-Baqara*.

Several rhetorical levels can be distinguished in this text. The basic level is that of the *members*, corresponding to the lines in Figure 19.1. Each member is a syntagma (a word or phrase forming a syntactic unit). At the second level, members are grouped into five *segments*, each consisting of two semantically related members (1–2, 3–4, 5a–b, 6–7a, 7b–c). There can also be segments of three members, but never more. In the third level of the *Fātiḥa*, the bimember segments are grouped into two *pieces* 1–4 and

– 1 In the name of	*God,*	the Mercy-giving,	the Merciful.
– 2 Praise be to	*God,*	Lord	of the worlds,
= 3		the Mercy-giving,	the Merciful,
= 4		Ruler	of the Day of Judgment.

+ 5a	**You** *do we worship,*
+ b and	**You** *do we ask for help.*

– 6 Guide us along the straight ***path***
– 7a the ***path*** of those whom You have favored,
= b *not [ghayr]* of those who earn (Your) anger,
= c *nor [wa lā]* who are lost.

FIGURE 19.1 The composition of *Sūrat al-Fātiḥa's* according to Semitic Rhetoric

6–7. The central piece (5) contains only one bimember segment. At the top level, that of the whole sura, the text is thus composed of three pieces: two including two bimember segments, and one including only one bimember segment. The *Fātiḥa* is structured into four levels: members, segments, pieces, and the whole sura. Longer texts, such as long Medinan suras, can include up to eleven levels, which were given the names of member, segment, piece, part (here corresponding to the whole *Fātiḥa*), passage, sequence, section, book (or long sura), with possibly, if necessary, sub-part, sub-sequence, and sub-section. It is noteworthy that the lower levels (segment, piece, and part) can only contain one, two, or three elements of the next lower level, and never more.

Each of those rhetorical levels, from the segment on, may be structured according to one of the three following composition figures:

1. *Parallelism*, or parallel construction, when related units of text (by synonymy, antithesis, or complementarities) reappear in the same order (A//A′, AB//A′B′ or ABC//A′B′C′). All the bimember segments of the *Fātiḥa* are synonymic parallels (1//2; 3//4; 5a//5b; 6//7a; 7b//7c): both members that compose them have similar meanings. But the two segments of the first piece in turn form a synonymous parallelism (1–2//3–4), while the two segments of the last piece form an antithetic parallelism (6–7a ↔ 7b–c). And at the third level, that of the sura or 'part', there is a complementary parallelism between the first and the last piece (1–4/6–7): from the semantic point of view, the first piece is a praise or a prayer of adoration while the last piece is a prayer of demand; praise and demand are the two essential and complementary forms of prayer.
2. *Mirror construction*, when related units of text reappear in inverted order (AB/B′A′). Sura 12 (*Yūsuf*) is a section composed of twelve sequences distributed, according to a mirror composition, into two subsections of six sequences (Figure 19.2).

A Prologue	1–3
B Vision of Joseph	4–7
C Joseph's contention with his brothers: their ruse against Joseph	8–18
D Comparative promotion of Joseph	19–22
E Attempted seduction of Joseph by the woman	23–34
F Joseph in prison interpreting the visions of the two prisoners, and prophet of monotheism	35–42
F' Joseph in prison interpreting the vision of the king	43–49
E' Unwinding of the seduction of the woman: Joseph rehabilitated	50–53
D' Definitive promotion of Joseph	54–57
C' Joseph's contention with his brothers: Joseph's ruse towards them	58–98
B' Fulfilling of Joseph's vision	99–101
A' Epilogue	102–111

FIGURE 19.2 Mirror composition of *Sūrat Yūsuf.*

3. *Concentric construction* or *ring composition*, when the units of text are arranged concentrically around a centre (ABC/×/C′B′A′). The *Fātiḥa* is constructed according to the simplest form of concentric construction A/×/A′: two extreme pieces (1–4 and 6–7) are connected by a short central piece (5), the first member of it ('You do we worship') refers to the foregoing piece, which is a prayer of adoration, and the second member ('You do we ask for help') introduces the following piece, which is a prayer of petition.

Figure 19.3 shows a slightly more complicated form of ring composition (AB/×/B′A′) (sura 81:19–25). Corresponding terms are highlighted by same characters.

We notice the importance of the central member which certifies the authenticity of the Prophet's vision.

Concentric construction is very common in the Qur'an, especially at higher text level. The centre is most often of particular importance for the understanding of the whole concentric construction. But it is noteworthy that the provision of verses or groups of verses in mirror or ring composition blurs the logic of a linear reading of the text, giving an impression of disorder. They should be read according to their own Semitic logic, quite different from the Greek logic we all inherited (including Arabs).

These three compositional figures locate fairly easily when they relate to whole texts ('total symmetries' between members, segments, or whole pieces). Often, however, symmetries will be indicated only by a word or a few words, as indices of composition, at the beginning, the middle, or the end of the corresponding units, or the extremities of a unit to delimit it, or at the end of a unit and at the start of a following unit, to show that they must be taken together. These compositional indices may also be added to total symmetries, as is the case in some of the following examples.

A Verily THIS IS THE SPEECH OF A NOBLE MESSENGER,
Powerful, beside the Lord of the Throne established,
Obeyed there and trustworthy.

B And your comrade **is not** mad,

x *He saw him on the clear horizon,*

B' and he **is not** regarding the unseen uncommunicative,

A' and THIS IS NOT THE SPEECH OF A SATAN STONED!

FIGURE 19.3 Ring composition of *Sūrat al-Takwīr*, verses 19–25.

- The two members of segment 5a–b of the *Fātiḥa* begin with the same initial term, the pronoun 'you': *iyyāka*.
- The two members 7b and 7c both begin with a negation: *ghayr*, *wa mā*.
- The members 7a and 7b end with the same final term *ʿalay-him*.
- Members 6 and 7a are connected by the repetition of the median or hook word *ṣirāṭ*.
- The piece 6–7 is framed by two antithetical extreme terms: 'guide us' ↔ 'lost'.

The composition indices may be of all kinds. There may be repetition of the same term or synonymies or antitheses, or the same grammatical form, a rhyme, assonance, or paronomasia, etc.

According to recent studies, Semitic rhetoric appears to be the typical mode of composition or syntax of the sacred texts of the ancient Middle East. In itself it owes nothing to Greek or Arabic rhetoric. This does not mean that those rhetorics cannot be applied equally to the Qur'anic text. In the biblical field, the current school of 'critical rhetoric' applies the categories of Graeco-Roman rhetoric, alongside a 'new rhetoric', to the biblical text. Some people suggest doing the same for the Qur'an, which is perfectly possible, and may illuminate other aspects of the text, in particular persuasive texts. Rhetorical analysis of the Qur'anic text according to the principles of Semitic rhetoric, however, should be primordial, to the extent that the structure of the text, its 'syntax', carries in itself the essential sense or 'intention' (*qaṣd*) of the text.

Bibliography

Abdul-Raof, Hussein. 'Conceptual and Textual Chaining in Qurʾānic Discourse', *Journal of Qur'anic Studies* 5/2 (2003), 72–94.

al-Biqāʿī, Ibrāhīm Burhān al-Dīn. *Naẓm al-durar fī tanāsub al-āyāt wa'l-suwar.* Cairo: Dār al-Kitāb al-Islāmī, 1992.

Cuypers, Michel. *The Banquet: A Reading of the Fifth Sura of the Qurʾān*. Miami: Convivium Press, 2009 (trans. from French: *Le Festin: une lecture de la sourate al-Māʾida*. Paris: Lethielleux, 2007).

Cuypers, Michel. *The Composition of the Qur'ān*. London: Bloomsbury, 2015 (trans. from French *La composition du coran. Naẓm al-Qur'ān*. Pendé: Gabalda, 2012).
Cuypers, Michel. *A Qur'ānic Apocalypse: A Reading of the Last Thirty-Three Suras*. Exeter: Lockwood Press, 2018 (trans. from French *Une apocalypse coranique: une lecture des trente-trois dernières sourates du Coran*. Pendé: Gabalda, 2014).
Farrin, Raymond. *Structure and Qur'ānic Interpretation: A Study of Symmetry and Coherence in Islam's Holy Text*. Ashland, OR: White Cloud Press, 2014.
Ḥawwā, Saʿīd. *Al-Asās fi'l-tafsīr*. 6th edn. Cairo: Dār al-Islām, 2003.
Meynet, Roland. *Treatise on Biblical Rhetoric*. International Studies in the History of Rhetoric 3. Leiden and Boston: Brill, 2012.
Mir, Mustansir. *Coherence in the Qur'ān: A Study of Iṣlāḥī's Concept of Naẓm in Taddabur-i Qur'ān*. Indianapolis: American Trust Publications, 1986.
Mir, Mustansir. 'The Sūra as Unity: A Twentieth Century Development in Qur'ān Exegesis'. In: G. R. Hawting and Abdul-Kader A. Shareef (eds.). *Approaches to the Qur'ān*, pp. 211–24. London and New York: Routledge, 1993.
Mir, Mustansir. 'Language'. In: A. Rippin (ed.). *The Blackwell Companion to the Qur'ān*, pp. 88–106 Malden, Oxford, and Victoria: Blackwell Publishing, 2006.
Neuwirth, Angelica. *Studien zur Komposition der mekkanischen Suren*. Studien zur Sprache, Geschichte und Kultur des islamischen Orients 10. Berlin and New York: Walter De Gruyter, 1981.
Neuwirth, Angelica. 'Form and Structure', In: Jane Dammen McAuliffe (ed.). *Encyclopaedia of the Qur'ān*. 6 vols., 2:245–66. Leiden: Brill, 2001–6.
Neuwirth, Angelica. 'Structure and the Emergence of Community'. In: Andrew Rippin (ed.). *The Blackwell Companion to the Qur'ān*, pp. 140–58. Oxford: Blackwell Publishing, 2006.
Neuwirth, Angelica. *Der Koran: Frühmekkanische Suren. Poetische Prophetie*. Berlin: Verlag der Weltreligionen, 2011.
Robinson, Neal. 'Hands Outstretched: Towards a Re-reading of Sūrat al-Mā'ida', *Journal of Qur'anic Studies* 3/1 (2001), 1–19.
Robinson, Neal. *Discovering the Qur'an: A Contemporary Approach to a Veiled Text*. London: SCM-Press, 2003.
al-Suyūṭī, Jalāl al-Dīn. *Al-Itqān fī ʿulūm al-Qur'ān*. Cairo: Maktaba Dār al-Turāth, 1967.
Zahniser, Mathias. 'Sūra as Guidance and Exhortation: The Composition of *Sūrat al-Nisā'*'. In: A. Afsaruddin and A. H. M. Zahniser (eds.). *Humanism, Culture and Language in the Near East: Studies in Honor of Georg Krotkoff*, pp. 71–85. Winona Lake, IN: Eisenbrauns, 1997.
Zahniser, Mathias. 'Major Transitions and Thematic Borders in Two Long Suras: *al-Baqara* and *al-Nisā'*'. In: Issa J. Boullata (ed.). *Literary Structure of Religious Meaning in the Qur'ān*, pp. 26–55. London and Richmond: Curzon Press, 2000.
al-Zarkashī, Muḥammad ibn Bahādir. *Al-Burhān fī ʿulūm al-Qur'ān*. Vols. 1–4. Beirut: Dār al-Kutub al-ʿIlmiyya, 2007.

CHAPTER 20

RHETORICAL DEVICES AND STYLISTIC FEATURES OF QUR'ANIC GRAMMAR

MUHAMMAD ABDEL HALEEM

THE language and style of the Qur'an have attracted a large amount of work by Western scholars of the Qur'an, as will be seen from the works cited in this chapter. However one important branch of traditional Arabic Qur'anic Studies has been largely neglected, that is *balāgha* in Arabic (normally translated as 'rhetoric'). There are also certain aspects of Qur'anic style which have not been given sufficient attention. *Balāgha* and these particular stylistic features of the Qur'an are fundamental aspects of its language and are interrelated in their functions. Understanding how they work is essential to the appreciation of the Qur'an. In this short chapter there is only room for an overview of the subject. We will deal first with *balāgha* and then with these stylistic features.

RHETORIC (*BALĀGHA*)

In the Arabic tradition, the study of *balāgha* was started and developed to understand and appreciate the finer qualities of the Qur'anic language which made it so effective to Arabs, both Muslims and non-Muslims. Al-Suyūṭī (d. 911/1515) explained that all Arabic and Islamic studies stemmed from the Qur'an, and were started and developed to serve the Qur'an (al-Suyūṭī, *al-Itqān*, 2:350–5). Phonetics started in order to enable people to articulate the Qur'an accurately, and grammar to provide a basic level to read and understand the text. The study of *balāgha* functions at a higher, more aesthetic level.

Importance of *Balāgha*

This crucial role of *balāgha* can be understood from the following statement made by a leading figure in grammar, *tafsīr* (Qur'anic exegesis), and *balāgha*, al-Zamakhsharī (d. 538/1144):

> As al-Jāḥiẓ stated in his book *Naẓm al-Qurʾān*, the discipline of *tafsīr* contains subtlety of language and secrets that are not easily obtained and not everyone should engage in it. A jurist, even if he excels all his peers in giving fatwas and rules; a theologian, even if he excels everyone in the craft of *kalām* (speculative theology); a man who learns stories and accounts, even if he knows more of this than Ibn al-Qarriyya; a preacher, even if he is better than al-Ḥasan al-Baṣrī in preaching; a grammarian, even if he is more knowledgeable than Sībawayhi; a philologist, even if he has digested much knowledge: none of these would engage in seeking to discover the truth of *tafsīr*, except a man who has excelled in two disciplines particular to [the study of the] Qurʾān: *ʿilm al-maʿānī* ('the science of meanings') and *ʿilm al-bayān* ('the science of eloquence'). Such a man returns time and again to go into these subjects, exerts effort to unearth their secrets, is driven to seek them by zeal to know the subtlety of the Qurʾān, God's conclusive argument, and is eager to discover the miracle of the Prophet. (Al-Zamakhsharī, *Kashshāf*, 1:15–16)

The importance of *balāgha* in appreciating aspects of *iʿjāz al-Qurʾān* (the inimitability of the language of the Qur'an) can be seen most prominently in the works of the eminent scholar of *balāgha*, ʿAbd al-Qāhir al-Jurjānī (d. 471/1078). Its importance for *tafsīr* in general is universally recognized in Arabic by such commentators as al-Zamakhsharī and Fakhr al-Dīn al-Rāzī (d. 606/1210), and by eminent literary scholars such as al-Jāḥiz (d. 255/868 or 869), but the pre-eminent scholar of *balāgha* is al-Jurjānī, particularly in his great work *Dalāʾil al-iʿjāz*.

Lack of *Balāgha* Studies in English Compared with Grammar

Whereas *balāgha* is studied as a separate subject from grammar in Arabic secondary schools, the crucial importance of *balāgha* for *tafsīr* and the appreciation of the Qur'an in the Arab-Islamic tradition does not appear to have been given a proper place in the schooling of Arabists in universities in the United Kingdom with which I am familiar. However, there has long been a plethora of grammar texts available to first-language English-speaking undergraduates in Arabic, including W. Wright et al. (1859) which was a translation from the German, with additions and corrections, of P. C. Caspari's *Grammatica Arabica* in 1854. G. W. Thatcher's *Arabic Grammar of the Written Language* was published in 1911, D. Cowan's *Introduction to Modern Literary Arabic* was published in 1958 and Haywood and Nahmad's *New Arabic Grammar of the Written Language* in 1962. These were the textbooks used for the BA and beyond. Understandably the time available for students who had to learn the language from scratch and study the literature, religion, history, and so on did not leave time to study *balāgha*. The BA and MA curricula in British universities, apart from the School of Oriental and African Studies (SOAS), even now do not include *balāgha*.

Theodor Nöldeke

The neglect of the study of Arabic *balāgha* appears to have had a clear effect on the appreciation of the style of the Qur'an. An obvious example of this can be seen in the work of even such a great scholar of the Qur'an as Theodor Nöldeke, who remains a towering figure in Qur'anic Studies, starting with his book *Geschichte des Qorâns*, published in 1860. Although I confine my discussion mostly to the English tradition with which I am familiar, I will make reference here to the works of Theodor Nöldeke (d. 1930) as his main work has now been translated into English and Arabic.

In his pioneering study, *Neue Beiträge zur semitischen Sprachwissenschaft*, Theodor Nöldeke 'discussed in detail the 'Stylistische und syntaktische Eigentümlichkeiten der Sprache des Korans' (1910: 5–23) thereby collecting together everything that had occurred to him in this respect during his protracted and intensive study of the Holy Book of the Muslims' (Paret 1983: 205). Nöldeke mentions, at the beginning of his article (Nöldeke 1910: 13–14), examples of what is known in *balāgha* as *iltifāt*. *Iltifāt* is a stylistic feature, involving a shift or departure from what is normally expected. There are countless examples of it in both the Qur'an and Arabic literature. It is a very old feature of Arabic usage, and is still used in modern Arabic (El-Sakkout 1970: 115, 141). However, Nöldeke seems to have been unfamiliar with it (as has been observed, he does not mention the term *iltifāt* in discussing the examples he cites) and appeared to view them from a purely formal, grammatical point of view, according to which he considered the feature as bad grammar.

Unlike Nöldeke, Arab critics, rhetoricians, and exegetes have long appreciated the rhetorical purpose of the grammatical shift. *Iltifāt* is discussed in *balāgha* books in Arabic. According to the rules of *balāgha*, *iltifāt* must be used for specific reasons, otherwise it is *mumtāniᶜ* ('inadmissible'). *Balāgha* is divided by al-Sakkākī (d. 626/1229) into three sciences: *ᶜilm al-maᶜānī* ('the science of meanings'), *ᶜilm al-bayān* ('the science of eloquence'), and *ᶜilm al-badīᶜ* ('the science of embellishment'). Of these the most neglected and sorely needed by Western scholars is *ᶜilm al-maᶜānī* (Al-Sakkākī, *al-Īḍāḥ*).

Regrettably A. F. von Mehren, who translated into German a major text on *balāgha*, in 1853 (*Die Rhetorik der Araber*), seven years before Nöldeke's *Geschichte des Qorâns* (1860), completely skipped the part on *ᶜilm al-maᶜānī*. Otherwise Nöldeke probably would not have made his comments on *iltifāt* and the other features which he considered as 'unusual and not beautiful' (Nöldeke 1910: 13) in the Qur'an, comments which were handed down to generations of students afterwards, so that for example Rudi Paret refers to such features without questioning Nöldeke's opinion (Paret 1983).

Scholars in English

Significantly, Montgomery Watt and Richard Bell's *Introduction to the Qur'ān* (Watt and Bell 1997: 69–82), which is mainly a student textbook, mentions nothing about *balāgha*. Bell's discussions of the text of the Qur'an in his translation (Bell 1937) and his commentary (Bell 1991) would also have been likely places to discuss *balāgha* and its importance to understanding the Qur'an, but he does not mention it at all. Nor did Watt in his *Companion* to Arberry's translation (Watt 1967). Regrettably too, in his extensive, generally good article on the Qur'an in the *Encyclopaedia of Islam*, second edition, Alford T. Welch did not mention *balāgha* in his discussion of the style of the Qur'an either. Nor does Rosalind Ward Gwynne in her *Logic, Rhetoric and Legal Reasoning in the Qur'ān* (Gwynne 2004) discuss *balāgha*. The bibliographies of such important works on the Qur'an as *Discovering the Qur'an* by Neal Robinson (Robinson 1996: 224–53) and *How to Read the Qur'an* by Carl Ernst (2011) show no mention of *balāgha* books. In two major collections of articles (Bijlefeld 1974 and Turner 2001: 89–115) on the Qur'an, *balāgha* is not mentioned apart from my own article on *iltifāt* in Colin Turner's book. Angelika Neuwirth, in her discussion on 'Rhetoric and the Qurʾān' in the *Encyclopaedia of the Qurʾān* (Neuwirth, *EQ* 4:461–76) does not touch on *ʿilm al-maʿānī* nor is there any mention of this in her article on 'Form and Structure of the Qurʾān' in the *Encyplopaedia of Islam* (Rippin, *EI*² 2:245–66). Even as late as 2006, the 'Tools of the Scholarly Study of the Qurʾān' listed by Andrew Rippin in the *Encyclopaedia of the Qurʾān* (Rippin, *EQ* 5:294–300) include 'The Text of the Qurʾān', 'Concordances', 'Dictionaries', 'Grammar', 'Thematic Indices', 'Commentaries', 'Approaches to the Qurʾān' and 'Bibliographical Aids'—a very useful guide for students but the entry does not include *balāgha*.

Quranic Studies by John Wansbrough (Wansbrough 1977: 227ff.) was the most likely work to refer to *balāgha* sources. He concentrated instead on *Majāz al-Qurʾān* by Abū ʿUbayda (d. 209/824–5) (Abu ʿUbayda, *Majāz*, 1:8), but the word *majāz* as used in Abū ʿUbayda's work does not mean 'figurative language' as normally understood in *balāgha*, as Wansbrough acknowledged. Abū ʿUbayda explains some Qur'anic statements by giving basic information. Thus in *wa-isaʾal al-qaryata* ('ask the town', Q. 12:82) he said that its *majāz* is *wa's'al ahl al-qarya* ('ask *the people of* the town'). No Arab would need such an explanation. Abū ʿUbayda also feels it necessary to explain the statement of God in the plural of majesty, 'We have created [everything] (*khalaqnāhu*) in due measure' (Q. 54:49), by saying, 'the Creator is only God, who is one' (*Majāz*, 1:9). Wansbrough's bibliography mentions *Kitāb al-Badīʿ* (Ibn al-Muʿtazz, *Kitāb al-Badīʿ*, ed. Kratchkovsky, 1935), but *badīʿ* means 'embellishment'. Embellishment attracted the attention of English scholars as seen in references to *jinās* ('homonymy') and *ṭibāq* ('antonymy' or 'contrast') (Arberry 1965: 63, n. 5; 68, n. 45; 66, n. 31; 69, n. 52). Wansbrough's bibliography also mentions al-Jurjānī's *Dalāʾil al-iʿjāz* and *Asrār al-balāgha* (Secrets of rhetoric), and there are detailed discussions in his work on *majāz* and *bayān* (Wansbrough 1977: 227–41), so he was clearly aware of the import of the subject, but al-Jurjānī's name does not appear in the Index, nor does von Mehren's (see above) and, like Nöldeke, he does not mention *ʿilm al-maʿānī*.

European Classical Sources

The following statement by Roland Meynet seems to indicate the general picture of Arabic studies in Europe and how important it was to read the works of Arab scholars:

> In Algiers I at first studied Arabic grammar in Arabic with manuals written by Arab authors. At the University of Aix-en-Provence I had to resume the study but with grammars by western scholars. I could then see that our grammatical categories, inherited from the Greek and Latin tradition were much less effective than those that had been worked out by the Arabic grammarians, from within their own language (Meynet 2012: 7).

Some attention has been given to *balāgha* more recently. In the second edition of *The Encyclopaedia of Islam*, there is an article on *balāgha* by Schade and von Grünebaum, surveying Arab scholarship but with references listed mainly to German scholars. On *al-maʿānī wa'l-bayān* the *Encyclopaedia* has an article by Bonebakker and Reinert, which surveys some mainly classical Arab works on the subject in an attempt to provide 'a few practical hints by way of introduction to the vast and little-known literature on the *maʿānī* and the *bayān*'. They are still confused by the term *maʿānī* and find both terms awkward (Bonebakker and Reinert, '*al-Maʿānī wa 'l-Bayān*').

Kees Versteegh, in the index of his *Encyclopedia of Arabic Language and Linguistics*, refers to scattered short mentions of *balāgha* and gives one reference to *ʿilm al-maʿānī* (Versteegh 2009: 51). The *Oxford Handbook of Arabic Linguistics* (Owens 2013), Chapter 8 on 'Arabic Linguistic Tradition II: Pragmatics' (Larchier 2013: 188–212) has a section (8.2.2.) on *ʿilm al-maʿānī*.

Recent Arab Writing on *Balāgha* in English

This is all very useful but nevertheless, the applied study of Qur'anic *balāgha* in English has until recently been left to scholars of the Qur'an trained in the Arabic-Islamic tradition, such as:

- Muhammad Abdel Haleem
  - *Understanding the Qur'an: Themes and Style*. London: IB Tauris, 2010;
  - 'Grammatical Shift for Rhetorical Purposes: *Iltifāt* and Related Features in the Qurʾān', *BSOAS* 55/3 (1992), 407–32;

- 'Arabic of the Qur'ān: Grammar and Style'. In C. Versteegh (general ed.). *Encyclopedia of Arabic Language and Linguistics*, vol. 4 (Q–Z), Qur'ān, pp. 21–32. Leiden: Brill, 2009.
- Hussein Abdul-Raof
  - *Arabic Rhetoric: A Pragmatic Analysis*. London and New York: Routledge, 2006;
  - *Exploring The Qur'ān*. Dundee: Al-Maktoum Institute Academic Press, 2003.
- Mustansir Mir. He brought to light in English Ḥamīd al-Dīn Farāhī, *Jamharat-al-Balāgha* (Manual of Qur'anic rhetoric) written in Urdu;
  - *Coherence in the Qur'ān*. Indianapolis: American Trust Publications, 1986.
- Bāsil Ḥātim
  - *Arabic Rhetoric: The Pragmatics of Deviation from Linguistic Norms*. Munich: Lincom Europa, 2010.
- Abd al-Rahim Ibrahim
  - *The Literary Structure of the Qur'ānic Verse*. Birmingham: Qur'ānic Arabic Foundation, 2005.
- Mahmoud M. Ayoub
  - 'Literary Exegesis of the Qur'ān: The Case of al-Sharīf al-Raḍī'. In Issa J. Boullata (ed.). *Literary Structures of Religious Meaning in the Qur'ān*', pp. 292–309. London: Curzon, 2000.

Issues Discussed Under *ʿIlm al-Maʿānī*

As already indicated, according to traditional categorizations of Arabic rhetoric, *balāgha* comprises three branches, *ʿilm al-maʿānī* ('the science of meanings'), *ʿilm al bayān* ('the science of eloquence'), and *ʿilm al-badīʿ* ('the science of embellishment'). *Bayān* deals mainly with factual and figurative language, including simile, metaphor, and *kināya* ('metonymy'). *Badīʿ* attracted Western Arabist writers in English with such verbal features as alliteration, assonance, and *jinās* ('homonymy'). These features do not seem far different from those in the rhetorical traditions of European languages. It is, therefore, the study of *ʿilm al-maʿānī* that is particularly needed (Baalbaki 1983: 7–23).

Under *ʿilm al-maʿānī*, important issues are discussed in the Arabic *balāgha* tradition, for example by al-Ṭībī (d. 743/1342) (al-Ṭībī, *Kitāb al-Tibyān*), al-Qazwīnī (d. 793/1338) (al-Qazwīnī, *al-Īḍāḥ*, 1–130) and, in the last century, by al-Hāshimī (d. 1943) (al-Hashimī, *Jawāhir al-balāgha*, 1–173), starting with *muṭābaqat al-kalām li-muqtaḍā al-ḥāl* ('conformity of speech to the context of the situation'). This was one of the crucial discoveries of Arab rhetoricians. According to Tammām Ḥassān (Ḥassān 1973: 337, 372), this preceded modern European linguistics by over 1,000 years. Much of what has been criticized about the text of the Qur'an is perfectly appropriate in the context of the situation, as explained in *ʿilm al-maʿānī*. *ʿIlm al-maʿānī* also analyses the different parts of the sentence: the subject, predicate, and complementary parts. In terms of the subject, for instance, there is discussion as to whether it is stated or omitted, and why; whether it is definite or indefinite; its placement in the sentence; whether it is restricted by adjectives or other elements, or not—all in great detail and with purposes and justification. For instance, the definition of the subject by a relative clause can be done for eleven reasons (Hashimi, *Jawāhir*, 130–2). Similarly detailed treatment is given to the predicate and complements. Another full chapter is dedicated to *al-qaṣr* ('restricting statements'), followed by a chapter on *al-faṣl wa'l-waṣl* ('disjoining and joining' of parts of the sentence using conjunctions like *wa* ('and') and *fa* ('so')). There is a chapter dedicated to *ījāz* ('brevity'), *iṭnāb* ('expansion'), and *musāwā* ('equality').

Departure from What is Expected

This all concluded with the crucial subject of *ikhrāj al-kalām ʿalā khilāf muqtaḍā al-ẓāhir* (departure from what is expected). This can apply to the various elements above. *Al-amr* ('command'), for instance, can range, according to the context, from being a mere request to twenty-one other things, such as permission (i.e. in Q. 2:187, *'Eat and drink until the white thread of dawn can be distinguished from the black'*). Likewise, *al-istifhām* ('question') can depart from being a mere question to twenty-four other meanings (Ḥātim 2010: 151–68). In al-Hāshimī, the number of derivations/departures varies slightly (*Jawāhir al-balāgha*, 78–9, 93–6). *Ikhrāj/khurūj al-kalām ʿalā khilāf muqtaḍā al-ẓāhir* is a distinguishing feature of Arabic rhetoric and is very common in Qur'anic discourse.

Without sufficient awareness of this, many expressions would appear as wrong or bad grammar or difficult to explain. Nöldeke's reaction to *iltifāt*, mentioned above, is an obvious example. Similar was his reaction to *ḥadhf* ('omission'), which is another feature studied under *ʿilm al-maʿānī* (Rahman 2000: 277–91); referring to Q. 24:10, 'if it were not for God's bounty and mercy towards you, if it were not that God accepts repentance and is wise . . .! It was a group from among you that concocted the lie', which omits to state what would have happened, Nöldeke notes that the omission of a 'continuing clause' is strange, and is 'followed by all sorts of strange things' (Nöldeke 1910:19). However, this feature is normal in Arabic and is still used now, even in daily language. A man who has been offended or insulted by someone would say, 'If it were not for the sake of his father . . .', stating the important consideration but 'leaving every possibility open' to people's imagination. In parsing a sentence like this, Arab students would be expected to say, *li-tadhhab al-nafs fī taqdīrihi kulla madhhab* ('so that, in assessing it, the mind may go in every possible direction'). Richard Bell, however, comments only: 'It is an incomplete sentence' (Bell 1991: 595). Now, as Ibn Mālik (d. 672/1273) declares, in his *Alfiyya*: *ḥadhf mā yuʿlam jāʾiz*—'it is permissible to omit what is understood' (Ibn Mālik, *Alfiyya*, 18). ʿIzz al-Dīn ibn ʿAbd al-Salām (d. 660/1262), in his book *Majāz al-Qurʾān*, dedicates more than 200 pages (pp. 261–478) just to examples in the Qur'an of the omission of the first part of the *iḍāfa* construct, the *muḍāf*. All this goes to show the pressing need for introducing *balāgha*, especially *ʿilm al-maʿānī*, into the teaching of Arabic in Western universities.

Having finished with *balāgha* we now move to deal with the second part of this chapter, Stylistic Features.

Stylistic Features

In their useful, well-written book, *[Bell's] Introduction to the Qur'ān*, under 'Features of Qurʾānic Style' (1997: chapter 5), Richard Bell and Montgomery Watt have various sections that deal with 'Rhymes and Strophes', 'Various Didactic Forms', and 'The Language of the Qurʾān'. These are useful but the discussion is very brief and they do not deal with many of the important features discussed in this chapter, which are essential to understanding the Qur'an, showing its dynamism, and explaining some of the means by which it achieves its impact in Arabic. Some of these features are:

Logical Arguments Blended with Emotion

The Qur'an gives arguments for the claims it makes: even the existence of God has to be proved by arguments and so do His unity and care. When asking people to do something or refrain from something, it presents some powerful reasoning to persuade the listener or reader. This stylistic feature is particularly obvious in the discussion on the Resurrection. To the Arabs' arguments against the possibility of the Resurrection it replies:

> Can man not see that We created him from a drop of fluid? Yet—lo and behold!—he disputes openly, producing arguments against Us, forgetting his own creation. He says, 'Who can give life back to bones after they have decayed?' Say, 'He who created them in the first place will give them life again: He has full knowledge of every act of creation. It is He who produces fire for you out of the green tree—lo and behold!—and from this you kindle fire. Is He who created the heavens and earth not able to create the likes of these people? Of course He is! He is the All Knowing Creator: when He wills something to be, His way is to say, "Be"—and it is! So glory be to Him in whose Hand lies control over all things. It is to Him that you will all be brought back.' (Q. 36:77–83).

In this passage, the Qur'an provides three logical answers: (1) God has created man before, so He can do it again; (2) He is able to produce things from their opposites, including life from dead bones; (3) He has done even greater work than the creation of man. This logical construct is clothed in strong emotional and dramatic language: rhetorical question (*'Can man not see...?'*); plural of majesty (*'We created him...'*); exclamation (*'lo and behold!'*); and paradox (from such a small beginning, *'he disputes openly producing arguments against Us, forgetting his own creation'*, followed by a powerful statement, *'He Who created them in the first instance'*, removing any possibility that someone else had created them). He is very knowledgeable in all acts of creation, not just of humans. Then follow the beautiful images of things coming from their opposite, fire from green trees and further exclamation, 'lo and behold!—and from this you kindle fire'. Then comes the very powerful rhetorical question, 'Is He who created the heavens and earth not able to create the likes of these small creatures?' The answer comes emphatically, 'Of course He is!' He is the all-knowing, ultimate creator (intensive form, *khallāq*) of all things. Then comes the dismissal of their conception of how God acts by saying, 'Whenever He wills something to be, His way is to say, "Be", and it is!' This is all followed by 'glory be to Him in whose Hand lies control over all things' and a stunning statement to disbelievers, 'it is to Him that you will all be brought back', in the passive, and not by their own choice. All this is expressed in a few short lines in Arabic, using compelling, brief, memorable words.

Affective Sentences (*jumal inshāʾiyya*) and Verbal Sentences (*jumal fiʿliyya*)

In addition to the more neutral declarative sentence (*khabariyya*, e.g. 'they arrived'), the Qur'an frequently uses affective sentences to persuade and convey its message: commands, prohibitions, and questions, which do not give information but initiate a new situation. For instance:

> Say [Prophet], 'Consider those you pray to other than God: show me which part of the earth they created or which share of the heavens they own; bring me a previous scripture or some vestige of divine knowledge—if what you say is true.' Who could be more wrong than a person who calls on those other than God, those who will not answer him till the Day of Resurrection, those who are unaware of his prayers, those who, when all mankind is gathered, will become his enemies and disown his worship? (Q: 46:4–6).

> If you wish to replace one wife with another, do not take any of her dowry back, even if you have given her a great amount of gold. How could you take it when this is unjust and a blatant sin? How could you take it when you have lain with each other and they have taken a solemn pledge from you? (Q. 4:20–1).

This explains the frequent occurrence in the Qur'an of the imperative and interrogative, as well as the many persuasive prohibitions, propositions, exhortations, supplications, exclamations, and oaths. In Q. 52:30–43, for instance, there are fifteen rhetorical questions in a row, addressed to the disbelievers, about God, the Prophet, and the Qur'an. The *jumla inshāʾiyya* serves to make the Qur'anic discourse dynamic and vibrant, involving the readers or listeners, rather than throwing statements over their heads—a very important consideration in Qur'anic discourse.

In its use of the verbal sentence the Qur'an also utilizes the tense of the verb rhetorically, for example using the past tense normally used for historical accounts also when discussing the afterlife. This is effective in making such momentous events as those in the afterlife (mentioned directly or indirectly on almost every page of the Qur'an) seem as if they are already here, a device common in Qur'anic discourse and techniques of persuasion. This may involve *iltifāt* or shift in tense as, for example, in Q. 20:125–6 and Q. 40:48–50.

Frequent Use of Descriptive Attributes (*ṣifāt kathīra*)

The use of descriptive attributes is an important means of Qur'anic persuasion and argument, noticeable from the very beginning: 'Praise be to God, Lord of the worlds, the Lord of Mercy, the Giver of Mercy' (Q. 1:2–3). Because He has such attributes (*ṣifāt*) He is worthy of praise and worship. The path required for believers is the 'straight' one, the one 'whose followers are blessed and not the object of anger' or 'those who are astray' (Q. 1:6–7), so qualified the path is worthy of asking God's guidance to it.

The believers, too, are described in many ways:

> The believers will succeed: those who pray humbly, who shun idle talk, who pay the prescribed alms, who guard their chastity except with their spouses or their slaves—with these they are not to blame, but anyone who seeks more than this is exceeding the limits—who are faithful to their trusts and pledges and who keep up their prayers, will rightly be given Paradise as their own, there to remain (Q. 23:1–11, see also Q. 70:22–9).

This is an important feature of Qur'anic rhetoric and style, according to which God is often defined by multiple adjectives, normally in the intensive form, such as *ʿalīm*, *qadīr*, *ghafūr*, or *tawwāb*, many of which are referred to as the names of God. Furthermore, the names of God, which are themselves adjectival, are normally accompanied by further attributes describing His acts, such as *khalaqakum* ('He created you') or *razaqakum* ('He provided for you'), used to illustrate God's power and care towards His creatures, thereby making the point that He is the only one worthy of worship, whereas other deities who do not share these attributes are not worthy of worship. Sometimes the longer suras contain lengthy glorifications of God and take many pages, as in large parts of *Sūrat al-Anʿām* (Q. 6) and *Sūrat al-Naḥl* (Q. 16). These attributes and acts are used evidentially since the Qur'an bases its message on evidence, reasoning, and argumentation. This aspect of 'argumentation' can be seen to dominate the discourse surrounding other important issues, such as the discussions of the Resurrection in *Sūrat Yāsīn* (Q. 36:77–83) and *Sūrat al-Wāqiʿa* (Q. 56:57–74).

Generalization (*taʿmīm*)

The Qur'an frequently uses generalization, since it maintains that it is for all people. It classifies people, using such plurals as *al-muʾminūn* ('the believers'), *al-muttaqūn* ('those who are mindful of God'), *al-kāfirūn* ('the non-believers'), *al-ẓālimūn* ('evildoers') and so on, and employs conditional sentences with grammatical particles like *man*, *mā*, *ayyu*, *haythumā*, *aynamā* ('whoever, whatever, whichever, wherever, whenever'), and also the indefinite noun. This serves to bring in all that are included under the relevant class, which also helps brevity.

Contrast (*taḍādd*)

Contrast is another central feature of Qur'anic style: the Book juxtaposes this world with the next (each occurring exactly 115 times); believers and disbelievers; Paradise and hell. Many other patterns of contrast have been observed: angels and devils; life and death; secrecy and openness, and so on, occurring exactly the same number of times (Nawfal 1976). One of the linguistic habits of the Qur'an is also to contrast two classes of a given thing, and their respective destinies, as a persuasive rhetorical device. Grammatically this contrast is achieved by such devices as '*man*... *wa-man*' ('those who... and those who') as, for example, in Q. 4:123–4 ('anyone who does wrong will be requited for it... anyone, male or female, who does good... will enter Paradise.... ') and Q. 92:5–8. Another device is '*ammā*... *wa-ammā*', as in Q. 3:106–7 ('On the day when some faces brighten and others darken, as for those with darkened faces it will be said... and as for those with brightened faces...') and Q. 79:37 and 40. Sometimes the contrasted elements follow each other without any conjunction, which shows the contrast even more powerfully: for example, Q. 89:25–7, 'On that day, no one will punish as He punishes, and no one will bind as He binds. [But] you, soul at peace, return to your Lord, well pleased and well pleasing, go in among my servants and into my Garden.'

Rhyme and Rhythm (*fāṣila wa-īqāʿ*)

Rhyme at the end of verses is a stylistic feature in the Arabic Qur'an, which has an aesthetic effect. It also gives finality to statements and accords with the general feature of classification and generalization, frequently using the plural endings *-ūn* and *-īn*. The ending of the verse can be an integral part of the sentence (as in sura 1) or a final comment on it (e.g. Q. 4:34–5, '... God is most high and great (*ʿaliyyan kabīr*)... He is all knowing, all aware (*ʿalīman khabīr*)'), but the rhyme is not just for embellishment (Omar 1999: 264–9).

Dialogue and Direct Speech (*ḥiwār wa-kalām mubāshir*)

The Qur'an frequently uses direct speech to bind each person by what he or she utters rather than in reported speech, and it also often presents itself as a conversation between God and the Prophet, and/or God and humanity, through the device of direct speech and dialogue. There is striking dialogue between people in hell (e.g. Q. 7:37–9, 40:47–50); there is even dialogue between people and their own organs (eyes, ears, and skins,

Q. 41:19–23), which testify against them in the next life: 'They will say to their skins, "Why did you testify against us?" and their skins will reply, "God, who gave speech to everything, gave us speech . . ."'. There is dramatic dialogue between characters in stories like that of Joseph (Yūsuf, Q. 12). Arabic grammar allows shifts between direct and reported speech within a sentence after such verbs as *qāla* ('he said'), one aspect of *iltifāt*. The fact that this verb occurs in the Qur'an more than 300 times is some indication of how frequently direct speech and dialogue are used, adding to dynamism and liveliness of the Qur'anic discourse.

Effective Repetition (*takrār muʾaththir*)

Repetition is an obvious feature of the language of the Qur'an. It may repeat what it considers essential to its message. Thus, the story of Adam and Eve occurs a number of times (Abdel Haleem 2010: 126–60). Material is not just repeated verbatim, but in different suras the Qur'an employs certain elements at various lengths as suits the context. The deception of Adam and Eve by Satan, swearing that he will use every possible means to mislead their children (e.g. Q. 7:17 and 17:62–4), is repeated to warn and explain why disbelievers behave in the way they do. Similarly, stories of prophets and how they argued with their people, how they suffered, and how God saved the believers in the end, all serve to encourage the Muslims and warn their opponents (Abdel Haleem 2006: 38–57). The lengthy descriptions of Paradise and Hell are used repeatedly, like the frequent mention of God's attributes, to impress the message, relating such descriptions to teachings, to create an impact which could not be achieved by a single mention of the fundamental components. It also has to be kept in mind that the whole of the Qur'an was revealed in stages over a period of more than twenty years, to different audiences in different situations, using oral delivery. Some employment of earlier material was needed to impress the message on these new situations and audiences, especially as that message dealt with matters of faith and practices that sought to break ingrained habits.

Suspension of Composition Patterns (*taʿlīq al-nasaq*)

Fakhr al-Dīn al-Rāzī in his *Tafsīr* writes about the stylistic habits of the Qur'an (*ʿādāt al-kitāb al-ʿazīz*). He explains why the Qur'an brings together various subjects in the same sura (e.g. Part 9, p. 133; Part 17, p. 86; Part 18, pp. 8–9, 55; Part 20, pp. 83; Part 20, p. 214). The various subjects reinforce each other and are not simply a conglomeration of unrelated material. This feature can be extended to include suspension of composition patterns for rhetorical purposes. At times the Qur'an interrupts the flow of discourse-mode, theme, sentence structure, rhythm, and rhyme and so on for considerations of context-specific purposes more important than maintaining form, before returning to the original discourse. It is in fact a form of *khurūj*, departing from what is expected. For example, in Q. 2:228–37 there is a long discussion on divorce and the rights of divorced women as well as the financial rights of widows, ending with the suggestion to both parties in these difficult emotional situations not to 'forget to be generous to each other: God sees what you do' (2: 237). This verse presents encouragement and warning, but the Qur'an adds to this, giving practical advice on steps that people can take to help them obey this teaching. Thus in 2: 238–9 the parties are reminded, 'Take care to do your prayers in the best way and stand before God in devotion. If you are in danger, pray when you are out on foot or riding, when you are safe again, remember God, for He has taught you what you did not know' before resuming the original theme, the rights of widows and divorced women. The idea behind this interruption and suspension of composition pattern is that undertaking the prayer at pertinent times is likely to reduce bitterness and bring people to a proper frame of mind. This effect of prayer is confirmed in Q. 5:107–8, in which it is recommended that legal testimony should be given after undertaking prayer, in the hope that it will make the witnesses give proper testimony. In my village in the Nile Delta, when two families are in dispute, it is common practice to decide to meet to settle the dispute in the afternoon, but to first go to the mosque together and perform the *ʿaṣr* prayer, shoulder to shoulder before God, as it is seen to put both parties in a more conciliatory frame of mind. The introduction of these two verses which comprise a more general instruction to perform prayer at difficult times into a section on the specific theme of divorce has been commented on by Richard Bell, who considered it had no connection with the context and seems designed for those on some military expedition (Bell 1991: 1:49). However, the underlying point of these two verses is to stress that even at war, not just in personal disagreement, believers should keep up the prayer so that it might have a beneficial effect on one's behaviour at times when it might be easy to act unjustly. For this reason, when the Qur'an provides a list of the qualities of believers, as in Q. 23:1–10 and in Q. 70:23–34, it puts observing the prayer first: this is the bedrock of Islamic practice on which everything else is built, and if the believers observe the prayer they are more likely to observe everything else. As the Prophet said: 'The first thing a person will be asked about on the Day of Judgement is the prayer. If it is good (*idhā ṣalaḥat*), the rest of his deeds will be affected, and if it is bad, the rest of his deeds will also be affected' (*Sunan al-Nasāʾī, Kitāb al-ṣalāt* 6; Wensinck 1992: 1–2:134).

In another example of this feature of Qur'anic style, sura 5 starts by urging the believers to fulfil their pledges, including observing the rites of the *ḥajj* and refraining from forbidden foods. Then in v. 5 it informs the believers, in answer to a question, that chaste Muslim women are lawful for them, and that so are the chaste women of the People of the Book, provided a dowry is paid and they are taken in marriage, not as lovers or secret mistresses. Then comes the warning: 'Whoever disregards the obligations of the faith, his deeds will come to nothing and he will be among the losers'. Following this warning, the composition pattern is interrupted, and the subject of prayer is brought in to heighten its impact. It enables people to obey but in the atmosphere of talking about forbidden foods and forbidding illicit sexual relations it asks the believers, when they stand to do the prayer, first to cleanse themselves, considering the instruction of cleansing as part of perfecting the blessing of God on them (v. 6). Then the sura returns to the original theme of keeping pledges. Thus the original discourse is interrupted and the prayer and purification interjected, as in the previous example, in order to encourage the believers to adhere to Qur'anic teachings.

In some other examples the Qur'an seizes a chance to introduce a piece of important teaching by attaching it to another teaching, even by interrupting a pattern. Thus while explaining the fast of Ramadan, during which believers should refrain during daytime from consuming lawful food and drink, they are told that at night it is lawful to eat and drink, and to lie with their spouses: 'thus God makes clear His revelation to people so that they be mindful of Him' (Q. 2:187). Immediately after this verse comes the rejoinder: 'Do not consume your property wrongfully, nor use it to bribe judges so that you may deliberately consume some of other people's property' (v. 188). This important piece of teaching comes after training the believers to refrain for a whole month from eating what is lawful during daytime and after reminding them of God's leniency during the night. *Wa-kulū wa'shrabū* is followed by *wa-lā taʾkulū amwālakum baynakum bi'l-bāṭil.* Again, Richard Bell sees this verse as quite detached (Bell 1991: 1:39) and other readers may also see it in this way, but the Qur'an has higher objectives and knows where to introduce teachings so that they are more likely to be obeyed.

One final example of this stylistic feature of suspending the flow of discourse for considerations more important than maintaining form is sura 33 (*al-Aḥzāb*) which introduces teachings to do with family relationships, particularly the banning of adoption of children as was practised, divorcing by *ẓihār*, and later on teachings to do with the Prophet's wives, as the sura tries to restrain the Muslims from practices very much part of Arab life at the time. After v. 8, a full two pages are introduced on the episode of the joint forces that came to invade Medina: 'Believers, remember God's favour to you when mighty armies massed against you...from above and below you and your eyes rolled with fear, your hearts rose to your throats...' (vv. 9–10). So, here, God reminds the believers how He saved them in this desperate situation so that they may now listen to the teaching in this sura. Even if it interrupts the original pattern, the importance of reminding the believers of God's favour so that they obey the teaching is more important than the consideration of maintaining formal aspects of the discourse.

Instilling the Desire to Obey and the Fear of Disobedience (*Targhīb wa-Tarhīb*)

Another important feature of the style of the Qur'an is that it is passionate in presenting its message. It is very keen for people to obey its *hudā* ('guidance'), as can be seen in, for example, Q. 49:7–8, 'God has endeared faith to you and made it beautiful to your hearts. He has made disbelief, mischief and disobedience hateful to you. It is such people who are rightly guided, through God's favour and blessing.' On the basis of this it uses *targhīb* ('awakening desire to obey') and *tarhīb* ('awakening fear of disobedience'). This involves contrast as mentioned earlier. Al-Shāṭibī (d. 790/1388) rightly observed:

> When *targhīb* occurs it will be accompanied by *tarhīb* in the subsequent or earlier material or in the same place. Thus when it mentions the people of Paradise it also mentions the people of hell, and vice versa, because mentioning the people of Paradise with their deeds instils hope and mentioning the people of hell with their deeds instils fear (al-Shāṭibī, *Muwāfaqāt*, 3:358).

Al-Shāṭibī further observed: 'One of the two may predominate in one place according to the requirement of the context' (*Muwāfaqāt*, 3:360). An obvious example is seen in *Sūrat al-Raḥmān* (Q. 55) which contains 78 verses: vv. 39–45 are dedicated to the guilty, and the rest of the sura to the *muttaqīn* ('the God-conscious'), which is appropriate for a sura that bears the title 'The Merciful'. In contrast to that, *Sūrat al-Qamar* (Q. 54) contains 55 verses, starting (vv. 2–3) with the disbelievers, 'Whenever the disbelievers see a sign, they turn away and say, "Same old sorcery." They reject the truth and follow their own desires.' Most of the sura after this concentrates on the guilty, with only the last two verses (vv. 54–5) showing the rewards of the *muttaqūn*. These are two stark examples, but the feature can be observed in various degrees throughout the Qur'an.

Distribution of Related Material (*Tawzī*ʿ *al-Mādda*)

In the Qur'an it is noticeable that sometimes material dealing with one specific subject may be distributed into different places for different reasons, two examples of which can be mentioned here. The first is its habit of introducing legislation gradually to make it more likely to be obeyed in a society which would otherwise reject a sudden wholesale change. The prohibition of alcohol is the example normally quoted, which was revealed in four stages: first a slightly disparaging remark, contrasting what people make out of dates and grapes, *sakar* (what produces intoxication), with *rizqun ḥasan* ('wholesome provision') (Q. 16:67). Later, when asked about *khamr* ('wine') the Prophet was instructed to say, 'There is great sin in [it], and some benefit for people: the sin is greater than the benefit' (Q. 2:219). Then the Qur'an prohibited people from coming to prayer, which takes place five times a day, while drunk (*sukārā*) (Q. 4:43), and finally banned alcohol completely in Q. 5:90 and condemns it, along with gambling, as 'filth of the works of Satan'. This one theme was introduced over a number of years in different places. This cannot be easily dismissed as repetition. There is no abrogation; the description at every stage is still valid: alcohol is intoxicating, any Muslim who is drunk should not pray and alcohol is banned (al-Khuḍarī 1964: 5–21).

The second reason for distributing material is that the Qur'an employs teachings already mentioned in different situations for suitable contextual purposes. Thus, prayer is introduced in many places, one of which, already mentioned, is as a prop to secure obedience (Q. 2:238–9) (see 'Suspension of Composition Patterns for Rhetorical Purposes'). Another example is the battle of Badr (AH 2) mentioned at length in *Sūrat al-Anfāl* (Q. 8) and then again referred to twice in *Sūrat Āl ʿImrān* (Q. 3:13) to remind the disbelievers who were sure of their strength that they had a good example in what happened at Badr where their large numbers did not prevent their defeat. In vv. 118–20 it is used again in reverse to encourage the Muslims who were afraid of the disbelievers. Similarly, the Qur'an repeatedly employs stories of earlier prophets to strengthen the Prophet Muḥammad and his followers and warn their opponents, a constant need throughout his life.

Conclusion

It is clear from the foregoing that the Qur'an uses Arabic grammar and *balāgha* together to serve its own purposes. Grammar may follow the normal rule (a process known as *istiṣḥāb al-aṣl*). Considerations of *balāgha*, however, can give priority to *al-ʿudūl ʿan al-aṣl* ('departure from the original norm') or, as the scholars of *balāgha* say, *al-khurūj ʿalā muqtaḍā al-ẓāhir* ('departure from what is normally expected'), but only 'for considerations required by the situation in certain contexts' (al-Hāshimī, *Jawāhir al-balāgha*, 239). As seen for instance in *iltifāt*, *balāgha* overrules grammar. The *balāgha* of the Qur'an is part of the way the Arabs used their language in their literature. To ignore this would be to reduce the universally acknowledged eloquence of the Qur'an to a very basic level of communication. The tools of *balāgha* and the stylistic features explained above, more than just simile, metaphor, and embellishments, are essential to understand the way in which the Qur'an introduces its messages and creates impact.

Future Development in the Study of Qur'anic *Balāgha*

As we have seen, *balāgha*, especially *ʿilm al-maʿānī*, has long been neglected in Qur'anic Studies in English, despite its crucial importance for the study and appreciation of the language and style of the Arabic Qur'an. The impact of the language and style of the Qur'an even on Arabs and Muslims does not seem to have been given sufficient attention. Understandably, with the exception of very few individuals, Western scholars of the Qur'an in the past did not show interest in its effectiveness; from the beginning the intention was quite the opposite. Qur'anic Studies have come a long way beyond that.

It is a welcome development that some attention has been given to *balāgha* in recent years, as we have seen in the *Encyclopaedia of Islam* (second edition) and more recently Brill's *Encyclopedia of Arabic Language and Linguistics*, and the *Oxford Handbook of Arabic Linguistics*. More detailed studies of *balāgha* as applied to the Qur'an have been undertaken by Arab and Muslim scholars of the Qur'an, now in Western universities, who have been trained in the Arabic and Islamic tradition. The number of such scholars is on the increase as a result of the global movements in academia. A new trend is also witnessed among Arab and Muslim Ph.D. students in Western universities, many of whom come from departments of Linguistics in their own countries, and it has become a favourite subject for them to study the Qur'an in English translation. This normally involves *balāgha* and all aspects of Qur'anic style. Durham and Leeds Universities have recently witnessed a number of these. This all adds to the new trend towards giving *balāgha* its proper place at the centre of Qur'anic Studies in English. It would be useful to have more Arabic texts on *balāgha* and style translated into English and to have some of this incorporated into the teaching of Arabic and Qur'anic studies in Western universities. This can only add strength to the discipline.

Bibliography

ʿAbd Allāh b. al-Muʿtazz. *Kitāb al Badīʿ*. Ed. Ignatius Kratchkovsky. London: Luzac and Co., 1935.

Abdel Haleem, M. 'The Qurʾānic Employment of the Story of Noah', *Journal of Qur'anic Studies* 8/1 (February 2006), 38–57.

Abdel Haleem, M. 'Adam and Eve in the Qurʾān and the Bible'. In: *Understanding the Qurʾān: Themes and Style*. pp. 126–60. London: IB Tauris, 2010.

Abdel Haleem, M. 'Divine Oaths in the Qurʾān'. *Journal of Qur'anic Studies* Occasional Paper 1 (2013).

Abū ʿUbayda, M. *Majāz al-Qurʾān*. 2 vols. Ed. M. F. Sezgin. Cairo: al-Khanji, 1954.

ʿAkkāwi, Inʿām, *al-Muʿjam al-mufaṣṣal fi ʿulūm al-balāgha*. Beirut: Dār al-Kutub al-ʿIlmiyya, 1992.

Arberry, A. J. *Arabic Poetry: A Primer for Students*. Cambridge: Cambridge University Press, 1965.

Ibn al-Athīr, Ḍiyāʾ al-Dīn. *al-Mathal al-sāʾir fī ʿadab al-kātib wa'l-shāʿir*. Cairo: Maṭbaʿāt Muṣṭafā al-Bābī al-Ḥalabī, 1939.

Baalbaki, Ramzi. 'The Relation Between *naḥw* and *balāġa*: A Comparative Study of the Methods of Sībawayhi and Gurgānī', *Zeitschrift für Arabische Linguistik* 11 (1983).

Bell, Richard. *The Qurʾān Translated with Critical Arrangement of the Suras*. Edinburgh: T. & T. Clark, 1937; 1960.

Bell, Richard. *A Commentary on the Qurʾān*. 2 vols. Manchester: University of Manchester, 1991.

Bijlefeld, Willem. 'Some Recent Contributions to Qurʾānic Studies: Selected Publications in English, French, and German, 1964–1973, Parts I–III', *Muslim World* 64/2 (1974) and 64/4 (1974).

Bonebakker, S. A. and B. Reinert. '*al-Maʿānī wa 'l-Bayān*'. In: P. Bearman, Th. Bianquis, C. E. Bosworth, E. van Donzel, and W. P. Heinrichs (eds.) *Encyclopaedia of Islam*, Second Edition. Consulted on-line on 18 July 2017 < http://dx.doi.org/10.1163/1573-3912_islam_COM_0595> First published on-line: 2012. First print edition: ISBN: 9789004161214, 1960–2007.

El-Sakkout, H. *The Egyptian Novel and its Main Trends 1913–1952*. Cairo: American University of Cairo Press, 1970.

Ernst, C. *How to Read the Qurʾān*. Chapel Hill, NC: University of North Carolina Press, 2011.

al-Hāshimī, Aḥmad, *Jawāhir al-balāgha fī'l-maʿānī wa'l-bayān wa'l-badīʿ*. Beirut: Dār al-Fikr, 1986 and al-Maktaba al-Assriya, 2008.

Ḥassān, Tammām. *al-Lugha al-ʿarabiyya: maʿnāhā wa-mabnāhā*. Cairo: al-Hayʾa al-Miṣriyya al-ʿĀmma li'l-Kitāb, 1973.

Hatim, B. *Arabic Rhetoric: The Pragmatics of Deviation from Linguistic Norms*. Munich: Lincom Europa, 2010.

Ibn Mālik. *Alfiyyat Ibn Mālik fī'l-naḥw wa'l-ṣarf.* Cairo: Dār al-Kutub, 1932.

ʿIzz al-Dīn b.ʿAbd al-Salām. *Majāz al-Qurʾān*. London: Al-Furqan, 1999.

Jones, A. *The Qurʾān Translated into English*. Exeter: Gibb Memorial Trust, 2007.

al-Jurjānī, ʿAbd al-Qāhir. *Dalāʾil al-iʿjāz*. Cairo: Maktabat al-Khānjī, 1424/2004.

al-Khaṭīb al-Qazwīnī. *al-Īḍāḥ fī ʿulūm al-balāgha*, pp. 1–130. Cairo: Ṣubayḥ, 1971.

al-Khuḍarī, M. *Tārīkh al-Tashrīʿ al-Islām*. Cairo: al-Maktaba al-Tijāriyya al-Kubrā, 1964.

Larcher, P. 'Arabic Linguistic Tradition II: Pragmatics'. In J. Owens (ed.) *The Oxford Handbook of Arabic Linguistics*, pp. 185–212. Oxford: Oxford University Press, 2013.

McAuliffe, J. D. (ed.). *Encyclopaedia of the Qurʾān*. 6 vols. Leiden: Brill, 2001–06.

Meynet, R. *Treatise on Biblical Rhetoric*. Trans. Leo Arnold. Leiden and Boston: Brill, 2012.

Nawfal, ʿAbd al-Razzāq. *al-Iʿjāz al-ʿadadī li'l-Qurʾān al-Karīm*. Cairo: Dār al-Shaʿb, 1976.

Nöldeke, T. *Die Rhetorik der Araber*. Copenhagen and Vienna: Verlag von Otto Schwartz, 1853. With extracts from al-Suyūṭī's (d. 1505) versified presentation *ʿUḳūd al-Djumān*.

Nöldeke, T. *Geschichte des Qorâns*. Göttingen: Verlag der Dieterichschen Buchhandlung, 1860.

Nöldeke, T. 'Stylistische und syntaktische Eigentümlichkeiten der Sprache des Korans'. In: *Neue Beiträge zur semitischen Sprachwissenschaft*. Strassburg: Verlag von Karl J. Trübner, 1910.

Omar, A. M. 'The *fāṣila* in the Qurʾān: Word, Context and Meaning', *Journal of Qur'anic Studies* 1/1 (1999), 264–9.

Owens, J. *The Oxford Handbook of Arabic Linguistics*. Oxford: Oxford University Press, 2013.

Paret, Rudi. 'The Qurʾān'. In: A. F. L. Beeston, T. M. Johnstone, R. E. Serjeant, and G. R. Smith (eds.). *Arabic Literature to the End of the Umayyad Period*, pp. 186–227. Cambridge: Cambridge University Press, 1983.

Rahman, Y. 'Ellipsis in the Qurʾān: A Study of Ibn Qutayba's *Taʾwīl mushkil al-Qurʾān*'. In: Issa J. Boullata (ed.). *Literary Structures of Religious Meaning in the Qurʾān*, pp. 277–91. London: Curzon, 2000.

al-Rāzī, Fakhr al-Dīn. *Mafātīḥ al-ghayb/al-Tafsīr al-kabīr.* 32 vols. Beirut: Dār al-Iḥyāʾ al-Turāth al-ʿArabī, n.d.

Robinson, N. *Discovering the Qur'an*. London: SCM Press, 1996.

al-Sakkākī, Abū Yaʿqūb Yūsuf b. Abī Bakr. *al-Īḍāḥ fī ʿulūm al-balāgha: Mukhtaṣar talkhīṣ al-miftāḥ*. Cairo: Subaih, 1356/1971.

Schade, A. and G. E. von Grünebaum. 'Balāgha'. In: P. Bearman, Th. Blanquis, C. E. Bosworth, E. van Donzel, and W. P. Heinrichs (eds.). *Encyclopaedia of Islam*, Second Edition. Consulted online on 18 July 2018 <http://dx.doi.org/10.1163/1573-3912_islam_SIM_1123> First published online: 2012. First print edition: ISBN: 9789004161214, 1960–2007.

al-Shāṭibī, Abū Isḥāq. *al-Muwāfaqāt fī uṣūl al-sharīʿa*. 4 vols. Beirut: Dār al-Maʿrifa, 1975.

al-Suyūṭī, J. *al-Itqān fī ʿulūm al-Qurʾān*. Beirut: 1987. English translation by Hamid Algar, Michael Schub, and Ayman Abdel Haleem, *The Perfect Guide to the Sciences of the Qurʾān*, vol. 1. Reading: Garnet, 2011.
al-Ṭībī, Sharaf al-Dīn. *Kitāb al-Tibyān fī ʿilm al-maʿānī wa-badīʿ waʾl-bayān*. Ed. Hādī ʿAṭiya. Beirut: ʿĀlam al-Kutub, 1987.
Turner, Colin (ed.). *The Koran: Critical Concepts in Islamic Studies*. 4 vols. New York and London: Routledge-Curzon, 2001.
Versteegh, K. (ed.). *Encyclopedia of Arabic Language and Linguistics*. Leiden: Brill, 2009. Vol. 5, Index.
Wansbrough, J. 'Arabic Rhetoric and Qurʾānic Exegesis', *Bulletin of the School of Oriental and African Studies* (1968), 469ff.
Wansbrough, J. *Quranic Studies*. Oxford: Oxford University Press, 1977.
Ward Gwynne, R. *Logic, Rhetoric and Legal Reasoning in the Qur'ān*. New York: Routledge-Curzon, 2004.
Watt, William Montgomery. *Companion to the Qurʾān: Based on the Arberry Translation* London: Allen & Unwin, 1967.
Watt, William Montgomery and Richard Bell. *Introduction to the Qurʾān*. Edinburgh: Edinburgh University Press, 1997.
Wensinck, A. J. *Concordances et indices de la tradition musulmane*. 8 vols. Leiden: Brill, 1992.
al-Zamakhsharī. *al-Kashshāf*. 4 vols. Beirut: Dār al-Maʿrifa, n.d.

CHAPTER 21

INNER-QUR'ANIC CHRONOLOGY

NICOLAI SINAI

The Structure of the Qur'an and the Question of Inner-Qur'anic Chronology

THE standard recension of the Qur'an contains 114 textual units, the so-called suras, which, according to the Kufan system of verse divisions, consist of a total of 6,236 verses (*āyāt*). Since verses are generally marked off by rhyme, the partition of the Qur'anic corpus into verses is not merely an externally imposed system of reference (Neuwirth 1981: 3, 117–18), although some uncertainty remains in traditional Islamic scholarship as to where precisely many verses end (Spitaler 1935). The Qur'anic corpus opens with a brief prayer, *al-Fātiḥa*, formulated in the first person plural. From Q. 2 onwards, the order of the suras is partly based on the principle of decreasing length, although this appears to have been frequently modified by additional considerations, such as a reluctance to separate certain groups of suras beginning with the same or similar clusters of isolated letters (e.g., Q. 40–6, which open with the letters *ḥāʾ-mīm*); thematic and terminological links between neighbouring suras may also have played a role (Robinson 2003: 256–83; Bauer 1921; Mir 1986: 75–98).

This division into suras does not, however, endow the Qur'an with an easily discernible thematic structure: typically, a given sura will interweave diverse themes and registers, such as eschatology, narrative, polemics, paraenesis, and law. Conversely, it is often the case that one and the same topic—for example, the story of Moses, or the subject of marriage and divorce—is treated at several non-contiguous places of the corpus. Although current scholarship has increasingly come to acknowledge the literary coherence of Qur'anic suras (see e.g., Neuwirth 1981 and Cuypers 2009), the seemingly disjointed character of Qur'anic discourse has led many earlier Western readers to complain about the Qur'an's 'confused' organization (cf. Mir 1986: 2). Pre-modern Muslims, by contrast, were often (though by no means always) content to approach the text as an essentially unstructured repository of brief revelatory utterances communicated to Muḥammad at different times throughout his prophetic ministry. Such an atomistic vision of Qur'anic textuality is manifested, for example, by the well-known report that following Muḥammad's death the Qur'anic revelations had to be 'collected from palm-leaf stalks, stones, and the breasts of men' (al-Bukhārī, *Ṣaḥīḥ*, 3:337–8, no. 4986 = 66:3). It is true that some medieval commentators, such as Fakhr al-Dīn al-Rāzī (d. 606/1210) and al-Biqāʿī (d. 885/1480), did pay ample attention to the correspondences or interrelationships (*munāsabāt*) obtaining between adjoining verses and even suras (Mir 1986: 10–24; Saleh 2008). Yet many pre-modern Muslim exegetes arguably placed greater emphasis on assigning particular Qur'anic passages to the historical situation in which they were reportedly revealed than on systematically exploring their literary context within the Qur'an. As a result, the Islamic scripture came to enter a symbiotic relationship with a host of extra-scriptural traditions setting out the 'occasions of revelation' (*asbāb al-nuzūl*) of particular verses (Rippin 1988), thus positioning the text of the Qur'an against an external chronological schema. Interest in the diachronic order of the Qur'anic revelations was also stimulated by the fact that it formed a prerequisite for applying the hermeneutical technique of 'abrogation' (*naskh*), which served to defuse the apparent tensions and contradictions between some of the Qur'an's legal pronouncements by considering later verses to override earlier ones (Robinson 2003: 64–9).

The modern Western study of the Qur'an, born in the first half of the nineteenth century, inherited the traditional Islamic interest in a chronological reordering of the Qur'anic corpus. Among other things, discovering the original order of the Qur'anic proclamations held out the tantalizing promise of enabling scholars to trace their thematic, conceptual, and literary evolution, and perhaps Muḥammad's psychological development as well. At the same time, Western scholars' attention to the problem of intra-Qur'anic chronology was probably also fuelled by 'frustration with the existing arrangement of the Qur'an' (Mir 1986: 2). The task of the remainder of the present chapter will be to assess to what extent such a diachronic reordering of the Qur'an should still be considered a worthwhile scholarly endeavour. In so doing, I shall limit myself to the question of *relative* chronology, that is, to the attempt to discern relationships of temporal priority and posterity between different suras or passages, and omit the related but distinct problem of assigning an *absolute* date either to the Qur'an as a whole or to specific sections of it. By way of setting out the research buttressing a recent book chapter on the topic (Sinai 2017a: 111–37), I shall argue in favour of the possibility of making justifiable statements about the evolution of the Qur'anic proclamations.

Qur'anic Chronology and its Critics

Apart from anecdotes belonging to the *asbāb al-nuzūl* genre, Islamic scholarship also transmits lists of the suras that were allegedly revealed before and after the *hijra*, referred to as the 'Meccan' and 'Medinan' parts of the Qur'an (see al-Suyūṭī, *Itqān*, 1:43–113 = *nawʿ* 1).

It was one such list that formed the point of departure for Gustav Weil's subdivision of the Qur'anic suras into four consecutive periods (three Meccan and one Medinan), presented in his 1844 *Historisch-kritische Einleitung in den Koran* (Weil 1844: 54–80; Stefanidis 2008: 2). The same list is also quoted in Theodor Nöldeke's influential elaboration of Weil's chronology in his *Geschichte des Qorâns* (1860, revised edition by Friedrich Schwally 1909). Nöldeke himself acknowledges that his work could be seen as building on earlier Islamic observations about the characteristic stylistic and thematic features of the Meccan and Medinan parts of the Qur'an (Nöldeke 1860: 46–8, 50–1; Nöldeke/Schwally 1909: 59–65; see in detail Stefanidis 2008).

Rather than duplicating the existing discussions of Weil and Nöldeke's model and of the various alternative proposals that have been made in its wake (see Robinson 2003: 76–96; Böwering 2001: 322–6; Reynolds 2011: 485–94), I shall try to delineate the main contours of a chronological approach to the Qur'an by engaging with a recent critique of it (Reynolds 2011). For Reynolds, the continuity between Weil and Nöldeke's work and the earlier Islamic tradition is indicative of the fact that all Western attempts at a relative dating of Qur'anic texts are irredeemably reliant on Islamic reports about the biography (*sīra*) of Muḥammad: scholars who work with a chronological model perpetuate the established Islamic practice of making sense of the Qur'an by linking it up with apocryphal extra-Qur'anic traditions. Although Reynolds acknowledges that both Nöldeke and Régis Blachère profess to build their chronological reconstructions on observations internal to the Qur'anic text (Reynolds 2011: 486, 490–1), he is unconvinced that they succeed in implementing this principle. For example, Reynolds points out that Blachère's invocation of the terminological distinction between 'the Israelites' (*banū Isrā'īl*), considered to be a typically Meccan expression, and 'the Jews' (*al-yahūd*), considered to be Medinan, is anchored in the assumption that the Qur'anic texts revealed in Medina would naturally have been less interested in 'the ancient Hebrews and their descendants' than in 'the small Jewish communities of that town' (Reynolds 2011: 491, quoting Blachère). Blachère's neat assignment of two easily identifiable terms to the Qur'an's two main stages of composition thus turns out to be predicated on extra-Qur'anic information about the Medinan suras' confessional environment: the terminological observation that certain suras prefer the expression 'Israelites' to 'Jews' becomes chronologically relevant only by covertly hooking it up with the historical power generator of the *sīra*. Chronological readings of the Qur'an, as portrayed by Reynolds, invariably seem to proceed in this fashion: Qur'anic terms, themes, and stylistic peculiarities are more or less uncritically assigned to the stages of Muḥammad's career as known from the *sīra* tradition. Whether a consistent bracketing of the *sīra* would leave behind any foundation on which to base meaningful chronological statements must thus appear doubtful.

It would be futile to deny that Nöldeke's original work and even its 1909 revision by Schwally utilized post-Qur'anic sources in a much less critical fashion than one would prefer to see today, despite their own insistence that a chronological periodization of the Qur'an be primarily based on 'the scrupulous observation of the meaning and language of the Qur'an itself' and on 'differences of style' (Nöldeke/Schwally 1909: 63, 72).

Nonetheless, Nöldeke and Schwally may be read as having had at least an intuitive grasp of what I take to be the central argument supporting a chronological reading of the Qur'an, namely: the fact that the Qur'anic corpus displays a striking 'convergence of style (including verse length and rhyme), literary structure, terminology, and content' (Sinai 2010: 410, 412; see also Sinai 2017a: 188, 122). Such a robust covariance of formal and contentual features that are not inherently interdependent is best viewed as raising an explanatory challenge: the phenomenon being too conspicuous to be coincidental, one may legitimately demand an explanation for it; and an evolutionary hypothesis arguably supplies such an explanation (Sadeghi 2011: 218). In sum, a chronological approach to the Qur'an does not have to consist in (although it may of course degenerate into) arbitrarily mapping isolated stylistic, terminological, and thematic peculiarities of the Qur'an onto the *sīra*.

Somewhat unhelpfully, Reynolds's critique of diachronic approaches to the Qur'an nowhere engages with this phenomenon of covariance, in spite of the fact that it occupies a central position in one of the publications he discusses.[1] Where it would have been imperative either to show that the explanandum identified above does not obtain or to sketch out an alternative explanation, he confines himself to the remark that while the chronological model may be a 'plausible' way of reading the Qur'an it is by no means 'well established' (Reynolds 2011: 501). Yet if we are faced with a phenomenon requiring an explanation, and if the only plausible and well-developed explanation that has so far been put forward consists in the hypothesis of a unilinear literary evolution, then it may well be argued that the latter can count as reasonably 'well established'. Naturally, it is impossible to rule out that someday an equally powerful, or even superior, theory could be devised, perhaps by analysing the Qur'anic corpus into several source strata that were editorially spliced into one another, in a way similar to Pentateuchal source criticism. However, merely to suggest that there *could* be an alternative theory, without undertaking any effort to adumbrate what it might look like, is ultimately to say very little.

The Covariance of Stylistic, Thematic, and Terminological Features

In order to corroborate my assertion that the Qur'an exhibits a significant covariance of formal and contentual features that are not inherently interdependent, it is useful to begin with some general patterns with which many readers of the Qur'an may be intuitively familiar. First, while verse length varies greatly across the Qur'anic corpus, it is generally much more consistent within individual suras (although there are conspicuous

[1] Namely, in Sinai 2010. Reynolds finds fault with my appraisal of Nöldeke as having contributed to removing the study of the Qur'an from the orbit of the *sīra* (Reynolds 2011: 495–6). While one can have legitimate disagreements on this question, it is clearly a distraction, the main issue being whether my attempt to restate Nöldeke's case for chronology is persuasive.

exceptions, such as Q. 73:20 and 74:31). Secondly, verse length appears to be linked with particular literary features, terms, and themes. For instance, suras with short verses tend to shift between different rhymes rather than retaining the same rhyme throughout an extensive portion of text, and they also display a wide variety of rhyme patterns (Neuwirth 1981, fold-out table 1). Furthermore, the distinctive oath introductions opening a significant number of Qur'anic suras are limited to texts with relatively brief verses. Thematically, many suras with short verses are dominated by eschatology. At the other end of the spectrum, suras with very long verses exhibit a significantly impoverished spectrum of rhyme schemes—mostly *ī/ū +n/m*, with occasional substitution of *ā* for *ī/ū* and of various other consonants for *n/m*. In terms of their content, suras with long verses contain detailed quasi-legal prescriptions, calls to arms, polemics against the Jews Sic! and a group referred to as the *munāfiqūn* (the 'hypocrites' or 'lukewarm ones'), refer to the Qur'anic messenger as a 'prophet' (*nabiyy*), and regularly enjoin their audience to 'obey God and his messenger' (cf. Sinai 2010: 411–12; see also Sinai 2015–16).

It is worthwhile examining some of these correlations in more detail. I shall begin with verse length, which may justifiably be regarded as the Qur'an's most fundamental stylistic feature (Nöldeke/Schwally 1909: 63). Instead of vaguely contrasting the 'passionate excitement' of certain suras with the 'dull and prosaic' language of others, as Nöldeke and Schwally do (Stefanidis 2008: 6, citing Nöldeke/Schwally 1909: 98, 143), it seems preferable to provide a straightforward quantitative inventory of what is after all a quantitative phenomenon. I have therefore conducted an electronic count of the mean verse length (henceforth: MVL) of all Qur'anic suras based on a transliteration of the Qur'an (according to the Kufan system of verse divisions) for which I am beholden to Prof. Hans Zirker.[2] Zirker's transliteration follows the conventions of the *Deutsche Morgenländische Gesellschaft* (i.e., it uses ǧ and ḏ, etc.; word-initial glottal stops are also transcribed). I have transformed all verse endings into pausal forms (by omitting brief vowels and *-un/-in*, changing the accusative ending *-an* to *-ā*, and omitting gemination) and counted all letters excluding hyphens and space characters. The results are given in Figures 21.1 and 21.2, which rearrange the suras by increasing MVL; values are rounded to the second decimal place (note the deliberate overlap between both figures). Figures 21.1 and 21.2 also give every sura's standard deviation (SD), which measures how much the length of individual verses strays from the sura mean; a low SD indicates relatively consistent verse length in a sura, while a high value indicates relatively large variation.[3] In order to compare the standard deviations of different suras, it is useful to

[2] See <http://duepublico.uni-duisburg-essen.de/servlets/DocumentServlet?id=10802> (8 August 2013). The currently most recent version of this transliteration, involving several corrections, was uploaded in November 2018, postdating the submission of the present chapter. One may quibble as to whether Zirker has produced a transliteration or a transcription of the Qur'an, since he (helpfully) takes into account certain features of the Qur'an's received pronunciation. Obviously, verse length could be measured in different ways, which will yield slightly different rankings—for example, in words (see Sadeghi 2011: 231) or in syllables (thus Schmid 2010). Especially for short suras, adopting a different division of verses than the Kufan system would have some effect on my results. It would clearly be desirable for my computations to be repeated based on a critical evaluation of all verse dividers along the lines of Neuwirth 1981: 11–62.

[3] For accessible explanations of basic statistical concepts like the standard deviation, see Kenny 1982.

introduce the concept of a sura's coefficient of variation (CV), defined as the ratio of its SD to its MVL, multiplied by 100. Whereas the SD is a measure of the number of characters by which verses in a sura deviate from their mean value in the sura, the CV is a measure of the percentage by which verse lengths deviate from the mean. Eighty-four suras have a CV of 50 per cent or less; for 20 suras the CV lies between 51 per cent and 60 per cent; five suras (Q. 20, 78, 33, 2, and 24) have a CV between 61 per cent and 70 per cent; and for another five suras the CV lies between 76 per cent and 164 per cent (Q. 85, 103, 53, 73, 74). Since the entire Qur'an has a MVL of 79.48 and a SD of 60.29, which yields a CV of 75.85 per cent (all values rounded), the foregoing values bear out the impression that verse length within most suras is considerably more consistent than within the Qur'anic corpus as a whole.

Interestingly, all five suras with a CV above 76 per cent as well as a few other short and medium-sized suras contain a small number of verses that are conspicuously longer than those surrounding them. The passages concerned are Q. 52:21, 53:23, 53:26–32, 69:7, 73:20, 74:31, 74:56, 78:37–40, 81:29, 84:25, 85:7–11, 87:7, 89:15–16, 89:23–24, 89:27–30, 90:17–20, 95:6, 97:4, and 103:3. A close examination of these verses makes it plausible to consider them as later insertions, many of which serve to comment on or qualify other parts of the sura in which they occur.[4] Since at least some of these verses have a significant impact on the MVL and SD of their suras, I have listed each of these texts twice, once with and once without the putative additions. The shortened—and most likely original—versions of the respective suras are distinguished by an asterisk: 'Q. 84*' thus refers to Q. 84 without v. 25. It is beyond the scope of this chapter to assess how widespread such insertions are in other parts of the Qur'an. Especially the long suras located at the beginning of the Qur'an, whose structure and editorial history is still not fully understood, are highly likely to be redactionally composite, and it is possible that further research will succeed in identifying discrete redactional layers in them. If this is the case, my figures will need to be revised in a way that takes such findings into account (e.g., by distinguishing between different parts of Q. 2, or between an original core and later expansions thereof). However, it is noteworthy that even Q. 2 has a CV (namely, 66.14 per cent) that is lower than that of the Qur'an as a whole, in contrast to suras like 85 or 74. Consequently, even if Q. 2 forms a redactional composite (as argued in Sinai 2017a: 97–104), its different strata generally seem to have a more consistent MVL than, say, the original core of Q. 73 (vv. 1–19) as opposed to its later appendix Q. 73:20.[5]

Obviously, not every minute discrepancy in MVL should be regarded as statistically significant. In order to assess whether two suras exhibiting different MVLs can be considered to constitute samples drawn from the same population (in which case

[4] For detailed comments on these passages, see Neuwirth 1981: 201–3; Sinai 2011 (for Q. 53); Sinai 2012 (for Q. 97); Sinai 2017b: 73–5 (for Q. 74); Sinai 2018: 261 (for Q. 73). My list of likely insertions omits Q. 70:4, excising which would have no noteworthy impact on the sura's MVL. Even if the entire passage 70:22–35 were considered to be an addition, which is far from certain (see Neuwirth 1981: 201–2), the text's MVL would not change significantly: thus shortened, the sura would rank before 69*, moving up a mere three places.

[5] However, see now Sinai 2017a: 100–1.

their difference in MVL would not be statistically relevant but could merely result from sampling variation), Figures 21.3 and 21.4 give the 95 per cent confidence limits for every sura's MVL (values are again rounded).[6] A quick way of making use of Figures 21.3 and 21.4 would be to assume that when the confidence intervals of two suras do not overlap, there is a very high probability that their divergence in MVL is not due to chance variation within one and the same population, meaning that the two suras in question are likely to originate from different sura populations. Their difference in MVL thus requires an explanation—for example, to the effect that the two suras date from different stages of a process of stylistic evolution.[7] If, as I shall go on to argue, a sura's MVL is a chronologically significant stylistic marker, two suras whose confidence intervals do not overlap would therefore normally—*ceteris paribus*—be considered not to be contemporaneous.

As Figures 21.1–21.4 show, (i) the variation in MVL between different suras is very considerable, ranging from fourteen to more than 179 letters, yet (ii) the individual values can be arranged to yield a continuous upward slope. Although there are a few perceptible gaps—e.g., between suras 15 and 50—only in two cases (between Q. 66 and 5, and Q. 65 and 60) is there a leap of more than eight letters; and in all cases—even for suras 15 and 50—the 95 per cent confidence intervals of the neighbouring suras in our graph show at least minimal overlap. As Behnam Sadeghi has underscored on the basis of a different breakdown of the variation of MVL across the Qur'an (Sadeghi 2011: 240), this combination of (i) and (ii) is by no means trivial and most naturally suggests an underlying process of gradual stylistic evolution. By contrast, had an examination of the MVL of Qur'anic suras yielded discrete clusters of suras, a source-critical model assigning a different origin to each cluster would have been the most obvious (although perhaps not the only possible) choice. (Note that the non-discrete behaviour of MVL across all 114 suras could be reconciled with a source-critical model by positing that each sura contains material from more than one source stratum in gradually changing proportions. However, such a scenario seems rather far-fetched and would need to be verified by a close textual analysis of a sufficient number of suras.) In any case, it would be insufficient to ascribe the divergences in MVL merely to the suras' different thematic profiles. It is true that legal regulations tend to be couched in relatively long verses. However, the verse length of the Qur'an's narrative, eschatological, and polemical

[6] See Kenny 1982: 95–7. To attempt a brief explanation, consider a population for which one is trying to determine the mean value of some parameter P by sampling. Naturally, the true mean of P for the entire population might differ from the mean value that P takes in a sample. The 95% confidence limits—which are computed on the basis of the size of the sample and the respective standard deviation—define an interval around the sample mean within which, at a probability of 95%, the true mean of P for the entire population can be assumed to be located. (Alternatively, the 95% confidence limits define an interval around the sample mean within which we can assume the mean of 95% of repeated further samples from the same population to be located.)

[7] Even if there is overlap, the difference in verse length might still be statistically significant. This could be assessed by performing a t-test.

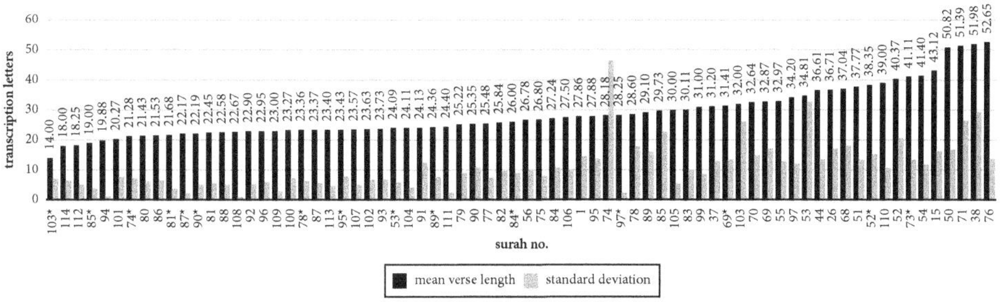

FIGURE 21.1 The suras ordered by increasing MVL, part 1.

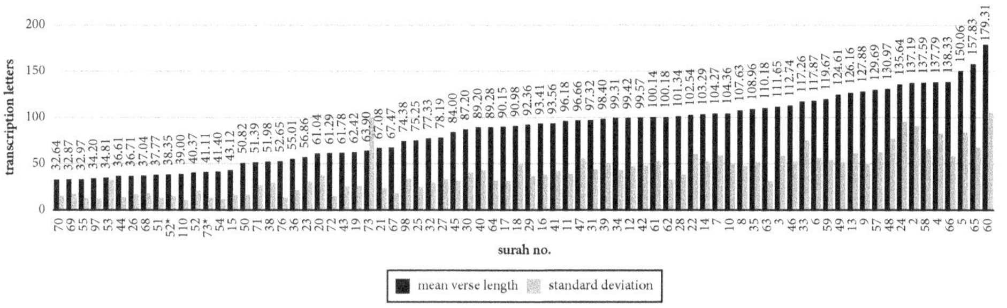

FIGURE 21.2 The suras ordered by increasing MVL, part 2.

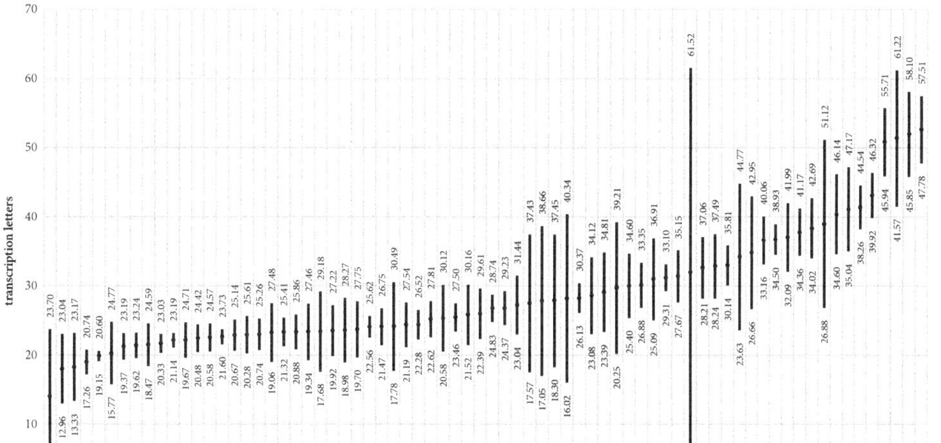

FIGURE 21.3 MVL and 95 per cent confidence intervals, part 1.

passages exhibits very significant fluctuation. Thus, MVL is not simply dictated by genre (cf. Sadeghi 2011: 286–7).

How, then, is MVL linked to other features of the text? Let us examine the following six typical components of sura introductions (a given sura opening can contain more than one of them): oaths; eschatological *idhā* clauses (which exclude non-eschatological

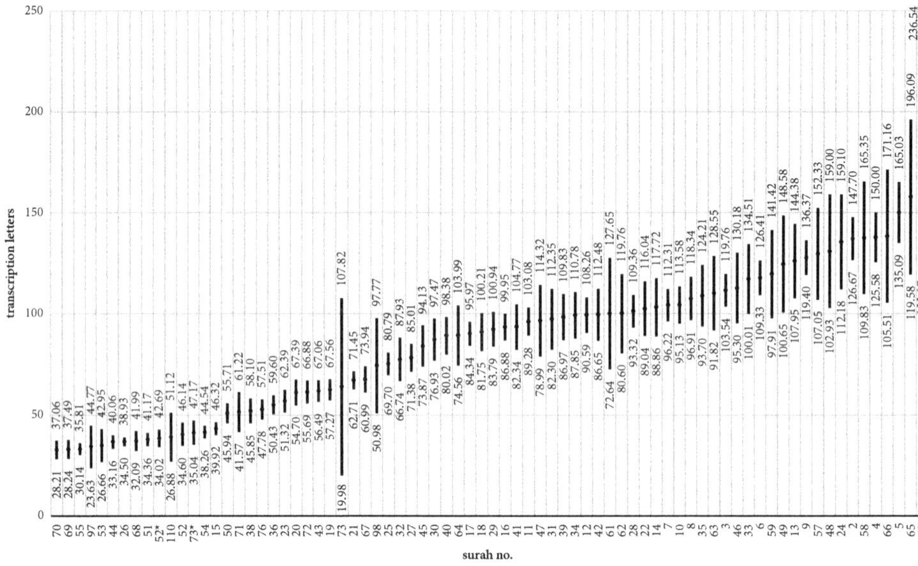

FIGURE 21.4 MVL and 95 per cent confidence intervals, part 2.

occurrences of *idhā* such as Q. 63: 1); isolated letters (*ḥā-mīm* and the like); self-referential statements or superscripts containing the terms *kitāb* and/or *nazzala/anzala* (e.g., *tilka āyātu l-kitābi l-ḥakīm*, *tanzīlu l-kitābi* etc.); derivatives of the roots b-r-k, ḥ-m-d, or s-b-ḥ (i.e., doxologies and eulogies); and vocatives. Figure 21.5 correlates the distribution of these introductory elements with verse length: suras are rearranged according to increasing MVL along the *x*-axis,[8] while the occurrence of a particular introductory element is marked on the *y*-axis. The fact that suras with similar introductions are often densely clustered together reveals a perceptible correlation between MVL and certain types of introductions. The general pattern is only disrupted by the considerable overall spread of doxologies/eulogies and vocatives. In both cases this is caused by two outliers on the left side.

Figure 21.6 presents a similar diagram for three additional terminological features: the divine name *al-raḥmān* occurring outside the *basmala* (which may have been prefixed to many suras retrospectively); the root sh-r-k, which almost always occurs in polemics against the 'association' of other beings with God; and references to the *munāfiqūn*, or 'hypocrites'. Once again, suras are rearranged according to increasing MVL along the *x*-axis; suras that contain at least one occurrence in a given category are marked on the *y*-axis. Apart from the last three occurrences of *al-raḥmān* and the first instance of *munāfiqūn*, the resulting diagram has no genuine outliers and is marked by even denser clustering than Figure 21.5. If one were to examine the occurrence of specific quasi-legal prescriptions (as opposed to general moral injunctions) across the

[8] Note that Figures 21.5 and 21.6 only take account of the asterisked (i.e. presumably original) versions of suras 52, 53, 69, 73, 74, 78, 81, 84–5, 87, 89–90, 95, 97, and 103, whereas in Figures 21.1–21.2 and 21.3–21.4, each of these suras was listed twice.

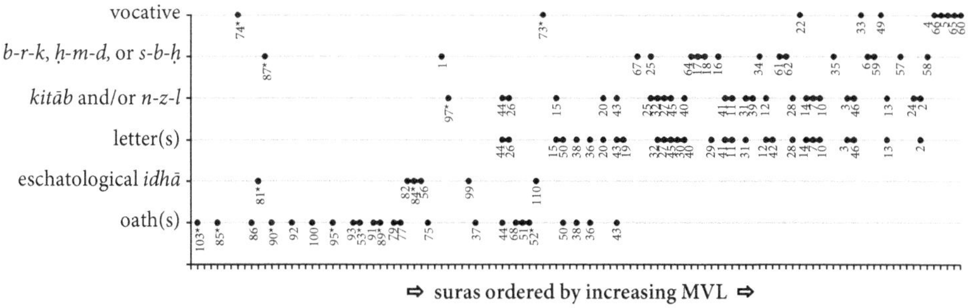

FIGURE 21.5 The correlation of MVL and characteristic introductory elements (data labels specify suras).

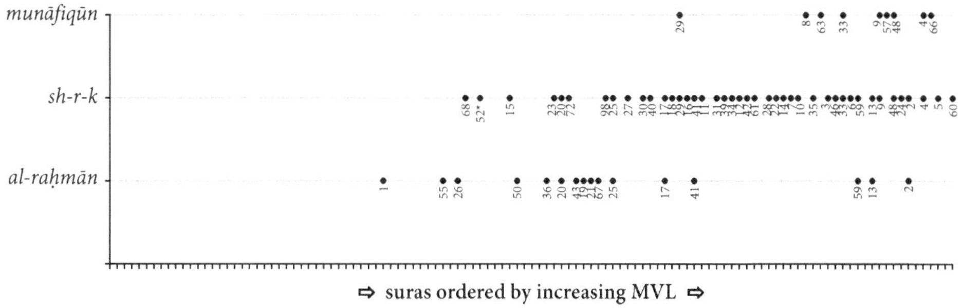

FIGURE 21.6 MVL correlated with three important Qur'anic terms (data labels specify suras).

Qur'anic corpus, a very similar pattern would be discerned: suras containing a substantial amount of quasi-legal material (especially Q. 2–5 and Q. 65) tend to be positioned towards the right-hand side of the spectrum (see Sinai 2015–16).

Figure 21.7 charts yet another correlation: that between a sura's MVL and its formulaic density. Formulaic density, measured in per cent, specifies to what extent a given sura consists of phraseology that recurs elsewhere in the Qur'anic corpus (Bannister 2014). The ultimate inspiration for Figure 21.7 is Andrew Bannister's observation that the formulaic density of suras customarily considered to be Meccan is noticeably lower than that of suras thought to be Medinan (Bannister 2014: 141–6). This suggests that formulaic density could be correlated with MVL, given that the suras customarily classed as Medinan are distinguished by their high verse length. As demonstrated by Figure 21.7, such a correlation does indeed exist. For the present purposes, I define a formula as a succession of three 'bases' (i.e., words stripped of any articles, prefixes, and suffixes, but still inflected for verb type, number, person, or gender) that recurs four times or more in the Qur'an (see Bannister 2014: 138–41 for more details). Figure 21.7 correlates MVL and formulaic density thus defined, based on an unpublished run of data kindly provided by Bannister. As it turns out, a high MVL normally entails high formulaic density. For instance, no sura with a MVL of 100 or more has a formulaic density below 23, although there are suras with a low MVL but high formulaic density, such as Q. 55 (MVL: 32.97,

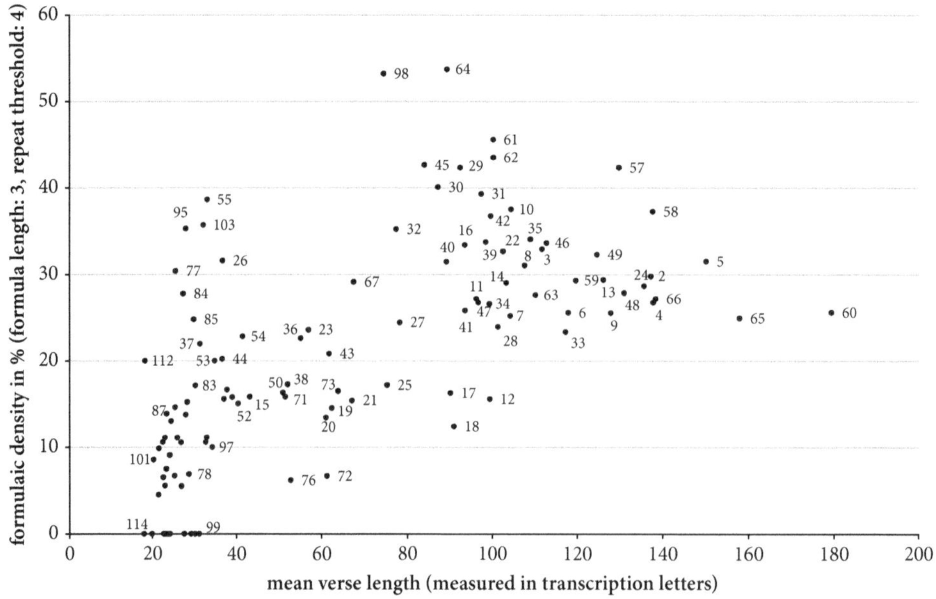

FIGURE 21.7 MVL correlated with formulaic density (data labels specify suras). Values for the *y*-axis were kindly provided by Andrew Bannister.

formulaic density: 38.64). More generally, the correlation coefficient of both arrays of data, MVL and formulaic density, is 0.65 (where a value of 1 would indicate perfect positive correlation, a value of 0 would indicate no correlation, and a value of −1 would indicate perfect negative correlation). Thus, for two suras that differ in MVL, there is a noticeable, albeit blurred, tendency for the sura with the higher MVL to be more formulaic.

Figures 21.5–21.7 document a clear correlation between the MVL of individual suras and a small number of highly visible formal, terminological, and stylistic parameters. The general upshot of these figures is confirmed by a statistically sophisticated appraisal of the relationship between MVL and Qur'anic diction undertaken by Behnam Sadeghi. Its starting point is the chronological model of Mehdi Bazargan (d. 1995), who subdivides the Qur'an's 114 suras up into 194 textual blocks that exhibit relatively consistent verse length and can be seen as thematically self-contained.[9] Bazargan then arranges these by increasing MVL, claiming that this order corresponds to the temporal sequence of the Qur'anic proclamations. Sadeghi proposes to test Bazargan's chronology by applying what he calls the 'Criterion of Concurrent Smoothness': 'if different, independent markers of style vary in a relatively continuous fashion over a particular ordering, then that sequence reflects the chronological order' (Sadeghi 2011: 218). For purposes of convenience, Sadeghi aggregates Bazargan's 194 blocks into twenty-two larger groups, grouping together blocks that, if arranged by increasing MVL, are consecutive and thus

[9] Note that in cases 'where he divides a sūra into more than two blocks, if two or more blocks in the sūra display similar verse length profiles, then because they belong to the same period in Bazargan's scheme, he combines them into a single block, even if they do not form a contiguous passage' (Sadeghi 2011: 232).

similar in verse length. Sadeghi then counts the lexical frequencies of three lists of Qur'anic morphemes: the twenty-eight most common morphemes (including such high-frequency words and suffixes as *wa-*, *fa-*, *min*, *fī*, *-hum*, *-ka*, *inna*, *mā*, *allāh*), 114 further common morphemes, and the 3,693 morphemes occurring more than once and fewer than twenty times. As it turns out, if Sadeghi's twenty-two groups are arranged by MVL, adjacent groups frequently exhibit a markedly more similar lexical profile than those further apart: MVL and diction thus display concurrent smoothness. This trend is extremely pronounced for Groups 1–5, whereas Groups 6–11, 12–19, and 20–2 form larger lexically similar clusters. Sadeghi accordingly concludes that, on average, groups 2, 3, 4, 5, and the larger clusters consisting of groups 6–11, 12–19, and 20–2 are chronologically consecutive, an ordering he refers to as the 'Modified Bazargan Chronology' (note that Sadeghi does not commit himself to the temporal priority of Group 1).[10] As Sadeghi points out, his results should not be viewed as corroborating the Modified Bazargan Chronology over and against similar chronologies that accord an equally fundamental role to MVL (Sadeghi 2011: 219, n. 13, and 237). Rather, the essence of Sadeghi's work consists in his demonstration of a continuous covariance between the MVL of Qur'anic passages and their lexical profile.

In view of Figures 21.5–21.7 as well as the comprehensive scope of Sadeghi's inquiry, the explanatory challenge formulated earlier becomes acute: the convergences between MVL, on the one hand, and various literary, stylistic, and lexical features, on the other hand, are far too conspicuous to be coincidental, and ascribing them to a process of literary development, in the course of which a host of formal and contentual features of the Qur'anic recitations would have naturally changed in a concurrent fashion, is arguably the most economical way of accounting for the evidence. Having established MVL as an effective chronological marker, it can be shown, even without having recourse to any extra-Qur'anic data, that a development from short to long verses makes much more sense than one unfolding in the inverse direction. For example, if verses such as Q. 73:20 and 74:31, which stand out from their context by virtue of being strikingly longer than the verses surrounding them, are later insertions designed to supplement or clarify statements made in other verses of the sura, then this entails that long verses postdate short ones, rather than the other way round (Sadeghi 2011: 283; see also Sinai 2010: 415). Nöldeke's conjecture that Qur'anic verses became longer over time is therefore solidly based on inner-Qur'anic evidence.

Incidentally, it is worthwhile to underscore that Sadeghi's argument is not vulnerable to an objection that has been raised against Nöldeke, namely, that the latter's chronology, which is largely a chronology of entire suras, naively assumes that material contained in

[10] This is to be applauded, as many members of group 1 are simply amputated introductions (Sadeghi 2011: 287). Even the Modified Bazargan Chronology divides a number of suras up among subsequent periods without there being, in my view, sufficient literary indications for considering them to have undergone later expansion (e.g. Q. 79, 70, 68, 65, and 55). However, Sadeghi's results are explicitly statistical (Sadeghi 2011: 228: 'the claim is not that the passages in one cluster all came after those in the preceding clusters, but that only *on average* they did so'; see also Sadeghi 2011: 237–8 and 284). And even if one were to retain the above suras as unities, the overall outcome of Sadeghi's lexical profiling would probably be very similar.

the same sura normally dates from the same period (Reynolds 2011: 492–3; but note that even Nöldeke recognizes the existence of later insertions). This is so because Sadeghi establishes a covariance between MVL and lexical profile for textual groups consisting, in many cases, not of entire suras but of smaller sura parts (where these show a palpable difference in verse length from what comes before or after). The argument for a chronological significance of MVL does not therefore depend on uncritically treating suras as unities.

Conclusion and Open Questions

It is vital to appreciate that the idea of stylistic and literary development is not an eccentricity born from the *sīra*. For instance, a similar model of linear development is commonly applied to the Platonic dialogues, supported by a 'striking coincidence of three independent sets of criteria, dramatic, philosophical, and stylometric' (Kenny 2004: 40). That gradual stylistic development is a perfectly real phenomenon is illustrated by the plays of the seventeenth-century French dramatist Pierre Corneille, about the date of whose composition we possess independent information and which have been found to exhibit a progressive increase in the mean number of words per verse (Kenny 1982: 74–5). Evolutionary hypotheses should therefore be seen as a legitimate part of the literary scholar's toolkit. As I have argued, an evolutionary model is well suited to making sense of the phenomenon of systematic covariance between stylistic, lexical, and other parameters that are exhibited by the Qur'anic corpus. A diachronic approach to the Qur'an receives additional confirmation from the fact that Q. 25:32 explicitly highlights the temporal spread of Muḥammad's proclamations: 'Why was the *qurʾān* not sent down to him as a single whole (*jumlatan wāḥidatan*)?' (see also Saleh 2015). Finally, one should also accord due weight to the fact that rearranging the Qur'an's pronouncements on various issues by increasing MVL of the respective suras frequently produces eminently plausible thematic trajectories (Robinson 2003: 87–92; Böwering 2001: 326–31; Sadeghi 2011: 216).

There is little reason to be daunted by the charge that a chronological approach to the Qur'an illicitly assumes that stylistic development must be irreversible (Stefanidis 2008: 5, citing Sprenger). For in view of the extensive covariation of different textual parameters reviewed above, such an objection can only be construed as inviting one to envisage an extremely far-reaching stylistic reversion, encompassing a large number of independent markers, including MVL and lexical profile—in fact, a throwback so complete and multi-dimensional as to have left virtually no traces that would give it away. This possibility only seems likely in cases of deliberate and extremely well-researched self-imitation and can, in my view, be regarded as remote (Sadeghi 2011: 287; Sinai 2010: 417–18, n. 21).

The present chapter has limited itself to a general plea for the methodological validity of viewing the Qur'an through a diachronic lens. Although I am sympathetic to the basic plot of the Islamic narrative of origins, I have not tried to determine how long the hypothesized process of literary development may have lasted, nor when and where it may have taken place: to a large degree, the question of whether a diachronic reading of the Qur'an makes sense is perpendicular to the problem of determining the text's spatial and temporal origin. Thus, the principal argument of this chapter by itself would be compatible with Tommaso Tesei's hypothesis that most of the suras that Weil and Nöldeke consider to be early Meccan—a sura group whose stylistic and thematic homogenity as well as temporal priority to the remainder of the Qur'an Tesei accepts—may hail from a different historical context and period than chronologically later parts of the Islamic scripture (Tesei forthcoming; but see my alternative account in Sinai 2017a: 40–77). I have also not attempted to derive a particular chronological sequence of Qur'anic texts: it would be simplistic to equate the above reordering of suras by increasing MVL with a strict diachronic series. Nevertheless, numerically precise comparisons of MVL have an important role to play in determining questions of relative chronology. For instance, in spite of certain literary affinities between Q. 74* and Q. 73* their difference in MVL makes it rather unlikely that they could be contemporaneous.

I should note that the above rearrangement of suras by increasing MVL raises a number of specific questions requiring more detailed discussion. For example, the rearrangement creates difficulties for Nöldeke's dating of particular texts, foremost among them Q. 110 and Q. 98, which both the Islamic tradition and Nöldeke assign to the Medinan period, in spite of their comparatively short verses (Sinai 2017a, 130–2; see also Robinson 2003: 80–2 and Reynolds 2011: 489–90). Yet even if the covariance of MVL and certain terminological markers may be seriously disrupted for particular suras, this does not undermine the diachronic approach in general. Similarly, while it is tempting to identify the leap in MVL between Q. 15 and Q. 50 with the end of the early Meccan phase (assuming of course that one locates the earliest period of the Qur'an's emergence in Mecca), it appears questionable whether the mostly continuous behaviour of MVL supports Nöldeke's division of the Qur'anic suras into four clearly demarcated periods. Lastly, one should give consideration to the possibility that the handful of very brief communal or individual prayers and creeds included in the Qur'anic corpus—suras 1, 109, and 112–14—could stand apart from the main evolutionary trajectory of the Qur'anic proclamations (Sinai 2017a: 131). This would imply that the brevity of their verses might indeed more properly be seen as a function of genre rather than of chronological position.

Bibliography

Bannister, Andrew. *An Oral-Formulaic Study of the Qur'an*. Lanham, MD: Lexington Books, 2014.

Bauer, Hans. 'Über die Anordnung der Suren und über die geheimnisvollen Buchstaben im Qoran', *Zeitschrift der Deutschen Morgenländischen Gesellschaft* 75 (1921), 1–20.

Böwering, Gerhard. 'Chronology and the Qurʾān.' In: Jane Dammen McAuliffe (ed.). *Encyclopaedia of the Qurʾān*. 6 vols., 1:316–35. Leiden: Brill, 2001–6.

al-Bukhārī. *al-Jāmiʿ al-ṣaḥīḥ*. Ed. Muḥibb al-Dīn al-Khaṭīb and Muḥammad Fuʾād ʿAbd al-Bāqī. 4 vols. Cairo: al-Maṭbaʿa al-Salafiyya, AH 1400.

Cuypers, Michel, *The Banquet: A Reading of the Fifth Sura of the Qurʾan*. Trans. Patricia Kelly. Miami: Convivium Press, 2009.

Kenny, Anthony. *The Computation of Style: An Introduction to Statistics for Students of Literature and Humanities*. Oxford: Pergamon Press, 1982.

Kenny, Anthony. *A New History of Western Philosophy*, vol. 1: *Ancient Philosophy*. Oxford: Oxford University Press, 2004.

Mir, Mustansir. *Coherence in the Qurʾān: A Study of Iṣlāḥī's Concept of* Naẓm *in* Tadabbur-i Qurʾān. Indianapolis: American Trust Publications, 1986.

Neuwirth, Angelika. *Studien zur Komposition der mekkanischen Suren*. Berlin: De Gruyter, 1981.

Nöldeke, Theodor. *Geschichte des Qorâns*. Göttingen: Verlag der Dieterichschen Buchhandlung, 1860.

Nöldeke, Theodor and Friedrich Schwally. *Geschichte des Qorāns. Erster Teil: Über den Ursprung des Qorāns*. Leipzig: Dieterich'sche Verlagsbuchhandlung, 1909. English translation in: Theodor Nöldeke, Friedrich Schwally, Gotthelf Bergsträßer, and Otto Pretzl, *The History of the Qurʾān*. Trans. Wolfgang H. Behn. Leiden: Brill, 2013.

Reynolds, Gabriel S. 'Le problème de la chronologie du Coran', *Arabica* 58 (2011), 477–502.

Rippin, Andrew. 'The Function of *Asbāb al-Nuzūl* in Qurʾānic Exegesis', *Bulletin of the School of Oriental and African Studies* 51 (1988), 1–20.

Robinson, Neal. *Discovering the Qur'an: A Contemporary Approach to a Veiled Text*. 2nd edn. London: SCM Press, 2003.

Sadeghi, Behnam. 'The Chronology of the Qurʾān: A Stylometric Research Program', *Arabica* 58 (2011), 210–99.

Saleh, Walid A. *In Defense of the Bible: A Critical Edition and an Introduction to al-Biqāʿī's Bible Treatise*. Leiden: Brill, 2008.

Saleh, Walid A. 'A Piecemeal Qurʾān: *Furqān* and its Meaning in Classical Islam and in Modern Qurʾānic Studies', *Jerusalem Studies in Arabic and Islam* 42 (2015), 31–71.

Schmid, Nora K. 'Quantitative Text Analysis and Its Application to the Qur'an: Some Preliminary Considerations.' In: Angelika Neuwirth et al. (eds.). *The Qurʾān in Context: Historical and Literary Investigations into the Qurʾānic Milieu*, pp. 441–60. Leiden: Brill, 2010.

Sinai, Nicolai. 'The Qur'an as Process.' In: Angelika Neuwirth et al. (eds.). *The Qurʾān in Context: Historical and Literary Investigations into the Qurʾānic Milieu*, pp. 407–39. Leiden: Brill, 2010.

Sinai, Nicolai. 'An Interpretation of *Sūrat al-Najm* (Q. 53)', *Journal of Qur'anic Studies* 13/2 (2011), 1–28.

Sinai, Nicolai. '"Weihnachten im Koran" oder "Nacht der Bestimmung"? Eine Deutung von Sure 97', *Der Islam* 88 (2012), 11–32.

Sinai, Nicolai. 'The Unknown Known: Some Groundwork for Interpreting the Medinan Qur'an', *Mélanges de l'Université Saint-Joseph* 66 (2015–16), 47–96.

Sinai, Nicolai. *The Qur'an: A Historical-Critical Introduction*. Edinburgh: Edinburgh University Press, 2017 (= Sinai 2017a).

Sinai, Nicolai. 'Processes of Literary Growth and Editorial Expansion in Two Medinan Surahs.' In: Carol Bakhos and Michael Cook (eds.). *Islam and its Past: Jahiliyya, Late Antiquity, and the Qur'an*, pp. 69–119. Oxford: Oxford University Press, 2017 (= Sinai 2017b).

Sinai, Nicolai. 'Two Types of Inner-Qurʾānic Interpretation', In: Georges Tamer et al. (eds.). *Exegetical Crossroads: Understanding Scripture in Judaism, Christianity and Islam in the Pre-Modern Orient*, pp. 253–88. Berlin: De Gruyter, 2018.

Spitaler, Anton. *Die Verszählung des Koran nach islamischer Überlieferung*. Munich: Verlag der Bayerischen Akademie der Wissenschaften, 1935.

Stefanidis, Emmanuelle. 'The Qur'an Made Linear: A Study of the *Geschichte des Qorâns*' Chronological Reordering', *Journal of Qur'anic Studies* 10/2 (2008), 1–22.
al-Suyūṭī, Jalāl al-Dīn. *al-Itqān fī ʿulūm al-Qurʾān*. 7 vols. Medina: Majmaʿ al-Malik Fahd li-Ṭibāʿat al-Muṣḥaf al-Sharīf, AH 1426.
Tesei, Tommaso. 'The Qurʾān(s) in Context(s)'. *Arabica*, forthcoming.
Weil, Gustav. *Historisch-kritische Einleitung in den Koran*. Bielefeld: Velhagen & Klasing, 1844.

CHAPTER 22

THE STRUCTURE OF THE QUR'AN

The Inner Dynamic of the Sura

MUSTANSIR MIR

A number of modern scholars, non-Muslim as well as Muslim, have come to view Qur'anic suras as possessing significant structure (Mir 1993; Rippin 2013). A specific way in which they investigate that structure is by studying the dynamic of the Qur'anic sura. This chapter examines the views of a number of such scholars—Angelika Neuwirth, Mathias Zahniser, Michel Cuypers, Muhammad Abdel Haleem, Salwa M. S. El-Awa, Neal Robinson, David E. Smith, Raymond K. Farrin, and Amīn Aḥsan Iṣlāḥī—and concludes with a few general observations. The discussion is brief rather than exhaustive, each of these scholars deserving a more elaborate treatment; also, some scholars are discussed in more detail than others. The views of the last four writers—Robinson, Smith, Farrin, and Iṣlāḥī—are examined with reference to *Sūrat al-Baqara* (Zahniser also looks at the sura).

Neuwirth

Angelika Neuwirth has made a major contribution to the subject of the structure of the Qur'anic suras. She argues for 'a reading of the Qur'an which studies the sura as a communication process and thus respects this redactionally-warranted unit as a genuine literary text'. The suras are 'essentially liturgical units that have developed...through a liturgical or communicational process that transpired within the emerging Islamic community' (Neuwirth 2002: 250). Making a stylistic analysis of Qur'anic suras—key to that analysis being considerations of rhyme—Neuwirth arrives at 'a typology of sura structures: Most Meccan suras display fixed sequences of formally and thematically defined verse groups distinctly separated by a change of rhyme or other clearly discernable, sometimes formulaic markers of caesurae' (Neuwirth 2002: 252). But while the short and medium-sized Meccan suras are well structured and 'technically sophisticated pieces' (Neuwirth 2002: 264), the long Medinan suras are characterized by 'loosely composed passages and often unframed, conceptually isolated communications' (Neuwirth 2002: 247; also 262, 264). Her application of literary criteria to the Qur'anic text highlights the building blocks, *enjeux*, of the sura (oaths, eschatological passages, signs (*āyāt*), debate, apologetics, and other *enjeux* found in Medinan suras).

Neuwirth's focus on rhyme, which she calls 'the fundamental characteristic of the Qur'anic discourse', and which she considers the necessary starting-point for both the style and the composition of the Qur'an (Neuwirth 2007: 117), leads her to discover remarkable structural patterns in the Meccan, especially in the early Meccan, suras (Neuwirth 2007: 204ff.). One cannot, however, help asking the following question: How is it that the same Qur'an includes some suras (Meccan, that is) that are neatly structured but others (Medinan, that is) that are haphazard compilations? How could the Meccan suras alone be intended units (Neuwirth 2002: 255)? For, if 'stylistic developments in any literature, once attained, are not deemed reversible' (Neuwirth 2002: 251), then some of the structural features of the chronologically prior Meccan suras should have rubbed off, so to speak, on the Medinan suras. Also, in her general approach, Neuwirth, it seems, is unable to break free of the iron grip of the biblically based approaches to the Qur'an (she, of course, is not the only one about whom this may be said). Of the two approaches she outlines and turns away from, the first is informed by (my emphasis) '*the older, more traditional biblical scholarship*,' the second, 'by *a more modern trend in biblical scholarship*' (Neuwirth 2002: 245), but, in following a third way, which involves shifting the focus from a 'canon from above' to 'a canon from below' (Neuwirth 2002: 246), she draws on 'the new approaches developed in *recent biblical studies*,' invoking Brevard S. Childs (Neuwirth 2002: 249). But the application of biblically informed literary methodologies to the Qur'an has limits. One wonders if it would not be more appropriate to regard the Qur'an as a *sui generis* text that ought to be studied on its own terms. Perhaps a fundamental shift of focus in Qur'anic studies is called for, the shift, namely, from form to thought, for, in the final analysis, literary form has only instrumental significance. The Qur'an brought about a radical transformation of Arabian society and culture primarily by means of its thought, by means of its dynamic worldview taken both in its entirety and in its integrality, not by means of its isolated literary features or its atomized *enjeux*. In practice, it is true, study of thought cannot be divorced from study of form, but while the horse and the cart will move together, it is the horse that must pull the cart.

Zahniser

In his study of *Sūrat al-Nisā'*, Mathias Zahniser remarks that, 'since position is hermeneutic, attention to composition and structure can contribute significantly to understanding the meaning of the sūra' (Zahniser 1997: 72). Zahniser employs both thematic and formal analysis (Zahniser 1997: 74) to discover the sura's 'overall structure' (Zahniser

1997: 73). The five sections into which he divides the sura (verses 1–43, 44–70, 71–104, 105–26, 127–66) are seen as having thematic continuities, with literary devices such as phrasal repetition, formulaic address, doublet, and concatenation serving to highlight the sura's structure. Zahniser applies the same analytical methods in another paper, reiterating his belief in the unity and coherence of the longer Qur'anic suras (Zahniser 2000: 27, 29), but paying greater attention to 'the borders between major sections of long suras and the transitions that cross them' (Zahniser 2000: 29). Zahniser sees cohesion in the six thematic units into which he divides the *Baqara*, three of these preceding and three following a transitional hinge (verses 1–39, 40–121, 122–52, 153–62 [hinge], 163–242, 243–83, 284–6). His study of suras 2 and 4 is meant to show that the Qur'an's longer suras are marked by coherence, that a literary device like chiasmus can signal 'the beginning and end of a meaningful span of oral discourse' (Zahniser 2000: 43), and that formulas of address can serve 'as indicators of thematic unit boundaries' (Zahniser 2000: 34). Zahniser, quite modestly, adds a few caveats to his findings (Zahniser 2000: 48).

Zahniser's study of the composition of the Qur'anic suras, while certainly not without merit, is a little too generalized in its approach and in the results it achieves. For example, suras 2 and 4 both have sizeable legislative sections (sura 2, verses 163–242; sura 4, verses 1–43). It is not enough to link up these sections with the preceding and following sections in the suras; it is also necessary to explain the logic of the sequence of the individual laws and regulations within those sections. Likewise, it is not enough to say that 'Adam stories [Q. 2:30–9] seem thematically appropriate for a section focusing on humankind in general' (Zahniser 2000: 31); it is necessary to explain why a specific portion or incident, and no other, of an Adam story was considered relevant for narration in the place in which it appears (cf. Mir 2009). Also, Zahniser appears to undercut his main thesis when he remarks that the Qur'an's long suras are 'loosely structured' (48), their distinctness being 'more obvious than their unity' (Zahniser 2000: 47).

Cuypers

Michel Cuypers is a distinguished participant in the conversation on the structure of the Qur'anic sura. His specific contribution to the subject consists in 'applying to the Qurʾanic text the different rules and characteristics of Semitic rhetoric first rediscovered by biblical studies' (Cuypers 2011: 1). The principles of Semitic rhetoric, with symmetry serving as the overarching principle (Cuypers 2011: 4), also apply to 'non-biblical Semitic texts' and to the hadiths of Muḥammad (Cuypers 2011: 3), and stand in contrast to those of the Greek 'logical and rhetorical tradition', in which 'ideas... succeed one another in a progressive linear continuity' (Cuypers 2011: 5). Cuypers distinguishes between several types of symmetry—parallelism, ring or concentric composition, and chiasmus—and symmetry indicators—outer terms; initial, central, and final terms; and median terms, or link-words, the relationship between these terms being that of identity, synonymy, antithesis, homophony, or paronymy (Cuypers 2011: 4). The symmetries and their indicators exist at four lower levels—those of member, segment, piece, and part; at four higher levels—those of passage, sequence, section, and book; and, sometimes, at intermediary levels—those of sub-part, sub-sequence, and sub-section (Cuypers 2011: 5). Employing this analytical scheme, Cuypers examines some thirty Qur'anic suras—including one of the longest, the fifth, *al-Māʾida*, in a book-length study—and concludes that the Qur'an has 'a very sophisticated composition, according to a rhetoric widespread in the antique world of the Middle East, but later forgotten, even by the Arabs, most probably under the influence of Hellenistic culture' (Cuypers 2011: 5). This composition, Cuypers stresses, has not only aesthetic, but also interpretive, significance (Cuypers 2011: 6).

The results yielded by Cuypers's analysis are indeed noteworthy, and his attempt to situate Qur'anic composition within the larger Near Eastern literary tradition provides a very wide context for comparing texts of various types, sacred and secular. Cuypers's account of Semitic and Qur'anic composition, however, raises a few questions.

To begin with, Cuypers's method, which stresses the commonality of form found in texts of various kinds, runs the risk of serving as a leveller, of consigning to the background precisely what is distinctive or characteristic of a text: it may blur the distinction between literary genres—between a hymnic text and a historical text, between an allegorical text and a legal text. On a higher level, it may blur the distinction between, for example, the Hebrew Scriptures or the New Testament on the one hand and Akkadian, Ugaritic, and Pharaonic texts on the other. In fact, use of the formal principle of, for example, symmetry in two ancient Near Eastern texts for widely divergent purposes—for, say, laying down high moral principles in one text and recording mythical history in the other—may turn the principle's use in the former case into a critical or ironic comment on its use in the latter case. Also, within the ambit of the scriptures of the monotheistic religions, in terms of form, in notable ways, the New Testament is significantly different from the Hebrew Scriptures, the Qur'an being yet quite different from both.

Furthermore, could the privileging of form over content result in a skewed interpretation of the content? The possibility exists. For example, Cuypers's analysis of *Sūrat al-Māʾida* leads him to think that verse 69 of the sura (like the very similar Q. 2:62), in which salvation is promised to all those—including Jews, Christians, and Sabeans—who hold the simple, no-frills-added twin belief in God and the Last Day (19–21), represents the definitive Qur'anic position on salvation, overriding those verses, such as Q. 3:85, which restrict salvation to those who subscribe to the religion of Islam. Interfaith courtesy aside, this view raises major problems of Qur'an interpretation. For one thing, a major theme of the Qur'an is belief in prophecy in general, and belief in the Prophet Muḥammad specifically. Cuypers's view would render both these beliefs, and a number of other basic Islamic beliefs—such as belief in revealed scriptures—redundant.

Cuypers's defence of Semitic, symmetry-oriented rhetoric, made at the expense of Greek, linearity-oriented rhetoric, is problematic. That the two types of rhetoric are fundamentally different may be granted, but why does symmetry have to be achieved at the expense of linearity? After all, an average reader of a text like the Qur'an cannot be told to ignore the question of linear coherence in the text and content himself with the feature of symmetrical coherence in it. In fact, the issue of linear coherence is the first one naturally to arise for the reader of a text. The 'sins' of a linearly disconnected text cannot be atoned for by reference to the text's presumed symmetrical coherence.

Finally, where is the historical evidence for the large claim that the 'rhetoric widespread in the antique world of the Middle East' was known to the Arabs, who, unfortunately, forgot it 'most probably under the influence of Hellenistic culture'? The impact of Hellenistic culture on Islam happened in the broad daylight of history, and history should have preserved at least some factual information about the supposed Arab amnesia concerning Semitic rhetoric.

Abdel Haleem

In his study of *Sūrat al-Raḥmān* (55), Muhammad Abdel Haleem, employing the 'two key concepts' of context (*maqām*) and internal relationships (*al-Qurʾān yufassiru baʿḍuhu baʿḍa*) (Abdel Haleem 2001: 158), notices a 'pairing structure' that, taking diverse forms, runs throughout the sura (Abdel Haleem 2001: 168, 174; also 164, 165, 169, 175), unifying the sura's three sections (verses 1–30, 31–45, 46–77; verse 78, the last, is a comment glorifying the Divine name *al-Raḥmān*) (Abdel Haleem 2001: 162; 181). Abdel Haleem's study seeks to invalidate theories of 'juxtaposition of variant traditions or paraphrasing of versions which may have had a liturgical or exegetical origin,' the positing of speculative grammatical constructions (Abdel Haleem 2001: 177–81), the explanation of the sura's well-known refrain as a litany (Abdel Haleem 2001: 167–8), or the comparison of the sura with Psalm 136 (Abdel Haleem 2001: 158–9, 181–3). Abdel Haleem persuasively argues that context and intertextuality govern sura 55's content, language, and structure (Abdel Haleem 2001, 165, 179; also 164, 170, 171–2, 179–80), and that intertextuality affects the choice of vocabulary and material in the sura as well. But while the study is an effective rejoinder to views held by such scholars as Richard Bell and John Wansbrough, one is tempted to ask, how does it help the reader negotiate the thematic or structural complexity of a long Medinan sura, since, quite clearly, sura 55 poses no special difficulties of thematic or structural interpretation of its own?

El-Awa

In her *Textual Relations in the Qurʾān*, Salwa El-Awa, taking a linguistic approach, examines, 'according to principles derived from modern pragmatic theory, the type of textual relations in the Qurʾān and the way in which verses of one *sura* relate to each other and to the wider context of the total message of the Qurʾān' (El-Awa 2007: 1–2). She maintains that '[Qur'anic] textual relations are not best explained in terms of the topics of thematic unity but rather in terms of the contextual thrust of verses, which may, or may not, be related to a single theme' (El-Awa 2007: 162). Employing Relevance Theory, El-Awa emphasizes the importance of contextual effects or assumptions; distinguishes between and explains, on the one hand, the concepts of explicature and implicature and, on the other, the inferential and decoding processes (for further explanation of El-Awa's method, see El-Awa 2007: 40).

One can only admire El-Awa's painstaking efforts to elucidate Qur'anic textual relations by applying a carefully laid out set of principles derived from Relevance Theory. And her discussion of suras 33 and 75 (El-Awa 2007: chapters 3 and 4, respectively) deserves attention. One feels, however, that there are some fundamental flaws in her approach, which includes a critique of what she calls the traditional view of the sura as a unity. Ignoring, for the moment, her rather hasty glossing over the issue of Qur'anic orality and the issue of the application of a theory originating in the study of modern Western language to a classical *literary* (the word 'divine', used by El-Awa, can be left out of the discussion) Arabic text like the Qur'an (El-Awa 2007: 7–8)—and ignoring also her rather limited and narrow view of what she calls 'the old thematic unity or linear connectivity' (El-Awa 2007: 39), a view responsible for her commission of the strawman fallacy against linear connectivity—one can make the following observations.

The opposition set up by El-Awa between the approach of thematic unity (as found in Sayyid Quṭb and Amīn Aḥsan Iṣlāḥī, two of the authors cited by El-Awa in this connection) and that of linguistic and pragmatic textual analysis is questionable. It is not correct to assume that, in the first approach, the only—and quite inadequate—tool for discovering a sura's theme is reading the sura thoroughly and repeatedly (El-Awa 2007: 21). For one thing, the proposal to read the sura in this way is not mystical or ambiguous in character, but is—at least in Iṣlāḥī—shorthand for a fairly systematic analytical method, and is, moreover, one that yields results that El-Awa is likely to approve of. Consider, for example, that El-Awa's analysis of sura 75 gives the following paragraph division: verses 1–6, 7–10, 11–15, 16–19, 20–5, 26–35, 36–40, a division similar to Iṣlāḥī's: verses 1–6, 7–15, 16–19, 20–5, 26–30, 31–5, 36–40. The only, and not so crucial, difference between the two divisions is that the second and third paragraphs in El-Awa are combined into one in Iṣlāḥī, and the sixth paragraph in El-Awa is divided into two in Iṣlāḥī. Either Iṣlāḥī's method is not as 'ambiguous' as El-Awa assumes (El-Awa 2007: 23) or the claim that the pragmatic method, when applied to the Qur'an, yields novel or superior results is exaggerated.

The view that if a portion of a sura cannot be shown to be thematically relevant to the sura but still may be thematically relevant to some other part of the Qur'an undermines any project of demonstrating a sura's coherence because it renders such a search practically unnecessary. It is true that El-Awa questions whether a 'text has to be coherent in the conventional sense in order to possess textuality or to achieve successful communication' (El-Awa 2007:8), but if so, then the textual relations established within a sura through the instrumentality of Relevance Theory might be too broad, diluted, and nebulous. As Deirdre Wilson and Dan Sperbar, proponents of Relevance Theory, acknowledge, 'pragmatic explanations are more general, albeit vaguer' (El-Awa 2012: 2). Actually, it seems that El-Awa is ambivalent about the notion of coherence within a sura.

On the one hand, she is interested in exploring 'relations that hold together the variety of topics within one *sura*, in most cases raising the major question as to why those topics are parts of one particular unit of the Qurʾān (El-Awa 2007: 3) and speaks of a sura's overall message, even though she adds that such a 'final message... is a total of a number of smaller messages' (El-Awa 2007: 46; see also 47–8). On the other hand, if one or more verses do not seem to belong to a sura's theme or themes, then, in El-Awa's view, as mentioned earlier, it would suffice to show that it is relevant to some part of the general message of the Qur'an.

Finally, El-Awa's claim that 'pragmatic principles explain a number of problematic aspects of the meaning of the Qurʾānic text' (El-Awa 2007: 2) does not succeed in showing the relevance of verses 16–19 to the sura's overall message—as El-Awa reluctantly seems to admit (El-Awa 2007: 156–9), and the attempt to redeem Relevance Theory (El-Awa 2007: 159, last paragraph) despite the admission of the claim's failure in this test case remains weak.

Robinson

Neal Robinson discusses *Sūrat al-Baqara* at length in his *Discovering the Qur'an*, a book full of insights into several aspects of the Qur'an. The *Baqara* has 'a coherent structure' (Robinson 1996: 201). It establishes Muslims, called a 'middle nation' in verse 143, as 'a separate community distinct from the Jews and Christians... with their own cultic regulations and legal code' (Robinson 1996: 201–2). Robinson divides the sura into five main sections and an epilogue—verses 1–39, 40–121, 122–52, 153–242, 243–83, 284–6—and undertakes to explain the rationale of the sequence of these sections and also of the verses within the individual sections (Robinson 1996: 203). Robinson establishes, quite plausibly in most cases, continuity in the sura by noting how ideas in the sura follow one another in accordance with considerations of contrast, reaction, extension, and so on. Also important to his method is the role of verbal echoes and correspondence in connecting the various parts of the sura's discourse. One wonders, though, if this role is exaggerated in Robinson, for not all verbal echoes and correspondences can be thematically significant. For example, Robinson speculates that 'the temptation for Muhammad to pray in the same direction as the People of the Scripture was as serious as Adam's temptation to approach the forbidden tree' (Robinson 1996: 211). Not only is there no basis in the Qur'anic text for this observation, the Qur'an specifies (Q. 2:144) that, after the Muslim emigration to Medina, Muḥammad was hoping that the *qibla* would be changed from Jerusalem to Mecca, and that God commanded Muḥammad to change the *qibla* in fulfilment of Muḥammad's wish (*fa-la-nuwalliyannaka qiblatan tarḍāhā*). Also, at times, it seems that these echoes and correspondences—for example, in Robinson's explanation of the links between the Adam story in verses 30–9 and the preceding material (Robinson 1996: 206)—tend to substitute for more substantive thematic links between verses and passages.

Smith

In his 'The Structure of *al-Baqarah*', David E. Smith says that the sura has 'evidence of genuine structure' (Smith 2001: 133). Like the rest of the Qur'an, the sura is structured, in general terms, 'by thematic repetition', but, in specific terms, by the principle of the Allah-Qur'an-Muḥammad authority. This principle is key to the sura's structure, but is to be distinguished from the sura's structure itself, which is 'cyclical in nature' (Smith 2001: 134, n. 12). Smith shows the recurrence of the principle in the four sections into which he divides the sura (verses 2–39, 40–118, 119–67, 168–286; verse 1, consisting of the so-called broken letters, is left aside). One cannot help feeling, though, that the structural principle of the Allāh-Qur'an-Muḥammad authority is a little too generalized, and that its application to the rest of the Qur'an, if at all possible, might be due to its overly inclusive non-specificity. One is tempted to ask whether one may speak of the God-Gospels-Jesus authority structure as the organizing principle of the New Testament, or whether a similar, albeit a qualified, statement may be made of the much more diverse Hebrew Scriptures, especially if such organizing principles yield notable formal structures. Smith's thesis, though not unworthy of consideration, needs to have greater rigour if it is to explain the distinctive structure of *al-Baqara*, and if, furthermore, the possibility of its relevance to the rest of the Qur'an is to be entertained.

Farrin

In '*Sūrat al-Baqara:* A Structural Analysis', Farrin examines the sura from a literary standpoint. Building on the views of Amīn Aḥsan Iṣlāḥī, Neal Robinson, Mathias Zahniser, and David Smith on the structure of the sura, and drawing on the theoretical framework of Mary Douglas's work on ring composition, Farrin divides the sura into nine sections (verses 1–20, 21–39, 40–103, 104–41, 142–52, 153–77, 178–253, 254–84, 285–6), divides the sections into subsections, identifies the ring structures of the sections (the first four being chiastically related to the last four, with the fifth, or middle, section (pertaining to the Ka'ba and calling the Muslims the median community) holding the sura's main message, and draws attention to 'the correspondence in section lengths and the appropriateness of the central section's dimension', arriving at the conclusion that the sura has 'marvelous justness of design' (Farrin 2010: 30).

Farrin's article is an important contribution toward understanding the structure of *Sūrat al-Baqara*. But Farrin's preoccupation, again in rather generalized terms, with the sura's ring structure leaves several questions unanswered. For example, how compelling is the point of correspondence between equality in retribution and bequests (verses 178–82) on the one hand and orphans, marriage and divorce, and widows (verses 220–42) on the other, or between fasting and superstition (verses 183–9) on the one hand and drinking wine and gambling (verse 219) on the other (27)? More important, what about the linear progression of ideas and themes in the sura? Why are certain subjects introduced in the particular places where they occur? For example, does the material in the 'long, legislative section' consisting, in Farrin's outline, of verses 178–253 (Farrin 2010: 26ff.) have a logical sequence?

IṢLĀḤĪ

Applying—and amplifying—the exegetical principles enunciated by his teacher Ḥamīd al-Dīn Farāhī (d. 1930), Amīn Aḥsan Iṣlāḥī wrote a multivolume Urdu commentary on the Qur'an, *Tadabbur-i Qur'ān* (literally, 'Reflection on the Qur'an'). Farāhī's original contribution to Qur'anic exegesis consists in his theory of Qur'anic *naẓm* (coherence or organic unity), which views the Qur'an, in its received recension, as possessing an orderly arrangement, both in respect of the verses in the individual suras and in respect of the larger units of what he calls sura-groups. Qur'anic *naẓm*, according to Farāhī, is hermeneutically significant, and is, therefore, integral to the task of Qur'anic interpretation. Farāhī did not live to complete his proposed *tafsīr* of the Qur'an in light of his understanding of Qur'anic *naẓm*; Iṣlāḥī's *Tadabbur* aims to complete the project.

Basic to the Farāhī-Iṣlāḥī *naẓm* theory is the idea of the *ʿamūd*—the central theme or axis—of a sura: every sura revolves around its particular *ʿamūd*, and a sura's verses, taken together, represent a systematic unfolding of that *ʿamūd* from the beginning of the sura to the end of the sura. Understanding a sura's *ʿamūd* is, therefore, key to understanding the sura's dynamic. *Sūrat al-Baqara*, according to Iṣlāḥī, replaces the Jews with the Muslims as the elected religious community. This replacement entails that the Jews, like the Muslims, accept Muḥammad as their prophet (hence the prominence of the Jews as addressees in the sura), that the Muslims receive a new Sharīʿa (code of law) that would supersede the previous, Torah-based Sharīʿa (hence the sura's detailed legislation for the newly elected Muslim community), and that the new community have their distinctive physical symbol of unity and spiritual centre of worship (hence the important change of the *qibla*, direction of prayer, made in the sura, from the Temple of Jerusalem to the Kaʿba in Mecca). In light of this, the sura's *ʿamūd* can be described as *īmān bi'l-risāla*, that is, an invitation to believe in Muḥammad's prophecy (Iṣlāḥī 2000: 1: 75; also 1: 94), the invitation being extended to the Jews (and, secondarily, to the Quraysh and other Ishmaelite Arabs), and also as the preparing of Muslims to receive the new Sharīʿa; and since the Sharīʿa forms an important part of *al-Baqara*, the sura may also be called the sura of Sharīʿa.

The aforestated *ʿamūd* of *al-Baqara* is brought into relief by Iṣlāḥī's verse analysis of the sura, which consists of an Introduction (1–39), four sections (40–121, 122–62, 163–242, 243–83), and a conclusion (284–6). The Introduction distinguishes between those who will believe and those who will not believe in Muḥammad's prophecy. Section 1 makes a critique of the Jews, and section 2 replaces them with a new community—that of Muslims, who, as true heirs of Abraham, shall have the Kaʿba—built by Abraham—as their *qibla*, which comes to replace the Temple of Jerusalem as *qibla*, and which, by clear implication, Muslims shall have to wrest from the hands of its present custodians, the idolatrous Arabs of Mecca. Section 3 furnishes details of the code of law—Sharīʿa—needed by the newly elected community, and section 4 prepares Muslims for the upcoming struggle for the liberation of the Kaʿba. The concluding part of the sura states the essence of revealed religion and reminds the members of the new community of the heavy responsibility they have to fulfil. Incidentally, a parallelism is noticeable in this division of the sura: section 1, which is about Jews, a Law-oriented community, parallels section 3, which is about a Law-oriented community in the making, and section 2, which is about the Kaʿba as the legacy of Abraham, parallels section 4, which is about liberation of the Kaʿba.

The foregoing should suggest, in broad terms, that the sura is a connected whole. A study of Iṣlāḥī's commentary on the sura will show that he offers a fairly cogent explanation of the linear relationship, with reference to the sura's *ʿamūd*, between the sura's verses from beginning to end, even though it is not possible to provide here details of his treatment of the sura. It is, nevertheless, necessary to make the following point: according to Iṣlāḥī, the dynamic of a Qur'anic sura reflects the dynamic of real life as lived and experienced by the sura's characters, whether individuals or groups, under a given set of circumstances. The events of real life have a logic of their own and do not necessarily follow the logic of an academic model conceived in the abstract. They are embedded in a living context, in all its variety and complexity, and an understanding of that context is essential to understanding why a sura treats certain themes in a certain order. For example, a panoramic view of *Sūrat al-Baqara's* contents shows that several of the sura's major themes are Kaʿba-related: Muḥammad has been raised as a prophet by God in response to Abraham's prayer (verse 129), and the Kaʿba, built by Abraham, shall serve as the *qibla* of the newly elected Muslim community, which means, on the one hand, that the Kaʿba shall replace Jerusalem's Temple as *qibla*, just as the Muslims shall replace the Jews as the elected community, and, on the other, that the Muslims shall replace the Ishmaelite idolaters—the Quraysh, more specifically—as custodians of the Kaʿba. The replacement of Jews with Muslims as elected community requires the dispensation of a new Sharīʿa, and the sura, consequently, provides legislation on a series of matters. And the replacement of the Ishmaelite Quraysh by Muslims requires that Muslims fight to gain control of the Kaʿba, since the Quraysh would not surrender the Kaʿba to the Muslims easily, the sura, therefore, enjoins Muslims to prepare for war, stressing the need to fund the war, and addresses several issues related directly or indirectly to war. The sequence of events in the sura's structure reflects the logic of the living context both in regard to the Jewish-Muslim trajectory and in regard to the Muslim-Ishmaelite trajectory.

Though highly plausible, Iṣlāḥī's explanation of the linear connection between the verses and passages of *al-Baqara* (and, for that matter, of the other suras) faces a potential theoretical objection—that of reckoning, in the main, without the existing exegetical literature on the Qur'an. In particular, Iṣlāḥī, one feels, gives short shrift to the so-called *asbāb al-nuzūl* (occasions of revelation). He does deal with the issue in the Introduction to his Qur'anic commentary: following his teacher, Farāhī, he seeks to derive the occasion of revelation of a verse or a passage from the Qur'anic text itself (Iṣlāḥī 2000: 1: 31–2).

But such an approach, besides being in tension with historical mainstream exegesis, might not be proof against the charge of subjectivity.

Concluding Observations

An overall view of the foregoing will suggest the following by way of conclusion. (1) The structure of the Qur'an, already a subject of considerable interest in modern Qur'anic scholarship, is likely to gain in importance in the coming years and to engage the attention of more scholars. (2) It is the structure of the thematically complex longer Medinan suras that will mainly claim this attention, since the structure of most of the Meccan suras does not, relatively speaking, raise many difficult issues. (3) The structure of the Qur'anic sura has been looked at in modern Qur'anic scholarship from different perspectives, some approaches stressing form (which itself is understood in more than one sense), others, theme, and yet others, intertextuality or textual relations. While the multiplicity of approaches currently in use in the study of the structure of the Qur'an will probably not resolve into a unified approach, future work in the area is likely to move in the direction of what Cuypers calls 'a general theory of composition' of the Qur'an (Cuypers 2011: 2). (4) The hold of biblically inspired approaches to the Qur'an has weakened but is still strong in some quarters; the structure of the Qur'anic suras has, as Cuypers has rightly observed, not only aesthetic but also interpretive significance. (5) A positive view of the structure of the Qur'anic sura weakens considerably the case for disjointedness in the Qur'anic text.

Modern Qur'anic scholarship seems to be attaching considerable attention to a synchronic study of the Qur'an, and it is not inconceivable that the hitherto dominant diachronic study of the Qur'an will require a re-examination of its results and conclusions. Neuwirth's statement, 'Any assessment of Qur'anic form and structure depends on the position chosen by the researcher as to the redaction and the canonization of the Qur'anic corpus' (Neuwirth 2002: 245), can, at least theoretically, be stood on its head for the following reason: if an independent analysis of the Qur'anic corpus in its received form shows this corpus to be possessed of significant and sophisticated structure, then either the validity of some aspects of the redactional approaches will be called in question or the redactional approaches may have to be critically modified to accommodate the results of such independent analysis. After all, why must a historically oriented redaction process alone supply the starting-point in studying the Qur'an?

Bibliography

Abdel Haleem, Muhammad. 'The Qur'an Explains Itself: *Sūrat al-Raḥmān*'. In: *Understanding the Qur'an: Themes and Style*, pp. 158–83. London: I. B. Taurus, 2001.

El-Awa, Salwa M. S. *Textual Relations in the Qur'ān*. New York: Routledge, 2007.

Cuypers, Michel. 'Semitic Rhetoric as a Key to the Question of the *naẓm* of the Qur'anic Text', *Journal of Qur'anic Studies* 13/1 (2011), 1–24.

Farrin, Raymond K. '*Surat al-Baqara:* A Structural Analysis', *Muslim World* 100/1 (2010), 17–32.

Iṣlāḥī, Amīn Aḥsan. *Tadabbur-i Qur'ān*. 9 vols. Lahore: Faran Foundation, 2000.

Mir, Mustansir. *Coherence in the Qur'anic: A Study of Iṣlāḥī's Concept of Naẓm in Tadabbur-i Qur'ān*. Indianapolis: American Trust Publications, 1986.

Mir, Mustansir. 'The *sūra* as a Unity: A Twentieth Century Development in Qur'ān. Exegesis.' In: G. R. Hawting and Abdul Kader A. Shareef (eds.). *Approaches to the Qur'ān*, pp. 211–24. London and New York: Routledge, 1993.

Mir, Mustansir. 'Some Aspects of Narration in the Qur'ān'. In: Roberta Sterman Sabbath (ed.). *Sacred Tropes: Tanakh, New Testament, and Qur'ān as Literature and Culture*, pp. 93–106. Leiden: Brill, 2009.

Mir, Mustansir. 'Continuity, Context, and Coherence in the Qur'ān: A Brief Review of the Idea of *Naẓm* in *Tafsīr* Literature', *Al-Bayān: Journal of Qur'ān and Ḥadīth Studies* 11/2 (2013), 15–29.

Neuwirth, Angelika. *Studien zur Komposition der mekkanischen Suren*. 2nd enlarged edn. Berlin and New York: Walter de Gruyter, 2007.

Neuwirth, Angelika. 'Form and Structure in the Qur'ān'. In: Jane Dammen McAuliffe (ed.). *Encyclopaedia of the Qur'ān*. 6 vols., 2:245–66 Leiden: Brill, 2001–6.

Rippin, Andrew. 'Contemporary Scholarly Understandings of Qur'ānic Coherence', *Al-Bayān* 11/2 (2013), 1–14.

Robinson, Neal. *Discovering the Qur'an: A Contemporary Approach to a Veiled Text*. London: SCM, 1996.

Smith, David. "The Structure of *al-Baqarah*', *Muslim World* 91/1–2 (2001), 121–36.

Wilson, Deirdre and Dan Sperbar. *Meaning and Relevance*. Cambridge: Cambridge University Press, 2012.

Zahniser, A. H. Mathias. 'Sūra as Guidance and Exhortation: The Composition of *Sūrat al-Nisā'*'. In: *Humanism, Culture, and Language in the Near East: Studies in Honor of George Krotkoff*, pp. 71–85. Winona Lake, IN: Eisenbrauns, 1997.

Zahniser, A. H. Mathias. 'Major Transitions and Thematic Borders in Two Long Sūras: *al-Baqara* and *al-Nisā'*'. In: Issa J. Boullata (ed.). *Literary Structures of Religious Meaning in the Qur'ān*, pp. 26–55. Richmond: Curzon, 2000.

CHAPTER 23

DISCUSSIONS OF QUR'ANIC INIMITABILITY

The Theological Nexus

AYMAN A. EL-DESOUKY

I must begin here by naming the fundamental premise in the following account of the theological nexus of *iʿjāz* discussions in classical and modern scholarship. The premise centres on the question, and the challenge, of how a modern literary scholar may approach the fact of the absolute singularity of Qur'anic revelations, both as a mode of composition, its formal arrangements and language style, and as a unique history of reception. The challenge of how to understand the powerful hold of Qur'anic recitations is not limited to the time of revelation, as archetypally represented by the Bedouin who upon hearing a single verse (*faʾṣdaʿ bi-mā tuʾmar*, Q. 15:94), retorted '*sajadtu li-faṣāḥatihi*' (I prostrated before its eloquence) and the numerous early accounts of conversion upon hearing single verses or clusters of verses (cited in al-Qāḍī ʿIyāḍ, *al-Shifā*, 1: 262; Kermani 1999: 257). The challenge has continued historically, even when theological debates over the status of the Qur'an seemed to have been settled by the authority of the caliph al-Mutawakkil in 232/847 on the side of the Ḥanbalī view of the Qur'an as eternal (*qadīm*) and uncreated. And just as the first attempts at explaining the miraculous nature of the Qur'an had naturally to develop a new language of systematic reflection that is fundamentally linguistic and rhetorical in nature but theological in its thrust, so too did the literary approaches that began to emerge early in the twentieth century. Modern literary approaches have since had to face the same double challenge: literarily, the challenge is how to develop a critical theoretical language with which to approach the singularity of a text (let alone its unique modes of reception), but hermeneutically, the challenge emerges in the struggle to account for the theological dimension of the experience that such an exceptionally matchless text elicits. My aim is therefore not so much to rehearse the full history of *iʿjāz* discussions, already well covered in Qur'anic Studies, as to revisit the discussions from the centralizing challenge of the unique nexus of the theological and the literary in Islamic traditions.

Iʿjāz al-Qurʾān: the Originating Contexts of *Taḥaddī*

The question of *iʿjāz al-Qurʾān*, or the inimitability of the Qur'an, from the time of the first revelations and to this day, has been central both to the formulation of Islamic theological thought, or *kalām*, and to the emergence and development of classical Arabic literary and rhetorical theories. The translation of *iʿjāz* as inimitability already serves to highlight the incomparability of the unique styles of the Qur'an, its composition (*taʾlīf*) and its rhetorical thrust and textual arrangement (*naẓm*), that is, the *form* of its revelations. The Arabic word *iʿjāz* connotes also the miraculous nature of the revelation as a foundational event, the very fact of revelation, of the Qur'an as *kalām Allāh* or divine speech. From the very beginning, however, the very fact of revelation as a miraculous event, restricted only to prophets in the classical scholarship, has been inseparable from its form and content, a conception that was developed into a creedal reflections on *tathbīt dalāʾil al-nubuwwa*, or authenticating the signs of Muḥammad's prophethood, in the third/ninth century, perhaps earlier, and settled into a distinct genre by fourth/fifth century (in the authoritative works of the Muʿtazilī al-Qāḍī ʿAbd al-Jabbār (d. 415/1025). The theological nexus of Islamic thought on the nature of *iʿjāz* has therefore emerged first in the early reflections on the originary contexts of revelation as confirming the status of the Prophet and the authenticity of his message. The Qur'an itself attests to these contexts in the well-known *taḥaddī* or challenge verses (Q. 2:23–4; 10:38; 11:13; 17:88; 52:33–4) in which doubters and detractors of the Prophet are challenged to produce similar verses or suras. The doubters are declared incapable of doing so, even if they were to help one another by inspiring humans or inspiring jinn (Q. 17:88; 2:23–4).

This context of *taḥaddī* brings the very fact of revelation as a metaphysical force of divine origin to the fore, drawing on and radically transforming established cultural attitudes towards language in the milieu of revelation and among the Qurayshis, particularly noted for poetic and linguistic genius. The established practice of *muʿāraḍa*, in which a well-known poet produces similar or even more accomplished poems and thereby establishing not only his poetic genius but also the status of his tribe, is already radically transformed in this context (van Ess 1981). In this context, the Qur'an also denies that Muḥammad is a soothsayer (*kāhin*), a madman (*majnūn*), or a poet (*shāʿir*), not only clearing such charges directly levelled at the Prophet but also addressing the mysterious force of such radically new language which was clearly felt by individuals in a culture that prided itself on its linguistic genius as one of its most defining traits (Q. 52:29–31; 69:41–2). The form of the word *iʿjāz* does not itself appear in the Qur'an, though the fourth form verb *aʿjaza* and variously derived forms occur as many as sixteen times, mostly in the context of humankind's inability to thwart God's will (cf. Q. 8:59; 9:2, 3; 34:5, 38; 72:12). The opening of *Sūrat Yūnus* (Q. 10:1–2) offers some of the most often quoted verses in confirming both the Qur'anic revelations and the status of the Prophet: '*Alif Lām Rā*ʾ. These are the verses of the decisive Scripture. Is it so surprising to people that We have revealed to a man from among them that he should warn people, and give glad news to those who believe, that they are on a sure footing with their Lord?' (Martin, '*Iʿjāz*', *EI*²; cf. 1980; 1988). The expression *āya* or sign from God confirms the transcendent source of the revelation, while the expression *ʿajab*, or wonder, and its cognate *ʿajība*, or miracle, became technical terms in the theological discourses referring to the type of miracles that is restricted only to prophets, as opposed to human made wonders.

Theological reflection originated in the early debates over the nature and power of the speech of God, or *kalām Allāh*, and subsequently settled into the two schools of traditionalists, Ashʿarī Sunnīs, those who based their arguments on the metaphysical fact of revelation, and rationalists, the Muʿtazilīs, those who argued for the evidence of reason and supporting speculative thought. The consensus of the scholarship has it that the theological theories of *iʿjāz* have reached their fullest doctrinal expression in the classical *tafsīr* (exegesis) and *sīra* (biography of the Prophet) genres by the end of the fourth/tenth century, with classical literary approaches following in the fifth/eleventh century. Modern thought in the late nineteenth and early twentieth centuries and in contemporary scholarship seems to have turned more to the literary and rhetorical aspects of the Qur'an when reflecting on its uniqueness and foundational status as text. The classical formulations of the doctrine began in the folds of early third-/ninth-century debates over prophethood and the authenticity of the Prophet's miracle, compared to those of Moses and Jesus, settling into the dominant Sunnī doctrine through theological, legal, and rhetorical/literary arguments. The force of Qur'anic revelations and their hold on believers (and non-believers), however, continued in more experiential contexts and in daily Muslim practices, confirming Islam as a religion of the Word and Islamic cultures as text-based. Still, following the lines of argument and authoritative stance of the classical debates over *al-iʿjāz al-bayānī* (rhetorical/literary) and *al-iʿjāz al-tashrīʿī* (legal/doctrinal), varieties of popular and pseudo-scientific ideological discourses that look for signs of *iʿjāz* outside of the text began to appear in the nineteenth century, interpreting some of the Qur'an's references to natural and human phenomena as divinations of scientific truths or current events and major ethical debates of the day—what is now generally known as *al-iʿjāz al-ʿilmī*. In this brief and general sketch, it has been a constant historical reality that approaches to both the form and content of Qur'anic revelations must first contend with the theological nexus and the authority of its historical and traditional institutional hold.

Richard Martin has made convincing arguments crediting the circle of Abū ʿAlī al-Jubbāʾī (d. 303/915) and the Basran Muʿtazilīs—al-Jubbāʾī was also the teacher of two important leaders of *kalām*, his son Abū Hāshim (d. 321/933); and the founder of the Ashʿarī school, Abū'l-Ḥasan al-Ashʿarī (d. 324/935)—with the earliest debates (Martin 1980: 174). It was during the time of al-Jāḥiẓ that critical formulations of the literary dimensions of the questions of *iʿjāz* were initially set forth. The work of Ibn Qutayba (d. 276/889), *Taʾwīl mushkil al-Qurʾān*, is cited by Khalafallāh as being significant for the study of the relations between *iʿjāz* studies and literary criticism (Khalafallah 1976:5). Abū Hāshim ibn al-Jubbāʾī, as Abū Zayd has argued, offers a good useful transition from the extrinsic to the intrinsic approaches through the argument that if the Qur'an were unique and incomparable only in form (*nawʿ* and *jins*), this would make it completely beyond the realm of humans and therefore may not offer us the provenance of *iʿjāz*. He then proposes *faṣāḥa* (eloquence, defined by al-Jubbāʾī in the two features of excellence in meaning and precision in expression, or *ḥusn al-maʿnā wa jazālat al-lafẓ*) as the rhetorical feature wherein human language (crossing the genres of *khaṭāba*, *rasāʾil* and *shiʿr*) and divine speech may be compared to prove the *iʿjāz* of the Qur'an. This argument also leads by extension to locating *iʿjāz* in the realms of meaning or divine knowledge, which no human can attain (Abū Zayd 1994: 153). As scholars have noted, it was al-Qāḍī ʿAbd al-Jabbār, a Muʿtazilī and a *mutakallim*, who took the arguments further, arguing that meanings cannot be compared: that *faṣāḥa* is not to be restricted to individual words or components of speech, but in the special arrangement or order of words in the expression: '*Iʿlam anna al-faṣāḥa lā taẓhar fī afrād al-kalām, wa-innamā fī'l-ḍamm ʿalā tarīqa makhṣūṣa*' (ʿAbd al-Jabbār, *al-Mughnī*, 16:200; Abū Zayd 1994: 153–17). This view anticipates the later crucial and systematic theories of *naẓm* developed by ʿAbd al-Qāhir al-Jurjānī (d. 471/1078).

Kalām Allāh and the Theological Nexus

As discussed earlier, however, the originary context of *taḥaddī* offers a further and most crucial theological as well as literary fact regarding the divine origin of the aesthetic force of *iʿjāz*: it reveals the very fact of revelation to be its most salient content. Scholars of the Qur'an, notably Navid Kermani (1999; 2006), have attempted to understand this seemingly simple fact in aesthetic terms, though the French philosopher Emmanuel Levinas has also remarked the same of Jewish revelation from a hermeneutical angle (Levinas 1994). It is in reflecting on the signs contained in the situation of *taḥaddī* as a foundational event, and on the miraculous accounts of conversion by such notoriously stolid figures as ʿUmar ibn al-Khaṭṭāb, that theological discourse, known as *kalām*, began systematically. Beyond early discussions such as to be found in al-Ṭabarī's introduction to his famous third-/ninth-century book of *tafsīr* (*Jāmiʿ al-bayān ʿan taʾwīl ayy al-Qurʾān*), theological reflection in the fourth/tenth century began to crystallize around the three aspects most defining of the theological view of *iʿjāz*: the Qur'an as *Kalām Allāh* is *muʿjiz* (inimitable and miraculous), *maqrūn bi'l-taḥaddī* (divinely marked by a challenge), and *sālim min al-muʿāraḍa* (matchless or immune to emulation). This is the doctrine that has settled in Sunnī Islamic traditions, very often precisely in refutation of diverse Shīʿī and Sufi views on revelation and prophecy, and the arguments of non-Muslim scholars. But it is in the shift away from the debates over the authenticity of the divine knowledge and message (*maʿnā*), the ideological act of *taḥaddī* and the rhetorical polemics of the status of the poetic, and toward the understanding of the Qur'an's unique *naẓm*, that the concept of *iʿjāz* began to develop conceptually as both a literary and a theological tenet.

The theological debates over *iʿjāz* led to the formulation of the first views on the nature of language, human and divine. The key tenets of *tawḥīd*, or the absolute unity of God, which constitutes the central doctrine of Islamic theological thought—uniqueness, transcendence, and incomparability—were sought not only in the Qur'an's proclamations but also in its unique style and language. If theology offers systematic reflection on the unity and existence of the Divine and of humanity's relation to their creator, the thought of language in Islamic theology is inseparable from such reflection on the nature of the Divine and its attributes (Shah 2019). The conception of the Qur'an as the unique miracle of Islam, compared to those of Judaism and Christianity, lies in its uniqueness as both *the proof* of the authenticity of the Prophet and his message and *the embodiment* of the message (of God and absolute oneness), unlike the cases of Judaism and Christianity in which the proof of revelation is conceived of materially as other than the source of revelation.

In *kalām* literature, or theological discourses, the Qur'an becomes the Prophet's miracle, comparable with miracles associated with the monotheistic prophets, the parting of the sea by Moses, and the miracles of healing by Jesus. In classical studies on *iʿjāz*, the key insight, at once centralizing and contextualizing the range of differing arguments, is that while the miracles of Moses and Jesus, and other prophets, are material and extrinsic to the fact of revelation, the miracle of the Prophet and of Islam is the very form of revelation as the confirmation of its transcendent source. The superiority of the Qur'an as the miracle of Islam is seen precisely in the way the transcendent sign that confirms the fact of revelation is none other than the very revelation and not outside it: 'The Qurʾān is itself the revelation that it reveals, and it is the miraculous occurrence, for its sign is in itself and does not seek proof outside of itself as in previous miracles. It is therefore the most incisive of proof, as it contains 'both the sign and the content of revelation in itself'—in Ibn Khaldūn's words (*Muqaddima*, 1:59; cf. Abū Zayd, 1994: 137–9). This unique status of the Qur'an as both the very fact of revelation and its content, as it was already clearly conceived and articulated by the third/ninth century, lies at the very heart of the differences between the Muʿtazilī and Ashʿarī *mutakallimūn*, or theologians. But it also informs the literary approaches that sought to confirm how the form of *iʿjāz* is itself the content, aside from the usual content as we know it in the spheres of religious practice, jurisprudence, divine knowledge, and knowledge of human affairs. In the debates over *iʿjāz*, disagreements have not emerged over the actual meaning and knowledge contained in the Qur'an but rather the tension arose over the postulate that the transcendent sign of revelation, or the form of revelation, is itself the content or sign, and the implication of such a postulate for the status of the Qur'an: is it created (*makhlūq*), as a sign of revelation, or eternal, as the very speech of God, that is, what is the nature of divine speech as a divine act? This question also informs traditional Jewish thought on the nature of revelation, and in Christian theology, it comes back with hermeneutical force in the work of kerygmatic theologians such as Karl Barth and after him in the work of existential theologians such as Rudolf Bultmann and in the philosophical hermeneutics of Paul Ricoeur (El-Desouky 2007; 2013; 2014).

Both Temporal and Eternal: On the Aesthetic Force of Revelation

With the early phase of *taḥaddī* over, the shift from *maʿnā* to *naẓm* led to later significant developments such as the attempt by Abū Bakr al-Bāqillānī (d. 403/1013) to thematize that which lies in-between the *matlū* (the content of what is recited or *anbāʾ al-ghayb*, news of the unknown), and the *tilāwa* (the recitation itself or the annunciated word in the revelations of the Qur'an). It is significant in this context that al-Bāqillānī was among the first to consider the question of *iʿjāz* in relation to the earlier holy books (El-Desouky 2013). That which lies in-between is the direct experience with the word of God, and the most fundamental tenet of Arabic and Islamic theological thought. It is this unique aesthetic experience that has led to the subsequent development of both Islamic theology and classical rhetorical theories, as well as to a whole range of philosophical and literary theologies such as Ibn Ṭufayl's (d. *c.*580/1185) literary form of the theological thesis as to whether one can attain knowledge of God without language: the language of humans that is (in his famous philosophical narrative *Ḥayy ibn Yaqẓān*). The thought of the word of God as both temporal (conceivable by humans) and eternal (divine speech or *Kalām Allah*) has demarcated the critical reach of literary approaches since the third/ninth century (Abū Zayd 2003), and until the twentieth century when different conceptions of the literary and different hermeneutical approaches developed in the attempt to understand literarily the uniqueness of the Qur'an as text.

Retracing Ibn Khaldūn's terse formula of the unity of the signifier and the signified (*ittiḥād al-dāl wa'l-madlūl*) reveals the history of the nexus of the theological and the literary in *iʿjāz* debates in crucial and pertinent ways (especially to the dilemmas of modern literary approaches). The terse formula encapsulates the tension between extrinsic and intrinsic approaches to the Qur'an. The tension becomes hermeneutical and theological in nature when it touches on the question of the Qur'an's divine source, and literary when it touches on its singularity as a text and its unique modes of composition. The early approach represented in issues of *taḥaddī* signals the understanding of *iʿjāz* from the extrinsic view that rests on the conception of sheer human inability and the impossibility of understanding the *muʿjiz* dimensions of divine speech from within history or human reason. The external context of *taḥaddī* reached its strongest expression in the well-known debate initiated by al-Naẓẓām's postulate of *ṣarfa*, or turning away, that God had turned away humans, the Arabs at the time of revelation in their highest capacity of rhetorical eloquence (not to be matched by succeeding generations or ages as al-Qāḍī ʿAbd al-Jabbār and others have later argued), and disengaged their ability to match the revelations by an act of Divine Will. Related to this theory is also the argument from '*maʿnā*' or divine knowledge as the purport of the revelations and their inimitability. Al-Naẓẓām's theory is ultimately related to the Muʿtazilī theory of the divine attributes, and specifically that of *tawḥīd* or absolute unity and oneness of God. From *ʿadl* to *tawḥīd*, God is just and it is in the attribute of justice that God would not impose such a condition of *ṣarfa* on humans. It is not necessarily the case, however, as some modern scholars have argued, that such an attempt constitutes a refutation of the concept of *iʿjāz*. Moreover, the theory was refuted almost immediately and by fellow Muʿtazilīs as is well known. But a later scholar such as al-Bāqillānī (d. 403/1013), in his detailed arguments over the nature of *iʿjāz*, determining that the Qur'an is unique in form and stylistically unmatchable, unwittingly also offered ultimately an equally extrinsic reason for the explanation of *iʿjāz*. In *Iʿjāz al-Qurʾān*, as Abū Zayd has reasoned, al-Bāqillānī advances his own refutations of *ṣarfa* beginning with the text itself, arguing for its inimitability on the levels of form (*nawʿ* and *jins*) and stylistics (its being neither rhyming prose, *sajʿ*, nor poetry) as well as on the level of divine knowledge as imparted in meaning. All such attributes—comparable only to the Divine attributes of uniqueness, transcendence, and incomparability—reveal the nature of *iʿjāz* in the end as beyond the realm of humans. Such a conclusion significantly comes close to the argument of *ṣarfa*, as both arguments confuse the human inability to produce anything like the Qur'an with the ability to fathom the secrets of *iʿjāz* (Abū Zayd 1994: 145–7). Both approaches therefore seem to look for *iʿjāz* from outside of the text, so to speak.

The distinction between extrinsic and intrinsic conceptions of *iʿjāz* will prove most crucial in the intellectual and scholarly shifts between the theological and the literary approaches, both in the classical sources and in modern scholarship. The intrinsic approaches, which focus on the text itself and the linguistic dimensions of *iʿjāz*, was the achievement of the Muʿtazilīs, and was made possible as a line of investigation owing to the less drastic division between human utterance (*muwāḍaʿa*) and divine speech (*kalām*). Divine speech is both temporal and eternal; otherwise no human would have the capacity of belief in God's unity and transcendence. Maintaining both attributes is most crucial in understanding the limitations of some modern approaches to the Qur'an, which have undermined the transcendent possibility in the attempt to examine the literary nature of Qur'anic revelations, and it is what led a scholar such as Abū Zayd to call for a theology of the literary, a conceptually sound and unique postulate, as I shall explain later, if we are to begin to outline a unique hermeneutics of Islamic provenance (as opposed to some recent literary approaches that are primarily based on biblical hermeneutics).

Scholarship on *iʿjāz* has barely begun to extend its provenances to include modern literary approaches and to recognize them as possibly offering more than literary or aesthetic insight, that is, as offering the possibility of a theology of *iʿjāz* that supports literary approaches, a type of sacred hermeneutics. Such approaches are received mainly as interpretive calls for the historicity of meaning of Qur'anic revelations, they are not received as possibly offering a theology of the literary that may expand on the classical literary approaches, while not contesting the divine status of the Qur'an as *kalām Allāh*. In other words, the door of *ijtihād* on the question of *iʿjāz* was closed when the Abbasid caliph al-Mutawakkil settled the matter in support of the view of the eternity of the Qur'an, first propounded by Ibn Kullāb (d. 258/854), and ended the *miḥna* or strife that ensued when al-Maʾmūn (r. 198–218/813–33) officially supported the Muʿtazilī view of *ḥudūth* or *khalq* (creation of the Qur'an). Since then the doctrine continues in the form of iconoclastic attitudes, disregarding the fact that in substance, *iʿjāz*, as a direct experience of that which lies between *tilāwa* and *matluw*, is arguably a living trans-historical phenomenon. The rhetorical force of inimitability (*balāghat al-iʿjāz*), which constituted the thrust of early literary approaches, soon developed at the hands of traditional theologians into an institutionally powerful hold over the inimitability of the rhetorical construct itself, that is, the primacy of linguistic understanding began to settle into a form of *iʿjāz al-balāgha*, or the inimitability, hence sacral force, of rhetorical understanding (ʿAyyāsh 2013 and ʿArafa 1985). This historically settled approach, backed by official institutions since the fourth/tenth century, has tended to foreclose the development of conceptions of literature and the literary that are unique to Qur'anic *naẓm* and the possibility of a uniquely Islamic hermeneutics of proclamation, one, I have argued, that could be sought hermeneutically in the aesthetic force of the single standing verse (El-Desouky 2013, 2014).

Dilemmas of the Literary in Modern Approaches

For the modern literary scholar, as for the traditionalist theologian, the Qur'an offers a unique and singular instance of composition. At the source, the challenge of transcendence holds true for both. The disciplinary tension occurs at the level of conceptions of language, of textuality, and of the aesthetics and history of reception. Qur'anic revelations have such a unique style of composition and language modes that classical scholars had to devise new terminology, other than that used in reference to poetry; therefore, new branches of scholarship were developed out of interpretive approaches: the so-called *ʿulūm al-Qurʾān* (sciences of the Qur'an), as well as literary critical studies such as al-Jurjānī's *Dalāʾil al-iʿjāz*. Ṭāhā Ḥussain's statement regarding the uniqueness of the Qur'an still captures the fundamental dilemma that all literary approaches, including those at the disposal of theological speculation, have had to face: 'But you know that the Qur'an is not prose and that it is not verse either. It is rather Qur'an, and it cannot be called by any other name but this' (Boullata 2000: ix). The Qur'an's structure and composition, its division into suras and *āya*s and its rhetorical modes, mix of genres, and syntactic arrangements have all been without precedence (notwithstanding recent attempts in modern scholarship to identify precedence of phraseological or lexical or syntactic provenance in other surrounding linguistic and textual practices at the time). Most modern literary approaches, on the other hand, have had to derive methods and analytical tools from other traditions: narratology, classical rhetorical analysis, textuality and canonical criticism, form criticism, the ring theory of textual cultural anthropology, and so on, all of which belong to Western approaches and to the writerly domain of textuality. Modern Western-based scholarship has on the whole revived classical rhetorical approaches with the addition of textual and form critical approaches inspired by biblical studies in the attempt to offer new literary approaches to the Qur'an. The *Blackwell Companion to the Qur'ān* (Rippin 2006) offers a synopsis of the new approaches, focusing on the Qur'an's historical contexts, composition and language styles, and modes of interpretation (El-Desouky 2014: 16–24; see also Boullata 1988 and 2000; Wild 1996 and 2006; Johns 2011). It is arguable, however, that while these studies have shed significant light on the nature of the Qur'an as text, they remain strictly within the domain of extrinsic, textual approaches, so far as they are not able to articulate a clear hermeneutical postulate as to how to conceive of the Qur'anic utterance as at once divine in origin and temporal in its modes of composition and reception, and how the temporality of such modes demands the articulation of a different aesthetic (perhaps excepting studies on sound and syntactic features such as Sells 2000 and 2007, Stewart 2009 and 2013, and Toorawa 2005). The nexus of the theological and literary provenances of *iʿjāz* is perhaps the most constitutive of Islam as a religious experience, beyond the historically developed practices of the faith.

Arabic-based approaches have rather sought to tackle the necessity of a hermeneutical understanding as the basis of approaching the Qur'an as literature. From a theological point of view, the task is fundamentally hermeneutical, and a number of strong modern theorists, such as Abū Zayd, Mohammed Arkoun, Abdolkarim Soroush, Ṭāhā ʿAbd al-Raḥmān, Farid Esack, Ebrahim Moosa, Fazlur Rahman, and other contemporary theorists working mostly from within the Arabic and Islamic cultural spheres, have offered formidable interpretive and culturally revisionist approaches. These interpretive approaches vary significantly in their critical assumptions and modes of analysis, but fundamentally acknowledge the divine and transcendental source of Qur'anic voice. There remains, however, the task of facing the theological and institutional challenges. As Navid Kermani has put it: 'They know that if the Qur'an is accepted as a revelation and as a literary monument and body of sound, this will open up a whole cosmos of signs, meanings, and interpretations, and allow it to be read in a multitude of different ways' (2006: 18).

A Supportive Theology for Literary Approaches?

The hermeneutical provenances of systematic reflection on *iʿjāz* have traditionally been divided between theological or *kalām* discourses and rhetorical (theories of *majāz* and *balāgha*) as well as literary (from al-Jāḥiẓ through to al-Jurjānī to Ibn Khaldūn) discourses. The tension between these two provenances (theological and rhetorical/literary) seems to have settled by the fourth/tenth century, only to be renewed in the twentieth. The well-known debates over Ṭāhā Ḥussain's work, *Fī'l-shiʿr al-jāhilī*, in the 1920s and then again over Muḥammad Aḥmad Khalafallāh's *al-Fann al-qaṣaṣī fī'l-Qurʾān* in the 1940s served to renew attention to the literary features of the Qur'an. Sayyid Quṭb's literary studies and *tafsīr* works followed in the 1960s (including ʿĀʾisha ʿAbd al-Raḥmān's study on *al-Tafsīr al-bayānī*, 1990), offering a freshly engaged approach to the phenomena of sound and image. In the 1990s, Naṣr Ḥāmid Abū Zayd's hermeneutical studies, combining philological method and theological considerations, were again misinterpreted as questioning the eternal provenance of Qur'anic revelations. Abū Zayd, on the contrary, sought to re-engage the literary approaches by renewing attention to the most fundamental assumption in classical *iʿjāz* studies, that the word of God is both eternal and temporal. A tenet of modern thought (though also of al-Jāḥiẓ (d. 255/868–9) in his discussion of the figure of the *turjumān* as the one able to compose and think in more than one language, in *Kitāb al-ḥayawān*) is that linguistic understanding is fundamentally cultural, but the question for Abū Zayd is not only how to understand the Qur'an culturally but how to do so 'within its divine nature as a text revealed by God?' (Abū Zayd 2003: 35). One of Abū Zayd's most significant conclusions in his study on 'The Dilemma of the Literary Approaches to the Qur'an', and later work, as I have noted, is that 'the literary approach suffers from the absence of a new supportive theology' (2003: 34). This insight offers in turn one of the most significant contributions to the theological nexus of *iʿjāz* in modern and contemporary scholarship (El-Desouky 2013 and 2014).

Were we to pursue the hermeneutical implications of such a call for a supportive theology, the tension between the theological and the literary, I would argue, would begin to emerge as resting on a paired misconception. The first misconception rests on the view that modern literary approaches, advancing modern postulation and methods of literary criticism and theory, can only be pursued on the assumption that a sacred book or sacred scriptures are historical texts in their composition, language, and authorial voice. Such a view would clearly threaten both the divine provenance of revelations and the authority of historically established institutions. The second misconception also rests on the authority of traditional rhetorical conceptions of *iʿjāz*, that is, the rhetorical theories advanced primarily in *tafsīr* work and their linguistic modes of explanation have acquired a similar sanctity, one that cannot afford to admit new conceptions of language or of metaphoricity (*majāz*). A corollary assumption behind both views is that an individual act of interpretation, one that is pursued outside the established institutions and their modes of classical training, is an inherent call for all Muslims to follow its insights and conclusions, which is contrary to the individualist impulse in modern literary theory. The tension is also complicated by the self-positioning by many Arab theorists in a perceived direct line with the long-suppressed intellectual traditions of the Muʿtazilīs and later Ibn Rushd's legacy. This is not always true, as Abū Zayd notes, for example, Muḥammad ʿAbdūh sought to combine the Muʿtazilī doctrine of *ʿadl* or divine justice and that the Ashʿarī doctrine of *tawḥīd* or divine unity, indicating how the choice of theological doctrines carries certain fundamental assumptions that the modern theorist must be able to examine closely in order to avoid confusion (2003: 40).

An equally crucial dimension of the history of *iʿjāz* debates is the inescapability of a founding and legitimating act of interpretation, regardless of the institutional or ideological context. The theological speculative reflection on the word of God or *kalām Allāh*, whether Ashʿarī or Muʿtazilī, is also at once a reflection on the numinous immediacy of the experience of the divine in Islam. What is at stake in the historical and theological debates is not so much the conception of the status of language, whether it is divine in origin or human, as Shah has convincingly argued (2011). Nor is it even the miraculous status of the Qur'an. Rather what is at stake is the unique aesthetics of a numinous immediacy that is received in and through language, one that would further offer the basis of a supportive theology of the literary by admitting the dimensions of subjectivation and individuation through language experience. Similar debates issued in modern Christian kerygmatic theologies, from Karl Barth to Rudolf Bultmann, and eventually led a literary critic of the calibre of Northrop Frye to articulate the postulate of a kerygmatic and proclamatory word that is neither poetic nor dialectical but rather 'on the other side of the poetic' (El-Desouky 2007). In the Christian theological and the literary approaches that inform biblical studies, however, the experience of numinous immediacy through the word is narrative-based, following the unique modes of the New Testament.

What is different in the case of Qur'anic revelations is not only the untranslatability of its language in its history of reception but also, and just as fundamentally, the singularity of its formal structures and composition. As with the classical *iʿjāz* studies, a literary or a philological approach is always already theological in its thrust. In considering the nexus of the theological and the literary, the question of *iʿjāz*, however, may be reconceived in light of the larger Muslim religious experience of the word of revelation in daily practice, historical and collective imagination, and ethical vision. That is, the history of lay individual and communal reception of the word (in its emotive and aesthetic force) should also be considered in the attempt to understand the unique aesthetic experience of Qur'anic revelations. Such an approach, building on arguments for an aesthetics of reception and a hermeneutics of the temporal and eternal in the conception of voice, would not only explain the aesthetic hold of Qur'anic revelations on the first believers, it would also enable a new hermeneutics of the sacred word that may have further explanatory power for the Qur'an's unique literary nature and aesthetic force.

Bibliography

Primary Sources

Abdel-Haleem, Muhammad. *The Qur'an: English Translation with Parallel Arabic Text*. Oxford: Oxford University Press, 2010.

Abū'l-Faḍl ʿIyāḍ, al-Qāḍī. *Al-Shifā bi-taʿrīf ḥuqūq al-Muṣṭafā*. 2 vols., vol. 1. Beirut: Dār al-Kutub al-ʿIlmiyya, 1969.

ʿAbd al-Jabbār, al-Qāḍī, Aḥmad al-Asadabādī *Tathbīt dalāʾil al-nubuwwa*, 2 vols. Ed. ʿAbd al-Karīm ʿUthmān. Beirut: Dār al-ʿArabiyya, 1966.

ʿAbd al-Jabbār, al-Qāḍī, Aḥmad al-Asadabādī. *Sharḥ al-uṣūl al-khamsa*. Ed. Bidair ʿAwn. Kuwait: Maṭbaʿat Jāmiʿat al-Kuwait, 1998. (The text is often attributed to ʿAbd al-Jabbār, but is a commentary by Mānkdīm Shashdīw, Aḥmad b. al-Ḥusayn).

ʿAbd al-Jabbār, al-Qāḍī, Aḥmad al-Asadabādī. *Kitāb al-Mughnī fī abwāb al-tawḥīd wa'l-ʿadll-ʿadl*, 16 parts, 10 vols. Ed. Khiḍr Muḥammad Nabhā. Beirut: Dār al-Kutub al-ʿIlmiyya, 2011.

al-Bāqillānī, Abū Bakr Muḥammad ibn al-Ṭayyib. *Iʿjāz al-Qurʾān*. Ed. Sayyid Aḥmad Ṣaqr. Cairo: Dār al-Kutub, 1954.

al-Jurjānī, ʿAbd al-Qāhir. *Dalāʾil al-iʿjāz*. Ed. M. al-Tunjī. Beirut: Dār al-Kitāb al-ʿArabī, 1995.

Ibn Khaldūn, ʿAbd al-Raḥmān. *Muqaddimat Ibn Khaldūn*. Vol. 1 of 7. Beirut: Dār al-Fikr, 2001.

Ibn Qutayba, Abū Muḥammad ʿAbd Allāh ibn Muslim. *Taʾwīl mushkil al-Qurʾān*. Ed. al-Sayyid Aḥmad Saqr. Cairo: Maktabat Dār al-Turāth, 1973.

al-Sharīf al-Raḍī, Muḥammad ibn al-Ḥusayn. *Talkhīṣ al-bayān fī majāzāt al-Qurʾān*. Ed. Muḥammad ʿAbd al-Ghanī Ḥasan. Cairo: ʿĪsā al-Bābī al-Ḥalabī, 1955.

al-Ṭabarī, Abū Jaʿfar Muḥammad ibn Jarīr. *Jāmiʿ al-bayān ʿan taʾwīl āyy al-Qurʾān*. 36 vols. Ed. Muḥammad Aḥmad Shākir and Aḥmad Muḥammad Shākir, 2:34–57. Cairo: Dār al-Maʿārif. 1969.

Thalāth rasāʾil fī iʿjāz al-Qurʾān: Al-Rummānī, al-Khaṭṭābī, al-Jurjānī. Ed. M. A. Khalafallāh and M. Z. Salām. Cairo: Dār al-Maʿārif, 1976.

al-Zamalkānī, Kamāl al-Dīn, ʿAbd al-Waḥid ibn ʿAbd al-Karīm. *al-Burhān al-kāshif ʿan iʿjāz al-Qurʾān*. Ed. Khadīja al-Ḥadīthī and Aḥmad Maṭlūb. Baghdad: al-Jumhūriyya al-ʿIraqiyya, Riʾāsat Diwān al-Awqaf, 1974.

Secondary Sources

ʿAbd al-Raḥmān, ʿĀʾisha. *Al-Tafsīr al-bayānī li'l-Qurʾān*. 2 vols. Cairo: Dār al-Maʿārif, 1990.

Abū Zayd, Naṣr Ḥāmid. *Falsafat al-taʾwīl: dirāsa fī taʾwīl al-Qurʾān ʿinda Muḥyī al-Dīn Ibn ʿArabī*. Beirut: Dār al-Tanwīr, 1993.

Abū Zayd, Naṣr Ḥāmid. *Mafhūm al-naṣṣ: dirāsa fī ʿulūm al-Qurʾān*. Beirut: al-Markaz al-Thaqāfī al-ʿArabī, 1994.

Abū Zayd, Naṣr Ḥāmid. 'The Dilemma of the Literary Approach to the Qur'an', *Alif: Journal of Comparative Poetics* 23, special issue on 'Literature and the Sacred' (2003), 8–47.

Abū Zayd, Naṣr Ḥāmid. *Al-tajdīd wa'l-taḥrīm wa'l- taʾwīl: Bayna al-maʿrifa al-ʿilmiyya wa'l-khawf min al-takfīr*. Beirut: al-Markaz al-Thaqāfī al-ʿArabī, 2010.

ʿArafa, ʿAbd al-ʿAzīz ʿAbd al-Muʿṭī. *Qaḍiyyat al-iʿjāz al-Qurʾānī wa-āthāruhā fī tadwīn al-balāgha al-ʿarabiyya*. Beirut: ʿālam al-Kutub, 1985.

Arkūn, Muḥammad. *Al-Qurʾān: min al-tafsīr al-mawrūth ilā taḥlīl al-khiṭāb al-dīnī*. Trans. Hāshim Ṣāliḥ. Beirut: Dār al-Ṭalīʿa, 2005.

ʿAyyāsh, Mundhir. 'Al-Qurʾān: Iʿjāz am iblās?', *Fuṣūl* 85–6 (Spring/Summer 2013), 15–28.

Boullata, Issa. 'The Rhetorical Interpretation of the Qurʾān: Iʿjāz and Related Topics'. In: Andrew Rippin (ed.). *Approaches to the History of the Interpretation of the Qurʾān*, pp. 139–57. Oxford: Clarendon Press, 1988.

Boullata, Issa J. (ed.). *Literary Structures of Religious Meaning in the Qurʾān*. London: Curzon, 2000.

El-Desouky, Ayman. '*Ego eimi*: *Kerygma* or Existential Metaphor? Frye, Bultmann and the Problem of Demythologizing', *Canadian Review of Comparative Literature/Revue canadienne de littérature comparée* 34/2 (2007), 131–71.

El-Desouky, Ayman. '*Naẓm, Iʿjāz*, Discontinuous Kerygma: Approaching Qur'anic Voice on the Other Side of the Poetic', *Journal of Qur'anic Studies* 15/2 (2013), 1–21.
El-Desouky, Ayman. 'Between Hermeneutic Provenance and Textuality: The Qurʾān and the Question of Method in Approaches to World Literature', Special Issue on the Qur'an and Modern Literature, *Journal of Qur'anic Studies*. (ed.). Helen Blatherwick and Shawkat Toorawah 16/3 (2014), 11–38.
Johns, Anthony. 'A Humanistic Approach to *iʿjāz* in the Qurʾān: The Transfiguration of Language', *Journal of Qurʾānic Studies* 13/1 (2011), 79–99.
Kermani, Navid. 'Revelation in its Aesthetic Dimension'. In: Stefan Wild (ed.). *The Qurʾān as Text*, pp. 214–24. Leiden: E. J. Brill, 1996.
Kermani, Navid. *Gott ist schön: Das ästhetische Erleben des Koran*. Munich: Becck, 1999.
Kermani, Navid. 'Poetry and Language'. In: Andrew Rippin (ed.). *The Blackwell Companion to the Qur'ān*, pp. 107–19. Oxford: Blackwell Publishing Ltd, 2006.
Khalafallāh, M. A. *al-Fann al-qaṣaṣī fī'l-Qurʾān al-karīm*. Cairo: Sīnā li'l-Nashr, 1999.
Larkin, Margaret. 'The Inimitability of the Qurʾān. Two Perspectives', *Religion and Literature* 20 (1988), 31–47.
Levinas, Emmanuel. *Beyond the Verse: Talmudic Readings and Lectures*. Trans. Gary D. Mole. London: Continuum, 1994.
Martin, Richard. 'Inimitability'. In: *Encyclopaedia of the Qurʾān*. 2nd edn. Brill online.
Martin, Richard. 'The Inimitability of the Qurʾān: Two Perspectives', *Religion and Literature* 20 (1988), 31–47.
Martin, Richard. 'The Role of the Baṣrah Muʿtazila in Formulating the Doctrine of the Apologetic Miracle', *Journal of Near Eastern Studies* 39 (1980), 175–89.
Neuwirth, Angelica. *Scripture, Poetry and the Making of a Community: Reading the Qur'an as a Literary Text*. Qur'anic Studies Series. London: Oxford University Press and the Institute of Ismaili Studies, 2014.
al-Rāfiʿī, Muṣṭafā Ṣādiq. *Iʿjāz al-Qurʾān*. Beirut: al-Maktaba al-ʿAṣriyya, 2003.
Rahman, Yusuf. 'The Miraculous Nature of Muslim Scripture: A Study of ʿAbd al-Jabbār's *Iʿjāz al-Qur'ān*', *Islamic Studies* 35/4 (1996), 409–24.
Rippin, Andrew (ed.). *The Blackwell Companion to the Qur'ān*. Oxford: Blackwell Publishing Ltd, 2006.
Sells, Michael. *Approaching the Qur'ān: The Early Revelations*. Ashland, OR: White Cloud Press, 1999; 2007.
Sells, Michael. 'A Literary Approach to the Hymnic Sūras of the Qur'ān: Spirit, Gender, and Aural Intertextuality'. In: Issa J. Boullata (ed.). *Literary Structures of Religious Meaning in the Qurʾān*, pp. 3–25. London: Curzon, 2000.
Shah, Mustafa. 'Classical Islamic Discourse on the Origins of Language: Cultural Memory and the Defense of Orthodoxy', *Numen* 58 (2011), 314–43.
Shah, Mustafa. 'The Word of God: The Epistemology of Language in Classical Islamic Theological Thought'. In: Robert Yelle, Courtney Handman, and Christopher Lehrich (eds.). *Language and Religion*, pp. 158–92. Berlin: De Gruyter Mouton, 2019.
Stewart, Devin J. 'Poetic License in the Qur'an: Ibn al-Ṣāʾigh al-Ḥanafī's *Iḥkām al-rāy fī aḥkām al-āy*', *Journal of Qur'anic Studies* 11/1 (2009), 1–56.
Stewart, Devin J. 'Divine Epithets and the *Dibacchius*: *Clausulae* and Qur'anic Rhythm', *Journal of Qur'anic Studies* 15/2 (2013), 22–64.
Toorawa, Shawkat. 'Modern Arabic Literature and the Qur'an: Creativity, Inimitability... Incompatibilities?' In: Glenda Abramson and Hilary Kilpatrick (eds.). *Religious Perspectives in Modern Muslim and Jewish Literatures*, pp. 239–57. London: RoutledgeCurzon, 2005.

van Ess, Josef. 'Some Fragments of the *muʿāraḍat al-Qurʾān* Attributed to Ibn al-Muqaffaʿ'. In: Wadād al-Qāḍī (ed.). *Studia Arabica et Islamica: Festschrift for Iḥsān ʿAbbās on his Sixtieth Birthday*, pp. 151–63. Beirut: American University of Beirut, 1981.
van Ess, Josef. 'Verbal Inspiration? Language and Revelation in Classical Islamic Theology'. In: Stefan Wild (ed.). *The Qurʾān as Text*, Islamic Philosophy, Theology, and Science: Texts and Studies, 27, pp. 177–94. Leiden: Brill, 1996.
Wild, Stefan (ed.). *The Qurʾān as Text*. Islamic Philosophy, Theology, and Science: Texts and Studies 27. Leiden: E. J. Brill, 1996.
Wild, Stefan (ed.). *Self-Referentiality in the Qurʾān*. Wiesbaden: Harrassowitz Verlag, 2006.

CHAPTER 24

THE QUR'AN AND THE ARABIC MEDIEVAL LITERARY TRADITION

GEERT JAN VAN GELDER

THE UNIQUENESS OF THE QUR'AN

THE medieval Arabic literary tradition, which owes its existence to the revelation of the Qur'an to the Prophet Muḥammad, could not but be influenced heavily and profoundly by it. Even when we take 'literature' in the restricted sense of texts that aim to entertain, delight, and move by their language and style and which are not exclusively scholarly or technical, it would be difficult to find works of some length that do not quote or refer to the holy text. Even in Arabic poetry, which is predominantly secular and profane, there are many such references and allusions.

There is, nevertheless, a paradox: whereas Qur'anic ideas, idioms, expressions and allusions are ubiquitous, the influence of the Qur'an as a 'genre' is slight. This may sound strange; large claims have been made for the opposite. In a recent handbook it is stated that

> The Qur'an has enriched Arabic poetry more than any other Arabic literary genre. Apart from frequent references to qurʾānic verses or images throughout Arabic or Persian literature, the Qur'an liberated Arabic poetry from the narrow framework of existing genres and inspired new approaches to language, imagery and the use of motifs. Conventional standards, and the theoretical analysis of language and literature, can both be traced to the hermeneutics of the Qur'an.
>
> (Graham and Kermani 2006: 131)

However, it can be argued that all these changes in poetry and new approaches in literature were not caused directly by the Qur'an but rather, and overwhelmingly, by the changing nature of society and culture, by the contacts with and adaptations from other civilizations, notably Persian and Graeco-Byzantine, whereas the direct influence of the Qur'an remained relatively minor. This is, firstly, because the Qur'an, being *sui generis*, is not properly a genre (it cannot even properly be called a 'work'),[1] and secondly, because attempts at close imitation of its form and style are considered doomed from the start, as the Qur'an itself pronounces it to be, subsequently confirmed in the Muslim dogma of the inimitability (*iʿjāz*) of the Qur'an. It is true, of course: a perfect imitation cannot equal the original precisely because it is an imitation. This is valid not only for the Qur'an but for any work of literature; and if one, moreover, believes that the text is God's literal speech it is obvious that one cannot but consider it superior to anything else. The uniqueness of the Qur'an is reflected in the usage of key terms: *qurʾān*, 'recited text' or 'recitation' cannot be used for any other recited text or recitation, sura and *āya* cannot be used for any 'chapter' or 'verse', the verb *talā* 'recite' only refers to the Qur'an, and *tafsīr*, 'commentary, exegesis' is but rarely employed for anything but the Qur'an.

Parody of the Inimitable

Among the earliest traces of the impact of the Qur'an is in fact such an attempt at imitation, if the reports about the 'false prophet' Musaylima are authentic. The preserved fragments of his 'anti-Qur'an' may be his or they may have been put into his mouth by his Muslim adversaries, but they are clearly a parody of the Qur'an, using its kind of prose with rhyme and assonance, oaths, and imagery, as in the following 'agricultural, anti-pastoral' passage (al-Ṭabarī, *Tārīkh*, 1:1934, al-Bāqillānī, *Iʿjāz al-Qurʾān*, 157):

> *wa-'l-mubdiyāti zarʿā * wa-'l-ḥāṣidāti ḥaṣdā * wa-'l-dhāriyāti qamḥā * wa-'l-ṭāḥināti ṭaḥnā, * wa-'l-khābizāti khubzā * wa-'l-thāridāti thardā * wa-'l-lāqimāti laqmā * ihālatan wa-samnā * laqad faḍaltum ʿalā ahli 'l-wabar * wa-mā sabaqakum ahlu 'l-madar * rīfukum fa-'mnaʿūh * wa-'l-muʿtarru fa-āwūh * wa-'l-bāghī fa-nāwiʾūh*
>
> By the seed-sowing women * and the crop-reaping women * and the wheat- winnowing women * and the flour-milling women * and the bread-baking women * and the bread-broth-sopping women * and the women gobbling morsels * of fat and butter: * You are better than the dwellers in tents of hair. * Nor do the village dwellers take precedence over you. * Your cultivated fields, defend them! * He who addresses you humbly, harbour him! * And the oppressor, oppose him!

Compare this with, for example, the beginning of sura 100 (*al-ʿĀdiyāt*):

> *wa-'l-ʿādiyāti ḍabḥā * fa-'l-mūriyāti qadḥā * fa-'l-mughīrāti ṣubḥā * fa-atharna bihī naqʿā * fa-wasaṭna bihī jamʿā * inna 'l-insāna li-rabbihī la-kanūd * wa-innahū ʿalā dhālika la-shahīd *...*

[1] Either, from the traditional Muslim point of view, because the Qur'an is uncreated, or, from a non-religious scholarly viewpoint, because it was composed as more or less loose fragments over the course of more than twenty years.

> By the snorting chargers, * by the strikers of fire, * by the dawn-raiders * blazing a trail of dust, * cleaving there with a host! * Surely Man is ungrateful to his Lord, * and surely he is a witness against that! (Arberry's translation).

The passage attributed to Musaylima may be parody and naturally it has been ridiculed by Muslims—a later writer mentions this as an example of the 'amusing nonsensical utterances' (*khuzaʿbilāt*) of Musaylima (al-ʿĀmilī, *Kashkūl*, 634)—but an unbiased reader could perhaps see some literary qualities in it. Some other cases of reputed emulation of the Qur'an are discussed below.

The Qur'anic text is explicit about its rhetorical and 'literary' qualities, not only by the repeated challenges to produce ten suras (11:13–14) or even one (2:23, 10:38), but also when it depicts the effect on the listener as causing a true frisson: (39:23) 'God has sent down the best (or: the finest) discourse (*aḥsana ḥadīthin*) . . . at which the skins of those who fear their Lord shiver'; the *Sūrat Yūsuf* (Joseph) is 'the finest of stories (*aḥsana l-qaṣaṣ*)'. The Qur'an was certainly novel, but whereas novelty may wear off, thorough familiarity never diminished its literary qualities for Muslims through the centuries. The precise nature of its inimitability (*iʿjāz*) became a matter of theological and doctrinal discussions,[2] but the consensus that prevailed in the end was that this inimitability lay in its style and use of language. There are some amusing stories about people who confuse Qur'an with poetry. A Bedouin, hearing verses by Dhū'l-Rumma (d. 117/735), thinks he is reciting the Qur'an (al-Iṣfahānī, *Aghānī*, 18:7); someone quotes a verse by the pre-Islamic poet ʿAdī ibn Zayd when delivering a sermon thinking it is a Qur'anic verse (al-Jarīrī, *Jalīs*, 3:365); the wife of the poet ʿAbd Allāh ibn Rawāḥa, suspecting her husband of adultery, asks him to recite the Qur'an to prove his ritual purity, upon which he fools her by quoting a few pious lines of poetry (Ibn Manẓūr, *Lisān*, s.v. *ʿRḌ*, al-Ḥuṣrī, *Jamʿ*, 38, Ibn ʿAbd al-Barr, *Bahja*, 2:36, etc.); the wife of Abū Lahab, hearing sura 111, thinks that the Prophet has lampooned her in verse (Ibn Hishām, *Sīra*, 1:355–6, trans. Guillaume, 161). But all these anecdotes are intended to show the ignorance of the people involved, who are blind and deaf to what should be obvious.

Qur'an and Poetry

According to an often-quoted saying by al-Aṣmaʿī (d. *c.* 213/828) poetry and religion do not go well together: 'Poetry is harsh (*nakid*); when it is introduced to the Good it becomes weak' (Ibn Qutayba, *Shiʿr*, 305; cf. al-Marzubānī, *Muwashshaḥ*, 85, 90, al-Murtaḍā, *Amālī*, 1:269). He said this when comparing the poetry of the most important of the poets supporting the Prophet and his mission, Ḥassān ibn Thābit, before and after his conversion, adding, 'Ḥassān was among the best poets in pre-Islamic times; but when Islam came his poetry went downhill.' Al-Aṣmaʿī clearly hints at the fact that the

[2] See Chapter 23 in this volume.

often scurrilous and virulent invective in which Ḥassān excelled, but which was frowned upon by the pious early Muslims, was part and parcel of being a good poet. In fact, Ḥassān's pro-Islamic verse preserved more of this invective style than that of his colleagues and was all the more effective for it. Nevertheless, it is true that poetry in general was suspect among many of the pious, for this and other reasons (Bonebakker 1976), not least because the Qur'an itself, in a famous and often-discussed passage (Q. 26:224–7), condemns poets, 'who say what they do not do', even though it excepts 'those who believe and perform good deeds and think of God often'.

While there are many literary traditions in the world in which religious poems are counted among the greatest and most esteemed works, the same cannot be said of Arabic. It may be true that the most popular Arabic poem by far is a religious one, al-Būṣīrī's (d. *c*.694/1294) ode on the Prophet (part of which deals with the Qur'an), yet its fame is found mostly among the devout and is due more to its contents than its poetic qualities, even though it is by no means a bad poem. It is also true that some splendid religious poetry was composed by mystical poets, above all Ibn al-Fāriḍ (d. 632/1235); yet on the whole literary critics and literati would give pride of place to non-religious verse, whether from the pre-Islamic period or later. Treatises on poetics, rhetoric, and stylistics usually ignore religious verse and draw on other genres: panegyric, elegy, love lyric, invective, and descriptive poetry; naturally, they also take their illustrations from the Qur'an.

However, much of the enormous body of 'secular' poetry is influenced by religion and indirectly or directly by the Qur'an. On the level of ideas and doctrines any direct influence is difficult to pinpoint because Islamic beliefs, values, and attitudes do not derive from the Qur'an alone. Influence is easier to discern in allusions and the occurrence of Qur'anic phrases and idioms. A panegyric poem by Bakr ibn al-Naṭṭāḥ (d. *c*. 196/808) on Abū Dulaf, an Abbasid general, contains several such phrases, as Claude France Audebert shows (Audebert 2000: 461–5; Ibn al-Muʿtazz, *Ṭabaqāt*, 223), for instance *ṣārū aʿẓuman nakhirātī* ('they have become decayed bones', cf. Q. 79:11 *a-idhā kunna ʿiẓāman nakhira*) and *wirdu ujāji 'l-shurbi ghayri furātī* ('a watering of bitter drink, not palatable', cf. Q. 25:53 *hādhā ʿadhbun furātun wa-hādhā milḥun ujāj*). Another example is a long poem by a Khārijite poet, composed on the occasion of a battle in 130/748 between the Khārijites and an Umayyad army, which has been studied in detail by Wadād al-Qāḍī (al-Qāḍī 1994: 162–81, *Shiʿr al-Khawārij* n.d.: 223–7, al-Iṣfahānī, *al-Aghānī*, 22:250–4). This battle poem is at the same time secular (it opens with a dialogue between the poet and a woman; it is an elegy on the fallen heroes) and religious, as could be expected from a militant sectarian poet. It refers to the Qur'an (*al-Kitāb*, *al-Dhikr*) and in listing the virtues of the fallen it echoes Qur'anic ideas and diction in numerous places, creatively reshaping the material according to the requirements of metre and rhyme. But in the battle scenes the poet relies much more on the rich poetic tradition in this theme.

Another poetic genre on the borderline of the religious and the secular is gnomic and 'ascetic' (*zuhd*) verse. A prominent representative is Abū'l-ʿAtāhiya (d. 211/826), many of whose ascetic poems are not particularly religious: with their obsession with mortality and the evils of the temporary world, and with surprisingly little about a Hereafter, they could have been composed by an atheist or agnostic. His piety was suspect; he is reported to have said casually that after reciting Qur'an he composed a poem that was even better (al-Iṣfahānī, *Aghānī*, 4:34). But when he does mention the Hereafter the diction and the imagery are inevitably heavily Qur'anic, as in (Abū'l-ʿAtāhiya, *Dīwān*, 291):

Console yourself for the world and its shade,
for in the Garden there is dense shade,
And surely in the Garden there is comfort and
fragrance and repose and (the well called) Salsabīl.[3]

In a long 'cosmological' poem by Ibn al-Shibl al-Baghdādī (d. 474/1081–2) he depicts the end of the world by means of many Qur'anic images and phrases (Ibn Abī Uṣaybiʿa, *ʿUyūn al-anbāʾ*, 2:263–266, Yāqūt, *Muʿjam al-udabāʾ*, 10:24–30):

When the enveloping snatches the sun (cf. Q. 81:1) away from us
and a scattering snatches the night's stars, (Q. 82:2),
And this earth is replaced for us by another earth (Q. 14:48)
and a splitting flings the heavens away (Q. 82:1)
And nursing mothers will be distracted from their children (Q. 22:2)
in their bewilderment, and camels ten-months pregnant
are left untended (Q. 81:4)...

Ibn al-Jawzī condemns the poem for its allegedly heretical content (Ibn al-Jawzī, *Muntaẓam*, 16:214), but it is possible that he also objected to the extreme quasi-quotation, or *iqtibās*, of Qur'anic material, just as Shams al-Dīn al-Ṭībī (d. 717/1317) was blamed for his poem rhyming on *-iyyā*, based on *Sūrat Maryam* (al-Ṣafadī, *Wāfī*, 8:299–300, 30:130–2). Al-Ṣafadī, quoting it, says he does not mind such versification of Qur'anic phrases when it concerns one or two *āyas*, but applying it to a complete sura he finds rather in bad taste. The phenomenon of *iqtibās* in prose and poetry was discussed in detail and at length, and its frivolous use, in improper context, often twisting the original sense, was naturally condemned in strong terms, even though it is by no means uncommon (Macdonald and Bonebakker 1970; Gilliot 2000; van Gelder 2002–3). A humorous example, relatively innocent, is the use of Qur'anic sentences in a dialogue about food (al-Baghdādī, *Taṭfīl*, 121, trans. al-Baghdadi, *Selections*, 82–4; on the Qur'an in jocular contexts see also Tamer 2009: 24–8).

Later 'imitations'

Such quotations, even when on a large scale, do not amount to a wholesale imitation of the Qur'an, or an attempt to emulate or even surpass it, which would of course be considered blasphemous. The fragments attributed to the 'false prophet' Musaylima have

[3] cf. Q. 4:57 *wa-nudkhiluhum ẓillan ẓalīlā*, 56:89 *fa-rawḥun wa-rayḥānun wa-jannatu naʿīm*, 76:18 *ʿaynan fīhā tusammā salsabīlā*.

been mentioned above; later names of those who are reputed to have made similar attempts include the important prose writer Ibn al-Muqaffaʿ (d. *c.*137/755), the celebrated poet al-Mutanabbī (d. 354/965), and the maverick poet and prose writer Abū'l-ʿAlāʾ al-Maʿarrī (d. 449/1057). Some fragments attributed to Ibn al-Muqaffaʿ read very much like a pastiche of Qur'anic phrases and formulas (van Ess 1981). Al-Mutanabbī earned his nickname, 'the would-be prophet', to his youthful exploits among Qarmaṭī sectarian Bedouin tribes (Heinrichs 1990); an example of his 'Qur'an' is (al-Tanūkhī, *Nishwār*, 8:198–200):

> *wa-'l-najmi 'l-sayyār * wa-'l-falaki 'l-dawwār * wa-'l-layli wa-'l-nahār * inna 'l-kāfira la-fī akhṭār * imḍi ʿalā sabīlaka wa-'qfu athara man kāna qablaka mina 'l-mursalīn fa-inna 'llāha qāmiʿun bika zaygha man alḥada fī dīnihī wa-ḍalla ʿan sabīlihī*
>
> By the moving Star[4] * and the revolving Sphere * and day and night * the unbeliever is truly in danger *. Go forth on your path and follow the tracks of those who were sent before you. God will subdue, through you, the aberration of those who deviated from His religion and went astray from His path.

It has often been said that with his *al-Fuṣūl wa'l-ghāyāt* (Paragraphs and periods) al-Maʿarrī intended to surpass the Qur'an; the title is said to be modelled on *suwar*, 'suras' and *āyāt*, 'Qur'anic verses' (Peltz 2013: 1:16, 20–1). This collection of pious, homiletic texts is composed in an extremely ornate and often obscure style, employing *sajʿ* (prose rhyme) on different levels; the author regularly interrupts the text with passages (tellingly called *tafsīr*) containing an explanation of the difficult words. It is true that in rhetorical artifice, variety of vocabulary, style, and imagery, this work indeed far surpasses anything found in the Qur'an; it is not surprising that the combination of form and content led people to believe that al-Maʿarrī, notorious for his heterodox views, consciously sought to surpass the holy text (Peltz 2013: 1:20–4). What is clear, however, is that the 'imitations' attributed to Ibn al-Muqaffaʿ, al-Mutanabbī, and al-Maʿarrī are in no way intended to polemicise against the Qur'an or Islam. It is true, however, that the last-mentioned, especially in some of his poems, shows himself to be critical of accepted doctrines and the authority of the Qur'an, as when he says—and one should be aware that the Qur'anic word *furqān* is often taken to refer to the Qur'an itself—(al-Maʿarrī, *Luzūmiyyāt*, 2:183; cf. Nicholson 1921: 174),

> Religion, unbelief, related stories,
> a fixed Revelation (*furqān yunaṣṣu*), a Torah, a Gospel:
> In every generation there are falsehoods (*abāṭīl*) judged to be true.
> Was there ever a generation that was the sole possessor of true guidance?

Al-Maʿarrī's most famous work is his *Risālat al-ghufrān* (Epistle of forgiveness), in which he imagines how his correspondent, the pedantic and self-righteous Ibn al-Qāriḥ, after the Resurrection, has reached Paradise (with some difficulty) and has many discussions,

4 *Al-najm* often refers specifically to the Pleiades.

mostly with poets and grammarians, in heaven and, peeping down into hell (cf. Q.7: 47–51), with its inhabitants, including Satan. With his descriptions of Paradise, with rivers of wine, fowls that offer themselves to be roasted or marinated, and beautiful damsels either growing from trees or having been rewarded for a pious life on earth, it is fairly obvious that al-Maʿarrī is mocking popular beliefs about the Hereafter (he seems to have been very sceptical of the bodily resurrection). Nevertheless, he does not include any description that cannot not found either in the many Qur'anic depictions of heaven and hell or in widely accepted traditional accounts. Needless to say, the work also contains many Qur'anic quotations.

In spite of the many clear references and partial quotations of the Qur'an in poetry, especially in gnomic and 'ascetic' verse (*ḥikma*, *zuhd*), in general poetry kept a certain distance from religion. For religious purposes various prose forms were preferred, such as the sermon (*khuṭba*) and the treatise or epistle (*risāla*). Poets continued pre-Islamic usages such as railing against *al-dahr* ('Fate') or *al-zamān* ('Time') even though the pious might argue that this smacks of blasphemy since reviling Fate amounts to blaming God. Whereas it is customary for Muslims to open any speech or text with 'in the name of God the Merciful, the Compassionate', some people frowned on writing this formula before a poem, as the poet and critic Ibn Rashīq al-Qayrawānī (d. 456/1063 or 463/1071) said (Ibn Rashīq, *ʿUmda*, 2:309). Another poet and critic (and *qāḍī* or religious judge), ʿAlī ibn ʿAbd al-ʿAzīz al-Jurjānī (d. 392/1002) defended al-Mutanabbī, attacked for some doctrinally dubious verses, by stating that poets should not be condemned as poets because of showing their irreligiosity in their verse, or else the names of the pre-Islamic poets or Abū Nuwās should be wiped from all literary records (al-Jurjānī, *Wasāṭa*, 64): 'Religion is detached from poetry (*al-dīn bi-maʿzil ʿan al-shiʿr*).' But one has to qualify this bald statement: it applies to the critical appreciation of poetry rather than to poetry itself, for the detachment between the two domains is by no means strict. Abū Nuwās certainly produced much excellent verse that is deplorable from a Muslim, religious point of view, what with the abundance of Bacchic, homoerotic, and obscene poems in his collected works, but even in those poems he often refers to the Qur'an (Kennedy 1997; Montgomery et al. 1994).

Qur'an and Literary Criticism

Moreover, in the extensive body of literary criticism, poetics, rhetoric, and literary stylistics (fields that are difficult to distinguish and which combine in various shapes) the Qur'an has an important place and to some extent lies at its origins: in order to explain puzzling expressions in the Qur'an, in particular those referring to God in anthropomorphic terms, some exegetes and commentators developed ideas about figurative language and metaphor. Thus Ibn Qutayba (d. 276/889), who was a religious scholar as well as a literary critic and a philologist, wrote *Ta'wīl mushkil al-Qur'ān* ('Explanation of Problematic Passages in the Qur'an') which contains sections on *istiʿāra* ('metaphor'), *majāz* (roughly 'figurative speech'),[5] and *kināya wa-taʿrīḍ* (approximately, 'metonymy and allusion'). The Abbasid prince ʿAbd Allāh ibn al-Muʿtazz (d. 247/908), an important poet, wrote a short but seminal work on figures of speech, *al-Badīʿ*. It is obvious that he was chiefly interested in poetry: he was inspired to write his treatise by the 'novel' (*badīʿ*) traits in 'modern' poets such as Abū Tammām (d. 232/845), but for the main figures that he discusses he also provides Qur'anic illustrations. This became standard in the many subsequent works on literary criticism and stylistics. One of these, *Kitāb al-Ṣināʿatayn al-kitāba wa-'l-shiʿr* (The two arts: Epistolography and poetry) by Abū Hilāl al-ʿAskarī (d. after 395/1005) is written for would-be prose writers and poets, or anyone with literary interests; but on the first page he justifies his writing of the book by saying that 'after knowledge of God, praised be He, the discipline most worthy of study is the knowledge of eloquence (*balāgha*) and elocution (*faṣāḥa*), with which one gets to know the inimitability (*iʿjāz*) of the Book of God the Exalted' (al-ʿAskarī, *Ṣināʿatayn*, 7). He may merely be paying lip-service to the primacy of the Qur'an, but it demonstrates the importance of the Qur'an in literary studies, for by Abū Hilāl's time the idea of the Qur'an's stylistic uniqueness and inimitability had crystallized to a dogma, through such works as *al-Nukat fī iʿjāz al-Qurʾān* by al-Rummānī (d. 384/994) and *Iʿjāz al-Qurʾān* by al-Bāqillānī (d. 403/1013).

These works discuss the figures of speech and tropes, yet state that the unique character of the Qur'an cannot be explained merely in these terms. Obviously, many literary works are far more 'artful', in their verbal and rhetorical brilliance and ingenuity, than the Qur'an and therefore its inimitability should not be sought there. This did not prevent scholars from devoting works to the figures and tropes in the Qur'an. Ibn Abī'l-Iṣbaʿ (d. 654/1256), author of a general work on *badīʿ* entitled *Taḥrīr al-taḥbīr* (which contains the usual share of Qur'anic examples) also wrote a book especially devoted to the Qur'an, *Badīʿ al-Qurʾān*. It lists 109 different figures, slightly fewer than *Taḥrīr al-taḥbīr*, which has 125 chapters, for some figures are said not to occur in the Qur'an, such as *al-hazl alladhī yurādu bihi 'l-jidd*, 'jesting with a serious purport', varieties of hyperbole or exaggeration (*ighrāq*, *ghuluww*), or some figures involving poetic prosody. A somewhat similar work also on *badīʿ* in the Qur'an, published as *al-Fawāʾid* and attributed to Ibn Qayyim al-Jawziyya (d. 751/1350) but in fact the introduction to a Qur'anic commentary by Ibn al-Naqīb (d. 698/1298), goes even further in identifying in the Qur'an several literary themes and modes such as praise and blame, lament, and love (*ghazal* and *tashbīb*, terms usually reserved for poetry, but here applied to the description of women in Paradise).

Qur'an and Literary Anthologies

It is clear that in spite of the Qur'an's unique character it was incorporated in literary and stylistic studies. It has a regular place in literary anthologies. The famous collection of

[5] Before him, the philologist Abū ʿUbayda (d. 209/824) had used the term *majāz* in a somewhat broader sense in his *Majāz al-Qurʾān*, which deals with difficult and idiomatic expressions.

stories with a happy ending, *al-Faraj baʿd al-shidda* (*Relief after Distress*) by al-Muḥassin al-Tanūkhī (d. 384/994), opens with a chapter on the Qur'anic stories about the prophets from Adam to Muḥammad (al-Tanūkhī, *Faraj*, 1:59–108). Their stories are not told in any detail and the most prominent example of a happily ending story in the Qur'an, that of Jacob/Yaʿqūb and Joseph/Yūsuf, is summarized in a few lines. For nicely fleshed-out versions of this and similar stories one should turn to the genre of *qiṣaṣ al-anbiyāʾ*, 'the stories of the prophets'. The most famous example is that by al-Thaʿlabī (d. 427/1035), which he composed as a kind of background literature to his Qur'anic commentary. The large anthology of literary prose compiled by al-Ābī (d. 421/1030), entitled *Nathr al-durr* (A scattering of pearls),[6] is largely a secular work. It includes long chapters that are basically a series of jokes and amusing anecdotes, but it also contains serious matter and it naturally begins with a chapter on the Qur'an (al-Ābī, *Nathr*, 1:29–150), thematically subdivided into forty-one sections, so that a reader can easily find, for instance, 55 passages on 'injustice' (*ẓulm*) or 24 passages on 'fortitude, patience' (*ṣabr*). Such combinations and stark juxtapositions of secular (sometimes even irreligious) and Qur'anic material is common. Many scholars combined in themselves the qualities of the *ʿālim* (the religious scholar) and the *adīb* (the basically secular 'man of letters'). Two founders of Arabic prose style and prose genres, al-Jāḥiẓ (d. 255/868–9) and Ibn Qutayba (d. 276/889), in spite of the great differences between their outlooks and styles, already exemplify this trend. The same combination of the secular and the religious can be seen in many works that belong to the interesting genre called *amālī* ('dictations') or *majālis* ('sessions'), lectures and lecture notes written down by teachers or sometimes their students. They tend to be rather disordered, without clear progression or structure, and they often jump from topic to topic. Al-Sharīf al-Murtaḍā (d. 436/1044), Shīʿī and Muʿtazilī scholar and poet, at least gave some structure to his *Dictations*, for he opens each of his eighty sessions with Qur'anic exegesis, followed by anything that takes his fancy, be it a discussion of poetry, historical events, anecdotes, or of prophetic tradition (hadith).

The Omnipresence of Qur'an in Prose and Poetry

The Qur'an is present in all forms of literary Arabic prose. A detailed study (al-Qāḍī 1993) of the epistles of another founder of Arabic prose, ʿAbd al-Ḥamīd ibn Yaḥyā (d. 132/749) discusses the quotations and how they are fitted in, the allusions, rephrasings, amplifications, and reductions of Qur'anic material. Narrative literature is replete with references to the Qur'an, either by means of direct quotation or through allusions to motifs and stories, sometimes obviously and at other times more obliquely. Thus al-Hamadhānī's entertaining *maqāma* on the dish called *maḍīrah* may have been modelled to some

[6] The word *nathr*, literally 'scattering', is also the technical term for 'prose' as contrasted with *naẓm* ('stringing' and 'verse').

extent on the story of Yūsuf/Joseph of the twelfth sura (Hämeen-Anttila 2002: 112–14; for the many references to the Qur'an in al-Ḥarīrī's *Maqāmāt* see Zakharia 1987). What is valid for the *maqāma* is equally valid for less consciously artful narratives such as those of the *Thousand and One Nights*.

It was mentioned above that al-Būṣīrī's famous *al-Burda* (Mantle ode) contains a passage in praise of the Qur'an, in the context of the Prophet's miracles (see e.g. Stetkevych 2010: 121–7). A very different, possibly unique, kind of poetry inspired by the Qur'an is found in the extensive *Dīwān* (collected poems) by the great mystical writer Ibn al-ᶜArabī (d. 638/1240), who composed a series of poems inspired by the Qur'an, or more precisely by the 'spirit' (*rūḥ*) of the individual suras (Ibn al-ᶜArabī, *Dīwān*, 130–70, McAuley 2012: 59–92). One or more poems are devoted to each of the 114 suras; one poem is on the 'mysterious letters' that open some suras. Whatever these often baffling poems contain, they are certainly neither straightforward poetic paraphrases of the Qur'anic material, nor attempts to rival the holy text; rather, they are mystical effusions that demonstrate one extreme of the extraordinary range of Qur'anic influence on Arabic literature.

Bibliography

Primary Sources

al-Ābī, Abū Saᶜd Manṣur ibn al-Ḥusayn. *Nathr al-durr*. 7 vols. Ed. Muḥammad ᶜAlī Qurana, Cairo: al-Hayʾa al-Miṣriyya al-ᶜĀmma, 1980–90.

Abū 'l-ᶜAtāhiya. *Dīwān*. Ed. Shukrī Fayṣal. Beirut: Maktabat Dār al-Mallāḥ, n.d.

Abū ᶜUbayda. *Majāz al-Qurʾān*. 2 vols. Ed. Fuʾād Sazkīn (Fuat Sezgin). Cairo: Maktabat al-Khānjī, 1955, 1962.

al-ᶜĀmilī, Bahāʾ al-Dīn. *Al-Kashkūl*. Beirut: Dār al-Kitāb al-Lubnānī, 1983.

al-ᶜAskarī, Abū Hilāl. *Kitāb al-Ṣināᶜatayn al-kitāba wa-'l-shiᶜr*. Ed. ᶜAlī Muḥammad al-Bajāwī. Cairo: ᶜĪsā al-Bābī al-Ḥalabī, 1971.

al-Baghdadi, al-Khatib. *Selections from the Art of Party-Crashing in Medieval Iraq*. Trans. Emily Selove. New York: Syracuse University Press, 2012.

al-Baghdādī, al-Khaṭīb. *Al-Taṭfīl wa-ḥikāyāt al-ṭufayliyyīn wa-akhbāruhum wa-nawādiruhum wa-ashᶜāruhum*. Ed. ᶜAbd Allāh ᶜAbd al-Raḥīm ᶜUsaylān. Jedda: Dār al-Madanī, 1986.

al-Bāqillānī. *Iᶜjāz al-Qurʾān*. Ed. al-Sayyid Aḥmad Ṣaqr. Cairo: Dār al-Maᶜārif, 1963.

al-Ḥuṣrī, *Jamᶜ al-jawāhir fī 'l-mulaḥ wa-'l-nawādir*. Ed. ᶜAlī Muḥammad al-Bajāwī, repr. Beirut, 1987.

Ibn ᶜAbd al-Barr. *Bahjat al-majālis wa-uns al-mujālis*. 2 vols. Ed. Muḥammad Mursī al-Khūlī. Beirut: Dār al-Kutub al-ᶜIlmiyya, 1981–2.

Ibn Abī 'l-Iṣbaᶜ al-Miṣrī. *Taḥrīr al-taḥbīr fī ṣināᶜat al-shiᶜr wa-'l-nathr wa-bayān iᶜjāz al-Qurʾān*. Ed. Ḥifnī Muḥammad Sharaf. Cairo: Lajnat Iḥyāʾ al-Turāth al-Islāmī, [1963].

Ibn Abī 'l-Iṣbaᶜ al-Miṣrī. *Badīᶜ al-Qurʾān*. Ed. Ḥifnī Muḥammad Sharaf. Cairo: Maktabat Nahḍat Miṣr, 1957.

Ibn Abī Uṣaybiᶜa. *ᶜUyūn al-anbāʾ fī ṭabaqāt al-aṭibbāʾ*. 5 vols. Ed. ᶜĀmir al-Najjār. Cairo: Dār al-Maᶜārif/al-Hayʾa al-Miṣriyya al-ᶜĀmma, 1996–2001.

Ibn al-ᶜArabī, Abū Bakr Muḥyī 'l-Dīn. *Dīwān*. Ed. Aḥmad Ḥasan Basaj. Beirut: Dār al-Kutub al-ᶜIlmiyya, 1996.

Ibn Hishām. *Al-Sīra al-nabawiyya*. 2 vols. Ed. Muṣṭafā al-Saqqā, Ibrāhīm al-Abyārī, and ʿAbd al-Ḥafīẓ Shalabī. Cairo: Muṣṭafā al-Bābī al-Ḥalabī, 1955.
[Ibn Hishām] *The Life of Muhammad. A Translation of Isḥāq's* [*sic*] Sīrat Rasūl Allāh. Trans. with an introduction and notes by A. Guillaume. Karachi: Oxford University Press, 1955.
Ibn Isḥāq *see* [Ibn Hishām]
Ibn al-Jawzī. *Al-Muntaẓam*. Ed. Muḥammad ʿAbd al-Qādir ʿAṭā and Muṣṭafā ʿAbd al-Qādir ʿAṭā. 19 vols. Beirut: Dār al-Kutub al-ʿIlmiyya, 1992–3.
Ibn Manẓūr. *Lisān al-ʿArab*. 20 vols. Cairo: al-Dār al-Miṣriyya li-l-Taʾlīf wa-ʾl-Tarjama, n.d. (= repr. ed. Būlāq, AH 1308).
Ibn al-Muʿtazz, ʿAbd Allāh. *Al-Badīʿ*. Ed. Ignatius Kratchkovsky. London: Luzac, 1935.
Ibn al-Muʿtazz, ʿAbd Allāh. *Ṭabaqāt al-shuʿarāʾ*. Ed. ʿAbd al-Sattār Aḥmad Farrāj. Cairo: Dār al-Maʿārif, 1968.
Ibn al-Naqīb, Muḥammad ibn Sulaymān. *Muqaddimat Tafsīr Ibn al-Naqīb fī ʿilm al-bayān wa'l-maʿānī wa'l-badīʿ wa-iʿjāz al-Qur'ān*. Ed. Zakariyyā Saʿīd ʿAlī. Cairo: Maktabat al-Khānjī, 1995.
Ibn Qayyim al-Jawziyya (attrib.). *Kitāb al-fawāʾid al-mushawwiq ilā ʿulūm al-Qurʾān wa-ʿilm al-bayān*. Ed. Muḥammad Badr al-Dīn al-Naʿsānī. Cairo: al-Khānjī, n.d.
Ibn Qutayba. *Al-Shiʿr wa-ʾl-shuʿarāʾ*. 2 vols. Ed. Aḥmad Muḥammad Shākir. Cairo: Dār al-Maʿārif, 1966–7.
Ibn Qutayba. *Taʾwīl mushkil al-Qurʾān*. Ed. al-Sayyid Aḥmad Ṣaqr. Cairo: ʿĪsā al-Bābī al-Ḥalabī, [1954].
Ibn Rashīq. *Al-ʿUmda fī maḥāsin al-shiʿr wa-ādābihi wa-naqdih*. 2 vols. Ed. Muḥammad Muḥyī ʾl-Dīn ʿAbd al-Ḥamīd. Beirut: Dār al-Jīl, 1972.
al-Iṣfahānī, Abū ʾl-Faraj. *Al-Aghānī*. 24 vols. Cairo: Dār al-Kutub/al-Hayʾa al-Miṣriyya al-ʿĀmma, 1927–74.
al-Jarīrī, al-Muʿāfā ibn Zakariyyāʾ. *Al-Jalīs al-ṣāliḥ al-kāfī wa-ʾl-anīs al-nāṣiḥ al-shāfī*. 4 vols. Ed. Muḥammad Mursī al-Khūlī and Iḥsān ʿAbbās. Beirut: ʿĀlam al-Kutub, 1993.
al-Jurjānī, al-Qāḍī ʿAlī ibn ʿAbd al-ʿAzīz. *Al-Wasāṭa bayn al-Mutanabbī wa-khuṣūmihi*. Ed. Muḥammad Abū ʾl-Faḍl Ibrāhīm and ʿAlī Muḥammad al-Bajāwī. Cairo: Dār Iḥyāʾ al-Kutub al-ʿArabiyya, n.d.
al-Maʿarrī, Abū ʾl-ʿAlāʾ. *Al-Luzūmiyyāt*. 2 vols. Ed. Amīn ʿAbd al-ʿAzīz al-Khānjī. Cairo: Maktabat al-Khānjī, AH 1342.
al-Maʿarrī, Abū ʾl-ʿAlāʾ. *Risālat al-ghufrān/The Epistle of Forgiveness*, vol. 1: *A Vision of Heaven and Hell*. Ed. and trans. Geert Jan van Gelder and Gregor Schoeler, New York: New York University Press, 2013.
al-Marzubānī, Muḥammad b. ʿImrān. *Al-Muwashshaḥ fī maʾākhidh al-ʿulamāʾ ʿalā ʾl-shuʿarāʾ*. Ed. ʿAlī Muḥammad al-Bijāwī. Cairo: Dār Nahḍat Miṣr, 1965.
al-Murtaḍā, ʿAlī ibn al-Ḥusayn al-Sharīf. *Al-Amālī (Ghurar al-fawāʾid wa-durar al-qalāʾid)*. 2 vols. Ed. Muḥammad Abū ʾl-Faḍl Ibrāhīm. Cairo: ʿĪsā al-Bābī al-Ḥalabī, 1954.
al-Ṣafadī. *Al-Wāfī bi-ʾl-Wafayāt*. 30 vols. Beirut, Wiesbaden, and Berlin: Franz Steiner—Klaus Schwarz, 1931–2005.
Shiʿr al-Khawārij. Collected and ed. Iḥsān ʿAbbās. Beirut: Dār al-Thaqāfa, n.d. (date of preface: 1974).
al-Ṭabarī, Muḥammad ibn Jarīr. *Tārīkh Tārīkh al-rusul wa-ʾl-mulūk*. 3 vols. Ed. M. J. de Goeje et al. Leiden: Brill, 1879–1901.
al-Tanūkhī, al-Muḥassin ibn ʿAlī. *Al-Faraj baʿd al-shidda*. 5 vols. Ed. ʿAbbūd al-Shāljī. Beirut: Dār Ṣādir, 1978.

al-Tanūkhī, al-Muḥassin ibn ʿAlī. *Nishwār al-muḥāḍara*. 8 vols. Ed. ʿAbbūd al-Shāljī. Beirut: Dār Ṣādir, 1973.

al-Thaʿlabī, Abū Isḥāq Aḥmad ibn Muḥammad. *Qiṣaṣ al-anbiyāʾ (ʿArūs al-majālis)*. Cairo: Dār Iḥyāʾ al-Kutub al-ʿArabiyya, n.d.

al-Thaʿlabī, Abū Isḥāq Aḥmad ibn Muḥammad. *ʿArāʾis al-majālis fī qiṣaṣ al-anbiyāʾ, or 'Lives of the Prophets'*. Trans. and annotated by William M. Brinner. Leiden: Brill, 2002.

Yāqūt. *Muʿjam al-udabāʾ*. 20 vols. Ed. Aḥmad Farīd Rifāʿī. Cairo, 1936–8, repr. Beirut: Iḥyāʾ al-Turāth al-ʿArabī, n.d.

Secondary Sources

Audebert, Claude France. 'Emprunts faits au Coran par quelques poètes de IIe/VIIIe siècle', *Arabica* 47 (2000), 457–77.

Bonebakker, S. A. 'Religious Prejudice Against Poetry in Early Islam'. In: Paul Maurice Clogan (Ed.). *Medievalia et Humanistica: Studies in Medieval and Renaissance Culture*. NS 7: *Medieval Poetics*, pp. 77–99. Cambridge: Cambridge University Press, 1976.

Gilliot, Claude. 'Un florilège coranique: le *Iqtibās min al-Qurʾān* de Abū Manṣūr al-Ṯaʿālibī (*ob.* 430/*init.* 3 oct. 1038 ou 429)', *Arabica* 47 (2000), 488–500.

Graham, William A. and Navid Kermani. 'Recitation and Aesthetic Reception'. In: Jane Dammen McAuliffe (ed.). *The Cambridge Companion to the Qurʾān*, pp. 115–41. Cambridge: Cambridge University Press, 2006.

Hämeen-Anttila, Jaakko. *Maqama: A History of a Genre*. Wiesbaden: Harrassowitz, 2002.

Heinrichs, Wolfhart. 'The Meaning of *Mutanabbī*'. In: James L. Kugel (ed.). *Poetry and Prophecy: The Beginnings of a Literary Tradition*, pp. 120–39, 231–9. Ithaca, NY: Cornell University Press, 1990.

Kennedy, Philip F. *The Wine Song in Classical Arabic Poetry: Abū Nuwās and the Literary Tradition*. Oxford: Oxford University Press, 1997.

Macdonald, D. B. and S. A. Bonebakker. 'Iḳtibās'. In: *Encyclopaedia of Islam*, second edition. 13 vols., 3:1091–2 (fascicle published in 1970). Leiden: Brill, 1960–2009).

McAuley, Denis E. *Ibn ʿArabī's Mystical Poetics*. Oxford: Oxford University Press, 2012.

Montgomery, J. E. et al. 'Revelry and Remorse: A Poem of Abū Nuwās', *Journal of Arabic Literature* 25/2 (1994), 116–34.

Nicholson, Reynold A. 'The Meditations of Maʿarrī'. In: Reynold A. Nicholson (ed.). *Studies in Islamic Poetry*, pp. 43–289. Cambridge: Cambridge University Press, 1921, repr. 1979.

Peltz, Christian. *Der Koran des Abū l-ʿAlāʾ. Teil 1: Materialien und Überlegungen zum K. al-Fuṣūl wa-l-ġāyāt des al-Maʿārrī; Teil 2: Glossar*. Wiesbaden: Harrassowitz, 2013.

al-Qāḍī, Wadād. 'The Impact of the Qurʾān on the Epistolography of ʿAbd al-Ḥamīd'. In: G. R. Hawting and Abdul-Kader A. Shareef (eds.). *Approaches to the Qurʾān*, pp. 285–313. London: Routledge, 1993.

al-Qāḍī, Wadād. 'The Limitations of Qurʾānic Usage in Early Arabic Poetry: The Example of a Khārijite Poem'. In: Wolfhart Heinrichs und Gregor Schoeler (eds.). *Festschrift Ewald Wagner zum 65. Geburtstag. Band 2: Studien zur arabischen Dichtung*, pp. 162–81. Beirut and Stuttgart: Franz Steiner, 1994.

Stetkevych, Suzanne Pinckney. *The Mantle Odes: Arabic Praise Poems to the Prophet Muḥammad*. Bloomington and Indianapolis: Indiana University Press, 2010.

Tamer, Georges, 'The Qurʾān and Humor'. In: Georges Tamer (ed.). *Humor in der arabische Kultur/Humor in Arabic Culture*, pp. 3–28. Berlin and New York: Walter de Gruyter, 2009.

van Ess, J. 'Some Fragments of the *muʿāraḍat al-Qurʾān* Attributed to Ibn al-Muqaffaʿ'. In: *Studia Arabica et Islamica: Festschrift for Iḥsān ʿAbbās on his sixtieth birthday*, pp. 151–63. Beirut: American University of Beirut, 1981.
van Gelder, Geert Jan. 'Forbidden Firebrands: Frivolous *iqtibās* (Quotation from the Qurʾān)'. *Quaderni di Studi Arabi* 20–1 (2002–3), 3–16.
Zakharia, Katia. 'Les Références coraniques dans les *Maqāmāt* d'al-Ḥarīrī: éléments d'une lecture sémiologique', *Arabica* 34 (1987), 275–86.

CHAPTER 25

THE QUR'AN AND ARABIC POETRY

STEFAN SPERL

THE relationship between the Qur'an and Arabic poetry is rich, complex, and enduring. It ranges from antagonism and ambivalence to mutually reinforcing interdependence, has gone through many phases, and remains to this day a pivotal aspect of poetic writing. In the absence of a full-length study, its range and significance can only be gleaned through a limited number of articles and the references to the Qur'an which figure in much secondary literature on Arabic poetry.

This chapter is a preliminary attempt to identify some of the most salient aspects of this relationship.[1] The focus is on three historical periods: the early first/seventh century, which saw the genesis of the Qur'an and its confrontation with pre-Islamic poetry; the medieval period, starting from the third/ninth century, when a new style arose which brought classical Arabic poetry to its apogee; and the modern period, starting from the outbreak of the First World War up to the present, when poetry is transformed in the wake of European colonial dominance. The available material is so vast and varied that only a limited number of sources could be selected for reference. The resulting observations cannot but be tentative and must await verification by a more detailed study. They are intended to illustrate the diverse range of poetic responses to the Qur'an over this long period, as well as the persistence of certain themes which re-emerge throughout in ever new guises.

Poetry and Prophecy

Pre-Islamic poetry is a very substantial body of high-quality verse which was collected and edited by Muslim philologists more than a century after the rise of Islam. Its mainstay is the *qaṣīda*, a polythematic mono-rhymed ode (on its origin and significance see

[1] This chapter is to be read in conjunction with Geert Jan van Gelder's chapter in this volume, which also discusses poetry.

inter alia Hamori 1974; Stetkevych 1993; Jakobi 1996; and Montgomery 1997). Its themes and literary form appear to have very little in common with the Qur'an, a fact which helps to explain why studies of pre-Islamic poetry and Qur'anic studies have for long existed side by side with relatively little overlap. The disconnect between the two types of text was deepened further by the suggestion put forward early last century by Margoliouth and Ṭāhā Ḥussain that pre-Islamic poetry was a later forgery. While their theory has been largely abandoned, doubts about the authenticity of the corpus have continued to persist.

One counter-argument to the forgery thesis has always been that the notion of poetry figures quite prominently in the Qur'an. The text emphasizes repeatedly that Muḥammad is not a poet and in one instance launches a much discussed attack on poets about which more will be said below. So poetry clearly existed, but what evidence is there to prove that it was the pre-Islamic poetry transmitted by later sources? This question has been newly addressed in recent scholarship. Thomas Bauer (2010) argues that Qur'anic diction deliberately avoids any semblance with the form, style, or content of the poetry of its time. As a result of this 'negative intertextuality', a text came into being which 'is, in many ways, the complete antithesis of contemporary poetry' (2010: 705–6). Bauer points out, however, that there are instances where the Qur'an, in a tone of disparagement, appears to evoke phrases found in pre-Islamic verse. These passages suggest that the poetry from which the Qur'an seeks to distance the Prophet is indeed identical with the type of verse collected and transmitted by the Arabic tradition.

Bauer's findings corroborate the work of earlier scholars, notably Toshihiko Izutsu (1959), who have argued that the Qur'anic message was intended to overcome the tribalist ethos of pre-Islamic Arabia. It centred on the concept of *muruwwa*, a term akin to the Latin *virtus* since it conjoins the notions of manliness and virtuous behaviour. Echoing Hamori (1974: 3–30) and Montgomery (1986), Neuwirth describes *muruwwa* as 'excessive hospitality, extravagance, grandiloquence, boastful attachment to one's tribe and extreme prowess in battle' and notes that 'it was particularly powerful due its artistic representation in the most prestigious literary genre, the ancient Arabic *qaṣīda*' (2014: 76). Having, like Bauer, established poetry as the repository of the ethos to which the Qur'an is opposed, Neuwirth repeatedly highlights how standard poetic themes are countered and implicitly nullified by passages in the Qur'an. Thus the transitory bliss of lost love conjured up by the *nasīb*, the erotic prelude of the *qaṣīda*, is inverted by the 'counter-image of everlasting bliss' and amorous delight granted to the souls in Paradise (2014: 79).[2] Similarly, the *aṭlāl*, the ruins of the abandoned campsite bemoaned by the pre-Islamic poet, have a superior Qur'anic counterpart in the *umam khāliya*, the communities destroyed by divine retribution (2014: 26). These and numerous other examples in Neuwirth's work show that in the Qur'an, a pessimistic, anthropocentric world-view internalized by the tribal ethos of *muruwwa* and voiced through the medium of

[2] A similar observation is also made by Duraković (2015: 129–36). His study on *The Poetics of Ancient and Classical Arabic Literature* contains much relevant material on the interface between the Qur'ann and poetry.

poetry is effectively and deliberately countered by a theocentric vision in which the individual is answerable only to God and faced with the prospect of eternal punishment or reward.

The crucial role of pre-Islamic poetry as a 'foil' to the Qur'anic 'fact' is further documented in the writings of Georges Tamer and Ghassan El Masri, where a more differentiated picture arises. Tamer uses the Qur'anic concept of *dahr* (time) to probe the 'deep connection between pre-Islamic poetry and the Qur'an' and to demonstrate that both emanate from 'the Hellenistic context of Late Antiquity' (2011: 24). In a similar vein, El Masri's study of poetry and Qur'anic eschatology (2015) demonstrates that a more precise understanding of pivotal Qur'anic terms such as *al-ākhira* (the hereafter) can be obtained by recourse to pre-Islamic verse. In a more recent study he uses the pervasive interface between a pre-Islamic poem and the Qur'an as evidence that 'pre-Islamic poetry can play a major role in revealing the intellectual situation of the first audience of the Qur'an' (El Masri 2017: 97). Commenting on the authenticity debate, El Masri concludes that pre-Islamic poems are not forgeries but result from 'a selective act of cultural reclamation' largely determined by 'the poetry's thematic relevance to the Qur'an' (El Masri 2017: 128).

With the recent work of Bauer, Neuwirth, and El Masri, a scholarly consensus emerges which confirms Kermani's view that the conflict between the Prophet and the poets was in essence 'a struggle over leadership' (2000: 352). A telling sign of this is the prominence in both pre-Islamic poetry and the Qur'an of the imperative mode. As custodian of tribal honour, the poet speaks with authority and addresses friend and foe with commanding urgency. The first Qur'anic revelation also begins with a command, but it emerges from a higher sphere (Q. 96:1–2):

> *Iqraʾ bi-smi rabbika lladhī khalaq * khalaqa ʾl-insāna min ʿalaq*
> Recite in the name of your Lord, who created, created man from a clot of blood

These words suffice to distance the Prophet's authority immeasurably from those of the poets: he speaks not in the name of a tribe, but of the Creator of mankind. Significantly, the issue of authority is the principal theme of the *Sūrat al-Shuʿarāʾ* (Q. 26), as indicated by the eightfold repetition of the imperative phrase 'fear God and obey me' (*ittaqū l-Lāha wa-aṭīʿūni*) with which prophets of all ages are shown to have warned their disbelieving contemporaries. The verses berating the poets (26:224–6) occur at the end of the sura and have been much discussed (e.g. Zwettler 1990; Montgomery 1997: 210–16; Bauer 2010; Duraković 2015: 45–53). Seen in the context of the pattern of admonition, rejection, and punishment established by the sura as a whole, the poets appear as just one more example of all those who fail to 'fear God and obey'. Their description as being followed by the wayward (*ghāwūn*) and saying 'what they do not do' (Q. 26:224–6) is all the more damning and their punishment a foregone conclusion. A stark warning is delivered, and the much repeated prophetic command is powerfully thrown into relief against the misguided authority of the poets—except for those 'who believe, do good work and often mention God', as stressed in the final verse (Q. 26:227).

To contrast the prophetic imperative with a sarcastic poetic counterpart we may turn to the *Muʿallaqa* of ʿAmr ibn Kulthūm in which the martial zeal of the pre-Islamic ethos is most vehemently expressed. Turning to his adversary, the poet exclaims (ʿAmr, *Muʿallaqa*, 1971: 98):

Abā Hindin fa-lā taʿjal ʿalaynā wa-ʾanzirnā nukhabbirka l-yaqīnā
Bi-ʾannā nūridu l-rāyāti bīḍan wa-nuṣdiruhunna ḥumran qad rawīnā

Abū Hind, don't make us hurry!
Give us the time to tell you a certitude:

Our banners are white when we bring them to the drinking fount [of battle]
And red when we bring them back, satiated [with blood].

Like the prophet in sura 26, so the poet here acts as a messenger passing on a warning of certain doom (*yaqīn*). As the poem progresses, it is repeated with increasing ardour, but the like of it must pale in comparison with the prophetic warning of eternal doom addressed to all mankind. Indeed, the term *al-yaqīn* ('the certitude') appears repeatedly in the Qur'an where it conveys not only death but the certain truth of the soul's encounter with divine judgement (e.g. Q. 56:95).

The rivalry between pre-Islamic poetry and the Qur'an is further accentuated by the fact that the authority of both derives from the mastery of language. Both convey a code of ethics whose credibility and impact depends on the aesthetics of delivery. The respective literary merits of poetry and the Qur'an, and the inherent superiority and inimitability of the latter, have accordingly been a pivotal theme in classical Arabic literary sciences and theology, as discussed by Geert Jan van Gelder in this volume. Symptomatic of this is the debate over the *Muʿallaqa* by Imrūʾ 'l-Qays (d. 542), arguably the most famous pre-Islamic poem ever written. Its lasting allure was such that the medieval theologian al-Bāqillānī (d. 403/1013) subjected the poem to a fierce critique in order to prove its failings, though his heavy-handed methodology has been compared to 'taking a butterfly through a carwash' (Mir 1990: 119).

The *Muʿallaqa's* strikingly antithetical relationship to the Qur'an is best illustrated by comparing it with sura 24 with which it shares numerous themes, though from opposing perspectives. The poet vaunts himself for trespassing into women's chambers, seducing them into adultery and disclosing their charms which are described in exquisite detail. True to the ethos of *muruwwa*, he glories in risking his life to transgress the boundaries of decorum. Sura 24, by contrast, appears designed to impose limits upon just such behaviour: adultery and indecent talk are proscribed, female charms are to be veiled in public, homes should not be entered without permission, and men and women are to lower their gaze in chastity.

Of particular note is that both texts are ring compositions, a fact which points to a structural parentage between sura and *qaṣīda* that merits more extensive research.[3] As

[3] In this context reference must be to Stetkevych's observation that the 'expression of the Qur'anic ideology of salvation' and the Arabic three-part *qaṣath* share the same 'archetypal pattern' (Stetkevych 2017: 25).

Farrin (2011) and others have shown, the tears shed by Imrūʾ 'l-Qays when faced with the ruined abode at the beginning of the poem are countered at the end by the rain storm which brings both destruction and hope for renewal. In the sura, beginning and end are linked by verses on themes of conviviality and social interaction. Remarkably, a juxtaposition of darkness and light is centrally positioned in both texts. Here, Imruʾ al-Qays describes his beloved as a shining light, before plunging into a dark night of solitude and tribulation. By contrast, the famous light verse of the sura (Q. 24:35) shows God to be the true source of illumination, while wave upon wave of darkness symbolize the perdition of those led astray (Q. 24:40). The difference here is symptomatic of a new attitude to nature championed by the Qur'an. For the pre-Islamic poets, nature is sufficient unto itself and represents both their salvation and their undoing. In the Qur'an all natural phenomena are but signs (*āyāt*) pointing to the Creator and reminding man that his salvation lies elsewhere.

The new outlook brought about by the Prophet's message, coupled with the political success of his mission, could not fail to have an impact on poetry, but the result was 'complex' and 'occasionally contradictory' (Montgomery 1997: 254). Some poets appeared to pay mere lip-service to the new creed. Others became subservient, as best illustrated in the panegyric *qaṣīda*s addressed to the Prophet, notably the famous *burda* by Kaʿb ibn Zuhayr (Stetkevych 2010: 30–69). These were polythematic *qaṣīda*s in the old style in which the key ingredients of *muruwwa*—generosity and death-defying valour—are integrated into the new ethics of Islam. Alongside them we also find a new type of monothematic war poem composed in simpler language. A notable example inspired by Qur'anic punishment narratives is the ode by Kaʿb ibn Mālik on the expulsion of the Jewish Banū al-Naḍīr which portrays the Muslim warriors as agents of divine retribution (Imhoff 2010). It anticipates the politico-religious poetry of the early Islamic period in which Qur'anic references play a significant role, as illustrated in Wadād al-Qāḍī's (1994) analysis of a long *qaṣīda* by the Khārijī poet ʿAmr al-ʿAnbārī (d. after 130/749). Her findings still provide the most detailed insight into the techniques employed by early Muslim poets to adapt Qur'anic material to the constraints of rhyme and metre and integrate it into the conventional thematic structure of the *qaṣīda*. The resulting fusion of missionary zeal and martial prowess anticipates all later Arabo-Islamic war poetry, from Abbasid times to the present day.

The Abbasid Period

By the third/ninth century the influence of the Qur'an on Arabic poetry is all-pervasive. This does not mean that poetry has become religious or that the form and themes of inherited convention are abandoned, nor does poetry aspire to imitate the Qur'an, an impossibility by definition (on this see Van Gelder in this volume). Citations of the Qur'an, known as *iqtibās*, which proliferate in the poetry of the time (Zubaidi 1983: Van Gelder 2002–3) are the most visible but not the most important sign of this influence.

The thrust of it resides in a new, theocratic understanding of human history, individual destiny, and the natural environment which is implicit even in works devoid of reference to scripture. This understanding gained in complexity by association with the philosophical theories and scientific insights made available in Arabic by the translation movement sponsored by the early Abbasid caliphs. As Stetkevych has shown, it led to the rise of a new mode of thought—'abstract, dialectical, metaphorical'—which created a new style of poetic expression known as *badīʿ* (Stetkevych 1991: 37). It was to dominate Arabic poetry until the modern age.

The theocratic understanding generated by the Qur'an and refined by speculative thought, in particular the philosophical cosmology of Neoplatonism, left a diverse range of imprints on Abbasid poetry. As illustration, four types of verse will be briefly discussed hereunder.[4] The first and most prolific is the panegyric mode. Here, the recipient of praise and his exploits are placed into a teleological framework of history which sees the establishment and expansion of a just Islamic order as the fulfilment of the Prophetic mission and the pathway to communal salvation. To this effect the ethical virtues championed by the pre-Islamic code are recast and elevated from a tribal to an imperial context. The poet who more than any other forged this new language of praise and led it to a level of hitherto unparalleled intellectual sophistication was Abū Tammām (d. 232/845). In an incisive study, Stetkevych has documented how his work legitimizes Abbasid statehood through the skilful fusion of Qur'anic and pre-Islamic concepts (1991, see index, 'Qurʾān').

The mutually reinforcing combination of Islamic and ancient Arabian themes was to remain a hallmark of the panegyric tradition and exemplifies the subservience of poetry to prophecy. A hidden element of rivalry nevertheless subsisted. Convinced of his genius, al-Mutanabbī (d. 354/965) in his youth felt impelled to compose verses in emulation of the Qur'an which earned him his sobriquet 'the would-be prophet' (see Van Gelder in this volume). The mature panegyrics of this master of eulogy illustrate the careful positioning of Qur'anic allusions in the structure of the panegyric. His famous *qaṣīda* on the recapture of the frontier-post of al-Ḥadath from the Byzantines begins by endowing his patron Sayf al-Dawla with the classical Arabian virtues of resolve (*ʿazm*) and nobility (*karam*). The climactic conclusion by contrast grants him quasi-prophetic, if not quasi-divine, status in verses redolent with Qur'anic references, such as the following (al-Mutanabbī, *Dīwān*, 3:392):

> O sword (*sayf*) which is never sheathed
> About which no one is in doubt (*murtāb*) and from which there is no protector (*ʿāṣim*)

The sovereign's might is here associated with the Qur'an 'in which there is no doubt' (*lā rayba fīhi*, Q. 2:2) and with God 'from whom there is no protector', a thrice repeated Qur'anic phrase bound to evoke the destruction of the people of Noah (*lā ʿāṣima*, Q. 11:43).

[4] For a different approach to Abbasid poetry and the Qur'an see Beatrice Gruendler (2017) which examines the Qur'an's appearance in recorded events (*akhbār*) about the poets.

Thus the sovereign's victory re-enacts a Qur'anic punishment narrative, and herein lies his historic mission. Of special note is the fact that his elevation from heroic to quasi-divine status first occurs in the central line of the poem where he is described as transcending the bounds of courage as though he knew the unseen (*al-ghayb*)—a prerogative only of God.

Al-Mutanabbī's depiction of the sovereign in such hyperbolic terms makes sense if it is seen in the context of the Neoplatonist cosmology which had become widely accepted by this time. It views the cosmos as a hierarchy of being whose components stand in a mirroring relationship to each other, hence God's human agents may be validly endowed with attributes that reflect those of the Creator. This way of thinking is relevant also for the understanding of the next two types of poetry I wish to discuss. Unlike the panegyric which portrays the role of communal leadership in the teleology of history, these are concerned with the fate of the individual: his emancipation by spiritual ascent; or his captivation by worldly delights. The former is the subject of ascetic and mystical poetry, starting with Rābiᶜa al-ᶜAdawiyya (d. *c.*180/796) and culminating with Ibn al-Fāriḍ (d. 632/1235), Ibn ᶜArabī (d. 638/1240), and al-Būṣīrī (d. *c.*694/1294) whose panegyric of Muḥammad marked the onset of flourishing tradition of prophetic eulogy (Stetkevych 2010: 70–150). The latter, rather more abundant, is the poetry of wine, love, and indecent revelry (*mujūn*) made famous by Abū Nuwās (d. 199/813). In both types the Qur'an is present as implicit normative framework and as source of citations and allusions.

As discussed by McAuley, Ibn ᶜArabī's thought on the function of poetry provides an instructive insight into the ongoing debate over the relative merits of poetry. In keeping with most classical commentators, Ibn ᶜArabī does not see the negative Qur'anic verdict on the poets as an all-out condemnation of their art. Rather, poetry has a distinct function. Unlike the Qur'an, which is revealed in clear language, poetry is 'a deliberate act of encoding', whose structure and symmetry 'reflects the workings of the cosmos' and acts as 'a vehicle of secret knowledge' accessible to an elite (McAuley 2012: 44–6). The cosmic order here alluded to is the emanatory world of Neoplatonism which Ibn ᶜArabī came to know through intermediate sources and whose concepts he saw embodied in Qur'anic terms and images (McAuley 2012: 17). His ample poetic production, examined for the first time in English by McAuley, is a tour de force of mystical hermeneutics which includes a series of poems on every Qur'anic sura (McAuley 2012: 59–92, republished in McAuley 2017). The exploration of Qur'anic concepts is equally prominent in the rather more accessible poetry of Ibn al-Fāriḍ, where such citations have a climactic structural function, like in al-Mutanabbī's verse. One of his major works, discussed by Homerin (2007), ends with an imaginary voice that welcomes the mystical wayfarer to his long-aspired goal with the following words (Ibn al-Fāriḍ, *Dīwān*, 165; Homerin 2007: 396):

> Good news for you, so strip off what is on you (*ikhlaᶜ mā ᶜalayka*)
> You have been remembered despite your crooked ways.

ᶜAbd al-Ghanī al-Nābulusī's interpretation of the verse points to the Qur'anic verse 'remember me and I will remember you' (Q. 2:152) as the explanation for the welcome granted (Homerin 2007: 397). The command to 'strip off' what is on him—and hence divest himself of his worldly apparel—furthermore evokes a rhyming parallel with the divine command to Moses to strip off his sandals as he enters upon the sacred ground of Ṭuwā (*ikhlaʿ naʿlayka*, Q. 20:12). The poem thus ends with the adept given access to the divine presence, like Moses stepping into the precinct of the sacred fire.

While Qur'anic associations are to be expected in religious poetry it may be surprising to see them in the poetry of revelry, including sexually explicit verses such as those by Ibn al-Rūmī discussed by Smoor (2014). That multiple allusions to scripture can serve as subtext to an entire poem of this kind is documented in detail in Montgomery's (1994) study of a bacchanal by Abū Nuwās.[5] Montgomery notices the paradox of 'positive Koranic terms' being applied to 'morally negative activities' (1994: 127)—a paradox whose skilful exploitation is a hallmark of this entire genre. While the amorous exploits of the pre-Islamic poet were outdone by the Qur'an's depiction of eternal bliss, here the opposite process is at work, as Qur'anic images serve as a means to conjure up a sinful Paradise on earth. The aim is not just to shock by parodying the sacred, or to render earthly temptation irresistible by giving it the lure of Eden. At work here is a vision warranted by the cosmology of the time in which the earthly represents an imperfect mirror image of the heavenly—a contrasting parentage moreover fully in keeping with the Qur'anic message. The reveller's principal sin—as well as his claim to salvation—may reside precisely in his awareness that the source of his seduction carries an imprint of Heaven.

The fusion of medieval cosmology and the Qur'anic way of seeing enables the Abbasid poet to discern a spark of the sublime even in the most ordinary of things, as illustrated in the fourth type of Abbasid poetry I wish to mention, the ekphrastic epigram. It is a type of miniature in which the object of description is woven into the cosmic fabric by mining and combining the associative potential of poetic and Qur'anic language. Thus a five-line epigram on the pen is enough for Ibn al-Muʿtazz (d. 296/908) to reveal hidden parallels between courtly and religious spheres, macrocosm and microcosm, human action and divine ordinance. What comes to the fore is the object's semiotic quality in the hierarchy of being—in short its quality as a sign (*āya*) in the Qur'anic sense (Sperl 2009). Sumi's study shows that this analogical, metaphorical style is a feature of Abbasid descriptive poetry also in longer structures (Sumi 2004).

The Modern Period

Abbasid poetry emanates from a culture at the pinnacle of its power. Arabic verse of the modern age reflects a culture shaken to its foundations by colonial subjugation, dictatorship, internal fragmentation, and war. Central to these foundations are language and

[5] Considering the frequent allusions to the story of Jonah detected by Montgomery, it is to be noted that the poem's central lines may contain a further hint at the same tale. Here the wine is described as having been concealed as though 'buried inside a coffin' (1994: 118), which brings to mind Jonah's sojourn in the belly of the whale, including the death and rebirth symbolism conveyed by the tale.

prophecy, shards of identity which poets seize upon to confront the trauma. It is therefore not surprising that the Qur'an is a pivotal subtext also in modern Arabic poetry. Stefan Wild's survey of eight modern poets identifies a continuum in the use of Qur'anic citations which ranges from the reassertion of inherited values to their subversion 'by a flippant, nostalgic or even destructive counterpoint' (Wild 2001: 145). Despite the widely different messages proffered, the poets Wild studied have one point in common. All of them 'in one way or another assume the role of the poet-prophet' (144). The brief chronological overview given hereunder dwells on this association and its role in the confrontation with social, political, and cultural upheaval.

The existential challenge represented by colonialism and modernity is tangible in a famous poem composed in 1903 by the Egyptian Ḥāfiẓ Ibrāhīm (d. 1932) in which the Arabic language is cited as bemoaning its own demise. Incredulously it exclaims (Ibrāhīm, *Dīwān*, 253):

> I have been broad enough to comprise the Book of God in word and meaning
> I was not too narrow for any verse or admonition.
>
> How then should I be too narrow to designate a tool
> And string up names for new inventions?

In anti-colonial poetry the Qur'an appears repeatedly as the key repository of arguments to delegitimize the occupier and rally the forces of resistance. How rich and skilful the use of Qur'anic allusions to this end can be is shown in Hussein Kadhim's (1997) analysis of two poems by Aḥmad Shawqī (d. 1932), including the famous 'Farewell to Lord Cromer'. Here, Qur'anic references form the bedrock of a 'counter-discursive strategy' which results in 'casting the struggle between Egypt and Cromer/Colonialism as one between belief/Islam and infidelity, as a conflict between good and evil, between the forces of life and those of death and degeneration' (Kadhim, 1997: 194).

Confronted with French colonial rule and what he saw as the submissiveness and ignorance of his people, the Tunisian Abū'l-Qāsim al-Shābbī (d. 1934), not only resorted to Qur'anic paradigms like Shawqī, but assigned to poetry a role analogous to prophecy. His composition 'Al-Ṣayḥa' ('The Scream', 1925) concludes with the following Qur'anic imperatives addressed to the art of poetry (al-Shābbī, *Dīwān*, 47):

> *Wa'ṣbir ʿalā mā tulāqī*   *wa'ṣdaʿ wuqīta'l-ʿithārā*
>
> Bear up to what you are faced with
> And comply—may you be guarded from failure.

In the Qur'an, both imperatives are addressed to the Prophet in order to strengthen and comfort him in the face of his detractors (see Q. 15:94, 20:130). By association, al-Shābbī urges poetry—and, by implication, himself—to emulate the prophetic model, be steadfast, and trust in eventual triumph.

Following the watershed year of 1948, the sense of existential crisis deepens and the search for poetic renewal leads to a rupture with the past. The two-hemistich mono-rhymed verse form which had persisted since pre-Islamic times was abandoned in favour of free verse. The change is symptomatic of the collapse of inherited certainties brought about by the upheavals of the time. Unfettered forms of expression were needed to erect new foundations. For the Iraqi Badr Shākir al-Sayyāb (d. 1964), one of the pioneers of free verse, the transformation of poetic form is concomitant with a sea change in ideological consciousness. For him the teleology of history is no longer Qur'anic but Marxist and encompasses elements of ancient Mesopotamian mythology. Scriptural themes and images nevertheless persist as symbolic fragments, like the mention of Thamūd, which figures in his masterpiece 'The Rain Song' (1960). In the Qur'an it designates a community destroyed by divine wrath, but here the agent of destruction is 'not nature and not God', but man (Deyoung 1993: 58).

For the Syrian poet Adonis (b. 1930) the Qur'an remained a seminal point of reference in his search for a new poetic language, though less on account of its message than on account of its unprecedented literary qualities which he saw as emblematic of the renewal he was himself aiming for (Mersal 2016). His *Introduction to Arabic Poetics* describes the Qur'an as 'a radical and complete departure' which in the Abbasid period 'led indirectly to the opening up of unlimited horizons in poetry and the establishment of a genuine literary criticism' (Adonis, *Introduction*, 37, 42). By analogy, Adonis posits a similarly radical innovative surge for his own time to which his poetic work is intended to point the way. His classic compendium *Songs of Mihyār the Damascene* (1961) adopts a mantic and prophetic tone, but carries no religious denomination. As Kermani remarks, his poems 'are oriented towards Heaven but not towards God' (2000: 361). Wild goes further and declares that Adonis' language 'evokes a religious, Islamic and inevitably Koranic spectre, only to immediately and deliberately counteract it, undermine it and fight it' (2001: 159).

In the Middle East the cultural dislocation brought about by modernism has been aggravated as though epitomized by the physical dislocation of the Palestinian people and the denial of its identity. In response, a new Palestinian literature arose which aimed to reassert that identity and root it both in the soil of the land and in the foundation of its culture. Its most notable representative is the poet Maḥmūd Darwīsh (d. 2008) whose work draws upon the Palestinian heritage in its entirety, including the New Testament and the Hebrew Bible. Among the countless Qur'anic allusions in his poetry one is of particular relevance here for it harks back to the above-mentioned command 'recite' which marked the onset of divine revelation. In a long poem composed under the impression of the Sabra and Shatila Massacre and the expulsion of the Palestinian fighters from Beirut he exclaims (Darwīsh, *Madḥ al-Ẓill al-ʿĀlī*, 28):

> These are our 'verses' (*āyātunā*)[6]
> So recite (*iqraʾ*)
> In the name of the fighter (*fidāʾī*) who created

[6] The term *āyāt* means both signs and Qur'anic verses but never, in normal usage, refers to poetry. By being qualified as *āyāt* these 'verses' are put on a par with Scripture.

An horizon out of a boot (*jazma*)
(...)
In the name of the fighter who begins,
Recite (*iqraʾ*):
Beirut—our image (*ṣūra*)
Beirut—our sura.

Faced with extreme violence and catastrophic defeat the poet resorts to the Qur'anic paradigm and inverts it in an act of supreme defiance. Agency is wrested from God, as the freedom fighter assumes the role of the Creator and reveals a new sacred text in the form of a poem cast into the image of Beirut. In the process, the expulsion of the fighters from the city is transformed into a new beginning, a re-enactment of the prophetic *hijra*, as documented in Anette Månson's insightful discussion of the passage (2003: 230–1). The example shows how a moment of utmost despair brings about a return to, and recasting of, the most seminal of Qur'anic phrases.

Notwithstanding his frequent reference to scripture, Darwīsh's poetry is non-denominational, unlike the politico-religious verse spawned by the Islamist movements that have proliferated in recent decades and seek to counter modernity and secularism by reasserting the Qur'anic teleology of history, often by recourse to traditional poetic forms. As shown in Alshaer's studies of the poetry of Hamas and Hizbullah (2009, 2014), it plays a major role in the propaganda war and casts a revealing light on the cultural dimension of the conflicts involved. Thus the Syrian poet ʿUmar al-Farrā (d. 2015) sanctifies the earth of South Lebanon in his poem *Men of God* composed to celebrate Hizbullah's resistance against the Israeli incursion in 2006 (Alshaer 2014: 134–6). Upon entering the land, the poet draws on the same Mosaic image which served Ibn al-Fāriḍ to validate his entry into the realm of enlightenment:

Here we have reached our journey's end
Come take [them] off (*ikhlaʿ*)
I might even ask you to bow down (*tarkaʿ*)—
Come take off your sandals! (*ikhlaʿ niʿālaka*)
We are walking on holy land...

The power of the association is undiminished, as shown by the immense popularity achieved by the poem.

Despite his endorsement of Hizbullah, al-Farrā was in the first instance not a political writer, unlike Abū Yaḥyā al-Lībī, a senior al-Qaeda operative killed by a US drone strike in 2012 who was also one of the movement's leading poets. Of particular relevance for the purpose of this chapter is his poem *The Cry of Faith Arose in Us* which is composed in the same rhyme and metre as the above-cited *Muʿallaqa* by ʿAmr ibn Kulthūm. Though couched in far simpler language, it evokes the ferocity of the pre-Islamic ethos at its most death-obsessed and rallies it into the service of totalizing religious warfare. In the following lines the poetic imperative reappears once more, invoking 'the promise of God' (*waʿd Allāh*), a phrase repeated numerous times in the Qur'an. Like in ʿAmr's poem, the word *yaqīn* ('certain') supplies a rhyme:[7]

> *Fa-yā man qad ghadaw li'l-kufri ḥarban*
> *bi-waʿdi l-Lāhi kūnū wāthiqīnā*
>
> *Fa-ṣabran fī majāli l-mawti ṣabran*
> *fa-inna n-naṣra ātīnā yaqīnā*
>
> O you who have turned into warriors against unbelief
> Put your trust in the promise of God.
>
> Be steadfast on the path of death, be steadfast
> Victory will come your way for certain.

The combined veneer of pre-Islamic heroism and religious zeal harks back to the early Muslim war poetry by the likes of Kaʿb ibn Mālik. It is symptomatic of the categorical return to an idealized past championed by Islamist ideology which gains in appeal by the lasting resonance of this form of poeticized rhetoric. As pointed out by Elisabeth Kendall in her study of al-Qaeda poetry in Yemen, 'jihadist acts thus become the natural culmination of a long chain of seemingly comparable acts from Islam's glorious past' (2015: 260). Her study documents the crucial functions—'practical, ideological and emotional' (255)—performed by poetry in the jihadists' struggle and shows it to be a principal and hitherto not sufficiently recognized weapon in their arsenal.

To conclude I would like to turn to the Egyptian Muḥammad ʿAfīfī Maṭar (d. 2010) whose hermetic style is a world away from the reactionary pastiche of Islamist poetics, though no less steeped in Qur'anic assonance. His work is perhaps the most outstanding example of the search for a new expressive medium which has dominated much of Arabic poetry since 1948. Composed between 1975 and 1988, his *Quartet of Joy* charts the rebirth of poetic language through a panoramic web of associations that deeply probe the fusion between nature and culture, world and word, which makes us human. The explanatory notes to the prize-winning English translation by Ferial Ghazoul and John Verlenden (1997) point the reader to the many Qur'anic allusions whose richness and complexity would merit a study in its own right.

In the following example, which ends the third prelude (*muftataḥ*), we encounter once more the notion of certitude, though here it does not relate to certain death or triumph but to the poet's certainty of his task as their witness. Having recalled the Adamic covenant between God and human kind (Q. 7:172–3) and found it 'sealed with the blood of my tattoo and clay', he has the strength to put forth his message, like the trumpet of Judgment Day (*ṣūr*, Q. 6:73; Maṭar, *Quartet* (1997), 7–8 [English], 9 [Arabic]):

> *Fa-nṭiq yā yaqīnī*
> *wa-nfukh damī fī'l-ṣūri wa'l-tashhad yamīnī*

[7] For the Arabic text see <http://www.kurdname.org/2014/01/blog-post_7190.html> consulted on 10 August 2015. The translation is mine.

anna l-madā'ina wa'l-madāfina taḥta maḥḍi l-lamsi yarjufu
min rawājifihā nfijāru l-mashhadi l-yawmī bi'l-ru'yā

So speak up O my Certitude,
And blow my blood in the Trumpet.
Let my right hand attest that cities
of the living and the dead
under the pure touch quiver,
stirring the eruption of the daily scene
with apocalyptic vision.[8]

Bibliography

Primary Sources

Abū'l-Qāsim al-Shābbī. *Dīwān*. Beirut: Dār al-ʿAwda, 1972.

Adonis. *An Introduction to Arabic Poetics*. Translated by Catherine Cobham. London: Saqi Books, 1990.

ʿAmr b. Kulthūm. 'Muʿallaqa'. In: *Sharḥ al-Muʿallaqāt al-Sabʿ* by Abū ʿAbd Allāh al-Zawzanī. Cairo: al-Maktaba al-Tijāriyya al-Kubrā, 1971.

Darwīsh, Maḥmūd. *Madḥ al-Ẓill al-ʿĀlī*. Beirut: Dār al-ʿAwda, 1984.

Ibn al-Fāriḍ. *Dīwān*. Edited by Giuseppe Scattolin. Cairo: Institut français d'archéologie orientale, 2004.

Ibrāhīm, Ḥāfiẓ. *Dīwān*. Edited by Aḥmad Amīn, Aḥmad al-Zayn, and Ibrāhīm al-Abyārī. Cairo: al-Mu'assasa al-Miṣriyya li'l-Kitāb, 1980.

Maṭar, Muḥammad ʿAfīfī. *Rubāʿiyyāt al-Faraḥ/Quartet of Joy: Poems*. Arabic text and English translation by Ferial Ghazoul and John Verlenden. Fayetteville: University of Arkansas Press, 1997.

Al-Mutanabbī. *Dīwān bi-Sharḥ Abī l-Baqā' al-ʿUkbarī*. Edited by Muṣṭafā al-Saqqā, Ibrāhīm al-Abyārī, and ʿAbd al-Ḥafīẓ Shalabī. Cairo: Muṣṭafā al-Bābī al-Ḥalabī, 1956.

Secondary Sources

Alshaer, Atef. 'The Poetry of Hamas', *Middle East Journal of Culture and Communication* 2 (2009), 214–30.

Alshaer, Atef. 'The Poetry of Hizbullah'. In: Lina Khatib. Dina Matar, and Atef Alshaer (eds.). *The Hizbullah Phenomenon: Politics and Communication*. London: Hurst & Company, 2014.

Bauer, Thomas. 'The Relevance of Early Arabic Poetry for Qur'ānic Studies Including Observations on *kull* and on Qur'ān 22:27, 26:225 and 52:31.' In: Angelika Neuwirth, Nicola Sinai, and Michael Marx (eds.). *The Qur'ān in Context: Historical and Literary Investigations into the Qur'ānic Milieu*, pp. 699–732. Leiden: Brill, 2010.

[8] Muhammad Afifi Matar, excerpt from 'Third Prelude' from *Quartet of Joy*, translated by Ferial Ghazoul and John Verlenden. Translation copyright © 1997 by the University of Arkansas Board of Trustees. Reprinted with the permission of The Permissions Company, Inc., on behalf of the University of Arkansas Press, <http://www.uapress.com>.

Deyoung, Terry. 'A New Reading of Badr Shākir al-Sayyāb's "Hymn of the Rain"', *Journal of Arabic Literature* 24/1 (1993), 39–58.
Duraković, Esad. *The Poetics of Ancient and Classical Arabic Literature: Orientology*. Trans. Amila Karahasanović. London and New York: Routledge, 2015.
El Masri, Ghassan. '*Min al-Baʿad ilá al-āḫira*: Poetic Time and Qurʾānic Eschatology'. In: François Déroche, Christian Robin, and Michel Zink (eds.). *Les Origines du Coran, le Coran des origins*, pp. 129–49. Paris: Fondation Del Duca et Académie des Inscriptions et Belles-Lettres, 2015.
El Masri, Ghassan. 'The Qurʾān and the Character of Ancient Arabic Poetry'. In: Nuha Alshaar (ed.). *The Qur'an and Adab: The Shaping of Literary Traditions in Classical Islam*, pp. 93–135. Oxford: Oxford University Press in association with the Institute of Ismaili Studies, Qur'anic Studies Series, 2017.
Farrin, Raymond. *Abundance from the Desert: Classical Arabic Poetry*. Syracuse, NY: Syracuse University Press, 2011.
Gruendler, Beatrice. 'Abbasid Poets and the Qurʾān'. In: Nuha Alshaar (ed.). *The Qur'an and Adab: The Shaping of Literary Traditions in Classical Islam*, pp. 137–69. Oxford: Oxford University Press in association with the Institute of Ismaili Studies, Qur'anic Studies Series, 2017.
Hamori, Andras. *On the Art of Medieval Arabic Literature*. Princeton: Princeton University Press, 1974.
Homerin, Th. Emil. '"On the Battleground": Al-Nābulusī's Encounters with a Poem by Ibn al-Fāriḍ', *Journal of Arabic Literature* 38/3 (2007), 352–410.
Imhof, Agnes. 'The Qurʾān and the Prophet's Poet: Two Poems by Kaʿb b. Mālik'. In: Angelika Neuwirth, Nicola Sinai, and Michael Marx (eds.). *The Qurʾān in Context: Historical and Literary Investigations into the Qurʾānic Milieu*, pp. 389–403. Leiden: Brill, 2010.
Izutsu, Toshihiko. *The Structure of the Ethical Terms in the Koran*. Tokyo: Keio University, 1959.
Jakobi, Renate. 'The Origins of the Qasida Form'. In: Stefan Sperl and Christopher Shackle (eds.). *Qasida Poetry in Islamic Asia & Africa*, 1:1–34. Leiden: Brill, 1996.
Kadhim, Hussein N. 'The Poetics of Postcolonialism: Two Qaṣīdahs by Aḥmad Shawqī', *Journal of Arabic Literature* 28/3 (1997), 179–218.
Kendall, Elisabeth. 'Yemen's al-Qa'ida and Poetry as a Weapon of Jihad'. In: Elisabeth Kendall and Erwan Stein (eds.). *Twenty-First Century Jihad: Law, Society and Military Action*, pp. 247–69. London: I. B. Taurus, 2015.
Kermani, Navid. *Gott ist schön: das ästhetische Erleben des Koran*. Munich: C. H. Beck, 2000.
McAuley, Denis. *Ibn ʿArabī's Mystical Poetics*. Oxford: Oxford University Press, 2012.
McAuley, Denis. 'Ibn ʿArabī (d. 637/1240) and the Qur'an: A Series of Poems'. In: Nuha Alshaar (ed.). *The Qur'an and Adab: The Shaping of Literary Traditions in Classical Islam*, pp. 495–544. Oxford: Oxford University Press in association with the Institute of Ismaili Studies, Qur'anic Studies Series, 2017.
Mersal, Iman. 'Reading the Qur'an in the Poetry of Adonis'. In: *Middle Eastern Literatures*, 19/1 (2016), 1–33.
Månson, Anette. *Passage to a New World: Exile and Restauration in Mahmoud Darwish's Writings 1960–1995*. Uppsala: Uppsala University, 2003.
Mir, Mustansir. 'Bāqillānī's Critique of Imruʾ al-Qays'. In: James E. Bellamy (ed.). *Studies of Near Eastern Literature and Culture in Memory of Ernest T.Abdel-Massih*. Ann Arbor: University of Michigan, 1990.
Montgomery, James E. 'Dichotomy in *Jāhilī* Poetry', *Journal of Arabic Literature* 17 (1986), 1–20.

Montgomery, James E. 'Revelry and Remorse: A Poem by Abū Nuwās', *Journal of Arabic Literature* 25 (1994), 116–34.

Montgomery, James E. *The Vagaries of the Qaṣīdah: The Tradition and Practice of Early Arabic Poetry*. E. W. Gibb Memorial Trust, 1997.

Neuwirth, Angelika. *Scripture, Poetry and the Making of a Community: Reading the Qurʾān as a Literary Text*. Oxford: Oxford University Press in association with the Institute of Ismaili Studies, 2014.

al-Qāḍī, Wadād. 'The Limitations of Qurʾānic Usage in Early Arabic Poetry: The Example of a Khārijite Poem'. In: Wolfhart Heinrichs and Gregor Schoeler (eds.). *Festschrift Ewald Wagner zum 65. Geburtstag*, pp. 162–81. Beirut: Franz Steiner Verlag, 1994.

Smoor, Peter. 'A Suspicion of Excessive Frankness'. In: Adam Talib, Marlé Hammond, and Arie Schippers (eds.). *The Rude, the Bad and the Bawdy: Essays in Honour of Professor Geert Jan van Gelder*. Gibb Memorial Trust, 2014.

Sperl, Stefan. 'Darkness Transformed into Light: Ibn al-Muʿtazz on the Pen'. In: Christine Allison, Anke Joisten-Pruschke, and Antje Wendtland (eds.). *From Daena to Din: Religion, Kultur und Sprache in der iranischen Welt—Festschrift für Philip Kreyenbroek zum 60. Geburstag*, pp. 457–64. Wiesbaden: Harrasowitz, 2009.

Stetkevych, Suzanne Pinckney. *Abū Tammām and the Poetics of the ʿAbbāsid Age*. Leiden: Brill, 1991.

Stetkevych, Suzanne Pinckney. *The Mute Immortals Speak: Pre-Islamic Poetry and the Poetics of Ritual*. Ithaca, NY, and London: Cornell University Press, 1993.

Stetkevych, Suzanne Pinckney. *The Mantle Odes: Arabic Praise Poems to the Prophet Muḥammad*. Bloomington, IN, and Indianapolis: Indiana University Press, 2010.

Stetkevych, Suzanne Pinckney. 'Solomon and Mythic Kingship in the Arabic-Islamic Tradition: *Qaṣīdah*, Qurʾān and *Qiṣāṣ al-anbiyāʾ*', *Journal of Arabic Literature* 48 (2017), 1–37.

Sumi, Akiko Motoyoshi. *Description in Classical Arabic Poetry: Waṣf, Ekphrasis, and Interarts Theory*. Leiden: Brill, 2004.

Tamer, Georges. 'Hellenistic Ideas of Time in the Qur'an'. In Lothar Gall and Dietmar Willweit (eds.). *Judaism, Christianity and Islam in the Course of History: Exchange and Conflicts*, pp. 21–41. Munich: Oldenbourg, 2011.

Van Gelder, Geert Jan. 'Forbidden Firebrands; Frivolous "Iqtibās" (Quotation from the Qurʾān) according to Medieval Arabic Critics', *Quaderni di Studi Arabi* 20/1 (2002–3), 3–16.

Wild, Stefan. 'The Koran as Subtext in Modern Arabic Poetry'. In: Gert Borg and Ed de Moor (eds.). *Representations of the Divine in Arabic Poetry*, pp. 140–60. Amsterdam and Atlanta: Rodopi, 2001.

Zubaidi, A. M. 'The Impact of the Qurʾān and *Ḥadīth* on Medieval Arabic Literature'. In: A. F. L. Beeston, T. M. Johnstone, R. B. Serjeant, and G. R. Smith (eds.). *Arabic Literature to the End of the Umayyad Period*. Cambridge: Cambridge University Press, 1983.

Zwettler, Michael. 'A Mantic Manifesto: The Sūra of "The Prophets" and the Qurʾānic Foundations of Prophetic Authority'. In: James L. Kugel (ed.). *Poetry and Prophecy: The Beginnings of a Literary Tradition*, pp.75–119. Ithaca, NY, and London: Cornell University Press, 1990.

PART V

TOPICS AND THEMES OF THE QUR'AN

CHAPTER 26

REVELATION AND PROPHECY IN THE QUR'AN

ULRIKA MÅRTENSSON

THE English term 'revelation' refers to events and concepts in the Hebrew Bible, the New Testament, and the Qur'an, which describe how a deity communicates with a group of people, by prophets, angels, and seers. These three canons are thematically connected. The New Testament refers to the Hebrew Bible's prophets, kings, and the Law of Moses; and the Qur'an shares many of the two Bibles' prophets and kings. Given that canon as a genre serves to demarcate communities through doctrine, the Hebrew Bible, the New Testament, and the Qur'an would have similar but slightly different concepts of revelation. According to Toshihiko Izutsu's path-breaking study of Qur'anic divine-to-human communication (1964), it shares the biblical worldview but is in a unique way concerned with linguistic communication. Naṣr Ḥāmid Abū Zayd (1992) has applied Izutsu's linguistic model in his equation of Christ with the Qur'an as God's word (*kalām*), and Mary with Muḥammad as mediums conveying God's word to the community. Stefan Wild (1996), on the other hand, argues that the Christian term 'revelation' connotes the manifestation of things concealed (Greek *apokalypsis*), which does not correspond with the relevant Qur'anic concepts. Consequently, this chapter compares Qur'anic, biblical, and Greek concepts related to revelation, in order to bring out what is specific about the Qur'anic ones.

BIBLICAL AND GREEK CONCEPTS

According to Karel van der Toorn (2007), the Hebrew Bible comprises 'books' dating between Antiquity and Late Antiquity, which evince different concepts of divine communication. The redacted canon, however, was produced by a scribal institution, which associated all concepts of divine communication with 'writing': the scribal profession. Thus, in 2 Moses, God addresses Moses directly in a dialogue, persuading Moses to save His enslaved people by giving him signs (Hebrew *ʾothôt*, sing. *ʾôth*; cf. Moberly 2011) to persuade the people that he is speaking on behalf of God. This narration—Torah—reflects a third-person description of God's dialogue with Moses. In the later 5 Moses (early 500 BCE) God commands Moses to recount to the people their history as God reads it to him, to remind them (*zekôr*) that worship is restricted to the Temple in Jerusalem. Moses reads the divine account from a *written* scroll (*sefer*), making it 'the second Torah' (Deuteronomy). In the Book of Jeremiah, God places His word in Jeremiah's mouth, who communicates it to his scribe Barukh, who writes it in a scroll (*sefer*). The prophet Hezekiel even eats a scroll, handed to him by the Lord's messenger, then communicates the Lord's message to the people.

In the Hellenistic wisdom and apocalyptic literature of the Bible, the communicators are sages who have visions, sometimes mediated by angels, which enable them to explain a divine writing. The apocalyptic genre is the one that corresponds with the English term 'revelation' (Greek 'apocalypse'), referring to divine disclosure of concealed events and agents, including eschatology. As Stefan Wild (1996) points out, this apocalyptic concept of revelation implies an 'epiphany', that is, God's becoming manifest and visible. In early 2 Moses, God lets Moses see Him, if only in a fleeting glimpse of His blue mantle, and from behind. In the Hebrew Bible's apocalypse, the Book of Daniel, the divine self-manifestation involves no meeting. The verb here is *niglā* of the root *gālā* (Dan. 2:19, 22; cf. 1 Mos. 35:7; 1 Sam. 14:8–11; Isa. 49:9), 'to become manifest', now through dream visions. Some of Daniel's dream visions are obscure; these are explained by the angel Gabriel, who informs Daniel that they concern the messianic promise and the end of time (Dan. 8:15–27; 9:20–7). The New Testament apocalypse, the Book of Revelation, describes how the seer John hears a voice commanding him to write down the visions he is about to see and hear (Rev. 1:11, 19). By comparison, in the Gospels, Jesus is the manifest word of God and teaches the people. The notion of written text appears in Luke 1:1–4, in the context of assuring that the events accounted for are reliable. Furthermore, the Acts and Epistles are written, as accounts and guidance for the early communities.

A heuristic comparison is Gregory Nagy's study (1990) of the Oracle of the god Apollo at Delphi. The god communicates his guidance by 'indicating', *semainei*, a verb derived from the noun *sema*, 'sign'. Sign-making is done from a hilltop or mountain, symbolizing the deity's supreme overview. The meaning that is communicated derives from the god's inner vision, which he signals to an inspired *mantis* or seer, who signals it to the non-inspired *prophetes*, who makes rational sense of it. In linguistic terms, the *mantis* controlled the contents (semantics) of the god's signs while the *prophetes* controlled its verbal form, usually the dactylic hexameter. The *prophetes* verbalizes the message to a *theoros*, who in his turn repeats the message *verbatim* to the community (*polis*) in the forum. In some significant cases the distinction between *prophetes* and *theoros* was collapsed, notably the lawgiver-*prophetes* Lycurgus who gave the Spartans their law code directly from the *mantis* of Apollo at Delphi without the medium of a *theoros*.

Another important aspect of the divine communication concerns prophetic subjectivity. Comparing Plato's *Phaedrus* and the Hebrew Bible's concepts of inspiration, Abraham Avni (1968) finds that *Phaedrus*' notion of the poet who expresses the muse's inspiration agonistically through his own personality, matches the biblical books where each prophet expresses the divine message through his unique personality and concerns.

The following parallels appear between the Greek and biblical cases: God's elevated vantage point and supreme knowledge; divine communication consisting in signs; the vision; a messenger between God and the prophet; repetition of the divine message to the community in order to decide on a course of action; insistence on *verbatim* transmission; and the giving of the law. The Bible, however, appears to stress the evidentiary nature of writing. The following survey of Qur'an research below will bring out points of comparison with these cases, as avenues for further research.

Qur'anic Concepts

According to Toshihiko Izutsu, the Qur'anic concepts related to revelation signify functions of the divine communication, namely *tanzīl*, *āya*, *kalām*, *waḥy*, *kitāb*, and *qur'ān*. In Izutsu's view, *āya* refers to both linguistic and non-linguistic 'signs' which God 'makes descend' (*nazzala*, noun *tanzīl*) to His prophets to guide their peoples. *Tanzīl* is a term exclusive to the Qur'anic divine communication, which moves from God 'on high' to man below. The downward movement of the divine signs has been further explored by Stefan Wild (1996), who identifies *tanzīl* as the key concept of revelation in the Qur'an, and which differs from the biblical concept of revelation as the seeing of previously concealed things (*apokalypsis*), or the divine self-manifestation (*epiphaneia*).

Izutsu, however, sees the distinguishing trait of the Qur'anic revelation as consisting in its linguistic character. Applying Ferdinand de Saussure's (d. 1913) distinction between *langue* (language) and *parole* (speech) to the Qur'anic terms *lisān* and *kalām*, Izutsu argues that *lisān* refers to the Qur'an's self-identification as the clearest and most intelligible form of the Arabic language of the Prophet's people, and *kalām* to the Qur'an's identity as God's spoken word with specific meaning contents or semantics (cf. Abū Zayd 1992). With Izutsu's linguistic terminology, the *āyāt* or signs are the semiotics of the divine *kalām*.

In further contrast to Wild (1996), Izutsu distinguishes *waḥy* as the 'revelation concept' par excellence in the Qur'an. Yet, Izutsu points out, unlike the exclusively Qur'anic term *tanzīl*, *waḥy* occurs also in non-Quranic contexts, including poetry (*shiʿr*), where it is sometimes used also for communication between humans and animals, or among animals. The basic meaning of *waḥy* is 'to signify', referring to the non-verbal act of communicating the meaning of the signs after which they can be verbalized. While this may appear like a mystical concept, Izutsu stresses that the whole point of the Qur'anic *waḥy* is to communicate a clear message to the rational faculty of men, which is intelligible to anyone who knows the Arabic language. Thus, Izutsu points out, Qur'anic *waḥy* is not semantically identical with Arabian poetry (*shiʿr*) because it identifies as a prophetic *true* message from God, whereas the poets freely make up their messages; nor is the Qur'anic form like the poetic metres. The communication scheme of Qur'anic *waḥy* also differs from the three-step communication that characterizes *shiʿr* (*jinn* → *shāʿir* → community) since it involves four steps: God → messenger (in Medina also identified as Gabriel) → prophet → community. The scheme resembles the lawgiver-prophet at the Delphi Oracle of Apollo, and thus differs from Moses' Sinai revelation, where the Lord spoke directly to Moses; his unique status in this respect is mentioned in the Qur'an as well (Q. 4:164).

Izutsu's approach contradicts identifications of the Qur'anic *waḥy* with Arabic poetic inspiration. The same point was made by Theodor Nöldeke, who defined the Qur'anic genre overall as didactic rhetoric, not poetic metre (Nöldeke-Schwally 2013/1909). Similarly, Michael Zwettler (1990) has showed how Q. 26 (*al-Shuʿarāʾ*) employs the character of Moses to distinguish between the Qur'an as a prophetic medium about the truth and poets who speak on fictive topics. Also unlike poetry, the prophetic speech is matched by ethical actions, specifically the giving of the law to the community in Medina (cf. Waldman 2013; Tottoli 2002).

A particular strand of research concerns the rhetorical and logical aspects of the Qur'anic language. Rosalind Ward Gwynne (2004), Geneviève Gobillot (2004), and Jacques Jomier (2005) have found that the Qur'an rhetorically employs the syllogistic demonstration (*enthymeme*) to prove the truth of its arguments. Jomier and Gobillot find parallels in the Church Fathers and Hermetic tradition, while Gwynne compares Qur'anic syllogism heuristically with Aristotelian models, and defines the central truth that is demonstrated as the human obligation to recognize and fulfil the divine covenant. Ulrika Mårtensson (2008) has further qualified the Qur'anic demonstration regarding the covenant as the *semeion*, 'sign *enthymeme*'. According to Aristotle's *Rhetoric*, *semeion* is a demonstration adapted for deliberative speech in the public forum, which uses narrative examples as 'signs' (i.e. *āyāt*) instead of the abstract syllogistic demonstration used in philosophical discourse. This result agrees with another of Izutsu's points, that although some suras resemble the Arab soothsayers *sajʿ*, or rhyming prose, the dominant form is narrative accounts (*qiṣaṣ*).

Marilyn Waldman (2013) has pointed out that the Arabic word for prophet (*nabī*) signifies contrariness and being at odds with society. The prophetic experience of being obligated by God to rhetorically persuade their communities in the face of adversity is also brought out by Anthony Johns (2011) and Muhammad Abdel Haleem (2006) in respective studies of the Qur'anic prophets Shuʿayb and Nūḥ (Noah). According to Johns (2011), Shuʿayb serves as the generic model for Muḥammad's identity as the Arab prophet whose rhetorical skills surpass all other prophets, admonishing his people about the urgency of justice. Thus, Moses is a model primarily of the prophetic lawgiver, while Shuʿayb primarily represents the Arab rhetorician.

Johns's approach to Qur'anic prophet personalities could fruitfully be further pursued with reference to Avni's (1968) comparative study of *Phaedrus*' poets and the

Hebrew prophets, as well as the Islamic concept of *iʿjāz*. Angelika Neuwirth (1983, 1987) has argued that the post-third/ninth-century doctrine of the Qur'an's linguistic 'inimitability' (*iʿjāz*) is reflected in the literary, poetic form of the Qur'an itself. Questioning Neuwirth's approach, Mattias Radscheit (1996) has argued that while *iʿjāz* does indeed have a foundation in the Qur'an, it refers here to God's mastery of nature in His 'inimitable' capacity as Creator. As the Creator's signs, the *āyāt* constitute God's proof (*ḥujja*). The defining framework for this concept of *āyāt* is the Qur'anic covenant (*mīthāq*), which is modelled according to Moses' Sinai revelation and reception of the written law. Radscheit's view of *āyāt* matches the Hebrew Bible's *ôthôt*, that is, signs exclusive to God as Creator (Moberly 2011). However, Izutsu (1964/2002) actually synthesized the linguistic and 'Creator performer' inimitability as two aspects of the inimitable *āyāt*. This approach was further elaborated by Mårtensson (2008), who argues that in the Qur'anic *rhetoric*, the *topic* of God's inimitable mastery of creation 'signals' and persuades of the divine nature of the communication.

Another important non-linguistic form of Qur'anic revelation are visions, such as Q. 53 and Q. 81. Josef van Ess (1999) argues that these suras describe visions, most likely of God, who has descended to earth to manifest Himself, and perhaps even dwells there. Van Ess's view challenges the common exegetical understanding inspired by the *sīra*, which locates the Prophet's visions in heaven subsequent to his ascension (*miʿrāj*), but is in line with the Qur'anic *tanzīl* movement, according to which God always signals downwards (Wild 1996). Geo Widengren made the same point in his comparative studies of Near Eastern messengers and prophets (1946–55): some ascend to heaven to fetch divine writing, but the Prophet Muḥammad remains on earth and divine *kitāb* is made to descend to him. Nevertheless, Kevin van Bladel (2007) claims the Qur'anic term *sabab* (pl. *asbāb*, 'cause') refers to cosmic cords, by which prophets ascend to heaven in order to bring down signs; that is, rather than God sending down the signs the Prophet ascends and then brings them down.

It is also worth noting that the biblical verb *niglā* ('divine manifestation'; see above) has a Qur'anic Arabic cognate: *jallā*, 'God makes something manifest' (Q. 7:187); *tajallā*, 'God made Himself fully manifest' (Q. 7:143); and the noun *jalāʾ*, 'banishment, exile at God's command' (Q. 59:3). This Qur'anic concept is close to the biblical 'apocalyptic' sense of 'revelation'.

Oral or Written?

According to Izutsu, the Bible describes God's speech as events observed from an external viewpoint, while the Qur'an also self-identifies with it, as the divine *kalām*, *kitāb* (writing, scripture), and *qurʾān* (reading, recitation). The conceptual pair *kitāb* and *qurʾān* has generated a debate whether *qurʾān* refers to *kalām* as reading or recitation of a written text (*kitāb*), or as an oral communication written down in the process of canonization. Early consensus held that *kitāb* referred to a written text

(Madigan 2001: 13–23). More recently, Wild (1996; 2006) and Mårtensson (2008) too argue that Qur'anic references to itself as signs which are interpreted (Q. 3:7) imply identification with an interpreted scripture (*kitāb*).

An early representative of the opposite view is Tor Andrae (1933). Andrae concluded that the Prophet Muḥammad never perceived the Qur'an as a read scripture but as a liturgical recitation, patterned on the Syriac churches' *qeryāna*, 'lecture' (cf. Graham 1984; Gilliot 2004). Accordingly, the Qur'anic term *kitāb* originated within an oral discourse *about* scripture, not *as scripture*. The same basic idea has been developed by Richard Martin and William Graham. Angelika Neuwirth has taken an evolutionary approach to the issue, arguing that the Qur'anic text displays development from an original oral, liturgical recitation to the notion of a written text. The argument follows Nöldeke's (2013/1909) dating of suras and his argument that the contents of the Qur'anic message changed as the Prophet encountered new religious communities. In the late Meccan period and especially in Medina the Prophet met Jews and Christians and accommodated their view of scripture (*kitāb*), unknown to him in Mecca. Similarly, Alford Welch, in a study of the so-called 'punishment stories' in Q. 26, 54, 7, and 11, finds that they contain specific formulaic features, which vary somewhat depending on the context, all of which support the notion of evolving oral speech.

The arguments for the oral nature of the Qur'an culminate with Daniel Madigan's monograph on the subject (2001). *Kitāb*, Madigan argues, refers to the divine, living *logos*, the Platonic concept of discursive exposition of teachings that corresponds to Christ (cf. Abū Zayd: 1992) and was popularized in the Syriac and Egyptian ascetic Christian communities, and in the rabbinical concept of oral and written Torah (cf. Graham: 1984). In these traditions, 'text' is perceived dialogically as 'that which speaks to the scholar's queries'. Against the developmental approach of Neuwirth (1996), however, Madigan shows that *kitāb* cannot be a late Meccan and Medinan concept, since it spans the canonical corpus. Madigan (2006) has also questioned Wild's (1996) conclusion that Qur'anic references to itself as interpreted signs (Q. 3:7) mean that it was a written text, suggesting instead that signs could just as well refer to events, which are alluded to in the oral narrative. Subsequently, Neuwirth has accepted Madigan's argument that *kitāb* appears across the canon, but within her paradigm of the evolution of an oral pre-canonical Qur'an, of the prophetic-mantic genre, to a canonical scripture that now overlays the whole corpus (cf. the approach to the Hebrew Bible by van der Toorn 2007). Devin Stewart's (2011) analysis of formal similarities between Greek and Babylonian oracle texts, and Qur'anic suras and the 'mysterious letters', also suggests that some suras should be understood as mantic speech, which voices the silent heavenly divine writing (cf. Widengren 1955). Stewart, however, presupposes a generic difference between oracle and prophecy, and suggests that formal differences between early and late suras reflect a transition from oracle to prophecy. From the perspective of Nagy (1990), however, prophecy *is* a form of oracle, and the main distinction is between lawgiver prophets and others.

While Madigan's approach to *kitāb* as discursive exposition (*logos*) appears to converge with the rhetorical studies of the Qur'an, none of these finds the demonstrative nature of the text to require an oral form (Gobillot 2004; Gwynne 2004; Jomier 2005). Mårtensson (2008) even argues that rhetorical speech requires a written template, and that the legal-contractual nature of the Qur'anic self-identity as a message about covenant explains its insistence on being 'writing' (cf. Radscheit 1996). Moreover, the 'Semitic rhetoric' method developed by Michel Cuypers describes the composition of Qur'anic suras around conceptual pairs, which constitute elaborate ring-structures that give coherence even to the long Medina suras. Cuypers's analysis of Q. 5 (2009) suggests that the ring structures must have been composed in writing, which, if correct, complicates the argument in favour of an original oral reading without any textual basis. Finally, Andrew Bannister (2014) turns the matter on its head. Tentatively (and controversially), he proposes that the long formulaic suras are more characteristic of oral, mnemonic techniques than the short, terse suras, which are more typical of written poetry.

The Politics of Revelation

Shabbir Akhtar (1991) has drawn attention to the political implications of debates about the oral or written nature of the Qur'anic revelation. The interfaith scholar Kenneth Cragg had claimed that Muslims must rethink their concept of the Qur'an as a divine revealed *text*, because it precludes politically desirable changes in the understanding of Qur'anic commands. If Muslims could recognize that the Prophet Muḥammad was the divinely inspired speaker of the Qur'an, and thus its human author, they could view the text as historically bounded and fallible. In Akhtar's view, Cragg advances a common Christian polemic against the Muslim creed, since the scholars have always made new interpretations of the Qur'an without having to renege on the belief that it is the sent-down divine *kitāb*.

Other scholars have made similar points as Cragg. Josef van Ess (1996) argues that while the Qur'an presents itself as the *verbatim* word of God, the theologians always distinguish between the word of God and the word of the Prophet, and the reading (*qirāʾa*) and what is read (*maqrūʾ*), lest any human claim to be speaking God's word. Modern 'fundamentalists' reject these theological traditions because they claim to appropriate God's word. While van Ess's approach is descriptive, Madigan has taken a prescriptive turn, claiming that the concept of *kitāb* as 'book' is dangerous because it legitimizes the fundamentalist strategy of cutting itself 'adrift from the evolving wisdom of the tradition'. He appoints Mohammed Arkoun as an exemplary Muslim academic rethinking the Qur'an as a living, oral address and 'a power with an infinite capacity to signify things' (2001: 191). Similarly, although in individually distinct ways, Fazlur Rahman (1966, 1978), Abdelmajid Charfi (2004), Abū Zayd (2004; cf. Rahman 2007), Amina Wadud (1999/1992), Abdolkarim Soroush (Amirpur 2011), and Massimo Campanini (2016) argue that socio-political reform in Islamic societies requires conceiving of the Qur'an not as a closed text, but as a living source of divine manifestation, which speaks to each believer. Since these scholars frame their studies of Qur'anic revelation with reference to current philosophy and literary theory, they also represent important new approaches to the topic. For example, Campanini's (2016) analysis of the Qur'an as a philosophy of Being as language illustrates how engagement with *both* a range of medieval and contemporary exegetes *and* modern philosophy, particularly phenomenology, pushes, for example, Izutsu's language-oriented approach to revelation further.

For followers of E. D. Hirsch, Jr., *Validity in Interpretation* (1967), however, it is disquieting when the current political issue of *which* new meanings *ought* to be derived from the Qur'an, is confounded with, for example, the historical question of the meaning of *kitāb*. To premise the outcomes of historical research on current affairs transforms the intent of research from description into prescription, that is, normative theology.

Conclusion

While some have claimed that Qur'anic concepts of divine-to-human communication differ from biblical 'revelation', closer scrutiny of the several concepts involved both in the Bible and the Qur'an reveals several parallels, some of which correspond also with ancient Greek theory. The common Greek and Near Eastern lawgiver prophet's rhetorical communication of the divine law and signs to the people appears to be the Qur'anic *generic* concept of revelation, which is complemented by the legitimizing prophetic vision of the manifest divinity. Further research is required to substantiate these preliminary findings, including the contested issue of *kitāb* and *qur'ān*. For example, 'mantic speech' approaches to the Qur'anic genre appear to contradict claims that *qur'ān* parallels Syriac *qeryānā*, that is, liturgical-textual portions, as Neuwirth points out (2014).

The Qur'an's Arabic linguistic universe and internal structures and generic forms can also still yield new insights. Given the continuous politicization of Qur'an research, and of the Islamic scholarly disciplines and legacies, efforts to systematically analyse the medieval Qur'an scholars' concepts of 'revelation', and compare them with modern research and theories, appear important. This line of enquiry would advance research into Qur'anic concepts of 'revelation', and into similarities and differences between medieval and modern research paradigms.

Bibliography

Abū Zayd, Naṣr Ḥāmid. *Naqd al-khiṭāb al-dīnī*. Cairo: Dār Ṣināʿa li'l-Nashr, 1992.

Abū Zayd, Naṣr Ḥāmid. *Rethinking the Qur'ān: Towards a Humanistic Hermeneutics*. Utrecht: Humanistics University Press, 2004.

Akhtar, Shabbir. 'An Islamic Model of Revelation', *Islam & Christian-Muslim Relations* 2 (1991), 95–105.
Amirpur, Katayun. 'The Expansion of the Prophetic Experience: Abdolkarim Soroush's New Approach to Qurʾānic Revelation', *Die Welt des Islams* 51 (2011), 409–37.
Andrac, Tor. 'Muhammad' Doctrine of Revelation', *Muslim World* 23 (1933), 252–71.
Avni, Abraham. 'Inspiration in Plato and the Hebrew Prophets', *Comparative Literature* 20/1 (1968), 55–63.
Bannister, Andrew. *An Oral-Formulaic Study of the Qur'an*. Plymouth: Lexington Books, 2014.
Campanini, Massimo. *Philosophical Perspectives on Modern Qurʾānic Exegesis: Key Paradigms and Concepts*. Sheffield: Equinox, 2016.
Charfi, Abdelmajid. *L'Islam entre le message et l'histoire*. Paris: Albin Michel, 2004.
Cuypers, Michel. 'Structures rhétoriques dans le Coran: une analyse structurelle de la sourate "Joseph" et de quelques sourates brèves', *MIDEO* 22 (1994), 107–95.
Cuypers, Michel. 'Une analyse rhétorique de début et de la fin du Coran'. In: D. De Smet, G. de Callataÿ, and J. M. F. Van Reeth (eds.). *Al-Kitāb: la sacralité du texte dans le monde de l'islam*, pp. 233–72. Brussels: D. De Smet, 2004.
Cuypers, Michel. *The Banquet: A Reading of the Fifth Sura of the Qurʾān*. Series Rhetorica Semitica. Rome: Convivium Press, 2009.
Gilliot, Claude. 'Le Coran, fruit d'un travail collectif?' In: D. De Smet, G. de Callataÿ, and J. M. F. Van Reeth (eds.). *Al-Kitāb: la sacralité du texte dans le monde de l'islam*, pp. 185–231. Brussels: D. De Smet, 2004.
Gobillot, Geneviève. 'La Démonstration de l'existence de Dieu comme élément sacré d'un texte'. In: D. De Smet, G. de Callataÿ, and J. M. F. Van Reeth (eds.). *Al-Kitāb: la sacralité du texte dans le monde de l'islam*, pp. 103–42. Brussels: D. De Smet, 2004.
Graham, William A. 'The Earliest Meaning of "Qurʾān"', *Die Welt des Islams* 23–4 (1984), 361–77.
Graham, William A. 'Qurʾān as Spoken Word: An Islamic Contribution to the Understanding of Scripture'. In Richard Martin (ed.) *Approaches to Islam in Religious Studies*, pp. 23–40. Tucson: University of Arizona Press, 1985, reprinted in: Mona Siddiqui (ed.) *Islam*, vol. 1: *Qur'ān and Prophecy*, pp. 23–45. London: SAGE, 2010.
Gwynne, Rosalind Ward. *Logic, Rhetoric, and Legal Reasoning in the Qur'ān: God's Arguments*. London: Routledge, 2004.
Haleem, M. A. S. 'The Qurʾānic Employment of the Story of Noah', *Journal of Qur'anic Studies* 8/1 (2006), 38–57.
Izutsu, Toshihiko. *God and Man in the Qur'ān: Semantics of the Qur'ānic Weltanschauung*. Kuala Lumpur, 2002/Keio University, 1964.
Johns, Anthony. 'Shuʿayb, Orator of the Prophets: Reflections on Qurʾānic Narrative', *Journal of Qur'anic Studies* 13/2 (2011), 136–48.
Jomier, Jacques. 'L'Évidence de l'Islam'. In: Geneviève Gobillot (ed.) *L'Orient chrétien dans l'empire musulman: hommage au professeur Gérard Troupeau*, pp. 23–36. Versailles: Éditions de Paris, 2005.
Madigan, Daniel. *The Qurʾān's Self-Image: Writing and Authority in Islam's Scripture*. Princeton: Princeton University Press, 2001.
Madigan, Daniel. 'The Limits of Self-Referentiality in the Qurʾān'. In: Stefan Wild (ed.). *Self-Referentiality*, pp. 59–69. Wiesbaden: Harrassowitz Verlag, 2006.
Mårtensson, Ulrika. '"The Persuasive Proof": A Study of Aristotle's Politics and Rhetoric in the Qurʾān and al-Tabari's Commentary', *Jerusalem Studies in Arabic and Islam* 34 (2008), 363–420.

Martin, Richard. 'Understanding the Qurʾān in Text and Context', *History of Religions* 21/4 (1982), 361–84, repr. in Mona Siddiqui (ed.). *Islam*, vol. 1: *Qur'ān and Prophecy*, pp. 1–21. London: SAGE, 2010.

Moberly, Walter L. 'Miracles in the Hebrew Bible'. In G. H. Twelftree (ed.). *The Cambridge Companion to Miracles*, pp. 57–74. Cambridge: Cambridge University Press, 2011.

Nagy, Gregory. 'Ancient Greek Poetry, Prophecy, and Concepts of Theory'. In: James L. Kugel (ed.). *Poetry and Prophecy: The Beginnings of a Literary Tradition*, pp. 56–64. Ithaca, NY: Cornell University Press, 1990.

Neuwirth, Angelika. 'Das islamische Dogma der "Unnachahmlichkeit des Korans" in literaturwissenschaftlicher Sicht', *Der Islam* 60 (1983), 166–83.

Neuwirth, Angelika, 'Iʿjāz al-Qurʾān'. In: Helmut Gätje (ed.). *Grundriss der arabischen Philologie*, vol. 2: *Litteraturwissenschaft*, pp. 126–8. Wiesbaden: Reichert, 1987.

Neuwirth, Angelika. 'Vom Rezitationstext über die Liturgie zum Kanon'. In Stefan Wild (ed.) *The Qur'ān as Text*, pp. 69–105. Leiden: Brill, 1996.

Neuwirth, Angelika. 'Orientalism in Oriental Studies? Qurʾānic Studies as a Case in Point', *Journal of Qur'anic Studies* 9/2 (2007), 115–27.

Neuwirth, Angelika. *Scripture, Poetry, and the Making of a Community: Reading the Qur'ān as a Literary Text*. Oxford: Oxford University Press, 2014.

Nöldeke, Theodor, Friedrich Schwally, Gotthelf Bergsträsser, and Otto Pretzl. *The History of the Qurʾān*. Ed. and trans. Wolfgang H. Behn. Leiden: Brill, 2013 [Leipzig, 1909–38].

Radscheit, Matthias. 'Iʿjāz al-Qurʾān im Koran?' In: Stefan Wild (ed.). *The Qur'ān as Text*, pp. 113–23. Leiden: Brill, 1996.

Rahman, Fazlur. *Islam*. Chicago: University of Chicago Press, 1966.

Rahman, Fazlur. 'Divine Revelation and the Prophet', *Hamdard Islamicus* 2/1 (1978), 66–72.

Rahman, Yusuf. 'The Qurʾān in Egypt III: Naṣr Abū Zayd's Literary Approach'. In: Khaleel Mohammed and Andrew Rippin (eds.). *Coming to Terms with the Qurʾān* pp. 227–65. North Haledon, NJ: Islamic Publications International, 2007.

Stewart, Devin. 'The Mysterious Letters and Other Formal Features of the Qur'an in Light of Greek and Babylonian Oracular Texts'. In: Gabriel S. Reynolds (ed.). *New Perspectives on the Qurʾān: The Qurʾān in its Historical Context 2*, pp. 323–48. New York: Routledge, 2011.

Tottoli, Roberto. *Biblical Prophets in the Qur'ān and Muslim Literature*. Richmond: Curzon, 2002.

van Bladel, Kevin. 'Heavenly Cords and Prophetic Authority in the Qurʾān and its Late Antique Context', *Bulletin of the School of Oriental and African Studies* 70/2 (2007), 223–46.

Van der Toorn, Karel. *Scribal Culture and the Making of the Hebrew Bible*. Cambridge, MA: Harvard University Press, 2007.

van Ess, Josef. 'Verbal Inspiration? Language and Revelation in Classical Islamic Theology'. In: Stefan Wild (ed.). *The Qur'ān as Text*, pp. 177–94. Leiden: Brill, 1996.

van Ess, Josef. 'Vision and Ascension: *Surat al-Najm* and its Relationship with Muhammad's *miʿraj*', *Journal of Qur'anic Studies* 1/1 (1999), 47–62.

Wadud, Amin. *Qur'ān and Woman: Rereading the Sacred Text from a Woman's Perspective*. Oxford: Oxford University Press, 1999/1992.

Waldman, Marilyn. *Prophecy and Power: Muhammad and the Qur'ān in the Light of Comparison*. Sheffield: Equinox, 2013.

Widengren, Geo. *King and Saviour*. 4 vols. Uppsala: Lundequistska bokhandeln, 1946–55.

Wild, Stefan. '"We have sent down to thee the book with the truth...": Spatial and Temporal Implications of the Qurʾānic Concepts of nuzûl, tanzîl and 'inzâl'. In: Stefan Wild (ed.). *The Qurʾān as Text*, pp. 137–53. Leiden: Brill, 1996.
Welch, Alford, 'Formulaic Features of the Punishment Stories'. In: Issa J. Boullata (ed.). *Literary Structures of Meaning in the Qur'ān*, pp. 77–116. Richmond: Curzon, 2000.
Zwettler, Michael. 'A Mantic Manifesto: The Sura of "The Poets" and the Qurʾānic Foundations of Prophetic Authority'. In: James L. Kugel (ed.). *Poetry and Prophecy: The Beginnings of A Literary Tradition*, pp. 75–119. Ithaca, NY: Cornell University Press, 1990.

CHAPTER 27

DOCTRINE AND DOGMA IN THE QUR'AN

STEPHEN R. BURGE

THERE have been a number of different reflections and approaches to the issue of doctrine and dogma in the Qur'an, and in Islam more broadly; and, consequently, it is necessary to distinguish between those studies which have examined the reception, elaboration, and discourses of Muslim scholars and those which have studied the Qur'an directly. Inevitably, it is not always possible to distinguish the two, but this chapter will focus on studies of dogma in the Qur'an, rather than those that explore later Muslim discussions, either medieval or modern.

To talk of dogma and doctrine in relation to a scripture, rather than to a faith, can sometime be difficult, as scriptures do not always provide clear and unambiguous statements on all theological issues. So, whilst the Qur'an is explicit and unequivocal in its espousal of monotheism, the Muslim doctrine of *tawḥīd* (divine 'unicity' or 'oneness'), other doctrines are less clearly stated. This is best illustrated by the complex array of sources in Muslim literature on the problem of predestination and free will found in the Qur'an, the hadith, and theology—conveniently collected in a number of old but helpful sources (e.g. Salisbury 1866; de Vlieger 1903). For example, whilst there are verses in the Qur'an which clearly advocate divine predestination (Q. 51:22; 56:60; 57:22; 68:25, etc.), there is also a strong sense of *taklīf*—human responsibility for actions (Q. 2:25; 5:9; 10:9, etc.). This has led many scholars to engage with both the medieval Muslim theological responses to this problem (Wolfson 1976: 601–719; De Cillis 2014), and to reflect on the relationship between Muslim theology and the dogmatic statements found in the Qur'an (Gardet 1967). Furthermore, different theologians and groups within Islam also use the same verses of the Qur'an to advocate contradictory positions (Hamza et al. 2008: 455–89). However, Muslim thinkers did develop a series of ideas or beliefs, known as the *uṣūl al-dīn* ('the roots of the faith'), that were deemed to form a central core, to which all Muslims should adhere. The Muslim theologian Ibn Rushd (d. 595/1198), for example, gives the core beliefs in his *al-Kashf ʿan manāhij al-adilla fī ʿaqāʾid al-milla* as (i) the existence of God, (ii) the oneness of God, (iii), the attributes of

God, (iv) the transcendence of God, and (v) the actions of God, which includes creation, interaction with humanity through prophets, predestination and free will, divine justice, and the resurrection and judgement of the dead (Ibn Rushd/Averroës 2001; see also Watt 1994). It is, therefore, necessary to be a little cautious about describing 'Qur'anic dogma', since there is little that is held in common by all Muslims, past and present. In recent years many Muslim scholars have tried to re-evaluate doctrinal positions in light of contemporary society, a process which began with the modernist movement and figures such as Muḥammad ʿAbdūh and Rashīd Riḍā. For example, Munʾim Sirry has presented a study of modernist and reformist interpretations of Qur'anic passages relating to inter-faith concerns (2014) and Abdulaziz Sachedina has explored the idea of democratic pluralism in light of the Qur'an (2001). Both of these works can be seen as contemporary engagements with Qur'anic dogma and belief.

The dichotomy between those who believe and those who do not believe is a predominant theme, which reveals the importance of *tawḥīd* in the Qur'anic worldview. There are a number of words used in the Qur'an to describe believers and non-believers, particularly *muʾmin* ('believer'), *muslim* ('Muslim' or literally 'one who submits'), *mushrik* ('one who associates [something with God]'), *ḥanīf* ('a pre-Islamic monotheist') amongst others. Some of the precise meanings of these words are contentious, especially *ḥanīf*, which has generated much discussion (Rubin 1990). Most recently Fred Donner has argued that the use of the term *muslim* to refer to the contemporary concept of a 'Muslim' was developed at a later date, during the reign of the Umayyad Caliph ʿAbd al-Malik (r. 65–86/685–705). Donner argues that statements that Abraham was both a *muslim* and a *ḥanīf*, suggest that the term *muslim* did not necessarily denote what we mean by it now (see Donner 2010: 57–8 and 203–4). Qur'anic dogma is the means by which people can be divided into the categories of 'believer' and 'non-believer'.

This chapter will begin by exploring four areas of dogma that are used to distinguish Muslims from others as believers. The four areas concern different beliefs or attributes of God: (i) the Qur'anic views on divine unity (*tawḥīd*), which is expressed often, but most clearly in the statement, 'Say: "He is God, One"' (Q. 112:1); (ii) the belief that God is the creator of the heavens and the earth (cf. Q. 2:29; 6:1–2; 7:54 etc.), and the theological beliefs that emerge from this view of God, namely that God is also 'ruler' or 'sovereign' of the created order; (iii) a belief in divine mercy and communication with the created order; and (iv) the belief that God also created other supernatural beings, such as the jinn, angels (*malāʾika*), and devils (*shayāṭīn*).

God as One

Monotheism or 'Oneness' (*tawḥīd*) is a central tenet in Islam, and different scholars have approached the question of *tawḥīd* in different ways. Much time and energy has been spent in Islamic studies in attempts to understand the theology of the Qur'an, and especially the emergence of *tawḥīd* in the context of pre-Islamic Arabia: why did monotheism develop in Arabia, and how can the Arabian context help frame our interpretation of the Qur'anic *tawḥīd*? (Welch 1979). There have been a number of different ways in which this subject has been approached by historians of religion. The field is extremely complex, partly because of the paucity of sources for first-/seventh-century Arabia, but also because of the various responses scholars have made regarding the authenticity and accuracy of the Muslim accounts of its early development. Although it is something of an oversimplification, it is possible to separate studies of the development of Qur'anic dogma into two main approaches: (i) that Qur'anic dogma should be viewed as a product of its Arabian context; and (ii) that late-ancient Christian and Jewish thought had a profound influence on Qur'anic monotheism.

The study of the Qur'an and the emergence of Islam in its Arabian context has been the focus of a number of studies, but it is necessary to place any modern studies in the context of the work of early figures such as Julius Wellhausen (1897/1927), and Josef Henninger (1959/1981) who set the tone for much of the work that has followed them. Scholars such as M. M. Bravmann (1972) and Jacques Ryckmans (1989) developed the study of pre-Islamic religion; their studies, although more directly concerned with pre-Islamic paganism, provide the religious context in which Islamic dogma emerged, and such studies continue to be of interest (e.g. Hoyland 2001). Of those who have discussed Islam in its Arabian context more specifically, Jacques Chelhod, Toufic Fahd, and W. Montgomery Watt deserve particular attention, since it was these sorts of studies that 'revisionist' views of early Islamic history and doctrine reacted against.

Jacques Chelhod's work of the 1950s and 1960s viewed Muslim doctrines as developing out of pre-Islamic belief systems (Chelhod 1955; 1964). Influenced by the development of the anthropology of religion, he argues that Arabian religion underwent a process of theological development, which showed increasing monotheism. He and other scholars argued that the Qur'an bears witness to this process, with the Qur'an displaying stronger monotheist statements over time (Welch 1980; Waardenburg 1984). Toufic Fahd's work places Islam and Qur'anic theology within the milieu of pre-Islamic religion, exploring the social and religious structures and beliefs of pre-Islamic paganism and their relationship to the Qur'an (Fahd 1968). This approach continues to garner great interest and a number of studies exploring the Qur'an in light of late antique Arabia (de Blois 2010).

Whereas Chelhod approaches Qur'anic *tawḥīd* from an anthropological perspective, Montgomery Watt's 'High God' theory attempted to present a historical account for the emergence of *tawḥīd* in Arabia (Watt 1971, 1979; Rubin 1984), which developed earlier studies of pre-Islamic Arabian monotheism (Gibb 1962). The theory argues that as Arabian society became more integrated, with a particular focus on the Kaʿba in Mecca, Arab religious thinking began to coalesce around Allāh, the 'High God' of the Arabian pantheon. Qur'anic *tawḥīd*, then, was part of this gradual movement towards the worship of a single deity within the region. Watt's position that Allāh was the pre-eminent divinity of the Arabs gained some support (e.g. Pavlovich 1982), but recently it has been critiqued by G. R. Hawting (1999: 20–44), Patricia Crone (2010), and Aziz al-Azmeh (2014). For example, al-Azmeh argues that archaeological evidence suggests the persistence of pagan cultic worship in Central Arabia (2014: 279). More widely al-Azmeh argues that it is necessary to place pre-Islamic paganism in its late ancient context, particularly the fact that late ancient paganism also went through a monotheizing process, without being Judaeo-Christian (2014: 47–99, 279–357). The benefits of utilizing both Muslim and non-Muslim sources to understand aspects of Qur'anic and early Muslim dogma has been stressed by Robert Hoyland (1997: 523–98).

Many of these studies based their ideas on the later Muslim understanding of its early history, typified by Ibn Isḥāq's *Sīrat Rasūl Allāh,* which contains many stories about pre-Islamic religion, and Ibn al-Kalbī's *K. al-Aṣnām* (1952); however, such assumptions were challenged by John Wansbrough (1977, 1978). Regarding the Qur'anic doctrine of *tawḥīd*, the most important contribution is Hawting's *The Idea of Idolatry and the Emergence of Islam* (1999). Hawting argues that the polemics against idolatry (*shirk*) in the Qur'an do not necessarily suggest an Arabian context; rather, he argues, the discourse is similar to other inter-monotheist disputes, in which certain monotheist rituals and beliefs are declared 'idolatrous' by a reforming party (1999: 67–87). The religious history of Islam subsequently went through a process of Arabization (1999: 88–110), which located the origins in the Arab heartlands, rather than in Mesopotamia. Although not all will be convinced by Hawting's arguments, *The Idea of Idolatry* emphasizes the importance of viewing Qur'anic *tawḥīd* in conjunction with its discourse against *shirk*: the two cannot, and should not, be viewed separately. More recently Michel Cuypers has presented an analysis of *Sūrat al-Māʾida*, in which he argues that the whole sura should be read in terms of a Qur'anic engagement with Christian, and to a lesser extent, Jewish, beliefs, and their incompatibility with the new religion given in the Qur'an (Cuypers 2007/2009).

In recent years, the idea of 'Late Antiquity' has developed significantly in relation to the Qur'an and beliefs such as *tawḥīd*, although it is important to place these modern works in the context of the scholarship that preceded it. The material in the Qur'an that is related to the Bible solicited much interest from non-Muslim scholars, who attempted to read the Qur'an and its beliefs in light of Judaism and/or Christianity. Although there are many examples, the early works of Richard Bell (1926), Charles Cutler Torrey (1933), and James Sweetman (1947–55) are notable examples. In more recent scholarship, the interest has shifted from a Jewish and/or Christian 'origin' of Muslim beliefs, to a contextualization of the Qur'an and its beliefs, within a wider scope of Late Antiquity. In relation to *tawḥīd*, the focus has often been on the Qur'anic attacks on the Trinity and the Incarnation, both of which it describes as *shirk*. Much research has focused on the interpretation of Q. 112 (*Sūrat al-Ikhlāṣ*), and what this sura says about both Trinitarian beliefs and pre-Islamic religion (Kropp 2011). Although this sura does present some interpretative challenges, the studies show the importance and benefits of placing the Qur'anic belief in the oneness of God in the context of interlocutors, whether they are Jewish, Christian, or pagan. Indeed, Angelika Neuwirth, who advocates a kind of *lex orandi, lex credendi*, has shown that the use of suras such as *al-Fātiḥa* and *Sūrat al-Ikhlāṣ* in the devotional and liturgical life of the nascent Muslim community reveals the importance of theological concepts of ideas such as *tawḥīd* (2010: 451–509).

God as Creator and Ruler

The fact that Allāh was the 'creator of heaven and earth' is a dominant theme in the Qur'an. Some scholars, such as al-Azmeh, have argued that such a position has elements of *henotheism*, in which other gods are accepted as existing but whose power is meaningless in comparison to the authority of *Allāh* (al-Azmeh 2014: 293–315; Watt 1971). It is, however, extremely difficult to assess such theories, as the evidence for such a belief in the Qur'an can only be made through inferences. For example, the so-called 'Satanic verses', which are part of the hadith literature and are not in the Qur'an, suggest that nascent Islam did accept the existence of other goddesses (the *banāt Allāh*; 'daughters of God'; viz. *al-Lāt, al-ʿUzzā,* and *al-Manāt*). However, these 'verses' present a number of difficulties for interpretation (cf. Ahmed 1998). Nevertheless, it is important to emphasize that God's creative power is an integral part of the Qur'anic understanding of God, and a number of other religious beliefs develop out of reflections on God's role as the creator.

The Qur'anic view of the universe is cosmically dualist, in the sense that heaven and earth form two distinct realms: God and the angels reside in heaven, humans, animals, and jinn on earth. This is not to be confused with *ethical* dualism, in which good and evil are equal opponents competing for control over the universe, as can be found in Zoroastrianism and Gnosticism (see Gammie 1974). Although it has not received significant attention, particularly in relation to the Qur'an specifically, it must be remembered that heaven and hell are part of the created cosmos (cf. Rustomji 2009), and contribute to the Qur'anic view of the created order. Whilst the earth, the 'lower world' is temporal and has a specific time of existence (an *ajal*), heaven and hell are often believed to be eternal, although the eternality of hell is often debated. As with other areas of theological belief, the focus of the secondary literature is more interested in later Muslim reflections on this idea (e.g. Abrahamov 2002).

Many scholars have reflected on the nature of creation in Islam, and whether God created *ex nihilo* (out of nothing). There have been some studies of this concerning the Qur'an directly, principally by O'Shaughnessy (1985: 1–11), and it has received more interest recently. However, since the Qur'an does not engage with the belief in *creatio ex nihilo* explicitly, the focus in the secondary literature is often on later discussions in exegesis, Islamic philosophy, and theology (al-Alousi 1965; Wolfson 1976: 355–409). The Qur'an is, however, much more explicit in the descriptions of God creating human life, particularly Adam, but also all creatures. The Qur'an provides a basic outline of the development of the embryo within the womb (Q. 23:12–14), which has received some attention in the secondary literature (O'Shaughnessy 1985: 10–19; Bakker 1965: 9–19). Such description is also used in *tafsīr ʿilmī* (or 'scientific exegesis'), to argue that the Qur'an (and the hadith) and modern scientific advances are comptatible (e.g. Albar 1986). Similar approaches to the Qur'an have been used to argue for or against the idea of evolutionism (cf. Shanavas 2005), and there are numerous studies on these discussions (Ayoub 2005).

God's act of creation also makes God sovereign or ruler over creation. This sovereignty is symbolized in the Qur'an with the image of God sitting upon a throne (*'arsh*; Q. 25:59; 32:4 etc.), often with attendant angels (e.g. Q. 39:75; 69:17). Such imagery has much in common with biblical and Judaeo-Christian motifs (see O'Shaughnessy 1973), and these images generated much discussion in medieval Muslim thought, since they could lead to a belief in anthropomorphism (see Gimaret 1997: 123–261). Although some read the references to God's throne literally, both in the medieval and modern periods, the Qur'an clearly uses the image to describe God's authority and 'kingship', indeed, the same word is used to describe both heavenly and human, kingly thrones (Q. 27:23–42; 38:34 etc.). Although the uses of the imagery of divine kingship do not properly constitute dogmatic statements, the concept of divine sovereignty is an essential element in Islamic doctrine; and a number of critical and definitive beliefs flow out from the notion of divine authority, which warrant discussion.

First, one consequence of the view of God as the sovereign and creator of all things, both heavenly and divine, is that God is able to subvert the natural order of creation when events necessitate. This manifests itself in a number of different ways: first, there is a theological and semantic link between God's creative and destructive power (Makino 1970; Smith and Haddad 1981); second, God can create life and so is able to create Adam and Jesus without there being a process of divine incarnation (Robinson 1990: 156–66). Third, God is able to give this ability to subvert the natural order to the prophets, so Jesus is able to create birds from clay (Q. 5:110; Robinson 1989; Dzon 2011); prophets are able to raise the dead (Q. 2:259; O'Shaughnessy 1969: 45–49; Reynolds 2009: 167–85); Moses can part the Red Sea (Q. 20:77–8), and so on. The study of the supernatural elements of the Qur'anic and Muslim worldview has recently gained the interest of scholars, and is being continually developed (Williams 2013).

As the creator of all things, what God creates, God is also able to destroy; indeed the companion pair of life and death is common throughout the whole of the Qur'an. The belief that death is generated by God is central to Muslim belief and forms a break from what is known about pre-Islamic beliefs, which appear to have been much vaguer and abstract (Homerin 1985). The Qur'an makes frequent reference to the *ajal*, the 'moment of death' or the 'span of a life', which is decreed by God and under God's authority. This theme is developed in great detail in the hadith literature (see Smith and Haddad 1981) and beyond, with the remembrance of death (*dhikr al-mawt*) becoming a focus of Islamic piety (Winter 1989: i–xxx). The sense of ending and completion is not just applicable to human life, but is also seen in the end of time and the cataclysmic events that accompany it: creation has a violent end and the natural order is subverted through the authority of God (Smith and Haddad 1981: 31–62, 127–46). More importantly, the earth also has a fixed time for existence, that is, an *ajal* (Q. 30:8; 46:3), and all of creation is geared towards the completion of the *ajal*.

After the 'death' of the world, there comes judgement, and the subsequent consignment to hell (*jahannam*) or admittance into the Garden. The Qur'an is quite clear about when judgement will take place—on the Day of Resurrection—and that judgement is based on the actions committed by each individual, principally belief in God and His messenger (Smith and Haddad 1981: 62–98). The belief in the two Muslim angels, Munkar and Nakīr, who come to visit the grave after death, is a much later development (see Burge 2012: 190–2). In recent years, there has been much reflection on whether non-Muslims are able to enter heaven; Mohammed Hassan Khalil in particular, highlights a number of Muslim theologians who have argued for a pluralistic approach to salvation (Khalil 2012) that engages with Qur'anic understandings of salvation and the afterlife.

Such approaches highlight the main problem with considering a scripture such as the Qur'an and questions of 'dogma' and 'doctrine'. At a basic level, the Qur'an is clear about the need for humans to acknowledge divine authority and to behave accordingly, since judgement is based on these criteria; but the application of such a belief is much more complex and no answer is provided within the text. In this respect, dogma always remains fluid and susceptible to change; but, nevertheless, it is possible to draw out overarching themes, of which God's ultimate sovereignty over the universe, through God's own creative power, is a central belief. Other considerations, such as whether God is actually seated on a throne, or who precisely will gain admittance into heaven, can tend to miss the main, wider point being made: namely, that God holds authority over the universe and acts accordingly.

God's Mercy

The extent to which divine mercy can constitute a matter of dogma or doctrine is hard to say, but the concept of mercy forms an essential element of the Qur'anic worldview; and, furthermore, certain ideas flow out from the belief in divine mercy, particularly the Qur'anic view of salvation, prophethood, and revelation. Although these three ideas can be treated individually, they are all manifestations of divine mercy.

God's mercy is expressed in the forgiveness of humans who commit sins and the human inclination to be ungrateful for the benefits that God bestows on them. Hamartiology, the study of sin, has received relatively little consideration in comparison to other areas of Qur'anic theology, although there are some short early surveys of the theme (e.g. Rahman 1980: 17–36). The focus has tended to be on legal aspects and the categorization of different types and classes of sins. However, sin is a central theme in the Qur'an, with the sin of Adam in the Garden providing an account of why humans can and do sin (e.g. Neuwirth 2000). It is through an acknowledgement of God's sovereignty, as well as God's beneficence, that sins can be forgiven by God. This is illustrated clearly throughout *Sūrat Yūnus* (Q. 10), in which unbelief (*kufr*) and 'associationism' (*shirk*) are linked theologically to a failure to see God's signs (*āyāt*) in creation and to give thanks to God for them. As has been mentioned above, the Qur'an envisions a universe in which the divine and earthly worlds are separate and distinct spheres and the expulsion of Adam from the Garden marks human separation from God. However, whilst sin abides in the earthly world, God, through kindness and mercy, sends messengers to humans in order to provide them with an opportunity to be shown God's *āyāt*. Prophecy and prophethood are consequently an essential component in the articulation of divine mercy.

The role of prophets in the Qur'an has generated much discussion in the secondary literature. Many of the early studies of the prophets in the Qur'an were made as they provided a bridge between the Muslim and Judaeo-Christian traditions. Some early scholarship includes an element of anti-Muslim polemic, but more recent studies have highlighted the centrality of the prophets within Qur'anic discourse. Studies have looked at prophecy and prophethood in general (e.g. Rahman 1980: 80–105; Tottoli 2002), while others have looked at the portrayals of specific prophets, such as Abraham, Moses, and Solomon (Firestone 1990; Wheeler 2002; Lassner 1993). This recent scholarship has tended to focus on the way the Qur'an makes use of prophets within a wider theological discourse, rather than source-critical comparisons with Jewish and Christian material, and these studies aim to gain a deeper understanding of what prophecy and prophethood means in the Qur'anic worldview. Some of the wider implications of prophethood have also been given some attention in the secondary literature. For example, God's use of angels and men as messengers of God's word also establishes a link between God and humanity that forms an essential part of the Qur'anic worldview. Toshihiko Izutsu has explored the patterns of communication between God and prophets in the most detail (Izustu 2002: 133–97; see also Wild 1996). The giving of revelation (*tanzīl, inzāl*) is not simply a private experience for the prophet, but is something that needs to be passed on to the prophet's audience as a divine proclamation. This relationship is also embodied in the idea of covenant (*mīthāq*, *ʿahd*), of which the covenant made between God and the Children of Israel is the most significant (Humphreys 1989; Mårtensson 2008). The idea of making oaths and covenant also had an impact on early Muslim politics, in which the giving of an oath to a caliph formed an important part of the acknowledgement of political leadership (Marsham 2009).

Just as God is merciful, there is an expectation that humans will also behave in a like manner, although this moves away from the realm of doctrine into the sphere of ethical thought. Although, it should be noted that an interesting trend in the discussion of divine mercy has recently emerged, in which the Qur'anic concepts of mercy and forgiveness are used to aid conflict resolution within the contemporary world (Abu-Nimer and Nasser 2013). In many respects, this illustrates that doctrine and dogma are not isolated academic issues, but are ones that can have an important impact on a community as a whole.

The Otherworldly

The Qur'an clearly describes a created universe which incorporates both human and supernatural elements, of which angels, jinn, and devils are the most notable. The study of Qur'anic angelology and demonology has received much less attention than other aspects of Qur'anic doctrine, but more recently a number of new works have begun to open out the study of the supernatural in the Qur'an.

In many early studies of Qur'anic angelology scholars have often posited a strong influence of Jewish and Christian ideas (Fahd 1971). Although there is, undoubtedly, much in common between Qur'anic angelology and that of sixthcentury Judaism and Christianity (both biblical and extra-biblical), scholars have begun to acknowledge that there are some unique elements to Islamic and Qur'anic angelology (Burge 2012: 52–69; cf. O'Shaughnessy 1953: 33–42). The role of angels as 'messengers' has also been stressed throughout the literature, with scholars often asserting that the Arabic for angel (*malak*, pl. *malāʾika*) should be interpreted in light of its verbal root (*alaka* or *laʾaka*), meaning 'to send'; *malāʾika* are, therefore 'sent things' or 'messengers'. However, *malak* is frequently glossed with *rasūl* ('messenger'), which implies that role of angels as messengers had to be spelt out (Burge 2008: 51–4). This means that the Qur'anic *malak* is conceived as a divine creature, rather than as a 'messenger'. This view of angels as a species of supernatural being, rather than functionaries, fits in with the ways in which other supernatural creatures, such as the jinn and the *shayāṭīn*, are conceived (El-Zein 2009: 32–52). Angels also have a clear role in both worship (Burge 2009) and the eschatological events of the Last Day (Smith and Haddad 1981), which are not strictly 'messenger' roles.

One of the most difficult issues to deal with concerning angelology is the prostration of the angels to Adam in Q. 2:34. It is an issue that presented many problems for medieval Muslims and it still remains largely unresolved and continues to generate debate (Tottoli 1998; Chipman 2002). The angelic prostration to Adam is important since it provides a confluence of the supernatural, as it involves God, the angels, Adam, Iblīs, and jinn. It is worth discussing the episode in a little detail as it illustrates the problems that can be encountered with aspects of dogma in the Qur'an, as well as Qur'anic beliefs about angels, jinn, and devils. The Qur'anic narrative appears to be relatively straightforward: God commands the angels to prostrate to Adam, but Iblīs refuses (Q. 2:34; 7:11), and then subsequently vows to lead humans astray (Q. 7:16; 20:117). After this Iblīs becomes known as Shayṭān ('Satan'), who then gains fellow 'devils' (*shayāṭīn*; Q. 2:14, 257 etc.). This simple story provides a mythical-historical account of the origin of evil; but on closer inspection it can open wide a number of theological problems, but two are worthy of mention and have a bearing on Qur'anic doctrine.

First, why did God command the angels to prostrate to something that was not God? The most common response has been that the prostration was not an act of worship, but is related to Adam's, and by extension human, superiority over other created beings (Tottoli 1998). However, the reason humans are hierarchically higher than other creations is unclear. Numerous reasons have been posited: first, the designation of Adam as the *khalīfa* ('representative' or 'vice-regent') of God; but even the meaning or significance of this title is unclear and it has generated much discussion in both medieval and contemporary scholarship (Crone and Hinds 1986). Second, Adam is able to use reason (cf. Q. 2:31); this is used to distinguish and promote Adam above other creations, particularly angels, jinn, and *shayāṭīn*, but also animals (El-Zein 2009: 24–31; Burge 2012: 88–108). Third, the substance out of which creatures are created influences their place in the hierarchy of the universe: angels are made of light, jinn are made out of 'smokeless fire' (Q. 15:27), Adam is made out of mud, into which God breathes the divine spirit (Q. 15:28–29). Iblīs' protestations to God focus on the question of physical substance (Q. 17:61; 38:76); but why does the matter out of which creations are made create a hierarchy? Reynolds, drawing on Syriac texts, has argued that the prostration is a result of the divine spirit that is placed with Adam (Reynolds 2009: 29–54). Fourth, the prostration to Adam is in anticipation of human faith in God and the moral responsibility (*taklīf*) that is imposed on humans despite God's hiddenness, unlike the angels who see and know God's existence (Burge 2012: 93–7). All of these solutions are consonant with wider Qur'anic theology, but the Qur'an does not provide a full account of the reasons behind the prostration to Adam, revealing the problems of reflecting on Qur'anic dogma: something theological and 'dogmatic' is clearly intended by the episode, but exactly what it is remains difficult to establish.

The prostration to Adam has also raised debates about the justice of God, since Iblīs is dealt with harshly (Awn 1983; Neuwirth 2000). However, these debates are more concerned with later Muslim reflection on the episode than on specifically Qur'anic dogma. The *rūḥ al-qudus* ('the holy spirit') mentioned in Q. 19:17 and identified by both the *tafsīr* tradition and many secondary commentators with the angel Gabriel (cf. Luke 1:26) has also generated much discussion in the scholarly literature (MacDonald 1932; O'Shaugnessy 1953; Hawting 2011); however these discussions are more concerned with later interpretation.

The Qur'an also accepts the presence of other, supernatural creatures on earth: the jinn and the *shayāṭīn* ('devils'). These have both received relatively little attention in the secondary literature, save where they become relevant in other discussions (such as the prostration to Adam). Since Eichler's early monograph, which includes specific discussions of the Qur'anic representation of jinn (1928: 8–39) and *shayāṭīn* (1928: 40–80), there have only been a few articles on either species in the Qur'an (e.g. Fahd 1971; Welch 1979; Waardenburg 1984). The focus of scholarly attention has often been focused on the belief that mental illness is derived from jinn possession, and the only recent monograph on the jinn focuses on jinn in medieval Arabic literature (El-Zein). However, the stories in the Qur'an that feature jinn, particularly their involvement with Solomon have been treated more fully (Klar 2004). Above all, the Qur'an stresses that the revelation was not given just to humans but also to the jinn, and that the jinn are subject to judgement on the Day of Resurrection (Waardenburg 1984: 276–278).

Conclusion

Any discussion of dogma and doctrine in the Qur'an is likely to prove problematic: the many different groups and schools within Islam have interpreted the same text in widely different ways. This is a problem shared by most, if not all, religions with a written scripture. The controversies of later dogmatic theology (*kalām*) often arose as differing responses to linguistic and syntactic ambiguities within the Qur'anic text. Nevertheless, there remains a core set of beliefs which are central to all Muslim groups. First, the Qur'an espouses strict monotheism (*tawḥīd*), which is placed in contrast to its religious environment. This has been an area of Qur'anic studies that has and will continue to generate much discussion. Second, that God is creator of the universe; and from this a number of other beliefs and doctrines emanate, such as divine sovereignty and eschatology. Third, in the Qur'an God is merciful and interacts with creation and sends messengers. Lastly, the Qur'an envisions a cosmic order in which there are a number of different species of being, each having a different relationship between God and humans.

Bibliography

Primary Sources

Ibn Isḥāq, Muḥammad. *Sīrat Rasūl Allāh*. Trans. A. Guillaume. *The Life of Muhammad*. Reprinted Lahore: Oxford University Press, 2006.

Ibn al-Kalbī. *Kitāb al-Aṣnām*. Trans. Nabih Amin Faris. *The Book of Idols*. Princeton: Princeton University Press, 1952.

Ibn Rushd/Averroës. *Al-Kashf ʿan manāhij al-adilla fī ʿaqāʾid al-milla*. Trans. Majid Fakhry, *Faith and Reason in Islam: Averroës Exposition of Religious Arguments*. Oxford: Oneworld, 2001.

Secondary Sources

Abrahamov, Binyamin. 'The Creation and Duration of Heaven and Hell in Islamic Theology', *Der Islam* 79 (2002), 87–102.

Abu-Nimer, Mohammed and Ilham Nasser. 'Forgiveness in the Arab and Islamic Contexts: Between Theology and Practice', *Journal of Religous Ethics* 41/3 (2013), 474–94.

Ahmed, Shahab. 'Ibn Taymiyya and the Satanic Verses', *Studia Islamica* 87/2 (1998), 67–124.

Albar, M. A. *Human Development as Revealed in the Holy Qurʾān and Ḥadīth*. Jeddah: Saudi Publishing and Distributing House, 1986.

al-Alousi, Ḥusām Muḥyī al-Dīn. *The Problem of Creation in Islamic Thought*. Baghdad: National Print and Publishing Company, 1965.

Awn, Peter J. *Satan's Tragedy and Redemption: Iblīs in Sufi Psychology*. Leiden: Brill, 1983.

Ayoub, Mohammed M. 'Creation or Evolution? The Reception of Darwinism in Modern Arab Thought'. In: Zainal Abidin Baghir (ed.). *Science and Religion in a Post-Colonial World: Interfaith Perspectives*, pp. 173–90. Hindmarsh: ATF Press, 2005.

al-Azmeh, Aziz. *The Emergence of Islam in Late Antiquity: Allah and his People*. Cambridge: Cambridge University Press, 2014.

Bakker, Dirk. *Man in the Qurʾān*. Amsterdam: Drukkerij Holland NV, 1965.

Bell, Richard. *The Origins of Islam in its Christian Environment*. London: Macmillan, 1926.

Bravmann, M. M. *The Spiritual Background of Early Islam: Studies in Ancient Arab Concepts*. Leiden: Brill, 1972.

Burge, S. R. 'The Angels in *Sūrat al-Malāʾika*: Exegeses of Q. 35:1', *Journal of Qur'anic Studies* 10/1 (2008), 50–71.

Burge, S. R. 'Angels, Ritual and Sacred Space in Islam', *Comparative Islamic Studies* 5/2 (2009), 221–45.
Burge, S. R. *Angels in Islam: Jalāl al-Dīn al-Suyūṭī's* al-Ḥabāʾik fī akhbār al-malāʾik. London: Routledge, 2012.
Chelhod, Jacques. *Le Sacrifice chez les Arabes: recherches sur l'évolution, la nature, et la fonction des rites sacrificiels en Arabie occidentale.* Paris: n.p., 1955.
Chelhod, Jacques. *Les Structures du sacré chez les Arabes.* Paris: Maisonneuve et Larosse, 1964.
Chipman, Leigh N. B. 'Adam and the Angels: An Examination of the Mythic Elements in Islamic Sources', *Arabica* 49 (2002), 429–55.
Crone, Patricia. 'The Religion of the Qurʾānic Pagans: God and the Lesser Deities', *Arabica* 57/2 (2010), 151–200.
Crone, Patricia and Martin Hinds. *God's Caliph: Religious Authority in the First Centuries of Islam.* Cambridge: Cambridge University Press, 1986.
Cuypers, Michel. *The Banquet: A Reading of the Fifth Sura of the Qur'an.* Miami: Convivium, 2009. Originally published as *Le Festin: une lecture de la sourate al-Māʾida.* Paris: Lethiellieux, 2007.
de Blois, François. 'Islam in its Arabian Context'. In: Angelika Neuwirth, Nicolai Sinai, and Michael Marx (eds.). *The Qurʾān in Context: Historical and Literary Investigations into the Qurʾānic Milieu*, pp. 615–24. Leiden: Brill, 2010.
de Cillis, Maria. *Free Will and Predestination in Islamic Thought: Theoretical Compromises in the Works of Avicenna, al-Ghazālī and Ibn 'Arabī.* London: Routledge, 2014.
de Vlieger, Anthonin. *Kitâb al Qadr: matériaux pour servir à l'étude de la doctrine de la prédestination dans la théologie musulmane.* Leiden: Brill, 1903.
Donner, Fred McGraw. *Muḥammad and the Believers: At the Origins of Islam.* Cambridge, MA: Harvard University Press, 2010.
Dzon, Mary. 'Jesus and the Birds in Medieval Abrahamic Traditions', *Traditio* 66 (2011), 189–230.
El-Zein, Amira, *Islam, Arabs, and the Intelliogent World of the Jinn.* Syracuse, NY: Syracuse University Press, 2009.
Fahd, Toufic. *Le Panthéon de l'Arabie centrale à la veille de l'Hégire.* Paris: Institut Français d'Archéologie de Beyrouth, 1968.
Fahd, Toufic. 'Anges, démons et djinns in Islam'. In: D. Meeks (ed.). *Génies, anges et démons: Égypt, Babylone, Israël, Islam, Peuples Altaïques, Inde, Birmanie, Asie du Sud-Est, Tibet, Chine*, pp. 155–213. Paris: Éditions du Seuil, 1971.
Firestone, Reuven. *Journeys in Holy Lands: The Evolution of the Abraham-Ishmael Legends.* Albany: State University of New York Press, 1990.
Gammie, John G. 'Spatial and Ethical Dualism in Jewish Wisdom and Apocalyptic Literature', *Journal of Biblical Literature* 93/3 (1974), 356–85.
Gardet, Louis. *Dieu et la destine de l'homme.* Paris: Librarie Philosophique J. Vrin, 1967.
Gibb, H. A. R. 'Pre-Islamic Monotheism in Arabia', *Harvard Theological Review* 55/4 (1962), 269–80.
Gimaret, Daniel. *Dieu à l'image de l'homme: les anthropomorphismes de la sunna et leur interpretation.* Paris: Cerf, 1997.
Hamza, Feras, Sajjad Rizvi, with Farhana Mayer (eds.). *An Anthology of Qur'anic Commentaries*, vol. 1: *On the Nature of the Divine.* Oxford: Oxford University Press, in association with the Institute of Ismaili Studies, 2008.
Hawting, G. R. *The Idea of Idolatry and the Emergence of Islam: From Polemic to History.* Cambridge: Cambridge University Press, 1999.

Hawting, G. R. '"Has God sent a Mortal as a Messenger?" (Q. 17:95): Messengers and Angels in the Qurʾān'. In: Gabriel Said Reynolds (ed.). *New Perspectives on the Qurʾān: The Qurʾān in its Historical Context 2*, pp. 372–89. London: Routledge, 2011.

Henninger, Josef, 'La Religion bédouine préislamique'. In: Francesco Gabrielli (ed.). *L'antica società beduina*, pp. 115–40. Rome: Università di Roma, 1959; trans. Merlin L. Swartz, 'Pre-Islamic Bedouin Religion'. In: Merlin L. Swartz (ed.). *Studies on Islam*, pp. 3–22. Oxford: Oxford University Press, 1981.

Homerin, T. E. 'Echoes of a Thirsty Owl: Death and the Afterlife in pre-Islamic Arabic Poetry', *Journal of Near Eastern Studies* 44/3 (1985), 165–84.

Hoyland, Robert. *Seeing Islam as Others Saw It: A Survey and Evaluation of Christian, Jewish, and Zoroastrian Writings on Early Islam*. Princeton: Darwin Press, 1997.

Hoyland, Robert. *Arabia and the Arabs: From the Bronze Age to the Coming of Islam*. London: Routledge, 2001.

Humphreys, R. Stephen. 'Qurʾānic Myth and Narrative Structure in Early Islamic Historiography'. In: F. M. Clover and R. S. Humphreys (ed.). *Tradition and Innovation in Late Antiquity: Seminar entitled 'Cultural Change in the Mediterranean World and the Near East in Late Antiquity': Revised papers*, pp. 271–90. Madison: University of Wisconsin Press, 1989.

Khalil, Mohammed Kassan. *Islam and the Fate of Others*. Oxford: Oxford University Press, 2012.

Klar, M. O. '*And We cast upon his throne a mere body*: A Historiographical Reading of Q. 38:34', *Journal of Qur'anic Studies* 6/1 (2004), 103–26.

Kropp, Manfred. 'Tripartite, but anti-Trinitarian Formulas in the Qurʾānic Corpus, Possibly pre-Qurʾānic'. In: Gabriel Said Reynolds (ed.). *New Perspectives on the Qurʾān: The Qurʾān in its Historical Context 2*, pp. 247–67. London: Routledge, 2011.

Lassner, Jacob. *Demonizing the Queen of Sheba: Boundaries of Gender and Culture in Postbiblical Judaism and Medieval Islam*. Chicago: University of Chicago Press, 1993.

MacDonald, D. 'The Development of the Idea of Spirit in Islam', *Muslim World* 22/1 (1932), 25–42.

Makino, Shinya. *Creation and Termination: A Semantic Study of the Structure of the Qurʾānic World View*. Tokyo: The Keio Institute of Cultural and Linguistic Studies, 1970.

Mårtensson, Ulrika. '"The persuasive proof": A Study of Aristotle's Politics and Rhetoric in the Qurʾān and in al-Ṭabarī's Commentary', *Jerusalem Studies in Arabic and Islam* 34 (2008), 363–420.

Neuwirth, Angelika. 'Negotiating Justice: A Pre-Canonical Reading of the Qur'anic Creation Accounts', *Journal of Qur'anic Studies* 2/1 (2000), 25–41 and 2/2 (2000), 1–18.

Neuwirth, Angelika. *Der Koran als Text der Spätantike: Ein europäischer Zugang*. Berlin: Verlag der Weltreligionen, 2010.

O'Shaughnessy, Thomas. *The Development of the Meaning of Spirit in Islam*. Rome: Pontificum Institutum Orientalium Studiorum, 1953.

O'Shaughnessy, Thomas. *Muhammad's Thoughts on Death: A Thematic Study of the Qur'anic Data*. Leiden: Brill, 1969.

O'Shaughnessy, Thomas. 'God's Throne and the Biblical Symbolism of the Qurān', *Numen* 20/3 (1973), 202–21.

O'Shaughnessy, Thomas. *Creation and the Teaching of the Qurʾān*. Rome: Biblical Institute Press, 1985.

Pavlovich, Pavel. '*Qud kunnā lā naʿbudu 'llāha wa lā naʿrifuhu*. On the Problem of the Pre-Islamic Lord of the Kaʿba', *Journal of Arabic and Islamic Studies* 2 (1982), 49–74.

Rahman, Fazlur. *Major Themes of the Qur'an*. Chicago: University of Chicago Press, 1980.
Robinson, Neal. 'Creating Birds from Clay: A Miracle of Jesus in the Qurʾān and Classical Muslim Exegesis', *Muslim World* 79/1 (1989), 1–13.
Robinson, Neal. *Christ in Islam and Christianity*. Albany: State University of New York Press, 1990.
Reynolds, Gabriel Said. *The Qurʾān and its Biblical Subtext*. London: Routledge, 2010.
Rubin, Uri. '*Al-Ṣamad* and the High God: An Interpretation of sūra CXII', *Der Islam* 61/2 (1984), 197–217.
Rubin, Uri. '*Ḥanīfiyya* and Kaʿba: An Inquiry into the Arabian Pre-Islamic Background of *Dīn Ibrāhīm*', *Jerusalem Studies in Arabic and Islam* 13 (1990), 85–112.
Rustomji, Nerina. *The Garden and the Fire: Heaven and Hell in Islamic Culture*. New York: Columbia University Press, 2009.
Ryckmans, Jacques. 'Le Pantheon de l'Arabie sud préislamique: état des problèmes et brève synthèse', *Revue de l'histoire des religions* 206/2 (1989), 151–69.
Sachedina, Abdulaziz. *The Islamic Roots of Democratic Pluralism*. Oxford: Oxford University Press, 2001.
Salisbury, Edward E. 'Materials for the History of the Muhammadan Doctrine of Predestination and Free Will', *Journal of the American Oriental Society* 8/1 (1866), 105–82.
Shanavas, T. O. *Creation and/or Evolution: An Islamic Perspective*. Philadelphia: XLibris, 2005.
Sirry, Mun'im A. *Scriptural Polemics: The Qur'an and Other Religions*. Oxford: Oxford University Press, 2014.
Smith, Jane Idleman and Yvonne Yazbak Haddad, *The Islamic Understanding of Death and Resurrection*. Albany: State University of New York Press, 1981.
Sweetman, J. W. *Islam and Christian Theology: A Study of the Interpretation of Theological Ideas in the Two Religions*. London: Lutterworth Press, 1947–55.
Torrey, C. C. *The Jewish Foundation of Islam*. New York: The Jewish Institute of Religion Press, 1933. Repr. Jerusalem: Ktav, 1967.
Tottoli, Roberto. 'Attitudes to Prostration (*sujūd*). 1: Arabs and Prostration at the Beginning of Islam and in the Qur'an', *Studia Islamica* 88 (1998), 5–34.
Tottoli, Roberto. *Biblical Prophets in the Qurʾān and Muslim Literature*. Trans. Michael Roberston. Richmond: Curzon, 2002.
Waardenburg, J. D. Jacques. 'Changes of Belief in Spiritual Beings, Prophethood, and the Rise of Islam'. In: Hans G. Kippenburg (ed.). *Struggles of Gods: Papers on the Groningen Work Group for the Study of the History of Religions*, pp. 259–90. Berlin: Mouton, 1984.
Wansbrough, John. *Quranic Studies: Sources and Methods of Scriptural Interpretation* Oxford: Oxford University Press, 1977.
Wansbrough, John. *The Sectarian Milieu: Content and Composition of Islamic Salvation History*. Oxford: Oxford University Press, 1978.
Watt, W. Montomgery. 'Belief in a "High God" in Pre-Islamic Arabia', *Journal of Semitic Studies* 16/1 (1971), 35–40
Watt, W. Montgomery. 'The Qur'an and Belief in a "High God"', *Der Islam* 56/2 (1979), 205–11.
Watt, William Montgomery. *Islamic Creeds: A Selection*. Edinburgh: Edinburgh University Press, 1994.
Welch, Alford T. 'Allāh and Other Supernatural Beings: The Emergence of the Qurʾānic Doctrine of *Tawḥīd*', *Journal of the American Academy of Religion* 47 (1979), 733–58.
Wellhausen, Julius. *Reste arabischen Heidenthums—Gesammelt und erläuert (2nd Edition)*. Berlin: n.p., 1897; trans. M. G. Weir, *The Arab Kingdom and its Fall*. Calcutta: University of Calcutta, 1927.

Wheeler, Brannon M. *Moses in the Quran and Islamic Exegesis*. London: Routledge Curzon, 2002.

Wild, Stefan. '"We have not sent down to thee a book with truth"... Spatial and Temporal Implication of the Qurʾanic Concepts of *nuzul, tanzīl*, and *inzāl*'. In Stefan Wild (Ed.) *The Qurʾan as Text*, pp. 21–40. Leiden: Brill, 1996.

Williams, Rebecca R. *Muḥammad and the Supernatural: Medieval Arab Views*. London: Routledge, 2013.

Winter, T. J. *The Remembrance of Death and the Afterlife: Kitāb dhikr al-mawt wa-mā baʿdahu—Book XL of the Revival of the Religious Sciences (Iḥyāʾ ʿulūm al-Dīn) of al-Ghazālī; translated, with an introduction and notes*. Cambridge: Islamic Texts Society, 1989.

Wolfson, Harry A. *The Philosophy of the Kalam*. Cambridge, MA: Harvard University Press, 1976.

CHAPTER 28

LAW AND THE QUR'AN

JOSEPH E. LOWRY

Introduction: Problems, Approach, Outline

THE Islamic legal tradition views the Qur'an as the primary source of Islamic law. How the Qur'an's earliest audiences understood the legislative passages, in a text that has been increasingly recognized as shaped on the one hand by its homiletic character and performance dynamics and on the other by complex and obscure processes of editing and redaction, is not clear. Nonetheless, both specific rules of conduct and larger ideas about law constitute important features of the Qur'anic text.

This chapter will focus on the Qur'an's legislative passages and survey their positive legal content. Qur'anic law will be treated here as emerging from the Qur'anic text through its various lexical, linguistic, rhetorical, thematic, formal, and other features. Then, the Qur'an's role in Islamic law and legal thought will be discussed. Finally, a brief overview will be given of some trends in modern Islamic thought (broadly defined) that reflect contemporary perceptions of Qur'anic legislation.

Law and Positive Legislation in the Qur'an

Two critical threshold questions must be answered before surveying Qur'anic legislation. First, does the Qur'an have a general term for 'law'? Second, by what criteria can one recognize the passages in the Qur'an that were intended as legislative, or received by the original Qur'anic audience as legislative?

The Qur'an uses several terms that might be translated as 'law'. The most frequent such term is the Arabic word *ḥaqq*, which occurs well over 200 times in the Qur'an in various senses. It has a semantic field similar to French *droit*, German *Recht*, but also English 'truth', and is etymologically and semantically related to the biblical Hebrew word *ḥuqq* ('statute', e.g. Exod. 30:21). It often has a legal connotation of something due, a duty, or a right (e.g. Q. 6:141, of agricultural produce paid as alms, or 30:38, in regard to the claim of the less fortunate to charity) and also has the sense of 'legal justification' in a way reminiscent of the modern principle of legality (e.g. Q. 6:151, no one should be killed except '*bi'l-ḥaqq*', 'according to law'). It is also used to refer to 'correct' (or possibly 'just') adjudication together with the roots ḥ-k-m (e.g. Q. 38:26, of King David) and q-ḍ-y (e.g. Q. 40:20, where God is the adjudicator).

An especially common term that may have a legal valence in some contexts is *dīn*. Jeffery suggests that it has two overlapping semantic fields, 'religion' and 'religious law', and notes the similarity of the Qur'anic *yawm al-dīn* (e.g. Q. 1:4) to the Rabbinic Hebrew and Aramaic *yom ha-ddīn/yom dīnā*, all meaning 'Day of Judgement' (the significance of the parallel remains unclear, however, since the Talmud uses the phrase in question to refer to the New Year; Jeffery 1938: 131–3). Muqātil ibn Sulaymān (d. 150/767) also notes that *dīn* can mean 'final reckoning' (*ḥisāb*) (*Ashbāh*, 133). Although *dīn* often seems to have a very general sense of 'religion', there are a few passages in which it may connote something like 'law'. In Q. 9:11 and 98:5 *dīn* may be equated with the obligations to pray and give alms. In Q. 22:78, the *dīn* is said not to contain anything difficult (*ḥaraj*) for its adherents; elsewhere, *ḥaraj* is part of the Qur'anic lexicon of legal excuse (e.g. Q. 9:91). In Q. 24:2 (*dīn Allāh*) and 12:76 (*dīn al-malik*), *dīn* seems to refer to something like 'law and legal system' (noted by Muqātil, *Ashbāh*, 133–4). In Q. 42:21, *dīn* is the object of the verb *sharaʿa* ('promulgate', 'institute'). In most of these cases, however, the word *dīn* could refer to something more general than 'rule', 'obligation', 'judgement', or 'law'.

The root ḥ-k-m also does legal work in the Qur'an. Most often terms derived from this root, especially verbs, refer to adjudication, by God (usually in an eschatological context, e.g. Q. 2:113) and Muḥammad (Q. 5:42). The noun *ḥukm* vacillates somewhat between 'rule', 'ruling', or even 'law', and 'wisdom' (e.g. 'those whom we gave the Book, the *ḥukm*, and prophecy', Q. 6:89). Sometimes it clearly refers to God's judgement or ruling (e.g. Q. 27:78: 'your lord will render His judgement', *yaqḍī... bi-ḥukmihi*) and expressions such as 'God possesses the *ḥukm*' or 'the *ḥukm* of your Lord' could well refer to the final judgement (e.g. Q. 28:88, 68:48).

The root sh-r-ʿ, from which the word *sharīʿa* is derived, may also refer to law in general. The two occurrences of the phrase '*sharaʿa... min al-dīn*' could mean something as broad as 'institute... a religion' though it could also have a more narrowly legal connotation, such as 'reveal... as a religious law' (Q. 42:13, 21), especially if one is inclined to see a legal valence in the term *dīn*. The word *sharīʿa* also appears once, in the phrase 'We have set you upon a *sharīʿa min al-amr*, so follow it...' (Q. 45:18). The italicized phrase makes the passage difficult. Jones, emphasizing the base meaning of the root ('to go') has 'set you on a clear way [that comes] from [Our] affair' while Paret, emphasizing the idea of a religious dispensation unique to the Qur'anic audience and distinct from Judaism, has 'auf einen (eigenen) Ritus festgelegt' ('laid down for you your own rite'). Finally, in a passage that is structurally similar to Q. 45:18, the term *shirʿa* is used in conjunction with the word *minhāj* in a context where both could mean something as specific as 'religious law' or as broad as 'religious dispensation': 'For each of you [pl.] we have made a *shirʿa* and a *minhāj*, and had God wished, He could have made each of you a separate religious community [*umma*]' (Q. 5:48). The conjunction of the terms *shirʿa* (which Paret claims as an Ethiopic borrowing) and *minhāj* (which Jeffery accepts as a 'borrowing from the Jews', and which does have a strong resonance with Rabbinic law; 1938: 273), may be suggestive of religious law in particular.

The modern English phrase 'religious law' may, however, suggest a kind of bifurcation of religion and law that is foreign to the Qur'an's thought-world. The word *dīn*, for example, need not be resolved into specifically legal and broader religious significations. Moreover, terms derived from the root sh-r-ʿ seem to be used in contexts in which the *separate character* of specific communities' religious dispensations receives more emphasis than the idea of legislation. Therefore, when attempting to isolate a specifically Qur'anic notion of law, it is probably safest to concentrate on individual obligations that are imposed in the text, while bearing the semantic range of the above terms in mind. Accordingly, in the following survey of Qur'anic legislation, such law is defined as any passage that enjoins specific, repeatable conduct (that is not purely mental) on a reasonably identifiable person or persons likely to be aural recipients of the Qur'an. Although this working definition of 'Qur'anic law' may seem both overly broad and narrowly positivistic, it will help isolate Qur'anic legislation if used with sensitivity to the Qur'an's language of obligation and attentiveness to its invocation of obvious areas of legal subject matter.

Space precludes a complete list, discussion, or analysis of all the Qur'an's rules of law, so the following survey is abbreviated. It is heuristically useful to divide Qur'anic legislation into three categories: (1) ritual, (2) rules that are not necessarily ritual-related but that affect the contours of the community in other ways, and (3) rules governing matters that correspond more or less to secular legislation in modern legal systems. These divisions are admittedly artificial, but they provide a convenient set of rubrics for considering individual Qur'anic laws.

Rules Relating to Ritual

The Qur'an's injunctions relating to ritual and worship cover the following topics: purity, prayer, pilgrimage, fasting, sacrificial offerings, and diet.

Purity: pre-prayer ritual cleansing is required; urination and defecation, sexual activity, and menstruation are all identified as necessitating such cleansing. Symbolic cleansing using clean earth is possible in the absence of water (Q. 2:222, 4:43, 5:6) (see generally Katz 2001–6; Reinhart 2001–6; and Lowry 2001–6).

Prayer: the five daily prayers do not appear in the Qur'an. The command to perform the prayer termed *ṣalāt* is frequently paired with the injunction to give alms ('pray and give alms!', *aqīmū'l-ṣalāt wa-ātū'l-zakāt*, e.g. Q. 2:43). The Qur'an often urges frequent performance of prayer and supplication, usually by suggesting that one pray 'day and night'. A variety of terms is used for prayer in such contexts, including: *sabbiḥ* (extol, Q. 33:41–2), *daʿā* (supplicate, Q. 6:52), *dhakara* (recollect, Q. 33:41), and *tahajjada* (pray or keep vigil during the night, Q. 17:79). Whether the injunctions to pray in the morning and evening indicate specific prayer times or merely the desirability of frequent prayer remains unclear. The Qur'an enjoins attendance of a congregational prayer on Fridays (*jumuʿa*) using the term *ṣalāt* (Q. 62:9–10).

Fasting: The Qur'an requires fasting for two different purposes: a fast during the month of Ramadan (Q. 2:183–5) and fasting as penance for specific kinds of unlawful behaviour or ritual non-compliance (e.g. Q. 4:92, for accidental death). It is also listed as a general attribute of the pious (e.g. Q. 33:35). The term *sāʾiḥ*, which etymologically seems likely to refer to travel, is understood to mean 'fasting' (*ṣāʾim*) in two passages that contain lists of such general attributes of pious persons (Q. 9:112, 66:5), though perhaps fasting in the wider sense of ascetic abstention is meant (Paret 1980: 213–14; Wagtendonk 1968: 128).

Pilgrimage: the Qur'an mentions two different pilgrimages, *ʿumra* and *ḥajj* (Q. 2:158, 196), which may be combined, and the latter of which is required (Q. 3:97). Pilgrims must shave their heads and bring an offering (usually understood to be an animal to be sacrificed, most likely a camel), and certain locales are identified as places of procession (Q. 2:191–200, 3:97, 22:25–37). The pilgrimage, or its object, the Kaʿba (or 'sacred temple' or 'sacred house', *al-masjid al-ḥarām, al-bayt al-ḥarām*), often appears in contexts in which conflict over the pilgrimage site is emphasized, and in which fighting is either enjoined or discouraged (e.g. Q. 2:191, 9:5–7, 22:25). The acts that make up the pilgrimage are in general referred to as *shaʿāʾir* ('rites', 'ceremonies', Q. 2:158). Finally, in regard to the sacred calendar, which was lunar, intercalation (presumably for the sake of keeping rituals in the same season), is strongly discouraged (Q. 9:36–7) and the ritual importance of the lunar months affirmed (Q. 2:189).

Diet, slaughter, and sacrifice: The Qur'an's main dietary restrictions encompass the following prohibited items: carrion, blood, pork, pagan sacrifices, animals that have been strangled, beaten, gored, or that have fallen to their death, and animals killed by predators; there is an exception for necessity (Q. 5:3, 6:145) Otherwise, frequent reference is made to 'the good things' (*al-ṭayyibāt*) that have been 'made lawful' (*uḥillat*, e.g. Q. 5:5) in proximity to lists of dietary restrictions. No guidelines for ritual slaughter appear, but certain problems of ritual slaughter are addressed. Animals that have been wounded by predators may be eaten if still amenable to ritual slaughter (Q. 5:3) and trained hunting animals may be used (Q. 5:4). Fishing is also expressly made lawful (Q. 5:96). Hunting is proscribed for pilgrims in the sacred precinct, but if one kills a game animal, appropriate compensation will be determined (Q. 5:1, 95). Sacrifice occurs within the context of the pilgrimage. Sacrificial animals, termed *hady* and *budn* (Q. 2:196, 22:36), were marked by garlanding (*qalāʾid*, Q. 5:2, 97). Conversely, pagan taboos against the slaughter of certain camels (*baḥīra, sāʾiba, waṣīla, ḥām*) and pagan rites relating to other animals are denounced (Q. 5:103, 6:138–44). Jewish dietary laws are characterized as punitive (e.g. Q. 6:146).

Other Rules Governing Life in the Qurʾānic Community

Many matters discussed under 'ritual' above undoubtedly contributed to the demarcation, visually and otherwise, of a nascent religious community, and probably many non-ritual related rules did so as well. Nevertheless, the rules discussed under this subheading treat the following topics: charity and alms; family law; slavery; war; and those rules dealing specifically with Muḥammad and his household.

Charity and alms: alms-giving and charity are prominent themes. Regular alms-giving must have been seen as integral since the paired injunction to 'pray and give alms!' (e.g. *aqīmū al-ṣalāt wa-ātū al-zakāt*, Q. 2:43) occurs frequently. Repetition of this vocabulary so often perhaps suggests (as with prayer) a recurring obligation. A levy on agricultural produce at the time of harvest is mentioned (Q. 6:141) and the term *ṣadaqāt* is used for a levy on property generally (Q. 9:103). The Qur'an expressly identifies the *ṣadaqāt* as being for 'the poor, the destitute, those who collect alms, those whose hearts are to be reconciled, for (the freeing of?) slaves, creditors, debtors, God's cause, and travellers' (Q. 9:60). Lists similar to this one also appear in regard to the distribution of inheritance and voluntary charity, as well as war booty, sometimes with the addition of parents, orphans, and (poor) relations (*wālidān, yatāmā, dhū'l-qurbā*, e.g. Q. 2:83, 4:8, 8:41). Charity is sometimes required as penance or as a substitute for another obligation (e.g. Q. 2:196, for certain aspects of the pilgrimage, and 5:89, for breaking a vow). Conversely, the forgiveness of certain legal liabilities is characterized as charity (e.g. *an yaṣṣaddaqū*, of tort liability, Q. 4:92). Alms-giving appears in lists of attributes of the pious (e.g. Q. 33:35, *al-mutaṣaddiqīn wa'l-mutaṣaddiqāt*). Finally, there are recurring injunctions to 'spend (charitably)' or to do so 'in God's way' (e.g. *anfiqū fī sabīl Allāh*, Q. 2:195). The many injunctions to give charitably must have met with some resistance, which is reflected in a few passages (e.g. Q. 9:60, 79).

Rules governing family law—marriage, divorce, orphans, and inheritance—are discussed at length in the Qur'an.

Marriage: Men are allowed to marry Jewish and Christian women (Q. 5:5). A ban on women marrying pagan men suggests that at one point women may have been able to marry non-Qur'anic monotheists as well (Q. 2:221). Marriage to one's slaves may be encouraged in some circumstances (Q. 4:3, 4:25 and also 2:221). There is a list of persons whose marriage is prohibited by reason of family or other relationships (Q. 4:22–4), and it is expressly prohibited to forcibly bequeath wives to others (Q. 4:19). A dowry must be paid to the bride (Q. 4:4), and it becomes the bride's property, not to be interfered with in general (Q. 2:229); it is at least partly refundable prior to consummation (Q. 2:237), though it is meritorious to make some provision for the woman in such cases (Q. 2:236–7).

Divorce is extensively regulated, and one has the impression that it must therefore have been a common practice. Divorce pronouncements are made twice and then either retracted or finalized (Q. 2:229). Remarriage is only possible after the woman has had an intervening marriage (Q. 2:230). As that rule suggests, the male prerogative to divorce should not be abused (Q. 2:231), and former husbands should not interfere with their ex-wives' attempts to remarry (Q. 2:232). However, the husband is allowed to discipline the wife if she misbehaves, which may be done verbally, by banishing her from the marital bed, or by hitting her (Q. 4:34). After a divorce, the woman waits three menstrual cycles before remarrying (Q. 2:228). Marriage proposals to divorced women may not be finalized until that waiting period has concluded (Q. 2:235, presumably to be understood in the context of divorce). Many of the rules in *Sūrat al-Baqara* (2) are further elaborated in *Sūrat al-Ṭalāq* (65), the title of which means 'Divorce'. Apart from divorce, two other methods of marriage dissolution are mentioned. Men may take an oath of sexual abstinence for four months, but must then either divorce or return to their wives (Q. 2:226–7). In addition, men who, in order to dissolve their marriage, compare their wives to their mothers in a way suggesting that their wives are forbidden to them must do penance by freeing a slave before returning to their wives (Q. 58:3).

Mothers may nurse their infants for as long as two years; divorced mothers are to receive support from their former husbands during that time (Q. 2:233, 65:6). It is also lawful to hire a wet nurse (Q. 2:233, 65:6). Possibly the rules on nursing and weaning are to be understood primarily in the context of divorce.

Children are commanded to treat their parents with respect (Q. 17:23–4). Treatment of orphans is the subject of extensive regulation. Their guardians are enjoined to fulfil their fiduciary duties fairly (e.g. Q. 6:152), and the orphans are identified as specific objects of charity (e.g. Q. 76:8) and of kind treatment (e.g. Q. 2:83). The well-known verse that is considered to allow polygynous marriage is connected somehow with the treatment of orphans (Q. 4:3), but its original significance is obscure. Adoption seems to be prohibited (Q. 33:5).

Inheritance: the Qur'an has two different inheritance regimes. One encourages the making of a will, which should be duly witnessed, in favour of certain relatives, especially those who may be economically or socially vulnerable (Q. 2:180, 240, 5:106). The other requires fixed shares of the estate to be distributed to certain named relatives in fractions specified by the Qur'an (Q. 4:11–12, 176). Those heirs who receive fixed shares are a combination of agnates, presumed to reflect pre-Islamic Arabian customary law, and female cognates, thought to represent a Qur'anic attempt to reform Arabian customary law. Expressly named heirs are children, parents, brothers, and sisters; males receive twice the shares of females of equivalent degree. The estate may only be distributed once any outstanding claims against it are settled.

Slavery: Qur'anic law implicitly recognizes slave ownership, but also generally encourages the freeing of slaves (*taḥrīr raqaba*) as a religiously meritorious act, in particular as penance for certain kinds of wrongdoing, such as accidental homicide (Q. 4:92), likening one's wife to one's mother in order to effect a divorce (Q. 58:3), or breaking an oath (Q. 5:89). In some cases (such as Q. 4:92), the freeing of a 'believing' slave is specified. Good treatment of slaves is encouraged (Q. 4:36). Marriage to slaves is also discussed. The Islamic legal tradition understands one verse as authorizing contracts in which the slave purchases his or her freedom in instalments (Q. 24:33), but the context may suggest that the contract in question (*kitāb*) is a marriage contract (Crone 1994). Prostituting one's female slaves is outlawed (Q. 24:33), but men may use their female slaves as concubines (Q. 4:24).

Communal defence and warfare: The Qur'an contains many passages that require the Qur'anic audience to 'kill' (*uqtulū*), 'fight' (*qātilū*), and 'give to the cause' (*anfiqū*) or 'give to God's cause' (*anfiqū fī sabīl Allāh*). The objects of the commands to 'kill' and 'fight' are generally those who fight the Muslims (Q. 2:190–1), the unbelievers (*kāfirūn*) (Q. 4:76, 89), and the pagans (*mushrikūn*) (Q. 9:5, 36). The term *jihād* and the related verb *jāhada*, often in the imperative, appear several times as obligations of the Prophet or the community at large (e.g. Q. 9:41) in ways similar to the use of the imperative verb *qātilū*. The frequent injunctions to 'give to the cause' or 'contribute' (*anfiqū*) sometimes refer to charitable giving (e.g. Q. 36:47), but sometimes seem, from context, to have to do with what might be called the war effort (e.g. Q. 2:195). Justifications for fighting include the fact that the enemy are the aggressors, that they have expelled the Qur'anic audience from their homes (e.g. Q. 22:39–40), and that they bar the way to the pilgrimage (e.g. Q. 2:217).

Some very specific aspects of the conduct of warfare are regulated. The Qur'an seems to reflect its audience's concerns about the lawfulness of fighting during the sacred Arabian months (*al-ashhur al-ḥurum*); such fighting is implicitly prohibited in one passage (Q. 9:5) but then justified as legitimate retaliation in others (Q. 2:194, 217). The Qur'anic audience is urged to fight even when outnumbered ten-to-one, but then this obligation is lightened to two-to-one (Q. 8:65–6). The Prophet is expressly given power over prisoners (Q. 8:71), but prisoners also appear in a list of persons whom it is meritorious to feed, along with the other usual named recipients of charity (Q. 76:8). Payment of tribute (*jizya*) may apparently be accepted from defeated enemies (Q. 9:29).

Rules governing the conduct of warfare frequently appear in proximity to discussions of the pilgrimage and the Kaʿba (e.g. Q. 2:217 and prominently in *Sūrat al-Ḥajj* (22), the title of which is 'The Pilgrimage'). There are also rules for a shortened ritual prayer in battle conditions (Q. 2:238–9) with specific mandated procedures (Q. 4:101–3). *Sūrat al-Anfāl* (8) (Spoils) and *Sūrat al-Tawba* (9) (Repentance) seem particularly concerned with communal defence and warfare, though injunctions to 'fight' and to 'kill' appear reasonably often also in *Sūrat al-Baqara* (2), *Sūrat Āl ʿImrān* (3), and *Sūrat al-Nisāʾ* (4).

Torts: injuries to the person, including accidental and intentional wounding and accidental and intentional homicide, are dealt with as torts under Qur'anic law, that is, as private injuries with private remedies and, in some cases, penance. Rules governing wounding and homicide do not seem to contemplate prosecution by a state authority. The Qur'an outlaws intentional homicide in its paraphrases of the Decalogue (e.g. Q. 17:33) and also identifies intentional homicide as sinful and leading to perdition (Q. 4:93). In cases of intentional homicide, the Qur'an allows retaliation (*qiṣāṣ*) against socially equivalent individuals but also suggests that forgiveness in exchange for payment may be appropriate (Q. 2:178). Deterrence is implicitly identified as the policy for this rule (Q. 2:179). Unintentional killing requires penance (freeing a slave) and the payment of a blood price (*diya*) (Q. 4:92). One passage paraphrases the biblical *lex talionis* (retaliation for homicide and wounding: a life for a life, an eye for an eye, etc.; compare Exod. 21:24–5), expressly identifies the rules in question as from the Torah, suggests that those rules applied to the Jews in the biblical past, and allows for the charitable waiver of retaliation (Q. 5:45). In context, it is not clear whether the passage is meant as legislation for the Qur'anic audience or instead as an allusion to biblical law.

Crimes: the Qur'an also describes a small number of 'crimes', that is, specified unlawful behaviour that incurs a defined, earthly corporal or capital punishment that, from context, seems intended to be carried out by a person or persons in a position of political authority. The Islamic legal tradition generally came to define the elements of all these offences extremely narrowly and erected high evidentiary bars to conviction. Thus, the Qur'anic statutory language is in all the following cases considerably broader than later juristic doctrine and practice. Theft is punishable by amputation of the hand (Q. 5:38). Unlawful sexual intercourse is punishable by indefinite house arrest according to one passage (Q. 4:15) but adulterers (*zānī, zāniya*) are given 100 lashes in another (Q. 24:2). Accusations of adultery are discouraged since those who bring such accusations without being also able to support them with four witnesses receive 80 lashes (Q. 24:4). Those who accuse their wives of adultery may, together with the wife, swear an oath that they are truthful, a procedure that presumably ends the marriage but that also averts the punishment specified in 24:4 (Q. 24:6–9). Finally, the offence of 'warring against God and the Prophet' incurs the alternative punishments of death, crucifixion, amputation of limbs on alternate sides, or banishment, in addition to punishment in the next world (Q. 5:33). This last offence may be meant more as a stern warning to obey the Prophet rather than as a specific crime, since both the unlawful conduct and the punishment are vague and non-specific, respectively. Several of the above passages seem to contemplate the possibility that repentance could avert punishment (e.g. Q. 5:39 for theft, 5:34 for warring against God and the Prophet).

Certain other unlawful behaviours are named, but no punishment specified for them. These include drinking grape wine (*khamr*, Q. 2:219, 'a major sin'), and certain Arabian games of chance involving the drawing of lots (*maysir*, Q. 2:219, also 'a major sin'; *azlām*, Q. 5:3, 'sinful', *fisq*). Arguably, the declaration of certain behaviours as sinful rather than as incurring specific earthly punishment takes those behaviours out of the narrowly legal sphere.

Other Rules

Commercial Law

The Qur'an expressly makes sales transactions licit (Q. 2:275). Sales should be based on the parties' mutual consent (Q. 4:29). Lending money for a defined term is also permitted, provided the transaction is reduced to writing and witnessed (Q. 2:282). Pawns or pledges may be entrusted to the obligor or a third-party trustee (Q. 2:283). *Ribā*, which is generally understood to mean 'usury', but is never defined, is strictly prohibited (Q. 2:275). The Qur'an makes *ribā* the moral opposite of charity; usury is said to be morally unprofitable, but charitable giving will lead to an increase in the wealth of the persons who give charitably (e.g. Q. 2:276), and contributions to God's cause are portrayed as a loan that will be repaid many times over (e.g. Q. 57:11). The Qur'an often uses commercial imagery to express theological ideas though it remains unclear whether such vocabulary is simply a common Middle Eastern metaphor or a reflection of economic life in Mecca and Medina (Rippin 1996).

Legal System and Procedure

The Qur'an refers on one occasion to adjudicators (*ḥukkām*, 2:188, forbidding bribing tribunals) and once to an arbiter in marital disputes (*ḥakam*, Q. 4:35). Several legal procedures expressly require witnesses (sg. *shāhid*): accusations of adultery (four witnesses, Q. 4:15), drawing up contracts of indebtedness (two male witnesses, or one male and two female witnesses, Q. 2:282), and assessing equivalent livestock for game unlawfully killed by pilgrims (two just persons, *dhawā ʿadl*, Q. 5:95). It is suggested that Muḥammad acted as ạ judge (Q. 4:65, 5:43) and disputes are required to be referred to God and to Muḥammad (Q. 4:59).

Muḥammad and his household: a number of Qur'anic injunctions seem to apply exclusively to Muḥammad and/or his household. *Sūrat al-Aḥzāb* (33), for example, although it describes God's Messenger as an 'excellent example for you' (*lakum... uswa ḥasana*, Q. 33:21), contains a sustained set of injunctions addressed directly to the Prophet concerning his wives and household (Q. 33:28–38). Then, beginning at v. 49, there is a series of verses that alternate between rules ostensibly for the Prophet and other rules that seem directed at the community at large, all dealing with matters of family law. The Islamic legal tradition did recognize that such passages posed a hermeneutical problem and pondered whether they were meant exclusively for the Prophet or for the wider community (Ibn ʿAqīl, *Wāḍiḥ*, 3:7–9).

Legal Language, Themes, and Ideas

One especially prominent and recurring idea in the Qur'an is that a day will come when the world will end and humans will be judged. However, this theological theme occurs at a much higher level of abstraction than the Qur'an's positive legislation, even though one presumes the relevance of adhering to that legislation in order to receive a positive judgement at the end of time.

The Qur'an's rhetorical strategies for indicating legal obligations are various. Imperative verbs furnish one common marker of obligation, as in the frequent injunctions to pray and give alms (*aqīmū al-ṣalāt wa-ātū al-zakāt*, e.g. Q. 2:43), as do negative imperatives (e.g. *wa-lā tankiḥū al-mushrikāt*, 'do not marry pagan women', Q. 2:221). Particularly powerful markers of lawfulness and unlawfulness are the verbs *aḥalla* ('God has made lawful') and *ḥarrama* ('God has made unlawful'), sometimes also used in the passive voice (e.g. Q. 5:3–4) (see Lowry 2001–6). Another frequent marker is the phrase 'it is prescribed for you' (*kutiba ʿalaykum*, e.g. Q. 2:178). In some instances, the Prophet is provided with rulings about which people seem to be enquiring, always introduced by the phrase 'They ask you about...' (e.g. *yasʾalūnaka ʿan al-ahilla*, in regard to new moons and the ritual function of the lunar months, Q. 2:189; and with *yastaftūnaka*, 'they seek an opinion from you about...', in Q. 4:127, 176). The indefinite pronoun *man*, 'whoever', often introduces obligations (e.g. *man baddalahu*..., 'whoever changes it...', in regard to changing someone's will after the testator's death, Q. 2:181). In a similar fashion, rules are sometimes introduced with a definite relative pronoun (e.g. *alladhīna yutawaffawna minkum*, 'those of you who pass away', in regard to making provisions for widows, Q. 2:240). Finally, conditional sentences can introduce obligations (e.g. *wa-in ṭallaqtumūhunna*, 'if you divorce them, then...' Q. 2:237).

The Qur'an has a well-developed vocabulary for expressing exceptions to rules and denoting exculpation (Lowry 2015–16). The most common are *lā junāḥ*, 'it is not wrongful to...' (e.g. Q. 2:235, always in legal contexts); *lā ḥaraj*, 'there is nothing wrong with...' (e.g. Q. 24:61); *lā ithm*, 'it is not a sin to...' (e.g. Q. 2:203); *fa-man uḍṭurra*, 'whoever does so out of necessity...' (e.g. Q. 5:3). A phrase that indicates immunity from liability or legal proceedings is *lā sabīl ʿalā*..., 'there is no way to proceed against...' (e.g. Q. 4:34, *lā tabghu ʿalayhinna sabīl*, in regard to male authority in the marriage). Finally, there is a special turn of phrase for exemption from liability for pagan or pre-Qur'anic acts that are inconsistent with subsequent Qur'anic legislation: *illā mā qad salafa*, 'except for what has already occurred'. The phrase is not always used to exempt pre-Qur'anic behaviour from liability, but it is used to do so in reference to a couple of conspicuous areas of the law, such as the ban on usurious interest or on certain incestuous marriages (e.g. Q. 4:23, in regard to being married simultaneously to two sisters).

The many phrases that denote exceptions may be related to another Qur'anic idea, which is that God does not want the law to be burdensome for the believers (e.g. *yurīd Allāh... al-yusr wa-lā... al-ʿusr*, Q. 2:185). In a couple of passages, the Qur'an expressly refers to specific instances in which the law has been made less burdensome (using the verb *khaffafa*, 'to lighten', e.g. Q. 4:28, in regard to marrying concubines). And in several passages, the Qur'an appears to suggest that it has brought a less burdensome legal regime in general, as in the lists of dietary restrictions cited above, an idea that perhaps echoes Christian notions of the fulfilment of the law and is signalled by phrases such as 'today the good things have been made lawful for you' (*al-yawm uḥilla lakum al-ṭayyibāt*, Q. 5:5) (Zellentin 2013: 155–74).

The Qur'an alludes to and is polemically engaged with specific aspects of biblical law as it relates to the Jews, including dietary rules (Q. 6:146–7), torts (Q. 5:45), and the Decalogue (especially at Q. 6:152–3 and 17:22–3) (Lowry 2007; Zellentin 2013).

Notwithstanding its resonances with Rabbinic narratives (see e.g. Speyer 1930), the Qur'an seems uninterested in Rabbinic law. As noted above, certain aspects of biblical law are characterized as punishment for the Jews. One might also include as part of the theme of biblical law the history of the covenant (e.g. in sura 2, with the first of many references to it beginning at Q. 2:27). It is possible that the Qur'an's references to biblical law participate in a wider Near Eastern tradition of polemics over the meaning of biblical law for a spectrum of Jewish and Christian groups (see generally Zellentin 2013).

A contemporaneous reflection of some Qur'anic legal ideas is found in a text (or set of texts) referred to as the 'Constitution of Medina', which embodies an agreement or series of agreements between Muḥammad and his followers and the Medinan tribes (compare Serjeant 1978; Rubin 1985; and Lecker 2004). The 'Constitution' provides that no believer is to kill another believer in retaliation for the death of a non-believer (*kāfir*) and also that the unjustified killing of a believer makes the killer subject to retaliation (*qawad*) unless the victim's heir (*walī al-maqtūl*) agrees to accept compensation (Ibn Hishām, *Sīra*, 1:502). This provision generally reflects the rules of Qur'anic tort law which provide that only social equals are to be killed in retaliation for intentional homicide, that compensation may be accepted in lieu of retaliation (Q. 2:178–9) and that believers should not kill believers intentionally (Q. 4:92–3). Several terms found in the 'Constitution' do not appear in the Qur'an, including *yataʿāqalūn maʿāqilahum* ('bear responsibility for torts committed by one's tribe') and *qawad* ('retaliation'), for example (Ibn Hishām, *Sīra*, 1:502).

The 'Constitution' also provides that disputes over its interpretation be referred to 'God... and Muḥammad' (Ibn Hishām, *Sīra*, 1:503: *mahmā 'khtalaftum fīhi min shayʾin fa-inna maraddahu ilā Allāhi... wa-ilā Muḥammad*). The Qur'an also refers disagreements to God and Muḥammad, in two passages, using language that is very close to that of the 'Constitution' (Q. 42:10: *wa-mā 'khtalaftum min shayʾin fa-ḥukmuhu ilā Allāh*; and Q. 4:59: *fa-in tanāzaʿtum fī shayʾin fa-raddūhu ilā Allāhi wa'l-rasūl*).

Literary Form

The high frequency and distribution of rhyme and assonance in the Qur'an, the density of its oral-formulaic structures, and other formal properties characteristic of a homiletic or liturgical function suggest that the text was originally communicated orally and received aurally to some degree (Neuwirth 2007). How the Qur'an's original degree of orality affected the reception of its legislation remains unclear, but it would probably be unwise to imagine that, at the time of its reception by the original Qur'anic community, it was read and consulted in the manner of a written legal code. The Qur'an's suras are traditionally divided into those revealed in Mecca and those revealed in Medina, a distinction that may have relevance to Qur'anic legislation. Legislative passages that are particularly dense and technical, which are mostly Medinan, do not display the poetic elegance that is to be found, for example, in shorter and more dramatic suras, which are mostly Meccan (compare e.g. the legislation at Q. 2:282–3 and 4:11–12 with suras 54, 55, or 112). However, the careful formal construction of Medinan suras, considered as literary unities, is increasingly recognized (e.g. Zahniser 2000).

Legislative passages can play structurally meaningful roles in the composition of individual suras. For example, the two long lists of obligations that occur toward the end of *Sūrat al-Baqara* (2) that run from vv. 178 to 203 and vv. 215 to 242 may be meant as the conclusion to a retelling of the history of the covenant (from vv. 30 to 141), in which case those lists of rules, apart from their positive legal content, also symbolize the fact that the Qur'anic community is governed by divine law in the biblical-covenantal tradition. Under such a reading, *al-Baqara* could be understood as a condensed Qur'anic rewriting of Genesis and Exodus, or perhaps of the Torah or Pentateuch as a whole (Lowry 2017). The nature of legislative passages can also set the mood of a sura, as in *Sūrat al-Māʾida* (5), in which frequent references to the lawfulness of things at the sura's beginning and middle (Q. 5:1, 4, 5, 87, 88) could be understood as setting the scene for the sura's conclusion with an interpretation of the Last Supper as a banquet that provides miraculous evidence of, among other things, God's generosity (Q. 5:112–15, 119–20) (see Cuypers 2009).

Qur'anic legislation can also function figuratively or allusively, whereby its positive legal content may prove less important than its ability to communicate aspects of Qur'anic theology. For example, the Qur'an makes several allusions to the Decalogue, but those allusions occur in very different contexts; in some contexts, the rules' content is given more emphasis (e.g. Q. 6:151–2), but in others the mere fact of the biblical allusion may be more important (e.g. Q. 2:83) (Lowry 2007).

In some cases, specific legislative passages may indicate a late stage of sura redaction, especially where some legislative aspect of the sura is clarified or revised. For example in Q. 73:20, the final verse of the sura seems to refer to a modification of the obligation implied at the beginning of the sura (to recite the Qur'an during night-time vigils) and exhibits markedly different stylistic properties than the opening verses of that sura. In Q. 4:176, the verse seems to be offering a clarification of the term *kalāla* that appears in Q. 4:12. Both instances could be understood as late additions to these two suras that could not easily be integrated into their earlier sections.

Some Textual and Historical Problems

A small number of legislative passages seem to have occasioned interpretive difficulties at the very early stages of the emergence of the Islamic legal tradition. For example, in Q. 5:6, the word order of the consonantal skeleton (*rasm*) suggests that the verse should read in relevant part, concerning ablutions prior to prayer: 'wash (*fa-'ghsilū*) your faces and your hands to the elbows, and wipe (*wa-'msaḥū bi-*...) your heads and your legs to the ankles'. The Sunnī exegetical and legal tradition, however, generally assumes that the verb 'wash' also governs the phrase 'your legs to the ankles', seemingly ignoring what looks otherwise like an unproblematic parallelism, and vowels the text in accordance with that understanding. The conclusion that one should probably draw from this odd wrinkle is that the practice of ablutions may have begun with the text of Q. 5:6 but evolved away from it before the text became widely available for study and comparison with actual ritual practice. The Sunnī tradition is aware that its reading is not the most syntactically natural one (see e.g. al-Farrāʾ, *Maʿānī*, 1:302–3; al-Jaṣṣāṣ, *Aḥkām*, 2:433–6, 'Bāb ghasl al-rijlayn').

The word *kalāla* in Q. 4:12 offers a more intractable puzzle. The term is generally understood by the legal and exegetical traditions as an adverb meaning 'having no direct male heir': 'If a man, or a woman, has no direct heir (*in kāna rajulun yūrath kalālatan aw imraʾatun*), but has a brother or sister, each of the two gets a sixth' (Q. 4:12b, Jones, trans.; see also al-Farrāʾ, *Maʿānī*, 1:257–8, holding that it means to die without living male issue and without a living father). This reading makes a syntactically simple sentence into something grammatically difficult. A possibly more likely reading is, 'If a man makes a *kalāla* or a wife as his heir (*in kāna rajulun* yūrith *kalālatan aw* imraʾatan, emphasis added), and has a brother or sister, each of the two gets a sixth'. This speculative rereading makes for a more natural sentence, but it does not clear up who gets the one-sixth share of the estate. Since males are given twice the shares of females (Q. 4:11, 4:176), it seems that it cannot be the brother and sister, so perhaps the two recipients of the one-sixth share are the *kalāla* or wife on the one hand and the sister on the other, but a neat resolution remains elusive (see Powers 1986: 43, proposing that the brother and sister each take one-sixth). Unlike the case of the ablutions verse (Q. 5:6), the exegetical and legal traditions mostly did not preserve information about the syntactically more natural reading of this verse, or any other meaning of the word *kalāla*, but they did retain traditions about the difficulty people had interpreting that term (e.g. al-Jaṣṣāṣ, *Aḥkām*, 2:108–10). Powers interprets the term as referring to a daughter-in-law (1986: 40–3). In both Syriac and Jewish Babylonian Aramaic the word *kallūtā* means marriage and in Syriac it can refer to being a daughter-in-law in legal contexts (Sokoloff 2009: 626 and 2002: 583).

Most of the Qur'an's legislative passages are not so enigmatic. These two cases may, however, indicate that the early spread and availability of the Qur'anic text lagged to some extent behind the speculative elaboration of norms by early Muslims. Such a lag would not be surprising even if one accepts the traditional dating of the collection of the Qur'an during the caliphate of ʿUthmān ibn ʿAffān (r. 23–35/644–656) since the resources and technology for disseminating the text widely must have been limited and it is unlikely to have kept pace with the geographical spread of Muslims during the early conquests (see Crone 1994).

Reception in Islamic Law and Legal Theory

Islamic law, the body of positive legal doctrine (*fiqh*) developed by jurists in a scholastic context, is a post-Qur'anic phenomenon. It developed in tandem with the fortunes of the Muslim community as a result of geographic expansion under the Umayyads and early Abbasids, the rise of urban centres of study, the availability of resources to support such study, and the emergence of private and state-backed institutions for its elaboration and enforcement. The Qur'an's role in the rise of Islamic law has been variously characterized. Joseph Schacht held it to be minimal, but Wael Hallaq has taken strong exception to Schacht's views (Schacht 1950; Hallaq 2009a and 2012). How one approaches this question depends on what assumptions one makes about several different issues, chief among which are: (1) the de facto legislative role of the Qur'an in the original Qur'anic community; (2) the dissemination of the entire, integral Qur'anic text in the period after the death of the Prophet Muḥammad; (3) the extent of continuity or discontinuity of social structures and practices as between the original Qur'anic community and the beginning of the Islamic intellectual tradition in the Umayyad period; and (4) what constitutes an appropriate methodology for analysing the primary sources. One can in any event agree with Harald Motzki that the history of the origins and early evolution of Islamic legal doctrine remains to be written (Motzki 2002: 299).

A transitional period between the codification of the Qur'anic text (*c.*30/650) and the emergence of writing on legal doctrine (*c.*132/750 or perhaps slightly earlier?) witnessed the collection of a vast body of legal traditions, some preserving opinions of early Muslims with a pietistic and/or speculative interest in religious law and others relating all the legally relevant pronouncements and behaviour of Muḥammad. Such traditions, hadiths, and the doctrines that they preserved are collectively referred to as the Sunna, two terms that are used especially to refer to precedents traced or attributed directly to the Prophet. These traditions laid the foundation for much of Islamic legal doctrine, not only for areas of the law not dealt with in the Qur'an or dealt with only cursorily, but also for many topics squarely regulated by the Qur'an.

Many traditions suggested ways of interpreting Qur'anic legislation. For example, Muḥammad is reported to have said, 'No bequest to an heir'. This statement implicitly explains how to reconcile the Qur'anic regime of fixed inheritance shares (at Q. 4:11–12 and 4:176) with the several verses that urge one to make a will (*waṣiyya*, e.g. Q. 2:180) in favour of certain of the heirs named as recipients of those fixed shares. Although that particular tradition had the effect of making some Qur'anic rules ineffective, other traditions modified Qur'anic legislation. For example, the Prophet is reported to have limited application of the rule mandating amputation for theft at Q. 5:38 by imposing a *de minimis* exception of one-quarter dinar, an exception for food required for daily sustenance, and a requirement that the item stolen be in a place of safe-keeping (*ḥirz*) (on Muḥammad's modification of Qur'anic rules governing theft and inheritance, see al-Shāfiʿī, *Epistle*, trans. Lowry. 59–61, 105–11). The resulting doctrine of theft under Islamic law thus emerges out of a complex interweaving of Qur'an and prophetic Sunna, which is typical of many if not most areas of the law as elaborated by Muslim jurists.

The need to harmonize the Qur'an with hadiths provided a major impetus for the emergence of Islamic legal theory. The science of Islamic legal theory or legal hermeneutics (*uṣūl al-fiqh*, 'the bases of the law') defines the sources of the divine law and the literary and logical techniques used to derive the law from those sources. The earliest preserved theoretical treatment of the Qur'an was by the jurist al-Shāfiʿī (d. 204/820), who developed systematic techniques for harmonizing its legal provisions with the legal pronouncements found in prophetic hadiths (see generally Lowry 2007). This approach led, both as a matter of practical legal reasoning and in regard to theory construction, to the baseline assumption of the Qur'an's legislative incompleteness and fundamental ambiguity (on ambiguity, see Vishanoff 2011: esp. 50–6).

In fact, the enduring concern of Islamic legal theory in its mature phase with problems of epistemology—distinguishing both sources of law as well as individual rules that are certain from those only provisionally valid (Zysow 2013: 279–93)—stemmed in large part from the jurists' perception of Qur'anic language as suffused with ambiguity. While they considered the Qur'an to be linguistically and rhetorically normative in its use of Arabic, they also considered Arabic to be unusually rich in expressive possibilities. Thus, every aspect of the Qur'an's linguistic structure—from conjunctions to figurative language to communicative context—presented opportunities for the jurists to find and propose resolutions of ambiguities.

The legal theorists' definition of the Qur'an for legal purposes relativized its ontological authority by emphasizing the text's limited, earthly dimension in a way that implied a fuller but inaccessible heavenly recension. As al-Ghazālī (d. 505/1111) defines it, the Qur'an, or God's Book, is 'what has been transmitted to us between the two covers of the Qur'an-codex, in seven widely accepted versions, the transmission of which is uninterrupted and has multiple points of origin' (al-Ghazālī, *Mustaṣfā*, 81). This is a way of saying that it is only an earthly instantiation of God's (eternal) speech, that the text is authentic and reliable, but that it also has accepted variants (see Reinhart 2017: 434–5). At the same time, however, Islamic legal theory assumes the ontological and legislative primacy of the Qur'an. As Ibn ʿAqīl (d. 513/1119) puts it: 'The primary source for indicators of legal rules, and the most highly ranked place to begin looking for them, is God's Book... This is because it is epistemologically certain on account of its faultless transmission and its miraculousness, which guards against it being corrupted or improperly added to or subtracted from' (Ibn ʿAqīl, *Wāḍiḥ*, 3:1; and see generally Krawietz 2002: 87–114; on hermeneutics and the contours of the Qur'an for jurists generally, see Reinhart 2017).

The complexity of juristic attitudes toward the Qur'an as a legal source is well exemplified by the doctrine of abrogation. The Qur'an abrogates earlier scriptures (Torah and Gospels), but also on occasion abrogates itself, as in the case of the fixed inheritance shares and their supersession of the mandate to make a will in favour of one's parents noted above. According to one view of abrogation, some ostensibly Qur'anic rulings (e.g. the stoning of adulterers) remain in force even though the Qur'anic text on which they are based has disappeared from the earthly text (see Reinhart 2017: 436–7).

Despite its relative theological importance, the Qur'an's contributions to legal doctrine are far fewer than those of the hadiths (Hallaq 2001–6: 3:149). The legal theorists generally considered the number of specifically legislative verses—defined as those that must be known to qualify as a master jurist (*mujtahid*)—to be about 500. This number may have originated with Muqātil ibn Sulaymān, but was repeated by al-Ghazālī and others, according to al-Zarkashī (d. 794/1392) (*al-Baḥr al-muḥīṭ*, 4:490).

Some Modern Responses to the Qur'an as a Source of Law

A general survey of Islamic law and modernity is beyond the scope of this chapter. At most, it will be possible to identify a couple of points along a spectrum of distinctively modern attitudes towards the Qur'an as a source of law. One modernist current is Salafism, a partly textualist approach that elevates the Qur'an, the hadith, and the opinions of Muḥammad's Companions and the first three generations of Muslims generally (collectively referred to as the *salaf*, 'predecessors', or *al-salaf al-ṣāliḥ*, 'the righteous predecessors', who give the movement its name) at the expense of the legal tradition and its institutions, especially the schools of legal thought (*madhhab*s). It is, as originally formulated by one of its founding figures, Rashīd Riḍā (d. 1935), an anti-clerical trend that urges a return to the texts. It assumes, moreover, that the evolution of legal institutions represents decline and a specific dilution of revelation, which should be seen as the primary source of moral guidance and religious authority (see Hallaq 2009b: 504–8). Stripping away the legal tradition allows the reappropriation of revealed texts in the service of a highly flexible and seemingly potentially unconstrained utilitarianism (labeled *maṣlaḥa*, and prominent in Riḍā's thought as well as that of the scholar and *sharīʿa* judge ʿAbd al-Wahhāb Khallāf, d. 1956) (Hallaq 1997: 214–20, 222). Salafism is modern in its rejection of the scholastic hermeneutic, but remains traditional in its view of Islamic law as an amalgam of Qur'an and prophetic Sunna.

The approach of the Sudanese religious figure Maḥmūd Muḥammad Ṭāhā (d. 1985) entails, in sharp contrast to Salafism, a de-emphasis of the many prophetic hadiths that reinforce Qur'anic legislation, and a consequent re-emphasis of the Qur'an's non-legislative passages (An Naʿim 1988: esp. 12–17). The relegation of legislative hadiths to the margins and elevation of the non-legislative Qur'an has also been proposed by some other modern writers, such as the Egyptian chemist Rashad Khalifa (d. 1990), Malaysian politician Kassim Ahmad, and Turkish writer Edip Yuksel (Musa 2008: 83–97). Several groups have adopted the name *ahl al-Qurʾān* ('Qur'an-only adherents') or are referred to as *qurʾāniyyūn* ('Qur'anists') to indicate a Qur'an-only orientation in their ethical thought, an orientation that typically downplays both hadiths and the legal tradition as a whole. The first such movement in the modern period seems to have emerged in nineteenth-century India under the leadership of ʿAbd Allāh Chakralavi (d. 1930), though both early Khārijī and Muʿtazilī theology exhibited 'scripturalist' tendencies (van Ess 1991–7: 1:38, 4:595–6, 1094 (index, 'Skritpuralismus')). Such Qur'an-only ideas remain, in any event, firmly outside mainstream religious institutions (some of their adherents have been persecuted) but are apparently attractive to modern secular professionals (Musa 2008: 83, 103–4, on the *ahl al-Qurʾān* in Egypt). Although Qur'an-only views may share some affinities with Salafism in regard to interpreting the Qur'an without the lens of the pre-modern hermeneutic, they are at the opposite end of a spectrum of attitudes toward the prophetic Sunna.

Finally, the Qur'an is occasionally invoked in the legislation of modern domestic legal systems, although typically the Islamization of the legal system is heralded by references to the term Sharīʿa in constitutions or civil codes (as in Article 1 of Egypt's Civil Code or Article 2 of the Constitution of 1971, which is retained in the Constitution of 2014). Foremost among specific invocations of the Qur'an are two articles in the Saudi Arabian Basic Law (*al-niẓām al-asāsī li'l-ḥukm*) of 1992. Article 1 provides that the Saudi 'constitution is the Book of God (*dustūruhā kitāb Allāh*) and the Sunna of the Prophet' and Article 7 provides that 'Government in the Kingdom of Saudi Arabia derives its authority from the Book of God (*yastamidd al-ḥukm fī'l-mamlaka... sulṭatahu min kitāb Allāh*) and the Sunna of the Prophet, which are the ultimate sources of reference for this Law and the other laws of the State'. The constitution of the Islamic Republic of Iran also makes reference to the Qur'an in several key provisions. Article 1 refers to the Iranian people's belief in the principle of 'Qur'anic justice' (*ʿadl-i Qurʾān*) and Article 2.6.a describes the jurists' use of and expertise in scripture (*kitāb*) in their continuous practice of legal reasoning (*ijtihād*). Other articles refer to the institution of consultative bodies (citing Q. 42:38 and 3:159, both using words derived from the root sh-w-r, which connotes 'consultation') (Art. 7), the universal duty to enjoin the good and forbid evil (as in Q. 9:71) (Art. 8), and the importance of the transnational Islamic community (*umma*) (as described in Q. 21:92) (Art. 11).

It has been observed that in the religion of Islam, the Qur'an plays a role analogous to that of Jesus in Christianity (Esack 2009:18). Thus, however individual Muslim thinkers may interpret the Qur'an for their various aims and projects, it will remain the foundation for all claims of Islamic legitimacy, authority, and authenticity. It will therefore also continue to play a central role in all Muslim thinking about law and legislation, whether as a source, a reference, or a symbol.

Bibliography

Primary Sources

al-Farrāʾ, Abū Zakariyyā Yaḥyā ibn Ziyād. *Maʿānī al-Qurʾān*. 3 vols. Ed. Aḥmad Yūsuf Najātī and Muḥammad ʿAlī al-Najjār. Reprint Dār al-Surūr, n.p., n.d.

al-Ghazālī, Abū Ḥāmid. *al-Mustaṣfā fī [sic] ʿilm al-uṣūl*. Beirut: Dār al-Kutub al-ʿIlmiyya, 1993.

Ibn ʿAqīl. *al-Wāḍiḥ fī uṣūl al-fiqh*. 5 vols. Ed. George Makdisi. Stuttgart: Franz Steiner Verlag, 1996–2002.

Ibn Hishām. *Sīrat Rasūl Allāh*. 2 vols. Ed. Muṣṭafā al-Saqqā, Ibrāhīm al-Abyārī, and ʿAbd al-Ḥafīẓ Shalabī. Cairo: Muṣṭafā al-Bābī al-Ḥalabī wa-Awlāduhu, 1955.

al-Jaṣṣāṣ, Abū Bakr Aḥmad ibn ʿAlī. *Aḥkām al-Qurʾān*. 3 vols. Ed. ʿAbd al-Salām Muḥammad ʿAlī Shāhīn. Beirut: Dār al-Kutub al-ʿIlmiyya, 2003.

Muqātil b. Sulaymān. *al-Ashbāh wa ʾl-naẓāʾir fī al-Qurʾān al-karīm*. Ed. ʿAbd Allāh M. Shiḥāta. Cairo: al-Hayʾa al-Miṣriyya al-ʿĀmma li'l-Kitāb, 1994.

al-Shāfiʿī, Muḥammad ibn Idrīs. *The Epistle on Legal Theory*. Ed. and trans. Joseph E. Lowry. Library of Arabic Literature. New York: New York University Press, 2013.

al-Zarkashī, Badr al-Dīn. *Al-Baḥr al-muḥīṭ fī uṣūl al-fiqh*. 4 vols. Ed. Muḥammad Muḥammad Tamir. Beirut: Dār al-Kutub al-ʿIlmiyya, 2007.

Secondary Sources

Crone, Patricia. 'Two Legal Problems Bearing on the Early History of the Qur'ān', *Jerusalem Studies in Arabic and Islam* 18 (1994), 1–37.

Cuypers, Michel. *The Banquet: A Reading of the Fifth Sura of the Qur'ān*. Miami: Convivium Press, 2009.

Esack, Farid. *The Qur'ān: A Short Introduction*. Oxford: Oneworld, 2009.

Hallaq, Wael. *A History of Islamic Legal Theories: An Introduction to Sunnī* uṣūl al-fiqh. Cambridge: Cambridge University Press, 1997.

Hallaq, Wael. 'Law and the Qur'ān'. In: Jane Dammen McAuliffe (ed.). *Encyclopaedia of the Qur'ān*. 6 vols., 3:149–72. Leiden: Brill, 2001–6.

Hallaq, Wael. 'Groundwork of the Moral Law: A New Look at the Qur'ān and the Genesis of the Sharīʿa', *Islamic Law and Society* 16 (2009a), 239–79.

Hallaq, Wael. *Sharīʿa: Theory, Practice Transformations*. Cambridge: Cambridge University Press, 2009b.

Hallaq, Wael. 'Qur'ānic Constitutionalism and Moral Governmentality', *Comparative Islamic Studies* 8 (2012), 1–51.

Jeffery, Arthur. *The Foreign Vocabulary of the Qur'ān*. Baroda: Oriental Institute, 1938.

Katz, Marion Holmes. 'Cleanliness and Ablution'. In: Jane Dammen McAuliffe (ed.). *Encyclopaedia of the Qur'ān*. 6 vols., 1:341–4. Leiden: Brill, 2001–6.

Krawietz, Birgit. *Hierarchie der Reschtsquelllen im tradierten sunnitischen Islam*. Berlin: Duncker & Humblot, 2002.

Lecker, Michael. *The Constitution of Medina: Muhammad's First Legal Document*. Princeton: Darwin Press, 2004.

Lowry, Joseph E. 'Law, Structure, and Meaning in Sūrat al-Baqarah', *Journal of the International Qur'anic Studies Association* 2 (2017), 111–48.

Lowry, Joseph E. 'Exculpatory Language in the Qur'an: A Survey of Terms, Themes, and Theologies', *Mélanges de l'Université Saint-Joseph* 66 (2015–16), 97–120.

Lowry, Joseph E. *Early Islamic Legal Theory: The Risāla of Muḥammad ibn Idrīs al-Shāfiʿī*. Leiden: Brill, 2007.

Lowry, Joseph E. 'When Less is More: Law and Commandment in *Sūrat al-Anʿām*', *Journal of Qur'ānic Studies* 9 (2007), 22–4.

Lowry, Joseph E. 'Lawful and Unlawful'. In: Jane Dammen McAuliffe (ed.). *Encyclopaedia of the Qur'ān*. 6 vols., 3:172–6. Leiden: Brill, 2001–6.

Lowry, Joseph E. 'Ritual Purity'. In: Jane Dammen McAuliffe (ed.). *Encyclopaedia of the Qur'ān*. 6 vols., 4:498–176. Leiden: Brill, 2001–6.

Motzki, Harald. *The Origins of Islamic Jurisprudence: Meccan Fiqh before the Classical Schools*. Trans. Marion Holmes Katz. Leiden: Brill, 2002.

Musa, Aisha Y. *Ḥadīth as Scripture: Discussions on the Authority of Prophetic Traditions in Islam*. New York: Palgrave Macmillan, 2008.

An-Na'im, Abdullahi Ahmed. 'Maḥmūd Muḥammad Ṭāhā and the Crisis in Islamic Law Reform: Implications for Interreligious Relations', *Journal of Ecumenical Studies* 25/1 (1988), 1–21.

Neuwirth, Angelika. *Studien zur Kompositin der mekkanischen Suren*. 2nd edn. Berlin: Walter de Gruyter, 2007.

Paret, Rudi. *Koran: Kommentar und Konkordanz*. Stuttgart: Kohlhammer, 1980.

Paret, Rudi. *Koran: Übersetzung*. Stuttgart: Kohlhammer, 1983.

Powers, David S. *Studies in Qurʾān and Ḥadīth: The Formation of the Islamic Law of Inheritance.* Berkeley: University of California Press, 1986.
The Qurʾān. Trans. Alan Jones. Cambridge: Gibb Memorial Trust, 2007.
Reinhart, A. Kevin. 'Contamination'. In: Jane Dammen McAuliffe (ed.). *Encyclopaedia of the Qurʾān.* 6 vols., 1:410–12. Leiden: Brill, 2001–6.
Reinhart, A. Kevin. 'Jurisprudence'. In: Andrew Rippin (ed.). *The Blackwell Companion to the Qurʾān*, pp. 434–49. Oxford: Wiley Blackwell, 2017.
Rippin, Andrew. 'The Commerce of Eschatology'. In: Stefan Wild (ed.). *The Qurʾan as Text*, pp. 125–35. Leiden: Brill, 1996.
Rubin, Uri. 'The "Constitution of Medina": Some Notes', *Studia Islamica* 62 (1985), 5–23.
Schacht, Joseph. *Origins of Muhammadan Jurisprudence.* Oxford: Clarendon Press, 1950.
Serjeant, R. B. 'The *Sunna Jāmiʿah*: Pacts with the Yathrib Jews, and the *Tahrīm* of Yathrib: Analysis and Translation of the Documents Comprised in the So-Called "Constitution of Medina"', *Bulletin of the School of Oriental and African Studies* 41/1 (1978), 1–42.
Sokoloff, Michael. *A Dictionary of Jewish Babylonian Aramaic.* Bar Ilan: Bar Ilan University Press, and Baltimore: Johns Hopkins University Press, 2002.
Sokoloff, Michael. *A Syriac Lexicon.* Winona Lake, IN: Eisenbrauns, and Piscataway, NJ: Gorgias Press, 2009.
Speyer, Heinrich. *Die biblischen Erzählungen im Qoran.* Gräfenhainchen: C. Schulze & Co., 1930.
van Ess, Josef. *Theologie und Gesellschaft im 2. und 3. Jahrhundert Hidschra.* 6 vols. Berlin: Walter de Gruyter, 1991–7.
Vishanoff, David R. *The Formation of Islamic Hermeneutics: How Sunni Legal Theorists Imagined a Revealed Law.* New Haven: American Oriental Society, 2011.
Wagtendonk, K. *Fasting in the Koran.* Leiden: Brill, 1968.
Zahniser, Mathias. 'Major Transitions and Thematic Borders in Two Long Sūras: *al-Baqara* and *al-Nisāʾ*'. In: Issa J. Boullata (ed.). *Literary Structures of Religious Meaning in the Qurʾān*, pp. 26–55. Richmond: Curzon, 2000.
Zellentin, Holger. *The Qurʾān's Legal Culture: The* Didascalia Apostolorum *as a Point of Departure.* Tübingen: Mohr Siebeck, 2013.
Zysow, Aron. *The Economy of Certainty: An Introduction to the Typology of Islamic Legal Theory.* Atlanta: Lockwood, 2013.

CHAPTER 29

QUR'ANIC ETHICS

EBRAHIM MOOSA

Introduction

The place and importance of an ethics derived from the Qur'an or inspired by the revelation largely depends on the historical perspective adopted by the interpreter. If one views Islam as an event in history, then one will be prepared for the emergence into visibility over time of subterranean and circuitous Muslim discursive formations. In other words, the meaning and significance of concepts, ideas, and practices mutate and become thicker or thinner over time, depending on circumstances and contexts. Scholars who adopt a positivist approach to facts and data, on the other hand, are often suspicious of Muslim claims regarding the date of the origins of Islam. They, in turn, would challenge the idea of a Qur'anic ethics existing at the very inception of Islam. Some of these critics might be content to concede the emergence of ethics at a later date in Muslim history conceding to the view that Islam as an unfolding event in history. However, Muslim scholars, in turn, will claim that if the Prophet Muḥammad accomplished anything, as God's messenger armed with the revelation vouchsafed to him, then it would be the ethical template that he had established for his own community and for future communities adhering to his faith.

Keywords

A cluster of Qur'anic terms shapes the ethical desideratum of the Qur'an. These terms form part of a semiotic or meaning-making framework consisting of interrelated and overlapping terms. Together, they signify a subtly textured tableau of ethical practices, dispositions, and sensibilities. *Khuluq or khulq*, meaning moral behaviour or character, as well as ethos, is a term only used twice in the Qur'an, but it is an enormously significant keyword that establishes a foundational value. The Prophet Muḥammad is addressed in the Qur'an as displaying an 'exalted character—*khuluq ʿaẓīm*' (Q. 68:4). And in another place the term is used in the sense of 'ethos' and 'traits' (Q. 26:137). *Khuluq* etymologically signifies several things, among them, 'trait' (*sajīya*), 'nature' (*ṭabʿ*), 'manliness' (*murūʾa/muruwwa*), meaning the virtue of possessing the power of the soul in order to display courage, patience, generosity and to display a calm mind and demeanour, and it also refers to the 'salvation path' (*dīn*) constitutive of both the fundamental convictions and the practices of revealed teachings (al-Kafawī et al. 1419/1998) (Izutsu 2002). At the very heart of Qur'anic ethics is the conceptual paradigm of *dīn*.

Abū'l-Baqāʾ al-Kafawī (d. 1094/1683), the legendary Ottoman scholar and philologist-lexicologist, helpfully defines *dīn* as the 'divinely coined [order] that marshals intelligent/rational beings to utilize their admirable choice exclusively in pursuit of the good, irrespective whether that choice involves inwardly affirmed (*qalb*an) [convictions] or outwardly (*qālibī*yan) embodied [performative acts], such as beliefs (*iʿtiqād*), knowledge (*ʿilm*) and ritual prayers (*ṣalāt*)' (al-Kafawī et al. 1419/1998). And Muḥammad Aʿlā al-Tahānawī (d. *c*.1191/1777), the renowned Indian scholar and philologist-lexicologist, in his definition explains that those choices humans make in pursuit of *dīn* results 'in righteousness (*ṣalāḥ*) in the present and success in the future (*maʾāl*) [i.e. the hereafter]' (al-Tahānawī and al-ʿAjam, 1996).

The semiotic framework of the Qur'an on morals thus makes manifest a significant understanding of ethics: the intimacy of the divinely assigned order or salvation path (*dīn*) with its indissoluble link to the embodiment of character, excellences, or virtues (*khuluq*). *Dīn* in the Qur'anic lexicon is imagined to be almost identical to an approved ethos of how to do things in the right way. It is therefore not surprising that one of the literal meanings of *dīn* is *ʿāda*, custom and convention. Further meanings of *dīn*, among others, include accountability, decree, compulsion, obedience, the present, and recompense (al-Tahānawī and al-ʿAjam 1996). In its most explicit sense, *dīn* is about the everyday and regular living in accordance with a prevailing ethical standard or norm. To be a person of *dīn*, would in the lexicon of the Qur'an mean that one is a righteous person, one who combines convictions, excellence, and virtues in their ordinary performance of practices in a regular, but normative sense. To the first listeners of the Qur'an, the term *dīn* invoked a whole range of ethical registers of right living in an ordinary sense.

Other ethical categories in the Qur'an are terms like *khayr*, meaning 'good', which also occurs in different derivatives on more than 177 occasions in the Qur'an. Terms like *ḥusn* (beauty), *aḥsan* (best performance), *ḥasana* (good deeds), *iḥsān* (excellence and integrity), and *muḥsinūn* (those who strive to reach excellence) are all derivatives from ḥ-s-n root, which signifies beauty, good, and excellence. These terms equate a range of individual and social actions of good that are cognitively and aesthetically informed by notions of beauty. *Maʿrūf* is another well-known and often-used term for that which is good. Other terms frequently used include *taqwā*, awareness of God, *ṣalāḥ*, to make better through advancing the common good, and *ṣāliḥ*, a pious person who embodies the common good. Together these terms form a set of overlapping meanings and sensibilities. All these terms also link to conceptions of fairness such as the all-important *ʿadl* (justice), and *qisṭ* (equity) in order to form a complex and multi-layered framework for the habitations of the good as portrayed in the teachings of the Qur'an. There might be other more contextual terms signifying the pursuit of ethical life, but these cannot be pursued here.

Discourses on Qur'anic Ethics

Varieties of ethical treatises by philosophers, physicians, and mystics have in the history of Islam been authored over the centuries. But there were few that focused on the ethics of the Qur'an. The closest proximate source resembling such a Qur'an-based work on ethics is a treatise by Abū Ḥāmid al-Ghazālī (d. 505/1111) titled, The Jewels of the Qur'ān and its Pearls *(Jawāhir al-Qur'ān wa duraruhu)*. This is an early attempt to capture the verses relevant to ethics in two major categories: firstly, a cluster of verses that lead to the understanding of the divine and, secondly, those verses related to conduct (*sulūk*) (al-Ghazālī and Bījū 1428/2007). Al-Ghazālī also creates several subcategories of the verses (Whittingham 2007). However, a leading Egyptian scholar Muḥammad ʿAbd Allāh Darāz (d. 1958) lamented that the task of deriving an ethical manifesto from the teachings of the Qur'an was not really continued after al-Ghazālī's early efforts in that direction. Most subsequent compilations of Qur'anic verses were often collections of verses used to identify the various juristic rules (*aḥkām*), not so much ethics (*akhlāq*). However, it might be fair to say that al-Ghazālī's own Revivification of the Sciences of Religion (*Iḥyā' ʿulūm al-dīn*), is a monumental enterprise in ethics drawing on the Qur'an and other sources, but it cannot qualify as a treatise on Qur'anic ethics in the strict sense.

The Pakistani émigré scholar to the United States, Fazlur Rahman (d. 1988) would agree with Darāz on the absence of Islamic ethics as 'an independent discipline based on a systematic interpretation of the Qur'an' (Rahman 1980). One major twentieth-century contribution to the study of Qur'anic ethics was Toshihiko Izutsu's highly resonant semantic study of the Qur'an's ethico-religious concepts. Izutsu's point of departure was this: just as Qur'anic Arabic corresponded in its connotative aspect, namely its additional features and attributes, with a Qur'anic worldview, similarly the ethical language of the Qur'an reflected only a segment of the features evident in entirety of the Qur'anic worldview (Izutsu 2002). The Qur'anic conception of God, Izutsu said, is 'of an ethical nature and acts upon man in an ethical way' and it carried the 'grave implication that man, on his part, is expected to respond in an ethical way' (Izutsu 2002). Instead of distinguishing between 'good' versus 'evil', Izutsu pointed out, the Qur'an chose to frame its moral concepts into two radically opposed moral categories, namely, as a contestation between *īmān*, belief on the one hand, versus *kufr*, ingratitude and disbelief, on the other. This created a binary that served in his words as the 'keynote of the whole ethical system of Islam' (Izutsu 2002). While some might challenge the latter proposition, it does nevertheless lead Izutsu to conclude: 'And man's ethical response to God's actions is, in the Qur'anic view, religion itself' (Izutsu 2002). Most valuable is Izutsu's semantic map of ethico-theological categories and the various transitions certain concepts undergo from the pre-Islamic period via the tribal system of ethics to finally morph into a distinct Islamic vocabulary as emphasized in the Qur'an.

George F. Hourani also made a strong case to demonstrate that the Qur'an permitted the use of ethical judgement independent of revelation. Yet, at the same time the Qur'an itself required the Muslim to take some ethical guidance from the revelation, for without it one could cease to be a Muslim (Hourani 1980).

However, as opposed to a strictly historical approach, a modern Muslim account of faith has no difficulty in accepting the fact that Islam, as Fazlur Rahman stated, began as a community that pursues a 'social order based on *īmān*, *taqwā* and *islām*' (Rahman 1983) These three key terms are rooted in a Qur'anic vocabulary that forms the conceptual unity of ethics. In Rahman's view, *īmān*, as faith is rooted in the inner life of a believer; *islām* points to the outer surrender to God's Law or Sharīʿa and, finally *taqwā*, consciousness and awareness of the divine, serves as the driving force of action and also incorporates faith (*īmān*).

In theory, this triad of concepts—surrender to God, faith, and God-consciousness—form part of the Qur'an's theological ethics. For ethics in Islam at its core is theocentric. Thus, it is no surprise that the Qur'an as a revelation repeatedly rehearses these themes in multiple contexts. Hence, it might not be an exaggeration to say that the Qur'an is essentially an elaborate programme in theocentric ethics. Whether the story of ethics as told above unfolded in this manner in Muslim history is difficult to substantiate. But modern Muslim ethicists are clearly re-narrating the story of ethics drawing on early Islamic teachings and tracing back certain ethical practices to the Qur'an.

Fazlur Rahman in the twentieth century claimed that it was imperative for Muslims to work out a Qur'anic ethics. He provided several reasons why in his view such an approach was relevant. Among them were the fact that Muslims believed the Qur'an to be the very word of God, and they furthermore believed that the revelation could actually and potentially provide answers to the questions produced by everyday life, through the exercise of both the mind and spirit (Rahman 1985). The major shortcoming in achieving this goal, he pointed out, was the absence of a 'proper Qur'anic theology in order to define the God-man relationship', but one that remained elusive and, in his view, was 'never worked out by Muslims' (Rahman 1985). Ironically, Rahman did not formally construct a Qur'anic theology but one can clearly view his important work *Major Themes of the Qur'an* as groundwork in the direction of Qur'an-based theological ethics.

Already in the fifth/eleventh century, the illustrious Abū'l-Maʿālī al-Juwaynī (d. 478/1085) pointed out the interdependence of legal theory or moral philosophy and dialectical theology (*kalām*). Dialectical theology, al-Juwaynī said, meant to 'know the world, the division of the world, its realities, its origination and knowledge of its Originator as well as His mandatory attributes and which things are impossible to attribute to the Originator and which things are permissible for attribution.' Al-Juwaynī continued: 'And dialectical theology involves knowledge of prophecies and to adjudicate between them by way of miracles, the rules regarding prophecy and discussion as to what is permissible and impermissible in order to qualify under the rubric of the universals of revealed religions' (al-Juwaynī, *Nihāya*).

It is as if Fazlur Rahman acts on al-Juwaynī's description of the relationship of moral good to faith claims. Knowledge and the performance of moral acts, as Fazlur Rahman and before him al-Juwaynī would have it, are premised on a deep knowledge of the Creator, a commitment to prophecy, and some consensus as to which things form the universal good. These are precisely the narrative themes that frequently recur in the Qur'an and form the theological mainframe of the revelation. Among modern scholars Fazlur Rahman gave considerable attention to crafting certain theological and moral teachings from the Qur'an; these included beliefs about God, society, the individual, prophethood, eschatology, and evil (Rahman and Moosa 2009).

While the Qur'anic approach to ethics is, in the view of many people, a laudable move one should yet be cautious. The major reason for this caution is due to the fact that the emergence of the *fiqh* tradition often regulated by traditional scholars, the *ʿulamāʾ*, has become the dominant narrative for what is viewed as a default form of Islamic ethics. *Fiqh* literally means 'understanding and comprehension' and became the dominant vocabulary in which Islam's ethical teachings were articulated. Unfortunately, most interpreters describe the *fiqh* tradition as a legal or juridical tradition. Especially among moderns, very few have viewed the *fiqh* tradition as an ethical tradition or as a hybrid legal-ethical tradition.

Some early Muslim thinkers did view virtue ethics to be at the core of *fiqh*, for instance in the work of al-Ghazālī and even to some extent that of Ibn Rushd (d. 595/1198). The truth is that only a portion of Muslim ethical thinking gives rise to a law requiring a public authority to enforce it. The greater part of the ethical tradition is devoted to ethical formation, *akhlāq*. Often this ethical literature was viewed as part of the teachings deployed in the formation of an ethical self, but this material was not frequently deployed in the sense of public ethics. There was an unspoken assumption that the personal ethics of a moral subject would be in harmony with the public ethics adopted by the community. Nevertheless, for centuries, *fiqh* was also part of Muslim expressions of public ethics in the genre of Sharīʿa-derived political ethics, *al-siyāsa al-sharʿiyya*.

But over time *fiqh* became autonomous and developed into a hegemonic and elaborate discourse of deontological ethics, a duty-based system of obligations. Discontent about the mechanical nature of *fiqh* was expressed by no less an exemplary figure than al-Ghazālī, who argued that the true understanding of God's rules, namely the ethical importance of practices, was mistaken for legal hairsplitting by professional jurists. True 'understanding' (*fiqh*) was the 'understanding of the self (*fiqh al-nafs*)', al-Ghazālī lamented.

Centuries later, living in new and radically altered contexts in the modern period, the inheritance of deontological ethics (*fiqh*) has, in the view of many Muslims, become a challenge. Critics rightly argue that it is steeped in cultural presumptions and notions of selfhood that are at odds with the lived experiences of contemporary Muslims. Hence, there is a renewed attempt to access the ethical heritage of Islam beyond the *fiqh* tradition. To avoid the limits of *fiqh*, scholars turn to the Qur'an and the prophetic Sunna, the lived tradition of the Prophet that was documented in the hadith.

In the Muslim tradition, the Prophet Muḥammad was the ethical model par excellence. The Prophet is depicted in the Qur'an as an 'excellent exemplar (*uswa ḥasana*)' and anyone who anticipated an encounter with God and the Last Day would take his example seriously (Q. 33:21). Furthermore, the Prophet is hailed to be a moral archetype as the one who has 'a strong character, *khuluq ʿaẓīm*' (Q. 98:4). Therefore, anyone who claims to love the Prophet Muḥammad must affiliate themselves to him, as Q. 3:31 explains in pursuing the work of *ittibāʿ*. *Ittibāʿ* is often wrongly translated as 'emulation', a rather mechanistic and unthinking descriptor at odds with anything remotely resembling ethics. The truth is that the word *ittibāʿ* signifies meanings such as 'affiliate', 'catch up', as well as to 'attain' and 'perceive' (*al-luḥūq and idrāk*) (al-Kafawī et al: 1419/1998). *Ittibāʿ* sublimates a category of love in an ethical register. With this framework in mind, one can confidently suggest that *ittibāʿ* requires both an affective and intellectual relationship with the exemplary ethical and moral tradition embodied by the Prophet. Such an approach results in an engagement with prophetic morality itself, not a mere mechanistic replication of certain prophetic practices that have ceased to be contextually and socially relevant.

Thus when ʿĀʾisha, the Prophet Muḥammad's wife, is asked about his character she promptly replies, according to Muslim tradition, that his character was the embodiment of the Qur'an. In fact she said his character was identical to the requirements of the revelation; or put differently, she can be construed as having said that his character was attuned to revelation. This makes even better sense in so far as reports attributed to the Prophet explain that Muḥammad defined his entire prophecy in an ethical register, when he proclaimed: 'Indeed, I was sent to complete the nobility of character' (Mālik, *al-Muwaṭṭaʾ*).

Hence, in the teachings of the Prophet Muḥammad in both the Qur'an and the Sunna, the notion of ethics is central, writes ʿAbd al-Ḥayy al-Ḥasanī (d. 1923) the Indian author of a treatise on scriptural ethics. The refinement of character (*tahdhīb al-akhlāq*) and formation of the self (*tazkīya al-nufūs*) and the pursuit of wisdom (*ḥikma*) are characteristics of the Qur'an's ethical call. Various teachings in the Qur'an therefore warrant Qur'an-based ethics. For many authors the inspiration for the ethical comes from the prophet Abraham. After erecting the house of God, the Kaʿba for the people of Mecca, Abraham's prayer is encapsulated in Q. 2:129. Abraham asks God to send to the people of Mecca a messenger from among them who will 'recite [declare] Your signs to them and teach them the Book [scripture] and wisdom, and purify them'. These are all themes that are again repeated in Q. 2:151–2 and 2:164.

The keyword is *ḥikma*, meaning wisdom and its capaciousness to serve as the central theme for a Qur'anic ethics. It signifies both ways of performance (*adab* pl. *ādāb*) and the cultivation of virtues (*khuluq* pl. *akhlāq*). The prolific twentieth-century tradition-minded Indian scholar and preacher, Abū'l-Ḥasan ʿAlī al-Nadwī (d. 1999), the son of ʿAbd al-Ḥayy al-Ḥasanī, states that wisdom has an integral relationship with ethical virtues and they mutually reinforce each other in the Qur'an's semantic field, a point borne out by al-Kafawī too (al-Kafawī et al. 1419/1998) (al-Nadwī *c.*1972).

In very specific passages the Qur'an provides copious ethical proclamations that a human being ought to pursue. The Qur'an begins by obliging the worship of one God, then encourages a moral subject to show kindness to parents, to promote gentle speech, to display humility, to give freely to the poor, to assist the traveller, be generous in disposition, and then strongly forbids murder, back-biting, slander, and infanticide, while announcing stringent prohibitions against adultery and usury. The Qur'an urges its listeners and readers to earn the trust of people in monetary matters, and to conduct themselves responsibly and honestly as stated in Q. 17:23–40. Especially when making monetary sacrifices, the Qur'an in 2:264 cautions a donor from making any comments to a recipient that would amount to a rebuke (*mann*) and abuse (*adhā*) for the conferral of a favour. The Qur'an also teaches people to pardon one another and to promote virtuous speech, to shun arrogant conduct, to avoid disbelief in God, to seek the grace of God, and to permanently strive towards an order that cultivates a wholesome soul and to nurture that soul so that it consistently obeys God. Pardons involving the infringement of the rights of others and the public must be preceded by the full disclosure of the wrong committed and a compensation, if possible, before a full pardon can occur (Q. 2:160).

Darāz designs a hermeneutic or interpretive framework in order to extrapolate the key principles of ethics from the Qur'an. He complains that ethical debates were historically either advice literature or descriptive accounts about the nature of the soul drawn from multiple philosophical traditions. What he seeks is a purely Qur'an-centred ethics. The Qur'an, he explains, provides comprehensive frameworks of central themes, each of which are flexible. How does the Qur'an accomplish this feat, he asks? The methodology of the Qur'an is plain, he explains. The Qur'an provides multiple choices of principles that have a special effect on the practitioner and always provides a median path by navigating that space between abstraction and the sensory. The frameworks are both strict and flexible at the same time. In terms of its clarity of the substance of ethical themes, the Qur'an offers certain rules that suggest restraint in order to combat chaos and unbridled pleasures. Another compelling feature is the unspecified substance of the Qur'an's ethical themes, says Darāz, which allows every individual the freedom to choose a specific ethical form that represents the highest ideal (Darāz et al. 1974). Following this approach the Qur'an-based Sharīʿa (*al-sharīʿa al-qurʾāniyya*) reaches the unusual perfection not allowed its rivals, he argues. This results in an ethical framework with the following characteristics: grace in resoluteness, progress within stability, and diversity in unity. Few people grasp the delicate wisdom of the Qur'an, he argues, that allows submission within a paradigm of freedom, ease in serious endeavours, and initiative within a framework of continuity. In Darāz's view the Qur'an is primarily a teaching of ethics and deals with human existence. Good and bad are attributes of excellence within an individual person.

A plethora of studies on ethics has been published in recent years. These studies engage the general topic of ethics and then invariably turn to the Qur'anic references to ethics. Often these studies are fairly nominalist readings of Qur'anic passages and refer to the various moral codes that are enumerated. However, there is little attempt at the systematization of a Qur'anic ethics *per se*.

Bibliography

Darāz, M. ʿA. Shāhīn, and A. Badawī. *Dustūr al-akhlāq fī'l-Qurʾān: dirāsah muqāranah li'l-akhlāq al-naẓarīyah fī'l-Qurʾān: mulḥaq bihā taṣnīf li'l-āyāt al-mukhtārah allatī tukāwin al-dustūr al-kāmil li'l-akhlāq al-ʿamaliyyah.* Beirut: Muʾassasat al-Risāla (1974).

al-Ghazālī, Abū Ḥāmid, Muḥammad. *Jawāhir al-Qurʾān wa-duraruhu.* Damascus: Dār al-Taqwā, 1428/2007.

Hourani, George. F. 'Ethical Presuppositions of the Qurʾān', *Muslim World* 70 (1980), 1–28.

Izutsu, Toshihiko. *Ethico-religious Concepts in the Qur'ān.* Ithaca, NY, and Montreal: McGill-Queen's University Press, 2002.

al-Juwaynī, Abū'l-Maʿālī ʿAbd al-Malik. *Nihāyat al-maṭlab fī dirāyat al-madhhab.* Jidda: Dār al-Minhāj, 2007.

al-Kafawī, Ayyūb ibn Mūsā al-Ḥusaynī. *al-Kulliyāt: Muʿjam fī'l-muṣṭalaḥāt wa'l-furūq al-lughawīya.* Beirut: Muʾassasat al-Risāla, 1419/1998.

Mālik Ibn Anas. *al-Muwaṭṭāʾ.* Beirut: Dār al-Fikr, 1419/1998.

al-Nadawī, Abū'l-Ḥasan. *Tahdhīb al-akhlāq.* Introd. Abū'l-Ḥasan ʿAlī al-Ḥasanī. Lucknow: Maktaba al-Nadwa al-Tijāriya, *c.*1972.

Rahman, Fazlur. 'Islamic Studies and the Future of Islam'. In: M. H. Kerr (ed.). *Islamic Studies: A Tradition and its Problems.* Malibu, CA: Undena Publications, 1980.

Rahman, Fazlur. 'Some Key Ethical Concepts of the Qur'an', *Journal of Religious Ethics* 11 (1983), 173–85.

Rahman, Fazlur. 'Law and Ethics in Islam'. In: R. G. Hovannisian (ed.). *Ethics in Islam.* Malibu, CA: Undena Publications, 1985.

Rahman, Fazlur and Ebrahim Moosa. *Major Themes of the Qur'an.* Chicago and London: University of Chicago Press, 2009.

al-Tahānawī, Muḥammad ʿAlī and Rafīq al-ʿAjam. *Mawsūʿa kashshāf iṣṭilāḥāt al-funūn wa'l-ʿulūm.* Beirut: Maktaba Lubnān, 1996.

Whittingham, Martin. *Al-Ghazālī and the Qur'ān: One Book, Many Meanings.* London and New York: Routledge, 2007.

CHAPTER 30

ESCHATOLOGY AND THE QUR'AN

SEBASTIAN GÜNTHER

THE apocalyptic cessation of this world, the end of human life, and resurrection of the dead, divine judgement, and God's ultimate and eternal kingdom of the heavens and the earth (Q. 2:107; 48:14) to be established in a world-to-come, are issues central to the Qur'anic message. Indeed, confidence in the truth of these 'last things', expressed on numerous occasions in Islam's sacred scripture, forms the foundation of several articles of Islamic faith. Eschatological statements of this kind underscore the recognition of God's unity or 'oneness' (*tawḥīd*) and His omnipotence. They also provide the ground for Islamic creeds such as the belief in the immortality of the soul, in bodily resurrection and divine judgement, as well as in the existence of paradise and hell as real worlds. The eschatological developments heralded in the Qur'an are thus distinctive for their two-fold function: on the one hand, they are related as crucial warnings of the approaching end of the world and of life as it is known. On the other, they convey great hope and joy, with their promise of a new beginning for all existence after Doomsday and the reality of eternal life and human fulfilment.

Throughout history the Qur'anic concepts of the final things have fuelled intense debates in the Muslim world about accountability for deeds in this life, as effected through reward and punishment in the next. Thus, the Qur'anic concepts of 'the end' lend dynamic form and content to Muslim life, whether on religious, political, and cultural levels, or concerning individual, communal, and societal aspects. This is true of the eschatological theories advanced by Muslim scholars, and of related ideas current in Muslim 'lay piety' and in daily life. It applies to Sunnī, Shīʿī, and other Muslim identities past and present. Moreover, these ideas have also been critical points of encounter between the Muslim world and the 'West'.

Since E. Pococke's (1705) and Th. Arnold's (1746) treatments of the eschatology of Islam, probably the first such works of note in Western scholarship, a great number of studies have appeared in European languages, with various foci and approaches. Thematic overviews introduce the eschatology in the Qur'an, in the Sunna, and in the

Muslim dogmatic, philosophical, and apologetic writings (Rüling 1895; Stieglecker 1959–62; and van Ess 1991–7: 4:521–34, 543–561). Other examinations analyse more specific topics, such as the individual spiritual life in the context of eschatology (Massignon 1922; Corbin 1971), Shīʿī eschatological views (Ayoub 1978; Sachedina 1981), and Sunnī interpretations (Smith and Haddad 1981). The eschatological discourses in Qur'anic exegesis (Böwering 1980); Islamic history (Donner 2010; more radically by Shoemaker 2012); Islamic mysticism (Schimmel 1975; Ernst 1985); the Qur'an; and Babi thought (Lawson 2011) have been assessed; and the characteristics of suras with overarching eschatological themes have received brilliant elucidation (Neuwirth 2011, 2017). The provocative argument that sees the birth of Islam as an apocalyptic movement (Casanova 1911–13) was taken up recently (Cook 2002) and the view that the Qur'an as a whole is an apocalyptic text (Lawson 2012, 2017 a, b). The geographical and religious implications of realms in the world beyond sensory perception, the legal dimensions of reward and punishment in the hereafter, and the diversity and specifics of eschatological concepts in the Qur'an and Islamic traditions have received in-depth attention (Rustomji 2009; Lange 2008, 2015; and Günther/Lawson 2017, the latter with an extensive bibliography of primary and secondary sources on Islamic eschatology and concepts of the hereafter, in major European languages as well as in Arabic, Persian, and Turkish).

The End of This World

The Qur'an says more, comparatively, about the end of the world, resurrection, final judgement, and a world-to-come than any other sacred scripture. No fewer than fifty-six suras from an early stage of Muḥammad's prophethood, and eleven suras revealed later in Medina, address eschatological issues in various ways. Themes range from the initial signs of 'the Hour', or the 'End Time', to divine judgement, to rewards or punishment in the afterlife. (Particularly explicit and evocative portrayals are found in Q. 23:101–18; 37:31–49 and 60–6; 39:68–75; 69:13–37; 70:1–35, and 76:12–22.) Although no clear chronological order of the 'final events' is given, the Qur'an does indicate clearly that there will be an absolute termination of all life and existence (*fanāʾ*), as 'everything will perish' (if only even temporarily) except God's face (Q. 28:88; 55:26–7), to be followed by a second creation in the hereafter (Q. 29:20). (On 'the face (*wajh*) of God' as an image firmly rooted in the ancient Near Eastern heritage, see Rippin 2000).

While contemporary Western scholarship has a continued strong interest in an analytical 'mapping' of the Qur'anic hereafter (Rustomji 2009; Günther 2011), comparing these findings with statements in the Bible and other religious traditions (Bijlefeld 2004; Tubach et al. 2010), and a fresh scrutiny of major perceptions of Qur'anic eschatology based on their own merits (Günther/Lawson 2017), the focus has shifted to include the study of the characteristic and definitive structure of eschatological discourse in the Qur'an (Neuwirth 1984, 2011, 2017), the interrelation of apocalyptic and epic literary topics and motifs in Qur'anic eschatology (Lawson 2014, 2017 a, 2017b, and the understanding of eschatological themes in the Qur'an as foundational for the origins of Islam (Cook 2003, 2005; Donner 2010, 2017). Similarly innovative research has been done on the ways in which an individual's or a community's actions and existence on earth will be judged in the hereafter in relation to human existence in the here and now (Lange 2008, 2015), and the implications of Islamicate eschatological discourses for inter-religious dialogue (Khalil 2013).

The Final Hour and its Signs

Numerous Qur'anic statements warn of the '**the Hour**' (*al-sāʿa*), as the Qur'an frequently calls the all-decisive *eschaton* (from Greek ἔσχατα, 'the final things'). Other designations include *ghāshiya* (an 'overwhelming [hour of disaster and punishment]', Q. 12:107), *al-wāqiʿa* ('the occurring [hour of terror]', Q. 56:1), *al-ḥāqqa* ('the indubitable' or 'inevitable [reality of the hour]', Q. 69:1–3), and *al-qāriʿa* ('[the hour of] the crashing blow', Q. 101:1).

An especially evocative description of the signs and '**conditions of the Hour**' (*ashrāṭ al-sāʿa*) is included in *Sūrat al-Takwīr* (81) ('Shrouded in Darkness'), a Qur'anic chapter revealed in Mecca. Here humankind is warned:

> [1]When the sun is shrouded in darkness, [2]when the stars are dimmed, [3]when the mountains are set in motion, [4]when pregnant camels are abandoned, [5]when wild beasts are herded together, [6]when the seas boil over, [7]when the souls are sorted into classes, [8]when the baby girl buried alive is asked [9]for what sin she was killed, [10]when the records of deeds are spread open, [11]when the sky is stripped away, [12]when hell is made to blaze [13]and paradise brought near: [14]then every soul will know what it has brought about.

The Qur'an indicates that God has already determined the time of the Hour's occurrence; and that He is 'delaying it only for a specified period' (Q. 11:104). It is certain that the Hour 'draws near' (Q. 54:1). In fact, 'its signs are already here' (Q. 47:18). However, because God alone knows when exactly it occurs (Q. 43:85; 41:47) the Prophet Muḥammad was commanded to say: 'I do not know whether what you have been warned about is near, or whether a distant time has been appointed for it by my Lord' (Q. 72:25). In other words, the exact point in time when the Hour will occur is unknown to humankind; it may be in the near future or in a far-distant time. Muḥammad warns of severe punishment awaiting those who persist in blasphemy (Q. 10:70)—in which he is like Noah, warning of the Deluge (Q. 26:115; see also *Sūrat Nūḥ* [71]), or Moses and other messengers and prophets after him, who were sent to give their people 'a clear warning' of the torment to come 'on a painful Day', if they do not abandon their sinful ways and worship only God (Q. 11:25–6).

In modern scholarship, O'Shaughnessy (1969, 1991), for example, places the Qur'anic references to death (and killing) in a wider eschatological context and compares them with biblical concepts. Meier (1971) emphasizes the unique centrality of the eschatological concept of 'the Hour' for the Islamic religion, while Stieglecker (1959–62: 747–55) and Smith (2002) expose the characteristics of the signs and conditions of 'the Hour'.

Signs of the End Time in History

Muslim scholarship elaborates considerably on Qur'anic end-time scenarios of this kind. In the hadith literature—the prophetic tradition—for example, the Prophet Muḥammad is quoted as saying, 'The Hour and I have been sent like these two—and he pointed to [or 'joined'] his index and middle fingers' (Ibn Ḥanbal, *Musnad*, 3:124; see also Bashear 1993: 75–99). Thus Muḥammad is often seen as the quintessential 'apostle of the end of time', because the world's inexorable move towards the Day of Judgement began with the advent of his prophethood (Donner 2010: 78; and, with a number of controversial ideas, Shoemaker 2012: 118–36).

Although nothing in the Qur'an explicitly points to historical events that would indicate the advent of the beginning of the end of the world, it is stated that the Hour of the End Time will occur suddenly and quickly (Q. 7:187). An earthquake will shake the world so severely that 'every nursing mother will think no more of her baby, every pregnant female will miscarry, you will think people are drunk when they are not' (Q. 22:2).

Other Qur'anic statements specify certain 'major signs of the Hour' (*ʿalamāt al-sāʿa al-kubrā*): (1) Gog and Magog, two savage peoples whom Alexander the Great (Dhū'l-Qarnayn) had constrained by a huge iron barrier, will be released and 'race down from every slope' (Q. 18:93–9; 21:96; cf. also Ezek. 38:39). (2) God will bring 'a creature out of the earth (*dābbat al-arḍ*), which will tell them that people had no faith in Our revelations' (Q. 27:82; cf. also Rev. 13:13–16 and other parallels in Isaiah, Jeremiah, and minor prophets). Moreover, (3) the sky will bring forth 'clouds of smoke' (Q. 44:10) and (4) Jesus will appear as 'a portent of the hour' (Q. 43:61), alternatively, the pronoun *hu* can also be seen as referring to the Qur'an. The advent of the Antichrist (Dajjāl) and his killing by Jesus as signs of the approaching Hour are not mentioned in the Qur'an. These ideas are based on prophetic traditions, as is the oft-quoted eschatological view that at the dawn of the Last Day, the sun will rise in the West. (For the Jewish and Christian background of these ideas, see esp. Robinson 2001; the understanding of political events and movements in early and later Islamic history as typically apocalyptic in nature, and the ideological concerns prompting apocalyptical concepts in Islam, are advanced by Cook 2002; while Stowasser 2004 and 2014: 25–30, examines messianic claims and the end time in the Islamic calendar).

The appearance of a messianic figure, the *mahdī* or Guided One, who 'redeems' Islam, is significant in both Sunnī and Shīʿī sources of later times, even though the term *mahdī* as such does not appear in the Qur'an. Furthermore, in Shīʿī beliefs the *qāʾim* or 'one who will arise' (eventually identified as the *mahdī*) renews the lost sense of the sacred, and spreads justice and equity throughout the world (Ghaemmaghami 2017). After the *mahdī*'s death, either of natural causes or, according to some traditions, killed by the forces of darkness, a period of turmoil and chaos follows before the world collapses and the Day of Resurrection occurs.

The Hereafter

The Day of Judgment and its Many Names

The remarkable variety of Qur'anic designations for the Last Day illustrates both its general importance and the thematic scope of the 'events' which Islam's revealed scripture associates with it. It is called 'the Day of Doom' (*yawm al-dīn*, e.g. Q. 1:4; 13 times), 'the Day of Resurrection' (*yawm al-qiyāma*, e.g. Q. 2:85; 70 times), 'the Last Day' (*al-yawm al-ākhir*, e.g. Q. 2:8; 38 times), 'a mighty/dreadful day' (*yawm ʿaẓīm*, Q. 6:15; 10 times), 'a great day' (*yawm kabīr*, Q. 11:3), 'a painful day' (*yawm alīm*, Q. 11:26; 43:65), 'an encompassing, inevitable day' (*yawm muḥīṭ*, Q. 11:84), 'a tempestuous day' (*yawm ʿāṣif*, Q. 14:18), 'a day herein shall be neither bargaining nor befriending' (*yawm lā bayʿ fīhi wa-lā khulla/khilāl*, Q. 2:254; 14:31), the 'Day of the Appointed Time' (*yawm al-waqt al-maʿlūm*, Q. 15:38; 38:81), 'an [everything] destroying day' (*yawm ʿaqīm*, Q. 22:55), 'a hard day' (*yawm ʿasir/ʿasīr*, Q. 54:8; 74:9), 'an appointed day' (*yawm maʿlūm*, Q. 56:50); 'a frowning and wrathful day' (*yawm ʿabūs qamṭarīr*, Q. 76:10); 'a hard grievous day' (*yawm thaqīl*, Q. 76:27); and 'the Promised Day' (*al-yawm al-mawʿūd*, Q. 85:2), yet this is but a sampling of the many terms used in the Qur'an for this concept (Günther 1988).

The Blast of the Trumpet

Resurrection and divine judgement will be signalled by the blast of the divine Trumpet (*nāqūr* in 74:8; *ṣūr* in other suras). 'When the Trumpet is sounded a single time, when the earth and its mountains are raised high and then crushed with a single blow, on that Day the Great Event will come to pass' (Q. 69:13–15). On this Day of the Crushing Blow, 'people will be like scattered moths and the mountains like tufts of wool' (Q. 101:4–5). 'Wild beasts are herded together' and 'the seas boil over' (Q. 81:5–6). 'The mountains… will float away like clouds' (27:88). They will be blasted into dust and 'leave a flat plain with no peak or trough to be seen' (Q. 20:105–107).

Now, 'the sun is shrouded in darkness,… the stars are dimmed' (Q. 81:1–2); the moon is eclipsed and 'the sun and the moon are brought together' (Q. 75:8–9). The sky 'turns crimson, like red hide' (Q. 55:37). The sky will be like molten brass (Q. 70:8). It 'sways back and forth' (Q. 52:9) and will eventually be torn apart (Q. 78:18), apparently so that the angels will be 'sent down in streams' (Q. 25:25).

Resurrection

In stark contrast to the Qur'an's image of pre-Islamic Arabia where the belief in one life and one death prevailed, the Qur'anic creed that those 'turned to bones and dust, shall…be raised up in a new act of creation' (Q. 17:49) offers comfort, and the hope that death is not the end, but a new beginning. Moreover, the Qur'anic assurance of resurrection underscores God's omnipotence, as the dead shall be revivified even 'if you were [as hard as] stone, or iron, or any other substance you think hard to bring to life' (Q. 17:50–1). 'God is certainly able to bring [the dead] back to life' (Q. 86:8), since He is 'the one who created you from clay and specified a term [for you] to live and another fixed time [for you to be resurrected]' (Q. 6:2). He 'is the One who originates creation and will do it again [at the end of time]' (Q. 30:27). God causes a human being 'to die and be buried'. But 'when He wills, He will raise him up again' (Q. 80:21–22).

Proof of such divine miracles in the hereafter is, according to the Qur'an, plain to see in the here and now. The cycle of nature is mentioned to illustrate this: 'there is a sign…in the lifeless earth: We give it life and We produce grain from it…; We have put gardens of date palms and grapes in the earth, and We have made springs of water gush out of it' (Q. 36:33–34). In fact, this is an easy undertaking for God, as the Qur'an insists, since 'creating and resurrecting all of you is only like creating or resurrecting a single soul' (Q. 31:28).

The Qur'an supports the idea that human bodies will be recreated in the shape they had on earth. Those who doubt the resurrection should remember that God 'created you from dust, then a drop of fluid, then a clinging form, then a lump of flesh, both shaped and unshaped' (Q. 22:5). Moreover, man should know that God 'can reshape his very fingertips' (Q. 75:4) on the day when 'when souls are sorted into classes' (Q. 81:7) before they are reunited with their respective bodies.

On that Day of Resurrection, **the disbelievers'** 'hearts will tremble and eyes will be downcast' (Q. 79:8–9). Their 'eyes will stare in terror. They will rush forward, craning their necks, unable to divert their eyes, a gaping void in their hearts' (Q. 14:42–43). The sinful will be gathered sightless, not remembering how long they stayed on earth (or in the grave) (Q. 20:102–104; 46:35). The **believers**, though, and in fact 'all those who believe in God and the Last Day and do good'—here expressly including Jews, Christians, and Sabians—'will have their rewards with their Lord. No fear for them, nor will they grieve' (Q. 2:62). Along these lines, the disbelievers among the jinn as well are said to be doomed to hell (Q. 6:128; 11:119; 32:13), while it is implicit that the believers among the jinn will go to paradise.

As for the **signs** signalling resurrection, the Qur'an states that revivification of the dead will take place 'when the earth is levelled out, casts out its contents, and becomes empty' (Q. 84:3–4). It will occur 'on the Day when the blast reverberates and the second blast follows' (Q. 79:6–7). Resurrection is immediately connected to a single blast of the Trumpet in most Qur'anic passages. Only Q. 39:68 specifies that, when the Trumpet will be sounded for the first time, 'everyone in the heavens and earth will fall down senseless except those God spares'. Then, the Trumpet 'will be sounded once again and they will be on their feet, looking on'.

With the awakening of the dead, a 'caller' (archangel Isrāfīl, or archangel Gabriel, according to some exegetes) 'will call from a nearby place' (the Temple Mount in Jerusalem, as later Muslim tradition indicates) so that the dead come out from their graves (Q. 50:41).

Reckoning

On the Day of Reckoning, eight angels 'will bear the throne of your Lord above them' (Q. 69:17). The resurrected will be called to the place of judgement by an angel called 'the summoner from whom there is no escape' (Q. 20:108). 'Each person will arrive attended by one [angel] to drive him on and another to bear witness' (Q. 50:21), so that the resurrected line up to eventually meet their Lord (*liqāʾ* Allāh, as in Q. 6:31). God Himself will conduct the reckoning (*ḥisāb*) of each person. He will do so individually and instantly, as He 'is swift in reckoning' (Q. 2:202).

On that Day, 'the evildoers' excuses will be of no use to them: they will not be allowed to make amends' (Q. 30:57). But for those who are on God's side, who believe and are conscious of God, 'for them there is good news in this life and in the Hereafter—there is no changing the promises of God' (Q. 10:62–4).

Deeds and actions executed in this world will be reckoned as registered in heavenly books by 'watchers, noble recorders who know what you do' (Q. 82:11–12). Apparently, each person has his or her individual record, which will be brought out for each and 'spread wide open' so that he or she will be commanded 'read your record' (Q. 17:13–14). Nations also have a 'book' of their own, and on the Day of Reckoning, every community will be seen kneeling, 'summoned to its record', and be told, 'Today you will be repaid for what you did' (Q. 45:28). While the mouths of people shall be sealed up, 'their hands will speak' to God, and 'their feet bear witness to everything they have done' (Q. 36:65). Even the earth will bear witness. 'People will come forward in separate groups to be shown their deeds;' they will see the smallest good and the smallest evil they had done (Q. 99:6–8). Eventually, it is said, angels and prophets will bear witness for individuals and entire communities, respectively (Q. 2:143; 16:89).

The divine balance (*mīzān*) will be erected, and 'the weighing of deeds will be true and just. Those whose good deeds are heavy on the scales' will prosper, and 'those whose good deeds are light' will have lost their souls. Disbelievers in God and His messages 'will remain in hell' (Q. 7:8–9; 23:103; 23: 43–74; 101:6–9).

Judgement and Retribution

The Day of Judgement is a day of uncompromised ruling and final verdict, but it is apparently also a time of festive celebration and the triumph of divine power and justice.

'The earth will shine with the light of its Lord; the Record of Deeds will be laid open; the prophets and witnesses will be brought in' so that divine judgement may begin. 'Fair judgment will be given between them: they will not be wronged and every soul will be repaid in full for what it has done' (Q. 39:69–70). Hence, whoever arrives at the place of judgement (*maqām*) with a good deed will be 'rewarded with something better'. Such persons will be 'secure from the terrors of that Day' and enter paradise. Yet, anyone coming with evil deeds 'will be cast face downwards into the Fire' (Q. 27:89–90).

Consistent with the overall division of humankind and jinn into three classes—the disbelievers (Q. 55:41–5), the ordinary believers (55:62–77), and the best of the believers (55:46–61)—on the Day of Judgement people will be grouped in three classes: 'those on the Left' who will go to hell; 'those on the Right' who will go to paradise; and 'those in front—ahead indeed' in terms of faith and good works, who will be the first to enjoy the bliss of paradise (Q. 56:7–10).

Jews and Christians, along with the ancient monotheistic community of the Sabians, and the Zoroastrians (called Magians in the Qur'an) will also be resurrected and judged alongside the Muslims (Q. 22:17). In fact, 'all those who believe in God and the Last Day and do good' need not fear nor grieve, since God will reward them (Q. 2:62). Other Qur'anic statements similarly stress that all the monotheists may hope for paradise as long as they are virtuous and do good during their earthly lives (Q. 2:111–112). Furthermore, Jesus is quoted in the Qur'an as appealing to the Jews to 'worship God, my Lord and your Lord' so that they may be spared from hell and permitted entrance into the Garden (Q. 5:72). Belief in all of God's messengers is an essential precondition for entering paradise, because 'God will give [due] rewards to those who believe in Him and His messengers' (Q. 4:152). The idolaters, however, will be doomed to the torments of hell (Q. 2:165, 167; Günther 2017).

The bridge (or pathway) set up above and across hell, over which the faithful will reach paradise, is not expressly mentioned in the Qur'an. The expression *ṣirāṭ al-jaḥīm* is used in later Islamic tradition to speak, often in elaborate terms, of a bridge spanning over the Fire, which believers will cross effortlessly while all others slip downward into hell. This 'straight path' or 'bridge' (*ṣirāṭ*) (cf. Q. 1:6–7) appears to be a reflection of a pre-Islamic Zoroastrian concept (Tisdall 1905: 217, 251–3; for a general discussion, see Saleh 2010: 665–70).

Paradise and Hell

The Qur'an provides uniquely detailed descriptions of the geography of the world beyond human sensory perceptions. As for the structure of the heavens, it is recurrently stated, for example, that God created 'seven heavens' (Q. 67:3) or 'firmaments' (Q. 78:12). Hell, in turn, is said to have 'seven gates' (Q. 15:44). Paradise is said to consist of a multitude of luscious gardens, with lovely trees, an endless supply of food, and lofty buildings provided for believers (Q. 25:75; 29:58; 39:20). Green, the dominant colour of lavish garden landscapes, thus became a symbol in Islam of paradise itself, with all its delights and tranquillity. Other distinct features include invigorating beverages: water, a symbol of life in the Qur'an (Q. 21:30), is represented by heavenly rivers of fresh water, 'forever pure', and by 'rivers of milk forever fresh, rivers of wine, a delight for those who drink, and rivers of honey clarified and pure' (Q. 47:15), along with the numerous springs and fountains in the many gardens of paradise (Lawson 2008; Subtelny 2008). For the etymology of the word 'paradise' and its conception as a garden in the Bible and the ancient Near East, see Bremmer (2008: 36–55).

The generic name in the Qur'an for paradise is *janna* (used more than 66 times, including the dual *jannatān*, 4 times; plus 3 instances of the plural *jannāt*). Traditionally, *janna* is linked to the Hebrew word *gan* (Gen. 2:8), meaning 'garden' or 'enclosure', while more recent studies note that the Arabic root of the verb j-n-n indicates 'being covered and protected', and the related word *junna* means 'shield' and jinn, something 'unseen' (Kinberg 2004: 12–15).

Other names referring to paradise are 'abode of peace' (*dār al-salām*), 'gardens of refuge' (*jannāt al-maʾwā*), and 'gardens of comfort and happiness' (*jannāt al-naʿīm*). In addition, the high domain of 'equilibrium and perpetuity' (*ʿadn*) is believed to be the Qur'anic equivalent of the biblical Garden of Eden. Finally, there is, according to most commentators, the seventh, highest, largest, and most beautiful garden of paradise, *jannāt firdaws* (or just *al-firdaws*), where the throne of God floats and the rivers of paradise rise, to run through all gardens of paradise. According to Ibn ʿArabī (d. 638/1240), however, *ʿadn* is the highest of the heavens, or its citadel (*qaṣaba*) (Günther 2011).

The Qur'anic paradise is 'the garden of bliss' (*jannat naʿīm*, Q. 56:89), whose dwellers rest on 'couches lined with brocade' (Q. 55:54), on 'green cushions and lovely rugs' (Q. 55:76). The inhabitants of paradise will be invited to 'eat and drink with wholesome appetite!' (Q. 69:24), as paradise is a 'garden, in which they will delight' (*rawḍa yuḥbarūn*, Q. 30:15). This Qur'anic idea of reward in another life resembles the ancient Greek concept of eternal bliss, where the virtuous and blessed rest 'on couches at a feast, everlastingly drunk, crowned with garlands' (an image found, for example, in Plato, *The Republic*, book ii, p. 52).

Paradise in the Qur'an is also named 'the gardens of eternal retreat' (*jannat al-khuld*, Q. 25:15). It is 'recompense and homecoming', 'promised to the God-fearing' (Q. 25:15) and to 'those who suffered hurt in [God's] way, and fought, and were slain' (Q. 3:193). 'They shall have what they desire, dwelling [therein] forever' (Q. 25:15–16). This 'is a promise binding upon thy Lord', as the Qur'an confirms (Q. 25:16).

More evocative Qur'anic descriptions of paradise famously refer to 'purified spouses' (Q. 2:25) waiting in paradise as rewards for the believers. They are described as 'wide-eyed maidens, restraining their glances' (Q. 37:48; 55:56), and as maidens 'untouched beforehand by man or jinn'. However, the actual meaning of the Qur'anic expression in question here, *ḥūr ʿīn*, traditionally understood as 'wide-eyed [maidens] with a deep black pupil' or 'white skinned women', denoting 'virgins of paradise', has been discussed controversially in modern scholarship (Luxenberg 2007: 247–83 suggested the meaning 'white grapes' instead; for refutations of this reading, see Jarrar 2002 and Griffith 2017). Likewise, 'young boys serving wine' are mentioned on more than one occasion

(Q. 56:17; 76:19) to add to the image of a place where every desire of the body and wish of the mind will come true.

Hell is most frequently termed 'the Fire' (*al-nār*) in the Qur'an. Other designations are 'place (or state) of pain and torment' (*jahannam*; *gehenna* in Greek, and *gêhinnōm* in Hebrew) and, similarly, 'intense Fire' (*jaḥīm*). It is also termed 'abyss' (*hāwiya*), 'fierce blaze' (*saʿīr*), 'brightly burning, raging Fire' (*laẓẓā*), 'hot-burning Fire' (*saqar*), and 'crushing Fire' (*ḥuṭām*). Hell is the location of the 'Fire prepared for the disbelievers, whose fuel is men and stones' (Q. 2:24). Here, scalding water will be poured over the heads of the disbelievers, 'melting their insides as well as their skins; there will be iron crooks to restrain them; whenever, in their anguish, they try to escape, they will be pushed back in and told, "Taste the suffering of the Fire"' (Q. 22:19–22). Hell is an evil place, the site of agonizing torment, and burning in the flames (Q. 56:88–94). Hellfire is guarded by nineteen angels, while God made their number 'a test for the disbelievers' (Q. 74:30–1). The tree of Zaqqūm, which grows at the heart of the blazing Fire and has fruits shaped like devils' heads, will be the food for the sinners: hot 'as molten metal, it boils in their bellies like seething water' (Q. 37:62–8; 44:43–6). The unbelievers and sinners will experience in hell a symbolic 'second death', the death of the soul; as the Qur'an states that they 'have lost their souls, dwelling [in hell] forever' (Q. 23:103).

The pictorial style of the Qur'anic passages on paradise and hell perfectly fulfils its dual mission of reassuring Muslim believers on the one hand, and urging non-Muslims to convert to Islam on the other (see also Subtelny 2010: 56–9).

The Qur'an stresses that strict adherence to an ethical lifestyle is a precondition for divine reward, while disbelief and immoral behaviour lead straight to hell: paradise is the realm of eternal happiness promised to those men and women who obey God and his Messenger; to those who are righteous, truthful, and who bear witness to the truth (Q. 4:69), while hell is the abode of the damned, the site of physical torment, and 'a foul resting place' (Q. 3:12) for unbelievers, evildoers, and the wicked.

Whether paradise and hell, and thus divine reward and punishment, are eternal was a question of much concern to medieval Muslim scholars and seems to be answered in the positive: for example, the Qur'an states that evildoers will be punished in hell and 'remain in it eternally' (*khālidīna fīha*, Q. 3:88) and they will suffer a 'lasting torment' (*ʿadhab muqīm*, Q. 5:37). Similarly, God will admit the fortunate into paradise and it shall be their 'everlasting Home' (Q. 35:35) where 'they will remain forever' (Q. 4:57, 98:8) (see also Abrahamov 2002: 87–102).

Based on the respective Qur'an references, the various majoritarian (Sunnī) theological approaches share a belief in resurrection of the body. The spirit (*nafs* or *rūḥ*, depending on definition), which proceeds from God, rejoins the resurrected body and both become immortal (cf. Sells 2006: 116; Wensinck 1932: 129–30, 195, 268). The belief in bodily resurrection, where body and soul are reunited, is of principle theological and philosophical significance: it is seen as a powerful sign of God's omnipotence; it supplements and supports the overall human trust in the hereafter as a physical world; and it provides a basis for the idea of 'physical' reward and punishment of the resurrected in the hereafter. In addition, the return (*maʿād*, Q. 28:85) of the soul to the body is interpreted also as the return from annihilation into existence and the return to life after death in general, as, for example, the Ashʿarī theologians ʿAḍud al-Dīn al-Ījī (d. 756/1355) and Saʿd al-Dīn al-Taftāzānī's (d. 793/1390) reason in their examinations of certain Muʿtazilī and philosophical objections to this concept.

The classical Islamic philosophers, in turn, embrace the Qur'anic concept of paradise as a 'state of bliss'. Ibn Sīnā (d. 427/1037), for example, postulates a 'lower level of paradise' awaiting the souls of the virtuous, non-philosophical majority, where they will experience the physical delights promised in the Qur'an. The highest, the 'intellectual paradise', with the eternal light of God's infinite knowledge and goodness, will be attainable only to the souls of those who, in their earthly existence, pursued philosophy and worshipped the source of all truth, God.

Individual Death and Post-Mortem Existence

The Qur'an is quite clear about the course and final objective of life: birth, death, resurrection, and eternal reality. These are among the clearest manifestations of God's eternal existence, omnipotence, and mercy, allowing the question: 'How can you ignore God when you were lifeless and He gave you life, when He will cause you to die, then resurrect you to be returned to Him?' (Q. 2:28). Likewise, the unbelievers will appeal to God on the Day of Judgement, saying 'Lord, twice You have caused us to be lifeless and twice You have brought us to life' (Q. 40:11), a passage explained by one of the most popular exegetes, al-Bayḍāwī (d. *c.*719/1319), as divine 'signs' indicating that God creates human beings dead before granting them life in this world. When God causes humans to die, they experience lifelessness for the second time—until resurrection, which marks the beginning of their second life, this one eternal (al-Bayḍāwī, *Anwār*, on Q. 40:11; Rüling 1895: 8).

The Qur'an says little about individual human death. It is indicated that death is a distressing process, one which every person will experience, helplessly and individually, 'as the angels stretch out their hands' to the souls of the dying (Q. 6:93–94), and that the soul of the dying person 'comes up to his throat' (Q. 56:83).

The Condition of the Soul

There is much contemplation among medieval Muslim scholarship regarding the state of human existence between the moment of death and resurrection. Not untypically for medieval Muslim thought, al-Ghazālī (d. 505/1111) notes that the death of the individual is 'a minor return' to God, while that of the Universal Soul is 'the major return towards the Creator'. He supports this with reference to the prophetic saying, 'As soon as one dies,

Doomsday begins for him' (al-Ghazālī, *Mysteries*, 21). Al-Ghazālī explains furthermore that death occurs when the soul is separated from the body. Immediately after death, two angels 'with beautiful faces, wearing lovely clothes and sweet-smelling fragrances' receive the fortunate soul. They take it to the seven heavens, as far as the Throne of Mercy, before they return it to earth. In contrast, ugly, black-garbed guardians of hell will receive the soul of the profligate, and transport it to the first heaven where it will be denied entry (Q. 7:40). It will fall from heaven and be dropped by the wind in a far-distant place (Q. 22:31) so that the guardians of hell take charge of it. Eventually, all souls will be reunited with their respective bodies before burial. Each soul will attach itself to the deceased's 'breast from the outside' (*bi-ṣadr min khārij al-ṣadr*) and, thus reunited in the grave, body and soul shall await the Day of Resurrection (al-Ghazālī, *al-Durra*, 31; al-Ghazālī, *Pearl*, 32). Until that Day, the deceased experience scenes of paradise or visions of hell, depending on whether they had lived a pious or a sinful life on earth (Q. 40:46). Only 'the souls, or spirits, of the martyrs (*arwāḥ al-shuhadāʾ*) are allowed to remain at the highest heaven. They reside here in the crops of the green birds (*fī ḥawāṣil ṭuyūr khuḍr*), perched on the trees of the garden, to await the Hour'. The spirits of the believers, in turn, 'are gathered... in the form of green birds which fly freely in paradise until the Day of Resurrection, stamped (*marqūm*) with [the seal] of [God's] good pleasure (*riḍā*) and satisfaction (*riḍwān*)' (al-Ghazālī, *al-Durra*, 33; al-Tustarī, *Tafsīr*, 273; Günther 2019).

Existence in the Grave and the *Barzakh*

The Qur'an is ambiguous about the state in which the dead await resurrection. While there are clear differences between the living and the dead, it seems that the dead retain their senses in the grave to some degree, as the Qur'an insists that God can make anyone He wills hear His message, even those in their graves (Q. 35:22). However, there is little textual evidence in the Qur'an regarding the 'life in the grave' as expanded upon in later Islamic literature. Nothing explicit is mentioned here, except angels of punishment who appear and strike the disbelievers' faces and backs so that they may taste, while still in their graves, the torture that awaits them in the Fire (Q. 8:50). Yet, while believers and disbelievers alike remain in their graves until resurrection, martyrs are exempt from this waiting because 'those who are killed in God's cause are... alive' (Q. 2:154). Only once does the Qur'an mention the *barzakh* in the sense of an intermediate state or place in which the dead bridge the time between death and resurrection, stating that 'a barrier stands behind such people [i.e. the unbelievers, on the Day of Judgement] until the very Day they are resurrected' (Q. 23:100). It is only later that Muslim scholarship significantly elaborates on various concepts of the *barzakh*, assigning it such meanings as (a) a 'time barrier' between death and resurrection which prevents the dead from returning to the world of the living, (b) a 'time gap' (of forty years) between the first and the second blast of the Trumpet on the Day of Resurrection, and (c) a physical 'location' or 'grave' where the dead await resurrection, with the possibility of initial reward or punishment prior to Judgement Day, expressly including 'glimpses' of paradise and hell (Ibn al-Ḥabīb, *Waṣf*, 89–90, 104–7; see also Eklund 1941; Zaki 2001; and Rebstock 2003).

Contemporary liberal Muslim thinkers such as the Egyptian philosopher Ḥasan Ḥanafī (b. 1935), for instance, take the perceptions of an 'ideal world' expressed in the Qur'an concerning the hereafter as metaphors for their visions of an Islam-oriented civil society. In this spirit, the French-Moroccan publicist Nadia Tazi (b. 1953) utilizes them in her feminist critique of Islam (see Mas 2017). Although such ideas are exceptional among modern Muslim intellectuals, their innovative quality shows that the eschatological concepts in the Qur'an continue to play a vital role in the contemporary world not only as the foundation of conventional Muslim faith and spirituality, but also as powerful factors in an ever-expanding vision for the growth and development of culture and society. This highlights once again that references to the hereafter in Islam's sacred scripture retain their unparalleled authority and energy, not only because they are read by Muslims as sacred indicators of the grand finale and peak of humankind's long history of revelations, expected in a far-distant future. Rather, throughout history the Qur'anic promises of humankind's 'return' to God, along with the divine assurance of eternal life, justice, and complete fulfilment, appear to have a vital and definitive impact on Muslim life in the here and now.

Bibliography

Abdel Haleem, M. A. S. *The Qur'an: A New Translation*. Oxford: Oxford University Press, 2005.

Abrahamov, B. 'The Creation and Duration of Paradise and Hell in Islamic Theology', *Der Islam* 79 (2002), 87–102.

Arberry, A. The Koran Interpreted. New York: Touchstone, 1996.

Arnold, T. (trans.) *Der Koran, Oder insgemein so genannte Alcoran des Mohammeds*... Lemgo, Germany: J. H. Meyer, 1746.

Ayoub, M. *Redemptive Suffering in Islam: A Study of the Devotional Aspects of ʿāshūrāʾ in Twelver Shīʿism*. The Hague: Mouton 1978.

Bashear, S. 'Muslim Apocalypses and the Hour: A Case Study in Traditional Reinterpretation', *Israel Oriental Studies* 13 (1993), 75–99.

Bijlefeld, W. A. 'Eschatology: Some Muslim and Christian Data', *Islam and Christian-Muslim Relations* 15 (2004), 35–54.

Böwering, G. *The Mystical Vision of Existence in Classical Islam: The Qur'ānic Hermeneutics of the Ṣūfī Sahl al-Tustarī* (d. 283/896). Berlin and New York: de Gruyter, 1980.

Bremmer, Jan N. *Greek Religion and Culture, the Bible, and the Ancient Near East*. Leiden: Brill, 2008.

Casanova, P. *Mohammad et la fin du monde: étude critique sur l'Islam primitive*. Paris: Geuthner, 1911–13.

Cook, D. *Studies in Muslim Apocalyptic*. Princeton: Darwin Press, 2002.

Cook, D. *Contemporary Muslim Apocalyptic Literature*. Syracuse, NY: Syracuse University Press, 2005.

Corbin, H. *En Islam iranien: aspects spirituels et philosophiques*. 4 vols. Paris: Gallimard, 1971–2.

Donner, F. M. *Muhammad and the Believers: At the Origins of Islam*. Cambridge: Cambridge University Press, 2010.
Donner, F. 'A Typology of Eschatological Concepts'. In: S. Günther and T. Lawson (eds.). *Roads to Paradise*, 1:757–72. Leiden: Brill, 2017.
Eklund, R. *Life between Death and Resurrection according to Islam*. Uppsala: Almqvist & Wiksell, 1941.
Ernst, C. *Words of Ecstasy in Sufism*. Albany: State University of New York Press, 1985.
Ghaemmaghami, O. '"And the Earth will Shine with the Light of its Lord" (Q 39:69): *Qāʾim* and *qiyāma* in Shiʿi Islam'. In: S. Günther and T. Lawson (eds.). *Roads to Paradise*, 2:605–48. Leiden: Brill, 2017.
al-Ghazālī, Abū Ḥāmid. *Al-Durra al-fākhira fī kashf ʿulūm al-ākhira*. In: L. Gautier (ed.). *Ad-Dourra al-fākhira: La perle précieuse de Ghazālī: Traité d'eschatologie musulmane, avec une tradition française par Lucien Gautier*, Réimpression de l'Édition Genève 1878. Leipzig: Harrassowitz, 1925.
al-Ghazālī, Abū Ḥāmid. *The Precious Pearl:* al-Durra al-fākhira: *A Translation from the Arabic with Notes of the* al-Durra al-fākhira fī kashf ʿulūm al-ākhira *of Abū Ḥāmid Muḥammad b. Muḥammad b. Muḥammad al-Ghazālī*. Trans. J. I. Smith. Ann Arbor, MI: Scholars Press, 1979.
al-Ghazālī, Abū Ḥāmid. *The Mysteries of the Human Soul* (*al-Maḍnūn bihi ʿalā ghayr ahlihi*). Trans ʿA.Q. Shafaq Hazārvi. Lahore: Ashraf, 2001.
Griffith, S. 'St. Ephraem the Syrian, the Quran, and the Grapevines of Paradise: An Essay in Comparative Eschatology'. In: S. Günther and T. Lawson (eds.). *Roads to Paradise*, 2:781–805. Leiden: Brill, 2017.
Günther, S. 'Tag und Tageszeiten im Qurʾān', *Hallesche Beiträge zur Orientwissenschaft* 25 (1988), 46–67.
Günther, S. '"Gepriesen sei der, der seinen Diener bei Nacht reisen ließ" (Koran 17:1): Paradiesvorstellungen und Himmelsreisen im Islam—Grundfesten des Glaubens und literarische Topoi'. In: E. Hornung and A. Schweizer (eds.). *Jenseitsreisen*, pp. 15–56. Basel: Schwabe, 2001.
Günther, S. '"God Disdains not to Strike a Simile" (Q 2:26). The Poetics of Islamic Eschatology: Narrative, Personification, and Colors in Muslim Discourse'. In: S. Günther and T. Lawson (eds.). *Roads to Paradise*, 1:181–217. Leiden: Brill, 2017.
Günther, S. and T. Lawson (eds.). *Roads to Paradise: Eschatology and Concepts of the Hereafter in Islam. 1. Foundations and the Formation of a Tradition: Reflections on the Hereafter in the Quran and Islamic Religious Thought. 2. Continuity and Change: The Plurality of Eschatological Representations in the Islamicate World*. Leiden: Brill, 2017.
Günther, S. '"As the Angels Stretch out their Hands" (Quran 6:93): The Work of Heavenly Agents According to Muslim Eschatology'. In: S. Kuehn et al. (eds.). *The Intermediate Worlds of Angels: Islamic Representations of Celestial Beings in Transcultural Contexts* (*Beiruter Texte und Studien*). Beirut, Würzburg: Ergon (forthcoming 2019).
Ibn al-Ḥabīb, ʿAbd al-Malik ibn. Sulaymān al-Sulamī al-Andalusī al-Mālikī. *Kitāb Waṣf al-Firdaws*. Ed. ʿAbd al-Laṭif Ḥasan ʿAbd al-Raḥmān. Beirut: Dār al-Kutub al-ʿIlmiyya.
Ibn Ḥanbal, Aḥmad, *Musnad al-imām Aḥmad b. Ḥanbal wa-bi-hāmishihi muntakhab kanz al-ʿummāl fī sunan al-aqwāl wa-aʿmāl*, 6 vols., Beirut: al-Maktab al-Islāmī, 1969.
Jarrar, M. 'Houris'. In: Jane Dammen McAuliffe (ed.). *Encyclopaedia of the Qurʾān*. 6 vols., 2:456–7 Leiden: Brill, 2001–6.
Kinberg, L. 'Paradise'. In: Jane Dammen McAuliffe (ed.). *Encyclopaedia of the Qurʾān*. 6 vols., 4:12–20. Leiden: Brill, 2001–6.

Lange, C. 'The Eschatology of Punishment'. In: C. Lange, *Justice, Punishment, and Medieval Muslim Imagination*, pp. 99–175. Cambridge: Cambridge University Press, 2008.
Lange, C. *Paradise and Hell in Islamic Traditions*. Cambridge: Cambridge University Press, 2015.
Lawson, T. 'Divine Wrath and Divine Mercy in Islam: Their Reflection in the Qurʾān and Quranic Images of Water'. In: R. G. Kratz and H. Spieckermann (eds.). *Forschungen zum Alten Testament*, pp. 248–67. Tübingen: Mohr Siebeck, 2008.
Lawson, T. *Gnostic Apocalypse and Islam: Qurʾān, Exegesis, Messianism, and the Literary Origins of the Babi Religion*. London and New York: Routledge, 2011.
Lawson, T. 'Apocalypse'. In: G. Böwering et al. (eds.). *Princeton Encyclopedia of Islamic Political Thought*. Princeton: Princeton University Press, 2012.
Lawson, T. 'The Qurʾān and Epic', *Journal of Qurʾanic Studies* 16/1 (2014), 58–92.
Lawson, T. 'Paradise in the Quran and the Music of Apocalypse'. In: S. Günther and T. Lawson (eds.). *Roads to Paradise*, 1:93–135. Leiden: Brill, 2017a.
Lawson, T. *The Quran, Epic and Apocalypse*. London: Oneworld, 2017b.
Luxenberg, C. *The Syro-Aramaic Reading of the Koran: A Contribution to the Decoding of the Language of the Koran*. Berlin: Schiler, 2007.
Khalil, M. H. *Between Heaven and Hell: Islam, Salvation, and the Fate of Others*. Oxford: Oxford University Press, 2013.
McAuliffe, Jane Dammen (ed.). *Encyclopaedia of the Qurʾān*. 6 vols. Leiden: Brill, 2001–6.
Massignon, L. *La Passion de Husayn ibn Mansûr Hallâj: martyr mystique de l'Islam, exécuté à Bagdad le 26 Mars 922: étude d'histoire religieuse*. 4 vols. Paris: Geuthner, 1922 (repr. Paris: Gallimard, 1975; Eng.: Princeton: Princeton University Press, 1982).
Mas, R. 'Crisis and the Secular Rhetoric of Islamic Paradise'. In: S. Günther and T. Lawson (eds.). *Roads to Paradise*, 2:1290–321. Leiden: Brill, 2017.
Meier, F. 'The Ultimate Origin and the Hereafter in Islam'. In: G. L. Tikku (ed.). *Islam and its Cultural Divergence: Studies in Honor of Gustave E. von Grunbaum*, pp. 96–112. Urbana: University of Illinois Press, 1971.
Neuwirth, A. 'Symmetrie und Paarbildung in der Koranischen Eschatologie. Philologisch-Stilistisches zu Surat ar-Raḥman', *Mélanges de l'Université Saint-Joseph* 50 (1984), 443–80.
Neuwirth, A. Der Koran. *Frühmekkanische Suren, poetische Prophetie: Handkommentar mit Übersetzung*. Berlin: Verlag der Weltreligionen, 2011.
Neuwirth, A. 'Paradise as a Quranic Discourse: Late Antique Foundations and Early Quranic Developments'. In: S. Günther and T. Lawson (eds.). *Roads to Paradise*, 1:67–92. Leiden: Brill, 2017.
O'Shaughnessy, T. J. *Muhammad's Thoughts on Death: A Thematic Study of the Qurʾānic Data*. Leiden: Brill, 1969.
O'Shaughnessy, T. J. 'The Qurʾānic View of Youth and Old Age', *Zeitschrift der Deutschen Morgenländischen Gesellschaft* 141 (1991), 33–51.
Pocock. E. = Reineccius, C. (ed.). *Eduardi Pocockii lingvarum orientalium in academia Oxoniensi qvandam professoris notæ miscellaneæ philologico-biblicæ*... Leipzig: Lanckisch, 1705.
Rebstock, U. 'Das Grabesleben: Eine islamische Konstruktion zwischen Himmel und Hölle'. In: R. Brunner et al. (eds.). *Islamstudien ohne Ende: Festschrift für Werner Ende zum 65. Geburtstag*, pp. 371–82. Würzburg: Ergon, 2003.
Rippin, A. '*Desiring the Face of God*: The Qur'anic Symbolism of Personal Responsibility'. In: I. J. Boullata (ed.). *Literary Structures of Religious Meaning in the Qur'ān*, pp. 117–24. Richmond: Curzon, 2000.
Robinson, N. 'Antichrist'. In: Jane Dammen McAuliffe (ed.). *Encyclopaedia of the Qurʾān*. 6 vols., 1:107–11. Leiden: Brill, 2001–6.

Rüling, J. B. *Beiträge zur Eschatologie: Der Islam*. Leipzig: (Diss.) Universität Leipzig, 1895.

Rustomji, N. *The Garden and the Fire: Heaven and Hell in Islamic Culture*. New York: Columbia University Press, 2009.

Sachedina, A. *Islamic Messianism: The Idea of the Mahdī in Twelver Shīʿism*. Albany: State University of New York Press, 1981.

Saleh, W. 'The Etymological Fallacy and Qur'ānic Studies: Muhammad, Paradise, and Late Antiquity'. In: A. Neuwirth et al. (eds.). *The Qurʾān in Context: Historical and Literary Investigations in the Qur'ānic Milieu*, pp. 649–98. Leiden: Brill, 2010.

Schimmel, A. *Mystical Dimensions of Islam*. Chapel Hill: University of North Carolina Press, 1975.

Sells, M. 'Spirit'. In: Jane Dammen McAuliffe (ed.). *Encyclopaedia of the Qurʾān*. 6 vols., 5:114–17. Leiden: Brill, 2001–6.

Shoemaker, S. J. *The Death of a Prophet : The End of Muhammad's Life and the Beginnings of Islam*. Philadelphia: University of Pennsylvania Press, 2012.

Smith. J. 'Eschatology'. In: Jane Dammen McAuliffe (ed.). *Encyclopaedia of the Qurʾān*. 6 vols., 2:44–54. Leiden: Brill, 2001–6.

Smith, J. I. and Y. Y. Haddad. *The Islamic Understanding of Death and Resurrection*. Oxford and New York: Oxford University Press, 1981.

Stieglecker, H. *Die Glaubenslehren des Islam*. 4 parts. Paderborn: Schöningh, 1959–62.

Stowasser, B. F. 'The End is Near: Minor and Major Signs of the Hour in Islamic Texts and Contexts'. In: A. Amanat and J. Collins (eds.). *Apocalypse and Violence*, pp. 45–67. New Haven: Yale University Press, 2004.

Stowasser, B. F. *The Day Begins at Sunset: Perceptions of Time in the Islamic World*. London: Tauris, 2014.

Subtelny, M. 'The Traces of the Traces: Reflections of the Garden in the Persian Mystical Imagination'. In M. Conan (ed.). *Sacred Gardens and Imagination: Cultural History and Agency*, pp. 19–39. Washington, DC: Dumbarton Oaks Research Library and Collection, 2008.

Subtelny, M. 'The Jews at the Edge of the World in a Timurid-Era *Miʿrājnāma*: The Islamic Ascension Narrative as Missionary Text'. In: C. Gruber and F. Colby (eds.). *The Prophet's Ascension: Cross-Cultural Encounters with the Islamic* miʿrāj *Tales*, pp. 50–77. Bloomington: Indiana University Press, 2010.

Tisdall, W. St. Clair. *The Original Sources of The Qurʾān*. London: Society for Promoting Christian Knowledge 1905 (reprint 1911).

al-Tustarī, Sahl b. ʿAbd Allāh. *Tafsīr al-Tustarī: Great Commentaries on the Holy Qurʾan*. Trans. A. Keeler. Louisville, KY: Fons Vitae, 1905, repr. 1911.

Tubach, J. et al. (eds.). *Sehnsucht nach dem Paradies: Paradiesvorstellungen in Judentum, Christentum, Manichäismus und Islam. Beiträge des Leucorea-Kolloquiums zu Ehren von Walther Beltz*. Wiesbaden: Harrassowitz, 2010.

van Ess, J. *Theologie und Gesellschaft im 2. und 3. Jahrhundert Hidschra: Eine Geschichte des religiösen Denkens im frühen Islam*. 6 vols. Berlin: de Gruyter, 1991–7.

Wensinck, A. J. *Muslim Creed: Its Genesis and Historical Development*. Cambridge: Cambridge University Press. Repr. Abingdon: Routledge, 1932, repr. 2008.

Zaki, M. M. 'Barzakh'. In: Jane Dammen McAuliffe (ed.). *Encyclopaedia of the Qurʾān*. 6 vols., 1:203–4. Leiden: Brill, 2001–6.

CHAPTER 31

PROPHETS AND PERSONALITIES OF THE QUR'AN

ANTHONY H. JOHNS

THIS chapter is about personalities in the Qur'an, primarily the prophets, but also those associated with them, including angels and jinn, along with humankind, male and female, royalty and common people. For many years these personalities were regarded as of minor interest, and the Qur'an itself as of little more than an epigone that appeared without antecedents in first-/seventh-century Arabia. It is now seen on an equal footing with the Hebrew Bible and the New Testament as belonging to the cultural complex referred to as Late Antiquity. This has engendered new insights into the world behind the words of the Qur'an, and discloses the dramatis personae it shares with the Bible as exponents of a revised and revitalized theology, enduing them with a freshness and vigour that, as Geiger puts it, they had lost in crucial areas of the world of Late Antiquity (Geiger 1833). The chapter follows the stages of this transformation.

Pride of place belongs to the Prophets. A prophet/messenger is chosen to be close to God, and to receive something from God while remaining responsible to his immediate social context (Siddiqui 2013: 34). All have the responsibility to renew in their peoples, by threat and promise, an awareness of the ways in which they had been sinning, and recall them to the right path. The Qur'an names twenty-five of them. The first is Adam, the last and greatest is Muḥammad. They are Adam, Idrīs (Enoch), Nūḥ (Noah), Hūd, Ṣāliḥ, Ibrāhīm (Abraham), Ismāʿīl (Ishmael), Isḥāq (Isaac), Lūṭ (Lot), Yaʿqūb (Jacob), Yūsuf (Joseph), Shuʿayb (Jethro?), Ayyūb (Job), Mūsā (Moses) and Hārūn (Aaron), Dhū'l-Kifl, Dāwūd (David), Sulaymān (Solomon) Ilyās (Elijah), Ilyasaʿ (Elisha), Yūnus (Jonah) Zakariyāʾ (Zakarias), Yaḥyā (John), ʿĪsā (Jesus) and Muḥammad. Of these, nine are distinguished by the further designation of messenger (*rasūl*): Nūḥ, Lūṭ, Ismāʿīl, Mūsā, ʿĪsā, Shuʿayb, Hūd, Ṣāliḥ and Muḥammad. All have a counterpart in the Bible except five—Hūd, Ṣāliḥ, Shuʿayb, Dhū'l-Kifl, and Muḥammad. But these five enjoy a status equivalent to those with biblical counterparts—indeed Muḥammad is the last and greatest of prophets—together all are part of the design of salvation history—each sent to his own people. In general, the prophetic chronology of the Qur'an follows the same time line as that of the Bible.

Prophets are a community apart, and in *Sūrat Āl ʿImrān* (3:81), *Sūrat al-Muʾminūn* (23:51), and *Sūrat al-Māʾida* (5:109), God addresses them as such. All have a common role and responsibility. Some names appear in a single verse, or in one or a number of pericopes, as their roles are highlighted for reasons appropriate to the context established by the structure of the sura or suras in which they appear, or the time of their revelation.

Among other figures are Pharaoh, Haman, Goliath, Cain, Abel, as well as the individual sleepers in the cave, Dhū'l-Qarnayn, and the unnamed instructor of Moses. Of women, there are the wife of ʿImrān; mother of Mary, mother of Jesus; Sarah and Hagar, wives of Abraham; the mother and sister of Moses; and an allusion to Bilqīs, the Queen of Sheba. Several of these women have crucial roles, notably Mary, mother of Jesus, and Bilqīs, the equal of Solomon in all but prophecy. Three women are identified as being in hell, the wives of Noah, Lot, and Abū Lahab. Equally significant are the communities to whom the prophets were sent, and the divisions between them. In the case of Muḥammad, there were those who followed him, those who rejected or were disloyal to him, Jews, Christians, hypocrites, and unbelievers.

There are hosts of angels who praise and celebrate God, and serve as his messengers. Only two are named, Michael and Gabriel, and of them it is Gabriel who is singled out as having a pre-eminent role: he revealed himself to Muḥammad, and brought the divine words of the Qur'an to him. By nature angels cannot sin.

In addition, there are multitudes of jinn, 'created of smokeless flame', lower than the angels, but intelligent, morally responsible creatures. They may be believers or unbelievers. Their leader is Iblīs, also known as Satan, the only one of them to be named, who disobeyed God's command to bow in honour of Adam. He and his unbelieving followers are determined to waylay humankind and lure them into disbelief and disobedience. The teaching of every prophet is founded on three principles: that God is One (*tawḥīd*); that he sends prophets, each to preach (*nubuwwa*) to his own people; and that a day is to come when all will be resurrected for judgement (*qiyāma*).

God's providence is not limited to the sending of these twenty-five. He has sent myriads of others unnamed, to their individual peoples. Muḥammad, however, the last and 'seal of the prophets' has a universal mission. He was an Arab, sent to the Arabs with a revelation in Arabic not for the Arabs alone, but for all peoples. The prophets are presented in a discourse, the Qur'an, that in its own right and without dependence on any other authority, sets out God's will for humankind. By the very resonances of their names, they are the foundation of the *imaginaire* of the world, in which Muslims live, establishing a spiritual realm, in which Muḥammad and those who accept his message belong, and feel they are at home.

References to them are distributed among many suras, five of which have names of the prophets—Jonah (10), Hūd (11), Joseph (12), Abraham (14), and Muḥammad (47) and Noah (71). However only two, Joseph (12) and Noah (71) are devoted exclusively to the figures whose names they bear, though differing in length and the kind of information they provide.

The prophets with most attestations are Moses (502 verses), Abraham (235), Noah (131), and Jesus (93) (Moubarac 1954: 375). Those with the fewest are Idrīs (Enoch), Dhū'l-Kifl, Ilyās, and Ilyasaʿ (each also with two mentions). Of Dhū'l-Kifl, no information is given of his ethnicity, the people to whom he is sent, or his message. The two occasions on which he is mentioned are in the company of Ishmael and Elisha, 'All among the steadfast (*al-ṣābirīn*) and the righteous (*ṣāliḥīn*)' (Q. 38:48). Of Enoch (Idrīs) it is said only that 'He was *ṣiddīq*, he was a prophet, and we raised him to a high station'(Q. 19:56–7). The verse is devoted to him exclusively.

Compared to 'lesser' Judaic figures such as these, the Arabian prophets Hūd, Ṣāliḥ, and Shuʿayb have a far higher profile. Each is sent to his own people, ʿĀd, Thamūd, and Madyan respectively. Each proclaims the foundational doctrine, 'My people, worship God! You have no god but He,' and their principal sin condemned. The majority of their peoples, led by the elders, reject their messenger. They debate with them, but in vain, and the unbelievers are destroyed (Q. 7:59–94 and 11:25–95). Shuʿayb is distinctive in that his message explicitly condemns dishonesty in trading and robbing people of their due. This warning resonates with that given in the early suras (104:1–4 and 107:1–3) condemning abuse of the widow and orphan. The presence of these figures demonstrates that prophecy is not a monopoly of the Jews, and offers evidence for its presence among the Arabs as well as many other peoples not identified.

However, the overwhelming preponderance is of figures known in the Bible, and some of the great scenes of the Qur'an, such as the visit of angels to Abraham to tell him that he and Sarah are to have a son in their old age; God speaking to Moses from the burning bush; Moses and Aaron confronting Pharaoh; and the angelic announcement to Mary that without 'knowing man' she is to be the mother of Jesus; and others also have a counterpart in the Bible.

In comparing the Bible and Qur'an those brought up in the Western tradition generally have adopted the default position that the biblical presentation of these scenes is normative. This position is analogous to what Walid Saleh terms the 'Etymological Fallacy' (2010: 659–98), that is, the notion that just as words are presumed to be used correctly when they coincide in sense with that of the earliest known form to which their derivation can be traced, so the correct portrayal of these figures is that which derives from their role in the earliest canonical revelation in which they appear (Saleh 2010).

This being so, the Qur'an and its dramatis personae, including Muḥammad himself, have over the years attracted ample expressions of *odium theologicum*—Luther described the Qur'an as 'full of lies, fables and all abominations' (quoted by Ernst 2011: 70–1),—but little intrinsic, let alone sympathetic interest. In 1849 Washington Irving, in his *Life of Mohamet* apologizes for writing the book on the grounds that 'no new fact can be added to those already known concerning him' (Irving 1949: 1). It must have seemed at the time that the study of the foundations of Islam, and so its prophetology, had little to offer.

There are however other reasons. The Qur'an represented a textual world unfamiliar to biblical scholars. It appeared to originate from a place, the Ḥijāz, the geographical region in which Mecca and Medina are located, deemed to be culturally a *terra nullius*. Its content is divided into 114 suras of diverse content, not obviously related to each other, with the only apparent principle of order in their arrangement being that of decreasing length. For the most part they seemed to lack internal organization, and the word sura itself did not appear to correspond to any accepted sense of its common rendering 'chapter' in Western literature.

A number of suras include episodes from the lives of the prophets, but with the partial exception of the *Sūrat Yūsuf*/Joseph (12), are not biographical in character. Often, these episodes are not presented sequentially, but in different suras, sometimes in varying forms, appropriate to the emphases of the sura in question. Construction from them of synoptic narratives was not always straightforward, and this, together with variations when episodes were repeated, gave the impression that the book was a 'welter of confusion'.

Equally disturbing to scholars of biblical texts was the absence of genealogies, an absence that may be seen as a significant 'identity marker' distinguishing the Qur'an from the Bible. Alter remarks, 'Nothing reveals the difference of the biblical conception of literature from later western ones more strikingly than the biblical use of genealogies as an intrinsic element of literary structure' (Alter 2004: 34). In short, the organization of the Qur'an was found to be so unlike that of the Bible that philologists in non-Muslim academe, while recognizing that much of its content appeared cognate with that of the Judaeo-Christian scriptures, did not know how to approach it. The philological tools developed in biblical studies were of limited service for understanding the roles of its dramatis personae, or defining the linguistic, geographical, and historical parameters of the context in which it claimed to be situated.

Along with such issues was the question as to whether the episodes of lives of the prophets in the Qur'an and the roles they played were an integral part of an organic whole or simply eclectic items opportunistically occasioned by the circumstances Muḥammad encountered in his interactions with the communities to which he presented himself as a religious and political leader.

As long as this was the case, the perspectives from which prophetic figures and others of the Qur'anic dramatis personae might be viewed were limited. There seemed to be no definable place in history in which the Qur'an might be situated—and within it no temporal context in which the prophets played their parts. While it was clear that they were divinely sent messengers, of whom Muḥammad himself was reputedly the last and greatest, it was difficult to see them as individuals and personalities in a religious narrative that spoke with authority in its own right—hence Wansbrough could argue that it did not exist in its canonical form as the *muṣḥaf* until the second/eighth century (Wansbrough 1977).

Serious philological study of the Qur'an, of its background and the chronology of its revelation, did not begin in earnest until the time of Abraham Geiger (1833). He was not the first to draw attention to the presence of rabbinic elements in the Qur'an—at that time regarded simply as opportunistic borrowings. In 1734 George Sale, for example, in the notes to the first English translation of the Quran frequently refers to the *Midrash*, *Talmud*, apocryphal gospels, and assorted writings and commentaries as sources for episodes occurring in the Qur'an. In a note to Q. 3:81, for example, he draws attention to the fact that the perception of the prophets as a community in the Qur'an, is parallel to the notion of the Talmudists that the souls of all of the prophets, even of those not yet born, were present on Mount Sinai when God gave the law to Moses, and that they entered into this covenant with him (Sale 1939: 55). More recently, Jacob Lassner (1990: 210) documents this covenantal belief in greater detail, drawing on Hebrew and Arabic sources.

It is significant of Geiger's insights that, from his reading of the Qur'an, he identifies the son of Abraham called for sacrifice as Ishmael. The Qur'an does not identify the intended victim by name. On scriptural and theological grounds, Jews and Christians believe him to be Isaac. Up until around the seventh/thirteenth century, the question had not been perceived as important, but subsequently, identification with Ismāʿīl became virtually unanimous. Fontaine notes this, and taking Ibn Khaldūn (d. 808/1406) as a point of departure, attributes this consensus to social and historical factors (Fontaine 1966). Geiger, on the other hand, argues that the internal dynamic of the Qur'an itself—the ordering and contextual setting of verses relating to the *dhabīḥ*, indicate that it was Ishmael (Geiger 1898: 102–6). It may be observed that in this case it is a Jewish scholar who rejects an *isrāʾīliyya* identification of Isaac as the *dhabīḥ* that for centuries had contributed to ambivalence among exegetes down to and including Fakhr al-Dīn al-Razī (d. 606/1210).

Other scholars followed in Geiger's footsteps, exploring Midrashic and related sources for Jewish narrative, legal, and vocabulary references in the Qur'an. They included Weil (1844), Sprenger (1861), Horovitz (1926), Speyer (1931), and Torrey (1933). While from one point of view their approach was reductionist, downgrading Qur'anic studies to a discovery of sources, they had at least begun the work of situating it in a context, and of subverting the dominant narrative that the Qur'an had appeared in a region that culturally was *terra nullius*. Their work opened the door to exploration of the possibility that the Ḥijāz might be included in the broad area occupied by the widely diffused competing monotheistic religious traditions of Late Antiquity, traditions in which prophetic figures bearing the same names as those in the Qur'an had a part. An understanding of the ways in which the Qur'an and Islam might legitimately be seen as fitting into that tradition and in dialogue with it, however, was still a distant dream.

Along with the preoccupation with 'sources' for the Qur'an; however, there was painstaking work on the history of the text pioneered by Nöldeke (1860) and Schwally/Nöldeke (1919). This, in due course, would prepare the ground for a discussion of how the Qur'anic text was intertwined with the emergence of a Qur'anic community to the extent that this could be established, 'defined by its allegiance towards, and liturgical use of an open-ended series of divine communications promulgated by Muḥammad', establishing Muḥammad as a legitimate successor to Moses, Abraham, and Noah.

Régis Blachère (1947) continued a study of the history of the text, and also attempted to arrange the suras according to order of revelation. With his translation of the Qur'an he contributed to the diffusion of the view that revelation of the Qur'an might divide into four chronological periods, the first three in Mecca, and the fourth in Medina. Montgomery Watt used this periodization as a framework for his studies of Muḥammad as prophet and political leader (1953; 1956). Rodinson (1973), in a rather more engaged account of the life of the Prophet (Muḥammad) accepts the same framework, and the same biographical concerns.

Even though the primary concern of these authors was not the text of the Qur'an itself, these studies were significant and important despite carrying the burden of older attitudes, foremost among them that the Qur'an lacked internal organization and noteworthy originality. Bell (1937) hypothesizes that the suras, and the Qur'an as a whole, rest upon a 'confusion of written documents' (Bell 1937: 7). It is within this 'confusion' that references to the prophets and other personalities were to be found. As long as it was regarded as a 'dreary welter' of pericopes, 'a wearisome confused jumble', and 'not really a book at all', little could be done with the information it provided about prophets and other personalities other than to trace sources for the information given about them in the Talmud, the Midrash, apocryphal gospels, and other assorted writings. It was a general view that these elements had come to the prophet by chance; some of them he had misunderstood, others adapted as circumstances required, others he transformed by the power of his creative imagination and religious sensibility (Ernst 2011: 32). The narrative of the Ḥijāz as a culturally empty space in which the Qur'an appeared with few if any immediate antecedents died hard.

Judaic traditions used to complement the understanding of Qur'anic discourse were known to the exegetic tradition, and came to be referred to as *isrāʾīliyyāt*. An example of their use to particular effect is al-Ṭabarī's (d. 310/923) exegesis of two verses referring to Job in *Sūrat al-Anbiyāʾ* (Q. 21:83–4). Though they make it clear that Job is a model of patience, they are highly allusive. They do not indicate who he was, or why or how his patience was tested. Al-Ṭabarī's commentary establishes a context in which every element in these verses has a place and a meaning (Johns 2001, 2002). His exegesis draws on numerous passages from the biblical Job, mediated by Wahb ibn Munabbih. The distinction between prose and verse passages in the Hebrew is maintained by the use of the Arabic *khabar* (narrative) and *khaṭīb* (orator) registers respectively. The literary skill revealed in the Arabic is remarkable, and is worthy of the grandeur of the Hebrew in the description of the divine theophany that marks the climax of the book. It suggests that a literary form of the story was diffused in Mecca when the two verses were revealed, without which they would have had little meaning. While much of al-Ṭabarī's text follows the Hebrew closely, there is a significant difference between it and the biblical version: Job's challenges to God are put into the mouths of his companions, so that his charism of patience is not tarnished.

It is more difficult to be sure of the presence of other biblical figures with few attestations such as Elisha and Elijah in the *imaginaire* of the first hearers of the Qur'an. As already noted, they are overshadowed by the information given about the 'Arabian' prophets

Shuʿayb, Ṣāliḥ, and Hūd. *Isrāʾīliyyāt* were to lose favour as a tool to clarify pericopes relating to the prophets in Qur'anic exegesis. By the time of Fakhr al-Dīn al-Rāzī (d. 606/1210), they were widely viewed with suspicion and even hostility. Al-Rāzī had moreover developed a radical theory of prophetic impeccability, reflected in his interpretation of Q. 38: 21–5. These verses are widely understood as a presentation of the Prophet Nathan's parable to David (2 Sam. 12) condemning him for his seduction of Bathsheba, wife of the warrior Uriah. Al-Rāzī's interpretation of them excludes the possibility of any sin on David's part, and requires no reference to any extra-Qur'anic text. Furthermore, he argues that the account of David's sin in the bibilical text is proof of *taḥrīf*—that it is warped (Johns 1989). Despite al-Rāzī's convincing skill in dialectic, it is not unlikely that the traditional story of Nathan's condemnation of King David was known in Mecca, and reference to it could support Muḥammad's claim to a right to condemn the Meccan aristocracy for their misuse of authority.

This default position to the authority of the biblical tradition as a norm was still present during the 1950s. There is little evidence that the prophets in the Qur'an were recognized as figures with a role defined by the theology of the Qur'an, and legitimate claims to authority. Indeed lemmata on individual prophets in the first edition of the *Encyclopaedia of Islam* may be taken as a base line to illustrate this general attitude. Thus, B. Heller identifies Mūsā as 'the prophet Moses of the Bible'; there follows a summary of events in his life from the Qur'an, an account of differences between the biblical and Qur'anic accounts, and sources of some of the Qur'anic variants. Noah (Nūḥ), the Noah of the Bible, 'is a particularly popular figure in the Qurʾān'. They are identified first by their occurrence in the Bible, without reference to their relation to each other in the structure of salvation history presented by the Qur'an, and little, if any reference to the structure of the sura in which they are set, or the relevance of this to their personalities and the roles they play.

A stone was thrown into the relatively still pool of Qur'anic Studies with the publication of Wansbrough's *Quranic Studies* (1977) and *The Sectarian Milieu* (1978). By way of example he takes three presentations of Shuʿayb, aligning them to an ideal structure of a warning-punishment story following a biblical model (Wansbrough 1977) against which he assesses their completeness or otherwise. Thus he rejects Moubarac's (1958) account of a 'historical development of Abraham in the Qurʾān', as lacking a verifiable foundation—such as the structural unity of the Qur'anic canon. His theory of the internal composition of the Qur'an to account for the repetition and selection of episodes from lives of the prophets is then only marginally more sophisticated than that of Bell. This does not diminish the importance of his work, however, which lies in the uncovering of the richness and diversity of materials associated with what is referred to as Late Antiquity, even though he argued that this cultural diversity was part of the life of Baghdad, but unknown in the Ḥijāz. This was a view that even in his time was being increasingly questioned.

Meanwhile, largely unnoticed if not unknown among Western scholars, from the first half of the twentieth century, Muslim scholars had been discovering ways to demonstrate that far from being a confusion of written documents, order and coherence existed both within individual suras, even the longest, and in the arrangement of the suras within the *muṣḥaf*. Not that the text of the *muṣḥaf* had ever been perceived as disordered to Muslims. It was not a question of the fact that the Qur'an *had* coherence, but the ways in which this coherence might be recognized analysed and discussed. An understanding of the internal coherence of the sura adds a new dimension both of the roles of the prophets and other actors in the Qur'an, and the manner of their presentation might be perceived to develop in dialogue with the first generation of Muslims.

One of the first scholars to draw attention to this phenomenon was Mustansir Mir, who points out that an approach to the Qur'an centred on this concern is a twentieth-century development (Mir 1993: 211–24). One example is his reference to *taṣrīf* as a narrative principle, noting that the Qur'an may not present a story all in one place, but breaks it up into several portions to appear in different places 'in accordance with the thematic exigencies of the suras in which they occur' (Mir 1993).

One might consider the application of this principle to the Prophet Jonah. For a synoptic view of his prophetic role, it is necessary to refer to six suras (Johns 2003). Although only eighteen verses in all are explicitly devoted to him, his presence in each of them is suggested by a number of literary devices, related in one way or another to the emphases of the suras in which they occur. It follows from this that the frequency of attestation is not always a guide to the presence of a prophet in the Qur'an, and that Wansbrough's notion, that the repetition of various forms and portions of a narrative in a sura is derived from regional traditions and found its place in the canon because of regional rivalries, is not tenable.

Once this is realized, such references though few and brief, are sufficient for their significance in the revelation to be felt, both as they relate to the Prophet Muḥammad himself, and to every Muslim.

Following this line of enquiry, Mir remarks that most of the characters, good or bad, are presented as men and women of flesh and blood, and that Moses, Abraham, and Joseph are multi-dimensional figures (Mir 2003). One might add that the Queen of Sheba (*malikat Saba'*) is presented as a robust female character of wisdom and intelligence whom al-Rāzī accounts as Solomon's equal, except in prophecy (Johns 1986). It may be recalled that Sayyid Quṭb was educated in English literature and in his commentary he sees *Sūrat Yūsuf* (Joseph) as a drama, with its acts closing and opening with the lowering and raising of a curtain—articulating the shape of the sura, and highlighting the lessons to be learnt from it (Quṭb 1968). He and Mir have each come to a discussion of the dramatis personae of the Qur'an from the Western tradition of literary appreciation.

Awareness of the internal dynamics of the sura and its place and time of revelation, acceptance—as a credible working hypothesis—of the presence of the cultural traditions of Late Antiquity in the Ḥijāz, and attentiveness to the implications of the fact that the revelation of the Qur'an was in dialogue with the developing circumstances of Muḥammad's community: such awareness, acceptance, and attentiveness are characteristic of approaches to Qur'anic discourse from the 1990s on, and have made their mark on the appreciation of the text. They have opened a number of doors for fresh approaches to the significance of interactions between prophets, angels, common people, and communities in the Qur'an.

This may be illustrated by a number of examples from research completed since 2007. They are presented in roughly chronological order. The first is an article by Neal Robinson, 'Sūra Āl ʿImrān and Those with the Greatest Claim to Abraham' (Robinson 2004). In it he explores the contextual setting and layers of meaning beneath the verses: 'Abraham was not a Jew nor a Christian, but a *ḥanīf*, a man who submitted himself to God. He was not an idolater' (3:67), and 'Those with the greatest claim to Abraham are surely those who follow him and this prophet, and those who believe' (Q. 36:68). He brings into his reflections on these verses the claims that Jewish and Christian communities in Medina made to appropriate him for themselves, and the guidance God gives to the prophet Muḥammad to settle the issue in favour of the Muslims.

Robinson sees the sura as an echo and consolidation of *Sūrat al-Baqara* (2), set in Medina in the aftermath of the near defeat of the Muslims at the battle of Uḥud. This setback tempted a number of Muslims to abandon Islam, and provided an occasion for Jewish and Christian communities to compete both with each other and win back converts to Islam. It is in two parts. Part One (vv. 1–99), the focus of Robinson's article, is addressed to 'People of the Book' that is, Jews and Christians, countering the arguments they use to reject Muḥammad's claim to be a Prophet. Part Two (vv. 100–200) is directed to Muslims, whose faith may have been shaken by the near defeat.

Abraham is at the heart of these altercations. Robinson discusses four issues he sees as foregrounded in Part One: Abraham's religious identity, prophetology, dietary regulations, and the proper location of the Abrahamic sanctuary. He sets out a network of sources of subtexts to the debate, which draw on some knowledge (however acquired), of the Bible, the Mishnah, various apocryphal and pseudepigraphal writings, and Rabbinic and Patristic texts. As a point of departure, to frame a context for the debates, he points out that long before the rise of Islam, Jews and Christians had each tried to appropriate Abraham exclusively for themselves.

While these suggestions are speculative, they are credible. And the significance of the article is that in it, Robinson, taking into account the three insights mentioned above, succeeds in giving a historical depth to discussions and rivalries relating to Abraham among the communities to whom Muḥammad was preaching as the Qur'an reports them, and shows that they were at a higher level than mere polemic, that there are layers of meaning beneath what at first sight might appear a brilliant but superficial debating point, 'Abraham was neither a Jew nor a Christian' (Q. 3:67).

Mir approaches the characterization of various prophets and figures in the Qur'an from a largely Western rhetorical and literary tradition. Michel Cuypers, on the other hand, in *Le Festin* (2007), a book-length study of *Sūrat al-Māʾida* argues that the full panoply of Semitic rhetorical devices common in Hebrew, Akkadian, and Ugaritic—parallel, mirror, and concentric constructions—are present in it. Accordingly, the Qur'an is to be read, not only linearly, but with an awareness of these underlying structures. This brings to the surface numbers of subtexts—*contexts interscriptuaires*—that lie within and behind the Qur'anic discourse. This throws fresh light on the understanding of the significance of particular individuals in this discourse, and the scriptural context in which they should be seen. Thus the reference to Cain and Abel in 5:27–40 is not to be associated with Genesis 4, but with either Hebrews 11:4–5, or with Matthew 23: 33–8. A figurative reading of the Qur'an then becomes possible, and a new dimension of the significance of these figures is revealed. Thus—if this intertextual reading is accepted—'just as the persecuted Jesus was prefigured in Abel, so Muḥammad is prefigured both by Abel and by Jesus, two persecuted innocents. Behind Muḥammad, the bringer of *the light* to those in *darkness*, we accept the face of the Messiah described in the *Canticle of Zachariah*'. Then Cuypers continues, 'Jesus, giving his apostles food which has come down from heaven, prefigures Muḥammad handing on the Word sent down from heaven.' Finally, the way the text is viewed shows differences in the way relations between its dramatis personae may be understood.

Michael Marx, in 'Glimpses of a Mariology in the Qur'ān' (Marx 2010), raises a different but related issue. He remarks that 'the entire issue of how the figures of the prophets develop within the Qur'an has remained largely unexplored'. He points out that the majority of researchers still refuse to recognize that the chronology of the text still allows it to be recognized as a record of Muḥammad's proclamations, and that it can be interpreted as part of the process of establishing a community.

With this in mind he studies the figure of Mary, mother of Jesus, in the two major pericopes devoted to her, *Sūrat Maryam* 19:16–33, and *Sūrat Āl ʿImrān* 3:33ff. He points out that the reason for the repetition of the episode is a change in situation, a different contextual setting requiring different emphases. The first is Meccan, and largely hagiographic in character, the second is Medinan. As already observed by Robinson, this sura was revealed when the Muslim community was in disarray, Christians and Jews were in contention with each other, each concerned with reclaiming converts to Islam.

The second presentation of the episode then is occasioned by religious debate and the need for theological definition this required. Its starting point is Qur'an 3:33, 'God chose Adam, Noah and the family of Abraham and of ʿImrān, privileging them above all others.' The opening of the pericope, telling of the wife of ʿImrān pregnant with Mary, sets Mary and her son Jesus in an Aaronid line, a line part of, but distinct from the Abrahamic line, but equal in status with it.

By an exploration of a range of intertexts (Marx 2010: 542), he highlights the significance of the words 'Mary in an eastern place' (19:16) Here, Mary is not as the Gospel of Luke has it, in a private room (Luke 1:26–38) but in the temple by the eastern gate, closed and to be opened only by the Messiah, as recorded in the Gospel of James, and celebrated in the Syriac tradition as Rod of Aaron. Her womb is to be opened by the birth of Christ as the eastern gate of the temple is to be unlocked at the coming of the Messiah (Marx 2010: 542), hence in this text, Mary is referred to metaphorically as the temple.

The Aaronid line, he continues, with its matrilineal emphasis on the line of Jesus, and its recognition of the status of Jesus as the Messiah, is set over against the patriarchal Judaic line of Abraham, setting the Christian claims above those of the Jews, but de-mythifying the figure of Mary. In the Qur'anic narrative she is not the temple, but a figure in the temple, and in place of the appellative Rod of Aaron, she is described as 'sister of Aaron', and Jesus is son of Mary. She is presented as a figure of grace, as a figure to be revered, but without her Christian accoutrements. Her son is not divine. In this reading of the text, Mary is seen as indicating the superiority of the line of ʿImrān (i.e. the Christian tradition) over that of Abraham (the Judaic) and the Qur'an revealed to Muḥammad has given the true account of the nature of Jesus, about which Jews and Christians had disputed.

This Medinan retelling of the story of Mary, with the genealogical and theological elements built into it, is indeed appropriate to the situation in Medina, as outlined by Robinson. While it is not possible to be certain that the writings adduced are the direct source of the subtext detected behind the literal sense of these verses, the scenario of argument and debate they are used to construct is credible. The Qur'anic resolution of the issues is evidence of elements in the Late Antiquity mix, coalescing into a distinctive, creative, and powerful force, which as Geiger puts it, fitted the needs of the times (Geiger 1833), as it were making the old new, and became a world religion.

The final example of such approaches is Reynolds's *The Qurʾān and its Biblical Subtext* (2010). It is a work of wide learning, but very much *une etude à thèse*. Put at its simplest, the *thèse* is that the exegetic tradition, which was not born until a century or more after the death of the prophet, is not a reliable guide to the meaning of the Qur'an in cases of ambiguity or disagreement. Resolutions of ambiguity are to be found rather by uncovering subtexts derived from Jewish or Christian sources that are part of the cultural world of Late Antiquity in which the Qur'an was revealed, sources that the exegetic tradition had deliberately excluded. In so doing Reynolds finds an interpretive guide and clarification of the Qur'an's often brief and allusive references to facts in salvation history and uncovers *richesses* of Qur'anic discourse which had been overlooked. In his book, he uses thirteen case studies to illustrate what the classical exegete had allegedly missed, and the fuller understanding to be acquired by recourse to the past.

One of these case studies is Sarah's laughter referred to in *Sūrat Hūd* (Q. 11:69–71). Divine messengers come to Abraham; they do not partake of the food he has prepared for them. He is afraid. They say to him, Do not be afraid, we are sent to the people of Lot (v.70). His wife is standing nearby, and she laughs. 'Then we gave her good tidings of Isaac, and after Isaac of Jacob' (71).

The issue is, why did she laugh *before* hearing the extraordinary news that in her ninetieth year she was to become pregnant. Reynolds reviews the various explanations given by the exegetes, and concludes that those hearing the story would have known what was to follow, and be aware that she laughed at the thought that she might become pregnant. The episode recurs in slightly different forms on three other occasions in the Qur'an. Accordingly—and he applies similar reasoning to the other case studies—Reynolds sees the Qur'anic narrative as homiletic in character, clarifying and expanding lessons to be learned from the rich traditions subsumed in the subtext widely known and so retrievable from within it. In his view, this use of the word homiletic is justified by the fact that the Qur'an has little interest in narrative as such, but constantly returns to the same episode on numbers of occasions, as it were to preach on it, and reiterate the lessons it teaches. It is a view that bypasses Wansbrough's theory that such repetitions are variants carried by conflicting oral traditions. The internal coherence of the sura is not a concern in this work.

In his reflections on the scene, presented or referred to on four occasions, Reynolds discovers a typological relationship between Sarah and Mary (the mother of Jesus), each receives good tidings from angels, and each reacts in amazement at what had been promised them. Sarah, who in frustration and disappointment at not having conceived a child, beat her head and screamed, then laughed with delight and pleasure (if the traditional view is accepted) (Johns 1986: 10), and Mary was especially favoured 'over women of the worlds' (Reynolds 2010). It should not be overlooked, however, that the majority of exegetes understand the phrase 'of her time' (McAuliffe 1981) as ellipted. This leaves space for the broad consensus (universal among the Shīʿa and predominant among the Sunnī) of the superiority of Fāṭima, not withstanding that Mary is mentioned on thirty-four occasions (although in most cases in the phrase 'Mother of Jesus'), and Fāṭima's name never occurs.

It is of interest to contrast Reynolds' approach to the scene with that of the 'classical' exegete al-Rāzī, who sees no reason to look outside or behind the pericope to explain its meaning. He comments on the arrival of the visitors, speaks of the preparations that Abraham made to welcome them, even suggesting, in the context of desert life, how the lamb served to them was cooked. When they do not eat, he sees them as refusing hospitality, and therefore regards their arrival as ominous. He and Sarah are afraid. When the visitors identify themselves and he says to them, 'Do not be afraid', Sarah laughs. Of seven possible explanations, including a hyperbaton, an inversion of the order for rhetorical effect, his preference is that her laugh be interpreted as a psychological reaction to release from fear (Johns 1986: 105). He sees the story as complete in itself. While al-Rāzī too is driven by an *idée fixe*, it is clear that he has a different sense of what constitutes completeness in a story than Reynolds. It is further clear that al-Rāzī sees the event in a nomadic desert setting, is aware of Bedouin style cooking, and of the courtesies and conventions that govern nomadic life—perhaps as relevant to a fuller understanding of the story as subtexts. In Genesis too (18: 1–8), it may be noted, there is an account of Sarah's hurried activity to receive her guests with a suitable meal.

Conclusion

It has taken a long time for 'Western' scholars to recognize that, as Sidney Griffith puts it, 'Hermeneutically speaking, one should approach the Qurʾān as an integral discourse in its own right; it proclaims, judges, praises, blames from its own narrative centre. It addresses an audience which is already familiar with oral versions in Arabic of earlier scriptures and folklores' (Griffith 2008: 116). When Geiger published his study in 1833, the prophets in the Qur'an were widely regarded—and by Geiger himself for that matter—as figures opportunistically taken by Muḥammad from Judaic and Christian sources, and research was largely directed to identifying these sources. Now they are recognized as key figures in the dynamics of an integral discourse living in the hearts of the Islamic community it created, a discourse which has been the foundation of the continuing vitality of that community.

This survey has given a broad-brush account of developments in Qur'anic Studies over the past century and a half that have led to this significant change. While no ur-text of the *muṣḥaf* has been discovered, a plausible narrative of the history of the text has been established. Other studies relate to what kind of book it is, the rhetorical conventions behind its literary constructions, its internal structure, and how these changes are related to the way in which its dramatis personae are viewed. They are now widely recognized as playing roles in the dynamics of an integral discourse, living in the hearts of the community it created and the foundation of that community's continuing vitality.

Bibliography

Alter, Robert. *The Five Books of Moses: A Translation with Commentary*. New York and London: Norton, 2004.

Bell, Richard. *The Qurʾān Translated with a Critical Re-arrangement of the Surahs*. Vol. 1. Edinburgh: T. & B. Clark, 1937.

Blachère, Régis. *Le Coran: Traduction selon un essai de reclassement des sourates*. Paris: Editions G. P. Maisonneuve, 1947.

Ernst, Carl W. *How to Read the Qurʾān: A New Guide with Select Translations*. Edinburgh: Edinburgh University Press, 2011.

Fontaine, Jean. 'Ibn Khaldoun, penseur indépendant dans la question du dhabîḥ Allâh', *Revue de l'Institut des belles lettres arabes* (1966), 421–2.

Geiger, Abraham. *Was hat Mohammed aus dem Judenthume aufgenommen?* Berlin: Baaden, 1833.

Geiger, Abraham. *Judaism and Islam: A Prize Essay*. Trans. from the German by a member of the Ladies' League in aid of the Delhi Mission. Madras: Printed at the MDC RSPCK Press and sold at their Depository VEPREY, 1898.

Griffith, Sidney. 'Christian Lore and the Arabic Qurʾān: The "Companions of the Cave" in *Sūrat al-Kahf* and in Syriac Christian Tradition'. In Gabriel Said Reynolds (ed.). *The Qurʾān in its Historical Context*, pp. 109–137. London: Routledge, 2008.

Horovitz, Josef. *Koranische Untersuchunger*. Berlin: W. de Gruyter, 1926.

Irving, Washington. *Life of Mohamet*. Everyman's Library. London: J. M. Dent & Sons Ltd.; New York: E. P. Dutton & Co., 1949.

Johns, A. H. 'Solomon and the Queen of Sheba: Fakhr al-Dīn al-Rāzī's Treatment of the Qurʾānic Telling of the Story', *Abr-Nahrain* 24 (1986), 58–82.

Johns, A. H. 'Al-Rāzī's Treatment of the Qur'anic Episodes Telling of Abraham and His Guests: Qur'anic Exegesis with a Human Face', *Mideo* (Institut Dominicain d'Études Orientales du Caire) (1986), 81–114.

Johns, A. H. 'David and Bathsheba: A Case Study in the Exegesis of Qurʾānic Story-telling', *Mideo* (Institut Dominicain d'Études Orientales du Caire), 19 (1989), 225–66.

Johns, A. H. 'Three Stories of a Prophet: Al-Ṭabarī's Treatment of Job in Surah al-Anbiyāʾ 83–84', *Journal of Qur'anic Studies* 3/2 (2001), 39–61 (Part I) and *Journal of Qur'anic Studies* 4/1 (2002), 51–60 (Part II).

Johns, A. H. 'Jonah in the Qurʾān: An Essay on Thematic Counterpoint', *Journal of Qur'anic Studies* 5/2 (2003), 48–71.

Lassner, Jacob. 'The Covenant of the Prophets: Muslim Texts, Jewish Subtexts', *AJS Review* 15/2 (Autumn 1990), 207–38.

Lassner, Jacob. *Demonizing the Queen of Sheba: Boundaries of Gender and Culture in Postbiblical Judaism and Medieval Islam*, 2:36–46. Chicago and London: University of Chicago Press, 1993.
McAuliffe, Jane Dammen. 'Chosen of All Women: Mary and Fatima in Qurʾānic Exegesis', *Islamochristiana*, 7 (Rome 1981), 19–28.
Marx, Michael. 'Glimpses of a Mariology in the Qurʾān: From Hagiography to Theology via Religious Debate'. In: Angelika Neuwirth and Michael Marx (eds.). *The Qurʾān in Context: Historical and Literary Investigations into the Qurʾānic Milieu*, pp. 533–63. Leiden and Boston: Brill, 2010.
Mir, Mustansir. 'The Sura as a Unity: A Twentieth Century Development in Qurʾān Exegesis'. In: G. R. Hawting and Abdul-Kader A. Shareef (eds.). *Approaches to the Qurʾān*, pp. 211–24. London: Routledge, 1993.
Mir, Mustansir. 'Literature and the Qurʾān'. In: *Encyclopaedia of the Qurʾān*, 3:205. Leiden and Boston: Brill, 2003.
Moubarac, Youakim. 'Moise dans le Coran'. In: *Moise, l'homme de l'alliance*. Paris: Cahiers Sioniens, 1954.
Moubarac, Youakim. *Abraham dans le Coran*. Paris: Editions J. Vrin, 1958.
Nöldeke, Theodor. *Geschichte des Qorâns*. Göttingen: Dieterich, 1860.
Quṭb, Sayyid. *Fī Ẓilāl al-Qurʾān*. Cairo: Dār al-Shurūq, 1968.
al-Rāzī, Fakhr al-Dīn. *al-Tafsīr al-kabīr*. Beirut: Dar al-Kutub al-ʿIlmiyya, n.d.
Reynolds, Gabriel Said. *The Qurʾān and its Biblical Subtext*. London and New York: Routledge, 2011.
Robinson, Neal. 'Sūrat Āl ʿImrān and Those with the Greatest Claim to Abraham', *Journal of Qur'anic Studies* 6/2 (2004), 1–21.
Rodinson, Maxime. *Mohammed*. Middlesex: Penguin Press, 1973.
Sale, George. *The Koran*. London and New York: F. Warne, 1939.
Saleh, Walid A. 'The Etymological Fallacy and Qurʾānic Studies: Muhammad, Paradise and Late Antiquity'. In: Angelika Neuwirth, Nicolai Sinai, and Michael Marx (eds.). *The Qurʾān in Context Historical and Literary Investigations into the Qurʾānic Milieu*, pp. 659–98. Leiden and Boston: Brill, 2010.
Schwally, Friedrich and Theodor Noeldeke. *Geschichte des Qorāns*, rev. edn. Leipzig: Dieterich, 1919.
Siddiqui, Mona. *Christians Muslims and Jesus*. New Haven and London: Yale University Press, 2013.
Speyer, Heinrich. *Die Biblischen Erzählungen im Qoran*. Hildesheim: Georg Olms Verlag, 1931.
Sprenger, Aloys. *Das Leben und die Lehr des Mohammed*. Berlin: Georg Olms Verlag, 1861.
Torrey, Charles Cutler. *The Jewish Foundation of Islam*. New York: Jewish Institute of Religion Press, 1933.
Wansbrough, J. *Quranic Studies Sources and Methods of Scriptural Interpretation*. Oxford: Oxford University Press, 1977.
Wansbrough, J. *The Sectarian Milieu: Content and Composition of Islamic Salvation History*. Oxford: Oxford University Press, 1978.
Watt, W. Montgomery. *Muhammad at Mecca*. Oxford: Clarendon Press, 1953.
Watt, W. Montgomery. *Muhammad at Medina*. Oxford: Clarendon Press, 1956.
Weil, Gustav. *Historisch-kritische Einleitung in den Koran*. Bielefeld: Velhagen & Klasing, 1844.

CHAPTER 32

POLITICS AND THE QUR'AN

STEFAN WILD

Generalities

'Politics' is confined in this chapter to the question of legitimate versus illegitimate Muslim rule. This entry is in two sections: (a) the pre-modern era from the time of the revelation of the Qur'an up to the late eighteenth century and (b) modernity from the nineteenth century up to the present.

This distinction between pre-modernity and modernity is drawn along the historical/political line of colonialism and postcolonialism. Muslim scholars and intellectuals—like their Jewish and Christian forerunners—tended and tend to find in their scriptures what they look(ed) for. Mahmoud M. Ayoub (b. 1938), a specialist of Qur'anic exegesis, states the obvious: '(E)very legal or theological school, religious trend, or *political movement* in Muslim history sought to find in the Qur'an its primary support and justification' (Ayyoub 2004: 45, my emphasis). This is equally true for the present—with the exception of radical left-wing movements.

Pre-Modern Era

The Medinan period of Islam (1/622– 11/632) was a unique religious-political constellation. Muslims at the time of the Prophet did not live in a state but in a community (*umma*). After the *hijra*, the Prophet was the unquestioned ruler of a fast growing group of followers. The Medinan Muslim community was embedded in a tightly woven tribal setting: patriarchal, multi-religious, partly sedentary, partly Bedouin-nomad. Qur'anic stipulations sometimes overruled, more often modified and frequently confirmed pre-Islamic custom. The question if and to what degree commandments as proclaimed in the Qur'an and addressing the socio-political realities of Yathrib/Medina in the first/seventh century should be binding for later Muslim societies was and is a core question for Muslim political and religious thought.

The Qur'anic Text: Compilation, Canonization, and Exclusion

According to traditional Sunnī Muslim historiography, the third caliph ʿUthmān ibn ʿAffān (r. 23–35/644–56) was responsible for enforcing one single written version (*rasm*) of the Qur'an in the Muslim community. *Rasm* is the consonantal skeleton of the Qur'an that at the time lacked diacritics and vowel signs. Qur'anic recitation and oral transmission had preceded scripturalization. The written text was an underdetermined mnemonic aid for the reciter, not an easily readable text. ʿUthmān had all competing codices that showed variants in the *rasm* destroyed, a step resented by those reciters of the Qur'an who followed differing versions. The canonized text that eventually emerged became what is now known as the 'ʿUthmānic codex' (*al-muṣḥaf al-ʿUthmānī*). Under the Umayyads, al-Ḥajjāj ibn Yūsuf (d. 95/714), governor of Iraq and a fervent supporter of the Umayyads, had to contend with the competing Qur'an-version of the Prophet's companion ʿAbd Allāh ibn Masʿūd (d. 32/652). Al-Ḥajjāj 'wanted on the one hand to put an end to the quarrels of the theologians over the different readings and to produce a single text which the Islamic community should be obliged to use, and on the other hand to purge this text of any kind of anti-Umayyad allusions' (Dietrich, 'Ḥadjdjādj', 3:41r.) According to Omar Hamdan, al-Ḥajjāj's main aim in this step was 'to improve the political image of the Umayyads' (Hamdan 2010: 799).

While doubt remains about the historical details, the political advantage of having one and only one version of the Holy Book was evident. Imposing one single version of the Qur'an on the Muslim community aimed at more than achieving unity of liturgy and cult. It also intended to streamline and control the fledgling government and administration of the *umma*. The ruler ensured his status as leader of the Muslim community by asserting his competence to define Qur'anic canonicity. The caliph's suppression of competing versions of the holy text was as much political as it was religious.

The Qur'an in Early Twelver Shīʿī History

The question of who should legitimately rule the Muslim *umma* after the Prophet's death was linked to the question as to whether the Qur'an had said anything about a successor. This is evident in early Shīʿī doctrine on the shape and history of the Qur'an. Shīʿī scholars argued for centuries that the Qur'an had been first collected and written down by ʿAlī ibn Abī Ṭālib and not—as their opponents claimed—by Abū Bakr and ʿUthmān. A majority of Twelver Shīʿī scholars up to the third/ninth centuries were furthermore convinced that anti-Shīʿī readers had falsified or tampered with the

Qur'anic text. Some argued for example that in the original Qur'anic text the words of Q. 5:67: 'Messenger, proclaim everything that has been sent down to you from your Lord...' had been followed by the words 'with regard to ʿAlī' (*fī ʿAlīyyin*). This wording would have shown ʿAlī as the only worthy successor to the Prophet (Brunner 2001: 7). According to many Shīʿī Qur'an readers, their opponents had suppressed these two words. It was inconceivable for most of the Twelver Shīʿī at the time that the Qur'an should have failed to include a clear ruling that the Prophet's successor must come from ʿAlī ibn Abī Ṭālib or his descendants. It was only under the Buyids in the third/tenth centuries that a majority of Twelver Shīʿī scholars slowly came to accept that the Qur'anic text as we know it today was indeed the complete Qur'an. In any case, these controversies about the status of the Qur'an concerned the legitimacy of Muslim rule and were, therefore, eminently political.

The Battle of Ṣiffīn

After the Prophet's death, there was a period of turmoil. The Qur'an was silent on the topic of Muḥammad's succession and the Prophet had not unambiguously opted for a successor. The most symbolically charged inner-Muslim battle for the caliphate was that of Ṣiffīn (37/657). It was fought between the 'Iraqis' under the ruling fourth caliph ʿAlī ibn Abī Ṭālib (r. 35–41/656– 61) and the 'Syrians' under Muʿāwiya (r. 41–60/661– 80), who later became the first caliph of the Umayyad dynasty. When in a drawn-out battle the Syrian side faltered, Muʿāwiya stopped the fighting by using a ruse. He made his soldiers raise copies of the Qur'an on their lances and shout 'let the Book of God decide'. Ṣiffīn opened the way for the rift between two groups that were later called Sunnīs and Shīʿīs as well as for the emergence of the Khārijī sect. The political fight for the succession of the Prophet in the name of the Qur'an marked the first century of Islam.

Modern Era: Does the Qur'an Have a Political Message?

The underlying methodical precondition in this section is that developments in the reception of the Qur'an since the nineteenth century cannot be explained as resulting mainly from a philological or theological scrutiny of Qur'anic verses. Modern reception of the Qur'an, especially in the political realm, is better analysed as caused by colonial and postcolonial ruptures, the Palestinian/Israeli conflict, globalization, widespread poverty, the role of petroleum, and other political and socio-economic factors (Hroub 2010: 9ff.). Muslim scripture does play 'an almost exclusive role in the revitalization of Muslim religious thought' (Rahman 2009: xi). But this revitalization of Muslim exegesis usually has a strong political underpinning. Hermeneutics of

Qur'anic exegesis in modern times are more divergent, more multi-layered, and more controversial than Qur'anic exegeses in earlier periods ever were. Today, the Muslim scholar (*ʿālim*) versed in a venerable exegetical tradition competes with the Muslim intellectual (*muthaqqaf*) familiar with political science, sociology, text analysis, and other scholarly achievements of modernity.

Scholarship has no way to decide what the Qur'an 'really' says. But it can document and analyse what Muslims have said or say that the Qur'an says (Roy 2004: 10). The issue is, therefore, not the text of the Qur'an itself. At stake are the political discourses and practices of Muslims who refer to the Qur'an and base their actions on this reference. In contemporary Muslim and Muslim-majority societies, the question of how life according to Qur'anic prescriptions should be regulated in a rapidly modernizing world is urgent. In most Muslim majority-states, Qur'anic injunctions, as part of the Sharīʿa, are enforced in the realm of personal law and ritual law only. The Qur'anic insistence that socio-political prosperity and obedience to the Qur'anic message are indissolubly linked, resonates to this day in Muslim societies.

To some Muslims it seemed and seems obvious that there should be, at the least, a radically new beginning to the interpretation the Qur'an in modern times. Ashraf ʿAlī Thanāvī declared that '(I)f the goal is... to study the Qur'an not in the light of the long record of agreements and disagreements... but as if the Book had been revealed *to us*, as if it had come for our own generation... and as if the Prophet had died only recently after bringing the Book to us then such formal continuities as those constituted by the commentary or the study circle can barely conceal the reality of the fundamental rupture with the past' (Zaman 2002: 10).

Some contemporary Muslim scholars maintain that the Qur'an has no political message: 'Those who derive a political message from the Qur'ān exploit its verses out of context for their own goals' (Qamaruddin Khan 1973 quoted by Heck, 'Politics', *EQ* 4:126). The Turkish revisionist scholar Ömer Özsoy (b. 1963), professor of Muslim theology and representative of the Ankara school of Qur'anic exegesis, warns: '(T)he severest hermeneutic disease of Islam is the anachronism which wants the Koran to have literal answers for *today*'s questions...' (Körner 2005: 153). The South-African scholar Farid Esack (b. 1959) states: 'There is no direct reference in the Qur'ān to any notion of an Islamic state' (Esack 2007: 183). Already in 1925, the Egyptian judge ʿAlī ʿAbd al-Razzāq (d. 1966) had written a bitterly contested book *al-Islām wa-uṣūl al-ḥukum* (Islam and the foundations of political power). He claimed that the Qur'an was a spiritual message and concluded that Muslims could not opt for any specific form of political government on the basis of the Qur'an. These, however, are minority views.

Most Muslim scholars and many intellectuals are convinced that the Qur'an was and is 'the only possible basis for any renewal and development of Islamic religious, *political and social* thought, and that the Quran was the only resource for Muslim reinterpretation of traditional norms in Islam and Islamic thinking' (Poonawala 1963: 234, my emphasis). Muḥammad ʿIzzat Darwaza (d. 1984), an erstwhile Ottoman bureaucrat and Palestinian Arab nationalist, constructed 'a Qur'anic vision of political organization' (Heck, 'Politics' in *EQ* 4:126). Influential voices such as that of Mohammed Iqbal

(d. 1938), 'the father of Pakistan', insisted: 'According to the Qur'an, it is the religion of Islam alone which sustains a nation in its true cultural *or political* sense. It is for this reason that the Qur'an openly declares that any system other than that of Islam must be deprecated and rejected' (Zaman 2002: 34 fn. 81, my emphasis). On the radical side of the Islamic political spectrum, Abdessalam Yassine (d. 2012), one of the founders of the al-ʿAdl wa'l-Iḥsān movement in Morocco, writes: 'Let us read the Coran to recover from the secularist inanities teaching that Islam has nothing to do with politics. The Holy Book tells us the exact opposite...' (Yassine 1998: 28). The India-born scholar Fazlur Rahman (1919–88) concords: 'There is no doubt that the Qurʾān wanted Muslims to establish a political order on earth for the sake of creating an egalitarian and just moral-social order' (Rahman 2009: 62f.).

Ebrahim Moosa cautiously praises Fazlur Rahman's contextual approach: 'In his writings on ethics and morality he was acutely aware that changes in social values were informed by history, human experience, and altering human subjectivities' (Rahman 2009: xiv). But Moosa also points out what he considers weak points: 'Often, he used to mirror certain ideals that were more often the product of social change and human agency rather than the product of the Qur'an itself.... In doing so, he himself became vulnerable to the same critique he leveled at what he called 'neo-fundamentalist' tendencies, which he claimed had turned rules and norms derived from the teachings of the Qur'an into absolute imperatives' (Rahman 2009: xiv). The Egyptian philosopher Ḥasan Ḥanafī (b. 1935), a representative of the 'Islamic Left' argues that modern interpretation is a socio-political interpretation. It 'uses the text as a critical tool in order to measure the distance between the real and the ideal. Qur'anic interpretation is a social critique of Muslim societies' (Hanafi 1996: 201).

Evidently, the Qur'an as the most potent symbol of Islam has been used for and against the most divergent political views. Muḥammad Aḥmad Khalafallāh (1916–91) even put forward the surprising claim that only the Qur'an made a secular state possible. The Qur'an 'liberated the reason of mankind from the chains that were imposed on it in the name of religion... It is the first and the last heavenly book that contributes to the destruction of the religious state and to replacing it by a civil and democratic state. In this state, the president rules in the name of the people, elected by the people and for the good of the people' (Khalafallāh 1973: 65).

The Qur'an and Colonialism

At the turn of the nineteeth to the twentieth century, the majority of Muslims were under British, French, Dutch, etc. colonial rule or dominance. The Ottoman Empire, a Muslim multinational and multi-religious state, had become the 'Sick Man of Europe'. Its collapse after the First World War swept away the caliphate, the central symbol of Sunnī Islam, and sharpened many Muslims' awareness of their colonized status. It also gave the Qur'an a new role.

Among the first major voices to react to colonialism by promoting a specific political interpretation of the Qur'an were Sayyid Ahmad Khan (d. 1898) and Ameer Ali (d. 1928) in India. Sayyid Ahmad Khan urged Muslims to take over scientific achievements of the West and saw no disagreement between these achievements and the Qur'an. Moreover, he was sure that there was nothing in the Qur'an that could 'prevent Indian Muslims from coexisting and cooperating with the British' (Wielandt 2002: 2:126). He used the Qur'an to argue for full Muslim cooperation with British rule in India (Keddie 1968: 21). Ameer Ali founded a 'National Mahommedan Association' in India and a branch of the Muslim League in London. He wanted 'to promote good feeling and fellowship between the Indian races and creeds and at the same time to protect and safeguard Mahommedan interests and help their political training'. Timothy Winter (b. 1960), Dean of the Cambridge Muslim College, much later saw in Sayyid Ameer Ali one of those modernists who 're-examined the Qur'an, only to discover in its pages the entire moral code of Victorian England'. The Iranian pan-Islamic activist Jamāl al-Dīn al-Afghānī (1838–97) 'reserved his deepest hatred for Ahmad Khan' and his followers, whom he considered traitors (Keddie 1968: 42). Al-Afghānī's political life and his religious works were aptly called an 'Islamic response to imperialism'.

The Egyptian Muḥammad ʿAbdūh (1849–1905) and the Syrian/Lebanese Rashīd Riḍā (1865–1935) published a widely read reformist, and, at times, distinctly anti-colonial interpretation of the Qur'an. Their exegesis started being published in the journal *al-Manār* in 1898 and remained incomplete. It is still very popular between Turkey and Indonesia (Pink 2011: 45). Muḥammad ʿAbdūh's exegesis was rationalist. It opened up to findings of Western natural sciences, and was not adverse to modern socio-political ideas and thus represented a far cry from earlier traditional commentaries. He insisted that this commentary should react to the 'needs of the times' (*ḥājāt al-ʿaṣr*) and became an early proponent of the contextualization of Muslim scripture (Jansen 1974: 30). In a self-critical and anti-colonialist mood, he notes in a commentary to Q. 2:29: 'Yes, indeed the Muslims have become backward compared with other peoples in the world. They have fallen back into a state inferior to what they were in before the advent of Islam liberated them from their paganism. They have no knowledge of the world they live in, and they are unable to profit from the resources of their surroundings. Now foreigners have come, who snatch these riches away from under their noses. However, the Book [the Qur'an] interposes itself and exclaims: "He has subjected to you what is in the heavens"' (Jansen 1974: 30).

The Qur'an came to be seen by many Muslims as a barrier to colonization and as an effective weapon against the cultural, economic, and military hegemony of 'the West': 'as long as the Muslims persisted in their religion and as long as the Koran was read among them, it would be impossible for them to be sincere in their submission to foreign rule...' (Keddie 1968: 176).

The Qur'an as a Constitution

In May 1876, the British ambassador to Istanbul reported: 'the word "Constitution" was in every mouth...texts from the Koran were circulated proving to the faithful that the form of government sanctioned by it was properly democratic, and that the absolute authority now wielded by the Sultan was an usurpation of the rights of the people and not sanctioned by the Holy Law; and both texts and precedents were appealed to, to show that obedience was not due to a Sovereign who neglected the interests of the State' (Lewis 1961: 161). In 1908, Muḥammad ʿAbdūh congratulated the Ottoman Sultan on the new Ottoman constitution (Kawtharānī 1980: 130ff.), thereby rejecting the idea that such a constitution contradicted the Qur'an. But a number of Muslim scholars elsewhere did object. In Iran for example, many scholars violently opposed Iran's 1906/7 constitution on religious grounds (Bayat 1991: 130). Ayatollah Khomeini much later created an 'Islamic Constitution' for an 'Islamic Republic' (Krämer 1999: *passim*). But at this time, numerous scholars had already simply declared the Qur'an itself to be their constitution and claimed the Qur'an as their highest political authority.

Identifying the Qur'an with a national constitution seems possible only when the *umma*-ideal is made compatible with the reality of a multitude of different Muslim-majority national states and when a unified political order (*umma*) comprising all Muslims is renounced or postponed. The most famous scholar proposing a state comprising all Muslims was the Egyptian Sayyid Quṭb (executed 1966). His commentary *Fī ẓilāl al-Qurʾān* ('In the shadow of the Qur'an'), has been called 'the most widely translated and distributed Islamic book of all time' (Zaman 2002: 39). It is certainly one of the most influential, radical, and determinedly political exegeses of the Qur'an. Sayyid Quṭb teaches 'our ruler is God, our constitution is the Qurʾān' (1987: 160). He regards Arab nationalism and pan-Arabism as representing a relapse into heathendom (*jāhiliyya*) and incompatible with a truly Qur'anic government (Sivan 1985: 31). A comprehensive Islamic state must be established—if need be by force—to give the Muslim world community a home. All existing Muslim states and societies fail to be truly in line with the Qur'an and have to be viewed as pagan (*jāhilī*). The leaders of these pseudo-Muslim states are apostates; their rule, even if legitimated by corrupt Muslim scholars, is illegitimate. The main characteristic of the Muslim state to come is the adoption of what Sayyid Quṭb takes to be the complete Islamic law with the Qur'an at its centre. It has been rightly claimed that Sayyid Quṭb with some of his social concepts may be 'more indebted to modern Western ideas than to the Qur'an' (Zaman 2002: 8). Nevertheless, Sayyid Quṭb's Qur'anic exegesis has a distinctly retrogressive utopian quality. He describes in detail the Qur'an-centred religious-political system of the idealized community of 'the first generation of Muslims' in Medina. He claims that according to the Prophet's intention 'this group should dedicate itself purely to the Book of God…' (1978: 25) His activist ideology and his interpretation of the Qur'an were and are sources of inspiration for many revolutionary Islamic movements. His ideas influenced the Muslim Brothers within and outside of Egypt. They also inspired the militant splinter groups that claimed responsibility for the assassination of the Egyptian President Anwar al-Sadat (1981). Sayyid Quṭb's exegetical message had a lasting influence on the Iranian revolution (1979), the ideologies of Hizbullah in Lebanon, of Hamas in the West Bank, and in the Gaza Strip.

Abū'l-Aʿlā al-Mawdūdī's (d. 1979) vision of a new community of righteous individuals was close to Sayyid Quṭb's exegesis of the Qur'an and intended to lead human society to an 'Islamic revolution' (Zaman 2002: 103). Al-Mawdūdī, in his monthly *Tarjumān al-Qurʾān*, proclaimed his vision of an 'Islamic constitution' in the following way: 'The plan of action I had in mind was that I should first break the hold which Western culture and ideas had come to acquire over the Muslim *intelligensia*, and to instil in them the fact that Islam had a code of life of its own, its own culture, its own political and economic systems and a philosophy and an educational system which are all superior to anything that Western civilization could offer' (Abū Zayd 2004: 60). Al-Mawdūdī's booklet, *The Codification of the Islamic Constitution*, was a step in this direction.

Many Muslims who reject the identification of a political constitution with the Qur'an feel that at least the spirit of the Qur'an should reign in the way a Muslim state addresses its contemporary fundamental issues. Mahmoud M. Ayoub (b. 1938) writes: ' the Qur'an is not only the primary source of moral and religious guidance for the Muslim community; it is also its legal, political, and social constitution' (2004: 42). Evidently, he does not mean that the 'Constitution of the Islamic Republic Iran' (1980) is in fact identical with the Qur'an. Muslim authors call the Qur'an their constitution and at the same time affirm that the Qur'an as it stands cannot serve as a constitution. The Pakistani scholar Mawlana Taqi Usmani (b. 1943) distinguishes: 'When we say that Islam has provided us with directions for all spheres of life, we do not mean to suggest that the Qurʾān or the *Sunna* or Islamic Law has a ruling on every single particular of life. We mean, rather, that in all spheres of life, Islam has provided basic principles in whose light all the particulars can be determined' (quoted in Zaman 2002: 94). On the whole, Muslim scholars even in fairly traditional circles today seem today less prone to consider the Qur'an a modern constitution in a strict sense. However, there are still important exceptions such as Saudi Arabia and the Hamas movement.

The Kingdom of Saudi Arabia has claimed for a long time that the Qur'an alone was its constitution. In 1967, King Faisal confirmed this view (*Umm al-Qurā*, issue 2193, 20 October 1967). Often the Sunna of the Prophet is also mentioned as part of the constitution. Article 1 of the so-called Saudi Basic Law (*al-niẓām al-asāsī li'l-ḥukm*), promulgated by King Fahd in 1992, states: 'God's Book and the Sunna of the Prophet are the Saudi-Arab constitution' (*Middle East* 1992: 691).

An often-quoted slogan of the Muslim Brotherhood in post-Second World War Egypt was: 'God is our aim, the Prophet is our leader, the Qur'an is our constitution (*al-Qurʾānu dustūrunā*)...' (Krämer 2010: 66). It can be interpreted as a rejection of colonialism intended to show that Muslims did not need an imported document as the cornerstone of their political life. It also served as a device to avoid political discussion. Farid Esack (b. 1959), an advocate of a South African Qur'anic hermeneutic of religious pluralism and liberation, reports from inner-Muslim discussions in South Africa that the sentence 'the Qur'an is our constitution' was often used as stock-phrase to silence any further enquiry (1997: 219).

Nowadays, fewer members of the Muslim Brotherhood still opt for the Qur'an as their constitution—with the notable exception of its Palestinian branch and its Hamas Charter (1981). At present, all Muslim states have a national constitution that usually does not even mention the Qur'an. Apparently, it has become more important to define

Islam as the religion of the state and to underline the role of Sharīʿa in the constitution than to claim that the Qur'an itself is the constitution. Tariq Ramadan (b. 1962), however, speaks for many Muslims inside and outside the diaspora, when he says: 'It is impossible to understand, let alone literally enforce, the slogan "the Qur'an is our constitution"' (Ramadan 2012: 125). But the controversy is not yet over. Shaykh al-Azhar Maḥmūd Shaltūt (d. 1963) argued in his book *Min tawjīhāt al-Islām* (1982: 554): 'The Qur'an is a general, eternal, unchangeable constitution.'

Conclusion

Dealing with contemporary political issues, 'such as human rights, women's rights, how a society should be governed, the relationship of Muslims to non-Muslims and the questions of jihad and war, there has to be a new way of approaching, interpreting and understanding the Qurʾān' (Saeed 2006: 141). Muslims 'need to maintain a strong relationship between the solutions we are seeking and the Qurʾānic text' (Saeed 2006: 141). This avoids the double trap that either the Qur'anic text is seen as containing already all the answers to all modern questions, or that Muslims just 'discard the inheritance of the past and somehow develop what we think is appropriate for our own time' (Saeed 2006: 149). More than 1,400 years after the revelation of the Qur'an, Muslim debates on how to deal with Qur'anic verses that seem to have a socio-political message become more and more urgent. For the future of Muslims there is much at stake.

Bibliography

ʿAbdalrāziq, ʿAli. *al-Islām wa-uṣūl al-ḥukm. Baḥth fī'l-khilāfa wa'l-ḥukūma fī'l-Islām (Islam and the Roots of Political Authority)*. 3rd impression. Cairo: Maṭbaʿat Miṣr, 1344/1925.

Abū Zayd. Naṣr. *Rethinking the Qurʾān: Towards a Humanistic Hermeneutics*. Amsterdam: Humanistic University Press, 2004.

Ayoub, Mahmoud M. *Islam: Faith and History*. Oxford: Oneworld, 2004.

Bayat, Mangol. *Iran's First Revolution: Shi'ism and the Constitutional Revolution of 1905–1909*. Oxford: Oxford University Press, 1991.

Brunner, Rainer. *Die Schia und die Koranfälschung*. Würzburg: Ergon, 2001.

Dietrich, Albert. 'Ḥadjdjādj Ibn Yūsuf'. In: *EI*² 3:41r.

Esack, Farid. *Qurʾān, Liberation & Pluralism: An Islamic Perspective of Interreligious Solidarity against Oppression*. Oxford: Oneworld, 1997.

Esack, Farid. *The Qurʾān: A User's Guide*. Oxford: Oneworld, 2007.

Hamdan, Omar. 'The Second *maṣāḥif*-Project: A Step towards the Canonization of the Qurʾānic Text'. In: Angelika Neuwirth, Nicolai Sinai, and Michael Marx (eds.). *Historical and Literary Investigations into the Qurʾānic Milieu*, pp. 795–835. Leiden: E. J. Brill, 2010.

Ḥanafī, Ḥasan. 'Method of Thematic Interpretation of the Quran'. In: Stefan Wild (ed.). *The Qurʾān as Text*, pp. 195–211. Leiden: E. J. Brill, 1996.

Heck, Paul L. 'Politics and the Qurʾān'. In: Jane Dammen McAuliffe (ed.). *Encyclopaedia of the Qurʾān*. 6 vols., 4:126 Leiden: Brill, 2001–6.

Hroub, Khaled (ed.). *Political Islam: Context versus Ideology*. London: Saqi, 2010.
Jansen, Johannes J. G. *The Interpretation of the Koran in Modern Egypt*. Leiden: E. J. Brill, 1974.
Kawtharānī, Wajīh (ed.). *Mukhtārāt siyāsiyya min majallat al-Manār*. Beirut: Dār al-Ṭalīʿa, 1980.
Keddie, Nikki R. *An Islamic Response to Imperialism: Political and Religious Writings of Sayyid Jamāl ad-Dīn "al-Afghānī"*. Berkeley and Los Angeles: University of California Press, 1968.
Khalafallāh, Muḥammad Aḥmad. *Al-Qurʾān wa-l-dawla*. Cairo: Maktabat al-Anjlū al-Miṣriyya, 1973.
Khan, Qamaruddin. *Political Concepts of the Qurʾān*. Karachi: Institute of Islamic Studies, 1973.
Körner, Felix. *Revisionist Koran Hermeneutics in Contemporary Turkish University Theology: Rethinking Islam*, Würzburg: Ergon, 2005.
Krämer, Gudrun. *Hasan al-Banna*. Oxford: Oneworld, 2010.
Krämer, Gudrun. *Gottes Staat als Republik: Reflexionen zeitgenössischer Muslime zu Islam, Menschenrechten und Demokratie*. Baden-Baden: Nomos, 1999.
Lewis, Bernard. *The Emergence of Modern Turkey*. 2nd edn. Oxford: Oxford University Press, 1961.
Middle East Contemporary Survey, vol. 16. Boulder, CO: Westview Press, 1992.
Pink, Johanna, *Sunnitischer Tafsīr in der modernen islamischen Welt: Akademische Traditionen, Popularisierung und nationalstaatliche Interessen*. Leiden: E. J. Brill, 2011.
Poonawala, Ismail K. 'Muḥammad ʿIzzat Darwaza's *Principles of Modern Exegesis: A Contribution toward Quranic Hermeneutics*'. In: G. R. Hawting and Abdul-Kader A. Shareef (eds.). *Approaches to the Qurʾān*, pp. 225–46. London and New York: Routledge, 1963.
Quṭb, Sayyid. *Maʿālim fī al-ṭarīq*, 11th edn. Cairo: Dār al-Shurūq, 1987; Eng. trans.: *Milestones*. N.p., 1978.
Quṭb, Sayyid. *Fī ẓilāl al-Qurʾān*, Cairo, 1999.
Rahman, Fazlur. *Major Themes of the Qur'an*. 2nd edn. With a New Foreword by Ebrahim Moosa. Chicago: University of Chicago Press, 2009.
Ramadan, Tariq. *The Arab Awakening: Islam and the New Middle East*. London: Allen Lane, 2012.
Roy, Olivier. *Globalised Islam: The Search for a New Ummah*. London: C. Hurst, 2004.
Saeed, Abdullah. *Interpreting the Qurʾān: Towards a Contemporary Approach*. Abington: Routledge, 2006.
Sivan, Emmanuel. *Radical Islam: Medieval Theology and Modern Politics*. New Haven, CT: Yale University Press, 1985.
Wielandt, Rotraud. 'Exegesis of the Qurʾān: Early Modern and Contemporary'. In: Jane Dammen McAuliffe (ed.). *Encyclopaedia of the Qurʾān*. 6 vols., 2:24–42 Leiden: Brill, 2001–6.
Yassine, Abdessalam. *Islamiser la modernité*. Salé: al-Ofok Impressions, 1998.
Zaman, Muhamad Qasim. *The Ulama in Contemporary Islam: Custodians of Change*. Princeton: Princeton University Press, 2002.

CHAPTER 33

JIHAD AND THE QUR'AN: CLASSICAL AND MODERN INTERPRETATIONS

ASMA AFSARUDDIN

THE lexeme jihad and related verbs occur in the Qur'an in different contexts and have various significations. The basic connotations of the Arabic root j-h-d have to do with struggle, exertion, making an effort. The frequently encountered phrase *al-jihād fi sabīl allāh* ('struggling/striving in the path of God') is quite common in the extra-Qur'anic literature in general but does not occur in the Qur'an in this exact formulation. Instead, the Qur'an uses verbal forms derived from j-h-d with the phrase *fī sabīl allāh* and less frequently with *fī 'llāh*. Two other Qur'anic terms—*ṣabr* (patient forbearance) and *qitāl* (fighting)—are to be regarded as key components of the broader term jihad, as discussed below. *Ḥarb*, the Arabic word for 'war' in general is never used in the Qur'an with the phrase 'in the path of God' and is not related to the concept of jihad.

CONCEPTUALIZATIONS OF JIHAD IN THE WESTERN ACADEMY

A survey of key modern studies of jihad reveals that there are three primary conceptualizations of this term that are predominant in the Western academy. These are now discussed below.

The first such conceptualization is that the term jihad in general refers primarily, if not exclusively, to military activity against the non-Muslim enemy (Lewis 1988: 72; Lewis 1995: 233; Watt 1976: 143; Tyan 1998: 538; Morabia 1993: *passim*; Khadduri 1955: 51; Cook 2005: *passim*); according to this conceptualization, jihad essentially becomes conflated with *qitāl*. David Cook goes so far as to stridently maintain that only apologists,

Western and Muslim, emphasize the notion of an internal or spiritual jihad in order 'to present Islam in the most innocuous manner possible' (2009: 166).

Recently, Asma Afsaruddin has argued that these perceptions have developed in the Western academy due to the absence of a recognition of the importance of *ṣabr* and its cultivation as a constant feature of jihad—understood broadly as human striving—in the Qur'an and by downplaying or ignoring the verses that refer to jihad in the non-combative sense, especially in the Meccan period (*c*.610–622 CE). This situation, she says, is compounded by the fact that disproportionate scholarly attention is paid to the juridical literature which understandably focuses on the combative jihad as a state-sanctioned duty within the context of military security and international relations (Khadduri 1955; Morabia 1993; Peters 1996, among others). Afsaruddin points to pre-modern Muslim exegetical and edifying literature which, in contradistinction to the legal corpus, extols *ṣabr* as an essential ingredient of human striving, taking its cue from the Qur'an. Apart from Morabia, who briefly recognized *ṣabr* as an aspect of jihad (1995: 175, 293ff.), Western scholars in general have not taken account of this attribute as constituting a part of the Qur'anic jihad.

Afsaruddin notes that one particular Meccan verse—Q. 3:200—is often invoked in the sources to establish the importance of *ṣabr* as a constant feature of human striving in the face of life's vicissitudes. This verse states: 'O those who believe, be patient and forbearing (*iṣbirū*), outdo others in forbearance (*ṣābirū*), be firm (*rābiṭū*), and revere God so that you may succeed.' A survey undertaken by Afsaruddin of early commentaries on this verse produced by exegetes (Sunnī and Shīʿī) from the first three centuries of Islam—such as Mujāhid ibn Jabr (d. 104/722), Muqātil ibn Sulaymān (d. 150/767), ʿAbd al-Razzāq (d. 211/827), Hūd ibn Muḥakkam al-Hawwārī (d. *c*.290/903), Furāt ibn Ibrāhīm (*fl.* second half of third/ninth century), and Ibrāhīm al-Qummī (fl. late third/ninth century)—reveals a general uniform emphasis upon *ṣabr* and its derivatives as referring to patient forbearance in the carrying out of religious duties, such as prayer, particularly in the face of ill-treatment by others (see extensive discussion of their views in Afsaruddin 2013b: esp. 179–204). In the fourth/tenth century al-Ṭabarī (d. 310/923) in his well-known commentary quotes the early pietistic scholar Ibn Jurayj (d. 150/767) who remarked that this verse counselled believers to 'Remain steadfast in obedience and to be patient with the enemies of God, and be firm in the path of God' (al-Ṭabarī, *al-Jāmiʿ*, 3:562) In his commentary on this verse, the late sixth-/twelfth-century exegete al-Rāzī (d. 606/1210) comments that the first imperative in the verse—*iṣbirū*—relates to the individual while the second imperative *ṣābirū* deals with interactions between the individual and others. He notes further that the verbal noun *muṣābara* (related to the command *ṣābirū* in Q. 3:200) has to do with commanding the good and preventing wrong, which could possibly lead to fighting (jihad) in order to defend oneself from the harm of others (al-Rāzī, *al-Tafsīr*, 3:473).

The effort inherent in the inculcation of the Qur'anic virtue of *ṣabr* is renamed as *jihād al-nafs* in later typologies of jihad while the Qur'anic *qitāl* is termed *jihād al-sayf*. The scholars al-Ghazālī (d. 505/1111), an Ashʿarī theologian of a mystical bent, and Ibn Qayyim al-Jawziyya (d. 751/1350), a Ḥanbalī jurist, for example, wrote treatises in their respective centuries praising the cultivation and practice of patient forbearance as the best expression of jihad, indispensable for resisting the incitements of the lower self (*al-nafs al-ammāra*) (al-Ghazālī, *Iḥyā*ʾ, 84–100; Ibn Qayyim al-Jawziyya, *ʿUddat al-ṣabirīn*). Afsaruddin subsequently maintains that a clear Qur'anic genealogy can thereby be established for the conception of internal, spiritual jihad under the rubric of *ṣabr*, which pre-dates the combative jihad in the Qur'an. She therefore takes issue with some modern scholars who have maintained the opposite in order to establish, often in a polemical vein, that the concept of the internal, non-combative jihad is a later construction and has no basis in the Qur'an (Cook 2005: 32–48; Morabia 1993: 330–44; Peters 1996: 187).

Some modern scholars have furthermore drawn attention to the occurrence of the term jihad in some Meccan verses with clearly non-combative connotations (Abdel Haleem 2010: 147–8; Bonner 2006: 21–2; Picken 2015: 127–8; Afsaruddin 2013b: 16–25). One such verse—Q. 22:78—states: 'Strive in regard to God a true striving as is His due' (*Wa-jāhidū fī 'llāh ḥaqqa jihādihi*). The Arabic locution *fī-'llāh* ('in regard to God') in this precise formulation occurs only once in the Qur'an and tends to be overlooked in most discussions of the term jihad. Another verse (Q. 29:69) uses *fīna* ('in regard to us') with similar significations. The variant formulation in Q. 22:78 of what became the more common locution *al-jihād fī sabīl allāh* is worthy of closer attention.

A survey of some key commentaries establishes the non-combative nature of jihad in Q. 22:78. The second/eighth-century exegete Muqātil ibn Sulaymān understands this verse to exhort believers to excel in the performance of good deeds in general so as to earn divine approbation. Al-Ṭabarī in his commentary refers to the early authority al-Ḍaḥḥāk ibn Muzāḥim (d. 105/723) who interpreted this verse as 'Perform a deed appropriately as is His due [God].' Al-Ṭabarī himself however prefers to understand this verse as containing the imperative to 'Struggle against the polytheists (*al-mushrikīn*) for the sake of God (*fī sabīl allāh*) as is rightly due Him.' In al-Ṭabarī's *tafsīr*, therefore, the prepositional phrase *fī 'llāh* is now deemed to be the equivalent of *fī sabīl allāh* and therefore possibly connoting fighting in the context of struggling against the polytheists. After this decisive exegetical shift in al-Ṭabarī's commentary, both combative and non-combative meanings of jihad are included by later exegetes in relation to Q. 22:78. Al-Rāzī and al-Qurṭubī (d. 671/1273), for example, refer to two types of exertion as fundamentally and equally constitutive of jihad: (a) the spiritual exertion inherent in overcoming one's base desires in order to obey God; and (b) the general, physical exertion required to carry out one's religious obligations, including military activity (al-Rāzī, *al-Tafsīr*, 8:254–5; al-Qurṭubī, *al-Jāmiʿ*, 12:91–2).

Another relevant Meccan verse (Q. 25:52) states 'Do not obey the unbelievers and strive against them mightily with it (*wa-jāhidhum bihi jihādan kabīran*).' There is near-consensus among pre-modern and modern exegetes that 'it' refers to the Qur'an; jihad here is therefore an oral, discursive undertaking, in which the Qur'an is used as a *ḥujja* (proof) against those who opposed it (for some of these views, see Afsaruddin 2013b: 16–18).

A second pervasive assumption is that the military jihad is meant to be waged as expansionist war in order to aggressively promote and spread Islam. The opposite position—that the military jihad is primarily defensive—has been dismissed by some modern scholars, like Emile Tyan, as mere apologetics (1998: 539; cf. Peters 1996: 110, 148; Peters 1979: 163). Some have even gone as far as to state that in the Qur'an 'all war is assumed to involve religious issues' (Crone 2006: 5:456; cf. Bravmann 2009: 115; Firestone 1999: 88–90). As a consequence of this assumption, jihad is translated as 'holy war' in most Western works.

According to the classical exegetes, Q. 22:39–40 are widely regarded as the first revelation in the Medinan period (622–32 CE) that permitted Muslims to fight their Meccan enemies who had ruthlessly and violently persecuted them. These verses state:

> Permission is given to those who are fought against (*yuqātalūna*) because they have been wronged/oppressed, and God is able to help them. These are they who have been wrongfully expelled from their homes merely for saying 'God is our Lord.' If God had not restrained some people by means of others, monasteries, churches, synagogues, and mosques in which God's name is mentioned frequently would have been destroyed. Indeed God comes to the aid of those who come to His aid; verily He is powerful and mighty.

The defensive nature of fighting is underscored by the passive Arabic verb *yuqātalūna* ('those who are fought against') used in the verse, which however is erroneously translated in the active sense as 'those who fight' in a number of English translations, including those produced by George Sale, A. J. Arberry, and Muhammed Marmaduke Pickthall. The explicit reasons given in the verse for fighting are that the pagan Meccans had oppressed Muslims by driving the latter from their homes and subjecting them to physical torture and verbal abuse merely for asserting the oneness of God, as Muqātil ibn Sulaymān comments (Muqātil, *Tafsīr*, 3:130). The defensive nature of the fighting permitted in this verse is underscored by all subsequent major exegetes—al-Ṭabarī, al-Zamakhsharī, al-Rāzī, and others (for their views, see Afsaruddin 2013b: 35–43).

Q. 22:40 also suggests that Muslims may fight to prevent the destruction of monasteries, churches, and synagogues at the hands of the polytheists, in addition to mosques. This was the understanding of Muqātil ibn Sulaymān, who explicitly states that God defends all these places of worship through Muslims (Muqātil, *Tafsīr*, 3:129–30). Al-Zamakhsharī (d. 538/1144) understands this verse as referring to the polytheists during the time of Muḥammad, who would have triumphed over the Muslims and the People of the Book 'in their protection' (*fi dhimmatihim*) and whose houses of worship would have been destroyed if Muslims had not resorted to the military jihad (al-Zamakhsharī, *al-Kashshāf*, 4:199).

That fighting cannot be initiated by Muslims and can only be in response to a prior act of aggression is unambiguously stated in another Medinan verse, Q. 2:190. Together with the next four verses, this cluster (Q. 2:190–4) contains important injunctions for carrying out legitimate armed combat and form the nucleus for classical juridical discussions about the ethics of war and peace (e.g. al-Māwardī, *al-Ḥawī*, 14:102ff.). The exegetes are in general agreement that these verses refer to the events at al-Ḥudaybiyya in 8/628 in which year the Muslims were granted divine permission to defend themselves in the precincts of the Kaʿba in the event of an attack upon them by the pagan Meccans during one of the pre-Islamic sacred months, something they were previously forbidden to do. Our earliest exegetes understand the interdiction in Q. 2:190 against committing aggression as a clear and general prohibition against initiating hostilities under any circumstance. The early exegete Mujāhid ibn Jabr (d. 104/722) thus unequivocally subscribed to the view that Q. 2:190 explicitly forbids Muslims from ever initiating aggression against anyone, including obvious wrongdoers/oppressors (*al-ẓālimīn*), in any place, sacred or profane (Mujāhid, *Tafsīr*, 23). In the fourth/tenth century, al-Zamakhsharī similarly maintained that Muslims may not ever initiate fighting on the basis of Q. 2:190 (*Kashshāf*, 1:395–6) as did al-Rāzī in the early sixth/twelfth century (*al-Tafsīr*, 2:288).

So unambiguous is the Qur'anic proscription against initiating fighting in Q. 2:190 that some exegetes from the second/eighth century onward who wished to allow for expansionist military activity felt impelled to resort to "abrogation" (*naskh*) as a hermeneutic tool to nullify this explicit command. Al-Ṭabarī documents a lively debate among early exegetes concerning the implications of Q. 2:190. He notes that certain unnamed exegetes understood the verse as commanding the believers to fight the pagan Meccans only after the latter had initiated hostilities and to desist from combat when they (sc. the pagan Meccans) refrained from fighting. However, the Successors al-Rabīʿ ibn Anas (d. 139/756) and Ibn Zayd (d. 183/798) had been of the opinion that the ninth chapter (*al-Tawba or al-Barāʾa*) of the Qur'an had abrogated this verse. In opposition to them, other exegetes (unnamed by al-Ṭabarī) had maintained that no part of this verse was abrogated and that the aggression forbidden in it, which was a categorical prohibition, applied specifically to non-combatants, especially women and children. Al-Ṭabarī himself accepts this latter exegesis as the most fitting—rather than being abrogated, he says the command 'Do not commit aggression' should be understood to mean that one should not kill children or women; additionally, those who pay the *jizya* from among the People of the Book and the Zoroastrians are similarly protected. Exceeding these limits constitutes aggression (al-Ṭabarī, *al-Jāmiʿ*, 2:196–7). It should be noted that al-Ṭabarī's reconstrual of the aggression clause in this manner became quite influential after him and became reflected in the classical laws of war and peace formulated by many jurists (cf. al-Sarakhsī, *Kitāb al-Mabsūṭ*, 10:6–8; Saḥnūn, *al-Mudawwana*, 2:587; al-Māwardī, *al-Ḥāwī*, 14:192–4; Ibn Qudāma, *al-Mughnī*, 13:138ff.) Accordingly, these jurists also came to understand the non-aggression clause in this verse as primarily setting up a prohibition against fighting non-combatants, and not as a categorical prohibition against initiating fighting under any circumstance, as was clearly the view of several early exegetes.

Understood in this larger context, the next verse Q. 2:191 need not be understood to contain a general injunction to 'slay the polytheists' *qua* polytheists; it may instead be understood as calling for retaliation against the polytheists on account of their having resorted to persecution and prior aggression against Muslims, to which a proportional response is warranted according to Q. 2:194. Pre-modern exegeses actually record a range of views on the interpretation of this verse (for this discussion, see Afsaruddin 2013b: 43–58). The gradual understanding of the terms *fitna* and *ẓulm* occurring in this verse cluster as specifically referring to 'associationism' (*shirk*) and/or 'unbelief'(*kufr*) rather than broadly to 'discord/trials' and 'wrongdoing' respectively also allowed a significant number of pre-modern exegetes to make the case that the profession of polytheism in itself rather than the aggression of the polytheists was the *casus belli*. Al-Ṭabarī, for example, notes that the root meaning of *fitna* is 'tribulation' but goes on to express a preference for imputing the meaning of 'polytheism' to it (al-Ṭabarī, *al-Jāmiʿ*, 2:197–8). This interpretation has been subjected to severe criticism by modern scholars (Riḍā 1999: 2:170–1; Abdel Haleem 2010: 151–4; al-Dawoody 2011: 60–3).

Similar reasons which legitimate an armed response to the adversary are contained in another important group of verses—Q. 9:12–13—which state:

> If they break their pacts (*aymānāhum*) after having concluded them and revile your religion, then fight the leaders of unbelief. Will you not fight a people who violated their oaths and had intended to expel the Messenger and commenced [hostilities] against you the first time?

The overwhelming majority of exegetes stress that the violation of pacts by the polytheists, their denigration of Islam, hostile intent toward Muḥammad, and their initial act of aggression towards Muslims had made fighting necessary against them (see an account of some of these views in Afsaruddin 2013b: 58–63). In his commentary on Q. 9:12, al-Ṭabarī says that it is a critique of those among the Quraysh who violated the terms of their pact with Muḥammad according to which they had agreed not to fight the Muslims nor provide aid to their enemies (al-Ṭabarī, *al-Jāmiʿ*, 6:330).

Another verse Q. 4:75 exhorts Muslims to defend militarily those who are among 'the feeble of men and of women and children who cry out, "Our Lord! Deliver us from this town in which the people are oppressors!"' In the understanding of pre-modern jurists, this verse establishes humanitarian reasons for military intervention to aid those who are defenceless against their oppressors and who specifically call upon Muslims to provide them with help (e.g. al-Sulamī, *Aḥkām*, 610); a point stressed in modern juridical discourses (al-Qaraḍāwī 2009: 1:240–3; al-Zuḥaylī 1981: 93–4).

One verse that could be and has been understood by certain modern scholars (Peters 1996: 49; Firestone 1999: 88; Landau-Tasseron 2003: 3:39) as allowing fighting for the sake of religion is Q. 8:39 which states: 'And fight them until persecution/trials (*fitna*) is/are no more, and religion is entirely for God. But if they cease, then indeed God sees what they do' (cf. also Q. 2:193). Reading it with its preceding verse provides more context however: Q. 8:38 states: 'Tell those who disbelieve that if they cease [from persecution of believers] then that which is past will be forgiven them; but if they return [to it], then the example of the men of old has already gone before them as a warning.' As was the case with Q. 2:193, an overwhelming majority of exegetes from the second/eighth century onward understand *fitna* in Q. 8:39 to mean polytheism (*shirk*) which must be extirpated so that Islam may prevail. 'If they cease' is consequently understood to refer to the pagan Arabs who abandon polytheism. This is, for example, al-Ṭabarī's preferred understanding; in his comprehensive listing of various interpretations of this verse, he, however, indicates that some earlier commentators had held markedly different views. Thus, according to the Successor al-Ḥasan al-Baṣrī (d. 110/728) *fitna* refers to tribulation (*balāʾ*) so that fighting is thereby understood to be undertaken to put an end to persecution and strife, not to uproot polytheism. Al-Ṭabarī also refers to a group of unnamed exegetes who were of the view that the phrase 'If they cease' refers to pagan Arabs who desist from fighting, not from polytheism, a position with which he disagrees (al-Ṭabarī, *al-Jāmiʿ*, 2:245–7).

Al-Rāzī, like al-Ṭabarī, is of the opinion that the verse refers to pagan Arabs who abandon their polytheism. But he also goes on to cite the views of ʿUrwa ibn al-Zubayr (d. 93/711–2 or 94/712–3) who interpreted *fitna* in this verse to refer to the trials and persecution faced by the early Muslims in Mecca which aimed 'to lure them away from God's religion'. After the *hijra* (migration) to Medina, Muslims were given the divine command to fight the polytheists because they were persecuting Muslims and obstructing them from the free practice of their religion. According to ʿUrwa, 'So that religion may be entirely for God' expresses the purpose of this sanctioned fighting which is to ensure the free and unfettered practice of religion in the absence of persecution (al-Rāzī, *al-Tafsīr*, 5: 483–4).

Modern Muslim scholars largely agree with al-Ḥasan al-Baṣrī's and ʿUrwa's interpretations. Thus Muḥammad ʿAbdūh in the late nineteenth century emphasizes that this verse specifically relates to the circumstances during the Prophet's time when he and his Companions were subjected to much hardship on account of their public profession of their faith. Fighting commanded in it was intended to put an end to this hardship and thus 'to ensure freedom of religion' (*wa-yakūn al-dīn ḥurran*) so that no one may be coerced into abandoning his or her religion and/or face persecution on account of it. This position, he comments, is in full conformity with Q. 2:256 which states, 'There is no compulsion in religion.' ʿAbdūh, like ʿUrwa and others in the first century of Islam, thus infers no broader mandate in this verse to continue to wage war so that Islam eventually supplants all other religions (Riḍā 1999: 9:554; cf. Sachedina 1990: 39–40).

The third widely-held assumption among Orientalist scholars is that, according to a final set of revelations which effectively 'abrogate' earlier conciliatory verses, the Qur'an calls for all-out aggressive war against non-Muslims until they see the error of their ways and convert to Islam or accept Muslim political domination. Thus Emile Tyan states, 'the fight (*d̲jihād*) is obligatory even when they (the unbelievers) have not themselves started it' and that 'the d̲jihād is nothing more than a means to effect conversion to Islam or submission to its authority' (Tyan 1998; cf. Khadduri 1955: 59). David Cook asserts that the Qur'an itself mandates expansionist military conquest (Cook 2005: 7ff.) while Reuven Firestone describes jihad in the Qur'an as 'a ruthless ideological war of religion against those labeled as unbelievers' (Firestone 1999: 90). Other modern scholars point out that although such perspectives can be encountered in the *kitāb al-jihād/siyar* sections of many legal manuals as a concession to Realpolitik, they cannot be justified on the basis of the Qur'an. Such views in fact countermand the overall tenor of relevant Qur'anic injunctions which sanction fighting only in limited circumstances and as defensive military activity (Mahmassani 1966: 321; Shaltūt, *Al-Islam wa'l-ʿAlāqāt al-Dawliyya*, 37–8; Abū Zahra 1964: 47–52, 89–94; Hamidullah 1977: 174–7; Esposito 2002: 26–46; Afsaruddin 2013a: 45–63).

The Qur'an does exhort able-bodied men to fight as an obligatory duty when legitimate cause exists and the acknowledged leader of the community proclaims the military jihad, as happened during the time of the Prophet. Q. 2:216 states: 'Fighting has been prescribed for you even though you find it displeasing. Perhaps you dislike something in which there is good for you and perhaps you find pleasing that which causes you harm. But God knows and you do not.' It is significant however that several exegetes were of the opinion that the plural 'you' (*kum*) in the phrase 'prescribed for you' (*kutiba alaykum*) occurring in the verse referred only to the Companions of the Prophet and that it did not constitute a normative command binding upon subsequent generations of Muslims. In his commentary, al-Ṭabarī notes that when ʿAṭāʾ [ibn Abī Rabāḥ; d. 115/733] was asked whether Q. 2:216 made fighting (*ghazw*) obligatory for people in general, he replied that it did not and that 'it was prescribed only for those [*ulāʾika*, sc. Companions] at that time (*ḥīnaʾidhin*)' (al-Ṭabarī, *al-Jāmiʿ*, 2:357). In the fifth/eleventh century, al-Wāḥidī continues to endorse the early position that fighting as a religiously prescribed duty was restricted to the time of the Prophet, quoting ʿAṭāʾ ibn Abī Rabāḥ as his source (al-Wāḥidī, *al-Wasīṭ*, 1:319). Al-Rāzī acknowledges that widely divergent opinions have historically existed among the scholars. Thus the Syrian Umayyad jurist Makḥūl al-Shāmī (d. *c*.119/737) is said to have sworn at the Kaʿba that *ghazw* (military campaign) was a continuing religious obligation. According to the Medinan scholars ʿAbd Allāh Ibn ʿUmar (d. 73/693) and ʿAṭāʾ, however, this verse imposed the duty of fighting on the Companions of Muḥammad 'at that time only' (*fī dhālika 'l-waqt faqaṭ*), that is, during the lifetime of the Prophet (al-Rāzī, *al-Tafsīr*, 2:384). We may deduce from al-Rāzī's exegesis that Syrian jurists like Makḥūl who supported Umayyad wars of expansion allowed for a general injunction to fight to be read into this verse in contradistinction to Medinan scholars not generally supportive of the Umayyads, such as ʿAṭāʾ ibn Abī Rabāḥ and Ibn ʿUmar, who inferred no such broad religious mandate and restricted the imposition of the duty of fighting on the Companions of the Prophet alone (cf. Mottahedeh and al-Sayyid 2001: 23–9).

Q. 9:5 AND 9:29

In support of the position that the Qur'an mandates continuous warfare against non-Muslims *qua* non-Muslims, two verses in particular are often cited in the secondary literature on jihad: 9:5 which is understood to mandate fighting against all non-Abrahamic non-Muslims until they convert and 9:29 understood to require fighting against the People of the Book who refuse either to submit to Muslim rule, signified by their payment of the *jizya*, or embrace Islam (Firestone 1999: 88–90; Cook 2005: 10; Landau-Tasseron 2003: 3:39–40; Rubin 1984: 17ff.). These verses are also sometimes presented in modern scholarly literature (Peters 1996: 2–3; Rubin 1984: 18–20) and modern militant writings (e.g. Faraj 1986: 195–7) as having abrogated the more numerous irenic verses in the Qur'an. Other modern scholars have argued that these verses engaged in isolation from others that have much to say about the parameters of legitimate armed combat can be highly misleading and distorting of the ultimate purpose of *qitāl* in the Qur'an (al-Ghunaimī 1968: 165–71; Abdel Haleem 2008: 307–40; Esposito 2002: 64–8; Afsaruddin 2013b: 65–94).

A survey of key exegetical works on these verses reveals in fact a broad spectrum of views on the meaning of these verses in the pre-modern period, as follows.

Q. 9:5 states: 'When the sacred months have lapsed, then kill the polytheists (*al-mushrikīn*) wherever you may encounter them. Seize them and encircle them and lie in wait for them. But if they repent and perform the prayer and give the *zakāt*, then let them go on their way, for God is forgiving and merciful.' Most pre-modern exegetes, particularly before the Mamluk period, restrict the applicability of this verse to the Arab polytheists (*mushrikūn*) of the first/seventh century with whom there is no pact (*ʿahd*) and who may be fought wherever they are to be found and whenever, except for the three sacred months of Dhū'l-Qaʿda, Dhū'l-Ḥijja, and al-Muḥarram when fighting was traditionally forbidden in the pre-Islamic period. It is significant that pre-Mamluk exegetes, like al-Ṭabarī, al-Zamakhsharī, and al-Wāḥidī, tended not to pay much attention to this verse; they also do not maintain that Q. 9:5 had abrogated other verses in the Qur'an that counsel good relations with peaceful people, regardless of their religious affiliation. Al-Ṭabarī specifically states that it is not correct to assume that the verse commands the slaying of polytheists in every situation; he refers to Q. 47:4 which, in this context, unambiguously allows prisoners of war to be ransomed or released outright (al-Ṭabarī, *al-Jāmiʿ*, 6:320). In his brief commentary, al-Zamakhsharī identifies the intended polytheists in the verse as 'those who betray you and rise up against you' who may be killed in holy and non-holy places and taken captive, and restricted in their movements (al-Zamakhsharī, *al-Kashshāf*, 3:13–14). Like his predecessors, al-Zamakhsharī does not consider this to be an abrogating verse. Worthy of note is al-Zamakhsharī's depiction of the polytheists who should be fought against as specifically those who break their pledges and display *a priori* hostility to Muslims—not polytheists as a general collectivity.

With regard to the status and function of Q. 9:5, al-Qurṭubī in the seventh/thirteenth century, like al-Ṭabarī and al-Zamakhsharī before him, considers it to be neither abrogated nor abrogating (al-Qurṭubī, *al-Jāmiʿ*, 8:70). However, al-Qurṭubī spends more time explicating this verse than most of his predecessors, indicating that the need to justify military activity on the basis of scriptural warrants was more of a pressing issue in his time as Muslims in al-Andalus were confronted by advancing Christian armies from the north. It is also highly significant that none of the exegetes in this survey up to al-Qurṭubī had specifically dubbed this verse the *āyat al-sayf* ('sword verse'). Afsaruddin notes that although Muqātil ibn Sulaymān already uses the term *āyat al-sayf* in his commentary (Muqātil, *Tafsīr*, 4:301–2; although not in the section where he discusses Q. 9:5), none of the later commentators she surveyed used this designation specifically for Q. 9:5 until Ibn Kathīr (d. 774/1373) (Ibn Kathīr, *Tafsīr*, 2:322; cf. Afsaruddin 2013b: 75). Ibn Kathīr's commentary on this verse and his explicit designation of it as 'the sword verse' indicates to us that a partiality had developed by the eighth/fourteenth century during the Mamluk period for the derivation of an expansive general mandate from otherwise historically circumscribed Qur'anic verses—such as Q. 9:5—to fight or punish all those deemed enemies of Islam in the later period. In Ibn Kathīr's time, these enemies were the Crusaders as well as the Mongols.

The so-called *jizya* verse (Q. 9:29) was also understood by a number of influential exegetes as granting permission to Muslims to fight in general a different group of non-Muslims—the People of the Book—who refuse to accept Islam or submit to Muslim political rule. The verse states: 'Fight those who do not believe in God nor in the Last Day and do not forbid what God and His messenger have forbidden and do not follow the religion of truth from among those who were given the Book until they proffer the *jizya* with [their] hands in humility.' *Jizya* refers to a kind of poll-tax levied on financially solvent male scriptuaries (primarily Jews and Christians, but also extended in practice to Zoroastrians and others), usually in exchange for exemption from military service (cf. Cengiz Kallek, 'Jizya'). Mujāhid's extant brief comment on this verse merely identifies the occasion of revelation as the battle of Tabūk in 8/630 (Mujāhid, *Tafsīr*, 99). Exegetes after him identify the referents in this verse as Jews and Christians in general who pay the *jizya* willingly and humbly in return for their protection by Muslim rulers (al-Ṭabarī, *al-Jāmiʿ*, 6:349–50). Al-Ṭabarī says that the historical context for the revelation of this verse was war with Byzantium, and soon thereafter Muḥammad undertook the campaign of Tabūk, as briefly referenced by Mujāhid. But unlike Mujāhid who indicates the warring Byzantine Christians as the referent in this verse, al-Ṭabarī treats Jews and Christians as undifferentiated collectivities, making no distinction between hostile and peaceable factions within them. Furthermore, their legal subjugation and general doctrinal inferiority to Muslims are stressed (al-Ṭabarī, *al-Jāmiʿ*, 6:349)—these views are consistently replicated by later exegetes, with the notable exception of al-Qurṭubī, who vigorously advocates for compassionate treatment of the People of the Book under the protection of Muslims (al-Qurṭubī, *al-Jāmiʿ* 8:106; cf. Afsaruddin 2013b: 75–9 for a range of exegetical views).

Based on the historical context provided in some of the sources for Q. 9:29, modern scholars like Muḥammad Ṭalʿat al-Ghunaimī have arrived at the conclusion that the verse contains a specific reference to the Byzantine Christians of the time hostile to Muslims and not to the People of the Book in general (al-Ghunaimī 1968: 170–1). Muhammad Abdel Haleem has pointed out that the Arabic partitive preposition *min* in the verse indicates that specific contingents from among the People of the Book who are wrongdoers are being referenced here and not Jews and Christians in their entirety (Abdel Haleem 2012: 75).

Cessation of Fighting and Peacemaking

Some pre-modern and modern scholars (discussed below) further make the case that the apparent harshness of the commandments contained in Q. 9:5 and 9:29 can be considerably ameliorated and their applicability limited to specific conditions by reading the Qur'an holistically and without invocation of the concept of abrogation. The Qur'an after all in addition to stating who can be fought against and for what reasons also unambiguously refers to those who cannot be fought against. Thus, in several verses, the Qur'an states that Muslims cannot fight non-Muslims who are peaceful and show no hostile intent towards them. One verse (Q. 4:90) states: 'If they hold themselves aloof from you and do not wage war against you and offer you peace, then God does not permit you any way against them.'

Two significant verses (Q. 60:8–9) mandate kind and just interactions with those who are peaceful, regardless of their religious beliefs, in contrast to those who willfully commit aggression:

> God does not forbid you from being kind and equitable to those who have neither made war on you on account of your religion nor driven you from your homes; indeed God loves those who are equitable. God forbids you however from making common cause with those who fight you on account of your religion and evict you from your homes and who support [others] in driving you out.

Al-Ṭabarī in his exegesis dismisses the suggestion of others that Q. 60:8–9 are abrogated; instead he affirms that they clearly permit Muslims to be kind to all those who bear no ill-will towards them, regardless of their religion and creed. For God, he says, loves those who are equitable, who give people their due rights, are personally just to them, and do good to those who are good to them (al-Ṭabarī, *al-Jāmiʿ*, 12:62–3). These views were repeated by practically all the exegetes who came after him; among the later exegetes, al-Qurṭubī is the most adamant in maintaining that the exhortation in Q. 60:8 to be kind to those who had caused Muslims no harm was applicable to everyone who belonged in this category, regardless of their religious affiliation, and that the command was unambiguous and valid (*muḥkama*) for all time (al-Qurṭubī, *al-Jāmiʿ*, 18:54–5; cf. Afsaruddin 2013b: 82–7).

Another important verse—Q. 8:61—requires Muslims to cease fighting as soon as the other side desists from fighting and makes peaceful overtures. The verse states, 'And if they should incline to peace, then incline to it [yourself] and place your trust in God; for He is all-hearing and all-knowing.' This point is stressed by al-Ṭabarī who comments that when a people enters into Islam, or pays the *jizya*, or establishes friendly relations with Muslims, then the latter should do the same 'for the sake of peace and peacemaking' (al-Ṭabarī, *al-Jāmiʿ*, 6:278). Al-Ṭabarī notes that the Successor Qatāda ibn

Diʿāma (d. 118/736) had maintained that this verse had been abrogated by Q. 9:5 and 9:36 but he himself dismisses this interpretation as insupportable on the basis of the Qur'an, the Sunna, or reason (al-Ṭabarī, *al-Jāmiʿ*, 6:278–9). The unabrogated status of the verse was similarly affirmed by a majority of exegetes after him (see this discussion in Afsaruddin 2013b: 90–3). Modern scholars in particular have emphasized the continuing applicability of these conciliatory verses and criticized the principle of abrogation that was applied to them by some pre-modern exegetes (Jamāl al-Banna 1984: 54–7; Jumʿa 2005: 22–4; Zuḥaylī 1981: 106–20; al-Dawoody 2011: 63–9).

Conclusion

Despite the multivalence of the Qur'anic term jihad (and other derivatives from its root), academic (and popular) discussions of this term overwhelmingly emphasize its military dimensions, which are then projected onto the Qur'anic text itself. A detailed survey of relevant Qur'anic verses establishes the multiple inflections of jihad. The non-combative dimensions of jihad are encapsulated by the term *ṣabr* (patient forbearance) particularly in the Meccan period to connote internal, personal striving to fulfil God's commandments, such as prayer; this term is also invoked in the Medinan period, sometimes in conjunction with fighting. *Ṣabr* therefore may be regarded as the constant feature of jihad understood as human striving in general while *qitāl* is its conditional feature, restricted to certain circumstances outlined by the Qur'an. Jihad is then the broad umbrella term which encompasses these different modes of human striving on earth. A close study of these Qur'anic terms and the various contexts in which they are deployed allow us to identify a broader semantic landscape for jihad and to revise and correct certain construals of this term that invariably highlight its military component.

Two verses in particular—Q. 9:5 and 9:29—have received disproportionate attention in academic and non-academic circles as corroborating the view that the Qur'an itself requires adult Muslim men to fight the military jihad against non-Muslims *qua* non-Muslims until they convert to Islam or submit to Muslim rule. As demonstrated above, a much broader and contested spectrum of exegetical views on the purview of these verses and their abrogating status existed in the pre-modern period. This has led a significant number of modern scholars, mostly Muslim, to stress that the Qur'an read holistically—without considering any of its verses to be abrogated—can be understood to clearly advocate peaceful relations among humans regardless of their religious beliefs. Fighting when undertaken for principled reasons—primarily in response to prior aggression by the enemy; its violation of treaties; and persecution of defenceless people—is defensive and limited in nature. The Qur'anic jihad is therefore most categorically not 'holy war;' it is rather a broad term that refers to human striving on earth in all its various dimensions.

Bibiliography

Abdel Haleem, M. A. S. 'The Sword Verse Myth [El mito del "versiculo de la espada"]'. In: Salvador Peña Marín and Miguel Hernando de Larramendi (eds.). *El Coran ayer y hoy [The Quran Yesterday and Today]*, pp. 307–40. Cordoba: Berenice, 2008.

Abdel Haleem, M. A. S. 'Qur'anic "*jihād*": A Linguistic and Contextual Analysis', *Journal of Qur'anic Studies* 12 (2010), 147–66.

Abdel Haleem, M. A. S. 'The *jizya* Verse (Q. 9:29): Tax Enforcement on Non-Muslims in the First Muslim State', *Journal of Qur'anic Studies* 14/2 (2012), 72–89.

Abū Zahra. *al-ʿAlāqāt al-dawliyya fī'l-islām*. Cairo: Al-Dār al-Qawmiyya li-'l-Ṭibāʿa wa'l-Nashr, 1964.

Afsaruddin, Asma. 'The Siyar Laws of Aggression: Juridical Re-Interpretations of Qur'anic Jihād and their Contemporary Implications for International Law'. In: Marie-Louisa Frick and Andreas Th. Müller (eds.). *Islam and International Law: Engaging Self-Centrism from a Plurality of Perspectives*, pp. 45–63. Leiden: Martinus Nijhoff, 2013a.

Afsaruddin, Asma. *Striving in the Path of God: Jihād and Martyrdom in Islamic Thought*. Oxford: Oxford University Press, 2013b.

al-Banna, Jamal. *al-Farīḍa al-gha'iba: jihād al-sayf am jihād al-ʿaql?* Cairo: Dār Thābit, 1984.

Bonner, Michael. *Jihād in Islamic History*. Princeton: Princeton University Press, 2006.

Bravmann, M. M. *The Spiritual Background of Early Islam: Studies on Ancient Arab Concepts*. Leiden: E. J. Brill, 2009.

Cook, David. *Understanding Jihād*. Berkeley: University of California Press, 2005.

Crone, Patricia. 'War'. In: Jane Dammen McAuliffe (ed.). *Encyclopaedia of the Qur'ān*. Leiden: E. J. Brill, 2006.

Al-Dawoody, Ahmed. *The Islamic Law of War: Justifications and Regulations*. New York: Palgrave Macmillan, 2011.

Esposito, John. *Unholy War: Terror in the Name of Islam*. Oxford: Oxford University Press, 2002.

Faraj, Muhammad ʿAbd al-Salam. *al-Farīḍa al-ghā'iba*. Trans. Johannes J. G. Jansen in his *The Neglected Duty: The Creed of Sadat's Assassins and Islamic Resurgence in the Middle East*. London: Macmillan, 1986.

Firestone, Reuven. *Jihād: The Origin of Holy War in Islam*. Oxford: Oxford University Press, 1999.

al-Ghazālī, Abu Ḥāmid. *Iḥyā 'ulūm al-dīn*. Ed. ʿAbd Allāh al-Khālidī. Beirut: Dār al-Arqam, n.d.

al-Ghunaimi, Mohammad Ṭalaat. *The Muslim Conception of International Law and Western Approach*. The Hague: Martinus Nijhoff, 1968.

Hamidullah, Muhammad. *Muslim Conduct of State*. Lahore: Sheikh Muhammad Ashraf, 1977.

Ibn Kathīr, Ismāʿīl ibn ʿUmar. *Tafsīr al-Qur'ān al-ʿaẓīm*. Beirut: Dār al-Jīl, 1990.

Ibn Qayyim al-Jawziyya. *ʿUddat al-ṣabirīn wa-dhakhīrat al-shakirīn*. Ed. Muḥammad ʿAlī Quṭb. Beirut: Sharikat Dār al-Arqam Ibn Abī al-Arqam, n.d.

Ibn Qudāma. *Kitāb al-Mughnī*. Ed. ʿAbd Allāh ibn ʿAbd al-Muḥsin al-Turkī and ʿAbd al-Fattāḥ Muḥammad al-Ḥilw. Cairo: Hajar, 1990.

Jumʿa, ʿAlī. *al-Jihād fī'l-islām*. Cairo: Nahḍat Miṣr li'l-Ṭibāʿa wa'l-Nashr wa'l-Tawzīʿ, 2005.

Kallek, Cengiz. 'Jizya', *Oxford Islamic Studies Online*, available at <http://www.oxfordislamicstudies.com/article/opr/t343/e0147&p=emailAsiI5AjhyEVc2&d=/opr/t343/e0147>; (last accessed 18 April 2019).

Khadduri, Majid. *War and Peace in the Law of Islam*. Baltimore: Johns Hopkins University Press, 1955.

Landau-Tasseron, Ella. 'Jihād'. In: Jane Dammen McAuliffe (ed.). *Encyclopaedia of the Qur'ān*. Leiden: E. J. Brill, 2003.
Lewis, Bernard. *The Political Language of Islam*. Chicago: University of Chicago Press, 1988.
Lewis, Bernard. *The Middle East: A Brief History of the Last 2,000 Years*. New York: Scribner, 1995.
Mahmassani, Sobhi. 'The Principles of International Law in the Light of Islamic Doctrine', *Recueil des cours* 117 (1966), 201–328.
al-Māwardī, *al-Ḥāwī al-kabīr fī fiqh madhhab al-imām al-Shāfiʿī raḍī Allāhu ʿanhu wa-huwa Sharḥ mukhtaṣar al-Muzanī*. Ed. ʿAli Muḥammad Muʿawwad and ʿĀdil Aḥmad ʿAbd al-Mawjūd. Beirut: Dār al-Kutub al-ʿArabiyya, 1994.
Morabia, Alfred, *Le Ğihâd dans l'Islam medieval: le combat sacré des origines au XIIeme siècle*. Paris: Albin Michel, 1993.
Mottahedeh, Roy and Ridwan al-Sayyid. 'The Idea of the Jihād in Islam before the Crusades'. In: Angeliki E. Laiou and Roy Parviz Mottahedeh (eds.). *The Crusades from the Perspective of Byzantium and the Muslim World*, pp. 23–9. Washington, DC: Dumbarton Oaks, 2001.
Mujāhid ibn Jabr. *Tafsīr Mujāhid*. Ed. Abū Muḥammad al-Asyūṭī. Beirut: Dār al-Kutub al-ʿIlmiyya, 2005.
Muqātil ibn Sulaymān. *Tafsīr Muqātil ibn Sulaymān*. Ed. ʿAbd Allāh Maḥmūd Shiḥāta. Beirut: Muʾassasat al-Taʾrīkh al- ʿArabī, 2002.
Peters, Rudolph. *Islam and Colonialism: The Doctrine of Jihād in Modern History*. The Hague: Mouton, 1979.
Peters, Rudolph. *Jihād in Classical and Modern Islam: A Reader*. Princeton: Markus Weiner, 1996.
Picken, Gavin. 'The "Greater" Jihād in Classical Islam'. In: Elisabeth Kendall and Ewan Stein (eds.). *Twenty-First Century Jihād: Law, Society, and Military Action*, pp. 126–38. London: I. B. Tauris, 2015.
al-Qaraḍāwī, Yūsuf. *Fiqh al-jihād: dirāsa muqāranah li-aḥkāmihi wa-falsafatihi fī ḍawʾ al-Qurʾān wa'l-Sunna*. Cairo: Maktabat Wahba, 2009.
al-Qurṭubī, Muḥammad ibn Aḥmad. *al-Jāmiʿ li-aḥkām al-Qurʾān*. Ed. ʿAbd al-Razzāq al-Mahdī. Beirut: Dār al-Kitāb al-ʿArabī, 2001.
al-Rāzī, Fakhr al-Dīn. *al-Tafsīr al-kabīr*. Beirut: Dār Iḥyāʾ al-Turāth al-ʿArabī, 1999.
Riḍā, Rashīd. *Tafsīr al-Manār*. Beirut: Dār al-Kutub al-ʿIlmiyya, 1999.
Rubin, Uri. 'Barāʾa: A Study of Some Quranic Passages', *Jerusalem Studies in Arabic and Islam* 5 (1984), 13–32.
Sachedina, Abdulaziz A. 'The Development of Jihād in Islamic Revelation and History'. In: James Turner Johnson and John Kelsay (eds.). *Cross, Crescent, and Sword: The Justification and Limitation of War in Western and Islamic Tradition*, pp. 35–50. New York: Greenwood, 1990.
Sahnūn. *Al-Mudawwana al-Kubrā*. Ed. Ḥamdī al-Damardash Muḥammad. Beirut: al-Maktaba al-ʿAṣriyya, 1999.
al-Sarakhsī. *Kitāb al-Mabsūṭ*. Ed. Muḥammad Ḥasan Muḥammad Ḥasan Ismāʿīlī al-Shāfiʿī. Beirut: Dār al-Kutub al-ʿIlmiyya, n.d.
Shaltūt, Maḥmūd. *Al-Islām wa'l-ʿalaqāt al-dawliyya: fi'l-silm wa'l-ḥarb*. Cairo: Maktab Shaykh al-Jāmiʿ al-Azhar li'l-Shuʾūn al-ʿĀmma, n.d.
al-Sulamī, ʿIzz al-Dīn. *Aḥkām al-jihād wa-faḍāʾilihi*. Ed. ʿIyāḍ Khālid al-Tabbāʿ. Beirut: Dār al-Fikr al-Muʿāṣir, 1996.
al-Ṭabarī, Muḥammad ibn Jarīr. *Jāmiʿ al-bayān ʿan taʾwīl ayy al-Qurʾān*. Beirut: Dār al-Kutub al-ʿIlmiyya, 1997.

Tyan, Emile. 'Djihād'. In: B. Lewis et al. (eds.). *The Encyclopaedia of Islam*. Second edition, 2:538–40. Leiden: E. J. Brill, 1998.

al-Wāḥidī, ʿAlī ibn Aḥmad. *al-Wasīṭ fī tafsīr al-Qurʾān*. Ed. ʿĀdil Aḥmad ʿAbd al-Mawjūd. Beirut: Dār al-Kutub al-ʿIlmiyya, 1994.

Watt, W. Montgomery. 'Islamic Conceptions of the Holy War'. In: Thomas P. Murphy (ed.). *Holy War*. Columbus: Ohio State University Press, 1976.

al-Zamakhsharī, Maḥmūd ibn ʿUmar. *al-Kashshāf ʿan ḥaqāʾiq ghawāmiḍ al-tanzīl wa-ʿuyūn al-aqāwīl fī wujūh al-taʾwīl*. Ed. ʿĀdil Aḥmad ʿAbd al-Mawjūd and ʿAlī Muḥammad Muʿawwad. Riyadh: Maktabat al-ʿUbaykan, 1998.

al-Zuḥaylī, Wahba. *Athar al-ḥarb fī'l-fiqh al-Islamī: dirāsa muqārana*. Beirut: Dār al-Fikr, 1981.

CHAPTER 34

WOMEN AND THE QUR'AN

ASMA AFSARUDDIN

IN roughly the third or fourth year of the Islamic era (corresponding to 625–6 CE), the Medinan woman Companion Umm ʿUmāra from the first generation of Muslims is said to have remarked to the Prophet Muḥammad in connection with the Qur'anic revelations he had received up to that point, 'I see that everything pertains to men; I do not see the mention of women.' According to variant accounts, it was Umm Salama, the Prophet's wife, who wondered out loud why the revelation appeared to be primarily concerned with men. Regardless of who the Prophet's interlocutor was, the question posed to him foregrounded the concern that an explicit lack of reference to women believers might lead to the assumption that only men had a role to play in human soteriology and only their good deeds would earn fulsome rewards in the hereafter. Were women believers not to be recognized as equal participants in the grand unfolding drama of human agency, fulfilment, and salvation?

Our sources refer to this event as the 'occasion of revelation' for the following critical Qur'anic verse:

> Those who have surrendered to God among males and females; those who believe among males and females; those who are sincere among males and females; those who are truthful among males and females; those who are patient among males and females; those who fear God among males and females; those who give in charity among males and females; those who fast among males and females; those who remember God often among males and females—God has prepared for them forgiveness and great reward. (Q. 33:35)

In response to the female Companion's anxious query, this Qur'anic verse took an unequivocal position: women and men have equal moral and spiritual agency in their quest for the good and righteous life in this world for which they reap identical rewards in the afterlife. The other-worldly salvific efficacy offered by the Qur'an through its prescription for the well-ordered moral existence on earth was not inflected by gender. Muslim feminist scholars frequently point to this verse to underscore what they understand to be the uncompromising gender egalitarianism inherent in the Qur'an.

A common complaint on the part of these same scholars is that despite this verse and others like it, scriptural exegesis undertaken almost exclusively by men in the pre-modern period has all but occluded the gender egalitarianism of the Qur'an and undermined the impact of its gender-inclusive language. This has led to the creation of a moral and religious paradigm which privileges the male over the female and accords to the former 'guardianship' over the latter. As examples of such androcentric exegesis, they point to commentaries generated by male exegetes on specific verses that refer to male–female relations which have become influential and authoritative over the centuries.

One such cluster of verses refers to the creation of Adam and his wife before their earthly existence (Q. 2:30–9; 7:11–27; 15:26–43; 20:115–24; and 38:71–85). In contradistinction to biblical accounts, Adam's wife (unnamed in the Qur'an but named Ḥawwāʾ [Eve] in the exegetical literature) is not singled out for exclusive blame in these Qur'anic verses for having caused the 'Fall' of humankind. Instead, it is noteworthy that the Qur'an either (a) blames Adam exclusively for the Fall or (b) blames Adam and his wife equally for giving in to the blandishments of Satan. On balance, Adam in the Qur'an is the one who is morally culpable for failing to heed God's injunctions and succumbing to wrong-doing. He is however forgiven by God and both he and his wife are given equal opportunity to redeem themselves by establishing a righteous and God-fearing community on earth. In its creation accounts, the Qur'an therefore does not assign any kind of ontological moral failing to the woman companion of Adam and thus by extension to womankind in general (Hassan 1985: 124–55; Stowasser 1994: 25–38).

Recuperation of the meaning of these Qur'anic verses concerning Adam and his wife is highly important for it provides a corrective to a very different story that emerges from the prolific exegetical literature (*tafsīr*) concerning them. Commentaries from after the third/ninth century reveal that the Qur'anic assignment of blame primarily to Adam in the creation accounts proved unpalatable to a number of later Muslim male exegetes and they deliberately imported the biblical creation story into their interpretations to reassign the blame to his wife, whom they now call Eve. In addition to Eve's culpability, the creation story found in Genesis also refers to the story of her creation from the rib of Adam which allows one to conclude that the female is secondary to the male as a human being. Through the medium of hadith and the general importation of the *isrāʾīliyyāt* (materials relating to biblical stories and Jewish and Christian sacred history) into the *tafsīr* literature, the story of Eve's creation from Adam's rib took deep root in Muslim exegeses by al-Ṭabarī's time, especially since its overall implications nicely accorded with the growing patriarchalization of society in the third/ninth century.

Such exegetical construals are markedly in contrast to what the Qur'an actually states concerning the creation of humankind. The relevant verse is:

> O humankind! Be careful of your duty to your Lord Who created you from a single soul (*nafs wāḥida*) and from it created its mate and from the two a multitude of men and women has spread. (Q. 4:1)

Simultaneous creation from the *nafs wāḥida*, as described in this verse, negates the possibility of the male being granted an ontologically superior status by virtue of having been created first, from whose body is then derived the woman's. The Qur'an thus clearly undermines the notion of a hierarchical relationship between man and woman and grants them instead complete ontological equality.

Woman's Moral Agency in the Qur'an

Culturally derived attitudes which progressively undermined women's equal status in society in the formative period of Islam stand in tension with several passages in the Qur'an that affirm women's moral agency equal to that of men. A critical verse in the Qur'an (9:71) establishes equal and complementary moral agency for both men and women. The verse states:

> (Male) believers (*al-muʾminūn*) and (female) believers (*al-muʾmināt*) are the natural partners (*awliyāʾ*) of one another; they command the good and forbid wrong and they perform prayer, give the obligatory alms, and obey God and His messenger. They are those upon whom God has mercy; indeed God is Almighty, Wise.

Semantically, the obvious intent of the verse is to establish parity between men and women as partners in the common venture to promote the good, righteous society on earth and in the fulfilment of their individual and communal obligations towards God. As obvious as this meaning may seem to us, male interpreters from the pre-modern and modern periods have understood this verse in ways that more often than not were consonant with their own particular views of proper male–female relations and, especially from the Abbasid period on, subversive of its egalitarian thrust (Ahmed 1993; al-Hibri 1982: 207–19).

In the pre-modern period, the early exegete Muqātil ibn Sulaymān (d. 150/767) asserts the full and equal partnership of female and male believers in matters of religion (*fi'l-dīn*) and highlights their mutually reinforcing obedience to God in this verse (Muqātil ibn Sulaymān, *Tafsīr* 2:181). The celebrated late third-/ninth-century exegete al-Ṭabarī (d. 310/923) from the Abbasid period similarly emphasizes that righteous men and women 'who believe in God, His messenger and the verses of His book are each other's allies and supporters'. Their fundamental duty to promote what is right and prevent what is wrong consists in inviting people to monotheism and to abandon the worship of idols, and to carry out their fundamental religious obligations, such as offering prayers and paying alms (al-Ṭabarī, *al-Jāmiʿ*, 6:415). Similar views are offered by al-Wāḥidī (d. 468/1075) (al-Wāḥidī, *al-Wasīṭ*, 2:509) and al-Qurṭubī (d. 671/1273); the last, on the basis of this verse, characterizes the relationship between men and women as one of 'hearts united in mutual affection, love, and empathy' (al-Qurṭubī, *al-Jāmiʿ*, 8:186). The influential exegete Ibn Kathīr (d. 774/1373) in the eighth/fourteenth century also comments on the special bond existing among believers and invokes the hadith in which the Prophet describes the faithful as constituting 'a [single] edifice in which each strengthens the other' (Ibn Kathīr, *Tafsīr*, 2:353). Worthy of note is that Ibn Kathīr uses however only the masculine noun for believers (*al-muʾminīn*) in his commentary, in stark contrast to our earlier commentators who repeated the masculine and the feminine plural nouns occurring in Q. 9:71 that refer explicitly to believers of both sexes.

In the modern period, Rashīd Riḍā in the Qur'an commentary *Tafsīr al-Manār* states that the *wilāya* that exists, according to this verse, between believing women and men has to do in general with mutual support, solidarity, and affection. He goes further than his pre-modern predecessors in asserting that men and women collaborate equally in defending truth, justice, the community, and the nation, except in the realm of military defence of the polity, which remains a masculine preserve (Riḍā 1990: 10:471; see further Afsaruddin 2015: 89–92).

Male Guardianship Over Women?

Whereas Q. 9:71 has typically not been the focus of extensive exegetical attention, another verse—Q. 4:34—has been, and continues to be, the subject of prolific exegeses. The verb *qawwāmān* that occurs in the verse is deliberately left untranslated below because of its contested meanings, as we discuss shortly. Another verb in the verse that can be read either as *wa-ḍribuhunna* (majority classical reading) or *wa-ʾaḍribuhunna* (minority modern, particularly feminist, reading) is translated to reflect both possible meanings. The verse states,

> Men are *qawwāmūn* over women because God has preferred some of them over others and because of what they spend of their wealth. Virtuous women are devout, preserving that which is hidden according to what God has preserved. As for those women whose recalcitrance (*nushūz*) may be feared, reprimand them, banish them to their beds, and strike/avoid them. And if they obey you, then do not misbehave towards them at all; indeed God is majestic and great.

The Umayyad-era exegete Muqātil ibn Sulaymān proceeds to explain that *qawwāmūn* in this verse means that men have been granted general authority over women and that men have been granted greater rights over women by virtue of the fact that they pay the bridal gift (*mahr*) to them. Men also exercise their authority in regard to general discipline (*fī'l-adab*) according to this verse. The rest of the verse refers to virtuous women who are obedient (*qānitāt*) to God and *to their husbands* (emphasis added) and who guard their private parts and their wealth in the absence of their husbands. As for those who manifest disobedience (*nushūz*) to their husbands, comments Muqātil, they should first of all be given a warning, followed by abstention from intercourse with them. If these two measures do not achieve the desired result, then the wife may be struck in a way that does not cause any agony or disfigurement (*ghayr mubarriḥ yaʿnī ghayr shāʾin*). Once she has returned to proper wifely obedience, then she should not be burdened with showing affection to her husband 'more than she is capable of' (Muqātil, *Tafsīr*, 1:370–1).

Muqātil's exegesis became very influential and has been reproduced in many commentaries after him. Al-Ṭabarī in the late third/ninth to early fourth/tenth century refers to the occasion of revelation listed by Muqātil and provides it with several chains of transmission, thus documenting its widespread dissemination (al-Ṭabarī, *Jāmiʿ*, 4:60–1). In reference to the Arabic word *qānitāt* that occurs in the verse, al-Ṭabarī cites several authorities who understand it to mean women who are obedient to both God and their husbands. As for the women's *nushūz*, it consists of their haughtiness towards their husbands, 'rising up from their [husbands'] beds in disobedience', and contradicting their husbands in matters in which they should be obedient. This understanding, al-Ṭabarī notes, is consistent with the etymology of the Arabic word *nushūz*, which has to do with 'elevation'. Other authorities cited by al-Ṭabarī offer similar meanings. One early source however—ʿAṭāʾ ibn Abī Rabāḥ (d. 115/733)—maintained significantly that *nushūz* applied equally to the wife and husband and referred to the desire of each to separate from the other (al-Ṭabarī, *Jāmiʿ*, 4:62–4).

Al-Ṭabarī then elaborates upon what he understands to be the distinctive steps recommended by the Qur'an for dealing with a recalcitrant wife. Briefly, the first step for the husband is to counsel the wife to remember God and return to the marital bed. If the wife should fail to heed this counsel, the next step is for the husband to desist from having sexual relations with her and sleeping apart from her and/or avoid speaking to her. Should these first two steps not suffice, then the husband may lightly beat her (*ḍarabahā ghayr mubarriḥ*) which leaves no marks on the body until she returns to a state of wifely obedience; this was the predominant interpretation attributed to Ibn ʿAbbās and others. A more detailed commentary from Ibn ʿAbbās warns against striking the wife to the extent of breaking her bones, whether she acquiesces to her husband's entreaties or not. If she is physically hurt, then the husband must pay a compensation (*fidya*) for her injuries. Ibn ʿAbbās is also the main source for the view that a 'light beating' amounted to a more or less symbolic tapping with the equivalent of a toothbrush (*siwāk*). Al-Ṭabarī concludes by asserting that once the wife has returned to obedience, the husband is obligated to fulfil his duties towards her and he may not seek to cause her any kind of physical or emotional harm (al-Ṭabarī, Jāmiʿ, 4:465–71).

Similar interpretations are recorded by al-Wāḥidī in the fifth/eleventh century (al-Wāḥidī, *al-Wasīṭ*, 2:46–7) and al-Rāzī in the sixth/twelfth century (al-Rāzī, *Tafsīr*, 4:70–3) but with some noteworthy developments. In comparison with earlier exegetes who had emphasized the functional superiority of men over women primarily in a domestic context, both al-Wāḥidī and al-Rāzī now attribute an additional ontological superiority to men over women. Furthermore, al-Rāzī's list of reasons why men *qua* men are to be understood as superior to women has grown longer. Not only is the man able to work harder, and more skilled in writing, horsemanship, and spear-throwing, he also reminds that the prophets and scholars are all men, as are the rulers, prayer leaders, callers to prayers, orators, and so forth (al-Rāzī, *Tafsīr*, 4:70).

This ontological sense of male superiority over the female, in addition to the functional one, now becomes pervasive in the exegetical literature, as affirmed by al-Qurṭubī in the seventh/thirteenth century (al-Qurṭubī, *al-Jāmiʿ* 5:161–7). Ibn Kathīr in the eighth/fourteenth century also leaves no doubt that the guardianship that men are assumed to enjoy over women, based on Q. 4:34, is one of unassailable authority over every aspect of the latter's existence and conduct. The words he uses, largely unprecedented in comparison with previous exegeses, in order to describe this aggrandized hierarchical relationship are revealing of the extent to which the marital bond between man and woman has been reconfigured as one of essential domination and subjugation. Thus the man has become the woman's 'head' (*raʾsuhā*); her 'elder' (*kabīruhā*), her 'ruler/judge' *(al-ḥākim ʿalayhā)* and her 'discipliner if she should stray' (*muʿadhdhibuhā idhā iʿwajat*). Ibn Kathīr adduces as an authoritative proof-text the solitary report recorded by al-Bukhārī in which the Prophet warns that a nation governed by a woman will not prosper. This is a new proof-text that we encounter in Ibn Kathīr's commentary in the context of this verse, which is clearly being deployed to warn against the consequences of letting women get 'the upper hand' in any manner or form (not just in the domestic sphere) in relation to men. It is also in his commentary that we see the clearest iteration of the absolute nature of man's superiority over woman by virtue of being male (*fa-'l-rajul afḍal min al-marʾa fī nafsihi*) (Ibn Kathīr, *Tafsīr* 1:465).

Not surprisingly, Ibn Kathīr, like al-Wāḥidī, al-Rāzī, and al-Qurṭubī before him, glosses the *qānitāt* solely as women who are obedient to their husbands, citing Ibn ʿAbbās 'and others' as his source. He does not list the alternative interpretation, more prevalent in the earlier period, that it is a reference to women who are obedient to God as well. The nature of this unconditional obedience of wives to their husbands is driven home by the purported hadith in which Muḥammad declares, 'If I were to command anyone to prostrate himself before another [person], it would be the wife before her husband on account of the rights he enjoys in relation to her' (Ibn Kathīr 1990: 1:66). We had not encountered this hadith previously as proof-text in the exegetical discussions of Ibn Kathīr's predecessors, proving to us once again that male authoritarian attitudes towards women in the later period were progressively projected back to the time of the Prophet in the form of hadiths attributed to him, creating a powerful legitimizing source for such changed sensibilities (Abou El Fadl 2001: 65–6).

In the modern period, Riḍā very clearly articulates both the ontological and functional reasons for the superiority of the man over the woman. He introduces the word *fiṭrī* (ontological) in relation to certain attributes that are unique to men and which establish their preferred status vis-à-vis women. Riḍā also proceeds to reference the views of Muḥammad ʿAbdūh who had stated that the guardianship (*qiyāma*) of the husband over the wife did not imply that the latter was subjugated (*maqhūr*) and robbed of her will in general. Rather, the husband acts as a guide and counsellor for the general welfare of the family. The *qānitāt* are women who are obedient to God as well as to their husbands in matters which require their obedience (*bi'l-maʿrūf*). As for *nushūz*, Riḍā, like most of his predecessors, understands it as referring to the wife's 'rising up' in disobedience to her husband and denying him his rights over her. As before, he indicates the progressive stages available to the husband to bring his recalcitrant wife into line and takes care to emphasize that the final stage involves only a light beating. Such a situation is understood to be exceptional and represents a last resort for the restoration of domestic harmony (Riḍā, *al-Manār*, 5:55–63). Riḍā quotes ʿAbdūh in this context, who had stressed that the normal state of marital relations should be characterized by 'gentleness towards women, refraining from oppressing them, and treating them with respect and dignity' (Riḍā, *al-Manār*, 5:61).

It is worthy of note that when a majority of the exegetes above resorted to talking about the ontological superiority of the male over the female, they did not temper their discussion by referring to, for example, Q. 33:35, which posits the unequivocal spiritual and moral equality of men and women, or to Q. 9:71, which refers to the mutual partnership of men and women and their equal moral agency on the basis of righteousness. In fact the scant attention paid by most pre-modern male exegetes to these otherwise critical verses in comparison with the lavish attention given to Q. 4:34 is very revealing of the gendered identities and relationships envisioned by them through time. It is not until the modern period—when we encounter the exegeses of women scholars in particular who tend to focus on cross-referential reading of the Qur'an—that we are exposed to the fuller potential of Q. 33:35, 9:71, and other related verses, to ameliorate the narrow, androcentric readings of particularly their pre-modern male counterparts.

Feminist Hermeneutics of the Modern and Contemporary Periods

Beginning in the twentieth century, Muslim feminist scholars started going back to the Qur'anic text itself in order to circumvent what they perceived as the distinctively woman-unfriendly exegeses of specific verses generated by many influential male scholars. These feminist scholars hoped thereby to retrieve what they believed to be the original egalitarian élan of the Qur'an itself. Through their egalitarian lens, these women exegetes offer critiques of traditional methodologies of engaging the Qur'an and offer 'alternative' readings of verses that deal specifically with gendered relations. Their exegeses underscore the polyvalence of the Qur'anic text and the possibilities of extracting multiple meanings from scripture based on specific reading strategies that are fully cognizant of historical contexts and of the frequently broad semantic spectrum of key terms and concepts.

Thus, the well-known feminist exegete Amina Wadud suggests adopting what she calls a 'hermeneutics of *tawḥīd*', referring to a holistic method of reading the Qur'an that specifically challenged the line-by-line atomistic method of interpretation that was so popular among many medieval exegetes (and remains so till today). If the Qur'anic claim of establishing a 'universal basis for moral guidance' is to be taken seriously, comments Wadud, then Muslim exegetes must develop a hermeneutical framework that leads to 'a systematic rationale for making correlations [among Qur'anic verses] and [which] sufficiently exemplifies the full impact of Qur'anic coherence' (Wadud 1999: xii). Universals (*ʿāmm*) and particulars (*khāṣṣa*) must be distinguished from one another; time- and place-bound interpretations must be recognized as such and their limited applicability recognized. Wadud's interpretive venture is thus fundamentally concerned with retrieving an unending 'trajectory of social, political, and moral possibilities' that remain consistent with the overall 'Qur'anic ethos of equity, justice, and human dignity' in changing historical and socio-political circumstances (Wadud 1999: xii–xiii).

Asma Barlas similarly emphasizes the development of a new Qur'anic hermeneutics that would effectively challenge and undermine traditional understandings of key Qur'anic verses related to gender and women's roles in society. Barlas remarks, 'if we wish to ensure Muslim women their rights, we not only need to contest readings of the Qur'an that justify the abuse and degradation of women, we also need to establish the legitimacy of liberatory readings' (Barlas 2004: 3). In order to retrieve such an egalitarian perspective from within the Qur'anic text, Barlas and other contemporary feminist exegetes have typically resorted to a holistic reading of the text so that single verses, especially those that appear to be promoting gender inequity, may be read in conjunction with other verses that are thematically and semantically related, allowing for the emergence of other interpretive possibilities. A classic example of this would be the term *nushūz*, which, as we saw in reference to Q. 4:34, was understood primarily as a reference to a woman's arrogant demeanour and behaviour towards her husband by the male exegetes. Only one very early source—ʿAṭāʾ ibn Abī Rabāḥ—is quoted by al-Ṭabarī as understanding *nushūz* to refer to a constellation of negative traits in *both* men and women.

ʿAṭāʾ may have been among our very early feminist readers of the Qur'an who preferred to read the text cross-referentially because the Qur'an does in fact refer to *nushūz* on the part of both men and women. The corresponding verse in regard to men is Q. 4:128, which states, 'If a woman fears *nushūz* or rejection (*iʿrāḍ*) from her husband, there is no blame on them if they reach a settlement, and settlement is better, even though people's souls are miserly.' Al-Ṭabarī understands *nushūz* on the part of the husband to be similar to *nushūz* on the part of the wife—that it is an attitude of haughtiness and pride towards one's spouse and expression of distaste towards her, whether it is on account of her lack of comeliness, advancing years, or other reasons. *Iʿrāḍ* consists of turning away from her with his face or withholding certain benefits that she is accustomed to receiving from him. In such cases, the couple is exhorted to seek arbitration and reconciliation which, he comments, is better than separation and/or divorce (al-Ṭabarī, *al-Jāmiʿ*, 4:304ff.).

Highly noteworthy is the fact that even though the same term is used in both verses and may be understood to imply the same basic meaning in relation to the husband and wife, none of the exegetes discussed above referred to Q. 4:128 in connection with Q. 4:34. Instead, they showed a clear preference for explaining the term solely as it occurs in the latter verse to sharply demarcate gendered differences, with the earliest commentators delineating these differences within the domestic sphere, progressing to al-Ṭabarī and his successors, who extrapolated broad ontological differences between the male and the female. The result was the idealization of a highly patriarchal family with *nushūz* implying primarily wifely disobedience to her husband, who wielded considerable authority over her physical and emotional well-being. Reading the two verses which contain the term *nushūz* together allows one to retrieve a much more egalitarian and reciprocal concept of marital rights and duties.

The imperative *wa-ḍribuhunna* in Q. 4:34 provokes similar feminist anxiety—how can the concept of a loving, equal, and peaceful union between wife and husband be justified when the man possesses the exclusive right to 'beat' her (Chaudhry 2014: 1–22)? It is clear that the verb elicited concern on the part of the classical male jurists as well who did not under any circumstance condone violent retribution against the wilful and recalcitrant wife—a light tapping that caused no physical injury was the maximum discipline as a last resort that was practically unanimously considered permissible by them. The practice of this husbandly 'duty' did not then amount to wife battery, which the scholars regarded as a criminal, reprehensible activity and for which the husband would be required to pay a compensation to his wife.

At best a symbolic physical chastising, *ḍaraba* in the sense of beating—however light—still remains problematic for many Muslim feminist exegetes today. Surely, a number of them ask, an immensely just and infinitely benevolent God would not sanction an act that even hints at physical violence and implies a skewed relationship of power between the husband and wife? The answer for these scholars to such a theodicean question appears to lie in the rich polysemy of the Arabic root *ḍ-r-b* : besides to beat, the root in its various derivative forms can also mean to avoid or shun someone or to have sexual relations with a person. Thus, the two most plausible alternative meanings that could be applied to the imperative as occurs in this verse are (indicated in bold): (a) as for those women whose *nushūz* may be feared, reprimand them, banish them to their beds and **have sex with them**; and (b) as for those women whose *nushūz* may be feared, reprimand them, banish them to their beds and **avoid them/leave them alone**. The second meaning is generated by understanding the imperative as being derived from the fourth verbal form *aḍraba* rather than from the first verbal form *ḍaraba*; a slight change in orthography (with the addition of the *hamza* to the initial *alif*) credibly leads to the meaning of 'leave them alone' (Bakhtiar 2007: xxvi). This last reinterpretation is quite popular among a minority of feminist exegetes, women and men, because it further satisfactorily accords with what is known of Muḥammad's conduct towards his wives, whom he is not known to have ever struck or addressed harshly (Mernissi 1993: 155; Myrne 2014: 272–5).

Another verse (Q. 2:223) which reads, 'Your women are a tilth for you, so approach your tilth as you will and send [good deeds] in advance for your souls,' has been typically understood by male exegetes to imply that women are the sexual property of men. Feminist exegetes have argued that this masculinist reading can be circumvented by bringing in other relevant verses in this context that convey a fuller sense of the equal, complementary roles that men and women are expected to assume within an Islamic marriage. Prominent among them is Q. 2:187 which reads, '[wives] are your garments and you [husbands] are their garments'. 'Garments' (*libās*) here is understood to be a metaphor for mutual comfort and joy and the equal rights shared by wives and husbands vis-à-vis one another in the marital relationship. Another equally relevant verse is Q. 30:21 which states, 'And among His signs is this, that He has created for you mates from among yourselves, that you may dwell in tranquility with them; and He has put love and mercy between you,' as well as the aforementioned Q. 9:71 in which believing men and women are described as the equal partners or allies of one another. Read in conjunction with these verses, Q. 2:223 then is more properly interpreted not as mandating an unequal relationship between husbands and wives, but pointing to two of the fundamental purposes of the marital union within Islam—the enjoyment of licit sexual pleasure and generation of offspring. Feminist exegetes argue that there is nothing in the specific language of the verse to indicate—*prima facie*—that biological differences in themselves amount to an unequal relationship between the husband and wife. As Barlas comments, 'the Qur'an does not use sex to construct ontological or sociological hierarchies that discriminate against women' (Barlas 2004: 165).

As we know from our sources, such a holistic reading was not prevalent among pre-modern male exegetes of the Qur'an, who like other Muslim scholars, particularly jurists, regarded the patriarchal model of familial and marital relations as the ideal, no doubt because it was in conformity with the prevailing cultural notions and sensibilities of their day. Historicizing juridical and exegetical discourses as specific products of their time and milieu that often subverted the fundamental Qur'anic ethos of justice and equality is a major driving force behind feminist hermeneutics, and, one may add, its most persuasive and compelling feature.

Bibiliography

Primary Sources

Ibn Kathīr, Ismāʿīl ibn ʿUmar. *Tafsīr al-Qurʾān al-ʿaẓīm*. Beirut: Dār al-Jīl, 1990.

Muqātil ibn Sulaymān, *Tafsīr Muqātil ibn Sulaymān*. Ed. ʿAbd Allah Maḥmūd Shiḥāta. Beirut: Muʾassasat Taʾrīkh Al-ʿArabī, 2002.

al-Qurṭubī, Muḥammad ibn Aḥmad. *Al-Jāmiʿ li-aḥkām al-Qurʾān*. Ed. ʿAbd al-Razzāq al-Mahdī. Beirut: Dār al-Kitāb al-ʿArabī, 2001.

al-Rāzī, Fakhr al-Dīn. *Al-Tafsīr al-kabīr*. Beirut: Dār Iḥyāʾ al-Turāth al-ʿArabī, 1999.

Riḍā, Rashīd. *Tafsīr al-Manār*. Beirut: Dār al-Kutub al-ʿIlmiyya, 1999.

al-Ṭabarī, Muḥammad ibn Jarīr. *Jāmiʿ al-bayān ʿan taʾwīl ayy al-Qurʾān*. Beirut: Dār al-Kutub al-ʿIlmiyya, 1997.

al-Wāḥidī, ʿAlī ibn Aḥmad. *Al-Wasīṭ fī tafsīr al-Qurʾān*. Ed. ʿĀdil Aḥmad ʿAbd al-Mawjūd. Beirut: Dār al-Kutub al-ʿIlmiyya, 1994.

Secondary Sources

Abou El Fadl, Khaled. *And God Knows the Soldiers: The Authoritative and the Authoritarian in Islam*. Lanham, MD: University Press of America, 2001.

Afsaruddin, Asma. *Contemporary Issues in Islam*. Edinburgh: Edinburgh University Press, 2015.

Ahmed, Leila. *Women and Gender in Islam.* New Haven, CT: Yale University Press, 1993.
Bakhtiar, Laleh. *The Sublime Quran.* Chicago: Kazi Publications, 2007.
Barlas, Asma. *'Believing Women' in Islam: Unreading Patriarchal Interpretations of the Qur'an.* Austin: University of Texas Press, 2004.
Chaudhry, Ayesha S. *Domestic Violence and the Islamic Tradition.* Oxford: Oxford University Press, 2014.
Hassan, Rifaat. '"Made from Adam's Rib": The Woman's Creation Question', *al-Mushir* (1985), 124–55.
al-Hibri, Azizah. 'A Study of Islamic Herstory: Or How Did We Ever Get into This Mess?' In: *Women's Studies International Forum*, pp. 207–19. Oxford: Pergamon Press, 1982.
Mernissi, Fatima. *The Veil and the Male Elite: A Feminist Interpretation of Women's Rights in Islam.* Trans. Mary Jo Lakeland. Reading, MA: Addison-Wesley Publishing Co., 1993.
Myrne, Pernilla. 'Husband'. In Adam Walker and Coeli Fitzpatrick (eds.). *Muhammad in History, Thought, and Culture: An Encyclopedia of the Prophet of God.* Santa Barbara, CA: ABC-CLIO, 2014.
Stowasser, Barbara. *Women in the Qur'an, Traditions, and Interpretation.* Oxford: Oxford University Press, 1994.
Wadud, Amina. *Qur'an and Woman: Rereading the Sacred Text from a Woman's Perspective.* Oxford: Oxford University Press, 1999.

PART VI

THE QUR'AN IN CONTEXT: TRANSLATION AND CULTURE

CHAPTER 35

TRANSLATIONS OF THE QUR'AN: WESTERN LANGUAGES

ZIAD ELMARSAFY

Chronological Survey

The history of the translation of the Qur'an into Western languages is the product of multiple variables, including military conflict, religious polemic, and the advancement of learning, which was itself the product of complex institutional histories and politics writ large. None of this, however, prevented the translated Qur'an from being something of a long-term bestseller in Europe (Burman 2007: 1). One of the earliest and best-known surviving translations of the Qur'an emerged from the twelfth-century Renaissance; a period during which numerous Arabic works were translated into Latin. Robert of Ketton's *Lex Mahumet pseudoprophete* (*The Law of Muhammad the Pseudo-Prophet*), commissioned as part of an anthology co-ordinated by Peter the Venerable, presents a translation of the text of the Qur'an with numerous additions and interpolations to guide the Western reader through its complexities, framed by historical, biographical, and theological works, the whole intended to give a complete idea of Islam based on Arabic sources. In spite of its hostile tone and numerous inaccuracies, the Toledan Collection (alias the Cluniac Corpus, 1142–3) and Robert's version of the Qur'an became standard references for the Western understanding of Islam for several centuries, despite the existence of later, more accurate translations of the Qur'an into Latin.

Robert's approach—calling the Qur'an the 'Law of Muḥammad' rather than 'the liturgy' or 'the Book' of the Muslims, as well as his prioritizing the content rather than the form of the text—would set the tone for future Western translations of the Qur'an. Future translators would also adopt prescribed polemical roles in order to portray Islam in a negative light, while simultaneously paying careful attention to the text under scrutiny with the tools available (Burman 2007: 3). Since the word 'Qur'an' connoted controversy in many circles, especially in light of conflict between Muslims and non-Muslims, translators sometimes felt compelled to sharpen their attacks on Muḥammad and the Qur'an lest they be mistaken for Muslim sympathizers, often using prefaces, marginalia, notes, and illustrations as ways of compromising with the authorities and protecting themselves (Hamilton 2008).

Robert's translation would go on to become the first printed translation of the Qur'an. In 1543 Theodor Bibliander published a revised version of Robert's translation as part of a three-volume reference work entitled *Machumetis Saracenorum principis vita ac doctrina omnis* (*The Life and Teachings of Machumet, Prince of the Saracens*) (Bobzin 1995: 181–239). Bibliander claimed that his motive was to show where real heresy lay in the ongoing Catholic–Protestant polemic (Burman 2007: 111–13). The work is prefaced by Luther, together with a letter by Philip Melanchthon and an apology by Bibliander—a necessity in view of the authorities' opposition to its publication. Here Bibliander argues that although the Qur'an contained much that was heretical, it should not be ignored. Other parts of the Toledan Collection are included, as are countless refutations of Muslim doctrine by various hands. By the mid-sixteenth century, therefore, the translation of the Qur'an is not only a printed text that circulates widely in the Europe, it has also become part and parcel of polemics *within* Christianity. The existence of this text quickly engendered further translations into European vernacular languages. In 1547 Andrea Arrivabene retranslated Bibliander's Latin Qur'an into Italian (while claiming, falsely, to have produced a new translation from the Arabic text), and in 1616 Salomon Schweigger retranslated Arrivabene's retranslation from Italian into German under the title, *Der Türken Alkoran*, thereby indicating the extent to which 'Muslim' and 'Turk' were now synonymous (as opposed to the previously widespread term 'Saracen') as a result of the Ottoman military threat in central Europe. In 1641, an anonymous Dutch translator retranslated Schweigger's retranslation of Arrivabene's retranslation of Bibliander's version of Robert of Ketton's translation of the Qur'an, producing a text five times removed from the Arabic original.

As of the middle of the seventeenth century, then, no Western reader has what can properly be called a complete published translation of the canonical codex of the Qur'an—there were only paraphrases with interpolated exegeses, revised paraphrases, and retranslations increasingly distant from the Arabic text along with the occasional partial translation. All of this would change radically in 1647 with the publication of André Du Ryer's *Alcoran de Mahomet*. Du Ryer had a long career as a diplomat in the Middle East, with appointments in Alexandria, Cairo, and Istanbul. An exacting and gifted polymath fluent in Arabic, Persian, and Turkish, Du Ryer was far more attentive than his predecessors to the form and literary qualities of the Qur'an and more intelligent in his use of commentary (*tafsīr*). Du Ryer's translation conforms to the literary ideal of the age: he renders the Arabic text into the elegant French that would be deemed acceptable for a seventeenth-century *honnête homme* without being excessively concerned with a literal rendition of the content (Hamilton and Richard 2004: 93–103; Zuber 1995). Instead of providing the reader with voluminous compendia aimed at refuting the Qur'an, Du Ryer contents himself with a six-page summary of 'la religion des Turcs', openly derogatory in tone but arguably included to camouflage Du Ryer's sympathy with Islam.

All told, Du Ryer's translation is a vast improvement on Robert's and Bibliander's versions, taking the reader away from the register of conflict and polemic and towards a quieter, if troubled, understanding. Again, such was the demand for the Qur'an among Western readers that it was quickly retranslated into English (1649), Dutch (1658), German (1688), and Russian (1716, 1790). The English retranslation would eventually become the first one to be published in the United States (1806).

By the end of the seventeenth century, Arabic studies and library collections in the West finally reached a point that enabled a complete translation with a fuller set of annotations. Ludovico Marracci, one of the sharpest minds of the age, published his monumental *Alcorani textus universus* in Padua in 1698. This publication is striking on a number of levels: the reader is met with the fully vocalized Arabic text of the Qur'an, followed by a detailed translation, followed by an impressive set of scholarly notes adducing multiple Arabic sources, exegetical and historical, usually quoted in the original and then translated into Latin (Bevilacqua 2018: 57–69). The volume of all this valuable information is matched by the painstaking 'refutation' that Marracci adds to every translated passage. That the refutation was an important part of the project is evinced by his publication of a four-part *Prodromus ad refutatio alcorani* (*A Prologue to the Refutation of the Qur'ān*) in 1691 that was then republished alongside the translation of 1698. Despite the open hostility of Marracci's tone, and the often too literal quality of the translation, the sheer wealth of information contained therein made it a useful source for future scholars well into the nineteenth century.

Marracci's project was clearly inscribed within the complex politics of the Catholic reformation, and seems to have set off something of a translation arms race among Europe's Protestants (Hamilton 2014; Bevilacqua 2018: 55–63). In 1734, with the support of the Society for the Promotion of Christian Knowledge (SPCK), George Sale produced an excellent English translation of the Qur'an. Sale positions himself with respect to Marracci, clearly identifying his debt to him but taking the trouble to add:

> The writers of the Romish communion, in particular, are so far from having done any service in their refutation of Mohammedanism, that by endeavouring to defend their idolatry and other superstitions, they have rather contributed to the increase of that aversion which the Mohammedans in general have to the Christian religion, and given them great advantages in the dispute. The Protestants alone are able to attack the Koran with success; and for them, I trust, Providence has reserved the glory of its overthrow. (iii–iv).

Although he did not reproduce the Arabic text, Sale stopped at nothing to produce a balanced and informative rendition of the Qur'an, so much so that the few anti-Muslim statements that one runs across in his paratexts come across as being perfunctory and insincere. The translation, which is copiously annotated, is preceded by a long 'Preliminary Discourse' (the title is a riposte to Marracci's *Prodromus*) in which Sale presents the history and geography of seventh-century Arabia, the rise of Islam, the history of the revelation and collection of the Qur'an, as well as a cursory map of the doctrines and schools of thought of Islamic theology. Despite Sale's acknowledgement of Marracci, recent research indicates that his reliance on the *Alcorani textus universus* was far greater than he acknowledged (Bevilacqua 2013).

Over the course of the eighteenth century, all three translations (Du Ryer, Marracci, and Sale) would be retranslated in whole or in part, with Sale enjoying the widest diffusion of all and continuing to be published well into the twentieth century. By the mid-eighteenth century hybrid editions that combined a French translation of Sale's 'Preliminary Discourse' with the text of Du Ryer's translation of the Qur'an were common in France, indicating again the public's taste for translations that were not too onerous. The eighteenth century also saw the rapid rise of the Protestant parts of Germany as European centres of research and scholarship on the Qur'an. Although many German Arabists attempted to complete a translation of the Qur'an during the eighteenth century, only two succeeded. A third, Theodor Arnold retranslated Sale's version into German (1746), though the net effect of this translation seems to have been an accentuated demand for a proper German translation of the Qur'an from the Arabic. In 1772, David Megerlin's translation of the Qur'an was published. Entitled *Die türkische Bibel* (*The Turkish Bible*), he declared in his foreword that one of his aims was 'to save the honour of the Germans' in the matter of Arabic and Qur'anic studies (Hamilton 2014). Nevertheless, he failed to capture anything of the Qur'an's stylistic beauty, driving the young Goethe to describe his translation as being 'wretched' [*elend*]. Goethe's comment reflects the growing appreciation of Arabic culture in the West, as well as the recognition of the importance of the Qur'an's linguistic awe and majesty. Although earlier translators were aware of this aspect of the Qur'an, by the end of the eighteenth century it had become part of the public's expectation that a translation of the Qur'an should convey some of its formal magnificence (Loop 2009).

This expectation would eventually lead to a number of translations that attempted to live up to the Qur'an's literary qualities. Friedrich Boysen's 1773 translation, *Der Koran*, was accompanied by a preface in which the translator openly acknowledged his inability to translate the 'melodic' quality of the original. The second (1775) edition of Boysen's translation also departed from previous translations through its open and unquestioning admiration of Muḥammad and the Qur'an. In 1783, there appeared another French translation, ostensibly based on the Arabic, by Claude Savary. Savary claims to have published the text in Mecca, though this seems to be part of a consistent pattern of exaggeration, decoration, and fraud that one also finds elsewhere in his publications (Hamilton 2019). What the Savary translation lacks in critical and historical apparatus it makes up in notes devoted to local colour, yielding to an exoticizing aesthetic situated between rococo and romanticism. Its inaccuracies indicate that it is more of a retranslation of Marracci's text rather than a straight translation from the Arabic, though none of this has prevented its repeated republication. Joseph von Hammer-Purgstall's translation of the last forty suras of the Qur'an appeared in the *Fundgruben des Orients*, the journal that he founded in 1809. His presentation foregrounds his view of the Qur'an as a masterpiece of Arabic poetry, along with the imperative that the translator reproduce the form of the Qur'an. Friedrich Rückert continued the trend of poetic translation of the Qur'an from the Arabic, although he never completed his translation. The free-verse partial translation was published in 1888, marking a high-point in German verse translations from the Qur'an (Bobzin 2006).

During the nineteenth century, two key shifts affected the production and circulation of the translation of the Qur'an in the West: imperialism and historicism. Albin de Biberstein Kazimirski's lucid French translation of the Qur'an was first published in 1840 as part of a massive tome entitled, *Les Livres sacrés de l'orient* edited by a sinologist, Guillaume Pauthier, whose preface argues that a better understanding of the Qur'an would lead to better control over France's colonies. Kazimirski's sympathies on the matter are more difficult to pin down, and Pauthier adds to the political ambiguity by adding a French translation of Sale's 'Preliminary Discourse' to the volume. The Kazimirski translation also saw separate publication in 1840 as well as several revisions and corrections over the course of the decade, with the final edition going through multiple reprints well into the twentieth century and major specialists consistently attesting to its quality.

Qur'anic studies took a giant step forward with the philological and critical research of Heinrich Fleischer, Gustav Flügel, Theodor Nöldeke, and Gustav Weil. Armed with a better understanding of the order of revelations, and driven by the assumption that the best way to understand something must necessarily be to take it to its earliest known form, translations of the Qur'an with the suras arranged in chronological order start to appear in 1861, when John M. Rodwell published his English translation (albeit in a chronological order that differed from those proposed by Weil and Nöldeke). This trend would eventually peak with the English translation of Richard Bell, first published in 1937–9, though the full scholarly apparatus that went with his work would not be published until some forty years after his death in 1991. Bell's translation rearranges individual verses and parts of verses, often depicting his chronological theories through the arrangement of the text on the page. Régis Blachère's French translation (1947–9) of the Qur'an combines the Qur'an and its scholarly apparatus: the detailed and annotated translation presents the suras in the order suggested by Nöldeke with various thematic subheadings, taking variant readings into account and fully engaging with the genetic history of the text of the Qur'an, itself a major constituent of Blachère's introduction. A second edition of Blachère's translation, without the introduction and with the text arranged in traditional order, appeared in 1957. The last of the century's great historicist-philological translations was produced by Rudi Paret in 1962, followed by a commentary and concordance in 1971 and a new edition in 1982. Paret aimed at reproducing the meaning that the Qur'an had at the time when it was first heard, seeking to understand the Qur'an through the Qur'an itself. Part of the process involved a certain degree of scepticism towards exegetical texts composed long after the death of the Prophet and the compilation of the Qur'an.

The global transformations of the twentieth century—world war, decolonization, and large-scale immigration—have decisively shaped the development of the translation of the Qur'an into Western languages. Accordingly we find a chorus of assertive Muslim translators and non-Muslim sympathizers joined in the common pursuit of communicating the wonder of the Qur'an to a Western audience. The accusation of conversion that had once haunted translators and scholars of Islam during the early modern period now becomes a mark of honour for some translators and influence for their translations. One such translation, the immensely popular *Meaning of the Glorious Koran* (1930) by Muhammad Marmaduke Pickthall, takes the position that 'the Koran cannot be translated' and that his translation 'is only an attempt to present the meaning of the Koran—and peradventure something of the charm—in English' (vii). Pickthall's conviction is so strong that the translation contains very few explanatory notes; a significant difference from Sale's translation into English. Shortly afterwards, ʿAbdullāh Yūsuf ʿAlī published a larger translation, *The Holy Qur'ān* (1934) that includes detailed notes and a verse commentary, justifying his endeavour as a response to the 'amount of mischief done by these versions of non-Muslim and anti-Muslim writers [which] has led Muslim writers to venture into the field of English translation' (xv). Nevertheless, Yusuf ʿAlī's translation is remarkable for its broad-minded approach to translation, giving the reader a good idea of the multiple levels of meaning in play at any one textual moment and relying on a number of commentaries from across the cultural spectrum. A. J. Arberry's landmark 1955 translation, while continuing Pickthall's paucity of notes, uses layout, 'rhythmic patterns and sequence-groupings' in an attempt to echo 'however faintly the sublime rhetoric of the Arabic Koran' (x).

A comparable dynamic obtains in recent French translations of the Qur'an, all of which are, at least implicitly, in dialogue with France's large Muslim population. In his preface to Denise Masson's fluid and moving translation of the Qur'an (1967), Jean Grosjean (who would go on to publish his own translation in 1972) speaks of the Qur'an as a 'miracle' whose effects should be imparted to the reader (ix). Masson's notes repeatedly draw attention to the similarities between the Qur'an and the Bible with a view to implementing the hospitable ethics of appreciating the Other formulated by Louis Massignon: 'To understand the Other, one should not annex him or her, but rather become his guest [*hôte*]' (Massignon 2009, 2:248). The publication in 1972 of a translation with an extensive commentary and notes by Cheikh Si Hamza Boubakeur, the former Rector of the Paris Mosque (1957–82) is similarly inscribed within this postcolonial dynamic, seeking to save the Qur'an from 'defamation' and convince the non-Muslim reader of the coherence of its message. More recently, another convert, Muhammad Asad (né Leopold Weiss) published his *Message of the Qur'ān* (1980) where he makes many more concessions than Pickthall to the complicated history and reality of the Qur'an, its translation, and the relationship between Muslims and non-Muslims. Asad's foreword calls on the translator to 'reproduce within himself the conceptual symbolism of the language in question,' to hear it ' "sing" in his ear in all its naturalness and immediacy' (v) in order to produce a suitable translation. Grammar and literature alone are not enough: Asad calls for a 'communion' with the spirit of the language, something that can only be achieved by 'living with and in it', as he himself had done in Saudi Arabia, Pakistan, and elsewhere. The long-term trend in modern and contemporary translations of the Qur'an thus points towards foregrounding the ineffable language of the sacred.

The intersection of politics and language, or rather the politics *of* language, is evident in the history of Jacques Berque's important translation, *Le Coran: Essai de traduction* (1990). Published a little over a year after the furore surrounding Salman Rushdie's

Satanic Verses, and simultaneously with the Iraqi invasion of Kuwait, it was, perhaps inevitably, surrounded by controversy when it was first published. Unlike previous translators, Berque's intention was not the restitution of 'an archaeological object', but rather 'the interrogation of a living subject'; one which was thus re-inscribed in the ongoing affairs of the world (Berque 1994: 184). Among the consequences of this urge to communicate the Qur'an's importance to the here-and-now was a series of lengthy, real-time exchanges between Berque and his readers, culminating in a revised edition of his translation (1995) as well as multiple interventions on the linguistic and textual reality of the Qur'an (Berque 1993; Berque 1995: 711–95). More recently Muhammad Abdel Haleem's introduction to his English translation (2004) contains a review of previous translators evaluated according to their 'respect' for the language of the Qur'an and the prophet of Islam (xxvii–xxviii). Among contemporary English translations that successfully convey the lyrical force and emotional charge, of the Qur'an, Tarif Khalidi's (2008) is outstanding. The deft use of layout, language, and learning combine to move the reader in ways rarely attained by other translators. In a similar vein, Hartmut Bobzin's translation (2010) attempts to update and bring a contemporary linguistic and conceptual exactitude to the long tradition of German translations, especially with respect to Rückert's incomplete lyrical version which Bobzin himself reworked before embarking on his own. As of this writing there is no end in sight: as languages, audiences, and our knowledge of Islam evolve, so do the translations of the Qur'an.

Theoretical Issues

One useful point of departure might be that, when it comes to the Qur'an, the process of translation is always already under way. This is not only due to the salient feature of scripture—what Erich Auerbach called its *Deutungsbedürftigkeit*; its need for interpretation—but also to the more pragmatic reality that nobody speaks Qur'anic Arabic today (Auerbach 2003: 15–16; Wansbrough 2004: 100). Translation precedes and inhabits any encounter with the Qur'an.

Furthermore, this process entails much more than a translation of the Qur'an's textual 'content'. A holistic view of translation is required. In a recent lecture on the process of translating the Qur'an, Tarif Khalidi invoked Wittgenstein to describe the complexities involved:

> 'If a lion could speak, we could not understand him'[(Wittgenstein 2009, 235)] [...] If a lion could speak, he would speak 'Lionese.' And now that God has spoken, can we really understand Him? Can we really understand 'God-ese'? Nor is understanding 'God-ese' made any simpler by the fact that we do not, it seems to me, make enough allowance for the Qurʾān's often deliberate mystification. (Khalidi 2012)

There will always be something uncontainable about the message of God, an infinity that human language can only indicate. Khalidi goes on to delineate the effects of the

Qur'an's 'often deliberate mystification', the 'shudder' of the listener or reader before the *mysterium tremendum* of the divine, and the challenge of translating that shudder into another language. Wittgenstein's remark is related to his argument about forms of life (*Lebensformen*): we have to understand the form of life of a given being in order to understand its language (Glock 1996: 128; Descombes 1996: 93–4). Translating and understanding the Qur'an would not therefore be about listing the words that constitute it, analysing them and finding an equivalent in another language. What is required, instead, is an appreciation of what Descombes calls 'the institutions of meaning' at work in the Qur'an; not only Arabic language and grammar, but the social, political, and religious frameworks within which the Qur'anic utterance is embedded. The *mysterium tremendum* in Khalidi's account recalls Rudolf Otto's account of the sacred, the Wholly Other that generates the aforementioned shudder but defies analysis or understanding (1950: 12–30). The nexus of these two aspects defines the task of the translator of the Qur'an: reconstructing the institutions of Qur'anic meaning around the textual (oral and written) trace of the Wholly Other that manifests itself as much in the Qur'an's inimitable beauty (*iʿjāz*) as in the awestruck 'shudder' of its readers. The translator is thus caught in a double bind, engaged with a sacred text that simultaneously calls for and inhibits translation, while proclaiming both its clarity and its ambiguity (Derrida 1998: 234–5; Davis 2001: 10–12). The task of the translator, to borrow a phrase, is to present a record of this struggle.

Accounting for the institutions of meaning that frame the Qur'an has, as the above chronology indicates, been a consistent preoccupation of translators from the outset: the auxiliary texts in the Toledan Collection, Sale's 'Preliminary Discourse,' Marracci's encyclopaedic commentary and 'refutation', as well as the sizeable apparatus that accompanies many contemporary translations. One of the most impressive attempts at dealing with this aspect of the Qur'anic translation process is the Corpus Coranicum, a research project based at the Berlin-Brandenburg Academy of Sciences under the leadership of Angelika Neuwirth, Michael Marx, and Nicolai Sinai. The project treats the Qur'an as a text of Late Antiquity, carefully attempting to reconstruct its unfolding in a space bordered by Byzantium and Persia, and informed by sources composed in Ethiopic, Greek, Hebrew, and Syriac in addition to Arabic. By bringing together material from the recently recovered Qur'anic manuscript photo archive assembled by Gotthelf Bergsträsser and Otto Pretzl during the early twentieth century, along with additional documentation of the oral transmission of the Qur'an against a backdrop of Judaeo-Christianity and early Arabic poetry, the Corpus Coranicum promises to bridge the gaps that still exist between research into the Judaeo-Christianity on the one hand and Islam on the other (Marx 2008). Although the project is scheduled to run until 2025 in the first instance, it has already borne fruit in the form of Neuwirth's translation and commentary on the early Meccan suras as well as her detailed study of the Qur'an as a text of Late Antiquity (Neuwirth 2010; Neuwirth 2011).

The sheer volume of new material adduced to help us understand and translate the Qur'an, both in the Corpus Coranicum and elsewhere, raises the additional question of 'thickness', both literally and theoretically. The term 'thick translation', first coined by

Anthony Appiah in a seminal article published in 1993, pleads for a renewed understanding of what translation actually does. Responding to Paul Grice's work on the logic of conversation, and his claim that convention and belief guide understanding as much as the content of what is said (Grice 1989; Davis 2001: 61–3), Appiah argues in favour of value transmission through translation:

> A translation aims to produce a new text that matters to one community the way another text matters to another: but it is part of our understanding of why texts matter that this is not a question that convention settles; indeed, it is part of our understanding of literary judgement, that there can always be new readings, new things that matter about a text, new reasons for caring about new properties.
> (Appiah 1993: 816)

In other words, the use of auxiliary materials and notes may bring a given translation closer to the aim of persuading the reader in the target community about the importance of the Qur'an, but the evaluation of such a translation relies, in whole or in part, on criteria that are mainly literary rather than conventional. This is not to say that the Qur'an is literature, but it is to say that the literary competence of its translators and readers, and indeed the literary qualities of the translation, play a key part in conveying its value. It is the literary register, rather than the theological one, that moves the history of Qur'anic translation forward.

Bibliography

Translations of the Qur'an into Western Languages

Abdel Haleem, M. (trans.). *The Qur'an: A New Translation by M. A. S. Abdel Haleem*. Oxford: Oxford University Press, 2004.

Arberry, A. J. (trans.). *The Koran Interpreted*. Oxford: Oxford University Press, 1998, 1955.

Asad, M. (trans.). *The Message of the Qurʾān*. Gibraltar: Dar al-Andalus, 1980.

Bell, R. (trans.). *The Qurʾān: Translated with a Critical Rearrangement of the Surahs*. Edinburgh: T. and T. Clark, 1939.

Berque, J. (trans.). *Le Coran: Essai de traduction*. Paris, Albin Michel, 1990, 1995.

Bibliander, T. *Machumetis Saracenorum principis vita ac doctrina omnis, quae et Ismahelitarum lex, et Alcoranum dicitur, ex Arabica lingua ante CCCC annos in Latinam translata*... Basel: Johann Oporinus, 1543.

Bobzin, H. (trans.). *Der Koran, neu übertragen von Hartmut Bobzin*. Munich: Beck, 2010.

Blachère, R. (trans.). *Le Coran*. 3 vols. Paris: M. Besson, 1957.

Boubakeur, S. H. (trans.). *Le Coran: traduction française et commentaire d'après la tradition, les différentes écoles de lecture, d'exégèse, de jurisprudence et de théologie, les interprétations mystiques, les tendances schismatiques et les doctrines hérétiques de l'Islâm, et à la lumière des théories scientifiques, philosophiques et politiques modernes*. Paris: Maisonneuve et Larouse, 1995.

Boysen, F. (trans.). *Der Koran, oder Das Gesetz für die Muselmänner, durch Mohammed den Sohn Abdall*. Halle: Gebauer, 1773, 1775.

Du Ryer, A. (trans.). *L'Alcoran de Mahomet: translaté d'arabe en françois, par le sieur Du Ryer, sieur de la Garde Malezair*. Paris: Antoine de Somaville, 1647, 1651.

Grosjean, J. (trans.). *Le Coran*. Paris: Le Club du Livre, 1972.

Khalidi, T. (trans.). *The Qurʾān*. London: Penguin. 2008.

Les Livres sacrés de l'orient. Comprenant le Chou-king ou le livre par excellence;—les sse-chou ou les quatre livres moraux de Confucius et de ses disciples;—les lois de Manou, premier législateur de l'Inde;—le Koran de Mahomet. Ed G. Pauthier and trans. M. Kasimirski. Paris: Firmin Didot, 1840.

Marracci, L. (trans.). *Alcorani textus universus ex correctioribus Arabum exemplaribus summa fide atque pulcherrimis characteribus descriptus*. 2 vols. Padua, 1698.

Masson, D. (trans.). *Le Coran*. Bibliothèque de la Pléiade. Paris: Gallimard, 1967.

Megerlin, D. F. (trans.). *Die türkische Bibel, oder des Korans allererste Uebersetzung aus der Arabischen Urschrift selbst verfertiget...* Frankfurt: Johann Gottlieb Garbe, 1772.

Neuwirth, A. (trans.). *Der Koran: Handkommentar mit Übersetzung von Angelika Neuwirth. I. Poetische Prophetie. Frühmekkanische Süren*. Berlin: Insel, 2011.

Paret, R. (trans.). *Der Koran*. 2 vols. 1: Übersetzung 2: Kommentar und Konkordanz. Stuttgart, Berlin, and Cologne: W. Kohlhammer, 1966–71.

Pickthall, M. M. (trans.). *The Meaning of the Glorious Koran*. Des Plaines, IL: Library of Islam, 1930, 1992.

Rodwell, J. (trans.). *The Koran: Translated from the Arabic, the Suras Arranged in Chronological Order*. London and Edinburgh: Williams and Norgate, 1861.

Rückert, F. (trans.). *Der Koran in der Übersetzung von Friedrich Rückert*. Ed. H. Bobzin and W. Fischer. Würzburg: Ergon, 1995.

Sale, G. (trans.). *The Koran: Commonly called the Alkoran of Mohammed, translated into English from the original Arabic, with explanatory notes taken from the most approved commentators, to which is prefixed a preliminary discourse by George Sale*. London: J. Wilcox, 1734.

Savary, C. (trans.). *Le Coran*. Paris: Garnier, 1783, 1960.

Yusuf ʿAli, A. (trans.). *The Holy Qur'ān: Text, Translation and Commentary*. Lahore: Shaikh Muhammad Ashraf; rpt. Beirut, Dār al-ʿArabiyya, 1934, 1968.

Other Sources

Appiah, A. 'Thick Translation', *Callaloo* 16/4 (1993), 808–19.

Auerbach, E. *Mimesis: The Representation of Reality in Western Literature*. Trans. W. R. Trask. Princeton: Princeton University Press, 1953, 2003.

Bell, R. *A Commentary on the Qurʾān*. C. Bosworth and M. Richardson (eds.). 2 vols. Manchester: University of Manchester Press, 1991.

Berque, J. *Relire le Coran*. Paris: Albin Michel, 1993.

Berque, J. 'Autour d'une traduction du Coran', *Studia Islamica* 79 (1994), 181–90.

Bevilacqua, A. 'The Qurʾān Translations of Marracci and Sale', *Journal of the Warburg and Courtauld Institutes* 76 (2013), 93–130.

Bevilacqua, A. *The Republic of Arabic Letters: Islam and the European Enlightenment*. Cambridge, MA and London: Harvard University Press, 2018.

Bobzin, H. *Der Koran im Zeitalter der Reformation: Studien zur Frühgeschichte der Arabistik und Islamkunde in Europa*. Beirut and Stuttgart: Orient-Institut der Deutschen Morgenländischen Gesellschaft and F. Steiner, 1995.

Bobzin, H. 'Translations of the Qurʾān'. In: Jane Dammen McAuliffe (ed.). *Encyclopaedia of the Qurʾān*. Leiden: Brill Online, 2006, 5:340–58. <http://referenceworks.brillonline.com/entries/encyclopaedia-of-the-quran/translations-of-the-quran-COM_00208>.

Burman, T. *Reading the Qurʾān in Latin Christendom, 1140–1560*. Philadelphia: University of Pennsylvania Press, 2007.

Davis, K. *Deconstruction and Translation*. Manchester and Northampton, MA: St. Jerome Publications, 2001.

Derrida, J. *Psyché: inventions de l'autre*, Nouvelle édition augmentée. Paris: Galilée, 1987, 1998.

Descombes, V. *Les Institutions du sens*. Paris: Minuit, 1996.

Glock, H.-J. *A Wittgenstein Dictionary*. Oxford and Cambridge, MA: Blackwell, 1996.

Grice, P. *Studies in the Way of Words*. Cambridge, MA, and London: Harvard University Press, 1989.

Hamilton, A. *The Forbidden Fruit: The Koran in Early Modern Europe*. London: London Middle East Institute, 2008.

Hamilton, A. 'To Rescue the Honour of the Germans': Qurʾān Translations by Eighteenth- and Early Nineteenth-Century German Protestants', *Journal of the Warburg and Courtauld Institutes* 77 (2014), 173–209.

Hamilton, A. 'Claude-Etienne Savary: Orientalism and Fraudulence in Late Eighteenth-Century France', *Journal of the Warburg and Courtauld Institutes* 82 (2019) forthcoming.

Hamilton, A. and F. Richard. *André Du Ryer and Oriental Studies in Seventeenth-Century France*. London and Oxford: The Arcadian Library in association with Oxford University Press, 2004.

Khalidi, T. 'Reflections of a Qurʾān Translator', Inaugural Conference of the Centre for the History of Arabic Studies in Europe (CHASE). London: The Warburg Institute, School of Advanced Study, University of London, 2012. <http://warburg.sas.ac.uk/publications/online-colloquia/translating-the-quran/#c1550>.

Loop, J. 'Divine Poetry? Early Modern European Orientalists on the Beauty of the Koran', *Church History and Religious Culture* 89/4 (2009), 455–88.

Marx, M. 'The Lost Archive, the Myth of Philology and the Study of the Qurʾān'. In: *Corpus Coranicum*, in: *Berlin-Brandenburg Academy of Sciences*, 2008. <http://edoc.bbaw.de/volltexte/2009/830/pdf/29Ej10bKlM1b.pdf>.

Massignon, L. *Écrits mémorables*. C. Jambet (ed.). Paris: Robert Laffont, 2009.

Neuwirth, A. *Der Koran als Text der Spätantike: Ein europäischer Zugang*. Berlin: Insel, 2010.

Otto, R. *The Idea of the Holy*, 2nd edn. Trans. J. W. Harvey. London, New York, and Toronto: Oxford University Press, 1923, 1950.

Wansbrough, J. *Quranic Studies: Sources and Methods of Scriptural Interpretation*. A. Rippin(ed.). Amherst, MA: Prometheus, 1977, 2004.

Wittgenstein, L. *Philosophical Investigations*, rev. 4th edn. P. Hacker and J. Schulte (eds.). Trans. G. Anscombe, P. Hacker, and J. Schulte. Chichester, Oxford, and Malden, MA: Wiley-Blackwell 2009.

Zuber, R. *Les 'Belles infidèles' et la formation du goût classique*. Paris: Albin Michel, 1968, 1995.

CHAPTER 36

TRANSLATIONS OF THE QUR'AN: ISLAMICATE LANGUAGES

M. BRETT WILSON

FROM al-Azhar's burning of Ahmadiyya translations in 1925 and Mustafa Kemal Atatürk's experiments with reciting Turkish translations in mosques in the 1930s to the Indonesian state's censorship of Hans Bague Jassin's versified *Bacaan Mulia* (1978), translations have constituted a site of public contestation over Islamic authority, the meaning of the Qur'an, and the proper practice of Islam. According to certain narratives of the early Muslim community, the companions of the Prophet Muḥammad were the first to translate the Qur'an. The most famous account describes how Salmān al-Fārisī—the first Persian convert to Islam—translated the first chapter (*Sūrat al-Fātiḥa*) into the language of his people. Another story relates that in 628 CE the Prophet sent messengers to kings around the world to demand their embrace of Islam and to teach them about the Qur'an in their own languages (Zadeh 2012: 262). These accounts connect translation to the prophetic biography (*sīra*) and ostensibly seek to demonstrate the universal mission of the prophet and the revelation he conveyed.

Translating the Qur'an—whether in oral or written form—has been integral to the Muslim communities across Asia, Africa, and Europe who faced the task of communicating the Qur'an to a diverse variety of populations and linguistic groups over the past fifteen centuries. Contrary to the widespread idea that Muslims oppose all translation of the Qur'an, there is a robust history of rendering the text into the vernacular languages used by Muslim communities (languages that for the sake of simplicity we will refer to as 'Islamicate' languages). European and American studies of Qur'anic translation have focused largely on translations into European languages, often giving the impression that Muslim activity in the field was negligible in comparison with the efforts of Euro-American missionaries and scholars (Zwemer 1915; Bobzin 2014).

The challenge to effectively surveying the history of Islamicate translations is not only the relative paucity of available literature; it is also tied to an acute conceptual problem, namely how to define *translation*. The question of what qualifies as a translation of the Qur'an has posed difficulties for the field. In particular, the question of how to distinguish the genre of *tafsīr*—Qur'anic commentary and exegesis—from translations has been a thorny and persistent problem (Burman 1998). In both pre-modern and modern contexts, the dominant position among Muslim scholars has been that the Qur'an is truly *the* Qur'an only in Arabic, and most scholars argue alternately that either translation (*tarjama*) or perfect translation of the Qur'an is impossible. While there are significant exceptions and a diverse array of opinions on the matter, the strength of this view persists in the modern period among religious experts, the greater Muslim population, and academicians. Scholars often categorize translations as interpretive literature, in effect, denying them the possibility of replacing the original text. While early Muslim scholars discussed 'Qur'an translation'—its possibility, its desirability, and its permissibility—at length, it did not become a robust genre or field of knowledge in its own right. And since Qur'anic translations have usually not been considered a separate category from *tafsīr* in Islamicate literary taxonomies, they assumed an inconspicuous status and it has been more difficult for scholars to identify, categorize, and assess them. As a result, a large body of literature has been under-appreciated and understudied.

The emergence of translation as a distinct category of Islamic texts has been an incremental process that was observed in some regions during the eighteenth century, accelerated in the nineteenth century more broadly, and crystallized in the twentieth century on a global scale. Arguably, a milestone for the genre occurred during the eighteenth century with the Persian language work—*Fatḥ al-Raḥmān fī tarjamat al-Qurʾān*—by the South Asian scholar Shāh Wālī Allāh (1114–76/1703–62) of Delhi. Written by one of the most influential members of the *ʿulamāʾ* in the Subcontinent, the work openly proclaimed itself a translation (*tarjama*), not commentary (*tafsīr*), strove to address a broader audience of Persian literate readers, and inspired similar efforts in Urdu and Turkish. Though this work was not the first Persian translation to be published, it was by far the most frequently reprinted Persian version (Binark/Eren 1986: 356–64) and shaped the trajectory of South Asian and modern Persian translations. Regrettably, a full-length study of this important work has—to the author's knowledge—not been completed in a Western academic language.

During the eighteenth and nineteenth centuries, European lexicography and oriental studies flourished and Christian missions entered the Muslim world in force. European and American scholars and missionaries played an important role in carving out a space for considering renderings of the Qur'an an entity of their own and a subject for study. In particular, Protestant missionaries made translating the Qur'an an integral part of missionary work, using vernacular translations to encourage Muslims to compare the quality of the Bible to that of the Qur'an. It was assumed that translation would reveal the flaws and inconsistencies of the Qur'an and demonstrate the superiority of the

Christian scriptures (Jeffery 1924: 183–4). Parallel to their biblical translation work, missionary-scholars produced a number of original translations of the Qur'an in African and Asian languages (Lacunza-Balda 1997: 97). As will be examined below, Muslim missionary groups such as the Ahmadiyya also produced translations and shaped the development of a modern genre of Qur'anic renderings.

Since translations of the Qur'an were important for Christian missions and the emerging field of Oriental studies, missionaries and scholars began tracking the publication of translations and compiling bibliographies around the turn of the twentieth century. These represent some early attempts to survey existing works and provide bibliographies for 'translations' of the Qur'an. The Cairo-based missionary Samuel Zwemer's 1915 article 'Translations of the Qur'ān' is noteworthy in this regard as it attempted to list all printed translations in the most widely used Islamicate languages (Zwemer 1915). The journal *The Moslem World*—founded by Zwemer—assiduously tracked the publication of translations around the world, announcing new releases and highlighting the efforts of both Muslim and missionary translators to produce vernacular renderings for their target populations in Africa, Asia, and the Middle East (e.g. Birge 1938; Anon. 1935: 297–8). These efforts demarcated such works as a field of study of their own rather than as a subset of Qur'anic commentaries. Simultaneously with—and sometimes in response to—missionary engagements with the Qur'an, Muslims in British India, the Ottoman Empire, and Egypt reignited debates about the permissibility and possibility of Qur'anic *tarjama* in the late nineteenth and early twentieth centuries (Wilson 2014). These efforts accelerated over the course of the twentieth century, leading to the crystallization of Qur'anic translations as a genre and the prolific production of translations by Muslim and non-Muslim authors.

Following these early attempts at recording extant translations, the massive task of compiling comprehensive bibliographies has been carried forward, and it should be noted that the study of translations in many languages remains at the bibliographic stage. To date, *The World Bibliography of Translations of the Meanings of the Holy Qur'ān* (1986) is the most ambitious and comprehensive bibliographic project of its kind. Put together by scholars at the Istanbul-based Research Centre for Islamic History, Art and Culture (IRCICA), this work catalogues printed translations in 65 languages between the years 1515 and 1980, listing 551 complete and 883 partial translations. Including reprints, it records a total of 2,672 editions. Region-specific studies like Mofakhkhar Hussain Khan's *The Holy Qur'ān in South Asia: A Bio-Bibliographic Study of Translations of the Holy Qurān in 23 South Asian Languages* (2001) have refined and expanded the findings of the *World Bibliography*. Despite shortcomings in certain languages, the *World Bibliography* remains unsurpassed in terms of global coverage and stands as an indispensable reference work for research on Qur'anic translation. While the conception behind this volume is clearly that of translation, it is interesting that the very title of the work harks back to the dilemma of what to call a rendering of the Qur'an. In opting to call it a bibliography of 'Translations of the Meanings' rather than simply 'translations', the authors display uneasiness with the very category around which the entire project is based. The cumbersome and somewhat perplexing moniker 'Translations of the Meanings' (Ar. *tarjamat maʿānī al-Qurʾān*) is a mode of referring to translations without violating the taboo surrounding 'Qur'an translation'. This phrase has been adapted and translated in several different languages for designating a category of texts that are neither commentaries nor translations.

Bibliographies chart out the extant terrain of translation, providing a rough map of the vast terrain that remains to be studied. And given the vast amount of literature that exists in a variety of languages, bibliographical studies continue in the present, both for understudied as well as for widely researched Islamicate languages. Following the *World Bibliography*, IRCICA embarked upon a series of projects to catalogue manuscript versions of translations held in collections around the world (Sefercioğlu 2000; Khan 2010). These volumes enable scholars to gain a sense of the scope of translations, their chronology, and their history of composition and publication. Nevertheless, scholarly coverage of translations in Islamicate languages is highly uneven. Some languages have been the subject of several studies (Persian and Turkish), but even for the widely used vernaculars and scholarly languages (e.g. Urdu), there is a relatively meagre coverage and lesser known languages (e.g. Uyghur) often remain completely neglected.

Interlinear Works

Interlinear translations are the oldest type of translations and exist in many Islamicate languages, including Chagatay, Persian, Mandarin Chinese, and Turkish. These works come in a variety of formats and styles. Typically, the original Arabic text of the Qur'an stands in larger characters (and often in a different colour) above the translation. Frequently, these texts contain translations in more than one language—Persian and Turkish or Persian and Urdu works, for instance, were common. Some interlinear works simply list the definitions of Arabic words, acting as a kind of running glossary. Others paraphrase the text or provide cohesive translations, at times with stylistic flourishes such as rhyme.

Persian translations are the oldest and most numerous in this category and Persian interlinear translations—first produced in Central Asia—defined the genre for South Asian and the Turkic West Asian and later Ottoman domains. Most Persian translations were composed by anonymous authors and many of the early works lack dates (Zadeh 2012: 266–7). The oldest dated version is an interlinear translation with commentary likely composed during the reign of the Samanid ruler Abū Ṣāliḥ Manṣūr ibn Nūḥ (r. 350–65/961–76). Despite the fact that the work that accompanies the interlinear translation is titled *Tafsīr-i Tabarī*, it is not a translation of the famous commentary *Jāmiʿ al-bayān* by Muḥammad ibn Jarīr (Abū Jaʿfar) al-Ṭabarī, but rather a Persian commentary that focuses on history drawing upon and reworking extensive passages from al-Ṭabarī's universal history (*Tārīkh al-Ṭabarī* also known as *Mukhtaṣar tārīkh al-rusūl wa'l-mulūk wa'l-khulafā'*), blending Persian mythology with Islamic history—an important observation made by Zadeh (2012: 305). However, evidence suggests that a vernacular translation culture existed even before the fourth/tenth century. It is likely that the important legal thinker Abū Ḥanīfa Nuʿmān ibn Thābit's (d. 150/767) well-known opinion on the permissibility of obligatory prayer (*ṣalāt/namaz*) in Persian granted post-factum legitimacy to existing practices of vernacular ritual during the 700s (Zadeh 2006: 477–8). Persian interlinear works flourished from the fifth/eleventh to the thirteenth/nineteenth century, attesting to a vibrant vernacular reading culture and leaving behind hundreds of manuscripts. A bibliographical work on Persian translations has been completed (Khorram-Shahi 2010), but modern translations into Persian remain in need of further study.

Turkish and Turkic translations followed the model laid out by Persian texts. In fact, Persian translations and commentaries can be found at the important Anatolian shrine complexes of both Jalāl al-Dīn Rūmī in Konya and Hacı Bektaş (Zadeh 2012: 563). The Turkologist Zeki Velidi Togan theorized that the first Turkic translation was composed simultaneously with the Persian translation project commissioned by the Samanids in the fourth/tenth century (Togan 1964: 13–15). While oft repeated, this opinion was based on speculation, not textual or historical evidence, and appears unsound. Fuat Köprülü argued that the first Turkish translation was done based on a Persian translation in the fifth/eleventh century (Topaloğlu 1976: p. 2). Some of the earliest known translations were tri-lingual (Arabic-Persian-Turkish) with the Turkish text coming below the Persian, and, in some cases, actually translated from the Persian, rather than the Arabic. The ninth-/fifteenth-century trilingual Qur'an (Arabic MS 38 [773]) held by the John Rylands University Library is an excellent early example of such works (Eckmann 1976). The oldest dated translation in Old Anatolian Turkish, the forerunner of Ottoman and modern Turkish, is dated 826/1422, and Topaloğlu produced a study of a manuscript dated 827/1424 (Topaloğlu and bin Hamza 1976), locating the beginning of an active translation culture in the post-Anatolian Saljuq period and continuing into the Ottoman reign. Though not as numerous as Persian works, several hundred manuscripts have been catalogued and attest to the widespread use of interlinear works in the madrasas and courts of Turkophone Anatolia.

Interlinear works exist in many languages including Mandarin Chinese, Urdu, Malay, and Hausa, and they continued to be printed and even composed in the twentieth century. In certain languages, interlinear renderings survived the rise of print (e.g. Urdu and Persian) while in others (e.g. Turkish) the genre was relegated to artefact status as paraphrastic commentaries and modern translations came into broad circulation. The full scope of interlinear works should be better understood as ongoing bibliographic projects come to fruition. Unfortunately, relatively few studies of this vast corpus have been completed. Studies on Turkish works, for instance, have an overriding concern with linguistic elements treating the translations as artefacts of language, with little concern for content or context (e.g. Eckmann 1976; Karabacak 1994). The large corpus of Urdu works—often called 'Hindi' by early translators—awaits a comprehensive study (Khan 1996: 212). Zadeh's monograph *The Vernacular Qur'ān* (2012) is a seminal study of Persian translations and, additionally, provides a blueprint for the kind of scholarship that can address this abundant literature in other languages.

Commentary-Translations

The distinction between translation and commentary—*tarjama* and *tafsīr*—in Qur'anic literature is often hazy, and many renderings of the sacred book are embedded in a composite genre that blends paraphrase, exegesis, and translation proper. The translations of succinct commentaries such as *Tafsīr al-Jalālayn*, *Mavāhib-i ʿaliyya*, and *Anwār al-tanzīl* into vernacular languages across Asia and Africa played a key role in producing hybrid texts that not only translated, but also adapted important commentaries in ways that approximated and furthered the evolution of modern literary translations. Translations of these popular commentary works have confounded bibliographers and made the question of when the first 'translations' appeared difficult to answer. How should an adaptive Malay, Turkish, or Hausa translation of al-Bayḍāwī's *Anwār al-tanzīl* be considered in the history of vernacular Qur'anic translation? Pinpointing precisely when translation develops as a separate genre is an inexact science, and perhaps this approach is methodologically ill-advised. In any case, translation and commentary coexist in many works, often in the form of marginalia, and this is the case even after the widespread printing of commentary works during the nineteenth century. Whereas manuscript and lithographically printed works often paired an interlinear translation with a commentary in the margins, new works appeared that explicitly designated *tafsīr* and *tarjama* sections in moveable type printed works (e.g. al-Dihlawī 1294/1877). In the main, these were not voluminous, erudite commentaries but rather succinct translations and paraphrases with occasional commentarial digressions.

Spanning Islamicate regions, such composite works were produced in South Asia, South-East Asia, Africa, as well as the Turkophone Middle East and Iran. This genre—widespread prior to the nineteenth century—became yet more prominent with the printing of vernacular *tafsīr*, many of which were translations of well-known Arabic and Persian language commentaries.

According to the *World Bibliography* (*WB*), the first printed Turkish translation was Ayıntâbî Mehmet's (d. 1111/1698–9) commentary *Tefsir-i Tibyan* (published in 1257/1841–2) which drew heavily upon *Anwār al-tanzīl*, and the second was İsmail Ferruh's (d. 1840) *Mevakib* (1281/1864–5), an adaptive translation of *Mavāhib-i ʿaliyya*, a popular Persian language commentary. A mark of their popularity is that shortly after publication Ottoman madrasas incorporated them into their curriculum (Gunasti 2011: 52). Considering the nature of these works, the late Ottoman writer Ahmet Midhat (1844–1913) quipped that they were 'so succinct that they can be seen more as translations than commentaries' (Ahmet Midhat 1894–5: 99). Categorized as the first Malay translation by the *WB*, ʿAbd al-Rauf al-Singkili's (*c.* 1024–1105/1615–93) Malay language *Tarjumān al-Mustafīd* was a composite work based largely upon *Jalālayn*, but was printed in Istanbul under a title indicating that it is a translation of *Anwār al-tanzīl* (Riddell, *EI*³; Abd al-Raʾūf, 1324/1906). Additionally, *Jalālayn*, *Anwār*, and al-Qurṭubī's *al-Jāmiʿ li-aḥkām al-Qurʾān*, shaped the trajectory of vernacularization in various African languages, including Old Kanembu and Hausa (Tamari/Bondarev 2013: 11–13; Brigaglia 2005: 428–9).

While such renderings were composite and mediated by popular *tafsīr* works, they pushed Qur'anic commentary into increasingly succinct formats and, benefitting from print technology, they familiarized broader audiences with accessible paraphrases and renderings of the Qur'an. In the early twentieth century, an influential segment of readers—the non-*ʿulamāʾ* intelligentsia and reformist *ʿulamāʾ*—argued that the Qur'an should be translated directly, in clear and accessible language. In Russia and the Ottoman Empire, intellectuals called for translation because they held commentaries to be excessively scholastic and tied to traditional interpretations that stifled intellectual progress (e.g. Bigiyev 1912: 91–2).

Modern Translations

During the nineteenth and twentieth centuries, translations of the Qur'an achieved a new degree of independence from interlinear works and composite commentaries. Many authors openly proclaimed their works 'translations', defying the conventional taboo, and, gradually, modern-style renderings, which could be read independently from the Arabic original, came into widespread use. This break was not sudden and often times commentary-style translations persisted. Additionally, elements of *tafsīr* were incorporated in new forms (such as footnotes) and, in many cases, publishers have placed the Arabic text alongside the translation or maintained the interlinear format.

Several factors played a role in the evolution of a modern translation genre.

First, the spread of print technology and the florescence of print culture over the course of the nineteenth century redefined the shape of the modern book, made books more affordable, and spurred a push for more accessible works. Second, translations by Orientalists and Christian missionaries provided alternative models for Qur'anic translation that were more accessible (e.g. Biberstein-Kazimirski 1841) and more in tune with the trends in modern book culture. The polemic nature of some such works (e.g. Goldsack 1908–20) inspired Muslim authors to rectify the image of Islam and its scripture by composing translations. Muslim missionary efforts, in turn, came to use translations as tools for education and proselytization. Additionally, the spread of nationalism across large swaths of the Muslim world contributed to the push for renderings that spoke to the concerns of emergent nation states and their attendant ideologies. The rise of non-*ʿulamāʾ* intellectuals in the print-based public sphere brought new voices to Islamic debates, voices that challenged the authority of the *ʿulamāʾ* and made translating the Qur'an a key part of Muslim reformist agendas. Finally, important Islamic institutions—including various *ʿulamāʾ* corps—began to produce and distribute translations on a large scale.

The impact of Western scholarship and Christian missionary work in establishing new models for translation should not be underestimated. In the late Ottoman Empire for instance, a generation of intellectuals read French translations of the Qur'an due to the absence of a similar text in Turkish. *Le Coran* (1841) by Albert Biberstein-Kazimirski was immensely popular among late Ottoman intellectuals (Wilson 2014). Moreover, prominent devout intellectuals viewed Muhammad Ali's English translation (1917), which combines an Arabic-English interlinear layout with footnotes, as a model for contemporary Turkish translations (Wilson 2009). In South Asia, the missionary influence was more direct than in Turkey. The first published Urdu translations were printed at the Hindustani Press by the British Orientalist John Wilkins in 1802–3 (Khan 1982: 132), and the American Presbyterian Mission sponsored an Urdu translation in 1844 (Uddin 2006: 77). Nevertheless, the impact of these works was dwarfed by the seminal Urdu work *Muḍiḥ al-Qurʾān* (1828–9) by a son of Shah Wali Allah—Shah Abdul Qadir (1735–1815). The book was usually published together with an interlinear Urdu translation by Abdul Qadir's brother Rafīʿ al-Dīn al-Dihlawī (1750–1818) and the Persian rendering of their father. *Muḍiḥ al-Qurʾān* was widely reproduced with at least seventy editions published by 1977 (Khan 1997: 43). The use of translations by missionaries in South Asian polemics—such as William Goldsack's Bengali rendering (1908–20)—motived groups like the Ahmadiyya movement and a host of South Asian intellectuals to compose translations in response. In Sub-Saharan Africa and China as well, the presence of missionary groups played a pivotal role in sparking conversations over the need for Muslim translations of the holy book (Loimeier 2005: 410–11).

The interwar period (1919–39) witnessed a florescence of translations and seminal renderings that were published in a variety of languages. As a result of a culmination of earlier debates, nationalist currents, and post-war political configurations, this period experienced unprecedented activity and enthusiasm in the realm of Qur'anic translations. While in most cases these were not the first translations in their respective languages, the translations of this period exhibited independence from the commentary tradition and its format. Concise, inexpensive translations became available in Turkey, the Russian Empire, and South and South-East Asia. In some instances—e.g. Swahili (1923), Turkish (1926/7), Serbo-Croatian (1937), Malay (1938)—the Arabic text of the Qur'an is omitted as well, creating 'freestanding' translations. These freestanding translations embodied the evolution of a modern genre of Qur'anic translation, a genre that reflects prevalent contemporary understandings of translation as a book that can be read independently, privately, and—preferably—in a concise format. Concision was prized as means of making the books accessible, cheap, and distancing them from the voluminous commentaries. However, most twentieth-century works include the Arabic text, and the interlinear format of pre-modern works was readopted in many languages.

Translations were part of the zeitgeist of the interwar period and wide-ranging efforts to argue for and compose translations occurred across the Muslim world. Seminal translations in a variety of languages were published or embarked upon. For instance in 1932, the Chinese Muslim scholar Ma Jian (1906–78), sponsored by the Academic Association of Chinese Islam, was sent in a group of students to study Arabic with the aim of creating a modern Chinese translation. He produced one of the most influential Mandarin renderings which was published gradually over the course of several decades (1949–81) (Ma 2006: 55–8). In the 1930s, Muhammad Marmaduke Pickthall (1875–1936) and ʿAbdullāh Yūsuf ʿAlī (1872–1953) penned seminal English-language works and Yusuf ʿAlī voiced his aspiration to make English an Islamic language (Ali 1934: iv). It was during the interwar years that the two traditional centres of Sunnī authority in the Mediterranean weighed in on the issue. In 1925, the Turkish Parliament voted to sponsor a project to create a modern Turkish translation, commissioning the devout modernist poet Mehmet Akif Ersoy (1873–1936) to compose what was hoped to be a masterpiece of Turkish literature. After six years, Ersoy withdrew from the commission, and the translation along with an expansive commentary was completed by the Islamic scholar Elmalılı Hamdi Yazır (1878–1942) and published between 1935 and 1939. On the southern Mediterranean, the Turkish and English translations of the era embroiled the Egyptian *ʿulamāʾ* and intelligentsia in a debate on the merits of translation for modern Islam during the 1930s. The Rector of al-Azhar University Muṣṭafa al-Marāghī (1881–1945) argued that translations were essential to the vitality and well-being of Islam in the modern world (al-Marāghī 1936: 12–14). While he and his supporters met substantial opposition, ultimately these debates opened the way to extensive liberalization of translation activities for the latter half of the twentieth century.

By mid-century, the translations of the nineteenth and early twentieth centuries had begun to appear archaic in some languages and new efforts rose to modernize the language and style of such works. Meanwhile, a significant number of languages still lacked a printed translation or, at least, a suitably modern one. For instance, the Swahili translation (1953) by Mubarak Ahmad Ahmadi (1910–2001) sharply criticized earlier Christian missionary renderings and, unlike those works, his new translation included the Arabic text of the Qur'an—a common feature that maintained a tradition of emphasizing the subsidiary nature of the translated text. Mubarak Ahmad had come to East Africa in 1934 as a missionary of the Qadiani Ahmadiyya Muslim Mission and commenced his translation in the late 1930s. In this case as in many others, Ahmadiyya-affiliated authors played an important role in the composing translations for the twentieth century. They were among the first groups to implement an organized effort to translate and distribute the Qur'an in a variety of languages on a global scale. They not only produced texts but also ignited controversy and provoked responses. Supported by the Islamic Foundation of Nairobi, the *ʿulamāʾ* leader Shaykh Abdallah Saleh al-Farsy (1912–82) responded by composing a Swahili rendering that was initially published in newspapers in the 1950s and ultimately as a book in 1969. This work was intended to present a mainstream Sunnī rebuttal to the Ahmadi interpretations contained in Mubarak Ahmad's translation (Lacunza-Balda 1997: 100–12).

Twentieth-century translations in Hausa produced similar polarization. A Nigerian activist named Abu Bakr Mahmud Gumi (1922–92) composed the first complete Hausa rendering (1979) with the support of Saudi Arabia. Gumi's translation—written in accessible, common Hausa—reflected his Salafi and anti-Sufi views. It departed from the heavily *Jalālayn*-influenced interpretive tradition in Nigeria and attacked Sufi practices in footnotes. The book was widely distributed, and, given its polemic character, ignited substantial controversy. Sponsored by the Libyan Daʿwa Society, Nasiru Kabara (1925–96), a former teacher of Gumi and a major figure in the Qadiriyya order in Africa, responded with a poetic Hausa rendering that defended esoteric and Sufi-inflected interpretation (Brigaglia 2005: 428). Not only in Africa but across the Muslim world, translations increasingly became fora for polemics, Islamic outreach, and education during the twentieth century.

The adoption of translation by several important Islamic institutions—some with explicit state funding—paved the way for an explosion in publishing and distribution. And, increasingly, translations became a tool in the competition for Islamic authority in the late twentieth century. In South Asia, Egypt, Turkey, Iran, and—most importantly—Saudi Arabia, various groups adopted the globally oriented missionary model that the Ahmadiyya pioneered in the 1910s and 1920s. Continuing this trajectory, the King Fahd Complex for Printing the Holy Qur'an in Medina has become the largest publisher of Qur'anic translations in the world and produces original translations in a wide variety of languages. Additionally, the centre publishes *muṣḥafs* and is responsible for 'responding to false information and dispelling uncertainty' (*JOQS* 1999: 157). The translations it produces include footnotes supporting Saudi *ʿulamāʾ* approved interpretations of the text. Unfortunately, little scholarly attention has been paid to this institution and its activities, which are rather significant for the current state of translations and the modern shape of the Qur'an in general.

Related to the mass production and distribution of translations is the question of impact. What effect have renderings of the Qur'an had in shaping the contours of Islam? There is no global response to this query and, inevitably, answering this question depends largely on context, as translations have served diverse purposes. The formation of vernacular and/or national Islamic communities has been an issue of conversation for many scholars. Considering the formative period, Zadeh's research shows that Persian translations—oral and written—were pivotal in preaching, teaching, and spreading Islam during the second/eighth to seventh thirteenth centuries. Moreover, they assisted in the cultivation of a vernacular, Persianate Islam that involved not only the production and use of vernacular texts, but also fostered and solidified a Persian communal identity within the *umma* (Zadeh 2012: 583–4). However, even in the same context opinions diverge. Lacunza-Balda, for instance, credits translations with the development of Swahili Islam, whereas Van de Bruinhorst doubts that translations had much impact beyond limited scholarly circles (Van de Bruinhorst 2013: 207).

In Turkey, certain intellectuals such as Ziya Gökalp clearly hoped that translations would help form a nationally oriented 'Turkish Islam', in which the call to prayer, Qur'anic recitation and daily and communal rituals would be performed in Turkish, not Arabic. In the Turkish case, translations certainly contributed to a nationally oriented Islamic outlook, but their role should not be overstated. When the first translations in modern Turkey were published, they inspired not national devotion but rather widespread discontent due to the dubious credentials of the authors and the variable quality of the renderings (Wilson 2009). They were but one among several factors that helped cultivate nationalist

Islamic sentiments in Turkey. As in other contexts, Turkish translations have been marshalled for use in ongoing polemics and competition between Muslim groups in Turkey. The same holds true in South Asia, where—since the early nineteenth century—competing groups have published renderings that support their views, making translations an important vehicle of intra-Muslim polemics. At the same time, they—along with tracts written in simple Urdu—played a role in elaborating a more accessible textual tradition and cultivating Urdu as a language of Muslim elites across the Subcontinent (Metcalf 2002: 67, 208). Given the linguistic diversity of South Asian Muslim communities, two countervailing processes occurred simultaneously. Communities produced translations in their regional languages—Bengali, Gujarati, Marathi, Tamil, etc.—while scholars and elites in various locales composed Urdu translations with aspirations of a trans-regional audience. The role of translations in contributing to Muslim Indian national identity awaits further analysis.

Finally, the question of religious authority—in particular, the right to interpret the Qur'an—crops up in studies of translation in many contexts. In what ways—if any—do translations challenge traditional authorities and upset conventional modes of exegesis? Persianate and Turcophone translations from the fourth/tenth to tenth/sixteenth centuries appear not to have challenged traditional authority to a great extent as they were composed mainly by the *ʿulamāʾ* and often used in madrasa studies. The same appears to hold true in most pre-print Islamicate contexts when such translations circulated primarily in courtly and scholarly circles. In pre-modern South Asia, Central Asia, and Ottoman West Asia, interlinear translations were a largely uncontroversial genre—occasionally challenged but never suppressed.

On the other hand, during the nineteenth and twentieth centuries, translations were put to new uses in new formats often by reformist *ʿulamāʾ* and non-*ʿulamāʾ* intellectuals. They have been harnessed for promoting various agendas of Islamic reform, nationalism, sectarianism, and proselytization. Moreover, print technology enabled the mass production and distribution of these texts, spreading them far beyond the scholarly, courtly networks of earlier centuries. As a result, printed translations over the past two centuries have occasioned substantial and ongoing controversy. From the tenth century to the present, Islamicate translations of the Qur'an have served a variety of purposes in Muslim communities and their availability and importance has only increased with time.

Bibliography

Ahmet Midhat. *Beşair: Sıdk-ı Muhammediye*. Istanbul: Kırk Anbar Matbaası, 1312/1894–5.

[Anon.]. 'Yet Another Chinese Translation of the Qurʾān', *Muslim World* 25/3 (1935), 297–8.

Bigiyev, Musa Carullah. *Halk Nazarına bir Niçe Mesele*. Kazan: Mahmud ʿAlim Efendi Maqsudov, 1912.

Binark, İsmet, Halit Eren (authors), and Ekmeleddin İhsanoğlu (ed.). *World Bibliography of Translations of the Meanings of the Holy Qurʾān: Printed Translations, 1515–1980*. Istanbul: Research Centre for Islamic History, Art, and Culture, 1986.

Birge, John Kingsley. 'Turkish Translations of the Koran', *Muslim World* 28/4 (1938), 394–9.

Bobzin, Hartmut. 'Translations of the Qurʾān'. In: Jane Dammen McAuliffe (ed.). *Encyclopaedia of the Qurʾān*. Washington, DC: Georgetown University, Brill Online, 2014. Accessed 20 March 2014 <http://referenceworks.brillonline.com/entries/encyclopaedia-of-the-quran/translations-of-the-quran-COM_00208\>.

Brigaglia, Andrea. 'Two Published Hausa Translations of the Qurʾān and their Doctrinal Background', *Journal of Religion in Africa* 35/4 (Nov. 2005), 424–49.

Burman, Thomas E. ' Tafsīr and Translation: Traditional Arabic Qurʾān Exegesis and the Latin Qurʾāns of Robert of Ketton and Mark of Toledo', *Speculum* 73/3 (1998), 703–32.

al-Dihlawī, Muhammad Jamāl al-Dīn. *el-Tefsirü'l-Cemali*. Trans. Muhammad Khayr al-Dīn Hindī al-Haydarābādī. Cairo: Bulak Matbaası, 1294 [1877].

Eckmann, János. *Middle Turkic Glosses of the Rylands Interlinear Koran Translation*. Budapest: Akadémiai Kiadó, 1976.

Goldsack, William. *Korān*, Calcutta, 1908–20.

Gunasti, Susan. 'Approaches to Islam in the Thought of Elmalılı Muhammed Hamdi Yazır (1878–1942)', Ph.D. Dissertation, Princeton University, 2011.

Jeffery, Arthur. 'The Presentation of Christianity to Moslems', *The International Review of Missions* 13/2 (1924), 174–89.

Karabacak, Esra, *An Inter-Linear Translation of the Qurʾān into Old Anatolian Turkish*. Cambridge, MA: Harvard University Department of Near Eastern Languages and Civilizations, 1994.

Khan, Ahmad. *World Bibliography of Translations of the Holy Qurʾān in Manuscript Form II: Translations in Urdu*. (ed.). Ekmeleddin Ihsanoğlu. Istanbul: IRCICA, 2010.

Khan, Mofakhhar Hussain. 'A History of Bengali Translations of the Holy Qurʾān', *Muslim World* 72/2 (1982), 129–36.

Khan, Mofakhkhar Hussain. 'An Early History of Urdu Translations of the Holy Qurʾān: A Bio-Bibliographic Study, Part 1', *Islamic Quarterly* 40/4 (1996), 211–34.

Khan, Mofakhkhar Hussain. 'An Early History of Urdu Translations of the Holy Qurʾān: A Bio-Bibliographic Study, Part 2', *Islamic Quarterly* 41/1 (1997), 34–51.

Khan, Mofakhkhar Hussain. *The Holy Qur'ãn in South Asia: A Bio-Bibliographic Study of Translations of the Holy Qurãn in 23 South Asian Languages*. Dhaka: Bibi Akhtar Prakãsani, 2001.

Khorram-Shahi, Bahaeddin. بررسی ترجمه های امروزین فارسی قرآن کریم [A Survey of the Modern Farsi Translations of the Holy Qurʾān] (Qom: Center for the Translation of the Holy Qurʾān, 1388 (Persian Calendar)/2010).

Lacunza-Balda, Justo. 'Translations of the Quran into Swahili, and Contemporary Islamic Revival in East Africa'. In: Eva Evers Rosander and David Westerlund (eds.). *African Islam and Islam in Africa: Encounters between Sufis and Islamists*, pp. 95–126. Athens: Ohio University Press, 1997.

Loimeier, Roman. 'Translating the Qurʾān in Sub-Saharan Africa: Dynamics and Disputes', *Journal of Religion in Africa* 35/4 (2005), 403–23.

Ma, Haiyun. 'Patriotic and Pious Muslim Intellectuals in Modern China: The Case of Ma Jian', *American Journal of Islamic Social Sciences* 23/3 (2006), 54–70.

al-Marāghī, Muḥammad Muṣṭafā. *Baḥth fī tarjamat'il-Qurʾān al-karīm wa aḥkāmihā*. Cairo: Maṭbaʿat al-Raghāʾib, 1355/1936.

Metcalf, Barbara Daly. *Islamic Revival in British India: Deoband, 1860–1900*. New Delhi and New York: Oxford University Press, 2002.

Riddell, Peter G. 'Abdurrauf Singkili'. In *Encyclopaedia of Islam*, THREE. Brill Online, 2014. Accessed 24 June 2014 <http://referenceworks.brillonline.com/entries/encyclopaedia-of-islam-3/abdurrauf-singkili-COM_0149>.

Tamari, Tal and Dmitry Bondarev. 'Introduction and Annotated Bibliography', *Journal of Qurʾānic Studies* 15/3 (2013), 1–55.

Togan, Zeki Velidi. 'The Earliest Translation of the Qurʾān into Turkish', *İslam Tetkikleri Enstitüsü Dergisi* 4 (1964), 1–19.

Topaloğlu, Ahmet and Mehmet bin Hamza, *XV. Yüzyıl Başlarında Yapılmış Satır-Arası Kur'an Tercümesi*. Istanbul: Devlet Kitapları, 1976.

Sefercioğlu, M. Nejat. *World Bibliography of Translations of the Holy Qurʾān in Manuscript Form*. Ed. Ekmeleddin İhsanoğlu. Istanbul: IRCICA, 2000.

Uddin, Sufia M. *Constructing Bangladesh: Religion, Ethnicity, and Language in an Islamic Nation*. Chapel Hill: University of North Carolina Press, 2006.

Van De Bruinhorst, Gerard C. 'Changing Criticism of Swahili Qurʾān Translations: The Three "Rods of Moses"', *Journal of Qur'anic Studies* 15/3 (2013), 206–31.

Wilson, M. Brett. 'The First Translations of the Qurʾān in Modern Turkey', *International Journal of Middle East Studies* 41/3 (2009), 419–35.

Wilson, M. Brett. *Translating the Qurʾān in an Age of Nationalism: Print Culture and Modern Islam in Turkey*. Oxford University Press in association with the Institute of Ismaili Studies, 2014.

ʿAbdullāh Yūsuf ʿAlī. *The Holy Qurʾān*. Lahore: Shaikh Muhammad Ashraf, 1934.

Zadeh, Travis. 'Translation, Geography, and the Divine Word: Mediating Frontiers in Pre-Modern Islam'. Ph.D. Dissertation, Harvard University, 2006.

Zadeh, Travis. *The Vernacular Qurʾān: Translation and the Rise of Persian Exegesis*. Oxford: Oxford University Press in association with the Institute of Ismaili Studies, 2012.

Zwemer, Samuel M. 'Translations of the Koran', *Moslem World* 5/3 (1915), pp. 244–61.

CHAPTER 37

PRESENTING THE QUR'AN OUT OF CONTEXT

MUHAMMAD ABDEL HALEEM

Introduction

'You are quoting me out of context' is a familiar protest from public figures. Quoting out of context can become all the more serious when quoting religious texts and can be seen especially in academic, political, and media circles when quoting the Qur'an. In much *tafsīr* writing, and in most of the translations of the Qur'an into English, as well as in what is written about the Qur'an, insufficient regard to the context seriously mars understanding and misrepresents the Qur'anic message. The study of context (*siyāq*) has a central place in *balāgha* (rhetoric) and Qur'anic studies in Arabic but, as will be seen, it is hardly even mentioned in Qur'anic studies written in English. In this chapter we will discuss context in relation to the Qur'an—the types of context—and will confine the discussion to its role in determining the meaning of words and sentences. The discussion here will explore which linguistic features cause difficulties in determining meaning, and what clues are given in the Qur'an to help identify the context and the proper meanings. Examples will be given from translations of the Qur'an, *tafsīr*, and Qur'anic studies.

Context in Relation to the Qur'an

The Qur'an is above all a text rooted in context. It is not a book written in a philosophical way about the subject of religion, but according to the traditional accounts was revealed over twenty-three years, and on each occasion the revelation was responding to a specific situation. As the Qur'an itself says (Q. 17:106),

> it is a recitation that We have revealed in parts, so that you [Prophet] can recite it to people at intervals.

and in Q. 5:101:

> You who believe, do not ask about matters which, if made known to you, might make things difficult for you—if you ask them while the Qur'an is being revealed, they will be made known to you—for God has kept silent about them: God is most forgiving and forbearing.

Thus, it is clear that the importance of historical context, that is the causes/circumstances of revelation (*asbāb al-nuzūl*), was recognized within the Islamic tradition from the beginning, and has always been important in *tafsīr*. The Qur'an is a dialogic text which engages the audience, rather than a linear narrative. It frequently uses *jumal inshāʾiyya* (affective sentences), in which it orders, persuades, prohibits, and questions its audience rather than introducing detached general instructions that might go over their head. Because of its non-linear nature, a number of factors can cause difficulties in determining the meaning, and context provides the solution.

Pronouns and adverbs of place can cause difficulties. Since the Qur'an was talking to an audience, second person pronouns are frequently used to address people and third person pronouns to refer to others well known in the context. Take for instance the much-quoted phrase, 'slay them wherever you find them', which is often cut off from its context in Q. 2:191 and cited as a general maxim (Busuttil 1991: 113–40). The addressees of this verse are the Prophet and the believers and the 'them' referred to here is clarified in the previous verse ('those who fight you'). The adverbial phrase, 'Wherever you find them' is not a general dictum, but refers to a specific issue the addressees had asked about, the question of whether they were allowed to fight back if attacked when inside the prohibited areas (the *ḥaram*) (al-Bayḍāwī *Anwār*, 1:108). Clearly, the context is crucial here in aiding the correct identification of who is being addressed, who is to be fought, and where they are to be fought.

Furthermore, there are occasions on which the very concise nature of the Qur'anic discourse means that the meaning may not be clear, and so elaboration and reference to the context are required to help explain the text. The end-rhyme of verses and the short verses, especially where the authors of *tafsīr* were atomistic in their approach, led at times to the isolation of words from their context, which affected the interpretation of their meanings. One further complication can arise where there exists a multiplicity of potential meanings, known as *wujūh* and discussed below, in which case only the context can help determine which meaning is appropriate to the situation. For all of these reasons, the need for observing the context was felt from the beginning, and a whole theory of context was developed by scholars of *balāgha* as a result of their efforts to identify what makes the style of the Qur'an so special as to be inimitable.

The issue of context is clearly a major one in the Qur'an. The Qur'an recognizes that its own verses are of two types and shows an awareness of the fact that some people deliberately misquote it: 'It is He who has sent the scripture down to you [Prophet]. Some of its verses are definitive in meaning—these are the cornerstone of the scripture—and others are *mutashābih* (not so definite). The perverse at heart eagerly pursue the *mutashābih* in their attempt to make trouble and to pin down a specific meaning of their own' (Q. 3:7). Such people, it seems, have always been around, but there are, of course, others who are simply unaware of the context and so make genuine errors.

Textual and Situational Context

Let us now define what is meant by context. In the discussion that follows, context refers to two things:

- (i) Textual Context, that is:
  - (a) Parts of a statement that precede or follow a particular word or sentence and influence its meaning, referred to in Arabic as *siyāq* or *siyāq al-naṣṣ*, or
  - (b) More distant cross-references in the Qur'an which also have relevance to textual context (different parts of the Qur'an explain each other), and
- (ii) Situational Context, that is the context of the situation: the set of circumstances or facts that surround a particular statement in the Qur'an. This is known in rhetoric as *maqām*, in recent discussion in Arabic also referred to as *siyāq al-mawqif*. Both of these types will be seen to affect the meanings of words and statements. But it was situational context that was singled out for lengthy discussion in *balāgha*, and which requires some elaboration at the outset.

Maqām/siyāq al-mawqif

One of the important contributions of scholars of *balāgha* in *ʿilm al-maʿānī* was their recognition of the concept of *maqām* (situational context) and its role in determining the meaning of the utterance and providing the criterion for judging it. *ʿIlm al-maʿānī* was defined as the science that discusses *muṭābaqat al-kalām li-muqtaḍā'l-ḥāl* (the conformity of the utterance to the requirements of the situation). As al-Khaṭīb al-Qazwīnī (d. 793/1338) explains (Qazwīnī 1971: 7–8):

> The context (*maqām*) that demands the definition, generalisation, pre-positioning of part of a discourse, and inclusion (of particular words) differs from the context that demands the indefinite, specification, post-position and omission; the context of disjoining differs from that of joining; the situation that requires conciseness differs from that requiring expansiveness. Discourse with an intelligent person differs from discourse with an obtuse one. Each word with its companion is suited to a particular context. A high standard of beauty and acceptability of speech depends on its appropriateness to the situation and vice versa.

As Tammām Ḥassān (d. 2011) has pointed out (Hassān 1973: 337, 372), when the scholars of classical *balāgha* recognized the concept of *maqām*, they were 1,000 years ahead of their time, since the recognition of *maqām* and *maqāl* as two separate bases for the analysis of meaning has been arrived at only recently as a result of modern linguistic thinking. When they said *li-kulli maqām maqāl* and *li-kull kalima maᶜ ṣāḥibatihā maqām* ('every context has its own [mode of] expression and every pair of collocating words has its own context'), they hit on two remarkable statements that could equally apply to the study of other languages. When Malinowski (d. 1942) coined his famous term 'the context of the situation' he had no knowledge of this Arabic work. Yet, despite the importance of the concept of *maqām* and its role in the study of the Qur'an, as expressed in *balāgha*, it does not seem to have figured in discussions about the Qur'an in English (see Chapter 20 in this volume).

Context and *Wujūh* (Aspects of the Meaning of a Given Word)

Context becomes particularly important in determining the meaning of a word that has *wujūh*, that is, different aspects of meaning. As will be seen, a word such as *kitāb* is used in the Qur'an in ten different *wujūh*. *Wujūh* is a well-known phenomenon in Qur'anic studies in Arabic. It was recognized early in the first/seventh century: the caliph ᶜAlī is reported to have advised his emissary to the Khawārij, saying, 'Do not argue with them using the Qur'an because it is *ḥammāl dhū wujūh* (it is capable of being interpreted in different ways) (ᶜAbdūh (ed.), *Nahj al-Balāgha*, 2:75:7 *Bāb kutub wa rasāʾil*, 77). The study of *wujūh* became well developed, producing scores of texts over five or six centuries. However, the habits of some *mufassirūn*, as will be seen, deflected the reader from looking into *wujūh* because they were atomistic in their approaches, listing all possible meanings of a word from a dictionary, saying, 'It means either this or that or that or...' rather than looking at the meaning in context. The context often narrows the potential meanings down to one single meaning, making other dictionary meanings irrelevant. It will be useful now to discuss some examples of words that have *wujūh* and what translators made of them.

Ḥakīm

Let us start with the word *Ḥakīm*. It occurs ninety-seven times in the Qur'an, mostly referring to God, but it has more than one meaning. Morphologically it is an intensive form of the adjective, *ṣifa mushabbaha*, and this does not seem to present a problem. It is the lexical meaning that does. The word can be assumed to be derived from *ḥikma* 'wisdom' or from *ḥukm* 'decision/judgement'. English translators of the Qur'an have opted for the first meaning in all the various examples I cite below. This decision may have been based on the fact that this is the first meaning that occurs in dictionary entries. Translators may also have been influenced by al-Bayḍāwī's commentary, which was until recently the most readily available to Western scholars on the Qur'an, since it was edited and published in Europe (Watt and Bell 1970: 169). Al-Bayḍāwī (d. *c*.719/1319) takes the first occurrence of *al-ḥakīm* (Q. 2:32) to refer to God's wisdom but al-Bayḍāwī, as will be shown later, is known to be atomistic in much of his approach, concentrating on the word in hand, isolated from its surroundings, which does not help in identifying context. In addition to copying al-Bayḍāwī, translators, starting with Sale, seem to have copied from their predecessors without questioning whether the translation fits the context or not. A number of examples will be discussed here, for which all translators have rendered *ḥakīm* as 'wise'.

Take, for instance, 2:208–9, 'Believers, do not follow in the footsteps of Satan, for he is your sworn enemy. If you backslide after clear proof has come to you then be aware that God is Almighty (*ʿazīz*) and *ḥakīm*'. The context here is a threat that God has the power to decide to punish them if they backslide. An Arab Bedouin, who was not a reader of the Qur'an, had the quick common sense, when he heard a reciter misreading this verse saying *ghafūr* and *raḥīm* instead of *ʿazīz* and *ḥakīm* to say 'If this was the speech of God he would not say so. *Al-ḥakīm* would not mention forgiveness in the context of backsliding because this will encourage them to sin more.' When the reciter corrected it to *ʿazīzun ḥakīm* the Bedouin said, 'Yes, that is how it should be *ʿazza fa-ḥakama*—he possessed the might and so he passed judgement' (Abū Ḥayyān 1983: 2:123). A more fitting translation would thus be: 'if you backslide after clear proofs have come to you then know that God is mighty, decisive in judgement'.

Al-Raḥmān

Al-Raḥmān is another word, occurring fifty-seven times in the Qur'an, that expresses a divine attribute which has suffered in translation as a result of translators not paying due regard to context. Many translators have rendered this term as 'the Merciful', or 'the All-Merciful', but in many situations this does not fit. For instance, in 21:42 it has been translated by Khalidi as 'Who shall keep you safe from the All-Merciful by night or day? by Jones as Who will guard you night and day from the Merciful? and by Arberry as Who shall guard you by night and in the daytime from the All-merciful?' Clearly, the phrasing 'Keep you safe from the All-Merciful' sounds somewhat contradictory. Instead, I have translated this phrase as 'Who could protect you night and day from the Lord of Mercy?' on the basis that it is the lordly and powerful side of God that is operative in this context. There is Mercy but there is also Lordship with power and authority. Another example can be seen in Q. 19:45 where Jones renders Abraham's words as, 'My father, I fear that some punishment from the Merciful will touch you'. Punishment from the Merciful does not quite fit. Again, the context here demands something more like the Lord of Mercy (see also 67:20). Tammām Ḥassān has studied the various examples of *al-raḥmān* in the

Qur'an and also come to the conclusion that the meaning of this term involves power and sovereignty (2004: 74–7).

Walad

Walad is another example used twenty-nine times in the Qur'an in connection with God. Arberry's translation of Q. 19:88 runs as follows:

> 'They say, "The All-Merciful has taken unto Himself a son." You have indeed advanced something hideous! The heavens are wellnigh rent of it and the earth split asunder and the mountains wellnigh fall down crashing for that they have attributed to the All-merciful a son: and it behoves not the All-merciful to take a son.'

Arberry, Alan Jones, and Khalidi, among others, translate *walad* as 'son', but this is in fact a modern meaning of *walad*. In classical Arabic, *walad* denotes all offspring, *kull mā wulida*, whether singular, plural, male, or female (*al-Muʿjam al-wasīṭ*, 2:1056). In fact *walad* should not be translated as son anywhere in the Qur'an, even when it refers to Jesus earlier in the sura at Q. 19:35, *mā kāna li'llāhi an yattakhidha min waladin*. In this case, in addition to the strong negation, *min* is added for *taʿmīm al-nafī*, that is, the negation applies to every possible form of *walad*, be it girls or boys, it does not mean 'a son'. To say 'It is not for God to take a son unto Him' (Q. 43:15–16), as many translators have done, leaves the door open for understanding that He could take a daughter or daughters, as the pagan Arabs thought the angels to be and which the Qur'an rejects strongly. Later on in Q. 19 (v. 77ff.) the sura refers to the *mushrikīn* (polytheists) of Mecca, and again in verses 81–2, 'They have taken other gods beside God to give them strength, but these gods will reject their worship and will even turn against them.' The statement in verse 88 quoted above clearly refers to the same group of pagans. The wider context *siyāq al-naṣṣ* (vv. 77ff.) makes this very clear. The case of *walad* shows the importance of determining the meaning of Arabic words at the time of the revelation of the Qur'an, and in context.

Tamnun

So far the examples have been in connection with God. We shall now give some examples of *wujūh* connected with the Prophet Muḥammad. The first is at Q. 74:6, where the Prophet is instructed: *wa lā tamnun tastakthir*, for which translators have variously given, 'Give not, thinking to gain greater' (Arberry), 'Do not show favours seeking gain' (Jones), 'Give not, hoping to gain more' (Khalidi). So, *tamnun* has been understood here to mean 'give' or 'show favour'. This is indeed the first meaning that comes to mind, but it cannot be suitable for the *maqām* or the *siyāq al-naṣṣ* here. Sura 74 is a very early sura, and the fact is that the Prophet had little to give at that time in order to gain anything. The context is clearly explained in the neighbouring sura, Q. 73, when he is asked to keep vigil at night: 'We shall cast upon thee a weighty word' (Arberry); 'We shall send a momentous message' *down to you* (Abdel Haleem). The Prophet clearly felt awed by these numerous commands coming all at once and had to be told *wa-lā tamnun tastakthir*, that is, 'Do not weaken, feeling overwhelmed', by the many requests made of him here. This reading of the verse is confirmed by the following verse (7) which says, *wa-li rabbika faṣbir*, 'Be patient unto thy Lord' (Arberry). *Tamnun* has one other *wajh* related to *manna*, becoming weak. If a task *manna* a person, it weakens and tires him, hence the saying *ḥablun manīn*—a weak rope (al-Rāzī, *Tafsīr*, 30:194). Here the *siyāq* determines the meaning of 'weaken', supported by intratextual evidence in the previous sura relating to the Prophet and how he felt in his early calling.

al-ʿAḥdiyya

Also connected to the Prophet are two examples of *wujūh* involving the definite article *al-* which can be *jinsiyya* (generic, referring to everything covered by the following noun) or *ʿaḥdiyya* (referring to a specific entity already mentioned or known to the addressee). Take, for instance, Q. 17:94. This has been translated by Pickthall as 'And naught prevented mankind (*al-nās*) from believing when the guidance came unto them save that they said: Hath Allah sent a mortal as [His] messenger?' Arberry gives 'men' instead of 'mankind', while Khalidi gives 'mankind' and so does Jones. In my own translation, I instead give the translation 'these people' for *al-nās*. The fact is that 'mankind' could not be intended here, since we know that many peoples had already received human messengers and did not find it strange or a reason for not believing. The disbelievers of Mecca challenge the Prophet in the previous verse that they will not believe until he brings down God or the angels for them to see face to face. Many times in the Qur'an they demand that an angel should come down with the Prophet to support him, for example in Q. 15:7 and Q. 25:7. This request for an angel rather than a human being as a messenger means that the immediate and wider context *siyāq* of the Qur'an makes it clear that the *al-nās* who presented such challenges to the Prophet were specifically 'these people (of Mecca)' mentioned in the previous verse. This is just one example of the meaning and translation of *al-ʿaḥdiyya* but there are in fact numerous examples in the Qur'an where *al* is *ʿaḥdiyya*, not *jinsiyya* and I observed this in my translation.

Tafakkahūna

Similar to *tamnun* discussed above, it might be suitable here to give the example of 56:65.

God warns the disbelievers that he 'could make their Harvest fragments and you would still jest (*tafakkahūn*), we are burdened by debt. No we are deprived'. Jones takes *tafakkahūn* to mean jest, which is one of the *wujūh* but it could hardly fit people whose harvests had been totally destroyed and who say, 'We are burdened with debts…'. The contradiction does not arise if we use another meaning (*wajh*) of *tafakkahūn*, 'wail' or 'lament' (see Lane 1863: 6:2432).

Oaths in Context

One obvious case in which the crucial role of context can be seen is in a number of examples taken from suras which begin with an oath on the pattern *wa'l-fāʿilāt* (37, 51, 77, 79, and 100). These oaths raise an important issue, in view of the problems they seem to cause in Qur'an translations, which deserves some elaboration. These oaths take the form of an implied noun described in Arabic by an active participle. This is a common feature in Arabic when the meaning of the adjective in itself is obvious without the described noun. Thus, in *Sūrat al-ʿĀdiyāt* (100), the root of the implied noun used, *al-ʿādiyāt*, is ʿ-d-w (to run, speed, gallop, dash, race). Even without the noun being supplied, it is readily understood to refer to horses. This would not necessarily be so obvious in an English translation. Now al-Bayḍāwī, whose *tafsīr* many translators say they have consulted, is not helpful in these cases. His methodology was to look at individual words in isolation, as if in a dictionary. Thus, he was keen to supply all possible alternatives of the individual word, without reference to the context to eliminate unsuitable alternatives. In *al-Dhāriyāt* (51) four items are sworn by: *wa'l-dhāriyāti dharwan fa'l-ḥāmilati wiqran fa'l-jāriyāti yusran fa'l-muqassimāti amran.*

For the first oath, *wa'l-dhāriyāti dharwan*, al-Bayḍawī gives three alternative meanings: (1) Winds, because they scatter dust, (2) Women because they produce and spread children, (3) Causes, because they produce creatures, angels and others. For the second verse, *fa'l-ḥāmilāti wiqran*, he gives four possible explanations (1) Clouds because they carry rain, (2) Winds because they carry clouds, (3) Women because they carry children, (4) Causes... To him, *fa'l-jāriyāti yusran* meant either (1) Ships because they run in the sea (2) Winds because they run, or (3) Stars because they run on their courses. Finally, for the fourth and final item, *fa'l-muqassimāti amran*, he suggests (1) Angels because they share out the rain and other provisions, (2) Causes that distribute anything, and (3) Winds because they distribute rain (al-Bayḍāwī, *Anwār*, 2:247). Clearly this type of reasoning makes it possible to go on indefinitely suggesting words that happen to have a possible meaning that relates to individual words in the oath but in isolation from the context. However, the context in sura 51 is an oath to prove that the resurrection of the dead will happen, as is clear from verses 5 and 6. Al-Bayḍāwī did not relate the items sworn by, *al-muqsam bihi*, to the object of the oath, *al-muqsam ʿalayhi*. He gets distracted from seeing the objectives of the whole series. In fact, this passage is all one oath swearing by the wind that scatters rain, carries clouds, and speeds them easily to reach their destinations and distribute the rain there. This is very obvious from other parts of the Qur'an where this is stated explicitly, such as 7:57, 30:48, and 35:9. Al-Bayḍāwī himself was aware of the 'wind' meaning, and indeed lists it in his commentary on all four oaths, but he mixes this meaning up with others and so obscures the connection between them, and hence misses what the whole passage is driving at. In contrast, my translation of this verse shows the series as an argumentation oath to prove the Resurrection (Abdel Haleem 2013: 49) and renders it as follows: *By those [winds] that scatter far and wide, that are heavily laden, that speed freely, that distribute [rain] as ordained, what you are promised is true: the Judgement will come.*

The oath is meant to prove that just as winds drive clouds and rain to a dead land, which will sprout with life, as the Qur'an says, *kadhālika tukhrajūn*—'in this way you will be brought out [from the earth] (7:57)'. 'He who [sent the rains etc...] is the one who will bring the dead back to life (30:50)'. Ignoring the *maqām*, the *siyāq*, and intratextuality in all the oaths in the five suras listed above, makes the passages unclear and creates a non-sequitur with the object of the oath, unlike other parts of the Qur'an that clearly and specifically mention the simile of bringing plants out of the dead land and bringing people out of their graves.

The Sword Verse: *Wujūh*, Textual Context and Situational Context

The 'sword verse' is perhaps one of the most famous Qur'anic verses, and one of the most often quoted by propagandists, extremists, and by some modern orientalist academics. For example, in his *The Koran: A Very Short Introduction*, Michael Cook gives the following translation by Arberry of Q. 9:5:

> Then, when the sacred months are drawn away, slay the polytheists wherever you find them, and take them, and confine them, and lie in wait for them at every place of ambush. But if they repent, and perform the prayer, and pay the alms, then let them go their way: God is All-forgiving, All-compassionate.

But Cook goes on to interpret the verse as follows:

> In other words, you should kill the polytheists unless they convert. A polytheist (*mushrik*) is anyone who makes anyone or anything a 'partner' (*sharik*) with God; the term extends to Jews and Christians, indeed to unbelievers. (Cook 2000: 34).

This is an extraordinary assertion when applied to the Qur'an, which has very definite separate terms for Jews, Christians, and unbelievers. Moreover, as will be shown in the discussion below, the verse is talking about just one group of polytheists, not all of them, and the instruction absolutely does not 'extend to Jews and Christians, indeed to unbelievers'.

Cook uses Q. 9:5 in his discussion to contrast this interpretation of the Qur'anic verse with 'a modern Western society, where it is more or less axiomatic that other people's religious beliefs [...] are to be tolerated and perhaps even respected' (Cook 2000: 33).

However, his reading of this verse represents a very stark example of wrenching one verse out of its context and building a theory around it that has no foundation in the Qur'anic text. The fact is that the context of this verse (see Abdel Haleem 2016–17) deals with one specific group of polytheists who had broken their peace agreements with the Prophet many times, and attacked Muslims at the Kaʿba at night while some were sleeping and some were praying. The sword verse informs the believers that they should renounce the agreement this group of idolaters had broken, and give them four months' notice, after which the Muslims might attack them. Cook's view of this verse thus contradicts the *siyāq al-naṣṣ*, which is made very clear from vv. 1–16. *Al-mushrikīn* in v. 5 has the *al-ʿahdiyya* , meaning that it refers back to the particular *mushrikīn* mentioned in v. 1, not 'any idolaters'. The exception of other *mushrikīn* is made clear in vv. 4, 6, and 7, and the rest of the passage lists the misdeeds of the *mushrikīn* in question, singling them out for the treatment they are to receive. The discussion in Abdel Haleem (2016–17) shows Cook's interpretation of the verse to be inaccurate.

Consistency and *Wujūh*

It could be argued that paying regard to *wujūh* in translation could result in inconsistency in translating a given word. It should not. Once a translator has determined the meaning or *wajh* of a word, he or she should be consistent in using the same translation for the word whenever it occurs in that meaning (*wajh*). But automatically forcing one meaning on a word that has several *wujūh* would lead to inaccuracy or strange rendering. Take, for example, the word *al-ʿālamīn*. This can mean 'all worlds' as in Q. 1:2, or 'all women' in Q. 3:42, or 'all other people' in Q. 26:165. This last verse expresses Lot's objection to the practice of the men of his town. Alan Jones gives, 'Do you come to the males of created beings?', which encompasses much more than human males; Arberry gives, 'male beings'; while I render it as, 'Must you, unlike other people, lust after males'. *Min al-ʿālamīn* here applies 'you' [the people of Lot], not the males (see also Q. 29:28). *Al-ʿālamīn* occurs seventy-three times in the Qur'an, in different contexts and with different *wujūh*, so that a consistent translation using only one word would create many problematic renderings.

A second example of a polyvalent word is *al-kitāb,* which occurs 1,230 times with ten different meanings in the Qur'an, variously meaning 'scripture', 'writing', or the records of deeds or a legal document, such as manumitting a slave, or recording a debt (Ḥassān 2000: 429–30). To render it with the word 'book' consistently clearly would not work. (In fact in Abdel Haleem's OUP translation, the word *kitāb*, when referring to the Qur'an, is not rendered as a book on the ground that it clearly refers to the revelation of a particular passage or sura, revealed separately over twenty-three years, and not to a book as a bound volume in the modern sense.) So the cherished rule of consistency should not be applied mechanically and the Qur'an should be treated as a text on its own terms. A useful practice would be to pause when the translation seems strange, or to contradict common sense, as in the examples discussed above, and give consideration to the causes of the anomaly. In most cases it could have resulted from using the wrong *wajh* for a given word. Clearly some translators simply force a meaning, regardless, and move on, leaving some readers to think the Qur'an is an odd text.

Wujūh in Sentence Structure

Wujūh does not obtain only with individual words, but can be seen also to obtain in a larger lexical structure for which only the context can determine which option of interpretation or translation is correct. One example of such instances of *wujūh* can be seen in a situation where a statement can be read either as complete at a given point, or as continuing in a following statement. For example, in the case of Q. 5:97, 'God has made the Kaʿba—the Sacred House—a means of support for people, and the sacred months, the sacrificial animals, including the garlanded'... Normally translators continue in the same verse. Thus we have '... that is so that you may know that God knows all that is in the heavens and all that is in the earth and that God is aware of everything' (Jones); '... this is in order that you may know' (Khalidi); and '... so that you may know that God has knowledge of all that the heavens and the earth contain; that God has knowledge of all things' (Dawood). However, the Arabic here reads *dhālika li taʿlamū anna'llāha yaʿlamu mā fi'l-samāwāti wa'l-arḍ*... Exegetes understand this as a clause of purpose with *li* functioning as a *lām al-taʿlīl*, to give the sense '*in order that people should know that He knows*...'. Sensing perhaps that one may ask how God could establish the Kaʿba and the sacrificial animals 'so that we know that He knows what is in the heavens and earth', exegetes have tried to explain this in various ways, including asserting that His knowledge is important to determine that people need the Kaʿba and the sacred months and so on (e.g. al-Bayḍāwī 1988: 284). They take the context to be intending to demonstrate that God has extensive knowledge. However, my suggestion is that this is not the correct way of reading the text. Instead, the verse should stop at the garlanded animals, before *dhālika*. Then *dhālika* itself is a complete sentence, meaning '*He ordained all this*', which is followed by a separate order *lām al-amr* reminding the readers/listeners to bear in mind that God has knowledge of all things, including whether they will be obedient or not, and that He has power over everything and can punish those who infringe His orders. This reading can be supported for two reasons. In v. 2 of the same sura there is an enumeration of the things God has ordained and an order that they should not be violated, which ends with the warning '*beware of God because He is shadīd al-ʿiqāb*'. Then, in v. 198, immediately following the verse under discussion, the same wording *iʿlamū anna-llāha shadīd al-ʿiqāb* recurs. *Dhālika*, read as a full sentence, occurs similarly as a full sentence in other parts of the Qur'an, for instance Q. 22:30 and 22:60. It is the context of warning and threatening, rather than informing about God's extensive knowledge, that determines the segmentation of the material and the correct *wajh*, reading and translation of the passage.

In another example, in Q. 6:38 the disbelievers have rejected the Prophet and his teachings. In v. 36, God directs him not to worry about these people since they are like dead people who cannot hear. Then, in Arberry's translation, we read: 'They also say,

"Why has no sign been sent down to him from his Lord?" Say,...No creature is there crawling on the earth, No bird flying with its wings, but they are nations like unto yourselves. We have neglected nothing in the Book; then to their Lord they shall be mustered'. We are told that the obdurate disbelievers have demanded a sign and that they are shown one in the birds and other communities. In the Arabic text the verse continues, 'We have neglected nothing...to their Lord they will return.' This is normally understood to refer to the fact that even birds and animals are mentioned in the Qur'an and that they will be gathered on the Day of Judgement before God (al-Bayḍawī, *Anwār*, 1:300). This is incorrect: the sentence should stop before 'We have neglected nothing', which is a new statement referring not to birds and animals but directed to the disbelievers mentioned earlier as a warning that God has recorded everything in their records of deeds (see also Q. 18:49) and that they will be gathered before Him for Judgement. The following verse, 39, 'Those who deny Our signs are deaf and dumb, in darkness,' reiterates verse 36, 'Only those who can hear will respond, the dead will be raised by God and then will return to Him.' The context then is one of warning the obdurate deniers of God's revelation, rather than informing them about the resurrection of animals and birds. Those who disregard the context incorrectly segment the material and take *al-kitāb* to mean the Qur'an rather than the record of deeds. Even al-Suyūṭī (1987: 7:348) was of this opinion, but this produces an impression of incoherence in the text.[1]

Conclusion

The study of context was developed by Muslim scholars of *balāgha* and *ʿilm al-maʿānī* in their study of the language and style of the Qur'an. As seen in this chapter, context has a critical role in understanding Qur'anic material. Regrettably, like other aspects of *maʿānī*, it has not received sufficient attention in Qur'anic Studies in English, especially given its relevance to issues of translation. Although there is some discussion on *asbāb al-nuzūl*, context as such is not discussed, for example in R. Bell's *Introduction to the Qur'ān, in the Encyclopaedia of Islam*, or in Colin Turner's four-volume anthology, *The Koran: Critical Concepts in Islamic Studies* (apart from in my own article). The terms for context (*siyāq*, *maqām*) are not listed in the Index of Articles or the General Index in the *Encyclopaedia of the Qurʾān*. Only recently have authors, educated in the Arabic-Islamic tradition, where *balāgha* is central, written about context and its effect on *tafsīr* and translation (see sources under Abdel Haleem, Abdul-Raof, Mir, Hatim). It is hoped that more writing on *balāgha* and context will now appear in English and that the subject will find its rightful place in the curricula of Western Qur'anic Studies.

Nearly all English translations of the Qur'an to one degree or another contain errors resulting from insufficient regard to context. However, in spite of the fact that *wujūh* and

[1] Some readers may be disappointed that birds and animals here are not shown to be resurrected or gathered to God, but there are several examples in the hadith to suggest that they are.

conciseness of style may cause difficulties in understanding, as has been seen in the examples discussed, the Qur'an always provides clues either within the verse or the wider context surrounding it or in the Qur'an as a whole, to remove ambiguity or vagueness and guide to the meaning that the context demands. It becomes imperative to look for these clues when an interpretation or translation results in contradiction, awkwardness, or vagueness in a statement. As scholars of *maʿānī* have said, *li-kulli maqām maqāl* (each context has its own appropriate words). The context is the starting point and should be kept constantly in mind.

Bibliography

Abdel Haleem, M. *Divine Oaths in the Qur'an. Journal of Qur'anic Studies* Occasional Paper 1. London: SOAS, 2013.

Abdel Haleem, M. 'The "Sword Verse" Myth'. In: *Exploring the Qur'an.* London: I. B. Tauris, 2016–17.

Abū Ḥayyān Gharnāṭī, *al-Baḥr al-muḥīṭ.* Beirut: Dār Iḥyāʾ al-Turāth al-ʿArabī, 1983.

Academy of the Arabic Language. *al-Muʿjam al-wasīṭ.* 2 vols, Cairo: Academy of the Arabic Language, 1972.

al-Bayḍāwī, Nāṣir al-Dīn. *Anwār al-Tanzīl.* Beirut: Dār al-Kutub al-ʿIlmiyya, 1988.

Busuttil, J. J. 'Slay them wherever you find them: Humanitarian Law in Islam'. In: *Revue de droit pénal militaire et de droit de la guerre.* Oxford: Linacre College, 1991.

Cook, M. *The Koran: A Very Short Introduction.* Oxford and New York: Oxford University Press, 2000.

Ḥassān, Tammām. *al-Bayān fī rawāʾi ʿal-Qurʾān.* Cairo: ʿĀlam al-Kutub, 2000.

Ḥassān, Tammām. *al-Lugha al-ʿarabiyya: ma ʿanā wa mabnāhā.* Cairo: al-Hayʾa al-Miṣriyya al-ʿĀmm li'l-Kitāb, 1973.

Ḥassan, Tammām. *al-Sabʿ al-Mathānī. Journal of Qur'anic Studies* 6/2 (2004), 174–7.

Hatim, B. *Arabic Rhetoric: The Pragmatics of Deviation from Linguistic Norms.* Munich: Lincom Europa, 2010.

Nahj al-balāgha. Ed. Muḥammad ʿAbdūh. 1st edn. Beirut: Muʾassasat al-Taʾrīkh al-ʿArabī, 2013.

Lane, E. W. *An Arabic-English Lexicon.* 8 vols. London: Willams & Norgate, 1863.

al-Qazwīnī, al-Khaṭīb. *al-Īḍāḥ fī ʿulūm al-balāgha.* Cairo: Ṣubaiḥ, 1971.

al-Rāzī, Fakhr al-Dīn. *al-Tafsīr al-kabīr.* Lebanon: Dār Iḥyāʾ al-Turāth al-ʿArabī, n.d.

al-Suyūṭī, Jalāl al-Dīn. *al-Itqān fī ʿulūm al-Qurʾān.* 2 vols. Beirut: Dār Iḥyāʾ al-ʿUlūm, 1987.

Watt, W. M. and R. Bell *Introduction to the Qur'an.* Edinburgh: Edinburgh University Press, 1970.

Wehr, Hans. *A Dictionary of Modern Written Arabic.* (ed.). J. M. Cowan. 4th edn. Ithaca, NY: Spoken Language Services Inc., 1979.

CHAPTER 38

POPULAR CULTURE AND THE QUR'AN

Classical and Modern Contexts

BRUCE LAWRENCE

Overview

In writing about popular culture and the Qur'an over time, moving from classical to modern contexts, one has to establish balance from the outset. Where does the emphasis fall, on the classical or the modern? Is it origins or sequels that matter most in examining, and then interpreting how popular culture relates to the Qur'an?

The current chapter will explore the reciprocal but also ambiguous relationship between the Qur'an and popular culture. It will address the central question: how does a bound book in period-specific Arabic become a universal source of mercy in multiple dialects of Arabic but also in multiple non-Arabic languages, as also for oral cultures, semi-literate populations, and non-elite groups, all of whom draw upon and relate to its divine aura? Issues of language access/privilege, literacy in multiple registers, and the post-Enlightenment, colonial triad of reason/belief/magic—all have to be examined with attention to the central role of the Qur'an as both vehicle and transformer of popular culture, for Muslims and non-Muslims, from West Africa to South-East Asia.

A preliminary question concerns the distinction between popular culture and popular religion. Popular religion is deemed to be in conflict with the central message of the Qur'an: *tawḥīd*, or the unqualified oneness of the Absolute Other, the Eternal Source, Allāh. Popular religion is linked to idol worship of the *jāhiliyya*, or period of ignorance; it entails goddess worship, spirit intercession, sorcery, grave visitation, and relic adoration. In short, it derives from and perpetuates superstition, magic, and unbelief. Yet popular religion persists under Muslim rule in multiple Muslim societies, often through the rubric of *ʿādāt*, or local customs. And *ʿādāt*, in turn, almost always entails material objects: tomb-sanctuaries and sacred natural sites, along with clothing, writing, or amulets that relate to them and evoke their efficacy. It also can be, and sometimes is, linked to regional politics of identity as in Indonesia where *ʿādāt* encompasses both the laws and rights of indigenous people (Davidson and Henley 2007: esp. 1–42).

In what follows I want to distinguish popular culture from popular religion, even while noting where and how they elide. Instead of presuming that popular culture, like popular religion, is 'bad' and by nature un-Islamic, I will focus on the use of Qur'anic idioms, verses, and chapters in a variety of cultures across time. Islam, like any religion, involves continuity as well as discontinuity; its norms and values mark difference through borders and boundaries, separating Islam from its precursors and rivals, yet at the same time Islam relies on sameness for its emotive appeal, its social diffusion, and its historical survival. The central distinction, I want to argue, is not theological but social. It is the interface between high and low culture, between elites and non-elites. It is neither unique nor peculiar to Islam. It resonates in all periods and all places in global history. The esteemed fifth-/eleventh-century polymath al-Bīrūnī reviewed Greeks and Romans, Jews, Christians, and Mazdeans in their disposition to higher thought. All groups and communities, he observed, had elites and masses, the educated few and the uneducated many. About educated Hindu elites, he wrote: 'they believe with regard to God that he is one, eternal, without beginning and end, acting by free-will, all-wise, almighty, living, giving life, ruling, preserving; one who in his sovereignty is unique, beyond all likeness and unlikeness, and that he does not resemble anything nor does anything resemble him...' but their contemporaries, the large mass of uneducated Hindus, saw all things metaphysical as physical, beseeching not one but many gods, and accessing each in relation to material benefits, everyday desires, and inexhaustible needs (Embree 1971: 27, 111–12).

While one might disagree with al-Bīrūnī's assumption that religious instincts and practices among the masses are blameworthy, he has made a pivotal empirical claim, to wit, that the distinction between high/low, educated/uneducated, literate elites and illiterate masses persists across time, place, region, and culture. This is as true for Muslims as it is for other human social groups. Popular culture in all ages and all regions is deemed to reflect low rather than high culture. Popular equals plebian—at once reflexive and unexamined, everyday and unregulated, tethered by animal instinct. While elite culture encourages dispassionate, abstract thought, popular culture prizes the practical results of passionate engagement with material objects and pervasive spirits.

For the classical period of Islamic civilization the American cultural historian Kathleen O'Connor has offered a comprehensive survey of the many popular uses of the Qur'an over time. She has drawn special attention to the dichotomy presupposed in the use of 'popular' as a qualifier. Popular religion, she notes, 'usually is the second of a pair of opposite or complementary terms implying a hierarchical and dichotomized view of religion, such as official and popular religion, or normative and popular religion, paralleling other dichotomizations, such as orthodox and heterodox religion, and elite and folk religion'. She elaborates on how both authority and legitimacy are attached to these categories in scholarly literature. She notes the further irony that 'the vernacular religious creativity and interpretive negotiations of actual believers in the para-liturgical uses of the Qur'an include the *ʿulamāʾ* or Islam's religious hierarchy. Yet it is these same scholars who make elite materials available to the masses, especially through popular devotional material, like prayer manuals, prophetic medical texts, charm- and talisman-making booklets, as well as editions of the Qurʾān marked with methods for divination and dream interpretation.' While agreeing with her mode of analysis and conclusions, I want to emphasize that the high/low, elite/mass social distinction is itself the crucial catalyst for the dichotomized structures, judgements, and values that become evident in the dispersion and usage of Qur'anic dicta in parts of Asia and Africa (O'Connor 2014).

While one cannot examine popular culture in Muslim societies without also taking account of popular religion and material culture, it would be a mistake to look at either popular religion or material culture as equivalent to popular culture for Muslims. The added element is the Qur'an. One must take account of what is distinctive about the Qur'an *in* popular culture. To highlight the agency of the Qur'an as both text and icon I want to begin where most end. I want to pay special attention to the diffuse, often subversive use of Qur'anic idioms and citations in the contemporary period, that is, during the past twenty-five years. Qur'anic dicta have proliferated during the Information Age, especially due to the pervasive presence of the internet, founded by the British computer-scientist, Tim Benders-Lee in 1989. At the same time, both offline and online, there are commercially motivated and widely circulated uses of the Qur'an that permeate almost all modern societies. Beyond the horror stories of Qur'an burnings, there are the efforts of Muslim youth, video-bloggers, Facebookers, comedians, and others, to use Qur'anic passages or symbols to project their message, to attract audiences, and to secure commercial recompense for their creativity. On the one hand, there are Qur'anic themes in popular literature, whether graphic novels, comic books, or political cartoons, as also the use of Qur'anic letters, terms, passages by Muslim artists, both at the low end and high end of contemporary global art. But there is also the pivotal role of music—from whirling dervishes and sacred dance performances to Muslim heavy metal bands, hip hop artists, folk music, punk rock artists, and Islamic MTV. While this chapter must be selective, it will still try to account for popular use of the Qur'an by artists from India and Indonesia, as also from the Maghrib, Egypt, and the Mashriq during the past quarter of a century.

In the conclusion I will focus on the unending dialectic between iconic and disputatious invocations of Qur'anic themes, letters, and passages, highlighting the Qur'an's dual role as sacred source and public commodity via an Indonesian Sufi web master.

Introduction

Let me begin with an aphorism. Popular culture can be evoked by the three ms: music, magic, and medicine. It is not reduced to only these categories or practices, and other categories such as preaching or public *tafsīr* performance (see e.g. Brigaglia 2014: 379–415 on *qiṣāṣ* and *tafsīr* popularization in contemporary Nigeria) could be added, but without music, magic, and medicine popular culture becomes an abstract commentary on class or social difference, not an observation on its pragmatic, daily function.

Let me restate the novelty of my approach. I intend to suspend the teleological habit. Instead of trolling from the classical to the modern, from the first/seventh to the twenty-first century, I will fast forward from first-/seventh-century Arabia to twenty-first-century America.

One of the events defining twenty-first-century America and the Muslim world is 9/11. The event has been discussed in many forums often from competing perspectives, but in the domain of popular culture one approach that is often overlooked is the Muslim rapper response. It is not the event itself, but the American response, the twin wars, first in Afghanistan (after October 2001) and then in Iraq (after March 2003), that have become the focus of attention and criticism. Consider one example of Qur'an popularized protest rap which features the Egyptian-American linguist, Samy Alim, who takes as his Qur'an rapping subjects, JT Bigga Figga and Mos Def.

It was July 2006 when Fun^Da^Mental put out a track titled '786 All is War'. To any Muslim 786 immediately triggers, or should trigger, *abjād*, the system of calculating names via numbers, and in this case 786 as representing the *basmala*, or opening invocation of the Qur'an, '*Bismillāh al-raḥmān al-raḥīm*' (In the name of God, the Most Merciful, Ever Merciful). While that connection may be logical, reflexive, and natural for most Muslims, what was to follow took the listener in a novel direction. (See the discussion of these lyrics in Wilson 2006:133.)

Here is an Islamic sci-fi futuristic counterattack against the United States plotted by Muslim invaders/liberators. Beyond invoking the Qur'an in its opening stanza, it goes on to use other Qur'anic images, and to solicit the support of other citizen allies who while non-Muslim are equally troubled by the disconnect between the United States as a democratic, free, and just society and the role of American warriors and weapons, especially drone missiles, as perpetrators of destruction on a mass scale, mostly of Muslim populations, for more than a decade.

In a slamming electronic riff, with a background chorus, the track ends with a resounding plea, making dramatic use of the *basmala* formula.

Interestingly, the numerical code of the *basmala* is subsumed as an echo of the entire Qur'anic message but one that builds toward social justice. The tone is holistic in rhyme and in time. In the new century all is compressed, so that shorthand becomes code. Not just congregate or dominate or propagate but also, crucially, emancipate in the name of God, the most Merciful, ever Merciful.

To some, this link of the Qur'an to twenty-first-century American popular culture will seem strained and far-fetched at best, sacrilegious and defiling at worst. Yet the semiotic appeal to the Qur'an in American popular culture surfaces at one end of a long, diverse spectrum of performers who link the Qur'an to black rap. Samy Alim focuses on the American rapper JT Bigga Figga, who sees black street argot as an echo of the creative use of language in the Qur'an. Describing the inventive wordplay of fellow rapper E-40, JT says:

> It's almost like with Allāh how he'll describe his prophets as moonlight. He'll describe his word that he speaks in a metaphoric phrasing. Where he'll say the

> clouds and when they swell up heavy and the water goes back to the earth, distilling back to earth. The water's heavier than gravity so it distills back to the earth on dry land, producing vegetation and herbs comin' up out the ground, you feel me?...And that's kinda like what E-40 do when he take something and take a word and apply it, you feel me? (Alim 2005: 268).

Even more explicit in linking Qur'anic terminology to hip-hop scripts is the Muslim rapper Mos Def. Alim notes how Mos Def revels in knowledge of the Qur'an but also in its efficiency as a speedy way of providing vital information.

> 'How much information—vital information—could you get across in three minutes?!', he asks an interviewer. 'You know, and make it so that...I mean, the *Qurʾān* is like that. The reason that people are able to be *hafiz* [one who memorizes the entire Qur'an through constant repetition and study] is because the entire *Qurʾān* rhymes. [Mos Def begins reciting Islamic verses from the Qur'an] "*Bismillah Al-Raḥmān Al-Raḥīm. Al-hamdulillahi Rub Al-Alameen.*" Like everything, you see what I'm saying? I mean, it's any *sūra* [chapter] that I could name. "*Qul huwa Allahu Ahad, Allahu Samad. Lam yalid wa lam yulad wa lam yakun lahu kufwan ahad.*" It's all like that. Like, you don't even notice it. "*Idha ja'a naṣr Allahi wal fath. Wa ra'aita al-nas yadkhuluna fi dini Allahi afwajan. Fa sabbih bi hamdi rabbika wa istaghfiru innahu kana tawwab.*" Like, there's a rhyme scheme in all of it. You see what I'm saying? And it holds fast to your memory. And then you start to have a deeper relationship with it on recitation. Like, you know, you learn *Sūrat al-Ikhlas*, right. You learn *Al-Fatiha*. And you learn it and you recite it. And you learn it and you recite it. Then one day you're reciting it, and you start to understand! You really have a deeper relationship with what you're reciting. "*Aʿudhu billahi min al shaitān al-rajim...*" You be like, "Wow!" You understand what I'm saying? Hip Hop has the ability to do that—on a poetic level.' (Alim 2005: 267)

Qur'an and Popular Culture in Twenty-First-Century Africa/Asia

Like their American counterparts, hip-hoppers in Africa and Asia also relate the Qur'an to contemporary events and global crises. The Dutch trained ethnographer Miriam Gazzah looks at how Moroccan immigrants to the Netherlands coalesce around Maroc-hop. They refuse to accept stereotypical degradations of their origins, culture, and religion. They offer a defence of Arabic terms like jihad, especially as a personal name. The Moroccan-Dutch hip-hopper J-Rock (Jihad Rahmouni) also released his album Jihad in 2006, the same year as '786 All is War', but the tone was much more personal, defending his name and its associations in a lighter, even humorous vein. With echoes behind his voice, he asks the imaginary (female) listener questions as he endeavours to explore and expound jihad as an internal struggle, not a terrorist slogan.

The Qur'anic resonance of jihad as *jihād al-nafs* (Q. 91: 7–10), a non-violent struggle of the soul, pervades (Gazzah 2008: 225–77).

Also personal and affective rather than political and confrontational is the Qur'anic style of Indonesian painters and musicians. The cultural diversity and geographical expanse of the Archipelago renders any observation problematic, unless it is heavily qualified, contextualized, and localized, as American anthropologist, Kenneth George, has made clear. George has studied the acrylic artist Abdeljalil Pirous, and highlighted how Pirous's rendering of the Qur'anic text as artistic calligraphy is itself problematic. Pirous, a native of Banda Aceh, has produced extraordinary pictures of Qur'anic suras, yet some Indonesian religious authorities consider his art a profanation. Pirous himself was moved to link contemporary politics to Qur'anic dicta. He considered the terrible fate that befell Indonesians after the fall of Soeharto in 1998 during the struggle known as Reformasi, or the Period of Reform, through Qur'anic idioms. 'Has That Light Already Shown Down from Above?' was one such work based on *Sūrat al-Raᶜd* (Q. 13):

> God does not change the state of a people
> Until they change themselves.
> When God intends misfortune for a people
> No one can avert it
> And no savior will they have apart from Him.
> (Q. 13:11b, as quoted in George 2010: 125)

At the same time there are a group of Javanese musicians who have studied abroad yet remain so close to Indonesian cultural resources that they compose popular pieces bridging Islamic belief and modern entertainment. Again, it is an ethnographer, in this case, an Indonesian ethnomusicologist trained in the United States, who has studied the professional trajectory of her compatriot and co-religionist, Trisutji Kamal. A contemporary Indonesian composer, successful in both art and film music, she combined forms and techniques of European art music with Islamic ritual and performance, including stress on Qur'anic recitation. Her 1990s magisterial work, Persembhan, literally means worship. It blurs the boundaries between musical performance and religious ritual for her listeners. Not only does the composer introduce many Qur'anic phrases into the composition but she also makes the performance itself an echo of prayer, neither crossing into Western modes of expression nor voicing the combativeness of her American and Dutch-Moroccan contemporaries (Notosudirdjo 2011: 299–306).

From American hip-hop to Indonesian hybrid scores, the Qur'anic idiom suffuses the style of myriad Muslim performers. Not all strands of Islam accept parallels between hip-hop and Qur'anic recitations. To the orthodox minded, the suras of the Qur'an, like the performance of the *adhān*, or call to prayer, are meant to be chanted (*tilāwa*), a vocal practice related to but distinct from singing (*ghanniya*). These definitional boundaries break down across generational lines, with younger people embracing hip-hop as a boost to their understanding of Islam. Eman Tai, a female member of the Calligraphy of Thought spoken-word collective, connects hip-hop to Islam's history. 'It's part of our history and culture in Islam,' she muses. 'The traditional books of law and philosophy in Islam were written in poetry, and students memorize them with drums, basically singing out the poetry. And if you "beat" that up, it sounds just like rapping' (Liu n.d.).

Ibn Muqlah (d. 328/940) might not recognize himself in the Calligraphy of Thought, but others who relate to high culture in modern day Europe and America do look at calligraphy as expressive of Islam's deepest aesthetic tone. Mohamed Zakariya, having mastered the art of traditional Ottoman calligraphy, has also provided the Arabic design for the first Eid stamp issued from the US Postal Service (<http://www.zakariya.net/history>), while across the Atlantic Ocean in the United Kingdom the Egyptian born Ahmed Moustafa has produced a stunning set of Qur'anic evocations as well as a Kaʿba cube that reflect high calligraphy at its most creative zenith (Moustafa and Sperl 2014). Yet their work contrasts not just with the Calligraphy of Thought but also with the graffiti art emerging from the 2010–11 Arab uprisings. Even as the Arab Spring threatened to become a forlorn autumn, then a dark winter after the elected president of Egypt, Mohammed Mursi, was replaced with yet another military dictator, Egyptians continued to express hope in graffiti art that evoked not just resistance but also restraint, as in the Qur'anic dictum:

> If you raise your hand to kill me,
> I will not raise mine to kill you.
>
> (Q. 5:28, cited in Hamdy and Karl 2014)

Poets also responded to the first hope of regime change in Cairo with a Qur'anic trope. An American writer and journalist, Ursula Lindsay, captured the intensity of these now distant moments when she wrote about two subjects: Hasan Talab and Tamim Barghouti.

This is reflected in the lines with which Hasan Talab penned the opening (or *fātiḥa*) of his collection of verse titled *The Revolution's Testament and Its Qurʾān*, alluding to the revolution:

> At times the swiftness of change seemed to confound the imagination, producing tasteless results. The urge to comment on an event that augured uncertainty as well as portentous change often led to trite, bombastic statement art that inevitably appeared static and shortsighted.

Yet Egyptian-Palestinian poet Tamim Barghouti captured the heartbeat of the revolutionary spirit in his epic colloquial poem 'O People of Egypt' (*Yā Shaʿb Maṣr*), recited on several occasions. Barghouti, like Talab, uses Qur'anic references, but in his verses they suggest the restless motion of the future, how the revolution remains to be achieved, at once relived and retold (Lindsey 2012).

Qur'anic imagery evokes hope, even as it requires patience. To whatever period one turns or whatever place one visits, the same irony echoes. It is not just a generational but also a class distinction. The Qur'anic resource is used for multiple audiences with different aesthetic and social judgements about its validity. The major cleavage persists: hip hop and street graffiti are deemed to be low or popular culture while artful design and calligraphy are high culture, yet focus on the Qur'an connects one with the other.

The same cleavage permeates music and poetry in the public square where the Qur'an cannot escape the impact of globalized commodification. Both are defined as skirting the boundaries of permissibility in conservative Islamic circles. The Prophet, one can argue, prohibited music but allowed the beautiful voice. Hence Qur'anic recitation is permissible, while music for profane purposes is not. The line is hazy, however, and it has been made still hazier by global consumer culture which echoes the sacred yet always with commercial intent. *Qawwali*, celebrated throughout the Indian subcontinent, has become profane in Bollywood yet when a *qawwal* like Nusrat Fateh Ali Khan performs *Allah Hoo Allah Hoo Allah Hoo*, resonant with Qur'anic themes, he too is not simply applauded, but also handsomely paid. The same can be, and must be, said of the Mevlevis. Descendants of Mawlānā Jalāl al-Dīn Rūmī (d. 672/1273), the famed Whirling Dervishes celebrate music, as well as dance, in modern day Istanbul, but often they do so in settings where tourists are expected to attend and to pay for spiritual entertainment. A spiritual affinity with Islam may be moot but still present. Not only does an actual Qur'an recitation introduce each performance of dervish dance, but the one performing is said to mirror the nature of creation: the goal of the *semazen* or twirler is not to lose consciousness or to fall into a state of ecstasy. Instead, by revolving in harmony with all things in nature—from the smallest cells to the stars above—the *semazen* testifies to the existence and the majesty of the Creator, thinking of Him, praying to Him, and, above all, giving thanks to Him. In rapt performance the *semazen*, whatever the economic benefit, hopes to confirm the words of the Qur'an (Q. 64:1): 'Whatever is in the skies or on earth invokes God'.

Magic and Medicine

The pattern of a cleavage between high/low, elite/mass culture, as also between economic/spiritual motives, also pertains to magic and medicine: should it be allowed, and to what extent? And who benefits? While the role of magic changes across time, the Qur'an remains central to its practice, performance, and durability in Muslim societies.

Of special, often apotropaic value are certain verses, such as *Āyat al-Kursī* (Q. 2:255), *Āyat al-Nūr* (Q. 24:35), or the verse cited so often in Shīʿī *taʿwīdh* Q. 68: 50–2 ('They claim: Surely he is possessed while he is no more than a reminder to the worlds'). No one has examined their persistent appeal and repeated use more thoroughly than the literary/exegetical scholar Walid Saleh. 'Each of the 114 chapters of the Qur'an', observes Saleh in an astute summary of what he terms 'the theology of reading',

> has special powers of salvation. Each held a key to a certain aspect of the path to God, and each chapter came to have a specific *ḥadīth* (based on the authority of Muḥammad) that explicitly states what powers and benefits the act of reading it

> bestows on the believer. Reading chapter 91, for example, is equivalent to giving the whole earth as alms to the poor. Benefits from reading the chapters varied from success and rewards in this world, like wealth, good health, and absence of hardship, to pardon of sins, and admittance to paradise in the world to come. Reading, to take another example, chapter 95 assures the believer wealth in this world and certitude in his or her faith in God. While reading some of the chapters can assure material success, most of the promised rewards were to be attained on Judgment Day and in the afterlife. It is these kinds of traditions that predominate: the reader of chapter 98 will be in the company of those saved on the Day of Judgment; the power of reading chapter 101 is such that it can tilt the primordial scale of justice in favor of good deeds; by reading chapter 108 one gets to drink from the rivers of paradise, and so on. Reading the Qur'an has also the power of transporting the believer to the time of Muḥammad in order to partake of his blessed presence. (Saleh 2010: 364)

All of these acts are not just condoned but also supported, encouraged, and dispersed across time and space. Yet they are but one end of a spectrum for filling human needs that the Qur'an itself supports by 'magical' means. There is also attention to the disconnected letters (the famed *al-ḥurūf al-muqaṭṭaʿā* that appear at the beginning of twenty-nine Qur'anic suras), and much speculation has been directed to their significance as precisely symbols of the *mutashābih* or ambiguous level of Qur'anic dicta (see especially treatment of *al-Ḥawāmīm* in Dayeh 2010).

Whether theologically validated or juridically outlawed, uses of the disconnected letters are not far separated as functions from acts of reciting the Qur'an for purposes of gaining special power from specific words, that is, from practices known as divination, asking for divine direction through a sign or omen. O'Connor remains a valuable source for tracing these practices. Labelled as *faʾl*, a sign or omen; or *istikhāra*, 'seeking goodness and the best outcome', they all presuppose the Absolute Other, the Supreme Source, Allāh. This form also applies to dream interpretation. Dream interpretation rests on a single Qur'anic proof text, saying that believers will receive 'glad tidings (*al-bushrā*) in the life of this world and in the next' (Q. 10:64). Yet dream experiences are validated through, and also modelled on, prophetic characters in the Qur'an, whether Abraham, Joseph, or the Prophet Muḥammad, whose journey/ascent happened at night, and can be interpreted either as a physical miracle or a 'mere' dream experience (Q. 17:1, 17:60).

While the importance of dreams and visions is connected to Qur'anic prophets, and also extolled in interpretive commentaries, it is their popular use and their economic benefit for dream interpreters that needs to be stressed. Popular manuals of dream divining and encyclopaedias of dream interpretation abound in the public squares of major cities in North and West Africa. Because they require experts for their power to be channelled, they are also a source of income. Many are the professional readers, often women, who combine techniques of astrology and numerology with divining the Qur'an in order to assist believers with the decisions facing them, and to be paid for their services.

The Qur'an itself hints at the hidden knowledge and guidance inherent in its message: 'And with Him are the keys of the secret things; none know them but He: He knows whatever is on the land and in the sea' (Q. 6:59). It is the faithful practitioner, often assisted by an expert, who must find the keys, and the most frequent practice is to open the text of the Qur'an spontaneously, and then select a verse by pointing and not looking. What motivates the concern? Is it a prospective journey, an upcoming business or employment situation? Is it a health question, the timing of an event, perhaps a medical or surgical treatment, or a marriage, or even a divorce? In each instance, the reader is guided to interpret the Qur'anic verse(s), in order to learn the final outcome. Although sorcery was proscribed in the Qur'an, popular reliance on divination via the Qur'an was deemed not just lawful but useful, and for some necessary.

Intercession through the Qur'an is especially powerful in its numeric orchestration through water. Numerology or the science of numbers plays a crucial role in the prescriptions of mercy that diviner/saints make to dispel the evil one. Since every letter in the Arabic alphabet carries a value, those numbers when added up can give a total that symbolically represents the holy phrase. No phrase is deemed to be more important than the *Fātiḥa,* or opening chapter. A Sufi expert in medicine declared that these seven verses 'provide the key to acquiring riches, success and strength. They act as a medicine and a cure, dispelling sadness, depression, anguish and fear' (Chishti 1991: 159–62).

For many the meaning of the Opening Chapter is summed up in its first words: 'In the Name of God, the Most Merciful, Ever Merciful.' This phrase is known as the *basmala*, and since it represents 786, those numbers are thought to convey its power if correctly used. The number 786 may be written on a piece of paper or voiced as a silent prayer; it may be spoken aloud as though it were a prayer; it may be written on glass and the ink washed off, then drunk as medicine; or it may be affixed to some part of the body or, in the case of a corpse, it may be buried with the deceased in the ground.

Often 786 is written at the top of a paper or material conveying the *basmala*, but then applied to specific words that are written out in Arabic script, in order to make the prescription of mercy effective:

- If a woman suffers from headache, she might wear around her neck a prescription of mercy that reads 'O God' in symmetrical rows of three
- Or if her baby has measles, she might have an expanded diagram of O God 16 times that encompass the first nine numbers in Arabic.
- If it is eye pain that causes distress, then the form of 'O God' may be written as though it were the upper and lower eyelid, and on each corner within a rectangular box one of the mighty intervening angels is invoked: O Gabriel, O Michael, O Azrael, O Israfil!
- For beautiful women or women at risk because of their evident charm, the evil to ward off comes from the eye of others. It is known as the evil eye, and the defense against it is a Qur'anic prescription of mercy that numbers the *basmala* at top and then in even patterns of four invokes God by his pronominal referent 'O He!', 'O He!' 16 times.
- And for women who cannot conceive, there is a still more elaborate formula of the pronominal invocation. After invocation of 786, 'O He' has to be written 35 times, in

> 5 rows of 7 pronouns each. Once written, preferably in vegetable ink, it is then washed off and drunk by the woman hoping to conceive. (Chishti 1991: 134–40)

Still other formulae apply to amulets that cover a variety of distresses, from nosebleeds to labour pains, from toothaches to abscesses. Huge and varied is the inventory of Qur'anic invocations in use today throughout the Muslim world. Men may be the religious functionaries dispensing them, but many, if not most of their clients are Muslim women, and economic transaction is integral to their quest for health. Whether literate or illiterate, privileged or poor, these clients pay because they trust in the Qur'an as the medical mediation for whatever afflicts them or those closest to them.

O'Connor traces these reflexes back to the classical period, to the formation of Islam and also their rejection to declamations from medieval scholars such as Ibn Taymiyya and al-Suyūṭī. The forms from pre-Islamic to Islamic times remain remarkably similar. Specific objects are invested with special power, words/letters that epitomize all truth, health, and healing, but what matters most is not just reliance on professional healers but also intent or *niyya*.

Yet if intent becomes paramount, and purity of intent is known to God alone, then the scope of Qur'anic healing can be, and often is, vastly extended. Qur'anic authority pervades even without explicit citation of Qur'anic passages. Carla Bellamy, an anthropologist working in North India during the first decade of the twenty-first century, noted the story about Moses and Pharaoh's magicians had Qur'anic antecedents. It can be traced to Q. 7:109–26, 10:79–81, 20:43–7 and also 20:65–70, but its everyday use was more important than its scriptural citation. As William James has noted, the truest religion is one most beneficial to functioning in the real (meaning, the material, everyday) world, and so the assumption has been that magic is not a psychological heresy but a real force in the world of 'ordinary' believers. It can be, and is traced, indirectly to the Qur'an through the backstory of magic performed on the Prophet Muḥammad. As Saleh has noted, it is often understood, or presumed that magic was performed against the Prophet, that 'the final two sūras, or chapters, of the Qurʾān are understood to have been given to Muhammad to protect him from magic...' And why are they the final accents of the Noble Book? While some may complain that 'the order of chapters in the Qurʾān is not the order we would like to have,' observes Saleh, 'if a sacred text is to end with a potent charismatic finale, then there is nothing more potent than ascribing an apotropaic power to the words at the very end' (Saleh 2010: 367).

Hence, in contemporary India, as elsewhere, framed calligraphic renderings of these two suras can be found on the walls of Muslim (and occasionally non-Muslim) homes and businesses; these suras are also commonly placed in *taʿwīdh,* those small metal boxes containing Qur'anic verses in Arabic, worn on a string around the neck or upper right arm. And what gives these Qur'anic emblems power is not just their citation as scripture or their link to the Prophet. Rather, 'they are authoritative and popular simply because they are stories about people whose lives provide answers to the types of questions with which pilgrims (that is, those "ordinary" believers who go to saint's shrines) wrestle' (Bellamy 2011: 15–16).

Conclusion

And the wrestling for the hidden keys to health among Muslim consumers of the Qur'an extends to the internet. Since 1994 the sacred source has become a public resource, and also a further means to tap into global consumer culture. Not limited to believers or to one group of believers, the Qur'an functions in a broad arena of virtual access and unregulated use for Muslims and non-Muslims alike. One instance is the use of Qur'anic passages on the internet to cure AIDS victims. This unexpected and graphic use of protective prayer formulas derived from the Qur'an comes from Indonesia. There a Sufi master has devised a *taʿwīdh* that is posted on-line. It coordinates times of recitation with different locations around the globe. Its purpose is to assist and relieve those who suffer from HIV/AIDS. If one accesses the website, <http://www.all-natural.com/sufi.html>, the first announcement is:

> Sufi Healing
> A. HIV/AIDS TREATMENT
> WITH THE SUFI HEALING METHOD.

The service is offered free through the Barzakh Foundation, and yet one suspects that the domain web master gains some practical benefit from its availability. Muḥammad al-Zuhrī professes to be a Sufi master. Having practised the Sufi healing method for more than twenty years, he claims to have cured many people with cancer, mental illness, leukemia, impotency, and paralysis, and he does it not outside Islam or the Qur'an but within Islam by using the Qur'an. How does that work?

The very title of this group, the Barzakh Foundation, derives from a Qur'anic verse that confronts the fear of death:

> When death finally comes to one of them,
> He says: 'My Lord, send me back,
> That I may do right by what I neglected.'
> There is no way; for that is just talk.
> And before them is a barrier (*barzakh*)
> Until the day they will be resurrected.
>
> Q. 24:99–100

Barzakh is a word that Ibn ʿArabī (d. 638/1240) used repeatedly. For the Andalusian mystic, it became a key term connoting the passage from this physical world to the world beyond death that is spiritual, but also the space that each individual occupies after death and before the Day of Resurrection. Through their keen insight, Sufi masters, like Ibn ʿArabī and like Muḥammad Zuhrī, are able to see the passage awaiting each person as they leave the material realm and before they experience the blinding light of eternity. This practice relies not only on ritual prayer, or *ṣalāt*, but also on voluntary meditation, or *dhikr*. Though *dhikr* may be simply translated as 'divine remembrance', it is much more than isolated or random remembrance. It is a rigorous daily practice, common to all Sufi groups, but here it is also practised as a method to cure mental or physical illness. It requires repeating verses from the Qur'an or God's beautiful names, including the pronoun 'Hu' or 'He', under the supervision of Muḥammad Zuhrī, whether in person or by internet connection.

As a Sufi master, Muḥammad Zuhrī also uses some of the techniques described earlier. To mediate the divine will and understand the *barzakh* awaiting each patient/petitioner, he combines the uses of God's names and Qur'anic verses with prayer in a specific and complex method. The formulations may be written on a paper, bone, or leather. Those things are to be put in a glass of water to be taken by the patient or buried in the ground, or carried around by the patient. The formulations can also be spoken aloud or in the heart, or using many other ways.

Because this comes very close to magic, Muḥammad Zuhrī is careful to remind his audience that the practice he advocates 'uses power from God's angels for constructive purposes only, and it is not the same with voodoo, black magic, or witchcraft which use the power from jinn or evil spirits, often for destructive purposes.'

To the uninitiated, this may sound like white magic rather than black magic. Yet it is also a pervasive and powerful application of Qur'anic resources. It is popular religion projected transnationally with an appeal to a global consumerist culture. While intended mainly for a Muslim audience, it also offers hope to all who come to this therapy with the right intent (*niyya*), with sincerity and trust, whatever their religious background. Muḥammad Zuhrī's pledge is 'to cure the already infected patients using every way which is acceptable by human laws and morality or religion'. For those who suffer AIDS and exit this world on a path that parallels the Straight Path but does not intersect it, this is perhaps the most radiant light from the Qur'an, Sufi healing in its source but non-creedal in its expanse and seemingly without cost (Lawrence 2006: 184–92).

In multiple ways the temporal and spatial boundaries of the Qur'an have been expanded through popular culture. Reflected in magic, music, and medicine, popular uses of Qur'anic dicta and themes have also now been disseminated on the World Wide Web to encompass an audience unimaginable just twenty-five years ago, before the invention and proliferation of online resources. While the Qur'an itself remains stable, an anchor of authority and piety, it still resonates with different classes of consumers according to a pattern of taste and sensibility that has endured for more than a millennium, and will not likely be altered in the new millennium.

Bibliography

Alim, H. Samy. 'A New Research Agenda: Exploring the Transglobal Hip Hop Umma'. In: Miriam Cooke and Bruce B. Lawrence (eds.). *Muslim Networks from Hajj to Hip-Hop*, pp. 264–74. Chapel Hill: University of North Carolina Press, 2005.

Bellamy, Carla. *The Powerful Ephemeral; Everyday Healing in an Ambiguously Islamic Place*. Berkeley: University of California Press, 2011.

Brigaglia, Andrea. '*Tafsīr* and the Intellectual History of Islam in West Africa: The Nigerian Case'. In: Andreas Gorke and Johanna Pink (eds.). *Tafsir and Islamic Intellectual History: Exploring the Boundaries of a Genre*. Oxford and New York: Oxford University Press, 2014.

Chishti, Shaykh Hakim Moinuddin. *The Book of Sufi Healing*. Rochester, VT: Inner Traditions International, 1991.

Davidson, Jamie S. and David Henley (eds.). *The Revival of Tradition in Indonesian Politics: The Deployment of Adat from Colonialism to Indigenism*. London and New York: Routledge, 2007.

Dayeh, Islam, 'Al-Ḥawāmīm: Intertextuality and Coherence in Meccan Surahs'. In: Angelica Neuwirth, Nicolas Sinai, and Michael Marx (eds.). *The Qurʾān in Context: Historical and Literary Investigations into the Qurʾān Milieu*, pp. 461–98. Leiden: E. J. Brill, 2010.

Embree, Ainslee T. *Alberuni's India*. New York: Norton, 1971.

Gazzah, Miriam. *Rhythms and Rhymes of Life: Music and Identification Process of Dutch-Moroccan Youth*. Leiden: Amsterdam University Press, 2008.

George, Kenneth M. *Picturing Islam: Art and Ethics in a Muslim Lifeworld*. Oxford: Wiley-Blackwell, 2010.

Hamdy, Basma and Don Karl, *Walls of Freedom: The Book on Street Art of the Arab Revolution*; accessed online at <http://www.indiegogo.com/projects/walls-of-freedom>.

Lawrence, Bruce B. *The Qurʾān: A Biography*. London: Atlantic Books, 2006.

Lindsey, Ursula. 'Art in Egypt's Revolutionary Square'. January 2012. Available at <|http://www.merip.org/mero/interventions/art-egypts-revolutionary-square>, and also for the YouTube of the entire Maghrouti poem in Arabic, see <https://www.youtube.com/watch?v=LaeC83g1zZU>.

Moustafa, Ahmed and Stefan Sperl. *The Cosmic Script: Sacred Geometry and the Science of Arabic Penmanship*. New York: Inner Traditions, 2014.

Notosudirdjo, R. and S. Franki. 'Islam, Politics and The Dynamic of Contemporary Music in Indonesia'. In: David R. Harnish and Anne K. Rasmussen (eds.). *Divine Inspirations: Music and Islam in Indonesia*, pp. 297–317. New York: Oxford University Press, 2011.

O'Connor, Kathleen M. 'Popular and Talismanic Uses of the Qurʾān'. In: Jane Dammen McAuliffe (ed.). *Encyclopaedia of the Qurʾān*. 6 vols., 4:163–82 Leiden: Brill, 2001–6.

Saleh, Walid A. 'Word', In: Jamal J. Elias (ed.). *Key Themes for the Study of Islam*, pp. 356–76. Oxford: Oneworld, 2010.

Spooky, D. J. (ed.). *Fear of a Muslim Planet: The Islamic Roots of Hip-Hop*. Cambridge, MA: MIT Press, 2008.

Swedenborg, Ted. 'Fun^Da^Mental's "Jihad Rap"'. In: Linda Herrera and Asef Bayat (eds.). *Being Young and Muslim: New Cultural Politics in the Global South and North*, pp. 291–308. New York: Oxford University Press, 2010 and <http://swedenburg.blogspot.com/2006/10/fundamentals-786-all-is-war-sufi.html>.

Wilson, Scott. *Great Satan's Rage*. Manchester: Manchester University Press, 2006.

Zakariya, Mohamed. <http://www.zakariya.net/history>.

CHAPTER 39

THE WESTERN LITERARY TRADITION AND THE QUR'AN

An Overview

JEFFREY EINBODEN

The Qur'an and *The Canon*

Long regarded as one of America's leading literary critics, Harold Bloom published his *The Western Canon: The Books and School of the Ages* in 1994. Focusing on familiar figures, from Dante Alighieri to Emily Dickinson, Bloom concludes his study with long 'lists' of literary classics, cataloguing the canon from its antique origins to its tentative futures. Among expected choices—fictions such as *The Iliad*, *Hamlet*, *Middlemarch*—Bloom's appendix includes also a choice somewhat less expected: 'The Koran' (Bloom 1994: 497). Reflecting its growing recognition as not only 'spiritual' but 'aesthetic', the Qur'an's inclusion in the modern 'Canon' hints too at its consistent, though often concealed, contributions to 'Western' literary history, with Islamic allusions evident from the beginnings of Europe's vernacular traditions.

Of course, the Qur'an's addition to the 'Western Canon' is also provocative and problematic. Viewed traditionally not merely as inspired, but inimitable, the Qur'an's sacred provenance challenges secular norms of textual criticism and category. The Qur'an's own self-definitions resist the very terms of this present chapter's title, with my adjectives of region and genre—'Western' and 'literary'—newly complicated in light of Islamic revelation. Proclaimed as global and eternal, the Qur'an gestures beyond borders of geography and history, appealing to a divine sovereignty that extends equally to '*the east and the west*' (Q. 2:115). Challenging divisions of time and space, the Qur'an resists too literary division; opposing labels of art and artifice, the scripture distinguishes itself from created verse in particular, self-describing in *āyas* such as Q. 69:41: 'And it is not the word of a poet; little do you understand'.

Posing an interior challenge to exterior critique, the Qur'an's inimitability situates the scripture outside genealogic lines of textual influence. However, despite its extraordinary relationship to literary time and type, the Qur'an has nevertheless punctuated the unfolding of world literatures, its holy text infusing a range of artistic contexts. This chapter will survey the scripture's significant overlaps with the 'Western Literary', reading its interventions in imaginative writings from the late medieval to postmodernity. Although a detailed map of Qur'anic influence is beyond my scope, this chapter seeks to sketch a skeletal 'Overview', balancing broad outline with representative specifics. Illustrative examples from discrete eras and areas—Renaissance, Romantic, Postmodern; Europe, Britain, America—will serve to illumine the Qur'an's literary receptions, accounting for contemporary inclusion of 'The Koran' within the *Western Canon*.

Qur'anic Renaissance

While not the first of its authors, Dante Alighieri is rightly associated with Europe's poetic beginnings. A pioneer of literary practice—in his lyric *La Vita Nuova* (*c.*1295) and epic *Commedia* (*c.*1307–21)—Dante would pioneer also literary theory, defending the rise of the vernacular in his *De vulgari eloquentia* (*c.*1304–5). Helping to establish a self-reliant Western canon, Dante would also, however, help to establish Western reliance on the East, reaching to Islamic precedents even while advancing European poetics. Inscribing Muslim foundations into his *Inferno*, Dante notoriously places 'Mäometto' and 'Alì' in his Hell's Eighth Circle, in a *bolgia* reserved not for 'infidels', however, but for 'schismatics', portraying Islam as an errant sibling within Dante's own religious family. More consequentially, and also inspiring controversy, the very structure of this Italian epic has been traced to Islamic origins, with the Prophet's celestial ascent—his *miʿrāj*—claimed as a model for Dante's divine pilgrimage, positioning the *Commedia* as an unlikely successor to the Qur'an itself.[1]

This ambivalent appeal to Islam by Europe's medieval epic amplifies through the Italian Renaissance, culminating in explicit references to the Qur'an. Produced two centuries after Dante's death, Ludovico Ariosto's *Orlando Furioso* (1516–32), and its successor, Torquato Tasso's *La Gerusalemme liberata* (1581), advance Italy's tradition of narrative poetry, but also deepen this tradition's Islamic debts, grounding their dramatic action in Christian–Muslim warfare. In Canto 38 of his *Orlando Furioso*, Ariosto recounts preparations for a duel between delegates of Emperor Charlemagne and King

[1] For the controversial 'argument that Dante was beholden to Muslim sources', advanced especially by Miguel Asín Palacios, and his 1919 *La escatología musulmana de la Divina Comedia*, see Ziolkowski 2007: 7–9.

Agramant; after selecting their respective weapons, the opposing factions then embrace their respective scriptures:

> duo sacerdoti, l'un de l'una setta,
> l'altro de l'altra, uscîr coi libri in mano.
> In quel del nostro è la vita perfetta
> scritta di Cristo; e l'altro è l'Alcorano.
> Con quel de l'Evangelio si fe' inante
> l'imperator, con l'altro il re Agramante.
> [Two priests stepped forth book in hand,
> one from one sect, the other from the other sect,
> The book our priest held contained the unblemished life
> Of Christ; the other's book was the Koran
> With the priest of the Gospel stepped forward
> the Emperor; with the other, King Agramant.][2]

Distinguished first by their arms, Christian and Muslim adversaries are distinguished next by their 'books', this pageant of chivalry expressed through opposing religious testaments. And it is within this combative context that the Qur'an first surfaces, Ariosto juxtaposing '*l'Alcorano*' and '*l'Evangelio*' as symbolic vehicles of political and martial force. More interesting than its hostile frame, however, is the hospitable union of foreign name and domestic style in Ariosto's poetic form, his verses weaving an Arabic title into the very fabric of his Italian meter and rhyme. Contributing to Ariosto's *ottava rima*, the term '*l'Alcorano*' offers an end-line rhyme with '*mano*' two verses prior, allowing *Orlando Furioso* to resist the Qur'an as an adversary in its content, yet recruit the scripture's title as a partner in its prosody.

Migrating north from Mediterranean shores, the Islamic echoes of Italian romance are muffled, but not altogether muted, as they reach the British Isles. Enjoying an extensive afterlife in England, Dante's own verse would help inspire Britain's primary epic poets—Geoffrey Chaucer, Edmund Spenser, John Milton—whose English works also subtly feature Muslim influences. For example, parallels with Sufi poets have been identified in Chaucer's *Canterbury Tales* (*c.*1388–1400); Spenser's *Faerie Queene* invokes 'Turkes and Sarazins' (1596); while Milton's *Paradise Lost* recalls Islamic, as well as biblical, precedents (1667; 1674).[3] It is not English poetry, however, but English drama, that features the earliest and most direct allusions to the Qur'an. Islam merely surfaces on the margins of Shakespeare's plays, implied in Othello's Moorish heritage, for instance, or in passing references to 'Turks'; only once is the Prophet himself named, with 'Mahomet' mentioned in *Henry VI, Part 1* (1591).[4] But it is Shakespeare's contemporary, Christopher Marlowe, who overtly—indeed shockingly—introduces the Muslim scripture onto the London stage. Composed in the late 1580s, Marlowe's two-part *Tamburlaine the Great*

[2] The original Italian of this passage is sourced from Ariosto 1971: 1153; the provided English translation is adapted slightly from Ariosto 2008: 464.

[3] For Chaucer and ʿAṭṭār, in particular, see Shah 1977: 116–17. Spenser's 'Turkes and Sarazins' are treated by Heberle 1989. For Milton and Islamic parallels, see Maclean 2007.

[4] See Dimmock 2013: 7 for mention of 'Mahomet' in *Henry VI, Part 1*.

proved popular at home in Elizabethan England, but would borrow its subjects from abroad, dramatizing settings and characters native to the Muslim East. Centred on the historical Tīmūr Lang (d. 807/1405), Marlowe's play includes multiple Qur'anic mentions, with the scripture inhabiting his drama's conclusion and climax. Nearing both the dénouement of *Tamburlaine*, and Tamburlaine's own destruction, Marlowe's anti-hero denounces Islam, demanding that 'the Turkish Alcoran' and other 'superstitious books' be brought to his kindled fire:

> So Casane, fling them in the fire.
> Now Mahomet, if thou have any power,
> Come down thy selfe and work a myracle,
> Thou art not woorthy to be worshipped,
> That suffers flames of fire to burn the writ
> Wherein the sum of thy religion rests.
> Why send'st thou not a furious whyrlwind downe,
> To blow thy Alcaron up to thy throne,
> Where men report, thou sitt'st by God himselfe
>
> (Marlowe 2008: 1:210)

Recalling Dante, Marlowe again associates the Islamic sacred with an inferno, enacting the burning of Muslim 'books'. However, inverting Dante's own *Inferno*, Marlowe's *Tamburlaine* does not seem to endorse such desecration, but attributes this blasphemy instead to its antagonist, setting the villainous Tamberlaine against 'Mahomet' as well as the 'Alcaron'. Also surpassing his poetic predecessors, Marlow's theatrical production seems to imagine the Qur'an's own tangible presence, with Muslim 'writ' supposedly 'materializing' on the British stage, as Elizabeth Williamson has most recently discussed.[5] Verbally surfacing in Ariosto's fleeting rhymes, the 'Alcaron' surfaces bodily in Marlowe's theatrical space, occupying the final dramatic acts of *Tamburlaine*.

A creative caution against tyranny, Marlowe's appeal to the Qur'an in *Tamburlaine* seems not only performative, but also political, condemning despotism through Islamic allusion. And in the tumultuous century of British revolution and restoration that follows *Tamburlaine*, the Qur'an will likewise emerge through dramatic protests and polemics. Published anonymously in the climactic year of England's Civil War—1649—*The Famous Tragedie of Charles I* harshly condemns English republicanism, satirizing Oliver Cromwell as he reportedly addresses his co-conspirator, Hugh Peters:

> Thou art that Load-stone, which shall draw
> my sense to any part of policy I'the Machiavilian world,
> we two (like Mahomet and his pliant Monk) will frame
> an English Alchoran, which shall be written with the
> self-same pensil great Draco grav'd his Lawes.[6]

[5] See Williamson 2016: 182–3 for discussion of this quotation in the context of theatrical 'materiality', as well as Marlowe's 'play's sympathetic portrayal of its Muslim characters'.

[6] Quoted from Birchwood 2007: 59, whose Chapter 2 provides illuminating discussion of *The Famous Tragedie of Charles I* in general, and this passage in particular.

Criticizing the 'draconian' atmosphere of England's new Commonwealth, *The Famous Tragedie* equates Cromwell's 'Lawes' to 'an English Alchoran', recruiting the Islamic scripture as a mirror for British social commentary. Seeking to foreignize Cromwell as both 'Machiavilian' and a new 'Mahomet', *The Famous Tragedie* converts Muslim sacred writ for its domestic critique of Puritan politics—a strategy of Qur'anic conversion that also surfaces earlier in Britain's pivotal seventeenth century, informing an icon of English poetics: John Donne (d. 1631). Celebrated for his abstract metaphysics and physical eroticism, Donne gestures to the Qur'an not in his spiritual poetry, but in his spiritual prose. Dean of St. Paul's Cathedral through the last decade of his life, Donne's sermons occasionally fashion a Muslim lens to reflect on Christian doctrine, such as this 1621 defence of the Trinity:

> [...] and hence is it, that in the Talmud of the Jews, and in the Alcoran of the Turks, though they both oppose the Trinity, yet when they handle not that point, there fall often from them, as clear confessions of the three Persons, as from any of the elder of those philosophers, who were altogether disinterested in that controversy.
> (Donne 1953–62: 1:264)

Discovering traditional Christology endorsed in surprising sources, Donne reads 'the Talmud' and 'the Alcoran' against their normative traditions, hearing Christian truth 'confessed' by non-Christian content. Extending a revisionary trajectory begun in Dante's *Inferno*, the Muslim sacred is no longer dismissed as alien in the West, but is drafted as an ally, converted as a 'clear' witness for Donne's theology. Recruited to support his own Christian position, the Qur'an will be recruited also by Donne as he attacks his Christian peers. Exposing the supposed errors of the 'Roman Church' in 1626, Donne justifies his digression on the 'degrees of Glory' ascribed by Catholics to 'the Saints in Heaven' through citing an analogy:

> And so, as *Melancthon* said, when he furthered the Edition of the *Alcoran*, that hee would have it printed, *Vt videamus quale poema sit*, That the world might see what a piece of Poetry the *Alcoran* was; So I have stopped upon this point, that you might see what a piece of Poetry they have made of this Problematicall point of Divinity [...] (Donne 1953–62: 7:131)

Appealing to 'the *Alcoran*' and its publication as precedent for his own 'stopp[ing] upon this point', Donne integrates Arabic scripture and Latin quotation into his English sermon, citing an 'Edition' of the Qur'an even while criticizing Catholic doctrine. Intersecting polemics of religion and rhetoric, Donne's '*Alcoran*' is aligned here too with 'Poetry', citing Protestant understanding of the Muslim scripture as mere verse. Seeming to degrade the Qur'an, this aesthetic accusation is also complicated somewhat by its speaker: John Donne—not only a prominent Anglican priest who was himself born a Catholic, but also a premier English poet. Recalling criticism that reaches back to Europe's literary beginnings, Donne's cited definition of 'the *Alcoran*' as 'a piece of

Poetry' reaches also forward to the following centuries of Western reception, where Renaissance ambivalence towards an aesthetic Qur'an will begin to shift to Romantic admiration.

The Romantic Qur'an

Published in 1734, George Sale's *The Koran, Commonly Called The Alcoran of Mohammad* would mark a decisive shift in Western receptions, both in their quantity, and their character. Distinct from prior European translations—such as Robert of Ketton's Latin (1143), or André Du Ryer's French (1647)—Sale's *Koran* is less polemic in approach, rendering Islamic revelation through English expression that is both more neutral and more nuanced. It is not only the substance, however, but the scaffolding, of Sale's edition that invites literary interest. Introducing Qur'anic 'style' in his lengthy preface—his 'Preliminary Discourse'—Sale would suggest that:

> The style of the Korân is generally beautiful and fluent, especially where it imitates the prophetic manner and scripture phrases. It is concise, and often obscure, adorned with bold figures after the eastern taste, enlivened with florid and sententious expressions, and, in many places, especially where the majesty and attributes of GOD are described, sublime and magnificent; [...] (Sale 1801: 81)

Emphasizing its 'fluent' virtues, Sale presents a 'Korân' that is dynamically 'beautiful', not only 'adorned' but 'enlivened', featuring 'expressions' that are 'florid', and 'figures' that are 'bold'.

A sacred text defined through its 'style', Sale's *Koran* harks back to 'eastern taste', but seems to reflect also the eighteenth-century West, a century that will see the eventual ascendance of Romanticism—a literary school that is itself 'often obscure', even while aspiring to the 'sublime'. Attracted partly by its aesthetic framing, Sale's *Koran* will enjoy unprecedented popularity in Britain and America, with the most prominent Romantics on both sides of the Atlantic appealing to his translation, including Robert Southey, Thomas Moore, Percy Bysshe Shelley, Lord Byron, Washington Irving, R. W. Emerson, Lydia Maria Child, and Edgar Allan Poe.[7]

While Sale lauds 'attributes' that suit his literary age, his literary age will also fashion a Qur'an that suits its own attributes, approaching the Muslim scripture in ways that seem self-reflective. Distinct from the Renaissance Qur'an, Romantic receptions will appeal to the Muslim scripture through personal experience and passionate encounter, through intimate feeling and informal experience—an appeal best exemplified by Britain's most iconic Romantic: Lord Byron. Echoing Sale's 'Preliminary Discourse', the preliminaries

[7] For Romantic reliance on Sale's *Koran* see Sharafuddin 1994 and Einboden 2014.

of Byron's own literary life witness his aesthetic approach to the Qur'an; in 1807, not yet 20 years old, Byron would catalogue a preferred 'List of the different poets, dramatic or otherwise, who have distinguished their respective languages by their productions', which includes:

> *Arabia.*—Mahomet, whose Koran contains most sublime poetical passages, far surpassing European poetry. (Byron 2012: 100–1)

Recalling Sale, the 'Koran' is here characterized again as 'sublime' and 'poetical'. However, Byron advances slightly further in his youthful enthusiasm, finding 'Arabian' scripture to 'surpass' Western verse, 'poetically' privileging Eastern writ over mere 'European'. A literary appreciation, Byron's admiration for the Qur'an will find practical expression as his career unfolds, travelling to Muslim lands for inspiration and adventure. Forming the background to his autobiographic *Childe Harold's Pilgrimage* (1812), as well as his popular series of *Turkish Tales* (1813–16), Byron's mature poetry echoes his Eastern sojourns, with the Qur'an emerging audibly in his English verse. For example, Byron's first *Turkish Tale* concludes with the death of his tragic hero, Hassan, whose grave is inscribed with 'The Koran verse that mourns the dead', and whose piety recalls Islamic prayer, especially the 'solemn sound of "Alla Hu!"' (Byron 2009: 28–9). Integrating Arabic syllables into Romantic poetry, 'Alla Hu!' is also glossed by Byron in a prose footnote, defined as 'the concluding words of the Muezzin's call to prayer' whose 'effect' is often 'solemn and beautiful beyond all the bells in Christendom' (Byron 2009: 46). Associated with both advantage and aesthetics—with going 'beyond' and the 'beautiful'—Qur'anic traditions again 'surpass' the Christian, with European 'bells' hushed by the 'Muezzin's call'.[8]

During the very years Byron's *Turkish Tales* appear in Britain, the Qur'an will also impact the most renowned poet of the Continent: Johann Wolfgang Goethe. Reflecting a generation of German authors with 'Oriental' interests—including J. G. Herder and the Schlegel brothers—Goethe's appeal to the Qur'an dates from his career's beginnings in the 1770s. Revived by his reading of Hafez in 1814, Goethe would deepen his engagement with Muslim sources, investing not only in secondary translations, but in primary tongues. Manuscripts in the following years find the German poet practising Qur'anic calligraphy, scripting Arabic from multiple suras, including Q. 114.[9] This linguistic groundwork culminates in one of Goethe's final literary efforts—his 1819 *West-östlicher Divan*—a poetry collection indebted primarily to Persian poets, but which features also striking Qur'anic intersections. The fifth poem in Goethe's *Divan*, for example, opens with verses that sound distinctly familiar:

[8] My treatment of this specific passage from Byron's *The Giaour* is previously and more fully presented in Einboden 2014: 129–31.

[9] Goethe's inscription of Q. 114 is reproduced in Bosse 1999: 1:619, and receives prior treatment in Einboden 2014: 62–4.

Talismane	[Talismans
Gottes ist der Orient!	To God belongs the Orient!
Gottes ist der Okzident!	To God belongs the Occident!
Nord- und Südliches Gelände	The Northern and Southern lands,
Ruht im Frieden Seiner Hände.	Rest in the peace of His hands.]

Paraphrasing Q. 2:115—'*And to God belongs the east and the west*'—Goethe adapts and extends this single *āya* within his first two lines, producing a German couplet from one Arabic verse. And while lines three and four above are original to Goethe himself, this second half of Goethe's quatrain is also fashioned to balance his initial Qur'anic borrowing, doubling the cardinal directions of lines one and two, adding 'North' and 'South' to 'Orient' and 'Occident'. Practically performing what Donne had alleged in abstract two centuries before, Goethe here refashions the Qur'an into verse, generating a European 'piece of Poetry' from Islamic revelation.[10]

Published late in his career, Goethe's *Divan* would also coincide with an early landmark of American Romanticism: Washington Irving's *Sketch-Book of Geoffrey Crayon, Gent.* First appearing also in 1819–20, Irving's *Sketch-Book* includes his most celebrated fictions, tales such as 'The Legend of Sleepy Hollow' and 'Rip Van Winkle'. Hidden beneath these New England stories, however, would be Irving's attraction to the Muslim sacred—an attraction that develops in the following decade as Irving visits Andalucía, staying at the storied Alhambra Palace. Dazzled by the 'fanciful arabesques, intermingled with texts of the Koran' that 'cover the walls of the Alhambra', Irving will even endeavour to learn Arabic, as evidenced by a manuscript notebook now held by the New York Public Library.[11] Striving to read the wondrous 'texts of the Koran', Irving is led also to write a history of its worldly advent, penning a two-volume biography of Islamic origins, the 1850 *Mahomet and his Successors*. Dedicating his eighth chapter to 'Outlines of the Mahometan Faith', Irving concludes lastly with the Qur'an's own account of 'the *last day*':

> Nevertheless, the description of the *last day*, as contained in the eighty-first chapter of the Koran, and which must have been given by Mahomet at the outset of his mission at Mecca, as one of the first of his revelations, partakes of sublimity:
>
> 'In the name of the all merciful God! a day shall come when the sun will be shrouded, and the stars will fall from the heavens.
>
> 'When the camels about to foal will be neglected, and wild beast will herd together through fear.
>
> 'When the waves of the ocean will boil, and the souls of the dead again united to the bodies.

[10] For this opening quatrain to Goethe's 'Talismane', and its creative adaptation of Q. 2:115, see Mommsen 2012: 185–205. My own discussion of Goethe's efforts to 'complet[e] the Qur'ān's compass' in his 'Talismans' first appears in Einboden 2014: 73–5.

[11] For Irving's appreciation of Alhambra's 'fanciful arabesques', see Irving 1832: 55. For his Arabic Notebook, see Einboden 2009: 5–6 and Einboden 2016: 75–9.

> 'When the female infant that has been buried alive will demand, for what crime was I sacrificed? And the eternal books shall be laid open.
>
> 'When the heavens will pass away like a scroll, and hell will burn fiercely; and the joys of paradise will be made manifest.
>
> 'On that day shall every soul make known that which it hath performed'[12]

Echoing Sale's 1734 meditations on Qur'anic 'style', Irving too finds 'sublimity' in this sura, celebrating the 'eighty-first chapter of the Koran' even as he adapts it for his own chapter conclusion in 1850. Verses of disclosure and confession—in which 'eternal books shall be laid open' and 'every soul make known that which it hath performed'—these lines also conceal Irving's complicity in their fashioning. Although not 'manifest' to his reader, this English version of the 'eighty-first chapter' is rendered and revised by Irving himself; reflecting not merely 'eastern taste', but U.S. imagination, this 'description of the *last day*' witnesses Irving's own efforts to render Muslim scripture, becoming not only a founding father of his nation's fiction, but also one of its first Qur'an translators (Einboden 2009: 5). In associating Islam with apocalypse and the afterlife, this recent US reception also recalls the very 'outset' of Western literature, reaching back to Dante. However, inverting the *Inferno*, it is the eschatology of 'the Koran' itself which here speaks in literary translation, with a fuller Islamic spectrum informing this American vision, Irving's authorship appealing not only to the 'fierce' burning of 'hell', but also to 'the joys of paradise'.

The Qur'an's Postmodern Postscripts

With the advance of the nineteenth century and eclipse of Romanticism, literary investment in the Qur'an too would begin to wane. The view from Victorian Britain most often cited is Thomas Carlyle's, who would unsympathetically declare in 1840 that 'Nothing but a sense of duty could carry any European through the Koran', asserting that the scripture:

> [...] is as toilsome reading as I ever undertook. A wearisome, confused jumble, crude, incondite, endless iterations, long-windedness, entanglement; most crude, incondite [...]

Although 'sublime' and 'surpassing' for Romantics, the Qur'an seems merely 'confused' and 'crude' to Carlyle, who himself falls into 'incondite' repetition even as he alleges the scripture's 'endless iterations'. However, the very targets of Carlyle's complaint in

[12] For Irving's Q. 81 quotation, which continues on, almost to the end of the sura, see Irving 1970: 43. See Einboden 2016: 86–9 for extensive treatment of Irving's adapted version of Q. 81, including the manuscripts witnessing to his (re)fashioning of this sura's text.

1840—the Qur'an's non-linearity, its abrupt shifts in tone and topic—have more recently been refigured as aesthetic assets in light of Modernism and Postmodernism, with Western experimentalism ironically advancing stylistic appreciation of Islamic scripture. As suggested by studies since at least the 1980s, the supposed 'entanglement' of Qur'anic style intriguingly overlaps twentieth- and twenty-first-century trends, aligning secular literature and sacred revelation through a variety of shared tropes, including elliptical narrative, discontinuity, self-awareness, and self-reference.[13]

It is not the particular style, but the global reach, of the Qur'an, that seems most relevant to the West's unfolding literature, as well as its literary criticism. Recent decades have seen an unparalleled opening in the traditional canon, embracing new diversities of region, race, and religion, including authors from Muslim lineages and lands writing in European languages. Fictionalists such as Mohja Kahf in America, and Manzu Islam in Britain, are producing novels and short-stories indebted to Qur'anic traditions, complexly mirroring the scripture through explicit reference and implicit echo.[14] Paralleling this canonical opening has been an opening too in criticism, fostering fresh appreciation of the productive role played by Islam and its scripture in the West's imaginative writing—appreciation which breaks from reductive trends of scholarly recrimination that reach back to the late 1970s. In the wake of Edward Said's landmark *Orientalism* (1978), Western literary engagement with Islam has been regularly portrayed as 'Orientalist', with authors from Europe to America identified as complicit in colonialist and imperialist agendas. This Saidean tradition of literary criticism continues to unfold; however, attention has increasingly turned towards more creative and complex encounters between Western authors and Muslim sources, parsing cross-cultural transmissions that highlight aesthetic indebtedness, rather than merely political exploitation. The consolidation of this critical approach has advanced in recent years, evidenced in the appearance of 2012 studies including *'Orient und Okzident sind nicht mehr zu trennen': Goethe und die Weltkurlturen* (an essay compilation indexing the illustrious career of Katharina Mommsen, accenting especially Goethe's productive engagements with Islam), and Humberto Garcia's (2012) *Islam and the English Enlightenment 1670–1840* (offering a sympathetic account of Islam's political and literary influence on English authors, from Henry Stubbe to Mary Shelley). This inclination to read Islam alongside, rather than against, Western authorship, has led in 2014 alone to a conference on 'Reading Milton through Islam', held at the American University of Beirut; a special issue of the *Journal of Qur'anic Studies*, dedicated to 'The Qurʾān in Modern World Literature'; and my own monograph on *Islam and Romanticism*, spanning European, British, and American receptions.

[13] See Brown 2009: 48–9, who cites 'Carlyle on the Qur'ān' while discussing stylistic overlaps between the Qur'an and Joyce's modernist masterpiece, *Finnegans Wake*; Brown even frames the Qur'an as a 'modernist piece of literature'.

[14] Manzu Islam's literary engagement with the Qur'an has been treated by Shawkat Toorawa, who also serves as a co-editor of the 2014 special issue the *Journal of Qur'anic Studies* dedicated to 'The Qurʾān in Modern World Literature' (16/3).

Situated at the crux of a globalizing canon of literature and literary criticism, the Qur'an's twenty-first-century receptions have, of course, not escaped the impacts of global conflict, with 9/11 and its embattled aftermath sustaining more than a decade of Western literary response. Regarded as highly 'representative of contemporary post-modernist novelists', Don DeLillo chose 11 September 2001 as the background for his 2007 *Falling Man*, a novel that also features pivotal appeals to Islamic traditions and 'the Koran'.[15] Nearing its conclusion, *Falling Man* follows Lianne as she sifts her post-9/11 associations with Muslim life:

> People were reading the Koran. She knew of three people doing this. She'd talked to two and knew of another. They'd bought English-language editions of the Koran and were trying earnestly to learn something, find something that might help them think more deeply into the question of Islam. She didn't know whether they were persisting in the effort. She could imagine herself doing this, the determined action that floats into empty gesture. But maybe they were persisting. They were serious people perhaps. She knew two of them but not well. One, a doctor, recited the first line of the Koran in his office.
>
> *This Book is not to be doubted.*
>
> She doubted things, she had her doubts. She took a long walk one day, uptown, to East Harlem [...] (DeLillo 2008: 231)

Reflecting its place and period, this passage dramatizes a crisis of modern uncertainty, highlighting the epistemic problems that are so frequently the focus of twenty-first-century fiction. Opening with sentences that foreground his protagonist's uneasy search for knowledge—'She knew', 'She didn't know', 'She could imagine'—DeLillo's narrative suddenly fractures in sense and structure, importing an emphatic quotation, indented and italicized: '*This Book is not to be doubted*'. Cited from the opening to *Sūrat al-Baqara*, DeLillo's adapted *āya* not only intersects his postmodern narrative, but interrogates its scepticism, this supposed 'first line of the Koran' voicing a faithful conviction in *Falling Man*'s literary dialogue on American 'doubt'.[16]

A mirror for the postmodern condition, DeLillo's 'Koran' also unmistakably surfaces in the trauma of 9/11 New York, recalling the climates of conflict that prompted Ariosto's '*Alcorano*' to first appear in his *Orlando Furioso* nearly five centuries before. However, unlike Ariosto's poem, DeLillo's passage associates the Qur'an not with the exotic East, but with 'East Harlem', the scripture now inhabiting American spaces, both urban and domestic, equally 'uptown' and 'in [the doctor's] office'. Inscribed and indented within postmodern fiction, the Qur'an passes from Western exteriors to interiors, straddling thresholds of certainty and doubt, within and without. And it is precisely these polarities that allow our return to the 'Canon' itself—an internal 'rule' to establish exclusive

[15] See Connor 2004: 72 who notes that Dellilo 'has often been represented, alongside Salman Rushdie, as the most representative of contemporary postmodernist novelists'.

[16] DeLillo's '*This Book is not to be doubted*' is adapted not from Q. 1:1, but from Q. 2:1, which begins 'That is the Book, wherein is no doubt.'

standards, but which is also open to perpetual doubt and debate. Introducing his own canonical inclusion of 'the Koran' in 1994, Harold Bloom readily defended his choice, remarking that, after 'the Bible, Homer, Plato, the Athenian dramatists, and Virgil':

> the crucial work is the Koran. Whether for its aesthetic and spiritual power or the influence it will have upon all our futures, ignorance of the Koran is foolish and increasingly dangerous. (Bloom 1994: 497)

Gesturing to unknown 'futures', as well as 'ignorance' that is 'foolish', Bloom's remark seems to reach forward to DeLillo's 9/11 novel, anticipating both its 'dangerous' concerns and its 'doubtful' approach to 'the Koran'. It is, however, where Bloom begins here that seems best to reflect the Qur'an's 'crucial' role in shaping the Western literary tradition. A source of stylistic inspiration, as well as 'spiritual power', the Muslim scripture has intersected centuries of 'aesthetic' innovation in Europe, Britain, and America; yet, more global parameters are still opening for Qur'anic 'influence', advancing towards literary pluralities and possibilities that seem faintly implied in Bloom's gesture to 'all our futures'.

Bibliography

Ariosto, Ludovico. *Orlando Furioso*. 2nd edn. Ed. Lanfranco Caretti. Torino: Giulio Einaudi, 1971.

Ariosto, Ludovico. *Orlando Furioso*. Trans. Guido Waldman. New York: Oxford University Press, 2008.

Birchwood, Matthew. *Staging Islam in England: Drama and Culture, 1640–1685*. Cambridge: D. S. Brewer, 2007.

Bloom, Harold. *The Western Canon: The Books and School of the Ages*. New York: Riverhead Books, 1994.

Bosse, Anke. *Meine Schatzkammer füllt sich täglich…Die Nachlaßstüke zu Goethes 'West-östlichem Divan'*. 2 vols. Göttingen: Wallstein Verlag, 1999.

Brown, Norman O. *The Challenge of Islam: The Prophetic Tradition*. (ed.). Jerome Neu. Berkeley: North Atlantic Books, 2009.

Byron, Lord George Gordon. *Letters and Journals of Lord Byron: With Notices of his Life*. Cambridge: Cambridge University Press, 2012.

Byron, Lord George Gordon. *Selected Poetry*. Ed. Jerome J. McGann. New York: Oxford University Press, 2009.

Connor, Steven. 'Postmodernism and Literature'. In: Steven Connor (ed.). *The Cambridge Companion to Postmodernism*, pp. 62–81. Cambridge: Cambridge University Press, 2004.

DeLillo, Don. *Falling Man: A Novel*. New York: Scribner, 2008.

Dimmock, Matthew. *Mythologies of the Prophet Muhammad in Early Modern English Culture*. New York: Cambridge University Press, 2013.

Donne, John. *The Sermons of John Donne*. 10 vols. Ed. G. R. Potter and E. Simpson. Berkeley: University of California Press, 1953–62.

Einboden, Jeffrey. 'The Early American Qurʾān: Islamic Scripture and US Canon', *Journal of Qur'anic Studies* 11/2 (2009), 1–19.

Einboden, Jeffrey. *Islam and Romanticism: Muslim Currents from Goethe to Emerson*. London: Oneworld, 2014.

Einboden, Jeffrey. *The Islamic Lineage of America Literary Culture*. Oxford: Oxford University Press, 2016.

Garcia, Humberto. *Islam and the English Enlightenment 1670–1840*. Baltimore: John Hopkins University Press, 2012.

Heberle, Mark. 'Pagans and Saracens in Spenser's *The Faerie Queene*'. In: Cornelia N. Moore and Raymond A. Moody (eds.). *Comparative Literature East and West: Traditions and Trends*. Honolulu: University of Hawaii Press, 1989.

Irving, Washington. *The Alhambra: A Series of Tales and Sketches of the Moors and Spaniards*. 2 vols. Philadelphia: Carey & Lea, 1832.

Irving, Washington. *Mahomet and his Successors*. Ed. Henry Pochmann and E. N. Feltskog. Madison: University of Wisconsin Press, 1970.

MacLean, Gerald. 'Milton, Islam and the Ottomans'. In: Sharon Achinstein and Elizabeth Sauer (eds.). *Milton and Toleration*, pp. 284–98. New York: Oxford University Press, 2007.

Marlowe, Christopher. *The Complete Works of Christopher Marlowe*. 2 vols. 2nd edn. Ed. Fredson Bowers. Cambridge: Cambridge University Press, 2008.

Mommsen, Katharina. *'Orient und Okzident sind nicht mehr zu trennen': Goethe und die Weltkurlturen*. Göttingen: Wallstein Verlag, 2012.

Sale, George (trans.). *The Koran; Commonly Called The Alcoran of Mohammad*. 2 vols. London: T. Malden, 1801.

Shah, Idries. *The Sufis*. London: The Octagon Press, 1977.

Sharafuddin, Mohammed. *Islam and Romantic Orientalism: Literary Encounters with the Orient*. London: I. B. Taurus, 1994.

Williamson, Elizabeth. *The Materiality of Religion in Early Modern English Drama*. London: Routledge, 2016.

Ziolkowski, Jan M. 'Introduction'. In *Dante and Islam*. Special Issue of *Dante Studies* 125 (2007), 1–34.

PART VII

QUR'ANIC INTERPRETATION: SCHOLARSHIP AND LITERATURE OF EARLY, CLASSICAL, AND MODERN EXEGESIS

CHAPTER 40

EARLY QUR'ANIC COMMENTARIES

ANDREW RIPPIN

THE study of early Qur'anic commentaries (a genre of works known as *tafsīr*) is fundamentally an exercise in analysing the techniques of interpretation as they developed in the first three centuries of Islam. The goal is to elucidate the parameters within which understanding of the text of the Qur'an was taking place during that period. The focus on the early centuries of Islamic history is rewarding for two reasons. One, it provides us with a glimpse into the development of exegetical techniques in their isolated form; and, two, it allows insights into the procedures by which competing approaches to the Qur'an were assessed and incorporated into what became the mature form of the genre of *tafsīr* late in the third *hijrī* century.

For most scholars, the study of early *tafsīr* is not a search to uncover meanings of the Qur'an that might be hoped to reveal some primal sense of the text that has been lost or suppressed by the later community; the evidence available to us suggests very little that could support such a thesis, even if one were to try to engage in such an approach. Some might view the supposed purity of origins as the motivation behind the academic focus on formative period of *tafsīr*: the thought that one can somehow return to the early primitive Muslim community and recapture the impact of the Qur'an, and perhaps even its early meaning, through examination of these early works. Less romantic concerns do need to be given their rightful place, however, in understanding the attention that has been given to this field in scholarly work. The memory of many of the specifics contained within early texts from the period seems to have been lost within the mature genre of Muslim *tafsīr*. This is a result of the cumulative nature of the *tafsīr* enterprise. Important aspects contained within the early works became incorporated into later texts, rendering direct consultation with those early texts redundant. The late Ottoman exegete Ismāʿīl Ḥaqqī al-Bursawī (d. 1137/1725), for example, makes reference to and quotes from about thirty works of *tafsīr* in his compendium *Rūḥ al-bayān*. However, when it comes to early works, he makes no reference to them at all. There is no direct mention of Ibn Jarīr al-Ṭabarī (d. 310/923) in al-Bursawī's text, let alone any of the works which preceded al-Ṭabarī. Information valuable to the exegetical task found in such early works had already become a part of the exegetical tradition and thus had been incorporated into later works. For an author such as al-Bursawī there was no need to return to the original sources to gain those insights. This integration of early material was, of course, a gradual historical process. The library of the Shīʿī writer Ibn Ṭāwūs in the seventh/thirteenth century (Kohlberg 1992) shows that by that time some early books were still owned and being consulted (and also shows how the boundaries between Sunnī and Shīʿī exegesis were quite permeable). However, what this means is that, until very recently, the full dimensions of an important element of the Muslim cultural, intellectual, and theological heritage has been overlooked. It is that heritage that has been reanimated in the recent rediscovery of early texts of *tafsīr*.

Scholarly attention to the early period of the development of *tafsīr*, it has been suggested (Saleh 2010: 27), does fall prey to certain ideological perspectives stemming from the modern Muslim world, especially manifest in the industry that is evident in editing and publishing of early texts. The desire to return to the earliest generations of those closest to the Prophet as the source of the most reliable information is strongly felt in contemporary times and the widespread publication of works from the earliest period is certainly an outcome of that concern. It is also the case that the examination of early *tafsīr* inevitably involves difficult historiographical questions that are common to many facets of the study of the rise of Islam. In this sense then, the study of early *tafsīr* could indeed be portrayed as a part of the quest for 'origins', with all of the attendant (and fallacious) implications that seem to intimate the emergence of a historical phenomenon within a context that is somehow a 'clean slate'. Yet there definitely is a history to be recovered which does speak to the emergence of a distinct genre of Arabic writing related to the Qur'an. Much of the academic discussion of this particular issue of the emergence of these texts has revolved around questions of the mode of transmission of material from the earliest generations of Muslims into the later written works. This is a dispute that emphasizes the perceived relationship between the modes of transmission of hadith as compared to *tafsīr* and the entire historiographical problem of the origins of Islam; it turned on the extent to which later sources can be relied upon to provide an accurate historical picture of these formative times. Hand-in-hand with this has been a good deal of discussion concerning certain reports that seem to suggest that interpretation of the Qur'an was discouraged in the earliest period of Islam. Such debates as evidenced in the works of Goldziher (1920), Birkeland (1955), Abbott (1967), and Sezgin (1967), have yet to be settled to any degree. However, the study of early *tafsīr* also has other concerns that can motivate it without it being sidelined into these intractable issues.

The core of the study of early *tafsīr* is to be found in the history of the development of Islamic sciences that are contained in this sequence of works, both in terms of the emergence of grammar as the primary tool of mature exegesis and of attitudes towards the Qur'an itself. On the latter point, the richness of the Islamic tradition is evident, sometimes in surprising ways when the early exegetical texts are the focus of attention. In sum, the goal of the study of early *tafsīr* is to discover the early community's attitude towards the meaning of its scripture and the attitude towards the authority of the past and its structure. Such aspects are uncovered by attending to the processes by which meaning is asserted and determined. That reflection upon meaning raises questions of why and how the meanings arose as they did.

To achieve an analysis of early *tafsīr*, the contemporary study of the field employs an approach to the products of the discipline that has as its basis three factors that have influenced the investigation: the Muslim tradition, early twentieth-century academic scholarship, and existing literary evidence.

Muslim tradition tends to view the emergence of exegetical works through the tools of the discipline of hadith. The Prophet Muḥammad is the source of the most authentic exegetical material, supplemented by the information transmitted from his followers and then their successors. Relatively little material from the first two generations, that is Muḥammad and his followers, is available in authenticated hadith form and the emphasis thus tends to fall upon the reports that stem from the successors when, it would be deemed, knowledge of the context of revelation and of the Arabic language was still alive (Koç 2009). This, of course, refers to interpretation, *tafsīr*, as process rather than actual written books of exegesis. The compilation of this material, like the compilation of hadith reports in general, became a concerted activity in the third/ninth and fourth/tenth centuries and formed the basis of the massive works of *tafsīr* that we know—the genre of books as such—with the work of al-Ṭabarī being viewed as the significant starting reference point for the tradition. Alternative views do exist as to the first pivotal work that establishes the mature genre of *tafsīr*; other schemes reflecting variations according to geography and theological alignment have been noted and do need serious consideration in any conception of the emergence of the genre of *tafsīr* as we know it (Frolov 1997; Saleh 2011).

The foundational work for the academic study of *tafsīr* is that by Ignaz Goldziher *Die Richtungen der islamischen Koranauslegung*, lectures given in 1913 and published in 1920. Goldziher divided his treatment of *tafsīr* into seven classifications: formative, liturgical, traditional, dogmatic, Sufi, sectarian, and modernist. This first attempt to write a scholarly history of Qur'anic interpretation was a considerable achievement given the very limited number of sources that were available to Goldziher when he wrote his work; despite that, his conceptions have informed much subsequent scholarly writing on *tafsīr*. His discussion of the formative period and parts of his examination of traditional interpretation convey material of interest here. Central within Goldziher's concerns was the debate about whether *tafsīr* was an activity that was permitted in the early decades of Islam. This discussion picked up not only on material found within later Muslim literature but also reflected the significance of the apparent absence of a substantive body of exegetical material from the very earliest members of the Muslim community as evidenced in the hadith collections. This point provoked considerable interest and debate among some later scholars. The crux of the issue in the early Muslim centuries appears to have regarded what sort of information was going to be allowed to provide a basis of interpretation; this is often pictured as having centred on what has become the focal point of even later (as well as contemporary) disputes over whether to allow personal opinion (*raʾy*) or to rely only on transmitted material. Much of the discussion of this topic returns us to the debates about the mode of transmission of hadith literature and the role of orality and written material in the formative period of Islam.

The publication in 1967 of volume 1 of Fuat Sezgin's *Geschichte des arabischen Schrifttums* brought a new focus to the study of early *tafsīr*. Sezgin gathered material on fifty-seven authors writing books of Qur'anic interpretation in the period down to approximately the year 430/1038. While the core of Sezgin's work paid attention to manuscript copies of specific works, he also collated references to lost works of the early Muslim generations. Sezgin's support for the existence of written texts attributable to early authorities such as Saʿīd ibn Jubayr (d. 95/714) and al-Ḍaḥḥāk (d. 105/723) was to be found in classic bibliographical and biographical works. The existence of such works also fits into Sezgin's general understanding of how the proliferation of hadith reports resulted from multiple transmissions of written material. Many of the references to early texts found in Sezgin's work must be deemed speculative, however, and not based on firm textual evidence that is available to us today. Despite that, the accomplishment of Sezgin's work is apparent: for the first time he drew attention in a systematic fashion to the existence of manuscripts of Qur'anic exegesis attributed to authors from the second and third Muslim centuries, pre-dating the work of al-Ṭabarī. Part four of John Wansbrough's 1977 work, *Quranic Studies: Sources and Methods of Scriptural Interpretation*, was the first to take advantage of the significant scope of the resources that Sezgin had made apparent. In that section of his book Wansbrough divided the early exegetical texts typologically into haggadic (narrative), halakhic (legal), masoretic (textual), rhetorical, and allegorical types, the first step in providing a vision of the modes in which early exegesis operated.

As a result of all of these factors—the record of Muslim tradition, early twentieth-century academic approaches, and the recovery of early written sources—the study of early *tafsīr* has come to mean, for those involved in the discipline, analysis of works that pre-date al-Ṭabarī (with, as mentioned, alternative visions of the maturation process to be kept in mind with other figures playing this role thus being conceivable). These works are far from possessing a monolithic character; a simple picture as painted by the (retrospective) hadith approach is clearly not sufficient in order to characterize them. Sezgin's bibliographical survey uses later scholastic disciplines and the relative fame of an author within a discipline in order to gather the works together. Thus entries for early *tafsīr* are found not only in the Qur'an section but also in sections (and subsequent volumes of his *Geschichte des Arabischen Schrifttums*) devoted to topics such as history, law, lexicography, and grammar. Wansbrough's typological categorizations of texts of early *tafsīr*, while influential, have created some confusion and debate, partially because of the use of terminology from the Jewish exegetical tradition but also because they have frequently been interpreted as providing a rigid historical framework. Wansbrough certainly entertains the possibility of historical progression through the sequence of the various types but he also argues that the texts as we have them are likely later than their supposed authors and are full of intrusive elements that reflect an amalgam of exegetical tendencies. The historical progression of the types is, therefore, a sequence based on observations of the development of interpretive tendencies in general rather than purely on the textual record.

Employing Wansbrough's categories primarily as descriptions of hermeneutical approaches that had varying emphases in different contexts can help us make sense of the variety of *tafsīr* works in the early centuries, the characteristics of each of them, their range of concerns, and the logical sequence of their development (although not necessarily in their historical order, given the form in which we have the texts today). The categories certainly do suggest that certain external factors within the overall emergence of Islam as a closely defined and politically supported religious orientation need to be considered within the context of each work and that can lead to historical observations and a sense of likely sequencing. However, issues of authorship, compilation, and editorial intrusion must always be kept in mind and those concerns tend to prevent any easy reduction of the material into a linear sequence. The emphases in each of the categories of approach can also be correlated to some extent to various devices or procedures employed in the interpretive process; these characteristics again should not be expected to be applied consistently or systematically in any absolute sense but they do allow for some generalizations based on observations derived from the texts.

With all of these caveats duly recognized, it may be suggested that the early *tafsīr* texts that have come down to us today can be classified into three primary formative categories according to their goals: narrative, legal, and textual. Each of these terms encompasses a significant variety of material and should not be taken to suggest any strict limits that it might be thought those words convey. The exact character of the books within these categories continues to stimulate significant interest among scholars (e.g. Rippin 2001; Sinai 2009) and the full dimensions of the analysis are always being refined.

An initial emphasis in early commentaries is on narrative development, an approach that Wansbrough called haggadic. That is the style found in the work *Tafsīr al-Qurʾān* attributed to Muqātil ibn Sulaymān (d. 150/767), but also in other treatises which might be thought of as composed of a sequence of simple glosses (or periphrastic commentaries). The goal of such works is conveyed on several layers. There is an element that appears to reflect a preaching context in which the didactic level of the narrative dominates. There is a strong element of historical contextualization of the text in order to bring out the narrative structure. In this respect, there are similarities between such commentaries and texts as the *Sīra* of Ibn Isḥāq (d. 150/767) although there, because the Qur'an loses its foregrounding as the subject of the text and is replaced by the person of Muḥammad, the works do not fall into the genre of *tafsīr* as that is commonly understood; that is so even though the *Sīra* clearly has explicit exegetical content. In narrative exegesis no person and no thing remains unidentified; such a process often serves to provide connections between various stories in scripture and beyond. All of this acts to produce a cohesive narration that might be associated with an oral context. What unifies the expansive (in its attention to the entire Qur'an) text of Muqātil and those works of other early writers such as Mujāhid ibn Jabr (d. 104/722) which are fragmentary in their dealing with the text of the Qur'an, is the sense one has, especially if the text is conceived of as being received in an oral, preaching situation, that the canon of scripture is seemingly unrestricted and somewhat uncertain at its edges. All such texts undertake the basic exegetical task of filling in the apparent 'blanks' of scripture where it seems that the potential ambiguities of language need to be constrained by making explicit what is not said. Consider the following brief extract from Muqātil's work:

> Q. 2.151: *ka mā arsalnā fīkum rasūl*[an] *minkum* ['just as We have sent among you a messenger of your own']
> meaning Muḥammad, may the prayers and peace of Allah be upon him
> *yatlū ʿalaykum āyātinā* ['to recite Our revelation to you']
> the Qurʾān
> *wa yuzakkīkum* ['purify you']
> meaning purifies you from associating and disbelief
> *wa yuʿallimukum al-kitāb* ['and teach you the Scripture']
> meaning the Qurʾān
> *wa-l-ḥikma* ['and the wisdom']
> meaning the permitted and the forbidden
> *wa yuʿallimukum mā lam takūnū taʿlamūna* ['and [other] things you did not know']
> when I did that for you.

The implication that emerges from considering this brief passage is that the text of the Qur'an does not seem to say quite what it means; the Qur'an thus needs clarification either by completion of a thought, provision of a synonym, or substitution of something specific for something general. The question that lingers is how to differentiate scripture from commentary; it is easy to imagine that an audience listening to such a process of commentary would experience that ambiguity.

Some early commentaries display an interest in legal issues, a category termed 'halakhic' in Wansbrough's scheme. *Tafsīr khams mīʾa āya min al-Qurʾān*, ascribed again to Muqātil ibn Sulaymān, illustrates the desire to connect the Qur'an to the emerging legal structures of Islam. Muqātil organized Qur'anic verses under topics of law and provided some basic exegesis of them; studies of the content of the book suggest a direct relationship between this work and his larger *Tafsīr*. The particular significance of this text lies primarily in its early attempt at a classification scheme and the documentation of all those legal elements on the basis of scripture alone. The topics covered include faith, prayer, alms-giving, fasting, pilgrimage (thus drawing attention to the 'five pillars' of Islam), testaments, marriage, divorce, adultery, and jihad (see Rippin 2015a). Overall, it would seem that no overarching legal principles can be derived from Muqātil's analysis of the Qur'an; the topics are presented primarily as ethical directives and not prescriptive judgements. Furthermore, the citation of scripture is not systematic nor is it complete in comparison with what becomes the standard list of verses under many of the topics in later centuries. The absence of citation of some prominent verses is certainly notable in the text's treatment of jihad, for example. Muqātil does not cite either of the most aggressive of the Qur'anic verses, Q. 9:5 and 2:190–1, both of which talk about killing the unbelievers wherever they are found, nor does he cite the verses that are often cited as counselling patience. His ethical categories into which he organizes the Qur'anic verses do not find a place for these aspects of jihad; rather, he focuses on matters such as 'How those who kill and are killed among the fighters will share in the hereafter' and 'What will happen to those who cheat regarding the spoils of war'. In relationship to the Qur'an, legal exegesis works with a constrained canon, one recognized not to extend to all of the community's needs nor to the entire text of scripture, but one that has to be correlated to existing and developing legal systems (Gleave 2001).

Those commentaries that fall conveniently under the label of the textual category constitute the third group of early works. Texts here may be seen to incorporate into writings that have as their focus the specific areas of textual readings, grammar, linguistics, rhetoric, and even allegory. What they all have in common is an attitude towards scripture as being a textual unity and possessing self-consistency. Various techniques of interpretation are employed that both presume and emphasize such principles and, as such, they underpin every effort of the exegetes. This becomes increasingly apparent in these works as they develop through history, especially by the time they solidify into the continuous and complete coverage of the text of scripture in the mature genre of *tafsīr*. On the surface, the goal of an exegete in a work of this category is to uncover aspects of the text that the author thinks that Muslims (other than the writer himself) will have a problem with and may interpret inaccurately or read incorrectly; the author is thus asserting that he knows the answer to such issues. The concerns that arise within the text of scripture may well not have been noticed if attention had not been drawn to them but, the exegete would claim, he has a responsibility to linger over them, just in case someone else stumbles over the point. As time progresses the number of instances of perceived potential problems increases, not only because of change in language—that is, the context within which the exegete is writing, historically and geographically—but also from an increasing sensitivity to subtleties.

The notion of 'problems' here is, of course, the critical matter. What sort of concerns raise the potential issue of a lack of consistency in the Qur'an? What are the triggers of interpretation? Contemporary theorists have reflected upon this point because it is of concern in the interpretation of all types of literature. Tzvetan Todorov (1982: 37–8), for example, speaks of five such factors: contradiction, discontinuity, superfluity, implausibility, and inappropriateness. In biblical studies such reflections have also been insightful. Geza Vermes (1970) describes the factors that necessitate interpretation: when the exact meaning escapes the interpreter; the text lacks sufficient detail; the text appears to contradict another text; and the apparent meaning is unacceptable. Underneath all of this is the basic assumption that all of the content of the text must be there for a reason and it must make sense. At the same time it was recognized that any indeterminancy inherent in the text as a result of these interpretive triggers produced desirable flexibility in the resulting production of meaning, especially in the context of considering legal developments.

The responses to these dilemmas that require interpretation are generalizable as well and are demonstrated in works from the textual category of early *tafsīr*. All the strategies that deal with the need for interpretation aim to support the basic assumption that the text is coherent and unified. Textual variants must be defined and limited. Apparent oversights or omissions can be viewed as the attribute of brevity and thus seen as the employment of a rhetorical device; redundancy provokes exactly the same response and both features are argued by the exegetes to be practical benefits to the reader rather than negative attributes. A lack of order in the text and the perception of difficulties with the proper sense of the text evokes a catalogue of linguistic attributes that demonstrate that the text is, in fact, unified. A lack of consistency suggests different levels of meaning and encourages devices such as allegory; such a perception does, of course, depend upon the text having a plain sense which somehow does not convey the desired or needed meaning. Multivalency becomes the best response. Immorality in the text requires reinterpretation frequently through allegory but never through deletion or simple overlooking of the issue. Sections of the text which seem somewhat mundane can still be asserted to be valid even if other sections, deemed more profound, can be emphasized. Lack of clarity can be understood as sublimity or simply used to justify the exegetical task (Henderson 1991: chapters 4 and 5).

Works within the textual category (which Wansbrough termed masoretic) appear to commence from a rudimentary basis of wishing to demonstrate the conceptual unity of the Qur'anic text, an issue that is dealt with in a number of ways. A work again ascribed to Muqātil ibn Sulaymān, published under the title *Kitāb al-Ashbāh wa'l-naẓā'ir*, provides an example, although, here, knotty problems of ascription and transmission make this simply a convenient text to consider rather than viewing this as a firm historical point of departure for the category; a text ascribed to Hārūn ibn Mūsā (d. *c.*170/786), *al-Wujūh wa'l-naẓā'ir*, is virtually identical to that ascribed to Muqātil and issues of transmission become highly problematic as a result. Be that as it may, the text provides a rather arbitrary selection of vocabulary that is treated according to its semantic usage throughout the text of the Qur'an. One hundred and eighty-five lexical items are analysed; most of the words are of a theological character (guidance, disbelief, religion, sin, path) although some particles and prepositions are also added into the mix. The aim of the work is dominated by a sense of an elucidation of religious meanings, however. For example, the text divides up the word *īmān*, usually translated as 'faith' or 'belief', into four senses, *wujūh* (Muqātil 1975: 137–8; also see Hārūn 1988: 125–6):

(a) affirming faith while speaking hypocritically
(b) declaring the truth, either in secret or publicly
(c) declaring the oneness of God
(d) believing in polytheism.

For the most part, these divisions simply correspond to the context of usage of the word in the Qur'an. For example, under sense one (to affirm faith hypocritically) the following example is provided: '... because they confessed their faith (*āmanū*) and then rejected it. So their hearts have been sealed and they do not understand' (Q. 63:3). An analogy (*naẓīr*) is then provided to this first sense: 'Believers (*alladhīna āmanū*), do not let your wealth and your children distract you from remembering God: [those who do so will be the ones who lose.]' The point in both of these instances is to suggest that, even though the people are addressed as 'those who believe', they do not, in fact, believe sincerely. Analogues here are based on lexical equivalence in the usage of *āmanū*, 'they believe'. This approach to equivalence may be compared to the linguistic phraseology found in the text *Mutashābih al-Qurʾān* ascribed to al-Kisāʾī (d. 189/804) or the grammatical approach associated with the *Maʿānī al-Qurʾān* of al-Farrāʾ (d. 207/822). All such works are premised around a unity of scripture and employ very specific but varying tools of interpretation (Rippin 1995, 2015b). It is the recurring nature of semantic formulae and grammatical usages that are resolved through texts of this type into catalogues of usages. In the end they produce a vision of a unified canon of scripture that is, at the same time, reconciled with history in a theory of revelation that took place over time during the life of Muḥammad.

Rhetorical features of the Qur'an also provoked close attention and were driven by the same concerns of textual exegesis. The clearest example of this may be seen in the work of Abū ʿUbayda (d. 209/824–5), *Majāz al-Qurʾān*, where the word *majāz* is used not in its later application of 'figurative language' but in a more fundamental (and certainly not unrelated) sense of 'a text that needs restoring to its full sense' (the word *taqdīr* is also used in a similar sense of 'reconstruction'). Isolated passages are examined and then rephrased in order to resolve linguistic ambiguity. Abū ʿUbayda's work has been subjected to extended scholarly attention with the goal of establishing the purpose of the work in the context of the emergence of *tafsīr* as an enterprise (Wansbrough 1970; Almagor 1979; Heinrichs 1984); there is no doubt that this is one of the most significant works of *tafsīr* from the early period.

One of the developments that can be observed in these early texts is the gradual acceptance of the comparison of profane texts with the sacred for semantic and grammatical reasons. The most important element here is the use of Arabic poetry—both pre-Islamic and contemporary with Muḥammad—in order to clarify grammatical and lexicographical issues. This was a process that took some argumentation in order to be legitimated, as evidenced by the ascription of various works to the primal authority, Ibn ʿAbbās (d. *c.* 68/687) (Rippin 1981; Boullata 1991). This interpretive device gained its acceptance once the possibility of the act of comparison did not arouse any fears about 'contamination' of the sacred by the profane.

Finally, symbolic readings of the text also show a tendency to emerge early on and display commonalities with other works in the textual category. Here our attention shifts to Sufi- and Shīʿī-influenced works such as the books of *tafsīr* ascribed to al-Tustarī (d. 283/896) and Furāt al-Kūfī (d. *c.*310/922) respectively. In terms of structure and exegetical tools, such works do not differ from other early works; their distinctiveness arises in the way in which they use the implements of variant readings and reconstructed text to suggest a meaning of the text that marks their interests as distinct from other Muslim groups. Allegiances to Shīʿī authorities (Bar-Asher 1999; Rippin 2013) and mystical masters (Böwering 1980) are apparent. In mystical texts, the meditation upon the text, in a manner that might be considered parallel to the extraction of ethical principles from the text, provides the defining element.

As suggested above, one of the features of Wansbrough's analysis based on the bibliographical work of Sezgin is that he paid attention only to texts that actually exist in medieval manuscripts. However, the study of early *tafsīr* is dominated on occasion by concerns that drive broader historical studies especially those connected to hadith reports; that involves the matter of ascription of material that is found in the tradition format. The issue has been seen to emerge from the work of Sezgin in the tendency to assert the existence of texts for which no textual evidence currently exists. The central question this raises is of what relevance to the study of early *tafsīr* are the early works ascribed to prominent authors but texts of which no longer exist? To what extent can these works be reconstructed on the basis of later texts? (Conrad 1993; Schoeler 2006). If they are reconstructed to what extent can they be trusted to represent the views of that early authority? The issue is one that is at the heart of the debate concerning the authenticity of hadith reports and the mechanisms of ascription. These are hotly debated topics among specialists. As far as the study of early *tafsīr* goes, the issue might best be framed as one related to the issue of authorship. The reality, however, is that the attempt to analyse these texts with a biographical focus on the author does not solve the problem of the lack of a consistent point of view that would imply the presence of a single personality behind the text. Berg (2000) has attempted to address the question through a detailed analysis of the employment of certain tools and procedures used in the exegesis ascribed to an early authority (in his book, specifically Ibn ʿAbbās) to see if a consistent picture emerges; he judged the outcome negative. Other methods rely on the presence of technical terminology (Versteegh 1990, 1993, 2011), biographical reports (Gilliot 2013), conceptual content (Pregill 2014) and what Motzki (2010) has termed *isnād-cum-matn* analysis but the results continue to be subject to lively debate.

In addition, and in keeping with the contemporary ideological interest in a return to the earliest sources as the most genuine source of Qur'anic meaning, there has been a proliferation of modern reconstructed texts in the area of *tafsīr*. Relying on ascription, reports have been gathered from later sources and then organized in Qur'anic order, essentially (re)creating a work of *tafsīr*. Issues arise: there can be no certainty that all the reports have been collected or indeed that they were even transmitted completely in later sources. As mentioned, Berg has shown that the material rarely leads to definitive results in that no coherent vision or method that could be attributed to a single person seems to emerge. One problem that this enterprise raises, however, is that this is not necessarily solely a contemporary issue resulting from efforts made by editors today in support of the book publishing business. The fragmentary nature of the texts ascribed to Mujāhid and Sufyān al-Thawrī (d. 161/787) (see Wansbrough 1977: 137), for example, suggest that a similar process may well have taken place in medieval times and thus, while we have a manuscript with the name of an author attached, the sense in which this is an authored work by that figure (or even a work that has been written down by the person's students and thus we might deem the work to be orally delivered in content even if it is not necessarily in its complete *isnād* form) is open to question. It may well be argued that we should no more trust apparently medieval manuscripts that are full of late intrusions or that appear to have been compiled on the basis of extracted segments than we trust modern texts that are extracted from later sources. We simply do not have sufficient knowledge about the methods of composition and transmission from medieval times in order to settle such questions definitively. The very notion of authorship is complex and difficult when dealing with texts from the first three centuries of Islam, regardless of genre. Even those texts which seem securely authored frequently have apparent intrusions from later authors but still the sense of a 'voice' of the author remains. But should we, in fact even conceive of the notion of a 'voice' of an author as being applicable at this time and in this context (Günther 2005)? These are questions that will set the agenda for future research.

The future study of early *tafsīr* will be on more certain grounds if it is confined to dealing with texts that have come down to us from medieval times in manuscript form. There is a good deal of work still to be done in order to understand the composition, ascription, and nature of all of these texts, even though the body of works itself is relatively small.

Bibliography

Abbott, Nabia. *Studies in Arabic Literary Papyri. ii. Qur'ānic Commentary and Tradition.* Chicago: University of Chicago Press, 1967.

Abdel Haleem, M. A. S. *The Qur'an: A New Translation.* Oxford: Oxford University Press, 2004.

Abū ʿUbayda. *Majāz al-Qur'ān.* Ed. Fuat Sezgin. 2 vols. Cairo: al-Khānijī, 1955, 1962.

Almagor, Ella. 'The Early Meaning of *Majāz* and the Nature of Abū ʿUbayda's Exegesis'. In: S. Shaked, Joseph L. Blau, Shlomo Pines, and M. J. Kister (eds.). *Studia Orientalia Memoriae D. H. Baneth Dedicata*, pp. 307–26. Jerusalem: Magnes Press, 1979.

Bar-Asher, Meir M. *Scripture and Exegesis in Early Imāmī Shiism.* Leiden: E. J. Brill, 1999.

Berg, Herbert. *The Development of Exegesis in Early Islam: The Authenticity of Muslim Literature from the Formative Period.* Richmond: Curzon, 2000.

Birkeland, Harris. *Old Muslim Opposition against Interpretation of the Koran.* Uppsala: Almqvist & Wiksells, 1955.

Boullata, Issa J. 'Poetry Citation as Interpretive Illustration in Qur'ān Exegesis: *Masā'il Nāfiʿ ibn al-Azraq*'. In: Wael B. Hallaq and Donald P. Little (eds.). *Islamic Studies Presented to Charles J. Adams*, pp. 27–40. Leiden: E. J. Brill, 1991.

Böwering, Gerhard. *The Mystical Vision of Existence in Classical Islam: The Qur'ān Hermeneutics of the Ṣūfī Sahl al-Tustarī (d. 283/896).* Berlin: de Gruyter, 1980.

al-Bursawī, Ismāʿīl Ḥaqqī. *Rūḥ al-bayān.* 3 vols. Cairo: Būlaq, 1255/1839.

Conrad, Lawrence I. 'Recovering Lost Texts: Some Methodological Issues', *Journal of the American Oriental Society* 113 (1993), 258–63.

al-Farrā', Abū Zakariyyā' Yaḥyā ibn Ziyad. *Maʿānī al-Qur'ān.* Ed. Aḥmad Yūsuf Najātī and Muḥammad ʿAlī al-Najjār, 3 vols. Cairo: Dār al-Kutub al-Miṣriyya, 1955–72.

Frolov, Dimitry. 'Ibn al-Nadīm on the History of Qur'ānic Exegesis', *Wiener Zeitschrift für die Kunde des Morganlandes* 87 (1997), 65–81.

Gilliot, Claude. 'Mujāhid's Exegesis: Beginnings, Ways of Transmission and Development of a Meccan Exegetical Tradition in its Human, Spiritual and Theological Environment'. In: Karen Bauer (ed.). *The Aims and Methods of Qur'anic Exegesis (8th–15th Centuries)*, pp. 63–112. Oxford: Oxford University Press/Institute of Ismaili Studies, 2013.

Gleave, Robert. 'The "First Source" of Islamic Law: Muslim Legal Exegesis of the Qurʾān'. In: Richard O'Dair and Andrew Lewis (eds.). *Law and Religion: Current Legal Issues 2001, Volume 4*, pp. 145–61. Oxford: Oxford University Press, 2001.
Goldziher, Ignaz. *Die Richtungen der islamischen Koranauslegung*. Leiden: Brill, 1920; English trans., *Schools of Koranic Commentators*. Trans. Wolfgang H. Behn. Wiesbaden: Harrassowitz, 2006.
Günther, Sebastian. 'Assessing the Sources of Classical Arabic Compilations: The Issue of Categories and Methodologies', *British Journal of Middle Eastern Studies* 32 (2005), 75–98.
Heinrichs, Wolfhart. 'On the Genesis of the *Haqīqa–Majāz* Dichotomy', *Studia Islamica* 59 (1984), 111–40.
Henderson, John B. *Scripture, Canon and Commentary: A Comparison of Confucian and Western Exegesis*. Princeton: Princeton University Press, 1991.
Ibn Isḥāq, Muḥammad. *al-Sīra al-nabawiyya li-Ibn Hishām*. Ed. Muṣṭafā Saqqā et al. 4 vols. Cairo: al-Ḥalabī, 1955.
Koç, Mehmet Akif. 'A Contribution to the Discussion on "the Beginning Period and the Sources of *Tafsīr*" ', *Ankara Üniversitesi İlahiyat Fakültesi Dergisi* 50/2 (2009), 1–12.
Kohlberg, Etan. *A Medieval Muslim Scholar at Work: Ibn Ṭāwūs and his Library*. Leiden: Brill, 1992.
Motzki, Harald. 'The Origins of Muslim Exegsis: A Debate'. In: Harald Motzki with Nicolet Boekhoff-van der Voort and Sean W. Anthony (eds.). *Analysing Muslim Traditions: Studies in Legal, Exegetical and Maghāzī Ḥadīth*, pp. 231–9. Leiden: Brill, 2010.
Muqātil ibn Sulaymān. *Tafsīr Muqātil ibn Sulaymān*. Ed. ʿAbd Allāh Maḥmūd Shiḥāta. 5 vols. Cairo: Muʾassasat al-Ḥalabī, 1967–.
Muqātil ibn Sulaymān. *Al-Ashbāh waʾl-naẓāʾir fī l-Qurʾān al-karīm*. Ed. ʿAbd Allāh Maḥmūd Shiḥāta. Cairo: al-Hayʾa al-Miṣriyya al-ʿĀmma liʾl-Kitāb, 1975.
Muqātil ibn Sulaymān. *Kitāb tafsīr al-khams mīʾat āya min al-Qurʾān*. Ed. Isaiah Goldfeld. Shfaram: al-Mashriq Press, 1980.
Pregill, Michael. 'Methodologies for the Dating of Exegetical Works and Traditions: Can the Lost *Tafsīr* of Kalbī be Recovered from *Tafsir ibn ʿAbbās* (also Known as *al-Wāḍiḥ*)'. In: A. Görke and J. Pink (eds.). *Tafsīr and Islamic Intellectual History: Exploring the Boundaries of a Genre*, pp. 393–453. Oxford: Oxford University Press/Institute of Ismaili Studies, 2014.
Rippin, Andrew. 'Ibn ʿAbbās's *al-Lughāt fīʾl-Qurʾān*', *Bulletin of the School of Oriental and African Studies* 44 (1981), 15–25.
Rippin, Andrew. 'Studying Early *Tafsīr* Texts', *Der Islam* 72 (1995), 310–23.
Rippin, Andrew. *The Qurʾān and its Interpretative Tradition*. Aldershot: Variorum/Ashgate, 2001.
Rippin, Andrew. 'What Defines a (Pre-modern) Shiʿi *Tafsīr*? Notes towards the History of the Genre of *Tafsīr* in Islam, in Light of the Scholarly Study of the Shiʿi Contribution'. In: G. Miskinzoda and F. Daftary (eds.). *The Study of Shiʿi Islam: History, Theology and* Law, pp. 95–112. London: I. B. Tauris/the Institute of Ismaili Studies, 2013.
Rippin, Andrew. 'Reading the Qurʾān on *jihād*: Two Early Exegetical Texts'. In: R. Gleave and I. Kristo-Nagy (eds.). *Violence in Islamic Thought from the Qur'an to the Mongols*, pp. 31–46. Edinburgh: Edinburgh University Press, 2015a.
Rippin, Andrew. 'Al-Mubarrad and Polysemy in the Qurʾān'. In: A. Rippin and R. Tottoli (eds.). *Books and Written Culture of the Islamic World: Studies Presented to Claude Gilliot on the Occasion of his 75th Birthday*, pp. 56–69. Leiden: Brill, 2015b.

Saleh, Walid. 'Preliminary Remarks on the Historiography of *Tafsīr* in Arabic: A History of the Book Approach', *Journal of Qur'anic Studies* 12/1–2 (2010), 6–40.

Saleh, Walid. 'Marginalia and Peripheries: A Tunisian Historian and the History of Qurʾānic Exegesis', *Numen* 58 (2011), 284–313.

Schoeler, Gregor. *The Oral and the Written in Early Islam*. Trans. Uwe Vagelpohl. Ed. James Montgomery. London: Routledge, 2006.

Sezgin, Fuat. *Geschichte des Arabischen Schrifttums*. Vol. 1. Leiden, Brill, 1967.

Sinai, Nicolai. *Fortschreibung und Auslegung: Studien zur frühen Koraninterpretation*. Wiesbaden: Harrassowitz Verlag, 2009.

al-Ṭabarī, Abū Jaʿfar Muḥammad ibn Jarīr. *Jāmiʿ al-bayān ʿan taʾwīl āy al-Qurʾān*. Ed. ʿAbd Allāh al-Turkī. 26 vols. Riyadh: Dār ʿĀlam al-Kutub, 2003.

Todorov, Tzvetan. *Symbolism and Interpretation*. Ithaca, NY: Cornell University Press, 1982.

Vermes, Geza. 'Bible and Midrash: Early Old Testament Exegesis'. In: P. R. Ackroyd and C. F. Evans (eds.). *The Cambridge History of the Bible, vol. 1: From the Beginnings to Jerome*, pp. 199–231. Cambridge: Cambridge University Press, 1970.

Versteegh, Cornelis [Kees] H. M. 'Grammar and Exegesis: The Origins of Kufan Grammar and the *Tafsīr Muqātil*', *Der Islam* 67 (1990), 206–42.

Versteegh, Cornelis [Kees] H. M. *Arabic Grammar and Qurʾānic Exegesis in Early Islam*. Leiden: Brill, 1993.

Versteegh, Cornelis [Kees] H. M. 'The Name of the Ant and the Call to Holy War: Al-Daḥḥāk ibn Muzāḥim's Commentary on the Qurʾān'. In: Nicolet Boekhoff-van der Voort, Kees Versteegh, and Joas Wagemakers (eds.). *The Transmission and Dynamics of the Textual Sources of Islam: Essays in Honour of Harald Motzki*, pp. 279–99. Leiden: Brill, 2011.

Wansbrough, John. '*Majāz al-Qurʾān*: Periphrastic Exegesis', *Bulletin of the School of the Oriental and African Studies* 33 (1970), 247–66.

Wansbrough, John. *Quranic Studies: Sources and Methods of Scriptural Interpretation*. Oxford: Oxford University Press, 1977; reprint with Foreword, Translations and Extended Notes by Andrew Rippin. Amherst, NY: Prometheus Press, 2004.

CHAPTER 41

EXEGETICAL DESIGNS OF THE *SĪRA*

Tafsīr and Sīra

MAHER JARRAR

Introduction

This chapter aims at outlining the trends and methodological approaches pertinent to the developments concerning the question of the relation between the biography of Muḥammad (*sīra*), the Qur'an, and the field of Qur'anic exegesis (*tafsīr*). My intention is to point out the main trends and to offer a critical examination of present academic discourses.

Like all episodes of origins, modern Western research on the origin of Islam since the nineteenth century has been defined by a proliferation of hypotheses and related polemics. The debate centred around the authenticity of the early reports on Muḥammad, the early community, and the collection of the Qur'an. Strong doubts were expressed regarding the validity of the historical representations given by Muslim sources. The debate demonstrates how intimately entangled are the historical, religious, and ideological issues in the making of the Muslim narratives of self-origins. The Islamic literary sources imply that Muḥammad's Companions and the generations following them, the Successors, collected traditions and historical material (*akhbār*) about the life of the Prophet (*maghāzī-sīra* accounts), both as oral transmission and by use of written *aide-mémoire* or hypomnēmata (Schoeler 2006: 78–9). The first written biographies according to Muslim tradition were written down by the end of the first/seventh century (Horovitz 2002: 7–39).

Modern Western Scholarship

German scholarship in the early nineteenth century has given rise to serious studies and revisions of the origins of Islam and its Prophet within the enlightened circles of the movement for Jewish scholarly reform termed *Wissenschaft des Judentum* (Meyer 1971; Neuwirth 2007; Heschel 2012). A member of the group, Abraham Geiger (1810–74) studied the Jewish influence on Muḥammad and the Qur'an (1833), while Gustav Weil (1808–89) attempted a reconstruction of the biography of Muḥammad (1843), presenting a chronological order of the suras of the Qur'an (1844). The critical approach to the study of early traditions of Islam found momentum under the influence of the German 'high criticism' school which was an offshoot of biblical studies in scholarly liberal Protestant circles as the case of Julius Wellhausen demonstrates (van Ess 1980a: 40–3). With the Hungarian Ignaz Goldziher (1850–1921), the study of these early traditions reached a sophisticated level. In his two-volume book *Muhammedanische Studien* (1889–90), Goldziher arrived at negative results about the authenticity of early traditions in general and hadith in particular (Goldziher 1971: 18–19). Moreover, he argued that the Qur'an was first understood by the Prophet and the community to represent 'the most beautiful and perfect *ḥadīth*', and that eventually it came to be regarded as God's speech '*kalām Allāh*' (Goldziher 1971: 17–18). For Goldziher, 'the *maghāzī* of earlier times' as well as early exegesis 'old *tafsīr*', were both considered arbitrary already at an early time (Goldziher 1971: 191–3).

With the studies of the Belgian Jesuit Henri Lammens (1862–1937), the scholarship became more focused on the relation between the Qur'an and the biography of the Prophet (*sīra*). In his article, 'The Age of Muhammad and the Chronology of the Sira' (1910), Lammens set out his thesis concerning the dependence of the *sīra* on the Qur'an. For him, the *sīra* was less regarded as a source for the life of Muḥammad than as an adjustment of the Qur'an, 'servilely interpreted and developed by the Traditions from preconceived ideas' (Lammens 1910). He accepted the fact that 'for the Medinan period of the life of Muhammad a vague oral tradition existed from the beginning of the *hijra*', however, 'if this had been preserved in its integrity, it would be a valuable check to determine the soundness of the tradition. But from an early stage it was tampered with by being adjusted violently to the Koran, which had become the supreme rule of knowledge'.

Commenting on Lammens's thesis, Carl Heinrich Becker (1867–1933) contended that Lammens had said nothing about 'the real historical tradition; for while the historical interest that led to shape the *sīra* as a literary form emerged later, still a plethora of historical traditions are preserved in *Tafsīr* and in *Ḥadīth* that must be old, or in any case might be old'. Becker argued that: In *tafsīr* one must make a distinction between two things: 1. Vignettes, which have a dogmatic tendency and which try to interpret something into the text. These are unhistorical. 2. Vignettes, which are purely exegetical. For example, when in certain places the battles of Badr and Uḥud are alluded to, this proves that, apart from the text of the Qur'an, a historical tradition went parallel through which one wanted to illustrate the wording of the Qur'an. (1924: 526–7). These arguments of Becker support the premise that the materials of the *sīra* developed from tendentious hadith and *tafsīr* reports; nevertheless, the material of the three genres are organized according to different historical points of view; with the *sīra* having originated under pressure from Christian polemic.

With the second generation of Western scholars of Islam, the question of the Qur'an as a source for the life of Muḥammad remained fundamental. The German Islam scholar, Rudi Paret (1901–83), who is renowned for his German translation of the Qur'an and a concordance, noted in a study on Muḥammad that according to the Muslim understanding 'the Koran is a direct divine revelation, unchanging and timeless, which more or less has been fortuitously (zufällig) transmitted by Muḥammad to his compatriots, in which an appropriate Arab formulation was communicated for them and for their time'. Nevertheless, the Qur'an remains for the Western scholar of special interest as a historical source; Paret argues, 'While for the Muslim the historical perspective is thereby fixed and narrowed down by the fact that the Koran as source bears the character of a pre-existent, highest authority and thus remains removed from the human questions of origin and development, it is for our purpose a special interest, to trace based on the koranic evidence the history of Islam and the personal and contemporary history of the founder of this important religion' (1961: 26; and 1980: 166). Paret observes, however, that the Qur'an alone is not enough to draw up a biography of Muḥammad and suggests two other sources, hadith and historical writing, although they both date from a later time, namely, the first half of the second/eighth century, during a time when the image of Muḥammad had already been bedraggled with legends and also partially tendentiously distorted (1980: 168–9). Paret does not address thoroughly these serious issues that were ardently debated at the time.

The Scottish scholar William Montgomery Watt (1909–2006) kept a distance from the position of his contemporary Paret and from the scepticism of Goldziher, Lammens, and Becker. In an article on the materials used by Ibn Isḥāq (d. 150/767) in his biography of the Prophet, Watt acknowledges the arguments raised by Becker concerning the dependence of the *sīra* on exegetical elaborations of Qur'anic allusions and on dogmatic and juristic hadith; however, he adopts Schacht's position—regardless of whether this theory is correct or even roughly correct'—that it was during the era of al-Shāfiʿī (d. 204/820) that it became 'regular practice for legal rules to be justified by hadith reporting a saying or action of Muḥammad through a continuous line of transmission'. But such hadith 'as they are found in the canonical collections were not in existence in the time of Ibn Isḥāq' (1962: 23–4; see also Watt 1966: 336–7). As for the material taken from Qur'anic exegesis (*tafsīr*), Watt selects two types of material as relevant to the *sīra*. The first type is Qur'anic references to earlier prophets based on either biblical tradition or direct allusions in the Qur'an, as in the stories about Abraham and Ishmael. The other type is that of the 'occasions of revelation', which is concerned with specifying the alleged circumstances of the instances of revelation. In this sense it is closely related to the biography of Muḥammad. This material, maintains Watt, gives information about the life of Muḥammad himself; 'there are contradictions in it, as when the same verse is said to have been revealed on two different occasions. On the other hand, there are many cases where there is no reason to doubt the traditional account of the circumstances in which a verse was revealed; this is usually so in passages concerned with the main events of the Medinan period'. Watt posits that 'both types of *tafsīr*-material were the product of a genuine religious interest'. He argues further that 'the group of men who were primarily responsible for this were the *quṣṣāṣ* or "story-tellers"' (1962: 25). When considering the *maghāzī*, or Muḥammad's military expeditions during the Medinan period, he contends that 'little of this material can be derived from the Qur'an, where most of the expeditions are not mentioned' (1962: 27). All through his prolific research, Watt defended the acceptance of what he termed collectively 'the traditional historical material', which includes sources other than the Qur'an; he asserts that 'only where there is internal contradiction is it to be rejected; where "tendential shaping" is suspected it is as far as possible to be corrected' (1966: 336). In the generations of scholars following Watt, research on this subject became more sophisticated and scholars fathomed new dimensions and excavated new grounds.

It is hardly an exaggeration to state that much of the research on Qur'anic studies and the *sīra* in the last three decades has been deeply influenced by John Wansbrough's (1928–2002) two books that appeared in the late 1970s: *Quranic Studies* (1977) and *The Sectarian Milieu* (1978). The basic design of Wansbrough's thesis in both books could be delineated as follows: 'Both the quantity and quality of source material would seem to support the proposition that the elaboration of Islam was not contemporary with but posterior to the Arab occupation of the Fertile Crescent and beyond' (Wansbrough 1978: 99). Once separated from an extensive corpus of prophetical *logia* traditions circulating within a sectarian community, the Islamic revelation became scripture in time. Wansbrough perceived the entire process of canonization as a 'protracted one of community formation'. Accordingly, the Qur'an as a corpus, that is, the ʿUthmānic codex, belongs to the field of historical fiction. Moreover, following the pattern of a 'Rabbinic model', Wansbrough contended that the Qur'an was assembled by various anonymous editors in a polemical environment over the period of some 200 years and reached its canonical form at the beginning of the third/ninth century.

Furthermore, he argued against 'the tyranny of the Hijazi origins of Islam', purporting for the 'Mesopotamian environment' as the native habitat where the 'prophetical logia', the Muḥammadan *evangelium*, as well as the canonical scripture had undergone a process of literary stabilization (Wansbrough 1977: 43–52; Wansbrough 1978: 49; Motzki 2006: 59–63; Karcic 2006: 214–15). Wansbrough adds that 'It was by the membership of this clerical élite (*ʿulamāʾ/fuqahāʾ*) that the Islamic version of salvation history was composed, the prophetical Sunna compiled, Muslim scripture edited, and dogmatic theology expounded. It would not, in fact, be an exaggeration to speak of a professional monopoly of those various agencies responsible for the expression of "normative" Islam' (Wansbrough 1978: 123).

In all this Wansbrough did not consider Muḥammad as a necessary founding historical figure; rather, Muḥammad's image emerged in that polemic Judaeo-Christian 'sectarian milieu' by laying considerable significance on the imagery of covenant, especially the covenant with Moses which included the gifts of scripture and prophecy. 'Like its Mosaic *Vorbild* the portrait of Muḥammad emerged gradually and in response to the needs of a religious community' (1977: 56). 'From the point of view of a literary analysis', states Wansbrough, 'it can be argued that the principal difference between the text of scripture and the Muḥammadan *evangelium* lies merely in the canonical status of the former. Thematic and exemplary treatment of prophethood in the Qur'ān was reformulated in the *evangelium* (*sunna/sīra*) as the personal history of Muḥammad' (Wansbrough 1977: 65).

These highly speculative and elaborate hypotheses by Wansbrough posit the view that there was no kernel of truth behind the 'Islamic event', that it was merely a literary construct made up of the so-called prophetic *logia* and the Muḥammadan *evangelium*, both formulated and construed over a period of some 200 years; and that the Qur'an won its eminence as scripture in this development only as a secondary extrapolation of this process. Invariably, Wansbrough's observations are the consequences of abstract generalizations which led him to conclusions that are debatable. All this allusive amalgam of what Wansbrough perceives as literary, polemical topoi is, moreover, to be understood as salvation history (cf. Rippin 1985: 153–8). Since, as Wansbrough suggested, this process took form in the milieu of a clerical elite, he affirmed that we are not dealing with history, but with salvation history (Wansbrough 1978: 55). The aim of salvation history is 'kerygma' and 'kerygma' cannot be separated from myth (Wansbrough 1978: 1, 4). It could be argued that although the invocation of the somewhat complex construct of 'salvation history' offers one way of accounting for the formation of the *sīra*, the historian is still left with the difficult task of explaining the intrinsic historical value and constitution of the body of materials that make up these sources.

In both these books, Wansbrough employed methods advanced in the fields of German biblical criticism, form history, and French Structuralism (van Ess 1980b: 137). His thesis ushered in a novel approach in the field and simultaneously broached a new wave of intense scepticism. At the same time it opened up the field to more sophisticated approaches and to revisionist scholars who refined their critical methods of historical inquiry, using them in the study of the Qur'an and Muḥammad's biography.

Occasions of Revelation (*Asbāb al-Nuzūl*)

A main field of inquiry into the relation between the Qur'anic exegesis and *maghāzī-sīra* accounts is to be sought in *asbāb al-nuzūl*, which was briefly discussed by Watt. It is however, safe to say that this field gained importance only at a secondary stage

(Conrad 1998: 540). Pioneering work on the subject has been advanced by the studies of Andrew Rippin and Bassām al-Jamal. Rippin points out that 'such reports are cited in these instances, out of a general desire to historicize the text of the Qurʾān in order to be able to prove constantly that God really did reveal his book to humanity on earth' (Rippin 1988: 2). It is not clear how the field of 'occasions of revelation' began to take shape; Rippin and al-Jamal associate its beginnings with popular preachers and also to material derived from *maghāzī-sīra* reports (Rippin 1988: 19; 2003: 570; al-Jamal 2013: 56, 168, 411). Rippin elaborates that 'Historically, it is not certain how the compilation of the *asbāb al-nuzūl* occurred. The reports may have originated within the context of the life story of Muḥammad; they may have been found among the stock of material used by the popular preachers in early Islam; they may have been a part of the documentation used by legal scholars to understand how a qurʾānic law was to be applied; or they may have been a form of exegesis in and by themselves' (Rippin 2003: 570). Conversely, al-Jamal notices that a very large percentage of the material covering occasions of revelation relates to explanations of Qur'anic verses whose nature is narrational (*āyāt al-akhbār*, 2013: 173).

The late Egyptian scholar Naṣr Ḥāmid Abū Zayd (d. 2010) explains that Muslim scholars 'did not stop at the mechanical relation between the text and factual reality, else they would have remained in the framework of an immature concept of simulation, but they have realized that the text—on the level of its linguistic dimension—carries a special efficacy, which exceeds the partial facts to which it responded. They discussed this in detail in what they termed as specific and general. They realized that as recitation, the Qurʾān goes beyond such a mechanical association' (Abū Zayd 1994: 97). Likewise, Richard Martin addresses the issue that 'it is part of the litany of Quranic Studies to point out (sometimes in dismay) that the liturgical sequence of reciting the Qur'an (the 'Uthmānic "collection"), though exegetically tied to events in the life of the Prophet, do not appear within the text in the putative diachrony in which the biographical materials locate them. The textual order of *sūras* and *āyas* is vastly different from the order of "occasions" within the Prophet's biography during which they were "sent down"' (Martin 1982: 373–4).

One example suffices to illustrate, for the purposes of this chapter, the complexity that might be encountered in this branch of exegesis, namely, Q. 2:217 concerning fighting in the 'sacred month' (*al-shahr al-ḥarām*). As an occasion for the revelation of this *āya*, the *maghāzī-sīra* reports associate it with the expedition to Nakhla (Guillaume 2011: 286–9). The ostensibly earlier traditions go back to ʿUrwa ibn al-Zubayr (d. 93 /711–2 or 94/712–3) on the authority of two of his students, Ibn Shihāb al-Zuhrī (d. 124/742) and Yazīd ibn Rūmān (d. 130/747) (Görke and Schoeler 2008: 251–4). Al-Zuhrī does not specify the date of the expedition but only mentions that it occurred on the last day of the sacred month (al-Bayhaqī, *Dalāʾil*, 17). In Yazīd ibn Rūmān's version the date is specified as the last date of Rajab (al-Bayhaqī, *Dalāʾil*, 19). Mūsā ibn ʿUqba dates it 'in Rajab, two months before Badr', (al-Bayhaqī, *Dalāʾil*, 21), and in other accounts attributed to Yazīd ibn Rūmān as well as to other traditionists, the date is given as either Rajab or Jumādā or even Shaʿbān, both of which are not considered among the four 'sacred months' (al-Ṭabarī, *Taʾrikh*, 412, 414;

al-Ṭabarī, *Jāmiᶜ*, 653, 655, 656). Most of the accounts, apart from that of al-Zuhrī from ᶜUrwa, reveal additional explanatory elements (al-Jamal 2013: 413–17). The urge to specify the date arises from the fact that fighting was forbidden during the sacred months; hence, Muslims would have disrupted the inviolability of a sacred month. Moreover, there is yet another factor to be considered that also explains some fragments of the additional explanatory elements, namely, that this verse was considered by some scholars to be abrogated (*mansūkh*; see Burton 2001: 11–19) by Q. 9:5 and 9:36 (al-Ṭabarī, *Jāmiᶜ*, 662–5; al-Jamal 2013: 321). This also had to do with the fact that grammarians disagreed on how to explain the parsing of the syntax (al-Ṭabarī, *Jāmiᶜ*, 649, 660–2). This example evinces a complex case, in which more than one type of exegesis is involved and where the *narratio* is central as Wansbrough has argued (1977: 140–1); in this case, however, the original kernel that goes back to ᶜUrwa is most probably authentic.

The Biography of Muḥammad, the *Sīra*

The Qur'an as a devotional document has played a central role in the life of the individual and community: it shaped the moral values and piety of the early community and promoted study activities centred around the Qur'anic text (Donner 1998). It also left an impact on a variety of rhetorical forms in early Arabic poetry, epistolography, and other prose genres (al-Qāḍī 1993; Allen 2005: 52–64). One of the main points of controversy in modern Western scholarship relating to Islamic sources concerns the dating of the various emerging disciplines of religious knowledge. Recent studies on hadith, Qur'anic *tafsīr*, and on *maghāzī-sīra* narratives have shown that energetic activities in these fields that formed the 'living tradition' of the community (Leemhuis 1988: 22, 28) date back to the last quarter of the first/seventh century—first quarter of the second/eighth century (Leemhuis 1988: 27–8; Donner 1998: 39, 219, 256–8; Motzki et al. 2010: 232, 296–8). Many scholars of this generation were known to have partaken in these various fields of study as the example of two early transmitters and collectors of hadith, ᶜUrwa ibn al-Zubayr (d. 93/711–2 or 94/712–3) and his celebrated student Ibn Shihāb al-Zuhrī (d. 124/742), clearly illustrates.

In an attempt to advance our understanding of the correlation between *maghāzī-sīra* and Qur'an on the one hand, and the use of Qur'anic citations in constructing the *maghāzī-sīra* narratives on the other, I propose to confine the concern of this study to reports whose authenticity has been established from the aforementioned scholarship.

Based on a solid and thorough *sanad-cum-matn* study Andreas Görke and Gregor Schoeler have rounded off their studies on the early *maghāzī-sīra* corpus with a book on ᶜUrwa ibn al-Zubayr. ᶜUrwa's material covers numerous events (some eight tradition clusters, *Traditionskomplexe*) about the life of Muḥammad. Some of the main conclusions of this reconstruction of an earlier layer of the sources indicate that this material gives a general outline of the main events in Muḥammad's life and that it can be safely ascribed to ʿUrwa, who must have collected the material in the decades following the death of the Prophet (2008: 263–4, 267, 271; see Shoemaker review, 2011; and Görke, Motzki, and Schoeler's response, 2012).

Likewise a large portion of al-Zuhrī's *maghāzī-sīra* traditions, which is most probably a genuine attribution to al-Zuhrī (Boekhoff-van der Voort 2011: 41–3), has been preserved in the *Kitāb al-maghāzī* (Jarrar 1989: 26, 29–30; Schoeler 1996: 37, 40; Boekhoff-van der Voort 2011: 27–47) of the *Muṣannaf* work by ʿAbd al-Razzāq al-Ṣanʿānī (d. 211/827) (Motzki 2002: 54–74). These new findings consolidated our knowledge of the early *maghāzī-sīra* narratives which were taking shape during the late first/seventh and early second/eighth centuries; ʿUrwa's endeavours were thus concurrent with the second *maṣāḥif* project of the ʿUthmānic *textus receptus*. (See: Sadeghi and Bergmann 2010; Sadeghi and Goudarzi 2012).

The central themes of the *sīra* accounts focus on the person and the role of the Prophet, as the bearer of God's message, and as a charismatic leader of the new community of believers. In various ways the *sīra* elaborates a definite distinction between the Book of God and Muḥammad as Prophet of God (the episode of the so-called 'satanic verses' would be a good example). Hence, a central aspect is the depiction of the 'Time of the Prophet', as a *hierophanic* time (Eliade 1958: 2–10, 26–30, 462–4; Eliade 1969: 7, 31–3; see also Wielandt 1971: 39, who calls it a *Kairós* borrowing from St. Paul) when God was communicating his word to the emergent *umma* (for the communicative act, Abū Zaid 2004: 32–44; Wild 1993: 257–8).

Moreover, the *sīra* endeavours to articulate the attempts of the early community to constitute itself as a post-prophetic community (Graham 1977: 9–13) whose emerging consciousness was shaped not only by the word of God, but also within the concrete historical events of this *hierophanic* time, which became part of its living memory and served as a witness to the recited message (Jarrar 2014: 570–1). As I have argued elsewhere, the genre of *mashāhid* was also woven into the fabric of the *maghāzī-sīra* material; 'these comprise places in which events took place that were perceived by the community as 'founding' episodes because they were connected to historical signs that were associated with the activity of the Prophet. Such localities form a 'dynamic space' and carry an inherent symbolic potential and accordingly they acquire a certain reverence. Here, power bestowed on a place is meant to mobilize the symbolic energy' (Jarrar 2011: 217).

Perceived as such, the *sīra* does not represent a scheme of salvation history, but rather reveals communal 'cultural memory' (Assmann 2011: 23–44) which took on the form of a historical narrative preserved over time by way of a complex and complementary process of oral/written transmission (Schoeler 2006: 28–61; Görke and Schoeler 2008: 9).

In his admirable entry on 'Sīra and the Qurʾān', Wim Raven concludes that 'certain *sīra* texts originate from an exegetical impulse. They elaborate on qurʾānic passages by commenting, expanding, or historicizing them through episodes of the life of the Prophet and his entourage'. Although aware of the different and very heterogeneous genres and intentions that are brought together in the *sīra* (Raven 2006: 30a, 36a, 40–9), he generalizes his statement by indicating that, 'In its narrative parts, the *sīra* is to a large extent qur'ānic exegesis *(tafsīr)*'. Despite this sweeping statement, Raven delineates an industrious schema of the various practices of exegetical devices in the *sīra* (Raven 2006: 36–40).

Görke and Schoeler present a compelling argument to support the claim that ʿUrwa could be regarded as an outstanding traditionist whose methodological efforts set forth a systematic approach combining *matn* with *isnād* (which more often than not consist of statements of his Aunt ʿĀʾisha) in the transmission of reports about the life of the Prophet and his *maghāzī* (Görke and Schoeler 2008: 270–1). His endeavours represent thus a parting with the ways of earlier storytellers. They have shown that ʿUrwa establishes relations between a certain event and a Qur'anic verse; however, his reports do not emerge as interpretations and interpolations of Qur'anic verses (Görke and Schoeler 2008: 265–6). Traditions that refer to Qur'anic verses may be classified as follows: some traditions paraphrase certain verses of the Qur'an or attempt to explain them; other traditions aim at specifying the event of a certain Qur'anic verse, and finally traditions, in which for various reasons a Qur'anic verse had been quoted. Sometimes these traditions might also have a legal implication (Görke and Schoeler 2008: 15–16).

The correlations among the different branches of religious knowledge (*ʿilm*) within the emerging early Islamic 'living tradition', which must have begun in a mnemonic variety and in the form of written notes during the first/seventh century (Schoeler 1996: 5–9; Donner 1998: 219–56), can be seen to be complex. There has long been a debate since the turn of the twentieth century about the development and credibility of the material on early Islamic branches of knowledge as well as the mechanisms of tradition construction and its dissemination. The dispute pertains largely to the historicity of the traditions (hadith and *akhbār*) as sources for the biography of prophet Muḥammad (*sīra*) and their relationship to Qur'anic exegesis (*tafsīr*). Concluding one of his articles published in 1910, Lammens argued that as a product of exegesis, 'proceeding at random... the *sīra* remained to be written, just as the historical Muhammad remains to be discovered' (Lammens 2000: 183). Conversely, Wansbrough perceives the relation between Qur'anic *logia* and *sīra* (as part of the Muḥammadan *evangelium*) as complex and complementary; these had served as exegetical devices to each other throughout a long process of 'reification, and might be described as "symbolic literalism"' (1978: 138). This intricate process is, however, not necessarily exegetical but rather follows various styles among which the exegetical style forms only one type (Wansbrough 1978: 45, 57, 59, 138–42). Other Western scholars have tried to show that the sources of the *sīra* and its historicity are rooted in Qur'anic exegeses and/or legal thinking (Reynolds 2008: 9–18; Schöller 1998: 79–133; Berg 2000: 79–83, 106–10; and see Schoeler 1996: 9–10; Donner 1998: 19–25; Görke 2011); whereas Burton argues for exegetical origin (1993: 269–84), and Schöller for the priority of *tafsīr* and *fiqh* scholarly activities over *maghāzī-sīra* compilations (1998: 110–22, 132–3; 2000: 42), Rubin on the other hand takes another trajectory proposed by Wansbrough, namely, that *maghāzī-sīra* traditions have their origin neither in the Qur'anic text nor in history, but rather in the Jewish biblical tradition (1995; 2003: 40–64).

Conclusion

The discussions relating to Q. 2:217, aimed to demonstrate the correlation between *maghāzī-sīra* traditions and a Qur'anic verse. In a forthcoming study based on *sanad-cum-matn* analysis I seek to show the complexity of an exegetical report on Q. 30:1–5 in relation to *maghāzī-sīra*. Again, the oldest report on the occasion of revelation for this verse goes back in its earlier form to the end of the first/seventh (ʿUrwa) and early second/eighth (al-Zuhrī) centuries. The genres that made up the body of this particular *khabar* and informed its contextual meaning were various and displayed segments and threads from different narratives; as suggested by Tarif Khalidi, 'Traditions are untidy and the elements that enter into their make-up themselves belong to the debris of earlier traditions' (Khalidi 1994: 1).

As is the case of many narratives of origin, *maghāzī-sīra akhbār* developed around literary strategies and topoi imbued with mythical themes. In stressing that the *sīra* accounts had their origin in oral tradition and *aide-mémoire* (Schoeler 1996: 5–6, 29–34), this should not divert attention from the fact that it also draws its material from various other sources, and that the Qur'an constitutes a major element in its configuration. Spur-of-the-moment allusions to the Qur'an are frequent in *sīra* accounts. Other strategies were also employed, where the narrative expounds on specific instances of Muḥammad's reception of the revelation. Furthermore, since the events of the *hierophanic* time are congruent with both the life of the community and its social fabric, some *sīra* narratives are intended to explain the setting in which the communicative act took place. Occasionally, a narrative comes to serve exegetical purposes, especially when a certain Qur'anic word or expression remains vague and needs to be explained in relation to other literary genres or life situations. In all these cases, it should be kept in mind that although these various fields formed a 'ball of many colored threads' (Khalidi 1994: 18; Khalidi 2009: 37, 38, 59) and borrowed from each other, each buoyed, however, its own characteristics and features.

Bibliography

Abū Zayd, Naṣr Ḥāmid. *Mafhūm al-naṣṣ: dirāsa fī ʿulūm al-*Qurʾān. Beirūt: al-Markaz al-Thaqāfī al-ʿArabī, 1994.

Abū Zayd, Naṣr Ḥāmid. *Rethinking the Qurʾān: Towards a Humanistic Hermeneutics*. Utrecht: University of Humanistic, 2004.

al-Aʿẓamī, Muḥammad Muṣṭafā. *The History of the Qurʾānic Text: From Revelation to Compilation*. Leicester: UK Islamic Academy, 2003.

al-Bayhaqī, Aḥmad b. al-Ḥusayn. *Dalāʾil al-nubuwwa wa-maʿrifat aḥwāl ṣāḥib al-sharīʿa*. Ed. ʿAbd al-Muʿṭī Qalʿajī. Vol. 3. Beirut: Dār al-Kutub al-ʿIlmiyya, 1985.

Allen, Roger. *An Introduction to Arabic Literature*. Cambridge: Cambridge University Press, 2005.

Assmann, Jan. *Cultural Memory and Early Civilization: Writing, Remembrance, and Political Imagination*. Cambridge: Cambridge University Press, 2011.

Becker, Carl Heinrich. *Islamstudien: Vom Werden und Wesen der islamischen Welt*. Vol. 1. Leipzig: Quelle & Meyer, 1924.

Berg, Herbert. *The Development of Exegesis in Early Islam: The Authenticity of Muslim Literature from the Formative Period*. London: Curzon, 2000.

Berg, Herbert. 'Competing Paradigms in Islamic Origins: Qurʾān 15: 789–91'. In: Herbert Berg (ed.). *Method and Theory in the Study of Islamic Origins*, pp. 259–90. Leiden, Boston, and Cologne: E. J. Brill, 2003.

Berg, Herbert and Sarah Rollens. 'The Historical Muhammad and the Historical Jesus: A Comparison of Scholarly Reinventions and Reinterpretations', *Studies in Religion* 37 (2008), 271–92.

Boekhoff-van der Voort, Nicolet. 'The *Kitāb al-maghāzī* of 'Abd al-Razzāq b. Hammām al-San'ānī'. In: Nicolet Boekhoff-van der Voort, Kees Versteegh, and Joas Wagemakers (eds.). *The Transmission and Dynamics of the Textual Sources of Islam: Essays in Honour of Harald Motzki*, pp. 27–47. Leiden and Boston: Brill, 2010.

Burton, John. 'Law and Exegesis: The Penalty of Adultery in Islam'. In: G. R. Hawting and Abdul-Kader A. Shareef (eds.). *Approaches to the Qurʾān*, pp. 269–84. London and New York: Routledge, 1993.

Burton, John 'Abrogation'. In: Jane Damen McAuliffe (ed.). *Encyclopaedia of the Qurʾān*, 1:11–19. Leiden and Boston: Brill, 2001.

Conrad, Lawrence I. 'Muḥammad, the Prophet (d. 11/632)'. In: Julie Scott Meisami and Paul Starkey (eds.). *Encyclopedia of Arabic Literature*, 2:539–44. London and New York: Routledge, 1998.

Donner, Fred M. *Narratives of Islamic Origins: The Beginning of Islamic Writing*. Princeton: Darwin Press, 1998.

Eliade, Mercia. *Patterns in Comparative Religion*. London: Sheed and Ward, 1958.

Eliade, Mercia. *The Quest: History and Meaning in Religion*. Chicago: University of Chicago Press, 1969.

Encyclopaedia of the Qurʾān. (ed.). Jane Damen McAuliffe. 6 vols. Leiden and Boston: Brill, 2001–6.

Goldziher, Ignaz. *Muslim Studies*. (ed.). S. M. Stern. Trans. C. R. Barber and S. M. Stern. Vol. 2. London: George Allen and Unwin, 1971.

Görke, Andreas. 'The Relationship between Maghāzī and Ḥadīth in Early Islamic Scholarship', *Bulletin of the School of African and Oriental Studies* 74 (2011), 171–85.

Görke, Andreas, Harald Motzki, and Gregor Schoeler. 'First Century Sources for the Life of Muḥammad? A Debate', *Der Islam* 89 (2012), 2–59.

Görke, Andreas and Gregor Schoeler. *Die ältesten Berichte über das Leben Muḥammads: Das Korpus ʿUrwa ibn az-Zubayr*. Princeton: Darwin Press, 2008.

Graham, William A. *Divine Word and Prophetic Word in Early Islam*. The Hague and Paris: Mouton, 1977.

Guillaume, Alfred. *The Life of Muhammad: A Translation of Ibn Ishaq's Sirat Rasul Allah*. 2nd printing. Oxford: Oxford University Press Karachi, 2001.

Hamdan, Omar. 'The Second Maṣāḥif Project: A Step towards the Canonization of the Qurʾānic Text'. In: Angelica Neuwirth, Nicolai Sinai, and Michael Marx (eds.). *The Qurʾān in Context: Historical and Literary Investigations into the Qurʾānic Milieu*, pp. 795–835. Leiden and Boston: Brill, 2010.

Heschel, Susannah. 'German Jewish Scholarship on Islam as a Tool for De-Orientalizing Judaism', *New German Critique* 117/39 (2012), 91–107.

Horovitz, Josef. *The Earliest Biographies of the Prophet and their Authors*. Ed. Lawrence I. Conrad. Princeton: Darwin Press, 2002.

Hoyland, Robert G. *Seeing Islam as Others Saw it: A Survey and Evaluation of Christian, Jewish and Zoroastrian Writings on Early Islam*. Princeton: Darwin Press, 1997.

Hoyland, Robert G. 'The Earliest Christian Writings on Muḥammad'. In: Harald Motzki (ed.). *The Biography of Muhammad: The Issue of the Sources*, pp. 276–97. Leiden, Boston and Cologne: Brill, 2000.

Hoyland, Robert G. 'Writing the Biography of the Prophet Muhammad: Problems and Solutions', *History* Compass 5 (2007), 581–602.

Al-Jamāl, Bassām. *Asbāb al-nuzūl: ʿilman min ʿulūm al-Qurʾān*. 2nd edn. Beirut: al-Markaz al-Thaqāfī al-ʿArabī, 2013.

Jarrar, Maher. *Die Prophetenbiographie im islamischen Spanien: Ein Beitrag zur Überlieferungs- und Redaktionsgeschichte*. Frankfurt: Peter Lang Verlag, 1989.

Jarrar, Maher. 'Ibn Abī Yaḥyā: A Controversial Medinan *Akhbārī* of the 2nd/8th Century'. In: Nicolet Boekhoff-van der Voort, KeesVersteegh, and Joas Wagemakers (eds.). *The Transmission and Dynamics of the Textual Sources of Islam: Essays in Honour of Harald Motzki*, pp. 197–227. Leiden and Boston: Brill, 2011.

Jarrar, Maher. 'Sira'. In: Coeli Fitzpatrick and Adam Hani Walker (eds.). *Muhammad in History, Thought, and Culture: An Encyclopedia of the Prophet of God*, pp. 568–82. Santa Barbara, CA: ABC-CLIO, Greenwood, 2014.

Karcic, Fikret. 'Textual Analysis in Islamic Studies: A Short Historical and Comparative Survey', *Islamic Studies* 45 (2006), 191–220.

Khalidi, Tarif. *Arabic Historical Thought in the Classical Period*. Cambridge: Cambridge University Press, 1994.

Khalidi, Tarif. *Images of Muhammad: Narratives of the Prophet in Islam Across the Centuries*. New York and London: Doubleday, 2009.

Lammens, Henri. 'Koran and Tradition: How the Life of Muhammad Was Composed'. In: Ibn Warraq (ed.). *The Quest for the Historical Muhammad*, pp. 169–87. Amherst, NY: Prometheus Books, 2000.

Leemhuis, Fred. 'Origins and Early Development of the *Tafsīr* Tradition'. In: Andrew Rippin (ed.). *Approaches to the History of the Interpretation of the Qurʾān*, pp. 13–30. Oxford: Clarendon Press, 1988.

Martin, Richard C. 'Understanding the Qurʾān in Text and Context', *History of Religions* 21 (1982), 361–84.

Martin, Richard C. (ed.). *Approaches to Islam in Religious Studies*. Tucson: University of Arizona Press, 1985.

Meyer, Michael M. 'Jewish Religious Reform and *Wissenschaft des Judentums*: The Positions of Zunz, Geiger and Frankel', *Leo Baeck Institute Yearbook* 16 (1971), 19–41.

Motzki, Harald. *The Origins of Islamic Jurisprudence: Meccan Fiqh before the Classical Period*. Leiden, Boston, and Cologne: E. J. Brill, 2002.

Motzki, Harald. 'The Question of the Authenticity of Muslim Traditions Reconsidered: A Review Article'. In: Herbert Berg (ed.). *Method and Theory in the Study of Islamic Origins*, pp. 211–57. Leiden, Boston, and Cologne: E. J. Brill, 2003.

Motzki, Harald. 'Alternative Accounts of the Qurʾānic Formation'. In: Jane Dammen McAuliffe (ed.). *The Cambridge Companion to the Qurʾān*, pp. 59–75. Cambridge: Cambridge University Press, 2006.

Motzki, Harald, Nicolet Boekhoff-van der Voort, and Sean Anthony (eds.). *Analyzing Muslim Traditions: Studies in Legal, Exegetical and Maghazi Hadith*. Leiden and Boston: Brill, 2010.

Neuwirth, Angelika. 'Orientalism in Oriental Studies? Qur'ānic Studies as a Case in Point', *Journal of Qur'ānic Studies* 9 (2007), 115–27.

Neuwirth, Angelika. *Der Koran als Text der Spätantike: Ein europäischer Zugang*. Berlin: Verlag der Weltrelgionen, 2010.

Paret, Rudi. 'Der Koran als Geschichtsquelle', *Der Islam* 37 (1961), 24–42.

Paret, Rudi. *Mohammed und der Koran: Geschichte und Verkundigung des arabischen Propheten*. Stuttgart: Kohlhammer, 1980.

Al-Qāḍī, Wadād. 'The Impact of the Qur'ān on the Epistolography of ʿAbd al-Ḥamīd'. In: G. R. Hawting and Abdul-Kader A. Shareef (eds.). *Approaches to the Qur'ān*, pp. 285–313. London and New York: Routledge, 1993.

Raven, Wim. 'Sīra and the Qur'ān'. In: Jane Dammen McAuliffe (ed.). *Encyclopaedia of the Qur'ān*, 5:29–51. Leiden: E. J. Brill, 2006.

Reynolds, Gabriel Said. *The Qur'ān in its Historical Context*. London and New York: Routledge, 2008.

Rippin, Andrew. 'Literary Analysis of Qur'ān, *Tafsīr*, and *Sīra*: The Methodologies of John Wansbrough'. In: Richard C. Martin (ed.). *Approaches to Islam in Religious Studies*, pp. 151–63. Tucson: University of Arizona Press, 1985.

Rippin, Andrew. 'The Function of '*Asbāb al-nuzūl*' in Qur'ānic Exegesis', *Bulletin of the School of Oriental and African Studies* 51 (1988), 1–20.

Rippin, Andrew. 'Muhammad in the Qur'ān: Reading Scripture in the 21st Century'. In: Harald Motzki (ed.). *The Biography of Muhammad: The Issue of the Sources*, pp. 298–310. Leiden: Brill, 2000.

Rippin, Andrew. 'Occasions of Revelation'. In: Jane Dammen McAuliffe (ed.). *Encyclopaedia of the Qur'ān*, 3:569–72. Leiden: E. J. Brill, 2003.

Rubin, Uri. *The Eye of the Beholder: The Life of Muhammad as Viewed by the Early Muslims. A Textual Analysis*. Princeton: The Darwin Press, 1995.

Sadeghi, Behnam and Uwe Bergmann. 'The Codex of a Companion of the Prophet and the Qur'ān of the Prophet', *Arabica* 57 (2010), 343–436.

Sadeghi, Behnam.'The Chronology of the Qur'ān: A Stylometric Research Program', *Arabica* 58 (2011), 210–99.

Sadeghi, Behnam and Mohsen Goudarzi. "Ṣan'ā' 1 and the Origins of the Qur'ān," *Der Islam*, 87:1–2 (2012), 1–129.

al-Ṣāliḥ, Ṣubḥī. *Mabāḥith fī ʿulūm al-Qur'ān*. Beirut: Dār al-ʿIlm li'l-Malāyīn, 1977.

Schmid, Nora K. 'Quantitative Text Analysis and Its Application to the Qur'ān: Some Preliminary Considerations'. In: Angelica Neuwirth, Nicolai Sinai, and Michael Marx (eds.). *The Qur'ān in Context: Historical and Literary Investigations into the Qur'ānic Milieu*, pp. 441–60. Leiden and Boston: Brill, 2010.

Schoeler, Gregor. *Charakter und Authentie der muslimischen Üeberlieferungüber das Leben Mohammeds*. Berlin and New York: Walter de Gruyter, 1996.

Schoeler, Gregor. *The Oral and Written in Early Islam*. Trans. Uwe Vagelpohl, ed. James E. Montgomery. London and New York: Routledge, 2006.

Shoemaker, Stephen J. 'In Search of ʿUrwa's *Sīra*: Some Methodological Issues in the Quest for "Authenticity" in the Life of Muḥammad', *Der Islam* 85 (2011), 257–344.

Schöller, Marco. *Exegetisches Denken und Prophetenbiographie: Eine quellenkritische Analyse*. Wiesbaden: Otto Harrassowitz, 1998.

Stefanidis, Emmanuelli. 'The Qur'an Made Linear: A Study of the Geschichte des Qorâns' Chronological Reordering', *Journal of Qur'ānic Studies* 10 (2008), 1–22.

al-Ṭabarī, Muḥammad b. Jarīr. *Taʾrīkh al-rusul wal-mulūk*. Ed. Muḥammad Abū al-Faḍl Ibrāhīm. Vol. 2. Cairo: Dār al-Maʿārif, 1968.

al-Ṭabarī, Muḥammad b. Jarīr. *Jāmiʿ al-bayān ʿan taʾwīl ayy al-Qurʾān*. Ed. ʿAbd Allāh b. ʿAbd al-Muḥsin al-Turkī. Vol. 3. Cairo: Dār Hajar, 2001.

Van Ess, Josef. 'From Wellhausen to Becker: The Emergence of *Kulturgeschichte*'. In: Malcolm H. Kerr (ed.). *Islamic Studies: A Tradition and its Problems*, pp. 27–51. Malibu, CA: Undena Publication, 1980a.

Van Ess, Josef. 'The Sectarian Milieu: Content and Composition of Islamic Salvation History by John Wansbrough', *Bulletin of the School of Oriental and African Studies* 43 (1980b), 137–9.

Wansbrough, John. *Quranic Studies: Sources and Methods of Scriptural Interpretation*. Oxford: Oxford University Press, 1977.

Wansbrough, John. *The Sectarian Milieu: Content and Composition of Islamic Salvation History*. Oxford: Oxford University Press, 1978.

Wansbrough, John. Book review of van Ess's *Anfänge muslimischer Theologie*, *Bulletin of the School of Oriental and African Studies* 43 (1980), 361–3.

Watt, William Montgomery. 'The Materials used by Ibn Isḥāq'. In: Bernard Lewis and P. M. Holt (eds.). *Histories of the Middle East*, pp. 23–34. London: Oxford University Press, 1962.

Watt, William Montgomery. *Muhammad at Medina*. Guildford and London: Billing and Sons, 1966.

Wielandt, Rotraud. *Offenbarung und Geschichte im Denken moderner Muslime*. Wiesbaden: Franz Steiner Verlag, 1971.

Wild, Stefan. 'Die andere Seite des Textes: Naṣr Ḥāmid Abū Zaid und der Koran', *Die Welt des Islams* 33 (1993), 256–61.

Zebiri, Kate. 'Towards a Rhetorical Criticism of the Qurʾān', *Journal of Qurʾānic Studies* 5 (2003), 95–120.

CHAPTER 42

EARLY QUR'ANIC EXEGESIS

From Textual Interpretation to Linguistic Analysis

KEES VERSTEEGH

The First Exegetical Efforts

According to the Qur'an (Q. 16:44), the Messenger of God who brought the revelation to the Quraysh was the best authority on the meaning of the revelation. Al-Suyūṭī even claims to have written a book, *Tarjumān al-Qurʾān*, in which he collected more than 10,000 reports about the *tafsīr al-nabī* (al-Suyūṭī, *al-Itqān*, 2:404). And, indeed, most collections of hadith, such as al-Bukhārī's *Ṣaḥīḥ* (book 60), contain a section devoted to *tafsīr*. Yet, these reports do not involve many instances of text interpretation. The majority of these hadiths narrate the circumstances of revelation, or they concern verses used by the Prophet in sermons, for instance, about his journey to heaven or about other prophets. In some cases, a verse is revealed to confirm something the Prophet just said (*nazalat hādhihi ʾl-aya taṣdīqan li-qawl rasūl Allāh ṣlʿm*, al-Bukhārī, *Ṣaḥīḥ*, book 60, chapter 222, no. 284). In one instance, the Prophet corrects someone's recitation of Q. 54:17, 22, 23, 40 where he should say *muddakir* instead of *mudhdhakir* (al-Bukhārī, *Ṣaḥīḥ*, book 60, chapter 290, nos. 395, 396, 397). Other examples of exegetical *tafsīr* ascribed to the Prophet are cited by Abdul-Raof (2010:112–16).

Early hadith collections do contain, however, numerous reports about Companions or Successors being asked about the interpretation of specific verses, in which both legal and lexical matters are mentioned. One assumes that during the first decades of Islam the believers, many of whom were converts with insufficient command of Arabic, were puzzled by the meaning of certain verses and wished to know what God's message meant. Those in the community with first-hand knowledge of the circumstances of the revelation were the natural authority to turn to. In ʿAbd al-Razzāq's *Muṣannaf*, we find a large number of these questions and answers. The majority concern details of Islamic law, as in the following story, which hinges on the applicability of Q. 65:1 to an individual case of divorce (ʿAbd al-Razzāq, *Muṣannaf*, 6:320–1):

> ʿAbd al-Razzāq from Ibn Jurayj. He said: I asked ʿAṭāʾ 'A man divorces [his wife], but he doesn't make it final; where is she supposed to wait?' He said: 'In her husband's house, where she used to be.' I said: 'Do you think he could allow her to retire to her family's house?' He said: 'No, because then he would share in the guilt.' Then he recited: 'Let them not go away except when they commit a manifest abomination.' I said: 'Does this verse apply here?' He said: 'Yes, and ʿAmr [agrees]'. I said: 'Hasn't it been abrogated?' He said: 'No.'

Remarkably, only the younger Companions figure in these traditions (Berg 2000:39). According to Fück (1939), this could be an indication that only at a time when the older Companions had already passed away, before the end of the first century of the *hijra*, did people start to interview those who had known the Prophet themselves. They were not only interested in the meaning, but also in the background of the text and wished to know when the verses were revealed, and who the persons mentioned in the Qur'an were. In some cases, the memory of the Companions and the Successors could be of assistance, but in other cases, the help of others with more knowledge about the outside world and other religions was enlisted. Among the new converts, there were many Jews and Christians with first-hand knowledge of other religious scriptures, who could supply this kind of information.

Sinai highlights this function of the Qur'anic text in the early Muslim community (Sinai 2009: 9, 48). Since the verses that have a direct bearing on legal matters constitute only a tiny proportion of the total body of the text, Sinai regards as much more important the contribution of the Qur'an to what he calls the 'narrative imagination' of the believers, who were less interested in concrete precepts for their behaviour than in accounts that could feed into this imagination. Presumably, both functions were important in the early community.

The narrative background to the Qur'an was probably partly the domain of *quṣṣāṣ*, professional storytellers, who were also employed by the authorities for purposes of propaganda (Juynboll 1983: 11–15; Tottoli 2002). Qur'anic exegesis was a different matter. According to some accounts, the second caliph, ʿUmar, forbade all scholarly writing (*ʿilm*), no doubt because he felt that this would threaten the authority of the Qur'an (Schoeler 1996: 30–1). Nonetheless, the need for specialists grew as the living memory of the time of the Prophet and Meccan society faded. In the course of time, therefore, a special class of experts in the interpretation of the text in all its features, not just the narrative background, arose. They dedicated themselves to the explanation of the text of the Qur'an, just like others became adept at reciting the Qur'an, or at applying the rules of Islamic law in litigation.The name connected with the first *tafsīr* is that of Ibn ʿAbbās (d. *c.*68/687), who in the course of time acquired mythical status (Gilliot 1985). This makes it difficult to evaluate the numerous reports about his comments on the Qur'an. Goldfeld (1981) maintains that it is possible to reconstruct the *Tafsīr Ibn ʿAbbās*, while more sceptical scholars tend to disagree with this, either because they reject the testimony of the *isnād* entirely, or because they do not believe that it is possible to find the true Ibn ʿAbbās teachings among the multitude of reports going back to him. Berg (2000) compares the most important transmission lines from Ibn ʿAbbās in al-Ṭabarī's *Tafsīr* and shows that the data are inconsistent with a direct line from Ibn ʿAbbās to the later compilers. Accordingly, he rejects the reports about Ibn ʿAbbās' teachings (Berg 2003; but see Motzki 2003). On the basis of a detailed analysis of the transmission lines Motzki (2010) traces some exegetical accounts to scholars of the generation after Ibn ʿAbbās, at the end of the first/seventh century. Although some of them ascribe their comments to Ibn ʿAbbās, in most cases the link with Ibn ʿAbbās is made by later transmitters. Motzki leaves open the possibility that elements in these early commentaries go back to Ibn ʿAbbās, but these cannot be identified with certainty.

The *Tafsīr* transmitted under his name, *Tanwīr al-miqbās min tafsīr Ibn ʿAbbās*, dates from a later period (Berg 2004). It was ascribed by Wansbrough (1977) to al-Kalbī, and it has also been regarded as a work by al-Fīrūzābādī (d. 817/1414). Motzki (2006) has identified the text as *al-Wāḍiḥ fī tafsīr al-Qurʾān al-karīm* by ʿAbd Allāh ibn al-Mubārak al-Dīnawarī (*fl.* 300/912).

The treatises about loanwords (*lughāt*) and difficult words (*gharīb*) in the Qur'an that are also ascribed to Ibn ʿAbbās are of doubtful authenticity (see Rippin 1981, 1983). The same goes for the collection of lexical explanations transmitted under the title *Masāʾil Nāfiʿ ibn al-Azraq* (Baalbaki 2014: 39–41), which probably belongs to a much later period.

The First Collections of *Tafsīr*

According to Schoeler (1996: 53–7), at first writing was only used in the form of personal notes that scholars made in their so-called *ṣaḥīfas*. At a later stage, at first in Medina, such notes were made available to the students in the schools, even though teaching continued to be predominantly oral. Schoeler shows how the transmission of knowledge at this early period could take place simultaneously in written and oral form. This explains the sometimes contradictory reports about scholars like ʿUrwa ibn al-Zubayr (d. 94/712), who are said to have opposed the writing of texts other than the Qur'an and are at the same time credited with books, as in the case of ʿUrwa's treatise on the *maghāzī* of the Prophet.

The earliest collections of notes on Qur'anic exegesis by scholars may be reconstituted partially from quotations in later sources that go back to the students' revisions of these notes (Versteegh 1993: 93). A thorough study of the common features and differences in these quotations may still reveal some elements of their teachings (see Gilliot 2002). *Tafsīr*s in the form of collected comments have been published, for instance, from Sufyān al-Thawrī (d. 161/787), Ibn Jurayj (d. 150/767), al-Ḍaḥḥāk ibn Muzāḥim (d. 105/723; see Versteegh 2011; Gilliot 2013), and al-Suddī al-Kabīr (d. 128/745). In some cases, students may have reworked these notes into real publications. This applies for instance to the works of Mujāhid (d. 104/722), in the recension of Warqāʾ (d. *c*.160/776) *ʿan* Ibn Abī Najīḥ (d. 131/748) (see Leemhuis 1981; Sinai 2009: 171–2), of Maʿmar ibn Rāshid (d. 154/770) in the recension of ʿAbd al-Razzāq al-Ṣanʿānī (d. 211/827), of Muqātil ibn Sulaymān (d. 150/767; see Versteegh 1990; Gilliot 1991; Sinai 2009: 168–71; Sinai 2014b), and of Yaḥyā ibn Sallām (d. 200/815). Ibn Wahb's (d. 197/812) commentary constitutes a special case, because it is not arranged according to the order of the Qur'anic verses, but according to the author's primary sources (see Muranyi 1993: 10–11).

At a somewhat later stage, actual books with a definitive form, published by the author themselves, began to appear. Perhaps the *tafsīrs* by Zayd ibn ʿAlī (d. 122/740; see Versteegh 1999) and by Muḥammad ibn al-Sāʾib al-Kalbī (d. 146/763; but see Schöller 2000: 42–4) belong to this category. The latter has a convoluted history of identification. The name of al-Kalbī occurs at the end of the *isnād* of the commentary ascribed to Ibn ʿAbbās (< Abū Ṣāliḥ < Ibn ʿAbbās), but Pregill (2013) points out that none of the manuscripts actually identifies it as *Tafsīr al-Kalbī*. He concludes that the attribution to him should be abandoned, but draws attention to the presence in the text of authentic material from the mid-second/eighth century, which may well go back to al-Kalbī after all, in particular a considerable number of parallels with Muqātil's *Tafsīr* (see also Nilsaz 2018). It will be referred to here as the *Tafsīr* transmitted from al-Kalbī.

Both in this category and in the commentaries transmitted by students, the internal references show that they were indeed intended as coherent books. Yaḥyā ibn Sallām rather often refers to other passages in which he has given some comment, for instance when he says (*Tafsīr*, 1:398) 'we have explained all this in *Sūrat Hūd*' (*wa-qad fassarnā dhālika kullahu fī sūrat Hūd*).

In explaining the meaning of God's word, the early commentaries deal with all aspects of the text. Wansbrough (1977) distinguishes between three early types of exegesis with terms borrowed from the Jewish tradition of Torah interpretation: haggadic (narrative), halakhic (legal), and masoretic (textual) exegesis. In his view, these different types represent a chronological development in *tafsīr* writing. Yet, none of the early commentaries, from the end of the first/seventh till the end of the second/eighth century, fits his classification, since to varying degrees they deal with all exegetical modes (see also Muranyi 1993: xii). In addition to providing glosses for the text, they all transmit narrative material and provide alternative readings. They all point out occasionally what the legal implications of the text are. Thus, for instance, Yaḥyā ibn Sallām (*Tafsīr*, 1:442–3) cites a number of different interpretations of the Qur'anic verses about the permissibility of seeing a woman unveiled. But typically, there are no generalized discussions of legal arguments of the kind that later became current. Likewise, one finds no theological discussions in the commentaries, although theological implications are of course inherent in interpreting the text, and sometimes intrude in the glossing of the text, especially when the nature of God's attributes is at stake.

Within this common framework, commentaries may differ in their attention to each exegetical mode, and to different topics. The characteristic differences one finds between the individual commentaries concern, among other things, the way in which they deal with earlier authorities. Muqātil, for instance, does refer to earlier scholars, but in a rather haphazard way; in fact, later scholars criticized him for his cavalier treatment of the transmission etiquette (al-Baghdādī, *Taʾrīkh Baghdād*, 13:164). On the other hand, Maʿmar ibn Rāshid's *Tafsīr*, which has been preserved in the recension by ʿAbd al-Razzāq, almost always quotes Maʿmar's authorities (Motzki 2002: 58–64). The first commentary to give full attention to the transmission is that of Yaḥyā ibn Sallām, who cites complete *isnād*s throughout his commentary, referring to the *tafsīr* of earlier commentators, such as al-Suddī (al-Kabīr), Mujāhid, Qatāda ibn Diʿāma (d. 118/736), al-Ḥasan (al-Baṣrī) (d. 110/728), and (Muḥammad) al-Kalbī. The term *tafsīr* may refer to their interpretation of a passage, or perhaps in some cases to some kind of written commentary. Yaḥyā is also the first to systematically provide alternative explanations for each passage. On Q. 22:20 *yuṣharu bihi*, for instance, he (*Tafsīr*, 1:360) first paraphrases the verb *ṣahara* 'to liquefy, to melt' with *yuḥraqu bihi* and then adds three paraphrases from earlier exegetes: *wa-qāla 'l-Ḥasan [al-Baṣrī] yuqṭaʿu bihi wa-qāla Mujāhid yudhābu bihi wa-qāla 'l-Kalbī yunḍaḥu bihi*. The commentators also differ with respect to their attitude towards alternative readings. When the third caliph, ʿUthmān, ordered the collection of all extant fragments of the Qur'an and the establishment of a canonical text, the different readings must have been the subject of close scrutiny. There is no consensus about the historicity of this tradition but, after a careful review of all the evidence, Sinai (2014a) concludes that a strong argument can be made for the establishment of a canonical text in the first decades after the Prophet's death. This does not preclude the survival of alternative readings.

Choosing between variants inevitably led to discussions about the correctness of the text. Stories about mistakes in recitation abound, and there are even cases where the commentator assumes a scribal error in the text, for instance when al-Ḍaḥḥāk (*Tafsīr*, no. 1425) claims that in Q. 17:23, the scribes had mistaken *wa-waṣā* for *wa-qaḍā*, which then became the canonical text (Beck 1945: 363). Obviously, the codification of the text did not put an end to the existence of rival versions. Within the consonantal ductus of the ʿUthmānic codex, there still remained a wide variety of different vocalic readings, for which canonization in the form of the Seven Readings was not achieved until much later (Shah 2004; Nasser 2012). For some readers, this meant that even when they had a vocalized text at their disposal, they could still recite their own version (Shah 2003: 27).

Finally, individual commentators manifest a special interest in certain topics. Al-Ḍaḥḥāk ibn Muzāḥim seems to have been particularly interested in the topography of hell, about which he supplies a wealth of details (Versteegh 2011: 292), while Ibn Jurayj seems to have had concerns about angels (*Tafsīr*, pp. 29, 31, 43, 68, 78, 136, 145, 192, 209, 258, 288, 318, 335). Systematic comparison of the exegetical comments by different scholars is required to identify such individual preferences.

The Meaning of the Text

The first task of the commentator is to explain the meaning of a word, a phrase, or an entire verse (for a thorough analysis and classification of glossing types see Sinai 2009:

188–215). Sometimes, text and comment are simply juxtaposed, especially when individual lexical items are 'translated', but more often, the comments are introduced by an exegetical connector, such as *yaʿnī, yaqūlu, ay, maʿnāhu*. This type of explanation would seem to belong to the oldest layers of exegetical activities, although it would be wrong to regard their use as an indication of oral transmission of the comments (Sinai 2009: 182–3). Some words in the Qur'an must have become incomprehensible for the common believer, either because they were obsolete, or because the new converts' command of Arabic was insufficient. The commentator apparently adapted the language to more contemporary usage by substituting more current lexical items for those in the text (on the use of this method in Muqātil see Versteegh 1990). This applies to nouns, such as *nabaʾun*, replaced by *ḥadīthun* (Muqātil, *Tafsīr*, 2:399, l. 7), or *wābil*, replaced by *maṭar shadīd* (*Tafsīr*, 1:220, l. 13), and to verbs, such as *khalā* replaced by *maḍā* (*Tafsīr*, 4:23, l. 2). A similar effect is achieved by changing a grammatical constituent, for instance a relative pronoun, as in *aḥsana mā kānū yaʿmalūna* (Q. 9:121) paraphrased as *aḥsana alladhī kānū yaʿmalūna* (Muqātil, *Tafsīr*, 2:203, l. 5), or a verbal form, as in *yataʿārafūna baynahum* (Q. 10:45), paraphrased as *yaʿrifūna baʿḍuhum baʿḍahum* (Muqātil, *Tafsīr*, 2: 240, l. 1).

Sometimes, the text is made more comprehensible not by paraphrasing, but by adding words, as in the following example from Muqātil (*Tafsīr*, 3:528–9) on Q. 34:15: (*thumma qāla*) *jannatāni* (*aḥaduhumā*) *ʿan yamīnin* (*al-wādī*) *wa-* (*'l-ukhrā ʿan*) *shimālin* (*al-wādī*) '(Then, He says:) two gardens (one of them) at the right (of the river-bed) and (the other at) the left (of the river-bed).' The added words may also serve to identify the referents of the verbs and pronouns in the text, as in Q. 12:58 *fa-dakhalū ʿalayhi* (*yaʿnī ʿalā Yūsuf bi-Miṣr*) *fa-ʿarafahum* (*Yūsuf*) 'and they came upon him (i.e. upon Joseph in Egypt) and he (Joseph) recognized them' (*Tafsīr*, 2:341, l. 9).

Sometimes the commentators refer to other occurrences of a lexical item in the Qur'an (*naẓāʾir*) in order to support their interpretation. Such a comparison may also demonstrate that a word has different meanings (*wujūh, ashbāh*) (Wansbrough 1977: 208ff.). In some cases, these different meanings may lead to an exegetical problem because they are contradictory. In later lexicography, the term *ḍidd* (plural *aḍdād*) was commonly used for this category of words. In the early commentaries, cases of *ḍidd* were commonly identified, but only one exegete actually uses the term. In Zayd ibn ʿAlī's *Tafsīr*, it occurs three times as a technical term (Versteegh 1999: 20–5), for example on Q. 20:15 *akādu ukhfīhā* 'I barely hide it', which Zayd ibn ʿAlī interprets as 'I [almost] show it' (*uẓhiruhā*). In his view, the verb *akhfā* is a *ḍidd* because it can mean both 'to hide' and 'to show'. The extensive discussion of this item in Ibn al-Anbārī's (d. 328/939) treatise on this topic (*Aḍdād*, 95–9) reveals that the exegetical problem in this passage concerned the announcement of the Hour (*al-sāʿa*), which Zayd ibn ʿAlī apparently believed to be near.

Even more controversial is the matter of metaphorical interpretation, which usually serves the purpose of avoiding anthropomorphic readings of the text. Muqātil is regarded by later authors as a prime example of an early authority who had no qualms about interpreting in an anthropomorphic way those passages in the Qur'an which referred to God's attributes (al-Baghdādī, *Taʾrīkh Baghdād*, 13:163; see Gilliot 1991 40–51). Recent research has somewhat mitigated the negative portrayal of Muqātil (Saleh 2004; Koç 2008; Sirry 2012).

Sometimes, semantic explanations are connected with other considerations, rather than being just a context-free lexicographical exercise. A considerable number of glosses appears to have been connected with doctrinal discussions among the community. In some cases, the ideological background to the glosses is fairly obvious, while in other cases it is not immediately clear what the rationale is behind a gloss. An example is the interpretation of the term *jaʿala* when applied to the Qur'an (Q. 43:3). When al-Ḍaḥḥāk (*Tafsīr*, no. 34) glosses this verb as *khalaqa*, he probably wishes to emphasize that even though the verb *khalaqa* is not used in connection with the Qur'an, this does not imply that the Qur'an was uncreated. The systematic replacement of *laʿalla* with *li-kay* in phrases like *laʿallakum yaʿlamūna* 'perhaps they will know' (Muqātil, *Tafsīr*, 2:338, l. 7 on Q. 12:46) may also have a doctrinal motive, since *laʿalla* could be seen as suggesting doubt on God's part. Sometimes, etymological explanations are adduced to further the understanding of a word, for instance when Muqātil (*Tafsīr*, 1:127) explains the proper name Babel by adding 'because the tongues became confused' (*li-anna 'l-alsun tabalbalat*) or when Ibn Jurayj (*Tafsīr*, p. 35) explains *sabt* 'Sabbath, Saturday' as derived from the root s-b-t in the sense of *qaṭaʿa* 'to cut off', and states that it is a *qiṭʿa zamān* 'segment of time', presumably in order to avoid association with s-b-t in the sense of 'to rest', which might suggest that God needed a rest after the creation.

Likewise, the meaning of a word in a different Arabic variety than the Qur'anic language may help to understand a difficult passage in which the common meaning does not fit, for instance when al-Ḍaḥḥāk (*Tafsīr*, no. 1197) states that the people from Oman use *khamr* for 'grapes'. Actually, this is the only time this commentator refers to a tribal variety, and he probably does so in order to avoid confusion in the interpretation of Q. 12:36, where *aʿṣiru khamran* would otherwise be unclear because wine cannot be pressed. Dialectal varieties may also be adduced to solve a grammatical problem: the awkward case ending in Q. 20:63 *inna hādhāni la-sāḥirāni* with a nominative after *inna* is explained in the *Tafsīr* transmitted from al-Kalbī (*Tafsīr*, 131b27) as a *lugha* of the Bal Ḥārith ibn Kaʿb (see Rabin 1951: 56–7).

Some exegetes seem to find foreign words particularly interesting, because they never fail to refer to their foreign origin. The fact that the same examples of foreign words occur over and over again, suggests that there was a traditional stock list of such words, including, for instance, *ṭūr* 'mountain' (from Syriac, Mujāhid, *Tafsīr*, 1:77; or Nabataean, *Tafsīr* transmitted from Muḥammad al-Kalbī, 142a19) and *maqālīd* 'keys' (from Persian, Mujāhid, *Tafsīr*, 2:560; or Nabataean, Muqātil, *Tafsīr*, 3:765). Yet, the fact that the commentators cite a different provenance for some of the stock examples shows that even at an early time, a difference of opinion existed (Rippin 1981; Baalbaki 1983: 124–6; Versteegh 1993: 89–91). Not all commentators shared the interest in foreign words. Yaḥyā ibn Sallām, for instance, mentions only a few of them. Since Yaḥyā belonged to a later generation, his lack of interest may be explained by reluctance to deal with the issue of loanwords which at his time had become controversial.

The Structure of the Text

Although the main interest of the exegetes was the elucidation of the text of the Qur'an, they cannot have been entirely naive in linguistic matters. Yet, grammatical insights are presented only piecemeal in the early commentaries and, compared to the linguistic analysis in later grammatical works, the commentators had only a limited technical vocabulary at their disposal.

The most important grammatical terms in the early commentaries are connected with the vocalic readings of the text. Even within the consonantal ductus of the ʿUthmānic codex, ambiguities could easily arise with respect to the vocalic signs (see Abbott 1967; Shah 2003). The terminology for vowels reveals a fundamental difference with that of the grammarians, starting from Sībawayhi's (d. *c.*180/796) *Kitāb*. The commentaries use the same terms for declensional and non-declensional vowels, whereas in later theory a fundamental distinction is made between these two sets. The *Tafsīr* transmitted from Muḥammad al-Kalbī, for instance, uses both *kasr* and *khafḍ* to refer to internal *i*-vowels: *mukhliṣūna bi-khafḍ al-lām* (*Tafsīr*, 183a3); *mufriṭūna bi-kasr al-rāʾ* (*Tafsīr*, 115b10). Likewise, Yaḥyā ibn Sallām (*Tafsīr*, 1:258) remarks that in Q. 20:32 *ashrik* is normally read with *naṣb*, while al-Ḥasan used to read it with *rafʿ* (i.e. *ushrik*). Both terms are used in later grammar for case endings, but here, they refer to internal vowels.

In Sībawayhi's *Kitāb*, one set of terms (*rafʿ*, *jarr*, *naṣb*) is reserved for the case endings *-u*, *-i*, *-a* that are connected with the syntactic structure of the sentence, and one set for vowels that are not syntactically determined (*ḍamm*, *kasr*, *fatḥ*).This distinction is introduced right at the beginning of the *Kitāb* (1:13–23), in a chapter entited 'The Ways of the Endings of Words in Arabic' (*Bāb majārī awākhir al-kalim min al-ʿarabiyya*). It is commonly assumed that the introductory chapters of the *Kitāb*, in which Sībawayhi does not cite any of his predecessors, introduce fundamentally new notions in linguistic theory. Contemporary grammatical works from Kufa, such as al-Farrāʾ's *Maʿānī al-Qurʾān*, are still part of the exegetical tradition, because they tend to use both sets indiscriminately (Owens 1990; Talmon 2003).

After the reception and canonization of the *Kitāb Sībawayhi*, his terminological innovation was universally accepted, and in later texts, both grammatical and exegetical ones, the terminology is standardized. The indiscriminate use of both sets of terms is, therefore, one of the clearest indications of the antiquity of the texts (Versteegh 1993: 125–30), since it is hardly conceivable that later falsifiers would go to such lengths as mimicking the old terminology.

A further source of variant readings is gemination, which is not indicated in the consonantal ductus, either. Two terms are commonly used to denote geminated and non-geminated readings, *takhfīf* and *tathqīl*, for example when Sufyān al-Thawrī (*Tafsīr*, p. 268) reads Q. 42: 23 as *alladhī yabshiru 'illāhu ʿibādahu* instead of the canonical reading *yubashshiru* and calls this reading *mukhaffafa*.

The early commentaries do not have an elaborate terminology for sentence structure. Yet, they use a number of what Wansbrough (1977: 129) calls 'stage directions' to refer to text types in the Qur'an. The most systematic use of these connectors is found in Muqātil ibn Sulaymān (Goldfeld 1981; Versteegh 1990). In his catalogue of text types in the Qur'an (*Tafsīr*, 27), he includes that of *khabar* 'account', and in the *Tafsīr* the term *akhbara* is used to introduce a story about a preceding subject, as in Q. 15:80ff. Here, the people of al-Ḥijr are mentioned, who rejected the message of their prophet and turned away from God's signs. At this point Muqātil (*Tafsīr*, 2:435) states 'and then He tells about them and says' (*fa-akhbara ʿanhum fa-qāla*) to introduce the account of their fate. Another example is the connector *naʿata*, which introduces a new attribute of a preceding subject, as in Q. 13:27f. 'He leads to it whoever repents' (*wa-yahdī ilayhi man anāba*). The next verse 'who believe' (*alladhīna āmanū*) is interpreted by Muqātil (*Tafsīr*, 2:377) as an attribute of the repentant sinners, rather than the start of a new sentence, which he indicates with the connector 'then, He describes them and says' (*thumma naʿatahum fa-qāla*).

Some terms serve to disambiguate possible interpretations of a Qur'anic verse. Thus, for instance, *istaʾnafa* may be used to indicate a caesura in a verse. The term is used more than fifteen times by Muqātil (Versteegh 1993: 134–6), and only once by Muḥammad al-Kalbī (*Tafsīr*, 22a25), but the latter uses it in a way that shows very well the function of this connector. The verse Q. 3:7 contains the phrase *wa-mā yaʿlamu taʾwīlahu... illā ʾllāhu* 'only God knows its interpretation' and then proceeds with *wa'l-rāsikhūna fī ʾl-ʿilmi* 'and those steeped in knowledge'. The latter phrase might be read in coordination with the preceding part, but the commentator rejects this interpretation, regarding it as the beginning of a new sentence. He indicates this by his comment 'the speech is broken off, and then starts again and He says' (*inqaṭaʿa ʾl-kalām thumma ʾstaʾnafa fa-qāla*). Here, two general connectors are used to clarify the syntactic relation between the two parts of the verse.

The terminology of text types is also used by the commentators to refer to the pragmatic force of the text. The term *istifhām* 'questioning' is frequently used by Yaḥyā ibn Sallām to clarify that the form of the verse is interrogative, but that it is actually a rhetorical question. In Q. 19:65 *hal taʿlamu lahu samiyyan* 'do you know a namesake of Him?', he explains (*Tafsīr*, 1:234, l. 17) 'interrogative, i.e. you don't know one' (*ʿalā ʾl-istifhām ay innaka lā taʿlamuhu*). Elsewhere (*Tafsīr*, 1:193) on Q. 18:57 *wa-man aẓlamu mimman dhukkira bi-āyāti rabbihi* 'who is more sinful than someone who is admonished by the signs of his Lord?', he states even more explicitly that 'this is a question to which the answer is known' (*hādhā istifhām ʿalā maʿrifa*).

One of the ways in which the commentators explain the text is by 'correcting' the word order, replacing it by something that corresponds more to that of everyday language. This phenomenon is indicated with the term *taqdīm* or *muqaddam wa-muʾakhkhar* (Versteegh 1993: 121–4, 140–1). In such cases, the meaning of the text is usually clear, so that the paraphrase serves solely to draw the attention to the marked word order, for instance in Q. 25:59 *thumma ʾstawā ʿalā ʾl-ʿarshi ʾl-Raḥmānu*, which is interpreted in the *Tafsir* transmitted from al-Kalbī (*Tafsīr*, 152a6) as a case of *muqaddam wa-muʾakhkhar*. This device may also serve to clarify potentially difficult verses, in which the reversed sequence is of a semantic, rather than a syntactic nature, e.g. Q. 67:2 *alladhī khalaqa 'l-mawta wa-'l-ḥayāta*, which is likewise called a case of *muqaddam wa-muʾakhkhar* (*Tafsīr*, 233b14), apparently in order to avoid the impression that God created death before life.

A further category of terms deals with words in the text that are redundant in the syntactic structure, for which the term *ṣila* is commonly used. The preposition *min* in the expression *li-yaghfira lakum min dhunūbikum* (Q. 14:10) is called a *ṣila* by Muqātil (*Tafsīr*, 2:399). In the expression *wa-in kullun lammā jamīʿun* (Q. 36:32), the element *-mā* is analysed as a *ṣila* in the *Tafsīr* transmitted from Muḥammad al-Kalbī (*Tafsīr*, 181a11), and so is the *alif* in the word *aw* (Q. 20:44) by Yaḥyā ibn Sallām (*Tafsīr*, 1:261 on the authority of al-Suddī). The origin of this term lies probably in the fact that the redundant word serves to link two items, which is one of the meanings for which the term is used in later Kufan grammar (Versteegh 1993: 141–6).

The opposite phenomenon is that of words that need to be added to the text in order to make it comprehensible. Muqātil uses the term *iḍmār* for cases of ellipsis where the ellipted word is required to understand the full meaning of the verse, for example in Q. 16:96 *mā ʿindakum*, where Muqātil (*Tafsīr*, 2:485) adds *min al-amwāl iḍmār* (Versteegh 1993: 146–51). The term is also used by Yaḥyā ibn Sallām (e.g. *Tafsīr*, 1:458, l. 3). In later grammar, *iḍmār* is used for words that have been deleted by the speaker and have to be supplemented in the underlying structure in order to explain the syntactic connections. *Iḍmār* and *muḍmar* are also used to indicate pronominalization (for the connection between these two functions see Ayoub 1990).

The Context of the Text

The prototypical context of the revealed text is that of the circumstances in which a certain verse was revealed. This genre of information is called *asbāb al-nuzūl* and it is found in all commentaries. Determining these circumstances goes beyond identifying the referents of anaphors, because it aims at specifying the individual or individuals intended by general denominations such as 'polytheists' or 'believers' in the text.

Often, indicating the context has a specific function, because it allows the exegetes to determine the chronological place of the verse. This type of information is crucial for the issue of abrogation. Even at an early period readers and exegetes were concerned with the order of the revelation, for instance when they categorized the suras and the verses as Meccan or Medinan. In addition, the oldest commentaries explicitly refer to verses that have been abrogated. One example is that of al-Ḍaḥḥāk ibn Muzāḥim, who repeatedly points out that all peaceful verses in the Qur'an have been abrogated by the revelation of Q. 9:1–2 (e.g. *Tafsīr*, no. 947, 1417, 2223, 2244, 2357). In his view, this verse implied a temporary respite (*barāʾa*), after which all treaties with non-believers were abrogated; in fact, this view made him one of the most frequently cited exegetes on this point (Versteegh 2011: 293–4).

Apart from the legal implications of the circumstances of the text, commentators sometimes mention such details purely to satisfy the curiosity of the believers, who wished to know everything there is to know about the life of the Prophet. According to Rippin (1985, 1988), this biographical interest antedated the discussions about the legal consequences (Berg 2000: 80), and was only subsequently connected with the issue of abrogation in the revealed text. Details about the historical background of the text may then have found their way into the *sīra* of the Prophet (Schöller 2000: 41–2).

Curiosity may also have played a role in the accounts about the pre-Islamic history of the Arabs and the manners and customs of the old Bedouin society. It is known that some of the Umayyad caliphs requested the collection of data about this topic (Schoeler 1996: 46–8). This interest stretched even beyond the Arabian Peninsula to the accounts of earlier communities and prophets. One specific category of data is sometimes called *isrāʾīliyyāt*. The term itself is not used in the early commentaries, but dates from a later period, when it was used either for a genre of books or for general data about Judaism (Tottoli 1999). It is not clear from whom such information was received, if it was not invented outright. A name often mentioned in this connection is that of Wahb ibn Munabbih (d. 110/728 or 114/732), who is credited with the authorship of a book about the *maghāzī* and is considered the main authority for stories about the preceding prophets (*qiṣaṣ al-anbiyāʾ*), although his credibility was judged negatively by later authors (al-Suyūṭī, *al-Itqān*, 2:391; see Adang 1996: 10–13).

The status of such data varied; according to some hadiths, the Prophet himself had forbidden the use of information from Jews, but according to others using this information was acceptable as long as it did not contradict the Islamic sources (Kister 1972). Nonetheless, there was always a certain ambiguity in the attitude toward the use of these data, and commentators like Muqātil were often accused of overly relying on information from non-Muslims. This charge is associated with an unhealthy interest in trivia, for instance when Muqātil is said to have invented a colour for the dog of the Sleepers of the Cave in *Sūrat al-Kahf* (Q. 18:22; al-Baghdādī, *Taʾrīkh Baghdād*, 13:165); the dog's colour seems to have become a standard example of useless knowledge (al-Suyūṭī, *al-Itqān*, 2:391). Another example is the search for the name of the ant in Q. 27:18, about which several commentators claimed to have information: according to Muqātil (*Tafsīr*, 3:299), the ant was called al-Jarmī, but alternative names are given in the *Tafsīr* transmitted from al-Kalbī (*Tafsīr*, 157a7: Mundhira), and by al-Ḍaḥḥāk ibn Muzāḥim (*Tafsīr*, no. 731: Ṭāḥiya).

Exegesis and Grammar

The appearance of Sībawayhi's *Kitāb* is often regarded as the beginning of Arabic grammatical study. But there are many founding stories in which the beginning of grammar is situated much earlier, in the time of the fourth caliph, ʿAlī, who is sometimes portrayed as the real instigator. What is more, the many quotations in the *Kitāb* show that

Sībawayhi was well aware of the existence of predecessors in Basra and, to a lesser degree, in Kufa. According to Talmon's reconstruction of the development of the study of Arabic grammar, there existed an earlier tradition than the Basran one, which he called the Old Iraqi School (Talmon 2003). This tradition was connected with the study of language and the Qur'an in Kufa and was ultimately supplanted by the grammarians from Basra. Talmon (1985) also believes that prior to the Basran takeover, grammatical traditions not only existed in Kufa, but also in Medina, decades before the appearance of the *Kitāb*. The scarce data about these grammarians do not permit a complete evaluation of their contribution to the study of grammar, but it seems fair to say that it consisted mainly in linguistic observations related to the text of the Qur'an and the variant readings (*qirāʾāt*).

Whether the study of grammar started in the Ḥijāz, in Kufa, or in Basra, the connection between the early study of language and the study of the Qur'anic text is obvious. It is equally obvious that later sources did not always have a positive opinion about these early efforts. Shah (2003) is no doubt right when he asserts that these preceding generations of readers were connoisseurs of language in their own right and some of them no doubt developed fairly sophisticated reasoning in dealing with the text of the Qur'an. They may even have collected notes on topics closely connected with the reading profession, such as phenomena of pause (*waqf*) or the category of rare words (*nawādir*). Posterity has dealt rather harshly with these readers; without subscribing to the thesis developed by Shaban (1971) and Juynboll (1973), that the *qurrāʾ* had a poor reputation because they were only villagers (*ahl al-qurā*, see Shah 2005), one must concede that there is sufficient evidence of criticisms levelled against the readers, because of their lack of grammatical knowledge, to warrant the conclusion that they were indeed commonly held to be poor linguists.

In Kufa, there was a strong link between the earlier generations of readers and the later grammarians. Al-Kisāʾī (d. 189/804), al-Farrāʾ's (d. 207/822) teacher, was a respected reader himself. In Kufa, non-ʿUthmānic codices such as the one by Ibn Masʿūd (d. 32/652) remained popular for a longer period of time than in Basra (Nasser 2012: 56–7). But even in Kufa, there was a certain disdain for the linguistic expertise of earlier generations of readers. This is obvious, for instance, when al-Farrāʾ (*Maʿānī*, 2:75; Beck 1946: 190) refers to the *wahm* of the generation of readers of Yaḥyā ibn Waththāb (d. 103/721), and states that 'only very few of them were free of speculation' (*wa-qalla man salima minhum min al-wahm*).

The bias towards readers seems to have been particularly strong in Basra. For Sībawayhi, the ʿUthmānic codex was the only accepted form of the Qur'an, whereas his Kufan colleagues al-Kisāʾī and al-Farrāʾ maintained an interest in non-ʿUthmānic readings, if only to confirm their choice (*iʿtibār*) among alternative vocalic readings, Sībawayhi firmly embraced the canonical text. When dealing with the jussive in Q. 63:10 *wa-akun min al-ṣāliḥīna*, al-Farrāʾ (*Maʿānī*, 3:160) mentions (and rejects) an unorthodox reading *wa-akūna* by Abū ʿAmr, but Sībawayhi (*Kitāb*, 3:100) does not even bother to mention this reading (Beck 1945: 364). In this respect, he not only distanced himself from his Kufan colleagues, but also from predecessors like ʿĪsā ibn ʿUmar al-Thaqafī (d. 149/766) and Abū ʿAmr ibn al-ʿAlāʾ (d. *c*.154–6/770–2), who subjected the text of the

Qur'an to their views about the structure of Arabic (*qiyās al-ʿarabiyya*). A good example of Sībawayhi's attitude is a passage in which he discusses a verse with two alternative case endings (Beck 1946: 207; Shah 2003:16). According to him (*Kitāb*, 1:148), one of these conforms with the *ʿarabiyya*, yet, he admits only the canonical reading, because 'one cannot disagree with the canon since it is the custom' (*al-qirāʾa lā tukhālafu li-anna 'l-qirāʾa sunna*).

Having accepted the codex, Sībawayhi could proceed with his study of the Arabic language: for him, the Arabic language became the main focus rather than the text of the Qur'an. In this respect, he differed from his teacher al-Khalīl (d. 175/791), whose exegetical interests are manifest in the *Kitāb al-ʿAyn* (Khan 1994). This constituted a fundamental change in scope and approach. From now on, grammarians became linguists: their focus was the structure of the Arabic language itself. Grammar and exegesis became separate disciplines, and when grammarians occupied themselves with the text of the Qur'an, they did so because it was the prime example of the *ʿarabiyya*.

Bibliography

Primary Sources

ʿAbd al-Razzāq, Abū Bakr ibn Hammām al-Ṣanʿānī. *al-Muṣannaf*. 11 vols. Ed. Ḥabīb al-Raḥmān al-Aʿẓamī. Dabhel; Beirut, 1983.

ʿAbd al-Razzāq, Abū Bakr ibn Hammām al-Ṣanʿānī. *Tafsīr*. 3 vols. Ed. Maḥmūd Muḥammad ʿAbduh. Beirut: Dār al-Kutub al-ʿIlmiyya, 1999.

Abū ʿUbayda, Maʿmar ibn al-Muthannā. *Majāz al-Qurʾān*. 2 vols. Ed. Muḥammad Fuʾād Sazgīn. Cairo: Muḥammad Sāmī Amīn al-Khānjī, 1954.

al-Baghdādī, Abū Bakr Aḥmad ibn ʿAlī al-Khaṭīb, *Taʾrīkh Baghdād*. 14 vols. Beirut: Dār al-Kutub al-ʿIlmiyya, n.d.

al-Bukhārī, Abū ʿAbd Allāh Muḥammad ibn Ismāʿīl. *Kitāb al-jāmiʿ al-ṣaḥīḥ*. 4 vols. Ed. Christoph Ludolf Krehl and Theodoor Juynboll. Leiden: E. J. Brill, 1862–1908.

al-Ḍaḥḥāk ibn Muzāḥim, Abū Muḥammad al-Hilālī al-Khurāsānī. *Tafsīr al-Ḍaḥḥāk: Jamʿ wa-dirāsa wa-taḥqīq*. 2 vols. Ed. Muḥammad Shukrī al-Zāwiyyatī. Cairo: Dār al-Salāma, 1419/1999.

al-Farrāʾ, Abū Zakariyyāʾ Yaḥyā ibn Ziyād. *Maʿānī al-Qurʾān*. Ed. Muḥammad ʿAlī al-Najjār. 3 vols. Cairo: al-Dār al-Miṣriyya, 1966–72.

[Ibn ʿAbbās]. *Tanwīr al-miqbās min tafsīr Ibn ʿAbbās*. Beirut: Dār al-Kutub al-ʿIlmiyya, 1412/1992.

Ibn al-Anbārī, Abū Bakr Muḥammad ibn al-Qāsim. *Kitāb al-aḍdād*. Ed. Muḥammad Abū 'l-Faḍl Ibrāhīm. Kuwait: Wizārat al-Maṭbūʿāt wa-'l-Nashr, 1960.

Ibn Jurayj, ʿAbd al-Malik ibn ʿAbd al-ʿAzīz. *Tafsīr Ibn Jurayj*. Ed. ʿAlī Ḥasan ʿAbd al-Ghaniyy. Cairo: Maktabat al-Turāth al-Islāmī, 1992.

Ibn Wahb, Abū Muḥammad ʿAbd Allāh al-Fihrī. *al-Jāmiʿ*. Ed. Miklos Muranyi. Wiesbaden: Harrassowitz, 1993.

Maʿmar ibn Rāshid, see ʿAbd al-Razzāq. *Tafsīr*.

Muḥammad al-Kalbī, Abū'l-Naḍr ibn al-Sāʾib. *Tafsīr*. MS Chester Beatty, no. 4224. See Ibn ʿAbbās, *Tanwīr*.

Mujāhid ibn Jabr, Abū 'l-Ḥajjāj al-Tābiʿī al-Makkī al-Makhzūmī. *al-Tafsīr*. 2 vols. Ed. ʿAbd al-Raḥmān al-Ṭāhir ibn Muḥammad al-Sūrtī. Islamabad, n.d. (New edition by Muḥammad ʿAbd al-Salām Abū 'l-Nīl. Cairo: Dār al-Fikr al-Islāmī al-Ḥadītha, 1989.)
Muqātil ibn Sulaymān, Abū 'l-Ḥasan al-Balkhī, *Tafsīr*. 4 vols. Ed. ʿAbd Allāh Maḥmūd Shiḥāta. Cairo: al-Hayʾa al-Miṣriyya al-al-ʿĀmma li-'l-Kitāb, 1980–7.
Sībawayhi, Abū Bishr ʿAmr ibn ʿUthmān, *al-Kitāb*. 5 vols. Ed. ʿAbd al-Salām Muḥammad Hārūn. Cairo: vol. 1 Dār al-Qalam; vol. 2 Dār al-Kātib al-ʿArabī li-'l-Ṭibāʿa wa-'l-Nashr; vols. 3–5 al-Hayʾa al-Miṣriyya al-ʿāmma li-'l-Kitāb, 1966–7.
al-Suddī al-Kabīr, Abū Muḥammad Ismāʿīl ibn ʿAbd al-Raḥmān. *Tafsīr al-Suddī al-Kabīr*. 2 vols. Ed. Muḥammad ʿAṭāʾ Yūsuf. Mansoura: Dār al-Wafāʾ, 1993.
Sufyān al-Thawrī, Abū ʿAbd Allāh ibn Saʿīd. *al-Tafsīr*. Ed. Imtiyāz ʿAlī ʿArshī. Beirut: Dār al-Kutub al-ʿArabiyya, 1983.
al-Suyūṭī, Jalāl al-Dīn Abū'l-Faḍl ʿAbd al-Raḥmān ibn Abī Bakr. *Bughyat al-wuʿāt fī ṭabaqāt al-lughawiyyīn wa-'l-nuḥāt*. 2 vols. Ed. Muḥammad Abū 'l-Faḍl Ibrāhīm. Cairo: Maṭbaʿa ʿĪsā al-Ḥalabī, 1964–5.
al-Suyūṭī, Jalāl al-Dīn Abū'l-Faḍl ʿAbd al-Raḥmān ibn Abī Bakr. *al-Itqān fī ʿulūm al-Qurʾān*. 2 vols. 2nd edn. Beirut: Dār al-Kutub al-ʿIlmiyya, 1991.
Yaḥyā ibn Sallām al-Taymī al-Baṣrī al-Maghribī. *al-Tafsīr*. 2 vols. Ed. Hind Shalabī. Beirut: Dār al-Kutub al-ʿIlmiyya, 2004.

Secondary Sources

Abbott, Nabia. *Studies in Arabic Literary Papyri*. II. *Qurʾānic Commentaries and Tradition*. Chicago: University of Chicago Press, 1967.
Abdul-Raof, Hussein. *Schools of Qur'anic Exegesis: Genesis and Development*. London; New York: Routledge, 2010.
Adang, Camilla. *Muslim Writers on Judaism and the Hebrew Bible: From Ibn Rabban to Ibn Hazm*. Leiden: E. J. Brill, 1996.
Ayoub, Georgine. 'De ce qui "ne se dit pas" dans le livre de Sībawayhi: la notion de *tamṯīl*'. In: Michael G. Carter and Kees Versteegh (eds.). *Studies in the History of Arabic Grammar*, pp. 1–15. Amsterdam; Philadelphia: J. Benjamins, 1990.
Baalbaki, Ramzi. 'Early Arab Lexicographers and the Use of Semitic Languages', *Berytus* 31 (1983), 117–27.
Baalbaki, Ramzi. *The Arabic Lexicographical Tradition From the 2nd/8th to the 12th/18th Century*. Leiden: E. J. Brill, 2014.
Beck, Edmund. 'Der ʿuṯmānische Kodex in der Koranlesung des zweiten Jahrhunderts', *Orientalia* NS 14 (1945), 355–73.
Beck, Edmund. "ʿArabiyya, Sunna und ʿāmma in der Koranlesung des zweiten Jahrhunderts', *Orientalia* NS 15 (1946), 180–224.
Berg, Herbert. *The Development of Exegesis in Early Islam: The Authenticity of Muslim Literature from the Formative Period*. London; New York: RoutledgeCurzon, 2000.
Berg, Herbert. 'Competing Paradigms in Islamic Origins: Qurʾān 15: 89–91 and the Value of *Isnāds*'. In: Herbert Berg (ed.). *Method and Theory in the Study of Islamic Origins*, pp. 259–92. Leiden: E. J. Brill, 2003.
Berg, Herbert. 'Ibn ʿAbbās in ʿAbbasid-Era *Tafsīr*'. In: James E. Montgomery (ed.). *ʿAbbasid Studies: Occasional Papers of the School of ʿAbbasid Studies Cambridge 6–10 July 2002*, pp. 129–46. Leuven: Peeters, 2004.

Fück, Johann. 'Die Rolle des Traditionalismus im Islam', *Zeitschrift der Deutschen Morgenländischen Gesellschaft* 93 (1939), 1–32.

Gilliot, Claude. 'Portrait "mythique" d'Ibn ʿAbbās', *Arabica* 32 (1985), 127–84.

Gilliot, Claude. 'Muqātil, grand exégète, traditionniste et théologien maudit', *Journal Asiatique* 279 (1991), 39–92.

Gilliot, Claude. 'Exegesis of the Qurʾān: Classical and Mediaeval'. In: Jane McAuliffe et al. (Eds.) *Encyclopaedia of the Qurʾān*, 2:90–124. Leiden: E. J. Brill, 2002.

Gilliot, Claude. 'A Schoolmaster, Storyteller, Exegete and Warrior at Work in Khurāsān: al-Ḍaḥḥāk b. Muzāḥim al-Hilālī (d. 106/724)'. In: Karen Bauer (ed.). *Aims, Methods and Contexts of Qurʾānic Exegesis (2nd/8th–9th/15th c.)*, pp. 311–92. Oxford: Oxford University Press, 2013.

Goldfeld, Isaiah. 'The *Tafsīr* of Abdallah b. ʿAbbās', *Der Islam* 58 (1981), 125–35.

Juynboll, Gautier H. A. 'The *Qurrāʾ* in Early Islamic History', *Journal of the Economic and Social History of the Orient* 16 (1973), 113–29.

Juynboll, Gautier H. A. *Muslim Tradition: Studies in Chronology, Provenance and Authorship of Early* Ḥadīth. Cambridge: Cambridge University Press, 1983.

Khan, Mohammad-Nauman. *Die exegetischen Teile des* Kitāb al-ʿayn: *Zur ältesten philologischen Koranexegese*. Berlin: K. Schwarz, 1994.

Kister, M. J. '*Ḥaddithū ʿan banī Isrāʾīla wa-lā ḥaraja*: A Study of an Early Tradition', *Israel Oriental Studies* 2 (1972), 15–39.

Koç, Mehmet Akif. 'A Comparison of the References to Muqātil b. Sulaymān (d. 150/767) in the Exegesis of al-Thaʿlabī (d. 427/1036) with Muqātil's Own Exegesis', *Journal of Semitic Studies* 53/1 (2008), 69–101.

Leemhuis, Fred. 'Ms. 1075 *tafsīr* of the Cairene Dār al-Kutub and Muǧāhid's *Tafsīr*'. In: Rudolph Peters (ed.). *Proceedings of the Ninth Congress of the Union Européenne des Arabisants et Islamisants, Amsterdam 1st to 7th September, 1978*, pp. 169–80. Leiden: E. J. Brill, 1981.

Motzki, Harald. *The Origins of Islamic Jurisprudence: Meccan* Fiqh *before the Classical Schools*. Leiden: E. J. Brill, 2002.

Motzki, Harald. 'The Question of the Authenticity of Muslim Traditions Reconsidered: A Review Article'. In: Herbert Berg (ed.). *Method and Theory in the Study of Islamic Origins*, pp. 211–58. Leiden: E. J. Brill, 2003.

Motzki, Harald. 'Dating the So-Called *Tafsīr Ibn ʿAbbās*: Some Additional Remarks', *Jerusalem Studies in Arabic and Islam* 31 (2006), 147–63.

Motzki, Harald. 'The Origins of Muslim Exegesis: A Debate'. In: Harald Motzki, with Nicolet Boekhoff-van der Voort and Sean W. Anthony (eds.). *Analysing Muslim Traditions: Studies in Legal, Exegetical and Maghāzī Ḥadīth*, pp. 231–303. Leiden: E. J. Brill, 2010.

Muranyi, Miklos. *ʿAbd Allāh b. Wahb (125/743–197/812)*, al-Jāmiʿ: Tafsīr al-Qurʾān (Die Koranexegese), *herausgegeben und kommentiert*. Wiesbaden: Harrassowitz, 1993.

Nasser, Shady Hekmat. *The Transmission of the Variant Readings of the Qurʾān: The Problem of* Tawātur *and the Emergence of* Shawādhdh. Leiden: E. J. Brill, 2012.

Nilsaz, Nosrat. 'The *al-Wāḍiḥ Tafsīr*: Further Evidence for Author Identification, Relation with *Tafsīr al-Kalbī*, and Literary Analysis', *Der Islam* 95 (2018), 401–28.

Owens, Jonathan. *Early Arabic Grammatical Theory: Heterogeneity and Standardization*. Amsterdam; Philadelphia: J. Benjamins, 1990.

Pregill, Michael E. 'Methodologies for the Dating of Exegetical Works and Traditions: Can the Lost *Tafsīr* of al-Kalbī be Recovered from *Tafsīr Ibn ʿAbbās* also Known as *al-Wāḍiḥ*?'

In: Karen Bauer (ed.). *Aims, Methods and Contexts of Qurʾānic Exegesis (2nd/8th–9th/15th c.)*, pp. 393–453. Oxford: Oxford University Press, 2013.
Rabin, Chaim. *Ancient West-Arabian*. London: Taylor's Foreign Press, 1951.
Rippin, Andrew. 'Ibn ʿAbbās's *al-Lughāt fī l-Qurʾān*'. *Bulletin of the School of Oriental and African Studies* 44 (1981), 15–25.
Rippin, Andrew. 'Ibn ʿAbbās's *Gharīb al-Qurʾān*', *Bulletin of the School of Oriental and African Studies* 46 (1983), 323–33.
Rippin, Andrew. 'The Exegetical Genre *Asbāb al-Nuzūl*: A Bibliographical and Terminological Survey', *Bulletin of the School of Oriental and African Studies* 48 (1985), 1–15.
Rippin, Andrew. 'The Function of *Asbāb al-Nuzūl* in Qurʾānic Exegesis', *Bulletin of the School of Oriental and African Studies* 51 (1988), 1–20.
Saleh, Walid. *The Formation of the Classical Tafsīr Tradition: The Qurʾān Commentary of al-Thaʿlabī*. Leiden: E. J. Brill, 2004.
Schoeler, Gregor. *Charakter und Authentie der muslimischen Überlieferung über das Leben Mohammeds*. Berlin; New York: W. de Gruyter, 1996.
Schöller, Marco. '*Sīra* and *Tafsīr*: Muḥammad al-Kalbī on the Jews of Medina'. In: Harald Motzki (ed.). *The Biography of Muḥammad: The Issue of the Sources*, pp. 18–48. Leiden: E. J. Brill, 2000.
Shaban, M. A. *Islamic History A.D. 600–750 (A.H. 132): A New Interpretation*. Cambridge: Cambridge University Press, 1971.
Shah, Mustafa. 'Exploring the Genesis of Early Arabic Linguistic Thought: Qurʾanic Readers and Grammarians of the Kūfan Tradition, I, II', *Journal of Qurʾanic Studies* 5/1 (2003), 47–78, 5/2 (2003), 1–47.
Shah, Mustafa. 'The Early Arabic Grammarians' Contribution to the Collection and Authentication of Qurʾanic Readings: The Prelude to Ibn Mujāhid's *Kitāb al-Sabʿa*', *Journal of Qurʾanic Studies* 6/1 (2004), 72–102.
Shah, Mustafa. 'The Quest for the Origin of the *Qurrāʾ* in the Classical Islamic Tradition', *Journal of Qurʾanic Studies* 7/2 (2005), 1–35.
Sinai, Nicolai. *Fortschreibung und Auslegung: Studien zur frühen Koraninterpretation*. Wiesbaden: O. Harrassowitz, 2009.
Sinai, Nicolai. 'When did the Consonantal Skeleton of the Quran reach Closure?', *Bulletin of the School of Oriental and African Studies* 77 (2014a), 273–92, 509–21.
Sinai, Nicolai. 'The Qur'anic Commentary of Muqātil b. Sulaymān and the Evolution of Early *Tafsīr* Literature'. In: Andreas Görke and Johanna Pink (eds.). Tafsīr *and Islamic Intellectual History: Exploring the Boundaries of a Genre*, pp. 113-43. Leiden: E.J. Brill, 2014b.
Sirry, Munʿim. 'Muqātil b. Sulaymān and Anthropomorphism', *Studia Islamica* 3 (2012), 51–82.
Talmon, Rafael. 'An Eighth-Century Grammatical School in Medina: The Collection and Evaluation of the Available Material', *Bulletin of the School of Oriental and African Studies* 48 (1985), 224–36.
Talmon, Rafael. *Eighth-Century Iraqi Grammar: A Critical Exploration of Pre-Ḫalīlian Arabic Linguistics*. Winona Lake, IN: Eisenbrauns, 2003.
Tottoli, Roberto. 'Origin and Use of the Term *Isrāʾīliyyāt* in Muslim Literature', *Arabica* 46 (1999), 193–210.
Tottoli, Roberto. *Biblical Prophets in the Qurʾān and Muslim Literature*. Richmond: CurzonPress, 2002.

Versteegh, Kees. 'Grammar and Exegesis: The Origins of Kufan Grammar and the *Tafsīr Muqātil*', *Zeitschrift der deutschen morgenländischen Gesellschaft* 67 (1990), 206–42.
Versteegh, Kees. 'Zayd ibn ʿAlī's Commentary on the *Qurʾān*'. In: Yasir Suleiman (ed.). *Arabic Grammar and Linguistics*, pp. 9–29. London: CurzonPress, 1999.
Versteegh, Kees. *Arabic Grammar and Qurʾānic Exegesis in Early Islam*. Leiden: E. J. Brill, 1993.
Versteegh, Kees. 'The Name of the Ant and the Call to Holy War: al-Ḍaḥḥāk ibn Muzāḥim's Commentary on the Qurʾān'. In: Nicolet Boekhoff-van der Voort, Kees Versteegh, and Joas Wagemakers (eds.). *The Transmission and Dynamics of the Textual Sources of Islam: Essays in Honour of Harald Motzki*, pp. 279–99. Leiden: E. J. Brill, 2011.
Wansbrough, John. *Quranic Studies: Sources and Methods of Scriptural Interpretation*. London: Oxford University Press, 1977.

CHAPTER 43

EARLY MEDIEVAL *TAFSĪR* (THIRD/NINTH TO THE FIFTH/ELEVENTH CENTURY)

ULRIKA MÅRTENSSON

INTRODUCTION

THIS chapter deals with the period 'from the third/ninth to the fifth/eleventh century, within which a wealth of exegetical genres acquired their definitive forms: the encyclopaedic commentaries that cover the whole Qur'an and provide several different interpretations of each verse; the commentaries by specialized linguists; the thematically organized commentaries that seek to ground doctrine and law in the Qur'an and hadith; the *wujūh* works that list the different aspects of meaning that a Qur'anic word takes on in different contexts; and the *gharīb* works that translate the Qur'an's 'exceptional words'. In addition, there are the Sufi and Shīʿī treatises that aim at grounding their specific teachings in the Qur'an. The period is especially significant because the third/ninth century marks the systematization of all the Islamic disciplines, which now acquired their distinct methodologies. However, it is open to question whether the methodologies that were systematized in this period were actually new to the period, or whether they were rather systematizations of methodologies observable already in the preceding centuries. The answers determine how we date developments within *tafsīr* and write the history of this discipline (cf. Görke and Pink 2014). Since *tafsīr* aims at explaining the meaning of the Qur'an's language, the discipline that has had the most decisive influence on the exegetical methods and genres is linguistics. Of equal importance is legal methodology, since the Qur'an is the first source and principle of the legal methodologies (*uṣūl al-fiqh*), and exegetical aims and methods overlap with the broader objectives of deriving rulings and doctrine from scripture. Observations of this circumstance are as old as the modern study of *tafsīr* itself. What this chapter offers is an illustration of how linguistic and legal methodologies link *tafsīr* in the period from the third/ninth to the fifth/eleventh century with the preceding period, and provide a measure for developments of the exegetical genres and methods. The survey starts with an outline of *tafsīr* methodologies, and then proceeds to illustrate different genres and methods through six selected Sunnī exegetes and their works.

Methodologies

Feras Hamza (2013) has argued that modern *tafsīr* studies are founded on the assumption that *tafsīr* works do not provide historically valid explanations of the Qur'an's meaning, but only reflect the exegetes' aims and interpretations (whether these are seen as individual or depending on a school). The approach is evident in Ignaz Goldziher's *Die Richtungen der islamischen Koranauslegung* (1920), which seeks to identify the ways in which the Islamic schools and 'sects' shaped *tafsīr* methods and their development. At a later stage in the research history, Andrew Rippin (1988a) has reinforced the approach, arguing that the history of *tafsīr* should include hermeneutics, since the aim should be to study how exegetes constructed meaning in the Qur'an, not what they thought it meant. Except for Feras Hamza's critical contribution, Karen Bauer's volume (2013) further pursues Rippin's approach, exploring the significance of exegetes' aims, methods, and contexts for their interpretations. Yet Hamza, in spite of his critique, does not provide any concrete examples of exegetes who have produced historically valid explanations of the Qur'an. While still at the explorative level, Ulrika Mårtensson has argued that al-Ṭabarī's (d. 310/923) *tafsīr* represents his academic commitment to produce historically valid information about the Qur'an's rhetorical genre, concepts, and meaning (2008; 2009; 2016; cf. Heath 1989). With a similar aim, Ḥātim al-Tamīmī (2013) shows that al-Ṭabarī provided important historical information on the development of the ʿUthmānic established script, and that he worked with several different manuscript versions.

It is quite natural, given that *tafsīr* studies focus on the significance of the Islamic schools and disciplines for interpretation, that methods and hermeneutics are perceived as uniquely 'Islamic'. However, there have been attempts to compare or universalize *tafsīr* as well. Peter Heath's (1989) study of al-Ṭabarī's, Ibn Sīnā's, and Ibn ʿArabī's hermeneutics and methods aims at identifying their 'transcultural and metahistorical' dimensions, showing al-Ṭabarī's hermeneutics to be philological, historical, and inductive; Ibn Sīnā's rationalist, allegorical, and deductive; and Ibn al-ʿArabī's experiential, allegorical, and deductive. Mårtensson (2008, 2009) has taken the transcultural approach further, comparing al-Ṭabarī's historical-philological and empiricist hermeneutics 'positively' with that of E. D. Hirsch, Jr (1967) and 'negatively' with Ismāʿīlī hermeneutics and Hans-Georg Gadamer's idealism (1960).

Transcultural or comparative approaches are sometimes relevant for dating the development of *tafsīr* methods, which remains a contested issue, as Mustafa Shah's survey of *tafsīr* studies shows (2013a). Dating requires analysis of the relationship between *tafsīr* and the other disciplines. John Wansbrough (1977) started with the Qur'anic canonical text, which he understood as emerging out of a history of *tafsīr*, spanning Muqātil ibn Sulaymān (d. 150/767) and Ibn Qutayba (d. 276/889). Within this period, Wansbrough identified five method-related and consecutive stages of *tafsīr*: narrative, legal, lexical, rhetorical, and allegorical. In contrast to Wansbrough's approach, Yeshayahu Goldfeld (1988) identified an intrinsic relationship between early *tafsīr* and the derivation of rulings and doctrine in Ibn ʿAbbās's (d. *c.*68/687) exegetical reports, and he traced the contextualizing methodology reflected in these reports to rabbinical sources, which places the methodology in an epistemic continuum from before Islam. Kees Versteegh (1993) and Harald Motzki (2002) support Goldfeld's early dating of some exegetical traditions attributed to Ibn ʿAbbās—although not necessarily Goldfeld's conclusions. In sum: while Wansbrough dated legal *tafsīr* to the third/ninth century, Goldfeld, Versteegh and Motzki dated such reports to the late first/seventh century. The former implies that these methodologies were new to our period from the third/ninth to the fifth/eleventh century and the latter that they date at least to the late first/seventh century, possibly earlier if Jewish exegesis is considered. Andrew Rippin (1995, 1999) continued to defend a late date (*c.*third/ninth century) given that the *tafsīr* works in which the supposedly early reports are cited are from the later period and there are no preserved early compilations.

The genre that these exegetical reports represent reflects a methodology related to linguistics. According to Claude Gilliot (1990a; 'Exegesis', *EQ*), *tafsīr* proper begins in the third/ninth century with al-Kisāʾī's (d. 189/804) *Kitāb al-Maʿānī* when exegetes began to systematically use grammar, as distinct from earlier mere lexical analysis. In linguistics, this transition is identified with *Kitāb* Sībawayhi (d. *c.*180/796), which provides a methodology of Arabic linguistics and grammar. However, based on Sībawayhi's references to earlier grammarians, some argue that grammar emerged already in the late first/seventh century, with the Qur'an readers' efforts to preserve the canonical text, and that *tafsīr* depends on linguistics from the outset (Shah 2003a-b, 2004; cf. Leemhuis 1988; Versteegh 1990, 1993). This dating of linguistics within *tafsīr* coincides with the early dating of the legal *tafsīr* reports, and suggests that linguistic and legal methods coincided in time.

Gilliot (1990a; 2013) claims that another decisive change in *tafsīr* is represented by Abū ʿUbayda's (d. c. 209/824–5) *Majāz al-Qurʾān* and al-Farrāʾ's (d. 207/822) *Maʿānī al-Qurʾān* and their use of 'profane' Arabic linguistic conventions to explain the Qur'an, compared with the early Qur'an readers who conceptualized Qur'anic Arabic as divine speech. According to Gilliot, there remained a tension within *tafsīr* between profane and divine concepts of the Qur'anic language (cf. Rippin 1995). However, Shah's survey (2013a) suggests that already with Sībawayhi, profane linguistics became the established convention for examining the Qur'an's divine language, so that deliberations over what constituted its divine characteristics necessarily employed the terms of profane linguistics.

Recent research on Sībawahyi's linguistics has defined it as rhetorical and pragmatist. Meaning is both formal (grammatical) and substantial (semantic) and emerges in a speech-act in a given context. Within this rhetorical and pragmatist convention, the goal of *tafsīr* is identical with linguistic analysis, that is, to attain the *context-dependent meaning* (*maʿnā*, pl. *maʿānī*) of a speech act, which includes understanding why the speaker chooses a particular form to communicate the message (Carter 2007; Baalbaki 2007; Marogi 2010). This is why, as Goldfeld (1988) and Gilliot (2013) show, the earliest exegetes in the late first/seventh and early second/eighth century used hadith and history to provide contexts for the Qur'anic speech acts. The early context-based exegetical genre thus depends on an *implicit* rhetorical and pragmatist theory of language, which Sībawayhi's linguistics *explicitly* theorizes. Thus, an alternative to Rippin's (2013) argument, that contextualization is *the* distinguishing feature of *tafsīr* and constitutes an essentially Islamic response to the Qur'an's vagueness and lack of context, is that the method reflects a transcultural theory of language, that is, rhetoric and pragmatism. However, such a theory of continuous development of rhetorical linguistics contrasts with Rippin's dating (1994, 1995). In his view, references to early instances and authorities are retrospective projections from the fourth/tenth century when the disciplines were fully developed, and he is skeptical of the theory of early connections between *tafsīr* and linguistics.

David Vishanoff's (2011) study of *uṣūl al-fiqh* and linguistics from the third/ninth to the sixth/twelfth century provides a useful framework for understanding how *tafsīr* as context-oriented rhetoric develops in tandem with rhetoric as logical demonstration, the latter becoming increasingly prominent in our time period. As Vishanoff shows, al-Shāfiʿī's (d. 204/820) *al-Risāla* develops an exegetical methodology around the hermeneutical concept of *bayān*, 'clarification'. *Bayān* presupposed that scripture, consisting of the Qur'an and prophetic hadith, contains ambiguities emanating from the polyvalent character of its Arabic language. As exegetical method, 'clarification' means to bring out the complexity of a verbal expression and establish compatible meanings between the Qur'ān and prophetic hadith. Establishing meaning across the Qur'an and hadith involved correlating the textual meaning with the principles of a legal or doctrinal issue, through argumentation and demonstration. Al-Shāfiʿī's *bayān* hermeneutics thus combines rhetorical, context-oriented linguistics (hadith) with rhetorical argumentation and logical demonstration, a method which is prominent in some *tafsīr* works from the fourth/tenth century (Schöck 2006). Thus, as Mårtensson has shown (2008, 2009, 2016), the methodology that al-Ṭabarī defines and applies in his encyclopaedic *tafsīr* is built around *bayān* in this sense. According to Ahmed El-Shamsy (2013), al-Shāfiʿī's *bayān* methodology should even be seen as the cause that generated the encyclopaedic genre of *tafsīr*, exemplified most clearly by al-Ṭabarī's *tafsīr*. Where early *tafsīr* reflected local legal traditions with authoritative scholars simply stating their interpretations, the *madhāhib* as universalizing methodologies forced exegetes to demonstrate the validity of their interpretations against a range of alternative ones, employing hadith, linguistics, and logic. By comparison, Walid Saleh (2004) perceives the rationale of the encyclopaedic commentaries to be tools for including and excluding different Islamic traditions in a context of increasing scholarly and political diversity.

The incorporation of the *bayān*-demonstrative methodology into context-based *tafsīr* might explain the 'traditionist' critique of *tafsīr*, as described by Harris Birkeland (1955). Aḥmad ibn Ḥanbal (d. 241/855) rejected the use of unauthorized exegetical traditions and reasoning when deriving rulings and doctrine from the Qur'an, since it implied explaining scripture through sources extraneous to it (see also survey in Shah 2013a: 24–31). This early Ḥanbalī reluctance to equate the divine scripture with human interpretation and reasoning leads us over to another rhetoric-related feature of *tafsīr* from the third/ninth to the sixth/twelfth century, the theory of the Qur'an's inimitability (*iʿjāz*). As James Montgomery (2006) shows, al-Shāfiʿī's *bayān* concept implicitly assumes that Qur'anic *iʿjāz* consists in rhetorical supremacy, a theory which was explicitly elaborated in the Muʿtazilī al-Jāḥiẓ's (d. 255/868–9) *al-Bayān wa'l-tabyīn*. From the fourth/tenth century onwards, systematic treatises on *iʿjāz* were composed, including the Muʿtazilī al-Rummānī's (d. 384/994) *al-Nukat fī iʿjāz al-Qurʾān*; the Shāfiʿī al-Khaṭṭābī's (d. 388/998) *Bayān iʿjāz al-Qurʾān*; the Muʿtazilī al-Qāḍī ʿAbd al-Jabbār's work (d. 415/1025); and the Shāfiʿī al-Jurjānī's (d. 471/1078) *Dalāʾil al-iʿjāz* and *Asrār al-balāgha*. Sophia Vasalou has argued that as the theorists seek to define the nature of the Qur'an's inimitability, they are by necessity confined to the linguistic categories and therefore end up equating the Qur'an with human language, particularly the logical proof (Vasalou 2002). As Vasalou shows, the only theology that preserves the incomparably divine character of the Qur'an is the early Ḥanbalī one, which transcends and dispenses with linguistic comparisons through the concept of *bilā kayf*, 'without modality'. Accordingly, the Ḥanbalīs rejected *tafsīr* in the logical demonstrative sense but not in the early contextualizing sense.

The Exegetes

The following presentation of exegetes and genres seeks to place them within the framework developed above. For an overview of their place in the whole history of *tafsīr*, the reader may consult Mustafa Shah's survey (2013a).

ʿAbd al-Razzāq al-Ṣanʿānī (d. 211/827)

Al-Ṣanʿānī from Sanaa in Yemen is famous for works in *tafsīr* and hadith, which provide some of Harald Motzki's data on the beginnings of hadith, *fiqh*, and *tafsīr* in Ḥijāz and Iraq in the second half of the first/seventh century (1991; 2002; 2003). The *Tafsīr* was transmitted by al-Khushanī (d. 286/902), from al-Ṣanʿānī's students Ibn Shabīb (d. 247/861) and al-Ṭahrānī. Rippin (1995) has dated *tafsīr* al-Ṣanʿānī to the fourth/tenth century, i.e. al-Khushanī's time. Its genre pertains to the rhetorical paradigm of context-dependent meaning. It consists of exegetical reports by al-Ṣanʿānī's teacher Maʿmar ibn Rāshid, from Qatāda, some of which appear also in al-Ṭabarī's *tafsīr* (Versteegh 1993: 154–9; Motzki 1991; 2003). The reports cover the whole Qur'an in sequential order, but treat only selected phrases, presumably those considered relevant or in need of explanation. While these reports have been described as reflecting a pre-linguistic stage (al-Ṣanʿānī/Muhammad 1989: 6), Versteegh (1993) has identified several linguistic terms in them, which Rippin (1995) saw as further support for his late dating of the *tafsīr*.

As Versteegh shows (1993), al-Ṣanʿānī's reports in a unique way present his teachers in law and hadith as actively engaged in deliberating the meaning of Qur'anic words.

This method, built around the teachers' reasoning about the meaning of the Qur'an, reflects their methodology of deriving law from the Qur'an and hadith through 'the living *sunna*', associated especially with the teacher al-Awzāʿī's (d. 157/774) local Syrian school. By comparison, the Shāfiʿī al-Muḥāsibī's (d. 243/857) *tafsīr*, *Fahm al-Qurʾān*, is structured around legal-doctrinal topics deduced from corresponding Qur'anic verses, which are explained through exegetical hadith, including some from Maʿmar-Qatāda. A systematic comparison of al-Ṣanʿānī's and al-Muḥāsibī's methodologies would yield more insight into the relationship between legal and exegetical methods.

Two Mālikī Exegetes: Yaḥyā ibn Sallām and Ibn Abī Zamanīn

The works of Yaḥyā ibn Sallām (d. 200/815) were significant for *tafsīr* in North Africa and Umayyad Andalusia (see Shah 2013a: 10–11, on this region). Born in Kufa, Ibn Sallām studied in Basra, Medina, and al-Fusṭāṭ, and moved to Qayrawan to teach. Among his teachers in hadith and *fiqh* was Mālik ibn Anas (d. 179/795).

Two *tafsīr* works are attributed to Ibn Sallām: *al-Tafsīr* and *Kitāb al-taṣārīf*. Research on the *Tafsīr* consists mainly of Hind Shalabī's editorial introduction (Ibn Sallām/Shalabī 2004). It was transmitted by Muḥammad ibn Yaḥyā ibn Sallām (d. 262/876), and Aḥmad ibn Mūsā al-ʿAṭṭār (d. 274/888). According to al-Dānī (d. 444/1053; al-Dhahabī, 1:396–7), Ibn Sallām's *tafsīr* distinguished itself among contemporaries by its use of linguistics. It was cited by, among others, Ibn al-Jawzī (d. 597/1200), al-ʿAsqalānī (d. 852/1449), and al-Suyūṭī (d. 911/1505). The first modern scholar to study Ibn Sallām was the Tunisian historian Ibn ʿĀshūr (d. 1389/1973), who defined it as the earliest example of the critical (*naqdī*) and theoretical (*naẓarī*) *tafsīr* which al-Ṭabarī later perfected (Ibn ʿĀshūr 1970; Ibn Sallām/Shalabī 2004: 1:10; Saleh 2011). Shalabī shows that Ibn Sallām's *Tafsīr* is one of al-Ṭabarī's sources, which the latter studied in al-Fusṭāṭ with Ibn Sallām's student Muḥammad ibn ʿAbd Allāh, who in his turn transmitted al-Ṭabarī's *tafsīr*.

Shalabī's edition covers Q. 16–37 of a once complete *tafsīr*, the earliest of the encyclopaedic genre, as Saleh points out (2011). Ibn Sallām proceeded by first defining what parts of the sura are Meccan and Medinan, then explaining it phrase by phrase. Context is often implicit as his explanations mostly proceed by referencing other exegetes (including Ibn ʿAbbās, Qatāda, al-Suddī, Mujāhid, al-Kalbī, al-Ḥasan ibn Dīnār, al-Ḥasan al-Baṣrī), but sometimes it is made explicit by reference to prophetic hadith (Q. 16:8; 16:24). *Isnād*s are provided but are not as complete as those of Mujāhid and al-Ṭabarī. Sometimes Ibn Sallām gives different interpretations and readings (*qirāʾāt*), often the same as al-Ṭabarī, but without the latter's extensive linguistics-based argumentation and summary of the verse's correct meaning. Ibn Sallām defines the Qur'an's meanings more often in terms of doctrine and rulings than language analysis and grammar, and unlike al-Ṭabarī and the grammarians, he does not use poetry as evidence. His method thus harmonizes the Qur'an with prophetic hadith and with legal-doctrinal principles.

A similar objective is achieved through a different genre in *al-Jāmiʿ*, the *tafsīr* composed by the Mālikī ʿAbd Allāh ibn Wahb (d. 197/812), who was one of Ibn Sallām's students in Egypt. As described in Shah's survey (2013a: 10), Ibn Wahb's exegesis takes traditions on specific topics as a starting point and employs them to explain individual Qur'anic verses.

The meanings defined in Ibn Sallām's *Tafsīr* correspond to those in his second exegetical work, *al-Taṣārīf li-tafsīr al-Qurʾān* which belongs to the *wujūh/ashbāh* genre. *Al-Taṣārīf*'s written version is attributed to Ibn Sallām's grandson. The work is not mentioned in the medieval bibliographies and is consequently missing in surveys of *wujūh* pre-dating the finding of the manuscripts in Tunisia (Rippin 1988b). Shalabī shows that *al-Taṣārīf* partly overlaps with Muqātil's *al-Ashbāh wa'l-naẓāʾir fī 'l-qurʾān al-karīm*, an inter-dependence she traces to Basra where Muqātil (d. 150/767) spent his last years and Ibn Sallām studied with Muqātil's students (Ibn Sallām/Shalabī 1980: 7, 29–30, 43–5; Shah 2013a: 7; 10–11).

Al-Taṣārīf explains the aspects (*wujūh*) of selected concepts' meaning through *taṣrīf*, 'diversifying meaning'. According to Shalabī (Ibn Sallām/Shalabī 1980: 59–60), the concepts correspond to categories in *uṣūl al-dīn*: doctrine (*ʿaqīda*), eschatology (*ākhira*), and political authority (*siyāsa*), although no specific doctrinal position is expressed; yet Sammoud (2007) does detect the doctrine of *irjāʾ* in Ibn Sallām's text. For example, the concept of *hudā* is diversified into seventeen aspects. Each aspect is brought out through cross-references to other contexts where it has the same meaning; thus, *hudā* in the sense of *bayān* occurs in the following contexts:

> Guidance (*hudā*) means clarification (*bayān*). Thus (God) said in *al-Baqara* (5): 'Those have received guidance from their Lord', meaning 'they have received clarification from their Lord'. In *Luqmān* (5) He said; 'Those have received guidance', meaning 'clarification'. [...] And in *Ṭāhā* (128) He said: 'Did He not guide', meaning 'Did He not clarify', according to the explanation of Qatāda. Al-Ḥasan [ibn Dīnār *ʿan* al-Ḥasan al-Baṣrī] said: His speech 'Who measured the capacities and guided rightly' (Q. 87:3) means 'He clarified to him the path of right guidance and the path of error'. And in *al-Sajda* (26) He said: 'Did He not guide them?' meaning 'Did He not clarify to them?' And there are many similar cases.
>
> (Ibn Sallām, *Tafsīr*, 96–7)

Rippin (1988b) has defined *wujūh* as semantic lexicology based on the principle of context-dependent meaning, with antecedents in classical Greek linguistics. This aligns *wujūh* with the general paradigm of rhetorical and pragmatist linguistics. Thus, while Ibn Sallām's *Tafsīr* clarifies Qur'anic words verse by verse, *al-Taṣārīf* shows how key doctrinal concepts take on specific aspects of meaning in specific speech-contexts. As genre, *wujūh* provides a tool for harmonizing the Qur'an, hadith, and legal principles, which requires defining the exact meaning of a concept in its context.

Ibn Sallām's *Tafsīr* was abbreviated (*mukhtaṣar*) by Muḥammad ibn ʿAbd Allāh ibn Abī Zamanīn (d. *c*.399/1008), a Mālikī jurist of Umayyad Córdoba, and transmitted by his son. His Andalusian teachers included outstanding scholars such as Wahb ibn Masarra; and Ibn Waḍḍāḥ, who taught him the *Musnad* of Ibn Abī Shayba, which was influential in al-Andalus and Maghrib. Among his students were Abū ʿAmr al-Dānī; al-Qulaynī; and Ibn al-Ṣaffār, judge of Córdoba's *Jāmiʿ* (Ibn Abī Zamanīn/Ibn ʿAkkāsha and al-Kanz, 2002: 1:21–2; Campoy 1984; 1993; 2005).

Al-ʿAmrī (2004) shows that the *mukhtaṣar* genre gained currency during the fourth/tenth century, as teaching material in *fiqh* and *tafsīr*. Ibn Abī Zamanīn, who was teaching Mālikī *fiqh*, presumably produced his *Mukhtaṣar* for that purpose. Compared with other contemporary commentaries, Ibn Sallām's *tafsīr* and Ibn Abī Zamanīn's synopsis illustrate Mālikī hermeneutics as applied within the encyclopaedic genre and context-oriented linguistics (hadith), while other works are deductive commentaries on legal-doctrinal topics, or concerned with specific aspects of linguistic analysis (Shah 2013a: 14–15).

In a brief introduction, Ibn Abī Zamanīn explains the changes he made to Ibn Sallām's *tafsīr*: eliminating repetitions and superfluous hadith; tracing the *isnād*s of the remaining hadith; identifying the different readings (*qirāʾāt*); and updating Ibn Sallām's linguistics to state-of-the-art. He also presents a list attributed to Ibn Sallām (but missing from the manuscript of the latter's *tafsīr*) of twelve issues that the exegete must address: the Meccan and the Medinan contexts; abrogation; hyperbaton (*al-taqdīm wa'l-taʾkhīr*); the abbreviated (*maqṭūʿ*) and the fully developed (*mawṣūl*); the particular and the general; ellipsis; and Arabic linguistics (Ibn Abī Zamanīn, *Mukhtaṣar*: 1:114; Shah 2013a: 11). Some of these terms are rhetorical, corresponding with Ibn Abī Zamanīn's definition of the Qur'an as the divine rhetoric through which the Prophet persuaded his community: '[God] sent down the scripture to Muḥammad, His servant and messenger... [who] conveyed (*balagha*) the message as he advised those to who he was sent' (Ibn Abī Zamanīn, *Mukhtaṣar*, 1:111).

In terms of method, Ibn Abī Zamanīn proceeded by citing Ibn Sallām's reports, with *isnād*s, adding his own linguistic analysis, including different readings. But as al-ʿAmrī (2004) points out a *mukhtaṣar* is no longer the first scholar's work. Ibn Abī Zamanīn changed Ibn Sallām's text, omitting words (Q. 19:34), even whole sections of commentary (Q. 20:1). Reducing repetition also means that where Ibn Sallām gave different interpretations of a word, Ibn Abī Zamanīn gave only one, absorbing Ibn Sallām's *tafsīr* into his own definition of the correct meanings.

Muḥammad ibn Jarīr al-Ṭabarī (d. 310/923)

Al-Ṭabarī is the most prodigious of the selected exegetes. He was born in Āmūl in Tabaristan, studied in Rayy, Kufa, Basra, al-Fusṭāṭ, and in several Syrian cities, settling finally in Baghdad. Regarding his life, studies, teachers, and works, see Gilliot (1990b) and Rosenthal (1989). Twenty-seven works are attributed to al-Ṭabarī within *fiqh*, *ʿaqīda*, hadith, *tafsīr*, *taʾrīkh*, Arabic language, poetry, and ethics. Drawing on Shāfiʿī, Mālikī, and Ẓāhirī legal methodologies, al-Ṭabarī developed his own *madhhab jarīrī* (Rosenthal 1989: 101–5; Gilliot 1990b: 41–6; Stewart 2004; 2013; 2016). The *tafsīr*, *Jāmiʿ al-bayān ʿan taʾwīl ayy al-Qurʾān*, belongs to the encyclopaedic genre. The reference works on it are

Claude Gilliot's monograph (1990b), and Heribert Horst's (1953) survey of its 13,026 *isnāds*; of these, Mujāhid–Ibn ʿAbbās are among the most frequently attested.

Compared with Ibn Sallām and Ibn Abī Zamanīn's *tafsīr* method, which al-Ṭabarī formally shared, his methodology and method were much more systematically developed and demonstrative than theirs. Mårtensson (2016) argues this relates to the fact that al-Ṭabarī developed his own *madhhab* and doctrine. His exegetical method involved going through the whole Qur'an sura by sura and verse by verse. Nearly always he introduced each verse by giving his own comprehensive interpretation of its meaning. He then proceeded to break down the verse into its composite utterances, which he analysed through exegetical hadiths and reports, grammar, variant readings, and—unlike Ibn Sallām and Ibn Abī Zamanīn—poetry. He also frequently cited instances in the Qur'an in which the same word was used in different contexts. In the course of the analysis, he demonstrated the correctness of his own interpretation over alternative ones. This is why Ibn ʿĀshūr (1970) defined his *tafsīr* as *naqdī* ('critical') and *naẓarī* ('theoretical'). Shah (2013b) in particular brings out how al-Ṭabarī employed logical demonstration in the course of his exegesis. Disputing with a range of doctrinal positions within the Sunnī framework, he developed his own dogma by constructing meaning-contexts through selected hadith, combined with linguistic analysis and dialectical reasoning. His refutations of the grammarians' arguments, such as al-Farrāʾ's *Maʿānī al-Qurʾān* and Abū ʿUbayda's *Majāz al-Qurʾān*, appositely illustrate his use of hadith and reports (see also Gilliot 1990b: 165–203). Shah also suggests that al-Ṭabarī's use of hadith was a strategy to defend himself against traditionist critique against reasoning in *tafsīr* (2013a: 27–30). However, al-Ṭabarī's ambition to develop a *madhhab* also defined his use of hadith. He produced his own collection of prophetic hadith, *Tahdhīb al-āthār*, and Gilliot has showed that the doctrinal contents of those hadith al-Ṭabarī deemed sound match his interpretations in the *tafsīr* (1990b; 1994).

Al-Ṭabarī's method is grounded in a hermeneutics centred on the concept of *bayān*, which he developed in the long methodological introduction to *Jāmiʿ al-bayān*. Gilliot has applied his general argument about tensions in *tafsīr* between profane and divine concepts of the Qur'anic language (1990a) to al-Ṭabarī's concepts of *bayān* and *maʿānī*. According to Gilliot, al-Ṭabarī defined the Qur'an as inimitable divine linguistic excellence (*iʿjāz*), expressed through *maʿānī*, which Gilliot translates as the 'qualities' or generic forms of the divine Arabic. *Bayān* thus refers primarily to the elucidation of these qualities, rather than to explain intended meaning, which is the general linguistic sense of *maʿnā* (Gilliot 1990b: 73–86; cf. 'Exegesis', *EQ*).

Others understand al-Ṭabarī's methodology slightly differently. Provisionally, Hind Shalabī (Ibn Sallām/Shalabī 2004) and Hussein Abdul-Raof (2006) have defined it as *balāghī*, 'rhetorical'. Mårtensson (2008, 2016) shows that al-Ṭabarī's concept of the Qur'an as God's *bayān* and inimitably persuasive proof (*al-ḥujja al-bāligha*) is a rhetorical concept, which corresponds with his own use of argumentation and proof in exegesis. Hence, Mårtensson argues that al-Ṭabarī's *bayān* reflects a general theory of language communication, which refers to clarification of the speaker's intended 'meanings' (*maʿānī*) in the rhetorical, context-dependent sense described above. Consequently, al-Ṭabarī's aim is *taʾwīl*, that is, tracing meanings back to God's original intended meaning. By comparison, Gilliot (1990b) and Stewart (2016) stress that al-Ṭabarī located exegetical proof (*ḥujja*) in the authority of what he defined as the consensus-forming body of expert scholars.

Heath (1989) has noted that al-Ṭabarī strove to produce the most academically solid *tafsīr* imaginable given the standards of his day, and omitted folkloristic and edifying traditions (including Sufi and Shīʿī ones) because he considered them irrelevant for the historical understanding of the Qur'an (cf. Mårtensson 2008, 2009). In contrast, Saleh (2004) views al-Ṭabarī's omission of Shīʿī and Sufi materials as a Sunnī-orthodox, exclusive measure. For this reason, Saleh claims, al-Ṭabarī's *tafsīr* was superseded by al-Thaʿlabī's (d. 427/1035) highly popular *al-Kashf wa'l-bayān*, which included for example Sufi and folkloristic material. After falling into oblivion, al-Ṭabarī's *tafsīr* was resuscitated by Ibn Taymiyya (d. 728/1328), because of its 'Sunnī-exclusive' hadith approach. For the same reason, it was appreciated by Ibn Kathīr (d. 774/1373), al-Suyūṭī (d. 911/1505), and the modern Salafī movement (Saleh 2011: 298–9; 2004: 206–8). Yet al-Ṭabarī's *tafsīr* was cited by a number of *mujtahid*s, that is, jurists qualified to make legal rulings independently of their *madhhab*, who form a continuous tradition between al-Ṭabarī and Ibn Taymiyya (himself a *mujtahid* within the Ḥanbalī *madhhab*). These include the Mālikī Makkī ibn Abī Ṭālib (d. 437/(d. 189/804-5)), the Shāfiʿī *qāḍī* al-Māwardī (d. 450/1058), the Mālikī al-Qurṭubī (d. 671/1273), the Ḥanbalī Ibn al-Jawzī (d. 597/1200), the Shāfiʿī Fakhr al-Dīn al-Rāzī (d. 606/1210), and the Shāfiʿī ʿIzz al-Dīn ibn ʿAbd al-Salām (d. 660/1262) (al-Wuhaybī 1982). While it remains to be investigated, it appears that al-Ṭabarī's demonstrative yet historical-philological exegetical method, grounded in the rhetorical concept of *bayān*, was particularly useful for *mujtahid*s who, like al-Ṭabarī, had to prove the validity of their new interpretations before their peers. Other important research questions concern the place of his *tafsīr* and his exegetical methodology and method within his whole oeuvre; and the exact relationship of his methodology and *isnād*s to the field of *tafsīr*, linguistics, and the other disciplines.

Gharīb: Makkī and al-Iṣfahānī

An important aide-*tafsīr* is *gharīb*, a lexical genre, which lists 'exceptional' Qur'anic words and provides synonyms for them, as shown in Shah's survey (2013a: 11–16; cf. Carter 2006; Rippin 1988b; Makkī ibn Abī Ṭālib/al-Marʿashlī, 1988). Most extant *gharīb* works date to the late third/ninth century, although there are references to works from the late second/eighth century. Abū ʿUbayda's (d. 209/824–5) *Majāz al-Qur'ān* is an early example of *gharīb*, which proceeds sura by sura and selects only 'exceptional' words for explanation (not unlike al-Ṣanʿānī's procedure). Ibn Sallām and al-Ṭabarī included *gharīb* in the sense of non-Arabic words in their exegesis, the latter often referring to Abū ʿUbayda. Ibn Abī Zamanīn, however, omitted the non-Arabic words in his synopsis of Ibn Sallām. According to Michael Carter (2006), al-Ṭabarī explained the presence of non-Arabic words in the Arabic Qur'an in terms of linguistic universals (Arabic shares words with other languages), a theory which Rippin (1981) has identified with Ibn ʿAbbās's *gharīb* traditions. Here two *gharīb* authors will illustrate two distinct lexicographical approaches: contextual-historical *versus* rational-universal meanings.

Makkī ibn Abī Ṭālib (d. 437/1045) was a North African Mālikī jurist and *mujtahid*, settled in Córdoba. Farhāt (1997) has listed his works, showing the relationship between his *fiqh*, *kalām*, *tafsīr*, and *gharīb*. Makkī's *tafsīr* entitled *al-Hidāya ilā bulūgh al-nihāya* makes frequent use of the *tafsīrs* of al-Ṭabarī, Ibn Sallām, and al-Farrāʾ. The purpose of his *gharīb* works was to define a Qur'anic dictionary through Arabic linguistics and to clarify ambiguous words which hampered *bayān*, hence *Tafsīr al-mushkil min gharīb al-Qurʾān al-ʿaẓīm ʿalā'l-ījāz wa'l-ikhtiṣār*, a lexicon which influenced both the *gharīb* genre and the later dictionaries.

The most detailed study of Makkī's *Tafsīr al-mushkil* is al-Marʿashlī's introduction (1988). It is a *mukhtaṣar* of an early *gharīb* work, Ibn Qutayba's (d. 276/889) *Tafsīr gharīb al-Qurʾān*, and follows its structure, listing exceptional words—including non-Arabic ones—according to the canonical order of suras and *āyas*. Makkī explains the words within their verse contexts, through inter-Qur'anic referencing and hadith. However, he omitted Ibn Qutayba's poetic comparisons in favour of evidence from Companions, Successors, and scholars. His strict adherence to the Qur'anic context is apparent in, for example, his explanation of *azkā* (Q. 18:19):

> Q. 18:19: (*azkā ṭaʿāman*), that is, the choicest; the most tender; and the most lawful.

Compared with Ibn Qutayba, who attributed connotations of abundance and plenty to *azkā*, which he derived from its root *zakā*, Makkī ignored any meaning that was not borne out by the immediate Qur'anic context.

Another lexicographic methodology is that of al-Rāghib al-Iṣfahānī (d. early fifth/eleventh century) in *al-Mufradāt fī gharīb al-Qurʾān*. Al-Rāghib worked in Isfahan under the Buyids (322–447/934–1055), specializing in poetry, rhetoric, *adab*, and *fiqh*. In line with the increasing integration between *falsafa* and *kalām* in the fourth/tenth to the fifth/eleventh century (Wisnovsky 2004), al-Rāghib integrated Platonic philosophy and Aristotelian ethics into his Ashʿarī *kalām* and Shāfiʿī *fiqh*, influencing al-Ghazālī (d. 505/1111) as well as the *tafsīrs* of al-Rāzī (d. 606/1210) and al-Bayḍāwī (d. 719/1319) and later dictionaries.

Al-Rāghib's lexicon *al-Mufradāt* arranges words alphabetically, according to their consonant roots, and excluding non-Arabic words (Rippin 1988b). Al-Marʿashlī shows that this switch from context to root etymology allowed al-Rāghib to produce universal meanings, on the basis of which he connected Qur'anic words with *sharʿī* objectives (1988: 52; also see Key 2018). Concerning methodology, Mohamed (1995a, 1995b) has explored al-Rāghib's use of Aristotelian and Platonic epistemology and ethics to establish correspondences between Qur'anic words and law, in *al-Mufradāt* and *al-Dharīʿa ilā makārim al-sharīʿa*. Arif (2007) sums up al-Rāghib's method as morphological and etymological analysis, supported by intra-Qur'anic references, prophetic traditions, philosophy, and poetry. Further comparative studies of Ibn Qutayba's, Makkī's, and al-Rāghib's methodologies and linguistics along the line of al-Marʿashlī's provisional observations could yield important new insights into the detailed relations between exegetical, linguistic, and legal methodologies and methods.

Conclusion

As a specific pragmatist theory of language, rhetoric has been employed here to define methodologies and genres within *tafsīr* from the third/ninth to the fifth/eleventh century. The rhetorical methodology of contextualization can be attested at the latest with Sībawayhi's linguistics, possibly earlier, following Goldfeld's dating of hadith as an exegetical method to the late first/seventh century. This would imply that methodologies and genres pertaining to the period from the third/ninth to the fifth/eleventh century are not new but developments of earlier theories of language and interpretation. Al-Ṣanᶜānī, Ibn Sallām, Ibn Abī Zamanīn, al-Ṭabarī, and Makkī represent the contextualizing approach to language and meaning. The opposite approach is the one which seeks to define context-independent, universal meanings, here represented by al-Rāghib, whose lexicography and *fiqh* drew on Platonic and Aristotelian epistemologies. A similar approach appears to be at work in, for example, al-Muḥāsibī's *Fahm al-Qurʾān*, where the exegete defines legal topics and reads them into the Qur'an. The difference also appears to be a divide between inductive and deductive methods. The main conclusion is that a detailed history of *tafsīr* from the third/ninth to the fifth/eleventh century requires systematic research into the relationships between *tafsīr* and the other disciplines, and into how these relationships express themselves in the individual exegetes' methodologies and interpretations. Such research requires linguistics as its main analytical framework.

Bibliography

Abdul-Raof, H. *Arabic Rhetoric: A Pragmatic Analysis*. London: Routledge, 2006.

al-ᶜAmrī, ᶜA. *al-Ikhtiṣār fī'l-tafsīr*. Makka: Umm al-Qurā University, 2004.

Arif, S. 'Preserving the Semantic Structure of Islamic Key Terms and Concepts: Izutsu, al-ᶜAṭṭās, and al-Rāghib al-Isfahānī', *Islam & Science* 5/2 (2007), 107–16.

Baalbaki, R. 'Inside the Speaker's Mind: Speaker's Awareness as Arbiter of Usage in Arab Grammatical Theory'. In: E. Ditters and H. Motzki (eds.). *Approaches to Arabic Linguistics*, pp. 3–23. Leiden: Brill, 2007.

Bauer, K. (ed.). *Aims, Methods and Contexts of Qurʾānic Exegesis (2nd/8th—9th/15th C.)*. Oxford: Oxford University Press, 2013.

Birkeland, H. 'Old Muslim Opposition against Interpretation of the Koran'. In: *Avhandlinger Utgitt ab De Norske Videnskaps-Akademi i Oslo*, pp. 1–43. II Hist. Filos. Klasse 1. Oslo: Universitetsforlaget, 1955.

Campoy, M. A. 'Ibn Abī Zamanīn y su obra jurídica', *Cuadernos de historia del Islam* 11 (1984), 87–101.

Campoy, M. A. 'Teoría jurídica de la guerra santa: el "kitāb qidwat al-ghāzī" de Ibn Abī Zamanīn', *al-Andalus-Maghreb* 1 (1993), 51–65.

Campoy, M. A. 'Casuística sobre el perdón del talión en el *Muntajab al-ahkām* de Ibn Abī Zamanīn', *al-Qantara* 26/2 (2005), 387–403.
Carter, M. 'Foreign Vocabulary'. In: A. Rippin (ed.). *The Blackwell Companion to the Qur'ān*, pp. 120–39. Oxford: Blackwell Publishing, 2006.
Carter, M. 'Pragmatics and Contractual Language in Early Arabic Grammar and Legal Theory'. In: E. Ditters and H. Motzki (eds.). *Approaches to Arabic Linguistics*, pp. 25–44. Leiden: Brill, 2007.
El-Shamsy, A. *The Canonization of Islamic Law: A Social and Intellectual History*. Cambridge: Cambridge University Press, 2013.
Farhāt, A. H. *Makkī ibn Abī Ṭālib wa-tafsīr al-Qurʾān*. Amman: Dār "ʿAmmār, 1997.
Gilliot, C. 'Les Débuts de l'éxègese coranique', *Revue du monde musulman et de la Méditerranée* 58 (1990a), 82–100.
Gilliot, C. *Exégèse, langue et théologie en islam: l'exégèse coranique de Tabari*. Paris: Vrin, 1990b.
Gilliot, C. 'Le Traitement de "Ḥadīth" dans le "Tahdhīb al-āthār" de Ṭabarī', *Arabica* 41/3 (1994), 309–51.
Gilliot, C. 'A Schoolmaster, Storyteller, Exegete and Warrior at Work in Khurāsān: al-Ḍaḥḥāk ibn Muzāhim al-Hilālī'. In Bauer (ed.). *Aims, Methods and Contexts*, pp. 311–92. Oxford: Oxford University Press, 2013.
Goldfeld, Y. 'The Development of Theory on Qurʾānic Exegesis in Islamic Scholarship', *Studia Islamica* 67 (1988), 5–27.
Görke, A. and J. Pink (eds.). *Tafsīr and Islamic Intellectual History: Exploring the Boundaries of a Genre*. Oxford: Oxford University Press, 2014.
Hamza, F. '*Tafsīr* and Unlocking the Historical Qurʾān: Back to Basics?' In: Bauer (ed.). *Aims, Methods and Contexts*, pp. 19–37. Oxford: Oxford University Press, 2013.
Heath, P. 'Creative Hermeneutics: A Comparative Analysis of Three Islamic Approaches', *Arabica* 36/2 (1989), 173–210.
Horst, H. 'Zur Überlieferung im Korankommentar aṭ-Ṭabarīs', *Zeitschrift der Deutschen Morgenländischen Gesellschaft* 103 (1953), 290–307.
Ibn Abī Zamanīn, M. *Tafsīr*. Ed. H. Ibnʿ Akkāsha and M. al-Kanz. 6 vols. Cairo: al-Fārūq al-Ḥadītha li'l-Ṭibāʿa wa'l-Nashr, 2002.
Ibn ʿĀshur, Muḥammad al-Fāḍil. *al-Tafsīr wa-Rijāluhu*. Cairo: Silsilat al-Buḥūth al-Islamiyya, 1970.
Ibn Sallām, Yaḥyā. *al-Taṣārīf*. Ed. H. Shalabī. Tunis: al-Sharika al-Tūnisiyya li'l-Tawzīʿ, 1980.
Ibn Sallām, Yaḥyā. *Tafsīr*. Ed. H. Shalabī. 2 vols. Beirut: Dār al-Kutub al-ʿIlmiyya, 2004.
Key, Alexander. *Language between God and the Poets: Maʿná in the Eleventh Century*. Oakland, California: University of California Press, 2018.
Leemhuis, F., 'Origins and Early Development of the *tafsīr* Tradition'. In: A. Rippin (ed.). *Approaches to the History of the Interpretation of the Qurʾān*, pp. 13–30. Oxford: Clarendon Press, 1988.
Makkī ibn Abī Ṭālib. *Tafsīr al-mushkil min gharīb al-Qurʾān*. Ed. H. al-Marʿashlī. Beirut: Dār al-Nūr al-Islāmī, 1988.
Marogi, A. E. *Kitāb Sībawayhi: Syntax and Pragmatics*. Leiden: Brill, 2010.
Mårtensson, U. '"The Persuasive Proof": A Study of Aristotle's Politics and Rhetoric in the Qurʾān and in al-Ṭabarī's Commentary', *Jerusalem Studies in Arabic and Islam* 34 (2008), 363–420.
Mårtensson, U. 'Through the Lens of Modern Hermeneutics: Authorial Intention in al-Ṭabarī's and al-Ghazzālī's Interpretations of Q. 24:35', *Journal of Qur'anic Studies* 11/2 (2009), 20–48.

Mårtensson, U. 'al-Ṭabarī's Concept of the Qurʾān: A Systemic Analysis', ed. M. Klar, Special issue on al-Ṭabarī, *Journal of Qur'anic Studies*, 18/2 (2016), 9–57.

Mohamed, Y. 'The Ethical Philosophy of al-Rāghib al-Iṣfahānī', *Journal of Islamic Studies* 6/1 (1995a), 51–75.

Mohamed, Y. 'Al-Rāghib Al-Iṣfahānī's Classical Concept of the Intellect (*al-ʿaql*)', *Muslim Education Quarterly* 13 (1995b), 52–61.

Montgomery, J. E. 'Al-Jāḥiẓ's *Kitāb al-Bayān wa'l-tabyīn*'. In: J. Bray (ed.). *Writing and Representation in Medieval Islam: Muslim Horizons*, pp. 91–152. New York: Routledge, 2006.

Motzki, H. 'The Muṣannaf of ʿAbd al-Razzāq al-Ṣanʿānī as a Source of Authentic *Aḥādīth* of the First Century A.H.', *Journal of Near Eastern Studies* 50/1 (1991), 1–21.

Motzki, H. *The Origins of Islamic Jurisprudence: Meccan Fiqh before the Classical Schools*. Leiden: Brill, 2002.

Motzki, H. 'The Author and his Work in the Islamic Literature of the First Centuries: The Case of ʿAbd al-Razzāq's *Muṣannaf*', *Jerusalem Studies in Arabic and Islam* 28 (2003), 171–201.

Rippin, A. 'Ibn ʿAbbās's *Al-Lughāt fī'l-Qurʾān*', *Bulletin of the School of Oriental and African Studies* 44 (1981), 15–25.

Rippin, A. 'Introduction'. In: A. Rippin (ed.). *Approaches to the History of the Interpretation of the Qurʾān*, pp. 1–9. Oxford: Clarendon Press, 1988a.

Rippin, A. 'Lexicograpical Texts and the Qurʾān'. In: Rippin (ed.). *Approaches*, pp. 158–74. Oxford: Clarendon Press, 1988b.

Rippin, A. '*Tafsīr ibn ʿAbbās* and Criteria for Dating Early *Tafsīr* Texts', *Jerusalem Studies in Arabic and Islam* 19 (1994), 38–83.

Rippin, A. 'Studying Early *Tafsīr* Texts', *Der Islam* 72 (1995), 310–23.

Rippin, A. (ed.). *The Qurʾān: Formative Interpretation*. Aldershot: Ashgate Variorum, 1999.

Rippin, A. 'The Construction of the Arabian Historical Context in Muslim Interpretation of the Qurʾān'. In: Bauer (ed.). *Aims, Methods and Contexts*, pp. 173–98. Oxford: Oxford University Press, 2013.

Rosenthal, F. 'Introduction'. In: *The History of al-Ṭabarī*. Vol. 1: *General Introduction and From the Creation to the Flood*. Albany: State University of New York Press, 1989.

Saleh, W. *The Formation of the Classical Tafsīr Tradition: The Qurʾān Commentary of al-Thaʿlabī (d. 427/1053)*. Leiden: Brill, 2004.

Saleh, W. 'Marginalia and Peripheries: A Tunisian Historian and the History of Qurʾānic Exegesis', *Numen* 58 (2011), 284–313.

Sammoud, H. 'Un exegete oriental en Ifrīqiyya: Yaḥyā ibn Sallām (124/742–200/815)', *Revue IBLA*, Tunis 2/200 (2007), 263–78.

al-Ṣanʿānī, ʿAbd al-Razzāq. *Tafsīr al-Qurʾān*. Ed. Muṣṭafā Muslim Muḥammad. 3 vols. Riyadh: Maktabat al-Rushd, 1989.

Schöck, C. *Koranexegese, Grammatik und Logik: Zum Verhältnis von arabischer und aristotelischer Urteils-, Konsequenz- und Schlusslehre*. Leiden: Brill, 2006.

Shah, M. 'Exploring the Genesis of Early Arabic Linguistic Thought: Qurʾānic Readers and Grammarians of the Kufan Tradition (Part I)', *Journal of Qur'anic Studies* 5/1 (2003a), 47–78.

Shah, M.'Exploring the Genesis of Early Arabic Linguistic Thought: Qurʾānic Readers and Grammarians of the Basran Tradition (Part II)', *Journal of Qur'anic Studies* 5/2 (2003b), 1–47.

Shah, M. 'The Early Arabic Grammarians' Contributions to the Collection and Authentication of Qurʾānic Readings: The Prelude to Mujāhid's *Kitāb al-Sabʿa*', *Journal of Qur'anic Studies* 6/1 (2004), 72–102.

Shah, M. 'Introduction'. In: M. Shah (ed.). *Tafsīr: Interpreting the Qurʾān*. Vol. 1: *Tafsīr: Gestation and Synthesis*, pp. 1–157. London: Routledge 2013a.

Shah, M. 'Al-Ṭabarī and the Dynamics of *Tafsīr*: Theological Dimensions of a Legacy', *Journal of Qur'anic Studies* 15/2 (2013b), 83–139.

Stewart, D. J. 'Muḥammad ibn Jarīr al-Ṭabarī's *al-Bayān ʿan Uṣūl al-Aḥkām* and the Genre of *Uṣūl al-Fiqh* in Ninth Century Baghdād'. In: J. E. Montgomery (ed.). *'Abbasid Studies: Occasional Papers of the School of 'Abbasid Studies, Cambridge 6–10 July 2002*, pp. 321–49. Orientalia Lovaniensia Analecta 135. Cambridge: Cambridge University Press, 2004.

Stewart, D. J. 'Al-Ṭabarī's *Kitāb Marātib al-ʿUlamāʾ* and the Significance of Biographical Works Devoted to "the Classes of Jurists"', *Der Islam* 90/2 (2013), 347–75.

Stewart, D. J. 'Consensus, Authority, and the Interpretive Community in the Thought of Muḥammad ibn Jarīr al-Ṭabarī', *Journal of Qur'anic Studies* 18/2 (2016), 130–79.

al-Ṭabarī, Muḥammad ibn Jarīr. *Jāmiʿ al-bayān*. Ed. Ṣidqī Ḥamīd al-ʿAṭṭār. 15 vols. Beirut: Dār al-Fikr, 1995.

al-Tamīmī, H. J. *'al-Rasm al-ʿUthmānī min khilāl tafsīr al-Ṭabarī: ʿarḍ wa-naqd'*, *Majallat al-buḥūth wa'l-dirāsa al-Qurʾāniyya* 8/4 (2013), 77–122.

Vasalou, S. 'The Miraculous Eloquence of the Qurʾān: General Trajectories and Individual Approaches', *Journal of Qur'anic Studies* 4/2 (2002), 23–53.

Versteegh, K. 'Grammar and Exegesis: The Origins of Kufan Grammar and the *Tafsīr Muqātil*', *Der Islam* 67/2 (1990), 206–42.

Versteegh, K. *Arabic Grammar and Qurʾānic Exegesis in Early Islam*. Leiden: Brill, 1993.

Vishanoff, D. *The Formation of Islamic Hermeneutics: How Sunni Legal Theorists Imagined a Revealed Law*. New Haven: American Oriental Society, 2011.

Wansbrough, J. *Quranic Studies: Sources and Methods of Scriptural Interpretation*. Oxford: Oxford University Press, 1977/New York: Prometheus, 2004.

Wisnovsky, R. 'One Aspect of the Avicennian Turn in Sunni Theology', *Arabic Sciences and Philosophy* 14 (2004), 65–100.

al-Wuhaybī, A. *al-ʿIzz ibn ʿAbd al-Salām: ḥayātuhu wa-āthāruhu wa-minhajuhu fi'l-tafsīr*. Ph.D. thesis. Riyadh: University of Muḥammad ibn Saʿūd, Department of Tafsir Studies, 1982.

CHAPTER 44

MEDIEVAL EXEGESIS

The Golden Age of *Tafsīr*

WALID A. SALEH

JUST as theologians were making bold statements about *kalām* (theology), claiming that it is the queen of the religious sciences, so Qur'an commentators asserted that *tafsīr* is the most noble of religious sciences (Saleh 2004: 91). The case for *tafsīr*, however, was harder to argue, since *tafsīr* remained a discipline with little apparent practical function. It did not prepare one for a career in law, nor was it a discipline needed for guiding Muslims to the orthodox faith. To know God's law, a person studied *fiqh*, and to know Him one studied *kalām*; both disciplines included a hermeneutical approach to the Qur'an, but they were not disciplines that exclusively concerned themselves with the Qur'an (Vishanoff 2011). Moreover, after the victory of hadith in the debates about the sources of the law, *tafsīr* (and the Qur'an) had to vie with another scriptural competitor. Yet, I would argue that it is this very non-programmatic nature that is the secret of *tafsīr*'s longevity and cultural significance, if not centrality (Saleh 2004: 51). *Tafsīr* was the arena for the cultural appropriation and Islamization of other disciplines through their incorporation into a Qur'anic paradigm. Every discipline had to pass through a Qur'anic phase, in which *tafsīr* brought that discipline into conversation with the wider intellectual environment. Moreover, this process insured that the Qur'an remained central to the culture that the Qur'an produced and thus remained indispensable for making sense of the world. *Tafsīr*'s integrative nature—as a genre that made use of other disciplines and incorporated a variety of scholastic methods for its own ends—meant that it was always using the current languages of intellectuals and commoners alike to fashion a Qur'anic world that eventually made *tafsīr* the intellectual meta-language of Islam and the font of its pietistic sensibilities. The common trope of a dying luminary who on his deathbed regretted not dedicating his life to *tafsīr* reflected the notion of the Qur'an (through *tafsīr*) as the beginning and the end of all things. *Tafsīr* was the discipline that offered the possibility of making sense of the world through God's word. *Tafsīr* being the key to the Qur'an meant that the world was fashioned through *tafsīr*.

Tafsīr studies in Western academia has only recently achieved independence as a discipline, and as such is still a field in search of its own parameters (Rippin 1982;

Hamza et al. 2008; Saleh 2010; Shah 2013a). However, the last two decades have witnessed an increased production of specialized studies, facilitated by greater ease of acquiring manuscripts. As a result, our historical knowledge is now based on a more thorough investigation of the sources themselves. Yet any notion that we will soon be able to offer a detailed historical outline of the development of this textual genre is wildly inaccurate. Take a figure like ʿUmar ibn Muḥammad al-Nasafī (d. 537/1142), who wrote two Qur'an commentaries, both of which are available in manuscript form though as of yet unedited (Ziriklī 2002: 5:60)—but who has no place in our narrative of *tafsīr*. Or a figure like ʿAlī ibn Ibrāhīm al-Ḥawfī (d. 430/1039), a major Cairene Qur'an commentator who was a deciding influence on Abū Ḥayyān al-Gharnāṭī (d. 745/1344), and who is rarely even mentioned (Ziriklī 2002: 4:250; Rufaydah 1990: 1:641–53). The situation is no better when it comes to some major published works. Take, for example, the work of Ibn ʿAṭiyya (d. 546/1152), whose massive, fifteen-volume Qur'an commentary, *al-Muḥarrar al-wajīz*, has been available in print for over three decades. Yet, little has been said about him apart from cursory mention of his name in encyclopaedia entries, with the result that one has no clue as to how to understand his role in the history of *tafsīr* (Ziriklī 2002: 3:282; Ibn ʿAṭiyya 1977, vol. 1). Gilliot characterizes Ibn ʿAṭiyya *Muḥarrar* as an abridgement of previous works, a claim that could not be further from the truth (2002: 112). In fact, Ibn ʿAṭiyya was the major Qur'an commentator of the generation of al-Wāḥidī (d. 468/1075) and his *tafsīr* work was a turning point in the history of the genre in Andalusia and North Africa. Abū Ḥayyān al-Gharnāṭī deems his commentary as equal to that of al-Zamakhsharī (d. 538/1144) while being more comprehensive. This neglect of Ibn ʿAṭiyya is all the more surprising, given that the introduction to his Qur'an commentary was published by Arthur Jeffery (1954) over sixty years ago.

Contrast this with the state of the field in the Islamic world, where a more historical knowledge of *tafsīr* is not lacking, although it is marred by certain ideological outlooks (Saleh 2010). Much of our knowledge about the field in Western academia is dependent upon what is happening in the Islamic world. This overview is thus an attempt at bridging two worlds of the study of *tafsīr* in the hope of offering a fuller picture, and to open venues for further studies. The student or scholar who wants a more accurate picture of the historical development of *tafsīr* now has research tools that make her or his work more feasible. The most important of these is the twelve-volume catalogue of all existing *tafsīr* manuscripts, *al-Fihris al-shāmil* (1987, later editions in two massive volumes), and since then a three-volume work from Saudi Arabia, *Fihrist muṣannafāt tafsīr al-Qurʾān al-karīm* (2003). When used together, these resources offer exhaustive coverage of the field. They are especially helpful for locating extant materials available in libraries throughout the world.

Al-Dāwūdī's (d. 945/1538) two-volume *Ṭabaqāt al-mufassirīn* (1972) is a massive reference work that remains our most reliable medieval source on exegetes and their works. What is sorely needed is a study which collates the titles mentioned in it and those in the other two published biographical dictionaries of exegetes—namely by al-Suyūṭī (d. 911/1505) (1976) and al-Adnahwī (d. *c.*1700) (1997), though these are of less value—with the *tafsīr* works that have in fact reached us today. That is, we need to study not only the commentaries that have come down to us, but also to survey what has disappeared.

Only then will we be in a position to sketch a complete picture of the history of the genre, ensuring that we have encompassed as much as possible of the tradition. Our attempts to reconstruct the history of the genre of *tafsīr* thus have to be reconfigured on a more solid academic basis—one that avoids the all too common pitfalls of current approaches, which on the whole rely on published *tafsīr* works as our guide to the historical scope of the field.

In addition to these reference tools, the monographs produced in the Islamic world on individual exegetes are also essential, if grossly neglected. With certain recent (and encouraging) exceptions (Nguyen 2012), these are usually summarily dismissed by Western academics. These monographic studies offer the latest bibliographic and biographical material on individual exegetes, so they are extremely useful even when the analytical studies are heavily influenced by a Salafī historiographical paradigm.

Far more significant is the constant output of editions of Qur'an commentaries, which are the backbone of our work. The quality of editions coming out of the Middle East varies depending on several factors; however, even shoddy editions are indispensable. The Arabian Peninsula (Saudi Arabia and the Gulf states) is now producing critical editions of major *tafsīr* works, heralding a new phase in the history of book production in the Islamic world. Iran has been republishing Shīʿī Qur'an commentaries in new and critical editions. Remarkably, no Western scholar has ever bothered to review *tafsīr* editions coming out of the Islamic world—with the singular exception of Claude Gilliot, who reviews Qur'an commentaries published in Egypt. This is in itself an indication of the perfunctory interest taken in *tafsīr* as a discipline. There has been a veritable cascade of critical editions coming out in the Islamic world, but little heed is being paid to their significance to our field. By way of example, two major Qur'an commentaries edited in the past decade have transformed the field: *Taʾwīlāt ahl al-Sunna* by al-Māturīdī (d. 333/944), and *al-Basīṭ* by al-Wāḥidī (Saleh 2015 and 2016).

Collectively, these developments have revolutionized the field of *tafsīr* studies, necessitating a professional specialization in the field to keep pace with the developments. *Tafsīr* can no longer be studied on the side or as an afterthought, as was often the case in the past. The next logical step would be to connect the study of *tafsīr* to other fields in Islamic studies and Arabic studies. That some of the most influential thinkers of medieval Islam wrote *tafsīr* works is now common knowledge. Yet *tafsīr* has remained inconsequential to the writing of Islamic intellectual history, apart from al-Ṭabarī (d. 310/923), whose work as a historian made him an inescapable figure. The time has come to incorporate *tafsīr* into the history of Islam.

Tafsīr as a Genre

Tafsīr, in its classical phase (pre-1800), was a running interpretation of almost every verse and word in the Qur'an. The accumulation of such interpretations in the first 300 years of Islam was such that by the fourth/tenth century, one could draw upon a seemingly inexhaustible store in order to offer an analysis and commentary of the whole

Qur'an. The formal characteristics of this classical phase, evident in every major *tafsīr* of this period, include citations of authorities, polyvalent readings of the verses, and interpretive tools which Norman Calder (1993) divides into instrumental (orthography, lexis, syntax, rhetoric, symbol/allegory) and ideological (prophetic history, theology, eschatology, law, and mysticism) types. Such formal analysis, insightfully presented first by Calder, nonetheless came with its own presuppositions about *tafsīr*: that it could be studied by surveying a few authors (al-Ṭabarī, al-Qurṭubī, al-Rāzī, Ibn Kathīr, with occasional references to some others), and that it was a harmonious (if not irenic) and rich genre that subsequently came to be undone by Ibn Kathīr's unrepresentative methodology. Finally, Calder's presentation was squarely based on printed texts.

In contrast to this formal approach, *tafsīr* should be understood as a dynamic process within the genre itself. The textual tradition was internally riven by contradictions, bursting at the seams due to the use of incompatible methods, and always ready to come undone because of the various demands made on the genre. Thus, *tafsīr* is a genre that at every historical moment was a vehicle for efforts to smooth over or resolve the major dilemmas of Islamic religious tradition. Its seemingly peripheral position was precisely the cause of its pervasive influence. Every Qur'an commentary was an attempt at a resolution of certain problems. As a result, the genre cannot be reduced to its formal constitutive elements, nor can we proceed to take these elements as constituting an analysis of what *tafsīr* was or is. Every work was thus both coherent and contradictory, because *tafsīr* was always attempting to join incompatible ideas and resolve problems which were pulling at the tradition. *Tafsīr* studies maintains a romantic attachment to certain heroes, al-Ṭabarī and al-Rāzī (d. 606/1210) often favoured in this regard, and other villains, Ibn Kathīr (d. 774/1373) chief among them. Although, to his credit, Calder saw in al-Qurṭubī (d. 671/1272) the culmination of the potentialities of the genre, this resulted simply in an addition to the constellation of names (Calder 1993: 134) but not a transformation in the way we understand *tafsīr*. Yet Ibn Kathīr is more closely related to al-Ṭabarī than Calder realized, being just one belated manifestation (Saleh 2010: 21–31) of the *salaf* hadith-focused current which has a venerable history as the underbelly of the *tafsīr* tradition.

Al-Ṭabarī Read Through Al-Māturīdī

Until recently, one could do little without al-Ṭabarī. Not only was his the most exhaustive of all early classical *tafsīr* works, his was also the only example we have from that period; as such, any measure of the field was determined by what he offered us. We understood *tafsīr* through the lens of his Qur'an commentary. However, the recent publication of al-Māturīdī's massive *Ta'wīlāt al-Qur'ān* (2005–11), which is a work contemporaneous to that of al-Ṭabarī, has radically changed the situation. This work is not another addition to the list of works we have; rather, it proves an Archimedean point that allows us to penetrate beyond the fog of words that al-Ṭabarī surrounded us with. It is now clear that al-Ṭabarī was not compiling the tradition, but attempting a reconciliation between a more moderate reformed Sunnism and the radical Sunnī fringe that I term the *salaf* underbelly of Sunnī *tafsīr* tradition (Saleh 2010: 21).

Indeed, al-Ṭabarī's radical reconfiguring of what Sunnī *tafsīr* should look like is only apparent thanks to al-Māturīdī. There were two main approaches to exegesis that al-Ṭabarī attempted to establish as normative: first, the pretence that *tafsīr* was hadith-like, that is, that it depended on *isnāds* (and thus on oral transmission) rather than books; and second, an effacement of several major currents of *tafsīr*, in order to present a purified mode of *tafsīr* that was oblivious of its competitors. For example, he pretended that Muqātil ibn Sulaymān (d. 150/767) did not exist, that there was no Muʿtazilī tradition of Qur'an commentary, and that Sunnī *tafsīr* was at a standstill by the early third/ninth century. The *isnāds* given before every snippet of interpretation in al-Ṭabarī effect the impression that he had gathered all that there was to gather, with this mode of presentation implying that it was the sum total of what has so far been said about each verse. However, al-Māturīdī's Qur'an commentary challenges the implications of these reconfigurations. By building his work on Muqātil's exegesis, al-Māturīdī reaffirmed that Muqātil was and remained central to the mainstream Sunnī tradition, and that the deliberate neglect not to name him by al-Ṭabarī while using him was only cosmetic.

Moreover, al-Māturīdī clearly shows that the Sunnī tradition was more preoccupied with the challenge of the Muʿtazilī hermeneutical programme than al-Ṭabarī leads us to believe. The question is then what al-Ṭabarī attempted to do with his approach, which silenced the other exegetical activities of the whole third/ninth century. It should be clear that al-Ṭabarī was only willing to preserve a certain kind of Sunnī material, not its total sum. Al-Māturīdī's work makes evident the fact that the major threat to and interlocutor of the Sunnī hermeneutical project was the Muʿtazilī Qur'an commentarial tradition. The Muʿtazilī *tafsīr* tradition has now to be seen as the central tradition, not as a peripheral phenomenon, as has thus far been the case. For it was the dominant school to which the *ahl al-Sunna* were responding, and shaping their interpretive approach to accommodate this challenge (for a survey of the Muʿtazilī *tafsīr* tradition, see Fudge 2011: 114–42). By pretending that this competing commentary tradition did not exist, al-Ṭabarī presented Sunnism as the only (and thus necessary) voice that spoke for the meaning of the Qur'an. This reconfiguration was all the more urgent, since the radical camp among the *ahl al-Sunna* was claiming that *tafsīr* was not needed. In this light, the *isnāds* in al-Ṭabarī's exegesis appear a fetish-like device used to reconfigure *tafsīr* in the form of hadith, a small price to pay if it could manage to edge Sunnī *tafsīr* closer to modes that the *ahl al-Sunna* could endorse. Thus al-Ṭabarī attempted to present *tafsīr* in a manner that would be acceptable to the radical fringe of Sunnism, while making it a credible challenger to the Muʿtazilī professionalized craft of Qur'an commentary. His was an attempt to reconcile radical Sunnism to *tafsīr* as a major mode of scholarly activity (Shah 2013b).

Each Qur'an commentary was embedded within its historical moment and responded to challenges that it was attempting to overcome; each work was shaped far less by a defined script of a codified genre than by the cultural function of *tafsīr*. *Tafsīr* was never bound by a method or confined by certain features; it was rather bound by a function: to resolve the profound contradictions that faced each Islamic current and to offer a solution that would appear to emanate from the Qur'an. This was also the case for every Islamic period; modernity is not the only destabilizing and disorienting force in human history. This is the reason behind the ever-changing face of *tafsīr* as a genre: beyond the basic text of the Qur'an, one could never be certain what one would find in a *tafsīr* work. Even the enshrinement of philology as the bedrock of *tafsīr* did not necessarily mean that philological materials would appear in every Qur'an commentary; early Shīʿī, mystics, and Bāṭinists did not need philology to write *tafsīr* works. More significantly, ultra-Sunnī hadith-based interpretation never submitted to the unfettered authority of philology. A reading of al-Suyūṭī's Qur'an commentary *al-Durr al-manthūr* shows clearly that Sunnism in its extreme form was as non-philological as *ghulāt* (extremist) Shīʿī *tafsīr*. The *tafsīr* chapters in Sunnī hadith collections were the earliest example of the radical Sunnī camp's attempt to envision *tafsīr* (Saleh 2010: 26).

In the final analysis, contrary to the claims of the twentieth-century Salafi movement and modern Western scholarship alike, al-Ṭabarī's Qur'an commentary was never the bedrock of the classical exegetical tradition. His was only and merely a ring in a concatenation of works, and thus soon forgotten. As with all classics, there were periodic rediscoveries of his work, but he was never the dominant force scholars claim him to be. He was not the gateway to the tradition. That honour belonged to the Nishapuri school of authors.

Nishapur and its Centrality in the Classical *Tafsīr* Tradition

Isaiah Goldfeld's edition (1984) of the introduction to al-Thaʿlabī's *al-Kashf wa'l-bayān*, with its hundreds of footnotes, would not be recognized as a monument of scholarship for twenty years. The edition (and its title) was the first to call attention to the fact that the Islamic exegetical tradition had a major centre other than al-Ṭabarī's Baghdad; that the *tafsīr* output of Khurasan was highly significant was later confirmed by Claude Gilliot (1999). I have argued since then (Saleh 2004, 2006a) that al-Thaʿlabī (d. 427/1035) and his student al-Wāḥidī formed a Nishapuri school of *tafsīr* that reconfigured the genre such that they set the tone for the medieval period. Recently, Martin Nguyen has enlarged the scope of the notion of the Nishapuri school to include other figures from the city, such as al-Qushayrī (d. 465/1072) (2012). Travis Zadeh (2012) has demonstrated the centrality of Nishapur in shaping the Persian Qur'an exegetical tradition. When I published my monograph on al-Thaʿlabī, I was at the beginning of uncovering what turned out to be an extensive node of influence that radiated from al-Thaʿlabī and his student al-Wāḥidī (Saleh 2006) and indeed shaped the Sunnī classical mode of doing *tafsīr*. The resolutions set out by these two authors demarcated both the limits and the expanse of this genre.

Al-Thaʿlabī faced a host of problems when he took on the task of writing his Qur'an commentary. Not least among these was the cumulative accretion of works on the Qur'an over the preceding 400 years. To address these precedents, he carried out an assessment of at least 100 works on the Qur'an. This literature review remains the only classical instance of a comprehensive review of the genre carried out by a professional exegete, and is our most important witness to the existence of works that we might have suspected never existed (Saleh 2004). Together with the reports of Ibn al-Nadīm (d. 380/990), it confirms with certainty the existence of independent early works of *tafsīr*, regardless of whether these were 'authentic'. That they have disappeared is simply a matter of scholarly preferences and not because they never existed as independent books. It is clear that Sunnism at that moment was willing to act as a collective voice of the Muslims, pretending to be the *sawād al-aʿẓam* (the great multitude of the Muslims). However, al-Thaʿlabī was not a typical Sunnī, for he employed 'heretical' Sunnī authors, as well as Shīʿī and Muʿtazilī works, in the composition of his exegesis. His commentary also played a decisive role in ensuring that citations from al-Zajjāj (d. 311/923) would become a central feature of the classical *tafsīr* corpus. At times more comprehensive than al-Ṭabarī, al-Thaʿlabī's commentary is an instance of a collection of the *tafsīr* tradition that was independent of the former, and moreover not constrained by his exegetical programme. Given these distinctions, we can reach the broader methodological conclusion that the three Qur'an commentaries of al-Ṭabarī, al-Māturīdī, and al-Thaʿlabī should be used in conjunction when studying the early period of *tafsīr*, since each has preserved material that the others did not and each accessed the tradition independently of the others.

The other major problem that faced the *tafsīr* tradition was the place of philology in explicating the word of God. The philological revolution of early Islamic Arabic culture meant that philology grew to be the most dominant form of discourse, uncontrolled by religious inhibitions. The major intellectual problem faced by the craft of *tafsīr* was how to employ this independent discipline in exegesis without undermining long-established theological understandings of the Qur'an. *Tafsīr* could not be strictly haggadic, nor conversely could it abandon established traditional understandings en masse. A resolution was effected, in which *tafsīr* pretended to give philology free rein, yet through its polyvalent layering of meanings ensured that inherited interpretations were given a place. This also meant that *tafsīr* was intellectually capable of conversing with the dominant form of discourse in the education of the elites, who were first and foremost trained in all the arts of Arabic philology (Saleh 2004: 130–40).

Professionalizing *tafsīr*, however, carried with it the danger of alienating it from pietistic popular sensibilities that had grown up around the Qur'an. One can already detect that tone in al-Ṭabarī, where a professionalized craft was suffocating the pietistic relationship to the text. Al-Thaʿlabī was one of the early exegetes who sought to keep Sunnī pietism alive in the high style of *tafsīr*. This was effected by emphasizing the salvific powers of the Qur'an through various affective means, including illustrative stories, poetry, hagiographic narratives, tales of miracles effected by reading the Qur'an, and by marrying the act of reading the Qur'an to the act of interpreting it. Interpretation carried with it a salvific effect that gave this scholastic discipline a depth formerly only reserved for the reading of the Qur'an. This was necessary to combat the rise of Sufi modes of interpretation that were isolating themselves from the mainstream of Sunnī hermeneutics. Moreover, it was necessary to place the text in a frame that made it accessible to believers without the mediating powers of the Shīʿī discourse, where an Imam stood between the text and the believers who wanted access to it.

Al-Ṭabarī unlike al-Māturīdī, did not forthrightly present *tafsīr* as a theological battleground (Shah 2013b). Although he clearly belonged to the Sunnī fold, one has to tease out his theology from various statements made, and there is no reference to a named school of theology in his Qur'an commentary. This proves all the more effective a mode of theologizing, with al-Ṭabarī once again standing for the totality of the tradition (rather than, for instance, acknowledging and mediating disparate voices). But *tafsīr* was already manifestly contested, especially by the Muʿtazilīs, who presented a Qur'an that accorded with their doctrines. Al-Māturīdī was a formidable foe of Muʿtazilism, but his work took a unique trajectory, and its significance and influence has yet to be investigated. As late as the ninth/fourteenth century, Mamlūk Cairo was trying to obtain a copy of his work (Ragheb 2012). It is with al-Thaʿlabī that we witness the entrance into *tafsīr* of a distinctly Ashʿarī discourse—gingerly at first, and brought to full bloom by his student al-Wāḥidī, in his *al-Basīṭ*.

This brings us to a constant feature of *tafsīr*, namely the centrality in its discourse of *kalām* theology. *Tafsīr* became sectarian early on, and remained so despite the uniformity of its outlook due to professionalization and especially its use of philology. It is this proximity to theology, and the intimate connection between Sunnī and Muʿtazilī *tafsīr*, that explains the success of al-Zamakhsharī's work among Sunnīs. Al-Zamakhsharī mimicked the Sunnī resolutions, layering them over with a Muʿtazilī theology; yet the whole structure of his work was of such integrity that it was impossible to dismiss. But perhaps Sunnism needed to keep its foe alive, both close by and ever in intimate, adversarial conversation, to remind it of the dangers it risked and the triumphs it achieved against Muʿtazilism.

It is remarkable how little the medieval Sunnī exegetical tradition cared to rebut Shīʿī hermeneutics. This is one of the most intriguing aspects about the genre of *tafsīr*: the battles it chose to fight. Al-Thaʿlabī is here unique, because he did attempt to undermine Shīʿī claims about how to read the Qur'an, by appropriating and limiting the connection between the Qur'an and the *ahl al-bayt* (the family of Muḥammad) to pietistic (rather than political) terms. His approach was as daring as it was dangerous, for it backfired, and his commentary would become the most contested of works in the rising polemics between Sunnism and Shīʿism (Saleh 2004: 215–21). Indeed, the use of *al-Kashf* by Shīʿī scholars in their counterclaims over the Qur'an has had such a lasting effect that, in a singular instance of such effort, the modern edition of this massive Sunnī *tafsīr* work was a Shīʿī enterprise. The influence of al-Thaʿlabī is pervasive even when scholars are unaware of the connections between his work and Shīʿī scholarship, a connection that has left its trace far and wide and in many fields.

Lurking in the shadows of the genre was the question of the role of the corpus of prophetic traditions and its relationship to the Qur'an. The debate about *tafsīr bi'l-maʾthūr* (tradition-based interpretation) has clouded the field of *tafsīr* studies and has resulted in the notion that prophetic hadith was from the very beginning intimately tied to *tafsīr*. This is not the case. The relationship between the disciplines of hadith proper and *tafsīr* was complex and took centuries to develop (Saleh 2004: 189–98; Saleh 2010: 21–31). It remained a contentious relationship, taut and unresolved. On the one hand, there was the radical Sunnī pretence that only hadith could properly interpret the Qur'an; on the other, a full abeyance of this relationship in favour of philology (Saleh 2010). Sunnism, or at least the resolution that was fully articulated by al-Thaʿlabī, married the two, the Qur'an and the hadith, while preserving the pre-eminence of philology. The danger was always how much to concede to hadith as the key to God's word. The thoroughgoing philologist knew that any compromise was dangerous; it was simply a matter of time before hadith overwhelmed the tradition, should any concessions be given. Meanwhile, the radical camp started producing Qur'an commentaries that accorded with their vision of interpreting the Qur'an solely through hadith (Saleh 2010). Sunnism writ large, however, remained faithful—if not to the resolution of al-Thaʿlabī, then to the safe-guarding of the role of philology in interpretation.

The career of al-Wāḥidī (d. 468/1075) reflects the ever-complex history of *tafsīr*. He authored three Qur'an commentaries, each reflecting a resolution to a specific problem (Saleh 2006a). His *al-Wajīz*, the shortest of his commentaries, is the first single-volume Qur'an commentary that updated the work of Muqātil ibn Sulaymān and answered the need for a handy reference work. This work remained the undisputed single-volume Qur'an commentary for five centuries, until the appearance of al-Suyūṭī's (d. 911/1505) *Tafsīr al-Jalālayn*, but its popularity never waned. His third Qur'an commentary, *al-Wasīṭ*, was an attempt to present *tafsīr* as a Sunnī craft, fully conservative and entirely in accord with the tradition. It was also a harking back to al-Ṭabarī's pretence that Sunnism was the sole existing interpreter of the Qur'an.

It is his massive second commentary, his magnum opus *al-Basīṭ* (recently published in twenty-three volumes), that illustrates the radical swings at the heart of the history of *tafsīr* (Saleh 2006a, 2013b). The aim of this Qur'an commentary was to bring the craft of Sunnī *tafsīr* to the same level of sophistication that was evident in Muʿtazilī *tafsīr* compositions. Here an attempt was made to do *tafsīr* as if one were doing pure philological interpretation, to rid *tafsīr* of its weak points and indebtedness to sectarian identity. *Tafsīr* by this account was more akin to *shurūḥ* (commentary) on Arabic poetic compilations. It was also a magisterially failed attempt, for it was not then possible to fully — separate the two, *tafsīr* from a sectarian matrix (as would later be possible with Enlightenment notions of original meaning). Although an exegete could tip the balance in one direction or another, there was no possibility of composing a *tafsīr* without anchoring it in a sectarian environment. If anything, this showed the degree of maturity that Sunnism had to develop in order to win its battles, which it did by becoming ever more intellectual, ever more scholastic, and as such capable of persuading the literati to join its ranks. Finally, it is of note that al-Wāḥidī spent nineteen years writing this Qur'an commentary. This demonstrates the sort of time that medieval exegetes had to spend when they wrote such massive works.

These two exegetes had a pervasive influence on the medieval exegetical tradition, far more than al-Ṭabarī or any other exegete. They also stand at a turning point in the history of *tafsīr* writing, after which we start witnessing cookie-cutter type commentaries. That is, by that time the genre was mature enough and classical *tafsīrs* were sufficiently available that one could churn out a work in no time. That some post-Thaʿlabī works were hastily produced does not negate their influence, however. For example, al-Thaʿlabī's exegesis was bowdlerized by al-Baghawī (d. 516/1122) in his *Maʿālim al-tanzīl*, a work that proved extremely popular. These new commentaries have to be studied carefully, for they do not represent the same intellectually agonizing process of a work independently composed in response to a major cultural upheaval. Although not of the same calibre as the major works, they do answer a need, and it is this need that should guide our understanding of the process of compilation of these works as they partake in the culture of their times. Moreover, it is through the study of these second-hand works that we are able to gauge the influence of other works, since the former usually fell back on the most popular models available.

Al-Kashshāf of al-Zamakhsharī and *Anwār al-Tanzīl* of al-Bayḍāwī (d. c.719/1319)

These two works came to play a central role in the scholastic madrasa system of education. They were the basis of *tafsīr* education after the seventh/twelfth century, and a starting point for most of the Qur'an commentaries written afterwards. They would also spawn a massive literature of glosses (*ḥawāshī, ḥāshiya*) (Gunsati 2013; Naguib 2013; Saleh 2013a). The rise to prominence of *al-Kashshāf* is a turning point in the history of *tafsīr*, since now there was a Qur'an commentary that was known all over the Islamic world. This marked the end of regionalism in *tafsīr*, and the emergence of a universal point of reference for interpreting the Qur'an. It is remarkable that Sunnism allowed a Muʿtazilī work to obtain this rank. Moreover, these two works must be studied together with the literature that they engendered. Since *al-Kashshāf* was squarely based on al-Thaʿlabī's *al-Kashf wa'l-bayān* and al-Wāḥidī's *al-Basīṭ*, and since al-Bayḍāwī's work was based on *al-Kashshāf* and al-Rāzī's *Mafātīḥ al-ghayb*, we can see the far-reaching influence of the Nishapuri school of *tafsīr*. I have already argued that *al-Kashshāf* is based on the Nishapuri school (Saleh 2004: 209–14), which has since been confirmed by evidence from inside the tradition. For example, Abū Ḥayyān al-Gharnāṭī had a love-hate relationship with *al-Kashshāf*: he could not escape it, but he tired of al-Zamakhsharī's style and the latter's practice of not acknowledging his sources. At times he would lose patience and call him on his plagiarism, as when Abū Ḥayyān was interpreting Q. 3:179 (1993: 3:130). He accuses al-Zamakhsharī of stealing his interpretation from ʿAbd al-Raḥmān Ibn Kaysān (d. 225/840)—an interpretation that is only available through al-Thaʿlabī's *al-Kashf wa'l-bayān* (2002: 3:218–19). The degree of al-Zamakhsharī's dependence on the Nishapuri school is apparent through tracing such intertextual arguments.

To emphasize the transformative degree of this new universal mode of scholastic interpretation, we can take the Andalusi/North African Qur'an interpretive tradition as an example. This was a tradition that was based on the works of Baqiyy Ibn Makhlad (d. 276/889) and Yaḥyā Ibn Sallām (d. 200/815). One of the major figures of this school was a contemporary of al-Thaʿlabi of Nishapur, Makkī ibn Abī Ṭālib (d. 437/1045), whose work has only recently been published (Makkī 2008). The maturation of this tradition came with Ibn ʿAṭiyya (d. 546/1151), who married the Andalusi/North African tradition to al-Ṭabarī's work. This North African tradition would be united fully with the output of eastern Islam in the work of al-Qurṭubī (d. 671/1272), whose *al-Jāmiʿ li-aḥkām al-Qurʾān*, bringing together Qur'anic exegesis as practised at the two extremities of the Islamic world, relied primarily on Ibn ʿAṭiyya and al-Zamakhsharī, among others. It is, however, clear that he used al-Thaʿlabī as a scaffold for his work. In this sense we can see how cumulative and more truly representative works were being produced as time went on. *Tafsīr* works now operated within a fairly stable genealogical framework, which included al-Thaʿlabī, al-Wāḥidī, al-Zamakhsharī, al-Bayḍāwī, and al-Rāzī. Although this core varied slightly, occasionally including an exegete such as al-Ṭabarī, the scholastic tradition by that time had a fixed number of authors that it referred to consistently.

The same process occurred in the Shīʿī tradition of exegesis (Saleh 2010). Both al-Thaʿlabī and al-Zamakhsharī proved foundational in transforming medieval Shīʿī exegetical tradition, both in Arabic and Persian (Zadeh 2012). Reading any of the post-Buyid Shīʿī works, one finds the same methodological presuppositions as the works produced by Sunnism. This was despite the foundational premise of the *bāṭinī* (inner) theology of Shīʿī hermeneutics (Bar-Asher 1999; Rippin 2013). The prevailing sense that philology has to be given a proper role in the craft of *tafsīr* meant that a common language was adopted by all schools of Islam. One could argue for one's view as to the meaning of a given verse or passage, but not before parsing it in a manner that was common to and understood by all. This philological paradigm can also be seen at work in Zaydī works produced in Yemen. Indeed, with al-Shawkānī's (d. 1250/1834) Qur'an commentary, we have a complete reversal to a Sunnī model.

The dominance of al-Zamakhsharī's *al-Kashshāf* in the madrasa system is now clearly demonstrated (Naguib 2013). However, this total dominance would not last, and by the early tenth/sixteenth century we start witnessing competition from (if not displacement by) al-Bayḍāwī's *Anwār al-tanzīl* (Gunasti 2013). We are just at the beginning of investigating what was happening in the madrasa system at this juncture. The tens of *ḥāshiyya*s (glosses) written on both works have to be seriously investigated. Since some are already published, there is no reason why this should not now become the most important task for scholars who work on *tafsīr* (Saleh 2013a).

The *al-Kashshāf* and *Anwār al-tanzīl* would be joined by other works that were latecomers to the circle of glossed works. One was al-Suyūṭī's *Tafsīr al-Jalālayn*, which would slowly but assuredly compete with al-Wāḥidī's *al-Wajīz* as the first point of reference for any difficulty encountered in the Qur'an. Moreover, *Tafsīr al-Jalālayn* had the advantage of being taught and glossed in the madrasa system. Perhaps the most gaping hole that remains in this picture is the situation in Mughal and South-East Asia, where our knowledge of *tafsīr* is rather scanty.

The Use of Paper and the Encyclopaedic *Tafsīrs*

In the middle of composing his massive Qur'an commentary, al-Biqāʿī (d. 885/1480) heard that Ibn al-Naqīb (d. 698/1298) had employed the same method as he was using, and panicked. He rushed to the mosque library of al-Ḥākim in Cairo, where he knew that there was a copy of the text, but after inspecting it was reassured. No one has written anything of the like before, al-Biqāʿī bragged to his readers (*Naẓm*, 1:10). What is of significance for us in this anecdote is that the work in question was supposedly 100 volumes. This could have been dismissed as medieval exaggeration, were it not for the fact that Abū Ḥayyān al-Gharnāṭī, who was a student of Ibn al-Naqīb, specifically criticized his teacher for writing this unwieldy work (Abū Ḥayyān 1993: 1:114). *Tafsīr* works were always running the risk of becoming impossibly endless. Many scholars died before finishing their works. The tendency toward such voluminous output was a consequence of the underlying premise of *tafsīr*: that God's word is inexhaustible, and its interpretation is likewise inexhaustible (Saleh 2004: 1–2). Already, al-Ṭabarī's and al-Māturīdī's works were voluminous. But they were not that large when compared to al-Rāzī's *Mafātīḥ al-ghayb*, al-Biqāʿī's *Naẓm al-durar*, or al-Suyūṭī's *al-Durr*. This massive output was only conceivable because of the availability of the new technology of paper, which meant a democratization of the material tools of writing.

These encyclopaedic works represent the continuation of the high style of writing, in which an author takes on the challenge of interpreting the meaning of the Qur'an in light of major cultural developments. Al-Rāzī's work came at a momentous transitional point in Islamic intellectual history. Theology and Islamic philosophy were now married in a new formulation that necessitated a reworking of what the Qur'an was saying in light of this new cultural transformation (Jaffer 2015). What is most significant about al-Rāzī is that his Qur'an commentary joined the core group of works read all over the Islamic world, including the Shīʿī seminaries.

The periodic encyclopaedic reformulations of *tafsīr* were recognized by the intellectual world of Islam, and the currency of these works was such that they were available in almost every major cultural Islamic centre. Al-Biqāʿī's *tafsīr* was also a culturally momentous transformation: he not only opened up Qur'anic exegesis to the Bible, but also saw a cohesiveness in the Qur'an that he emphasized by foregrounding his new interpretive technique (*tanāsub*) (Saleh 2008a; Saleh 2008b: 7–20). By contrast, al-Suyūṭī's work was a culmination of a radical trend that was then on the margins of *tafsīr*, a trend that would eventually come to dominate the Sunnī hermeneutical paradigm: a complete and exclusive equation of the Qur'an with the Sunna. It is remarkable that the same radicalism would occur in Safavid Iran, which saw a resurgence of what seemed to be dead Akhbārī traditions of Qur'an interpretation (Lawson 1993).

Each of these works is now published, and they are being incrementally incorporated into the grand narrative of *tafsīr* history. A problem persists in that these works (apart from the work of al-Rāzī) are not generally studied in conjunction with the larger intellectual history of medieval Islam. Moreover, we remain woefully unaware of what other works were also foundational, whether the gloss of al-Ṭībī (d. 743/1342) on *al-Kashshāf* or the work of al-Iṣfahānī (d. 749/1349) (Saleh 2013a: 230, 244–5). These works were quoted and studied extensively in centuries past, yet their significance is not usually acknowledged today, due to the fact that they are not yet available in print.

The Rise of the Ottoman Research Libraries and the Ottoman *Tafsīr* Tradition

The sudden disappearance of the Ottoman Empire, and the radical cultural transformation brought about in the wake of the founding of the modern Turkish republic, severed the ties not only between modern Turkey and the Arabs but between Ottoman and Islamic and Arabic intellectual histories. The Ottomans are the domain of historians, and they hardly figure as players in studies written today of Islamic intellectual history. Yet, the culmination of the scholastic system of medieval *tafsīr* was apparently in Istanbul (the case of the Mughal Empire has to be studied further, and faces an absolute dearth of scholarship). Most of the surviving *tafsīr* works, including most of the marginal or obscure works available to us today, now reside in the libraries of Istanbul. This fact points to a systemic programme of gathering that goes beyond the coincidental. Such is the comprehensiveness of the titles in Istanbul libraries that they can only indicate an organized effort to gather all the works available on *tafsīr*, bespeaking a sophisticated understanding of the history of this textual genre (Saleh 2013a: 220). This aspect of *tafsīr* studies has never been examined to date: where works were preserved, and why. The publication of works in critical editions is only one aspect of studying the medieval heritage. We need to study the manuscripts themselves as part of our investigation of the history of their transmission and production. Moreover, Istanbul was the only place where vast quantities of the Islamic world's cultural production were increasingly being archived; works from Spain to Samarqand were gathered regardless of their origin or immediate usefulness.

In addition to this preservation and cataloguing of the *tafsīr* heritage of medieval Islam, the Ottoman Empire, after a period of translation of *tafsīr* works, soon became a centre of both *tafsīr* glosses and the production of new compositional works that became bestsellers in the Islamic world. We know of three major works that have been published and which remain hugely influential. The first is the Qur'an commentary of Abū 'l-Suᶜūd (d. 982/1574), the Sheikh al-Islām of Suleiman the Magnificent. This work became a staple of the Ottoman madrasa curriculum and was widely disseminated in the Islamic world (Naguib 2013). It was also published very early on in the history of the Arabic book. The second work to play a major role was al-Bursawī's (d. 1137/1725) *tafsīr*, which came to represent the pinnacle of Sufi *tafsīrs* and was the work most used for accessing the Sufi Qur'an interpretive tradition. This work was also published very early on in the history of the Arabic book. Finally, the massive gloss on al-Bayḍāwī's exegesis by Ismāᶜīl ibn Muḥammad al-Qūnawī (d. 1195/1781) was published in Istanbul soon after it was written. This work, which has since disappeared from the narrative of *tafsīr* history, was a staple in scholastic education. The Ottoman patronage of *tafsīr* extended to the Arab provinces of their empire, most notably to the work of Maḥmūd Shihāb al-Dīn al-Ālūsī (d. 1270/1854). Istanbul rivalled Cairo in its publishing of the medieval *tafsīr* tradition from the middle of the nineteenth century until the demise of the Ottoman Empire.

Bibliography

Abū Ḥayyān al-Gharnāṭī *al-Baḥr al-muḥīṭ*. 9 vols. Beirut: Dār al-Kutub al-ᶜIlmiyya, 1993.

Bar-Asher, M. M. *Scripture and Exegesis in Early Imāmī Shiism*. Leiden: Brill, 1999.

al-Biqāᶜī, Ibrāhīm Ibn ᶜUmar. *Naẓm al-durar fī tanāsub al-āyāt wa'l-suwar*. 22 vols. Hyderabad: Dāʾirat al-Maᶜārif al-ᶜUthmāniyya, 1976.

al-Dāwūdī, Muḥammad Ibn ᶜAlī. *Ṭabaqāt al-mufassirīn*. Ed. A. M. ᶜUmar. 2 vols. Cairo: Maktabat Wahbah, 1972.

Calder, N. 'Tafsīr from Ṭabarī to Ibn Kathīr: Problems in the Description of a Genre, Illustrated with Reference to the Story of Abraham'. In: G. R. Hawting and A. A. Shareef (eds.). *Approaches to the Qurʾān*, pp. 101–40. London: Routledge, 1993.

al-Fihris al-shāmil li'l-turāth al-ᶜarabī al-makhṭūṭ: ᶜulūm al-Qurʾān: makhṭūṭāt al-tafsīr, 12 vols. Amman: Muʾassasat Āl al-Bayt, 1987.

Fihrist muṣannafāt tafsīr al-Qurʾān al-karīm (1424/2003). 3 vols. Medina: Mujammaᶜ al-Malik Fahd li-Ṭibāᶜat al-Muṣḥaf al-Sharīf, 1424/2003.

Fudge, B. *Qurʾānic Hermeneutics*: al-Ṭabrisī *and the Craft of Commentary*. London: Routledge, 2011.

Gilliot, C. 'Exegesis of the Qurʾān: Classical and Medieval'. In: J. D. McAuliffe (ed.). *Encyclopaedia of the Qurʾān*, 2:99–124. 6 vols. Leiden: Brill, 2002.

Gilliot, C. 'L'exégèse du Coran en Asie Centrale et au Khorasan', *Studia Islamica* 89 (1999), 129–64.

Goldfeld, I. *Mufassirū sharq al-ʿālam al-islāmī fī arbaʿat al-qurūn al-hijriyya al-ūlā: nashr makhṭūtat muqaddimat al-Thaʿlabī (tāʾ: 427) li-kitāb al-Kashf waʾl-bayān ʿan tafsīr al-Qurʾān*, Acre: Maktabat al-Sarrūjī, 1984.

Gunasti, S. 'Political Patronage and the Writing of Qurʾān Commentaries among the Ottoman Turks', *Journal of Islamic Studies* 24 (2013), 335–57.

Hamza, Feras, Sajjad Rizvi, with Farhana Mayer (eds.). *The Anthology of Qurʾānic Commentaries: On the Nature of the Divine*. Oxford: Oxford University Press, 2008.

Ibn ʿAṭiyya, ʿAbd al-Ḥaqq ibn Ghālib. *al-Muḥarrar al-wajīz*. Ed. A. al-Anṣārī and A. Ibrāhīm. 15 vols. Cairo: Dār al-Fikr al-ʿArabī, 1977.

Jaffer, Tariq. *Rāzī: Master of Qurʾānic Interpretation and Theological Reasoning*. Oxford: Oxford University Press, 2015.

Jeffery, A. *Muqaddimatān fī ʿulūm al-Qurʾān*. Cairo: Maktabat al-Khānjī, 1954.

Lawson, T. B. 'Akhbārī Shīʿī Approaches to Tafsīr'. In: G. R. Hawting and A. A. Shareef (eds.). *Approaches to the Qurʾān*, pp. 173–210. London: Routledge, 1993.

Makkī ibn Abī Ṭālib. *al-Hidāya ilā bulūgh al-nihāya fī ʿilm maʿānī al-Qurʾān wa-tafsīrihi wa-aḥkāmihi wa-jumal min funūn ʿulūmihi*. 13 vols. United Arab Emirates: Shāriqa University, 2008.

al-Māturīdī, Abū Manṣūr *Taʾwīlāt al-Qurʾān*. Ed. A. Vanlioglu et al. 18 vols. Istanbul: Dār al-Mīzān, 2005–11.

Naguib, S. 'Guiding the Sound Mind: Ebu's-Suʿūd's Tafsīr and Rhetorical Interpretation of the Qurʾān in the Post-classical Period', *Journal of Ottoman Studies* 42 (2013), 1–52.

Nguyen, M. *Sufi Master and Qurʾān Scholar: Abū al-Qāsim al-Qushayrī and the* Laṭāʾif al-Ishārāt. Oxford: Oxford University Press, 2012.

Ragheb, F. 'In Search of a Māturīdī Manuscript', graduate seminar paper submitted to Maria Subtelny, University of Toronto, 2012.

Rippin, A. 'The Present Status of Tafsīr Studies', *Muslim World* 72/3–4 (1982), 224–38.

Rippin, A. 'What Defines a (Pre-modern) Shiʿī Tafsīr?' In: F. Daftary and G. Miskinzoda (eds.). *The Study of Shiʿi Islam: History, Theology and Law*, pp. 95–112. London: IB Tauris, 2013.

Rippin, A. (forthcoming). 'al-Bursawī's *Rūḥ al-bayān* and the Genealogy of the Tafsīr Discipline'.

Rufaydah, I. *al-Naḥw wa kutub al-tafsīr*. 2 vols. Benghazi: Dār al-Jamāhiriyya, 1990.

Saleh, W. A. *The Formation of the Classical Tafsīr Tradition: The Qurʾān Commentary of al-Thaʿlabī (d. 427/1035)*. Leiden: Brill, 2004.

Saleh, W. A. 'The Last of the Nishapuri School of Tafsīr: Al-Wahidi (d. 468/1076) and his Significance in the History of Qurʾānic Exegesis', *Journal of the American Oriental Society* 126 (2006), 223–43.

Saleh, W. A. 'A Fifteenth-Century Muslim Hebraist: al-Biqāʿī and his Defense of Using the Bible to Interpret the Qurʾān', *Speculum* 83 (2008a), 629–54.

Saleh, W. A. *In Defense of the Bible: A Critical Edition and an Introduction to al-Biqāʿī's Bible Treatise*. Leiden: Brill, 2008b.

Saleh, W. A. 'Preliminary Remarks on the Historiography of *Tafsīr* in Arabic: A History of the Book Approach', *Journal of Qurʾanic Studies* 12 (2010), 6–40.

Saleh, W. A. 'The Gloss as Intellectual History: The *Ḥāshiyah* on *al-Kashshāf*', *Oriens* 41 (2013a), 217–59.

Saleh, W. A. 'The Introduction of al-Wāḥidī's *al-Basīṭ*: An Edition, Translation and Commentary'. In: Karen Bauer (ed.). *Aims, Methods and Contexts of Qurʾanic Exegesis (2nd/8th–9th/15th Centuries)*, pp. 67–100. Oxford: Oxford University Press, 2013b.

Saleh, W. A. 'The Introduction to Wāḥidī's *al-Basīṭ*: An Edition, Translation and Commentary'. In: Andreas Görke and Johanna Pink (ed.). *Tafsīr and Islamic Intellectual History: Exploring the Boundaries of a Genre*, pp. 67–100. Oxford: Oxford University Press, 2015.
Saleh, W. A. 'Rereading al-Ṭabarī through al-Māturīdī: New Light on the Third Century Hijrī', *Journal of Qur'anic Studies* 18/2 (2016), 180–209.
Shah, Mustafa (ed.). *Tafsīr: Interpreting the Qur'ān. Critical Concepts in Islamic Studies*, 1:1–15. London: Routledge, 2013a.
Shah, Mustafa. 'Al-Ṭabarī and the Dynamics of *Tafsīr*: Theological Dimensions of a Legacy', *Journal of Qur'anic Studies* 15 (2013b), 83–139.
al-Thaʿlabī, Aḥmad ibn Muḥammad (2002). *al-Kashf wa'l-bayān*. Ed. Abī Muḥammad ibn ʿĀshūr. 10 vols. Beirut: Dār Iḥyāʾ al-Turāth al-ʿArabī.
Vishanoff, D. R. *The Formation of Islamic Hermeneutics: How Sunni Legal Theories Imagined Revealed Law*. New Haven, CT: American Oriental Society, 2011.
Zadeh, T. *The Vernacular Qur'ān: Translation and the Rise of Persian Exegesis*. Oxford: Oxford University Press, 2012.
al-Ziriklī, Khayr al-Dīn. *Al-Aʿlām*. 8 vols. Beirut: Dār al-ʿIlm li'l-Malāyyīn, 2002.

CHAPTER 45

THE CORPORA OF *ISRĀʾĪLIYYĀT*

ROBERTO TOTTOLI

The presence of narratives recounting biblical stories and Jewish and Christian sacred history in the Qur'an, ranging from the creation of Adam to Jesus, has prompted the circulation and diffusion of traditions and reports on these topics among early Muslim scholars. This material, today usually referred to as *isrāʾīliyyāt*, its origin, and its use in exegetical activities and in Muslim literary genres have been the topic of differing evaluations and various studies.

The beginnings of Muslim literary activity attest the large reception and inclusion of narrative enlargements and their use in almost all the genres in the form of extra-canonical reports and traditions. Narrative exegesis was most probably the first exegetical approach and the most popular topic of the new religion. However, with the emergence of hadith criticism in the early tradition, doubts were raised about the provenance of this material, and discussions about their reliability were given further impetus through the efforts of scholars such as Ibn Taymiyya (d. 728/1328) and his pupils, and further in modern times from the end of the nineteenth century till today, culminating in the complete rejection of the *isrāʾīliyyāt*. Western studies, on their side, while discussing and in general agreeing with this evaluation of the origin of the *isrāʾīliyyāt*, have adopted different approaches. Early studies focused in particular on the Qur'an narratives and later traditions, looking for parallels with Jewish, Christian, and Near Eastern beliefs. Only in the last decades, with the emergence of a differing attitude to the examination of the Qur'an and to later narratives, have studies started to consider the topic under differing terms and not only in terms of seeking parallels or examining issues of derivation.

Isrāʾīliyyāt as the Early Exegetical Approach

There is general agreement that the first exegesis of the Qur'an consisted of reports and traditions mainly concerned with the prophets and messengers preceding Muḥammad. It is commonly maintained that storytellers and converts from Judaism and Christianity in particular played a role in the diffusion of these topics among early Muslims. The aim was to explain the text and, along with this, circulate edifying stories about prophets together with the description of the acts of the Prophet Muḥammad. Scholars such as Ignaz Goldziher (1920: 1–54) and John Wansbrough (1977: 122–48) agree on this and though some Muslim traditions attest an early general hostility towards exegetical activity as such, other reports and attestations state that 'haggadic' exegesis (to use Wansbrough's words) formed the core of early exegetical activity.

Exegetical concern with elucidating Qur'anic passages accounted for the emergence and diffusion of this material. However, some other reasons have been suggested. Early Muslims also used the popular character of many of these early reports with the aim of spreading Islamic themes and conceptions. This attitude was also prompted by early converts to Islam and intermediaries who could not but introduce to the new religion their previous religious knowledge and sensibilities. Western studies, following Islamic data, mention and list the major figures quoted in this regard. Among the converts from Judaism one relevant name is that of ʿAbd Allāh ibn Salām (Wasserstrom 1995: 175–8), but the most important figure is Kaʿb al-Aḥbār, whose name appears in connection with many reports, and emerges in the criticism by Ibn Kathīr (d. 774/1373) and contemporary Muslim opponents of the *isrāʾīliyyāt* (Tottoli 1999: 209). One further name to quote is no doubt that of Wahb ibn Munabbih (d. 110/728 or 114/732), a Yemeni of Persian descent who gained wide renown for his knowledge of biblical lore and texts, to whom even a Book of *isrāʾīliyyāt* is attributed. This is not the original title but most probably a title attributed to it in later times (cf. Khoury 1972: 203f.). Along with converts, some companions of Muḥammad are also described as displaying a peculiar proficiency in the knowledge and thus diffusion of the *isrāʾīliyyāt*, such as Ibn ʿAbbās (Lowin 2006: 11–14).

Notwithstanding the question of the origin of this material, many scholars underline that the spread of the *isrāʾīliyyāt* reveals an early communality between Islam and other religious cultures. According to Wasserstrom (1995), for instance, the use of *isrāʾīliyyāt*, in the form of popular, widespread reports of Jewish and to a lesser extent Christian origin, in literary genres such as the *qiṣaṣ al-anbiyāʾ* underlines his theory of early symbiosis between Jews and Muslims. Other studies also suggest that this situation led to a real sharing of narratives and knowledge before the emergence of separating lines (Rubin 1999).

Regarding the specific question of attitudes, an early openness is no doubt a probable explanation for the diffusion of reports and the use of the materials later defined as *isrāʾīliyyāt* and their introduction into Islamic literary genres. There is a substantial agreement on this among scholars (cf. Kister 1972). This receptivity came to an end after the first centuries when new methods for evaluating religious traditions and the importance attached to sound sayings going back to the Prophet emerged. This most probably took place during the third/ninth to fourth/tenth centuries (cf. Pregill 2008: 221), while some other scholars have suggested an earlier date (Newby 1979), maintaining that this occurred after the time of Muḥammad ibn Isḥāq (d. 150/767), who was the author not only of the major biography of the Prophet but also a lost work on creation and the prophets.

Along with this, the use together with the spread of the *isrāʾīliyyāt* was no doubt inspired by inner Muslim dynamics. As suggested in more recent studies, the prophetic genealogy and competing views around it constituted contentious issues in Shīʿī-Sunnī rivalries (Rubin 1979; Kohlberg 1980). Political concerns in the definition of history as ranging from the creation of the world to the Muslim Empire must have been propelled by caliphal interests and this no doubt prompted the definition of pre-Islamic history around the stories of the prophets as mentioned in the Qur'an and enriched by *isrāʾīliyyāt*.

Muslim traditional criticism gives a partially similar portrait. Though usually imposing later criteria for assessing the soundness of reports, it nevertheless attests that the circulation of *isrāʾīliyyāt* in early Islam was prolific for a number of reasons, as underlined above by Western studies. Questions of soundness and formal criticism according to the criteria which came to be defined on how to appraise previous reports and traditions led to doubts being raised about this material. Later criticism thus erected a wall to the introduction of most of this material into hadith literature but it circulated in *tafsīr* works and in the collections of universal history along with other genres of religious concerns (*zuhd*, *faḍāʾil*, *qiṣaṣ al-anbiyāʾ* books, etc.) which have always displayed a more liberal attitude toward it.

Western Attitudes: Studies Between Qur'an Narratives and Later Traditions

The Qur'anic and extra-Qur'anic narratives on the *isrāʾīliyyāt* dealing with the biblical patriarchs and prophets have attracted the attention of scholars since the beginning of modern studies on Islam. The early approaches however focused on the Qur'an and discussed possible relations between holy texts and other religious literatures and traditions. These early studies sought to trace the relationship and thus possible connections between Qur'anic contents and biblical and other traditional lore with the aim of understanding the formative environment in which Islam emerged. This general concern was more the result of Western approaches towards the study of religions and their origin than a deliberate attempt to undermine the Islamic religious sources. Notwithstanding attitudes and concerns, this all resulted in scholars taking an avid interest in the study of the Qur'anic narratives on prophets and history preceding Muḥammad and the later literary traditions which augmented stories and reports around these Qur'anic narratives.

Following the tendency to connect the Qur'an to the figure of Muḥammad and to his milieu, early studies tended to display the same approach towards the Qur'an and the *isrāʾīliyyāt* that originated around the text, though a distinction between Qur'anic contents and later literature and traditions has always been clear. The first epoch-making essay by Abraham Geiger which appeared in 1833 traced motifs, concepts, and terms in the Qur'an displaying clearer Jewish parallels, although he refrained from speaking of absolute borrowing. As a matter of fact, this attitude—that is, connecting Judaism to an imperial religious community such as Islam—was the result of the process of the emancipation of European Jewish scholars such as Geiger rather than an overtly negative attitude towards Islam. The work of Ignaz Goldziher, for example, attests a general sympathy and admiration for Islam and in his writing he underlined similitudes and parallels between Judaism and Islam. Other works adopted this approach with less sensitivity, simply tracing back Qur'anic stories to biblical antecedents (cf. Speyer 1961); others highlighted a Christian nexus (Bell 1926). This approach, albeit applied with greater sophistication toward the Qur'anic narratives and the wide range of Jewish, Christian, and Near Eastern sources, is also displayed in more recent studies. Reynolds, for instance, has dedicated and collected various studies with a specific concern for the parallels between some Qur'anic contents and Eastern Christian literature, and he is among a long list of scholars producing this kind of research (cf. Reynolds 2010: 3–36).

A number of studies have analysed not only the Qur'an, but related topics which feature in Islamic literature. The first work of this kind was no doubt the collection of translated stories covering the creation to Jesus collected by Gustav Weil (1846) and mainly based upon the *Qiṣaṣ al-anbiyāʾ (Stories of the Prophets)* by al-Kisāʾī (*c.* sixth/twelfth century). Further studies examined parallels and common motifs of Muslim literature, usually underlining the strict relation and at times direct dependence of Muslim narratives and *isrāʾīliyyāt* upon Jewish and also, to a certain extent, Christian sources. The specific attitudes in this approach are however different from author to author though the general outline was common. Along with a more comprehensive and rich discussion such as in Max Grünbaum (1893), we have also a crude listing of Muslim reports and their supposed sources such as in Sidersky (1933), who firmly maintained that reports found in the work of the historian al-Ṭabarī (d. 310/923) derived directly from the Talmud or other Jewish sources. More recently, in this regard, not much difference can be found in the position of Schwarzbaum (1982) who still promoted the idea of derivation, maintaining that in any case Islamic reports bear testimony of now lost Jewish legends. Adopting a similar view, Adam Silverstein has posited that the Islamic *isrāʾīliyyāt* materials preserve ancient Jewish and pre-Islamic lost traditions (Silverstein 2018).

The Bible in Early Islam

The Qur'an and early Islamic society were aware of not only the circulation of reports, narratives, and traditions concerning biblical lore, but also were acquainted with the proper text of the Bible. Notwithstanding the differing opinions about the circulation of the early Arabic translation of the Bible, early Islamic traditions draw attention to Muslim authors who knew of biblical texts and even quoted passages. The *Kitāb al-dīn wa'l-dawla* by the Nestorian convert to Islam ʿAlī ibn Rabbān al-Ṭabarī (d. 251/865) and the *Aʿlām al-nubuwwa* by Ibn Qutayba (d. 276/889) are the first works to quote passages from the Bible in Arabic (Schmidtke 2011; cf. Burge 2017: 310–11). The circulation of these translations was no doubt prompted by the relevance that the biblical text has in the Qur'an, where it appears as a revealed scripture notwithstanding the Qur'anic concept that the actual Jewish and Christian communities had altered its content. As recent studies have demonstrated, however, the theory of the alteration or corruption of the early scriptures is not clear-cut in early exegetical interpretation and seems to point to the belief that a supposed faithful biblical text was used in polemics against Muḥammad by Jews and Christians of his time (Nickel 2011). Further, as rightly maintained by McAuliffe (1996), the acceptance of the Bible as a sacred text and one containing a revelation on one side and prevailing views concerning its corruption on the other, are no doubt at the origin of a contradictory attitude in Muslim traditions in regard to it: although scholars revered the text, they also showed caution and wariness when dealing with it. It is to be noted that the recent research of Saleh (2008) has contributed to highlighting how knowledge and use of the biblical texts survived in Islamic scholarship in later times.

In general terms, it appears that biblical quotations and passages attributed to the Bible in Islamic sources are not usually connected to the proper *isrāʾīliyyāt* and related Islamic reports. In fact Islamic literature and criticism very seldom connect later exegetical reports and traditions to the Bible. Though in early times all this material most probably circulated as a composite body of literary dicta, with the emergence of hadith criticism and a better knowledge of the Bible, notwithstanding the discussions about the origin of reports and narratives, Islamic authors and critics sought to isolate and distinguish the different materials.

The Emergence of the Term *Isrāʾīliyyāt* in Islamic Literature and Western Studies

The use of the term *isrāʾīliyyāt* in relation to the narratives and reports dealing with topics related to proper or supposed biblical prophets has a specific history which reflects changing Muslim attitudes through the ages. Early attestations date only from the fourth/tenth century and from then onwards the term appears regularly in later literature (see Tottoli 1999; Tottoli forthcoming). It came to be used with a strong polemical connotation only with Ibn Taymiyya and his followers (cf. Hoover 2019). They were the first to introduce the category of *isrāʾīliyyāt* as reports of foreign origins of which there is no need; the implication is that these reports proliferated over the centuries within exegetical literature and other genres. Their criticism stemmed from the fact that these reports were presented as emanating from converts and figures from the early tradition such as Kaʿb al-Aḥbār, ʿAbd Allāh ibn Salām, and Wahb ibn Munabbih; it was not just the contents of these reports that were being disputed (Firestone 1990: 14–19). In fact, notwithstanding his definition of *isrāʾīliyyāt*, the exegetical novelty connected to the use of the term in Ibn Kathīr (d. 774/1373) was underlined by Norman Calder and Andrew Rippin. Calder concluded that the term *isrāʾīliyyāt* as used by Ibn Kathīr has nothing to do with the origins of a story and reflects a theological attitude (Calder 1993: 137 n. 37). The same arguments are propounded by Rippin, who states that the term came into 'wide circulation as a pejorative term in *tafsīr*—material which is not to be accepted as valid in interpretation' (Rippin 1993: 253). Both of the contributions introduced for the first time the perspective of exegetical traditions emerging with Ibn Kathīr and thus identified a problem in its use in Western studies in connection to its diffusion in Muslim sources.

Ibn Kathīr's attitude, however, did not prevail in the following ages. In fact, after the eighth/fourteenth century Muslim authors continued to use the term though without implying a critical connotation, but in general simply to label unsound reports. Thus the term never went out of use but it was only towards the end of the nineteenth century that it came to the fore in the works of Muslim reformers and exegetes such as Siddiq Hasan Khan (d. 1890) and Muḥammad ʿAbdūh (d. 1905). It gained growing relevance after them, and according to Nettler (1999) it was Muḥammad Rashīd Riḍā (d. 1935) who renewed criticism of this source, pointing to supposed schemes prompted by converts from Judaism (such as Wahb and Kaʿb) against Islam. After Rashīd Riḍā, *isrāʾīliyyāt* became thus a sort of reference term; it came into general use, when rejecting early materials and reports, to dismiss them as *isrāʾīliyyāt*. In particular this took place in the second half of the twentieth century also in connection with a general polemical attitude connecting the role of the early converts from Judaism to the birth of the modern state of Israel.

Though not much attention has been devoted to this, modern Muslim and contemporary attitudes should be considered also in relation to the Western criticism of this material and it is not by chance that the use of the term acquired growing relevance when it also started to appear in Western studies. The first to make use of it in a systematic way appears to be Ignaz Goldziher (see e.g. 1878: 347) who was also the first scholar to give a definition of its meaning which has remained influential today. According to Goldziher (1902: 325), who relied upon primary sources, the term indicates firstly the post-Qur'anic stories about prophets and early history which found their way into serious commentaries and literature; secondly, stories and legends not properly related to prophets and to Jews, but which fit the chronology of early times; and thirdly, fantastic stories, such as those related to the marvels of the sea, as quoted by the classical works of the geographer and historian al-Masʿūdī (d. 345/956).

More recent works have glossed over the question of the meaning and use of the term *isrāʾīliyyāt*. Some scholars have in fact underlined how its meaning is not so clear and this is due to the fact that exegetes and works of Muslim literature made use of it in different ways (McAuliffe 1998: 146). Regarding this, we find the term mentioned by scholarly literature with differing meanings. *Isrāʾīliyyāt* is usually quoted in scholarly literature to identify narratives on creation and 'biblical and quasi-biblical material' (Pregill 2008: 215; cf. Firestone 1990: 13–14). But Maghen (2006: 73), for instance, simply states that the term is a synonym of the *qiṣaṣ al-anbiyāʾ* literary genre—a genre, in his definition, deemed to 'edify the Muslim masses for centuries after Muḥammad's death'. Among recent studies, the most comprehensive discussion of the meaning of the term is found in Shari Lowin (2006: 7–18). In her opinion the *isrāʾīliyyāt* are hadith-type accounts which function as narrative supplements, connected to Banū Isrāʾīl (Israelites) and narratives on the prophets, *qiṣaṣ al-anbiyāʾ*. However, Lowin does allude to problems in the definition of the proper meaning and use of the term.

Recent Approaches to Exegetical Narratives

The most relevant recent developments in the field of the study of *isrāʾīliyyāt* and exegetical narratives around biblical figures are represented by the general change of perspectives in approaches to the synthesis of this material. First of all scholars now prefer to trace a clear line between the Qur'anic contents and later traditions, fully recognizing the inner and historical differences and the specific peculiarities of them. In the study of the later traditions, ranging from exegetical literature to all the other genres, an approach which underlines the originality and creativity of Muslim versions in the re-elaboration of the Jewish, Christian, and other versions is now established. This attitude, though already dealt with and repeated in the works by Bernard Heller (cf. e.g. 1934) since the first half of the twentieth century (as already pointed out by Wheeler 1998a; Alexander 2000: 13), is common to many studies. These studies usually maintain how some rabbinical parallel traditions are not at the origin of the Islamic reports and lore, but were part of a dynamic dialogue to the extent that it is the later Jewish and Christian literatures which reflect Islamic influence in some cases (see e.g. Halperin 1995; Wheeler 1998a, 1988b). Intertextuality and synergy are the keywords to understanding this new approach to the history of early Islam and the relation of the *isrāʾīliyyāt* to Jewish and Christian lore and traditions. Major contributions in this line of thought are offered by Wasserstrom (1995), who discussed it in terms of symbiosis; and Rubin (1999), who underlined how the imagery of the Jews and biblical stories in early Islam remained functional to highlight the Arab origin of Islam. Scholars now prefer to speak of the Islamic versions in terms of the specific evolution of preceding themes (Lassner 1993: 125) or, for instance, of their specific creativity (Alexander 2000: 12).

Lowin dates this new perspective and approach stating that 'over the past 25 years or so, a shift toward a more nuanced view of the Muslim–Jewish exegetical relationship has been at work' (Lowin 2011: 224). Pregill, in fact, though underlining the relevance of the studies appearing in the second half of the twentieth century, noticed how until the 1960s scholars had reappraised but not changed attitudes in terms of accepting a Jewish and Christian influence on Islam (Pregill 2008: 219).

New Lines of Research and Perspectives

Notwithstanding the new attitude displayed by researchers and the refinement of approaches, many lines of further study and inquiry remain. A first point to underline is that though attitudes change, most scholars are still working on a narrow range of sources and the new tools of research (electronic databases, archives, etc.) are yet to provide common ground for scholars working in this field. Furthermore, but also a consequence of this, it is to be noted that Islamic studies have not produced reference works or indexes of motifs, narratives, and reports on these topics. An accessible record of the various versions and different narratives diffused in Muslim literature as a whole would be very helpful to Islamicists and scholars in general and would contribute to a more comprehensive evaluation of the meaning and extent of the diffusion of the *isrāʾīliyyāt* materials in exegesis and in the other literary genres. This question recalls other evident shortcoming in scholarly research in the field: a general indifference to the later augmentation of these narratives. Late medieval and early modern works, also including those produced in languages other than Arabic, have received little attention by scholars. This later literature attests to how the traditions about the prophets and the *isrāʾīliyyāt* were further elaborated and diffused in all Muslim societies (cf. Tottoli 2003).

Another issue arising from the study of the corpora of *isrāʾīliyyāt* is the fact that the discussion in scholarly literature of the question of *isrāʾīliyyāt* is typically broached in terms of the debate about the historicity of these materials or indeed their theological import. The question of borrowing, together with the counter-attempts to accentuate the influence of Islamic versions upon later rabbinical or Christian literature, draws attention to the role played by literary peculiarities. A new and much welcomed sensibility towards narratives as literature rather than historical attestations is starting to emerge in more recent studies and needs to be enhanced. For instance, pursuing this line of thought, Pregill (2008: 237) emphasized the need to understand the figure of Wahb in Muslim literature more as a symbolic role than a historical one. Furthermore, Marianna Klar (2009) has demonstrated how literature such as the *Qiṣaṣ al-anbiyāʾ* (Stories of the prophets) by al-Thaʿlabī can be analysed not only as a repository of previous reports but as an authorial construction reflecting specific attitudes in delineating the characters constituting it. Along with this, some other scholars have properly underlined how it is not only through high authorial lines that interconnections and interrelationship acted, but also at other levels. According to this conception, Goldman (1995) underlined the common traits in the Middle Eastern area through the ages and the various religious traditions in folkloric themes including narratives on biblical prophets and figures.

The new attitudes emerging and, above all, a new consciousness of the useful differing approaches needed in dealing with this literature are all promising developments. New studies are thus awaited to better understand across a range of historical contexts and settings the inner literary dynamics, theological import, and relevance of the so-called *isrāʾīliyyāt*.

Bibliography

Alexander, P. S. 'Jewish Traditions in Early Islam'. In: G. R. Hawting, J. M. Mojaddedi, and A. Samely (eds.). *Studies in Islamic and Middle Eastern Texts and Traditions in Memory of Norman Calder*, pp. 11–29. Oxford: Oxford University Press, 2000.

Bell, R. *The Origin of Islam in its Christian Environment*. London: Macmillan, 1926.

Burge, S. R. 'Islamic'. In: E. Ziolkowski (ed.). *The Bible in Folklore Wordwide: A Handbook of Biblical Reception Jewish, European Christian, and Islamic Folklores*, pp. 307–29. Berlin and Boston: De Gruyter, 2017.

Calder, N. 'Tafsīr from Ṭabarī to Ibn Kathīr. Problems in the Description of a Genre, Illustrated with Reference to the Story of Abraham'. In: G. R. Hawting and A.-K. A. Shareef (eds.). *Approaches to the Qurʾān*, pp. 102–40. London and New York: Routledge, 1993.

Firestone, R. *Journeys in Holy Lands: The Evolution of the Abraham-Ishmael Legends in Islamic Exegesis*. Albany: State University of New York Press, 1990.

Geiger, A. *Was hat Mohammed aus den Judenthume aufgenommen?* Bonn: Baaden, 1833 (Eng. trans. *Judaism and Islam*. Madras, 1898).

Goldman, S. *The Wiles of Women/The Wiles of Men, Joseph and Potiphar's Wife in Ancient Near Eastern, Jewish, and Islamic Folklore*. Albany: State University of New York Press, 1995.

Goldziher, I. *Die Richtungen der Islamischen Koranauslegung*. Leiden: Brill, 1920 (Eng. trans. *Schools of Koranic Commentators*, Wiesbaden, 2006).

Goldziher, I. 'Mélanges judéo-arabes. IX. Isrāʾīliyyāt', *Revue des études juives* 44 (1902), 63–6 (repr. in *Gesammelte Studien*. (ed.). J. Desomogyi, 4:323–6. Hildesheim, 1970).

Goldziher, I. 'Über muhammedanische Polemik gegen *ahl al-kitāb*', *Zeitschrift der Deutschen Mörgenlandischen Gesellschaft* 32 (1878), 341–87 (repr. in *Gesammelte Schriften*, 2:1–47. Hildesheim, 1968).

Halperin, D. J. 'Can Muslim Narrative be Used as Commentary on Jewish Tradition?' In: R. L. Nettler (ed.). *Medieval and Modern Perspectives on Muslim-Jewish Relations*, pp. 73–88. Luxembourg: Horwood, 1995.

Heller, B. 'The Relation of Aggadah to Islamic Legends', *Muslim World* 24 (1934), 281–6.

Hoover, J. 'What Would Ibn Taymiyya Make of Intertextual Study of the Qur'an? The Challenge of the *Isrāʾīliyyāt*'. In: H. Zellentin (ed.). *The Qur'an's Reformation of Judaism and Christianity: Return to the Origins*, pp. 25–30. London and New York: Routledge, 2019.

Khoury, R. G. *Wahb ibn Munabbih*. Wiesbaden: Harrassowitz Verlag, 1972.

Kister, Meir J. '*Ḥaddithū ʿan banī isrāʾīla wa-lā ḥaraja*: A Study of an Early Tradition', *Israel Oriental Studies* 2 (1972), 215–39.

Klar, M. O. *Interpretating al-Thaʿlabī's* Tales of the Prophets: *Temptation, Responsibility and Loss*. London and New York: Routledge, 2009.

Kohlberg, Etan. 'Some Shiʿi Views of the Antediluvian World', *Studia Islamica* 52 (1980), 41–66.

Lassner, J. *Demonizing the Queen of Sheba: Boundaries of Gender and Culture in Postbiblical and Medieval Islam*. Chicago: University of Chicago Press, 1993.

Lowin, S. L. *The Making of a Forefather: Abraham in Islamic and Jewish Exegetical Narratives*. Leiden and Boston: Brill, 2006.

Lowin, S. L. 'Abraham in Islamic and Jewish Exegesis', *Religion Compass* 5–6 (2011), 224–35.

Maghen, Z. *After Hardship Cometh Ease*. Berlin and New York: De Gruyter, 2006.

McAuliffe, J. D. 'Assessing the *Isrāʾīliyyāt*: and Exegetical Conundrum'. In: S. Leder (ed.). *Story-Telling in the Framework of Non-Fictional Arabic Literature*, pp. 345–69. Wiesbaden: Harrassowitz Verlag, 1998.

McAuliffe, J. D. 'The Qur'ānic Context of Muslim Biblical Scholarship', *Islam and Muslim-Christian Relations* 7 (1996), 141–58.

Nettler, R. L. 'Early Islam, Modern Islam and Judaism: The *Isrāʾīliyyāt* in Modern Islamic Thought'. In: *Muslim-Jewish Encounters: Intellectual Traditions and Modern Politics*, pp. 1–14. Amsterdam: Harwood Academic, 1999.

Newby, G. D. '*Tafsīr Isrāʾīliyyāt*', *Journal of the American Academy of Religion* 47 (1979), 685–97.

Nickel, G. *Narratives of Tempering in the Earliest Commentaries on the Qur'ān*. Leiden and Boston: Brill, 2011.

Pregill, M. '*Isrāʾīliyyāt*, myth, and Pseudoepigraphy: Wahb ibn Munabbih and the Early Islamic Versions of the Fall of Adam and Eve', *Jerusalem Studies in Arabic and Islam* 34 (2008), 215–84.

Reynolds, G. S. *The Qurʾān and its Biblical Subtext*. London and New York: Routledge, 2010.

Rippin, A. 'Interpreting the Bible through the Qur'ān'. In: G. R. Hawting and A.-K. A. Shareef (eds.). *Approaches to the Qur'ān*, pp. 249–59. London and New York: Routledge, 1993.

Rubin, U. *Between Bible and Qurʾān: The Children of Israel and the Islamic Self-Image*. Princeton: The Darwin Press, 1999.

Rubin, U. 'Prophets and Progenitors in the Early Shiʿa Tradition', *Jerusalem Studies in Arabic and Islam* 1 (1979), 41–65.

Saleh, W. 'A Fifteenth-Century Muslim Hebraist: al-Biqāʿī and his Defense of Using the Bible to Interpret the Qur'ān', *Speculum: A Journal of Medieval Studies* 83 (2008), 629–54.

Schmidtke, S. 'The Muslim Reception of Biblical Materials: Ibn Qutayba and his *ʿAlām al-nubuwwa*', *Islam and Muslim-Christian Relations* 22 (2011), 249–74.

Schwarzbaum, H. *Biblical and Extra-Biblical Legends in Islamic Folk-Literature*. Walldorf-Hessen: Verl. für Orientkunde H. Vorndran, 1982.

Sidersky, D. *Les Origines des légendes Musulmanes dans le Coran et dans les Vies des Prophètes*. Paris: Geuthner, 1933.

Silverstein, A. *Veiling Esther, Unveiling Her Story: The Reception of a Biblical Book in Islamic Lands*. Oxford: Oxford University Press, 2018.

Speyer, H. *Die Biblischen Erzählungen im Qoran*. Hildesheim: Olms, 1961 (1st edn. 1931).

Tottoli, R. 'New Material on the Use and Meaning of the Term *isrāʾīliyyāt*', *Jerusalem Studies in Arabic and Islam*, forthcoming.

Tottoli, R. 'Origin and Use of the Term *isrāʾīliyyāt* in Muslim Literature', *Arabica* 46 (1999), 193–210.

Tottoli, R. 'The Story of Jesus and the Skull in Arabic Literature: The Emergence and Growth of a Religious Tradition', *Jerusalem Studies in Arabic and Islam* 28 (2003), 225–59.

Wansbrough, J. *Quranic Studies: Sources and Methods of Scriptural Interpretation*. Oxford: Oxford University Press, 1977.
Wasserstrom, S. M. *Between Muslim and Jew: The Problem of Symbiosis under Early Islam*. Princeton: Princeton University Press, 1995.
Weil, G. *The Bible, the Koran, and the Talmud; or Biblical Legends of the Mussulmans*. London: Longman, Brown, Green, and Longmans, 1846 (trans. from German, *Die Biblischen Legenden der Muselmänner*. Frankfurt, 1845).
Wheeler, B. 'Moses or Alexander? Early Islamic Exegesis of Qur'ān 18:60–65', *Journal of Near Eastern Studies* 57 (1998a), 191–215.
Wheeler, B. 'The Jewish Origins of Qurʾān 18:65–82? Reexamining Arent Jan Wensinck's Theory', *Journal of the American Oriental Society* 118 (1998b), 153–71.

CHAPTER 46

CONTEMPORARY *TAFSĪR*

The Rise of Scriptural Theology

WALID A. SALEH

CONTEMPORARY *tafsīr* is a new and hybrid phenomenon. Despite its structural similarities to medieval *tafsīr*, it is markedly different, such that one has to reconsider its function and its very nature. This hybridity is the result of several factors. The manner in which *tafsīr* is accessed, utilized, and disseminated has been transformed. Through the print revolution since the mid-nineteenth century, followed by audio cassettes, TV shows, and finally the new medium of the internet, a new populist genre has emerged. The internet has also made the extant *tafsīr* corpus in its entirety available to researchers, which is unprecedented in the history of the tradition. Following upon (but distinct from) these developments in access, dissemination, and audience, *tafsīr* also has a new function, resulting from the new ideological uses to which it is being put in the modern Islamic world. These developments have transformed the genre and positioned it as the pre-eminent discipline in Islamic literatures, whether scholarly or populist.

In this chapter I make three main observations about the nature of contemporary Qur'anic interpretation in modern Islamic societies, which set it apart from the previous history of *tafsīr*. The first is the rise of scriptural theology in the Islamic world, which is performed mostly through *tafsīr*. The second is the availability of a meaningfully representative portion of the *tafsīr* corpus, first in print and then—and this is really the deciding factor—through the internet. The final characteristic of contemporary *tafsīr* is its proliferation in various Islamicate languages, on an equal footing with Arabic. These three characteristics of contemporary *tafsīr* have resulted in the formation of a generative and culturally central field. *Tafsīr* has become the major bearer and means of negotiating the cultural tribulations of modernity and its transformative powers in the Islamic world.

Most scholarship to date on 'modern' *tafsīr* covers what are in essence 'modernizing' approaches to *tafsīr*, while being oblivious to or unwilling to address texts that do not correspond to this outlook. This modernizing framework still holds sway over how we approach Islamic intellectual history. The conflation of contemporaneity with modernity has only recently been challenged by Johanna Pink (2010a, 2010b), who exposes this framework's unhistorical foundations and thus calls into question the presuppositions of how we study *tafsīr* in modern times. The first scholar to offer a more systematic analysis of modern *tafsīr* is Aḥmīdah Nayfar, whose book first appeared in Arabic and then was translated into French (Nayfar 1997; Ennaifer 1998). Pink and Nayfar have reopened the question of what modern *tafsīr* is, and have allowed us to look afresh at the modern period in a more global way. Indeed, the history of *tafsīr* in the modern Islamic world cannot suffice with a rehashed version of the story of Muḥammad ʿAbdūh or Naṣr Abū Zayd. Perhaps the most glaring blind spot in the historical investigation of *tafsīr* in the modern Islamic world has been the complete negligence of the print revolution and its impact on the nature of Islamic disciplines. Further, despite the fact that most of the widely read works of *tafsīr* in modern times are from the medieval past, no attempt has thus far been made to understand the place of the 'medieval' in a modern setting. Why are medieval works still able to command such attention and authority? More importantly, why is *tafsīr* so religiously central in the modern Islamic world?

The Demise of *Kalām* and the Rise of Scriptural Theology

The demise of *kalām* in the wake of modernity in the Islamic world was an unceremonious affair; indeed, no one has noticed its whimpering end. Of course, *kalām* is still studied, and one will come across the remnants of Ashʿarism here and there. Indeed, the claim is made that neo-Muʿtazilī Muslim theologians have recently emerged—but *kalām* has ceased to provide the language used to describe the world or to understand the Muslim's relationship to God. The most prevalent form of theological works (*ʿaqīda* literature) is Wahhabi pamphlets and books, but these are markedly anti-*kalām* and anti-Ashʿarī in method, style, and vocabulary. Most Muslims today are believers in free will, and would be horrified to realize the extent of predestination's roots in the mainstream Islamic past—although this is also the result of the inability of modern Muslims to understand what the medieval philosophers understood predestination to mean. The very nature of what constitutes proof of faith has now changed. Most prominently, the nature of the Qur'an and its miraculous characteristics, cast now in its predicative scientific powers rather than its *naẓm* (coherence), eloquence, or inimitability, has so reconfigured the proof of faith that one has to count the 'scientific miracle' of the Qur'an as a new universal Islamic dogma on a par with the prophetic mission of Muḥammad and the other cardinal beliefs of modern Muslims. The reconfiguration of Islamic theology and its total destabilization due to the atrophy of its older tools has meant that the new theological methods and modes of discourse have escaped our attention. Modern Islamic theology is a discipline still looking for a name and a study.

Yet, theology in the Islamic world is thriving, albeit in the different mode and through the different genre of scriptural interpretation. This scripturalist approach to theology was an important step in efforts to reconfigure Islamic faith in the wake of internal pressures, such as the Wahhabi movement (the first modern scriptural revolution in Islam), and external pressures, such as the impact of the scientific revolution. Nonetheless, one cannot ascribe this tendency to engage in theology through scriptural interpretation solely to the encounter with Europe. It is clear that the Islamic tradition has long had a periodically resurgent radical underbelly centred on literal readings of the Qur'an and Sunna. The most important results of this reconfiguring of theology is that we now have a democratization of theology, a falling back on Qur'anic terms to recast old concepts and to develop new ones. As a result, *tafsīr* has been repositioned as the central mode of theologizing in the Islamic world today.

I will give two examples of how this type of scriptural exegesis has replaced modes of knowledge that were previously based on *kalām*. One is the word *ḥākimiyya* ('sovereignty', my translation), which was first coined by Abū'l-Aʿlā al-Mawdūdī (1903–79) based on Q. 5:44–74. This word came to encapsulate both his understanding of modernity's radical rethinking of the role of the nation state and the place of the citizen in this totalizing hegemony of state power. It was reconceived in a Qur'anic matrix, in an attempt to wrest from Europe the power of the definition of sovereignty, and hence what it means to be human in a political world order whose dictates are based on political ideologies of European origin. Theology was being reconceived in a scriptural mode precisely to articulate a vision of the world through an Islamic understanding of reality. The other example is Sayyid Quṭb's deployment of the term *jāhiliyya* in order to redefine history and its meaning. These two terms as used by these two ideologues have nothing to do with how the Qur'an uses them; nonetheless, these two terms are inexplicably connected to its world. Everything was now open for debate and, more significantly, for reassessment through the Qur'anic lens, via interpretive discourse. This included issues such as the place of women in society, the role of education, and social order, among other things, but also the nature of sin, the consequence of diversity, and the place of minorities in a nation state. Notable in this trend is the drive to Islamize the social sciences and to speak of an Islamic science of knowledge. All these debates were searching for an overarching paradigm to give the new theological language legitimacy, and Qur'anic interpretive discourse was the umbrella that was employed to give all these efforts at rethinking the tradition in line with modern Muslims' concerns a much-needed authority.

It is this new mode of theology, in its primary reliance on the Qur'an (and to a lesser extent the hadith), that is re-energizing *tafsīr* and that has fostered the continued utilization of classical *tafsīr* literature. There was thus a modern scholarly need for the medieval literature on the meaning of the Qur'an, in order to enable the emerging new theologians to use it as a starting point for their discussions and further elaborations. As such, the interest in medieval literature was functional, and far less reactionary than first meets the eye. Yet, that in and of itself does not explain the continued authority of medieval *tafsīr* literature. It is conceivable that modern Muslims could have rejected it, as they did the *isrā'īliyyāt* (material derived from Jewish and Christian lore) in *tafsīr*. Indeed, the Salafi movement had no difficulty rejecting much of the traditional corpus and cleaving to a very restricted mode of *tafsīr*, which in practice (despite the constant insistence on its primacy) made much of the medieval literature redundant.

The answer to this question lies in the peculiar history of medieval *tafsīr*, which matured in the wake of the philological revolution of early Arab medieval intellectual history. The early Muslims invented a grammar of Arabic that remains the backbone of Arabic philological studies. The Qur'an as scripture was never dislocated from its primary language, and thus was never in need of rediscovery (as were the Hebrew Bible and Greek New Testament in Europe). There is thus a large part of the *tafsīr* tradition that remains philologically useful: there is an intrinsic value to medieval *tafsīr*, which was not primarily a typological reading of the Qur'an. This, I believe, is one of the main reasons for the enduring value of medieval *tafsīr* in modern times. Although its authority is never absolute, it becomes authoritative when and as a modern author sees the need to use it. Medieval *tafsīr* is now positioned as answering modern needs, which has meant a selective absorption of this massive literature on a functional basis. But to what degree does this usage of medieval literature affect the process of contemporary interpretation? In other words, how does the past come to haunt the present in modern *tafsīr*?

Writing *tafsīr* in the modern period is not primarily intended to explain the Qur'an. In this sense, it differs markedly from its medieval predecessor. Muslims are now interpreting the Qur'an in order to position themselves in the world, which is a process of continuous reinvention of what it means to be a Muslim subject in an ever-evolving modernity. The Qur'an was and is the only common denominator left in a world that is often experienced as fractured and profoundly forgetful of its past. Using medieval *tafsīr* provides a sense of authenticity through continuity, an image of firm foundations that can be re-established through the Qur'an. To modern authors reinterpreting the Qur'an fatwas seemed virtually obsolete and inadequate to the task of changing the world, while interpretive discourse appeared by comparison to be effective, decidedly democratic, and profoundly subjective—in a word, modern. Qur'anic interpretation aimed to convince, to win over, not to subdue. A person not considered a leading religious authority who issued a fatwa risked not being taken seriously, and in any case Muftis and their compromises cavorting with governments had made fatwas laughable to many. By contrast, publishing a Qur'an commentary would only require one's personal effort; an author stood a better chance of gaining a hearing if he were willing to carry the whole enterprise to its very end, resulting in a complete Qur'an commentary. But even topical treatises were far more effective than any *kalām* or jurisprudential work. The proliferation of *tafsīr* works is thus at the centre of the new Muslim theology, represented most dramatically by *al-tafsīr al-mawḍū'ī* (topical interpretation), where a purported topic (modesty, honesty, Islamic rule, etc.) is investigated in all its Qur'anic manifestations. This approach is nothing but a theological discussion, carried out through the thematic grouping of Qur'anic terms or verses. The implicit justification behind this approach is that only through a deciphering of the Qur'an can believers come to know anything about what confronts them.

The Print Revolution, The Internet, and the Dissemination of *Tafsīr* Works

The consequences of the print revolution for access to the medieval tradition and the education of scholars (*ʿulamāʾ*) has been as yet inadequately investigated. This new medium has had major effects on the availability of and access to *tafsīr* works. First, access to manuscripts became ever more restricted, with the establishing of national libraries that acted as depositories for private libraries that had been either purchased or dismantled. Ironically, these national libraries became centralized bureaucratic institutions that in fact hindered unfettered access to the manuscripts, as had not typically been the case in earlier mosque libraries. Second, as the publication rate increased, scholars grew to depend on printed works as their reference to the textual tradition. These factors resulted in a radical disconnect between the general public and this vast medieval literature. As access to this medieval Islamic literature became confined to published editions, a new hierarchy of texts was established that was based on the print history of *tafsīr* works (and not fully reflective of the pre-print history of the genre). Thus, while the al-Bayḍāwī–al-Zamakhsharī–al-Rāzī triad of Qur'an commentaries was the first to be published, which reflected the historical dominance of this configuration, a displacement was soon effected by the publication of al-Ṭabarī and Ibn Kathīr. Indeed, while al-Ṭabarī had previously been a rare and virtually unavailable manuscript, its printing granted it an unprecedented pre-eminence.

The increase in availability of printed *tafsīr* works was only marginally meaningful at first, in so far as a systematic publication programme of the medieval genre did not exist. But soon, the hierarchy of *tafsīr* texts was answering to a Salafī programme of interests, which resulted in the ubiquity of Ibn Kathīr's Qur'an commentary as the most widely available medieval work and al-Ṭabarī's as the default mainstream work. Meanwhile, newly published works by modern scholars were joining the classics. Their authority increased as time went by, aided by contingencies such as their publishers' range of distribution, with the result that certain modern authors have been granted a level of acceptance comparable to that of the classical printed works. These include al-Qāsimī's *Maḥāsin al-taʾwīl*, Muḥammad ʿAbdūh's *Tafsīr al-Manār* (albeit more often mentioned than consulted), and Sayyid Quṭb's *Fī ẓilāl al-Qurʾān*. Other works, such as al-Ṭāhir Ibn ʿĀshūr's *al-Taḥrīr wa'l-tanwīr*, were steadily moving forward. The scene was being transformed through the continuous publication and silent accumulation of *tafsīr* works.

With the recent uploading of *tafsīr* works onto the internet, however, the full range of the medieval genre of *tafsīr* is now being recreated online, and also made available once again to the general public. In this sense the internet is undoing some of the restrictions placed on public access due to the paucity of research libraries in the contemporary Islamic world. There are now dedicated websites that carry a full inventory of the printed *tafsīr* works that have been amassed since the nineteenth century. This is a qualitative leap and a radical shift, facilitating a level of access to the scholarly tradition that was recently quite inconceivable. Moreover, the internet is a stage for the debate over the scope of the *tafsīr* heritage, with internet *tafsīr* forums discussing manuscripts and authors that are still unknown or unpublished. Add to this the uploading of information about MA and PhD dissertations which are edited medieval Qur'an commentaries, and we have truly a transformed landscape in the scholarship on *tafsīr*. At present, the internet is the most important research tool available to scholars in the Islamic world for works that were previously hard to find. The internet has also guaranteed newly published *tafsīr* works the same level of exposure that was usually reserved for classics of the past. This levelling of the grounds of interpretive discourse has meant that modern *tafsīr* works are (by dint of their simpler language) more attractive to the general reader and far more consulted than the classics. This also holds true for works that are not in Arabic.

Typologies of Contemporary *Tafsīr*, According to Aḥmīdah Nayfar and Johanna Pink

In 1966, the Mufti of Tunisia, al-Fāḍil Ibn ʿĀshūr, published a short history of *tafsīr* that remains a classic and original study of the genre (reissued in Cairo in 1970: Saleh 2011). In 1997, another scholar from Tunisia published a small booklet, *al-Insān wa'l-Qurʾān wajhan li-wajh* ('Human Beings and the Qur'an: Face to Face'), which is to date the most important analysis of modern *tafsīr* in the Arab world (Nayfar 1997, reissued in Beirut in 2000 with the title 'Critique of the Modern Mind'; French translation: Ennaifer 1998). Nayfar offers a typology and analysis of the modern Muslim Qur'an commentary tradition. The title of the work expresses an important aspect of the new Muslim sensibility towards the Qur'an: the conceit of immediacy that modernity expects believers to maintain vis-à-vis their scriptures. The typology outlined by Nayfar is, however, Arabo-centric, and has recently been corrected and amplified by the work of Johanna Pink (as elaborated below).

Nayfar introduces his work by offering some general observations about the nature of *tafsīr* in modern times. A large number of modern exegetes, he notes, are not graduates of the usual institutions that train *ʿulamāʾ*. The Qur'an has become more central to Arabic cultural life, he continues, precisely because the Arab world is passing through a historical epoch of radical transitions (Nayfar 1997: 13–14). He then describes five major trends in modern *tafsīr*: the Salafī school (*al-madrasa al-turāthiyya*, or *al-taṣawwur al-salafī*), the Reformist Salafī movement (the *al-Manār* school, the Muḥammad ʿAbdūh school), the ideological current (*al-tayyār al-aydūlūjī*), the Modern School (*al-madrasa al-ḥadītha*), and finally the Postmodernist reading (or the radical reading, *al-qirāʾa al-taʾwīliyya*—while Nayfar does not call it postmodern, it is clear that he is giving the original Arabic term *taʾwīl* this dimension).

The Ultra-Conservative School: The Salafī Outlook

Nayfar discusses ten authors under this rubric, from al-Ālūsī (d. 1270/1854) to the Iranian al-Ṭabāṭabāʾī (d. 1404/1981). He characterizes this approach as based on its sanctification of the Qur'an as a document that is above history. According to Nayfar, this understanding of the Qur'an as ahistorical, eternal, and uncreated invariably results in an interpretive method that sees no need for a historical anchoring of the text in its environment in order to understand its meaning. Its meaning is thus not tied to history or contingency. This school's hermeneutics gives primacy to the early Muslim generations as the sole interpreters of the Qur'an, and has an obsession with purging the *isrāʾīliyyāt* from *tafsīr* (Nayfar 1997: 31). Nayfar appears unaware that this paradigm is based specifically on Ibn Taymiyya's interpretive programme (Saleh 2010; cf. Daneshgar and Saleh 2017). Nayfar includes most of the major works produced in the Sunnī, Shīʿī, and Ibāḍī worlds in this camp—even those by al-Ṭāhir Ibn ʿĀshūr and al-Ṭabāṭabāʾī, which, although they include material that escapes hermeneutical enclosure, in Nayfar's view are ultimately too closely bound to the tradition to carry out a different interpretive project. Unfortunately, Nayfar does not address the role of medieval Qur'an commentaries in this movement, nor does he explain how they are an active rather than simply passive component of the school.

The *Manār* Movement, or the Reformed Salafī School

In this chapter Nayfar presents twelve authors whom he aligns with al-Afghānī and Muḥammad ʿAbdūh. With these exegetes, the Qur'an is made to fit the demands of modern developments, there is an attempt to claim that there is no contradiction between living a modern life and the demands of the Qur'an, and the classical demands of the Sharīʿa are maintained. That they form a school discrete from the preceding one, however, is unconvincing. The degree of modernizing is certainly more evident in the authors grouped here, but hardly in a manner that changes the landscape or provides a substantively different method of interpretation.

The Ideological Current

Nayfar places in this category scholars who have used the Qur'an to justify totalizing ideological outlooks on the human condition. He considers this approach one that sees meaning as a fixed entity (*iʿtibār al-maʿnā amran thābitan muṭlaqan*), and as such connected to the Salafī paradigm in its reformist manifestation (Nayfar 1997: 57). The main distinction of this current is its concentration on the social and political above anything else, and its subordination of the Qur'an to the service of power (*fī khidmat al-sulṭa*) (Nayfar 1997: 58). Scientific interpretation is included here, as well as the approaches of Sayyid Quṭb and the Mujāhidīn-e Khalq (the Iranian revolutionary radical group). Immediacy is the hallmark of this current, which oscillates between an ahistorical approach and the modernist readings that historicize the Qur'an (Nayfar 1997: 72).

The Modernist School

This is more a trend than a school, since it is really made up of Amīn al-Khūlī, his wife, ʿĀʾisha ʿAbd al-Raḥmān, and his student, Muḥammad Aḥmad Khalafallāh. Its significance, according to Nayfar, is that it opened the way for the radical reinterpretations of the next group. These three authors attempted to treat the Qur'an as a literary text and as such the Qur'an is governed by the same rules of rhetoric and composition as any other text, practically removing the divine element from determinations of how one is to read it contextually. The most famous episode in the course of this school is Khalafallāh's forced resignation from Cairo University, due to his analysis of the mythical dimensions of the stories of the prophets in the Qur'an. Nayfar states that this modernist approach has recently begun to recover from its initial setbacks, in the form of the final school.

The Deconstructionist and Postmodernist Reading

Nayfar claims that the last two decades have witnessed a shift in *tafsīr* studies due to the rise of a new approach to the Qur'an. The main feature of this school is that it attempts to understand the Qur'an as it was understood at the time of its revelation. Since this is a human attempt, it will always by definition be incomplete, and thus capable of revision and generative of multiple meanings. That is why these are 'readings' of the text (*qirāʾāt*), which should not be employed for a purpose beyond the understanding of the text (Nayfar 1997: 92). The text is a cultural phenomenon which can be deconstructed (*tafkīk*) and can be read by using postmodernist approaches (*taʾwīl*) with the help of the latest in humanistic theories to discover the world and way of thinking that engendered this text (Nayfar 1997: 92–3). Three individuals are grouped in this section: Mohammed Arkoun (d. 2010), Naṣr Ḥāmid Abū Zayd (d. 2010), and Fazlur Rahman (Faḍl al-Raḥmān, d. 1988). It is this group that Nayfar considers to be the hope of *tafsīr* studies, since it truly revolutionizes and modernizes the reading of the Qur'an. He ultimately states that this is the proper way to read the Qur'an, and the one that carries with it the possibility of the renewal and rejuvenation of the Qur'anic message (Nayfar 1997: 108).

This five-part division of the lie of the land of modern *tafsīr* is one of the most exhaustive treatments that we presently have in the secondary literature. It does have several shortcomings, however, not least its Arabo-centrism and its disregard for most of the secondary literature in English or other European languages. This is Arab scholarship that is tangentially connected to Western academia but, more disturbingly, is unaware of the Islamic world at large. This is not meant to detract from its originality or its insights, but rather to highlight the lamentable situation in both the Arab world and the Western academy, which is the lack at present of communication between those studying *tafsīr* or the Qur'an in these two sectors. For example, Rotraud Wielandt's article (2002: 140–2) on modern *tafsīr* in the *Encyclopaedia of the Qurʾān* makes no mention of Nayfar's seminal book, despite the fact that it had by then been translated into French and reissued in Beirut in a second edition. The fact that Nayfar is from Tunisia is not insignificant. Its proximity to yet distance from Cairo arguably helps enable the analysis of the Islamic landscape from a different angle. One intriguing limit of Nayfar's approach is his inability to connect modern *tafsīr* to its historic roots; nor does he try to conceal his own missionary modernist outlook. Nayfar thus magnifies the significance of the modernist outlook, despite the fact that most of its practitioners either lived in the West or were ultimately banished from the Islamic world.

Johanna Pink's Typology of Modern *Tafsīr*

A new, corrective typology of modern *tafsīr* has been recently advanced by Johanna Pink in a series of articles as well as a monograph. A major flaw in the study of modern *tafsīr* thus far is the compartmentalization of different areas of the Islamic world, such that those who work on Arabic literature disregard other languages and those who work on non-Arabic languages are not allowed full access to the (Arabo-centric) academic narrative of what modern *tafsīr* is. Pink, by analysing modern Arabic, Turkish, Malay, and Indonesian *tafsīr* works, has done the field a major service; she has brought new names into the discussion, and introduced scholars of *tafsīr* to a wider audience than was previously the case. This is not merely a broadening of our horizons but rather a methodological shift, in which what constitutes *tafsīr* is no longer defined through the medium of Arabic (which practice is a carry-over from the study of medieval *tafsīr*). Indeed, one could argue that in modern times al-Mawdūdī's influence on Arabic *tafsīr* has been instrumental, as Arabic translations of his Urdu works have become bestsellers.

Pink divides modern *tafsīr* works into three categories: scholar's commentaries (composed by an individual scholar); institutional commentaries (commissioned by official Islamic bodies and usually executed by a committee of professional scholars); and popularizing commentaries (meant for the lay public and using methods of writing that are decidedly non-scholastic) (Pink 2010b). These three broad categories, having to do with agent and audience, can be further distinguished into ideologically conservative, moderately orthodox, and modernist types (Pink 2010a: 73–4; and Pink 2019). In addition, Pink notes the factor of regional and cultural influences on *tafsīr* works, which are the result of authors' training and political environment. Pink's work is a turning point in the study of modern *tafsīr*, building as it were on the work of Nayfar (through the French translation of his text), and exhaustive in its attention to the secondary literature from the Islamic world. The most significant contribution of her work is the provincialization of Arabic, as well as the incorporation of two major Islamicate languages (Turkish and Indonesian) into the picture. Clearly we need to include others as well, especially Persian and Urdu, which have seen a plethora of works published in the past three decades. Finally, Pink has made clear the deep connections between these modern works and their medieval models. Only by realizing the complexity of the *tafsīr* heritage are we capable of fully describing the modern phenomenon of Qur'anic interpretation.

Conclusion and Directions for Future Research

It is clear that we need to integrate the internet into our study of modern contemporary *tafsīr*. Websites like altafsir.com are veritable research tools that are now as essential as any other. The uploading of *tafsīr* works onto the internet is also dramatically changing the hegemonic dominance of research institutions in the West. Moreover, the study of *tafsīr* can no longer be limited to Arabic written works. Indeed, given the demographic realities of the Islamic world, studying other Islamicate languages is now as urgent as ever. The problem has not been a lack of studies on *tafsīr* in other Islamicate languages, but the absence of a synthetic narrative that is truly global (Pink 2019). Nayfar utilized Fazlur Rahman in his typology, but this is hardly sufficient, given that Rahman's works stem from the 1980s and they are not what most English Muslim readers today are reading. English has become an Islamic language, and therefore English works of *tafsīr*, whether original or translated, have to be accorded the same level of attention that we give Islamicate languages. Finally, as already singled out by Pink, Turkey and its academy are a site of resurgent activities in *tafsīr* (and other Islamic fields) after a hiatus of over ninety years, which is a momentous transformation requiring attention.

Bibliography

Daneshgar, Majid and Walid A. Saleh (eds.). *Islamic Studies Today: Essays in Honor of Andrew Rippin*. Leiden and Boston: Brill, 2017.

Ennaifer, H. *Les commentaires coraniques contemporains: analyse de leur méthodologie*. Trans. M. Guillaud. Rome: Pontificio Istituto di Studi Arabi e d'Islamistica, 1998.

Nayfar, A. *al-Insān wa'l-Qurʾān wajhan li-wajh*. Casablanca: Nashr al-Fann, 1997.

Pink, J. 'Tradition and Ideology in Contemporary Sunnite Qurʾānic Exegesis: Qur'ānic Commentaries from the Arab World, Turkey and Indonesia and their Interpretation of Q. 5:51', *Die Welt des Islams* 50 (2010a), 3–59.

Pink, J. 'Tradition, Authority and Innovation in Contemporary Sunnī Tafsīr: Towards a Typology of Qurʾān Commentaries from the Arab World, Indonesia and Turkey', *Journal of Qur'anic Studies* 12 (2010b), 56–82.

Pink, J. *Sunnitischer Tafsīr in der modernen islamischen Welt: Akademische Traditionen, Popularisierung und nationalstaatliche Interessen*. Leiden: Brill, 2011.

Pink, J. *Muslim Qurʾānic Interpretation Today: Media, Genealogies and Interpretive Communities*. Sheffield: Equinox, 2019.

Rippin, A. 'The Qurʾān on the Internet: Implications and Future Possibilities'. In: G. Larsson and T. Hoffman (eds.). *Muslims and the New Information and Communication Technologies*, pp. 113–26. Dordrecht: Springer, 2013.

Saeed, Abdullah (ed.). *Approaches to the Qur'an in Contemporary Indonesia*. Oxford: Oxford University Press, 2005.

Saleh, W. 'Ibn Taymiyya and the Rise of Radical Hermeneutics: An Analysis of an Introduction to the Foundations of Qurʾānic Exegesis'. In: Y. Rapoport and S. Ahmed (eds.). *Ibn Taymiyya and His Times*, pp. 123–62. Oxford: Oxford University Press, 2010.

Saleh, W. 'Marginalia and the Periphery: A Tunisian Modern Historian and the History of Qurʾan Exegesis', *Numen* 58 (2011), 284–313.

Wielandt, R. 'Exegesis of the Qurʾān: Early Modern and Contemporary'. In: J. D. McAuliffe (ed.). *Encyclopaedia of the Qurʾān*, 2:124–42. 5 vols. Leiden: Brill, 2002.

PART VIII

QUR'ANIC EXEGESIS: DISCOURSES, FORMATS, AND HERMENEUTICS

CHAPTER 47

TWELVER SHĪʿĪ EXEGESIS

SAJJAD RIZVI

Exegesis as Disclosing *Waṣāyā* and *Walāya*: Esoteric Hermeneutics

Imam Muḥammad al-Bāqir (d. 114/733) stated, 'Our teaching is difficult and arduous; the only ones who can bear it are a prophet sent to humanity, one of the cherubim, or an initiate whose heart has been tested for faith by God' (al-Ṣaffār 2010: 51). While the function of exegesis is to explain and gloss the revealed word, the manifestation of God and His plan in the form of scripture, the strategies of exegetes depend to a large extent on how they see the word of God and understand the authority to interpret. In the Shīʿī tradition, exegesis, like most other forms of Shīʿī literature, is concerned with revealing and proclaiming the special status of the imams as heirs of the Prophet (the *waṣāyā*) and friends of God chosen to deploy their authority on the earth (the *walāya*) (Amir-Moezzi 2011). The underlying reality of the cosmos and the totality of the divine revelation are both associated with proclaiming the importance of the *walāya* of the imams succeeding the Prophet. This requires an esoteric approach of going beyond the literal word of the text through recourse to the words of the imams (Corbin 1972, vol. 1). In a saying attributed to the sixth Imam Jaʿfar al-Ṣādiq (d. 148/765), it is stated that the nature of the *walāya* of the imams is 'the very truth, that much is apparent, but also the very inner matter, the secret, the secret of secrets, the innermost secret that itself veils the secret' (al-Ṣaffār 2010: 59). The ultimate truth of the status of the imams is, therefore, hidden and remains a secret to be preserved by their adherents. This explains why in the earliest period Shīʿī exegesis is very much addressing a particular elect and not appealing to a wide audience; Steigerwald and Bar-Asher, following Goldziher, focus on the sectarian aspects of the early tradition, which, according to Lawson, was consciously revived in the Safavid period (Steigerwald 2006; Bar-Asher 1999; Goldziher 1920: 263–309, Lawson 1993). Gleave argues that the authority of the imams means that their exegesis, as reported in early works, does not provide any justification for an esoteric reading of the scripture (Gleave 2013). Ayoub and Karīmī-Niā argue for the development of the genre due to the diversity and periods of encounter and exchange, followed in this by Rippin, who questions essentialist definitions of Shīʿī exegesis (Ayoub 1988; Karīmī-Niā 2012 and 2013; Rippin 2014). Nevertheless, there are elements of the relationship between the revelation and the imam that suggest a particular quality to the exegesis of esotericism that is argued in this piece.

What this esotericism makes clear is that the classical tradition privileges a clear epistemology and hermeneutics before an engagement with the scripture; for example, one of the earliest major hadith compilations, *al-Kāfī* of Abū Jaʿfar al-Kulaynī (d. 329/941), begins with chapters on the notion of the intellect and its absence as well as the excellence of knowledge, divine unicity, and the need for a divinely ordained guide (*ḥujja*) before it shifts to the Qur'an and other materials (cf. Amir-Moezzi and Ansari 2009).

But the fundamental theme goes back to a central proof-text for the Shīʿī tradition, namely the famous hadith *al-thaqalayn* narrated from the Prophet: 'I am leaving behind two weighty things, the book of God and my progeny; cleave to them as neither will forsake the other until they reach me at the pool (in the afterlife)' (*Ṣaḥīḥ Muslim*, hadith #4425; *Kitāb al-Jāmiʿ li'l-Tirmidhī*, hadith #3718; *Sunan al-Nasāʾī*, 5:130; al-Qummī 1966: 1:3; al-ʿAyyāshī 1991: 1:4; al-Mīlānī 1992; al-Hindī 1993). Both the imam and the Qur'an are personal guides that have complementary roles in facilitating faith and understanding of reality. Hence the person of the imam as manifest in this hadith is the basis for Shīʿī exegesis. Just as the Qur'an is directly associated with the Prophet, his successors inherit his special knowledge that includes his direct relationship to the revelation—in this sense the *walāya* of the imams as succession to the prophecy mirrors the relationship between the interpretation (*taʾwīl*) of the text and its actual revelation (*tanzīl*). The function of *taʾwīl* is to reveal the *walāya* of the imams; as al-ʿAyyāshī (*fl.* late third/ninth century) quotes from Imam Jaʿfar al-Ṣādiq: 'God made our *walāya* the pole of the Qurʾān and the pole of all scriptures; through it scriptures were elucidated and through it faith becomes manifest' (al-ʿAyyāshī 1991: 1:5; Ayoub 1988: 181). The notion of *taʾwīl*, or going beyond the literal word (in its minimal sense), is predicated on two principles: the first is the privileged knowledge (*ʿilm*) of the imams that is inherited from the Prophet and directly from God that testifies to the fact that the imams are those rooted in knowledge (*al-rāsikhūna fī-l-ʿilm*) mentioned in Q. 3:7 (al-Kulaynī 2005: 1:153–4, 159–61). The second is the idea expressed in a hadith narrated from the fifth Imam Muḥammad al-Bāqir (d. 114/733) that each verse of the Qur'an has an apparent (*ẓāhir*) and a hidden (*bāṭin*) aspect, and that even the hidden aspect has further aspects which suggests a hierarchy or multiplicity of esoteric meanings (al-ʿAyyāshī 1991: 1:12; al-Tustarī 2002: 16). Again the same imam states that none can claim to know the totality of the revelation, the apparent and the hidden meanings except for the successors to the Prophet (al-Kulaynī 2005: 1:165).

The Speaking and Silent Qur'an (*al-Qurʾān al-Nāṭiq wa'l-Ṣāmit*)

The *bāṭin* of the Qur'an has a symbiotic relationship with the imams: a number of narrations talk about the inner aspect of the Qur'an proclaiming the true imams of the community, as well as addressing themselves only to the imam (al-Kulaynī 2005: 1:152). Both the Qur'an and the imam are pre-existing and eternal manifestations of the divine: the text of the Qur'an is a historical expression of both the knowledge of the divine and of its heavenly exemplar in the 'preserved tablet' (*al-lawḥ al-maḥfūẓ*), and the historical imam is an expression of the pre-existence in the heavens or at the Throne of God of the Prophet and the imams (Amir-Moezzi 1994: 29–59). This relationship—whose initial formulation seems linked to a famous hadith that ʿAlī is with the Qur'an and the Qur'an with ʿAlī (al-Ḥākim al-Nīsābūrī 1997: 3:124 hadith no. 4628; Ibn al-Ḥaythamī 1934: 9:134; al-Kulaynī 2005: 1:136; Majlisī 1983: 22:222, 38:38)—becomes the basis for an important Shīʿī topos of exegesis: that the Qur'an is the silent (*ṣāmit*) imam, and the imam is the speaking Qur'an (*al-kitāb al-nāṭiq huwa-l-walī*) (Bursī 1978:135; Amir-Moezzi 2011). Many hadith indicate this including those that identify the imams with the speech, the words, and the spirit of God (al-Kulaynī 2005: 1:139, 149; al-Ṣaffār 2010: 94–102). Similarly another narration stresses that the Qur'an itself cannot speak (*laysa bi-nāṭiqin*) and hence requires those worthy of it, its folk (*ahl*, the imams) to make it enunciate (al-Kulaynī 2005: 1:176). The imam and the Qur'an reveal the hidden God but most people fail to see it: esoteric approaches to the text therefore can disclose what God is—as Imam Jaʿfar al-Ṣādiq is reported to have said: 'God has disclosed himself to his creation in his book but they do not have the insight (to perceive him)' (Ibn Abī Jumhūr, 5:116; Āmulī: 1:207). The same imam is also quoted as stating that a quarter of the Qur'an directly relates to the imams and another quarter to their enemies (not least because *walāya* has *barāʾa* or dissociation as its complementary opposite), and 'to us belong the favours of the Qurʾān' (al-ʿAyyāshī 1991: 1:9; Ayoub 1998: 183). Training in Shīʿī exegesis is a means of developing the insight to recognize the imam and God. It is in this sense that Amir-Moezzi has described the early phase of exegesis as 'personalised commentary' as they identify the figures, the good and righteous being the imams and the evil their enemies, who are 'hidden' beyond the letter of the scripture (Amir-Moezzi 2103:169).

Early Exegetical Strategies: ʿAlī Ibn Ibrāhīm and His Period

The narrations contrast the outward revelation of the Qur'an (its *tanzīl*) with the inner *taʾwīl* (al-Ṣaffār 2010: 196). Shīʿī sources cite a saying of the Prophet: 'There is one among you who will fight for the *taʾwīl* of the Qurʾān just as I myself fought for its revelation (*tanzīl*) and he is ʿAlī ibn Abī Ṭālib' (al-ʿAyyāshī 1991: 1:15). As inheritors (*awṣiyāʾ*) of the Prophet, the imams know the totality of what was revealed and what the interpretation is (al-Ṣaffār 2010: 229–35). The hadith compilations demonstrate a range of exegetical strategies in the words of the imams: explaining the words through 'meaning equivalence', explanatory glosses, linguistic explanations, and examples of the *taʾwīl* (Gleave 2013: 146–66). To these, one could add the correction of the way in which the text is recited.

Correcting the reading was one way of making sense of the many-revealed text against the enemies of the faith. The *Kitāb al-tanzīl wa-l-taḥrīf* of Aḥmad al-Sayyārī (*fl.* fourth/tenth century) brings out the contrast and presents a recitation/reading different to the ʿUthmānic recension and its recitations that were being codified at the same time (al-Sayyārī 2009). However, al-Sayyārī's work is not exegetical but merely attempts to correct the *ẓāhir* of the text, and thus is quite at odds with most early Shīʿī exegesis that fits the esoteric category of drawing the implications of the reading for *taʾwīl*. This early corpus purports to present the esoteric teachings and revelation of the Qur'an as transmitted from the imams to their followers: the early exegeses attributed to ʿAlī ibn Ibrāhīm al-Qummī (*fl.* late third/ninth century, a companion of the eleventh imam, and a tradent and source for the first major hadith compiler al-Kulaynī), Abū-Naḍr al-ʿAyyāshī al-Samarqandī (*fl.* late third/ninth century), Furāt al-Kūfī (d. *c.*310/922), as well as the exegeses attributed to Imam ʿAlī in the recension of al-Nuʿmānī (d. 360/971), to Imam Jaʿfar al-Ṣādiq also through al-Nuʿmānī, and to the eleventh Shīʿī Imam al-Ḥasan al-ʿAskarī (d. 860/874). Some recent attempts have been made to reconstruct early texts attributed to companions of the imams like Jābir al-Juʿfī (d. 128/746, *tafsīr*), Abān ibn Taghlib al-Jurayrī (d. 141/758, *Gharāʾib al-Qurʾān*, *Kitāb al-qirāʾāt*), Abū Ḥamza al-Thumālī (d. 148/765, *tafsīr*), and most famously Abū'l-Jārūd Ziyād ibn al-Mundhir (d. *c.*150/167, *Tafsīr ʿan al-Bāqir*). The material contained is very similar to these early exegeses: reading the text to vindicate the Shīʿī case and the counter-narrative to the early history of Islam. Al-Qummī, for example, in the course of a long introduction on the hermeneutics of the text, clarifies the need to write an exegesis to vindicate the Shīʿī position on *walāya*, and to show how the Qur'an as it is before the people refutes the various non-Shīʿī heresies of dualism, anthropomorphism, materialism, idolatry, determinism, the Muʿtazila, and so forth (al-Qummī 1966: 1:5–6). In particular, the exegete must emphasize the *taʾwīl* to demonstrate the rights of the imams and the usurpations of their enemies (al-Qummī 1966: 1:13–15). As with most introductions to exegeses, al-Qummī does not follow up on his explicit hermeneutical aims, but he nevertheless gives us a map of the polemics which he wishes to engage and many of those are followed up, as discussed by Bar-Asher.

In this early phase, Shīʿī exegesis attempted to make the text speak and express the Shīʿī truth about the role of the imams and their teachings about the divine that lie beyond the surface of the text. A number of studies have stressed how these works focus upon major Shīʿī theological issues: the *walāya* of the imams, the dissociation (*barāʾa*) from their enemies sometimes discussed with code-names stressing the *rāfiḍī* (rejectionist, anti-Sunnī) nature of early Shīʿī Islam, the infallibility (*ʿiṣma*) of the prophets and by implication the imams, the notion of *badaʾ* or how it seems that God's decree changes as grasped by human minds, and intercession (*shafāʿa*) as the status the imams have before God to obtain paradise for their followers and extricate them from the hellfire (Bar-Asher 1999). Rippin has cautioned against the essentialization of early exegesis as esoteric (Rippin 2014). However, as Muslim exegetical traditions developed and Twelver Shīʿī scholarly interactions with other Muslims increased, the major exegeses of the medieval period collated both lexical and narrative as well as esoteric features, often arranged by section. Esoteric commentary was thus woven into the fabric of texts in different disciplines—and by esoteric one merely means what is beyond the apparent surface of the text. An example of this is the early exegesis of al-Ḥibarī (d. 286/899) which seeks to vindicate a broadly Shīʿī case for revelation and does not involve esotericism in the sense of some occult or arcane knowledge that is transmitted (Amir-Moezzi 2104).

A key feature of these works is supposed to be their adherence to the notion that the ʿUthmānic recension has been corrupted (*taḥrīf*). But what does *taḥrīf* mean? In what sense did the hadith suggest that the words of the Qur'an had been altered, omitted, or supplemented? Some have suggested that the issue of what constituted the text of the Qur'an, famously exemplified in the debate over whether stoning was a mandated punishment in the text or not, was argued out in early hadith texts whether Sunnī or Shīʿī (Modarressi 1993). The question of whether the Shīʿa reject the ʿUthmānic recension has become a matter of modern anti-Shīʿī polemics and still begs the question of what we understand the Qur'an as text to be and how a text can be fixed and canonized around a series of 'recitations' and variants that in turn have been canonized in the classical Abbasid period (Brunner 2005: 29–38). On the whole the early Shīʿī community—including the imams—were outside the process of the collation, redaction, and then canonization of the inscribed text and its recitations, hence one might suggest that taking ownership of it would always have been under some duress; the Shīʿī cause as an alternative sacred history makes it clear (Amir-Moezzi 2013). One could classify *taḥrīf* to entail the following types of variants: differences in vocalization or recitation, word substitution, usually significant ones such as placing *umma* (community) instead of *aʾimma* (imams), rearrangement of word order, as well as omissions such as the name of ʿAlī (Bar-Asher 1999: 47). The exegeses show the imams speaking to define the revelation as privileged enunciators of the text whose relationship to the revelation authorized them to do so. Even if one assumes that the texts suggest that the imams possess the privileged and definitive recension redacted by ʿAlī (the so-called *muṣḥaf ʿAlī*), it is rare to see the exegetes attempt to define what that recension was, as it was deferred to the unveiling of the awaited *mahdī*. Part of the process of being a believer whose heart has been tested by God entails accepting a silent Qur'an that was not fully sanctioned by the speaking Qur'an, to enable the membership of a wider community, precisely because the community of faith still had the revelation in the person of the imam.

Medieval Scholasticism: al-Ṭūsī

The Twelver Shīʿī tradition moved to the task of systematic and comprehensive exegesis. The Baghdad theologians realized the importance to communicate their faith within a more cosmopolitan context—a process to which the earlier tradents such as al-Ṣadūq (d. 381/991) had been somewhat attentive (Sander 1994)—and they wrote important critiques of hadith-based studies on creedal matters, and emphasized the significance of a rational hermeneutics of the text that continued to vindicate the Shīʿī case but ignored issues such as the integrity of the Qur'an. Engagement with Muʿtazilī thought had already begun with the tradents, but is not evident in the earlier exegeses. Three major medieval exegeses, *al-Tibyān* of Abū Jaʿfar al-Ṭūsī (d. 460/1067), *Majmaʿ al-bayān* of al-Faḍl ibn al-Ḥasan al-Ṭabrisī (d. 548/1154), and *Rūḥ al-janān* of Abū'l-Futūḥ al-Rāzī (*fl.* sixth/twelfth century, the first major Persian Shīʿī exegesis) all influenced by Muʿtazilī theology and Ibn Sīnā's philosophy to an extent, represent the classical tradition and a standard structure: outward matters such as the lexical gloss and the reading (*qirāʾa*), followed by discussion of the relevant hadith and the meaning (*khabar*, *maʿnā*), where the esoteric aspects come to the fore (Fudge 2011; Mourad 2010; Karīmān 1962). This required certain elements of the classical exegesis genre to be established (though these categories are not mutually exclusive): works based on hadith or narrative-based opinion, studies of lexical meaning, language, and stylistics such as *Maʿānī al-Qurʾān* of al-Farrāʾ (d. 207/822) and *Maʿānī al-Qurʾān* of al-Zajjāj (d. 311/923), and the development of theological discourse especially in the works of Muʿtazilī authors such as Abū ʿAlī al-Jubbāʾī (d. 303/915), Abū Muslim al-Iṣfahānī (d. 323/934), and ʿAlī al-Rummānī (d. 384/994) (Gimaret 1994; Giyāsī Kirmānī 1999; al-Iṣfahānī 2009). Recent research suggests that the works of these medieval Shīʿī authors drew upon *al-Maṣābīḥ fī tafsīr al-Qurʾān* of al-Wazīr al-Maghribī (d. 418/1027) who lived around fifty years before al-Ṭūsī—we know that *al-Maṣābīḥ* was cited (Karīmī-Niā 2013). These comprehensive works were subsumed within the wider genre of exegesis and directly appealed to a non-Shīʿī audience, drawing upon Sunnī hadith as well as explicitly citing a range of extra-Qur'anic and extra-Shīʿī sources of authority including lexicography, belles-lettres, rational theology, and philosophy (Thaver 2018). Al-Ṭūsī says that until his time no one had written an exegesis that went beyond narrations and was comprehensive discussing language and meanings and the whole range of religious disciplines that a scholar should master; he explicitly cited non-Shīʿī sources approvingly, while insisting on the need to combat the heresies of the anthropomorphists, determinists, and other groups (al-Ṭūsī 1963: 1:1). Al-Ṭūsī has an extensive discussion of how variants might arise in the text with the clear implication of denying *taḥrīf* but also of rejecting the established notion of seven canonical recitations reflecting seven dialects that were promoted by Sunnī exegetes (al-Ṭūsī 1963: 1:5–10).

This development in exegesis mirrors the development in other disciplines such as jurisprudence in which one sees Shīʿī authors forsaking their earlier isolationism and staunchly rejectionist approach to non-Shīʿī traditions and joining existing Muslim institutions and genres of literature and following the rules of their structure, method, and goals. There was even a juristic exegesis, *Kanz al-ʿirfān fī fiqh al-Qurʾān* written by Miqdād al-Siyūrī (d. 826/1422). But the basic principle of understanding the text to elucidate the *walāya* of the imams remained a constant within a larger framework of a scholastic contribution that establishes the credentials of the exegete as theologian—al-Ṭūsī, like all Shīʿī exegetes to that date, does not forget to cite the authority of the hadith *al-thaqalayn* (al-Ṭūsī 1963: 1:3, 5).

The Akhbārī Turn to Scripture: Fayḍ Kāshānī

The Timurid and Safavid periods led to a more heightened sense of an oppositional Shīʿī identity, partly borne out of the conflict and persecution of Shīʿī communities and thinkers at the hands of various authorities in Central and West Asia and the coming to power of the Shīʿī Safavid dynasty in Iran. As a result, the early modern period saw two different tendencies. The first was a revival of traditional Shīʿī exegesis based on the sayings of the imams, a refocusing upon what constituted the authentic and original Shīʿī message based on a revival of the early heritage. Works such as *Manhaj al-ṣādiqayn fī ilzām al-mukhālifīn* of Fatḥullāh Kāshānī (d. 980/1570), *al-Ṣāfī* by Muḥsin Fayḍ Kāshānī (d. 1090/1680), *Nūr al-thaqalayn* by ʿAbd ʿAlī Ḥuwayzī (d. 1104/1693), *al-Burhān* by Sayyid Ḥāshim al-Baḥrānī (d. 1106/1695), *Tafsīr* of Sharīf-i Lāhījī also known as Quṭb al-Dīn Ashkivarī (d. *c.* 1095/1684), and *Mirʾāt al-anwār* of Abū'l-Ḥasan al-ʿĀmilī (d. 1139/1727) were Akhbārī attempts at restating the positions of the early period and presenting exegesis as an exteriorization of the inner teachings of the imams in a triumphalist manner through lists of hadith (Lawson 1993). One could only understand the Qur'an through the words of the imam—anything else was an arrogation that implied exegesis based on one's own whim. This was more than the hadith-based approach of the early texts in which the revelation was glossed through the living revelation of the imam: it took that approach a logical step further by denying any understanding of the Qur'an, either intra-textuality or inter-textuality, without the explicit gloss attributed to the imam. Fayḍ Kāshānī prefaces his exegesis with a numerically significant (for a Twelver Shīʿī) set of twelve introductions designed to establish the need to turn to the hadith of the imams because it is they alone who know what the Qur'an is (Fayḍ Kāshānī 1979: 1:19–20). One needs to understand that the Qur'an informs the imams and about their enemies (Fayḍ Kāshānī 1979: 1:24). Since the principle of the need for *taʾwīl* to uncode all that is within the revelation requires the imams, it is imperative not to seek other sources, and even the seemingly innocent act of following the lexicography and stylistics of Sunnī authors goes against the hadith of the imams because it involves following someone's (false) opinion (*raʾy*) (Fayḍ Kāshānī 1979: 1:29–37). This whole hermeneutical propaedeutic is further expressed in a series of hadith to emphasis the point for their need (Lawson 1993). However, it would be misleading to see these works as merely fulfilling a Safavid propagandist attempt to continue the conflict with the Ottomans in religious terms. Most of these exegeses were written in Arabic for scholars by scholars and reflected an intellectual shift in making sense of the Shīʿī tradition that, in the seventeenth century, took a turn away from the philosophical and mystical towards a recovery of the words and texts of the imams themselves.

The Mystical Tradition: Sayyid Ḥaydar Āmulī to Sulṭān ʿAlī-Shāh

Alongside the Akhbārī approach, there was a strong tendency of mystical and philosophical commentary influenced by the school of Ibn ʿArabī (d. 638/1240) starting with the incomplete *Tafsīr al-Muḥīṭ al-aʿẓam waʾl-baḥr al-khiḍam* of Sayyid Ḥaydar Āmulī (d. after 787/1385), the unusually un-dotted *Sawāṭiʿ al-ilhām* of the Indian poet Fayżī (d. 1004/1595), and the *Tafsīr* of Mullā Ṣadrā Shīrāzī (d. 1050/1640). Āmulī's work is incomplete: only the tantalizing seven introductions have survived, the first importantly being on the principle of *taʾwīl*. Early on in the text, he makes his intent clear: to write a work of *taʾwīl* according to the principles of the people of singular reality (the Sufis who adhere, like Ibn ʿArabī, to the notion of *waḥdat al-wujūd*) and the principles of the *ahl al-bayt* (the family of the Prophet, the imams), elucidating the three levels of understanding open to all things: the level of the *sharīʿa* (the outward practice of the faith), the *ṭarīqa* (the spiritual path), and the *ḥaqīqa* (the inner reality unveiled to mystics and to the imams) (Āmulī 2002: 1:195). Given Āmulī's position on the complete identity and complementarity between Sufism and Shīʿism, this approach is not surprising. While continuing the tendency to critique exegesis based on one's own opinion, he cites four major exegetical influences: *Majmaʿ al-bayān* of al-Ṭabrisī which he describes as the best Shīʿī commentary, *al-Kashshāf* of al-Zamakhsharī (d. 538/1144) is well respected and can be useful for polemics, and then the two '*taʾwīlāt*' works of Najm al-Dīn al-Rāzī (d. 617/1220) and ʿAbd al-Razzāq al-Qāshānī (d. *c.*730–6/1329–35) both major influential Sufi commentaries, the latter in some ways prefiguring Āmulī as a Shīʿī Sufi (Āmulī 2002: 1:231). The exegesis of Mullā Ṣadrā is also incomplete. Written later in life, it exhibits the influence of Ibn ʿArabī, but it cannot be reduced to the metaphysics of the Sunnī Sufi (*contra* Rustom 2012). Mullā Ṣadrā's exegesis is based on his metaphysics and arises, as he says, from a desire to understand what it means to be human and how, on the spiritual path, one follows the imams to become a saint (*walī*) who is also a sage whose exegesis and practice of philosophy is in complete harmony (Mullā Ṣadrā 2010: 1:2–3). This theme of becoming a Shīʿī sage is later taken up in the modern period by al-Ṭabāṭabāʾī.

Later exegeses with a more marked Sufi taste that fulfil the promise of these earlier works are *Bayān al-saᶜāda*, an extensive and scholarly exegesis in Arabic by the Niᶜmatullāhī Gunābādī Shaykh Muḥammad Sulṭān ᶜAlī Shāh (d. 1327/1909) who had studied the philosophy of Mullā Ṣadrā with Hādī Sabzavārī (d. 1289/1873), and *Tafsīr-i Ṣafī* of a rival Niᶜmatullāhī Sufi Mīrzā Ḥasan Iṣfahānī known as Ṣafī ᶜAlī Shāh (d. 1317/1899), a versified Persian work that is both Shīᶜī but also conciliatory towards other non-Shīᶜī Sufis perhaps influenced by his engagements with wider circles beyond Iran (Kumpānī-Zāriᶜī 2011; Cancian 2009 and forthcoming; Sarvatīyān 2010; Boylston 2019). Both of these works use the Qur'an to demonstrate the validity and spiritual superiority of the Shīᶜī Sufi path and continue the method of Āmulī, albeit with an eye to the new realities of a Qajar Iran that was opening up to external influences from Europe and India in particular. All these works share a view of the Qur'anic text as multivocal and open to a hierarchy of interpretations with a preference for the mystical and supra-rational, and put forward the claims of the exegete as a Shīᶜī sage (*ḥakīm*).

Embracing Modernism: Sayyid Faḍlallāh and ᶜAllāma Ṭabāṭabāʾī

In more recent times, akin to Sufi commentaries, we find a greater concern for the social context and a desire to engage with modernity, which is common to various exegetical approaches in the modern period. The desire to communicate to a wider audience, a feature of modern exegesis, means a turn towards the use of vernaculars and more accessible style and language. Voluminous exegeses continue to be published and the leading ones of the twentieth century arise out of a concern to make a Shīᶜī reading and vindication of the text relevant to the times: the teaching commentary in Persian *Tafsīr-i namūna* compiled by a team under the supervision of Āyatullāh Nāṣir Makārim Shīrāzī (b. 1924), the socially engaged and ecumenical (and arguably barely Shīᶜī) *Min waḥy al-Qurʾān* of Sayyid Muḥammad Ḥusayn Faḍlallāh (d. 2010), the scholarly *al-Mīzān fī tafsīr al-Qurʾān* of Sayyid Muḥammad Ḥusayn al-Ṭabāṭabāʾī (d. 1981), and the socially engaged and philosophical *Tafsīr-i Faṣl al-khiṭāb* of Sayyid ᶜAlī Naqī Naqvī (d. 1988) in Urdu. Other multi-volume exegeses associated with leading jurists include *Ālāʾ al-Raḥmān fī tafsīr al-Qurʾān* of Muḥammad Jawād al-Balāghī (d. 1933), *al-Ṣirāṭ al-mustaqīm* of Sayyid Ḥusayn Burūjirdī (d. 1962), and *Mawāhib al-Raḥmān fi tafsīr al-Qurʾān* of Sayyid ᶜAbd al-Aᶜlā al-Sabzawārī (d. 1998) all of which have been published in some format. All of these commentaries continue the atomistic approach of the classical tradition, glossing verse by verse; the one that stands out for its method (although it is questionable whether he succeeds) is al-Ṭabāṭabāʾī, who insists upon an intra-textuality in which the Qur'an glosses the Qur'an (*tafsīr al-Qurʾān bi'l-Qurʾān*) alongside the hadith with a strong attack on those exegetes who engage in eisegesis and hence impose their preconceptions and learning upon the Qur'an. One work that began as an introduction to an exegesis never written has become important because of its approach to the polemical accusation of *taḥrīf*: *al-Bayān fī tafsīr al-Qurʾān* of Sayyid al-Khūʾī (d. 1992) deals in detail with the accusation that the Shīʿī tradition holds the ʿUthmānic recension to be inauthentic, with the concomitant point about accepting the recitations canonized in the Sunnī tradition, and even goes on to deny any abrogation (*naskh*) in the Qur'an (al-Khūʾī 1974). Opponents of *taḥrīf* tend to point to the fact that scholars have yet to find a manuscript that constitutes a different Shīʿī Qur'an, and that the Shīʿī tradition since at least the time of al-Kulaynī and al-Ṣadūq have insisted upon affirming the same Qur'anic recension as the Sunnīs (Eliash 1969: 24; *contra* St Clair Tisdall 1913 and Goldziher 1920: 271–2; Lawson 1991).

A modern trend is 'topical exegesis' (*tafsīr mawḍūʿī*) in which the exegete selects topics of social and intellectual relevance and does not follow the order of the Qur'an itself: one famous example is the ongoing series alongside his atomistic commentary *Tafsīr-i tasnīm* by Āyatullāh ʿAbd Allāh Javādī Āmulī (b. 1933). Another aspect of the modern approach has been the phenomenon of women writing exegeses especially in Persian—although it would be misleading to define them necessarily as feminist—including most famously the extensive and scholarly fifteen-volume work of Nuṣrat Amīn Iṣfahānī (d. 1983) entitled *Makhzan al-ʿirfān*, the *Bayānī az Qurʾān* by Zahrā Rustā (b. 1975), and *Tafsīr-i ravān* of Sayyida Ṣiddīqa Khurāsānī (b. 1959) (Mihrīzī 2006; Bīd-Hindī 2003; Künkler and Fazaeli 2012). These still require further study, not least to make sense of a new emerging female voice in Shīʿī exegesis. Given their training in Islamic philosophy and mysticism, a comparison between the work of Nuṣrat Amīn and al-Ṭabāṭabāʾī could be quite fruitful. These modern exegeses demonstrate a desire to reach out and make connections with broader communal and national identities as well as engage with concepts central to the modern period such as rationalism, science, and the need to make religion compatible and relevant to the contemporary world. With the advent of new media and ways of dissemination, exegesis is no longer confined to books: popular TV programmes on the many satellite channels in numerous languages bring the processes of interpretation and debate into the homes of believers, who also engage with each other on social media and more generally online, making sense of the revelation and deploying it for their own ends to understand what it means to live authentically as a Shīʿī believer. Authority has become centralized in the institutions of learning but also dissipated to the individuals themselves—the one constant that remains is the refrain of many an introduction of a Shīʿī exegesis to revert to the imams as privileged enunciators of the revelation.

What this brief survey demonstrates is that the tradition of exegesis among the Shīʿa has remained vibrant and dynamic; what has developed and changed over time have been the different approaches and methods of glossing the revelation to make sense of it for Shīʿī believers with a strong central focus on how the Qur'an reveals the *walāya* of the imams—and hence the recourse to the sayings of the imams and the practice of exegesis reinforces the authority of the revelation. The context and the audience tends to define the extent to which the exegeses are open and outward looking or more narrowly focused and inward looking, which is partly expressed in how they negotiate the complementarity or binary opposition of the *ẓāhir* and the *bāṭin*. Thus the commonalities that various exegetical exemplars bear to other exegeses in the wider Muslim traditions—and since we know that the very act of commenting upon the text bestows authority on the word of God as well as implies the authority of the exegete who has the privileged status of one who can explain the text—are balanced by the particularities of Shīʿī exegesis as an explanatory practice designed to emphasize the central complementarity of authority in the tradition between the Qurʾan as a text revealed to and through the Prophet and his family and successors, the imams who personify, define, and explain the text. But above all, exegesis is a process of establishing authority—of the revelation, both the text and the person of the Prophet and the imams—and of course of the exegete himself who seeks to define what it means to be Shīʿī.

Bibliography

Primary Sources

al-Aḥsāʾī, Ibn Abī Jumhūr. *ʿAwālī al-laʾālī*. Ed. Mujtabā ʿIraqī. Qum: Kitābkhāna-yi Āyatullāh Marʿashī Najafī, 1986.

Āmulī, Sayyid Ḥaydar. *al-Muḥīṭ al-Aʿẓam wa-l-baḥr al-khiḍam*. Ed. Sayyid Muḥsin Mūsawī Tabrīzī. Qum: Daftar-i Tablīghāt-i Islāmī, 2002.

al-ʿAskarī, Al-Ḥasan. *Tafsīr mansūb ilāʾ l-Imām al-ʿAskarī*. Ed. Shaykh Muḥammad al-Ṣāliḥī al-Andīmashkī. Qum: Dhawī l-Qurbā, 2009.

al-ʿAyyāshī, Abū-l-Naḍr. *Tafsīr*. Ed. Sayyid Hāshim Rasūlī Maḥallāṭī. Tehran: Muʾassasat al-Biʿtha, 1991.

al-Baḥrānī, Sayyid Hāshim. *al-Burhān fī tafsīr al-Qurʾān*. Beirut: Muʾassasat al-Wafāʾ, 1973.

al-Bursī, Rajab. *Mashāriq anwār al-yaqīn fī asrār Amīr al-muʾminīn*. Beirut: Muʾassasat al-Aʿlamī, 1978.

Burūjirdi, Sayyid Ḥusayn. *al-Ṣirāṭ al-mustaqīm*. Beirut: Muʾassasat al-Wafāʾ, 1995.

Faḍlallāh, Sayyid Muḥammad Ḥusayn. *Min waḥy al-Qurʾān*. Beirut: Dār al-Malāk, 1998.

Fayżī, Abū-l-Fayż. *Sawāṭiʿ al-ilhām fī tafsīr kalām al-malik al-ʿallām*. Ed. Murtaḍā Shīrāzī. Qum: Jāmiʿat al-Mudarrisīn, 1996.

al-Ḥaythamī, Ibn. *Majmaʿ al-zawāʾid*. Cairo: ʿĪsā al-Bābī al-Ḥalabī, 1934.

Ḥuwayzī, ʿAbd ʿAlī. *Tafsīr Nūr al-thaqalayn*. Ed. Sayyid Hāshim Rasūlī Maḥallāṭī. Qum: Maṭbaʿat al-ʿIlmiyya, 1965.

al-Iṣfahānī, Abu Muslim. *Jāmiʿ al-taʾwīl li-muḥkam al-tanzīl*. Ed. Muḥammad Hādī Maʿrifat and Maḥmūd Sarmadī. Tehran: Shirkat-i Intishārāt-i ʿIlmī va Farhangī, 1388/2009.

Kāshānī, Fatḥullāh. *Manhaj al-ṣādiqayn fī ilzām al-mukhālifīn*. Ed. Sayyid Abū-l-Ḥasan Shaʿrānī. Tehran: Maṭbaʿ-yi ʿIlmī, 1965.

Kāshānī, Muḥsin Fayḍ. *Tafsīr al-Ṣāfī*. Ed. Ḥusayn al-Aʿlamī. Beirut: Muʾassasat al-Aʿlamī, 1979.

al-Kūfī, Furāt. *Tafsīr*. Ed. Muḥammad al-Kāẓim. Tehran: Pazhūhishgāh-i ʿUlūm-i Insānī, 1990.

al-Kulaynī, Abū Jaʿfar. *Uṣūl al-Kāfī*. Ed. ʿAlī-Akbar Ghaffārī, repr. Beirut: Muʾassasat al-Aʿlamī, 2005.

Lāhījī, Sharīf-i. *Tafsīr*. Ed. Sayyid Jalāl al-Dīn Muḥaddith Urmawī. Tehran: Muʾassasa-yi Maṭbūʿāt-i ʿIlmī, 1961.

Majlisī, Muḥammad Bāqir. *Biḥār al-anwār*. Beirut: Dār al-Aḍwā᾿, 1983.
Majlisī, Muḥammad Bāqir. 'Tafsīr Imām ʿAlī bi-riwāyat al-Nuʿmānī Munajjimī, ʿAlī-Riżā. *Sharḥ-i jāmiʿ-yi tafsīr-i ʿirfānī-yi Ṣafī ʿAlī Shāh*. Tehran: Intishārāt-i Abā Ṣāliḥ, 1385/2006.
Naqvī, Sayyid ʿAlī Naqī. *Tafsīr-i faṣl al-khiṭāb*. Lahore: n.p., 1991.
al-Nīsābūrī, al-Ḥākim. *al-Mustadrak ʿalā l-Ṣaḥīḥayn*. Riyadh: Dār al-ʿĀṣima, 1997.
al-Qummī, ʿAlī ibn Ibrāhīm (attr.?). *Tafsīr*. Ed. Sayyid Ṭayyib al-Jazā᾿irī. Najaf: al-Maṭbaʿa al-Ḥaydarīya, 1966.
al-Rāzī, Abū'l-Futūḥ *Rawż al-jinān wa-rūḥ al-janān fī tafsīr al-Qur᾿ān*. Ed. M. J. Yāḥaqqī and M. M. Nāṣiḥ. Mashhad: Bunyād-i Pazhuhish-hā-yi Islāmī, 1987–97.
Sabzawārī, Sayyid ʿAbd al-Aʿlā. *Mawāhib al-raḥmān fī tafsīr al-Qur᾿ān*. Najaf: n.p., 1984.
al-Ṣaffār al-Qummī. *Baṣā᾿ir al-darajāt*. Ed. Mīrzā Muḥsin Kūcha-bāghī, repr. Beirut: Mu᾿assasat al-Aʿlamī, 2010.
al-Sayyārī, Aḥmad. *Revelation and Falsification: The Kitāb al-qirā᾿āt of Aḥmad ibn Muḥammad al-Sayyārī*. Ed. Etan Kohlberg and Mohammad Ali Amir-Moezzi. Leiden: Brill, 2009.
Shīrāzī, Mullā Ṣadrā. *Tafsīr al-Qur᾿ān al-karīm*, general editor Sayyid Muḥammad Khāmenei. Tehran: Bunyād-i Ḥikmat-i Īslāmī-yi Ṣadrā, 2010.
Shīrāzī, Nāsir Makārim. *Tafsīr-i namūna* Qum: Dār al-Kitāb al-Islāmī, 1998.
Ṭabāṭabā᾿ī, Sayyid Muḥammad Ḥusayn. *al-Mīzān fī tafsīr al-Qur᾿ān*. Tehran: Maktabat-i Ismāʿīlīyān, 1973.
al-Ṭabrisī, al-Faḍl. *Majmaʿ al-bayān fī tafsīr al-Qur᾿ān*. Beirut: Mu᾿assasat al-Aʿlamī, 1961.
al-Thumālī, Abū Ḥamza. *Tafsīr Abī Ḥamza al-Thumālī*. Ed. ʿAbd al-Razzāq Ḥirz al-Dīn. Qum: Dalīl-i Mā, 2000.
al-Ṭūsī, Abū Jaʿfar. *al-Tibyān fī tafsīr al-Qur᾿ān*. General editor Āqā Buzurg al-Ṭihrānī. Najaf: al-Maṭbaʿa al-Ḥaydarīya, 1963.
al-Tustarī, Sahl ibn ʿAbd Allāh. *Tafsīr al-Qur᾿ān al-ʿaẓīm*. Ed. M. B. al-Sūd. Beirut: Dār al-Kutub al-ʿIlmiyya, 2002.

Secondary Sources

Amir-Moezzi, M. A. *The Divine Guide in Early Shīʿīsm*. Albany: State University of New York Press, 1994.
Amir-Moezzi, M. A. *The Spirituality of Shīʿī Islam: Beliefs and Practices*. London: I. B. Tauris in association with the Institute of Ismaili Studies, 2011.
Amir-Moezzi, M. A. *Le Coran silencieux et le coran parlant*. Paris: CNRS, 2011.
Amir-Moezzi, M. A. 'The Silent Qur᾿ān and the Speaking Qur᾿ān: History and Scripture through Some Ancient Texts', *Studia Islamica* 108 (2013), 143–74.
Amir-Moezzi, M. A. 'The *Tafsīr* of al-Ḥibarī'. In: Farhad Daftary and Gurdofarid Miskinzoda (eds.). *The Study of Shīʿī Islam: History, Theology and Law*, pp. 113–34. London: I. B. Tauris in association with the Institute of Ismaili Studies, 2014.
Amir-Moezzi, M. A. and H. Ansari. 'Muḥammad ibn Yaʿqūb al-Kulaynī et son *Kitāb al-Kāfī*: Une introduction', *Studia Iranica* 38 (2009), 191–247.
Ayoub, Mahmoud. 'The Speaking Qur᾿ān and the Silent Qur᾿ān: A Study of the Principles and Development of Imāmī Shīʿī tafsir'. In: Andrew Rippin (ed.). *Approaches to the History of the Interpretation of the Qur᾿ān*, pp. 177–98. Oxford: Oxford University Press, 1988.
Bāhir, Muḥammad. *Abū-l-Futūḥ al-Rāzī va tafsīr-i rawż al-jinān*. Tehran: Khāna-yi Kitāb, 2009.

Bar-Asher, Meir. *Scripture and Exegesis in Early Imami Shīʿīsm*. Leiden/Jerusalem: Brill/Magnes Press, 1999.

Bar-Asher, Meir. 'The Qurʾānic Commentary Ascribed to Imam Ḥasan al-ʿAskarī', *Jerusalem Studies in Arabic and Islam* 24 (2000), 358–79.

Bīd-Hindī, Nāṣir Bāqirī. *Bānū-yi nimūna: jilva-hā-yi az ḥayāt-i bānū-yi mujtahida Amīn Iṣfahānī*. Qum: Daftar-i Tablīghāt-i Islāmī, 1382/2003.

Boylston, Nicholas. 'Speaking the Secrets of Sanctity in the *Tafsīr* of Ṣafī ʿAlī Shāh'. In: Alessandro Cancian (ed.). *Approaches to the Qurʾān in Contemporary Iran*, pp. 243–70, London: Oxford University Press in association with the Institute of Ismaili Studies, 2019.

Brunner, Rainer. 'La Question de la falsification du coran dans l'exégèse chiite duodécimaine', *Arabica* 52 (2005), 1–42.

Cancian, Alessandro. 'L'esegesi dell'acqua nel sufismo sciita: il caso del *tafsīr* di Sulṭān ʿAlī Shāh Gonābādī', *Indoasiatica* 6 (2009), 69–103.

Cancian, Alessandro. 'Translation, Authority and Exegesis in Modern Iranian Sufism: Two Iranian Sufi Masters in Dialogue', *Journal of Persianate Studies* 7/1 (2014), 88–106.

Corbin, Henry. *En islam iranien*. 4 vols. Paris: Gallimard, 1972.

Eliash, Joseph. 'The Shīʿite Qurʾān: A Reconsideration of Goldziher's Interpretation', *Arabica* 16 (1969), 15–24.

Fudge, Bruce. *Qurʾānic Hermeneutics: al-Ṭabrisī and the Craft of Commentary*. London: Routledge, 2011.

Ghiyāsī Kirmānī, Muḥammad Riżā. *Barrasī-yi ārāʾ va naẓarāt-i tafsīrī-yi Abū Muslim Muḥammad ibn Baḥr al-Iṣfahānī*. Qum: Muʾassasa-yi Farhangī-i Ḥuḍūr, 1378/1999.

Gimaret, Daniel. *Une lecture muʿtazilite du Coran: le tafsīr d'Abū ʿAlī al-Jubbāʾī*. Leuven: Peeters, 1994.

Gleave, Robert. 'Early Shīʿī Hermeneutics: Some Exegetical Techniques Attributed to the Shīʿī Imams'. In: Karen Bauer (ed.). *Aims, Methods and Contexts of Qurʾānic Exegesis (2nd/8th—9th/15th c.)*, pp. 141–72. London: Oxford University Press in association with the Institute of Ismaili Studies, 2013.

Goldziher, Ignaz. *Die Richtungen der islamischen Koransauslegung*. Leiden: Brill, 1920.

al-Hindī, Sayyid Ḥāmid Ḥusayn. *ʿAbaqāt al-anwār*. Ed. Sayyid ʿAlī al-Mīlānī. 11 vols. Qum: Muʾassasat al-Nabaʾ, 1993.

Karīmān, Ḥusayn. *Ṭabrisī va majmaʿ al-bayān*. Tehran: Tehran University Press, 1962.

Karīmī-Niā, Murtaḍā. '*al-Maṣābīḥ fī tafsīr al-Qurʾān: kanz min turāth al-tafsīr al-shīʿī*', *Turāthunā* 113 and 114 (Jumādā II 1434/April 2013), 55–100.

Karīmī-Niā, Murtażā. 'Chahār pārādāyim-i tafsīr-i shīʿa: muqaddima-yi dar tārīkh-i tafsīr-i shīʿī bar Qurʾān-i karīm'. In: Rasūl Jaʿfarīyān (ed.). *Jashn-nāma-yi Ustād Muḥammad ʿAlī Mahdavī-rād*, pp. 425–43. Tehran: Khāna-yi Kitāb, 1391/2012.

al-Khūʾī, Sayyid Abū-l-Qāsim. *al-Bayān fī tafsīr al-Qurʾān*. Beirut: Muʾassasat al-Aʿlamī, 1974.

Kumpānī-Zāriʿī, Muḥammad. *Gunābādī va tafsīr-i Bayān al-saʿāda*. Tehran: Khāna-yi Kitāb, 1390/2011.

Künkler, Mirjam and Roja Fazaeli. 'The Life of Two Mujtahidahs: Female Religious Authority in 20th Century Iran'. In: Masooda Bano and Hilary Kalmbach (eds.). *Women, Leadership, and Mosques: Changes in Contemporary Islamic Authority*, pp. 127–60. Leiden: Brill, 2012.

al-Mīlānī, Sayyid ʿAlī. *Ḥadīth al-thaqalayn: tawāturuhu, fiqhuhu*. Qum: Markaz al-Ḥaqāʾiq al-Islāmiyya, 1992.

Lawson, Todd. 'Akhbārī Shīʿī Approaches to Tafsīr'. In: G. Hawting and A. Shareef (eds.). *Approaches to the Qurʾān*, pp. 173–210. London: Routledge, 1993.

Lawson, Todd. 'Notes for the Study of a "Shīʿī Qurʾān"', *Journal of Semitic Studies* 36 (1991), 279–95.

Maʿrifat, Muḥammad Hādī. *al-Tafsīr wa'l-mufassirūn fi thawbihi-l-qashīb*. Mashhad: Bunyād-i Pazhuhish-hā-yi Islāmī, 1997.

Mihrīzī, Mahdī. 'Zan dar tafsīr *Makhzan al-ʿirfān*-i Bānū Amīn Iṣfahānī', *āyīna-yi pazhūhish* 98 & 99 (Khurdād tā Shahrīvar 1385/May to September 2006), 16–23.

Modarressi, Hossein. 'Early Debates on the Integrity of the Qurʾān: A Brief Survey', *Studia Islamica* 77 (1993), 5–39.

Mourad, Suleiman. 'The Survival of the Muʿtazila Tradition of Qurʾānic Exegesis in Early Sunnī and Shīʿī *Tafāsīr*', *Journal of Qur'anic Studies* 12 (2010), 83–108.

Rippin, Andrew. 'What Defines a (Pre-modern) Shīʿī Tafsīr?' In: Farhad Daftary and Gurdofarid Miskinzoda (eds.). *The Study of Shīʿī Islam: History, Theology and Law*, pp. 95–112. London: I. B. Tauris in association with the Institute of Ismaili Studies, 2014.

Rustom, Mohammed. *The Triumph of Mercy: Philosophy and Scripture in Mullā Ṣadrā*. Albany: State University of New York Press, 2012.

Sander, Paul. *Zwischen Charisma und Ratio: Entwicklungen in der frühen imāmitischen Theologie*. Berlin: Klaus Schwarz Verlag, 1994.

Sarvatīyān, Bihrūz. *Ṣafī ʿAlī Shāh va tafsīrash*. Tehran: Khāna-yi Kitāb, 1389/2010.

Steigerwald, Diana. 'Twelver Shīʿī *taʾwīl*'. In: Andrew Rippin (ed.). *The Blackwell Companion to the Qurʾān*, pp. 373–85. Oxford: Blackwell, 2006.

Thaver, Tehseen. 'Language and Power: Literary Interpretations of the Qurʾān in Early Islam', *Journal of the Royal Asiatic Society* 28/2 (2018), 207–30.

Tisdall, W. St Clair 'Shiʿah Additions to the Koran', *Muslim World* 3 (1913), 227–41.

al-Zaydī, Kāṣid. *Manhaj al-Shaykh Abū Jaʿfar al-Ṭūsī fi tafsīr al-Qurʾān al-karīm*. Baghdad: Bayt al-Ḥikma, 2004.

CHAPTER 48

ISMĀʿĪLĪ SCHOLARSHIP ON *TAFSĪR*

ISMAIL POONAWALA

Introduction

The Ismāʿīlīs did not cultivate the science of *tafsīr*. That is to say that, unlike Sunnī Muslims and the Shīʿī branches of the Zaydīs and Imāmīs (Twelvers), they did not produce Qur'anic commentaries wherein the text of the scripture was explicated or interpreted verse by verse and chapter by chapter, from beginning to end. Ismāʿīlī literature is, however, very rich in *taʾwīl* (the esoteric and allegorical interpretation) of Qur'anic verses. Indeed, Ismāʿīlīs assiduously cultivated the discipline of *taʾwīl*, elaborated hermeneutical principles, and applied them systematically not only to certain key verses but also to a number of short and long chapters of the Qur'an and the stories of ancient prophets. It is no exaggeration to state that all books of Ismāʿīlī doctrine, including works on cosmology and the ultimate philosophical system called *al-ḥaqāʾiq* (the true reality of being; based on Neoplatonism and neo-Pythagoreanism), are replete with Qur'anic citations as proof-texts, with appropriate *taʾwīl* to justify their doctrines.

The immediate predecessors of the Ismāʿīlī practice of *taʾwīl* are found among the Shīʿī *ghulāt* (extremists) sectarian groups that flourished in Iraq, especially in Kūfa, in the early second/eighth century. These groups were small and marginal to the early development of Islam, but their intellectual impact on the growth of Shīʿī thought was considerable (Halm 1982; Tucker 2008). Meir Bar-Asher has correctly portrayed pre-Buyid/Buwayhid Qur'anic exegesis as proto-Ismāʿīlī *taʾwīl* (Bar-Asher 1999). The Zaydī Imam Qāsim ibn Ibrāhīm (d. 246/860) used *taʾwīl* as rational interpretation—as did Muʿtazilī scholars—to clarify anthropomorphic verses in the Qur'an consistent with their transcendental view of God and His unity (Götz 1999).

According to some early commentators, *taʾwīl* refers to the interpretation of allegorical passages which deal with metaphysical issues that are beyond the reach of human perception. In his book entitled *Taʾwīl Mushkil al-Qurʾān*, Ibn Qutayba (d. 276/889) asserts the view that *al-rāsikhūna fiʾl-ʿilm* indeed know the *taʾwīl* and his arguments closely resemble those of the Shīʿa. In his *Kitāb al-Azhār*, Ḥasan ibn Nūḥ al-Bharūchī (d. 939/1533) devoted several pages on this issue and cited both Ismāʿīlī and non-Ismāʿīlī sources to assert his view. Among the latter he mentions al-Naqqāsh, al-Baghawī, al-Bayḍāwī, and al-Zamakhsharī (Poonawala 1977: 183). However, the early history and development of *tafsīr* clearly indicates that in the beginning the terms *tafsīr* and *taʾwīl* were used synonymously. The fact that both al-Ṭabarī (d. 310/923) and al-Māturīdī (d. 333/944) use the word *taʾwīl* in the title of their Qur'an commentaries suggests that for them the primary meaning of the term *taʾwīl* was Qur'anic exegesis (*EI*[2] 10:390–2). Conversely, Muqātil ibn Sulaymān (d. 150/767) draws a clear distinction between *tafsīr* and *taʾwīl* and states with reference to Q. 3:7 that the *ʿulamāʾ* know its *tafsīr* but no one knows its *taʾwīl* except God. In other words, the former is known on the human level, while the latter is known to God alone. In this context it is worth noting that, in his magnum opus *Kitāb al-Zīna fī ʾl-kalimāt al-Islāmiyya al-ʿArabiyya* (The book of adornment on Islamic-Arabic words) which deals with the etymology of Islamic nomenclature, the early Ismāʿīlī author Abū Ḥātim al-Rāzī (d. 322/934) states on the authority of Ibn al-Aʿrābī (a philologist and a *rāwī*, d. *c.*231/845–6) that *taʾwīl*, *tafsīr*, and *maʿnā* are virtually identical; however, *taʾwīl* means knowledge of the true state of affairs (*maʿrifat al-ḥaqāʾiq*), which is the source (*al-ʿayn*), the reality (*al-ḥaqīqa*), and the end (*al-ʿāqiba*). Al-Rāzī then adds that those who contend that *taʾwīl* and *tafsīr* are different entities affirm that *tafsīr* is what the common people (*al-ʿāmma*, i.e. the Sunnīs) relate from the exegetes, while *taʾwīl* signifies the discovery of subtle, hidden meaning known only to eminent scholars. *Tafsīr* is thus appropriately described as concerned with *riwāya* (i.e. the transmission of reports), while *taʾwīl* has to do with *dirāya*: knowing the esoteric meaning of something by a sort of artifice or cunning skill.

The Ismāʿīlīs draw a fundamental distinction between the twin aspects of religion, the *ẓāhir* (exterior) and the *bāṭin* (interior), and as such differentiate between the apparent literal meaning of the Qur'an and Sharīʿa and their hidden, true meaning (*EI*[2] 11:389–90). The Ismāʿīlī classification of the religious sciences into two categories: the *ẓāhirī* (exoteric) sciences and the *bāṭinī* (esoteric) sciences, also reflects the above distinction. It is worth noting however that despite this twofold division of religion, Ismāʿīlīs stress that its exoteric and esoteric aspects are not only complementary to each other, but that they are intertwined with each other like body and soul. One without the other cannot be sustained (Poonawala 1988: 199–200).

This chapter is devoted to elaborating on Ismāʿīlī *taʾwīl* as a genre of Qur'anic exegesis/hermeneutics (Steigerwald 2006). The scope of this survey is limited to certain well-known and extant early works on *taʾwīl* along with brief descriptions of their contents. Space does not permit me to go beyond the works of al-Sijistānī (d. after 361/971) or the reign of the Fatimid caliph-Imam al-Muʿizz (r. 341–65/953–75). It is hoped that this will nonetheless give the reader a glimpse of what this corpus contains. I conclude with some observations by way of assessing Ismāʿīlī contributions to the field of exegesis.

The Ismāʿīlīs and Their *Taʾwīl*

In his *Kitāb al-Maqālīd al-malakūtiyya* (The book of the keys to the kingdom), the Neoplatonic thinker al-Sijistānī (d. after 361/971) states that:

> *Tanzīl* (revelation in its scriptural form) is similar to the raw materials, while *taʾwīl* resembles the manufactured goods. For example, nature produces various types of wood, but unless a craftsman works on them and gives them a specific shape, such as a door, a chest, or a chair, the wood is not worth more than simple firewood [to be consumed] by the fire. The wood's worth and benefit become manifest only after it receives the craftsman's craftsmanship... Unless a craftsman works on it, its worth and utility remain hidden... Similarly, *tanzīl* consists of putting ideas together in words. Beneath those words lie the treasured meanings. It is the practitioner of *taʾwīl* who extracts the intended meaning from each word and puts everything in its proper place. This is, then, the difference between *tanzīl* and *taʾwīl*.
>
> (Poonawala 1988: 206)

As the craftsman cannot practise his art without raw materials, the function of *taʾwīl* comes after that of *tanzīl*. Similarly, the rank of the practitioner of *taʾwīl* in the Ismāʿīlī hierarchy comes after that of the *nāṭiq* (lit. speaking prophet, lawgiver). It is the *nāṭiq* who receives the *tanzīl*, while it is the *waṣīy* (the deputy and successor of the prophet, legatee, plenipotentiary) who imparts its *taʾwīl* (Poonawala 1988: 206–8). The concepts of revelation, scripture, and its hermeneutics are firmly grounded in the Neoplatonic doctrine and cosmology adapted by the Ismāʿīlīs. Accordingly, the *nāṭiq* has a direct connection to emanation (*waḥy*) from God, while the legatee and the successive imams receive *taʾyīd* (divine support/inspiration) which provides access to the hidden inner meanings embedded in scripture. The Ismāʿīlīs further claim that they have inherited the discipline of hermeneutics ultimately from the Prophet, who passed it on to his *waṣīy*, who then transmitted it on to the imams from among his progeny. The Prophet was the recipient of *waḥy*, and the secrets of *waḥy* (and gnosis) were passed over to ʿAlī. There are several traditions wherein the Prophet is purported to have said: 'I am the city of knowledge, and ʿAlī is its gate; those who intend to enter it should enter through its gate.'

The fact that Ismāʿīlīs take great pride in their *taʾwīl* is obvious from the very title of al-Sijistānī's highly polemical work, *Kitāb al-Iftikhār* (The book of boasting). In it, after refuting his opponents' arguments, al-Sijistānī expounds his own doctrine and esoteric interpretation and then concludes by posing a rhetorical question: 'What pride is greater than the comprehension of reality (*ḥaqāʾiq*) and pursuing the [right] path?' This phrase, like a refrain, is repeated after each argument throughout the book.

How is *Ta*ʾ*wīl* Justified?

Al-Qāḍī al-Nuʿmān (d. 363/974), the founder of Ismāʿīlī jurisprudence and a prolific author, states that the two terms *ẓāhir* and *bāṭin* are generally used in the Qur'an as a pair (*zawj*). For example, God states (Q. 6:120), 'Abstain from sinning, be it openly or in secret (*ẓāhir al-ithm wa-bāṭinahu*),' and (Q. 31:20), '[God] has lavished upon you His blessings, both outward and inward (*ẓāhiratan wa-bāṭinatan*)' (Poonawala 1988: 208). With reference to these pairs, God states (Q. 51:49), 'And in everything We created pairs (*zawjayn*), so that you might bear in mind [that God alone is One]'. Al-Nuʿmān adroitly adds that this is to demonstrate that God alone is One and Unique while everything He created, He fashioned in pairs.

The Qur'an also contains parables (*amthāl*, pl. of *mathal*, see Q. 29:43 and Q. 39:27) which, al-Nuʿmān argues, obviously need interpretation (Poonawala 1988: 212). In the story of Joseph it is stated (Q. 12:6), 'For, [as thou hast been shown in thy dream,] even thus will thy Sustainer elect thee, and will impart unto thee some understanding of the inner meaning of happenings (*ta*ʾ*wīl al-aḥādīth*),' and (Q. 12:21), 'And thus We gave unto Joseph a firm place on earth; and [We did this] so that We might impart unto him some understanding of the inner meaning of happenings (*ta*ʾ*wīl al-aḥādīth*).'

Al-Nuʿmān then cites Q. 3:7, regarded as a key to understanding the Qur'an and decisive in the development of *ta*ʾ*wīl* not only for the Ismāʿīlīs but also for the Imāmīs (*EI*[2] 10:390–2). In contradistinction to the Sunnī exegetes, who tend to take a pause after 'God', al-Nuʿmān reads the pause as occurring after 'those who are deeply rooted in knowledge', rendering the verse as follows:

> He it is who has bestowed upon thee from high this divine writ, containing messages that are clear in and by themselves (*āyāt muḥkamāt*)—and these are the essence of the divine writ—as well as others that are allegorical (*mutashābihāt*)...; but none know its final meaning (*ta*ʾ*wīlahu*) save God and those who are deeply rooted in knowledge...

He adds: 'Those deeply rooted in knowledge' are none other than the legitimate imams (Poonawala 1988: 209). In his *Kitāb al-Zīna*, al-Rāzī also discusses this thorny issue. To support his reading of a pause after 'those who are deeply rooted in knowledge', he states that those who maintain that the Prophet did not know the *ta*ʾ*wīl al-mutashābih* have uttered a terrible thing. How could such a thing be true? The Prophet is said to have stated: 'I knew and saw everything as if I witnessed it with my own eyes.' ʿAlī is also reported to have said: 'Ask me before you miss me. By God, there is no verse in the Qur'an except that I knew it better, what was the occasion and when was it revealed' (*EI*[2] 10:390–2).

Al-Sijistānī also elucidates the source of *ta*ʾ*wīl* from the Qur'an in his *Kitāb al-Iftikhār*, but from a philosophical perspective. He states:

> The relationship of the [human] soul to the world of knowledge is more intimate than its [relationship] to the world of sensory perception. Indeed, the *nāṭiq*'s soul attains a high degree of knowledge which his peers and their like are incapable of

> [reaching]. Hence, [the fact that] his revelations are expressions of the incorporeal world and its spiritual, luminous forms, cannot be denied. [This being the case], how could it be correct to translate everything he transmitted to his *umma* [community] into physical, corporeal objects?...When the [above statement] is established then most of the well-known names used for the physical objects in the Qurʾān need to be interpreted spiritually, whether they are [the names] of trees, rivers, fruits or heavens, earth, mountains, oceans and its waters... applying them to physical objects appears especially dubious...The only way out of this literal [but ridiculous] meaning is to seek intelligible interpretation, i.e., *taʾwīl*.
>
> (Poonawala 1988: 201–2)

Thus al-Sijistānī makes the following points. First: the Prophet communicates with the higher, spiritual world—the fountain-head of his revelations. Second: the prophet's soul/intellect attains the highest attainable status of knowledge. Third: revelations, being representations of the spiritual world in human language, cannot be taken literally (Poonawala 1988: 201–5; Walker 1993: 124–33; Izutsu 1962; Abū Zayd 1996). In other words, *taʾwīl* means the return from the external form or image of a physical object, to the corresponding metaphysical meaning (and reality) of the divine revelation.

The second argument advanced by al-Sijistānī in defence of *taʾwīl* is based on the principle of disparity (*tafāwut*), which is also his main argument in defence of prophecy (*ithbāt al-nubūʾāt*). The basic postulate in this theory is that disparity prevails over everything in the universe except for God and the Intellect. Consequently, the affairs of the two realms, the intelligible and the impressionable, sustain their order. According to al-Sijistānī, it is because of this disparity that Creation (i.e. emanation) is in itself the principle and the order of Being. Accordingly, the higher is simpler, nobler, and more subtle than the lower. It is always the higher that influences the lower. The key to universal order, therefore, is the knowledge of each particular thing's proper place in the hierarchy to which it belongs. This is precisely what *taʾwīl* accomplishes.

Al-Sijistānī argues that two categories of verses are obviously in need of *taʾwīl*: first, verses with physical objects, such as heaven, earth, mountain, rivers, animals, trees, and fruits; second, the *mutashābihāt* (allegorical, ambiguous, unclear) verses. The former category should be treated figuratively, especially when the literal meaning appears dubious. The latter category is defined by al-Sijistānī as follows:

> When the listener hears the *mutashābihāt* verses, his intelligence disapproves of [their obvious meaning], and he becomes confused, because [their meaning] departs from [accepted] norms and customs, such as the ant's speech to Solomon, the hoopoe's bringing the news about the personal religious beliefs of the Queen of Sheba, the cooling off of fire for Abraham, the gushing forth of twelve fountains when Moses struck his staff on a rock, etc.... When an intelligent person is presented with those *mutashābihāt* verses, his faith is not reassured, because he finds [those stories] surrounded by an element of impossibility. (Poonawala 1988: 210–11)

After a lengthy discussion of the issues involved in the *mutashābihāt* verses, al-Sijistānī raises some philosophical questions: Why should one seek the *taʾwīl* of the uncommon phenomena mentioned in those verses? Does not the seeking of *taʾwīl* imply the denial of those occurrences and consequently infringe upon God's omnipotence? Al-Sijistānī defends the use of *ta'wīl* by stating that the literal interpretation of those unusual phenomena violates the law of nature. It further implies that God, who has willed the cosmos to function according to the laws of nature, could annul His own wisdom. Once this wisdom is nullified, then the whole of creation is invalidated, which leads to denuding God of all content (*ta'ṭīl al-khāliq*). It should be noted that al-Sijistānī's younger contemporary Sa'adyah Gaon (d. 942), the Babylonian rabbinic leader, justifies non-literal exegesis of the biblical text on similar grounds.

Principles of *Ta'wīl*

Ismā'īlī hermeneutical principles are tied to a theory called *al-mathal wa'l-mamthūl* (the metaphor, and the one represented by the metaphor), which is based on establishing parallelism between the spiritual, physical, and religious realms and their corresponding hierarchies. In his *Kitāb al-Iftikhār*, al-Sijistānī delineates some general principles of hermeneutics, whereby the *mutashābihāt* verses together with those wherein physical objects are mentioned are to be interpreted. Thus, for example, the term 'earth' (*arḍ*) could be substituted for 'knowledge' (*'ilm*). Al-Sijistānī notes that the Qur'an states (Q. 27:82): 'Now, when the word [of truth] stands revealed against [the deaf and blind of heart, see Q. 27:80–1], We shall bring forth unto them out of the earth a creature which will tell them that mankind had no real faith in Our messages.' He observes that the earth is an abode of all 'generated beings' (*al-mawālīd al-ṭabī'iyya*), and they cannot exist without it. Likewise, the soul's subsistence and that of all the 'spiritually-generated beings' (*al-mawālīd al-rūḥaniyya*) depend on true, spiritual knowledge. The term 'earth', therefore, signifies 'knowledge', and the true (hermeneutical) meaning of the above verse reads as follows:

> 'When the word falls on them' means 'When the community is confronted with the proof, they will know that what they believed was falsehood.'
>
> 'We shall bring forth unto them out of the earth a creature' means 'God shall bring forth for them a leader who is well-versed in knowledge.'
>
> 'A creature which will tell them' means 'who will deliver them from falsehood to guidance and from [the state of] doubt to that of certainty.'

Commenting on Q. 50:7, 'And the earth—We have spread it wide, set upon it mountains firm, and caused it to bring forth plants of all beauteous kinds,' al-Sijistānī states:

> Its *ta'wīl* is realised when the word 'earth' is exchanged for 'knowledge', or 'the one who is the source of knowledge'. Thus, the setting up of the *asās* (the deputy and successor of the prophet) and [his] promulgation of the *ta'wīl* is analogous with the earth's stretching, while the casting of firm mountains is similar to appointing

religious dignitaries to disseminate knowledge among the deserving. 'Causing every splendid species to grow in it,' means the growth of twofold knowledge, exoteric and esoteric.

Similarly, 'journey in the land' (Q. 22:46 and Q. 29:20) means 'journey seeking knowledge from its rightful possessors'. Those who succeed in obtaining that knowledge will know how creation originated. It is this knowledge which 'brings forth the second growth' of the soul and attains success in the hereafter. Commenting on Q. 57:17, 'God gives life to the earth after it has been lifeless,' al-Sijistānī argues that the verse denotes the bestowal of knowledge or its source, the *asās*. Hence God will revive knowledge after it has become extinct—referring to the period of the first three caliphs—and the *asās* (i.e. ʿAlī) will revive the practice of disseminating esoteric knowledge by designating his son to succeed him (Poonawala 1988: 214). 'Knowledge', then, is the primary meaning of 'earth' in *taʾwīl*. In its secondary meaning, the term 'earth' is applied to the *waṣīy* (the *asās*), since he is the source of *taʾwīl* and the true sciences.

The same principle can be applied to the word *samāʾ* (sky, heavens). This term is applied to a fine, rotating body studded with stars, but it is synonymous with the *nāṭiq*, who forms 'the sky of religion'. Thus Q. 13:17, '[Whenever] He sends down water from the sky, and [once-dry] river-beds are running high according to their measure, the stream carries scum on its surface', means that God revealed the Qur'an to Muḥammad's heart (literally, He brought it out from the Prophet's heart) so that the people would carry it, each according to his capacity and the purity of his soul. And 'the stream carries scum on its surface', refers to the differences and disputes that surfaced among the Muslim community with regard to Qur'anic exegesis and hermeneutics. In the continuation of the same verse, 'Likewise, from that [metal] which they smelt in the fire in order to make ornaments or utensils [there rises] scum,' but it passes away because it is of no use while that which is of benefit to man abides on earth. It means that the differences and disputes among the community shall vanish, but that which is useful to mankind [i.e. *taʾwīl*] remains with the *asās*, i.e. ʿAlī and the imams. In its secondary meaning, 'sky' is applied to the Sharīʿa promulgated by the *nāṭiq*. Q. 21:104, 'On that Day We shall roll up the skies as written scrolls are rolled up,' indicates the cancellation of the Sharīʿa and its abrogation by the *qāʾim* (Poonawala 1988: 215).

'Firmly established mountains' serve as signposts whereby travellers are guided and wherefrom streams gush forth. In *taʾwīl* they represent the *ḥujja* (pl. *ḥujaj*, a high rank in the *daʿwa* hierarchy) who are established in every region of the earth to guide the faithful with their knowledge. Streams gushing forth from the mountains are then analogous with the fountains of wisdom and knowledge radiating from the *ḥujaj*. Al-Sijistānī interprets the mountains in, for example, 'And We caused the mountains to join David in extolling Our limitless glory' (Q. 21:79), as referring to the *ḥujaj* and various *daʿwa* dignitaries (Poonawala 1988: 215–16).

'Godly trees' are the righteous, God-fearing, and virtuous people, while 'corrupt trees', or those uprooted from the earth, are the debauched. 'A blessed tree—an olive tree'(Q. 24:35), stands for the Imam ʿAlī Zayn al-ʿĀbidīn, the son of al-Ḥusayn (Poonawala 1988: 217), while 'the tree [of hell] cursed in the Qur'an' (Q. 17:60) can stand for the second

Umayyad caliph Yazīd (the son of Muʿāwiya) who was responsible for Imam al-Ḥusayn's massacre at Karbalāʾ, the Umayyads in general, or the adherents of Mazdaism.

Another interesting aspect of *taʾwīl* found in the works of al-Sijistānī is the technique of transposing the letters of certain verses to vindicate a particular Shīʿī tenet. Although the Ismāʿīlīs did not openly dispute the canonical validity of the ʿUthmānic codex, they did cast doubts on the quality of the version, alleging political tendentiousness on the part of the editors. The editors were accused of altering the sequence of the verses as well as the omission and addition of certain words and verses. To cite an example, Q. 108 is employed by al-Sijistānī to demonstrate ʿAlī's *waṣāyā* (the rank of plenipotentiary). Al-Sijistānī transposes the letters of the verses, such that instead of reading 'Behold, We have bestowed upon thee good in abundance: hence, pray unto thy Sustainer [alone], and sacrifice [unto Him alone]. Verily, he that hates thee has indeed been cut off [from all that is good!]', the sura can be seen to read: 'Behold, the pure good in abundance is your *waṣīy* ʿAlī, if you sacrifice [him] indeed, he that hates thee is Abū Bakr.'

Sources for the Corpus of Ismāʿīlī Exegetical Literature

In what follows I will enumerate some of the major extant pre-Fatimid and early Fatimid sources. Although space does not permit me to go beyond this period in the current chapter, two works from the later Yemeni and Indian periods should be noted. The first is entitled *Mizāj al-tasnīm* by Ḍiyāʾ al-Dīn Ismāʿīl ibn Hibat Allāh (d. 1184/1770), a Sulaymānī *dāʿī* from Yemen, which gives a verse-by-verse *taʾwīl* of Q. 9:94 to Q. 29:44. The second, by Aḥmad ʿAlī Rāj (d. 2008), is a *taʾwīl* of the entire Qur'an written in Bohra Gujarati (with Arabic script). The first two volumes of this work (covering up to *Sūrat Maryam*) have been published, with a translation, under the title *Ismāʿīlī Tafsīr*. I would also like to highlight two anti-Ismāʿīlī polemical works which contain numerous examples of *taʾwīl* reproduced exactly from authentic early Ismāʿīlī works. These are: *Min kashf asrār al-Bāṭiniyya wa-ʿawār madhhabihim* (From the exposure of the secrets of the *bāṭiniyya* and the flaw of their doctrine) by Abū'l-Qāsim al-Bustī (d. *c.*420/1029), the dogmatic Zaydī theologian and jurist, and the *ʿAqāʾid al-thalāth wa-sabʿīn firqa* (Tenets of seventy-three sects) by Abū Muḥammad al-Yamanī, who lived during the first half of the sixth/twelfth century.

The Pre-Fatimid Period

Kitāb al-Rushd wa'l-hidāya (The book of guidance and direction) exists only in a number of surviving fragments, edited by M. Kamil Hussein in 1948. The extant contents clearly indicate a pre-Fatimid provenance, and the work is ascribed to Manṣūr al-Yaman (d. *c.* 303/915), although there is no internal or external evidence to support this. The first part is devoted to the advent of the Mahdī, while the second part deals with the *taʾwīl* of various verses of the Qurʾān, especially *al-muqaṭṭaʿāt* (the detached letters). Michael Brett considers it to belong to the same school of messianic thought as the *Kitāb al-Kashf*, described below (Brett 2001: 124).

Kitāb al-Kashf (The book of revelation), ascribed to Jaʿfar ibn Manṣūr al-Yaman (d. *c.*346/957), consists of six unconnected *rasāʾil* (treatises) of unequal length. The fact that the second Fatimid caliph-Imam al-Qāʾim is referred to in the fifth *risāla* suggests that the tracts were probably collected during the latter's reign. Brett asserts his view that Jaʿfar ibn Manṣūr al-Yaman may have been the editor of these tracts (Brett 2001: 123–6), but there is no internal evidence to support this ascription, and it should be noted that it is listed neither in the early Ismāʿīlī sources nor in the Majdūʿ *Fihrist*, while Abū Muḥammad al-Yamanī (d. after 540/1145–6) mentions it by title alone. It contains the *taʾwīl* of innumerable verses of the Qur'an, and reflects typical Shīʿī/Ismāʿīlī interpretations. Some of those allegorical interpretations clearly reveal a pre-Fatimid layer of doctrine, such as the theme of an unbroken line of successors from Muḥammad to the Mahdī, and the latter's imminent appearance. It also contains *ghulāt* elements, for instance the concept of *maskh* or *masūkhiyya* (metamorphosis), the theory of the primordial light shown by the Prophet, ʿAlī, Fāṭima, al-Ḥasan, and al-Ḥusayn, and the principle of *mustawdaʿ* (temporary or trustee) vs *mustaqarr* (permanent). There is no trace of Neoplatonism. It is worth noting that the author uses a cryptic script based on old south Arabian and Hindi in order to indicate the names of those who usurped ʿAlī's right to succeed the Prophet, and to transcribe derogatory appellations for the enemies of the imams. It should be noticed that cryptic writing was developed quite early to disguise the names of the enemies of the imams. The first three caliphs who are viewed within Ismāʿīlī thought as having usurped the legitimate right of ʿAlī to succeed the Prophet are generally referred to as *al-awwal* (the First), *al-thānī* (the Second), and *al-thālith* (the Third).

The *Kitāb al-ʿĀlim wa'l-ghulām* (The book of the master and the disciple) is also ascribed to Jaʿfar ibn Manṣūr al-Yaman, although again there is no direct evidence to support this: the contents and cosmology indicate a pre-Fatimid provenance. It contains copious allusions to Qur'anic verses. In fact most of the dialogues are woven from central Qur'anic themes. The framework of the story is modelled on that of the *Kitāb al-Bilawhar wa-Būdhāsaf* (derived from the biography of Buddha, and subsequently provides a prototype for the Christian legend of Barlaam and Josaphat). Throughout the narrative the author highlights the superiority of esoteric knowledge (*taʾwīl*, *bāṭin*) over exoteric knowledge (*ẓāhir*). In fact, with regard to Q. 7:26 the author states that there are three levels of revealed knowledge: the outer aspect (*ẓāhir*), its inner dimension (*bāṭin*), and the inner aspect of the inner dimension (*bāṭin al-bāṭin*).

The Fatimid Period

One of the most important Ismāʿīlī authors of the Fatimid period is al-Qāḍī al-Nuʿmān. The first chapter on *walāya* (loyalty to the imams) in his *Daʿāʾim al-Islām* (The pillars of Islam) contains innumerable verses of the Qur'an that are interpreted to validate the imamate of ʿAlī and the descendants of his son al-Ḥusayn. It also deals with the ranks of the imams, their moral injunctions, their knowledge, etc. All these issues are interpreted in light of the Qur'anic injunction of *mawadda* (Q. 42:23) for the family of the Prophet, the desirability of seeking knowledge from the imams (Q. 16:43, 21:7), etc. The *Daʿāʾim* is, therefore, a significant source as to how these verses are interpreted not only by the Ismāʿīlīs but within a wider Shīʿī context. It is a *ẓāhirī* work, representing the first stage of teaching and the lowest level of knowledge and understanding (al-Nuʿmān, *Asās al-taʾwīl*, 23). In his *Taʾwīl al-daʿāʾim* (Hermeneutics of the pillars of Islam) al-Nuʿmān deals with the esoteric interpretations of the Islamic rituals illustrated in the previous work. *Taʾwīl* is multi-layered, and multiple levels of interpretations can be represented within the works of the same author (*EI*² 11:389–90).

The *Asās al-taʾwīl* (The foundation of hermeneutics) is another highly significant work compiled by al-Nuʿmān, although the 1960 edition by ʿĀrif Tāmir is unfortunately replete with major and minor errors. In the introduction, al-Nuʿmān justifies the use of *taʾwīl* based on evidence from the Qur'an and hadith, expounding on the *taʾwīl* of *islām* (submission), *īmān* (faith), the *shahāda* (creed), and basic Ismāʿīlī doctrine. This is followed by the esoteric interpretation of the stories of the prophets Adam, Noah, Hūd, Ṣāliḥ, Abraham, Lot, Joseph and Jacob, Job, Shuʿayb, Moses, Ṭālūt, David, Solomon, Jonah, Zakariyāʾ, Jesus, and Muḥammad. These are divided into the typical Ismāʿīlī notion of cyclical history, in which the first is the cycle of Adam (the first *nāṭiq*), the second of Noah (the second *nāṭiq*), the third of Abraham (the third *nāṭiq*), the fourth of Moses (the fourth *nāṭiq*), the fifth of Jesus (the fifth *nāṭiq*), and the sixth of Muḥammad (the sixth *nāṭiq*). The author states that Muḥammad gave good tidings for the coming of the *qāʾim/mahdī*, citing Q. 12:40 in this respect (al-Nuʿmān, *Asās al-taʾwīl*, 150, 319), but there is no chapter dedicated to the *qāʾim/mahdī* in the *Asās al-taʾwīl*. Some scholars speculate that this chapter is missing; others state that al-Nuʿmān never composed it.

The *Taʾwīl al-sharīʿa* (Hermeneutics of the Sharīʿa) is sometimes also ascribed to al-Nuʿmān. This seems doubtful, however, as it lacks the proper arrangement and tight organization one generally finds in al-Nuʿmān's works, and some of its *taʾwīl* is quite different from that provided by al-Nuʿmān. An ascription to the Fatimid caliph-imam al-Muʿizz seems more likely. As its title suggests, the *Taʾwīl al-sharīʿa* contains esoteric interpretation of the Sharīʿa and its real meaning and secrets. It also contains *taʾwīl* of numerous Qur'anic verses.

Another work whose importance for Ismāʿīlī *taʾwīl* cannot be overstated is the *Kitāb al-Iftikhār* by al-Sijistānī. This is a highly polemical work covering the Ismāʿīlī doctrine of hermeneutics in its entirety (Poonawala 1988). Other Fatimid works include the *Kitāb al-Iṣlāḥ* (The book of rectification) by Abū Ḥātim Aḥmad ibn Ḥamdān al-Rāzī. This is a refutation of parts of the *Kitāb al-Maḥṣūl* (The yield) written by al-Rāzī's contemporary Abū'l-Ḥasan Muḥammad al-Nasafī (d. 332/943). It discusses the precedence of *qaḍāʾ*

over *qadar*, the imperfect nature of the emanation of the Soul from the Intellect, and the dissociation of the Sharīʿa from the first *nāṭiq*. It also provides *taʾwīl* of the stories of the prophets and is a rich source for the retrieval of esoteric and allegorical interpretations of innumerable Qur'anic verses.

The *Sarāʾir al-nuṭaqāʾ* and *Asrār al-nuṭaqāʾ* (The secrets of the speaker-prophets), ascribed to Jaʿfar ibn Manṣūr al-Yaman, can be dated to after 380/990 on the strength of the statement, within a polemical section about the sects that emerged following Jaʿfar al-Ṣādiq's death, that 120 years have elapsed since the death of Ḥasan al-ʿAskarī (d. 260/873). The ascription is therefore incorrect. The works contain elements which indicate a pre-Fatimid origin (De Blois 2011: 9–11), but the author also makes oblique reference, as part of his *taʾwīl*, to unusual political events within the ruling Fatimid dynasty. The first volume (*Sarāʾir al-nuṭaqāʾ*) contains the stories of Adam, Idrīs, Noah, Hūd, and Abraham, and ends with the *taʾwīl* of Q. 111. The *Asrār al-nuṭaqāʾ* continues with the stories of Abraham, Lot, Isaac, Jacob, Joseph, Shuʿayb, Moses, David, Solomon, Zachariah, John, Jesus, and Muḥammad. The author frequently quotes the Torah. M. Ghālib has published a composite edition of both volumes. This is not, however, a critical edition and is replete with errors and lacunae.

The following five works are also ascribed to Jaʿfar without any convincing evidence. The *Kitāb al-Shawāhid wa'l-bayān* (The book of evidence and clarification) affirms ʿAlī's status as *waṣīy* and rightful successor to the Prophet, to be succeeded in turn by the imams from his progeny. Various verses of the Qur'an and the stories of the ancient prophets are interpreted in support of this claim. The *Kitāb al-Farāʾiḍ wa-ḥudūd al-dīn* (The book of divine precepts and the religious hierarchies) contains the *taʾwīl* of the creation of man at Q. 15:26, *Sūrat Yūsuf* (Q. 12), *Sūrat al-Kahf* (Q. 18) and the protocols of modesty for believing men and women at Q. 24:30–2. The *Kitāb al-Riḍāʿ fi 'l-bāṭin* (The book on the inner meaning of nursing) contains esoteric interpretations of verses to do with prayers, fasting, pilgrimage, etc., and ends with the *taʾwīl* of Q. 97 (*Sūrat al-Qadr*). The *Taʾwīl al-zakāt* (Hermeneutics of the alms tax) gives allegorical interpretations of Qur'anic verses and *aḥādīth* related to the *zakāt* (poor-tax), connecting this issue to figures in the *daʿwa* hierarchy. The *Taʾwīl Sūrat al-Nisāʾ* (Hermeneutics of the chapter on women) provides *taʾwīl* of Q. 4 (*Sūrat al-Nisāʾ*) (Poonawala 1977: 71–3).

Ismāʿīlī *Taʾwīl*: Major Themes

Taʾwīl serves to justify Ismāʿīlī doctrine and to instruct the initiated regarding the inner truth about the purpose of this life and the reason behind the creation of the universe. The Ismāʿīlī concept of the *daʿwa*, which began with Adam and will continue until the end of time or the appearance of the *qāʾim*, occurs as a frequent theme, as does the doctrine of hierarchy within the *daʿwa*. During the later Yemenī and Indian periods, the *ḥudūd* or *tartīb al-daʿwa* (ranking of the entire universe in its proper sequence) would change whenever a new *dāʿī* assumed his office.

The Ismāʿīlī concepts of prophethood and the imamate are among the central themes of their *taʾwīl*, and the primordial institution of the imamate is often elaborated in the *taʾwīl* of God's covenants with Adam and Abraham. The notion of the seven major cycles of the lawgiver prophets, and the seven minor cycles of the imams within each major prophetic cycle, are anchored in the stories of the prophets, as is discussion of the final messiah (the *qāʾim* or the *mahdī*), who will usher in the last millennium. Another notable theme is the interpretation of the Sharīʿa (Poonawala 1988: 219).

Ismāʿīlī authors also elaborate and articulate a parallel hierarchy called *ʿālam al-waḍʿ* (i.e. *ʿālam al-dīn*, 'the world of religion'), in which the universe is classified into three categories. The World of Nature is based on substance and the nine accidents. The World of the Soul attained a lofty position with the emergence of man, who is the noblest of the three (i.e. the mineral, the plant, and the animal) kingdoms. The conventional World of Divine Law (*ʿālam al-waḍʿ*), meanwhile, is based on ten ranks (*ḥudūd*). Five of these are spiritual and five physical.

Conclusion and Directions for Future Research

Henri Corbin, the leading French scholar of Shīʿī Islam during the twentieth century, emphasized the intimate entanglement of hermeneutics and philosophy in Islam, and argued that the teachings of Islamic philosophy were incomprehensible without being placed in the context of recognized exegetical practices. In his recent study entitled *Mysticism and philosophy in al-Andalus: Ibn Masarra, Ibn al-ʿArabī and the Ismāʿīlī tradition*, Michael Ebstein similarly argues that, despite the fact that the philosophical, the mystical, and the Ismāʿīlī traditions are part of the same intellectual heritage, the affinities between Ismāʿīlism and philosophical mysticism have gone unnoticed by scholars. Ebstein correctly observes that philosophical, mystical, and Ismāʿīlī thought drew from common Gnostic, Hermetic, and Neoplatonic sources.

Taʾwīl played an important role in the Ismāʿīlī formulation of a new synthesis of reason and revelation based on the foundations of Neoplatonism and Shīʿī doctrine, and it was used as a peg upon which to hang Shīʿī doctrine as well as Neoplatonic cosmology and eschatology, all under the garb of Qur'anic verses. Yet a comprehensive survey of the Ismāʿīlī exegetical corpus from the earliest times until the present remains sorely needed. Esoteric interpretations are scattered throughout Ismāʿīlī doctrinal works in addition to the volumes of *taʾwīl*. It should be plausible to construct an Ismāʿīlī exegesis of a major portion of the Qur'an from these sources.

Bibliography

Abū Zayd, Naṣr Ḥāmid. *Mafhūm al-naṣṣ: Dirāsa fī ʿulūm al-Qurʾān*. 3rd printing. Beirut: al-Markaz al-Thaqāfī al-ʿArabī, 1996.

Bar-Asher, Meir, M. *Scripture and Exegesis in Early Imāmī Shīʿism*. Leiden, Boston, and Cologne: E. J. Brill, and Jerusalem: Magnes Press, 1999.

Bar-Asher, Meir, M. 'Outlines of Early Ismāʿīlī-Fāṭimid Qur'an Exegesis', *Journal Asiatique* 296/2 (2008), 257–95.

Brett, Michael. 'The Mīm, the ʿAyn, and the Making of Ismāʿilism', *Bulletin of the School of Oriental and African Studies* 57 (1994), 25–39.

Brett, Michael. 'The Realm of the Imām: The Fāṭimids in the Tenth Century', *Bulletin of the School of Oriental and African Studies* 59 (1996), 431–49.

Brett, Michael. *The Rise of the Fatimids: The World of the Mediterranean and the Middle East in the Tenth Century* CE. Leiden, Boston, and Cologne: E. J. Brill, 2001.

De Blois, François. *Arabic, Persian and Gujarati Manuscripts: The Hamdani Collection*. London: I. B. Tauris Publishers in association with the IIS, 2011.

Ebstein, Michael. *Mysticism and Philosophy in al-Andalus: Ibn Masarra, Ibn al-ʿArabī and the Ismāʿīlī Tradition*. Leiden and Boston: E. J. Brill, 2014.

Götz, Manfred. 'Māturīdī and his *Kitāb Taʾwīlāt al-Qurʾān*'. In: Andrew Rippin (ed.). *The Qurʾān: Formative Interpretation*, pp. 181–214. Aldershot: Ashgate, 1999.

Halm, Heinz. *Die islamische Gnosis: Die extreme Schia und die ʿAlawiten*. Zurich: Artemis Verlag, 1982.

Ḥusayn, Muḥammad Kāmil, *Fī adab Miṣr al-Fāṭimiyya*. Cairo: Dār al-Fikr al-ʿArabī, 1950.

Ivanow, Wladimir. *Studies in Early Persian Ismailism*. 2nd edn. Bombay: Ismaeli Society, 1955.

Izutsu, Toshihiko. 'Revelation as a Linguistic Concept in Islam', *Studies in Medieval Thought* 5 (1962), 122–67.

Poonawala, Ismail K. *Biobibliography of Ismāʿīlī Literature*. Malibu, CA: Undena Publications, 1977.

Poonawala, Ismail K. 'Ismāʿīlī Taʾwīl of the Qurʾān'. In: Andrew Rippin (ed.). *Approaches to the History of the Interpretation of the Qurʾān*, pp. 212–22. Oxford: Clarendon Press, 1988.

Poonawala, Ismail K. 'Taʾwīl'. In *Encyclopaedia of Islam*. Second edn. 10:390–2. Leiden: E. J. Brill, 1960–2005.

Poonawala, Ismail K. 'al-Ẓāhir wa'l-Bāṭin'. In: *Encyclopaedia of Islam*. Second edn. 11:389–90. Leiden: E. J. Brill, 1960–2005.

Steigerwald, Diana. '*Ismāʿīlī Taʾwīl*'. In: Andrew Rippin (ed.). *The Blackwell Companion to the Qur'an*, pp. 386–400. Oxford: Blackwell Publishing, 2006.

Tucker, William. *Mahdis and Millenarians: Shīʿite Extremists in Early Muslim Iraq*. Cambridge: Cambridge University Press, 2008.

Walker, Paul. *Early Philosophical Shiism: The Ismaili Neoplatonism of Abū Yaʿqūb al-Sijistānī*. Cambridge: Cambridge University Press, 1993.

CHAPTER 49

IBĀḌĪ *TAFSĪR* LITERATURE

VALERIE J. HOFFMAN AND
SULAIMAN BIN ALI BIN AMEIR AL-SHUEILI

OVERVIEW OF IBĀḌĪ *TAFSĪR* LITERATURE

IBĀḌĪ literature is full of discussion on the principles of Qur'an interpretation and on the interpretation of particular verses. Even the *Musnad* of al-Rabīᶜ ibn Ḥabīb, which is generally described as the Ibāḍī hadith collection, has sayings that adduce a clearly Ibāḍī perspective on core doctrines. However, there is a near-dearth of complete Ibāḍī *tafsīrs* until the modern period, and Ibāḍī *tafsīr* in general is based on or responds to Sunnī *tafsīr* literature. There are no more than four extant and complete Ibāḍī *tafsīrs* of the Qur'an.

Although medieval Ibāḍī historians claimed that the Ibāḍī Imam, ᶜAbd al-Raḥmān ibn Rustam (d. 171/787), wrote a *tafsīr* (Kharusi 2004: 270), no trace of such a work exists, and Wilkinson considers it 'a fable' (Wilkinson 2010: 386). The earliest extant Ibāḍī *tafsīr* is *Tafsīr Kitāb Allāhi 'l-ᶜAzīz*, by the Berber scholar Hūd ibn Muḥakkam al-Hawwārī (d. *c.*290/903), a *qāḍī* for the Rustamid Imam Aflaḥ ibn ᶜAbd al-Wahhāb (r. 208–28/823–72). His commentary is essentially an abridged and doctrinally adapted version of the *tafsīr* of the Basran scholar Yaḥyā ibn Sallām. Hūd, a Berber of the Aurès mountains in north-eastern Algeria, met a grandson of Yaḥyā ibn Sallām during his studies in Qayrawan, and thanks to this encounter he gained access to Yaḥyā's *tafsīr* and 'added to it' (Hawwārī 2005: 1:9). Hūd's commentary is mainly based on hadiths and reports from the Companions and Successors, but on certain doctrinal issues, such as the relationship between faith and works and the anthropomorphic descriptions of God, he adheres to Ibāḍī doctrines, adducing proofs for his interpretations mainly from other Qur'anic verses and from sayings of the Prophet, Companions, and Successors. Like other Ibāḍī authors, he does not provide complete *isnāds*, contenting himself with the names of only one or at most two of the transmitters of the reports. His commentary is also marked by an abundance of *isrāʾīliyyāt*. It was first published in Algiers and Beirut in 1990 with thorough editing and annotation by Bālḥājj ibn Saʿīd al-Sharīfī. The value of Hūd's commentary lies not only in the fact that it is the earliest extant Ibāḍī Qur'an commentary, but also that it preserves much of Ibn Sallām's *tafsīr*, of which only fragments have survived (Gilliot 1997).

The next complete Ibāḍī *tafsīr* appears some 900 years later, written in 1181/1757 by the Omani scholar Saʿīd ibn Aḥmad al-Kindī (1718–40) and titled *al-Tafsīr al-muyassar li'l-Qurʾān al-karīm*. He says that he based his work on the *tafsīrs* of al-Nasafī (d. 701/1310), al-Baghawī (d. 516/1122), al-Bayḍāwī (d. *c*.719/ 1319), al-Zamakhsharī (d. 538/1144), al-Ṭabarsī (d. 548/1153), and Abū'l-Suʿūd al-ʿImādī (d. 982/1574), although it is clear that the commentaries of al-Zamakhsharī and al-Bayḍāwī were most important. His reliance on al-Zamakhsharī is evident in his commentary on Q. 5:77, where he failed to edit out a reference to 'the theologians of the People of Justice and Unity (*ahl al-ʿadl wa-'l-tawḥīd*)' (al-Kindī 2004: 1:331). He also cites works by Ibāḍī scholars of Oman, such as Abū Saʿīd Muḥammad al-Kudamī (d. 353/964–356/967), Muḥammad ibn Jaʿfar al-Izkawī (third/ninth century) and Muḥammad ibn Ibrāhīm al-Kindī (d. 508/1114–15). Unlike Hūd, al-Kindī utilizes hadiths and other reports sparingly, as his main interest is in clarifying the meaning of verses and words. His commentary was edited by Algerian scholars Muṣṭafā ibn Muḥammad Sharīfī and Muḥammad ibn Mūsā Bābāʿammī and was published in 1998 in Cairo and again in 2004 in Oman.

The great Algerian scholar, Muḥammad ibn Yūsuf Aṭfiyyash (sometimes rendered Aṭfayyish, Aṭfiyyāsh, or even Tfeiche) (1237–1332/1821–1914), known as *quṭb al-aʾimma* (axis of the imams) or simply as al-Quṭb, a scholar of prodigious scholarship and tremendous influence, wrote no fewer than three *tafsīrs*. He completed his first *tafsīr*, *Himyān* [often rendered *Hīmyān*] *al-zād ilā dār al-maʿād* (Abundant provision for the afterlife), in May 1855. It was first published in fourteen volumes by the press of the sultanate of Zanzibar from 1888 to 1897 and was republished in Oman in fifteen volumes in 1980, 1983, and 1988. He begins his commentary on each sura with an introduction in which he mentions the names of the sura, which parts of it are Meccan and which are Medinan, the number of its verses, words, and letters, and hadiths about the excellence of the sura. Then he moves through the chapter verse by verse, citing any variants in the reading of the verse and discussing the meanings of the words and points regarding their vocalization and morphology and the verse's rhetorical construction. He discusses anything in the verse that touches on *fiqh* or theology, discussing the proofs cited by various thinkers, while supporting the Ibāḍī perspective. He clarifies any stories told in the sura with reference to al-Thaʿlabī's *ʿArāʾis al-majālis*. He attempts to resolve ambiguities by utilizing the style of debate (*fa-in qulta... qultu*), following the style of al-Zamakhsharī.

Most scholars say that Aṭfiyyash's second *tafsīr*, *Dāʿī 'l-ʿamal li-yawm al-amal* (Inviting to work toward the day of hope), which was never published, remained incomplete, covering only suras 55 to 114—only four of the author's intended thirty-two volumes. Ouintin, however, points to evidence in the manuscripts and in Aṭfiyyash's introduction to his third *tafsīr* indicating that this *tafsīr* was, in fact, complete (Ouintin 1996: 483

n. 12); he therefore concludes that parts of it have simply gone missing. This *tafsīr* goes into more investigative depth than the *Himyān*, according to Aṭfiyyash's nephew, Abū Isḥāq Ibrāhīm Aṭfiyyash, although Yahia Bouterdin says it is comparable in length and breadth to the *Himyān* and was written to correct some errors in the earlier work (Bouterdin 1989: 195). It is being edited for publication by Muṣṭafā Bājū, under the supervision of Muḥammad Bābāʿammī and Muṣṭafā Sharīfī.

Aṭfiyyash's last and most popular *tafsīr* is *Taysīr al-tafsīr li-'l-Qurʾān al-karīm*, which the author completed when he was more than 80 years old (Aṭfiyyash 1996: 1:*ghayn*, n. 2). It was first published as a lithograph in Algiers in seven thick volumes in 1907–8, and republished in fifteen volumes by the Ministry of National Heritage and Culture in the Sultanate of Oman from 1981 to 1988. It was then edited by Ibrāhīm Muḥammad Ṭallāy and republished in Ghardaïa, Algeria in 1996. In his introduction to the *Taysīr*, Aṭfiyyash says that he wrote it because people were bewildered by the *Himyān* and too lazy to read the *Dāʿī*, so he decided to write a *tafsīr* that would be more appealing and accessible (Aṭfiyyash 1996: 1:1). In the *Taysīr* he takes a strong stand against those he deems to have interpreted the Qur'an according to their unsubstantiated opinions. Sometimes he takes the role of a trustworthy transmitter of traditional reports concerning the stories in the Qur'an, while other times he subjects these reports to a detailed deconstruction.

Perhaps the most popular Ibāḍī Qur'an commentary today is *Fī Riḥāb al-Qurʾān* (In the company of the Qur'an) by Shaykh Ibrāhīm ibn ʿUmar Bayyūḍ (1899–1981) of Qarāra (El Guerrara), Algeria. This work, which is published in nineteen volumes, is a transcription of tape recordings of Bayyūḍ's lessons on *tafsīr* given in the mosque. These lessons were only recorded beginning with Q. 17:70, so that is where the published work begins. It marks a departure from earlier Ibāḍī exegeses in that it features long discourses on contemporary issues, which has led contemporary Ibāḍīs to compare it to *Tafsīr al-Manār* by Muḥammad ʿAbdūh (d. 1905) and Rashīd Riḍā (d. 1935), although Bayyūḍ's reformist agenda was markedly more conservative than theirs. In preparing his lessons, he did consult *Tafsīr al-Manār*, in addition to the commentaries of Maḥmūd Shahāb al-Dīn al-Ālūsī (d. 1270/1854), Fakhr al-Dīn al-Rāzī (d. 606/1210), Sayyid Quṭb (d. 1966), and Aṭfiyyash's *Taysīr* (Bouterdin 1989: 171), but his work is both original and oriented toward a general audience. His commentary on a sura or on a portion of it would focus on its textual context in relation to the rest of the Qur'an. Seeing himself as a social reformer, Bayyūḍ focused on the doctrinal and practical lessons to be drawn from a passage.

The Mufti of the Sultanate of Oman, Shaykh Aḥmad ibn Ḥamad al-Khalīlī (b. 1943), began delivering lessons in *tafsīr* to students at the Institute of Sharīʿa Sciences in Muscat in 1980. These lessons were tape-recorded and four volumes have been published under the title *Jawāhir al-tafsīr: Anwār min bayān al-tanzīl*: vol. 1 (1984) is on the methodology of Qur'anic exegesis and on the Fātiḥa; vol. 2 (1986) is on Q. 2:1–9; vol. 3 (1988) is on Q. 2:30–96; and a special volume (2004) on Q. 3:7, in order to clarify the meaning of the 'categorical' or foundational verses (*muḥkamāt*) and the ambiguous verses (*mutashābihāt*), who may interpret the ambiguous verses, and the method of doing so. In his introduction to this special volume he expresses his regret that his responsibilities have kept him from continuing work on his commentary, leaving it to God to make that possible.

Shaykh al-Khalīlī begins his commentary on sura 2 with a discussion of the name of the sura, the time of its revelation, the number of its verses, the historical context in Medina at the time, and the major themes of the sura. He quotes thirty-three religious principles that Rashīd Riḍā laid out in the introduction to *Tafsīr al-Manār*, citing his agreement with them, and then adding to them further comments on *jihād*, *ijtihād*, the limitations of human reason in matters of jurisprudence, and quoting reports on the excellence of the sura. On page 56 he finally begins a detailed discussion of each verse, analysing its vocalization, morphology, and rhetorical style, citing any variant readings and their implications, the lessons of *fiqh* and theology that can be derived from it, and their social and pedagogical implications. He cites and occasionally critiques the commentaries of al-Ṭabarī (d. 310/923), al-Zamakhsharī, Abū'l-Suʿūd, Ibn ʿAṭiyya (d. 546/1152), Abū Ḥayyān al-Gharnāṭī (d. 745/1344), al-Ālūsī, Muḥammad al-Ṭāhir ibn ʿĀshūr (d. 1973), and *Tafsīr al-Manār*.

Other Ibāḍī works of *tafsīr* and glosses on existing commentaries include a gloss on Hūd's *tafsīr*, up to Q. 2:238, by Muḥammad ibn ʿUmar ibn Abī Sitta (d. 1088/1677) of Jirba; Abū Yaʿqūb Yūsuf ibn Muḥammad al-Malīkī (d. 1188/1774) of the Mzāb wrote a gloss on *Tafsīr al-Jalālayn* that remains unpublished (Ibn Yaʿqūb 1986: 133); Ibrāhīm ibn Bīḥmān al-Thamīnī (d. 1232/1817) of Mzāb wrote *tafsīr*s on suras 1 and 103 and a gloss on the *tafsīr* of al-Bayḍāwī (Bābāʿammī et al. 2000: 2:14); Muḥammad ibn Sulaymān ibn Idrīsū (d. 1313/1896) began a *tafsīr*, but completed only the first three suras (Bouterdin 1989: 182); Ṣāliḥ ibn ʿUmar Laʿlī (d. 1928) of Mzāb wrote *al-Qawl al-wajīz fī tafsīr kalām Allāh al-ʿazīz*, in which he interpreted two sections of the Qur'an, beginning with the *Fātiḥa* and ending with Q. 2:181 (Bouterdin 1989: 158–64); Abū Nabhān Jāʿid ibn Khamīs al-Kharūṣī (d. 1822) of Oman began a *tafsīr* titled *Maqālīd al-tanzīl*, but he did not get beyond the *Fātiḥa*; Abū Isḥāq Ibrāhīm Aṭfiyyash (d. 1965), who was originally from Wādī Mzāb but spent most of his life in exile in Egypt, wrote a *tafsīr* called *Ta'wīl al-mutashābih*, but it seems that he may not have completed it, and it has never been published. In addition, many scholars have written on the sciences of the Qur'an.

IBĀḌĪ *TAFSĪR* METHODOLOGY

The Ibāḍīs are no different from other Muslims in their general approach to Qur'an interpretation, with the possible exception of their attitude toward the efficacy of human reason in completing and clarifying the Sharīʿa and in interpreting 'ambiguous' verses (*mutashābihāt*) in the Qur'an, especially anthropomorphic descriptions of God, which they believe must be taken as metaphors. Faith in human reason is reflected in Hūd's commentary on Q. 24:35, in which 'he seems to suggest that the intellect is able to know right and wrong innately, almost without the need for divine revelation' (Hamza et al. 2008: 351).

Much space is devoted in exegeses to diverse definitions of the 'categorical' (*muḥkamāt*) and 'ambiguous' (*mutashābihāt*) verses referred to in Q. 3:7. Thanks to the lack of punctuation in Arabic and the subsumption of subject pronouns in the verb, the final sentence of the verse can be understood in two very different ways:

> No one knows its meaning except God. Those who are well-grounded in knowledge say, 'We believe in it...'.
>
> No one knows its meaning except God and those who are well-grounded in knowledge. They say, 'We believe in it...'.

The majority of Sunnī exegetes have understood this verse in the first manner, but al-Zamakhsharī and most Ibāḍī exegetes include 'those who are well-grounded in knowledge' among those who can understand the meaning of ambiguous verses. Although Hūd does not discuss the topic in a theoretical fashion, he consistently rejects a literal interpretation of anthropomorphic descriptions of God in the Qur'an (Gilliot 1997: 202–4). Muḥammad Aṭfiyyash and Aḥmad al-Khalīlī state that the existence of *mutashābihāt* encourages people to exercise their intellects in studying the Qur'an (Aṭfiyyash 1988: 4:15; al-Khalīlī 2004: 31–4). Interestingly, in the *Himyān*, Aṭfiyyash seems to favour the exclusion of human beings from knowledge of the meaning of ambiguous verses (Aṭfiyyash 1988: 4:19), but in *Tayṣīr* he unequivocally states that those who are well grounded in knowledge may know their meaning (Aṭfiyyash 1996: 2:244).

All Ibāḍī exegetes see 'There is nothing like Him' (42:11) as foundational (*muḥkam*) and require *ta'wīl* of any verses that appear to imply a likeness between God and creatures. The antiquity of this attitude is evident in the fact that the Ibāḍī hadith collection attributed to al-Rabīʿ ibn Ḥabīb (d. 170/786)—although Wilkinson (2010: 432–6) argues that it is not strictly a hadith collection and that it was not authored by al-Rabīʿ—includes a number of sayings on the proper interpretation of Qur'anic anthropomorphisms such as God's shin, face, eye, and hand. In an unattributed 'note' (*tanbīh*), the *Musnad* says that if someone asks how one can know that these metaphorical interpretations are correct, one should respond by saying that expressions used in the texts are meant to be understandable, so if they are illogical or violate fundamental principles of the faith, such as God's perfection and difference from all created things, a metaphorical interpretation is required, bearing in mind the words of the Prophet, 'Every word has two meanings [literally 'aspects', *wajhān*], so interpret speech according to the best meaning' (Azdī 1970: 3:39–42). *Musnad al-Rabīʿ* consistently attributes anthropomorphic interpretations to the Jews, who are described as God's enemies ((Azdī 1970: 3:40).

Therefore, God's face (28:88, 55:25) means God Himself or His essence; 'His hands are open wide' (5:64) refers to His generous provision, His eye (20:39) refers to His command (Hawwārī 2005: 3:33) or His care and preservation (Aṭfiyyash 1988); His coming (2:210) means His command or judgement; His nearness (2:186) refers to His hearing prayer and His presence with people in paradise (54:55) refers to the ranks of honour the blessed will enjoy.

The throne (*ʿarsh* or *kursī*) of God is sometimes seen as a real thing, although they do not speak of God sitting on it. Hūd contents himself with quoting various reports about it. In the *Himyān*, Aṭfiyyash interprets God's throne as an allusion to His dominion and denounces acceptance of its apparent meaning as *kufr*, but in his interpretation of Q. 20:5 in *Taysīr*, he says that one cannot say the throne is merely a metaphor, because that would contradict hadiths like the one that says that angels carry the throne above the heavens as if it were a dome. Nonetheless, in his commentary on Q. 2:255 in that work, he states, 'There is no seat and no sitting; God transcends all that' (Aṭfiyyash 1996: 2:142), and suggests that it means God's dominion or power. On Q. 20:5, 'On the throne He is firmly established (*ʿalā 'l- ʿarsh istawā*),' Bayyūḍ says, 'God transcends inherence in places; place and direction do not affect Him, because He is not a body with a form or a substance that can be measured. Being firmly established means to assume power over something,' as illustrated in the line of poetry, 'Bishr assumed power (*istawā*) over Iraq without sword or bloodshed' (Bayyūḍ 2009: 12:32–3). In his commentary in *Taysīr* on Q. 67:16, 'Are you confident that He who is in heaven will not cause the earth to cave in beneath you?,'' Aṭfiyyash decries belief that God is in heaven as sheer ignorance, affirming that *taʾwīl* is an obligation 'as long as there is knowledge and light'.

Q. 6:103, 'Eyes do not perceive/comprehend Him, but He perceives/comprehends all vision,' is another 'foundational' verse, requiring the interpretation of Q. 75:22–3, 'Faces that day will be radiant, looking at/toward their Lord' to mean something other than that believers will see God in the afterlife. Sunnī Muslims have generally embraced the idea that believers will see God in paradise, and this is confirmed by a number of hadiths, including one that says they will see God as clearly as they can see the moon on a night when it is full, and will not include anything else in their vision of God (Bukhārī n.d.: no. 4851), and another that says the vision of God will be the greatest reward given to believers in paradise (al-Qushayrī 2000: no. 297). The Ibāḍīs, like the Muʿtazila before them, see ocular vision of God as an impossibility, because the eye sees only bodies, or parts of bodies, which have finite dimensions, occupy space, are composed of parts, and have substance and accidents—all of which are impossible for God, who does not have a body. Ocular vision entails a number of stipulations regarding its object, including shape, colour, the positioning of the object in front of the viewer, and the ability of the viewer to encompass (*iḥāṭa*) the object, all of which are absurd with respect to God (Thamīnī 1986: 2:43).

The interpretation of Q. 75:22–3 revolves around three main issues: (1) the meaning(s) of looking (*naẓar*); (2) the attribution of looking to faces that are described as radiant; and (3) the use of the preposition *ilā* (at/to). Ibāḍīs, like the Muʿtazilī exegete al-Zamakhsharī, interpret 'looking' in this verse as 'waiting' or 'anticipating', and they do not hesitate to enumerate a large number of other ways that *naẓar* may be used in Arabic (Rāzī 1981: 30:226–7; Warjlānī 2006: 1:93; Saʿdī 1983–9: 5:347–8; al-Khalīlī 2001: 42–3), concluding that to insist that *naẓar* means sight is mere caprice. Sunnīs argue that the attribution of *naẓar* to faces indicates that it means seeing, since eyes are in the face, whereas waiting is in the heart, but Ibāḍīs say, from evidence drawn from other Qur'anic verses, that 'face' refers to the whole person, just as the neck is sometimes used to describe the whole person (e.g. 4:92), and that the description of faces in this verse as radiant is paralleled by other passages to the same effect (e.g. 80:38–41) and the gloominess of the faces of the infidels mentioned in the verses that immediately follow those under discussion

(75:24–5). Furthermore, in this last passage the faces of the unbelievers are described as thinking (*taẓunn*) that some calamity was about to fall upon them, 'but faces cannot be described as thinking; only hearts think' (Thamīnī 1986: 2:34; cf. Saʿdī 1983–9: 5:380 and al-Khalīlī 2001: 46). Ibāḍīs point out that al-Ghazālī also said that vision may be in the heart or the intellect, and may simply mean an increase in unveiling (*kashf*) or knowledge (*maʿrifa* and *ʿilm*) (Ghazālī 2003: 66–7).

Sunnīs say that the attachment of *ilā* to *naẓar* indicates that it can only mean that the believers are 'looking at' God, and excludes the meaning of waiting or expecting (Ashʿarī 2010: 46; Warjlānī 2006: 1:94). Ibāḍīs respond with a well-worn inventory of Qur'anic verses (e.g. 2:280, 36:49, 38:15, 57:13), old Arab sayings (Azdī 1970: 3:27, no. 855), and lines of poetry (Hoffman 2012: 113) that indicate otherwise. They also say that the positioning of *ilā rabbihā* ('to their Lord') before *nāẓira* ('looking') places the emphasis not on the looking of the believers, but on God Himself, indicating that He alone is the object of waiting—whereas He cannot be the sole object of sight, since the Qur'an makes clear that believers will be looking at many things on the Day of Resurrection (Thamīnī 1986: 2:34; Hoffman 2012: 112–13, 117).

Another verse often discussed on this topic is Q. 7:143, in which Moses asks God to show Himself to him and God replies, 'You will never see Me (*lan tarānī*). But look at the mountain: if (*law*) it remains in its place, then you will see Me.' When God showed Himself to the mountain, it crumbled into dust and Moses fainted; upon returning to his senses, he repented. This passage raises numerous questions: (1) If it is impossible to see God, why did Moses request this? As a prophet, shouldn't he have known it was impossible? (2) What is the significance of the particle *lan* in God's response, 'You will never see Me'? (3) What is the meaning of God's manifestation to the mountain, and what is the significance of the linkage of the possibility of seeing God with the stability of the mountain? And finally, (4) why did Moses repent?

Sunnīs argue that the fact that Moses asked God to show Himself to him indicates that the vision of God is possible (Ashʿarī 2010: 48; Rāzī 1981: 14:238). Hūd cites with apparent approval al-Ḥasan al-Baṣrī's opinion that Moses asked to see God because he thought this *was* possible for him (Hawwārī 2005: 2:44). Al-Warjlānī argued that Moses did not know all impossible things, and that the idea that prophets know all impossible things is negated by God's rebuke to Noah, 'Do not ask me about things of which you have no knowledge' (Warjlānī 2006: 1:92). Most Ibāḍīs, however, do not take this view; they generally agree that a prophet must know what is possible and impossible for God, but they argue that Moses made this request because his people had told him they would not believe him unless they saw God openly (2:55, 4:153). Since they would not listen to him, Moses hoped they would accept this response from God. Moses knew God's attributes well enough to realize that He cannot be seen; he did this for the benefit of his people, because of their demand to see God (Azdī 1970: 3:34, no. 869). As proof that Moses knew that God could not be seen, Ibāḍīs point out that Moses described those who made this request as foolish (Q. 7:155) (Saʿdī 1983–9: 5:412; al-Khalīlī 2001: 35). Curiously, Bayyūḍ wrote, 'Moses delighted in the sweetness of intimate conversation (*al-munājāt*) [with God] and wanted to prolong the conversation... He aspired to what was even greater than that, to see God.' Bayyūḍ said that Moses did not have the aptitude (*istiʿdād*) to see the divine light, though he did have exceptional aptitude to hear the divine speech (Bayyūḍ 2009: 8:354).[1] This interpretation is surprising, as it leaves open the possibility that God could be perceptible, something other Ibāḍī scholars vehemently deny. Whereas some Sunnīs argued that God's response to Moses' request, '*Lan tarānī*', is only a denial of vision in this life (al-Ālūsī 1970–7: 9:48), Ibāḍīs say that the particle *lan* implies categorical negation. In words echoed in later Ibāḍī works, *Musnad al-Rabīʿ* says, '*Lan* is one of the words that, according to grammarians, indicate deprivation of hope, meaning that no one will ever see Him—in this world or the next' (Azdī 1970: 3:34).

Sunnīs have argued that God's linkage of the possibility of seeing Him to the stability of the mountain, which is in itself possible, indicates that seeing God is also possible (Rāzī 1981: 14:240–1). The Muʿtazilī Abū Ṭāhir responded that, at the time that God said this, the mountain was already crumbling, so it was *not* possible (Saʿdī 1983–9: 5:392). Unlike the Muʿtazila, however, Ibāḍīs believe that God's decree determines what will happen, so some argue that, since God's decree had determined the crumbling of the mountain, it was, in fact, impossible for it to remain stable (Aṭfiyyash 1996: 5:175; al-Khalīlī 2001: 39). Aṭfiyyash writes that God made the mountain come alive and gave it an intellect before manifesting Himself to it (Aṭfiyyash 1996: 5:175). Hūd says that God showed the mountain some of His signs, since it is impossible for God to show Himself (Hawwārī 2005: 2:44). Al-Khalīlī points out that the word *law* is a conditional particle that actually excludes possibility (al-Khalīlī 2001: 39). Moses repented, say the Ibāḍīs, because he had asked to see God. As proof, they point to the fact that a thunderbolt struck the Children of Israel because they had asked to see God with their own eyes (Q. 2:55).

A doctrine of major importance to Ibāḍism is that good deeds and fulfilling religious obligations are essential to faith. Only those who fulfil their religious obligations may properly be called believers. But whereas radical Khawārij, such as the Azāriqa, condemned grave sinners as unbelievers (*mushrikūn*), the Ibāḍīs recognize two types of infidelity (*kufr*): (1) *kufr shirk*, unbelief, which refers only to those outside the Islamic umma; and (2) the unfaithfulness of unrepentant sinning monotheists. This last is called *kufr nifāq* (the infidelity of hypocrisy) or *kufr niʿma* (ingratitude for God's blessing). In their interpretations of the Qur'an, Ibāḍīs make clear that not all references to *kuffār* in the Qur'an mean people outside the *umma* of the Prophet. For this reason, we translate *kufr* here as 'infidelity' rather than as 'unbelief'.

On Q. 5:44, 'Those who do not judge by what Allah has sent down, such people are infidels,' Hūd cites a saying of Ḥudhayfa ibn al-Yamān indicating that this verse refers to Jews, Christians, and Muslims. Hūd adds, 'Anyone who does not follow the rules of his scripture is an infidel, an oppressor and a sinner. Nonetheless, the *kufr* of the People of the Book is unbelief (*shirk*), whereas the *kufr* of the people who confess faith in God and the Prophet is an infidelity of hypocrisy' (Hawwārī 2005: 1:426). Aṭfiyyash echoes this in

[1] This is similar to what al-Ālūsī says, although al-Ālūsī uses the word *qābiliyya* rather than *istiʿdād*; he says that Moses' request was a request to increase his *qābiliyya*, which he defines as *istiʿdād* (al-Ālūsī 1970–7: 9:45, 51). Al-Ālūsī states that Muḥammad was the only one ever to see God in this life (al-Ālūsī 1970–7: 9:50).

the *Himyān*: 'The infidels are those who gravely disobey God in a way that contradicts gratitude, either by the infidelity of unbelief (*kufr al-shirk*) or by the infidelity of hypocrisy.' And on Q. 14:28, 'Do you not see those who have exchanged Allah's blessing for *kufr*,' Hūd says, 'The infidelity of the unbelievers (*al-mushrikīn*) is denial (*takdhīb*), and the infidelity of the hypocrites is ingratitude for God's blessings. If there is no gratitude for blessings, they are covered up (*kufirat*)' (Hawwārī 2005: 2:327). On Q. 2:3, Aṭfiyyash in the *Himyān* cites a hadith indicating that those who do not fulfil their religious obligations have no faith; Hūd, Bayyūḍ, and al-Khalīlī all cite the hadith in which the Prophet describes faith as having more than sixty characteristics, the least of which is the removal of harm from the path. On Q. 32:19, 'Those who believe and do good deeds will dwell in the gardens of refuge as a reward for what they did,' Bayyūḍ says, 'Most of the time, when the Qur'an mentions faith, it joins it to good deeds, so no one should think that mere belief in the heart and profession with the tongue exempts a person from performing [religious duties] with the limbs, as some do' (Bayyūḍ 2009: 12:107). Elsewhere he writes, 'Every belief in the heart that is not manifested on the outside is null and void and has absolutely no value' (Bayyūḍ 2009: 9:19).

Hūd takes aim not only at those who would delink faith and works, but also at the radical Khawārij who deny that sinners constitute a legitimate part of the *umma*. On Q. 9:54, 'They come to prayer lazily, and they give only under compulsion,' Hūd says the fact that the hypocrites donate their wealth, however begrudgingly, to jihad is proof against the 'people of division' (*ahl al-firaq*, i.e. the radical Khawārij) that they are not unbelievers, because unbelievers would not be required to go to jihad or donate to the cause (Hawwārī 2005: 2:140).

Grave sinners who do not repent will not enter paradise. On Q. 4:123, 'Not according to your desires,' al-Kindī writes that this refers to the unbelievers and the hypocrites, adding that God's promise of reward is obtained only by faith and good deeds (al-Kindī 2004: 1:274). Ibāḍīs do not believe in a temporary punishment in hellfire for sinning Muslims. Al-Kindī attacks this belief, which is pervasive among both Sunnīs and Shīʿa, as the same satanic delusion from which the Children of Israel suffered when they claimed that 'the Fire will only touch us for a number of days' (Q. 2:80). But the Qur'an rejects this claim, insisting in the following verse (2:81) that sinners will remain in hellfire forever. Al-Kindī says that this judgement applies to both the unbelievers and to those who are guilty of *kufr niʿma* (al-Kindī 2004:, 1:313). In his commentary on Q. 11:106–7, 'Those who are wretched will be in the fire... they will dwell in it forever,' Aṭfiyyash writes in the *Himyān* that this pertains to both polytheists and to monotheists who persist in sin.

Ibāḍīs deny that the Prophet will intercede for grave sinners; his intercession is reserved for the faithful, and serves not to remove people from hellfire but to increase their rank in paradise. Thus, on Q. 2:254, Hūd says that the denial of intercession applies to infidels. On that same verse, Aṭfiyyash in *Taysīr* writes, 'The angels, prophets, martyrs and scholars will intercede with God's permission, but only for the person who is saved (*saʿīd*), in order to raise his status or enable him to avoid the computation [of sins] or to reduce it, or other such things that do not negate judgment' (Aṭfiyyash 1996: 2:137–8).

Ibāḍīs deny the reality of God's attributes and the possibility of any eternal being besides God's essence. As God is the only Creator, all else must be created, including the heavenly scriptures. Many Sunnī theologians have held that the written or spoken Qur'an is only an expression or imitation of God's speech, whereas His essential speech (*al-kalām al-nafsī*) is an idea subsistent in God and does not consist of sounds, words, or letters. Ibāḍīs often make a similar distinction between God's essential speech and the revealed scriptures, which are created indicators (*madlūlāt*) of His knowledge and consist of letters and words (Hoffman 2012: 99–100). As al-Khalīlī writes, there is no indication that God's essential speech should be identified with the Qur'an (al-Khalīlī 2001: 103). Aṭfiyyash, on the other hand, rejects the very concept of God's essential speech and denies that the Qur'an is an expression (*tarjama*) of the essential speech, denouncing such a teaching as unsubstantiated and ignorant (Aṭfiyyash 1980: 1:447–8; Aṭfiyyash 1996: 5:173). The doctrine of the miraculousness (*iʿjāz*) of the Qur'an also provides him with an argument against its eternity, because what is eternal cannot be called miraculous (Aṭfiyyash 1996: 8:255). Bayyūḍ says that Q. 43:3, 'We made it an Arabic Qur'an,' indicates that it is created, not eternal. But he adds, 'This is a dead issue and it should remain in books. One should avoid matters of dispute because there is no benefit to stirring them up. Rather, teachers and educated people should know the truth of the matter and then keep quiet. Matters of dispute like this, on which there are various perspectives, need not divide the *umma*' (Bayyūḍ 2009: 17:421–3).

Although a number of similarities between Ibāḍī doctrines and those of the Muʿtazila have been noted, on the question of God's decree and determination Ibāḍī doctrine is the same as that of the Ashʿarī school. On 18:28, 'Do not obey those whose heart We have made heedless of Our remembrance,' Aṭfiyyash says, 'The verse explicitly states that God creates disobedience, just as He creates obedience, and ignorance, just as He creates knowledge' (Aṭfiyyash 1996: 8:331). This is indicated by Aṭfiyyash's insistence that there is nothing in Q. 18:29, 'Whoever wills may believe, and whoever wills may disbelieve,' to indicate that human beings have autonomy in their actions, even if faith and infidelity depend on human will, because both human acts and human will are created by God; the human being merely acquires them (Aṭfiyyash 1996: 8:334). Bayyūḍ engages in a long discussion on the topic, ultimately saying that the truth lies in a middle course between two extremes of free will and compulsion (Bayyūḍ 2009: 14:58–67).

Conclusion

Just as the *tafsīr* of al-Bayḍāwī is a Sunnī corrective of the Muʿtazilī *tafsīr* of al-Zamakhsharī, the earliest Ibāḍī *tafsīr* was written as a doctrinal corrective on an early Sunnī *tafsīr*. The fact that there are few manuscripts of Hūd's *tafsīr* indicates that Ibāḍīs did not feel the necessity of consulting complete Ibāḍī *tafsīr*s in order to teach Ibāḍī doctrine and Qur'an interpretation. In general, although Ibāḍīs wrote frequently on philology, rhetoric, theology, and the sciences of Qur'an interpretation, there has been little interest in the composition of complete Ibāḍī *tafsīrs* until the modern period. Ibāḍī teachers taught Qur'anic interpretation to their students using Sunnī *tafsīrs* as their reference before the publication of Aṭfiyyash's *tafsīrs* in the nineteenth century. Ibāḍī commentators have based their works on Sunnī *tafsīrs*, inserting the distinct doctrinal perspectives of their school at relevant points.

Stylistically, the *tafsīr* of Hūd al-Hawwārī is based mainly on the sayings of early authorities, the *tafsīrs* of Saʿīd al-Kindī and Muḥammad ibn Yūsuf Aṭfiyyash share the philological orientation of the commentaries on which they are based (al-Zamakhsharī, al-Bayḍāwī, al-Baghawī, and al-Ṭabarsī), and Bayyūḍ's *tafsīr* eclectically draws on a broad spectrum of old and new sources and is distinct in its long digressions on moral and religious topics and its intention to reach a broad audience.

Regardless of these stylistic differences, all Ibāḍī *tafsīrs* share the perspective that their doctrines regarding God, faith, and the afterlife are based on sound Qur'anic interpretation; whenever the literal meaning of the Qur'an contradicts these doctrines, the text must be interpreted in a non-literal manner that accords with possible lexicographical meanings and common linguistic usage.

Bibliography

Albayrak, I. and S. Al-Shueili. 'The Ibāḍī Approach to the Methodology of Qurʾānic Exegesis'. *Muslim World* 105 (2015), 163–93.

al-Ālūsī, M. S. *Rūḥ al-maʿānī fī tafsīr al-Qurʾān al-karīm wa-ʾl-sabʿ al-mathānī*. 30 vols. Beirut: Dār al-Turāth al-ʿArabī, 1970–7.

Ashʿarī, A. *Al-Ibāna ʿan uṣūl al-diyāna*. Ed. A. Ṣabbāgh. Beirut: Dār al-Nafāʾis, 2010.

Aṭfiyyash, M. *Tafsīr al-Qurʾān al-musammā 'Hīmyān [sic] al-zād ilā dār al-maʿād'*. 2nd edn. 15 vols. Muscat: Wizārat al-Turāth al-Qawmī wa-l-Thaqāfa, 1980. Accessible at <http://www.altafsir.com>.

Aṭfiyyash, M. *Taysīr al-tafsīr*, 17 vols. Ed. I. Ṭallāy. Ghardaïa: al-Maṭbaʿa 'l-ʿArabiyya, 1996.

Azdī, R. *Al-Jāmiʿ al-ṣaḥīḥ: musnad al-imām al-Rabīʿ ibn Ḥabīb*. 4 vols. Cairo: Maktabat al-Thaqāfa 'l-Dīniyya, 1970.

Bābāʿammī, M. et al. *Muʿjam aʿlām al-Ibāḍiyya min al-qarn al-awwal al-hijrī ilā 'l-ʿaṣr al-ḥāḍir, qism al-maghrib al-islāmī*. 2nd edn. 2 vols. Beirut: Dār al-Gharb al-Islāmī, 2000.

Bayyūḍ, I. *Fī riḥāb al-Qurʾān*. Ed. I. Bālḥājj. 2nd edn. 19 vols. Al-Qarāra (El Guerrara): Jamʿiyyat al-Turāth, 2009.

Bouterdin (Būterdīn), Y. S. *Al-Shaykh Aṭfayyish wa-madhhabuhu fī tafsīr al-Qurʾān al-karīm bi-'l-muqārana ilā tafāsīr ahl al-sunna*. Unpublished MA thesis, Department of Arabic, Faculty of Arts, Ain Shams University, 1989.

al-Bukhārī, M. *Al-Jāmiʿ al-musnad al-ṣaḥīḥ al-mukhtaṣar min umūr rasūl Allāh (Ṣaḥīḥ al-Bukhārī)*. Beirut: Dār al-Arqam, n.d.

Ghazālī, M. *Al-Iqtiṣād fī 'l-iʿtiqād*. Ed. I. Ramaḍān. Damascus: Dār Quṭayba, 2003.

Gilliot, C. 'Le Commentaire coranique de Hūd ibn Muḥakkam/Muḥkim', *Arabica* 44 (1997), 179–233.

Hamza, F. and S. Rizvi (eds.), with F. Mayer. *An Anthology of Qurʾanic Commentaries*, vol. 1: *On the Nature of the Divine*. London: Oxford University Press/Institute of Ismaili Studies, 2008.

Hawwārī, H. *Tafsīr kitāb Allāhi'l- ʿazīz*. Ed. I. B. N. Sharīfī. 2nd edn. 4 vols. Algiers: Dār al-Baṣāʾir, 2005. Also available online at <http://www.altafsir.com>.

Hoffman, V. J. *The Essentials of Ibāḍī Islam*. Syracuse, NY: Syracuse University Press, 2012.

Ibn Yaʿqūb, S. *Tārīkh jazīrat Jirba*. Tunis: Dār al-Juwaynī li'l-Nashr, 1986.

al-Khalīlī, A. *Jawāhir al-tafsīr: anwār min bayān al-tanzīl*. Muscat: Dār al-Istiqāma, 1984, 1986, 1988, 2004. Also available online at <http://www.altafsir.com>.

al-Khalīlī, A. *Al-Ḥaqq al-dāmigh*. Sīb, Oman: Maktabat al-Ḍāmirī, 2001.

Kharusi, K. 'An Overview of Ibāḍī *Tafsīr*'. In: R. G. Hoyland and P. F. Kennedy (eds.). *Islamic Reflections, Arabic Musings: Studies in Honour of Professor Alan Jones*, pp. 268–78. Oxford: Gibb Memorial Trust, 2004.

al-Kindī, S. *Al-Tafsīr al-muyassar li'l-Qurʾān al-karīm*. Ed. M. Sharīfī and M. Bābāʿammī. Muscat: Maktab al-Mustashār al-Khāṣṣ li-Jalālat al-Sulṭān li-'l-Shu'ūn al-Dīniyya wa'l-Tārīkhiyya, 2004.

Ouintin (Wīntin), M. *Ārāʾ al-Shaykh Amḥammad ibn Yūsuf Atfiyyash al-ʿaqdiyya*. Al-Qarāra (El Guerrara): Jamʿiyyat al-Turāth, 1996.

al-Qushayrī, M. *al-Jāmiʿ al-ṣaḥīḥ* (*Ṣaḥīḥ Muslim*). 2 vols. Vaduz: Thesaurus Islamicus Foundation, 2000.

Rāzī, M. *Tafsīr al-Fakhr al-Rāzī al-mushtahir bi-'Al-Tafsīr al-Kabīr' wa-'Mafātīḥ al-ghayb'*. 32 vols. Cairo: Dār al-Fikr, 1981.

Saʿdī, J. *Qāmūs al-sharīʿa al-ḥāwī ṭuruqahā 'l-wasīʿa*. 21 vols. Muscat: Wizārat al-Turāth al-Qawmī wa'l-Thaqāfa, 1983–9.

Thamīnī, A. *Kitāb maʿālim al-dīn*. 2 vols. Muscat: Wizārat al-Turāth al-Qawmī wa'l-Thaqāfa, 1986.

Warjlānī, Y. *Al-Dalīl wa'l-burhān*. Ed. S. Ḥārithī. 2nd edn. 3 vols. in 2. Muscat: Wizārat al-Turāth al-Qawmī wa-'l-Thaqāfa, 2006.

Wilkinson, J. C. *Ibāḍism: Origins and Early Development in Oman*. New York and Oxford: Oxford University Press, 2010.

CHAPTER 50

SUFI COMMENTARY

Formative and Later Periods

ALEXANDER KNYSH

Sufism: an Overview

Sufism (Ar., *taṣawwuf*), an ascetic-mystical movement in Islam, emerged in Iraq under the early Abbasids (the first half of the third/ninth century). Its competitors in the provinces were later subsumed under the title 'Sufism'. By the fifth/eleventh century, Sufi leaders (*shaykhs*) had produced a substantial body of normative oral and literary lore that became the source of identity and building bricks for Sufism's followers of the Middle Ages and beyond. With the emergence of the first Sufi 'brotherhoods', or 'orders' (*ṭuruq*; sing. *ṭarīqa*) in the sixth/twelfth century, Sufism became part and parcel of the religious, social, and political life of Islamic societies. In the modern epoch, Sufism was harshly criticized by Muslim modernists, fundamentalists, and leftists as a relic of the past, responsible for perpetuating idle superstitions, social inactivity, and senseless rituals. Nevertheless, it has managed to survive this critical onslaught and to remain relevant to the life of Muslim communities worldwide (Knysh 2010 and 2017).

Ascetic-Mystical Piety and the Qur'an

From the outset, the Qur'an was the principal source of contemplation and inspiration for every pious Muslim, whether formally Sufi or not. Many Sufi concepts and terms take their origin in the Qur'anic text, which endows them with much needed legitimacy in the eyes of both Sufis and other Muslims. At the same time, Sufi interpretations of the scripture (as well as Sufi practices, values, and beliefs) have continually been challenged by influential representatives of the Sunnī and Shīʿī religious establishment, occasionally resulting in persecution of individual Sufi teachers (de Jong and Radtke 1999). Sufis have often been accused of overplaying allegorical-mystical aspects of the Qur'an, claiming privileged, intuitive understanding of its contents and ignoring its literal sense. To respond to their criticisms, advocates of Sufism have used carefully selected Qur'anic verses to legitimize their brand of Islamic thought and practice.

Such verses emphasize proximity and intimacy between God and his human servants (e.g. Q. 2:115, 2:186; 20:7–8, 58:7, etc.). Thus, in Q. 50:16 God's immediate presence among his faithful is forcefully brought home, as he declares himself to be nearer to his human servant than 'his jugular vein'. Intimacy between God and human beings is occasionally depicted in the Qur'an in terms of mutual love between them, as in Q. 5:54 (cf. Q. 3:31; 3:76; 3:134, 3:146; 3:148; 3:159; 5:93, etc.). Deeming themselves paragons of piety and devotion to God and true heirs of the Prophet, Sufis understood such verses primarily, if not exclusively, as referring to themselves. In shaping a distinctive mystical cosmology and metaphysics Sufi thinkers put the Qur'an to new, creative uses. Thus, the famous 'light verse' (Q. 24:35), which depicts God as a sublime and unfathomable light, is highly conducive to mystical elaborations on the theme of light and darkness and the eternal struggle between spirit and matter. According to early Sufi exegetes, God guides whom he wishes with his light (2:257). However, he has a special predilection for the pious, humble, and God-fearing individuals who devote themselves single-mindedly to worshipping him. In return, God assures them of salvation in the Hereafter (2:38; 2:262; 2:264, 3:170, etc.). Muslim ascetics and mystics have consistently identified themselves with God's 'friends' or 'God's protégés' (*awliyāʾ*), mentioned in 8:34; 10:62; and 45:19. In the Sufi tradition, these elect individuals are consistently depicted as guides and intercessors on behalf of ordinary believers and identified with authoritative Sufi masters (*shaykhs* or *pīrs*), both living and deceased.

The Qur'an also provides Sufis with justifications of their world-renouncing, penitent attitudes. Thus, Q. 7:172, which figures prominently in Sufi exegetical discourses, describes a pre-eternal covenant/pact (*mīthāq*) between God and his servants (Böwering 1980: 146–65). During this momentous event, the human race appeared before God as an assemblage of disembodied souls. God demanded that the souls bear witness to his absolute sovereignty (*rubūbiyya*), and they complied. However, once endowed by God with sinful and restive bodies, the majority of humans have forgotten their pledge and therefore should be constantly reminded about it by divinely commissioned messengers and prophets. The loyal servants of God recognize their bodily existence in this world as a test, so they strive to avoid its allure and return to the state of the pristine faithfulness to their Lord that they proclaimed on the day of the covenant/pact. This goal is to be achieved by minimizing the corruptive drives of the human lower soul (*nafs*) that 'prompts [believers] to evil' (*ammāra bi-sūʾ*; Q. 12:53). If successful, the Sufi's restive self is transformed into a soul 'at peace' (*al-muṭmaʾinna*; Q. 89:27) that is incapable of disobeying its Lord. The Sufi tradition offers the means to this end: an ascetic and frugal life, pious meditation, and a constant remembrance of God (*dhikr*), as explicitly enjoined in

Q. 8:87, 18:24, and 33:41. Finally, the verses describing the visionary experiences of the Prophet Muḥammad (namely, Q. 17:1 and Q. 53:1–18) have motivated Sufis to try to recapture his spiritual conditions, especially since the Qur'an repeatedly encourages the faithful to imitate him (Q. 2:143; 3: 20 and 31; 33:21, etc.)

While such verses resonated well with the aspirations of early Muslim ascetics and mystics, there were also those that did not, because they prescribe moderation in worship, enjoyment of family life, and fulfilment of social responsibilities, while also discouraging the 'excesses' of Christian monasticism (Q. 4:3–4, 25–8, 127; Q. 9:31; Q. 57:27). Yet, these passages, as well as numerous injunctions against world-renouncing behaviour found in the Prophet's Sunna, could be either ignored or allegorized away, especially since some of them are inconclusive or ambiguous (e.g. Q. 5:82, which can be interpreted as both criticism and praise of Christian monks). However, eventually the weight of scriptural evidence and social pressures has forced the majority of Sufis to steer a middle course—one that allowed them to participate in social life and raise families, while also pursuing their mystical vocation. As the body of Sufi lore grew with the passage of time and Sufism had become a distinctive system of practices and teachings, there emerged a specific Sufi exegesis aimed at justifying and encouraging adherents.

The First Sufi Exegetical Works and Principles of Sufi Exegesis

The earliest samples of Sufi exegesis were collected by a prolific Sufi writer from Nishapur Abū ʿAbd al-Raḥmān al-Sulamī (d. 412/1021) in his *Ḥaqāʾiq al-tafsīr* (True realities of [Qur'an] interpretation). This work is our principal source for the earliest stages of mystical exegesis in Islam. Its major representatives, al-Ḥasan al-Baṣrī (d. 110/728), Jaʿfar al-Ṣādiq (d. 148/765), Sufyān al-Thawrī (d. 161/787), and ʿAbd Allāh ibn al-Mubārak (d. 181/797) were not Sufis *stricto sensu*, since Sufism as a distinctive doctrine and practice had not yet emerged. Nevertheless, those pious individuals were 'co-opted' into Sufism by its later spokesmen, who portrayed them as Sufism's founding fathers before the name itself had come into wide circulation. Whereas their preoccupation with the spiritual and allegoric aspects of the scripture is impossible to deny, the authenticity of their exegetical logia, collected and transmitted by al-Sulamī a century and a half later, is far from obvious. The problem is particularly severe (and intriguing) in the case of the sixth Shīʿī imam Jaʿfar al-Ṣādiq, to the extent that some modern scholars attribute the exegetical material transmitted in his name to a certain 'Pseudo-Jaʿfar al-Ṣādiq', who 'flourished in fourth/tenth century' (Nguyen 2012: 94 and 182; based on Böwering 2001 and Bowering 1996). Jaʿfar al-Ṣādiq's role as a doyen of primeval esoteric-mystical exegesis is indeed difficult to ascertain, especially since his exegetical logia, as transmitted by al-Sulamī, are devoid of any distinctly Shīʿī themes (Nguyen 2012: 172, 177, 189, 196). It is, however, quite possible that elements of esoteric-mystical exegesis originated in the pious circles associated with the imam, who is frequently quoted in the standard Sufi manual of Abū'l-Qāsim al-Qushayrī (d. 465/1072), whereupon they were appropriated by two distinct traditions, Sunnī-Sufi and Shīʿī. If authentic, Jaʿfar al-Ṣādiq's statements at the beginning of al-Sulamī's *Ḥaqāʾiq al-tafsīr* are probably the earliest extant articulation of the methodological principles of esoteric-mystical exegesis. They describe the Qur'an as having four levels of meaning: *ʿibāra* (literal); *ishāra* (allegorical or allusive); *laṭāʾif* (subtle); and *ḥaqāʾiq* (real). Each of them has its own addressees, respectively: the common folk (*al-ʿawāmm*), the spiritual elite (*al-khawāṣṣ*.), God's friends (*awliyāʾ*), and the prophets (*anbiyāʾ*). More commonly, Sufi commentators discern only two aspects of the Qur'an: the outward/exoteric (*ẓāhir*) and the hidden/esoteric (*bāṭin*), thereby subsuming the moral/ethical/legal connotations of a given verse under 'literal' and its allegorical/mystical/anagogical ones under 'hidden'/'esoteric'. The former aspect is the domain of the ordinary believers, the latter of the Sufi 'friends of God' (*awliyāʾ*).

As demonstrated by Paul Nwyia, Jaʿfar's exegetical interests were worlds apart from those of his contemporary Muqātil ibn Sulaymān (d. 150/767), who represents a more conventional approach to the Qur'an that focuses on its historical and philological aspects. For example, unlike Muqātil, Jaʿfar al-Ṣādiq shows no interest in the historical circumstances surrounding the battle of Badr, as described in the Qur'an. When it says that 'God supported him [Muḥammad] with the legions you [his followers] did not see' (Q. 9:40), [Pseudo-]Jaʿfar interprets the 'legions' not as 'angels' (as argued by Muqātil and other exoterically minded exegetes), but as the spiritual virtues that the Sufi wayfarer acquires on his way to God (*ṭarīq*), namely, 'certitude' (*yaqīn*), 'trust in God' (*thiqa*), and submission to his will (*tawakkul*). Likewise, Jaʿfar interprets the Qur'anic injunction to 'purify My [God's] House (namely, the Kaʿba) for those who shall circumambulate it' (22:26) as a call upon the believer to 'purify [his] soul from any association with the disobedient ones and anything other than God'. Finally, Jaʿfar explains the phrase 'those who stay in front of it [the Kaʿba]' as an invitation for the ordinary believers to seek the company of 'the [divine] gnostics (*ʿārifūn*), who stand on the carpet of intimacy [with God] and service of Him'. The notion of the divinely bestowed 'gnosis', or mystical knowledge (*maʿrifa*), which Jaʿfar attributes to God's elect servants figures prominently in his exegesis (see e.g. his commentary on Q. 7:143; 27:34; 8:24; 7:160, etc). In later Sufi epistemology *maʿrifa* is consistently juxtaposed with both received wisdom (*naql*) and knowledge acquired through rational contemplation (*ʿaql*). For Jaʿfar and later Sufi commentators, the Qur'an is the only proper means of obtaining *maʿrifa*.

The next stage of the development of Sufi exegesis, or, in Nwyia's apt phrase, *une lecture introspective du Coran*, is associated with a cohort of individuals who lived in the third/ninth to early fourth/tenth centuries. Their Sufi credentials, with a few exceptions (e.g. al-Ḥakīm al-Tirmidhī, d. *c*.300/910), do not raise serious doubts. At least one of them (Aḥmad ibn ʿAṭāʾ al-Adamī, d. 311/ 922 or 923), and possibly also Dhū 'l-Nūn al-Miṣrī (d. 246/861), were involved in the transmission of Jaʿfar's exegetical *logia*, which seems to contradict Nguyen's dating of [Pseudo-]Jaʿfar's activities to the middle of the fourth/tenth century. The others—such as Sahl al-Tustarī (d. 283/896), Abū Saʿīd al-Kharrāz (d. 286/899), Abū'l-Ḥusayn al-Nūrī (d. 295/907), Abū'l-Qāsim al-Junayd (d. 298/910),

Abū Bakr al-Wāsiṭī (d. 320/932), and Abū Bakr al-Shiblī (d. 334/946)—are frequently cited in Sufi literature as authoritative sources of exegetical *logia* and, in the case of al-Tustarī, Ibn ʿAṭāʾ and al-Wāsiṭī, also as authors of Qurʾanic commentaries (Böwering 1987–9 and 1980). The Sufi Abū Saʿīd al-Khargūshī of Nishapur (d. 406/1015 or 407/1016) is also credited with a mystical *tafsīr* that still awaits its researcher (Nguyen 2012: 10).

The Growth of the Sufi Exegetical Tradition (From the Fifth/Eleventh to the Seventh/Thirteenth Centuries)

Al-Sulamī's collection of Sufi exegetical statements, which played the same role with regard to Sufi *tafsīr* as al-Ṭabarī's *Jāmiʿ al-bayān* with regard to traditional Sunnī exegesis (Böwering 1987–9: 265), laid the foundations for the subsequent evolution of this genre of Sufi literature. With time there emerged several distinct trends within the body of Sufi exegetical works that reflected the growing internal complexity of Sufi thought in the fifth/eleventh–seventh/thirteenth centuries. One such trend can be described as 'moderate', that is, aimed at bringing out esoteric/mystical aspects of the Qurʾanic text, while not neglecting its exoteric/literal sense. The moderate trend is represented by such Sufi luminaries as al-Qushayrī (d. 465/1072), Abū Ḥāmid al-Ghazālī (d. 505/1111), and Abū Ḥafṣ ʿUmar al-Suhrawardī (d. 632/1234).

Abūʾl-Qāsim al-Qushayrī of Nishapur is famous primarily as the author of the popular tract *al-Risāla [al-Qushayriyya] fī ʿilm al-taṣawwuf* that combines elements of Sufi biography with those of a Sufi manual (see Knysh (trans.), *Al-Qushayri's Epistle*, pp. xxv–xxvi). Like the *Risāla*, al-Qushayrī's Qurʾanic commentary *Laṭāʾif al-ishārāt* pursues a clear apologetic agenda: to advocate the teachings, values, and practices of 'moderate', Junayd-style Sufism. Combining elements of Sufi 'science', Shāfiʿī jurisprudence, hadith scholarship, and mystical exegesis (Nguyen 2012: 3 and 16), it seeks to demonstrate their complete harmony with Sunnī Islam. Started in 437/1045 (Nguyen 2012: 1, 101, and 254), this lengthy exegetical work consistently draws parallels between the gradual progress of the reader/listener from literal to subtler meanings (*laṭāʾif*) of the Qurʾanic text and the stages of the Sufi's experiential journey to God. The success of this exegetical progress, as well as that of the Sufi's journey on the path to God, depends on the wayfarer's ability to combine personal piety and spiritual purity with sound doctrinal convictions. Giving preference to one over the other will result in failure. Even after this felicitous combination of faith, beliefs, and practices is achieved, the mystical exegete still needs divine assistance in unravelling the deepest mysteries of the sacred text. The same applies, argues al-Qushayrī, to the Sufi wayfarer's striving on the path to God.

Al-Qushayrī's *Laṭāʾif al-ishārāt* describes the exegete's progressive immersion into the innermost meaning of the scripture as a movement, first, from the intellect to the heart, then to the spirit (*al-rūḥ*), then to the innermost secret (*al-sirr*) and, finally, to the secret of secrets (*sirr al-sirr*) of the Qur'an. Al-Qushayrī's approach to the Qur'an is marked by his meticulous attention to every detail of the Qur'anic word, from an entire verse to every single letter in it. Typical in this regard is his interpretation of the *basmala*, in which each letter of this phrase is endowed with an allegorical/esoteric meaning: the *bā'* stands for God's gentleness (*birr*) toward his 'saintly friends' (*awliyā'*); the *sīn*—for the secret (*sirr*) that he conveys to his chosen ones (*aṣfiyā'*); the *mīm*—for his bestowal of grace (*minna*) upon those who seek intimacy with him (*ahl wilayātihi*).

While such Kabbalistic speculations are not unique to al-Qushayrī, there is one feature that sets his *Laṭā'if* apart from them. For al-Qushayrī, the *basmala* is not a simple repetition of the same set of allegorical/esoteric meanings, because, in his view, the divine word allows no repetition. Rather, its meaning changes depending on the major themes contained in the particular suras that the *basmala* introduces. Thus, in discussing the symbolism of the *basmala* of Q. 7, al-Qushayrī implicitly links it to the themes of submission (*islām*), humility, and reverence required of the true believer as opposed to the rebellious behaviour of Iblīs, both of which are discussed in this sura (e.g. Q. 7:11–15, 31–3, 35–6, 39–40, etc.). Al-Qushayrī's interpretation of the *basmala* of sura 15 (*al-Ḥijr*) is quite different. The omission of the letter *alif* in the *basmala* of that sura without any rationally justifiable reason, either grammatical or morphological, according to al-Qushayrī, symbolizes God's arbitrary 'elevation' of Adam (despite his 'base' nature) and the concomitant 'humiliation' of the angels (despite their elevated status), as described in the main body of the sura in question.

Preoccupied as he is with the esoteric and symbolic aspects of the Qur'anic text, al-Qushayrī pays little heed to its historical and legal references, treating them primarily as windows onto Sufism's ideas and values. Thus, in discussing the spoils of war (*ghanīma*) mentioned in Q. 8:41 al-Qushayrī argues: '*Jihād* can be of two types: the external one [waged] against the infidels and the internal one [waged] against [one's] soul and Satan. In the same way as the lesser *jihād* involves [the seizure of] spoils of war after victory, the greater *jihad*, too, has the spoils of war of its own, that is, taking possession of his soul by the servant of God after it has been held hostage by its two enemies—passions and Satan.' A similar parallel is drawn between ordinary fasting, which involves abstention from food, sex, and drink, and the spiritual abstention of the Sufi from the allure of mundane life.

Despite its overall 'moderate' character, al-Qushayrī's *Laṭā'if al-ishārāt* is not devoid of the visionary and ecstatic elements found in more 'bold' Sufi commentaries. These 'bolder' aspects of al-Qushayrī's exegesis can be characterized as 'unitive', namely, alluding to the possibility of an ecstatic union between God and his chosen servants. As an example one can cite his interpretation of Q. 7:143, in which Moses requests that God appear to him only to be humbled by the sight of a mountain crumbling to dust, after God has shown himself to it. In the course of this fateful encounter, Moses' very personality is 'erased' in an act of [self-]annihilation in God (*fanā'*). In al-Qushayrī's words, 'Moses came to God as [only] those passionately longing and madly in love could. Moses came without Moses. Moses came, yet nothing of Moses was left to Moses. Thousands of men have traversed great distances, yet no one remembers them, while that Moses made [only] a few steps and [school]children will be reciting until the Day of Judgment: "When Moses came..."' Such ecstatic and potentially controversial passages notwithstanding, al-Qushayrī's *Laṭā'if al-ishārāt* can still be classified as 'moderate' in as much as the exegete strove to achieve a delicate balance between daring flights of mystical imagination and respect for the letter of the revelation, or, in the Sufi parlance, between the external law (Sharīʿa) of Islam and its esoteric aspect, or 'true reality' (*ḥaqīqa*). Overall, al-Qushayrī's exegetical works (for his *al-Tafsīr al-kabīr* see Nguyen 2012: 101–10) bear an eloquent testimony to his triple credentials: as a Sufi master, a Shāfiʿī *faqīh* and an Ashʿarī theologian (Nguyen 2012: 257–8).

Another example of 'moderate' Sufi *tafsīr* is *al-Kashf wa'l-bayān ʿan tafsīr al-Qur'ān* by Aḥmad ibn Muḥammad al-Thaʿlabī (d. 427/1035). Drawing heavily on al-Sulamī's *Ḥaqā'iq al-tafsīr*, al-Thaʿlabī meshes its Sufi exegetical *logia* with conventional exegetical materials culled from hadith as well as discussions of philological and legal intricacies of the Qur'anic text (Saleh 2004). Al-Thaʿlabī's work formed the foundation of the famous commentary *Maʿālim al-tanzīl fī tafsīr al-Qur'ān* by al-Ḥusayn al-Baghawī (*Tafsīr al-Baghawī*). Born in 438/1046 in Afghanistan, al-Baghawī distinguished himself primarily as a Shāfiʿī jurist and *muḥaddith*, whose thematically arranged collection of prophetic reports titled *Maṣābīḥ al-sunna* has become a standard work of this genre. Although al-Baghawī was not a fully-fledged Sufi, he led an ascetic and pious way of life and avoided contacts with temporal authorities. His *tafsīr* is marked by a meticulous concern for the exegetical materials going back to the Prophet and his companions (*al-tafsīr bi 'l-ma'thūr*) that he cites frequently throughout his work. Seeking comprehensiveness, al-Baghawī avails himself of diverse sources: from the leading Arab grammarians to the Shīʿī imams and legal scholars. To the same end, he quotes such proto-Sufi and Sufi figures as Ibrāhīm ibn Adham (d. 160/777), Fuḍayl ibn ʿIyāḍ (d. 188/803), al-Tustarī and al-Junayd (d. 298/910), whose exegetical *logia* may have reached him via al-Sulamī's *Ḥaqā'iq al-tafsīr* and al-Thaʿlabī's *al-Kashf wa'l-bayān*. Al-Baghawī's use of this material was probably dictated by his drive to furnish the entire range of possible interpretations of the sacred text without privileging anyone of them. Since, by his age, Sufism had established itself as a legitimate strain of Islamic theory and practice, he felt obligated to include Sufi views of the Qur'an into his *tafsīr* without necessarily sharing or condoning them. The same trend can be observed in many later exegetical works, such as *Lubāb al-ta'wīl* by ʿAlī ibn Muḥammad al-Baghdādī, better known as 'al-Khāzin' (d. 741/1341). The presence of Sufi elements in non-Sufi *tafsīrs* is indicative of the exegetes' desire for comprehensiveness—a trend that has gradually led to the blurring of the borderline between 'Sufi' and 'non-Sufi' exegesis and the inclusion of Sufi exegetical *logia* into conventional commentaries by both Sunnī and Shīʿī authors.

On the other hand, renowned Sufi masters produced quite conventional exegetical works that are practically devoid of esoteric elements. As an example, one can cite *Nughbat al-bayān fī tafsīr al-Qur'ān* by the renowned Sufi scholar ʿUmar al-Suhrawardī (d. 632/1234), which is sometimes classified under the rubric of 'moderate' Sufi exegesis (e.g. Böwering 1987–9: 257). This exegetical opus, which remains in manuscript (see

Düzenli 1994), furnishes a rather pedestrian, non-mystical commentary that is firmly grounded in the type of philological and situational exegesis represented in the standard Sunnī commentaries upon which al-Suhrawardī relied heavily (Ohlander 2008: 49, 143, and 250).

Our survey of 'moderate' Sufi exegesis would be incomplete without mentioning the Persian *tafsīr* by Rashīd al-Dīn Aḥmad al-Maybudī (d. 530/1135). Entitled *Kashf al-asrār*, it is based on the Qur'an commentary of the renowned Ḥanbalī mystic ʿAbd Allāh al-Anṣārī al-Harawī (d. 481/1089), as the author explicitly states in the introduction (Keeler 2006: 40). Born in a family renowned for its learning and piety in a town of Maybud (the province of Yazd in Iran), al-Maybudī combined the traditional education of a Shāfiʿī jurist and *muḥaddith* with a strong inclination to contemplative mysticism and ascetịcism (Keeler 2006:14–15). As the other 'moderate' Sufi commentaries discussed above, al-Maybudī's *Kashf al-asrār* provides conventional historical, philological, and legal exegesis alongside Sufi 'allusions' (*ishārāt*) and 'subtleties' (*laṭāʾif*). The commentator describes his method as consisting of three 'stages' (sing. *navbat*). The first involves a translation of selected Qur'anic verses from Arabic into 'literal Persian' (*fārsī-ya ẓāhir*); the second, a conventional historical, philological, and juridical commentary in Persian; while the third explores the mystical aspects of the revelation. The last 'stage', as mentioned, draws heavily on al-Anṣārī's mystical commentary, which, in its turn, is based on al-Sulamī's *Ḥaqāʾiq al-tafsīr* and the [proto-]Sufi authorities cited therein. It also makes use of the ideas of al-Qushayrī's *Laṭāʾif al-ishārāt* that is 'sometimes quoted word for word in Arabic, and at other times rendered in Persian' (Keeler 2006: 22). As befits a 'moderate' commentator, al-Maybudī avoids interpretations that may contradict the literal meaning of the Qur'anc text. His treatment of controversial issues, especially anthropomorphic features of God, the provenance of good and evil, and divine predetermination of all events, is that of a middle-of-the-way Ashʿarī theologian (Keeler 2006: 15). In this respect, al-Maybudī follows in the footsteps of his eminent predecessor al-Qushayrī.

Al-Maybudī explains the necessity of a mystical or esoteric *tafsīr* by the presence in the Qur'an of the 'obscure' or 'ambiguous' verses (*mutashābihāt*) alongside 'clear' or 'unequivocal' ones (*muḥkamāt*) (see Q. 3:7). The meaning of the former belongs to God alone (Keeler 2006: 42). This is not to say that the spiritual elite (*al-khāṣṣa*) of the Muslim community should not try to penetrate the mysteries of the *mutashābihāt*. On the contrary, the Sufi 'gnostics' (*ʿārifān*), according to al-Maybudī, 'are given illuminative vision (*dīda-yi mukashāfaʾī*) so that every veil between their hearts and the truth is lifted' (Keeler 2006: 49; cf. 44). They alone are capable of extracting (*istinbāṭ*) the hidden aspect of the revelation through exegetical unveiling (*taʾvīl kashfī*) granted to them by God. One of the most original aspects of al-Maybudī's exegetical method lies in his explanation of the universal functions of the 'ambiguous verses', as summarized by Annabel Keeler: (1) They challenge human beings to use their rational and spiritual faculties, thus separating them from animals; (2) They distinguish the learned (or spiritual) elite from the mass of ordinary believers; (3) They make 'wise men' aware of their weakness as they seek, in vain, to reach the depths of the divine word; (4) They cause interpreters to obtain a spiritual realization of the true reality (*ḥaqīqat*) instead of simply practising the outward law (Sharīʿa); (5) They guard the divine mystery that surpasses human understanding and requires that God's servants accept it unconditionally and unquestionably (Keeler 2006: 43–4). The keynotes of al-Maybudī's approach to the Qur'an, especially his constant references to the 'ambiguous' versus 'unequivocal' verses, are characteristic of Sufi exegesis as a whole.

A unique vision of the Qur'anic revelation is found in the *Jawāhir al-Qurʾān* (Jewels of the Qur'an) by the renowned Sunnī theologian and Shāfiʿī jurist Abū Ḥāmid al-Ghazālī (d. 505/1111). Although not exegetical in the conventional sense of the word, it explores the numerous layers of meaning embedded in Qur'anic chapters and verses. As with al-Maybudī, who had probably drawn on al-Ghazālī's ideas (Keeler 2006: 45–8), the latter considers the most elusive and subtle aspects of the revelation to be the exclusive domain of Sufi gnostics (*ʿārifūn*). He discerns several types of Qur'anic verses based on their contents and establishes a hierarchy whose ranks correspond to various types of precious stones, pearls, and rare substances. Thus, the knowledge (*maʿrifa*) of God is symbolized by the red sulphur (the precious substance which, according to medieval alchemy, could transform base metals into gold). The knowledge that Sufi gnostics have of God's essence, attributes, and actions is likened to three types of corundum. Below this realm of the supreme knowledge lies the knowledge of the path, that is, the verses of the Qur'an that elucidate the major stages of the believer's progress to God. Al-Ghazālī depicts this progress by using the common Sufi imagery of 'polishing the mirror of the heart'. This 'polishing' actualizes the divine nature (*lāhūt*) that, according to some Sufis, is inherent in every human being. Al-Ghazālī describes the Qur'anic verses pertaining to the knowledge of the mystical path as 'shining pearls'. The fourth type of knowledge corresponds to the verses that refer to the condition of humans after they have finally met God, that is, the resurrection, reckoning, reward and punishment, the beatific vision of God in the afterlife, and so on. This category, which al-Ghazālī likens to 'green emeralds', comprises one-third of the Qur'anic suras. The fifth category of verses describes the condition of 'those who have traversed [the path to God]', on the one hand, and 'those who have denied God and deviated from His path', on the other. Al-Ghazālī compares these verses to grey ambergris and fresh, blooming aloe-wood. The sixth group of verses contains 'the arguments of the infidels against the truth and clear explanation of their humiliation by obvious proofs'. Al-Ghazālī calls such verses the 'greatest antidote' (*al-tiryāq al-akbar*). The final category of verses again refers to the stages of human beings' journey to God and the management of its 'vehicle', the human body, with special reference to what constitutes its lawful means of sustenance and procreation. This type of verses is described as the 'strongest musk'. Upon establishing the types of knowledge and thematic categories of Qur'anic verses associated with them, al-Ghazālī proceeds to classify the 'outward' and 'inward' sciences associated with the Qur'an. To the former belongs (a) the art of Qur'an recitation represented by its readers and reciters; (b) the science of the Qur'anic language and grammar which al-Ghazālī attributes to philologists and grammarians; and (c) the science of the 'outward exegesis' (*al-tafsīr al-ẓāhir*) of the Qur'an which its practitioners, the *ʿulamāʾ*, consider to be the consummate knowledge available to human beings. Although al-Ghazālī recognizes the need for these 'outward' sciences of the Qur'an, he denies that they represent the ultimate human understanding of the divine word. In his view, this honour belongs to the 'sciences of the kernels of the Qur'an' (*ʿulūm al-lubāb*) as opposed to what he labels as its outer 'shell' (*ṣadaf*). The knowledge of the Qur'an's 'kernel' belongs exclusively to Sufi gnostics (*ʿārifūn*).

Al-Ghazālī then proceeds to lay down his exegetical method. He describes it as gaining insight into the allegorical and symbolic meaning of the divine revelation. Inscribed on the Preserved Tablet (*al-lawḥ al-maḥfūẓ*; based on Q. 22:70 and 85:22), it can be accessed by some divinely chosen individuals in their sleep. As any knowledge received in a dream, it requires interpretation. In al-Ghazālī's own words, 'The interpretation of the Qur'an (*taʾwīl*) occupies the place of the interpretation of dreams (*taʿbīr*).' Therefore, the exegete's task is to 'comprehend the hidden connection between the visible world and the invisible' in the same way as the interpreter of dreams interprets somebody's dream or vision. This idea is brought home in the following programmatic statement: 'Understand that so long as you are in this-worldly life you are sleeping, and you will wake up only after death at which time you will be able to see the manifest truth face to face. Before that time it is impossible for you to comprehend the [true] realities [of being], except when they are couched in the form of imagination-inspiring symbols.'

To gain the knowledge of the true reality of God's word one must, according to al-Ghazālī, renounce this world and focus one's thoughts on God and the afterlife. Those who seek 'the vanities of this world, eating what is unlawful and following [their] carnal desires' are barred from a proper understanding of the Qur'an. Their corrupt and sinful natures inevitably distort their perception of its true meaning. They see nothing in the Qur'an but contradiction and incongruence. In al-Ghazālī's view, the realization of the Qur'anic allegories and symbols by different people corresponds to their level of spiritual and intellectual purity. In commenting on the special virtue of the *Fātiḥa* (Q. 1), which many exegetes consider to be the key to paradise, al-Ghazālī argues that whereas an ordinary believer imagines paradise to be a place to satisfy his/her desires for food, drink, and sex, the perfected Sufi gnostic sees it as a realm of refined spiritual pleasures and 'pays no heed to the paradise of the fools.'

This idea is reiterated in al-Ghazālī's *Mishkāt al-anwār*—a deeply mystical reflection on the epistemic and ontological implications of the 'light verse' (Q. 29:35): 'The [Sufi] gnostics ascend from the foothill of metaphor (*majāz*) to the way-station of the true reality (*ḥaqīqa*). When they complete their ascension, they witness directly that there is nothing in existence except God Most High.' Therefore, for the Sufi gnostics, the Qur'anic phrase 'Everything perishes save His face' (Q. 28:88) means that 'Everything except God, when considered from the viewpoint of its essence, is but pure nonexistence (*ʿadam maḥḍ*)', because, in essence, God is the only true reality of the entire universe (al-Ghazālī, *Mishkāt*, 58). This daring and controversial idea prefigures the monistic/unitive metaphysics of Ibn [al-]ʿArabī (d. 638/1240) and his followers, who have made extensive use of exegesis to explicate and justify their esoteric cosmology and epistemology.

The Blossom of Ecstatic/Esoteric Exegesis

The writings of Persian Sufis Shams al-Dīn Muḥammad al-Daylamī (d. 593/1197) and Rūzbihān Baqlī (d. 606/1209) constitute a distinctive trend in Sufi exegesis that is characterized by 'intense visions and powerful ecstasies interpreted in terms of a Qurʾānically based metaphysics' (Ernst 1996: ix). The prevalence of such elements in the exegetical works of these two Sufis is taken by Gerhard Böwering as evidence of their more 'esoteric' character compared to that of their 'moderate' counterparts discussed above (Böwering 1987–9: 257). However, this distinction is more a matter of emphasis than of quality. The borderline between 'esoteric/ecstatic' and 'moderately mystical' types of exegesis is blurry and easily crossed.

Al-Daylamī, a little known, but original and prolific author, composed a mystical commentary entitled *Taṣdīq al-maʿārif* (occasionally referred to as *Futūḥ al-raḥmān fī ishārāt al-Qurʾān*) as well as a series of mystical treatises describing his auditory and visionary experiences (Alexandrin 2012: 216–18). Al-Daylamī's works creatively combine early Sufi exegetical logia borrowed from al-Sulamī's *Ḥaqāʾiq al-tafsīr*, which constitute about half of al-Daylamī's *Taṣdīq al-maʿārif*, with the author's own elaborations. His exegesis reflects his overwhelming preoccupation with 'the visionary world of the mystic', which 'is seen as totally real and fully identical with the spiritual world of the invisible realm' (Böwering 1987–9: 270). Böwering describes al-Daylamī's method as one of 'a continuous yet eclectic commentary on selected Koranic verses from all suras presented in sequence' (1987–9: 270). A striking characteristic of al-Daylamī's method is his consistent use of the Qur'an as the 'touchstone' to verify the authenticity of his mystical experiences and cosmological visions (Alexandrin 2012: 226). In the process of his personal engagement with the Qur'an, which often occurs in his dreams, the exegete avails himself of the verses that are commonly used by Sufis to validate their ideas and behaviour, namely, the 'light verse' (24:35), the verse of the 'night of [the Prophet's] ascension' (17:1), or the entire text of *Sūrat Yāsīn* (36) (Alexandrin 2012: 223–4). al-Daylamī's meditation on these and other Qur'anic passages, either in his wakeful states or in his dreams, allows him glimpses of the world of the spirits (*ʿālam al-arwāḥ*) and even of the afterlife (Alexandrin 2012: 220, 226). His experiential exegesis prefigures 'the ideas that emerged in the Kobrawi school' [of Sufism] (Böwering n.d.), whose exegetical production will be discussed further on.

Somewhat better known is the commentary of al-Daylamī's younger contemporary Rūzbihān [al-]Baqlī al-Shīrāzī entitled *ʿArāʾis al-bayān fī ḥaqāʾiq al-Qurʾān*. This lengthy opus reflects Rūzbihān's propensity to visions, dreams, powerful emotional raptures, and ecstatic utterances that have 'earned him the sobriquet "Doctor Ecstaticus" (*shaykh-i shaṭṭāḥ*)' (Ernst 1996). Like al-Daylamī's *Taṣdīq al-maʿārif*, *ʿArāʾis al-bayān* is composed in Arabic and consists almost equally of earlier exegetical material—mostly borrowed from al-Sulamī and al-Qushayrī—as well as of the author's own glosses.

Rūzbihān's uses of the Qur'an are much bolder than those of the Sufi exegetes already described. Not only does he constantly invoke the sacred text in describing his direct encounters with God, but he also claims to have symbolically 'eaten' it, along with the texts of the Jewish Torah and the Christian Gospel (Ernst 1996: 51). One can hardly be any 'bolder' than this. According to Carl Ernst, Rūzbihān's claims emphasize his 'complete internalization' of the divine inspiration inherent in these scriptures. The Qur'an and its imagery figure prominently in Rūzbihān's ecstatic visions. In one poignant passage he compares his condition in the presence of God with that of Zulaykha in the presence of Joseph (Q. 12:22–32). Couched in a Qur'anic idiom, such expressions of love and intimacy between God and his mystical lover constitute the hallmark of Rūzbihān's entire mystical worldview. Ernst suggests that the very title of Rūzbihān's commentary—*ʿArāʾis al-bayān* (The brides of explanation)—'invokes the unveiling of the bride in a loving encounter as the model of initiation into the esoteric knowledge of God' (Ernst 1996: 71). Rūzbihān's visionary and ecstatic experiences, inspired in part by those of his controversial predecessor al-Ḥusayn ibn Manṣūr al-Ḥallāj (d. 309/922), are virtually permeated by Qur'anic language and imagery. As with early Sufi masters, for Rūzbihān, the Qur'an becomes a powerful means of transforming his personhood and preparing it for the ultimate [re-]unification with the Divine already in this life.

Ibn [al-]ʿArabī and the Kubrawī Tradition

According to Böwering's classification (1980: 257), the subsequent stage in the development of Sufi exegesis was dominated by two major traditions: that of Ibn [al-]ʿArabī (d. 638/1240) and his followers and that of Najm al-Dīn Kubrā (d. 618/1221) and the Kubrawī school of Sufism.

Ibn [al-]ʿArabī drew on the rich tradition of Maghribi and Andalusi mysticism represented by Ibn Masarra al-Jabalī (d. 319/931), Ibn Barrajān (d. 536/1141), Ibn al-ʿArīf (d. 536/1141), Ibn Qasī (546/1151), and Abū Madyan (d. 594/1197) (Gril 2000: 521–2). Ibn Barrajān deserves special notice as the author of several exegetical works (Casewit 2017). As with earlier Sufi exegetes, Ibn Barrajān envisions the realization of the Qur'anic message by the mystic as his progressive immersion into its mysteries. This immersion results in what the Andalusi Sufi master calls 'the superior reading' (*al-tilāwa al-ʿulyā*) of the Qur'an. In the process, the personality of the mystic is transformed by the encounter with the divine word as he passes from its literal message (*ʿibāra; iʿtibār*) to the ultimate truth to which it alludes (*al-maʿbūr ilayhi*), or, in other words, from a literal perception of the sacred text to an interior, intuitive grasp of both its inner reality and of divine self-disclosures in the letters and sounds of the scripture (Gril 2000: 516; cf. McAuley 2012: 65; Casewit 2017: 145–6).

In the process of 'reciting' (*dhikr*) and contemplating the Qur'an the mystic acquires a veridical insight that allows him to reach the very kernel of the revelation. As a result, he is transformed into the 'universal servant' (*al-ʿabd al-kullī*), whose recitation of the sacred text is twice as effective as the recitation of the ordinary believer, or the 'partial servant' (*al-ʿabd al-juzʾī*). Ibn Barrajān's exegesis displays the following features that set it apart from the mainstream interpretive tradition whose elements are also present in his work: (1) the insistence on constant recollection or recitation (*dhikr*) as a means of achieving a total and undivided concentration on the sacred text; (2) the awareness of the subtle correspondences between the phenomena of the physical universe and the 'signs' (*āyāt*) of the scripture; (3) the belief that the heart of the 'universal servant' is capable of encompassing the totality of existence in the same way as it is contained in the 'Guarded Tablet' mentioned in the Qur'an (85:22); and (4) the notion that the divine word constitutes the innermost reality of human nature, which makes it possible for the servant of God to achieve a cognitive and experiential union with his/her Creator (Gril 2000: 520–1). Ibn Barrajān restricts this superior realization of the divine word and divinely created world (*iʿtibār*) to a small group of divinely elected individuals, whom he identifies as 'the veracious ones' (*ṣiddīqūn*) or those firmly rooted in knowledge, mentioned in the Qur'an, 4:162 (Casewit 2017: 266–75). His ideas were taken up and brought to fruition in the monistic/unitive metaphysics of Ibn [al-]ʿArabī and his school.

Ibn [al-]ʿArabī's relations with the Qur'an are rich and variegated. He claims to have composed a multi-volume Qur'anic commentary entitled *al-Jāmiʿ wa'l-tafṣīl fī asrār maʿānī 'l-tanzīl*, which seems to have been lost. However, his entire corpus of writings, including his influential masterpieces—*Fuṣūṣ al-ḥikam* and *al-Futūḥāt al-makkiyya*—can be seen as running commentaries on the foundational texts of Islam—the Qur'an and the Sunna of the Prophet. Ibn [al-]ʿArabī's attitude to the Qur'an should be considered within the overall context of his world-outlook, according to which the true realities (*ḥaqāʾiq*) of God and the universe are concealed from ordinary human beings behind a veil of distorting appearances. God discloses these hidden realities to 'the people of the true reality' (*ahl al-ḥaqīqa*) or 'divine gnostics' (*ʿārifūn*) by granting them a spiritual awakening and a revelatory insight, or 'unveiling' (*kashf*). These divinely given senses allow the *ʿārifūn* to decipher the true meaning of the symbols that constitute both the Qur'anic text and the empirical universe. In sum, for Ibn [al-]ʿArabī and his fellow 'gnostics', both the Qur'an and the universe are but God's 'writings'—assemblages of symbols concealing the ultimate realities of existence that, in the final account, take their origin in, and are somehow identical with, the only Real One (*al-ḥaqq*).

Because Ibn [al-]ʿArabī considered himself to be the greatest 'gnostic' (*ʿārif*) of his age (and possibly of all times) and the spiritual 'pole' (*quṭb*) of the universe, he saw no reason to legitimize his understanding of the scripture, or—in his own words, of the scripture's 'spirit' (*rūḥ*)—by citing any prior exegetical authority. He believed that his insights were bestowed upon him directly by God (Nettler 2003: 29). This belief underlies Ibn [al-]ʿArabī's commentaries on selected Qur'anic suras included in his poetic collection (*Dīwān*, 136–79). Ibn [al-]ʿArabī presents himself as a simple transmitter of the divinely induced insights that unveil the spiritual 'quintessence' (*rūḥ*) of the suras. The insights are a product of the 'mystical moment' (*wārid al-waqt*) in which the interpreter happens to find himself; he himself adds nothing to what has come to him from the divine source (Bachmann 2000: 503). Ibn [al-]ᶜArabī's exegetical use of poetry—an art associated with pre-Islamic paganism—and his occasional imitation of the metre and rhythm of Qur'anic chapters no doubt has raised many scholarly eyebrows both during his lifetime and after his death (McAuley 2012: 160–99). At the same time, his claim to be a simple mouthpiece of divinely induced insights has effectively absolved him of the necessity to justify his exegetical method or to comply with the conventions of an ordinary exegesis.

For Ibn [al-]ᶜArabī, poetry becomes a perfect vehicle for illuminating multiple senses of the Qur'anic verses. Moreover, because of the kindred nature of poetic inspiration and prophetic revelation, for the multiple layers of the Qur'anic meaning to be expressed or at least alluded to, one simply has no choice but to resort to poetry (McAuley 2012: 62). At the same time, Ibn [al-]ᶜArabī's 'daring interpretative flights' are always restrained by his 'rigorous commitment to the Qur'an as God's literal word' (McAuley 2012: 62).

Ibn [al-]ᶜArabī's exegesis operates on three distinct levels: the metaphysical and cosmological; the analogical (built around implicit or explicit correspondences between the universe and the human organism); and the existential-experiential that rests on his supersensory perception of the underlying unity of God, man, and the universe (Gril 1990: 180). In the *Fuṣūṣ al-ḥikam*, Ibn [al-]ᶜArabī's controversial meditation on the phenomenon of prophethood and his use of the Qur'an is particularly daring. He consistently uses its verses as show-windows for his monistic (unitive) metaphysics (Nettler 2003: 13–14). This kind of monistic commentary of the Qur'an 'may be considered an Islamic religious *genre* in its own right' that Ronald Nettler describes as 'Sufi metaphysical story-telling' (2003: 14).

As an example of Ibn [al-]ᶜArabī's daring exegesis one can cite his rendition of the story of Aaron, Moses, and the golden calf (Q. 7:148–55 and Q. 20:85–94). Contrary to the literal meaning of the Qur'anic narrative, Ibn [al-]ᶜArabī portrays Aaron and the worshippers of the golden calf as being innocent of idolatry. Unlike Moses, who exemplifies a conventional vision of monotheism, they realize that God can be worshipped in everything, because every object, including the golden calf, is but 'a site of divine self-manifestation (*baᶜḍ al-majālī al-ilāhiyya*)' (Ibn [al-]ᶜArabī, *Fuṣūṣ*, 192; Nettler 2003: 53). In Ibn [al-]ᶜArabī's audacious interpretation, the original Qur'anic condemnation of idolatry is inverted: the idolaters become 'gnostics', who '*know the full truth* concerning idolatry, but are honor-bound not to disclose this truth, even to the prophets, the apostles and their heirs, for these all have their divinely-appointed roles in curbing idolatry and promoting the worship of God *in their time and their situation*' (Nettler 2003: 67). The ultimate truth, however, is that God inheres in all things and thus can be worshipped in any object or site. In this exegetical gloss, and throughout the *Fuṣūṣ*, Ibn [al-]ᶜArabī's monistic (unitive) vision of God and the world is illustrated by Qur'anic accounts of prophetic missions from Adam to Muḥammad. In Ibn [al-]ᶜArabī's understanding, his exegesis is not just *his* personal vision, but, in fact, *the true and unadulterated* meaning of the divine word (Nettler 2003: 94).

The keynotes of Ibn [al-]ʿArabī's monistic (unitive) doctrine were taken up and elaborated by his foremost disciple Ṣadr al-Dīn al-Qūnawī (d. 673/1274). His exegetical work, *Ījāz al-bayān fī taʾwīl al-Qurʾān*, is a lengthy disquisition on the metaphysical, epistemological, and psychological implications of the first sura that, according to al-Qūnawī, captures the very gist of the divine revelation. The author's indebtedness to Ibn [al-]ʿArabī is obvious from the outset, when he states that 'God has made the primeval macrocosm (*al-ʿālam al-kabīr*)—from the viewpoint of its [outward] form—a book carrying the images of the divine names... and he [God] has made the perfect man—who is but a microcosm (*al-ʿālam al-saghīr*)—an intermediate book, from the viewpoint of [its] form, that combines in itself the presence of the names and the presence of the named [i.e. God]' (al-Qūnawī, *al-Tafsīr*, 98).

Al-Qūnawī identifies five levels (or realms) of existence that correspond to the five senses of the divine word. His description of the hierarchies of the divine names and their ontological counterparts (or realms of existence) is the most salient feature of his highly recondite mystical commentary that can be seen as a fitting tribute to Ibn [al-]ʿArabī's monistic (unitive) vision of existence.

In ʿAbd al-Razzāq al-Qāshānī (d. *c*.730–6/1329–35), a native of the Iranian province of Jibāl, we find another exponent of Ibn ʿArabī's spiritual and intellectual legacy. Al-Qāshānī's main achievement lies in his ability to present Ibn [al-]ʿArabī's ambiguous ideas in a lucid form that could easily be understood by everyone interested in the subject. Al-Qāshānī excelled in this task to such an extent that his mystical commentary, originally entitled *Taʾwīl al-Qurʾān*, was for several centuries treated as a work of Ibn [al-]ʿArabī himself (see e.g. McAuley 2012: 65, nn. 33 and 34). Its latest edition, published in Beirut in 1968, still carries Ibn [al-]ʿArabī's name (henceforth al-Qāshānī/Ibn ʿArabī, *Tafsīr*).

A systematic thinker, al-Qāshānī provides a self-reflective exposition of his exegetical method in the introduction to his commentary. Citing the famous prophetic hadith, according to which each Qur'anic verse has two aspects—the 'outward' (*ẓahr*) and the 'inward' (*baṭn*)—al-Qāshānī identifies the explication of the former as *tafsīr* and of the latter as *taʾwīl* (lit. 'tracing something back to its origin'; al-Qāshānī/Ibn ʿArabī, *Tafsīr*, 1:4). He defines his own exegetical method as *taʾwīl*. This choice of the term may indicate that, by al-Qāshānī's time, the *tafsīr/taʾwīl* dichotomy had become widespread, at least in Sufi circles. This is not to say that it has been universally accepted, though: such eminent exegetes as al-Ṭabarī (d. 310/923) and al-Bayḍāwī (d. *c*.719/1319) applied the word *taʾwīl* to their quite conventional commentaries. Likewise, the famous Indian reformer Shāh Wālī Allāh (d. 1176/1762) considered *taʾwīl* to be a regular historic and contextual commentary (Baljon 1986: 141).

In the introduction to his commentary al-Qāshānī describes his personal relationship with the Qur'an that finely captures the general Sufi attitude to the divine word:

> For a long time I made the recitation (*tilāwa*) of the Qurʾān my habit and custom and meditated on its meaning with the [full] strength of my faith. Yet, in spite of my assiduousness in reciting its passages (*awrād*), my chest was constrained, my soul

> troubled and my heart remained closed to it. However, my Lord did not divert me from this recitation until I had grown accustomed and habituated to it so as to begin tasting the sweetness of its cup and its drink. It was then that I felt invigorated, my breast opened up, my conscience expanded, my heart was at ease, and my innermost self was liberated...Then there appeared to me from behind the veil the meanings of every verse that my tongue is incapable of describing, no capacity able to determine and count, and no power can resist. (al-Qāshānī/Ibnʿ Arabī, *Tafsīr*, 1:4)

Unlike the authors of 'moderate' Sufi commentaries discussed above, al-Qāshānī consciously neglects those passages of the Qur'an that, in his view, are not susceptible to esoteric interpretation (*kull mā lā yaqbal al-taʾwīl ʿindī aw lā yaḥtāj ilayhi*). With five centuries of Sufi exegesis behind him, al-Qāshānī no longer feels obligated to pay tribute to the trivia of the conventional *tafsīr*, focusing instead only on those aspects of the sacred text that resonate with his mystical states and world of ideas. Even such favourite 'Sufi' verses as Q. 7:172 and Q. 85:22 are passed over in silence, possibly because al-Qāshānī believed that their interpretive potential had been exhausted by his predecessors (Lory 1980: 31). Addressed to his fellow Sufis, 'the people of [supersensory] unveiling' (*ahl al-kashf*), al-Qāshānī's exegesis brims with Sufi terminology and thematic keynotes borrowed from Ibn [al-]ʿArabī's monistic (unitive) metaphysics. In many cases, this terminology is left unexplained, presupposing its prior knowledge by the initiated reader (Lory 1980:30). Al-Qāshānī is completely at home with all of major exegetical topoi articulated by his predecessors: the monistic metaphysics with its tripartite division of existence into the empirical realm (*ʿālam al-shahāda*), the intermediate realm of divine power (*al-jabarūt*), and the purely spiritual realm of divine sovereignty (*al-malakūt*); the conceptual parallelism between the universe (the macrocosm) and its human counterpart (the microcosm); the major stages and spiritual states of the mystic's progress to God; the symbolism of the letters of the Arabic alphabet and numerology, and so on.

As a typical example of his method one can cite his glosses on Q. 17:1 (the Qur'anic verses are italicized): '*Glory be to Him, who carried His servant*, that is—He who purified him from material attributes and deficiencies associated with [his] created nature by the tongue of the spiritual state of disengagement [from the created world] (*al-tajarrud*) and perfection at the station of [absolute] servanthood... *by night*, that is, in the darkness of bodily coverings and natural attachments, for the ascension and rise cannot occur except by means of a body; *from the Holy Mosque*, that is, from the station of the heart that is protected from being circumambulated by the polytheism of carnal drives...' (al-Qāshānī/Ibn ʿArabī, *Tafsīr*, 1:705).

In this passage and throughout, correspondences between Qur'anic images and Sufi psychology, epistemology, and ontology are consistently pursued, leaving little room for the ambiguity of reference and referent (as well as the general opacity of discourse) that characterizes the works of Ibn [al-]ʿArabī himself. Thus, in al-Qāshānī's commentary the esoteric exegesis of the previous centuries receives a succinct, systematic and lucid articulation (Lory 1980: 31). The exegetical method harking back to Ibn [al-]ʿArabī and his predecessors is now routinized. Its subsequent [re-]appropriation by such later Sufis as Badr al-Dīn Simawī (d. 820/1420), Ismāʿīl Ḥaqqī al-Bursawī (d. 1137/1725), Shāh Wālī Allāh (d. 1176/1762), and Ibn ʿAjība (d. 1224/1809), to name but a few, demonstrates a remarkable continuity that some observers may construe as a lack of originality or even outright stagnation. In the case of the last two authors, mystical exegesis is offered alongside other types of commentary, of which Ibn ʿAjība, for example, cites as many as eleven in his *al-Baḥr al-madīd* (1:129–31).

The tradition of Qur'an interpretation associated with the Central Asian Sufi master Najm al-Dīn Kubrā (d. 618/1221) and his followers Dāya [al-]Rāzī (d. 654/1256) and ʿAlāʾ al-Dawla al-Simnānī (d. 736/1336) is sometimes treated as a separate school of Sufi exegesis (e.g. Böwering 1980: 257). However, this perception has more to do with two distinct spiritual and intellectual lineages (Akbarian—associated with Ibn [al-]ʿArabī, and Kubrawī—stretching back to Najm al-Dīn Kubrā) than with any substantive differences in their approaches to the Qur'an.

The Kubrawī tradition is represented by the collective exegetical work that was started by Kubrā himself, continued by Dāya [al-]Rāzī, and completed by al-Simnānī, although 'it is possible that there are two different continuations to Kubra's commentary, one by al-Simnānī and the other by Dāya' (Elias 1996: 205). In any event, this commentary remains unpublished and our knowledge of its content is derived from a study of al-Simnānī's oeuvre by Jamal Elias (1996: 107–10).

Like his predecessors, al-Simnānī discerns 'four levels of meaning [of the Qur'an] corresponding to four levels of existence' (Elias 1996: 108). Its exoteric dimension relates to the realm of 'humanity' (*nāsūt*); its esoteric dimension to the realm of divine sovereignty (*malakūt*); its limit (*ḥadd*) to the realm of divine omnipotence (*jabarūt*); and its point of ascent (*maṭlaʿ* or *muṭṭalaʿ*; cf. the Greek *anagoge*) to the realm of divinity (*lāhūt*) (Elias 1996: 108). These realms, in turn, correspond to the four levels of the human understanding of the Qur'an—that of the ordinary believer (*muslim*), who relies upon his faculty of hearing; that of the faithful one (*muʾmin*), who receives divine inspiration; that of the perfected one (*muḥsin*), who should not disclose his understanding of the Qur'an to anyone, except with the divine permission (*idhn*). The ultimate realization of the Qur'anic meaning is granted to the [divine] witness (*shāhid*); he should keep it secret at all times, because, if disclosed to the uninitiated, it may plunge them into confusion, disquiet, or even sedition (Elias 1996: 108)

God's purpose in sending down the revelation is to cleanse the hearts and souls of human beings from mundane distractions and thereby to lead them to salvation. To this end, God has supplied his human servants with 'subtle centers' (*laṭāʾif*) embedded in their bodies. They alert the faithful to God's immediate presence, thereby directing them to 'a complete revelation of the true nature of reality' (Elias 1996: 85). The familiar Sufi notion of the deeper meaning of the Qur'an granted by God to his chosen folk (*awliyāʾ Allāh*; *ʿārifūn*; *ḥukamāʾ*; *al-khāṣṣa*, etc.) is once again brought home forcefully and unequivocally.

Finally, mention should be made of the exegesis that combines mystical epistemology and metaphysics with Shīʿī theology. The main representatives of this Sufi-Shīʿī exegetical synthesis are Iranian thinkers Ḥaydar-i Āmulī (d. after 787/1385) and Mullā Ṣadrā (d. 1050/1640) and their followers. To this exegetical tradition belongs an extremely rare mystical commentary on the Qur'an by a female scholar from Iran named Nuṣrat bint Muḥammad Amīn, better known as Bānū-yi Iṣfahānī (d. 1403/1982) (Iyāzī, *al-Mufassirūn*, 310–15 and 629–33; Āmulī, *Jāmiᶜ al-asrār*; Mullā Ṣadrā, *Asrār al-āyāt*; Amīn, *Tafsīr-i makhzan*). This tradition requires a separate study.

Bibliography

Primary Sources

Amīn, Nuṣrat (Bānū-yi Iṣfahānī). *Tafsīr-i makhzan al-ᶜirfān*. 10 vols. Tehran: Nahẓat-i Zanān-i Musalmān, 1982.

Āmulī, Ḥaydar. *Jāmiᶜ al-asrār*. Ed. Osman Yahya and Henri Corbin. 2nd edn. Tehran and Paris: Intishrāt-i Ṭūs, 1988.

al-Baghawī, al-Ḥusayn. *Maᶜālim al-tanzīl*. Ed. Khālid ᶜAbd al-Raḥmān al-ᶜAkk and Marwān Sawār. Multān: Idārat Taʾlīfāt Ashrafiyya, 1988.

al-Ghazālī, Muḥammad. *Jawāhir al-Qurʾān*. Ed. Muḥammad Rashīd Riḍā al-Qabbānī. Beirut: Dār Iḥyāʾ al-ᶜUlūm, 1985 (Eng. trans by M. A. Quasem, *The Jewels of the Qurʾān*. London and Boston: Kegan Paul International, 1983).

al-Ghazālī, Muḥammad. *Mishkāt al-anwār*. Ed. Sāmiḥ Dughaym. Beirut: Dār al-Fikr al-Lubnānī, 1994.

Ibn ᶜAjība, Aḥmad. *Tafsīr al-Fātiḥa al-kabīr al-musammā bi'l-baḥr al-madīd*. Ed. Bassām Muḥammad Bārūd. 2 vols. Abu Dhabi: al-Majmaᶜ al-Thaqāfī, 1999.

Ibn [al-]ᶜArabī, Muḥammad. *Dīwān Ibn ᶜArabī*. Reprint. Beirut: Dār al-Maktaba, n.d.

Ibn [al-]ᶜArabī, Muḥammad. *Fuṣūṣ al-ḥikam*. Ed. Abū'l-ᶜAlāʾ ᶜAfīfī. Cairo: ᶜĪsā al-Bābī al-Ḥalabī, 1946.

Ibn [al-]ᶜArabī, Muḥammad. *al-Futūḥāt al-makkiyya*. 4 vols. Reprint. Beirut: Dār Ṣādir, 1968.

al-Khāzin al-Baghdādī. ᶜAlī ibn Muḥammad. *Lubāb al-taʾwīl*. 4 vols. Cairo: Muṣṭafā al-Bābī al-Ḥalabī, 1955.

al-Maybudī, Abū'l-Faẓl. *Kashf al-asrār wa ᶜuddat al-abrār*. Ed. ᶜAlī Asghar Ḥikmet. 10 vols. Tehran: Dānishgāh-i Tihrān, 1331–9/[1952–60].

Mullā Ṣadrā (Ṣadr al-Dīn Shīrāzī). *Asrār al-āyāt*. Ed. Muḥammad Khvājavā. Beirut: Dār al-Ṣafwa, 1993.

al-Qāshānī/Ibn [al-]ᶜArabī. *Tafsīr al-Qurʾān al-karīm*. Beirut: Dār al-Yaqẓa al-ᶜArabiyya, 1968.

al-Qūnawī, Muḥammad. *al-Tafsīr al-ṣūfī li'l-Qurʾān: Ījāz al-bayān fī taʾwīl al-Qurʾān*. Ed. ᶜAbd al-Qādir Aḥmad ᶜAṭā. Cairo: Dār al-Kutub al-Ḥadītha, 1969.

al-Qushayrī, ʿAbd al-Karīm. *Laṭāʾif al-ishārāt*. 6 vols. Ed. Ibrāhīm Basyūnī. Cairo: Dār al-Kātib al-ᶜArabī, 1968–71.

al-Qushayrī, ʿAbd al-Karīm. *Al-Qushayri's Epistle on Sufism*. Trans. Alexander Knysh. London: Garnet Publishing, 2007.

al-Sarrāj, ʿAbdallāh. *Kitāb al-Lumaᶜ fī'l-taṣawwuf*. Ed. Reynold A. Nicholson. Leiden and London: E. J. Brill, 1914.

al-Sulamī, ᶜAbd al-Raḥmān. *Ḥaqāʾiq al-tafsīr*. Ed. Sayyid ᶜImrān. 2 vols. Beirut: Dār al-Kutub al-ᶜIlmiyya, 2001.

Secondary Sources

Alexandrin, Elizabeth.'Witnessing the Lights of the Heavenly Dominion: Dreams, Visions and the Mystical Exegesis of Shams al-Dīn al-Daylamī'. In: Őzgen Felek and Alexander Knysh (eds.). *Dreams and Visions in Islamic Societies*, pp. 215–31. Albany: State University of New York Press, 2012.

ʿAlī Ayāzī, Muḥammad. *Al-Mufassirūn: ḥayātuhum wa-manhajuhum*. Tehran: Wizārat al-Thaqāfa wa'l-Irshād, 1414/[1994].

Bachmann, Peter. 'Un commentaire mystique du Coran', *Arabica* 47/3 (2000), 503–9.

Baljon, Johannes. *Religion and Thought of Shāh Walī Allāh Dihlawī, 1703–1762*. Leiden: E. J. Brill, 1986.

Böwering, Gerhard. *The Mystical Vision of Existence in Classical Islam*. Berlin and New York: Walter de Gruyter, 1980.

Böwering, Gerhard. 'Sufi Hermeneutics in Medieval Islam', *Revue des études islamiques* 55–7 (1987–9), 255–70.

Böwering, Gerhard. 'The Major Sources of al-Sulami's Minor Qur'an Commentary', *Oriens* 35 (1996), 35–56.

Böwering, Gerhard. 'The Light Verse: Qur'anic Text and Sufi Interpretations', *Oriens* 36 (2001), 113–44.

Böwering, Gerhard. 'Deylami'. In: *Encyclopaedia Iranica*, online edition: <http://www.iranicaonline.org/>.

Casewit, Yousef. *The Mystics of al-Andalus: Ibn Barrajan and Islamic Thought in the Twelfth Century*. Cambridge: Cambridge University Press, 2017.

Düzenli, Şihabuddin. 'Sühreverdi ve Nuğbetü 'l-beyan'. Unpublished PhD thesis, Marmara University, Istanbul, 1994.

Elias, Jamal. *The Throne Carrier of God*. Albany: State University of New York Press, 1995.

Ernst, Carl. *Rūzbihān Baqlī*. Richmond: Curzon, 1996.

Ernst, Carl. 'Rūzbihān Baḳlī'. In *Encyclopaedia of Islam*. second edn. <http://referenceworks.brillonline.com>.

Gril, Denis. 'Le Commentaire du verset de la lumière d'après Ibn ʿArabī', *Bulletin de l'Institut francais d'archéologie orientale* 90 (1990), 179–87.

Gril, Denis. 'La "Lecture supérieure" du Coran selon ibn Barrağān', *Arabica* 47/3 (2000), 510–22.

Jong, Frederick de, and Bernd Radtke (eds.). *Islamic Mysticism Contested: Thirteen Centuries of Controversies and Polemics*. Leiden and Boston: E. J. Brill, 1999.

Keeler, Annabel. *Sufi Hermeneutics: The Qur'ān Commentary of Rashīd al-Dīn Maybudī*. Oxford and London: Oxford University Press, 2006.

Knysh, Alexander. *Islamic Mysticism: A Short History*. 2nd edn. Leiden and Boston: E. J. Brill, 2010.

Knysh, Alexander. *Sufism: A New History of Islamic Mysticism*. Princeton: Princeton University Press, 2017.

Lory, Pierre. *Les Commentaires ésotériques du Coran d'aprés 'Abd al-Razzâq al-Qâshânî*. Paris: Les Deux Océans, 1980.

McAuley, Denis. *Ibn ʿArabī's Mystical Poetics*. Oxford: Oxford University Press, 2012.

Nettler, Ron. *Sufi Metaphysics and Qur'anic Prophets: Ibn ʿArabī's Thought and Method in the Fuṣūṣ al-ḥikam*. Cambridge: Islamic Texts Society, 2003.

Nguyen, Martin. *Sufi Master and Qur'an Scholar: Abū'l-Qāsim al-Qushayrī and the Laṭā'if al-ishārāt*. Oxford and London: Oxford University Press, 2012.

Nwyia, Paul. *Éxègese coranique et langage mystique*. Beirut: Dār al-Mashriq, 1970.

Nwyia, Paul. *Trois œuvres inédites de mystiques musulmans*. Beirut: Dār al-Mashriq, 1972.

Ohlander, Erik. *Sufism in an Age of Transition: ʿUmar al-Suharwardī and the Rise of the Islamic Mystical Brotherhoods*. Leiden and Boston: E. J. Brill, 2008.

Saleh, Walid. *The Formation of the Classical Tafsīr Tradition: The Qur'ān Commentary of al-Thaʿlabī (d. 427/1035)*. Leiden and Boston: E. J. Brill, 2004.

CHAPTER 51

THEOLOGICAL COMMENTARIES

TARIQ JAFFER

MUCH of the discourse within the expansive tradition of Qur'anic commentary attempts to elicit theological meaning from the Qur'an and to provide insight into its theocentric worldview. Within the practice of scriptural exegesis it is customary for Muslim commentators to augment the Qur'an's theological arguments, to explain its theological symbols, and to provide solutions to problems that concerned, broadly speaking, God's relationship to His creation. For the purposes of this chapter, 'theological commentaries' refer to the Qur'anic exegeses that give pride and place to theological considerations.

The aim of this chapter is to review the scholarly literature that deals with the theological activity that took place within the tradition of Muslim exegesis from the late first/seventh century until the early seventh/ thirteenth century. It focuses on the areas in which scholars have concentrated most of their efforts: the exegetical sayings of Ibn ʿAbbās (d. *c.*68/687), the 'ocean' of exegesis who was a Companion of Muḥammad for a short period of time; the exegetical sayings of Mujāhid (d. 104/722), whose exegesis was a source of inspiration for a variety of Muslim intellectual trends and schools of Qur'anic commentary; the guiding methodological principles that al-Ṭabarī (d. 310/923) devised for Sunnī exegesis; the 'rationalistic' Muʿtazilī approach to the Qur'an and its influence on the Imāmī Shīʿī tradition; the key terms and principles that make up al-Māturīdī's methodology in Qur'anic commentary; and the rationalizing theological (and philosophical) tendencies exhibited in al-Rāzī's (d. 606/1210) Ashʿarī/Sunnī commentary.

Theological Reflection within Traditional Exegesis

The earliest attempts to elicit theological meaning from the Qur'an can be traced to prophetic reports that date from the life of Muḥammad and his Companions. Traditionists, whose personal piety motivated them to master the prophetic Sunna, often travelled to Islamic centres of learning—Mecca, Medina, Kufa, Basra, Baghdad, Egypt, and Syria; and it was in such centres of learning that they produced a great number of reports, which they ascribed to Muḥammad and his Companions using the *isnād* institution.[1] When the earliest Muslims interpreted Qur'anic verses that relayed theological ideas they consistently appealed to prophetic traditions and invoked the authority of the Sunna.

Ibn ʿAbbās (d. c.68/687)

There is a consensus of opinion among scholars that Ibn ʿAbbās, the paternal cousin and Companion of the Prophet, made considerable efforts to elicit theological meaning from the Qur'an. According to Claude Gilliot's studies, Muslim tradition honoured Ibn ʿAbbās with the appellations 'the great doctor', the 'divine', the 'ocean' [of science], and the 'interpreter' of the Qur'an. These appellations are justified by his wealth of knowledge in various branches of learning, including poetry, genealogy of the Arabs, pre-Islamic poetry, military expeditions, traditions, and law.

Ibn ʿAbbās is considered an authority within both Sunnī and Shīʿī exegesis. The former recognizes him as a Companion of ʿAlī ibn Abī Ṭālib. Wilferd Madelung (1996) has shown that major points of Imāmī religious and legal doctrine betray his influence on five counts: the basic rules of ablutions; temporary marriage; divorce by triple repudiation pronounced on a single occasion; the legal status of a slave woman who has given birth to a child of her master; the wiping of shoes instead of the washing or wiping of the feet in ritual ablution.

For historians of Muslim exegesis, the task of determining the role that Ibn ʿAbbās played in the *tafsīr* tradition presents a major problem. According to Gilliot, because it is impossible to distinguish the material that is actually attributable to Ibn ʿAbbās from the material that has come from other early transmitters, Ibn ʿAbbās lies between 'Islamic imagination' and 'reality'. Gilliot's scholarship on Ibn ʿAbbās has established that the practice of extending chains of transmission back to Ibn ʿAbbās occurred in Iraq during his lifetime. And scholarship by Rippin (1994) has dealt with the problem of the many works that have been attributed to Ibn ʿAbbās.[2]

Mujāhid (d. 104/722)

The important role that Mujāhid—a pupil of Ibn ʿAbbās in Qur'anic exegesis and a popular preacher or storyteller in Mecca—played in the history of exegesis has been studied in detail by Gilliot (2015). Mujāhid's theological ideas, which are expressed

[1] On the role of the *isnād* institution in dating Muslim traditions, see Juynboll 1983: 9–76.

[2] For discussions on early *tafsīr* see the Chapters in the present volume by Rippin and Versteegh.

in the form of exegetical sayings, were developed by Qadarīs, the Muʿtazila, and predestinationists; and they also became a basis for later Sufi exegesis. Gilliot's article (2015) clarifies Mujāhid's role in the Islamic tradition by establishing what has been attributed to him in the various versions, recensions, and sub-recensions of his Qur'anic commentary.

John Wansbrough's monograph, *Quranic Studies: Sources and Methods of Scriptural Interpretation* (1977), marked a milestone in scholarship within the fields of Qur'anic studies and scriptural commentary. As pointed out most recently by Rippin, Wansbrough was the first scholar to examine a large body of literature that Muslim exegetes authored during the first four centuries of Islam, a period in which the Qur'an came to be seen as a 'canonical and authoritative scripture for the Muslim community'. While the body of literature that Wansbrough examined had been catalogued by Fuat Sezgin in his *Geschichte des arabischen Schrifttums*, it had not yet been studied.[3]

Working on the supposition that *Deutungsbedürftigkeit* ('the need for interpretation'), which can be traced back to Q. 3:7, was of primary interest to the early Islamic community, Wansbrough is mainly concerned with determining the 'formal properties of scriptural authority' that contribute to 'the emergence of an independent and self-conscious religious community'. He proposes that the concept of authority was articulated by means of several exegetical types—haggadic, halakhic, masoretic, rhetorical, and allegorical. These four exegetical types are the 'principal lines of inquiry' that Muslim exegetes applied to the Qur'an. Because such types emerged chronologically, they exhibit minimum overlapping.

To argue for this thesis Wansbrough examines a cross-section of Qur'anic commentary prior to the monumental work of al-Ṭabarī. Chapter IV, the most significant discussion in his work, is devoted to 'Principles of Exegesis'. In this chapter Wansbrough lists twelve procedural devices that were used to explicate scripture: *variae lectiones*; poetic *loci probantes*; lexical explanation; grammatical explanation; rhetorical explanation; periphrasis; analogy; abrogation; circumstances of revelation; identification; prophetic tradition; anecdote. In Wansbrough's view, these terms constitute the nomenclature of early Islamic exegesis. Al-Ṭabarī's monumental exegesis of the Qur'an eventually eclipsed debates surrounding them.

Wansbrough argues that the exegetical activities listed above make up the narrative framework of Qur'anic exegesis, and he argues that this narrative can be conveniently labelled as haggadic. To argue for a haggadic orientation of early Islamic exegesis, Wansbrough avails himself of Muqātil ibn Sulaymān's (d. 150/767) Qur'anic exegesis, which is the oldest full extant commentary on the Qur'an.[4] Considering Muqātil's Qur'anic commentary a representative of the early community of Islamic exegesis, Wansbrough shows how Muqātil explicates the entire content of Q.18 by relating it to a story of Abū Jahl

[3] See Andrew Rippin's Foreword to the edition published by Prometheus Books in 2004.

[4] Muqātil's Qur'anic commentary (*Tafsīr*) was unedited when Wansbrough wrote *Quranic Studies*. The work has since been edited by ʿAbd Allāh Maḥmūd Shiḥātah. The first volume of this edition is a study of Muqātil's Qur'anic commentary.

and the rabbis. He draws attention to the motif of the 'rabbinical test of prophethood' in Muqātil's exegesis of Q. 18, a motif that is consistently related to Jewish (if not always Meccan) resistance to Muḥammad. By comparing Muqātil's exegesis of this verse with Ibn Isḥāq's biography of Muḥammad, Wansbrough argues that this motif has a stylistic function, which is to confirm Muḥammad's status as a prophet. Such motifs testify to the haggadic orientation of Muslim exegesis.

Al-Ṭabarī (d. 310/923)

Al-Ṭabarī's exegesis, *Tafsīr al-bayān ʿan taʾwīl ayy al-Qurʾān*, is the largest full extant commentary on the Qur'an. In his foundational study of Muslim exegesis, *Die Richtungen* (1920), Goldziher called al-Ṭabarī's Qur'anic commentary a model of 'traditional' Qur'anic exegesis. Recent scholarship by Walid Saleh (2004) distinguishes 'encyclopaedic' Qur'anic commentaries from those authored within Islamic institutions of learning (*madāris*), rejecting the categories and labels—including 'traditional'—that Goldziher formulated when he wrote his pioneering work.

In the introduction to his Qur'anic exegesis, al-Ṭabarī contends that prophetic traditions constitute the central guiding principles of exegesis. Throughout his commentary, he consistently appeals to the divinely sanctioned Sunna as the ultimate source of authority in matters of Qur'anic interpretation. The vast number of prophetic traditions that al-Ṭabarī records in this work—traditions which reflect his learning and piety—were passed down within the genealogical tradition of *tafsīr* and subsequently became an enduring feature of Sunnī exegesis. Similarly, the heavy weight that al-Ṭabarī gives the authority of the Sunna became an enduring feature of Sunnī exegesis.

Mustafa Shah's recent scholarship confirms that al-Ṭabarī's 'integrated and wide-ranging approach' to the Qur'an brought a wider range of disciplines—literary, legal, grammatical, and theological—to the practice of Qur'anic exegesis. It also confirms that al-Ṭabarī brought unprecedented degrees of precision and levels of expertise in these disciplines to the practice of Qur'anic interpretation. Importantly, Shah's recent scholarship challenges the old and widespread idea that al-Ṭabarī's approach to the Qur'an is informed by a 'rigidly derived traditionalist strategy' (as opposed to a 'rationally-devised exposition of dogma') that served as a vehicle for Sunnī religious orthodoxy.

To be sure, Shah acknowledges that al-Ṭabarī's *Tafsīr* is 'a traditionalist expression of Sunnī orthodoxy'. In his view, al-Ṭabarī argues from a standpoint of Sunni traditionalism when he opposes the Muʿtazila on conventional points of theology, including the created status of the Qur'an, the divine attributes, predestination, and intercession, and the beatific vision. Furthermore, al-Ṭabarī uses his commentary as a forum to articulate an 'orthodox' Sunnī position on theological issues. But, as Shah argues, al-Ṭabarī also willingly critiques views that sit within the 'confines of a traditionalist-defined theology', for example, when he discusses the relationship between the *ism* 'nomen' and the *musammā* 'nominatum'. Shah concludes that it would be a mistake to think that al-Ṭabarī lacks 'intellectual autonomy' and that he adheres unreflectively to theological positions that were formulated by traditionalist Sunnī orthodoxy.

The most substantial study of al-Ṭabarī's Qur'anic commentary to date is Gilliot's *Exégèse, langue, et théologie en Islam* (1990). This penetrating monograph supersedes Goldziher's discussion of al-Ṭabarī's role within the tradition of Qur'anic exegesis in *Die Richtungen*. It analyses the methodological principles that al-Ṭabarī formulates in his 'introduction'—a 'veritable exegetical prolegomenon' that became known in the Islamic tradition as al-Ṭabarī's 'Treatise on exegesis' (*Risālatuhu fī tafsīr*).

Gilliot is primarily interested in clarifying the posture and theological orientation of al-Ṭabarī's Qur'anic exegesis and in showing how al-Ṭabarī's methodology of Qur'anic exegesis is informed by his posture and theological orientation. He accomplishes this goal by analysing the intimate and dynamic relationship between al-Ṭabarī's theological standpoint and the 'sciences of language' (*ʿilm al-lugha*). Gilliot is especially interested in illustrating how al-Ṭabarī's linguistic approach to the Qur'an is influenced by his theological views. Gilliot observes that on one hand al-Ṭabarī approaches the Qur'an using the diverse instruments of human and profane philology; and that on the other hand al-Ṭabarī begins his commentary with an exposition in which he argues that the Qur'an's divine eloquence (*bayān*) is unsurpassable.

How does al-Ṭabarī's conviction in the unsurpassable degree of the Qur'an's eloquence dovetail with the emphasis he places on the profane science of language?

Gilliot observes that al-Ṭabarī's valorization of the Qur'an's language is informed by his views on the human aptitude to achieve linguistic perfection—a perfection in the science of language. Al-Ṭabarī's objective in his introduction to the *Tafsīr* is to defend the claim that the Qur'an's eloquence is unsurpassable by deploying a theory of *bayān*. He proposes that God arranged human beings in a hierarchy with various abilities to produce clear expression so that the capability to express oneself clearly and to make others understand their speech—the gift of *ibāna*—is unevenly distributed among human beings. While some people are 'orateurs prolixes' others are 'la bouche cousue' and incapable of expressing the thoughts of their hearts.

Working on the assumption that human perfection is defined by linguistic ability, specifically the gift of *bayān*, al-Ṭabarī proposes that the highest echelon of the human hierarchy is occupied by a person whose capacity to express himself clearly surpasses an ordinary degree. Furthermore, he places the degree of such perfection on the level of a miracle so that the ultimate miracle, which is performed by the prophet who is endowed with the highest gift of *bayān*, is the Qur'an's unsurpassable eloquence.

It is al-Ṭabarī's view that the prophet's superlative gift of eloquence is corroborated by the undefeated linguistic challenge of *bayān* that he issued to his Arab countrymen. In al-Ṭabarī's analysis, the Arabs had mastered the arts of oratory and rhymed prose that were employed in divination; and the inability of the poets and masters of oratory to respond to Muḥammad's challenge by 'produc[ing] something like the Qurʾān' attests to the Qur'an's matchlessness in the area of clear expression—its rhetorical excellence.

Al-Ṭabarī employs the science of rhetoric—specifically his theory of language—to defend his theory of the Qur'an's inimitability (*iʿjāz*). He proposes that the stylistic and rhetorical particularities employed in the Qur'an contribute to its unequalled perfection. While such particularities are part of the common language of the Arabs and give Arabic a superiority over other languages, the Qur'an elevates the use of these tropes and figures to a perfect and unequalled rank.

In the introduction to *Tafsīr al-bayān*, al-Ṭabarī lists seventeen stylistic and rhetorical particularities of the Arabic language that the Qur'an employs to the degree of perfection: (1) concision and brevity; (2) the employment of veiled instead of clear expression; (3) the employment of minimal instead of extended speech; (4) the use of extended expression and added words; (5) repetition and varied expression for the same meaning; (6) the setting out of meanings by non-circumlocutory expressions; (7) the concealing of intended meanings with cryptic expressions; (8) synecdoche of the particular for the general; (9) synecdoche of the general for the particular; (10); metalepsis of an indirect expression for a direct expression; (11) substitution of the description for the thing described; (12) substitution of the thing described by the description; (13) hysteron proteron; (14) the inversion of logical order; (15) synecdoche of the part for the whole; (16) the replacement of an ellipsis with a clear expression; (17) expressing clearly what is normally in the domain of ellipsis.

Al-Ṭabarī postulates that the Qur'an employs the aforementioned stylistic and rhetorical particularities to the highest degree of perfection and that, consequently, the Qur'an is the archetype of Arabic idiom. Furthermore, he proposes that the Qur'an's perfection of these devices grants it a pre-eminent sublimity. Al-Ṭabarī's theory of language thus serves the apologetic function of corroborating his theological position, which is that the rhetorical discourse of the Qur'an's sacred nature is due to its unsurpassability.

In addition to arguing for the insuperability of the Qur'an's literary beauty and eloquence, al-Ṭabarī also argues for the insuperability of the Qur'an's conceptual content. From his theological standpoint, the Qur'an's inimitability (*iʿjāz*) is so from two perspectives. Within Ṭabarī's technical vocabulary of *tafsīr*, the term *maʿānī* ('qualities') is employed to refer to two indissociable forms of the Qur'an's inimitability—stylistic quality and theological quality. By stylistic quality al-Ṭabarī means the Qur'an's *bayān*; and by theological quality (*contenu sapiential*) he means the Qur'an's genres, motifs, and themes. The ideas that God has assembled for the Prophet and his community had not been revealed in any earlier scripture (Torah, Psalms, Gospels) or given to any earlier community. The qualities of such genres, motifs, and themes attest to the unmatchable ideas that are expressed in the Qur'an and that are absent from earlier scriptures.

Al-Ṭabarī's defence of the insurpassable nature of the Qur'an's eloquence and its theological ideas is the pivot of his *tafsīr* methodology. While the dynamic relationship between al-Ṭabarī's theological position on the Qur'an's inimitability and his theory of rhetoric have been researched in excellent detail, there remain important aspects of al-Ṭabarī's methodology that remain to be investigated. As noted by Gilliot, al-Ṭabarī expressed his views on the relationship between Arabic language and the Qur'an before many of the major treatises on the Qur'an's inimitability were composed. A study of the ways that early discussions of *iʿjāz* (and theories of rhetoric) influenced al-Ṭabarī's theological argumentation within his Qur'anic commentary would likely be fruitful.

Muʿtazila

It was the Hungarian orientalist Ignaz Goldziher who first attempted to analyse the rationalizing tendencies of the Muʿtazila in their theological commentaries on the Qur'an. In his pioneering study, *Die Richtungen der islamischen Koranauslegung* (1920), Goldziher presented evidence that the Qur'anic commentaries authored by the Muʿtazila marked an important intellectual trend, especially in the early Abbasid period. For Goldziher, the Muʿtazila set itself apart from the traditionalist trends of Qur'anic interpretation by opposing the anthropomorphizing tendencies that were current among scholars who beheld the Sunna as a divinely sanctioned source of authority.

To be sure, rationalist forerunners to the Muʿtazila such as Mujāhid (d. 104/722) opposed anthropomorphism (at least to a certain degree) and influenced the rationalist theological orientation of the Muʿtazila. In contrast to Mujāhid, the Muʿtazila dealt with the entire sphere of the Qur'an's anthropomorphism. They rejected the anthropomorphic sense of Qur'anic verses on principle, so that the inclination to reject anthropomorphism became a foundational rule of Muʿtazilī methodology. The Muʿtazila rejected the plain sense not only regarding the physical attributes of God that might lead one to conceive of God as a manlike, corporeal individual—Seeing, Hearing, Anger, Willing, Satisfaction, [God's] sitting on the Throne, and [His] descent—but also the apparent sense of ideas such as predestination and [God's] revenge.

To bring out the differences between the Muʿtazilī and traditionalist methods of Qur'anic interpretation Goldziher analyses the beatific vision, an enduring point of contention between the Muʿtazila and advocates of traditional Muslim exegesis. The beatific vision is expressed in Q. 75:22–3: 'Upon that day faces shall be radiant, gazing upon their Lord.' Al-Shāfiʿī, a representative of traditional exegesis, accepts the beatific vision (in its plain sense) when he implies that God will be seen by believers who are rightly guided and pious (and that His speech will be heard by them). To justify his interpretation, al-Shāfiʿī adduces Q. 83:15 ('but upon that day they [the unbelievers] shall be veiled from their Lord'), a verse which in his view, relates that unbelievers will be denied the beatific vision, their faces being 'veiled from their Lord'. The Muʿtazila attack the idea of the beatific vision by diverting the phrase, 'Gazing upon their Lord' (75:23), to a figurative sense, finding support for this idea in the Qur'anic verse, 'The eyes attain Him not, but He attains the eyes' (6:106).

Since the publication of Goldziher's monograph, *Die Richtungen* (1920), considerable advances have been made by scholars working in the field of Qur'anic commentary. Recent studies by Suleiman Mourad (2010a, 2010b) point to the ways that Muʿtazilī methods and ideas were absorbed by Imāmī Shīʿī and Sunnī exegesis and placed in service of these theological movements. Of particular importance for the reception of Muʿtazilī ideas in the Imāmī Shīʿī tradition is al-Jishumī's Qur'anic commentary, *Tahdhīb*, which is extant in manuscript form and remains largely unstudied. Of importance for the reception of Muʿtazilī ideas in the Ashʿarī/Sunnī tradition is al-Zamakhsharī's *Kashshāf*, which the Ashʿarī/Sunnī theologian Fakhr al-Dīn al-Rāzī relied on when he composed his Qur'anic commentary in the late sixth/twelfth to early seventh/thirteenth century. An edition of al-Jishumī's Qur'anic commentary together with a study of its place within the broader arc of the *tafsīr* tradition is a desideratum.

Bruce Fudge's monograph on the Shīʿī commentator and Imāmī theologian al-Ṭabrisī, *Qur'ānic Hermeneutics* (2011), provides an overview of the most eminent Qur'anic commentators who worked within the Muʿtazilī tradition from the early third/ninth to early sixth/twelfth century. These commentators include Abū Bakr ʿAbd al-Raḥmān Kaysān al-Aṣamm (d. 201/816); Abū ʿAlī al-Jubbāʾī (d. 303/915); Abū'l-Qāsim al-Balkhī al-Kaʿbī (d. 319/931); Abū Muslim Muḥammad Baḥr al-Iṣfahānī (d. 323/934); ʿAlī ibn ʿĪsā al-Rummānī (d. 384/994); al-Qāḍī ʿAbd al-Jabbār (d. 415/1025); and al-Ḥākim al-Jishumī (d. 494/1101).

Most importantly, Fudge's monograph ploughs through unexplored territory by charting the influence of Muʿtazilī theology on Shīʿī hermeneutics. Fudge focuses his attention on the ways that al-Ṭabrisī's (d. 548/1154) Qur'anic exegesis, *Majmaʿ al-bayān*, is indebted to Muʿtazilī methods of Qur'anic commentary that can be traced to al-Jishumī's exegesis, the *Tahdhīb*. Naturally al-Ṭabrisī also relied on works from the Twelver Shīʿī tradition including the Qur'anic commentary of Abū Jaʿfar al-Ṭūsī (d. 460/1067). By analysing the attitudes that al-Ṭabrisī and al-Jishumī take towards knowledge, Fudge highlights an important difference between the conceptions of knowledge that underlie (and are at work in) the Muʿtazilī and Shīʿī traditions of Qur'anic exegesis. He points out that although the commentaries of the Imāmī theologian al-Ṭabrisī (*Majmaʿ al-bayān*) and the Muʿtazilī theologian al-Jishumī are similar in content, they have disparate underlying conceptions of knowledge. Al-Jishumī, like many other Muʿtazilīs, insists that all parts of the Qur'an are accessible to human reasoning. In contrast, al-Ṭabrisī's commentary explicitly states that in certain cases, recourse to the authority (*naṣṣ*) of the imams is necessary.

In his monograph, Fudge also calls attention to the important internal debates surrounding the Qur'anic distinction between 'clear' and 'ambiguous' verses (Q. 3:7) among the Muʿtazila, who speculated about the nature and meaning of this division more than any other intellectual movement. He identifies the exegetical works that analyse and interpret this Qur'anic distinction, proposing that such works constitute a subgenre within *tafsīr*. Importantly, he shows how discussions surrounding this crucial Qur'anic distinction provide insight into the principles that underlie Muʿtazilī exegesis. As is evident in ʿAbd al-Jabbār's *Mutashābih al-Qurʾān*, the genre that analyses and interprets the Qur'anic contrast between 'clear' and 'ambiguous' verses is concerned with 'giving doctrinally correct explanation of those verses that seem to contradict their [Muʿtazilī] dogma' and 'how proof can be drawn from the Qurʾān'. (Fudge 2011, 126).

AL-MĀTURĪDĪ

Around the time of al-Ashʿarī, al-Māturīdī (d. 333/944) composed an extensive Qur'anic commentary that exhibited scholastic tendencies and gave prominence to theological considerations. He deployed methods of *kalām* to defend the teaching of the Sunna against camps that (in his view) had deviated from the Sunna. Al-Māturīdī hailed from Samarqand, and later generations of scholars from Transoxiana considered him a learned scholar who masterfully explained and interpreted the theological teachings of Abū Ḥanīfa (d. 150/767). Ulrich Rudolph wrote that al-Māturīdī thought that Abū Ḥanīfa provided the correct answers to all questions in matters of belief, since his successors in Bukhara and Samarqand transmitted his teachings without alteration (Rudolph 1997). The generations of students who traced their intellectual genealogy to al-Māturīdī deemed him the most knowledgeable person on the views of Abū Ḥanīfa. They also considered al-Māturīdī's Qur'anic commentary, which they completed on the basis of his lecture notes, to have reached a breadth and depth of knowledge that no previous commentary had attained.

The most informative study of al-Māturīdī's Qur'anic exegesis, *Taʾwīlat al-Qurʾān*, is Manfred Götz's lengthy article, 'Māturīdī und sein Kitāb Taʾwīlāt al-Qurʾān' (1965). Writing before al-Māturīdī's Qur'anic commentary was published, Götz examined full and partial manuscripts of al-Māturīdī's *tafsīr* as well as the commentaries on that work which were authored by scholars within the Māturīdī tradition. A complete but uncritical edition of the *Taʾwīlāt* appeared almost thirty years later in 2004. A critical edition of the *Taʾwīlāt al-Qurʾān* was carried out in Istanbul under the supervision of Bekir Topaloğlu from 2005 to 2011.

Götz's study focuses on several themes in al-Māturīdī's *Taʾwīlat al-Qurʾān* that cast light on the interface between theology and exegesis in al-Māturīdī's system of thought. The most significant theme explored by Götz centres on the term *taʾwīl*, a practice of interpretation which forms the basis of al-Māturīdī's methodology. In order to overcome a major obstacle that had troubled previous commentators, al-Māturīdī opens his commentary by distinguishing between two methods of interpretation—*tafsīr* and *taʾwīl*.

Al-Māturīdī gives precision to these terms and establishes a principle of scriptural interpretation by proposing that the method of *tafsīr* is the prerogative of Muḥammad's Companions, a group of authorities who personally witnessed the course of Muḥammad's revelation. He reasons that because such knowledge of the Qur'an is based on personal authority it admits of only a single meaning. In contrast, *taʾwīl* (which means 'to return to') is the prerogative of the learned (*fuqahāʾ*). Relying on the authority of Abū Zayd Aḥmad Sahl al-Balkhī (d. 322/934), al-Māturīdī proposes that the application of *taʾwīl* enables a commentator to posit multiple meanings (or senses) that are permissible with respect to the Qur'an's wording. Thus, while the exegetical act of *tafsīr* can clarify only the outward sense of a Qur'anic verse, the method of *taʾwīl* gives authority to divergent possibilities of meaning. Al-Māturīdī sometimes invokes the authority of traditional scholars—ʿAbd Allāh ibn ʿAbbās, al-Ḥasan al-Baṣrī, etc.—when he applies *taʾwīl*. At other times he refrains from naming or appealing to authorities and offers interpretations of Qur'anic verses 'anonymously'.

The confines of this chapter do not permit an analysis or explanation of other important aspects of Götz's article, but let me mention that Götz's seminal study also deals with al-Māturīdī's teaching on God's attributes, divine predestination and human responsibility, and the nature of religious belief. Finally, as a direction for further research, let me mention that a study of al-Māturīdī's technical terminology, epistemic scheme, and the literary devices or instruments that he employs in his Qur'an commentary would enhance our understanding of al-Māturīdī's system of thought and bring out the differences between various schools (or trends) of exegesis in medieval Islam.

Ashʿarī-Sunnī Commentaries: al-Rāzī and his Legacy

Goldziher (1920) proposed that Fakhr al-Dīn al-Rāzī was the last of the 'prolific' commentators of the classical period, and that his commentary—*Mafātīḥ al-ghayb*—marked the high point of rational-theological Qur'anic exegesis (*tafsīr bi'l-raʾy*). Although the history of the various ways that al-Rāzī's encyclopaedic work guided later commentaries has not yet been written, it is quite certain that the methodological principles which al-Rāzī devised and the theological ideas which he formulated in *Mafātīḥ al-ghayb* persisted until well into *tafsīr* works of the late nineteenth century.

Al-Bayḍāwī's Qur'an commentary, *Anwār al-tanzīl wa-asrār al-taʾwīl*, which became a standard work in the curricula of Islamic institutions of learning, incorporated philosophical and theological ideas that al-Rāzī formulated in his elaboration of the Qur'an. Morrison (2007) wrote that Niẓām al-Dīn al-Nīsābūrī's (d. *c*.730/1330) scientific exegesis of the Qur'an illustrates that the methodological principles which al-Rāzī devised for Qur'anic commentary endured until the eighth/fourteenth century. Setia (2005) noted that the Qur'anic commentary of the Meccan-based Javanese scholar al-Nawawī al-Bantanī (d. 1314/1897) contained ideas that can be traced to al-Rāzī's *Mafātīḥ al-ghayb*. (Additional examples could also be adduced.)

Our knowledge of the commentaries that were composed by Ashʿarī-Sunnīs during the post-classical period (*c*.seventh/thirteenth to fourteenth/twentieth century) is rudimentary. Since the field has not yet identified the major commentators who flourished in this lengthy period—many of whom probably worked in Islamic institutions of learning (*madāris*)—it is not possible to say much about the nature of Qur'anic commentary in this period. Moreover, since the commentaries that were authored during this time have not yet been studied, we cannot yet determine how they contributed to broader intellectual discussions within the Islamic tradition.

Recent scholarship on Fakhr al-Dīn al-Rāzī (d. 606/1210), the leading representative of the Ashʿarī-Sunnī trend in the post-classical time period, offers insight into the ways that the Qur'an inspired commentators to expatiate on both *ʿaqlī* ('rational') bodies of knowledge and *naqlī* ('traditional') bodies of knowledge (including law, hadith, and theology). Beholding the Qur'an as a 'book that encompasses all knowledge' commentators considered the Qur'an a treasure house of philosophical and scientific ideas that could be discovered through the application of intellect or discursive reasoning to the Qur'anic verses.

It was al-Rāzī's prolific exegesis of the Qur'an—the Cairene edition (1933) is published in thirty-two large volumes—that first bridged the classical and post-classical intellectual traditions of Islam. Fundamentally, al-Rāzī established a new systematic methodology for the Sunnī intellectual tradition by implementing new rules and principles that govern the interpretation of the Qur'an. The new rules and principles that he devised for the tradition, which Ibn Taymiyya (d. 728/1328) aimed to undermine from the perspective of Traditionalism, incorporated the old signature method of *taʾwīl*, which the Muʿtazila had employed as a means of demythologizing the Qur'an. But in contrast to the Muʿtazila, al-Rāzī argued for the *logical* necessity of this interpretive method; and he set this old celebrated method within a new Ashʿarī-Sunnī theological system that also imparted the Qur'an and prophetic Sunna with authority.

Equally fundamentally, al-Rāzī established an organizational framework and devised a method of enquiry for the practice of Qur'anic interpretation. He designed a methodical system that organized all knowledge which was available in his culture according to the order and arrangement of Qur'anic verses. It was by using this method that al-Rāzī aimed to integrate the entire sweep of the rational (*ʿaqlī*) sciences (logic, physics or natural sciences, metaphysics, astronomy, and medicine) and traditional (*naqlī*) sciences (law, hadith, mysticism, and theology, including its theories of physics, anthropology, and cosmology) into his commentary. And it was by using this method that al-Rāzī achieved one of his ultimate goals—to reach the profundity of knowledge that God has deposited in Qur'anic verses.

Finally, in his Qur'anic commentary, al-Rāzī succeeded in synthesizing ideas from disparate intellectual currents—Aristotelian-Avicennian philosophy, Muʿtazilism, and Sufism. Scholars have recently illustrated that al-Rāzī had a genius for adapting the heritage of Greek-Islamic philosophy, especially Ibn Sīnā's innovations in epistemology and metaphysics, into Ashʿarī-Sunnī theology. Furthermore, they have shown that al-Rāzī's efforts to carry out this process of adaptation are discernible in his Qur'anic commentary. And they have illustrated how al-Rāzī, by executing this component of his intellectual programme fundamentally altered the Sunnī worldview within medieval Islam.

Let me close by suggesting a direction for research within the field of al-Rāzī studies. Major problems within al-Rāzī studies have yet to be resolved. Unlike his predecessors within the tradition of Islamic exegesis, al-Rāzī was imbued with an Islamic education and inculcated with the heritage of Greek learning. The ways that these sources of knowledge—the rational and traditional sciences—interacted within al-Rāzī's commentary remains to be further investigated. Did al-Rāzī subordinate the traditional sciences to the rational by giving the former less epistemic value? Or is the relationship between the two *dynamic*—does al-Rāzī shift the weight of authority throughout the commentary? In what ways did he place the rational sciences (especially Avicennian wisdom) in service of the practice of Qur'anic commentary? Further studies of the complexity of al-Rāzī's overall methodology and thought will cast light on these questions.

Bibliography

Calder, N. '*Tafsīr* from Ṭabarī to Ibn Kathīr: Problems in the Description of a Genre, Illustrated with Reference to the Story of Abraham'. In: Gerald R. Hawting and Abdul-Kader A. Shareef (eds.). *Approaches to the Qur'ān*. London: Routledge, 1993.

Cooper, J. and W. F. Madelung. *The Commentary on the Qur'ān by Abū Jaʿfar Muḥammad Jarīr al-Ṭabarī being an Abridged Translation of Jāmiʿ al-bayān ʿan taʾwīl āy al-Qurʾān*. (eds.). W. F. Madelung, Alan Jones, and J. Cooper. Oxford: Oxford University Press, 1987.

Crone, P. 'A Note on Muqātil Ḥayyān and Muqātil Sulaymān', *Der Islam* 74/2 (1997), 238–49.

Fudge, B. *Quranic Hermeneutics: Al-Ṭabrisī and the Craft of Quran Commentary*. Oxford and New York: Routledge, 2011.

Galli, A. M. A. 'Some Aspects of al-Māturīdī's Commentary on the Qurʾān', *Islamic Studies* 21 (1982), 3–21.

Gilliot, C. 'ʿAbdallāh ʿAbbās'. In: *Encyclopaedia of the Qurʾān*, 32.

Gilliot, C. 'Portrait Mythique d'Ibn ʿAbbās', *Arabica* 32 (1985), 127–84.

Gilliot, C. *Exégèse, langue, et théologie en Islam: l'exégèse coranique de Tabari*. Paris: Librairie Philosophique J. Vrin, 1990.

Gilliot, C. 'Muqātil, grand exégète, traditionniste et théologien maudit', *Journal Asiatique* 279 (1991), 39–92.

Gilliot, C. 'L'Embarras d'un exégète musulman face a un palimpseste: Māturīdī et la sourate de l'Abondance (*Al-Kawthar*, sourate 108), avec une note savante sur le commentaire coranique d'Ibn al-Naqīb (m. 698/1298)'. In R. Arnzen and J. Thielmann (eds.). *Words, Texts and Concepts Cruising the Mediterranean Sea: Studies on the Sources, Contents and Influences of Islamic Civilization and Arabic Philosophy and Science Dedicated to Gerhard Endress on his Sixty-Fifth Birthday*, pp. 33–69. Leuven: Peeters, 2004.

Gilliot, C. 'Mujāhid's Exegesis: Origins, Paths of Transmission and Development of a Meccan Exegetical Tradition in its Human, Spiritual and Theological Environment'. In: A. Görke and J. Pink (eds.). *Tafsīr and Islamic Intellectual History. Exploring the Boundaries of a Genre*, pp. 63–111. Oxford: Oxford University Press, 2015.

Gimaret, D. *Une lecture muʿtazilite du Coran: le tafsīr d'Abū ʿAlī al-Djubbāʾī (m. 303/915) partiellement reconstitué à partir de ses citateurs*. Leuven and Paris: Peeters, 1994.

Goldziher, I. 'Aus der Theologie des Fachr al-Dīn al-Rāzī', *Der Islam* 3 (1912), 213–47.

Goldziher, I. *Die Richtungen der islamischen Koranauslegung*. Leiden: E. J. Brill, 1920.

Götz, M. 'Māturīdī und sein Kitāb Taʾwīlāt al-Qurʾān', *Der Islam* 41 (1965), 27–70.

Gwynne, R. 'The *Tafsīr* of Abū ʿAlī al-Jubbāʾī: First Steps Toward a Reconstruction, with Texts, Translation, Biographical Introduction and Analytical Essay' (PhD). University of Washington, Ann Arbor: UMI, 1982.

Jaffer, T. *Rāzī: Master of Qurʾānic Interpretation and Theological Reasoning*. Oxford: Oxford University Press, 2015.

Juynboll, G. H. A. *Muslim Tradition: Studies in Chronology, Provenance and Authorship of Early Ḥadīth*. Cambridge: Cambridge University Press, 1983.
Kinberg, L. '*Muhkamat and Mutashabihat* (Koran 3/7): Implications of a Pair of Terms in Medieval Exegesis', *Arabica* 35 (1988), 143–72.
Lagarde, M. 'De l'ambiguité dans le coran: tentatives d'explication des exégètes musulmans', *Quaderni di studi arabi* 3 (1985), 291–314.
Lagarde, M. *Les Secrets de l'invisible: essai sur le Grand Commentaire de Faḫr al-Dīn al-Rāzī*. Paris: Éditions AlBouraq, 2009.
Lane, A. *A Traditional Muʿtazilite Qurʾān Commentary: The Kashshāf of Jār Allāh al-Zamakhsharī (d. 538/1144)*. Leiden: Brill, 2006.
Lane, A. 'You Can't Tell a Book by its Author: A Study of Muʿtazilite Theology in al-Zamakhsharī's (d. 538/1144) *Kashshāf*', *Bulletin of the School of Oriental and African Studies* 75/1 (2012), 47–86.
Leemhuis, F. 'Origins and Early Development of the *Tafsīr* Tradition'. In: Andrew Rippin (ed.). *Approaches to the History of the Interpretation of the Qurʾān*, pp. 13–30. Oxford: Clarendon Press, 1988.
McAuliffe, J. D. 'Text and Textuality: Q. 3:7 as a Point of Intersection'. In: Issa J. Boullata. Richmond Curzon (ed.). *Literary Structures of Religious Meaning in the Qurʾān*. Richmond: Routledge, 2000.
McAuliffe, Jane Dammen (ed.). *Encyclopaedia of the Qurʾān*. 6 vols. Leiden: Brill, 2001–6.
Madelung, W. 'Imāmism and Muʿtazilite Theology'. In: Toufic Fahd (ed.). *Le Shīʾisme imāmite*', pp. 13–29. Paris: Presses Universitaires de France, 1970.
Madelung, W. 'ʿAbd Allāh ʿAbbās and Shiʿite law'. In: U. Vermeulen and J. M. F. Van Reeth (eds.). *Law, Christianity and Modernism in Islamic Society in 1996: Proceedings of the Eighteenth Congress of the Union Europeene des Arbisants et Islamisants*, pp. 13–25. Leuven: Katholieke Universiteit Leuven, 1996.
Mayer, T. *Keys to the Arcana: Shahrastānī's Esoteric Commentary on the Qurʾān. A Translation of the Commentary on Sūrat al-Fātiḥa from Muḥammad ʿAbd al-Karīm al-Shahrastānī's Mafātīḥ al-asrār wa maṣābīḥ al-abrār*. Oxford and London: Oxford University Press and the Institute of Ismaili Studies, 2009.
Morrison, R. G. *Islam and Science: The Intellectual Career of Niẓām al-Dīn al-Nīsābūrī*. London and New York: Routledge, 2007.
Morrison, R. G. 'Natural Theology and the Qur'an', *Journal of Qur'anic Studies* 15/1 (2013), 1–22.
Mourad, S. A. 'The Survival of the Muʿtazila Tradition of Qur'anic Exegesis in Shīʿī and Sunnī *tafāsīr*', *Journal of Qur'anic Studies* 12a (2010), 83–108.
Mourad, S. A. 'The Revealed Text and the Intended Subtext: Notes on the Hermeneutics of the Qur'an in Muʿtazila Discourse as Reflected in the *Tahdhīb* of al-Ḥākim al-Jishumī (d. 494/1101)'. In: Felicitas Opwis and David Reisman (eds.). *In the Shadow of the Pyramids: Festschrift in Honor of Dimitri Gutas on his 65th Birthday*. Leiden: Brill, 2010b.
Raḥman, M. M. *An Introduction to al-Maturidi's Taʾwīlāt Ahl al-Sunna*. Dacca, 1981.
Rippin, A. 'Tafsir'. In: M. Eliade (ed.). *Encyclopedia of Religions*. Vol. 14. London: Macmillan, 1981.
Rippin, A. 'Ibn ʿAbbās's *Al-lughāt fīʾl-Qurʾān*', *Bulletin of the School of Oriental and African Studies* 44 (1981), 15–25.
Rippin, A. 'Ibn ʿAbbās's *Gharīb al-Qurʾān*', *Bulletin of the School of Oriental and African Studies* 46 (1983), 332–3.

Rippin, A. (ed.). *Approaches to the History of the Interpretation of the Qurʾān*. Oxford: Clarendon Press/Oxford University Press, 1988.
Rippin, A. 'Tafsīr Ibn ʿAbbās and Criteria for Dating Early Tafsīr Texts', *Jerusalem Studies in Arabic and Islam* 19 (1994), 38–83.
Rippin, A. 'Mudjāhid Djabr al-Makkī'. In: *Encyclopaedia of Islam*, 7:295.
Rudolph, U. *Al-Māturīdī und die sunnitsche Theologie in Samarkand*. Leiden: E. J. Brill, 1997.
Saleh, W. *The Formation of the Classical Tafsīr Tradition: The Qurʾān Commentary of al-Thaʿlābī (d. 427/1035)*. Leiden: E. J. Brill, 2004.
Saleh, W. 'The Last of the Nishapuri School of Tafsīr: Al-Wāḥidī (d. 468/1076) and his Significance in the History of Qurʾānic Exegesis', *Journal of the American Oriental Society* 126 (2006), 223–43.
Saleh, W. 'Preliminary Remarks on the Historiography of *tafsīr* in Arabic: A History of the Book Approach', *Journal of Qurʾānic Studies* 12 (2010), 6–40.
Saleh, W. 'The Gloss as Intellectual History: The Ḥāshiyahs on al-Kashshāf', *Oriens* 41 (2013), 217–59.
Saleh, W. 'The Ḥāshiya of Ibn al-Munayyir (d. 683/1284) on al-Kashshāf of al-Zamakhsharī'. In: Andrew Rippin and Robert Tottoli (eds.) *Books and Written Culture of the Islamic World: Studies Presented to Claude Gilliot on the Occasion of his 75th Birthday*, pp. 86–90. Leiden: Brill, 2015.
Schmidtke, S. (ed. and trans.). *A Muʿtazilite Creed of az-Zamakhsharī (d. 538/1144) (Al-Minhāj fī uṣūl al-dīn)*. Stuttgart: Steiner, 1997.
Setia, A. 'The Theologico-Scientific Research Program of the Mutakallimūn', *Islam & Science* 3 (2005), 127–52.
Shah, M. 'Al-Ṭabarī and the Dynamics of *tafsīr*: Theological Dimensions of a Legacy', *Journal of Qur'anic Studies* 15/2 (2013), 83–139.
Sinai, N. 'Qurʾānic Self-Referentiality as a Strategy of Self-Authorization'. In: Stefan Wild (ed.). *Self-Referentiality in the* Qurʾān, pp. 103–34. Wiesbaden: Harrassowitz, 2006.
Sinai, N. 'The Qur'anic Commentary of Muqātil Sulaymān and the Evolution of Early *Tafsīr* Literature'. In: Andreas Görke and Johanna Pink (eds.) *Tafsīr and Islamic Intellectual History. Exploring the Boundaries of a Genre*, pp. 113–43. Oxford: Oxford University Press. 2015.
Syamsuddin, S. '*Muḥkam* and *mutashābih*: An Analytical Study of al-Ṭabarī's and al-Zamakhsharī's Interpretations of Q. 3:7', *Journal of Qur'anic Studies* 1/1 (1999), 63–79.
Van Ess, J. *Theologie und Gesellschaft im 2. und 3. Jahrhundert Hidschra: Eine Geschichte der religiösen Denkens im frühen Islam*. Vols. 1–6. Berlin: Walter de Gruyter, 1991–6.
Wansbrough, J. *Quranic Studies: Sources and Methods of Scriptural Interpretation. Foreword, Translations, and Expanded Notes by Andrew Rippin*. New York: Prometheus Books, 2004.

CHAPTER 52

PHILOSOPHICAL COMMENTARIES

JULES JANSSENS

SYNTHESES of the history of classical Qur'anic exegesis are often broached with reference to *kalām* (theology), *fiqh* (law), and *taṣawwuf* (mysticism) (Calder 1993: 105–6). However, to complete the picture one has also to take into account the science of *falsafa* (philosophy). Even if the production of purely philosophical commentaries in the classical period was very limited, it influenced in a significant way later Qur'anic exegesis, especially as practised by theologians and mystics. Research regarding both the specificities of this particular genre of Qur'anic exegesis, as well as its influence on the later exegetical tradition, has hardly begun. Hence, in what follows, I examine a number of the major contributions to philosophical exegesis and assess their significance, while suggesting avenues for further research.

AL-KINDĪ

Al-Kindī (d. *c.*256/870) is generally considered to be the founder of *falsafa* in the Islamic world. In three of his works one finds important sections relating to Qur'anic exegesis. Unfortunately, many of his works have been lost, intimating that his treatment of exegetical discussions may have been more extensive. As to the preserved material, it is striking to note that strong evidence of philosophical influence, most particularly of Philoponus (Adamson 2003: 62–4), is present. But there is more. In spite of his working in a Muʿtazilī milieu, and in spite of the fact that some of his ideas must be understood in the context of, or, more precisely against the background of, contemporary Muʿtazilī discussions, the very approach he uses in his Qur'anic comments is definitely philosophical (Janssens 2007: 6–15). This is most obvious in his treatise *On the Prosternation of the Outermost Body*, where he, after having given two lexical remarks, develops an outspoken philosophical explanation of Q. 55:6, an important part of which consists in the presentation of the Universe as construed out of two—sharply distinguished from each other—worlds, that is, a supra- and an infra-lunar world (al-Kindī, *Fī'l-ibāna*, 247–61). Also beyond any reasonable doubt is al-Kindī's interpretation of Q. 36:82, as given in his treatise *On the Reason why the Higher Air is Cold and that which is Near the Earth is Warm*. In that *āya*, al-Kindī detects the affirmation of two sharply distinguished modes of knowledge: one by inspiration, proper to the prophets, and another through a gradual process of acquiring science, characteristic of all other human beings (al-Kindī, *Fī'l-ʿilla*, 93). However, that a philosophical ideology guides al-Kindī's Qur'anic exegesis shows up most sharply in the very fact that he, in his treatise *On the Quantity of Aristotle's Books*, interprets Q. 36:82 in a quite different way from the one just discussed. In fact, he now presents the *āya* as expressing the idea that God creates out of nothing, while being in no need of time (al-Kindī, *Fī kammiyyāt*, 375–6). Since the *āya* refers to Allāh's creative command 'Be', this latter interpretation clearly fits the context better. This does not mean that the former is just at random. It has perhaps been inspired by the preceding *āya*, where it is said that God is 'the Creator (of all), the Knower', in which one may detect an intimate link between creation and knowledge. In this sense, it seems possible, or even probable, that al-Kindī has understood the creative imperative 'Be' as expressing also an immediate donation of knowledge. Anyway, this double explanation of the same *āya* in two senses totally different from each other can only be explained by philosophical motives, that is, epistemological, metaphysical ones, respectively. It is not arbitrary in so far as the Qur'an, at least in al-Kindī's view, uses a metaphorical language, and, as such, is in principle open to more than one single interpretation. Moreover, and more importantly, al-Kindī seems not to doubt that the Qur'an allows for the essentials of philosophy (Janssens 2007: 11). Hence, he clearly paved the way for a new kind of Qur'anic interpretation (i.e. the philosophical), and did pioneering work in this respect.

For two centuries it received almost no attention. But then Ibn Sīnā (d. 427/1037), one of the greatest philosophers not only of the Islamic world, but of humankind, largely used and substantially developed it. Before dealing with him, a brief remark is required with respect to that other great thinker of the Islamic East, al-Fārābī (d. 339/950). In his authenticated works, he never refers to the Qur'an. For him, the revelation is destined for the masses and there is no need to elaborate a philosophical exegesis.

Ibn Sīnā

As to Ibn Sīnā, he undoubtedly has to be considered the scholar who brought to fruition the genre of philosophical exegesis. He wrote by way of independent treatises extensive expositions of a number of suras, more precisely the last three of the Qur'an, as well as on Q. 41:11–12a (ʿĀṣī 1983: 104–25 and 89–93). One other independent treatise of Qur'anic commentary, that is, on the celebrated light verse (Q. 24:35), which has been attributed to him, looks spurious (Janssens 2004: 181–3), while still another, namely the one on sura 87, is revealed to have been written by Fakhr al-Dīn al-Rāzī (Sebti forthcoming).

However, in the light verse one finds a rather systematic explanation in two of his writings, *Ithbāt al-nubuwwāt* (Proof of prophecies) (Ibn Sīnā, *Ithbāt al-nubuwwāt*, 48–52) and *Ishārāt* (Pointers and reminders) (Ibn Sīnā, *Ishārāt*, 125–7). Furthermore, on different occasions in his writings Ibn Sīnā quotes Qur'anic *āyāt* in order to strengthen a given doctrine. Finally, it has to be observed that he regularly uses Qur'anic names of Allāh, such as *al-Ḥaqq*, to designate what in philosophical terms is called the 'First' or 'Highest Being' (Janssens 1987: 268). All this clearly indicates that he uses the Qur'an in a more than secondary way. His view is that for the attentive reader, it entails, hidden beyond the superficial sense of the outer wording, the truth, which he identifies on the rational level with the demonstrative and hence philosophical truth.

When we look at his independent treatises, it is obvious that the interpreted Qur'anic text always gives rise to the evocation of major philosophical ideas: the absolute ipseity of God, whose quiddity is fully identical with His existence, who is absolutely one in Himself notwithstanding His being principle of the existence of all other beings, and who is unique (Q. 112) (De Smet-Sebti 2009: 134–48); the justification of evil, both ontologically—the accidental appearance of evil on the level of the divine decree, *al-qadar*—and morally, due to man's submission to the animal powers of imagination and estimation (Q. 113); and the human soul, especially its desire to turn itself to the higher world (Q. 114) (Janssens 2004: 187–92). As to the commentary on Q. 41:11–12a, it highlights that the reception of the forms from above is spontaneous in the supra-lunar world, whereas it happens in a much more reluctant way in this world (Michot 1980: 326). Such outspoken philosophical interpretations are undoubtedly surprising, but when one carefully looks at them, one is immediately struck by how seriously Ibn Sīnā takes into account the very wording of the Qur'an. When he starts his explication of Q. 112, he discusses the three words of the first *āya*, '*huwa*', '*Allāh*', and '*aḥad*', in the very order in which they appear. That he finds in this *āya* a solid expression of God's absolute ipseity, that is, 'He' is 'He', becomes easily understandable if one valorizes with him the '*huwa*' as the first, and therefore most important word. At once, it becomes understandable that the word '*Allāh*' is considered to offer the explanation of this fundamental '*huwa*', namely as its most proximate concomitant. In Ibn Sīnā's view it is only in this way that Allāh can become the principle of all being without disrupting His unity and uniqueness. In other words, he takes very seriously the idea of divine *tawḥīd*—so central to the Islamic faith. Even if his exegesis has nothing, or almost nothing, in common with the different Qur'anic commentaries that preceded him, one has to admit that he always keeps a serious eye on the text itself. Let us illustrate this by quoting extensively his exegetical gloss on Q. 112:2. Since the first of its two words, '*Allāh*', had already been discussed, Ibn Sīnā limits himself to explain the second word, '*al-Ṣamad*'. This latter term, which is difficult to translate, expresses the idea of a Lord, upon whom everything is dependent, but also that of a being that is 'solid, not hollow' (Lane 1872: 4: 1727). This is immediately indicated by Ibn Sīnā: 'There exist in (ordinary) language two explanations for *al-ṣamad*: one is "what possesses no cavity"; the other "lord" (*sayyid*)' (Ibn Sīnā, *Tafsīr*, 20, 14–15; ʿĀṣī 1983: 110, 18–19). In classical times, a wide range of Qur'anic interpreters used this kind of lexical explanation (Wansbrough 1977: 201). But Ibn Sīnā uses it in a very particular way, namely as a basis for a purely philosophical view. 'With regards to the first explanation, its meaning is negative; namely it is the negation of (having) a quiddity, because everything that has a quiddity has a cavity, i.e. an inner (portion), which is that quiddity. That, on the contrary (*wa-*), has no inner portion, is existent, and thus has no mode, no aspect in its essence other than existence. And what has no other aspect than existence, cannot receive non-being, for in so far as something (*al-shayʾ*) exists (*mawjūd*), it is not (open to) the reception of non-being. Consequently (*fa-idhan*), *al-Ṣamad* is the truth of what is absolutely necessarily existent in all respects. Regarding the second explanation, its meaning is relative, namely that *al-Ṣamad* is the lord of everything, i.e. the principle of the Universe. It is conceivable that both (meanings) are intended by the *āya*, as if its meaning is that the deity is like this: namely, that the divinity is a consideration of the totality of both these aspects (*hadhayn al-amrayn*), (i.e.) negation and affirmation' (Ibn Sīnā, *Tafsīr*, 20, 15–21, 4; ʿĀṣī 1983: 110, 18–111, 6). In this commentary one easily recognizes two major ideas of Ibn Sīnā's philosophical theology: the absolute identity in the divine Being between essence and existence and the latter's being the ultimate cause of all that exists. In this respect, one may consult the *Metaphysics* of his major work *The Healing*, more precisely b. VIII, c. 4 and 7, and b. IX, c. 1 (Ibn Sīnā, *Metaphysics*, 273–8 and 291–307). Even those who find this interpretation of Q. 112:2 far-fetched must recognize that it respects the letter of the Qur'an. It expresses in philosophical terms the divine *tawḥīd* together with the divine Lordship over all things, ideas that clearly fit an Islamic framework of thought.

But one might judge that this is no longer the case when Ibn Sīnā comments on Q. 24:35, in his *Pointers and Reminders*. The *āya* is interpreted according to Ibn Sīnā's theory of intellect and intellection, so that the niche symbolizes the material intellect, the lamp the acquired intellect, etc. (Janssens 2004: 183–4). A very similar interpretation is also present in *Proof of Prophecies*—in all likelihood, a pseudepigraphical work (Gutas 2014: 485–9), albeit highly Avicennian inspired (Lizzini 2018: 82). But there exist also differences between the two works, the major of which consists in the absence of any reference to the notion of 'intuition' (*ḥads*) in the *Proof of Prophecies*. In the version of *Pointers and Reminders* 'intuition' is directly linked with the Qur'anic word 'oil' (*zaytu*). As to the specification of the olive, the blessed tree as one 'whose oil is well-nigh luminous', it is presented in *Pointers* as expressing a 'holy power', whereas in the *Proof of Prophecies* it is said—without any special attention being paid to the notion of 'oil'—to designate 'a glorification of the thinking power'. Nevertheless, it is striking that both works take the very wording of the Qur'an into consideration. One should also note moreover that both offer an overall psychologizing interpretation. Certainly, the latter looks artificial to our contemporary eyes, but it was not so strange for many Muslim scholars who lived a few, or even several centuries after Ibn Sīnā, as soon will become clear.

As to Ibn Sīnā's use of isolated Qur'anic *āyāt* in his different works, there is a temptation to just consider them as being rhetorical expressions that have no purpose other than to conceal the profoundly un-Islamic character of a given philosophical truth. When he exposes the divine knowledge of the particulars in terms of being in 'a universal way', Ibn Sīnā quotes in the *Metaphysics of the Healing* (Ibn Sīnā, *Metaphysics*, 288) the following part of Q. 34:3 'From whom is not hidden the least little atom in the heavens or on earth.' At first sight, Ibn Sīnā's view seems to exclude the possibility of individual beings that are subject to generation and corruption, in other words all earthly ones, in so far as their materiality is spread over multiple individuals and therefore is not open to a 'universal' knowledge. However, the very fact that Ibn Sīnā so often and systematically deals with this topic can hardly be explained on purely philosophical grounds alone; rather, it points to religious motives. Although he always tries to formulate a philosophically coherent answer, Ibn Sīnā seems to have been aware of the difficulty of providing one such in the present case. In fact, he stresses that the divine omniscience is 'one of the wonders whose conception requires the subtlety of an inborn, acute intelligence' (Ibn Sīnā, *Metaphysics*, 288). Moreover, it is worth noting that he discusses the issue in many of his other works. Whether Ibn Sīnā succeeded in offering a fully coherent doctrine is a matter open to question but not easy to answer, since scholars continue to demonstrate that Ibn Sīnā failed to explain how God knows particulars, not whether He knows them (Acar 2004: 153–6). Hence it is reasonable to accept that Ibn Sīnā is sincere when he says that God knows everything, and in this perspective the quotation of part of Q. 34:3 is seemingly more than rhetorical embellishment. In a similar way, the quotation at the end of Q. 6:76, 'I love not those that set', in the twelfth section of *Namaṭ* 5 of *Ishārāt*, has nothing to do with what is intimated by the revelation in the context of a particular story about Ibrāhīm. In fact, Ibn Sīnā's explanation omits any reference to the disappearance of a star due to the setting of the night, as evoked in the beginnings of the *āya*. Instead, he emphasizes that a sensible being cannot necessarily be existent by itself 'because the fall in the realm of the possible is a kind of setting' (Ibn Sīnā, *Ishārāt*, 154, 11). In other words, not only the sensible, but also every possible being—and outside God, the unique necessary being by itself, all other beings are possible—has no necessity in itself, that is, it cannot exist without its cause. Hence, in itself it has a tendency to disappear, or, to put it in philosophical terms, towards non-being, even if it is eternal according to a 'temporal' eternity that completely differs from God's eternity, which is 'above time'. From this point of view, Ibn Sīnā's explanation is undoubtedly acceptable as it stresses that no single being can equal the proper being of God. More research is needed to see whether Ibn Sīnā's use of Qur'anic verses can always be explained by a genuine will to valorize—be it in a philosophical way—the message included in them, or if sometimes purely strategic reasons lie at its base.

Anyway, the Qur'an is never totally absent in Ibn Sīnā's writings, even in the most outspoken philosophical ones. This sharply contrasts with the practice of his great predecessor al-Fārābī, but also with that of that other giant of *falsafa*, the Andalusian scholar Ibn Rushd (d. 595/1198). In line with al-Fārābī, Ibn Rushd never quotes the Qur'an in his philosophical commentaries. However, Qur'anic verses are discussed in some of his other works, such as the *Faṣl al-maqāl* (The decisive treatise), *al-Kashf ʿan manāhij al-adilla fī ʿaqāʾid al-milla* (Disclosure of the methods of proofs) and the *Tahāfut al-Tahāfut (Incoherence of the Incoherence)*. In these works, he uses them for one single, major purpose: to show the obligatory character of philosophy and, more specifically, the need to use the demonstrative method as claimed by the philosophers (needed to distinguish the apparent from the real sense of (some) Qur'anic verses). Illustrative of this attitude is his explanation of the final affirmation of Q. 59:2, 'Consider, you who have sight', as 'a text for the obligation of using both intellectual and Law-based syllogistic reasoning' (Ibn Rushd, *Decisive Treatise*, 2) and of the beginning of Q. 39:42, 'It is God that takes the souls (of men) at death, and those that die not (he takes) during their sleep', as a proof for the immortality of the soul, which in its apparent sense can be understood by all men, including the ignorant masses: this is achieved by likening the condition in death to that in sleep, showing the learned the ways by which the survival of the soul is ascertained (Ibn Rushd, *Tahāfut* (*The Incoherence of the Incoherence*), 2:843). For Ibn Rushd the Qur'an entails the same truth as philosophy, but its affirmations do not require exegetical qualification, not even a philosophical exegesis, since they express that truth in a manner understandable for the elite as well as for the masses; whereas, the latter are unable to grasp that same truth when philosophically expressed. Therefore, one looks in vain in Ibn Rushd for exegetical explication, and, as far as I can see, this is also the case for both Ibn Bājja (d. 533/1138) and Ibn Ṭufayl (d. *c.*580/1185), who also represented the currents of *falsafa* in Andalusia and who were more or less his contemporaries. But this does not mean that philosophical exegesis came to an end with Ibn Sīnā. On the contrary, it received serious attention and was partly integrated in different major fields of thought: *kalām*, *taṣawwuf* ('Sufism') and the Ishrāqī school in Iran. In what follows we will present a few major figures. This survey is certainly not exhaustive, but it is hoped that it offers a representative sample of the presence of elements of philosophical exegesis in the later tradition.

AL-GHAZĀLĪ

Abū Ḥāmid al-Ghazālī (d. 505/1111), according to his honorific title the 'Proof of Islam', is undoubtedly one of the greatest thinkers of all times in the Islamic world. He elaborated a complex and unarguably unique system, wherein are present elements of Ashʿarī *kalām*, moderate Sufism, and philosophy. One can qualify it, as Frank Griffel has done, as a 'philosophical theology' (Griffel 2009), but, in order to be complete, one probably has to add 'sufi-guided' to 'philosophical theology', since al-Ghazālī wavers many times between philosophy and Sufism (Janssens 2011: 632). However, in the present context we do not need to evaluate the precise weight of each of these composing elements. We will limit ourselves to showing that al-Ghazālī—at least, on occasion—interprets Qur'anic *āyāt*, or parts of them, according to the patterns of philosophical exegesis as creatively developed by Ibn Sīnā.

A first significant example of this can be derived from the second section (*bayān*) of the book *ʿAjāʾib al-qalb* (*The Marvels of the Heart*) of the *Iḥyāʾ ʿulūm al-dīn* (*The Revival of the Religious Sciences*). The section is entitled 'The armies of the heart' and opens directly by quoting a sentence near the end of Q. 74:31, 'And none knows the armies of thy Lord except He' (al-Ghazālī, *Iḥyāʾ*, 3:5). Having specified that there are many armies that are only known by God, al-Ghazālī states that of the armies we, humans, have access to, mainly two can be distinguished: one seen by the outer eye and one perceived by the inner eye. In full accordance with Ibn Sīnā's doctrine, al-Ghazālī evokes the perceptive faculty (together with the specification of the five outer and the five inner senses), as well as the inciting (desire and anger) and moving faculties; he even mentions such a technical issue as the specific location of the inner senses in the ventricles of the brain (Janssens 2011: 620–1). Note that in the present context 'heart' is synonymous with 'soul', hence it is used in its subtle meaning, namely 'a lordly, spiritual subtlety, which is *the* reality of man' (al-Ghazālī, *Iḥyā'*, 3:3). We do not have to concern ourselves here with the exact meaning of this latter definition, but we have to draw attention to the fact that al-Ghazālī explains the Qur'anic saying in an unexpected, namely psychologizing way, which was also encountered in Ibn Sīnā's philosophical exegesis. It must be stressed moreover that the complete section presents itself as a detailed interpretation of the Qur'anic expression 'armies of the Lord'. Finally, in spite of his criticism of several of the philosophical doctrines, al-Ghazālī fully accepts Ibn Sīnā's view on the animal faculties, and even does not hesitate to present it as a valuable explanation for what might appear as an enigmatic expression. Although the Qur'an insists that only God knows those armies, al-Ghazālī does not hesitate to express them, at least, in a way that is understandable for the weak (al-Ghazālī, *Iḥyā'*, 3:6)—suggesting that the Qur'an is open to a profounder (in all likelihood, philosophical-mystical) understanding, full access of which has to be reserved for the 'elite'.

In *al-Maqṣad al-asnā fī sharḥ ma ʿānī asmāʾ Allāh al-ḥusnā (The Ninety-nine beautiful names of God)*, al-Ghazālī, in the discussion of the divine name *al-Ḥaqq*, 'The Truth', quotes Q. 28:88: 'Everything (that exists) will perish except His own Face' . He explains the *āya* as follows: 'It is forever and eternally thus. It is not in one state to the exclusion of another for—forever and eternally—everything besides God is not deserving of existence with respect to its own essence. It deserves (of existence) in virtue of Him, and so it is vain (*bāṭil*) in itself, real (*ḥaqq*) through another. From this you will know the absolute True is the Being that exists through itself, from which every real (thing) gets its reality' (al-Ghazālī, *Maqṣad*, 127; *Ninety-nine*, 124 [translation modified]). At the background of al-Ghazālī's interpretation, one easily detects Ibn Sīnā's famous distinction between God, the only necessary Being by itself, and all other Beings which are 'possible in themselves, but necessary through another'. Although partly inspired by *kalām*, this latter characterization has justly been qualified as Ibn Sīnā's big idea (Wisnovsky 2003: 199). Certainly, al-Ghazālī has replaced Ibn Sīnā's usual terminology of 'possible' (*mumkin*) and 'necessary' with one of 'vain' (*bāṭil*) and 'real' (*ḥaqq*), but his explanation otherwise recalls Ibn Sīnā's exposition of Q. 6:76 in the twelfth section of *Namaṭ* 5 of *Ishārāt*, where, as we have seen, the latter also detects in the Qur'an the idea that everything outside God inclines to non-being. It is worth bearing in mind, moreover, that al-Ghazālī had already given an identical interpretation of the very same verse, that is, Q. 28:88, at the beginning of the proper discussion of the ninety-nine names. In a brief remark on the name 'Allāh', he states that it is 'the name for the real Existent who comprehends all divine attributes, is provided with the Lordly attributes and stands alone in being real', whereas all other beings must perish when abandoned to themselves, but exist when they 'face' God (al-Ghazālī, *Maqṣad*, 61; *Ninety-nine*, 51 [translation modified]). Hence, al-Ghazālī's interpretation of Q. 28:88 may undoubtedly be characterized as an instance of philosophical exegesis. In this case its use is more easily understandable given the presence of a *kalām* inspiration in Ibn Sīnā's philosophical articulation of the sharp distinction between God and His creatures, as noted above.

A last case worth considering is al-Ghazālī's explanation of Q. 24:35, the famous light verse, as given in *Mishkāt al-anwār (Niche of Lights)* (al-Ghazālī, *Mishkāt*, 79–81). Al-Ghazālī links with each of the five major terms, niche, glass, lamp, tree, and oil, five he calls 'spirits' (*arwāḥ*), namely sensory, imaginative, intellective, cogitative, and holy prophetic. In spite of differences in the wording, and perhaps also in some doctrinal issues, it is beyond any reasonable doubt that regarding this commentary, al-Ghazālī has been inspired by Ibn Sīnā's musings in *Ishārāt* (Whittingham 2007: 109–18). Again, a Qur'anic *āya* is read in a philosophically inspired way: it is understood as expressing a theory of intellection.

In sum, one finds on different occasions examples of philosophical exegesis in al-Ghazālī's writings. This does not mean that the philosophers, and particularly Ibn Sīnā, were always influencing him in his understanding of the Qur'an. They certainly were not. Nevertheless, al-Ghazālī did not reject all their interpretations outright; on the contrary, he found some of them valuable and did not hesitate to include them in his 'new synthesis'.

Fakhr al-Dīn al-Rāzī

Living one century after al-Ghazālī, Fakhr al-Dīn al-Rāzī (d. 606/1210), whose first writings were still strongly aligned with classical Ashʿarī *kalām*, finally constructed a new type of *kalām* that completely integrated elements of *falsafa*. In that final system, he insists that Revelation itself becomes primarily a means to the goal of intellectual perfection rather than to communicate theological (and, we would add: *a fortiori*, philosophical) knowledge to men (Shihadeh 2005: 174). However, in some of his works one finds elements of philosophical exegesis. In al-Rāzī's commentary on Ibn Sīnā's *Ishārāt* he does not just mention the latter's exegesis of Q. 24:35; he also makes precise comments, emphasizing mainly the double function of the human intellect: to take care of the body, as practical intellect, and to prepare the human soul to receive the sciences, as theoretical intellect (al-Rāzī, *Sharḥ*, 154). Hence, al-Rāzī does not reject Ibn Sīnā's exegesis as unacceptable, but judges it at least possible. Therefore, it is not really surprising that he includes it in the third part, entitled 'On the nature of the symbolism', of his commentary on the light verse in his great Qur'anic *tafsīr*, *Mafātīḥ al-Ghayb*, although only as a sixth possibility of interpretation—immediately after that given by al-Ghazālī in the *Mishkāt* (al-Rāzī, *Mafātīḥ*, 235). However, it is obvious that al-Rāzī does not consider it as the best one—that honour is reserved for the classical Ashʿarī *kalām* interpretation of the *āya* according to which the main concern is God's guidance (*hidāya*). Nevertheless, he finds it worth mentioning without formulating any explicit condemnation.

The three quotations of Q. 28:88 deserve special attention, more precisely of the saying 'Everything (that exists) will perish except His own Face', which are present in al-Rāzī's *al-Lawāmiʿ al-bayyināt fī sharḥ asmāʾ Allāh al-ḥusnā wa'l-ṣifāt* (Explanation of Allah's beautiful names). The first quotation occurs in the exposé on the divine name *al-ʿaẓīm*, 'the Supreme'. The Qur'anic saying is presented as expressing the fact that 'everything other than God becomes, in comparison to His perfection and supremacy, a pure non-being, a pure negation' (al-Rāzī, *Lawāmiʿ*, 259). This explanation recalls al-Ghazālī's synthesis in the *Maqṣad*, at the background of which we saw an idea ultimately derived from Ibn Sīnā, namely that all possible beings, that is, all beings outside God, incline to non-being. Anew, the saying is present in the section on the divine names *al-awwal wa'l-ākhir wa'l-ẓāhir wa'l-bāṭin*. It is used to show that 'God is free from destruction, non-being, (both) in the past and in the future' (al-Rāzī, *Lawāmiʿ*, 330). Although there is a difference in emphasis—non-being is radically excluded from God, whereas in the first instance the stress was on the inclination of beings outside God to non-being—and, moreover, an encompassing time framework is introduced, the basic understanding remains the same. At first sight, a quite different explanation is given the third time the saying is quoted more precisely, in the discussion of *al-shayʾ*, the first of the divine names of essence. Al-Rāzī states: 'By "Face" is meant His [= God's] essence. (God makes *shayʾ*, "thing", a name of exception); His essence has already been put apart based on the word *shayʾ*, "thing", and the putting apart based on a specific difference is (revealing) a fundamental difference' (al-Rāzī, *Lawāmiʿ*, 357). Here, a radical opposition is brought to the fore between God's essence and all that is a 'thing'. But in what follows al-Rāzī makes clear that 'thing' can encompass both the existent and the non-existent, namely when the non-existent can be said to be a 'thing' when 'thing' means 'what is permissible to be known, more precisely to be considered' (al-Rāzī, *Lawāmiʿ*, 357). Based on philosophical-logical considerations, al-Rāzī affirms that God, in so far as He is existent, may be designated by 'thing'. However, since there is a total incompatibility between non-existence and God's essence, 'thing' has to be understood as an 'exception', *istithnāʾ*. Moreover, al-Rāzī continues to interpret the saying along the philosophically inspired line of God as the only being that is existent by itself—which itself was not free of inspiration from *kalām*, as indicated earlier.

To conclude: al-Rāzī was not an unconditional adept of philosophical exegesis. Rather, he used it now and then, albeit in an encompassing *kalām* framework of Qur'anic interpretation. However, by channelling philosophical—especially Avicennian, albeit mediated by al-Ghazālī—ideas into Sunnī *tafsīr*, he gave them undisputed authority and made it possible for later Sunnī commentators to use them as a resource to interpret the Qur'an (Jaffer 2015: 159).

Ibn ʿArabī

Muḥyī al-Dīn ibn ʿArabī (d. 638/1240) is known by the Sufis as al-Shaykh al-Akbar, 'The Greatest Master' (Chittick 1996: 497). His overall system is mystical and has therefore little or nothing in common with philosophy, which is essentially reason based. Nevertheless, on occasion Ibn ʿArabī seems to have been influenced by philosophical exegesis, at least by its method. Because many difficulties still surround the precise interpretation of his thought, we shall concentrate on a single example taken from his major work, *al-Futūḥāt al-Makkiyya* (*The Meccan Revelations*). In chapter 63 of book I, the notion of *barzakh*, 'barrier', occupies a central place. Not unsurprisingly, Ibn ʿArabī almost immediately refers to Q. 55:19–20, since in these verses the very term of *barzakh* is mentioned (Ibn ʿArabī, *al-Futūḥāt*, 1:304, 17–18). But whereas the Qur'anic text mentions the existence of a barrier between 'two seas', Ibn ʿArabī moves from a physical to an intellectual, more precisely imaginary, level. Having insisted that the *barzakh* is in itself not perceptible by sensation, he continues: 'since the *barzakh* is a separating entity between the known and the unknown, the non-existent and the existent, the negated and the affirmed, the intelligible and the non-intelligible, it designates "barrier" (*barzakh*) as a *terminus technicus*, which is intelligible in itself, and is only (accessible to) imagination' (Ibn ʿArabī, *Futūḥāt*, 1:304, 20–2). In a way similar to that in which Ibn Sīnā has explained (the different ways and degrees of) intellection on the basis of the Qur'an, that is, Q. 24:35, Ibn ʿArabī explains here a Qur'anic conception, *barzakh*, in terms of modalities of human acquaintance with reality, by way of sensation, intellection, or imagination, even if nothing in the Qur'anic verse directly points in this direction. From what appears to be at first sight a reference to a natural phenomenon, the focus has been changed toward a special form of experience that is proper to imagination. Of course, Ibn ʿArabī understands this later not in the usually philosophical sense, but as being *the* separation line between being and non-being, yes and no, etc., and hence as a means to make people sensitive to the divine disclosures. We therefore can only conclude that more research is needed to see to what extent exactly Ibn ʿArabī has been influenced by the practice of philosophical comment on the Qur'an.

The Ishrāqī School

The inception of an entirely new kind of philosophy was presaged by the work of Shihāb al-Dīn al-Suhrawardī (d. 587/1191) in the world of Islam, and especially in Iran. Even if al-Suhrawardī's basic options were different from, and sometimes even highly critical of, those of Ibn Sīnā, he was not insensitive to the latter's thought and took over several of his ideas, including elements of his philosophical exegesis. A significant example is present in his work *al-Talwiḥāt al-lawḥiyya wa'l-ʿarshiyya* (The intimations of the tablet and the throne). Even if he himself affirms that the work has been written according to the manner of the Peripatetic schools (al-Suhrawardī, *Talwiḥāt*, 2), it is an integral part of those writings that present details of his Ishrāqī philosophy (Ziai 1990: 9–15). In the context of a discussion about the life in the hereafter, al-Suhrawardī stresses that the souls which have too close a link with the body will vehemently suffer because they, due to their imaginative inclinations, will not be able to grasp the universals. Only the souls that show no such tendencies will be fully contented, and therefore it is said in Q. 44:56: 'Nor will they taste death, except the first death' (al-Suhrawardī, *Talwiḥāt*, 84, 1–2). Certainly, with the Qur'an al-Suhrawardī understands the first death as referring to that of the body. With the Qur'an he links the 'second death'—a term not present, but clearly suggested by the *āya* —with the destiny of those who have failed. But, in sharp contrast with the Qur'an, he identifies that destiny not with the fire of Hell, but with a suffering due to a lack in the power of knowledge, and hence places the failure not on the level of 'righteousness', but on epistemological perfection. So, it is obvious that the broader framework in which the Qur'anic verse is interpreted is outspokenly philosophical.

With Mullā Ṣadrā Shīrāzī (d. 1050/1640) the philosophy of Illumination reached its zenith. In his immense corpus, he evokes—at least—twice an exegesis of the light verse. In *Iksīr al-ʿārifīn (The Elixir of the Gnostics)* (Mullā Ṣadrā, *Iksīr*, 33, § 60), Mullā Ṣadrā detects in the *āya* the expression of the illumination of the soul through God's light and of the linking of the material with the immaterial world. In spite of its profound departures from Ibn Sīnā's commentary, one indisputably recognizes elements of influence from the latter, such as the idea that 'the olive tree' symbolizes reflexive thought (*al-fikra*) and 'fire' the Agent Intellect. In his *Tafsīr āyat al-nūr* (Commentary on the light verse), Mullā Ṣadrā explicitly refers to Ibn Sīnā's *Pointers*, as well as to the related commentary of Naṣīr al-Dīn al-Ṭūsī (d. 672/1274) (Mullā Ṣadrā, *Tafsīr*, xxxviii). Strikingly, he presents it as one of three possible exegeses of the *āya*, namely one related to the world of the soul. The others are related to the 'bodily human world' and to the 'world of the horizons'. According to the first the 'niche' is a symbol of the heart, the 'glass' of the animal spirit, and the 'lamp' of the psychic spirit; the rest of the verse is explained according to the activities of both these spirits (Mullā Ṣadrā, *Tafsīr*, xxxvi). As to the second, it identifies the 'niche' with the world of bodies, that is, the material world; the 'glass' with the throne (of God); the 'lamp' with the 'great spirit', etc. (Mullā Ṣadrā, *Tafsīr*, xxxvii). In the former the idea of man as microcosm prevails, whereas in the latter the focus is on the higher, spiritual world. It has to be stressed that for Mullā Ṣadrā these three interpretations are not mutually exclusive. On the contrary, they supplement each other since they represent different points of view. He even adds a fourth exegesis, namely in a section entitled '*Ishrāqī* illumination' (Mullā Ṣadrā, *Tafsīr*, xxxix–xl). There he links the *āya*'s evoked ideas of 'Orient' and 'Occident' with the philosophical issues of 'necessity' and 'possibility'. Mullā Ṣadrā, in a clearly Neoplatonic inspired way, identifies the 'niche' now with the 'universal nature', the 'glass' with the 'universal soul' and the 'lamp' with the 'universal intellect'. But even when he identifies the Qur'anic terms 'olive' and 'oil' with the divine power, respectively the divine will, his major framework remains philosophical, in so far as he, for example, insists that God's power is one of His concomitants, i.e. inseparable accidents, and His will is free of any final causality.

However, of special significance is the way Mullā Ṣadrā quotes, approvingly, (Mullā Ṣadrā, *Asfār*, 2:298) the beginning of Ibn Sīnā's commentary on Q. 113:1, where it is said that God, the First principle, 'cleaves' the darkness of non-existence by the light of existence, and that there is no evil whatsoever in His decree, but that any kind of turbidity is concomitant to the quiddity originated from the divine Ipseity

(ʿĀṣī, 1983: 156). Mullā Ṣadrā herein detects an affirmation of the existence of the individual in its very ipseity, and the relegation of 'opaqueness' to the fundamentally possible character of the quiddities. According to Mullā Ṣadrā, this 'possibility' implies the negation of the necessity of existence, as well as the privation of the essence 'coloured' (*munṣabigha*) by the light of existence. He finds this latter idea, which remains fully in line with Ibn Sīnā's commentary on Q. 113:1, expressed in Q. 2:138, the only *āya* where one finds the word *ṣibgha*. Without any surprise, the latter term has given rise to many interpretations, but it is obvious that Mullā Ṣadrā interprets it as a symbolic, but highly philosophical way of illuminating existential colouring. All in all, Mullā Ṣadrā can be best qualified as a philosopher/mystic commenting upon scripture (Rustom 2010: 121).

Conclusion

In the Peripatetic tradition, philosophical Qur'anic exegesis seems only to have been present in the thought of two major figures, al-Kindī and, above all, Ibn Sīnā. Nevertheless, elements of it have been incorporated in *kalām* and mystical circles. In this respect, a lot of research has still to be done, but the few—we admit, very limited in number—cases we have evoked show that at least elements of it entered both traditions. With the Ishrāqī school an entirely new way of philosophical thinking entered the world of Islam. From what we detected in two of his major figures, it took over from the 'Peripatetic tradition' (in Ibn Sīnā's line) the typical method of philosophical Qur'anic interpretation. Hence, this latter development was perhaps not as marginal as one might be inclined to believe at first sight.

Bibliography

Primary Sources

Al-Ghazālī, Abū Ḥamīd. *Iḥyāʾ ʿulūm al-dīn*. 4 vols. Anonymous Edition. Al-Maghreb: Dār al-Rashād al-Ḥaditha n.d.

Al-Ghazālī, Abū Ḥamīd. *Al-Maqṣad al-asnā fī sharḥ maʿānī asmāʾ Allāh al-ḥusnā*. Anonymous edition. Limasol: al-Jaffān wa'l-Jābī, 1407/1987; *The Ninety-nine Beautiful Names of God*. Translation with notes by David B. Burrell and Nazih Daher. Cambridge: Islamic Texts Society, 1992.

Al-Ghazālī, Abū Ḥamīd. *Mishkāt al-anwār*. Ed. A. 'Afīfī. Cairo: Al-Dār al-Qawmiyya li'l-Ṭibāʿa wa'l-Nashr, 1383/1964.

Ibn ʿArabī, Muḥyī al-Dīn. *Al-Futūḥāt al-Makkiyya*. 4 vols. Anonymous edition. Beirut: Dār Ṣādir, n.d.

[Ibn Rushd, Abū'l-Walīd]. Averroes. *Decisive Treatise and Epistle Dedicatory*. Translation, with introduction and notes by Charles E. Butterworth. Provo, UT: Brigham Young University Press, 2001.

Ibn Rushd, Abū 'l-Walīd. *Tahāfut al-Tahāfut*. Ed. S. Dunya. 2 vols. Cairo: Dār al-Maʿārif, 1981.

[Ibn Sīnā, Abū ʿAlī] Avicenna. *The Metaphysics of* the Healing. A parallel English–Arabic text translated, introduced, and annotated by Michael E. Marmura. Provo, UT: Brigham Young University Press, 2005.

Ibn Sīnā, Abū ʿAlī. *Fī Ithbāt al-nubuwwāt*. Ed. Michael E. Marmura. Beirut: Dār al-Nahār, 1968.

Ibn Sīnā, Abū ʿAlī. *Kitāb al-Ishārāt wa'l-tanbīhāt*. Ed. J. Forget. Leiden: E. J. Brill 1892.

Ibn Sīnā, Abū ʿAlī. *Tafsīr al-ṣamadiyya*. In: M. D. S. al-Kurdī. Ed. *Jāmiʿ al-Badāʾiʿ*, pp. 15–24. Cairo: al-Saʿāda, 1335/1917.

Al-Kindī, Yaʿqūb ibn Isḥāq. *Fī kammiyyāt kutub Arisṭūṭālīs*. In: M. Abū Rīda Ed. *Rasāʾil al-Kindī al-falsafiyya*, 1:363–84. Cairo: Maṭbaʿat al-Jannat al-Taʾlīf wa'l-Tarjama wa'l-Nashr, 1369–72/1950–53.

Al-Kindī, Yaʿqūb ibn Isḥāq. *Fī'l-Ibāna ʿan sujūd al-jirm al-aqṣā*. In: M. Abū Rīda Ed. *Rasāʾil al-Kindī al-falsafiyya*, 1:238–61. Cairo: Maṭbaʿat al-Jannat al-Taʾlīf wa'l-Tarjama wa'l-Nashr, 1369–72/1950–53.

Al-Kindī, Yaʿqūb ibn Isḥāq. *Fī'l-ʿilla allatī lahā yabrudu aʿlā al-jaww wa-yaskhunu mā qaruba min al-arḍ*. In: M. Abū Rīda Ed. *Rasāʾil al-Kindī al-falsafiyya*, 2:86–100. Cairo: Maṭbaʿat al-Jannat al-Taʾlīf wa'l-Tarjama wa'l-Nashr, 1369–72/1950–53.

Mullā Ṣadrā Shīrāzī. *Al-Asfār arbaʿa*. Qum: *al-Muṣṭafāvī*. 1379 AH.

Mullā Ṣadrā Shīrāzī. *Tafsīr āyat al-nūr*. In: Mullā Ṣadrā Shīrāzī, *Tafsīr al-Qur'ān al-karīm*. 4 vols. Ed. Muḥammad Khājavī, 1:343–427. Qum: Intishārāt-i Bīdār 1403 AH, reprinted in Mullâ Sadrä Shîrâzî, *Le Verset de la lumière: commentaire*. French trans., introduction and notes by Christian Jambet, pp. iv–lxxxv. Paris: Les Belles Lettres, 2009.

Mullā Ṣadrā [Shīrāzī]. *The Elixir of the Gnostics*. A parallel English–Arabic text translated, introduced, and annotated by William C. Chittick. Provo, UT: Brigham Young University Press, 2003.

al-Rāzī, Fakhr al-Dīn. *Al-Lawāmiʿ al-bayyināt fī sharḥ asmāʾ Allāh al-ḥusnā wa 'l-ṣifāt*. Ed. Ṭāhā ʿAbd al-Raʾūf Saʿīd. Beirut: Dār al-Kutub al-ʿArabī, 1404/1984.

al-Rāzī, Fakhr al-Dīn. *Sharḥ al-Ishārāt*. In: *Sharḥ al-Ishārāt li-Khwāji Naṣīr al-Dīn Ṭūsī wa li-Fakhr al-Dīn al-Rāzī*. Anonymous edition. Qum: Manshūrāt-i Maktabat Ayatollah al-ʿAẓāmī 'l-Marʿashī 'l-Najāfī, 1404/1985.

al-Rāzī, Fakhr al-Dīn. *Tafsīr al-kabīr. Mafātiḥ al-Ghayb*. 32 in 16 vols. Anonymous edition. Beirut: Dār al-Fikr, 1981.

al-Suhrawardī, Shihāb al-Dīn. *al-Talwiḥāt al-lawḥiyya wa'l-ʿarshiyya*. In: Suhrawardī, *Opera metaphysica et mystica*. Vol. 1. Ed. Henri Corbin, pp. 1–121. Istanbul: Maṭbaʿat al-Maʿārif, 1945.

Secondary Sources

Acar, Rahim. 'Reconsidering Avicenna's Position on God's Knowledge of Particulars'. In: Jon McGinnis, with the assistance of David C. Reisman (eds.). *Interpreting Avicenna: Science and Philosophy in Medieval Islam. Proceedings of the Second Conference of the Avicenna Study Group*, pp. 142–56. Leiden and Boston: Brill, 2004.

Adamson, Peter. 'Al-Kindī and the Muʿtazila: Divine Attributes, Creation and Freedom', *Arabic Sciences and Philosophy* 13/1 (2003), 45–77.

ʿĀṣī, Ḥasan. *Al-Tafsīr al-qurʾānī wa'l-lugha al-ṣūfiyya fī falsafat Ibn Sīnā*. Beirut: Al-Muʾassasat al-Jāmiʿiyya li'l-Dirāsāt wa'l-Nashr wa'l-Tawzīʿ, 1403/1983.

Calder, Norman. '*Tafsīr* from Ṭabarī to Ibn Kathīr: Problems in the History of a Genre'. In: G. R. Hawting and Abdul-Kadeer A. Shareef (eds.). *Approaches to the Qurʾān*, pp. 101–40. London: Routledge, 1993.

Chittick, William C. 'Ibn ʿArabī'. In: Seyyed Hossein Nasr and Oliver Leaman (eds.). *History of Islamic Philosophy*. 2 vols. London: Routledge, 1996.

De Smet, Daniel and Meryem Sebti. 'Avicenna's Philosophical Approach to the Qur'an in the Light of his *Tafsīr Sūrat al-Ikhlāṣ*', *Journal of Qur'anic Studies* 11/2 (2009), 134–48.

Griffel, Frank. *Al-Ghazālī's Philosophical Theology*. Oxford: Oxford University Press, 2009.

Gutas, Dimitri. *Avicenna and the Aristotelian Tradition: Introduction to Reading Avicenna's Philosophical Works. Second, Revised and Enlarged Edition. Including an Inventory of Avicenna's Authentic Works*. Leiden and Boston: Brill, 2014.

Jaffer, Tariq. *Rāzī Master of Qur'ānic Interpretation and Theological Reasoning*. Oxford: Oxford University Press, 2015.

Janssens, Jules. 'Al-Ghazālī between Philosophy (*Falsafa*) and Sufism (*Taṣawwuf*): His Complex Attitude in the *Marvels of the Heart* (*Ajāʾib al-Qalb*) of the *Iḥyāʾ ʿUlūm al-Dīn*', *Muslim World* 101/4 (2011) (= Celebrating the 900th Anniversary of al-Ghazālī's Death. (ed.) M. Afifi al-Akiti), 614–32.

Janssens, Jules. 'Al-Kindī: The Founder of Philosophical Exegesis of the Qurʾān', *Journal of Qur'anic Studies* 9/2 (2007), 1–21.

Janssens, Jules. 'Avicenna and the Qur'ān: A Survey of his Qur'ānic Commentaries', *Mélanges de l'Institut Dominicain d'Études Orientales* 25–6 (2004), 177–92.

Janssens, Jules. 'Ibn Sīnā's Ideas of Ultimate Realities: Neoplatonism and the Qur'ān as Problem-Solving Paradigms in the Avicennian System', *Ultimate Reality and Meaning* 10 (1987), 252–71 (reprinted in his *Ibn Sīnā and his Influence on the Arabic and Latin World*. Aldershot and Burlington, VT: Ashgate, 2006).

Lane, Edward William. *An Arabic-English Lexicon*. 8 vols. London: Williams and Norgate, 1872.

Lizzini, Olga. 'Introduction', In: Avicenne (?), *Épitre sur les prophéties*. Texte arabe, introduction par O. Lizzini, traduction et notes par J.-B. Brenet, pp. 7–82. Paris: Vrin, 2018.

Michot, Jean. 'Le Commentaire avicennien du verset: *Puis il se tourna vers le ciel*', *Mélanges de l'Institut Dominicain d'Études Orientales* 14 (1980), 317–28.

Rustom, Mohammed. 'The Nature and Significance of Mullā Ṣadrā's Qur'ānic Writings', *Journal of Islamic Philosophy* 6 (2010), 109–30.

Sebti, Meryem. 'Le commentaire d'Avicenne à la sourate al-Aʿlā: un pseudépigraphe'. In: Ayman Shihadeh (ed.). *Late Ashʿarism*. Leiden: Brill (forthcoming).

Shihadeh, Ayman. 'From al-Ghazālī to al-Rāzī: 6th/12th Century Developments in Muslim Philosophical Theology', *Arabic Sciences and Philosophy* 15/1 (2005), 141–79.

Wansbrough, John. *Quranic Studies: Sources and Methods of Interpretation*. Oxford: Oxford University Press, 1977.

Whittingham, Martin. *Al-Ghazālī and the Qur'ān. One Book, Many Meanings*. London and New York: Routledge, 2007.

Wisnovsky, Robert. *Avicenna's Metaphysics in Context*. London: Duckworth, 2003.

Ziai, Hossein. *Knowledge and Illumination: A Study of Suhrawardī's* Ḥikmat al-Ishrāq. Atlanta: Scholars Press, 1990.

CHAPTER 53

AESTHETICALLY ORIENTED INTERPRETATIONS OF THE QUR'ĀN

KAMAL ABU-DEEB

Introduction

SOON after its delivery, the Qur'an challenged the Arabs with many problematic issues, amongst which three are extremely relevant for the present chapter. First, the ambiguity of some of its statements; second, verses which appear to be stating contradictory things about two crucial issues: the nature of God and the agency of man's actions in the world; third, the authenticity of its message, which produced the assertion by the Qur'an that even if the *ins* (humans) and jinn (genies) helped each other, they could not 'bring' something like it. This assertion was coupled with a repeated challenge to the people of Quraysh to author or 'bring' something like it, a challenge that came to be contemplated later as the question of *iʿjāz al-Qurʾān* (the miraculous nature or inimitability of the Qur'an).

Much of what was debated about the Qur'an before the age of writing related to these issues and much of what was written about it from the inception of the age of writing was determined and motivated by a desire to resolve the problems arising from them and their implications. In the process, the Arabs discovered the *majāzī* (non-literal) use, indeed nature, of language and many questions began to be answered in terms of this immense discovery. Gradually, textual analysis of the Qur'an and poetry began to turn into questions of beauty, artistic qualities, secrets of eloquence, and similar issues of a purely literary nature. Much of this activity involved the interpretation of verses that appeared problematic in various types of writing, from treatises on religion to books on poetry and from debates about Islam and other faiths to books on science. Specialized works began to appear and some major figures made significant contributions to the understanding of many complex issues relating to the Qur'an as well as to other forms of writing. In many works, the issues of beauty in the Qur'an and the enquiry into the language of *majāz* and the controversial statements of the Qur'an mingled and received attention to varying degrees of focus on one or the other. Amongst the many important figures who made valuable contributions in this domain are al-Jāḥiẓ (d. 255/868–9), Abū ʿUbayda (d. 209/824), al-Rummānī (d. 384/994), al-Khaṭṭābī (d. 388/998), Ibn Qutayba (d. 276/889), al-Bāqillānī (d. 403/1013), al-Qāḍī ʿAbd al-Jabbār (d. 415/1025), and al-Sharīf al-Raḍī (d. 406/1016). A trend began to take shape that attempted to explore beauty in the Qur'an and poetry in equal measure, reaching its maturity in the works of ʿAbd al-Qāhir al-Jurjānī (d. 471/1078), who produced a unified theory that sought beauty in the same terms both in the Qur'an and in poetry and prose. Al-Jurjānī assimilated the finest ideas in the 'great tradition' that had burgeoned in three different circles: the circle of linguists; the circle of poets; and the circle of Qur'anic commentators. In the process, he established an approach to the beauty of the Qur'an that revealed its secrets as residing in its *naẓm* (its intricate, exquisite interplay of semantic, syntactic and grammatical elements, from word order to elision, to *faṣl* and *waṣl*, etc.), as well as in localized, specific processes of creative activity, thereby covering the entire gamut of the formulation of experience into language.

In many ways, all these scholars were presenting *tafsīr* (interpretation) of the Qur'an on a limited scale, as they often dealt with the problematic issues and verses as part of their enquiries into the secrets of eloquence or developments of new *ʿulūm*, like *al-bayān*, *al-badīʿ*, *al-maʿānī*, and *al-balāgha*, as is the case, for instance, with Ibn Qutayba in his *Taʾwīl Mushkil al-Qurʾān*. Quite significantly, many figures contributing to this process were involved in literary studies as well as Qur'anic commentary. However, a more specialized, systematic, almost autonomous science of *tafsīr* had also been evolving as from the early days of Islam and many major works of *tafsīr* had been produced by the end of the fifth/eleventh century.

This chapter explores a vital current of thought in Arabic culture, one that aspired to produce fully-fledged interpretations oriented towards questions of beauty and *iʿjāz*, while at the same time dealing with the problematic questions outlined earlier in this opening discussion. It will focus on three major works representing three main intellectual and doctrinal currents in Arabic culture. These are al-Zamakhsharī's *al-Kashshāf*, Ibn ʿArabī's *al-Futūḥāt al-Makkiyya*, and Abū Ḥayyān al-Andalūsī's *al-Baḥr al-Muḥīṭ*.

It should be stressed right away that none of these interpretations gives *priority* to the aesthetic appeal despite the fact that their starting point is that the Qur'an is *muʿjiz* in its beauty, its superior *faṣāḥa*, *balāgha*, and artistic language. Their focus is usually on meaning, ideas, legal consequences of readings, etc. Even when they deal with instances of *majāz*, *istiʿāra*, or *tashbīh* or *tamthīl*, they seek *primarily* the semantic content in them. Nevertheless, they are remarkably rich with hints and occasional detailed analysis of instances that reveal the 'amazing' quality of the imaginative processes of many Qur'anic verses. Ibn ʿArabī pioneers a reading that involves and invokes the real richness of the text and its impact on the soul and visions of the recipient as well as on his sense of magic, beauty, and the beyond.

Yet, these outstanding works do have their own shortcomings which are evident in the comments they make on some of the Qur'an's most charming images and, especially, in their handling of suras like *Sūrat al-Raḥmān*, the 'bride of the Qur'an', as some call it, with its fabulous description of paradise. Al-Zamakhsharī (d. 538/1144) passes by its images without much comment. Aesthetically, he has little to say about the image of the ships like mountains in the sea (*al-jawārī al-munshaʾātu fī al-baḥri ka al-aʿlām*) or the sky splitting like a rose, '*faʾidhā ʾinshaqqati al-samāʾu fa kānat wardatan ka'l-dihān*.' (4:446, 449–50). His comments on the verses reach their height in observations about the syntax and why the text mentions *rummān* (pomegranate) after *fākiḥa* (fruits) and uses the conjunction (*wāw*) although pomegranate is a *fākiḥa*. Abū Ḥayyān (d. 745/1344) (8:193–4) has similar interests and goes into more detail on every level but without truly enhancing the aesthetic appeal of the images. However, precisely because he gives different views and meanings of each word, the image of the sky is massively enriched by what his details invoke: red roses, yellow roses, red paint, oil of different colours and in different states, red skin, a red mare undergoing seasonal change of its colours: red, yellow, dusty, etc., all as different meanings of the two key words: *wardatan* (rose; red) and *dihān* (pigment of paint; colour). This fills the imagination with a Salvador Dali composition with bright colours, shooting mares, roses of different colours blooming, mares changing colours from spring to autumn, and skins and red paint and glittering oil, all with a splintered, shattered sky attired in this vast magical cataclysmic explosion. Ibn ʿArabī (d. 638/1240) deals with some of the sura's statements in the context of his exploration of ideas and visions that are much wider in scope than the sura. However, all of them read the image according to their mindset, or the stereotype process of comparison inherent in their minds and their traditions, treating it as a comparison between the cracked sky and a red rose or red skin or take *wardatan* to mean red, no rose involved, or red rose, etc. None of them notices that the verse does not say: *fa kānat ḥamrāʾa ka'l-wardati* (red like a rose) but *fa kānat wardatan ka'l-dihān*. The sky (as I read it) is thus a *warda* and is like *al-dihān*, without the word red appearing anywhere. As significantly, they fail to capture the fact that the verse is depicting a scene never seen before by a human eye, an infinitely indefinable visual space and it brilliantly depicts that in a language itself infinitely indefinable in which the key words are impossible to fix and remain more than ambiguous, more than *absent*. If *dihān* is a colour then the simile is saying the sky is *wardatan* like a (red?) colour (while in reality the (red?) colour is a trait of the rose): a strange 'cracked' simile indeed, most unusual and never before seen or portrayed. The syntax, the imaginative process itself is thus *cracked*, *split open* in the middle, turned inside out and upside down. The *kāf* of comparison is split from *wardatan* and stuck to *dihān*. The surrealism and indefinability of the image are thus embedded both in the indefinability of language and the surrealism of the syntax and the structure of the mind imagining the sky when it gets split open in a future that remains *absent*. Not even Dali has managed such a perfect embodiment of his surrealist vision in a surrealist, disorganized structure. One more sign or *āya* of the superiority of Qur'anic language and aesthetic power.

Some Focal Points of Interest

The texts I have chosen to work with in this chapter represent the zenith of the efforts to present interpretations of the Qur'an that are aesthetically oriented, viewing the Qur'an not only as a statement of dogma and call for belief in God as the only God and in Muḥammad as his prophet but as a text with superior artistic qualities arising from its language. And they are all works by open-minded, questioning, and courageous thinkers albeit belonging to competing schools of thought within Islam. Ibn ʿArabī noted in fact that various schools of thought form a unified whole despite their contrasting views. He thought of himself as belonging there too, despite considering himself one of a few people who really understand and have visions of the Truth. Their courage shows itself precisely in their differences and in the views they express, which often enough go against dominant trends. Al-Zamakhsharī was so faithful to his rationalist Muʿtazilī approach that he invoked harsh criticism by Abū Ḥayyān; furthermore, he made his imaginary interlocutor ask questions that implied negative views of some aspects of Qur'anic expression, of course, using that to validate the Qur'anic choices, no matter how unconvincingly, but he *did ask* the awkward questions. Ibn ʿArabī risked a great deal, but wrote, taught, and preached his ways to all; Abū Ḥayyān opened up fresh areas for questioning and included the views of critics of the Qur'an, whose thought he totally rejected; he also acknowledged that the Qur'an has *tasjīʿ* (rhymed prose), a view that was dismissed by most if not all others. Collectively, their studies of the artistic language of the Qur'an were and remain a fabulous achievement. When added to works on metaphorical language in specialized books such as those of Abū ʿUbayda, Ibn Qutayba, al-Sharīf al-Raḍī, and others, including the towering figure of al-Jurjānī, we can see clearly that the ancients produced remarkable and full enquiries into the Qur'an as a text of artistic qualities; these represent the best we have of their kind in the Arabic tradition of Qur'anic commentary. Of the many summits of excellence their works have reached, I would select what may be justifiably called a 'proto-Structuralist' approach embodied at its finest in Abū Ḥayyān's exploration of the *relational* principle that permeates the entire text of the Qur'an, which he calls *al-munāsaba* (suitability; harmony). This has its roots in the work of people like al-Jurjānī and al-Zamakhsharī, often under other names, but in Abū Ḥayyān's analysis it reaches degrees of depth, sophistication, and detail that can compete with some of the finest acts of analysis in modern literary studies. Abū Ḥayyān divides each sura into groups of verses exactly in the order in which they exist in the Qur'an. In his mind, between all groups of verses there is a *munāsaba* or *tanāsub* that embodies an inner link, interconnectedness, between each group and what precedes it. What this suggests is that the sura represents a chain of rings, each interconnected to what is before it and after it. In other words, the sura forms one coherent, interlacing structure. But more revolutionary in fact is his tireless effort to show that the *munasaba* exists also between each sura and the sura that precedes it and the one that follows it. This means that the entire text of the Qur'an, not only of each sura, is a unified, coherent, and tightly knit structure.

The types of bonds that create the *munāsaba* as seen by Abū Ḥayyān vary; some relate to individual words or semantic links; others to larger aspects of discourse: a character, a narrative episode, a legal doctrine, and many other such things. In some cases, his identification of the link is so subtle, so difficult to have conceived of, that a pleasure of discovery similar to what al-Jurjānī had called *hazzatun fi'l-nafs wa-irtiyāḥ* (a phrase almost identical with what Roland Barthes was to call 1,000 years later '*le plaisir du texte*' (the pleasure of the text) is generated. I am not aware that anyone else had actually conceived of the Qur'an in this fashion before Abū Ḥayyān and had tried to demonstrate the validity of this principle in practice through minute textual analysis. In this light, Abū Ḥayyān's achievement appears truly outstanding and leaves one even more puzzled that no one, as far as we now know, has benefited from his approach in the analysis of poetry and prose texts outside Qur'anic studies.

By comparison with these scholars and their collective achievement, contemporary scholarship on the Qur'an *from this specific angle* is poor, fragmentary, and mostly superficial. Despite great advances in linguistic and literary analysis, there is not a single fully-fledged study of the Qur'an as a whole text that is both a *tafsīr* and an exploration of its literary merits. One of the greatest and richest literary treasures in the world has thus been left almost untouched by scholarship for the past seven centuries or so, that is since Abū Ḥayyān produced his great work. This is not to say that literary aspects of the Qur'an have not been examined; not at all. For, there have been studies of specific aspects, such as the stories of the Qur'an, *al-taṣwīr al-fannī* in it (artistic portrayal?), and the like. But these are specialized studies in narrowly selected aspects of this treasure trove of literary and artistic phenomena. What has been lacking is a comprehensive modern work, armed with all the knowledge we have today, on the Qur'an as a text to be interpreted and to have its artistic constituents revealed by one scholar—or a group of scholars—dealing with the totality as a totality, exploring questions of interconnectedness, interlacing, unity, imagery, significance of metaphorical language and the language of the imagination, and tens of other features. Hundreds of thousands of pages on the internet now offer students of the Qur'an infinite resources but most of them produce almost the same material under different names or categories or websites. Throughout the Arab world, the most widely published books are religious works on the Qur'an, but nowhere is there a modern text to rival Abū Ḥayyān's or compete with al-Zamakhsharī's or be as courageous, visionary, intellectually stimulating, and meticulous as Ibn ʿArabī's. There have been some attempts, and some have had the courage to suggest a fresh look at certain aspects of the Qur'an (Naṣr Ḥāmid Abū Zayd stands out here) but again these are fragmentary, narrowly focused, and are not of a literary or aesthetically oriented nature. One book stands out in its scope and impressionistic responses, that of Sayyid Quṭb, *Fī Ẓilāl al-Qurʾān*, but not in much more; its analysis of the artistic language of the Qur'an is limited (his comment on '*wardatan ka al-dihān*' is a simple '*wardatan sāʾilatan ka al-dihān*' (a liquid rose like *al-dihān*) (6:456) and the literary training of its author, though at times sensitive and clever, was limiting and it lacks the questioning, acceptance of multiplicity, and open-minded touches we find in the works of the ancients. It is almost a feeling of what Ibn ʿArabī calls *tawahhum* that we are, after so many centuries of activity, standing on virgin ground, moving in an unexplored space or rather one that was invaded centuries ago and has remained as it was left by the last significant invader, Abū Ḥayyān al-Andalūsī.

Broaching the Unity of Structure in the Qur'an

Taking our cue from Abū Ḥayyān's effort to establish *munāsaba*, we need to further explore questions of the unity of structure in the Qur'an, within the individual suras and within the text as a total structure. We need to explore issues such as, 'why do the same epithets of Allāh close a verse in two or more different positions? Why does the same verse end with two different epithets in two different positions? Does this variation serve a specific purpose in the places where it occurs?' Abū Ḥayyān and al-Zamakhsharī both make some significant hints at such an approach, but they do not ask enough questions and do not go far enough in scope. The former makes the brilliant statement that in one verse a specific epithet is used in order to achieve *tasjīᶜ*, but does not ask about the aesthetic or semantic value of the *tasjīᶜ* that is achieved in the manner, for instance, of al-Jurjānī asking whether *tajnis* (paronomasia) in many places he examines is artistically good or bad. For instance: verse 34 in *Sūrat Ibrāhīm* occurs again as verse 18 of *Sūrat al-Naḥl*, but ends in different epithets in these two positions. The version in *Sūrat Ibrāhīm* (14) ends with '*inna al-insāna la ẓalūmun kaffār*', while the version in *Sūrat al-Naḥl* (16) ends with '*inna Allāha la ghafūrun raḥīm*':

> 'If you numerate the beneficence of Allāh you will not be able to quantify it; man indeed is unjust unbelieving.'
>
> (Q. 14:34)
>
> 'If you numerate the beneficence of Allāh you will not be able to quantify it; Allāh indeed is forgiving merciful.'
>
> (Q. 16:18)

The first version occurs after two verses ending with the phonemes/sounds *ār* (*anhār*, *nahār*), so it rhymes with what is before it and, importantly, it completes a pattern of three, whereas the second version falls between verses ending with *ūn* (*tadhkurūn*/*tuᶜlinūn*), so it does not rhyme with them, yet it is the closest rhyming sound in the Qur'an to them. However, perhaps immensely significantly, it repeats the word *raḥīm* that occurs in v. 7 as *raʾufun raḥīm*, and comes again in v. 18 *ghafūrun raḥīm*, then in 47, 58, 60, 63, 76, 94, 98, 104, 106, 110, 115, 117, 119, 121.

In other words, in a sura consisting of 128 verses, *ghafūrun raḥīm*/*raʾūfun raḥīm* occurs six times, at certain distances, and a very close rhyme *īm* occurs with it ten times, with only two occurrences (in 70, 77) of not so different a rhyming element *īr* (*qadīr*) that relates to *ghafūrun raḥīm* in meaning. What is truly stunning about these *facts* of the text, and no metaphysics here, is that the text almost in its entirety, that is, 110 verses, with the exception of 2 *qadīr*, is based on a single rhyme: *īn, ūn*, and variations come with a close phoneme *īm* to form a structure of 126 harmonious, extended, relaxed sound effects free even of a single hard rhyme like *ḥadda, azza*, etc. (which we see in the debating parts of *Sūrat Maryam*). Now as we look at the semantic structure of *Sūrat al-Naḥl*, at its emotional ambience or climate, so to speak, do we not find the *message* (as the jargon of linguistics propagated by Roman Jakobson goes nowadays) exactly of the same nature?

Further, the *ghafūrun/raʾūfun raḥīm* attributed to Allāh occurs in this relaxed content while *ẓalūmun kaffār* as epithets of man occurs in *Sūrat Ibrāhīm* within a much different content packed with arguments against the unbelievers, with tensions and infighting over the authenticity of God's message, with threats by Him to people who reject this message as well as with tensions between other people holding to the ideas of their fathers and the new religions being preached to them. Add to these the implicit tension, possibly within Ibrāhīm's inner world but certainly between his action here and his action in other suras (as here he asks for forgiveness for his parents who were *kuffār*, a questionable act noted by commentators including al-Zamakhsharī). As significantly, the immediate contexts of the version in *Sūrat Ibrāhīm* and the version in *Sūrat al-Naḥl* are *diametrically opposed*: in the former, God has already referred to those who 'changed the beneficence of God into infidelity (*kufr*) and landed their people in the abode of bareness which is Jahannam (Hell) into whose fires they will go; they established false deities whom they deemed as God's equals in order to lead people astray from His path. Tell them: 'Take your pleasure now, for truly your destination is the Fire' (Q.14:31), then addressed the Prophet telling him to command the believers to act in accordance with His teachings and mentioning his *niʿam* (beneficence) upon them. As opposed to that, in the version in *Sūrat al-Naḥl* the sura opens with '*atā amru Allāhi*' (God's command has come) followed by three verses which glorify God, then from 5 to 17 He counts *niʿam* that He bestowed upon the believers, then comes no. 18 to crown the beautiful sense of harmony between the believers and God with *ghafūrun raḥīm*. Moreover, the central figure in *al-Naḥl* is God and His actions, whereas the central figure in *Sūrat Ibrāhīm* is man and his actions. This is evident even in the name given to each sura, be it *tawqīf* or *tawfīq*: Ibrāhīm is a man, *al-naḥl* is symbolically the embodiment of the Creator, who presents bees as a central icon of His power as well as of His being the Creator of the world, who has created these small creatures who themselves are active creators in the way they construct their amazingly intricate beehives, mirroring the intricate construction of everything He has created in His world, as well as in creating honey (*niʿam*) to enrich and help preserve the life of man. Furthermore, bees actually receive *waḥī* (inspiration to act) from God (*awḥaynā ilā'l-naḥli*) and they are the *only living* creatures of the non-human world who receive *waḥī* from Him, as though they were in the rank of prophets, which places them in a special bond with God and elevates them above mere symbolism. And the verses describing the bees are amongst the most beautiful in the Qur'an. That centrality of figure is thus embodied in *Sūrat al-Naḥl* in two of God's most caring attributes, *ghafūrun raḥīm*, and in the *Sūrat Ibrāhīm* it is embodied in two of man's most negative attributes in the eyes of God, *ẓalūmun kaffār*, epithets repeatedly used throughout the

Qur'an by God to describe man (a centrality which is also embodied, in a most striking, incomprehensible manner, by the fact—no metaphysics here either—that the verse which has man as *ẓalūmun kaffār* is almost exactly in the *middle, the centre*, of *Sūrat Ibrāhīm* (no. 24 out of 52). Similarly, God as *ghafūrun raḥīm* not only occurs close to the centre of *al-Naḥl* but also permeates the entire texture of the sura (and at *symmetrical positions* from the beginning and end of the sura: 7, 121 out of 128).

Does all this tell us anything? What do we learn from it? Are we faced with a single, unified totality in *al-Naḥl*? Well, we are, although historical data tells us that *al-Naḥl* is Meccan except for the last three verses, which are Medinan. Separated by time, but not so separated by rhyme and harmony. How did they fit there? By accident? Who fitted them there? Why? What determines these choices? Are they determined by any factors within their immediate context or the context of each sura as a whole? Are they simply formulaic events which occur for no specific structural reasons? Let us contemplate such features, such *facts*, as part of a total, comprehensive, new aesthetically oriented *tafsīr* of the Qur'an. We need one. But, alas, we do not find it here.

Do Other Suras Present Such Well-Wrought Urns? How?

As a crucial part of such an approach we need to go far beyond ancient and modern studies in handling all elements of the text but specifically the elements of *majāz*, *badīʿ*, *bayān*, etc. and poetic imagery in all its forms. It is not sufficient to say this is an *istiʿāra*: we must do what we do in all other texts and ask: what is the structural role of this *istiʿāra* in the context in which it appears. And do the group of images in a sura form a network of relationships, illuminating one another, enriching, as a formative part of the text, a texture that vitalizes the text more, enhances its aesthetic appeal, or do they stand as autonomous images each serving only its localized context? Approaches like the one outlined here are amongst the best ways to understand, appreciate, and feel confident that we have a better comprehension of the mysteries and power of one of the most influential texts in human history.

I have sketched some of the questions that modern scholarship needs to raise and seek answers to. But I shall raise now what I believe to be the most important single question about the Qur'an, a question that I have raised in my studies in Arabic and tried to answer indirectly by exploring the nature of poeticality. The question is about the rhythm of the Qur'an or, more precisely, *its rhythmic structure*, sura by sura. Qur'anic scholarship has covered immensely rich and complex aspects of the text but I am not aware that anyone has busied himself/herself with its rhythmic structure, part of which I have explored in a study of *Sūrat Maryam* and other shorter suras. A fundamental aspect of that rhythmic structure is generated by the sound patterns woven into sharp, strong beats and patterns of stress on individual words and on the entire series of verses in the early shorter suras as distinct from the contrasting, more extended and relaxed patterns in the longer suras; such patterns are extremely prominent in particular in the paired last words of the verses that produce *sajᶜ*. Studying the *sajᶜ* across the whole of the Qur'an is a task that has been rendered difficult to carry out by purely ideological beliefs related to what has been interpreted as a prohibition of *sajᶜ* in a hadith attributed to the prophet. Nevertheless, it is an immensely important, albeit difficult, and highly rewarding task that will enhance not only our understanding of its powerful aesthetic impact but also of aspects of its authenticity and the historical evolution of its language and its message. There are documented reports about people crying when reading the Qur'an; the Arabs called the Qur'anic verses they first heard poetry. What is it that drove them, the very people who took so much pride in their poetic traditions and had instinctive feelings for what was poetry and what was not, to respond by saying that the Qur'an was poetry and Muḥammad was a poet, a response that ultimately invoked the counter-response: 'this is not poetry, Muḥammad is not a poet, *wa-mā ᶜallamnāhu al-shiᶜra wa mā yanbaghī lahu*. We did not teach him poetry' (Q. 21:5; 26:224; 36:69; 37:36; 52:30; 69:41). These exchanges generated ultimately the challenge by the Qur'an to people to bring something like it and led to the inception and evolution of the science of *iᶜjāz al-Qurʾān*; some of its fruits this study has revealed. But I am not aware that any of the old commentators dealt with this question of the presumed poeticality of the Qur'an with a view to understanding it. This is a task that modern scholarship needs to undertake, an undertaking which might bear far more fruit than any that we have seen since al-Jurjānī brought to a high degree of maturity the idea of *iᶜjāz* residing in the *naẓm* of the Qur'an and nowhere else. It is a huge task, but great texts deserve huge undertakings to understand and appreciate them. It is certainly worthy of a great text like the Qur'an: that Book that is the 'Grand World', as Ibn ᶜArabī has beautifully described it.

The Quest for Aesthetic Effect

The point I have made above about understanding and appreciation is crucial for my argument. Modern scholarship needs to prioritize understanding as opposed to glorification. Much of the explicit and implicit motive of work on the Qur'an by devout Muslim scholars is meant to affirm, prove, and glorify the divine qualities of every aspect of the Qur'an. This is a perfectly legitimate cause and some wonderful works have been produced with this motive. But such works fail to show how this superiority is achieved, why a certain feature of the Qur'anic text is inimitable, brilliant, amazingly beautiful, etc. This is especially true of the way metaphorical language (and poetic imagery in all its forms) is treated. In most cases, scholars simply identify a linguistic item as an *istiᶜāra*, a *tamthīl* or a *tashbīh* or a *majāz*, but with few, yet significant exceptions, they do not explore the *aesthetic* effect of what they identify or try to reveal their significant role within the structures in which they occur. We need to go far beyond that in understanding, allowing the affirmation of superiority to come as a result of this understanding not to be a motive for seeking it. We also need to look at new approaches that can enhance the understanding regardless of whether or not that leads to glorification. One domain of study of great interest and value in this respect is the untouched exploration of the sources of poetic images, the domains from which the constituents of a *tashbīh*, a *tamthīl*, or an *istiʿāra*, for instance, come from throughout each sura then throughout the Qur'an. The consequences of understanding such aspects can be hugely significant not only on an aesthetic level but on a much more crucial level: that of the *authenticity* of the text. Vicious things have been said about the Qur'an and many things have been fabricated to undermine its authenticity, but no one has carried out exhaustive analysis of the domains of its imagery to see where they belong and from what environment they flow. I have tried to do some of this in a forthcoming book of mine and some results have proved to be extremely interesting. But a lot more needs to be done. When the Qur'an, for instance, uses the language of commerce, of writing, of gardens and farms and when its images derive from a desert environment and scenes deeply rooted in pre-Islamic poetry, does this have serious implications for fantasies about it having been composed by people around the Dead Sea or by ʿAbd al-Malik ibn Marwān in Damascus at the end of the first/seventh century? We need to see. Take this image from *Sūrat al-Muddaththir*, said to be the first sura to be delivered to Muḥammad:

> What is the matter with them, away from piety they turn, like startled wild asses escaping from a group of hunters, yet each of them wants to be sent open sheets of paper; no they do not; they just do not fear the last day. (Q. 74:49–53)

Al-Zamakhsharī portrays the setting of this verse as follows:

> The word *al-mustanfira* means that their *nifār* (shooting out running) is very strong and hard, as though they were seeking *nifar* from their inner selves and urging them to perform it; . . . *al-qaswara* is a group of hunters chasing them to hunt them, He compared them in avoiding to listen to the Qur'an and turning away from it to wild asses running hard when terrified; in comparing them to wild asses a satire for them and assertion of their foolishness, stupidity and lack of reason as is the case in His saying 'like an ass carrying books' . . . You never see anything faster than wild asses when suspicious of something dangerous; that is why you see most similes by the Arabs describing camels comparing them to wild asses if they sense a hunter when they come to a water source to drink. (al-Zamakhsharī, 4:656)

The domains of the images in this early sura are striking: first the *tashbīh* of the unbelievers to the wild asses startled and running in fear of the hunters; second the reference to the open pages each inscribed with the name of a person. Two contrasting images from two different domains of existence: an almost purely pre-Islamic desert scene and an urban one in which writing is a very common activity. Similarly, when *Sūrat al-Raḥmān* (55:72–6) describe the scenes in paradise they create a context for the beautiful women who will be enjoyed by the [male] believers in the following terms: 'They are *ḥuriyyāt* housed in tents . . . never taken before them by human or jinn . . . [the males] reclining on green rugs of fabulous beauty.' One wonders where else, other than in Mecca and its environment, or the pre-Islamic setting of Arabia generally, could an image like this have originated with its description of the ultimate luxury as a green rug and nice *ʿabqarī ḥisān*; *ʿabqarī* is attributed to *wādi ʿabqar*, the land of the jinn in pre-Islamic Arabia which we encounter in the poetry of the period. From it comes the meaning of *ʿabqarī* as fantastic, fabulous, brilliant, genius. Furthermore, in the many *tamthīls* in the Qur'an where natural elements are used to represent the believers and unbelievers using very limited items of plant life and scenes of lighting fire in a dry landscape (e.g. *Sūrat Ibrāhīm* 14:18, 14:24–6, discussed above) do we have material evidence to support claims that the Qur'an was composed in fertile lands where people were farmers who raised cattle, produced various crops, had irrigation systems running across vast areas of rich soil with olive groves and vineyards and woodlands? Or do we have evidence to the contrary?

I am not suggesting anything here, because single images can come into a text from countless directions and sources without them having any definite physical relationship with the producer. But systematic analysis of such things can reveal dominant images or clusters of images in a text, and dominance cannot be accidental or infiltrate a text via outside influence; dominance is the nearest thing we can get to an authentic source. And exploring the Qur'anic text from such a perspective may lead to some remarkable hypotheses and further exploration. It is a task as important as it is fascinating. And the Qur'an is one of the richest texts in the world that lends itself to such a fascinating exploration with a promise of rich, seductive harvests.

Conclusions

Thus we are still waiting for a new *tafsīr* of the Qur'an that foregrounds those aspects of it which are—or are believed to be—the causes of its superiority, its *iʿjāz*. The main glimpses of such a *tafsīr* that relate to aesthetic appeal are those in al-Jurjānī's studies of a limited number of verses. But al-Jurjānī was not writing a *tafsīr*, he was writing a study of *asrār al-balāgha* and the secrets of beauty that arise in texts wholly from their linguistic properties. Perhaps we need a new al-Jurjānī who looks at the Qur'an from the same perspective and has the same type of interest in it but who also wants to write a systematic *tafsīr* in the light of the advances which have been made in the analysis of poetics and aesthetics as well as linguistics and stylistics and other semiotically based approaches. Will we ever have one? I doubt it.

Bibliography

Abū-Deeb, Kamāl. *Al-Jurjānī's Theory of Poetic Imagery*. Warminster: Aris and Phillips, 1979.

Abū-Deeb, Kamāl. 'Studies in the *Majāz* and Metaphorical Language of the Qurʾān: Abū ʿUbayda and al-Sharīf al-Raḍī.' In: Isa Boullata (ed.). *Literary Structures of Religious Meaning in the Qurʾān*, pp. 310–53. London: Curzon Press, 2000.

Abū Ḥayyān al-Gharnāṭī Athīr al-Dīn Muḥammad. *Tafsīr al-baḥr al-muḥīṭ*. Ed. ʿĀdil Aḥmad ʿAbd al-Mawjūd et al. 3rd edn. (in 9 vols.). Beirut: Dār al-Kutub al-ʿIlmiyya, 2010.

Ibn ʿArabī Muḥyī al-Dīn. *al-Futūḥāt al-Makkiyya*. 4 vols. Beirut: Dār Ṣādir, n.d.

Quṭb, Sayyid. *Fī Ẓilāl al-Qurʾān*. 6 vols. 17th edn. Cairo: Dār al-Shurūq. Published in the 1960s in thirty volumes as was the 2nd edn. Beirut: Dār Iḥyāʾ al-Turāth al-ʿArabī, 1967.

Al-Rummānī, Abū'l-Ḥasan ʿAlī ibn ʿĪsā. *al-Nukat fī iʿjāz al-Qurʾān*. Published with two other monographs on the inimitability of the Qur'an by al-Jurjānī and al-Khaṭṭābī. Ed. Muḥammad Khalafallāh Aḥmad and Muḥammad Zaghlūl Sallām. Cairo: Dār al-Maʿārif, 1991.

Al-Zamakhsharī Maḥmūd ibn ʿUmar. Al-Kashshāf *ʿan ḥaqāʾiq ghawāmid al-tanzīl wa ʿuyūn al-aqāwīl fī wujūh al-taʾwīl*. 4 vols. Beirut: Dār al-Kitāb al-ʿArabī, 1947.

CHAPTER 54

TAFSĪR AND SCIENCE

ROBERT MORRISON

This chapter will discuss the role of science in the history of Qur'an interpretation (*tafsīr*). At times this chapter uses the word *tafsīr* to refer to exegesis of the Qur'an even if that exegesis is not in a book devoted to *tafsīr*. Modern terms such as 'religion' and 'science' as well as the terms for the different sciences serve as shorthands for the question of these terms' historical development. Noting Ahmad Dallal's extensive, authoritative article 'Science and the Qur'an' in the *Encyclopaedia of the Qur'ān*, this chapter will focus on commentators' responses to science's epistemological claims (Dallal 2004: 540–58). The chapter begins by looking at discussions of the natural world in early *tafsīr* before moving to three pre-modern Qur'an commentaries that, without privileging science as a hermeneutic tool, made extensive use of science to interpret the Qur'an's references to the natural world. From there, the discussion examines the extent to which some modern Qur'an commentaries have addressed the challenges of scientism, the preference for the findings and methodology of the modern natural sciences as the criterion of the Qur'an's truth. Despite some continuities between pre-modern and modern commentators, there are significant differences between the way pre-modern and modern *tafsīr* make use of scientific information.

The Qur'an's references to the natural world have attracted much attention, even from commentators less concerned with science *per se*, because the references serve a variety of functions, including evoking humans' *fiṭra*, as in *Sūrat al-Rūm* Q. 30:30 (So set thy face to the religion, a man of pure faith (*ḥanīfan*)—God's original (*fiṭrat Allāh*) upon which He originated mankind *faṭara l-nās ʿalayhā*. There is no changing God's creation. That is the right religion; but most men know it not).[1] Fazlur Rahman commented that the order observed in the cosmos is a 'natural' sign; the Meccans, though, had demanded more from Muḥammad (Rahman 1980: 69). The explicit connection that the Qur'an made between God's work in creation and humans' *fiṭra* meant that the Qur'an's references to God's signs (*āyāt*) in nature gave commentators scope for reflection

[1] All translations from the Qur'an come from Arberry 1955. On the Qur'an's references to nature with regard to *fiṭra*, see Morrison 2013: 1–2.

upon or investigation of nature. In addition, Dallal has noted that the use of science in *tafsīr* of these references to creation is not necessary, even for a scholar well-versed in science. A figure such as al-Bīrūnī noted, approvingly, the separation (or what Stephen Jay Gould (1999: 49–67) would call the non-overlapping magisteria) of the areas of the Qur'an and astronomy (Dallal 2004: 540). In the modern era too, references to nature have not always been understood as eliciting scientific material. Jamāl al-Dīn al-Qāsimī (d. 1914) commented, in his *Maḥāsin al-taʾwīl*, on Q. 6:2 (It is He who created you of clay, then determined a term and a term is stated with Him) without mentioning evolution or any other theory about *how* God created humankind from mud. Al-Qāsimī's comment stands, in its disinterest in science as an interpretive tool, as a reminder that discussions of Islam and science, this one included, tend to focus on thinkers who thought that religion and science had something to say to each other. But a position such as al-Qāsimī's insinuation that science was not relevant, akin to Gould's non-overlapping magisteria, is, in fact, a position on the relationship between religion and science.

To turn to the earliest Qur'an commentaries, al-Ṭabarī's (d. 310/923) *Jāmiʿ al-bayān* contains a number of discussions of astrology all of which are attributed to figures who pre-dated al-Ṭabarī, with some going back to the companions of the prophet. Though the authenticity of such reports could be questioned, doing so would imply that either al-Ṭabarī or his earlier informants were aware of what was at stake (e.g. questions of fate, foreknowledge, and the existence of intermediate causes) with discussions of astrology. These early *tafsīr* presumed connections between heaven and earth that humans could understand, at least in part, in order to use astrological forecasting to argue for Islam's status. For example, an ancient king's astrologers predicted Muḥammad's advent and mission, meaning that Islam was, even to non-Muslims, clearly the will of the heavens. Or, another hadith-style report, going back to the companion Jābir ibn ʿAbd Allāh (d. 78/697), recounted how a Jew asked Muḥammad about the eleven stars mentioned in the Qur'an's account of Joseph's dream in Q. 12:4. When Muḥammad provided the correct answer, the Jew converted to Islam. Early Christianity and late antique Judaism also had acknowledged some validity in astrology; the positions of the early *mufassirūn* make sense in that context. *Kalām* was another field of scholarship that paid attention to the natural world and to astrology's claims. That some early *tafsīr* was comparatively less critical of astrology than contemporary works of *kalām* (rational speculation into the nature of God) foreshadows the relative positions of *tafsīr* and *kalām* on the astral sciences a few centuries later.[2] The connections between heaven and earth, posited by these early *tafsīr*, remained a medium for God's control over the terrestrial realm in the next three *tafsīr* to be discussed.

Fakhr al-Dīn al-Rāzī's (d. 606/1210) *Mafātīḥ al-ghayb* (a.k.a. *al-Tafsīr al-kabīr*) was the first *tafsīr* to incorporate a great deal of scientific content throughout. The presence of the scientific content was due to al-Rāzī's wish to write an encyclopaedic *tafsīr* which

[2] Early *kalām* texts criticized astrological forecasting, though not the concept of connections between heaven and earth. See e.g. al-Jāḥiẓ 1933: 137–8.

included any information that might lend insight into the Qur'an; scientific interpretations were not privileged over those based on, say, hadith or grammar. The purpose of all of the information that al-Rāzī brought to bear on the Qur'anic text was to show that God was a wise, perfect, and omnipotent creator.[3] At rare, but notable instances, al-Rāzī undercut the claims of scientists in order to uphold his understanding of a wise creator. For instance, al-Rāzī, in his pages-long comments on Q. 2:164 ('Surely in the creation of heavens and earth and the alternation of night and day...'), posited a physical model for the motion of the fixed stars, the stars that comprised constellations, that took as its foundation skepticism about the accuracy of astronomers' observations.[4] Al-Rāzī did so in order to show that human wisdom had limits. But, as Dallal has shown, al-Rāzī was also willing to disagree with certain *mutakallimūn* who upheld occasionalism, commenting that the existence of intermediate causes could actually enhance God's omnipotence because the presence of intermediate causes would necessitate even more reflection on the details of creation.

Niẓām al-Dīn al-Nīsābūrī's *Gharāʾib al-Qurʾān wa-raghāʾib al-furqān* drew heavily on al-Rāzī's *Mafātīḥ al-ghayb*, at times reproducing passages verbatim. In large part, al-Rāzī and al-Nīsābūrī agreed that the purpose of including scientific information in the *tafsīr* was to enhance the reader's appreciation of the Qur'anic text and of God's omnipotence and creative power (Morrison 2005: 203). But al-Nīsābūrī's *tafsīr* accorded even more hermeneutic power to science than al-Rāzī's in that al-Nīsābūrī's *tafsīr* clearly upheld sciences' conclusions where al-Rāzī had contested or nuanced them. For instance, al-Nīsābūrī, in his own comments on Q. 2:164, accepted the astronomers' observations of the motions of the fixed stars (al-Nīsābūrī, *Gharāʾib al-Qurʾān* 2:84). A key issue that scientifically informed commentators probed was that of causality; in particular, how might intermediate causes exist without compromising God's omnipotence? Al-Nīsābūrī's position emerged via his exegesis of two verses. In his comments on *Sūrat Sabāʾ* Q. 34:2 ('Praise belongs to God to whom belongs whatsoever is in the heavens and whatsoever is in the earth... He knows what penetrates into the earth and what comes forth from it, what comes down from heavens, and what goes up to it,') al-Nīsābūrī categorized as *shirk* the view that God, in order to control terrestrial events, entrusts (*tafwīḍ*) certain outcomes to the stars (*Gharāʾib al-Qurʾān*, 22:58). Also unacceptable, of course, were astral worship and presuming that the stars acted wholly independently. Thus, it was the independence of intermediate causes that was problematic, not their existence. Now, consider al-Nīsābūrī's comments on *Sūrat Fāṭir* (Q. 35:13). The verse reads: 'He makes the night to enter into the day, and makes the day to enter into the night, and He has subjected [*sakhkhara*- I prefer 'subjugated'] the sun and the moon, each of them running to a stated term.' The difference was whether God subjugated the stars to God's desires or if God merely entrusted the stars with God's desires (*Gharāʾib al-Qurʾān*, 22:80–1). Al-Nīsābūrī took subjugation to mean that the stars were a true intermediary but did not enjoy any independence. Al-Rāzī's own comments on the same verse had not made that precise distinction (*al-Tafsīr al-kabīr*, 26:11).

[3] On al-Rāzī's *tafsīr*, see Dallal 2004: 543–52 and, more generally, Jaffer 2015.

[4] Fakhr al-Dīn Rāzī, *al-Tafsīr al-kabīr*, 4:181. My discussion of al-Rāzī and al-Nīsābūrī's *tafsīr* also relies on Morrison 2002.

The fully subjugated existence of the intermediate causes meant that they could be seen as a dimension of God's activities in creation. For al-Nīsābūrī, religious and scientific thought were in a conversation not so much because religion and science were two versions of the same truth, but because religious scholars were interested in rationalist approaches to interpreting (but not validating) the Qur'an.

A third commentator who should be classified along with al-Rāzī and al-Nīsābūrī is Nāṣir al-Dīn al-Bayḍāwī (d. *c.* 719/1319). His *Anwār al-tanzīl* has stereotypically been known as an Ashʿarī version of al-Zamakhsharī's (d. 538/1144) *al-Kashshāf*, but the reality is more complex, not the least because the contents of the *Kashshāf* have been reappraised (see now Lane 2006). In many cases, al-Bayḍāwī did not adopt from the *Kashshāf* the scientific material which he included (Morrison 2013: 19). Despite *Anwār al-tanzīl*'s relative concision, al-Bayḍāwī made use of science and *falsafa* in many of the same places that al-Nīsābūrī and al-Rāzī did.[5] Regarding *Sūrat al-Aʿrāf* Q. 7:54 ('and the sun, the moon, and the stars subservient, by His command') al-Bayḍāwī wrote that God conducted the affair (*dabbara al-amr*) from the heavens to the earth by moving the orbs and by causing the stars and planets to travel.[6] Once more, the heavens were the means for God's control over the terrestrial realm and for God's creation of the three kingdoms of nature (animal, vegetable, and mineral) by compounding their matter (*tarkīb mawāddihā*). Al-Bayḍāwī was a well-known *mutakallim* whose *kalām* texts appropriated material and terminology from science and philosophy in order to make arguments about God without relying on revealed texts (Sabra 1994: 13). His rationalist language here and focus on *istidlāl* (reasoning from evidence), in his comments on Q. 7:54, were part of his argument for God's supreme power which would entail the ability to create *ex nihilo*. Here, al-Bayḍāwī's language and approach mirrored that found in his *kalām* text, *Ṭawāliʿ al-anwār*.

Elsewhere, al-Bayḍāwī's *tafsīr* could be remarkably accepting of science's conclusions and epistemological claims in a way distinct from the approach of his work on *kalām*. Let us consider al-Bayḍāwī's comments on *Sūrat al-Ḥijr* Q. 15:16: 'We have set in heavens constellations *(burūj)* and decked them out fair to the beholders.' He wrote that the word *burūj* referred to the twelve different signs, the definition of the technical term in astronomy, each with its own configurations (*hayʾāt*) and particulars (*khawāṣṣ*). Absent from al-Bayḍāwī's comments was linguistic analysis or consideration of any other possible meaning for *burūj*, especially material that was found in al-Rāzī's *tafsīr* (for al-Rāzī's comment on Q. 15:16, see Dallal 2004: 550). Then, he explained that humans' knowledge of these particulars has depended on observation and experience (*tajriba*). This comment suggests that these observations and experiences, which were the basis of astrological forecasting, might provide insight into the text of the Qur'an. Al-Bayḍāwī's *Ṭawāliʿ al-anwār* said nothing like that about *tajriba*.

This idea that a systematic rationalist investigation of God's signs in nature could lead one to important truths about God came out of the intellectual context of transformations

[5] On science in al-Bayḍāwī's *tafsīr*, see al-ʿAzīz Ḥājī 2000: 377.

[6] Al-Bayḍāwī, *Anwār al-tanzīl*, 1:342.

in the field of *kalām*, an area in which al-Rāzī and al-Bayḍāwī wrote pioneering works.[7] al-Nīsābūrī and al-Bayḍāwī's careers, in turn, were connected in that they both occurred in the context of the Ilkhanid Mongol court at Tabriz.[8] That court was a context in which scholars proficient in fields such as astronomy also wrote on topics such as *kalām*, *fiqh*, and *tafsīr*. The discussion in that intellectual milieu about the role of science in religious scholarship went beyond the question of whether intermediate causes existed, or whether God was the only cause, to a debate about whether the conclusions of science inspired enough confidence to be a or the foundation of religious knowledge. Scientific information which could not be demonstrated deductively could not necessarily provide the certainty that *kalām* demanded (Sabra 1994: 37). But scholars proficient in science, such as Muʾayyad al-Dīn ʿUrḍī (d. 665/1266) made a contrasting argument (Eichner 2009: 285). For ʿUrḍī, astronomy proved the greatness of the creator. Al-Nīsābūrī, on his part, included a two-page excursus on the wonders of God's creation in the middle of his own comments on retrograde motion (Morrison 2011: 88).

In that context of a debate about the role of science in religious thought, specifically competing claims of epistemological certainty, al-Bayḍāwī's comments on Q. 2:164 are fascinating because they made an argument that reflected ʿUrḍī's position more than the scepticism of some *mutakallimūn*. In his *tafsīr*, al-Bayḍāwī argued that the fact that things were created with a discernible order in a certain way indicated a wise creator. Al-Bayḍāwī wrote that 'it is possible that the [celestial] equator becomes a circle passing through the poles and that they [the heavens] do not have an apex and nadir at all'. The celestial equator is a projection of the earth's equator out towards the heavens. Any circle passing through the north and south poles of the heavens would be perpendicular to the celestial equator. There was more than one way to conceive of these circles as they were mathematical abstractions. But al-Bayḍāwī commented that God's decision to place the equator where it was and the circles running through the celestial poles where they actually were could not have been capricious. He wrote: '[it is] in this way owing to its simplicity and the equivalence of its parts'. Al-Bayḍāwī took a mathematical convention, the relative location of the equator, which could not be demonstrated deductively, to be sufficiently real as to be a sign of God's wisdom.

Al-Bayḍāwī did not make such an argument in his *kalām* text, and ʿAḍud al-Dīn al-Ījī (d. 756/1355), in his *al-Mawāqif fī ʿilm al-kalām* explicitly questioned the reality of astronomy's mathematical constructions: '[All] these are imaginary things (*umūr mawhūma*) that have no external existence. [Religious] prohibition does not extend to them, being neither an object of belief nor subject to affirmation or negation' (as cited in Sabra 1994: 37). Many of astronomy's conclusions could not be established deductively, that is, they could not meet the standards of demonstration that the *mutakallimūn* ostensibly set for themselves. Yet astronomy would have seemed to be an impressive science that could serve religious purposes. Astronomy's causal explanation of eclipses, though the premises

[7] Sabra's article that investigated these developments was path-breaking (Sabra 1994).

[8] Al-Bayḍāwī dedicated his *tafsīr* to the Ilkhanid ruler Arghun. See al-Bayḍāwī 2002: 1:xxxiii. On al-Nīsābūrī's connection to the Ilkhanids, see Morrison 2011: 38–41.

had to be intuited, was difficult to contest, a fact that al-Ghazālī noted in the *Tahāfut* (al-Ghazālī 1997: 6). A contemporary commentator, Ibn ʿĀshūr (d. 1973), borrowed from al-Rāzī an anecdote in his comments on Q. 2:164 in which ʿUmar ibn al-Ḥusām was teaching (*yaqraʾ ʿalā*) *The Almagest* to ʿUmar al-Abharī, and some (or one) jurists asked them what they were doing.[9] Al-Abharī said that he was interpreting the verse (Q. 50:6) 'What, have they not beheld heaven above them, how We have built it?' Heidrun Eichner has pointed out that the *Almagest*'s geometrical demonstrations must have been particularly compelling within the intellectual context of *kalām* (Eichner 2009: 377). The fact that al-Bayḍāwī used astronomy differently in his *tafsīr* than he did in his work on *kalām* supports Eichner's position. While pre-modern *mufassirūn* did not have to negotiate epistemological debates nearly on the scale of those posed by modern science and by scientism, pre-modern *mufassirūn* who provided scientific information did so from within an intellectual context in which the metaphysical and epistemological challenges of science were recognized and contested. Compared to *kalām*, *tafsīr* conceded more epistemological power to science in order to afford the reader greater insight into the Qur'an. In the period of al-Rāzī, al-Bayḍāwī, and al-Nīsābūrī though, science did not have the status of being the unique arbiter of truth.

The relative disinterest of the aforementioned commentators in mathematical solutions to the *qibla* problem, determining the direction of prayer enjoined in Q. 2:144, is a strong indication of how they used science selectively. After the translation movement, mathematical methods for determining the *qibla* appeared and proliferated (Dallal 1995: 145–93; see also King 1999). Once the general trigonometric solution became clear, increasingly refined approaches continued to emerge. Chapters on *qibla* computation appeared in what would otherwise be characterized as purely scientific texts such as Naṣīr al-Dīn al-Ṭūsī's (d. 672/1274) *Tadhkira* (al-Ṭūsī, *Tadhkira*, 1:306–9). All of these texts and solutions were *tafsīr* in the broad sense of the word because they expounded an obligation mentioned in the Qur'an. But when one turns to the comments on Q. 2:144 ('We have seen thee turning thy face about in the heaven; now We will surely turn thee to a direction that shall satisfy thee. Turn thy face towards the Holy Mosque') in the scientifically informed texts of *tafsīr* just surveyed, science was barely applied as a hermeneutic device even though mathematical methods clearly provided the most precise interpretation of the legal obligation. Al-Bayḍāwī's *Anwār al-tanzīl* (2:92) confined itself solely to the question of what the Qur'an *meant* by the new *qibla* (the Kaʿba), separating that question from the matter of computing the direction of the *qibla*.

Al-Rāzī, characteristically, commented more extensively on the verse and acknowledged that the direction from Medina to Mecca could be known only through geometrical methods (*al-Tafsīr al-kabīr*, 2:113: '*Wa-muqābalat al-ʿayn lā tudrak illā bi-daqīq naẓar handasī*'). But al-Rāzī did not make that point in the course of an argument for the

[9] Ibn ʿĀshūr, *al-Taḥrīr wa-'l-tanwīr*, 2:76. Ibn ʿĀshūr wrote that he found the anecdote in al-Rāzī's *tafsīr* (cf. al-Rāzī, *al-Tafsīr al-kabīr*, 4:176). Ibn ʿĀshūr noted that many of the Qur'an's references to celestial phenomena could be understood with respect to the sphericity of the heavens, perhaps implying that the spherical astronomy of the *Almagest* was still relevant for understanding the Qur'an in modernity.

mandatory application of mathematical methods for *qibla* determination. Rather, al-Rāzī held that since the mathematical method of *qibla* determination was not available to Muḥammad and his early followers, it was impossible that the verse unconditionally enjoined mathematical determination of the *qibla*. In fact, there were some instances, such as when one was in a dark room or if one was blind and alone, when prayer in any direction would be permissible (*al-Tafsīr al-kabīr*, 2:118). The possibility of imprecision in the direction of prayer did not eliminate the requirement of prayer. Implicit in al-Bayḍāwī's comments, and explicit in al-Rāzī's, was that the purpose of the verse was not to enjoin contemplation of the natural world but to differentiate Muḥammad's community from earlier religious groups. As the purpose of Q. 2:144 was not to encourage contemplation of the natural world, the absence of scientific material in exegeses of that verse reinforces the conclusion that the introduction of scientific material into pre-modern *tafsīr* would seem to have been driven by the concerns of *kalām*, learning about God through rationalist investigation, and not by those of *fiqh*, specifying one's religious obligations.

Some modern commentators have used science in a way similar to that of the pre-modern commentators. Ibn ʿĀshūr's exegesis of Q. 2:164 where he integrated modern astronomy into an attempt to place the verse in the Qur'an's historical context. He began his comments by saying that the purpose of the verse was to affirm God's existence and unity to the infidels of the Quraysh and to anyone else who held their materialist views.[10] Ibn ʿĀshūr suggested (*laʿalla*) that, in order to rebut and refute the infidels, the verse referred to the findings of astronomy (*ʿilm al-hayʾa*) and the solar system (*al-niẓām al-shamsī*). Then he suggested (again, *laʿalla*) that the seven heavens and the throne comprised Mercury, Venus, Mars, the Sun, Jupiter, Saturn, Uranus, and Neptune. It is interesting that either Uranus or Neptune, both planets not known at the time of the Qur'an's appearance, corresponded to the heavenly throne. Despite the reference to the solar system, Ibn ʿĀshūr has, nevertheless, put the Sun back in motion. But that slip was irrelevant to Ibn ʿĀshūr's broader argument that astronomy reveals God's creation of and enduring presence in the natural order (Ibn ʿĀshūr, *al-Taḥrīr*, 2:78). Ibn 'Āshūr went on to explain how the daily rotation of the spherical earth produced the regular processes of the passage of day and night. Thus modern scientific information could certainly serve non-scientistic ends in *tafsīr*.

In contrast, other recent commentators have made much of what they perceive to be the Qur'an's amenability to a scientifically informed interpretation. Some modern Qur'an commentary has understood the Qur'an's truth to be evidenced mostly by having predicted certain discoveries of modern science, unknown at the time of the Qur'an's emergence (Dallal 2004: 553). The paradigmatic work in linking the truth of the Qur'an with those of modern science is Maurice Bucaille's *The Bible, The Qur'an, and Science*.[11] Although written with the express aim of showing that there is no conflict between

[10] Ibn ʿĀshūr, *al-Taḥrīr wa-'l-tanwīr*, 2:75–6.

[11] Bucaille 1986: 107. There Bucaille draws on modern astronomy to explain how the sun is, indeed, moving in the solar system, thus demonstrating the truth of the Qur'an.

Islam and science, Bucaille's book has the effect of making the achievements of modern science the touchstone for the Qur'an's truth. Since science will continue to change, Bucaille's approach would imply that the truth of the Qur'an (and not simply people's understanding of it) would continue to change. Mohammed Arkoun has noted the great extent to which modern attempts to understand Islam's relationship to science were conditioned by external forces, and particularly by a scientific enterprise in which Muslims had not participated for centuries.[12] Drastic shifts in the relative position of traditionally Islamic societies relative to Europe and North America go a long way in accounting for approaches like Bucaille's.

That said, the modern context has yielded less scientistic modern approaches to the question of Islam and science, such as the work of Ismail Faruqi, in developing an Islamic scientific epistemology, and Seyyed Hossein Nasr's advocacy of an earlier, traditional scientific metaphysics (Kalin 2002: 59 (Faruqi) and 63 (Nasr)). Another recent proponent of an Islamic epistemology, Ziauddin Sardar, has written, 'The Qur'an, however, does not simply suggest, in general terms, that science is important. It points towards methods for doing science. First, it urges the reader to appreciate the importance of observation' (Sardar 2011: 351). Sardar's challenge, like Faruqi's, would be clarifying how a particular religion has played a distinctive role in shaping an increasingly global scientific enterprise.

An influential twentieth-century figure to pay attention to the relationship between Islam and science was Said Nursi (d. 1960), who worked in Turkey at the time of the rise of the Republic. Although Nursi has attracted attention from scholars, there has been inadequate attention paid to his use of science in interpreting the Qur'an. Ibrahim Kalin, a scholar of the discourse between Islam and science has characterized Bucaille's work as a vulgarized version of Nursi's.[13] In *Sözler* (Words), Nursi argued that an indication of the Qur'an's miraculousness was that it alluded to everything; along those lines, Q. 24:35 (the Light Verse), alluded to electricity (Nursi 1992: 260–1). There Nursi, like Bucaille, went beyond applying science as a hermeneutic tool to use science as a touchstone for the Qur'an's status. Characterizing Nursi as a more refined Bucaille may be a simplification. Other comments that Nursi made, to be discussed shortly, portrayed nature as a divine book that could yield religious truths through the application of human reason, but not as a divine book that was the *same* as the Qur'an. Other modern Muslim scholars have taken similar positions. For example, Tariq Ramadan has written that nature is a revealed book, like the Qur'an (March 2010: 253–73). Muḥammad ʿAbdūh and Rashīd Riḍā (1906–27: 2:68) wrote that it was insufficient to see the references to nature in Q. 2:164 simply as signs of the truths of the revealed Qur'an, but that one had to read them as their own parallel truth. Other Muslims' references to a book of nature posed hermeneutic questions that use nature as a religious text and that make

[12] It is not clear whether Arkoun thought the science associated with colonialism was qualitatively different from the earlier scientific culture of Islamic civilization.

[13] Kalin 2002: 55. See also p. 53 on remarks that Nursi made in *Gleams* that explain the connection between him and Bucaille.

sense in light of the role of science in pre-modern *tafsīr* and *kalām*. What Nursi did was to pursue this idea of a book of nature further than most, explaining, for example, that each scientific discipline explores a particular name of God (Nursi 1992: 270).

In *Sözler*, Nursi rejected Darwin's principle that random variations accounted for important changes in nature: 'Anyone with a grain of intelligence would know how contrary to reason is their attributing creatures adorned with infinite instances of wisdom to something based on purposeless, meaningless coincidence which is quite clear without order. Whereas, from the point of view of the wisdom of the All-Wise Qur'an, the transformations of particles have many purposes and duties, and demonstrate many instances of wisdom' (Nursi 1992: 574; Nursi quoted Q. 17:44 in support). Nursi was not necessarily arguing for the creationist views that eventually appeared in Turkey in the past few decades (Numbers 2006: 399–431). Rather, elsewhere in his copious writings, Nursi explained that the real problem was the place of evolution in arguments against God. For example, a long, discrete comment on the role of science in understanding the Qur'an's references to nature is in the twenty-third gleam of his *Lemalar* (The Gleams). Entitled 'On nature, or refuting naturalistic atheism', the comment takes as its point of departure *Sūrat Ibrāhīm* Q. 14:10: 'Their Messengers said: "Is there any doubt regarding God, the Originator of the heavens and the earth"'. The twenty-five-page chapter was an argument for design in nature. For instance, Nursi wrote, 'attributing any existent being, which has a unique individuality because of being a work of the Single One of Unity and Uniqueness, to the innumerable atoms that form it is an obvious hundred-fold impossibility.' Nature's marvellous composition and order could not be due to anything material. Thus, nature's composition and order, as well as its existence must be due to something immaterial: God. Darwin's fault was deifying evolution (Turner and Korkuc 2009: 49). The argument from design was central to Nursi's understanding of the Qur'an's portrayal of nature, as it was for pre-modern *mufassirūn* (and *mutakallimūn*). Nursi understood and rejected scientism not only as an *a priori* positioning of science's epistemological supremacy, but also for its premise that the cosmos can be understood only on science's wholly materialist terms (Nursi 2008: 339; see also Turner and Korkuc 2009: 80).

Nursi was not at all alone in attacking materialism; Jamāl al-Dīn al-Afghānī's (d. 1897) treatise against materialism is well known (see Keddie 1968). Yet Aziz al-Azmeh has found that all dimensions of Darwinism were not always understood to be materialist. Al-Afghānī (d. 1897) and his disciple Muḥammad ʿAbdūh (d. 1905) used concepts from social Darwinism in their interpretation of verses from the Qur'an such as *Sūrat al-Baqara* Q. 2:251. The verse reads: 'Had God not driven back the people, some by the means of others, the earth had surely corrupted.' ʿAbdūh wrote: 'For God says that the nature of men is such as to prevent each other from achieving rectitude and human interest; this is the obstacle to the corruption of the world, that is, it is the reason for the survival of rectitude and the survival of goodness' (Azmeh 2009: 121). Thus, when a dimension of Darwinism could be used to argue for God and God's design, Darwin could be acceptable to some. Along those lines, in a tantalizing passage in *Gleams*, Nursi described events which could be easily explained through evolutionary biology, though he himself did not do so, as a demonstration of God's power and providence. Nursi told of a moment when he was imprisoned and the shared jail cell was overrun by flies (2008: 373–4). Prison officials applied a pesticide, but the flies responded by breeding more furiously than ever. Said Nursi saw the flies' survival as a triumph of God's creation, and God's ability to intervene in the normal course of events, over the will of the jailers. A professional biologist would conclude, *contra* Nursi, that the flies had evolved a resistance to pesticides. What is now explicable as a process of evolution, to Nursi reflected God's providence and design. Recently, Sardar has commented that accepting the Qur'an's arguments about God's control over nature does not mean rejecting evolution (Sardar 2011: 359–62). In particular, it is impossible to know how ʿAbdūh, Riḍā, or Nursi would have responded to hard-core creationist arguments had they been alive in the late twentieth century.

More research on Nursi and others is necessary to determine the extent to which these modern recognitions of the epistemological challenges of science led to a deeper conversation between Islam and science in works of *tafsīr*. And, while the pre-modern scientifically informed commentators were eminent scholars in other fields including the sciences, thoughtful modern commentators have other religious agendas which shaped the use of science in their *tafsīr*. Moreover, because of scientism and the awareness of how science has and will continue to change, one scholar has argued that the ever-changing nature of modern science renders modern *tafsīr* futile (Mir 2004: 33–42). Commentators may sense that there is a risk of making science the arbiter of the Qur'an's truth. The picture may, however, be more complicated because modern science has, in some cases, changed standards of evidence in modern Islamic law. Specifically, DNA testing has brought new ways to prove paternity and neuroscience has brought new insights into the definition of death; scriptural definitions of death and paternity have been held to be insufficient in certain cases.[14] Research is necessary into whether these scientific developments have been reflected in interpretations of the Qur'an in the same way that they have been in Islamic law. Conversely, with the rise of creationism in some parts of the Islamic world, are commentators relying more on biblical materials and/or on creation science? Finally, the Qur'an itself reflected an understanding of nature that was just as historically conditioned as the scientific background of the scientifically informed commentators. As the context of the Qur'an is harder to determine than that of the commentators', penetrating studies on the Qur'an's own statements about the natural world are all the more fascinating.

Bibliography

ʿAbdūh, Muḥammad and Rashīd Riḍā. *Tafsīr al-Manār*. Vol. 2. Cairo: Dār al-Manār, 1906–27.
Arberry, A. J. *The Koran Interpreted*. New York: Collier Books, 1955.
al-Azmeh, Aziz. *Islams and Modernities*. 3rd edn. London and New York: Verso, 2009.
al-ʿAzīz, Ḥājī. *al-Bayḍāwī mufassiran*. Damascus: Dār al-Ḥasanayn, 2000.

[14] On DNA testing, see Shaham 2010: ch. 6. On brain death, see Brockopp 2003: 177–93.

al-Bayḍāwī, ʿAbd Allāh ibn ʿUmar. *Anwār al-tanzīl*. 2 vols. Beirut: Dār al-Kutub al-ʿIlmiyya, 1988.

al-Bayḍāwī, ʿAbd Allāh ibn ʿUmar. *Nature, Man, and God in Medieval Islam*. 2 vols. Leiden, Boston: Brill, 2002.

Bladel, Kevin van. 'Heavenly Cords and Prophetic Authority in the Quran and its Late Antique Context', *Bulletin of the School of Oriental and African Studies* 70 (2007), 223–46.

Brockopp, Jonathan E. 'The "Good Death" in Islamic Theology and Law'. In: Jonathan E. Brockopp (ed.). *Islamic Ethics of Life*, pp. 177–93. Columbia: University of South Carolina Press, 2003.

Bucaille, Maurice. *The Bible, The Qur'an, and Science: The Holy Scriptures Examined in Light of Modern Knowledge*. Trans. Alastair Pannell. Paris: Seghers, 1986.

Dallal, Ahmad. 'Ibn al-Haytham's Universal Solution for Finding the Direction of the Qibla by Calculation', *Arabic Sciences and Philosophy* 5 (1995), 145–93.

Dallal, Ahmad. 'Science and the Qurʾān'. In: Jane Dammen McAuliffe (ed.). *Encyclopaedia of the Qurʾān*, 6 vols., 4:540–58. Leiden: Brill, 2001–6.

Eichner, Heidrun. *The Post-Avicennian Philosophical Tradition and Islamic Orthodoxy: Philosophical and Theological Summae in Context*. Habilitationsschrift: Martin-Luther-Universität Halle-Wittenberg, 2009.

al-Ghazālī. *The Incoherence of the Philosophers*. Trans. and introd. Michael Marmura. Provo and London: Brigham Young University Press, 1997.

Gould, Stephen Jay. *Rocks of Ages: Science and Religion in the Fullness of Life*. New York: Ballantine Group, 1999.

Ibn ʿĀshūr. *Al-Taḥrīr wa'l-tanwīr*. Vol. 2 of 12. Tunis: Dār Saḥnūn li-l-Nashr wa-l-Tawzīʿ, 1997.

Jaffer, Tariq. *Rāzī: Master of Qur'anic Interpretation and Theological Reasoning*. New York: Oxford University Press, 2015.

al-Jāḥiẓ. '*Min Kitāb ḥujaj al-nubuwwa*'. In: Ḥasan al-Sandūbī (ed.). *Rasāʾil al-Jāḥiẓ*, pp. 117–54. Cairo: al-Maktaba al-Tijāriyya al-Kubrā, 1933.

Kalin, Ibrahim. 'Three Views of Science in the Islamic World'. In: Ted Peters, Muzaffar Iqbal, and S. Nomanul Haq (eds.). *God, Life, and the Cosmos*, pp. 43–76. Aldershot and Burlington, VT: Ashgate, 2002.

Keddie, Nikki. *An Islamic Response to Imperialism: Political and Religious Writings of Jamāl al-Dīn al-Afghānī*. Berkeley: University of California Press, 1968.

King, David. *World-Maps for Finding the Direction and Distance to Mecca*. Leiden and Boston: Brill, 1999.

Lane, Andrew. *A Traditional Muʿtazilite Qur'an Commentary: The* Kashshāf *of Jār Allāh al-Zamakhsharī (d. 538/1144)*. Leiden: Brill, 2006.

March, Andrew. 'The Post-Legal Ethics of Tariq Ramadan: Persuasion and Performance in Radical Reform: Islamic Ethics and Liberation', *Middle East Law and Governance* 2 (2010), 253–73.

Mir, Mustansir. 'Scientific Exegesis of the Qur'ān—A Viable Project?' *Islam and Science* 2 (2004), 33–42.

Morrison, Robert. 'The Portrayal of Nature in a Medieval Qur'an Commentary', *Studia Islamica* 94 (2002), 115–38.

Morrison, Robert. 'Reasons for a Scientific Portrayal of Nature in Medieval Commentaries on the Qur'ān', *Arabica* 52 (2005), 182–203.

Morrison, Robert. 'Discussions of Astrology in Early Tafsir', *Journal of Qur'anic Studies* 11/2 (2009), 49–71.

Morrison, Robert. *Islam and Science*. London: Routledge, 2011.
Morrison, Robert. 'Natural Theology and the Qur'an', *Journal of Qur'anic Studies* 15/1 (2013), 1–22.
al-Nīsābūrī, Niẓām al-Dīn. *Gharāʾib al-Qurʾān wa-raghāʾib al-furqān* (in the margins of al-Ṭabarī's *Jāmiʿ al-bayān*). Beirut: Dār al-Maʿrifa, 1992.
Numbers, Ronald. *The Creationists: From Scientific Creationism to Intelligent Design*. Cambridge, MA, and London: Harvard University Press, 2006.
Nursi, Bediuzzaman Said. *The Words*. Trans. Şükran Vahide. Istanbul: Sözler Neşriyat, 1992.
Nursi, Bediuzzaman Said. *The Gleams: Reflections on Qur'anic Wisdom and Spirituality*. Trans. Hüseyin Akarsu. Somerset, NJ: Tughra Books, 2008.
Rahman, Fazlur. *Major Themes of the Qur'an*. Minneapolis, MN: Bibliotheca Islamica, 1980.
al-Rāzī, Fakhr al-Dīn. *al-Tafsīr al-kabīr*. 3rd edn. Beirut: Dār Iḥyāʾ al-Turāth al-ʿArabī, n.d.
Sabra, A. I. 'Science and Philosophy in Medieval Islamic Theology', *Zeitschrift für Geschichte der arabisch-islamischen Wissenschaften* 9 (1994), 1–42.
Sardar, Ziauddin. *Reading the Qur'an*. London: Hurst and Company, 2011.
Shaham, Ron. *The Expert Witness in Islamic Courts: Medicine and Crafts in the Service of Law*. Chicago and London: University of Chicago Press, 2010.
Turner, Colin and Hasan Korkuc. *Said Nursi*. Oxford: Oxford University Press and I. B. Tauris, 2009.
al-Ṭūsī, Naṣīr al-Dīn. *Naṣīr al-Dīn al-Ṭūsī's Memoir on Astronomy (al-Tadhkira fī ʿilm al-hayʾa)*. Ed., trans., and comm. F. J. Ragep. 2 vols. New York, Heidelberg, Berlin: Springer-Verlag, 1993.

CHAPTER 55

CLASSICAL QUR'ANIC HERMENEUTICS

JOHANNA PINK

THIS chapter aims to provide an overview of the current state of scholarship on classical Qur'anic hermeneutics. The term 'classical' is used here to denote a period that roughly starts in the fourth/tenth century with efforts by scholars like al-Ṭabarī (d. 310/923), al-Māturīdī (d. 333/944), and al-Thaʿlabī (d. 427/1035) to present synopses of the state of the art of their field. The difficulty of defining the transition from the 'classical' into a 'post-classical' or 'modern' period will be discussed below.

As the field of Qur'anic hermeneutics is a vast one, potentially encompassing everything from the *iʿjāz al-Qurʾān* doctrine to the *qirāʾāt*, some limitation seems required. From among the many genres that could be subsumed under the label 'exegesis' (McAuliffe 2003a), this chapter will focus on Qur'anic commentaries (*tafsīr*). While these commentaries take into account hermeneutical discourses and usually explain the hermeneutical theories upon which they are based, several studies have shown that the influence of such discourses and theoretical expositions on the actual work that Qur'anic commentators perform is somewhat limited (Bauer 2013b: 52; Forster 2001: 117; Saleh 2004: 77,101). The focus of this chapter will therefore be on applied hermeneutics as evidenced in Qur'anic commentaries, while Chapter 56 will give an overview of theoretical hermeneutical discourses.

Given the fact that the field of *tafsīr* has received little serious and systematic attention for a long time and given the current dynamic development of *tafsīr* studies, any attempt at providing an overview of applied Qur'anic hermeneutics in the classical period can only be provisional and fragmentary. Many attempts at generating typologies and theories have at a closer glance proved dissatisfying. Based on the realization that we do not know nearly enough, current scholarship increasingly focuses on detailed studies of individual exegetes or comparative studies of exegetical problems, generating a wealth of new insights that, in turn, allow us to propose new hypotheses and develop new categories.

A good example of this process is the debate on the typology of pre-modern Qur'anic exegesis, which has a direct bearing on the assumptions that govern the study of hermeneutics. Goldziher, in his classic *Die Richtungen der islamischen Koranauslegung*, categorized *tafsīr* works, first, according to the period in which they had been written, and second, according to the religious agenda ascribed to their authors (Goldziher 1920). For instance, he distinguished between 'traditional' Qur'anic commentaries, by which he meant Sunnī works with a linguistic or hadith-based methodology, 'dogmatic' commentaries that were involved in theological disputes, 'mystical', and 'sectarian' commentaries. This categorization is quite similar to the one used in the standard Arabic work on the historiography of *tafsīr* by Muḥammad al-Dhahabī (1961). John Wansbrough, on the other hand, distinguished five modes of interpretation: haggadic (narrative), halakhic (legal), masoretic (lexical), rhetorical, and allegorical; a distinction that was meant to be both typological and chronological. Both Goldziher's and Wansbrough's typologies were based on a relatively limited amount of sources and were criticized by more recent scholars for being too rigid and impossible to uphold in the light of more detailed comparative studies of works of Qur'anic exegesis (Bauer 2013a: 5–11). Such studies have shown the remarkable degree to which there have been reciprocal influences as well as common themes and methods across religious fault lines, calling into question a division based on such fault lines (Fudge 2011: 147; Saleh 2004: 22–3). While Goldziher's and Wansbrough's categories continue to be in use with modifications and reservations—such as a greater awareness of the possibility that Sunnī *tafsīr* might be sectarian, too—recent scholarship has proposed other analytical perspectives that often cut across sectarian and theological boundaries and shed doubt on the usefulness of clear-cut typologies. By focusing less on categories and more closely on the internal workings of Qur'anic exegesis, the main interest is shifted to factors that help to explain the form and function of *tafsīr* works.

The increasing number of serious and detailed studies on the mechanisms of Qur'anic exegesis have highlighted the specificities and differences of individual exegetes' hermeneutics, making it impossible to generalize about Qur'anic hermeneutics in the classical period. At the same time, a number of central themes have emerged that will be the focus of the following sections.

Individual Approaches and Genre Constraints

As Bruce Fudge (2011: 145) has aptly stated, 'Qurʾānic commentary may well be shaped more by the nature of commentary than by the nature of the Qur'an.' Exegetes in the classical period often present distinctive hermeneutical visions; but at the same time, their hermeneutics have to fit into the framework of a well-established genre. Thus, there is a constant tension between their individual priorities and the standards that they have to follow for their works to become part of this genre.

A constitutive element of the genre of *tafsīr* was the fundamental organizational principle according to which a segment of the Qur'an—a verse, or even part of a verse—would be followed by commentary (Calder 1993: 101). This basic structure had far-reaching hermeneutical implications, as it usually meant that the detailed analysis of small segments had precedence over the establishment of a larger context (Fudge 2011: 146; Mir 1993: 211–12).

Introductions to Qur'an commentaries reveal how much emphasis exegetes place on the aims of their commentaries and the hermeneutical tools they consider appropriate for reaching those aims. These are the criteria by which, above all others, they seek to distinguish themselves from existing works and to justify the relevance of their exegetical endeavour. Most Qur'anic commentaries, therefore, open with lengthy introductions that expound, among other things, the characteristics of the exegete's individual approach to the interpretation of the Qur'an and the importance of this approach as opposed to those of previous commentators, who are often accused of lacking a proper understanding of hermeneutics. While in the fourth/tenth century, such statements are still fairly unsystematic and offer little more than an explanation of an author's interests and concerns, by the fifth/eleventh century they have evolved into lists of methods and hermeneutical principles that reflect the consolidation and growing sophistication of the genre. These lists are relatively similar to each other, but a comparative reading can nevertheless reveal points of interest for individual exegetes (Bauer 2013b: 49–51).

The common elements contained in these lists could be considered the theoretical hermeneutical foundations of *tafsīr* as defined by pre-modern Qur'anic exegetes. They include the knowledge of the Arabic language, aspects of grammar and philology, the *qirāʾāt*, the abrogating and the abrogated verses, the unambiguous (*muḥkam*) and ambiguous (*mutashābih*) verses, and legal rulings in the Qur'an. These hermeneutical concepts are what exegetes at least claim to base their Qur'anic commentaries upon. Apparently, the genre required them to state their aims and methods in inclusive terms shared with other Qur'anic commentaries, even if they proceeded to denounce their predecessors for their lack of hermeneutical understanding and even if their applied methodology differed vastly from the methodological framework described in the introduction (Bauer 2013b: 52; Forster 2001: 117; Saleh 2004: 101). This might potentially be understood as a natural consequence of the emergence of *tafsīr* as a mature genre of scholarship; it had evolved into an academic discourse which, like every academic discourse, was based on rules that could not simply be ignored if one was to be taken seriously.

Besides listing hermeneutical topics and tools, most Qur'anic commentators also engage in broader hermeneutical discourses. These include, for example, discussions of the differences between *tafsīr* and *taʾwīl* and their merits and disadvantages. These are somewhat related to the questions raised by Q. 3:7 that divides the verses of the Qur'an into those that are *muḥkam* ('clear, unambiguous') and those that are *mutashābih* ('unclear, ambiguous, problematic') (Wild 2003; Thaver 2016). Another fundamental hermeneutical discourse concerns the distinction between an exegesis based on authentic, reliable traditions and one based on the exegete's own reasoning. The way exegetes situate themselves in such exegetical discourses—most commonly by claiming to follow a middle path between extremes—is noteworthy, but not necessarily an indicator of their exegetical practice. This is especially true for the dichotomy between exegesis based on tradition and exegesis based on reason which will be discussed in the section 'Tafsīr as a "Genealogical Tradition"'.

Beyond a basic set of common elements, both the self-stated and the implicit aims of exegetes vary, and their hermeneutics vary accordingly. What they are trying to achieve almost always goes beyond a text-centric explanation of the meaning of verses. Exegetical interests may include, for example, the defence of a doctrinal position (Bauer 2013b: 47f.; Shah 2013: 113f.), the uncovering of a deeper layer of meaning (Saleh 2004: 97), the interpretation of the Qur'an in the light of other fields of knowledge (Calder 1993), the affirmation of the Qur'an's exalted status (Fudge 2011: 144) or the piety involved in the very act of exegesis (Elias 2010).

While exegetes thus pursue individual aims and follow an individual self-stated or implicit hermeneutical approach, the genre of *tafsīr* provides boundaries that most are careful not to cross. Some of these will be explored in the following sections.

TAFSĪR AS A 'GENEALOGICAL TRADITION'

In terms of genre constraints, the most noticeable hermeneutical principle that an exegete was obliged to adhere to, at least to a certain extent, if he wanted his work to be taken seriously as part of the *tafsīr* genre, was the engagement with the interpretive tradition from the formative period up to his own time. 'The nature of the commentary necessitated and perpetuated the ongoing interaction with the earlier work in the field' (Fudge 2011: 145).

Thus, it was not sufficient for an exegete to read the Qur'an on its own terms, according to his own ideas or in the light of other fields of scholarship, but he had to take into account the sum of previous interpretations (Calder 1993). He could, of course, make a conscious selection, criticize or reject some interpretations, and ignore others. If his commentary was—to follow the distinction made by Walid Saleh (2004: 16)—a short and concise madrasa-style one, the author would usually offer a digest of previous exegetical debates, only referring to that opinion or those few opinions that he deemed plausible. But he could not act as if the tradition did not exist if he wanted his work to be accepted as part of the genre (see Saleh 2004: 101).

Thus, regardless of differences in their hermeneutical approach, the sources that Qur'anic commentators refer to remain fairly consistent. Interpretations are related on the authority of a specific group of persons deemed to be knowledgeable in and relevant for the field of Qur'anic studies. This group expands with every new Qur'an commentary, but older authorities do not fade into the background or disappear. It is usually not the sources, but what exegetes do with the sources that distinguishes them from each other (Bauer 2013b: 40).

For a long time, the pervasive assessment of this aspect of *tafsīr* has been negative. The genre was considered to be repetitive, even 'sclerotic' (Gilliot 2001: 189; Saleh 2004: 15 n. 26). Calder (1993), on the other hand, has drawn attention to the often creative methods that exegetes employ in dealing with earlier authorities' interpretations. The exegetical tradition did exercise 'a strong and constraining influence' (El Cheikh 2004: 210) on the works of exegetes, but it did not predetermine their results or inhibit the development of an individual hermeneutical outlook. Indeed, by engaging with the tradition of *tafsīr*, scholars could actively establish their own authority over that of earlier exegetes by pointing to the latters' shortcomings with respect to methodology or knowledge. Far from allowing previous interpretations to determine their exegesis, they implicitly or explicitly aimed at determining the validity of previous interpretations by measuring them against the Qur'an, the Sunna, and—potentially—other criteria (see e.g. Jaffer 2013; Pink 2014).

One extremely important result of this type of interaction with earlier authorities is the 'anthological nature' (Saleh 2004) of most works of *tafsīr*. Demonstrating one's mastery of the multitude of previous interpretations was essential, while stating a preference for one of these interpretations was optional; 'process... [was] much more important than conclusion' (Fudge 2011: 146). The hermeneutics of *tafsīr* were based on a polyvalent reading of the text (Calder 1993), which was not necessarily, but often a result of the citation of named authorities (Saleh 2004: 152). The multitude of potential meanings could be restricted, but it was not fundamentally questioned. Even the firmly monovalent concise *madrasa*-style commentaries are ultimately based on the sum of the anthological *tafsīr* tradition and serve as introductions to it, rather than replacement for it (Calder 1993: 104). Thus, the object of Qur'anic hermeneutics is not merely to understand the text of the Qur'an, but also to make sense of the entirety of its previous interpretations.

The ultimate authority, of course, would be the Prophet Muḥammad, which made hadith an especially important source of exegesis.

The Role of Hadith

Rejecting hadith as a source of exegesis was not an option any longer in the classical period of Qur'anic exegesis. The degree to which it was incorporated into individual works of *tafsīr* and the authority it possessed in relation to other methods and sources, however, vary greatly.

Like other branches of religious scholarship, *tafsīr* was caught up in debates about the legitimacy of exegetical methods that are not based on tradition. The tendency in recent scholarship is to exercise great caution with respect to the adoption of the assumptions underlying these debates. Specifically, the construction of a dichotomy between exegesis based on sound traditions and exegesis based on arbitrary, personal reasoning has been shown to be of a very ideological nature. It has its uses in exegetes' self-descriptions and in their polemics against other exegetes, but tells us little about their actual hermeneutics; moreover, its construction as the defining element of hermeneutical tension—a battle between *al-tafsīr bi'l-raʾy* and *al-tafsīr bi'l-maʾthūr*—is largely a twentieth-century phenomenon (Saleh 2010a). The possibility of writing a Qur'anic commentary that is truly based on no other source but hadith has been explored by al-Suyūṭī (d. 911/1505) in his *al-Durr al-manthūr*; this work also shows the limits of such an enterprise and demonstrates that most of the exegetes who advocate a purely tradition-based *tafsīr* or who have been labelled by others as proponents of a *tafsīr bi'l-ma'thūr* do, in actual fact, use a repertoire of methods beyond the selection and quotation of hadith material (see e.g. Shah 2013: 115). Thus, rather than trying to determine whether an exegete follows a traditionalist agenda or not, it seems more fruitful to ask what role, if any, hadith plays in his work.

The question of the exegetical functions of hadith sparked an ongoing scholarly debate on the evolution of the genre of *tafsīr* and on the question whether markedly traditionalist hermeneutical models—models that based their Qur'anic hermeneutics exclusively on hadith and traditions going back to the first generations of Muslims—existed in the core or on the margins of the genre, whether they were exceptional and isolated phenomena or an organic part of the genre's development. A case in point are the divergent views of Ibn Kathīr's Qur'anic commentary, which is usually taken to be a staunchly traditionalist work. McAuliffe (1991) stresses the fact that Ibn Kathīr, though firmly relying on hadith, also takes into consideration non-prophetic exegetical authorities and non-Muslim sources; she considers his hermeneutics consistent, his exegesis original and independent, and she seems to situate him in the mainstream of the *tafsīr* tradition. Calder (1993), conversely, regards Ibn Kathīr's exegesis as narrowly dogmatic and disinterested in both polyvalent readings and hermeneutical frameworks other than hadith studies; his analysis evokes the impression that Ibn Kathīr set off a paradigm shift in *tafsīr*. Adding to the debate from the angle of intellectual history, Saleh (2010a) contends that Ibn Kathīr's hadith-centred approach has always been a marginal phenomenon in the history of *tafsīr* until it received support from Saudi Arabia and other Salafī circles in the twentieth century. This controversy is important because it highlights some general features of *tafsīr* studies that have consequences for our understanding of Qur'anic hermeneutics. First, especially in comparative studies of large Qur'anic commentaries, the amount of material that the analysis is based on is by necessity limited. It cannot be taken for granted, however, that exegetes use a uniform methodology and that their commentary on specific verses reliably reflects their overall approach. Their methodology might have changed over time, creating differences between their treatment of the first and the last suras, or it might differ according to the type of Qur'anic material they comment upon. This may lead researchers to come to divergent conclusions on the same exegete, depending on whether they focus on his treatment of narrative, legal, or exhortational segments in the Qur'an. Second, different disciplinary perspectives—religious studies, literary studies, intellectual history—are involved in *tafsīr* studies; for an appropriate and holistic understanding of classical hermeneutics, they all have to be taken into consideration.

What certainly stands out in Ibn Kathīr's *tafsīr* work in comparison to others of the genre is the strong emphasis he places on the authenticity of the hadiths he uses. Generally, hadith criticism did not play an important role in Qur'anic exegesis, certainly a much lesser one than in law (Fudge 2006: 119–24). In this context, an interesting phenomenon that is only beginning to receive scholarly attention is the fact that from a relatively early time onward, *tafsīr* seems to have established a genre-specific corpus of exegetical hadiths that were typically quoted in Qur'anic commentaries while other readily available traditions, for example in hadith collections, were ignored. Conversely, most exegetes readily quoted hadiths that were considered questionable by hadith scholars, even if the same exegetes were clearly experts in hadith scholarship (Jaffer 2013; Tottoli 2013; Tottoli 2014). On a more general level, this fact points to an at least partial boundary between *tafsīr* and other genres of scholarship that has as yet only partly been explored.

One particular aspect of this issue is the way in which many exegetes used traditions going back to non-Muslims fairly uncritically, but also fairly unsystematically. The polemical use of the term *isrāʾīliyyāt* to denote unreliable traditions of Jewish or Christian origin, with the aim of preventing the use of such traditions, probably goes back to Ibn Taymiyya (d. 728/1328) and only became a widespread phenomenon in the nineteenth (Tottoli 1999), or possibly the eighteenth century. Conversely, the systematic use of the Bible as a source of exegesis was just as exceptional a phenomenon (Saleh 2008; Mirza 2017) as the dogmatic rejection of the so-called *isrāʾīliyyāt*.

Exegesis and The Defence of Dogma

The degree to which dogma—whether it be Ashʿarī, Shīʿī, Muʿtazilī, or traditionalist—influenced specific exegetes has long been at the focus of studies of *tafsīr*; arguably, this focus has hindered, rather than helped, a proper understanding of the exegetes' hermeneutical concerns. It has led to a neglect of the exegetes' aims and methods in the study of the text; it has also led many scholars to overlook the importance of intellectual discourses related to non-doctrinal matters such as language or rhetoric, which could be just as bitterly and polemically contested as theology (cf. Naguib 2013). For example, Goldziher's (1920) description according to which the entire exegetical field after al-Ṭabarī, who is taken to be the last representative of 'traditional exegesis', is committed to 'dogmatic' exegesis, especially related to either the defence or the rejection of Muʿtazilī doctrines, has largely been called into question by more recent scholarship. His description does not take into consideration the degree to which supposedly traditionalist exegetes like al-Ṭabarī—or, more generally, mainstream Sunnī scholars—were, in fact, relying on a dogmatic framework (Shah 2013); likewise, it does not take into account the important non-dogmatic concerns of 'post-traditional' exegetes, which were often the same regardless of whether they were Sunnī or Shīʿī, pro- or anti-Muʿtazila (Bauer 2013a: 13). A very good example of this is al-Zamakhsharī's (d. 538/1144) *al-Kashshāf* which has long been considered to be an exclusively Muʿtazilī Qur'an commentary. Contemporary scholarship, however, highlights the multitude of sources it uses, including hadith, and the emphasis it places on philology, which accounts for the *Kashshāf*s popularity throughout the pre-modern period (Lane 2006).

That said, dogma is clearly an important factor in hermeneutics, and the *Kashshāf* is a case in point. Instead of considering religious doctrines the sole driving force behind most mainstream exegetes' Qur'an interpretations, recent studies suggest they rather functioned as a framework that determined the limits of what was possible but not to the point where the results would have been entirely predetermined and predictable. Doctrinal commitments did not preclude independent reasoning (Shah 2013: 114–15); neither did they preclude an engagement with intellectual debates upon which religious doctrines had no bearing. Dogma could be important in setting boundaries to the multitude of possible interpretations that a purely text-immanent, linguistic approach would allow for (Saleh 2004: 98). Seeking 'confirmation of and support for, [*sic*] a community's current opinion' in the Qur'an was an important aspect of exegetical activity, often outweighing the search for a mere explanation of the Qur'anic text (Fudge 2011: 144). Nevertheless, few exegetes went to the extreme of making it their supreme purpose to search the Qur'an for support for their dogmatic agenda. The rule was for exegetes to use religious dogma as a guideline that helped them determine, among the range of plausible interpretations identified by other hermeneutical tools, those that were doctrinally acceptable (Fudge 2011: 147).

Bauer suggests that 'at its essence, *tafsīr* is each scholar's... attempt to relate his intellectual, political and social contexts to the Qur'an's text.... It is a genre that creates and imposes meaning on the Qur'an; it is also a genre that takes meaning from the text of the Qur'an, expanding it with all the methods at an exegete's disposal' (2013a: 8). Thus, there is a dialectical relationship between the Qur'anic text and an exegete's extra-Qur'anic worldview, dogmatic or otherwise; just as dogmatic considerations set boundaries to the range of possibly valid interpretations, the Qur'anic text sets boundaries to the extent to which an exegete may plausibly impose dogmatic interpretations onto the text.

Philology

One of the main hermeneutical tools, possibly the most important one, was the study of language (Fudge 2011: 145). By the fourth/tenth century, philology had developed into a fully-fledged discipline of scholarship. The use of the techniques it offered posed its own problems, however; it was bound to clash with pre-existing interpretations that were tradition-based, narrative, doctrinal, or all of those. By the onset of the classical period, the exegetical tradition was too strong to be discarded, but at the same time, philology was considered too important a discipline to be ignored. In some cases, this resulted in a conflict between the claim of performing a philologically sound analysis of the 'literal meaning' of the text and the dogmatic framework in which that analysis was taking place (Saleh 2004: 98). Exegetes had to find solutions for this dilemma. One such solution was a case-by-case approach where they would weigh the interpretive tradition against the philological approach with respect to each individual verse or exegetical problem, sometimes giving preference to tradition, sometimes to philology (Saleh 2004: 132). Sometimes the solution lay in extensive discussions of the formal aspects of language while neglecting its semantic dimension (Fudge 2011: 146). Philology was often treated as an end in itself; in the course of the fourth/tenth century, discussions of lexicography, morphology, and etymology became part of the craft of commentary, whether they had any bearing on the Qur'anic meaning or not (Saleh 2004: 132–4).

At the same time, philology is instrumental in bridging the disjuncture between the Qur'anic text itself and the tradition of its interpretation that had occurred by the advent of the classical period. It was language that served to preserve the connection between *tafsīr* and the Qur'anic text despite the exegetes' involvement with larger religious and intellectual debates (Bauer 2013a: 8). The interest in language was also one of the main themes that connected exegetes across ideological, dogmatic, or denominational fault lines although debates on language and rhetoric could create fault lines of their own (Naguib 2013).

Qur'anic Hermeneutics and other Fields of Scholarship

As the Qur'an was elevated to a central position in the Islamic system of scholarship and learning, it was natural for its exegesis to become part of other branches of scholarship—besides philology—which, in turn, led to the incorporation of those other disciplines into Qur'anic commentaries. The specific dynamics, the interaction and boundaries between *tafsīr* and other genres, especially with respect to their hermeneutical implications, have as yet only partially been explored, as has already been shown with respect to hadith. The disciplines of scholarship certainly belong to the instrumental structures against which, according to Calder (1993), the Qur'an is measured by exegetes; but more detailed case studies are needed to theorize the extent and nature of the interaction between Qur'anic exegesis and other fields of knowledge.

One such study shows how Fakhr al-Dīn al-Rāzī (d. 606/1210) imported a whole system of enquiry from philosophy to *kalām* and from there to Qur'anic exegesis, offering a fresh analytical structure that allowed him to organize existing exegetical knowledge, systematically deriving from the text new exegetical questions and new possible interpretations, and to expand on these using philosophical methods (Jaffer 2013). This approach exposed al-Rāzī to criticism for having too heavily imposed his extra-Qur'anic concerns upon the text, but that hardly detracted from the immense popularity of his commentary.

Law was another discipline that was of great importance to the exegesis of the Qur'an, and legal discourses often informed exegetes' treatment of the legal content of the Qur'an. Nevertheless, detailed case studies show that, while there is interaction, there is no real overlap between the genres of *tafsīr* and law. Exegetes may reproduce legal debates in their works of *tafsīr*, but they may just as well choose to ignore legal terminology and debates in their interpretation of verses that are usually taken to contain clear legal rulings; their choice does not necessarily have any bearing on the acceptance of their *tafsīr*. Obviously, in the classical period, law and Qur'anic commentary were separate, if interconnected, genres (Sauer 2014).

One product of the interaction between law and Qur'anic exegesis was the doctrine of *naskh* (abrogation), which brought forth its own genre of Qur'anic scholarship. In a similar way, the *tafsīr* tradition generated a number of other genres which remained part of Qur'anic commentaries, but also existed as a distinct type of scholarship. The ongoing interaction between works of *tafsīr* and these emerging subgenres became an integral part of Qur'anic hermeneutics.

Of particular importance, in this respect, was the *asbāb al-nuzūl* literature. Exegetes used it in order to create a historical context for specific verses which would allow them to explain their meaning. The historical context provided by the *asbāb al-nuzūl* could assume various functions—narrative, philological, legal—and could, accordingly, yield various results, but it was an indispensable part of exegesis in any case (Rippin 1988; Rippin 2013).

Piety and the Sanctity of the Qur'an

For many exegetes, the interpretation of the Qur'an was not just a scholarly, but also a religious endeavour. In a study of the Sufi exegete al-Simnānī (d. 736/1336), Elias (2010: 52) comes to the conclusion that for al-Simnānī, writing a *tafsīr* was first and foremost an act of piety, rather than a way to explain his religious ideas. He raises the question whether this is a factor in the composition of *tafsīr* works in general and whether this has any bearing on the treatment of the genre.

One hermeneutical implication of conceptualizing *tafsīr* as a pious activity might be that the process of exegesis becomes more important than the actual result. This assumption is underscored by the presence of elements, in many Qur'anic commentaries, that have a primarily devotional function. One such element is the merit-of-sura preamble introduced by al-Thaʿlābī and adopted by many later exegetes (Saleh 2004: 103–8); trying to understand their function as interpretive in a narrow sense would be pointless. Beyond those preambles, Saleh shows to what extent al-Thaʿlabī's exegesis is guided by the notion of the salvific nature of the Qur'an (Saleh 2004: 108) and by the intention to admonish and exhort the believers (Saleh 2004: 167). The same has been demonstrated by Burge for al-Suyūṭī's use of merit-of-sura (or merit-of-verse) traditions (Burge 2013: 291–5).

In the classical period, the doctrine of the inimitability and perfection of the Qur'an (*iʿjāz al-Qurʾān*) was firmly established, which had marked consequences for the commentary tradition. It was inconceivable, for example, that the historical predictions made in the Qur'an had not come true (El Cheikh 2004). It was just as inconceivable that the Qur'an's grammar was incorrect; in the places where it did not seem to fit the system created by the grammarians, many exegetes felt a need to defend the Qur'an against what they saw as attacks on its integrity and perfection. *Tafsīr* can thus be understood as an attempt to make the scripture immune to criticism. The polyvalent reading of the Qur'an might be one of the strategies used to achieve this, for the sum of possible interpretations is more difficult to discard than a specific one (Fudge 2011: 144–5). The assumption of the Qur'an's perfection as a guiding principle might, hermeneutically, often necessitate the adaptation and even critique of discourses imported from other fields of knowledge, in which the integrity of the Qur'an is not as paramount as in *tafsīr*. For many Qur'anic commentators, the question in what way a particular verse manifests the Qur'an's rhetorical power and beauty was an integral part of exegesis (McAuliffe 2003b: 317).

New Directions in the Study of Applied Hermeneutics

Current *tafsīr* scholarship increasingly strives to comprehend the hermeneutical preoccupations of classical exegetes on their own terms and to identify the questions that preoccupied them (McAuliffe 2003b: 316–17), rather than looking for answers to the questions modern scholars might ask. At the same time, it is important to move beyond the categories that pre-modern exegetes explicitly used because that would pose the risk of being caught up in analytically fruitless debates or staying on the level of theoretical hermeneutical considerations which have little bearing on actual exegetical practice; in the worst case, it would mean falling prey to ideological claims such as the ones involved in the dichotomy between *tafsīr bi'l-raʾy* and *tafsīr bi'l-maʾthūr*. For example, the debate around the *muḥkamāt* and *mutashābihāt* is widely discussed in introductions to Qur'anic commentaries and other hermeneutical treatises (Kinberg 1988), but many exegetes hardly ever transfer this debate to their commentary on specific verses.

Bauer (2013a: 12) proposes to analyse the exegetes' use of particular terminology as a node for the study of *tafsīr*. One example for this would be the term *ẓāhir*, which is a complex notion referring roughly to the outward, obvious meaning of the text. While it is not very useful as an analytical category, since what one exegete considers *ẓāhir* might be considered implausible by others, the study of the use and function of the term in particular Qur'anic commentaries can offer new insights (Zamah 2013). Other technical terms that would merit a closer comparative analysis are the opposites *ʿāmm* and *khāṣṣ*, which differentiate between the specific reference a Qur'anic verse makes and its general applicability. Just like with the term *ẓāhir*, the interest would be in the function of this concept for particular exegetes' hermeneutics.

The End of Classical Qur'anic Hermeneutics?

It has already been mentioned that it is difficult to define the time in which the 'classical' period of Qur'anic hermeneutics ended. This is partly due to the fact that there is very little research, so far, on Qur'anic exegesis between the eighth/fourteenth and thirteenth/nineteenth centuries, based on the assumption that the scholarly output in that period was repetitive and unoriginal (Naguib 2013: 2). However, recent research suggests that new hermeneutical developments occurred in this period, which might therefore be labelled 'post-classical'. Notably, it witnessed the emergence and growth of a strong supercommentary tradition that has barely been studied so far (Saleh 2013).

Furthermore, starting in the eighth/fourteenth century, the exegetical genre seems to have taken new directions in the attempt to solve the dilemma between religious dogma and philology. One such direction was the methodology proposed by Ibn Taymiyya (d. 728/1328) and adopted by Ibn Kathīr (d. 774/1373), which ultimately resulted in the dismissal of philology in favour of hadith and of the doctrines of Sunnī traditionalism (Saleh 2010b). A different strand of the scripturalist tradition, represented by al-Shawkānī (d. 1250/1834), shares Ibn Taymiyya's mistrust of philosophy, scholastic theology, *isrāʾīliyyāt*, and 'heretical' opinions, but places more emphasis on the 'literal meaning' of the Qur'an, frequently elevating it above dogmatic considerations (Pink 2014).

An entirely different direction is represented by the eminent, yet little-studied Qur'anic commentary of Abū'l-Suʿūd (d. 982/1574), which emphasizes and theorizes the Qur'anic rhetoric while other disciplines fade into the background. A notable feature in this type of post-classical commentary is the near absence of named authorities; the interpretations of preceding exegetes are synthesized in a way that underlines the autonomy and dominance of the commentary's author vis-à-vis the diachronic exegetical community (Naguib 2013: 44–5), but might also reflect the degree to which the *tafsīr* tradition had developed a canon of exegetical opinions that was taken to be known and accepted.

An idea that was increasingly pursued by individual exegetes from the seventh/thirteenth century onwards was the search for a thematic connection between the verses of the Qur'an and for unifying principles structuring the suras, although that idea did not reach prominence until modern times (Mir 1993: 211–12).

In the second half of the thirteenth/nineteenth century, radically new modes of exegesis and hermeneutical paradigms entered the domain of Qur'anic exegesis. At the same time, the classical hermeneutical tradition has persisted until the present day. Classical Qur'anic hermeneutics are therefore of far more than merely historical interest; they very much inform contemporary Muslim scholarship.

Bibliography

Secondary Sources

Bauer, Karen. 'Introduction'. In: Karen Bauer (eds.). *Aims, Methods and Contexts of Qur'anic Exegesis (2nd/8th–9th/15th C.)*, pp. 1–16. Oxford: Oxford University Press, 2013a.

Bauer, Karen. 'Justifying the Genre: A Study of Introductions to Classical Works of *Tafsīr*'. In: Karen Bauer (eds.). *Aims, Methods and Contexts of Qur'anic Exegesis (2nd/8th–9th/15th C.)*, pp. 39–65. Oxford: Oxford University Press, 2013b.

Burge, S. R. 'Jalāl al-Dīn al-Suyūṭī, the *Muʾawwidhatān* and the Modes of Exegesis'. In: Karen Bauer (eds.). *Aims, Methods and Contexts of Qurʾanic Exegesis (2nd/8th–9th/15th C.)*, pp. 277–306. Oxford: Oxford University Press, 2013.

Calder, Norman. 'Tafsīr from Ṭabarī to Ibn Kathīr: Problems in the Description of a Genre, Illustrated with Reference to the Story of Abraham'. In: G. R. Hawting and A. Sharif Abdul-Kader (eds.). *Approaches to the Qur'ān*, pp. 211–24. London: Routledge, 1993.
al-Dhahabī, Muḥammad. *Al-Tafsīr wa'l-mufassirūn*. Cairo: Dār al-Kutub al-Ḥadītha, 1961.
El Cheikh, Nadia Maria. '*Sūrat Al-Rūm*: A Study of the Exegetical Literature'. In: Colin Turner (ed.). *The Koran: Critical Concepts in Islamic Studies*, pp. 210–24. London: RoutledgeCurzon, 2004.
Elias, Jamal J. 'Ṣūfī *tafsīr* Reconsidered: Exploring the Development of a Genre', *Journal of Qur'anic Studies* 12/1–2 (2010), 41–55.
Forster, Regula. *Methoden mittelalterlicher arabischer Qur'ānexegese am Beispiel von Q 53, 1–18*. Berlin: Klaus Schwarz, 2001.
Fudge, Bruce. 'Qurʾānic Exegesis in Medieval Islam and Modern Orientalism', *Welt Des Islams* 46/2 (2006), 115–47.
Fudge, Bruce. *Qurʾānic Hermeneutics: Al-Ṭabrisī and the Craft of Commentary*. London: Routledge, 2011.
Gilliot, Claude. 'Évolution ou sclérose de la tradition'. In: Jean-Claude Garcin (ed.). *États, sociétés et cultures du monde musulman medieval. Xe–XVe siècle*, 3:183–94. Paris: Presses universitaires de France, 2001.
Goldziher, Ignác. *Die Richtungen der islamischen Koranauslegung*. Leiden: Brill, 1920.
Jaffer, Tariq. 'Fakhr al-Dīn al-Rāzī's System of Inquiry'. In: Karen Bauer (ed.). *Aims, Methods and Contexts of Qurʾanic Exegesis (2nd/8th–9th/15th C.)*, pp. 241–61. Oxford: Oxford University Press, 2013.
Kinberg, Leah. '*Muḥkamāt* and *Mutashābihāt* (Koran 3/7): Implication of a Koranic Pair of Terms in Medieval Exegesis', *Arabica* 35/2 (1988), 143–72.
Lane, Andrew J. *A Traditional Muʿtazilite Qurʾān Commentary: The Kashshāf of Jār Allāh al-Zamakhsharī*. Leiden: Brill, 2006.
McAuliffe, Jane Dammen. *Qurʾānic Christians: An Analysis of Classical and Modern Exegesis*. Cambridge: Cambridge University Press, 1991.
McAuliffe, Jane Dammen. 'The Genre Boundaries of Qur'ānic Commentary'. In: Jane Dammen McAuliffe, Barry D. Walfish, and Joseph W. Goering (eds.). *With Reverence for the Word: Medieval Scriptural Exegesis in Judaism, Christianity, and Islam*, pp. 445–61. Oxford: Oxford University Press, 2003a.
McAuliffe, Jane Dammen. 'An Introduction to Medieval Interpretation of the Qur'ān'. In: Jane Dammen McAuliffe, Barry D. Walfish, and Joseph W. Goering (eds.). *With Reverence for the Word: Medieval Scriptural Exegesis in Judaism, Christianity, and Islam*, pp. 311–19. Oxford: Oxford University Press, 2003b.
Mir, Mustansir. 'The *Sūra* as a Unity: A Twentieth-Century Development in Qur'ān Exegesis'. In: G. R. Hawting and A. Sharif Abdul-Kader (eds.). *Approaches to the Qurʾān*. London and New York: Routledge, 1993.
Mirza, Younus. 'Ibn Taymiyya as Exegete. Moses' Father-in law and the Messengers in *Sūrat Yā Sīn*', *Journal of Qur'anic Studies* 19 (2017), 39–71.
Naguib, Shuruq. 'Guiding the Sound Mind: Ebu's-Suʿūd's *Tafsir* and Rhetorical Interpretation of the Qurʾān in the Post-Classical Period', *Journal of Ottoman Studies* 27 (2013), 1–52.
Pink, Johanna. 'Where Does Modernity Begin? Muḥammad al-Shawkānī and the Tradition of *tafsīr*'. In: Andreas Görke and Johanna Pink (eds.). *Tafsīr and Islamic Intellectual History: Exploring the Boundaries of a Genre*. Oxford: Oxford University Press, 2014.

Rippin, Andrew. 'The Function of "*Asbāb al-Nuzūl*" in Qur'ānic Exegesis', *Bulletin of the School of Oriental and African Studies* 51/1 (1988), 1–20.
Rippin, Andrew. 'The Construction of the Arabian Historical Context in Muslim Interpretation of the Qur'ān'. In: Karen Bauer (ed.). *Aims, Methods and Contexts of Qur'anic Exegesis (2nd/8th–9th/15th C.)*, pp. 173–98. Oxford: Oxford University Press, 2013.
Saleh, Walid A. *The Formation of the Classical Tafsīr Tradition: The Qur'ān Commentary of al-Thaʿlabī (d. 427/1035)*. Leiden: Brill, 2004.
Saleh, Walid A. 'A Fifteenth-Century Muslim Hebraist: Al-Biqāʿī and his Defense of Using the Bible to Interpret the Qur'ān', *Speculum* 83/3(2008), 629–54.
Saleh, Walid A. 'Preliminary Remarks on the Historiography of *tafsīr* in Arabic: A History of the Book Approach', *Journal of Qur'anic Studies* 12 (2010a), 6–40.
Saleh, Walid A. 'Ibn Taymiyya and the Rise of Radical Hermeneutics: An Analysis of *An Introduction to the Foundations of Qur'ānic Exegesis*'. In: Yossef Rapoport and Shahab Ahmed (eds.). *Ibn Taymiyya and his Times*, pp. 123–62. Oxford: Oxford University Press, 2010b.
Saleh, Walid A. 'The Gloss as Intellectual History: The *ḥāshiyahs* on *al-Kashshāf*, *Oriens* 41 (2013), 217–59.
Sauer, Rebecca. '*Tafsīr* between Law and Exegesis: The Case of Q. 49:9'. In: Andreas Görke and Johanna Pink (eds.). *Tafsīr and Islamic Intellectual History: Exploring the Boundaries of a Genre*. Oxford: Oxford University Press, 2014.
Shah, Mustafa. 'Al-Ṭabarī and the Dynamics of *tafsīr*: Theological Dimensions of a Legacy', *Journal of Qur'anic Studies* 15/2 (2013), 83–139.
Thaver, Tehseen. 'Encountering Ambiguity: Muʿtazilī and Twelver Shīʿī Approaches to the Qur'an's Ambiguous Verses', *Journal of Qur'anic Studies* 18 (2016), 91–115.
Tottoli, Roberto. 'Origin and Use of the Term *Isrā'īliyyāt* in Muslim Literature', *Arabica* 46/2 (1999), 193–210.
Tottoli, Roberto. 'Methods and Contexts in the Use of Ḥadīths in Classical *tafsīr* Literature: The Exegesis of Q. 21:85 and Q. 17:1'. In: Karen Bauer (ed.). *Aims, Methods and Contexts of Qur'anic Exegesis (2nd/8th–9th/15th C.)*, pp. 199–215. Oxford: Oxford University Press, 2013.
Tottoli, Roberto. 'Interrelations and Boundaries between *tafsīr* and *Ḥadīth* Literature: The Exegesis of Mālik B. Anas' *Muwaṭṭa'* and Classical Qur'ānic Commentaries'. In: Andreas Görke and Johanna Pink (eds.). *Tafsīr and Islamic Intellectual History: Exploring the Boundaries of a Genre*. Oxford: Oxford University Press, 2014.
Wild, Stefan. 'The Self-Referentiality of the Qur'ān. Sura 3:7 as an Exegetical Challenge'. In: Jane Dammen McAuliffe, Barry D. Walfish, and Joseph W. Goering (eds.). *With Reverence for the Word: Medieval Scriptural Exegesis in Judaism, Christianity, and Islam*, pp. 422–35. Oxford: Oxford University Press, 2003.
Zamah, Ludmila. 'Master of the Obvious: Understanding *ẓāhir* Interpretations in Qur'ānic Exegesis'. In: Karen Bauer (ed.). *Aims, Methods and Contexts of Qur'anic Exegesis (2nd/8th–9th/15th C.)*, pp. 263–76. Oxford: Oxford University Press, 2013.

CHAPTER 56

SUNNĪ HERMENEUTICAL LITERATURE

MARTIN NGUYEN

The Sunnī tradition has developed an array of strategies for interpreting the Qur'an, which in turn has been discussed and refined across a number of genres of hermeneutical literature. In his examination of Muslim principles of exegesis, Wansbrough delineates twelve procedural devices used by the exegetes: '1) *Variae lectiones.* 2) Poetic *loci probantes.* 3) Lexical explanation. 4) Grammatical explanation. 5) Rhetorical explanation. 6) Periphrasis. 7) Analogy. 8) Abrogation. 9) Circumstances of revelation. 10) Identification. 11) Prophetic tradition. 12) Anecdote' (1977: 121). These interpretive tools were derived from his analysis of a broad swath of the Muslim hermeneutical literature. Hadith collections frequently contained transmitted reports in which the Prophet Muḥammad explained the meaning of a verse. Sections consisting exclusively of exegetical prophetic reports are included in the *Ṣaḥīḥ* hadith collections of al-Bukhārī (d. 256/870) and Muslim (d. 261/875) and al-Tirmidhī's (d. 279/892) *al-Jāmiʿ al-ṣaḥīḥ*. The elliptical prophetic narratives in the Qur'an were also elaborated upon in the *qiṣaṣ al-anbiyāʾ* literature. The foremost genre, however, at least in terms of proliferation, is undoubtedly *tafsīr* or exegetical commentaries of the Qur'an. These commentaries largely proceed through scripture on a verse-by-verse basis and employ a variety of exegetical techniques. Classic Sunnī exemplars of *tafsīr* include the encyclopaedic commentaries of al-Ṭabarī (d. 310/923), *Jāmiʿ al-bayān ʿan taʾwīl ayy al-Qurʾān*, and al-Thaʿlabī (d. 427/1035), *al-Kashf waʾl-bayān ʿan tafsīr al-Qurʾān*. Wansbrough begins his study by closely analysing one of the earliest extant commentaries, the *tafsīr* attributed to Muqātil ibn Sulaymān (d. 150/767). The wide-ranging and voluminous *tafsīr* genre, however, is extensively explored elsewhere in this collection.

The present study instead focuses on the complementary field or, by some measures, the wider, encompassing field of *ʿulūm al-Qurʾān*, literally the 'sciences of the Qur'an.' As with the *tafsīr* genre, classic *ʿulūm al-Qurʾān* texts also emerged, though relatively late in comparison. The two most prominent examples are undoubtedly *al-Burhān fī ʿulūm al-Qurʾān* by al-Zarkashī (d. 794/1392) and *al-Itqān fī ʿulūm al-Qurʾān* by al-Suyūṭī (d. 911/1505) (other contributions to the genre are enumerated at the end of the section 'Disciplinary Diversity within *ʿUlūm al-Qurʾān*'). While earlier *ʿulūm al-Qurʾān* texts preceded these, none appears to have attained and sustained the curricular prominence that these two works eventually achieved.

Disciplinary Diversity Within ʿUlūm al-*Qurʾān*

The field of *ʿulūm al-Qurʾān* is exceedingly diverse since it comprises a large number of sub-disciplines, many of which developed their own sub-genre of literature. Two of the works mentioned above, *al-Kashf wa'l-bayān* and *al-Itqān fī ʿulūm al-Qurʾān*, provide further insight into the disciplinary diversity involved in Sunnī traditions of Qur'anic exegesis. Both al-Thaʿlabī and al-Suyūṭī enumerate the many exegetical sources available to them in the introductions to their respective works. Al-Thaʿlabī's introduction to *al-Kashf wa'l-bayān* has been edited and published separately from the main commentary twice (Goldfeld ed. 1984; al-ʿAnazī ed. 2008). In it, the author lists not only the titles of the works with which he was familiar, but also details the manner by which he came to know the various works, typically with a chain of transmission, as a means of foregrounding his commentary's exegetical authoritativeness. The titles are further grouped by genre. Al-Thaʿlabī begins with older *tafsīr* works, which are linked to notable personages from the earliest generations of the Muslim community, before describing the compositions of his contemporaries (*muṣannafāt ahl al-ʿaṣr*). This latter section also begins with *tafsīr* works but then switches to more specialized texts. These include treatises on Qur'anic homonyms and synonyms (*kutub al-wujūh wa'l-naẓāʾir*), linguistic analyses, especially syntactical ones (*kutub al-maʿānī*), by grammarians, treatises on obscure and difficult passages (*kutub al-gharāʾib wa'l-mushkilāt*), compilations of variant Qur'anic recitations (*kutub al-qirāʾāt al-majmūʾāt*), and historical chronicles of the early Muslim community, namely *Kitāb al-Mubtadaʾ* by Wahb ibn Munabbih (d. 110/728 or 114/732) and *Kitāb al-Maghāzī* by Ibn Isḥāq (d. 150/767).

Five centuries later the conceived scope of hermeneutical literature had increased manifold as evidenced by al-Suyūṭī's substantially lengthier list of textual sources. He similarly begins his list with *tafsīr* works, but restricts himself to books based upon transmitted traditions (*al-kutub al-naqliyya*). Aside from a dozen *tafsīr* works, he includes under this classification treatises on merits connected with the Qur'an (*faḍāʾil al-Qurʾān*), studies on the compilation of Qur'anic codices (*al-maṣāḥif*), Qur'anic etiquette handbooks (*ḥamalat al-Qurʾān*), and Ibn Ḥajar al-ʿAsqalānī's (d. 852/1448) commentary on the hadith collection *Ṣaḥīḥ al-Bukhārī*. Al-Suyūṭī immediately mentions afterwards that he also relied on other hadith collections, which is unsurprising given the inclusion of exegetical sections in hadith collections like *Ṣaḥīḥ al-Bukhārī* and *Ṣaḥīḥ Muslim.*

Al-Suyūṭī's remaining sources are divided into more specific exegetical categories. First are books discussing variant readings of the scripture (*kutub al-qirāʾāt*). Various linguistic studies follow that include examinations of the languages and dialects appearing in the Qur'an, studies of the scripture's syntax and structure, and meticulous analyses of Qur'anic vocabulary, which focus on different aspects such as homonyms and synonyms, obscure terms, singular and plural form, Arabized words, and so on (*kutub al-lughāt wa'l-gharīb wa'l-ʿarabiyya wa'l-iʿrāb*). Next are treatises concerned with Qur'anic legal prescriptions (*aḥkām al-Qurʾān*) and then works on Qur'anic inimitability (*iʿjāz*), rhetoric (*balāgha*), and figurative expressions (*majāz*). Al-Suyūṭī then lists texts that deal with specific types of Qur'anic verses, such as seemingly equivocal ones (*mutashābihāt*) and those pertaining to divine attributes (*ṣifāt*). Books on the orthography of the Qur'an (*kutub al-rasm*) are then named. The penultimate section consists of general works of knowledge (*al-kutub al-jāmiʿa*). Al-Suyūṭī concludes the disclosure of his sources with a series of Qur'an commentaries that are notably not included at the beginning with *al-kutub al-naqliyya*. These authors include al-Wāḥidī (d. 468/1075), al-Qushayrī (d. 465/1072), Ibn Barrajān (d. 536/1141), al-Zamakhsharī (d. 538/1144), Ibn ʿAṭiyya (d. 546/1151), Ibn al-Jawzī (d. 597/1200), and Fakhr al-Dīn al-Rāzī (d. 606/1210).

As this brief survey of sources demonstrates, the Sunnī tradition of exegesis had recourse to a large number of hermeneutical techniques and approaches. Many of the genres named by al-Thaʿlabī and al-Suyūṭī notably correspond with the procedural devices derived by Wansbrough listed above. Because of the wide breadth of the hermeneutical literature that developed, exegetes could include and incorporate various forms of analytical minutiae into their interpretive frameworks. Some of the more significant sub-genres of hermeneutical literature are more closely examined in the following sections. These include abrogation (*naskh*), occasions of revelation (*asbāb al-nuzūl*), variant readings (*qirāʾāt*), lexicography, *obscuriantia* (*muskhil*), inimitability (*iʿjāz*), and recitational elocution (*tajwīd*).

Al-Thaʿlabī and al-Suyūṭī also engaged with a number of non-Sunnī sources. Among these are exegetical works composed by Muʿtazilī and Shīʿī scholars. For example, al-Thaʿlabī references the Muʿtazilī ʿAbd al-Raḥmān ibn Kaysān al-Aṣamm (d. 200–1/816–17) and al-Suyūṭī mentions the Muʿtazilī scholars al-Rummānī (d. 384/994) and al-Zamakhsharī and the Shīʿī theologian al-Sharīf al-Murtaḍā (d. 436/1044). The inclusion of this other material points to the important role played by both polemics and cross-pollination in shaping the Sunnī hermeneutical literature. Okumuş's study demonstrates Abū Ḥāmid al-Ghazālī's (d. 505/1111) hermeneutical indebtedness to Ibn Sīnā (d. 427/1037) despite the former's noted opposition to the latter's tradition of *falsafa* (2012). Similarly, Shīʿī exegesis made use of Sunnī sources as demonstrated by al-Ṭabrisī's (d. 548/1154) usage of material from al-Thaʿlabī's commentary (Mourad 2010).

An *ʿulūm al-Qurʾān* treatise by al-Thaʿlabī's teacher Abū'l-Qāsim Ibn Ḥabīb (d. 406/1016) provides another case in point. Ibn Ḥabīb's *Kitāb al-Tanbīh ʿalā faḍl ʿulūm al-Qurʾān* was composed sometime in the late fourth/tenth to early fifth/eleventh century, marking it as a relatively early *ʿulūm al-Qurʾān* work, especially when compared to the later compositions of al-Zarkashī and al-Suyūṭī (Nguyen 2018). The present significance of the *Kitāb al-Tanbīh*, however, rests with its author's scholarly identity. According to biographical records, Ibn Ḥabīb was a Karrāmī who converted to the Shāfiʿī *madhhab*. The Karrāmiyya would eventually be excised from the Sunnī fold, as the heresiographical literature demonstrates, but during this era they were deeply invested in Qur'anic scholarship (van Ess 1980; Zysow 1988; Gilliot 1999; Zadeh 2012). Unfortunately it is unclear when Ibn Ḥabīb's supposed conversion took place and how the *Kitāb al-Tanbīh* aligns with this change in affiliation. Despite the uncertainty, al-Thaʿlabī cites his teacher unhesitatingly throughout the introduction of *al-Kashf wa'l-bayān*. Ibn Ḥabīb's Karrāmī training does not appear to have been an issue for al-Thaʿlabī. Reinforcing this point, Walid Saleh has delineated a Nishapuri school of exegesis that begins with Ibn Ḥabīb, continues with al-Thaʿlabī, and ends with al-Wāḥidī (Saleh 2004: 4, 28; Saleh 2006: 225–6; Gilliot 1999; Nguyen 2012: 88; Nguyen 2018: 47–50). Four to five centuries later both al-Zarkashī and al-Suyūṭī quote Ibn Ḥabīb's *Kitāb al-Tanbīh* at considerable length. It is the first text quoted in *al-Itqān* immediately after al-Suyūṭī's introduction. Again, Ibn Ḥabīb's Karrāmī past does not appear to have been a cause for concern for any of these Sunnī scholars.

An examination of the treatise's contents further reveals the trace effects of scholarly cross-pollination. While only a fragment of the *Kitāb al-Tanbīh* survives in quotation and manuscript, it nonetheless provides an important window into early *ʿulūm al-Qurʾān* concerns. The text is primarily occupied with two matters: (1) the chronological order of the Qur'anic revelation (*tartīb al-nuzūl*) and (2) types of divine address (*mukhāṭibāt*) that appear in the scripture. There is also a section that deals with the various issues related to Meccan and Medinan verses of the Qur'an and occasions of revelation (*asbāb al-nuzūl*). But most tellingly Ibn Ḥabīb spends some time detailing the precise number of verses, words, and letters that appear for specific suras. This is a common feature of Karrāmī works of Qur'anic exegesis. Whether the *Kitāb al-Tanbīh* was written before or after the author's conversion, this Karrāmī predilection persisted and found its way into later Sunnī hermeneutical works.

Concerning compilatory *ʿulūm al-Qurʾān* texts several other important compositions were produced in the interim between Ibn Ḥabīb and the eras of al-Zarkashī and al-Suyūṭī four and five centuries later. The Ḥanbalī scholar al-Ṭūfī (d. 716/1316) composed *al-Iksīr fī ʿilm al-Qurʾān* and the Ḥanafī scholar Ibn al-Naqīb (d. 698/1298) composed *al-Fawāʾid al-mushawwiq ilā ʿulūm al-Qurʾān wa-ʿilm al-bayān*, which served as an introduction to his Qur'an commentary and has been falsely attributed to the Ḥanbalī scholar Ibn Qayyim al-Jawziyya (d. 751/1350). Although al-Suyūṭī laments the apparent dearth of *ʿulūm al-Qurʾān* works in his introduction to *al-Itqān*, he nonetheless lists those works that he was aware of prior to writing *al-Itqān*: two short, unnamed treatises by his senior contemporaries Abū ʿAbd Allāh Muḥyī al-Dīn al-Kāfījī (d. 879/1474) and Jalāl al-Dīn al-Bulqīnī (d. 824/1421), al-Zarkashī's *al-Burhān*, and al-Suyūṭī's own earlier work *al-Taḥbīr fī ʿulūm al-tafsīr*. Al-Kāfījī's treatise *Kitāb al-Taysīr fī qawāʾid ʿilm al-tafsīr* survives and is an *iṣṭilāḥāt* work that defines the technical terminology of the Sunnī *ʿulūm al-Qurʾān* tradition. Al-Suyūṭī's *al-Taḥbīr* is also extant and lists 102 kinds of *ʿulūm al-Qurʾān*. Ibn ʿAqīla al-Makkī (d. 1150/1737–8) composed the voluminous *al-Ziyāda waʾl-iḥsān fī ʿulūm al-Qurʾān*, which brings together the typologies of al-Zarkashī and al-Suyūṭī and then adds to them.

Qur'anic Arrangement and Chronology

As the *Kitāb al-Tanbīh* demonstrates, the chronological order in which the Qur'an was revealed has been a persistent concern within Sunnī hermeneutics. That the arrangement of suras does not match the Qur'an's historical unfolding has driven studies in both how the Qur'an was arranged and composed as well as chronological analyses of the Qur'anic revelation. The narratives of the Qur'an's arrangement, collection, and composition that are found in commentaries and *ʿulūm al-Qurʾān* works largely depend on earlier hadith collections and historical chronicles for their information. For example, the Mālikī traditionalist Abū Jaʿfar al-Gharnāṭī (d. 708/1308), also known as Ibn al-Zubayr, opens his work *al-Burhān fī tartīb suwar al-Qurʾān* by emphasizing the Prophet's role in setting the Qur'an's arrangement. He then proceeds through each sura to address the known circumstances of a sura's arrangement and contextual address. Contemporary Sunnī treatments have largely followed the traditional historical narrative (al-Abyārī 1982; von Denffer 2000). Several theories have appeared from revisionist historians that challenge the Sunnī narrative entirely (Crone and Cook 1977; Wansbrough 1977; Nevo and Koren 2003).

Regarding chronology, Muslim scholars have recounted numerous possibilities. Ibn Ḥabīb's list differs from others presented by al-Zarkashī and al-Suyūṭī. Ibrāhīm al-Jaʿbarī (d. 732/1333) versified his efforts to set an order by composing a twenty-one-line didactic poem called *Taqrīb al-maʾmūr fī tartīb al-nuzūl*. An earlier work entitled *Tanzīl al-Qurʾān bi-Makka waʾl-Madīna* is ascribed to the influential early scholar al-Zuhrī (d. 124/742) and is primarily a listing of the suras in their supposed order of historical appearance. The title of the work, however, also points to an important means of chronological classification that has persisted down through the hermeneutical literature, namely whether a verse is Meccan (*makkī*) or Medinan (*madanī*). What this classification means, however, varies. The Meccan-Medinan distinction may refer to (1) whether a verse was revealed before or after the *hijra*, (2) the geographic location of a verse's revelation, or (3) the audience to which a verse is addressed. Yet even this breakdown of the classification is not exhaustive.

The scope of chronological investigations went beyond merely classifying a verse as either Meccan or Medinan. Analytical considerations could be more nuanced and particularized as attested by Ibn Ḥabīb's enumeration of such concerns in his *Kitāb al-Tanbīh*:

-The order of what was revealed in Mecca in the beginning, middle, and end,
-The order of what was revealed likewise in Medina,
-What was revealed in Mecca but whose ruling is Medinan,
-What was revealed in Medina but whose ruling is Meccan,
-What was revealed in Mecca for the people of Medina,
-What was revealed in Medina for the people of Mecca,
-What resembles Medinan revelations in Meccan surahs,
-What resembles Meccan revelations in Medinan surahs,
-What was revealed in Juḥfa,
-What was revealed in Jerusalem,
-What was revealed in al-Ṭāʾif,
-What was revealed in Ḥudaybiyya,
-What was revealed at night,
-What was revealed accompanied [by angels],
-Medinan verses in Meccan surahs,
-Meccan verses in Medinan surahs,
-That which was conveyed from Mecca to Medina,
-That which was conveyed from Medina to Mecca,
-That which was conveyed from Medina to Abyssinia. (Ibn Ḥabīb 1988: 307)

By the time of al-Zarkashī and al-Suyūṭī, the discussions of verse types had expanded considerably to include other temporal, spatial, and circumstantial distinctions such as whether a verse was revealed during the night or day, in a specific season, in wakefulness or sleep, while travelling or at home, and so on.

European language scholarship has similarly made the chronology of the Qur'an a major point of discussion. Gustav Weil and Theodor Nöldeke presented a chronological framework that has seen widespread engagement within the field (Weil 1844; Nöldeke 1908–38; Watt and Bell 1970; Neuwirth 1981). The Weil-Nöldeke scheme adopts the Muslim convention of classifying verses as either Meccan or Medinan, but further subdivides the former type into the First Meccan, Second Meccan, and Third Meccan periods. Nöldeke used variances in length and style as his measure for determining the historical order of the suras. Other scholars scrutinized passages within the suras in order to trace thematic commonalities and developments (Hirschfeld 1902; Watt and Bell 1970).

Challenging many of these theories is the statistical analysis of Behnam Sadeghi (2011), whose stylometric study of the Qur'an was inspired by the earlier Persian-language work of Mahdī Bārzagān, *Sayr-i taḥawwul-i Qurʾān*, which was published from 1976 to 2007. Bārzagān established a more finely particularized seven-phase chronological schema of the Qur'an based on a quantitative analysis of stylistic features. Sadeghi affirms and modifies Barzagan's chronology through a more rigorously developed stylometric study.

Additionally Sadeghi's study argues for the stylistic continuity of the Qur'anic text and its single authorship.

Asbāb al-Nuzūl

Works of *asbāb al-nuzūl* or 'occasions of revelation' have traditionally been closely associated with those on Qur'anic chronology. *Asbāb al-nuzūl* reports purportedly relate on the basis of transmission the circumstances of the Prophet's life and community that prompt the sending down of specific verses and passages, though earlier works also reported on the circumstances contemporaneous with past events talked about in the Qur'an. In addition to works of *asbāb al-nuzūl*, occasions of revelation could also appear in other genres like verse-by-verse scriptural commentaries, *aḥkām al-Qurʾān* treatises, and *naskh* works (discussed below). The texts that collected these reports did not necessarily furnish occasions of revelation for every verse or sura. And while many compilations provided supporting chains of transmission, some works did not, like *Asbāb al-nuzūl wa-qiṣaṣ al-furqāniyya* by Muḥammad ibn Asʿad al-ʿIrāqī (d. 567/1171 or 667/1268).

Andrew Rippin (1985) has provided an important overview of the major compositions within the *asbāb al-nuzūl* genre covering both texts that were allegedly produced and those that have survived. Included in his treatment are works ascribed to ʿIkrima (d. 105/723), al-Ḥasan al-Baṣrī (d. 110/728), ʿAlī ibn al-Madīnī (d. 234/848), Abū'l-Muṭarrif al-Andalusī (d. 402/1011), Ismāʿīl ibn Aḥmad al-Ḥīrī al-Nīsābūrī (d. 430/1038), Abū Jaʿfar al-Māzandarānī (d. 588/1192), and Ibn al-Jawzī (d. 597/1200), though none of these is extant. The four that do survive are *Asbāb al-nuzūl* by al-Wāḥidī (d. 468/1075), al-ʿIrāqī's work, a manuscript by a pseudo-al-Jaʿbarī (MS Berlin 3578), and *Lubāb al-nuqūl fi asbāb al-nuzūl* by al-Suyūṭī. Al-Wāḥidī's composition enjoyed popularity and was versified by Muḥammad ibn Tāj al-ʿĀrifīn in 1094/1682. Taking into account false ascriptions and non-extant works, the *asbāb al-nuzūl* genre appears to have emerged late. The technical meaning of *sabab* does not crystallize until the early fourth/tenth century and then only finds regular usage with al-Jaṣṣāṣ (d. 370/981). Hans-Thomas Tillschneider's monograph *Typen historisch-exegetischer Überlieferung* (2011), which investigates the development of *asbāb al-nuzūl* reports, places the genesis of *asbāb al-nuzūl* reports parallel with the ascendancy of prophetic hadith near the end of the second/eighth century.

Concerning the exegetical import of *asbāb al-nuzūl* reports, Wansbrough (1977) believed them to be halakhic or legalistic in nature, though Rippin (1987) has argued that they are more appropriately understood as haggadic or homiletic in function. Alternatively, Rubin (1995), working with the early *sīra* literature, dismisses the exegetical function of *asbāb al-nuzūl* reports. Motzki (2010) judiciously notes the relative soundness of each scholarly opinion if each respective theory is not over-generalized for all such reports. Tillschneider (2011) adds to this field of enquiry by problematizing how

Western scholars have tried to use *asbāb al-nuzūl* reports to reconstruct the Qur'an's historical context. In line with Rippin's understanding, Tillschneider instead contends that the *asbāb al-nuzūl* are more helpful for understanding the theological fault lines of medieval exegesis. The early appearance of *asbāb al-nuzūl* reports among hadith scholars appears to have been a means of selectively critiquing the work of Qur'anic exegetes. Moreover, the *asbāb al-nuzūl* genre by al-Wāḥidī seems to have formed as a Sunnī rejoinder to Shīʿī forms of exegesis.

Naskh

The study of the term *naskh*, commonly translated as 'abrogation', and its linguistic derivatives *nāsikh* ('abrogating') and *mansūkh* ('abrogated') constitute another major field of Qur'anic investigation. Three more technically precise interpretations of *naskh* are suppression, transcription, and supersession, the last of which constitutes the central concern of works dealing with *naskh* and is mainly based upon Q. 2:106 and Q. 22:52. As such *naskh* could entail the abrogation of the Qur'an by another verse of the Qur'an, the Sunna by the Qur'an, or even possibly the Qur'an by the Sunna, as in the case of the punishment for adultery (Burton 1985; Burton 1987: 24–42). In respect to Qur'an, the exegetes delineated several modes of *naskh*: (1) *naskh al-ḥukm wa'l-tilāwa* where both the ruling and recitation of a Qur'anic verse is abrogated by another verse, (2) *naskh al-ḥukm dūna al-tilāwa* where only the ruling of the Qur'an or Sunna is abrogated by the Qur'an or Sunna, and (3) *naskh al-tilāwa dūna al-ḥukm* where only the recitation of a Qur'anic verse has been suppressed though the ruling remains (Burton 1985; Powers 1988). Key to considerations of *naskh* is the chronology of the Qur'an since the relative appearance of a verse would need to be known in order to determine whether it was *nāsikh* or *mansūkh*.

The majority of the works dealing with *naskh* in the Qur'an do so with the express purpose of extrapolating the procedural boundaries within which to derive legal rulings. One of the most important of such *uṣūl al-fiqh* works is al-Shāfiʿī's (d. 204/820) *Risāla*. Other allegedly early works have also been studied. Rippin (1984) has carefully examined a short work entitled *Kitāb al-Nāsikh wa'l-mansūkh* attributed to al-Zuhrī (d. 124/742) and Burton (1987) has edited the *Kitāb al-Nāsikh wa'l-mansūkh* of Abū ʿUbayd (d. 224/838). David Powers (1988) has also provided a survey of this hermeneutical genre. Works attributed to early figures like Qatāda (d. 118/736), al-Ḥārith ibn ʿAbd al-Raḥmān (d. 130/747), ʿAṭāʾ al-Khurasānī (d. 135/757), Muqātil ibn Sulaymān (d. 150/767), and ʿAbd al-Raḥmān ibn Zayd (d. 183/798) are noted, however, his study focuses on several extant texts. He makes use of al-Zuhrī's treatise and Ibn Khuzayma al-Fārisī's *Kitāb al-mujāz fī'l-nāsikh wa'l-mansūkh*, but pays special attention to the *nāsikh al-Qurʾān* works of al-Naḥḥās (d. 338/949), Hibat Allāh ibn Salāma al-Baghdādī (d. 410/1020), and Ibn al-ʿAtāʾiqī (d. *c.*970/1308). According to Powers, a typical work in the genre begins with a theoretical discussion of *naskh* followed by a more detailed examination of the relevant suras following the order of the Qur'an. When examining an individual sura the author typically discusses whether it contains *nāsikh* verses, *mansūkh* verses, both, or none and if they are Meccan or Medinan. The author will also weigh in on the veracity of the *naskh* claims. Powers also notes that the number of verses considered to be *naskh*-related varies dramatically among the exegetes, from as few as five, twenty-five, or forty-two to more than 200. A minimalist example is found with the Andalusian mystic Ibn Barrajān (d. 536/1141), who severely delimits instances of *naskh* to possibly only five instances, namely those in which the abrogating verse is sequentially proximate to the abrogated one (Casewit 2014).

Other extant *nāsikh al-Qurʾān* works have been edited and published. These texts are generally a single volume and largely follow the above-described pattern. Examples include *al-Nāsikh wa'l-mansūkh* by ʿAbd al-Qāhir al-Baghdādī (d. 429/1037), *al-Īḍāḥ li-nāsikh al-Qurʾān wa-mansūkhihi* by Abū Muḥammad Makkī ibn Abī Ṭālib al-Qaysī (d. 437/1045), *al-Nāsikh wa'l-mansūkh fī'l-Qurʾān al-karīm* by Abū Bakr Ibn al-ʿArabī (d. 543/1148), *al-Muṣaffā bi-akuff ahl al-rusūkh min ʿilm al-nāsikh wa'l-mansūkh* by Ibn al-Jawzī (d. 597/1200), *Nāsikh al-Qurʾān al-ʿazīz wa-mansūkhuhu* by Ibn al-Bārizī (d. 738/1337–8), and *Qalāʾid al-marjān fī'l-nāsikh wa'l-mansūkh min al-Qurʾān* by Zayn al-Dīn Marʿī ibn Yūsuf al-Ḥanbalī (d. 1033/1623).

Qur'anic Lexicology

Qur'anic lexicology may be understood as 'the field which attempts to look at the morphological structure and the semantic function of lexical units and to analyse the use of vocabulary' found within the Qur'an (Rippin 1988: 158–9). Muslim scholars have accumulated a substantial body of literature concerned with this wide-ranging field. Wansbrough classified lexicological treatments as part of the Qur'anic masorah and included under this broad rubric *variae lectiones* or *qirāʾāt*, semantic collations, and periphrastic restoration (1977: 202–27). Rippin expands upon this research in his examination of several subgenres of Qur'anic lexicology: *gharīb* works that focus on 'difficult' or 'obscure' words, *al-wujūh wa'l-naẓāʾir* compilations of Qur'anic homonyms and polysemes, and *mushtabihāt* texts that examine Qur'anic diction (1988).

Gharīb al-Qurʾān texts generally sought to catalogue and examine 'difficult' words in the Qur'an. The range and approach, however, could vary and compositions alternatively looked at non-Arabic words, differences in dialect, bedouin usages, and the obscure. *Gharīb* works could be organized according to sura appearance or by some alphabetical scheme and entries could range from glosses specific to the Qur'anic context to lengthier discussions entailing supporting intra-Qur'anic citations and poetic attestations. These lexicological treatments were largely ahistorical as well, though *al-Lughāt fī'l-Qurʾān* attributed to Ibn ʿAbbās, might be considered an exception because of its concern for the tribal dialects contemporaneous with the revelation (Rippin 1981; Rippin 1988). The three major works detailed by Rippin are *Tafsīr gharīb al-Qurʾān* by Ibn Qutayba (d. 276/889), *Nuzhat al-qulūb fī gharīb al-Qurʾān* by al-Sijistānī (d. 330/942), and *al-Mufradāt fī gharīb al-Qurʾān* by al-Rāghib al-Iṣfahānī (d. early fifth/eleventh century). The first text proceeds through the suras providing succinct definitions or grammatical precedents for its chosen set of words. The same author also composed a similar work for prophetic reports, *Gharīb al-ḥadīth*. Al-Sijistānī's composition organizes its content alphabetically. Al-Rāghib al-Iṣfahānī's work is less a dictionary of difficult words and more of a comprehensive Qur'an glossary. The manuscript evidence further points to the work's wide dissemination (Key 2012; Key 2018). Perhaps an extension of *gharīb* lexicological works is the commentary of the grammarian Maḥmūd ibn Ḥamza al-Kirmānī (d. after 500/1106), *Gharāʾib al-tafsīr wa-ʿajāʾib al-taʾwīl*. Rather than dealing strictly with precise lexical units the work seeks to provide proper explanations for verses whose initial reading may appear astonishing or peculiar.

Concerning foreign vocabulary, Muslim positions differed (Jeffery 1938; Wansbrough 1977). Abū ʿUbayda (d. 209/824) in *Majāz al-Qurʾān* envisioned the language of the Qur'an to be pure Arabic (Wansbrough 1977: 219). Along similar lines, the *Kitāb Gharīb al-Qurʾān* ascribed to Ibn ʿAbbās argues that the Qur'an can be Arabic only. The main scriptural basis for the position was verse Q. 41:44 which inveighs against the notion of a foreign (*aʿjamī*) Qur'an. Others, however, pointed to specific scriptural examples to argue for the presence of other languages. Arthur Jeffery compiled such information in *The Foreign Vocabulary of the Qur'ān* (1938) by consulting the relevant section of al-Suyūṭī's *al-Itqān* and *al-Muhadhdhab fī mā waqaʿa fīʾl-Qurʾān min al-muʿarrab*, which served as the basis for his later work *Mutawakkilī*. Jeffery identifies the following languages, as classified by al-Suyūṭī: Ethiopic (*lisān al-ḥabasha*), Persian (*al-lugha al-fārisiyya*), Greek (*al-lugha al-rūmiyya, yūnāniyya*), Indian (*al-lugha al-hindiyya)*, Syriac (*al-lugha al-suriyāniyya*), Hebrew (*al-lugha al-ibrāniyya*), Nabataean (*al-lugha al-nabaṭiyya*), Coptic (*al-lugha al-qibṭiyya*), Turkish (*al-lugha al-turkiyya*), Negro (*al-lugha al-zinjiyya*), and Berber (*al-lugha al-barbariyya*) (1938). The secondary scholarship on foreign vocabulary and etymological analyses of the Qur'an has been relatively prolific as seen with the works focused on the single word *al-Ṣamad* alone (Ambros 1986). Luxenberg goes so far as to claim that the Qur'an should be reread and reinterpreted in accordance with Syriac, which he claims properly underlies the entirety of the scripture (2000). Saleh, among others, have offered critiques of this theory. Indeed Saleh has provided an in-depth critical review of the 'etymological fallacy' inherent to these revisionist approaches (2010a).

Qur'anic polysemes, homonyms (*wujūh*), and synonyms (*naẓāʾir*) were the subject of *al-wujūh waʾl-naẓāʾir* texts. Because these texts were concerned with the diversity of meaning, Rippin classifies the genre as semantic lexicology and then discusses the *Kitāb al-wujūh waʾl-naẓāʾir* attributed to Muqātil ibn Sulaymān (d. 150/767), Ibn Qutayba's *Taʾwīl mushkil al-Qurʾān*, al-Damaghānī's (d. 478/1085) *Iṣlāḥ al-wujūh waʾl-naẓāʾir fīʾl-Qurʾān al-karīm*, and Ibn al-Jawzī's two works *Nuzhat al-aʿyun al-nawāẓir fī ʿilm al-wujūh waʾl-naẓāʾir* and *Muntakhab qurrat al-ʿuyūn al-nawāẓir fīʾl-wujūh waʾl-naẓāʾir* (Rippin 1988). Nabia Abbott studied the first text and believed the work to be an original work of Muqātil (Abbott 1967). Wansbrough differed and instead dated the text later to approximately the beginning of the third/ninth century (1977). Regardless, a clear theological concern is discernible in the text's preoccupation with certain words like *waḥy* and *dīn*. Ibn Qutayba's *Taʾwīl mushkil al-Qurʾān*, which was written prior to *Tafsīr gharīb al-Qurʾān*, not only deals with *wujūh* material but also addresses figures of speech. Muhammad Abdus Sattar (1978) references several other works from the genre in his study of the literature: *Wujūh wa'l-naẓāʾir fī'l-Qurʾān* by Abū ʿAbd Allāh Hārūn ibn Mūsā al-Qāriʾ, *Kitāb wujūh al-Qurʾān* by Ismāʿil ibn Aḥmad al-Nīsābūrī al-Ḥīrī (d. 430/1038), and *Wujūh al-Qurʾān* by Abū'l-Faḍl al-Tiflīsī (d. sixth/twelfth century).

Mushtabihāt or *mutashābih* texts are works of phraseological lexicology. Wansbrough describes the approach as 'a distributional analysis of Qur'anic diction' and examines one such work attributed to al-Kisāʾī (d. 189/804) as the earliest example of the genre (Wansbrough 1977). In it the author discusses unique phraseologies and textual variations and repetitions across the Qur'an by means of exegesis. Wansbrough further believed later works adopted rhetorical analyses of such dictions because of the influence of the doctrine of *iʿjāz* or inimitability of the Qur'an. Rippin (1988) alternatively proposes that the genre's method of enumerating scriptural examples is a form of homiletic indexation.

Most works of *mushtabihāt/mutashābih* reference Q. 3:7, which delineates *muḥkam* and *mutashābih* verses in the Qur'an, as central to their respective analyses. Indeed, many of the later works understand it to indicate the need for metaphorical exegesis. Al-Zarkashī and al-Suyūṭī list several titles: *al-Burhān fī mutashābih al-Qurʾān* by Maḥmūd ibn Ḥamza al-Kirmānī (d. after 500/1106), *Durrat al-tanzīl wa-ghurrat al-taʾwīl* by Abū ʿAbd Allāh al-Rāzī (d. 420/1026), better known as al-Khaṭīb al-Iskāfī, *al-Milāk al-taʾwīl* by Abū Jaʿfar Ibn al-Zubayr (d. 708/1308), and *Kashf al-maʿānī ʿan mutashābih al-mathānī* by Badr al-Dīn ibn Jamāʿa. Each of these works went beyond merely addressing recognized instances of the *mutashābih*. Kinberg has investigated some of the larger discussions surrounding Q. 3:7 (Kinberg 1988).

MISCELLANY

Several other subgenres of Sunnī hermeneutical literature warrant brief mention. A number of works were composed on specific verses or suras of the Qur'an, a genre that has been studied by Afsaruddin (2002). For instance, Abū Ḥāmid al-Ghazālī's (d. 505/1111) *Mishkāt al-anwār* deals squarely with the light verse (Q. 24:35). In the work, al-Ghazālī explicates aspects of Sufi doctrine with philosophical undertones (Whittingham 2007: 102–25; Griffel 2009: 245–64). A similar work that also helps to allude to the *faḍāʾil al-Qurʾān* literature is *al-Mawrid al-khāṣṣ bi'l-khawāṣṣ fī tafsīr sūrat al-ikhlāṣ* by Muḥammad Kamāl al-Dīn al-Ḥarīrīzāde (d. 1299/1882). The merits inhering in *Sūrat al-Ikhlāṣ* (Q. 112) and in its recitation are described in this work are typical for other works in the *faḍāʾil* genre. Also helpful for appreciating the performative hermeneutics surrounding the Qur'an is the sub-genre of texts dealing with Qur'anic etiquette or *ādāb al-Qurʾān*. The most famous example is al-Nawawī's *al-Tibyān fī ādāb al-Qurʾān*, which delineates the proper comportment required when engaging with the Qur'an. *Tajwīd* texts are yet another form of performative hermeneutics in that they describe the rules of pronunciation and recitation. Some works of this sort include *Kitāb fīʾl-tajwīd al-qirāʾa wa-makhārij al-ḥurūf* by Ibn Wathīq al-Ishbīlī (d. 654/1256) and *Muqaddima al-Jazariyya fīʾl-tajwīd* by Ibn al-Jazarī (d. 833/1429), the latter of which has been the subject of numerous commentaries. While studies on *tajwīd* are limited, Nelson (1985) and Elashiry (2008) have provided insightful analyses of recitational practices in modern-day Egypt.

Certain works focused on only one aspect of the Qur'an. Ibn Qayyim al-Jawziyya (d. 751/1350) addressed only scriptural parables (*amthāl*) in his *Amthāl fīʾl-Qurʾān al-karīm*. The opening invocation for nearly every sura, the *basmala*, was the subject of Fakhr al-Dīn al-Rāzī's *Aḥkām al-basmala* and ʿAbd al-Karīm al-Jīlī's (d. *c.*832/1428) mystical treatise *al-Kahf waʾl-raqīm fī sharḥ bismillāh al-raḥmān al-raḥīm*. Treatises were also composed on *al-asmāʾ al-ḥusnā* or the beautiful names of God, which were traditionally reported to be ninety-nine and based upon the divine appellations appearing in the Qur'an. The scholars who wrote in this subgenre were many and included al-Mubarrad (d. 285/989), al-Zajjāj (d. 311/923), al-Naḥḥās (d. 338/949), Ibn Ḥazm (d. 456/1064), Abū Bakr al-Bayhaqī (d. 458/1066), Abūʾl-Qāsim al-Qushayrī (d. 465/1072), Abū Ḥāmid al-Ghazālī, Ibn Barrajān (d. 536/1141), al-Qūnawī (d. 673/1264), and Ibn ʿAbbād al-Rundī (d. 792/1390). Gimaret's monograph, which surveys the major works and trends in the *asmāʾ* literature, brings forward the highly theological nature of these exegetical enterprises (1988). Moving beyond the purely explanatory, these works were composed to assert particular doctrinal or mystical perspectives.

Other works of Qur'anic hermeneutics developed out of other fields of religious knowledge. For example, *Kitāb al-Muwāfaqāt allatī waqaʿat fīʾl-Qurʾān al-ʿaẓīm li-amīr al-muʾminīn abī Ḥafṣ ʿUmar ibn al-Khaṭṭāb al-ʿAdawī al-Qurashī* combines aspects of *asbāb al-nuzūl* with the *faḍāʾil al-ṣaḥāba* genre in that the text compiles reports detailing when the revelation of a verse corresponded with the views of ʿUmar. Al-Suyūṭī composed a similarly spirited poem called *Fatḥ al-wahhāb fī muwāfaqāt Sayyidinā ʿUmar ibn al-Khaṭṭāb*. Rippin believes that these Sunnī *muwāfaqāt* texts developed in response to Shīʿī works that did likewise with ʿAlī (Rippin 1985: 8, 10–11). From the field of disputative theology, there is al-Bāqillānī's *al-Intiṣār liʾl-Qurʾān* which aims to answer various theological questions concerning the Qur'an. Finally, recall further that the *asbāb al-nuzūl* genre appears to have developed in parallel with the ascendancy of hadith literature (Tillschneider 2011).

Hermeneutic Principles

Compositions detailing the hermeneutical principles of Qur'anic exegesis are scattered across a number of genres. Shah has provided an extensive study and bibliographic record of the primary and secondary literature on Qur'anic hermeneutics in the introduction to the first volume of *Tafsīr: Interpreting the Qur'ān* (Shah 2013). Classically, treatments of hermeneutics were sometimes detailed at the beginning of a *tafsīr*, as with the commentaries of Ibn ʿAṭiyya (d. 546/1151) and Ibn Kathīr (Jeffery 1972; McAuliffe 1988) or embedded within a wider ranging work, as in al-Ghazālī's *Iḥyāʾ ʿulūm al-dīn*, where the rules for Qur'anic recitation and interpretation are discussed in book eight of forty (Abul Quasem 1979). Works dedicated solely to explicating hermeneutical principles are rare and they generally do not follow a standard format as found with many other exegetical genres. Al-Ghazālī, who wrote several hermeneutical works, is a case in point (Heer 1999; Whittingham 2007; Griffel 2009; Okumuş 2012). In *Jawāhir al-Qurʾān* he takes a Qur'an-centric approach to hermeneutics and examines the Qur'an through the lens of the Qur'an whereas in *al-Qānūn al-kullī fī l-taʾwīl*, he more broadly looks at revealed texts, so as to include hadith, and schematizes the relationship between the intellect (*ʿaql*) and transmitted knowledge (*naql*) in the process of interpretation.

In fact, the *Qānūn* appears to have been formulated as a reply to a student, the jurist Abū Bakr Ibn al-ʿArabī (d. 543/1148), who himself went on to compose the similarly named *Qānūn al-taʾwīl*. In this latter work, Ibn al-ʿArabī takes up the same hermeneutical questions as al-Ghazālī, but delves more deeply into *ʿulūm al-Qurʾān* while also describing his own search for knowledge. In the earlier theologically oriented work of al-Ḥārith al-Muḥāsibī (d. 243/857) *Kitāb Fahm al-Qurʾān* the author not only explores the connection between the intellect (*ʿaql*) and the Qur'an, he also addressed *faḍāʾil al-Qur'ān*, *naskh*, and various linguistic considerations rooted in the *ʿulūm al-Qurʾān*.

Ibn Taymiyya's *Muqaddima fī uṣūl al-tafsīr* is another important work that has fortunately been carefully studied by Saleh (2010b). This brief treatise is both a critique of the preceding *tafsīr* tradition and the formulation of a new exegetical methodology altogether, what Saleh terms 'radical hermeneutics'. Ibn Taymiyya argues that the explanations presented by the Successors and Companions, collectively referred to as the *salaf*, is based upon prophetic knowledge and hence rooted in a distinct Sunna of the Prophet. Ibn Taymiyya then works to minimize the seeming differences of opinion among the *salaf* especially with respect to *asbāb al-nuzūl*. Saleh also notes the omission of philology from Ibn Taymiyya's enterprise. Instead, Ibn Taymiyya aligns scriptural exegesis with Sunnī juristic practices. The *tafsīr* of Ibn Kathīr (d. 774/1373) and *al-Durr al-manthūr* of al-Suyūṭī were clearly influenced by Ibn Taymiyya's treatise. In fact, the former reproduces wholesale sections of the *muqaddima* in his *tafsīr*'s introduction. Turning to the present, Brown identifies with many modern Muslim thinkers a tendency towards Qur'anic 'scripturalism', which he attributes to the enduring influence of Ibn Taymiyya's work (1996).

Also within this genre is *al-Fawz al-kabīr fī uṣūl al-tafsīr* by the South Asian scholar Shāh Walī Allāh (d. 1176/1762). In this work the author takes an *ʿulūm al-Qurʾān* approach to hermeneutics, addressing various aspects of the Qur'anic sciences and their bearing on exegesis. Notably, Shāh Walī Allāh frequently distinguishes between the views of earlier and later scholars on these matters. Baljon has traced the influence of Shāh Walī Allāh's hermeneutics on the *tafsīr* of one of his students ʿUbayd Allāh Sindhī (1977).

Bibliography

Abbott, Nabia. *Studies in Arabic Literary Papyri II: Qurʾānic Commentary and Tradition*. Chicago: University of Chicago Press, 1967.

Abdus Sattar, Muhammad. 'Wujuh al-Qurʾān: A Branch of Tafsir Literature', *Islamic Studies* 17/1 (1978), 137–52.

Abul Quasem, Muhammad. *The Recitation and Interpretation of the Qurʾān: al-Ghazālī's Theory*. Kuala Lumpur: University of Malaysia Press, 1979.

Al-Abyārī, Ibrāhīm. *Tārīkh al-Qurʾān*. Beirut: Dār al-Kutub al-Islāmiyya, 1982.

Afsaruddin, Asma. 'The Excellence of the Qurʾān', *Journal of the American Oriental Society* 122 (2002), 1–24.

Ambros, Arne A. 'Die Analyse von Sure 112: Kritiken, Synthesen, neue Ansätze', *Der Islam* 63 (1986), 219–47.

Baljon, J. M. S. 'A Comparison between the Qurʾānic Views of ʿUbayd Allāh Sindhī and Shāh Walī Allāh', *Islamic Studies* 16/3 (1977), 179–88.

Brown, Daniel W. *Rethinking Tradition in Modern Islamic Thought*. Cambridge, New York: Cambridge University Press, 1996.

Burton, John. 'The Exegesis of q. 2:106 and the Islamic Theories of naskh: mā nansakh min āya aw nansahā naʾti bi khairin minhā aw mithlihā', *Bulletin of the School of Oriental and African Studies* 483 (1985), 452–69.

Burton, John (ed.). *Abū ʿUbaid al-Qāsim ibn Sallām's k. al-nāsikh wa-l-mansūkh*. Cambridge: E. J. W. Gibb Memorial Trust, 1987.

Casewit, Yousef. *Ibn Barrajān and the Revolution in Sufi Thought*. PhD, Yale University, 2014.

Crone, Patricia and Michael Cook. *Hagarism: The Making of the Islamic World*. Cambridge: Cambridge University Press, 1977.

Elashiry, Mohammed R. *Sounds of Qurʾānic Recitation in Egypt: A Phonetic Analysis*. Lewiston, NY: Edwin Mellen Press, 2008.

Gilliot, Claude. 'L'Exégèse du Coran en Asie Centrale et au Khorasan', *Studia Islamica* 89 (1999), 129–64.

Gimaret, Daniel. *Les Noms divins en islam: exégèse lexicographique et théologique*. Paris: Les Éditions du Cerf, 1988.

Griffel, Frank. *Al-Ghazālī's Philosophical Theology*. Oxford: Oxford University Press, 2009.

Hirschfeld, Hartwig. *New Researches into the Composition and Exegesis of the Qoran*. London: Royal Asiatic Society, 1902.

Heer, Nicholas. 'Abū Ḥāmid al-Ghazālī's Esoteric Exegesis of the Koran'. In: Leonard Lewisohn (ed.). *The Heritage of Sufism*, vol. 1: *Classical Persian Sufism from its Origins to Rumi (700–1300)*, pp. 235–57. Oxford: Oneworld, 1999.

Ibn Ḥabīb. *Kitāb al-Tanbīh ʿalā faḍl ʿulūm al-Qurʾān li-Abī al-Qāsim al-Ḥasan ibn Muḥammad ibn al-Ḥasan ibn Ḥabīb al-mutawwafā sanna* 406 h. Ed. Muḥammad ʿAbd al-Karīm Kāẓim al-Rāḍī, *al-Mawrid* 17/4 (1988), 305–22.

Jeffery, Arthur. *The Foreign Vocabulary of the Qurʾān*. Baroda: Oriental Institute, 1938.

Jeffery, Arthur (ed.). *Two Muqaddimas to the Qurʾānic Sciences: The Muqaddima to the kitab al-mabani and the Muqaddima of ibn ʿAtiyya to his tafsir, Edited from the MSS in Berlin and in Cairo*. Cairo: Maktabat al-Khānjī, 1972.

Key, Alexander. *A Linguistic Frame of Mind: Ar-Raġib al-Iṣfahānī and what it Meant to be Ambiguous*. PhD, Harvard University, 2012.

Key, Alexander. *Language between God and the Poets: Maʿná in the Eleventh Century*. Oakland, California: University of California Press, 2018.

Kinberg, Leah. '*Muḥkamāt* and *Mutashābihāt* (Koran 3/7): Implications of a Koranic Pair of Terms in Medieval Exegesis', *Arabica* 35 (1988), 143–72.

Luxenberg, Christoph. *Die syro-aramäische Lesart des Koran: Ein Beitrag zur Entschlüsselung der Koransprache*. Berlin: Das Arabische Buch, 2000.

McAuliffe, Jane Dammen. 'Quranic Hermeneutics: The Views of al-Ṭābarī and Ibn Kathir'. In: A. Rippin (ed.). *Approaches to the History of the Interpretation of the Qurʾān*, pp. 46–62. Oxford: Oxford University Press, 1988.

Motzki, Harald. 'The Origins of Muslim Exegesis: A Debate'. In: *Analysing Muslim Traditions: Studies in Legal, Exegetical and Maghāzī Ḥadīth*, pp. 231–303. Leiden: Brill, 2010.

Mourad, Suleiman Ali. 'The Survival of the Muʿtazila Tradition of Qurʾānic Exegesis in Shīʿī and Sunnī *Tafāsīr*', *Journal of Qurʾānic Studies* 12 (2010), 83–108.

Nelson, Kristina. *The Art of Reciting the Qurʾān*. Austin: University of Texas Press, 1985.

Neuwirth, Angelika. *Studien zur composition der mekkanischen suren*. Berlin: Walter de Gruyter, 1981.

Nevo, Yehuda D. and Judith Koren. *Crossroads to Islam: The Origins of the Arab Religion and the Arab State*. Amherst, NY: Prometheus Books, 2003.

Nguyen, Martin. 'Exegetes of Nishapur: A Preliminary Survey of Qur'anic Works by Ibn Ḥabīb, Ibn Fūrak, and ʿAbd al-Qāhir al-Baghdādī', *Journal of Qur'anic Studies* 20/2 (2018), 47–73.

Nöldeke, Theodor, Friedrich Schwally, et al. *Geschichte des Qorāns*. 3 vols. Leipzig: T. Weicher, 1909–38.

Okumuş, Mesut. 'The Influence of Ibn Sīnā on al-Ghazzālī in Qurʾānic Hermeneutics', *Muslim World* 102/2 (2012), 390–411.

Powers, David S. 'The Exegetical Genre *nāsikh al-Qurʾān wa mansūkhuhu*'. In: A. Rippin (ed.). *Approaches to the History of the Interpretation of the Qurʾān*, pp. 117–37. Oxford: Oxford University Press, 1988.

Rippin, Andrew. 'Ibn ʿAbbās's *al-lughāt fī'l-Qurʾān*', *Bulletin of the School of Oriental and African Studies* 44/1 (1981), 15–25.

Rippin, Andrew. 'Al-Zuhrī, *naskh al-Qur'ān* and the Problem of Early *Tafsīr* Texts', *Bulletin of the School of Oriental and African Studies* 47/1 (1984), 22–43.

Rippin, Andrew. 'The Exegetical Genre of *asbāb al-nuzūl*: A Bibliographic and Terminological Survey', *Bulletin of the School of Oriental and African Studies* 48/1 (1985), 1–15.

Rippin, Andrew. 'The Function of *asbāb al-nuzūl* in Qurʾānic Exegesis', *Bulletin of the School of Oriental and African Studies* 51/1 (1988), 1–20.

Rubin, Uri. *The Eye of the Beholder: The Life of Muḥammad as Viewed by the Early Muslims*. Princeton: Darwin Press, 1995.

Sadeghi, Behnam. 'The Chronology of the Qurʾān: A Stylometric Research Program', *Arabica* 58 (2011), 210–99.

Saleh, Walid A. *The Formation of the Classical Tafsīr Tradition: The Qur'ān Commentary of al-Tha'labī (d. 427/1035)*. Leiden: Brill, 2004.

Saleh, Walid A. 'The Last of the Nishapuri School of Tafsīr: al-Wāḥidī (d. 468/1076) and His Significance in the History of Qurʾānic Exegesis', *Journal of the American Oriental Society* 126/2 (2006), 223–43.

Saleh, Walid A. 'The Etymological Fallacy and Qurʾānic Studies: Muhammad, Paradise, and Late Antiquity'. In: Angelika Neuwirth, Nicolai Sinai, and Michael Marx (eds.). *The Qurʾān in Context: Historical and Literary Investigations into the Qur'ānic Milieu*, pp. 649–98. Leiden: Brill, 2010a.

Saleh, Walid A. 'Ibn Taymiyya and the Rise of Radical Hermeneutics: An Analysis of an Introduction to the Foundations of Qur'ānic Exegesis'. In: Yossef Rapoport and Shahab Ahmed (eds.). *Ibn Taymiyya and his Times*. Oxford: Oxford University Press, 2010b.

Shah, Mustafa. 'Introduction'. In: M. Shah (ed.). *Tafsīr: Interpreting the Qur'ān*, vol. 1: *Tafsīr: Gestation and Synthesis*, pp. 1–157. London: Routledge, 2013.

al-Suyūṭī. *al-Itqān fī ʿulūm al-Qur'ān*. Ed. Muḥammad Abū'l-Faḍl Ibrāhīm. 4 vols. Cairo: Maktabat Dār al-Turāth, n.d.

al-Thaʿlabī. *Qur'ānic Commentary in the Eastern Islamic Tradition of the First Four Centuries of the Hijra: An Annotated Edition of the Preface to al-Tha'labi's "kitab al-kashf wa'l-bayan an Tafsir al-Qur'ān*. Ed. Isaiah Goldfeld. Acre: Srugy Printers and Publishers, 1984.

al-Thaʿlabī. *Muqaddimat al-kashf wa'l-bayān ʿan tafsīr al-Qur'ān*. Ed. Khālid ibn ʿAwn al-ʿAnazī. Riyadh: Kunūz Ishbīlyā, 1429/2008.

Tillschneider, Hans-Thomas. *Typen historisch-exegetischer überlieferung*. Würzburg: Ergon, 2011.

van Ess, Josef. *Ungenützte texte zur Karrāmīya*. Heidelberg: Carl Winter, Universitätsverlag, 1980.

Von Denffer, Ahmad. *ʿUlūm al-Qur'ān: An Introduction to the Sciences of the Qurʿān*. Leicester: The Islamic Foundation, 2000.

Wansbrough, John. *Quranic Studies: Sources and Methods of Scriptural Interpretation*. Oxford: Oxford University Press, 1977.

Watt, W. Montgomery and Richard Bell. *Bell's Introduction to the Qur'ān: Completely Revised and Enlarged*. Edinburgh: Edinburgh University Press, 1970.

Weil, Gustav. *Historisch-kritische einleitung in den Koran*. Bielefeld: Velhagen & Klasing, 1844.

Whittingham, Martin. *Al-Ghazālī and the Qur'ān: One Book, Many Meanings*. London: Routledge, 2007.

al-Zarkashī. *al-Burhān fī ʿulūm al-Qur'ān*. Ed. Muṣṭafā ʿAbd al-Qādi ʿAṭā. 4 vols. Beirut: Dār al-Fikr, 1988.

Zadeh, Travis. *The Vernacular Qur'ān: Translation and the Rise of Persian Exegesis*. Oxford: Oxford University Press, 2012.

Zysow, Aron. 'Two Unrecognized Karrāmī Texts', *Journal of the American Oriental Society* 108/4 (1988), 577–87.

CHAPTER 57

MODERN QUR'ANIC HERMENEUTICS

Strategies and Development

MASSIMO CAMPANINI

The Problem of Hermeneutics

This chapter sets off from the radical assumption by Friedrich Nietzsche that there are no facts but only interpretations (Nietzsche 1999:§ 481). This negation of the objective reality of things has potential nihilistic implications, for it seems to assume that the 'real' world is a production of the mind. However, we communicate—and act accordingly—not by 'things', but by 'signs' and 'words' that substitute, so to speak, for the 'things'. It follows that it is interpretation which builds up the sense of the world in all thinking. In particular, philosophical hermeneutics, as a peculiar key of interpretation of the holy scriptures, can be the very propelling power of a renewed exegetic faculty, as will be argued below (see also Leaman 2016). The danger of idealism is obviously implicit in a potential negation of the objective reality of things. So it is necessary to offer precautionary corrections and distinctions. In this framework, the problem of the use of contemporary hermeneutics in the analysis and commentary of the Qur'an appears as a very complex and many-sided issue. It actually implies the answer to at least three questions.

First of all, which hermeneutics is this? Literary or philosophical hermeneutics? Or religious and spiritual hermeneutics, which, being such, is not always performed on a homologous level. What scientific quality criteria does it, or should it, meet? I should exclude from my analysis the last esoteric level straight away, because spirit is not definable and quantifiable, while literature and philosophy are, and can be systematized, or better, rationalized within well-defined boundaries. This may imply a painful renunciation: that is, giving up mysticism (*taṣawwuf*) as a mode of interpretation—an interpretation mode widespread within the history of Islamic thought: yet here we must leave room for a future exegesis that will want to be considered a science (paraphrasing Kant). Maybe, mystical exegesis is not strictly speaking 'irrational', but critical reason (again in Kantian terminology) must be at the centre of hermeneutical (and especially philosophical hermeneutics) enquiry.

Secondly, and as a direct derivation of the first argument, does the term *ta'wīl*, which is frequently rendered as hermeneutics in translation, adequately encapsulate the technical thrust of the Arabic word? Certainly, it cannot be limited to being the allegorical or metaphorical interpretation of some ambiguous verses. The Arabic word connotes the attempt to go back to 'sources', to the original foundation of language, so *ta'wīl* represents the process by which the exegete tries to grasp the profound, innermost meaning of a verse without resorting to literality. The discipline of *ta'wīl* enjoys a distinguished history in classical Islamic religious thought. Contemporary hermeneutics, though, goes well beyond the limits of classicism, and somehow updates or even reverses them. Thus *ta'wīl* assumes a philosophical process, far beyond the literary starting point, that tries to harmonize the results of theoretical and intellectual research with the appearance (*ẓāhir*) of a text such as the Qur'an, which for Muslims articulates, without any interpretive doubt, God's very word uttered in clear Arabic so that it is immediately understood by everybody. If we try to understand better which kind of *ta'wīl* we are speaking of, we have to distinguish our position from Seyyed Hossein Nasr's. For while he maintained that Islamic philosophy is essentially a philosophical hermeneutics of the sacred text, he meant 'prophetic philosophy' grounded upon 'spiritual hermeneutics' (*ta'wīl*). This perspective is discarded here, as we explained above.

In this context, 'truth' (*ḥaqq*) is 'disclosure' (*kashf*), that is *aletheia*. A Qur'anic verse is worth quoting: 'We shall show them Our signs in the material world and within themselves, until it becomes manifest to them that He is the Truth' (Q. 41:53). This Qur'anic utterance does not mean only that there is a connection between the external and internal dimensions of man, but also that knowledge is emerging from a disclosure of Truth. Moreover, this does not merely mean removing the veil that conceals the truthful nucleus, but rather, using Heidegger-derived terms, the phenomenological showing and disclosing itself of the Being (in this case God). The statement by Maḥmūd Muḥammad Ṭāhā (1909–85), who was executed for his beliefs, must be understood in this sense: the process leading the individual to transform one from 'believer' (*mu'min*) into 'Muslim' (*muslim*) is based on a 'truth of certainty' (*'ilm ḥaqq al-yaqīn*) which points to God as the goal of our progress (Ṭāhā 1996: 46). Being certain that Truth (*ḥaqq*) has come and has defeated falseness (*bāṭil*) (cf. Q. 21:18) implies the fact that God spread some signs (*āyāt*) that reveal Him in the cosmos, in the soul, and in the Book. In this way, the veil of 'appearance' is actually removed to show Truth. 'Signs' clearly refer to a world of symbols that must be decoded, that is, interpreted.

Thirdly, when hermeneutics is applied to the Qur'an, does it possess an exclusively theoretical worth and what are its unintended political consequences? These issues are particularly important if one bears in mind that contemporary Islamic thought is eminently a praxis thought. Thinking is not solely and exclusively done as a mental exercise, but rather to affect reality and change it. If a relevant part of contemporary Islamic thought is an *idéologie du combat*, as Mohammed Arkoun posited, it is evident that interpretation is defined through reference to society and history in order to determine the scope of its application. This fact leads us to suppose that, at the very moment Muslim thinkers concretely perform hermeneutics, that is they interpret the holy text, they also theorize it on a methodological level.

Answering these questions (see also Campanini 2016 and 2018), I will try to offer a critical reading of contemporary Islamic hermeneutics and the features of its discourses.

Main Trends of Contemporary Hermeneutics

Contemporary Muslim hermeneutics of the Qur'an has explored many approaches of interpretation: literary, historical, philosophical, of gender, and so on (Taji Farouki 2004; Benzine 2004; Campanini 2011; Taji Farouki 2015). A survey of all these approaches is impossible here. The reader must consider that the outcomes of these endeavours are sometimes contradictory; but the most open-minded Muslim exegetes are intensely searching for new paths towards understanding the Qur'an in the light of contemporary necessities and challenges. Traditional hermeneutics is still alive, however, as is demonstrated, among others, by the commentaries of figures such as Ibn ʿĀshūr, Maḥmūd Shaltūt, and ʿAllāma al-Ṭabāṭabāʾī (Ibn ʿĀshūr 1979; Shaltūt 1968; al-Ṭabāṭabāʾī 1983), although traditional commentaries are still more influential on public opinion than innovative ones.

Anyway, it is important to distinguish between literary and philosophical hermeneutics, identifying the field of application of each. This issue becomes contentious if we consider that for Muslims the Qur'an is simultaneously both a 'literary miracle' (it is an untranslatable and inimitable text) and a deposit of theological truths that inevitably require a philosophical foundation. Well then, literary hermeneutics seems ultimately to be connectable to the field of *tafsīr* rather than that of *taʾwīl*. Nevertheless, the Egyptian triad of famous literary hermeneuts—Amīn al-Khūlī (d. 1967), his wife ʿĀʾisha ʿAbd al-Raḥmān Bint al-Shāṭīʾ (d. 1999), and his disciple Muḥammad Aḥmad Khalafallāh (1916–98)—proposed an extremely innovative exegetic method for their time (the 1950s). The Qur'an was to be considered as a normal literary text (*adabī*) and the rules of modern literary criticism were to be applied to it (Bint al-Shāṭīʾ 2004). This led to a different approach to the text, with serious consequences, for example the negation of the historicity of the Qur'anic tales (*qiṣaṣ*) about prophets by Khalafallāh (Khalafallāh 1999). The emerging question, in addition to discussing the Muslim dogma of the inimitability of the Qur'an (*iʿjāz*) and far beyond the authors' intentions, was the possibility of considering the Qur'an as a system of linguistic relations whose components do not exist by themselves but only in reciprocal connection. In this sense, in Ferdinand de Saussure's terminology, the Qur'an is not a *parole* but a *langue*, that is a system whose single component keeps its specific value in relation to other components and in relation to the history of the text, that is the history of revelation itself. The first is synchronic in terms of its thrust, while the second forms a diachronic approach. These are two angles that converge situating the text within a temporal context, which is an essential element of hermeneutics.

The literary level may be propaedeutical but not decisive, however. The philosophical level claims to be indeed authentically analytical. To discover the way to harmonize 'prejudice' and textual wholeness is a central issue for the point of view of philosophical hermeneutics which is being discussed here. One of the essential problems of philosophical hermeneutics is that of the relation between text objectivity and the interpreter's subjectivity. Up to what point does the interpreter's 'prejudice' allow him to determine what are the objective and objectifiable contents of the text? Clearly, here reference is made to Hans-Georg Gadamer, who from this point of view goes beyond the rather existentially overbalanced Heideggerian positions. Gadamer indeed translates on an epistemological level what for Heidegger remains entirely metaphysical. Many contemporary Muslim hermeneuts have discussed Gadamer and his analysis. The category which might be chosen to build up a common framework among exegetes and exegesis is probably that of *historicity*. The question about the relation with history is central for any hermeneutics, beginning from the very *Truth and Method* by Gadamer (Gadamer 1960). It is even more important within Islam because of tradition's (*turāth*) weight in the development of an Islamic worldview. ʿAbdallāh Laroui (b. 1933) has described the influence *turāth* has over the perception of history by Muslims (Laroui 1999). The burden of the past hovers over interpretations and decisions of the *homo islamicus* especially when he is facing modernity's challenges. It is here that the peculiar mental attitude I consider as widespread in the majority of Muslims (and particularly in the majority of Islamists) is moulded: the retrospective utopia thanks to which the construction of the future needs the past to be recovered, in particular the Prophet's and the *salaf's* (pious ancestors) example, that is, that perfect generation who lived following God's dictates. It is a well-known fact that many Muslims (and, most of all, many Islamists) deem the course of human history after the Prophet's unswerving time as a continuous involution that must be redeemed by the return to original perfection. Islam is bound—more tightly than it would wish to be—to history and its determinism. Philosophical interpreters particularly insist on the fact that the revelation (and its language) must be contextualized as it was transmitted to a definite people that spoke a definite language at a definite time.

The Pakistani scholar Fazlur Rahman (1919–88) may be considered the first to develop a self-aware philosophical Qur'anic hermeneutics. He confronted Gadamer directly, whose theoretical attitude he criticized, being, in his opinion, conditioned by an excessive subjectivity. Rahman rather endorsed Emilio Betti's method, originally applied to case law but which the Muslim thinker claims he can extend to philosophy. As we can once more see, the central problem is that of the interaction between subjectivity (the interpreter's view) and objectivity (the scriptural data in its literality). We ought to consider Rahman's belief that God's word, objectively revealed, unveils itself through the Prophet's subjective experience. The Qur'an—states Rahman—is God's word, but it is so profoundly bound to the Prophet's personality that it may not have a purely mechanical relationship of communication and reception with it: the divine Word passes through the Prophet's heart. Rahman especially criticizes the 'atomistic' approach to the Qur'an, to which he opposes the necessity to study the text transversally, not in a chronological sense but in a theme-based one. Moreover, Rahman does not consider the Qur'an as a theological book, but a book on ethics, because it is the instrument that informs the behaviour of men, encouraging them to build a fair and well-balanced society. His book, *Major Themes of the Qur'an* (Rahman 1980), a text in which the author puts his own method to the test, opens with the innovating acknowledgement that in Islam, God is the dimension that makes all other dimensions possible. God is the object of a diuturnal research and the demonstration of His existence is to be found in the continuous perception of His 'signs'. The issue, so important for Western philosophy, about the demonstration of God's existence, is bypassed in favour of a vision of divinity as a transcendental guarantee of all reality and its harmonious workings. The classical cosmological, ontological, and intelligent design proofs, applied in philosophical and rational Muslim discourses, *kalām*, in the classical Islamic world, or at least in the part thereof most strictly involved with the assimilation of the Greek rationalistic heritage, are no longer necessary: God's existence is *a priori* obvious.

In a similar framework of thought, the Syrian Muḥammad Shahrūr (b. 1938) emphasized the necessity that the Qur'anic reading ought not to be 'atomistic', separated into single, isolated verses. A thematic hermeneutics is needed in order to keep the stability of the textual form with the mobility of its content. There are immutable intentions in God's revelation, but they are expressed in a text that must be adaptable to the requirements and challenges of modernity. Thematical hermeneutics is particularly fitted for this goal (Shahrūr 1990 and 2012; and see Ḥanafī 1995).

The Algerian, naturalized French scholar, Mohammed Arkoun (1928–2010) acquired great fame on the grounds of his innovative methodology. Being convinced of the necessary historization of the holy Book, which remains the compulsive starting point of any critical reading and reconstruction of Arabic-Islamic thought, Arkoun complains that a great part of the 'unthought-of' has remained in this thought due to the predominance of a tradition enclosing all that is 'thinkable'. Moreover, the unthought-of has become 'unthinkable' and modernity and knowledge's conquests (democracy, historicity, gender equality...) are ghettoized in the limbo of impossibility (Arkoun 2002). This obviously makes all relations with modernity difficult. On the one hand, it is impossible to face tradition constructively if you do not accept modernity; on the other, you cannot actually adhere to modernity if you continue to side with a mythologized and timeless tradition rather than with a historically connoted, and thus criticizable, tradition. Arkoun applies these assumptions to the Qur'an, whose interpretation needs to be based on three main pillars: linguistics and semiotics; social criticism; and historical psychology (Arkoun 1982). Arkoun's reflection represents one of the most interesting, albeit only theoretical, attempts to overcome the *impasse* of that part of Islamic thought which idealizes the past at the expense of a constructive, future-bound projection. He nevertheless did not supply systematic applications of his method, which hence remains idealistic and excluded from its translation into praxis. I mean that his analysis of the Qur'an has been methodological more than factual, so that, for example, Farid Esack charged him with not foreseeing the building up of a new world starting from the holy book, while Muḥammad Ṭalbī charged him with denying the sacredness of the Book.

The third exegete whose contributions warrant separate consideration is the Egyptian scholar Naṣr Ḥāmid Abū Zayd (d. 2010). In what is probably his best-known piece of writing, *Mafhūm al-Naṣṣ* (The concept of the text), Abū Zayd grappled with the problem of an updated reading of the Qur'an. The Holy Book is properly a text, precisely located in history, so it must be analysed with suitable instruments that include linguistics, history, and anthropology. Far from constituting a negation of the text's holiness, this hermeneutic and historicist approach must help to multiply meanings and potential interpretations of the Qur'an, so as to make it fit to meet the needs of the current world. In a more recent articulation of his thought, though, Abū Zayd believed that even considering the Qur'an purely as a text risks making its interpretation more rigid, as, if the Qur'an were only a text, it would nonetheless transmit a unique message and not a plural intention. It is therefore necessary to consider the Qur'an as a 'discourse', or even better a set of discourses so as to reconsider its dialogic and dialectic and non-dogmatic aspects. The Qur'an must stay at the centre of Islamic culture, even if the traditional religious discourse (concerning which Abū Zayd wrote a *Naqd al-khiṭāb al-dīnī* (Critique of religious discourse) (Abū Zayd 1992) has exaggerated, for instance, the importance of the hadith and of the Sunna, elevating them at the expense of the very revealed Book. In addition to that, the religious discourse must be freed of all impediments that made it a closed and conservative system, such as the depreciation of scientific knowledge, excessive subordination to the old classics, the trend to reduce reality and its explanation to a sole cause. In this thought framework, two central contributions to the hermeneutic research on the Qur'an by Abū Zayd emerge: the distinction between sense and meaning in the light of Saussure's semiotics and language philosophy; and the foundation of 'humanist' hermeneutics. On the one hand, indeed, one must be aware of the distinction of linguistic levels in which the scripture is displayed: the 'sense' represents the unchangeable part, fixed in time and space of the text, its literality which, since the prophecy's closing, is unchangeable; the 'meaning' is mobile, plural, and flexible, allowing it to interpret the various historical circumstances which the community of believers encounters. On the other hand, God's revelation is *for* mankind; the dialogue between man and God constitutes an impulse to a self-aware action to fully realize history's humanity (Abū Zayd 2004). Unfortunately, Abū Zayd's untimely death prevented him from further developing these constructs.

Having briefly described the thought of three prestigious Muslim intellectuals of the twentieth century, it appears self-evident that new contents of *ta'wīl* must be found, and go beyond the criticality of the famous verse Q. 3:7. As known, the verse identifies two levels of meaning in the Qur'anic text: that of 'solid' expressions, which must be taken in their literality (*muḥkamāt*), and that of ambiguous or allegorical expressions (*mutashābihāt*) which must be interpreted. The fact is that interpretation (*ta'wīl*) is considered a source of schism and dissent (*fitna*), so that only God may exercise it. Men of solid science rather confess their dependence on divinity. It is also well known that philosophers, for example Ibn Rushd (Averroes) (d. 595/1198), have taken onto themselves the exclusive practice of *taʾwīl*, being certain of the fact that philosophy's rational rigour allows an exegesis which is perfectly fit to decode God's intentions. And all of the most audacious Muslim thinkers (not to mention many Sufi mystics and Shīʿī scholars) thought they could or should claim exoteric exegesis, not only of ambiguous expressions, but often also of the 'solid' ones. The mere literality of the text (*ẓāhir*) is unsatisfactory both to understand the mysteries of nature and, *a fortiori*, God's design. Now, the Salafī and the 'scientific' commentaries constitute two examples of how, in a conceptually traditional framework, one may indicate potentially meditated directions of the Qur'anic exegesis.

By Salafī commentary I mean in particular the exegetic work by Muḥammad ʿAbdūh (1849–1905) and Rashīd Riḍā (1865–1935). Their famous commentary, the so-called *Manār*, moves between the limits of the Q. 3:7 issue, although it emphasizes the role of rationality. Exegesis however knows insuperable boundaries because human reason is not capable of penetrating the most intimate secrets of God's will. And yet, especially in ʿAbdūh's opinion, the Qur'anic message is essentially rational, it does not require blind faith but rather encourages reasoning and reflection. ʿAbdūh's attitude has been defined as neo-Muʿtazilī in so far as it accepted some of the theoretical principles of that early theological school, from the Qur'an's created status to human free will. ʿAbdūh's disciples, on the grounds of this conceptual openness, stood out for the autonomy of their world vision, from the defence and re-evaluation of women's role by Qāsim Amīn to Luṭfī al-Sayyid's political liberalism. Riḍā's attitude, on the contrary, has been more conservative since it emphasized the authentically traditionalistic aspects of the *salaf*'s return to the past, so much so that his thought is reported to have inspired the Muslim Brotherhood movement and its desire to resurrect the Islamic concept of state. ʿAbdūh's and Rashīd Riḍā's heritage has been vindicated recently by the outstanding Azhari scholar Maḥmūd Zaqzūq who claimed that the problems of philosophy are the same problems of the Qur'an; that the conceptual order (*tartīb*) of philosophy is the same conceptual order of the Qur'an. Moreover, since intellect is derived from God's light, using it is a religious duty (*farīḍa dīniyya*) when interpreting scripture (Zaqzūq 2016).

The scientific commentary (*tafsīr ʿilmī*) is one of the most curious enterprises of Qur'anic exegesis. It is about understanding whether the Holy Book contains scientific information and whether this is in harmony with the more and more extraordinary discoveries made vis-à-vis the natural world. The debate arose as far back as the so-called Middle Ages, which correspond to the classical phase of Islamic civilization, during which many (e.g. the great al-Ghazālī (d. 505/1111)) claimed that the Qur'an contains the key to all sciences, while others, just as famous (e.g. al-Shāṭibī), underlined most of all the methodological impossibility of reconciling science with Scripture. In reality, no Islamic thinker has ever said that the Qur'an is in contradiction with scientific research or rationality. Rather, sometimes the desire to agree has caused some utterly surprising outcomes, such as when, for instance, ʿAbd al-Raḥmān al-Kawākibī (d. 1903) suggested that the Qur'anic Noah's Ark anticipated steamships! Scientific commentary is sound to this day, and there are numerous Muslim scientists and scholars who defend the idea that the Qur'an contains precise biological, geological, and astronomical data revealed in the remote past but confirmed by modern science. From a hermeneutic point of view and for its intrinsic features, scientific commentary obviously implies an epistemological debate on the relationship between religion and natural sciences, particularly concerning Darwinism. Indeed, the theory of evolution (we are here referring to Islam but in the Christian context very much the same happens) is considered by traditionalists as the most dangerous attempt by 'atheists' to dispute the Intelligent Design according to which God has created the world and sustains it. Irrespective of the most reactionary and backward positions, for example those who still claim today that the Earth is flat because the Qur'an says several times that God has literally 'spread it out', hermeneutics must find a way to cooperate between science and revealed Scripture, preserving the former's autonomy and falsifiability, and the latter's feature as a divine message transmitted to guide mankind to act appropriately in this world and attain salvation in the next. The challenge is extremely open and there are a number of medical doctors, physicists, and chemists who are trying to understand the natural world in ways which comply with religious teachings. Nidhal Guessoum, for example, a physicist, discussed extensively the problem of the relation between faith and science, showing not only that reason is not in contradiction with revelation, but also that the autonomy of reason can be a support for revelation (Guessoum 2011 and Bigliardi 2014).

As I mentioned above, contemporary Islamic thought must be understood as praxis driven and its performing intention represents the actual leitmotif of contemporary exegesis. This is even more the case for those authors who have put the Qur'an at the centre of their reflection. The Pakistani scholar Abū'l-Aʿlā al-Mawdūdī (1903–79) and the Egyptian Sayyid Quṭb (1906–66) are probably the two most important thinkers who have tried a revolutionary reading of the Qur'an. The thread binding them is the concept of God's sovereignty (*ḥākimiyya*): God is the only authentic lawgiver and the Islamic state must be realized on the grounds of the application of the Divine Law (Sharīʿa). The theorization of the *ḥākimiyya* is based on a forcible and surreptitious reading of some Qur'anic expressions: the term *ḥukm*, for example, which the Qur'an uses to express God's 'judgement' (e.g. in Q. 5:49 and Q. 12:40) is understood in the sense of 'government', so it implies, as a point of fact, the realization of an Islamic state based on the Sharīʿa. In this case, the exegesis reverses the primary sense of a term, rendering it consistent with an implied meaning. Hermeneutics forces God's intentions, so to say. Both al-Mawdūdī and Quṭb wrote lengthy Qur'anic commentaries. The former states that he wrote it to facilitate the comprehension (*tafhīm*) of scripture in order to bring it closer to human needs; the latter, to set the milestones for an action subverting the existing political order.

The efforts of female and feminist hermeneutics can be connected hereto, as well as hermeneutics as an instrument of liberation. Gender equality or even female demands for a more active role in society in the name of the Qur'an have been supported by many

Muslim women such as Asma Barlas or Asma Lamrabet (Barlas 2002). But Amina Wadud's (b. 1952) exegetic intention stands out as a more original effort. It has been supported by the belief that Islam may represent a privileged way to fight for women's liberation and the acknowledgement of their rights within a society where the patriarchal and chauvinist role is questioned more and more. The imperative is not only theoretical since Wadud has stood out also for acts considered controversial by conservatives, such as leading the prayer in a New York mosque in 2005, a highly symbolic undertaking that challenged the convention that this function is reserved for men only. On the theoretical level, though, the work that made Amina Wadud famous, the book *Qur'an and Woman* (Wadud 1992), which the author presents as a 'gender' study related to the tradition of *cultural studies*, reveals her mature awareness of the need to exploit linguistics and hermeneutics so as to offer not an atomistic, but rather a theme-based reading of the holy text. The author admits her debt to Fazlur Rahman and more generally to Gadamer's philosophical hermeneutic method, suggesting that the modernized and historically aware reading of the Qur'an uses a process of analysis of words and their context in order to derive text comprehension (*naṣṣ*) therefrom. Hermeneutically speaking, every reading partially reflects the text's intentions and partially the self-evident intentions of the person performing the reading. Every exegete makes subjective decisions: some details of their interpretation reflect these subjective decisions and not necessarily the intentions of the text. By this method, Wadud 'demolishes' the male chauvinist interpretation of certain sensitive passages of the Qur'an (such as the famous and controversial verse Q. 4:34 which appears to institutionalize the husband's 'right' to 'correct' his wife even using physical violence) claiming that Islam's God transcends gender: He is a loving God who wants the best for His creatures who are equal before Him. It is an audacious exegesis, founded on semiotics, even if it does not question the universality of the text, *as it is*, at any time and in any place. Only by exploiting the arguments of Abū Zayd or Maḥmūd Ṭāhā though, can the thorny issue of female subordination really be solved. However, Wadud shows that she appreciates the difference between the Qur'an's universal prescriptions and those historically determined, such as those concerning the Prophet's family or wives. In a wider sense, a typically feminine point of view should be applied to Qur'anic hermeneutics—a necessity which the author now feels is more and more crucial.

A South African Muslim who witnessed the hardships of apartheid, Farid Esack said that the Qur'an must be the means of liberation (Esack 1997). First from a methodological point of view, Esack privileges the dimension of historicity in the religious approach and introduces the concept of 'progressive revelation' (*tadrīj*). Revelation has not been an event given once and for all, but it unfolded in time in connection with precise circumstances and precise events. This is why the text is bound to a context. The fact that the Qur'an is a contextualized text makes the interpretive activity more and more fundamental. The features of the interpretive activity concern the interpreted, the interpreter, and the interpretation. The interpreted, that is the text, often sidesteps the author's intentions. God is the Qur'an's author, but men may in no way claim they know His ends and His motives. In this way, the text retains a purely objective character. As far as the interpreter is concerned, following Gadamer's line of argument, Esack thinks that each interpreter enters the interpretive process with some preconceptions of the questions treated in the text. A number of hermeneutic keys allow the interpreter to work out an interpretation with a concern for praxis. They are the following: *taqwā*, literally in Arabic 'piety' or 'fear of God', which the author suggests is an 'assumption of liability'; God's Uniqueness, in Arabic *tawḥīd*, which Esack does not apply in an ontological sense, but rather as a symbol of the interconnection Islam establishes between the various aspects of reality; humanity: the interpreter has a duty to side with the oppressed (*mustaḍʿafūn*), because God and the prophets sided with the oppressed; the concept of justice (*ʿadl* and *qisṭ*) enjoins all men to fight to redress wrongs; and finally *jihād* is defined by Esack as 'fight and praxis'. Certainly, the goal of *jihād* is to eradicate injustice, but in no way must its aim be the realization of a religiously connoted 'Islamic' state: it must not exchange one oppression for another. In addition to that, it is an acknowledgement, a way to understand and to know; it seemingly has an 'epistemological' value.

Conclusion: Towards a Contemporary Hermeneutics

In conclusion to this analysis, we may state that hermeneutics—and especially philosophical hermeneutics—applied to the Qur'an is a world yet to be discovered. There does not exist, at least as far as I know, a body of secondary literature which summarizes and synthesizes the hermeneutical situation of Qur'anic studies. This may issue from the fact that philosophical hermeneutics is not a popular means of discussing religious texts: the risk of research elitism is likely. In the meantime, at least two points remain open for discussion: what is the destiny of the text once the author has abandoned it? What is the author's destiny after the text has abandoned him/her, closing up on itself? Leaving aside all metaphors, what is God's destiny once the Qur'an appears sealed in its contents, since the prophecy after Muḥammad is inexorably over? Ḥasan Ḥanafī (b. 1935) suggested putting the author between brackets, meaning that we have to pronounce the epoché (in Husserl's terms): God is living, but out of our grasp. Using Roland Barthes's paradigm, the author of the text of the Qur'an is, so to speak, 'dead'. It embodies the consequence of the translation of theology into anthropology. God, the author of the text, cannot intervene to change the text itself; it produces its effects without the author's intervention. Human beings cannot be so arrogant as to understand the intentions of God, however. Simply, He let the text speak within history, at the level of human beings. The text sounds derated. God is living but the text is working within the human sphere. All this implies a weakening of thought: the metaphysical truths are derated in favour of an open hermeneutics.

Moreover: how can we suppose the Qur'an, having been revealed in a precise historical context, is able to solve the problems of modernity? God indeed speaks through the

Qur'an, but the Qur'an's *muṣḥaf* is inexorably closed. Hermeneutics is thus utterly necessary, or rather, if we want to pursue a real widening of knowledge, hermeneutics (in the *ta'wīl* sense) must dethrone *tafsīr* from the central seat it has enjoyed up to now. Muḥammad Ḥamza argued that, in order to open new horizons to hermeneutics, it is necessary to lighten, so to speak, the text's 'weight', without fear of offending its holiness, supporting *ta'wīl* over *tafsīr* (Ḥamza 2011). Moreover, philosophical hermeneutics of the Qur'an represents a newly developing strategy (Akhtar 2008), one that we may expect to receive more attention and one that more thinkers will practise with the aim of broaching modernity through the holy book.

To this end, an important step has been made by those exegetes who, refusing to consider the Qur'an as an untidy and botched book, have on the contrary tried to show its internal coherence and its rhetorical and conceptual structure. To identify cohesive compositional structures within the Qur'an is an exegetical effort that helps thematic interpretation. Neal Robinson (Robinson 1996) or Michel Cuypers (Cuypers 1995, 2007, 2011) among orientalists or Iṣlāḥī (see Mir 1986) and Abdel Haleem (Abdel Haleem 1999) among Muslims have made important contributions to this quest. An exegetical strategy in which the hermeneutic approach is balanced with the thematization of the Qur'anic text appears to provide a way of setting the Qur'an into contemporary reality and opening it up to historical and historicized interpretation. True, the stern traditionalists do and will resist, but contemporary Qur'anic exegesis must explore all possible ways so that the Qur'an is located at the centre of the future evolution of Muslim peoples.

Bibliography

Abdel-Haleem, Muhammad. *Understanding the Qur'an*. London: Tauris, 1999.

'Abduh, Muhammad. *The Theology of Unity*. London: Allen and Unwin, 1966.

Abū Zayd, Naṣr. *Naqd al-khiṭāb al-dīnī*. Cairo: Dār al-Thaqāfa al-Jadīda, 1992.

Abū Zayd, Naṣr. *Mafhūm al-Naṣṣ*. Beirut: al-Markaz al-Thaqāfī al-ʿArabī, 2000.

Abū Zayd, Naṣr. *Rethinking the Qur'ān: Towards a Humanistic Hermeneutics*. Amsterdam: Humanistic University Press SWP, 2004.

Akhtar, Shabbir. *The Qur'an and the Secular Mind*. London and New York: Routledge, 2008.

Arkoun, Mohammed. *Lectures du Coran*. Paris: Maisonneuve, 1982.

Arkoun, Mohammed. *The Unthought in Contemporary Islamic Thought*. London: Al-Saqi Books, 2002.

Barlas, Asma. *Believing Women in Islam: Unreading Patriarchal Interpretations of the Qur'an*. Austin: University of Texas Press, 2002.

Benzine, Rachid. *Les Noveaux Penseurs de l'Islam*. Paris: Albin Michel, 2004.

Bigliardi, Stefano. *Islam and the Quest for Modern Science*. Swedish Research Institute in Istanbul, Transactions vol. 21, 2014.

Bint al-Shāṭiʾ, ʿĀʾisha ʿAbd al-Raḥmān. *Al-Tafsīr al-bayānī li'l-Qur'ān al-Karīm*. Cairo: Dār al-Maʿārif, 2004.

Campanini, Massimo. *The Qur'an: Modern Muslim Interpretations*. London and New York: Routledge, 2011.
Campanini, Massimo. *Philosophical Perspectives on Modern Qur'anic Exegesis*. Sheffield and Bristol, CT: Equinox, 2016.
Campanini, Massimo. 'Towards a Philosophical Qur'anology', *Journal of Qur'anic Studies* 20/2 (2018), 1–18.
Cuypers, Michel. 'Structures rhétoriques dans le Coran: une analyse structurelle de la sourate Joseph et de quelques sourates brèves', *MIDEO* 22 (1995), 107–95.
Cuypers, Michel. *Le Festin: une lecture de la surate al-Ma'ida*. Paris: Lethiellieux, 2007.
Cuypers, Michel. 'Semitic Rhetoric as a Key to the Question of the *naẓm* of the Qur'anic Text', *Journal of Qur'anic Studies* 18/1 (2011), 1–24.
Esack, Farid. *Qur'ān: Liberation and Pluralism*. Oxford: Oneworld, 1997.
Gadamer, Hans-Georg. *Wahrheit und Methode*. Tubingen: Mohr, 1960.
Guessoum, Nidhal. *Islam's Quantum Question: Reconciling Muslim Tradition and Modern Science*. London: Tauris, 2011.
Ḥamza, Muḥammad. *Āfāq al-taʾwīl fī'l-fikr al-Islamī*. Beirut: Muʾassasat al-Intishār al-ʿArabī, 2011.
Ḥanafī, Ḥasan. 'Method of Thematic Interpretation of the Qur'an'. In: *Islam in the Modern World*, 1:407–28. Cairo: Anglo-Egyptian Bookshop, 1995.
Khalafallāh, Muḥammad Aḥmad. *Al-Fann al-Qaṣaṣī fī'l-Qurʾān al-Karīm*. London, Cairo, and Beirut: Muʾassasat al-Intishār al-ʿArabī, 1999.
Laroui, Abdallah. *Islam et Histoire*. Paris: Albin Michel, 1999.
Leaman, Oliver. *The Qur'an: A Philosophical Guide*. London: Bloomsbury, 2016.
Mawdūdī, Abū'l-A'la. *Towards Understanding the Qur'ān*. (ed.). Zafar Ishaq Ansari. Leicester: The Islamic Foundation, 1999.
Mir, Mustansir. *Coherence in the Qur'ān: A Study of Iṣlāḥī's Concept of Nazm* in Tadabbur-i Qurʾān. Indianapolis: American Trust Publications, 1986.
Nietzsche, Friedrich. *La Volontà di Potenza [Wille zur Macht]*. Milan: Bompiani, 1999.
Quṭb, Sayyid. *The Islamic Concept and its Characteristics*. Indianapolis: American Trust Publications, 1991.
Rahman, Fazlur. *Major Themes of the Qur'an*. Minneapolis: Bibliotheca Islamica, 1980.
Rahman, Fazlur. *Islam and Modernity*. Chicago and London: University of Chicago Press, 1984.
Robinson, Neal. *Discovering the Qur'an: A Contemporary Approach to a Veiled Text*. London: SCM, 1996.
Saeed, Abdullah. *Interpreting the Qur'an: Towards a Contemporary Approach*. London and New York: Routledge, 2006.
Shahrūr, Muḥammad. *al-Qur'ān wa'l-Kitāb: Qirāʾa Muʿāṣira*. Damascus: Dār al-Ahālī, 1990.
Shahrūr, Muḥammad. *Al-Qaṣas al-Qurʾānī: Qirāʾa Muʿāṣira*. Beirut: Dār al-Sāqī, 2012.
Shaltūt, Maḥmūd. *Min hudā al-Qur'ān*. Cairo: Dār al-Kātib al-ʿArabī, 1968.
Ṭabāṭabāʾī, Muḥammad Ḥusayn. *al-Mīzān: An Exegesis of the Qur'ān*. Trans. S. Akhtar Rizvi. Tehran: World Organization for Islamic Services, 1983.
Ṭāhā, Maḥmūd M. *The Second Message of Islam*. Syracuse, NY: Syracuse University Press, 1996.
Taji-Farouki, Suha (ed.). *Modern Muslim Intellectuals and the Qur'ān*. Oxford, New York, and London: Oxford University Press and the Institute of Ismaili Studies, 2004.

Taji-Farouki, Suha (ed.). *The Qur'an and its Readers Worldwide: Contemporary Commentaries and Translations*. London, Oxford, and New York: Oxford University Press in association with the Institute of Ismaili Studies, 2015.
Wadud, Amina. *Qur'an and Woman*. New York and Oxford: Oxford University Press, 1992.
Wild, Stefan (ed.). *The Qur'ān as Text*. Leiden: Brill, 1996.
Zaqzūq, Maḥmūd. *Al-Fikr al-Dīnī wa-Qaḍāya al-ʿAṣr*. Cairo: Dār al-Quds al-ʿArabī, 2016.

Index of Qur'an Verses

Note: Figures are indicated by an italic "*f*", respectively, following the page number.

1: *Sūrat al-Fātiḥa* 10, 73, 156, 317, 322–325, 323*f*, 346, 359, 433, 737, 755
1:1 602 n.16
1:2 574
1:2–3 336
1:4 446, 476
1:6–7 336, 479
2: *Sūrat al-Baqara* 73, 156, 175, 244, 317, 318, 321, 322, 346, 351, 355, 362, 364, 368, 369, 370, 371, 450, 451, 455, 456, 496, 602, 737, 814
2:1 602 n.16
2:1–9 736
2:2 406
2:3 742
2:5 657
2:8 476
2:14 438
2:16 156
2:23 390
2:23–24 375
2:24 481
2:25 430, 480
2:27 455
2:28 123, 482
2:29 431, 507
2:30–39 364, 368, 528
2:30–96 736
2:30–141 456
2:31 438
2:32 569
2:34 438
2:38 747
2:43 447, 449, 454
2:55 740
2:61 146, 149
2:62 85, 144, 147, 161, 365, 477, 479
2:63–66 148, 149
2:67 123
2:80 146, 742
2:81 742
2:83 146, 449, 450, 456
2:85 148, 476
2:87–91 146
2:89 149
2:89–90 149
2:94 149
2:105 149
2:106 839
2:107 472
2:109 148
2:111 161
2:111–112 479
2:113 161, 446
2:115 592, 599, 747
2:116 176
2:120 149, 161
2:124 132
2:125 248
2:127 131, 248
2:127–129 132
2:129 469
2:133 248
2:135 149, 161
2:136 248
2:138 133, 791
2:140 149, 161, 248
2:142 149
2:143 368, 478, 748
2:144 368, 811, 812
2:146 146
2:151 612

2:151–152 469
2:152 407
2:154 483
2:158 448
2:159 149
2:160 470
2:163–242 364
2:164 469, 808, 810, 811, 812, 813
2:165 479
2:167 479
2:174 149
2:175 156
2:178 451, 454
2:178–179 455
2:178–182 369
2:178–203 456
2:178–253 370
2:179 451
2:180 450, 458
2:181 454, 737
2:183 147
2:183–185 448
2:183–189 369
2:185 454
2:186 738, 747
2:187 333, 340, 535
2:188 340, 453
2:189 448, 454
2:190 515, 516
2:190–191 451, 612
2:190–194 515
2:191 448, 516, 566
2:191–200 448
2:193 517
2:194 451, 516
2:195 449, 451
2:196 448, 449
2:198 156
2:202 478
2:203 454
2:208–209 569
2:210 738
2:215–242 456
2:216 519
2:217 451, 625, 629
2:219 341, 369, 452
2:220–242 369
2:221 449, 454
2:222 447
2:223 535, 536
2:225 123
2:226–227 450
2:228 450
2:228–237 338
2:229 449, 450
2:230 450
2:231 450
2:232 450
2:233 450
2:235 450, 454
2:236–237 449
2:237 339, 449, 454
2:238 737
2:238–239 339, 342, 451
2:240 450, 454
2:251 814
2:254 476, 742
2:255 [*āyat al-kursī;* throne verse] 241, 248, 585, 739
2:256 241, 518
2:257 438, 747
2:259 435
2:262 747
2:264 470, 747
2:275 171, 452, 453
2:276 453
2:280 740
2:282 452, 453
2:282–283 456
2:283 453
3: *Sūrat Āl ʿImrān* 74, 131
3:3 146
3:3–4 147
3:7 424, 567, 642, 708, 722, 724, 736, 737, 753, 768, 773, 820, 842, 853, 854
3:12 481
3:13 342
3:14 145, 247
3:19 244
3:20 748
3:31 469, 747, 748
3:33 497
3:33ff. 497
3:35 131
3:42 574
3:45 160

3:50 146
3:52 146, 161
3:65 149
3:67 161, 496
3:67–68 149
3:70 149
3:71 146
3:76 747
3:79 145
3:81 146, 489, 492
3:84 248
3:85 365
3:85–86 241
3:88 481
3:91–92 241
3:91–99 241
3:93 146
3:93–94 141
3:95–97 240
3:96–97 241
3:97 448
3:98 149
3:99 148
3:106–107 337
3:110 146
3:113 148
3:113–114 147
3:118–120 342
3:123 100
3:129 177
3:134 747
3:144 98
3:146 747
3:148 747
3:159 461, 747
3:170 747
3:179 676
3:181 148
3:183 149
3:184 147
3:187 149
3:193 480
3:199 147, 149
3:200 513
4: *Sūrat al-Nisāʾ* 131, 175, 321, 355, 363, 364, 451, 731
4:1 528
4:1–43 364
4:3 449, 450
4:3–4 748
4:4 449
4:8 449
4:11 457
4:11–12 450, 456, 458
4:12 57, 304, 456, 457
4:12b 457
4:15 452, 453
4:19 449
4:20–21 335
4:22–24 449
4:23 57, 454
4:24 451
4:25 449
4:25–28 748
4:28 454
4:29 452
4:34 450, 454, 530, 532, 533, 534, 535, 856
4:34–35 337
4:35 453
4:36 450
4:43 341, 447
4:46 144, 146
4:47 148
4:49 149
4:54 145, 148
4:57 392 n.3, 481
4:59 453, 455
4:65 453
4:69 481
4:75 517
4:76 451
4:89 451
4:90 522
4:92 448, 449, 450, 452, 739
4:92–93 455
4:93 451
4:101–103 451
4:123 248, 742
4:123–124 337
4:127 454, 748
4:128 534
4:152 479
4:153 146, 149, 740
4:154 146
4:154–155 149
4:155 146

4:157 160
4:160 144
4:160–161 146, 149
4:162 758
4:163 146
4:164 422
4:171 160, 244
4:171–172 242*f*
4:172 160
4:176 57, 304, 450, 454, 456, 457, 458
5: *Sūrat al-Māʾida* 290, 321, 339, 352, 355, 365, 425, 433, 456, 496
5:1 448, 456
5:1–30 281
5:2 448
5:3 448, 452, 454
5:3–4 454
5:4 448, 456
5:5 147, 339, 448, 449, 454, 456
5:6 205, 339, 447, 456, 457
5:7 281
5:9 430
5:13 146
5:14 161
5:17 160
5:18 149, 156, 161
5:19–21 365
5:27–40 497
5:28 584
5:33 452
5:34 452
5:37 481
5:38 452, 458
5:39 452
5:42 446
5:43 453
5:43–44 146
5:43–46 146
5:44 144, 145, 146, 741
5:44–74 695
5:45 452, 454
5:48 447
5:49 855
5:51 149, 161
5:54 747
5:55 246
5:57 149
5:60 [Flügel system] 246
5:63 145
5:64 148, 738
5:67 504
5:69 85, 147, 161, 365
5:72 479
5:72–75 141
5:72a 160
5:72b 160
5:75 160
5:77 735
5:78 160
5:82 149, 161, 748
5:87 456
5:88 456
5:89 449, 450
5:90 103, 341
5:93 747
5:95 448, 453
5:96 448
5:97 131, 448, 575
5:101 566
5:103 448
5:106 450
5:107–108 339
5:109 489
5:110 157, 435
5:112–115 456
5:119–120 456
6: *Sūrat al-Anʿām* 233, 336
6:1–2 431
6:2 477, 807
6:6 134
6:15 476
6:25 99
6:31 478
6:38 575
6:52 448
6:59 586
6:73 412
6:76 784, 786
6:85 159
6:86 248
6:89 446
6:91–93 147
6:93–94 482
6:99 102, 103

6:103 739
6:106 772
6:120 724
6:128 477
6:138–144 448
6:141 446, 449
6:145 448
6:146 448
6:146–147 454
6:147 148
6:151 446
6:151–152 456
6:152 450
6:152–153 454
7: *Sūrat al-Aʿrāf* 424, 751, 809
7:8–9 478
7:10 134
7:11 438
7:11–15 751
7:11–27 528
7:16 438
7:17 338
7:26 729
7:31–33 751
7:35–36 751
7:37–39 337
7:39–40 751
7:40 483
7:47–51 394
7:54 431, 809
7:54–61 248
7:57 572, 573
7:59–94 490
7:65–102 99
7:96 288
7:109–126 588
7:131 123
7:143 423, 740, 749, 751
7:146 172
7:148 172
7:148–155 759
7:150 146
7:155 740
7:157 146, 157, 158
7:160 749
7:163 148
7:172 747, 761
7:172–173 412
7:187 423, 475
8: *Sūrat al-Anfāl* 342, 451
8:8 147
8:24 749
8:31 99
8:34 747
8:35 89
8:38 517
8:39 517
8:41 449, 751
8:50 483
8:59 375
8:61 522
8:65–66 451
8:71 451
8:87 748
8:193–194 796
9: *Sūrat al-Tawba* 451
9:1–2 643
9:2 375
9:3 375
9:5 451, 519–521, 522, 523, 573, 612, 626
9:5–7 448
9:11 446
9:12 517
9:12–13 517
9:18 247, 248
9:25 100
9:29 301, 451, 519, 521, 522, 523
9:30 148, 160, 161
9:31 148, 160, 748
9:33 175, 246
9:34 145
9:35 135
9:36 451, 523, 626
9:36–37 448
9:37 88
9:40 749
9:41 451
9:54 742
9:60 449
9:71 461, 529, 530, 533, 536
9:79 449
9:91 446
9:94 728
9:103 449

9:107 176
9:112 448
9:121 639
10: *Sūrat Yūnus* (Jonah) 375, 436, 490
10:1–2 375
10:9 430
10:19 481
10:38 375, 390
10:45 639
10:62 747
10:62–64 478
10:64 586
10:70 474
10:79–81 588
10:94 145
11: *Sūrat Hūd* 424, 490
11:3 476
11:13 375
11:13–14 390
11:25–26 474
11:25–95 490
11:26 476
11:43 406
11:58–68 99
11:69–71 498
11:71 47
11:84 476
11:84–95 99
11:104 474
11:106–107 742
11:119 477
12: *Sūrat Yūsuf* (Joseph) 99, 323, 324*f*, 338, 390, 397, 489–490, 491, 731
12:1–30 281
12:4 807
12:6 724
12:21 134, 724
12:22–32 757
12:31 288
12:36 640
12:40 730, 855
12:46 640
12:53 747
12:56 134
12:58 639
12:76 446
12:82 330
12:107 474
13: *Sūrat al-Raʿd* 583
13:11 583
13:17 727
13:25 146
13:27f. 642
13:43 145
14: *Sūrat Ibrāhīm* 799, 800–801, 814
14:10 643, 814
14:18 280, 287, 290, 476, 804
14:24–26 804
14:28 742
14:31 476
14:34 799
14:37 243
14:39 248
14:42–43 477
14:48 392
15: *Sūrat al-Ḥijr* 359, 751, 809
15:7 571
15:16 809
15:26 135, 731
15:26–43 528
15:27 439
15:28 135
15:28–29 439
15:33 135
15:38 476
15:44 479
15:80ff. 642
15:94 374, 409
16: *Surat al-Naḥl* 336, 799, 800
16:8 656
16:10–11 243
16:18 799
16:24 99, 656
16:43 730
16:43–44 145
16:44 634
16:67 341
16:89 478
16:96 643
16:101–103 142
16:103 285, 287, 288
16:114–118 141
17: *Sūrat al-Isrāʾ*
17:1 243, 586, 748, 756, 761

17:2 146
17:13–14 478
17:22–23 454
17:23 638
17:23–24 450
17:23–40 470
17:33 451
17:44 814
17:45 136
17:49 477
17:50–51 477
17:58 183
17:60 586, 727
17:61 439
17:62–64 338
17:70 736
17:78–79 247, 248
17:79 448
17:80 247
17:81 247
17:88 375
17:94 571
17:106 316, 565
17:107 145
17:107–108 148
17:110 122
18: *Sūrat al-Kahf* 99, 129, 134, 137, 731, 768, 769
18:9 129
18:18 130, 131
18:19 130, 661
18:21 130
18:22 131, 644
18:24 748
18:26 130, 131
18:28 743
18:29 743
18:31 278
18:49 576
18:57 642
18:57–68 195*f*
18:83–84 134
18:83–102 133
18:85 132
18:85–91 136
18:86 134, 136
18:86–88 134, 135
18:90 136
18:93–99 475
18:99 136
18:99–102 136
19: *Sūrat Maryam* 131, 175, 392, 570, 800, 801
19:1–98 250, 251*f*
19:16 131, 497
19:16–33 159
19:16:33 497
19:17 439
19:22–26 132
19:28 131
19:34 159, 658
19:35 250, 570
19:45 569
19:54 248
19:56–57 490
19:65 642
19:77ff. 570
19:81–82 570
19:88 570
20: *Sūrat Ṭaha* 351
20:1 658
20:5 739
20:7–8 747
20:9–99 99
20:12 408
20:15 639
20:32 641
20:39 738
20:43–47 588
20:44 643
20:63 640
20:65–70 588
20:77–78 435
20:85–94 759
20:102–104 477
20:105–107 476
20:108 478
20:115–124 528
20:117 438
20:125–126 336
20:128 657
20:130 409
21: *Sūrat al-Anbiyā*ʾ
21:5 802
21:7 730
21:18 849

21:30 480
21:42 569
21:79 727
21:83–84 493
21:85 248
21:92 461
21:96 475
21:104 727
22: *Sūrat al-Ḥajj* 451
22:2 392, 475
22:5 243, 477
22:17 85, 161, 479
22:19–22 481
22:20 638
22:25 448
22:25–37 448
22:26 749
22:30 575
22:31 483
22:36 448
22:39–40 451, 515
22:40 148, 515
22:41 134, 247
22:46 727
22:52 839
22:55 476
22:60 575
22:63 243
22:70 755
22:78 446, 514
23: *Sūrat al-Mu'minūn*
23:1–10 339
23:1–11 336
23:12–14 434
23:20 146
23:43–74 478
23:50 159
23:51 489
23:80 123
23:83 99
23:87 176
23:89 176
23:100 483
23:101–118 473
23:103 478, 481
23:112 176
23:114 176
24: *Sūrat al-Nūr* 351, 404
24:2 446, 452
24:4 452
24:6–9 452
24:10 333
24:30–32 731
24:33 305, 451
24:35 [*āyat al-nūr;* light verse] 247, 248, 252, 405, 585, 727, 737, 747, 756, 781, 783, 787, 789, 813, 842
24:40 405
24:61 454
24:99–100 589
25: *Sūrat al-Furqān* 185
25:5 99
25:7 571
25:15 480
25:15–16 480
25:16 480
25:25 476
25:32 315, 316, 358
25:50 243
25:52 514
25:53 391
25:59 435, 642
25:75 479
26: *Sūrat al-Shuʿarā'* 175, 403, 404, 422, 424
26:67 146
26:89 248
26:115 474
26:137 465
26:165 574
26:192–197 140
26:193–195 184
26:195 287
26:224 802
26:224–226 403
26:224–227 391
26:225 133
26:227 403
27: *Sūrat al-Naml* 422
27:18 644
27:23–42 435
27:34 749
27:44 129
27:68 99

27:78 446
27:80–81 726
27:82 475, 726
27:87 136
27:88 476
27:89–90 479
28: *Sūrat al-Qaṣaṣ*
28:6 134
28:38 129
28:52–53 147
28:54–55 148
28:85 481
28:88 446, 473, 738, 755, 786, 787, 788
29: *Sūrat al-ʿAnkabūt*
29:20 473, 727
29:28 574
29:35 755
29:43 724
29:44 728
29:58 479
29:69 514
30: *Sūrat al-Rūm* 806
30:1–5 629
30:3–4 247
30:8 435
30:15 480
30:21 536
30:27 477
30:30 806
30:38 446
30:48 572
30:50 573
30:57 478
31: *Sūrat Luqmān*
31:5 657
31:20 724
31:28 477
32:4 435
32: *Sūrat al-Sajda*
32:13 477
32:19 742
32:26 657
32:27 243
33: *Sūrat al-Aḥzāb* 320, 340, 351, 367, 453
33:5 450
33:6 57
33:8 340
33:9–10 340
33:13 100
33:21 453, 469, 748
33:28–38 453
33:33 100, 246, 246*f*
33:35 448, 449, 527, 533
33:36–40 57
33:40 98
33:41 448, 748
33:41–42 448
33:49 453
33:64 123
34: *Sūrat Sabāʾ* 808
34:2 808
34:3 784
34:5 375
34:15 639
34:15–17 84
34:38 375
35: *Sūrat Fāṭir*
35:9 572
35:13 808
35:22 483
35:35 481
36: *Sūrat Yāsīn* 233, 756
36:32 643
36:33–34 477
36:47 451
36:48 248
36:49 740
36:51 136
36:65 478
36:68 496
36:69 802
36:77–83 334, 336
36:82 54, 781
37: *Sūrat al-Ṣāffāt* 572
37:31–49 473
37:35–37 133
37:36 802
37:48 480
37:60–66 473
37:62–68 481
37:106 132
38: *Sūrat Ṣad*
38:4 133
38:15 740

38:21–25 494
38:26 446
38:34 435
38:48 490
38:71–85 528
38:76 439
38:81 476
39: *Sūrat al-Zumar*
39:20 479
39:23 390
39:27 724
39:42 785
39:68 136, 477
39:68–75 473
39:69–70 479
39:75 435
40: *Sūrat Ghāfir* 346
40:11 482
40:20 446
40:36–37 129
40:46 483
40:47–50 337
40:48–50 336
41: *Sūrat Fuṣṣilat* 346
41:3 183
41:11–12a 781, 782
41:19–23 338
41:22 136
41:42 245
41:44 288, 841
41:47 474
41:53 849
42: *Sūrat al-Shūrā* 175, 346
42:10 455
42:11 738
42:13 159, 446
42:15 149
42:21 446
42:23 641, 730
42:28 243
42:38 461
43: *Sūrat al-Zukhruf* 346
43:3 640, 743
43:15–16 570
43:57 159
43:61 475
43:63 159
43:65 476
43:85 474
44: *Sūrat al-Dukhān* 346
44:10 475
44:43–46 481
44:54 283
44:56 790
45: *Sūrat al-Jāthiyya* 346
45:18 149, 446
45:19 747
45:28 478
46: *Sūrat al-Aḥqāf* 346
46:3 435
46:4–6 335
46:17 99
46:35 477
47: *Sūrat Muḥammad* 489
47:2 98
47:4 520
47:15 480
47:18 474
48: *Sūrat al-Fatḥ* 233, 244
48:1 244, 247
48:14 472
48:18 103
48:24 100
48:29 98, 175
49: *Sūrat al-Ḥujurāt*
49:7–8 340
50: *Sūrat Qaf* 359
50:6 811
50:7 726
50:9 243
50:16 747
50:21 478
50:38 141
50:41 478
51: *Sūrat al-Dhāriyyāt* 572
51:22 430
51:49 724
52: *Sūrat al-Ṭūr* 354 n.8
52:9 476
52:20 283
52:21 351
52:29 133
52:29–31 375
52:30 133, 802

52:30–43 335
52:33–34 375
53: *Sūrat al-Najm* 351, 351 n.4, 354 n.8, 423
53:1–18 748
53:19–20 86, 124
53:19–22 124
53:21 124
53:23 351
53:26–32 351
54: *Sūrat al-Qamar* 341, 424, 456
54:1 474
54:2–3 341
54:8 476
54:17 634
54:22 634
54:23 634
54:40 634
54:49 330
54:54–55 341
54:55 738
55: *Sūrat al-Raḥmān* 233, 341, 355, 357 n.10, 366, 456, 796
55:6 780
55:19–20 789
55:25 738
55:26–27 473
55:37 476
55:39–45 341
55:41–45 479
55:46–61 479
55:54 480
55:56 480
55:62–77 479
55:72–76 803
55:76 480
55:78 122
56: *Sūrat al-Wāqiʿa* 233, 317
56:1 474
56:7–10 479
56:17 481
56:22 283
56:50 476
56:57–74 336
56:60 430
56:65 571
56:77–79 184
56:77–80 245
56:83 482
56:88–94 481
56:89 392 n.3, 480
56:95 404
56:96 317
57: *Sūrat al-Ḥadīd* 317
57:1 317
57:2 243, 250
57:11 453
57:13 740
57:17 727
57:22 430
57:27 748
58: *Sūrat al-Mujādala*
58:3 450
58:7 747
59: *Sūrat al-Ḥashr*
59:2 785
59:3 423
59:21 101
60: *Sūrat al-Mumtaḥana* 352
60:8 522
60:8–9 522
61: *Sūrat al-Ṣaff*
61:6 98, 146, 157
61:6b 158
61:9 157
61:13 247
61:13–14 161
61:14 161, 186
62:5 146
62: *Sūrat al-Jumuʿa*
62:6 149, 177
62:9–10 448
63: *Sūrat al-Munāfiqūn*
63:1 354
63:3 614
63:10 645
64: *Sūrat al-Taghābun*
64:1 243, 250, 585
65: *Sūrat al-Ṭalāq* 352, 355, 357 n.10, 450
65:1 635
65:6 450
66: *Sūrat al-Taḥrīm* 352
66:5 448
66:12 131

67: *Sūrat al-Mulk* 233
67:2 643
67:3 479
67:16 739
68: *Sūrat al-Qalam* 357 n.10
68:4 465
68:15 99
68:25 430
68:48 446
68:50–52 585
69: *Sūrat al-Ḥāqqa* 354 n.8
69:1–3 474
69:7 351
69:13–15 476
69:13–16 136
69:13–37 473
69:17 435, 478
69:24 480
69:41 593, 802
69:41–42 375
69:44–6 158
70: *Sūrat al-Maʿārij* 357 n.10
70:1–35 473
70:4 351 n.4
70:8 476
70:22–29 336
70:22–35 351 n.4
70:23–34 339
70:40 123
71: *Sūrat Nūḥ* (Noah) 474, 490
71:23 86
72: *Sūrat al-Jinn*
72:2 171
72:12 375
72:25 474
73: *Sūrat al-Muzzammil* 351, 351 n.4, 354 n.8, 359, 571
73:1–19 351
73:20 350, 351, 357, 456
74: *Sūrat al-Muddaththir* 351, 351 n.4, 354 n.8, 359
74:6 570
74:8 476
74:9 476
74:30–31 481
74:31 350, 351, 357, 785
74:33 186
74:49–56 803
74:56 351
75: *Sūrat al-Qiyāma* 122, 320, 367
75:4 477
75:8–9 476
75:16–18 158
75:21–25 121
75:22–23 739, 772
75:23 772
75:24–25 740
76: *Sūrat al-Insān*
76:8 450, 451
76:10 476
76:12–22 473
76:18 392 n.3
76:19 481
76:27 476
77: *Sūrat al-Mursalāt* 572
78: *Sūrat al-Nabāʾ* 233, 351, 354 n.8
78:12 479
78:18 136, 476
78:37–40 351
79: *Sūrat al-Nāziʿāt* 357 n.10, 572
79:6–7 477
79:8–9 477
79:11 391
79:37 337
79:40 337
80: *Sūrat ʿAbasa*
80:11–16 184
80:21–22 477
80:38–41 739
81: *Sūrat al-Takwīr* 325*f*, 354 n.8, 423, 474, 600
81:1 392
81:1–2 476
81:4 392
81:5–6 476
81:7 477
81:19–25 324, 325*f*
81:29 351
82:1 392
82: *Sūrat al-Infiṭār*
82:2 392
82:11–12 478
83: *Sūrat al-Muṭaffifīn*
83:13 99

83:15 772
83:22 252
83:24–25 252
84: *Sūrat al-Inshiqāq* 122, 354 n.8
84:3–4 477
84:16–23 122
84:25 351
85: *Sūrat al-Burūj* 351, 354 n.8
85:2 476
85:7–11 351
85:22 183, 755, 758, 761
86: *Sūrat al-Ṭāriq*
86:8 477
87: *Sūrat al-Aʿlā* 121, 354 n.8, 781
87:3 657
87:7 351
87:19 146
88: *Sūrat al-Ghāshiyya*
88:4 135
89: *Sūrat al-Fajr*
89 354 n.8
89:15–16 351
89:23–24 351
89:25–27 337
89:27 747
89:27–30 351
90: *Sūrat al-Balad* 354 n.8
90:17–20 351
91: *Sūrat al-Shams* 100, 132
91: 7–10, 583
92: *Sūrat al-Layl*
92:5–8 337
95: *Sūrat al-Tīn* 354 n.8
95:2 146
95:6 351
96: *Sūrat al-ʿAlaq* 98
96:1–2 403
97: *Sūrat al-Qadr* 351 n.4, 354 n.8, 731
97:4 351
98: *Sūrat al-Bayyina* 359
98:4 469
98:5 446
98:8 481
99: *Sūrat al-Zalzala*
99:6–8 478
100: *Sūrat al-ʿĀdiyāt* 389, 572
101: *Sūrat al-Qāriʿa*
101:1 474
101:4–5 476
101:6–9 478
101:11 135
103: *Sūrat al-ʿAṣr* 351, 354 n.8, 737
103:3 351
104: *Sūrat al-Humaza*
104:1–4 490
105: *Sūrat al-Fīl* 98
106: *Sūrat Quraysh*
106:1 100
107: *Sūrat al-Māʿūn*
107:1–3 490
108: *Sūrat al-Kawthar* 728
109: *Sūrat al-Kāfirūn* 359
109:1 186
110: *Sūrat al-Naṣr* 359
110:1 161
111: *Sūrat al-Masad* 317, 731
112: *Sūrat al-Ikhlāṣ* 156, 175, 250, 317, 359, 433, 456, 582, 782, 842
112:1 431
112:2 301, 782, 783
113: *Sūrat al-Falaq* 359, 782
113:1 790, 791
114: *Sūrat al-Nās* 359, 598, 782

Index of Bible References

Acts 161, 420
7:53 149
9:2 161
11:26 161
14:2 148
22:4 161
22:5 162
22:8 161
24:5 161
26:28 161
Col.
1:14–20 141
1:15 87
2 Cor.
11:32 162
Dan.
2:19 22, 420
8:15–27 420
9:20–27 420
Deut.
6:4 156
6:14 141
14:3–21 141
18:15–19 157
18:18–20 158
Epistles 420
Exod.
20:11 141
21:24–25 452
30:21 446
31:17 141
Ezek.
38–39 137
38:39 475
Gal.
1:17–18 162
3:6–14 141
Gen.
1:26 159
2:8 480
3 284
4 497
18:1–8 499
22 131–132
22:15–18 132
Heb.
8:6–13 141
8:13 147
11:4–5 497
Isa.
11:1 162
40:3 158
49:9 420
James 497
John 161
1:21 160
1:46 162
4:25 160
14:8–9 87
14:16–17 157
14:23 159
14:23–26 157
15:26 157
16:7–14 157
16:13 159
19:19 162
20:7 137
Lev. 11, 141

Luke 161, 497
1:1–4 420
1:26 439
1:26–38 497
Mark 161
1:3 158
12:29 156
Matt. 161
1:21 159
2:23 162
6:9–14 156
23:13–14 148
23:30–31 149
23:33–38 497
1 Pet.
4:16 161
Ps.
135:15–21 141
Rev. 160
1:11 19, 420
13:13–16 475
Rom. 160
4:29 149
11:7 149
15:4 158
1 Sam.14:8–11 420
2 Sam. 12 494
2 Timothy 160

Index of Hadith Citations

'ʿAlī is with the Qur'an and the Qur'an with ʿAlī..' 709
'As soon as one dies, Doomsday begins for him,' 482–483
...each Qur'anic verse has two aspects—the 'outward' *(ẓahr)* and the 'inward' *(baṭn)*... 760
'Every word has two meanings [lit. 'aspects,' *wajhān*], so interpret speech according to the best meaning' 738
[the faithful are described as constituting] 'a [single] edifice in which each strengthens the other,' 530
'The first thing a person will be asked [about] on the Day of Judgement is the prayer...,' 339
God made our *walāya* the pole of the Qurʾān 708
'He will be raised and judged as a whole nation by himself on the Day of Judgement,' 92
'The Hour and I have been sent like these two—and he pointed to [or 'joined'] his index and middle fingers' 475
'I am leaving behind two weighty things, the book of God and my progeny...,' 708
'I am the city of knowledge, and ʿAlī is its gate; those who intend to enter it should enter through its gate,' 723
'If I were to command anyone to prostrate himself before another [person],' 532
'I have heard that these seven *ḥarfs*...,' 186–187
'Indeed, I was sent to complete the nobility of character,' 469
'May God torment the Jews and the Christians for making the graves of their prophets and holy people into places of prayer,' 130
'No bequest to an heir,' 458
The Prophet describes faith as having more than sixty characteristics, the least of which is the removal of harm from the path 742
The Prophet warns that a nation governed by a woman will not prosper 532
...of the Qur'an being revealed in seven *ḥurūf* or modes 209
[Qur'an having been sent down] 'on seven edges... 185–186
[Qur'anic revelations had to be] 'collected from palm-leaf stalks, stones, and the breasts of men...,' 347
'There is one among you who will fight for the *taʾwīl* of the Qurʾān just as I myself fought for its revelation *(tanzīl)* and he is ʿAlī ibn Abī Ṭālib,' 709–710
...those who do not fulfil their religious obligations have no faith 742

Index of Places

Note: Figures are indicated by an italic "*f*", respectively, following the page number.

A

Abyssinia 297
Afghanistan 250, 263, 581
  Bust 231
  Jām 250
Africa 554, 557, 580
  central 235
  hip-hoppers in 582
  Muslim communities across 552
  Sub-Saharan 559
  West Africa 578, 586
    reading in 196
Agra, and Taj Mahal 233
Aleppo
  citadel of 248
  congregational mosque of 246
Alexandria 82
Algeria
  Aurès mountains 734
  Qarāra (El Guerrara) 736
Almaqah 87
Āmūl 658
Anatolia 556
Andalusia/al-Andalus/Andalucía 520, 599, 658
  Alhambra Palace 599
  tafsīr in 656, 667
Antioch 81–82, 161
Arabia/Arabian Peninsula 41, 45, 46, 84–85, 89, 92, 98, 102, 105, 111, 112, 114, 115, 118, 123–124, 143, 285, 297, 307, 488, 581
  ancient 87, 116
  Central 115, 432
  and divination 89
  nomadic societies of 115, 117
  North/northern 85, 114, 115, 124
    graffito from 245
    inscriptions in 118, 125
    oases of 114–115, 117
  north-west 87, 91, 117–118, 124
  pre-Islamic 98, 288, 431–432, 477, 804
    linguistic map of 111
  religion/beliefs of 85, 154
  South 90–91, 105, 116, 121
    inscriptions in 117, 122
    states of 86–87
  tafsīr produced in 668
  West/western 88, 98, 99, 101, 105–106, 115–116, 117
  written records in 116
Asia 152, 554, 580. *See also* South Asia
  hip-hoppers in 582
  Muslim communities across 552
ʿAthtar 87
al-Azhar 269

B

Badr 100
Baghdad 153, 228, 231, 494, 658
  Abbasid 225
  centres of learning in 767
Banda Aceh 583
Basel 256
Basra 169, 204, 656, 657, 658
  centres of learning in 767
  codices sent to 198
  grammarians from 645
  Great Mosque 190
  readings of 221
  school of 189
Beirut 263, 410–411

Berlin
library 267
Qur'anic fragments held in 197
Bosphorus 82
Bukhara 263
Buṣrā 83
Byzantium 82, 83, 521, 548

C

Cairo 263, 269, 673, 679, 701. *See also* al-Fusṭāṭ
al-Azhar mosque 232
ʿAmr ibn al-ʿĀṣ mosque (in al-Fusṭāṭ) 206, 208, 221, 224
Aqmar Mosque 246*f*
Biʾr al-Waṭāwiṭ 253
Dar al-Kutub 219
library of 267
mosque of al-Ḥākim 247
mosque of Ibn Ṭūlūn 244
Nilometer 243
Royal Library at 298
Calcutta 263
Cambridge, Mingana palimpsest in 222
Central Asia 555, 561
expansion of Russia into 263–264
Chicago, library 267
China 231, 235, 559
Silk Route to 84
trade with 260
Constantinople 82. *See also* Istanbul
fall of 256
Cordoba/Córdoba 235, 248, 658
Crimea 260
Ctesiphon, ruins of 153

D

Dadān 115, 124
Damascus 153, 155, 161, 162, 204, 219, 224
codices sent to 198
Great Mosque of 218–219, 224
Qur'an fragments in 169, 173
readings of 221
Umayyad codex/Qur'an of 174, 224
Dead Sea 118, 803
Delhi, Jamʿa Mosque in 241
Dhāt Ḥimyam 87
Dhū al-Majāz 88
Doha 265
Dublin 224
Chester Beatty Library 219
Dūmat al-Jandal 88, 119

E

Edessa 82–83
Edirne, Selimiye Mosque 248
Egypt 40, 82–83, 135, 206, 231, 268, 287, 318, 461, 554, 561. *See also* Cairo; al-Fusṭāṭ
artists from 580
centres of learning in 767
'Exodus' from 92
and Mamluks 230, 252
Emesa (modern Ḥomṣ, Syria) 87
England 595. *See also* United Kingdom
Ephesus 130
Europe 45, 224, 256
encounter with 695
modern day 584
Muslim communities across 552

F

Fertile Crescent 85, 91
France, Bibliothèque nationale de France 170, 219, 220, 304
al-Fusṭāṭ 287, 656, 658
ʿAmr ibn al-ʿĀṣ Mosque 206, 208, 221, 224
Qur'an fragments in 169, 173
Umayyad codex of 174, 224

G

Gaza Strip 508
Germany 266
Corpus Coranicum project 219
Ghur [region] 250
Greece 90
Gentile-orientated Churches 152
Gulf (al-Baḥrayn) 84

H

al-Ḥadath 406
Ḥarrān 91, 119

Ḥegrā (modern Madāʾin Ṣāliḥ) 85, 118, 120, 124
inscription from 113
Ḥijāz 34, 100–101, 104–105, 119, 196, 233, 263, 285, 306, 491–494, 645, 655
history of 98
late antique/antiquity 98, 495
northern, dialects in 114
oases of 102
pre-Islamic 103
Qur'an revealed in 42
urban centres of 287
Ḥimà (north of Najrān) 119 n.3
Hims, readings of 221
Ḥimyar 86, 89
Ḥirāʾ, Mount 51–52, 92
al-Ḥudaybiyya, events at 515
Ḥunayn 100

I

Iberia 225, 233. *See also* Andalusia
India 231, 233, 263, 588
artists from 580
under British 554
-Pakistan 318
trade with 260
western coast of 84
Indonesia 75, 231, 579, 589
artists from 580
Iran 85, 225, 231–232, 233, 249, 263, 268, 318, 557, 561, 789
constitution of (1906/7) 508
Islamic Republic of 461
National Library of 228
trade with 260
Turbat-i Shaykh Jām (eastern Iran) 228
Iraq 188, 196, 225, 232, 264, 581
northern 90
southern 85
Sufism in 746
Isfahan 228, 661
inscriptions in 240
Masjid-i ʿAlī 248, 249*f*
Israel 143, 687
Istanbul 200, 219, 224, 263, 585, 678–679
Evkaf Museum 219
Süleymaniye complex 241
Topkapı Sarayı [Palace] 169, 219
Turkish and Islamic Arts Museum 169, 176
Italy 256, 258

J

Jām 250–251
minaret of 251*f*
al-Jawf (Dūmat al-Jandal) 85
Jazira 232
Jeddah 269
Jerusalem 81, 153, 154, 155, 368
Aqsa Mosque 243
Dome of the Rock 174, 224, 242
inscription on 155, 175, 244, 250
milestones around 224
temple/Temple in 132, 370, 420
Jirba 737
Jordan 114
Northern, texts collected in 175
Judaea, northern 162

K

Kaʿba 86, 88, 93
Karbalā 728
Kashan (central Iran) 252
Kazan 261, 263
Khurasan 671
Konya 556
Kufa 169, 188, 204, 222, 656, 658
centres of learning in 767
codices sent to 198
grammatical traditions of 645
readings of 221
school of 189

L

Lebanon 285, 508
Leiden, library 267
Leningrad 267
Institute of Oriental Studies 265
Levant 83, 86, 112, 196
southern 117
London 222
first publication of Arabic Qur'an in 263
Khalili Collection 219

Lower Volga (region) 265
Lucknow 263

M

Madaba, inscription in 118
Maghrib 225, 229, 658. *See also* North Africa
  artists from 580
Majanna 88
Malay Peninsula 235
Manbij (Syria) 87
Mārib 84
Marrakesh, Almoravid Mosque 248
Mashhad 234
  Haram at 246
  shrines at 219
Mashriq, artists from 580
Mecca 32, 34, 58, 70, 100–102, 156, 169–170, 204, 368, 474, 491, 493–494, 804, 811, 837
  as an Aramean settlement 57
  beginning of revelation in 316
  centres of learning in 767
  disbelievers/polytheists/idolaters of 371, 570, 571
  economic life in 453
  Kaʿba in 88, 98, 370, 432
  language in 279
  and pilgrimage 88, 240
  readings of 221
  school of 189
  trade fairs 88
Medina 32, 101–102, 105, 153, 156, 169–170, 204, 269, 270, 320, 340, 348, 422, 424, 491, 493, 496, 498, 561, 656, 811, 837
  centres of learning in 767
  codices sent to 198
  Constitution of 455
  economic life in 453
  end of the revelation in 316
  grammatical traditions of 645
  Mosque of Prophet 245
  Muslim emigration/migration to 154, 368, 518
  readings of 221
  religious-political system of 508
  school of 189
  trade fairs 88
Mesopotamia 82–83, 86, 90, 280
  northern 91
Middle East 554, 557
  polytheism in 91
  Roman 82
Morocco 75, 506
Moscow, mosques in 260
Mosul, ʿUmariyya Mosque 245
Mount Sinai 492
al-Mushaqqar 88
Mzāb 737

N

Nabataea 90–91, 120, 124
Najrān 84, 88, 118, 119 n.4
Nakhla 625
Nazareth/Nazara/Nazaret (village in Galilee) 161
Near East 225. *See also* Middle East
Negev, dialects in 114
Nejd 279
Netherlands 582
Nigeria 75, 560
  contemporary 580
Nishapur 228, 750
North Africa 225, 247, 269, 586. *See also* Maghrib
  reading in 196
  tafsīr in 656, 667

O

Oman 84, 735
  Peninsula 115
Oxford 221

P

Pakistan 546
Palermo 245
Palestine 82, 84, 154
  West Bank and Gaza Strip 508
Palmyra 81–82, 85, 90–91
Paris 175, 221, 224
Persia 153, 297, 548. *See also* Iran
Persian Gulf 115
Petra 118, 121
  Greek papyri of 120

Philadelphia, library 267
Phoenicia 87

Q

Qaryat al-Fāw 85, 115
Qatar 40
Qayrawan (Tunisia) 656, 734
 Great Mosque of 235, 245
 Qur'an fragments in 169, 173
Qum 235
 shrines at 219
Qumran 154, 162

R

Rayy 658
Riyadh 269
Rome 82, 90, 152
Russia 258, 260, 264–265, 558, 559
 publication of Qur'an in 261

S

Saba 86
Samarqand 263, 774
 congregational mosque in 231
 Khwāja Akhrār Mosque in 264
Sanaa (Yemen) 218, 220, 224, 288, 655
 Great Mosque of 207, 219, 222
Saragossa (northern Iberia) 233
Sarāy-Bātū 265
Saudi Arabia 231, 265, 269, 461, 509, 546, 560–561, 823. *See also* Arabia
 al-Ḥaṣā (north-eastern) 115
Sicily 245
Sin 87
Sinai 85, 118, 119
 dialects in 114
Sindād 88
Socotra 84
South Asia/South-East Asia 235, 557, 559, 561–562, 578
Soviet Union 267. *See also* Russia
St. Petersburg 221, 224, 260, 265
Sultaniyya 230
Suqām (near Mecca) 86
Syria 83, 85, 86, 87, 114, 118–119, 196, 225, 231, 297
 centres of learning in 767
 inscriptions in 119, 121
 Mamluk court in 252
 school of 189
 southern, dialects in 114

T

Tabaristan 658
Tabriz 810
Tabūk 521
al-Ṭāʾif (south-east of Mecca) 86, 89, 102, 837
Tashkent 263, 265, 267
Taymāʾ 85, 115
Ṭayyʾ 86
Terengganu (north-west Malay Peninsula) 235
Tiberius, Masoretic school in 155
Transoxiana 774
Tucson 221
Tunisia 225–226, 269, 701
 manuscripts in 657
Turin, Shroud of 221
Turkestan 260, 265
Turkey 261, 268, 559, 561–562, 703, 813
 Ottoman 256, 268
 secular orientation of 40
Tyre 225

U

Ufa 265
 Russian fortress of 260
ʿUkāẓ 88
United Kingdom 584
 Britain 597
United States/America 581, 597
 modern day 584
Usays 119
Uzbekistān 265

V

Venice 235, 256
Vienna
 library of 267
 siege of 255
Volga basin 263

W

Wādī Mzāb 737
West Asia (Ottoman) 561
West Bank 508

Y

Yamama 279
Yathrib/Medina 100, 503. *See also* Medina
Yemen 75, 84, 90–91, 113, 278, 285
  dialect of 278
  languages of ancient 112
  manuscripts found in 187, 288
  urban centres of 287

Z

Zebed 119
Zurich 221

Index of People

A

Aaron [Prophet] 131, 490, 759
Abān ibn Tahglib al-Jurayrī (d. 141/758)
  Gharā'ib al-Qur'ān 710
  Kitāb al-qirā'āt 710
Abbott, Nabia 11, 608, 841
Abboud, Hosn; *Mary in the Qur'an* 70
Abboud-Haggar, Soha 277
ʿAbd Allāh Ibn ʿUmar (d. 73/693) 519
Abdel Haleem, Muhammad 8 n.19, 12, 303, 362, 422, 521, 571, 858
  Arabic-English Dictionary of Qur'anic Usage 71
  on context 565ff.
  Exploring the Qur'an 65
  on repetition 338
  on rhetoric *(balāgha)* 327ff., 331
  on the structure of suras 366
  on translations of Qur'an 16, 547, 574, 576
  Understanding the Qur'an 65, 331
ʿAbd al-Ḥamīd ibn Yaḥyā (d. 132/749) 396
ʿAbd al-Malik (r. 65–86/685–705) 58, 243, 431
  coinage under 175, 224
  scripts under reign of 172–173, 174, 201
ʿAbd al-Malik Ibn Marwān 803
ʿAbd al-Qāhir al-Baghdādī (d. 429/1037); *al-Nāsikh wa'l-mansūkh* 840
ʿAbd al-Raḥmān ibn Abi Bakr ibn ʿAbd al-Raḥīm 232
ʿAbd al-Raḥmān ibn Rustam (d. 171/787) 734
ʿAbd al-Raḥmān ibn Zayd (d. 183/798) 516, 839
ʿAbdūh, Muḥammad (d. 1905) 383, 431, 508, 518, 687, 694
  al-Manār [journal]/*Tafsīr al-Manār* 507, 697, 736, 854
  on marital relations 532–533
  on nature and man 813–815
  school of 699
Abdul Qadir, Shah (1735–1815); *Muḍiḥ al-Qur'ān* 559
Abdul-Raof, Hussein 321, 576, 634, 659
  Arabic Rhetoric: A Pragmatic Analysis 332
Abdus Sattar, Muhammad 842
ʿAbd al-Wahhāb Khallāf (d. 1956) 460
Abel 489, 497
al-Ābī (d. 421/1030); *Nathr al-durr* 396
Abraha al-Ashram 89, 98
Abraham/Ibrāhīm [Prophet] 47, 64, 132, 149, 431, 492, 499, 569, 586, 623, 725, 800
  God's covenants with 732
  and Hagar (Hajār) 154, 489
  line of 497–498
  Muslims, as true heirs of 370
  as named in Qur'an 488–490
  People of *(āl ibrāhīm)* 145
  prayer of 371, 469
  and Sarah, wife of 489
  stories of 437, 495–496, 622, 730–731, 784
Abū ʿAbd Allāh Harūn ibn Mūsā al-Qāri'; *al-Wujūh wa'l-naẓā'ir fi'l-Qur'ān* 842
Abū ʿAbd Allāh Muḥyī al-Dīn al-Kāfijī (d. 879/1474); *Kitāb al-Taysīr fī qawā'id ʿilm al-tafsīr* 835–836
Abū ʿAbd Allāh al-Rāzī (d. 420/1026) (known as al-Khaṭīb al-Iskāfī); *Durrat al-tanzīl wa-ghurrat al-ta'wīl* 842
Abū ʿAlī al-Ḥasan ibn Muḥammad al-Mālikī (d. 438/1047); *Rawḍa* of 190
Abū ʿAmr ibn al-ʿAlā' (d. *c.*154–6/770–2) 190–191, 196 n.1, 286–287, 645
Abū Bakr [caliph] 168, 178, 503, 728, 729
Abu Deeb, Kamal 19
Abū Dulaf 391
Abū Ḥanīfa Nuʿmān ibn Thābit (d. 150/767) 556, 774
Abū Hāshim (d. 321/933) 376

Abū Ḥayyān al-Gharnāṭī (d. 745/1344) 299, 667, 675–676, 677, 737, 796, 799
al-Baḥr al-Muḥīṭ 19, 795
on *munāsaba* 797–798
Abū Jaʿfar (d. 130/747) 190
Abū Lahab 489
wife of 390
Abū'l-ʿAtāhiya (d. 211/826) 391
Abū'l-Fidāʾ (d. 732/1331) 6
al-Mukhtaṣar fī akhbār al-bashar 4
Taqwīm al-buldān 4 n.9
Abū'l-Ḥusayn al-Nūrī (d. 295/907) 749
Abū'l-Muṭarrif al-Andalusī (d. 402/1011) 838
Abū'l-Raddād 243
Abū'l-Sammāl 189
Abū'l-Suʿūd al-ʿImādī (d. 982/1574) 318, 679, 735, 737, 829
Abū Madyan (d. 594/1197) 757
Abū Muslim Muḥammad Baḥr al-Iṣfahānī (d. 323/934) 712, 773
Abū Nabhān Jāʿid ibn Khamīs al-Kharūṣī (d. 1822); *Maqālīd al-tanzīl* 737
Abū-Naḍr al-ʿAyyāshī al-Samarqandī (fl. late third/ninth century) 710
Abū Nuwās 394, 408
Abū Saʿīd al-Khargūshī (of Nishapur) (d. 406/1015 or 407/1016) 750
Abū Saʿīd al-Kharrāz (d. 286/899) 749
Abū Ṣāliḥ Manṣūr ibn Nūḥ (r. 350–65/961–76); *Tafsīr-i Tabarī* 555
Abū Shāma al-Dimashqī; *Ibrāz al-maʿānī min ḥirz al-amānī* 211
Abū Ṭāhir 741
Abū Tammām (d. 232/845) 395, 406
Abū ʿUbayd (d. 224/838)
Kitāb al-amthāl 4 n.9
Kitāb al-Nāsikh wa'l-mansūkh 839
Abū ʿUbayda (d. 209/824–5) 208, 795, 797
Majāz al-Qurʾān 330, 395 n.5, 615, 653, 659, 660, 841
Abū Yaḥyā al-Lībī; *The Cry of Faith Arose in Us* 411
Abū Yaʿqūb Yūsuf ibn Muḥammad al-Malīkī (d. 1188/1774) 737
Abū Zayd, Naṣr Ḥāmid (d. 2010) 42, 72, 377, 380, 382, 383, 419, 425, 625, 694, 701, 798, 856
Mafhūm al-Naṣṣ (The Concept of the Text) 853
Naqd al-khiṭāb al-dīnī (Critique of Religious Discourse) 853
Adam 47, 51, 131, 135, 436, 488–489, 497
angels prostrate to 438–439
creation of 434–435
cycle of (as first *nāṭiq*) 730
daʿwa began with 731
'elevation' of 751
stories of the prophets 338, 730–732
al-Adamī, Aḥmad ibn ʿAṭāʾ (d. 311/922 or 923) 749
ʿAdī ibn Zayd 390
Adler, Jacob Georg Christian 11, 167
al-Adnahwī (d. *c.*1700) 667
Adonis (b. 1930)
Introduction to Arabic Poetics 410
Songs of Mihyār the Damascene 410
al-Afghānī, Jamāl al-Dīn (d. 1897) 507, 699, 814
Afsaruddin, Asma 15, 513–514, 520, 842
Agramant [King] 593–594
Aḥīqār (and nephew Nādān/Hāmān) 129
Ahmad, Kassim 460
Ahmadi, Mubarak Ahmad (1910–2001) 560
Aḥmad ibn Aḥmad [Sufi] 75
Aḥmad Jām 228
Aḥmad ʿAlī Rāj (d. 2008); *Ismāʿīlī Tafsīr* 728
Ahrens, Karl 10, 295
al-Ahwāzī (d. 446/1055)
Kitāb al-Iqnāʾ 211
Kitāb al-Wajīz 211
ʿĀʾisha ʿAbd al-Raḥmān 700
al-Tafsīr al-bayānī 383
ʿĀʾisha [wife of Muḥammad] 52, 469, 628
Akasoy, Anna 9
al-Akhfash al-Awsaṭ (d. 215/830) 208
Akhtar, Shabbir 425
Alexander the Great (d. 323 BCE) 81, 134–136
re. Dhū'l-Qarnayn 475
Alexander VII [Pope] (1599–1667) 258
Ali, Ameer (d. 1928) 506–507
Ali, Muhammad 559
ʿAlī ʿAbd al-Razzāq (d. 1966); *al-Islām wa-uṣūl al-ḥukum* (Islam and the foundations of political power) 505

ʿAlī ibn ʿAbd al-Raḥmān 231
ʿAlī ibn Abī Ṭālib 169, 218, 234, 246, 503–504, 644, 709, 710–711, 724, 767, 843
as *asās* 727
as gate of knowledge 723
recension of *(muṣḥaf ʿAlī)* 711
status of 730–731
as successor to Muḥammad 729
waṣāyā of 728
ʿAlī ibn Ibrāhīm al-Ḥawfī (d. 430/1039) 667
ʿAlī ibn al-Madīnī (d. 234/848) 838
ʿAlī ibn Muḥammad al-Baghdādī (d. 741/1341); *Lubāb al-taʾwīl* 752
Alim, Samy 581–582
ʿAlī Shāh, Muḥammad Sulṭān (d. 1327/1909) [Niʿmatullāhī Gunābādī Shaykh]; *Bayān al-saʿāda* 715
ʿAlī Zayn al-ʿĀbidīn 727
Al-Jallad, Ahmad 10
Almagest [Claudius Ptolemy] 811
Alshaer, Atef 411
Alter, Robert 491
Altıkula, Tayyar 169
al-Ālūsī, Maḥmūd Shahāb al-Dīn (d. 1270/1854) 318, 679, 699, 736–737, 741 n.1
Amājūr [governor of Damascus] 225
Amari, Michele 6, 11, 167, 170
al-Aʿmash (d. 148/765) 190
Ambros, Arne 303
al-ʿĀmilī, Abūʾl-Ḥasan (d. 1139/1727); *Mirʾāt al-anwār* 713
ʿĀmir ibn al-Ṭufayl 133
Amir-Moezzi, Mohammad Ali 709
Revelation and Falsification 70
al-ʿAmrī 658
ʿAmr ibn Ḥazm 184
ʿAmr ibn Kulthūm 412
Muʿallaqa of 404, 411
ʿAmr ibn Rabīʿa ibn Luḥayy 86
Āmulī, ʿAbdullāh Javādi (b. 1933); *Tafsīr-i tasnīm* 716
Āmulī, Ḥaydar-i (d. after 787/1385) 715, 763
Tafsīr al-Muḥīṭ al-aʿẓam waʾl-baḥr al-khiḍam 714
al-ʿAnbārī, ʿAmr (d. after 130/749) 405
Andrae, Tor 7, 10, 424
Der Ursprung des Islams und das Christentum 295
Anthony, Sean W. 133, 137
Appiah, Anthony 549
Arberry, A. J. 330, 515, 546, 569, 570, 571, 574, 575
Aresmouk, Mohamed Fouad; *The Immense Ocean* 75
Arif, S. 661
al-ʿĀrifīn, Muḥammad ibn Tāj 838
Ariosto, [Ludovico] 593–595
'Alcorano' 602
Orlando Furioso 593–594, 602
Aristotle; *Rhetoric* 422
Arkoun, Mohammed (d. 2010) 28 n.2, 382, 425, 701, 813, 850, 852
Arnal, William E. 53
Arnold, Theodor 472, 544
Arrivabene, Andrea 542
Asad, Muhammad (né Leopold Weiss); *Message of the Qurʾān* 546
al-Aṣamm, Abū Bakr ʿAbd al-Raḥmān Kaysān (d. 201/816) 773
al-Ashʿarī, Abūʾl-Ḥasan (d. 324/935) 376
ʿĀṣim ibn Abī al-Najūd (d. 127/745) 190, 196
lectio of 208
Asín Palacios, Miguel; *La escatología musulmana de la Divina Comedia* 593 n.1
al-ʿAskarī, Abū Hilāl (d. after 395/1005); *Kitāb al-Ṣināʿatayn al-kitāba wa-ʾl-shiʿr* 395
al-ʿAskarī, al-Ḥasan (d. 860/874) 710
al-Aṣmaʿī (d. *c.*213/828) 300 n.4, 390
al-ʿAsqalānī (d. 852/1449) 656
Assmann, Jan, 32
ʿAtāʾ ibn Abī Rabāḥ (d. 115/733) 519, 531, 534
ʿAṭāʾ al-Khurasānī (d. 135/757) 839
Aṭfiyyash, Abū Isḥāq Ibrāhīm (d. 1965) 736
Taʾwīl al-mutashābih 737
Aṭfiyyash, Muḥammad ibn Yūsuf (d. 1332/1914) 735, 738, 741, 743, 744
Dāʿī ʾl-ʿamal li-yawm al-amal [second *tafsīr*] 735
Himyān [often rendered *Hīmyān*] *al-zād ilā dār al-maʿād* 735, 736, 738, 742
Taysīr al-tafsīr li-ʾl-Qurʾān al-karīm 736, 738–739, 742

al-ʿAṭṭār, Aḥmad ibn Mūsā (d. 274/888) 656
ʿAṭṭār 594 n.3
Audebert, Claude France 391
Auerbach, Erich 547
Avni, Abraham 421, 422
al-Awzāʿī (d. 157/774) 655
Ayoub, Mahmoud M. (b. 1938) 332, 502, 509, 708
The Qurʾan and its Interpreters 73
al-ʿAyyāshī (fl. late third/ninth century) 708
al-Aʿẓamī, Muḥammad 35
al-Azmeh, Aziz 432, 814

B

Bābāʿammī, Muḥammad ibn Mūsā 735–736
Badawi, Elsaid M.; *Arabic-English Dictionary of Qurʾanic Usage* 71
al-Baghawī, al-Ḥusayn (d. 516/1122) 197, 722, 735
Maʿālim al-tanzīl fī tafsīr al-Qurʾān = Tafsīr al-Baghawī 7, 675, 752
Maṣābīḥ al-sunna 752
al-Baghdādī, Hibat Allāh ibn Salāma (d. 410/1020) 839
Baḥīrā [monk] 83
al-Baḥrānī, Sayyid Hāshim (d. 1106/1695); *al-Burhān* 713
Bājū, Muṣṭafā 736
Bakhos, Carol; (ed.) *Islam and Its Past. Jahiliyya, Late Antiquity, and the Qurʾan* 66
al-Balāghī, Muḥammad Jawād (d. 1933); *Ālāʾ al-Raḥmān fī tafsīr al-Qurʾān* 715
Baljon 844
al-Balkhī, Abū Zaid Aḥmad Sahl (d. 322/934) 774
Banī Ḥārith ibn Kaʿb 640
al-Bannāʾ (d. 1117/1705); *Itḥāf* 190
Bannister, Andrew 355, 425
al-Bāqillānī, Abū Bakr (d. 403/1013) 317, 379, 404, 795
Iʿjāz al-Qurʾān 13, 380, 395
al-Intiṣār li'l-Qurʾān 843
al-Bāqir, Muḥammad (d. 114/733) 707–708
Baradaeus, Jacob 83
Bar-Asher, Meir 707, 710, 721
Barghouti, Tamim 584
'O People of Egypt' *(Yā Shaʿb Maṣr)* 584
Bar Hebraeus (1226–86) [Syriac Orthodox Prelate] 6
Barlas, Asma 43, 534, 536, 856
Believing Women in Islam 76
Barr, James 307
Barth, Jacob
Etymologiscke Studien zum Semitischen 295
Sprachwissenschaftliche Untersuchungen zum Semitischen 295
Barth, Karl 384
Barthes, Roland 798, 857
Barukh [scribe] 420
Bārzagān, Mahdī; *Sayr-i taḥawwul-i Qurʾān* 837
Bathsheba [wife of Uriah] 494
Bauer, Karen 76, 652
(ed.), *Aims, Methods and Contexts of Qurʾanic Exegesis* 74
Gender Hierarchy in the Qurʾān 71
Bauer, Thomas 133, 402, 403, 825, 827
Baybars [Egyptian sultan] 265
Baybars II al-Jāshnakīr (r. 708–9/1309–10) 252
al-Bayḍāwī, Nāṣir al-Dīn (d. *c.*719/1319) 2–3, 17, 197, 297, 482, 569, 572, 697, 722, 760, 810–812
Anwār al-tanzīl wa-asrār al-taʾwīl 4, 6 n.12, 557–558, 675–677, 775, 809, 811
exegesis/*tafsīr* of 6–7, 679, 735, 737, 743–744
al-Bayhaqī, Abū Bakr (d. 458/1066) 843
Bayyūḍ, Ibrāhīm ibn ʿUmar (1899–1981) 740–743
Fī Riḥāb al-Qurʾān 736
tafsīr of 744
Bazargan, Mehdi (d. 1995) 356
Beck, Edmund 200 n.3
Becker, Carl Heinrich (1867–1933) 621–622
Bedwell, William (1563–1632) 1
Arabian Trudgman 296
Beeston, A. F. L. 90
Bektaş, Hacı 556
Bell, Richard (1876–1952) 7, 32, 58–59, 168, 296, 308, 333, 339–340, 366, 433, 545
Introduction to the Qurʾān 65, 330, 334, 576

The Origin of Islam in its Christian Environment 58, 295
studies/approach of 31–32, 56, 493–494
Bellamy, Carla 588
Bellamy, James A. 130, 301–302
Benders-Lee, Tim 580
Berg, Herbert 9, 29 n.3, 615, 636
Bergmann, Uwe 68, 221–222
Bergsträsser, Gotthelf (1886–1933) 6, 11, 35–36, 44, 200–203, 212, 264, 266, 548
'Korankomission' (of Bavarian Academy of Sciences) 200
on variant readings/*qirāʾāt* 197–200, 202, 204, 210
Berke 265
Berque, Jacques 547
Le Coran: Essai de traduction 546
Betti, Emilio 851
Bevilacqua, Alexander; *The Republic of Arabic Letters* 77
al-Bharūchī, Ḥasan ibn Nūḥ (d. 939/1533); *Kitāb al-Azhār* 722
Bibliander, Theodor (d. 1564) 3, 258, 543
Cribatio 3
Machumetis Saracenorum principis 3, 257*f*, 542
Bijlefeld, Willem A. 64
Bilqīs [Queen of Sheba] 489, 495
Bint al-Shāṭīʾ, ʿĀʾisha ʿAbd al-Raḥmān (d. 1999) 850
al-Biqāʿī, Burhān al-Dīn (d. 885/1480) 318, 347, 677–678
Naẓm al-durar fī tanāsub al-āyāt wa'l-suwar 317, 677
Birk, Sandow 218
Birkeland, Harris 608, 654
al-Bīrūnī 579, 807
Blachère, Régis (1900–73) 31, 261, 348, 493, 545
Blair, Sheila S. 11, 217
Blau, [J.] 119
Bloom, Harold 603
The Western Canon 592, 593
Bloom, [Jonathan M.] 228
Bobzin, Hartmut 547
Der Koran im Zeitalter der Reformation 76–77
Bodman, Whitney 130
Bonebakker, [S. A.] 331
Bonnet-Eymard, [B.] 154
Book of Tobit 129
Boubakeur, Cheikh Si Hamza 546
Boullata, Issa J.; (ed.), *Literary Structures of Religious Meaning in the Qurʾān* 72
Bouterdin, Yahia 736
Böwering, Gerhard 74, 756
classification of 757
Bowker, John W. 71
Boyle, Helen N.; *Quranic Schools* 75
Boys, Thomas (1792–1880) 322
Boysen, Friedrich; *Der Koran* [1773 translation] 544
Bravmann, Meïr 303, 432
Bremmer, [Jan N.] 480
Brett, Michael 729
Brockelmann, Carl; *Grundriss der vergleichenden Grammatik der semitischen Sprachen* 295
Brown, [Daniel] 844
Brunschvig, Robert 306
Bucaille, Maurice 813
The Bible, The Qur'an, and Science 812
Buchman, Theodor (Bibliander) (d. 1564); *Corpus Toletanum* 256. *See also* Bibliander, Theodor
Buddha 729
Buhl, Franz 303
al-Bukhārī (d. 256/870) 144, 532
Ṣaḥīḥ al-Bukhārī 51–52, 634, 832, 833–834
al-Bulqīnī, Jalāl al-Dīn (d. 824/1421) 835
Bultmann, Rudolf 384
Burge, Stephen 14, 827
(ed.), *The Meaning of the Word: Lexicology and Qur'anic Exegesis* 71
Burman, Thomas E.; *Reading the Qurʾān in Latin Christendom, 1140–1560* 76
al-Bursawī [Tk. Bursevi], Ismāʿīl Ḥaqqī (d. 1137/1725) 608, 679, 762
Rūḥ al-bayān 607
Burton, John 203, 204, 205, 305, 628, 839
Burūjirdī, Sayyid Ḥusayn (d. 1962); *al-Ṣirāṭ al-mustaqīm* 715
al-Būṣīrī (d. *c*.694/1294) 391, 407
al-Burda [Mantle ode] 397

al-Bustī, Abū'l-Qāsim (d. *c.*420/1029); *Min kashf asrār al-Bāṭiniyya wa-ʿawār madhhabihim* 728
Byron [Lord] 597–598
Childe Harold's Pilgrimage 598
Turkish Tales 598

C

Cahen, Claude 303
Cain 489, 497
Calder, Norman 18, 669, 687, 821, 823, 826
Campanini, Massimo 20, 425
Philosophical Perspectives on Modern Qurʾānic Exegesis 75
The Qur'an: Modern Muslim Interpretations 75
Carlyle, Thomas 600
Carter, Michael 299, 660
Casanova, Paul 57
Casaubon, Isaac 4 n.8
Caspari, Carl (1814–92) 4
Grammatica arabica [Grammar of the Arabic Language] 297, 328
Castell, Edmund; *Lexicon Heptaglotton* 296
Catherine II (1729–96) 258, 260–261
decree of 262*f*
Cellard, Éléonore; Codex Amrensis 1, 68–69, 208
Chakralavi, ʿAbd Allāh (d. 1930) 460
Charfi, Abdelmajid 425
Charlemagne [Emperor] 593
Chaucer, Geoffrey; *Canterbury Tales* 594
Chelhod, Jacques 432
Child, Lydia Maria 597
Childs, Brevard S. 363
Christ 419, 424, 594. *See also* Jesus
Christos *(Māshīaḥ; Mshīḥ)* 160
Cilardo, Agostino 304
Comerro, Viviane 176
Constantine [emperor] 82, 152
Cook, David 512, 518
Cook, Michael 57–58, 154–155, 222, 574
(ed.), *Islam and Its Past. Jahiliyya, Late Antiquity, and the Qur'an* 66
(ed.), *Law and Tradition in Classical Islamic Thought* 68
Hagarism 59
The Koran: A Very Short Introduction 65, 573
Corbin, Henri 732
Corneille, Pierre 358
Corriente, Federico C. 281–282, 285, 289, 290
Cowan, D.; *Introduction to Modern Literary Arabic* 328
Cragg, Kenneth 425
Cromwell, Oliver 595–596
Crone, Patricia 34, 67, 154–155, 309, 432
Hagarism 59
studies of 102, 104–105, 305–306
Cuypers, Michel 143, 321, 362, 433, 858
on composition of Qur'an 12, 290, 372, 425
The Composition of the Qur'an 72
Le Festin 496–497
on structure of suras 364–366
on syntax in Qur'an 315ff.

D

Dagli, Caner K.; (ed.) *The Study Quran* 74
al-Ḍaḥḥāk ibn Muzāḥim (d. 105/723) 514, 610, 636, 638, 640, 643–644
Dakake, Maria Massi; (ed.), *The Study Quran* 74
Dali, Salvador 796
Dallal, Ahmad 806–808
al-Damaghānī (d. 478/1085); *Iṣlāḥ al-wujūh wa'l-naẓāʾir fī'l-Qurʾān al-karīm* 841
al-Dānī, Abū ʿAmr (d. 444/1053) 177, 197, 225, 656, 658
Jāmiʿ al-bayān fī'l-qirāʾāt al-sabʿa al-mashhūra 211
Kitāb al-Muqniʿ fi rasm al-maṣāḥif 197
al-Taysīr 211
Daniel [Prophet] 420
Dante Alighieri 592
Commedia 593
De vulgari eloquentia 593
Inferno 593, 595–596, 600
La Vita Nuova 593
al-Dāraquṭnī 51
Darāz, Muḥammad ʿAbd Allāh (d. 1958) 466, 470
Darwaza, Muḥammad ʿIzzat (d. 1984) 318, 505
Darwin 814
Darwīsh, Maḥmūd (d. 2008) 410–411

David/Dāwūd [Prophet] 488, 494, 727
descendant of 160
stories of the prophets 730–731
al-Dāwūdī (d. 945/1538); *Ṭabaqāt al-mufassirīn* 667
Dayeh, Islam 303
al-Daylamī, Shams al-Dīn Muḥammad (d. 593/1197) 756
Taṣdīq al-maʿārif = Futūḥ al-raḥmān fī ishārāt al-Qurʾān 756
de Blois, François 133, 309
de Caprona, Pierre Crapon; *Le Coran: aux sources de la parole oraculaire* 319–320
Decius [emperor] 129
de Gifis, Vanessa; *Shaping a Qurʾānic Worldview* 75
DeLillo, Don 603
Falling Man 602
de Prémare, Alfred-Louis 57
Derenbourg, Hartwig (1844–1908) 4, 297
Déroche, François 11, 35, 217, 245, 267
The Abbasid Tradition: Qurʾāns of the 8th to the 10th Centuries AD 68
La Transmission écrite du Coran dans les débuts de l'islam 68
on material evidence/manuscripts of Qur'an 167ff., 206, 207–208, 219, 220–222, 225, 265
Nasser D. Khalili Collection of Islamic Art 68
Qur'ans of the Umayyads: A Preliminary Overview 68
de Saussure, Ferdinand (d. 1913) 421, 850
Descombes, V. 548
De Smet, Daniel 304
de Voragine, Jacobus (d. 1298) 130
al-Dhahabī, Muḥammad 819
D'Herbelot de Molainville (1625–95); *Bibliothèque Orientale of Barthélemy* 6
Dhū'l-Kifl 488, 490
Dhū'l-Nūn al-Miṣrī (d. 246/861) 749
Dhū'l-Qarnayn 99, 489
narrative 132–136
Dhū'l-Rumma (d. 117/735) 390
Dhū Nuwās 84
Dickinson, Emily 592
Dieterici, Friedrich; *Arabisch-deutsches Handwörterbuch zum Koran* 297
al-Dihlawī, Rafīʿ al-Dīn (1750–1818) 559
al-Dimyāṭī (d. 1117/1705); *Itḥāf fuḍalāʾ al-bashar* 211
al-Dīnawarī, ʿAbdallāh b. al-Mubārak (fl. 300/912); *al-Wāḍiḥ fī tafsīr al-Qurʾān al-karīm* 636
Ḍiyāʾ al-Dīn Ismāʿīl ibn Hibat Allāh (d. 1184/1770); *Mizāj al-tasnīm* 728
Dominicus Germanus of Silesia (d. 1670) 2 n.4
Donne, John (d. 1631) 596, 599
Donner, Fred 7, 54, 56, 59, 304–305, 431
Douglas, Allen; *Arab Comic Strips* 69
Douglas, Mary 369
Dozy, Reinhart; *Supplément aux dictionnaires Arabes* 297
Duderija, Adis 76
Duraković; *The Poetics of Ancient and Classical Arabic Literature* 402 n.2
al-Dūrī 196 n.1
Du Ryer, André (1580–1660) 2 n.4, 544, 597
Alcoran de Mahomet [translation] 542–543
Dutton, Yasin 11, 68, 69, 207
Dvořák, Rudolf
Ein Beitrag zur Frage über die Fremdwörter im Koran 295
Über die Fremdwörter im Koran 295

E

E-40 [rapper] 581
Ebstein, Michael; *Mysticism and philosophy in al-Andalus* 732
Eichhorn, Johann Gottfried (1752–1827) 5 n.11
Eichler 439
Eichner, Heidrun 811
Einboden, Jeffrey 16
Islam and Romanticism 601
Elashiry, Mohammed R. 843
El-Awa, Salwa M. S. 362, 366–368
Textual Relations in the Qurʾān 320, 366
El-Badawi, Emran; *The Qurʾān and the Aramaic Gospel Tradition* 68
El-Desouki, Ayman 13
Elias, Jamal 762, 827
Elijah [Prophet] 493

Elisha [Prophet] 490, 493
Elmarsafy, Ziad 15
The Enlightenment Qur'an 77
El Masri, Ghassan 403
El-Shamsy, Ahmed 654
Emerson, R. W. 597
Epiphanius 162
Erasmus (1469–1536) 256, 258
Ernst, Carl W. 757
How to Read the Qur'an 65, 330
Erpenius, Thomas (1584–1624) 1, 2, 4 n.9, 7, 296, 303
Grammatica arabica 2, 297
Historia Iosephi Patriarchae ex Alcorano 2
Ersoy, Mehmet Akif (1873–1936) 560
Esack, Farid (b. 1959) 43, 382, 505, 509, 853, 856–857
The Qur'an: A Short Introduction 65
Esau (Ar. ʿIsaw) 159
Ettinghausen, Richard 244
Eusebius 162
Eve/Ḥawwāʾ 338, 528
Ewald, Heinrich (1803–75) 6–7
De metris carminum Arabicorum (1825) 6 n.12

F

Faḍlallāh, Sayyid Muḥammad Ḥusayn (d. 2010); *Min waḥy al-Qurʾān* 715
Fahd, Toufic 432
Fahd [king] 509
Faisal [king] 509
al-Fārābī (d. 339/950) 781, 784
Farāhī, Ḥamīd al-Dīn (d. 1930) 13, 318, 370–371
Jamharat al-Balāghah 332
Farhad, [M.] 219
Farhāt, [A. H.] 661
al-Fārisī, Abū ʿAlī (d. 377/987) 210
al-Farrāʾ (d. 207/822) 208, 645, 661
Maʿānī al-Qurʾān 202, 615, 641, 653, 659, 712
al-Farrā, ʿUmar (d. 2015); *Men of God* 411
Farrin, Raymond K. 362, 369–370, 405
al-Farsy, Shaykh Abdallah Saleh (1912–82) 560
Faruqi, Ismail 813
Fāṭima 499, 729
Fayżī (d. 1004/1595); *Sawāṭiʿ al-ilhām* 714
Fedeli, Alba 208
Ferruh, İsmail (d. 1840); *Mevakib* 557
Firestone, Reuven 10, 518
Jihad: The Origin of Holy War in Islam 71
al-Fīrūzābādī (d. 817/1414) 636
al-Qāmūs al-muḥīṭ 296
Fitzgerald, Michael Abdurrahman; *The Immense Ocean* 75
Fleischer, Heinrich (1801–88) 4, 6–7, 297, 545
Kleinere Schriften 297 n.2
Flood, Finbarr 250
Flügel, Gustav (1802–70) 7 n.17, 209, 266, 545
Concordantiae Corani arabicae 297
edition of the Qur'an 241
Fontaine, [Jean] 492
Foucault, Michel 53
Fraenkel, Siegmund
De vocabulis in antiquis Arabum carminibus et in Corano peregrinis 295
Die aramäischen Fremdwörter im Arabischen 295
Freytag, Georg (1788–1861) 5–7, 30
Lexicon Arabico-Latinum 296, 297
Frobenius, Leo (1898) 143
Frye, Northrop 384
Fuʾād I [Egyptian king] (1868–1936) 268–269
Fück, [Johann] 635
Fudge, Bruce 36, 73, 819
Qurʾānic Hermeneutics 74, 773
Furāt ibn Ibrāhīm (fl. second half of third/ninth century) 513

G

Gadamer, Hans-Georg 652, 851, 856–857
Truth and Method 851
Gade, Anna M.; *Perfection Makes Practice* 75
Galal, Ehab 75
Gallez, [Edouard-Marie] 154
Garcia, Humberto; *Islam and the English Enlightenment 1670–1840* 601
Gazzah, Miriam 582
Geiger, Abraham (1810–74) 6–7, 9, 31, 488, 498
on Jewish influence on Muḥammad/Qur'an 33, 60, 142, 491–492, 499, 621, 685
Was hat Mohammed aus dem Judenthume aufgenommen? 5, 33, 58, 129, 142, 294

Geissinger, Aisha; *Gender and Muslim Construction of Exegetical Authority* 76
George, Alain 217
George, Kenneth 583
Ghālib, M. 731
al-Ghazālī, Abū Ḥāmid (d. 505/1111) 459, 513, 661, 740, 750, 834, 843, 854
 ʿAjāʾib al-qalb (Marvels of the Heart) 785
 on death and the soul 482–483
 on ethics 766, 768
 Iḥyāʾ ʿulūm al-dīn (The Revival of the Religious Sciences) 466, 785, 844
 Jawāhir al-Qurʾān wa duraruhu (The jewels of the Qur'an and its pearls) 466, 754, 844
 al-Maqṣad al-asnā fī sharḥ maʿānī asmāʾ illāh al-ḥusnā (The Ninety-nine Beautiful Names of God) 786, 788
 Mishkāt al-anwār (Niche of Lights) 755, 787, 842
 on mystical path 754–755
 on philosophy 785–787
 al-Qānūn al-kullī fī'l-taʾwīl 844
 Tahāfut [al-falāsifa] 811
Ghazoul, Ferial 412
Ghiyāth al-Dīn, Muḥammad ibn Sām 228, 251*f*
al-Ghunaimī, Muḥammad Ṭalʿat 521
Giggei, Antonio; (ed.) *Thesaurus Linguae Arabicae* 296
Gilliot, Claude 57, 280, 281, 284, 667, 671, 768
 Exégèse, langue, et théologie en Islam 770
 on Ibn ʿAbbās 767
 on *tafsīr* 653, 658–660, 668
Gleave, [Robert] 708
Glei, Reinhold F.; *Ludovico Marracci at Work* 77
Gobillot, Genévìeve 422
Goering, Joseph W.; (ed.), *With Reverence for the Word* 73
Goethe, Johann Wolfgang 544, 601
 Divan 598–599
Gökalp, Ziya 561
Goldfeld, Yeshayahu/Isaiah 635, 652–653, 662, 671
Goldman, [S.] 690
Goldsack, William 559
Goldziher, Ignaz (1850–1921) 4, 36, 51, 608, 621–622, 683, 685, 687, 707, 775, 824
 on authenticity of early traditions 621
 categories of 819
 Die Richtungen der islamischen Koranauslegung 4, 609, 652, 769–770, 772, 818
 Muhammedanische Studien 621
 on Muʿtazila 772
 Schools of Koranic Commentators 73
 on variants and Arabic script 198–199
Goliath 489
Golius, Jacobus 7, 303
 Lexicon Arabico-Latinum 296
Goossens, Eduard 302, 303
Görke, Andreas 52, 626, 628
 (ed.), *Tafsīr and Islamic Intellectual History* 73
Götz, Manfred 774–775
Goudarzi, Mohsen 68, 173, 207, 208, 221, 283
Gould, Stephen Jay 807
Graham, William 306, 424
Gregory XV [pope] 3 n.6
Grice, Paul 549
Griffel, Frank 785
Griffith, Sidney 129–130, 137, 499
Grimme, Hubert 295, 302, 308
Grohmann, Adolf 11
Grosjean, Jean 219, 546
Gruber, Christiane 70
Gruendler, Beatrice 406 n.4
Grünbaum, Max 685
Guadagnoli, Filippo (1596–1656) 3 n.5
Guessoum, Nidhal 855
 Islam's Quantum Question 76
Guidi, Ignazio; *Delia sede primitiva dei popoli semitici* 295
Gülen, Fethullah (b. 1941) 40
Gumi, Abu Bakr Mahmud (1922–92) 560
Gunasti, Susan 75
Günther, Sebastian 14–15, 472
Gwynne, Rosalind Ward 422
 Logic, Rhetoric, and Legal Reasoning in the Qur'ān 71, 330

H

al-Ḥaḍramī, Yaʿqūb (d. 205/820) 211
Haffner, August (1869–1941) 300, 300 n.4
Ḥāfiẓ 598
Ḥafṣa, *ṣaḥīfa* of 176
Ḥafṣ ibn Sulaymān (d. 180/796), transmission/recension of 190, 196, 208–209
al-Ḥajjāj ibn Yūsuf (d. 95/714) 57–58, 171, 177, 188, 201, 225, 503
al-Ḥakīm al-Tirmidhī (d. *c.*300/910) 749
al-Ḥallāj, al-Ḥusayn ibn Manṣūr (d. 309/922) 757
Hallaq, Wael 458
al-Hamad, Muntasir 9
al-Hamadhānī, Badīʿ al-Zamān 396
Haman 489
Hāmān 47, 129
Hamdan, Omar, 58 177, 188, 503
Hamori 402
Hamza, Feras 652
  (ed.), *An Anthology of Qur'anic Commentaries* 74
Ḥamza, Muḥammad 858
Ḥamza (d. 156/773) [one of the seven readers] 190
Ḥanafī, Ḥasan (b. 1935) 43, 484, 506, 857
al-Harawī, ʿAbdallāh al-Anṣārī (d. 481/1089) 753
al-Ḥarīrīzāde, Muḥammad Kamāl al-Dīn (d. 1299/1882); *al-Mawrid al-khāṣṣ bi'l-khawāṣṣ fī tafsīr sūrat al-ikhlāṣ* 842
al-Ḥārith ibn ʿAbd al-Raḥmān (d. 130/747) 839
Hārūn (Aaron) 488
Hārūn ibn Mūsā (d. *c.*170/786); *al-Wujūh wa-l-naẓāʾir* 614
Ḥasan al-ʿAskarī (d. 260/873) 731
al-Ḥasan al-Baṣrī (d. 110/728) 57, 188, 190, 278, 328, 638, 641, 656–657, 740, 775, 838
  on fighting 518
  mystical exegesis of 748
al-Ḥasanī, ʿAbd al-Ḥayy (d. 1923) 469
Ḥasan [ibn ʿAlī] 729
al-Ḥasan ibn Dīnār 656–657
al-Hāshimī (d. 1943) 332
Ḥassān, Tammām (d. 2011) 332, 568, 569
Ḥassān ibn Thābit 390–391
Hatim, Basil 576
  Arabic Rhetoric 332
Hawting, Gerald R. 34, 58, 154, 432
  The Idea of Idolatry and the Emergence of Islam 433
Ḥawwā, Saʿīd; *al-Asās fī l-tafsīr* 319
al-Hawwārī, Hūd ibn Muḥakkam (d. *c.*290/903) 513, 737–738, 744
  interpretations of 735, 737, 740–743
  Tafsīr Kitāb Allāhi 'l-ʿAzīz 18, 734–735
Haywood, John; *New Arabic Grammar of the Written Language* 329
Healey, John F. 9, 124
Heath, Peter 652, 660
Heidegger, M. 851
Heller, Bernard 688
Henninger, Josef (1959/1981) 432
Henry Stubbe 601
Heraclius 137
Herder, J. G. 598
Hezekiel [Prophet] 420
al-Ḥibarī (d. 286/899) 711
Hilali, Asma 208
  The Sanaa Palimpsest 68
Hinckelmann, Abraham (1652–95) 6, 258
Hippolytus of Rome 157
Hirschfeld, Hartwig 10, 296, 302
  Beiträge zur Erklärung des Korân 294
  Jüdische Elemente im Korân 294
  New Researches into the Composition and Exegesis of the Qoran 294
Hirsch Jr., E. D. 652
  Validity in Interpretation 425
Hitchens, Christopher 54
Hoffman, Valerie J. 18
Hoffmann, Thomas; *The Poetic Qurʾān* 73
Homer 603
Homerin, [Th. Emil.] 407
Horovitz, Josef 308, 492
  Koranische Untersuchungen 295
Horst, Heribert 659
Hottinger, Johann Heinrich (1620–67); *Promtuarium sive Bibliotheca Orientalis* 6 n.12
Hourani, George F. 467

Houtsma, Martinus Theodorus (1851–1943) 300
Hoyland, Robert 244, 433
Hūd 99, 488–490, 494
  stories of the prophets 730–731
al-Hudhalī (d. 465/1072); *Kitāb al-Kāmil* 211
Ḥudhayfa ibn al-Yamān 741
Hunarfar, [Luṭfallah] 240
al-Ḥusayn ibn ʿAlī ibn Abī Ṭālib 169, 727, 729, 730
  massacre at Karbalā 728
Hussein, M. Kamil (ed.) 728
Husserl 857
Ḥuwayzī, ʿAbd ʿAlī (d. 1104/1693); *Nūr al-thaqalayn* 713

I

Ibn ʿAbbād al-Rundī (d. 792/1390) 843
Ibn ʿAbbās, ʿAbd Allāh (d. *c.*68/687) 19, 531, 615, 656, 659, 775
  commentary of 635–636, 637, 767
  exegetical traditions of 653, 661, 766
  and *isrāʾīliyyāt* 683
  Kitāb Gharīb al-Qurʾān [attrib.] 841
  al-Lughāt fiʾl-Qurʾān [attrib.] 840
Ibn ʿAbd al-Salām, ʿIzz al-Dīn (d. 660/1262) 660
  Majāz al-Qurʾān 333
Ibn Abī Dāwūd; *Kitāb al-Māṣāḥif* 201
Ibn Abīʾl-Iṣbaʿ (d. 654/1256)
  Badīʿ al-Qurʾān 395
  Taḥrīr al-taḥbīr 395
Ibn Abī Najīḥ (d. 131/748) 637
Ibn Abī Shayba; *Musnad* 657
ibn Abī Sitta, Muḥammad ibn ʿUmar (d. 1088/1677) 737
Ibn Abī Zamanīn, Muḥammad ibn ʿAbd Allāh (d. *c.*399–1008) 3, 657, 658, 659, 660, 662
ibn Adham, Ibrāhīm (d. 160/777) 752
Ibn ʿAjība (d. 1224/1809); *al-Baḥr al-madīd* 762
Ibn ʿĀmir (d. 118/736) [one of seven readers] 190–191, 196
Ibn al-Anbārī (d. 328/939) 299, 639
  Kitāb al-Aḍdād (ed. Theodorus Houtsma) 300
  Kitāb al-Waqf waʾl ibtidāʾ 187
Ibn al-Anbārī, Abūʾl-Barakāt (d. 577/1181); *Asrār al-ʿarabiyya* 300
Ibn ʿAqīl (d. 513/1119) 459
Ibn ʿAqīla al-Makkī (d. 1150/1737–8); *al-Ziyāda waʾl-iḥsān fī ʿulūm al-Qurʾān* 836
Ibn [al-]ʿArabī, Muḥyī al-Dīn (d. 638/1240) 19, 480, 714, 788–789, 796, 797–798, 802
  on *barzakh* 589, 789
  Dīwān 397
  Fuṣūṣ al-ḥikam 758, 759
  al-Futūḥāt al-Makkiyya (The Meccan Revelations) 19, 758, 789, 795
  hermeneutics of 652
  influence on Shīʿī thought 714
  al-Jāmiʿ waʾl-tafṣīl fī asrār maʿānī ʾl-tanzīl 758
  and Kubrawī tradition 757–758
  monistic (unitive) doctrine of 755, 758–761
  on poetry 407, 759
Ibn al-ʿArabī, Abū Bakr (d. 543/1148)
  al-Nāsikh waʾl-mansūkh fīʾl-Qurʾān al-karīm 840
  Qānūn al-taʾwīl 844
Ibn al-Aʿrābī [philologist and *rāwī*, d. *c.*231/845–6] 722
Ibn al-ʿArīf (d. 536/1141) 757
Ibn ʿĀshūr, al-Fāḍil 698
ibn ʿĀshūr, Muḥammad al-Ṭāhir (d. 1973) 656, 659, 737, 811–812, 850
  al-Taḥrīr waʾl-tanwīr 697
ibn ʿĀṣim, Naṣr 188
Ibn ʿAṭāʾ 750
Ibn al-ʿAtāʾiqī (d. *c.*970/1308) 839
Ibn ʿAṭiyya (d. 546/1151) 676, 737, 834, 844
  al-Muḥarrar al-wajīz 667
  Tafsīr 187
Ibn Bājja (d. 533/1138) 785
Ibn al-Bārizī (d. 738/1337–8); *Nāsikh al-Qurʾān al-ʿazīz wa-mansūkhuhu* 840
Ibn Barrajān (d. 536/1141) 757–758, 834, 840, 843
Ibn al-Bawwāb, ʿAlī ibn Hilāl 219, 226, 227*f*, 228, 231
Ibn Ezra (d. *c.*1167) 30
Ibn al-Fāriḍ (d. 632/1235) 391, 407, 411

Ibn al-Fayyād 235
Ibn al-Furāt 253
Ibn Ghalbūn, Abū'l-Ṭayyib (d. 389/998)
al-Irshād fī'l-qirā'āt ʿan al-a'imma al-sabʿa 211
ibn Ghalbūn, Ṭāhir (d. 399/1008)
al-Tadhkira fī'l-qirā'āt al-thamān 190, 211
Ibn Ḥabīb, Abū'l-Qāsim (d. 406/1016) 20, 836
Kitāb al-Tanbīh ʿalā faḍl ʿulūm al-Qur'ān 834–835, 836–837
Ibn Ḥabīb, Ḥamza (d. 156/773 or 158/775) 196
Ibn Ḥabīb, al-Rabīʿ (d. 170/786) 738
Musnad al-Rabīʿ 734, 738, 741
Ibn Ḥajar al-ʿAsqalānī (d. 852/1448) 833
commentary on *Ṣaḥīḥ al-Bukhārī* 833–834
Ibn Ḥakīm = Hishām ibn Ḥakīm ibn Ḥizām 185
ibn Ḥanbal, Aḥmad (d. 241/855) 654
Ibn Ḥazm (d. 456/1064) 843
Ibn Hishām, ʿAbd al-Malik (d. 213/828–9 or 218/833) 55
redaction of Muḥammad ibn Isḥāq 97
Sīra of 153
ibn Idrīsū, Muḥammad ibn Sulaymān (d. 1313/1896) 737
Ibn ʿĪsā (d. 335/946) 202
Ibn Isḥāq, Muḥammad (d. 150/767) 55, 91, 97–98, 622, 684
Kitāb al-Maghāzī 833
Sīrat Rasūl Allāh 433, 611, 622, 769
ibn ʿIyāḍ, Fuḍayl (d. 188/803) 752
Ibn Jamāʿa, Badr al-Dīn; *Kashf al-maʿānī ʿan mutashābih al-mathānī* 842
Ibn al-Jawzī (d. 597/1200) 299, 392, 656, 660, 834, 838
Muntakhab qurrat al-ʿuyūn al-nawāẓir fī'l-wujūh wa'l-naẓā'ir 841
al-Muṣaffā bi-akuff ahl al-rusūkh min ʿilm al-nāsikh wa'l-mansūkh 840
Nuzhat al-aʿyun al-nawāẓir fī ʿilm al-wujūh wa'l-naẓā'ir 841
Ibn al-Jazarī (d. 833/1429) 182
Ghāyat al-nihāya fī ṭabaqāt al-qurrā' 196 n.1, 197
Muqaddima al-Jazariyya fī'l-tajwīd 843
al-Nashr fī'l-qirā'āt al-ʿashr 209–210
Ibn Jinnī (d. 392/1002); *Kitāb al-Muḥtasab* 191, 197
ibn Jubayr, Saʿīd (d. 95/714) 610
ibn al-Jubbā'ī, Abū Hāshim 377
Ibn Jurayj (d. 150/767) 16, 513, 635, 636, 640
Ibn al-Kalbī 86, 88–89
Kitāb al-Aṣnām 84, 433
Ibn Kathīr (d. 774/1373) 130, 521, 660, 669, 683, 697, 829, 844
on *isrā'iliyyāt* 687
views on exegesis of 823, 844
on women 529–530, 532
Ibn Kathīr (d. 120/738) [one of seven readers] 190–191, 196
Ibn Kaysān, ʿAbd al-Raḥmān (d. 225/840) 676
Ibn Kaysān al-Aṣamm, ʿAbd al-Raḥmān (d. 200/816) 834
Ibn Khālawayhi (d. 370/980) 210
Laysā fī kalām al-ʿArab 300
Mukhtaṣar fī shawādhdh al-Qur'ān 191, 197, 200
Ibn Khaldūn (d. 808/1406) 378, 379, 383, 492
Ibn Khallikān (608–81/1211–82) 243
Ibn Khuzayma al-Fārisī; *Kitāb al-mujāz fī'l-nāsikh wa'l-mansūkh* 839
Ibn Kullāb (d. 258/854) 381
Ibn Makhlad, Baqiyy (d. 276/889) 676
Ibn Mālik (d. 672/1273); *Alfiyya* 333
Ibn Manẓūr (d. 711/1311) 283
Ibn Marzūq al-Ḥafīd 232
Ibn Masarra al-Jabalī (d. 319/931) 757
Ibn Masʿūd, ʿAbd Allāh (d. 32/652) 191, 198–199, 205, 503, 645
codices of 207–208
muṣḥaf 186–187
reading of 188
recensions of 176
Ibn Mihrān (d. 381/991)
al-Ghāya 211
al-Mabsūṭ fī'l-qirā'āt al-ʿashr 190, 211
al-Shāmil 211
Ibn Miqsam (d. 354/965) 191, 202
ibn al-Mubārak, ʿAbd Allāh (d. 181/797) 748
Ibn Muḥayṣin (d. 123/741) 190
Ibn Mujāhid (d. 324/936) 202, 208
Kitāb al-Sabʿa fī'l-qirā'āt 8 n.20, 182, 188–191, 194, 196, 199, 206, 209–210, 286

ibn al-Mundhir, Abū'l-Jārūd Ziyād (d. *c.*150/167); *Tafsīr ʿan al-Bāqir* 710
Ibn al-Muqaffaʿ (d. *c.*137/755) 393
Ibn Muqla (d. 328/940) 202, 584
ibn Muṣarrif, Ṭalḥa (d. 112/730) 189
Ibn al-Muʿtazz, ʿAbd Allāh (d. 247/908) 408
Kitāb al-Badīʿ 330, 395
Ibn al-Nadīm (d. 380/990) 173, 175, 672
al-Fihrist 7, 169
Ibn al-Naqīb (d. 698/1298) 677
al-Fawāʾid al-mushawwiq ilā ʿulūm al-Qurʾān wa-ʿilm al-bayān 395, 835
ibn al-Naṭṭāḥ, Bakr (d. *c.*196/808) 391
Ibn al-Qāriḥ 393
Ibn al-Qarriyya 328
Ibn Qasī (546/1151) 757
Ibn Qayyim al-Jawziyya (d. 751/1350) 513, 835
Amthāl fī'l-Qurʾān al-karīm 843
al-Fawāʾid 395
Ibn Qutayba (d. 276/889) 299, 396, 652, 795, 797
Aʿlām al-nubuwwa 686
Gharīb al-ḥadīth 841
Tafsīr gharīb al-Qurʾān 661, 840–842
Taʾwīl mushkil al-Qurʾān 376, 394, 722, 795, 841–842
Ibn Rashīq al-Qayrawānī (d. 456/1063 or 463/1071) 394
ibn Rawāḥa, ʿAbd Allāh 390
ibn Rūmān, Yazīd (d. 130/747) 625
Ibn al-Rūmī 408
Ibn Rushd (Averroes) (d. 595/1198) 19, 383, 468, 854
Faṣl al-maqāl (The decisive treatise) 784–785
al-Kashf ʿan manāhij al-adilla fī ʿaqāʾid al-milla (Disclosure of the methods of proofs) 430, 784
Tahāfut al-Tahāfut (Incoherence of the Incoherence) 784–785
Ibn al-Ṣaffār 658
ibn Salām, ʿAbd Allāh [Companion] 683, 687
Ibn Sallām, Muḥammad ibn Yaḥyā (d. 262/876) 656
Ibn Sallām, Yaḥyā (d. 200/815) 16, 18, 640, 641–643, 659, 660–661, 662, 676, 734–735
interpretations/*tafsīr* of 637–638, 656–658
Kitāb al-taṣārīf 656
al-Taṣārīf li-tafsīr al-Qurʾān 656–657
Ibn al-Samayfaʿ (d. early second/eighth century?) 189
Ibn al-Sarrāj (d. 316/928) 210
Ibn Shabīb (d. 247/861) 655
Ibn Shanabūdh (d. 328/939) 191, 202
Ibn al-Shibl al-Baghdādī (d. 474/1081–2) 392
Ibn Shihāb al-Zuhrī (d. 124/742) 168, 186, 625–626
Ibn al-Sikkīt 300 n.4
Ibn Sīnā (d. 427/1037) 19, 482, 652, 781, 787–788, 789, 791, 834
commentary of 790–791
doctrine of 786
Ishārāt (Pointers and Reminders) 782–784, 786, 787, 790
*Ithbāt al-nubuwwāt (*Proof on prophecies*)* 782–783
al-Shifāʾ (The Healing) 783–784
Ibn Ṭāwūs 608
Ibn Taymiyya (d. 728/1328) 74, 588, 660, 682, 687, 699, 776, 824, 829
Muqaddima fī uṣūl al-tafsīr 844
Ibn Ṭufayl (d. *c.*580/1185) 785
Ḥayy ibn Yaqẓān 379
Ibn ʿUmar, 519
ibn ʿUqba, Mūsā 625
Ibn Waḍḍāḥ 657
Ibn Wahb, ʿAbd Allāh (d. 197/812) 637, 657
al-Jāmiʿ 656
Ibn Warraq [pseud.] 35, 48
(ed.), *The Origins of the Koran* 67
Ibn Wathīq al-Ishbīlī (d. 654/1256); *Kitāb fī'l-tajwīd al-qirāʾa wa-makhārij al-ḥurūf* 843
ibn Waththāb, Yaḥyā (d. 103/721) 645
ibn Yaʿmur, Yaḥyā 188
Ibn al-Zubayr = Abū Jaʿfar al-Gharnāṭī (d. 708/1308)
al-Burhān fī tartīb suwar al-Qurʾān 317, 836
al-Milāk al-taʾwīl 842
Ibrahim, Abd al-Rahim; *The Literary Structure of the Qurʾānic Verse* 332
Ibrāhīm, Ḥāfiẓ (d. 1932) 409
Ibrāhīm [Prophet]. *See* Abraham

Idrīs (Enoch) 488, 490
stories of the prophets 731
Iēsous/Yēshūaʿ/Yasūʿ 159
al-Ījī, ʿAḍud al-Dīn (d. 756/1355) 482
al-Mawāqif fī ʿilm al-kalām 810
ʿIkrima (d. 105/723) 838
Ilyās (Elijah) 488, 490
Ilyasaʿ (Elisha) 488, 490
al-Imam, Ahmad ʿAli; *Variant Readings of the Qurʾān* 69
Imbert, Frédéric 105
ʿImrān 131
family/line of 497–498
wife of 489
Imrūʾ ʻl-Qays (d. 542) 405
Muʿallaqa 281, 404
Innocent XI [pope] (1611–89) 258
Iqbal, Mohammed (d. 1938) 505–506
al-ʿIrāqī, Muḥammad ibn Asʿad (d. 567/1171 or 667/1268); *Asbāb al-nuzūl wa-qiṣaṣ al-furqāniyya* 838
Irving, Washington 597, 600
Life of Mohamet 490
Mahomet and his Successors 599
Sketch-Book of Geoffrey Crayon, Gent. 599
ʿĪsā. *See* Jesus
Isaac/Isḥāq 47, 131–132, 145, 488, 492, 498
stories of the prophets 731
Isaiah 475
Iṣfahānī, Nuṣrat Amīn (d. 1983); *Makhzan al-ʿirfān* 716
al-Iṣfahānī (d. 749/1349) 678
al-Iṣfahānī (d. after 360/970–1); *Kitāb al-Aghānī* 282
Ishoʿ [as pronunciation of Jesus] 160
Iṣlāḥī, Amīn Aḥsan (d. 1997) 13, 318–319, 362, 367, 369, 370–371, 858
Taddabur-i Qurʾān 318, 370
Islam, Manzu 601
Ismāʿīl, Mullā ʿUthmān 260
Ismāʿīl ibn Aḥmad al-Ḥīrī al-Nīsābūrī (d. 430/1038) 838
Kitāb Wujūh al-Qurʾān 842
Ismāʿīl/Ishmael 132, 145, 488, 490, 492, 623
as Messenger 489
Ismāʿīl [Shāh] (r. 907–30/1501–24) 249*f*
Israeli, Raphael 74
al-Izkawī, Muḥammad ibn Jaʿfar (third/ninth century) 735
Izutsu, Toshihiko 34, 306, 402, 419, 426, 437
Ethico-Religious Concepts in the Qurʾān 71
God and Man in the Koran 71
on Qurʼanic concepts 421–423, 466

J

al-Jaʿbarī, Ibrāhīm (d. 732/1333)
Kanz al-maʿānī fī sharḥ ḥirz al-amānī 211
Taqrīb al-maʾmūr fī tartīb al-nuzūl 836
Jābir ibn ʿAbd Allāh (d. 78/697) [Companion] 807
Jacob (of Serugh) 130, 132
Jacob Lassner 492
Jacob/Yaʿqūb [Prophet] 47, 145, 396, 488, 498
stories of the prophets 730–731
Jaʿfar ibn Manṣūr al-Yaman (d. *c.*346/957)
Asrār al-nuṭaqāʾ [attrib.] 731
Kitāb al-ʿālim waʾl-ghulām ascribed to 729
Kitāb al-Farāʾiḍ wa-ḥudūd al-dīn [attrib.] 731
Kitāb al-Kashf [attrib.] 729
Kitāb al-Riḍāʿ fiʼl-bāṭin [attrib.] 731
Kitāb al-Shawāhid waʼl-bayān [attrib.] 731
Sarāʾir al-nuṭaqāʾ [attrib.] 731
Taʾwīl Sūrat al-Nisāʾ [attrib.] 731
Taʾwīl al-zakāt [attrib.] 731
Jaʿfar al-Ṣādiq (d. 148/765) 74, 707–708, 709, 710, 731
interpretations/exegesis of 748–749
Jaffer, Tariq 19
al-Jāḥiẓ (d. 255/868–9) 396, 795
al-Bayān waʼl-tabyīn 655
Dalāʾil al-iʿjāz 328
Kitāb al-Ḥayawān 383
Naẓm al-Qurʾān 328
Jakobson, Roman 800
al-Jamal, Bassām 625
James, David
After Timur: Qurʾāns of the 15th and 16th Centuries 69
Manuscripts of the Holy Qurʾān from the Mamlūk Era 231
The Master Scribes: Qurʾāns from the 10th to 14th Centuries AD 69
Qurʾāns of the Mamlūks 231
James, William 588

Janssens, Jules 19
Jarrar, Maher 17
al-Jaṣṣāṣ (d. 370/981). 838
Jassin, Hans Bague; *Bacaan Mulia* 552
al-Jawāliqī (d. 539/1144); *Kitāb al-Muʿarrab min al-kalām al-aʿjamī ʿalā ḥurūf al-muʿjam* 300
al-Jawharī (d. *c.*400/1010); *Tāj al-lugha wa'l-ṣaḥāḥ* 296
Jebb, John (1775–1833) 322
Jeffery, Arthur 11, 12, 212, 303, 304, 306, 308, 667
  on *dīn* 446
  on Egyptian edition 209
  on foreign vocabulary in Qur'an 297–299, 447
  The Foreign Vocabulary of the Qurʾān 201, 841
  Materials for the History of the Text of the Qur'an 201
  on standarization of Qur'an text 200–203, 204, 266
Jeremiah 420, 475
Jesus/ʿĪsā [Prophet] 47, 60, 64, 131–132, 157, 158–159, 161–162, 420, 435, 488, 490, 497, 570
  and Antichrist *(dajjāl)* 475
  disciples, and teachings of 152–153
  as fifth *nāṭiq* 730
  as human 152
  life of 93
  al-Masīḥ Ibn Maryam 159–160
  as Messenger 157, 489
  as 'Messiah' (al-Masīḥ or al-Masīḥ ʿĪsā) 130, 154, 159, 162, 497
  miracles of 376, 378
  nature of 498
  prayer of 156
  sayings attributed to 157
  as son of God 83, 152
  stories of the prophets 730–731
al-Jīlī, ʿAbd al-Karīm (d. *c.*832/1428); *al-Kahf wa'l-raqīm fī sharḥ bismillāh al-raḥmān al-raḥīm* 843
al-Jishumī, al-Ḥākim (d. 494/1101) 773
  Tahdhīb 773
Job/Ayyūb [Prophet] 488, 493
  stories of the prophets 730
John (of Damascus) 155
Johns, Anthony 15, 73, 422
John/Yaḥyā [Prophet] 160, 488
  the Baptist 158
  stories of the prophets 731
Jomier, Jacques 306
  The Great Themes of the Qur'an 70
Jonah/Yūnus [Prophet] 47, 488, 490, 495
  stories of the prophets 408 n.5, 730
Jones, Alan 446, 569, 570–571, 574, 575
Josephus (37–c. 100 CE) 48, 81
Joseph/Yūsuf [Prophet] 134, 324*f*, 396, 397, 488–490, 495, 586, 757, 807
  stories of the prophets 99, 724, 730–731
Joyce, James; *Finnegans Wake* 601 n.13
J-Rock (Jihad Rahmouni) 582
JT Bigga Figga 581
al-Jubbāʾī, Abū ʿAlī (d. 303/915) 376, 712, 773
al-Juʿfī, Jābir (d. 128/746) 710
al-Junayd, Abū'l-Qāsim (d. 298/910) 749, 752
al-Jurjānī, ʿAbd al-Qāhir (d. 471/1078) 317, 328, 377, 383, 795, 797–798, 799, 802, 804
  Asrār al-balāgha 330, 655
  Dalāʾil al-iʿjāz 13, 330, 381, 655
al-Jurjānī, ʿAlī ibn ʿAbd al-ʿAzīz (d. 392/1002) 394
al-Juwaynī, Abū'l-Maʿālī (d. 478/1085) 467–468
Juynboll, G. H. A. 59, 645

K

Kaʿb al-Aḥbār 683, 687
Kabara, Nasiru (1925–96) 561
al-Kaʿbī, Abū'l-Qāsim al-Balkhī (d. 319/931) 773
Kaʿb ibn Mālik 405, 412
Kaʿb ibn Zuhayr 405
Kadhim, Hussein 409
al-Kafawī, Abū'l-Baqāʾ (d. 1094/1683) 465, 469
Kahf, Mohja 601
Kahle, Paul E. (d. 1964) 199, 279
al-Kalbī, Muḥammad ibn al-Sāʾib (d. 146/763) 16, 636, 637–638, 642, 656
  Tafsīr [transmitted from] 640, 641, 643, 644

Kalīla wa-Dimna 281
Kalin, Ibrahim 813
Kamal, Trisutji 583
Kant 849
Karimi-Nia [Karīmī-Niā], Morteza 708
  Bibliography of Qurʾānic Studies in European Languages 65
Kāshānī, Fatḥullāh (d. 980/1570); *Manhaj al-ṣādiqayn fī ilzām al-mukhālifīn* 713
Kāshānī, Muḥsin Fayḍ (d. 1090/1680) 713
  al-Ṣāfī 713
Kātib Çelebi; *Kashf al-ẓunūn ʿan asāmī al-kutub waʾl-funūn* 7 n.15
al-Kawākibī, ʿAbd al-Raḥmān (d. 1903) 855
Kazimirski, Albert [Albin de] Biberstein-
  Le Coran 559
  Les Livres sacrés de l'orient 545
Keeler, Ali; *Tafsīr al-Tustarī by Sahl b. ʿAbd Allāh al-Tustarī* 75
Keeler, Annabel 753
  Sufi Hermeneutics 75
  Tafsīr al-Tustarī 74–75
Kendall, Elisabeth 412
Kermani, Navid 377, 382, 403, 410
  God is Beautiful 72
Khalaf (d. 229/844) 190
Khalafallāh, Muḥammad Aḥmad (d. 1991) 376, 506, 700, 850
  al-Fann al-qaṣaṣī fīʾl-Qurʾān 383
Khāled, ʿAmr (b. 1967) 40–41
Khalidi, Tarif 547, 548, 569, 570, 571, 575, 629
Khālid ibn al-Walīd 86
Khalifa, Rashad (d. 1990) 460
Khalil, Mohammed Hassan 436
al-Khalīlī, Aḥmad ibn Ḥamad (b. 1943) 737, 738, 741–743
  Jawāhir al-tafsīr: Anwār min bayān al-tanzīl 736–737
al-Khalīl (d. 175/791); *Kitāb al-ʿAyn* 646
Khan, Mofakhkhar Hussain; *The Holy Qur'ān in South Asia* 554
Khan, Nusrat Fateh Ali 585
Khan, Sayyid Ahmad (d. 1898) 506–507
Khan, Siddiq Hasan (d. 1890) 687
al-Khaṭṭābī (d. 388/998) 795
  Bayān iʿjāz al-Qurʾān (Proof of the inimitability of the Qur'an) 316–317, 655
Khomeini [Ayatollah] 508
Khorchide, Mouhanad 42
al-Khūʾī, Sayyid (d. 1992); *al-Bayān fī tafsīr al-Qurʾān* 716
al-Khūlī, Amīn (d. 1967) 700, 850
Khurāsānī, Sayyida Ṣiddīqa (b. 1959); *Tafsīr-i ravān* 716
al-Khushanī (d. 286/902) 655
Khwāja Aḥrār 265
al-Kindī (d. *c.*256/870) 19, 742, 780
  On the Prosternation of the Outermost Body 780
  On the Quantity of Aristotle's Books 781
  On the Reason why the Higher Air is Cold and that which is Near the Earth is Warm 781
al-Kindī, Muḥammad ibn Ibrāhīm (d. 508/1114–15) 735
al-Kindī, Saʿīd ibn Aḥmad (d. 1740) 744
  al-Tafsīr al-muyassar liʾl-Qurʾān al-karīm 735
al-Kirmānī, Maḥmūd ibn Ḥamza (d. after 500/1106)
  al-Burhān fī mutashābih al-Qurʾān 842
  Gharāʾib al-tafsīr wa-ʿajāʾib al-taʾwīl 841
al-Kisāʾī (d. 189/804) 190, 196, 645, 842
  Kitāb al-Maʿānī 653
  Mutashābih al-Qurʾān [attrib.] 615
al-Kisāʾī [c. sixth/twelfth century]; *Qiṣaṣ al-anbiyāʾ (Stories of the Prophets)* 685
Kister, M. J. 303
Kitāb al-Bilawhar wa-Būdhāsaf 729
Kitāb al-Muwāfaqāt allatī waqaʿat fīʾl-Qurʾān al-ʿaẓīm li-amīr al-muʾminīn 843
Klar, Marianna 10, 689
Knauf, Ernest Axel 284–285, 289
Knysh, Alexander 19
Koffler, Hans 278
Kohlberg, Etan; *Revelation and Falsification* 70
Kopf, Lothar 307
Köprülü, Fuat 556
Koren, [J.] 155

Kubrā, Najm al-Dīn (d. 618/1221) 757, 762
al-Kudamī, Muḥammad (d. 353/964–356/967) 735
al-Kūfī, Furāt (d. *c.*310/922) 615, 710
al-Kulaynī, Abū Ja^cfar (d. 329/941) 710, 716
al-Kāfī 708

L

Labīd 133
Lacunza-Balda 561
La^clī, Ṣāliḥ ibn ^cUmar (d. 1928); *al-Qawl al-wajīz fī tafsīr kalām Allāh al-^cazīz* 737
Lammens, Henri (d. 1937) 621, 622, 628
Lamrabet, Asma 856
Lane, Andrew J.; *A Traditional Mu^ctazilite Qur^ɔān Commentary* 74
Lane, Edward William; *Arabic English Lexicon* (d. 1893) 296
Larcher, Pierre 280, 281, 284
Laroui, ^cAbdallāh (b. 1933) 851
Lawrence, Bruce 16
The Qur'an: A Biography 65
Lawson, Todd 708
The Crucifixion and the Qur'an 70
Lazarus-Yafeh, Hava (1992) 30
Leaman, Oliver 9
(ed.), *The Qur'an: An Encyclopedia* 66
Leemhuis, Fred 306
Lenin 265
Levi Della Vida, [Giorgio] 255
Levinas, Emmanuel 377
Lincoln, Bruce 60
Lindsay, Ursula 584
Lord, Albert 282–283
Loth, Otto 302
Lot/Lūṭ 488–489
stories of the prophets 730–731
Lowin, Shari 688, 689
Lowry, Joseph 14
Lowth, Robert (1710–87) 322
Lüling, Günter 33, 57, 154, 199, 281
Über den Ur-Koran (A Challenge to Islam for Reformation) 67, 280
Lumbard, Joseph E. B.; (ed.), *The Study Quran* 74
Luther, Martin 257, 490, 542
Luxenberg, Christoph 33, 48, 57, 154, 199, 284, 309, 841
Die syro-aramäische Lesart des Koran 59
The Syro-Aramaic Reading of the Koran 67, 283
Lycurgus 420

M

al-Ma^carrī, Abū'l- ^cAlā^ɔ (d. 449/1057) 394
al-Fuṣūl wa-'l-ghāyāt 393
Risālat al-ghufrān 393
Macdonald, Michael C. A. 112, 116–117, 118, 278, 289
Madelung, Wilferd 767
Madigan, Daniel A. 66, 424, 425
The Qur^ɔān's Self-Image 72
Madjid, Nurcholish (1939–2005) 42
Maghen, Z. 688
al-Mahdī (Abbasid caliph, r. 158–69/775–85) 225
al-Mahdī, ^cAbd Allāh (Fatimid caliph, r. 297–322/909–934) 247
Maḥfūẓ, Naguib 281
Majdū^c; *Fihrist* 729
Ma Jian (d. 1978) 559
Makḥūl al-Shāmī (d. *c.*119/737) 519
Makkī ibn Abī Ṭālib al-Qaysī, Abū Muḥammad (d. 437/1045) 662, 676
al-Hidāya ilā bulūgh al-nihāya 661
al-Īḍāḥ li-nāsikh al-Qur^ɔān wa-mansūkhihi 840
Kitāb al-Kashf ^can wujūh al-qirā^ɔāt al-sab^c 211
Tabṣira 211
Tafsīr al-mushkil min gharīb al-Qur^ɔān al-^caẓīm ^calā'l-ījāz wa'l-ikhtiṣār 661
Malcolm X 54
Mālik ibn Anas (d. 179/795) 168, 184, 656
Muwaṭṭa^ɔ 191
Malikshāh 246
Malinowski, [Bronisław Kasper] (d. 1942) 568
Malti-Douglas, Fedwa; *Arab Comic Strips* 69
Ma^cmar ibn Rāshid (d. 154/770) 16, 637, 655–656
Tafsīr 637–638
al-Ma^ɔmūn (caliph, r. 189–218/813–33) 242–243, 381

Mandelbrote, Scott; (ed.), *Nature and Scripture in the Abrahamic Religions* 71
Mani (215–75 CE) 85
Månson, Anette 411
Manṣūr al-Yaman (d. *c.*303/915); *Kitāb al-Rushd wa'l-hidāya* [attrib.] 728, 729
Manzoor, Parvez 66
al-Marāghī, Muṣṭafa (d. 1945) 560
al-Marʿashlī 661, 662
Margoliouth, David 308, 402
Mark, of Toledo (fl. 1193–1216) 2 n.4
Mark [apostle] 158
Marlowe, Christopher; *Tamburlaine the Great* 594–595
Marracci, Ludovico (1612–1700) 3, 4, 7, 77, 258, 544, 548
  Alcorani textus universus 3, 259*f*, 296 n.1, 543
  Latin translation of Qur'an 6
  Prodromus ad refutatio alcorani 543
Marshall, David; *Muhammad and the Unbelievers* 70
Mårtensson, Ulrika 14, 17, 422–423, 424–425, 652, 654, 659
Martin, Richard 376, 424, 625
Martin Luther. *See* Luther
Marx, Michael 33, 131, 137, 283, 497, 548
  (ed.), *The Qurʾān in Context* 67, 290
Mary (Maryam) 47, 131, 159, 419, 489–490, 497–499
Masāʾil Nāfiʿ ibn al-Azraq 636
al-Masīḥ ('The Messiah') 160. *See also* Jesus
Massey, Keith 303
Massignon, Louis 546
Masson, Denise 546
al-Masʿūdī (d. 345/956) 687
Masuzawa, Tomoko 53
Maṭar, Muḥammad ʿAfīfī (d. 2010); *Quartet of Joy* 412
Matthew [apostle] 162
Mattson, Ingrid; *The Story of the Qur'an: Its History and Place in Muslim Life* 65
al-Māturīdī (d. 333/944) 19, 670, 673, 677, 722, 766, 774–775, 818
  Taʾwīlāt ahl al-Sunna 668
  Taʾwīlāt al-Qurʾān 669, 774
Mavāhib-i ʿaliyya 557
al-Mawdūdī, Abū'l-Aʿlā (d. 1979) 508–509, 695, 702, 855
  The Codification of the Islamic Constitution 509
  Tarjumān al-Qurʾān [journal] 509
al-Maybudī, Rashīd al-Dīn Aḥmad (d. 530/1135) 75, 754
  Kashf al-asrār 753
Mayer, Farhana
  (ed.), *An Anthology of Qur'anic Commentaries* 74
  Spiritual Gems 74
Mayer, Toby; *Keys to the Arcana* 74
al-Māzandarānī, Abū Jaʿfar (d. 588/1192) 838
McAuley, [Denis] 407
McAuliffe, Jane Dammen 686, 823
  (ed.), *Encyclopaedia of the Qurʾān* 66
  (ed.), *The Cambridge Companion to the Qurʾān* 66
  (ed.), *With Reverence for the Word* 73
  Qurʾānic Christians 70
Megerlin, David; *Die türkische Bibel* 544
Mehmet, Ayıntâbî (d. 1111/1698–9); *Tefsir-i Tibyan* 557
Mehmet II (sultan, r. 1451–81) 256
Meier, [F.] 475
Melanchthon, Philip (d. 1560) 256, 542
  (ed.), *Mahumetis Saracenorum principis* 257*f*
Melchert, Christopher 69, 209
Mendelsohn, I. 264
Mettinger, T. N. D. 87
Meynet, Roland 331
  Treatise on Biblical Rhetoric 322
Michaelis, Johann David 4 n.8
Midhat, Ahmet (1844–1913) 557
Milo, Thomas 269
Milton, John; *Paradise Lost* 594
Mingana, Alphonse 199, 295
Mir, Mustansir 13, 73, 318–319, 495–496, 576
  Coherence in the Qurʾān 72, 332
  Understanding the Islamic Scripture 65
  Verbal Idioms of the Qurʾān 71
Mohamed, Y. 661
Mommsen, Katharina 601
da Monte di Croce, Riccoldo 3
Montgomery, James 402, 408, 654

Moore, Thomas 597
Moosa, Ebrahim 14, 70, 382, 506
Morabia, [Alfred] 513
Morrison, Robert 19, 71, 775
Mos Def 581, 582
Moses/Mūsā [Prophet] 99, 128, 131, 157–158, 160, 420, 437, 474, 488–490, 495
  covenant with 624
  dialog with God/divine command 408, 490, 740–741, 751–752
  as fourth *nāṭiq* 730
  Law of 419
  miracles of 376, 378, 435
  people of *(qawm mūsā)* 145
  Sinai revelation 422–423, 492
  story of 346, 725, 730–731, 759
Motzki, Harald 51, 58, 68, 168, 177, 458, 616, 636, 653, 655, 838
Moubarac, [Youakim] 494
Mourad, Suleiman 131–132, 772
Moustafa, Ahmed 584
Muʿāwiya (r. 41–60/661– 80) 504
al-Mubarrad (d. 285/989) 843
Muḥammad ʿAlī [re. Egypt] 268
Muḥammad [Prophet] 54, 59, 70, 142, 144, 157, 184, 371, 419, 425, 475, 488–490, 494–496, 499, 586, 611–612, 812
  acts/behaviour of 458, 683
  admiration for 544
  agreements/pact with 455, 517
  attacks/polemics against; hostility toward 517, 542, 686
  authority of 403
  as author of Qur'an 35, 43, 142
  biography *(sīra)* of 52, 83, 97, 348, 493, 611, 620, 621, 623–624, 628, 644, 684
  and campaign of Tabūk 521
  and Constitution of Medina 100
  and ethics 464, 468–469
  as a *ḥanīf* 92
  heart of 727
  heirs of 747
  hermeneutics ultimately from [re. Ismāʿīlīs] 723
  and his household/wives 449, 453, 535
    marriage to Zaynab 57
  identity of/as a historical figure 154–155, 624
  idiolect of 282, 290
  intercession of 742
  is not/was a poet 402, 802
  and issue of Christian sources 142, 499
  Jewish resistance to 769
  as judge/arbiter 446, 453
  language/dialect of 277, 278, 279, 285, 286, 308
  as last prophet/messenger 51, 489, 491
  as legitimate successor [to other prophets] 492
  life of 32, 98, 103, 622, 625, 626–627, 628
    to explain revelation 46
    traditional Muslim accounts of 56
  and magic 588
  as messenger 51, 250, 489
  miracle(s) of 328, 376, 378, 397
  mission of 246, 694
  on nature of Jesus 498
  Night Journey of 243
  and poets 403
  as political/spiritual leader 33, 42, 493
  predictions/prophecies of advent 83, 146, 157, 807
  primordial light of 729
  proclamations of 358, 497
  prophecy/prophethood of 370, 375, 473, 797
  psychological development of 347
  and *qibla* 368
  and Qur'an 32, 157, 183–184, 301, 342, 685, 708
    certifies he was a genuine prophet 280
    disseminated after death of 458
    as written during his lifetime 167
  and seeing God 741 n.1
  as sixth *nāṭiq* [re. Ismāʿīlīs] 730
  as a soothsayer *(kāhin),* Qur'anic denial of 375
  as source of exegetical material 609, 832
  stories of the prophets 730–731
  succession of 504
  sura (47) named after 489
  on the time of the Hour 474, 475
  traditional history of 44
  as 'unlettered' *(ummī)* 184
  on women 527
  and *wujūh* 570

al-Muḥāsibī, al-Ḥārith (d. 243/857); *Fahm al-Qur'ān* 656, 662, 844
al-Mu'izz ibn Badīs 235
al-Mu'izz li-Dīn Allāh (r. 341–65/953–75) 247, 722, 730
Mujāhid ibn Jabr (d. 104/722) 19, 513, 521, 611, 616, 637–638, 766, 767–768, 772
  and *isnāds* 656, 659
  on jihad/aggression 516
Mullā Ṣadrā Shīrāzī (d. 1050/1640) 19, 715, 763, 791
  Asfār 790
  Iksīr al-'ārifīn (The Elixir of the Gnostics) 790
  Tafsīr āyat al-nūr (Commentary on the light verse) 714, 790
Müller, David Heinrich (1846–1912) 4
  Epigraphische Denkmäler aus Arabien 295
  Südarabische Studien 295
al-Munajjid, Ṣalāḥ al-Dīn 169
Munt, Harry 9
Muqātil ibn Sulaymān (d. 150/767) 16, 459, 611–612, 644, 652, 670, 674, 749, 832, 839
  exegesis/commentary of 513–515, 521, 639–640, 768–769
  Kitāb al-Ashbāh wa'l-naẓā'ir fī 'l-qur'ān al-karīm 446, 614, 657
  Kitāb al-Wujūh wa'l-naẓā'ir [attrib.] 614, 841
  on men and women 529, 530–531
  on *tafsīr* and *ta'wīl* 722
  Tafsīr khams mī'a āya min al-Qur'ān [attrib.] 612
  Tafsīr al-Qur'ān [attrib.] 611, 637
  terminology of 642–643
Mursi, Mohammed 584
al-Murtaḍā, al-Sharīf (d. 436/1044) 834
Musa (B. Heller) 494
Musaylima ('false prophet') 389–390, 392
Muslim (d. 261/875); *Ṣaḥīḥ Muslim* 51–52, 832, 834
Musnad al-Rabī' 738, 741
al-Mutanabbī (d. 354/965) 393–394, 406–407
al-Mutawakkil [caliph] 243, 374, 381

N

al-Nābulusī, 'Abd al-Ghanī 407
al-Nadwī, Abū'l-Ḥasan 'Alī (d. 1999) 469
Nāfi' ibn Abī al-Nu'āym (d. 169/785) 190–191, 196
Nafīsa, Sayyida; mausoleum of 246
Naguib, Shuruq 74
Nagy, Gregory 420, 424
al-Naḥḥās (d. 338/949) 839, 843
Nahmad, H. M.; *New Arabic Grammar of the Written Language* 329
Nallino, C. H.; *Chrestomathia Qorani Arabica* 297
al-Naqqāsh 722
Naqvī, Sayyid 'Alī Naqī (d. 1988); *Tafsīr-i Faṣl al-khiṭāb* 715
al-Nasafī (d. 701/1310) 735
al-Nasafī, Abū'l-Ḥasan Muḥammad (d. 332/943); *Kitāb al-Maḥsūl* 730
al-Nasafī, 'Umar ibn Muḥammad (d. 537/1142) 667
al-Nāṣir Muḥammad [Mamluk sultan] 232, 252
Nasr, Seyyed Hossein 813, 849
  (ed.), *The Study Quran* 74
Nasser, Shady Hekmat; *The Transmission of the Variant Readings of the Qur'ān* 69
Nathan [Prophet] 494
al-Nawawī al-Bantanī (d. 1314/1897) 775
al-Nawawī; *al-Tibyān fī ādāb al-Qur'ān* 843
Nayfar, Aḥmīdah 694, 698, 699, 700, 702
  al-Insān wa'l-Qur'ān wajhan li-wajh 698
al-Naẓẓām 379–380
Necipoğlu, Gülru 241
Nehmé, Laila 118
Nelson, Kristina 843
Neṣḥānâ = Alexander Legend (Neṣḥānā dileh d-Aleksandros) 133–137
Nestorius (Patriarch of Constantinople 428–31) 83
Nettler, Ronald 687, 759
Netton, Ian 130
Neuwirth, Angelika 67, 100–101, 280, 283, 289, 330, 402–403, 433, 548
  (ed.), *The Qur'ān in Context* 67, 290
  approach of 32–34, 46, 284, 423, 424
  Der Koran als Text der Spätantike: Ein europäischer Zugang 44, 67
  (ed.) *Qur'anic Studies Today* 65
  Scripture, Poetry, and the Making of a Community 67

on structure of suras 101, 362–363
Studien zur Komposition der mekkanischen Suren 32, 284, 319–320
Nevo 155
Nguyen, Martin 20, 749
Sufi Master and Qur'an Scholar 75
Nicholas, of Cusa (d. 1464) 2
Cribratio Alcorani 2–3, 256
Nicholas I [tsar] (1796–1855) 263
Nietzsche, Friedrich 53, 848
al-Nīsābūrī, Abū Bakr (d. 324/936) 317
al-Nīsābūrī, Muḥammad ibn ʿAlī 228
al-Nīsābūrī, Niẓām al-Dīn (d. *c.*730/1330) 775, 810
Gharāʾib al-Qurʾān wa-raghāʾib al-furqān 808
Noah/Nūḥ [Prophet] 128, 131, 422, 488, 489, 492, 494, 497
God's rebuke to 740
as Messenger 489
as second *nāṭiq* 730
stories of the prophets 730–731
sura (71) named after 490
Nöldeke, Theodor (d. 1930) 6–7, 11, 31–32, 176, 308, 329, 348–349, 350, 357–358, 492
approach of 46, 545
on chronology/framework of suras 32, 359, 424, 545, 837
Geschichte des Qorâns 5–7, 32, 97, 197, 202, 210–211, 266, 295, 329, 348
influence of 9, 13, 97, 298
language of Qur'an 279, 281, 286, 300, 302–303, 333, 422
Neue Beiträge zur semitischen Sprachwissenschaft 295, 298, 300, 329
on *variae lectiones* 202, 203
Noseda, Sergio Noja 207, 219, 267
al-Nuʿmān 247
Asās al-taʾwīl 730
Taʾwīl al-sharīʿa [attrib.] 730
al-Nuʿmānī (d. 360/971) 710
Nuovo, Angela 256
Nūr al-Dīn [Zangid ruler] 248
Nursi, Said (1878–1960) 40, 813–815
Lemalar (The Gleams) 814
Sözler 813–814
Nuṣrat bint Muḥammad Amīn = Bānū-yi Iṣfahānī (d. 1403/1982) 763
Nusrat Fateh Ali Khan; *Allah Hoo Allah Hoo Allah Hoo* [song] 585
Nwyia, Paul 749

O

O'Connor, Kathleen 579, 586, 588
Ohlander, Erik 75
Okumuş, [Mesut] 834
Orient und Okzident sind nicht mehr zu trennen: Goethe und die Weltkurlturen 601
O'Shaughnessy 434, 475
Otto, Rudolf 548
Ouintin, M. 735
Owens, Jonathan 282, 285–287, 289
Özsoy, Ömer (b. 1963) 505

P

Paganini Brixiensis (Paganino de Bresla/ Paganino de Paganini; d. 1538) 3 n.7, 256
Paraclete 158, 159
Paret, Rudi (1901–83) 31, 303, 329, 446–447, 545, 622
Parry, Milman 282–283
Paul [apostle] 152–153, 158, 161, 162
letters of 52
Pausanias 87
Pauthier, Guillaume 545
Pavlovitch, Pavel 304
Pennacchio, Catherine 299
Penrice, John; *Dictionary and Glossary of the Koran* 297
Peter (the Venerable) 541
Peters, F. E. 105
Peters, Hugh 595
Pharaoh 129, 489, 490
Philoponus 780
Pickthall, Muhammad Marmaduke (d. 1936) 16 n.24, 515, 560, 571
Meaning of the Glorious Koran (1930) 546
Pink, Johanna 20, 694, 698, 701–702, 703
(ed.), *Tafsīr and Islamic Intellectual History* 73

Pirous, Abdeljalil 583
Pisarev, S. I. 264
Pius II [pope] (1405–64) 256
Plato 603
Phaedrus 421, 422
Pococke, Edward (1604–91) 6, 472
Poe, Edgar Allan 597
Poonawala, Ismail 18
Postel, Guillaume (1510–81) 258
Powers, David S. 52, 57, 59, 304, 457, 839, 840
Pregill, [Michael E.] 637, 689
Pretzl, Otto (1893–1941) 6, 11, 35, 44, 197, 198, 199, 200, 201, 202, 203, 204, 209, 212, 266, 548
Kitāb al-Taysīr 197
[Pseudo-] Jaʿfar 748–749
Puin, Elizabeth 173
Puin, Gerd-R. 283
Putin 265

Q

al-Qāḍī, Wadād 391, 405
al-Qāḍī, ʿAbd al-Jabbār (d. 415/1025) 375, 377, 380, 655, 773, 795
Iʿjāz al-Qurʾān 13
Mutashābih al-Qurʾān 773
al-Qāḍī al-Nuʿmān (d. 363/974) 724
Daʿāʾim al-Islam 730
al-Qāʾim 247
Qālūn (d. 220/835), transmissions of 190
al-Qaraḍāwī, Yūsuf (b. 1926) 40–41
al-Qāshānī, ʿAbd al-Razzāq (d. *c.*730–6/1329–35) 714, 761
Taʾwīl al-Qurʾān 760
Qāsim Amīn 854
al-Qāsimī, Jamāl al-Dīn (d. 1914); *Maḥāsin al-taʾwīl* 697, 807
Qāsim ibn Ibrāhīm (d. 246/860) 721
Qatāda ibn Diʿāma (d. 118/736) 522–523, 638, 655, 656, 657, 839
Qawṣūn, Sayf al-Dīn 252
al-Qazwīnī, al-Khaṭīb (d. 793/1338) 332, 567
al-Qulaynī 658
al-Qummī, ʿAlī ibn Ibrāhīm (fl. late third/ninth century) 513, 710
al-Qūnawī, Ismāʿīl ibn Muḥammad (d. 1195/1781) 679
al-Qūnawī, Ṣadr al-Dīn (d. 673/1274) 17, 843
Ījāz al-bayān fī taʾwīl al-Qurʾān 760
al-Qurṭubī, Abū ʿAbd Allāh Muḥammad ibn Aḥmad (d. 671/1273) 514, 520–521, 522, 529, 532, 660, 669
al-Jāmiʿ li-aḥkām al-Qurʾān 558, 676
al-Qushayrī, Abū'l-Qāsim (d. 465/1072) 75, 671, 749, 751, 756, 834, 843
Laṭāʾif al-ishārāt 750–753
al-Risāla [al-Qushayriyya] fī ʿilm al-taṣawwuf 750
al-Tafsīr al-kabīr 752
Quss ibn Sāʿida 92
Quṭb, Sayyid (d. 1966) 318, 367, 383, 695, 700, 736, 855
Fī ẓilāl al-Qurʾān 495, 508, 697, 798

R

Rabb, Intisar A. 69, 207, 222
Rābiʿa al-ʿAdawiyya (d. *c.*180/796) 54, 407
al-Rabīʿ ibn Anas (d. 139/756) 516
Rabin, Chaim; *Ancient West-Arabian* 278
Radscheit, Mattias 423
al-Rāghib al-Iṣfahānī (d. early fifth/eleventh century) 299, 662
al-Dharīʿa ilā makārim al-sharīʿa 661
al-Mufradāt fī gharīb al-Qurʾān 661, 841
Rahman, Fazlur (1919–88) 41, 382, 425, 466, 468, 506, 701, 702, 806, 851, 856
Major Themes of the Qur'an 70, 467, 852
Rāj, Aḥmad ʿAlī (d. 2008) 728
Ramadan, Tariq (b. 1962) 41, 510, 813
Raphelengius, Franciscus (1539–97); *Lexicon Arabicum* 296
Rasmussen, Anne K.; *Women, the Recited Qurʾān, and Islamic Music in Indonesia* 75
Raven, Wim 627–628
[al-]Rāzī, Dāya (d. 654/1256) 762
al-Rāzī, Abū Ḥātim (d. 322/934)
Kitāb al-Iṣlāḥ 731
Kitāb al-Zīna 722, 724
al-Rāzī, Abū'l-Futūḥ (fl. sixth/twelfth century); *Rūḥ al-janān* 712
al-Rāzī, ʿAlī ibn Shādhān 226

al-Rāzī, Fakhr al-Dīn (d. 606/1210) 19, 317–318, 328, 347, 492, 499, 513, 660, 661, 669, 676, 678, 697, 736, 766, 773, 781, 834
Aḥkām al-basmala 843
commentary/methodology of 775–777, 787–788, 807–809, 811–812, 826
on jihad 514–516, 518–519
*Lawāmiʿ al-bayyināt sharḥ asmāʾ Allāh taʿalā waʾl-ṣifāt (*Explanation of Allāh's beautiful names*)* 788
Mafātīḥ al-ghayb (= *al-Tafsīr al-kabīr*) 338, 675, 677, 775, 787, 807–808
on men and women 531–532
on prophets 494–495
al-Rāzī, Najm al-Dīn (d. 617/1220) 714
Reckendorf, Hermann (d. 1875) 2 n.4
Reckendorf, Hermann Solomon (d. 1923) 2 n.4
Redslob, G. 266
Reeves, John C.; (ed.), *Bible and Qur'an* 68
Reinaud, Joseph Toussaint (1795–1867) 297
Reineccius, Christian (1668–1752) 258
Reinert, [B.] 331
Reinink, [G. J.] 133–134
Reiske, Johann Jakob (1716–74) 4, 7
Reland, Adriaan (1676–1718) 3 n.5
De religione Mohammedica libri duo 3 n.5
Retsö, Jan, 12 280, 288, 289
Rettig, [S.] 219
Reynolds, Gabriel Said 104, 130, 283, 309, 348–349, 439, 498–499, 685
(ed.), *New Perspectives on the Qurʾān* 67
(ed.), *The Qurʾān in its Historical Context* 67
and Christian texts 34, 46–48, 57, 59, 101
The Qurʾān and its Biblical Subtext 59, 67–68, 498
Rezvan, Efim 11, 209
Rice, D. S. 219
Riḍā, Muḥammad Rashīd (d. 1935) 431, 460, 532–533, 687, 813, 815
al-Manār [journal] 507
Tafsīr al-Manār 530, 736, 737, 854
Rink, [Friedrich Theodor] 260
Rippin, Andrew 9, 16, 98, 330, 644, 653–654, 655, 687, 708, 711, 767, 843
on academic scholarship 27–31
on approaches to Qur'an 34–36
on *asbāb al-nuzūl* 625, 838–839
on early Qur'an commentaries 607–617
on *gharīb* 660–661, 840
on hermeneutics and history of *tafsīr* 652
on historical formation of Qur'an 32–33
on *isrāʾīliyyāt* 687
on modern academic study of *tafsīr* 609–610
on terms in Qur'an 308–309
(ed.), *The Blackwell Companion to the Qurʾān* 66, 382
(ed.), *The Qur'an: Formative Interpretation* 66
(ed.), *The Qur'an: Style and Contents* 65, 66
on *wujūh* 657, 841–842
Ritter, Helmut (1892–1971) 200
Rizvi, Sajjad 18
(ed.), *An Anthology of Qur'anic Commentaries* 74
Robert of Ketton (fl. 1136–57) 2, 543
Latin [translation of Qur'an] 541–543, 597
Lex Mahumet pseudoprophete 541
Robin, Christian 267
Robinson, Chase 58
Robinson, Neal 10, 129, 321, 362, 368, 369, 496, 497–498, 858
Discovering the Qur'an 65, 68, 330
Rodinson, Maxime 56, 493
Rod of Aaron 497
Rodwell, John M. 13, 545
Roper, Geoffrey 255
Rosenthal, Franz 300–301, 305, 308, 658
Rosenthal, Irwin 142
Roxburgh, David J.; *Writing the Word of God* 69
Rubin, Uri 303, 305, 308, 628, 688, 838
Between Bible and Qur'ān 70
Rückert, Friedrich (1788–1866) 2 n.4, 545, 547
Rudolph, Ulrich 774
Rudolph, Wilhelm; *Die Abhängigkeit des Qorans von Judentum und Christentum* 295
Rūmī, Jalāl al-Dīn (d. 672/1273) 556, 585

al-Rummānī, ʿAlī ibn ʿĪsā (d. 384/994) 712, 773, 795, 834
al-Nukat fī iʿjāz al-Qurʾān 395, 655
Ruqayya, Sayyida, mausoleum of 246
Rushdie, Salman 602 n.15
Satanic Verses 546–547
Rustā, Zahrā (b. 1975); *Bayānī az Qurʾān* 716
Rustom, Mohammed; (ed.), *The Study Quran* 74
Rūzbihān [al-]Baqlī al-Shīrāzī (d. 606/1209) 233, 756, 757
ʿArāʾis al-bayān fī ḥaqāʾiq al-Qurʾān 756, 757
Ryckmans, Jacques 432

S

Saʿadyah Gaon (d. 942) 726
al-Ṣabbāgh 87
Sabzavārī, Hādī (d. 1289/1873) 715
al-Sabzawārī, Sayyid ʿAbd al-Aʿlā (d. 1998); *Mawāhib al-Raḥmān fī tafsīr al-Qurʾān* 715
Sachau, Eduard (1845–1930); al-Jawāliqī's *Kitāb al-Muʿarrab* 300
Sachedina, Abdulaziz 431
al-Sadat, Anwar (1981) 508
Sadeghi, Behnam 68, 173, 207, 208, 221, 222, 283, 352, 356, 357, 358, 837, 838
al-Ṣadūq (d. 381/991) 712, 716
Saeed, Abdullah
(ed.), *Approaches to the Qurʾān in Contemporary Indonesia* 75
The Qurʾan: An Introduction 65
al-Ṣafadī 392
al-Saffāḥ (r. 132–6/749–54) [caliph] 245
Ṣafī ʿAlī Shāh (d. 1317/1899) = Mīrzā Ḥasan Iṣfahānī; *Tafsīr-i Ṣafī* 715
Said, Edward; *Orientalism* 28, 601
al-Sakkākī (d. 626/1229) 329
al-Sakūnī, Yazīd (fl. early second/eighth century?) 189
Sale, George (d. 1736) 4, 492, 515, 543, 544, 545–546, 569, 600
The Koran, Commonly Called The Alcoran of Mohammad 597
'Preliminary Discourse,' 545, 548
Saleh, Walid 36, 73–74, 132, 137, 307–309, 490, 585, 588, 654, 656, 660, 686, 769, 821, 823, 827, 835, 841, 844
The Formation of the Classical Tafsīr Tradition 74
Ṣāliḥ [Prophet] 99, 488–490, 494
stories of the prophets 730
Salman al-Fārisī 552
Salmān Āl Saʿūd [Saudi prince] 269
al-Samīn al-Ḥalabī (d. 756/1355); *ʿUmdat al-ḥuffāẓ fī tafsīr ashraf al-alfāẓ* 299
Samir, Samir Khalil 131
Sammoud, [H.] 657
al-Ṣanʿānī, ʿAbd al-Razzāq (d. 211/827) 513, 635, 637, 638, 655, 656, 660, 662
Muṣannaf 51, 627, 634
Sands, Kristin Zahra; *Ṣūfī Commentaries on the Qurʾān in Classical Islam* 74
Sarah 47–48, 490, 498, 499
Sardar, Ziauddin 813, 815
Reading the Qurʾan 76
Savary, Claude-Étienne 2 n.4, 544
Sawma, [G.] 154
Sayf al-Dawla 406
al-Sayyāb, Badr Shākir (d. 1964) 410
al-Sayyārī, Aḥmad (fl. fourth/tenth century); *Kitāb al-tanzīl wa-l-taḥrīf* 710
al-Sayyārī, Muḥammad (d. c. third/ninth century); *Kitāb al-Qirāʾāt* [attrib.] 206
al-Sayyid, Luṭfī 854
Scaliger, Joseph (1540–1609) 1, 4 n.9
Schacht, Joseph 51, 204, 458, 622
Schade, A. 331
Schaefer, Karl 255
Schnoor, J. K. 260
Schoeler, Gregor 52, 58, 280, 283, 289, 626, 628, 636
Schöller, [Marco] 628
Schultens, Albert (1686–1750); *Dissertatio theologico- philologica de utilitate linguae Arabicae in interpretenda sacra lingua* 1
Schwally, Friedrich (1863–1919) 6, 36, 197, 203, 266, 348, 349, 350, 492
revised edition of the *Geschichte* 302
Schwarzbaum, [H.] 685

Schweigger, Salomon; *Der Türken Alkoran* 542
Sebti, Maryem 304
Seddik, Youssef; *Si le Coran m'était conté* 69
Seetzen, Ulrich (1767–1811) 7 n.16
Selim II (r. 974–82/1566–74) 248
Sells, Michael Anthony
(ed.), *Qur'anic Studies Today* 65
Approaching the Qur'ān: The Early Revelations 65, 72
Serjeant, R. B. 59
Setia, [A.] 775
Seybold, Christian Friedrich (1859–1921) 300
Sezgin, Fuat 608, 615
Geschichte des arabischen Schrifttums 610, 768
Sha'ar, Nuha; (ed.), *The Qur'an and Adab* 72
Shaban, [M. A.] 645
al-Shābbī, Abū'l-Qāsim (d. 1934) 409
Shady Nasser 190–191, 210
al-Shāfiʿī (d. 204/820) 458, 622, 772
al-Risāla 654, 839
Shah, Mustafa 11, 12, 69, 74, 205, 289, 384, 645, 652–653, 655, 657, 659, 660, 769–770, 843
(ed.), *Tafsīr: Interpreting the Qur'ān* 73, 844
and *Kitāb al-Sabʿa* 210
Shahrūr, Muhammad (b. 1938) 852
Shāh Wālī Allāh (d. 1176/1762) 760, 762
Fatḥ al-Raḥmān fī tarjamat al-Qurʾān 553
al-Fawz al-kabīr fī uṣūl al-tafsīr 844
Shakespeare; *Henry VI* 594
Shalabī, Hind 656–657, 659
Shaltūt, Maḥmūd (d. 1963) 850
Min tawjīhāt al-Islām 510
Shariati, Ali 43
Sharīfī, Muṣṭafā ibn Muḥammad 735–736
al-Sharīfī, Bālḥājj ibn Saʿīd 735
Sharīf-i Lāhījī (also known as Quṭb al-Dīn Ashkivarī; d. *c.*1095/1684) 713
al-Sharīf al-Murtaḍā (d. 436/1044) 396
al-Sharīf al-Raḍī (d. 406/1016) 795, 797
al-Sharkawi 285, 287
al-Shāṭibī (d. 790/1388) 341, 854
al-Shāṭibī, al-Qāsim ibn Firruh (d. 590/1193); *Ḥirz al-amānī wa-wajh al-tahānī* (referred to as the *Shāṭibiyya*) 211
al-Shawkānī (d. 1250/1834) 676, 829
Shawqī, Aḥmad (d. 1932) 281, 409
Sheba, Queen of 129, 489
Shebunin, A. F. (1867–?) 264
Shelley, Mary 601
Shelley, Percy Bysshe 597
al-Shiblī, Abū Bakr (d. 334/946) 750
Shiḥātah, ʿAbd Allāh Maḥmūd 768 n.4
Shīrāzī, Nāṣir Makārim (b. 1924) [Āyatullāh] 715
al-Shirbīnī, al-Khaṭīb (d. 977/1569) 318
Shuʿayb [Prophet] 99, 422, 488, 490, 494
stories of the prophets 730–731
as warning-punishment story 494
Shuʿba (d. 193/809), transmissions of 190
al-Shueili, Sulaiman 18
Sībawayhi (d. *c.*180/796) 286, 288–289, 328, 645, 646
Kitāb 285, 297, 641, 644, 653
linguistics of 653, 662
Sibṭ al-Khayyāṭ (d. 541/1146); *Kitāb al-Mubhij* 211
Sidersky, D. 685
al-Sijistānī (d. after 361/971) 722
Kitāb al-Iftikhār 723, 724, 726, 730
Kitāb al-Maqālīd al-malakūtiyya 723
on *taʾwīl* 725–728
al-Sijistānī (d. 330/942); *Nuzhat al-qulūb fī gharīb al-Qurʾān* 841
Silverstein, Adam 129, 137, 685
Silvestre de Sacy, Antoine-Isaac (d. 1838) 7, 29, 297
Grammaire arabe 4, 297
Lexicon Arabico-Latinum 5
Sima, [A.] 115
Simawī, Badr al-Dīn (d. 820/1420) 762
Simelidis, Christos 303
al-Simnānī, ʿAlāʾ al-Dawla (d. 736/1336) 762, 827
Sinai, Nicolai 12–13, 33, 132, 137, 280, 283, 288, 548, 635, 638
(ed.), *The Qurʾān in Context: Historical and Literary Investigations into the Qurʾānic Milieu* 67, 290
The Qur'an: A Historical-critical Introduction 65
Sinan 241

al-Singkili, ʿAbd al-Rauf (d. *c.*1105/1693); *Tarjumān al-Mustafīd* 557
Sirry, Munʾim 431
al-Siyūrī, Miqdād (d. 826/1422); *Kanz al-ʿirfān fī fiqh al-Qurʾān* 713
Small, Keith E.; *Textual Criticism and Qurʾān Manuscripts* 68
Smith, David E. 362, 369
Smith, J. 475
Smoor, Peter 408
Socin, Albert (1844–99) 4
Soeharto, fall of 583
Solomon/Sulaymān [Prophet] 129, 437, 439, 488
  ant's speech to 725
  equal of 495
  stories of the prophets 730–731
Soroush, Abdolkarim 43, 382, 425
Southey, Robert 597
Spenser, Edmund; *Faerie Queene* 594
Sperbar, Dan 367
Sperl, Stefan 13
Speyer, Heinrich 10, 492
  Die Biblischen Erzählungen im Qoran 129, 295
Spinoza (d. 1677) 30
Spitaler, Anton 202–203, 207
Spitta, Wilhelm 300 n.4
Sprenger, Aloys 5–6, 295, 303, 492
Steigerwald, [Diana] 707
Stein, [P.] 116, 117
Stetkevych, [Suzanne Pinckney] 404 n.3, 406
Stewart, Devin 303, 424, 660
Stieglecker, [H.] 475
Stowasser, Barbara Freyer; *Women in the Qur'an, Traditions, and Interpretation* 71
al-Suddī al-Kabīr (d. 128/745) 636, 638, 656
Sufyān al-Thawrī (d. 161/787) 16, 615, 636, 641, 748
al-Suhrawardī, Shihāb al-Dīn (d. 587/1191) 19
  al-Talwiḥāt al-lawḥiyya wa'l-ʿarshiyya (The intimations of the tablet and the throne) 789–790
al-Suhrawardī, ʿUmar (d. 632/1234) 750, 753
  Nughbat al-bayān fī tafsīr al-Qurʾān 752
al-Sulamī, ʿAbd al-Raḥmān (d. 412/1021) 75, 750, 756
  Ḥaqāʾiq al-tafsīr 748, 749, 752, 753, 756
Suleman, Fahmida; (ed.) *Word of God, Art of Man* 69
Sumi, Akiko Motoyoshi 408
al-Surābādī, Abū Bakr ʿAtīq ibn Muḥammad (d. *c.*495/1101) 228, 250
al-Sūsī 196 n.1
al-Suyūṭī, Jalāl al-Dīn (d. 911/1505) 2, 3, 20, 197, 327, 576, 588, 634, 656, 660, 667, 678, 827, 834, 835, 837, 842
  al-Durr al-manthūr 671, 677, 823, 844
  Fatḥ al-wahhāb fī muwāfaqāt Sayyidinā ʿUmar ibn al-Khaṭṭāb 843
  al-Itqān fī ʿulūm al-Qurʾān 187, 318, 833, 835, 841
  Lubāb al-nuqūl fi asbāb al-nuzūl 838
  al-Muhadhdhab fī mā waqaʿa fī'l-Qurʾān min al-muʿarrab 298, 841
  al-Mutawakkilī 299, 841
  Tafsīr al-Jalālayn 557–558, 674, 677, 737
  al-Taḥbīr fī ʿulūm al-tafsīr 835, 836

T

al-Ṭabarī, ʿAlī ibn Rabbān (d. 251/865); *Kitāb al-dīn wa'l-dawla* 686
al-Ṭabarī, Muḥammad ibn Jarīr (Abū Jaʿfar) (d. 310/923) 17, 19, 55, 74, 283, 302, 608–610, 655, 656, 662, 668, 697, 737, 768, 818, 824
  on *gharīb* 660–661
  hermeneutics of 652
  and *isrāʾīliyyāt* 493, 685
  on jihad 513–519, 520
  on *jizya* 521, 522
  on men and women 529, 531, 534
  methodology of 654, 766, 770–771
  tafsīr of 652, 654, 658–660, 672–673, 769–772
  and *tafsīr* studies 669–671, 674–675
  Tafsīr al-Ṭabarī or *Jāmiʿ al-bayān ʿan taʾwīl ayy al-Qurʾān* 377, 555, 636, 658–659, 750, 769–771, 807, 832
  Tahdhīb al-āthār 659
  Tārīkh al-Ṭabarī = *Mukhtaṣar tārīkh al-rusūl wa'l-mulūk wa'l-khulafāʾ* 555

on *ta'wīl* 722, 760
on variants 210
al-Ṭabarsī (d. 548/1153) 735
al-Ṭabāṭabā'ī, Muḥammad Ḥusayn (d. 1981) 318, 699, 714, 716, 850
al-Mīzān fī tafsīr al-Qur'ān 715
Tabbaa, Yasser 228
al-Ṭabrisī, al-Faḍl ibn al-Ḥasan (d. 548/1154) 74, 834
Majmaʿ al-bayān fī tafsīr al-Qur'ān 18, 712, 714, 773
Tafsīr Ibn ʿAbbās 635
Tafsīr-i namūna 715
Tafsīr al-Kalbī 637
al-Taftāzānī, Saʿd al-Dīn (d. 793/1390) 482
Ṭāhā, Maḥmūd Muḥammad (d. 1985) 42, 460, 849, 856
Ṭāhā, ʿUthmān 270
Ṭāhā ʿAbd al-Raḥmān 382
Ṭāhā Ḥussain 381, 402
Fī'l-shiʿr al-jāhilī 383
al-Tahānawī, Muḥammad Aʿlā (d. *c.*1191/1777) 465
al-Ṭāhir Ibn ʿĀshūr 699
al-Ṭahrānī 655
Tai, Eman 583
Taji-Farouki, Suha
(ed.), *Modern Muslim Intellectuals and the Qur'an* 75
(ed.), *The Qur'an and its Readers Worldwide* 77
Talab, Hasan; *The Revolution's Testament and Its Qur'ān* 584
Talat Halman, Hugh; *Where the Two Seas Meet* 74
Talbī, Muhammad 853
Tale of Aḥīqār the Sage 129
Ṭallāy, Ibrāhīm Muḥammad 736
Talmon, Rafael 278, 645
Ṭālūt 730
Tamer, Georges 403
Humor in der arabischen Kultur 73
al-Tamīmī, Ḥātim 652
al-Tanūkhī, al-Muḥassin (d. 384/994); *al-Faraj baʿd al-shidda* 396
Tanwīr al-miqbās min tafsīr Ibn ʿAbbās 636
Tarjumān al-Qur'ān 634
Ta'wīl al-daʿā'im 730
Tazi, Nadia (b. 1953) 484
Tertullian 162
Tesei, Tommaso 134–137, 359
al-Thaʿlabī, Aḥmad ibn Muḥammad (d. 427/1035) 3, 74, 396, 672, 674, 675, 818, 827, 834
al-Kashf wa'l-bayān ʿan tafsīr al-Qur'ān 660, 671, 673, 675–676, 752, 832, 833, 835
Qiṣaṣ al-anbiyā' or *ʿArā'is al-majālis* (Stories of the prophets) 689, 735
al-Thamīnī, Ibrāhīm ibn Bīḥmān (d. 1232/1817) 737
Thanavī, Ashraf ʿAlī (d. 1943) 318, 505
al-Thaqafī, ʿĪsā ibn ʿUmar (d. 149/766) 645
Thatcher, G. W.; *Arabic Grammar of the Written Language* 328
Theodora (wife of emperor Justinian, r. 527–65) 83
Theodore of Mopsuestia (*c.*350–428) 83
Theodosius I (r. 379–95 CE) 82
Theodosius II [emperor] 130
Theophanes the Confessor (d. 818) 144
Thomas [apostle] 157
Thousand and One Nights 397
al-Thumālī, Abū Ḥamza (d. 148/765) 710
al-Ṭībī (d. 743/1342) 332
gloss on *al-Kashshāf* 678
al-Ṭībī, Shams al-Dīn (d. 717/1317) 392
al-Tiflīsī, Abū'l-Faḍl (d. sixth/twelfth century); *Wujūh al-Qur'ān* 842
Tillschneider, Hans-Thomas 839
Typen historisch-exegetischer Überlieferung 838
Tīmūr Lang (d. 807/1405) 231, 265, 595
al-Tirmidhī (d. 279/892); *al-Jāmiʿ al-ṣaḥīḥ* 832
Tisdall, William St. Clair 10
The Original Sources of the Qur'an 295
Todorov, Tzvetan 613
Togan, Zeki Velidi 556
Toorawa, Shawkat 302, 601 n.14
Topaloğlu, [Ahmet] 556
Topaloğlu, Bekir 774
Torquato Tasso; *La Gerusalemme liberata* 593

Torrey, Charles Cutler 7, 142, 296, 433, 492
The Commercial-Theological Terms in the Koran 295
The Jewish Foundation of Islam 295
Tottoli, Roberto 17
Biblical Prophets in the Qurʾān and Muslim Literature 70
Ludovico Marracci at Work 77
al-Ṭūfī (d. 716/1316); *al-Iksīr fī ʿilm al-Qurʾān* 835
Turner, Colin 330
The Koran: Critical Concepts in Islamic Studies 66, 576
al-Ṭūsī, Abū Jaʿfar (d. 460/1067) 713, 773
al-Tibyān fī tafsīr al-Qurʾān 18, 712
al-Ṭūsī, Naṣīr al-Dīn (d. 672/1274) 790
Tadhkira 811
al-Tustarī, Sahl (d. 283/896) 615, 749–750, 752
Tyan, Emile 515, 518
Tychsen, Thomas Christian (1758–1834) 6 n.12
Grammatik der arabischen Schriftsprache 297

U

ʿUbayd Allāh Sindhī 844
Ubayy ibn Kaʿb (d. 29/649 or 35/656) 157, 198–199, 205
codices of 207–208
muṣḥaf of 187
recensions of 176
al-ʿUkbarī, Abū'l-Baqāʾ (d. 616/1219); *Iʿrāb al-qirāʾāt al-shawādhdh* 191, 211
Uljaytū 230
ʿUmar al-Abharī 811
ʿUmar ibn ʿAbd al-ʿAzīz (r. 99–101/717–20) 188
ʿUmar ibn Abī Rabīʿa; *Diwān* 281
ʿUmar ibn al-Khaṭṭāb 153, 185, 218, 377, 635
views of 843
Umayya ibn Abī'l-Ṣalt 132
Umbreit, Friedrich Wilhelm (1795–1860) 5, 7
Umm Salama [Prophet Muḥammad's wife] 527
Umm ʿUmāra [Medinan Companion] 527
Urban VIII [Pope] (1623–44) 258
ʿUrḍī, Muʾayyad al-Dīn (d. 665/1266) 810
ʿUrwa ibn al-Zubayr (d. 93/711–2 or 94/712–3) 52, 518, 625–626, 627, 629, 636
ʿUthmani, Mawlana Taqi (b. 1943) 509
ʿUthmān ibn ʿAffān (r. 23–35/644–56; d. 35/656) 168–169, 176–178, 182, 186–187, 206, 225, 288–289
and destruction of non-conforming *muṣḥaf*s 188, 201, 503
edition of Qur'an promulgated/canonized by 153–154, 194, 198, 201, 206–208, 457, 503, 638
manuscripts attributed to 154, 169
Qur'an of 265
ʿUthmān ibn Muḥammad 231
ʿUzayr 148

V

van Berchem, Max (1894–1903) 240
van Bladel, Kevin 132, 133–137, 423
Van de Bruinhorst, Gerard 561
van der Toorn, Karel 419, 424
van Erpen, Thomas. *See* Erpenius, Thomas
van Ess, Josef 304, 423, 425
van Gelder, Geert Jan, 13
Vasalou, Sophia 655
Verlenden, John 412
Vermes, Geza 613
Versteegh, Kees 17, 285, 653, 655
Encyclopaedia of Arabic Language and Linguistics 331
Virgil 603
Vishanoff, David 654
Vollers, Karl (d. 1909) 199, 277, 279, 281, 286
Volkssprache und Schriftsprache 12, 284
Voltaire; *Dictionnaire philosophique* 12
von Grünebaum, G. E. 331
von Hammer-Purgstall, Joseph (d. 1856) 5 n.11, 544
Fundgruben des Orients 5 n.11
von Kaufmann, K. P. (d. 1882) 264–265
von Mehren, A. F. 331
Die Rhetorik der Araber 329

W

Wadud, Amina (b. 1952) 43, 425, 533, 534
Qur'an and Woman 76, 856

Wahb ibn Masarra 657
Wahb ibn Munabbih (d. 110/728 or 114/732) 493, 644, 687, 689
  Book of the Isrāʾīliyyāt [attrib.] 683
  Kitāb al-Mubtadaʾ 833
al-Wāḥidī (d. 468/1075) 519, 520, 529, 531, 532, 667, 671, 675, 676, 834–835, 838–839
  al-Basīṭ 668, 673–674, 675
  al-Wajīz 674, 677
  al-Wasīṭ 674
Wahl, Günther (1760–1834) 6
Waldman, Marilyn 422
Walfish, Barry D.; (ed.) *With Reverence for the Word* 73
al-Walīd (r. 86–96/705–15) [caliph] 224
Wansbrough, John (d. 2002) 16, 36, 98, 100, 101, 287, 366, 433, 495, 498, 616, 626, 636, 642, 834, 840–842
  approach of, re. historical treatment of Qur'an 32–34, 623–624
  on Arabic 280
  on dating of Qur'an 288, 305–306, 491, 841
  on Muḥammad 154, 624, 769
  Quranic Studies 59, 66, 267, 289, 330, 494, 610, 623, 768
  as revisionist 56–57
  The Sectarian Milieu 59, 494, 623
  on *sīra* 628
  on stages of *tafsīr*/exegesis 652–653, 832
  typologies/categories of 611–612, 614, 624, 637, 683, 768, 819, 838
  on *variae lectiones* 203–204, 768, 832
al-Wāqidī 55
Waraqa ibn Nawfal (d. 619) [cousin of Khadīja] 92
al-Warjlānī, Y. 740
Warqāʾ (d. *c.*160/776) 637
Warsh (d. 197/812) 196, 269
  transmissions of 190
al-Wāsiṭī, Abū Bakr (d. 320/932) 750
Wasserstrom, S. M. 683, 688
Watt, William Montgomery (1909–2006) 55, 56, 58–60, 334, 432, 493, 622–623
  biography of Muḥammad 55
  Companion to Arberry's translation 330
  Introduction to the Qur'ān 65, 330
al-Wazīr al-Maghribī (d. 418/1027); *al-Maṣābīḥ fī tafsīr al-Qurʾān* 712
Weil, Gustav (d. 1889) 5, 7, 9, 10, 359, 492, 545, 621, 685, 837
  Biblische Legenden der Muselmänner (1845) 5
  German translation of the *One Thousand and One Nights* 5
  Historisch-kritische Einleitung in den Koran 5, 12, 32, 348
Welch, Alford 55–56, 98, 303, 316, 330, 424
Wellhausen, Julius (1897/1927) 432, 621
Wheeler, Brannon M. 129
  Moses in the Quran and Islamic Exegesis 70
  Prophets in the Quran 70
Whelan, Estelle 209
Widengren, Geo 423
Wielandt, Rotraud 701
Wild, Stefan 15, 409, 410, 419, 420, 421, 424
  (ed.), *Self-Referentiality in the Qurʾān* 72
  (ed.), *The Qurʾān as Text* 71
Wilkins, John 559
Wilkinson, [J. C.] 734, 738
Williams, Wesley 303
Williamson, Elizabeth 595
Wilson, Brett 15–16
Wilson, Deirdre 367
Winter, Timothy (b. 1960) 507
Wittgenstein 547–548
Witztum 132, 137
Wright, W. 328
Wright, William 297
Wüstenfeld, Ferdinand 97

Y

al-Yamanī, Abū Muḥammad (d. after 540/1145–6) 729
  ʿAqāʾid al-thalāth wa-sabʿīn firqa 728
Yaʿqūb (d. 205/821), reading of 190
Yāqūt 231
Yassine, Abdessalam (d. 2012) 506
Yazicioglu, Isra; *Understanding the Qurʾānic Miracle Stories in the Modern Age* 76
Yazīd (son of Muʿāwiya) 728
al-Yazīdī (d. 202/817–18) 190
Yazır, Elmalılı Hamdi (1878–1942) 560

Yuksel, Edip 460
Yūsuf ʿAlī, ʿAbdullāh (d. 1953) 560
The Holy Qurʾān 546

Z

al-Zabīdī (d. 1205/1790); *Tāj al-ʿarūs* 296
Zaborski, Andrzej 307
Zachariah/Zakariyāʾ/Zakarias [Prophet] 488, 731
stories of the prophets 730
Zacharias of Mitylene (d. 536) 130
Zadeh, Travis 69, 556, 561, 671
The Vernacular Qurʾān 74, 556–557
al-Zahir [caliph] 243
Zahniser, Mathias 12, 321, 362, 363–364, 369
al-Zajjāj (d. 311/923) 672, 843
Maʿānī al-Qurʾān 712
Zakariya, Mohamed 584
al-Zamakhsharī (d. 538/1144) 2, 3, 17, 197, 263, 317, 667, 673, 675–676, 697, 722, 735, 737, 743, 796, 797–798, 799, 800, 834
on *balāgha* 328
interpretations of 738–739, 803
on jihad 515–516, 520
al-Kashshāf ʿan ḥaqāʾiq ghawāmiḍ al-tanzīl wa-ʿuyūn al-aqāwīl fī wujūh al-taʾwīl 6 n.12, 19, 303, 675–677, 714, 773, 795, 809, 824
Zammit, Martin R.; *A Comparative Lexical Study of Qurʾānic Arabic* 71
Zaqzūq, Maḥmūd 854
al-Zarkashī (d. 794/1392) 20, 318, 459, 835, 836, 837, 842
al-Burhān fī ʿulūm al-Qurʾān 317, 832–833, 835
Zayd ibn ʿAlī (d. 122/740) 637
Tafsīr 639
Zayd ibn ʿAmr ibn Nawfal 91
Zayd ibn Ḥāritha [adopted son of Muḥammad] 57
Zayd ibn Thābit (d. 42 or 57/662 or 676) 59, 176–177, 302, 304
Zayn al-Dīn Marʿī ibn Yūsuf al-Ḥanbalī (d. 1033/1623); *Qalāʾid al-marjān fī al-nāsikh waʾl-mansūkh min al-Qurʾān* 840
Zechendorff, Johannes (1580–1662) 2 n.4
Zellentin, Holger 306
Zenderoudi, Charles 219
Zirker, Hans 350
al-Zuhrī (d. 124/742) 627, 629
Kitāb al-Nāsikh waʾl-mansūkh [attrib.] 839
Tanzīl al-Qurʾān bi-Makka waʾl-Madīna 836
al-Zuhrī, Muḥammad 589–590
Zulaykha 757
Zwemer, Samuel 554
Moslem World 554
Zwettler, Michael (d. 2010) 72, 283, 422
The Oral Tradition of Classical Arabic Poetry 282

Index of Subjects and Terms

9/11, 581, 602
786 [number], 581, 587. *See also* numerology
as representing the *basmala* 581

A

Aaronid (line/genealogy) 131, 497
Abbasid(s) 153, 410, 746
artistic style of 225
abbreviated *(mukhtaṣar; maqṭūʿ)* 657–658
abjād (system of calculating names via numbers) 581
ablutions 123, 205, 456–457, 767
ʿabqarī (fantastic; fabulous; brilliant; genius) 804
Abrahamic Legacy 318
abrogated *(mansūkh)* 626, 839
abrogation 341, 518, 520, 522–523, 658, 768, 832
naskh 347, 516, 716, 834, 839–840
principle/issue of 459, 523, 643–644
by *qāʾim* 727
abstention 448
from food, sex, and drink 751
abstract/abstraction 470
theologizing 91
abuse *(adhā)* 470
academia/academy
global movements in 343
Western 512–513, 701
and *tafsīr* 666, 668
academic
discourse/study, and *tafsīr* 35–36, 820
scholarship/approaches
early twentieth-century 609–610
nature of/defined 27–31
to Qur'an 8, 40, 43, 64
accidents 732, 739
Achaemenid (era) 129
ʿĀd (tribe, people) 99, 490
ʿāda, pl. *ʿādāt* (custom(s); convention(s)) 465, 578–579
adab 661
*ādāb al-Qurʾān (*Qur'anic etiquette) 842–843
addition(s) 199, 456
and omissions 173, 728
and revisions 57
addressee [re. changes in person addressed], 321
adhān (call to prayer) 583. *See also* prayer(s)
adīb (man of letters) 396
adjudication, correct/just 446
adjudicators *(ḥukkām)* 453
ʿadl (justice) 465. *See also* justice
divine, doctrine of 383
al-ʿAdl wa-l-Iḥsān (movement) 506
admonition (in Qur'an) 403, 827. *See also* exhortations
adoption 340, 450
adulterers 452, 459
adultery 404, 612
accusations of 452, 453
prohibitions against 470
punishment for 839
aesthetic(s) 8, 327, 337, 377, 381–382, 601, 603, 804
appeal 795–796
approach to Qur'an 19, 598, 798, 804
of books 224
calligraphy as expressive of 584
of delivery [re. poetry], 404
effect 802–803
exoticizing 544
of Qur'an/revelation 12, 19, 72, 384, 597
and study of *balāgha* 327
value (of *tasjīʿ)* 799
afterlife 14, 335, 527, 586, 600, 755, 756. *See also* hereafter
Qur'anic understandings of 436, 744
seeing God in 739

agency 794
 human 506
 moral 527, 529, 533
 of Qur'an, as text and icon 580
Agent Intellect 790
aggression 515–516, 522, 523. *See also* fighting
 against Muslims 516–517
 of polytheists 517
agnates 450
agreements (with Muḥammad) 455, 574. *See also* pacts; treaty(ies)
agriculturalists 102
ʿaḥdiyya [re. a specific known entity], 571, 574
ahistorical (approach/view) 700, 840
 of Qur'an 99, 699
aḥkām al-Qurʾān 210, 466, 834, 838. *See also* law(s); rule(s)
ahl al-bayt (people of the [Prophet's] House) 673
 and the imams, principles of 714
 inscriptions with 246
ahl al-Qurʾān ('Qur'an-only adherents') 460
ahl al-Sunna 670
aḥmad, and *muḥammad* (in four verses of Qur'an) 98
Ahmadiyya (movement) 554, 559, 560–561
aḥsan (best performance) 465
aide-mémoire 233, 629
ʿajab (wonder) 376
ajal (moment of death; span of a life) 434–435
ʿAjam (non-Arabs) 285
ʿajība (miracle) 376
akhbara 642
ākhira 403, 657
ākhūnd 261
Akkadian 304, 496
ʿālamīn 574
ʿālam al-waḍʿ (world of religion) 732
Alcaron/Alchoran/Alcoran 595–596
alcohol, prohibition of 341
aletheia (disclosure) 20, 849
ʿālim (religious scholar) 396. *See also ʿulamāʾ*
Allāh. *See also* God
 as Absolute Other, Supreme Source 586
 Arabic equivalent *(al-Raḥmān)* 122
 as 'creator of heaven and earth,' 434
 as the High God 432
 -Qur'an-Muḥammad (authority) 369
al-Lāt (deity; idol) 124, 434
allegorical
 /esoteric meanings 19, 747, 749, 751
 as mode/stage of interpretation [re. Wansbrough], 652, 819
 mutashābihāt 724, 853–854
 type of exegesis 610, 768
allegory(ies) 613–614, 669
 Qur'anic 755
alliteration 332
allusions 391, 396, 595
 biblical 456
 ishārāt 749, 753
 in Qur'an 407, 409, 412, 622
  and *sīra* 622, 629
  as ubiquitous 388
 to Qur'an (in English poetry) 594
alms 573, 586
 -giving 449, 612
 injunction/obligation to give 446, 447, 529
 tax 731
alphabet(s)
 Ancient North Arabian (ANA) 114
 Ancient South Arabian (ASA) 112–113
 Arabic (language) 303, 761
 proto-Sinaitic 112
 West Semitic 112
amālī (dictations) 396
ambiguity(ies) 177, 548, 577, 641, 644, 654, 735, 794
 of language/linguistic 440, 612, 615
 in Qur'an, resolutions of 459, 498
ambiguous *(mutashābih*, pl. *mutashābihāt)* 737
 expressions 853–854
 verses/passages 736, 738, 748, 753–754, 820
 words 661
ʿāmm, and *khāṣṣ* 828
amr (command) 333
ʿamūd (central theme or axis [of a sura]) 13, 318–319, 370–371
amulet(s) 247, 268, 578
 block-printed *(ṭarsh)* 247

cases 235
formulae applied to 588
anachronisms 177
analogy(ies) 768, 832
naẓīr 614–615
anaphors 643
Ancient North Arabian (ANA) 112
alphabets 114
script(s) 113, 115, 117
Ancient South Arabia (ASA) 112–113
anecdote(s) 396, 768, 832. *See also* stories
angelology 437–438
angel(s) 47, 102, 130, 419, 420, 434, 435, 437–438, 476, 570, 571, 638, 749, 837
and Adam 751
archangels (Gabriel, Isrāfīl) 478
carry the throne 478, 739
at death/and punishment 483
and devils 337
Gabriel 184, 420, 439, 478, 489
good tidings from 499
guarding hellfire 481
intercession of 742
Isrāfīl 478
and magic 590
malak, pl. *malāʾika* 431, 438
as messengers 438
Michael 489
Munkar and Nakīr 436
nature of 439, 489
as noble/virtuous scribes/recorders 184, 478
in Qur'an 488
role of, on Day of Reckoning 478
Anglican Church 152
aniconic, *vs.* iconoclastic 218
aniconism (worship of uncarved or geometrically carved stones) 87, 93
animal(s) 220, 434, 725, 753, 796
and bad luck 89
birds 576
created from clay [re. Jesus], 435
green *(fī ḥawāṣil ṭuyūr khuḍr)* 483
hoopoe 725
calf (golden) story of 759
camels 448, 474
and dietary restrictions 448
dog(s) 130
of the Sleepers of the Cave [re. *Sūrat al-Kahf]*, 644
faculties 786
and human superiority to 438
pigs, flesh of *(laḥm al-khinzīr)* 141
sacrifices 89, 123, 448, 575
spirit 790
wild asses 803
Ankara School (of Qur'anic exegesis) 42, 505
annihilation (of self) in God (*fanāʾ*) 751
anṣāb (idols) 86
anṣār (helpers) 161
anthological (approach) 307, 822
anthropology 36, 142, 853, 857
of religion 432
anthropomorphic
descriptions of God 734, 737–738, 753
readings, avoiding 639
verses in Qur'an 721
anthropomorphism 435, 710, 738, 772
anthropomorphists, heresies of 712
Antichrist *(dajjāl)* 475
anti-colonial (interpretation of Qur'an) 507
anti-Islamic
propaganda/polemic 256, 258
tone 59
anti-Muslim
polemic 155, 437
statements, in Qur'an translations 543
antithesis/antitheses 318, 323, 325, 364
anti-Umayyad (allusions) 503
antonyms *(aḍdād)* works on 300
ant(s)
called al-Jarmī 644
and speech to Solomon 725
apocalypse
associating Islam with 600
in Hebrew Bible 420
apocalyptic 420. *See also* eschatology
apocryphal
extra-Qur'anic traditions 348
gospels 492–493
texts of Syriac Christianity 128
apokalypsis (concealed things) 421
apologetic(s) 35, 363, 515, 750
apologists 512

apostolic (tradition) 153
apparatus criticus 198, 266
  based on Ḥafṣ's version 201
apparent *(ẓāhir)* and hidden *(bāṭin)* 708
appearance *(ẓāhir)* 849
appositeness and correlations, science of 317
aptitude *(istiʿdād)* 741
ʿaqīda 657, 658. *See also* belief(s); doctrine(s); faith
ʿaqlī (rational) (bodies of knowledge) 776
ʿArab 285
Arabic (language) 47, 114, 118, 120, 409, 422, 548, 598, 599, 646, 658, 668, 702, 820. *See also* grammar; inscription(s); *iʿrāb;* translations
  alphabet 303, 761
  -Aramaic, bilingualism 119–120
  -based approaches 382
  and Bible, key to understanding 29
  in biblical philology 4
  Christian 133
  Classical 278, 279, 282, 283
  as clear 140, 142
    ʿarabī mubīn 28, 287
  computer typography/typefaces 261, 269
  and converts' command of 639
  definitions 555
  dialects/colloquial varieties of 121, 277, 278, 283, 285
  diction, classical 199
  Early Standard Arabic (as lingua franca) 284
  exegeses, for scholars by scholars 714
  -Greek contact 121
  and Hebrew 1, 155
  history of 285
  vs. Indo-European languages 281
  intellectual histories 678
  -Islamic tradition, scholars of 331
  as medium of administration 119, 174
  Modern Standard Arabic 279
  Old 113, 114, 115, 277, 278, 281, 289
    and *ikhtilās/takhfīf* feature 287
  poetry, and Qur'an 13–14, 544
  polyvalent character of 654
  pre-diasporic 285–286
  in pre-Islamic period 111, 113, 299
  of the Prophet's people 421
  pure 841
  and Qur'an 101, 255, 263, 547, 553, 555, 771
    genre 608
  script 118, 174, 270
    development/emergence of 10, 111, 114
  scripture 280, 596
  and Shīʿī exegetical tradition 676
  sources 6
    primary 2–3, 296, 458
    translated into Latin 541, 543
  structure of *(qiyās al-ʿarabiyya)* 646
  superiority of 771
  tafsīr works, modern 701–702
  teaching of, in Western universities 333
  text of Qur'an
    European edition of 256
    in translations 560
  tribal varieties of 279
  vernacular 155
Arabicisation/Arabization 280, 287, 433, 834
Arabic Studies 4, 15, 29, 76, 296, 331, 543, 668
Arabist(s) 328
ʿarabiyya 281, 285, 287, 646
  Qur'an as 283
Arabo-centric/centrism 698, 701
Arab(s)/Arabian
  and anti-Arabian (tone) 59
  backdrop 98–99
  -Christian treatises 228
  civilization/heritage 137, 143
  as ethno-cultural group 285
  expansion/conquests 285–286, 287
  name/term defined 287
  pre-Islamic 59, 644
  Spring (uprisings of 2010–11) 584
  world, popularizers from 40
Aramaic 81–82, 115, 119, 120, 153, 308
  Achaemenid Official 117
  -Arabic hybrid (language) 57
  culture 57
  loan words 295
  morphology 121
  Nabataean 123
  Old 112
  origins (of words in Qur'an) 33, 306
  and Qur'an 48

-speaking Christian communities 68
Syriac and Jewish Babylonian 457
/Syriac words 304
texts in 115–116
western 118
Aramean settlement 57
arbiter *(ḥakam)* (in marital disputes) 453
arbitration 534
archaeology 85
evidence from 432
archangels. *See* angel(s)
archetypal pattern 404 n.3
architecture 218, 224
and decoration 231
inscriptions on 11
archival (evidence/material) 206–208
archive(s) 203
argumentation 336, 659. *See also* debate(s)
Aristotelian (models) 422
armed combat 520. *See also* fighting; wars/warfare
arrangement (of Qur'an) 836. *See also* chronology(ies); order
syntactic 381
tartīb (of suras) 317
arrogance [re. *nushūz*], 534
art/artistic 583–584. *See also* graffito
contemporary global 580
expression, and Qur'an 11, 235
historians 218, 225, 231–232
history 11, 170, 232
language (in Qur'an) 795, 797
production 231
qualities 794, 797
Qur'an as object of 36
artists 231–232, 583
asās (deputy; successor of the Prophet) 726–727
asbāb al-nuzūl (occasions of revelation) 576, 624–625, 643, 838–839
genre of 838, 843
literature 827
asbāb [re. Dhū'l-Qarnayn], 132
ascension *(miʿrāj)* (of Prophet) 423, 593, 756. *See also* night (journey)
ascetic 448, 747–748
communities, Egyptian 424
poems/verse 391, 394
asceticism 753
of late antique Christianity 132
ascription, mechanisms/problems of 614, 616
Ashʿarī 824
and anti-Ashʿarī (method) 694
school 743
ashbāh 639
Asiatic Press (St. Petersburg) 260–262, 262 (fig. 16.3)
al-asmāʾ al-ḥusnā (beautiful names [of God]) 843
aspects *(wajh,* pl. *wujūh)* 657, 738. *See also wujūh*
asrār al-balāgha (secrets of beauty) 804
assassination, of Anwar al-Sadat 508
association (of other gods with Allāh) 93
associationism *(shirk)* 436, 517. *See also* idolatry; polytheism; *shirk*
associators *(mushrikūn)* 154
assonance 325, 332, 389, 455
Qur'anic 412
astrology 586, 807
astronomers 808
astronomy 2, 776, 809–812
and Qur'an 807
spherical 811 n.10
ateliers 231, 233
atheists 855
atomistic 347, 856
approach(es) to Qur'an 318, 566, 568, 569, 852
i.e., glossing verse by verse 715
attack, of Muslims (against idolaters) 574. *See also* fighting
attributes
descriptive *(ṣifāt kathīra)* 336
divine/of God 336, 338, 430–431, 467, 639, 740, 743, 754, 769, 786, 834
Muʿtazilī theory of 380
nature of 637
physical 772
audience 28–29
European [re. popularizers], 41
of Qur'an 46–47, 68, 101–102, 105, 493
to which a verse is addressed 836
audio cassettes 693

aural, shift to read 228
authenticity 51, 53, 57, 636, 696, 794, 802
  of early reports/traditions 620, 621
  of God's message 800
  of hadiths 616, 823
  of Muḥammad, Qur'an as proof of 378
  of pre-Islamic poetry 402–403
  of text [i.e., Qur'an], 140, 158, 461, 803
authority(ies) 569, 669, 716, 768, 776–777, 822, 829
  of *Allāh* 434
  chain *(sanad)* of 191
  divine 435–436
  of exegetes 717
  Islamic 41, 461, 552, 561
  of medieval *tafsīr* literature 695
  of men over women 530
  misuse of, by Meccan aristocracy 494
  of Muḥammad, *vs.* poets 403
  political 452, 657
  Qur'anic/of Qur'an 588, 716–717
  religious 562
  Shīʿī 615
    of imams 707, 773
  sources of
    extra-Qur'anic 97–98, 712
    extra-Shīʿī 712
    from mastery of language 404
    scriptural 13, 768
  for stories of prophets *(qiṣaṣ al-anbiyāʾ)* 644
  of Sunna 767, 769
author(s)/authorship 210, 299
  of Gospels 45
  issues/notion of 30, 611, 616–617
  of Qur'an 301, 838, 857
    Muḥammad as 43
    translations 558
  of Qur'anic commentaries/*tafsīr* 697, 750
  Sunnī 713
  Western 600, 601
āya, pl. *āyāt* (or *āyas*) 593, 599, 602, 781. *See also* verse(s)
  divisions into/of 381
  of God 437
  Heb. *ôthôt* 423
  meaning of 389
  muḥkamāt 724
  order of 625, 661
  al-sayf (sword verse) 520–521
  as sign/Qur'anic verse 376, 393, 410 n.6, 421, 796, 849
  use of isolated 782–783
Ayyubids 252
Azāriqa 741
al-Azhar University 560

B

Babi (thought) 473
back-biting, as forbidden 470
badaʾ, 711
badīʿ (embellishment) 330, 332, 801
  in Qur'an 395
Baha'i (scriptures) 59
Bahrid (dynasty) 265
balāgha (rhetoric) 12, 330, 331, 383, 565, 567, 658
  Arabic, neglect of study of 329, 342
  asrār al- (secrets of beauty) 804
  classical 568
  importance of, for *tafsīr* 328–329
  in Qur'an 342–343, 795
  scholars of 566, 576
balāghī (rhetorical) 659
balance *(mīzān)* divine 478
banāt Allāh (daughters of God; viz. al-Lāt, al-ʿUzza and al-Manāt) 434. *See also* deity(ies)
bans (of Qur'an) 258, 263
Banū al-Ḥārith (in Najrān) 88
Banū Isrāʾīl (Israelites; Children of Israel) 144, 688. *See also* Children of Israel; Jews
Banū al-Naḍīr (Jewish tribe) 405
Banū Qaynuqāʿ, 84
Banū Qurayẓa 84
Banū Thaʿlaba 84
baptist (movement) 85
barzakh (barrier) 483, 589–590, 789
Barzakh Foundation 589
basmala (*bismillah al-raḥmān al-raḥīm;* in the name of God, the Most Merciful, Ever Merciful) 172, 250, 354, 581, 587, 843
  interpretation/symbolism of 751

as invocation formula 221, 302, 581
late pre-Islamic variant of 123
[number] 786 as representing 581
bāṭin (inner; interior; esoteric) 252, 709, 717, 724, 749
and/*vs. ẓāhir* (exoteric) 252, 729
Ismāʿīlīs on 722
tafsīr of 671
theology (of Shīʿī hermeneutics) 676
battle(s)
of Badr 342, 622, 749
of Ṣiffīn 504
of Tabūk 521
of Uḥud 496, 622
bayān (clarification; eloquence) 330, 331, 654, 657, 659, 770–771, 801
concepts of 332, 659–660
ʿilm al- (science of) 328, 329, 332, 795
methodology/hermeneutics, of al-Shāfiʿī 654
bayt (house) 131–132, 137
beatific vision 769, 772. *See also* vision(s)
of God in the afterlife 754
beating 531, 535. *See also* violence
beauty 233, 465, 567, 794–796, 804. *See also* *iʿjāz*
of the book 224
iʿjāz 548, 795
of/in Qur'an 544, 597, 771, 794–795, 828
Bedouin 285, 290, 502. *See also* nomad(s)
dialects 279, 840
manners and customs of 644
bees 800
behaviour. *See also* conduct
immoral 481
Islamic 339
limits of *(ḥudūd)* 191
of Muḥammad 458
unlawful 452
being(s)
generated *(al-mawālīd al-ṭabīʿiyya)* 726
of God 784
as necessary Being 786
individual 468, 784
and non-being 789
spiritually-generated *(al-mawālīd al-rūḥāniyya)* 726
Bēl and Baalshamin 91
belief(s) 549, 742, 746, 750, 774. *See also* faith
in all God's messengers 479
Christian and Jewish 682
Qur'anic engagement with 433
core 430–431, 440
in God 380, 431, 436
vs. infidelity 409
before Islam 85
Islamic, and modern entertainment 583
iʿtiqād 465
in Muḥammad's prophecy 365
īmān bi'l-risāla 370
Near Eastern 682
religious 35, 102, 725, 775
believers 146–147, 336, 614, 634–635, 643–644, 740–741, 800, 827
common/ordinary 479, 639
on Day of Resurrection 477
of different faiths 103
female/women *(muʾmināt)* 527, 529
hostility towards 149
and Jews, as not true 146
male 529, 803
muʾmin, pl. *muʾminīn* 529–530, 849
muslim 762
and non-believers/unbelievers/disbelievers 337, 431, 804
progress of, to God 754
proto-Muslim(s) 59
qualities of 339–340
and role of Imam (in Shīʿī discourse) 673
tested by God 711
belles-lettres 712
Bengali (language) 562
rendering (of Qur'an) 559
bequests 369, 458
Berber (language) *(al-lugha al-barbariyya)* 841
Bible(s) 45, 46–47, 420–421, 496, 603, 686
books, of Daniel, Jeremiah, Revelation 420
of Christians and Jews 45, 46–47
figures in 490
Hebrew 39, 128, 141, 146–147, 410
and revelation 419
stories from, in Qur'an 144
Jewish explanations of 48

Bible(s) (*contd.*)
knowledge of 142
and pre-Islamic Arabic version of 101
pre-Qur'anic Ethiopic 129
and Qur'an(ic)
approaches to 363, 372
compared to 490, 553
counterparts to prophets of 70
exegesis 678
influences, on 5, 295
intertextuality 143
personae 15
use of, as source of exegesis 824
biblical
accounts/records
of fall of mankind 528
vs. Qur'an 35, 493–494
figures 128, 493, 688
Hebrew 154
ideas, philosophies, legends (late antique) 101
law 452, 454–455
presentation, seen as normative 490
and quasi-biblical material 688
and Qur'anic concepts 14
studies/scholarship 1, 5, 8, 280, 296, 321, 363, 364, 382, 384, 621
German 266
methodologies of 45
themes/motifs 435
in Semitic cultures 143
word
niglā (divine manifestation) 423
for revelation 423, 426
bibliography(ies) 65, 554–555
on individual exegetes 668
on Persian translations 556
of Sezgin 610, 616
World Bibliography of Translations of the Meanings of the Holy Qur'ān 554, 555, 557
bibliomancy 234
bilā kayf (without modality) concept of 655
bilingualism, Arabic-Aramaic 119–120
binarity 322
binary 466
biographical
dictionaries/material [re. exegetes], 667–668
reports 616
biography *(sīra)* (of Muḥammad) 33, 52, 56, 97–98, 280, 620, 621–623, 626, 628, 769. *See also sīra*
and commentaries *(tafsīr)* 17
for dating Qur'an 348
Muslim accounts of 56
order of occasions in 625
and translation 552
by Watt 55
blame [re. for fall of mankind], 528
blasphemy 218, 394, 474. *See also* heresy(ies)
blessings 123, 242–243
block prints 255, 268
blood 141
price *(diya)* 452
body(ies) 790
celestial 87
in paradise 481
recreated 477
and souls reunited 481, 483
as 'vehicle,' 754
Bohra Gujarati 728
Book [re. Qur'an], 42, 316, 461, 849. *See also* Qur'an
composer/author of 47–48
al-kitāb 145–146 (*See also kitāb*)
book(s) 224, 365, 584, 595, 670. *See also kitāb*, pl. *kutub* (book(s))
artists 231
based upon transmitted traditions *(al-naqliyya)* 833
bindings 170, 232
covers, leather, stamped 224
culture, modern 558
-hand 118
handwritten 268
heavenly 478
of Hebrew Bible 419–420
'Index of forbidden books' *(Index Librorum Prohibitorum)* 3, 256
on Islam, in Russia 263–264
market 264
and preservation of 184
production, history of 668

borders, *vs.* boundaries 579
borrowing 689
  Thesis of 10, 142, 144
bowing (to Adam) 489. *See also* prostration
boxes, to store early manuscripts 218, 232, 234
bracketing
  of Qur'an 244
  of *sīra* 348
bridal gift *(mahr)* 530
bridge/pathway *(ṣirāṭ)* (over Fire) 479
British 507, 601
b-r-k [root], 354
brotherhoods (Sufi) 746
building(s) 246–247. *See also* architecture
  function of 247
  inscriptions on 239–240, 242–243, 250
  religious, patronized by Fatimids 246
burial sites, material aspects of 249
burūj (constellations) 809
Buyids (322–447/934–1055) 504, 661
Byzantine
  Christians, hostile to Muslims 521
  Church 83
  Empire/period 82–84, 113

C

cabbalistic ciphers 302
caesura/caesurae *(istaʾnafa)* 642
  formulaic markers of 320, 362
calendar 86
  lunar 448
caliphal (interests) 684
caliphate 506
  of ʿAbd al-Malik 57
caliph(s) first three 729
calligraphers 226, 228, 229, 233
  famous 229, 231
calligraphy
  as high culture/aesthetic 584–585
  Islamic and Arabic 217
  of Qur'an 8, 583, 598
  script, classical 118
  traditional Ottoman 584
  traditions, development of 69
  in Umayyad times 175
Calligraphy of Thought (spoken-word collective) 583–584
canon 176, 419
  of scripture/Qur'an 34, 612, 615
  'Western Canon,' Qur'an's addition to 592–593
canonical (readings/text) 196, 268
  establishment of 189, 638
  form of *muṣḥaf* 491
  and non-canonical systems 198, 205, 289
canonicity, Qur'anic 503
canonization 58. *See also* readings
  from below, *vs.* above 32
  of orthography, structure, rules of reading 268
  processes of 198, 284, 623
  of Qur'an 101, 306
  re. Seven Readings 638
  of script [re. Six Pens], 226
  of text, by ʿUthmān 201
cartoons, political 580
carvings 112, 225. *See also* inscription(s)
casus belli 517
catalogues 219
  of manuscripts [re. *al-Fihris al-shāmil; Fihrist muṣannafāt tafsīr al-Qurʾān al-karīm]*, 667
  of *tafsīr* 679
categorical (*muḥkamāt* [verses]) 736, 737. *See also muḥkam;* verse(s)
Catholic(s) 542–543, 596
causality 790, 808
cause(s)
  of God 449, 453
  intermediate, existence of 807, 808–809, 810
  philosophical 784
censorship 263
ceremonial, or presentation copies 228
certainty 726, 810
  and doubt 602
certitude *(yaqīn)* 749
  (certain) doom 404
Chagatay 555
chanting (*tilāwa* [of Qur'an]) 583
character (of Muḥammad)
  as embodiment of Qur'an 469
  exalted/strong *(khuluq ʿaẓīm)* 465, 469
  refinement of *(tahdhīb al-akhlāq)* 469

charity 449, 450
cherubim 707. *See also* angel(s)
chiasmus 321, 364
children 120, 149, 247, 338, 340, 392, 516–517, 572, 614
  and treatment of parents 450
Children of Israel 140, 149, 741–742. *See also* Jews
  banū isrāʾīl 144
  and God, covenant between 437
Chinese, Mandarin 555–556
  renderings (of Qur'an) 560
choice *(iʿtibār)* 645
chosen
  folk *(awliyāʾ Allāh)* 762
  ones *(aṣfiyāʾ)* 751
Christendom, *vs.* Ottoman Empire 255
Christianity 53, 58, 60, 90–92, 113, 144, 157, 256, 378
  in Arabia 84, 143
  Arian 154
  converts from 635, 683
  early, and astrology 807
  Ethiopic 128, 137
  and fracturing of the Middle Eastern Church 82
  and image of Jesus 87
  and Islam/Qur'an 10, 33, 295
  late antique 132
  Orthodox 263
  Pauline and pre-Constantinian 153
  polemics within 542
  Protestant 42
  as a 'world' religion 82
Christian(s) 10, 53–54, 58–60, 82–84, 147, 161–162, 365, 489, 520–521, 573, 579, 741
  Arabic koine 280
  christianoi 161
  claims [re. specific verses], 496
  doctrine/teachings 3, 131, 153, 479
  dogma, challenges to 243
  era, beginning of 93
  influence
    on Islam/Muḥammad 58, 142, 689
    on Qur'an 67, 101, 295, 432
  on Last Day 477
  legend of Barlaam and Josaphat 729
  and name of Jesus 159
  Nestorian 160
  non-trinitarian 56
  origins 53, 60
    of Qur'an 154
  Prophet met 424
  and sleepers of the cave 130–131
  in Talmud 159
  terms used 308
    'revelation,' 419
    ṣibgha (baptism) 133
  Trinitarian 157
Christmas 92
Christology(ical) 10, 83–84
  traditional 596
chronicles, historical 833
chronological
  approach to Qur'an 348–349
  criteria 32
  marker, MVL as 357–358
  order (of Qur'an) 316, 356–357, 359, 621, 835, 836
  periods of revelation 493
  progression, linear 222
  schema, seven-phase 837
  theories 545
chronology(ies) 357, 687
  of Bazargan 356–357
  of handwritten transmission 178
  inner-Qur'anic/internal 12–13
  intra-Qur'anic 347
  of manuscripts 170–171
  of Qur'an 5, 7, 32, 101, 306, 491, 497, 838, 839
    four consecutive periods of 13
    prophetic 489
    textual transmission of 11
    translations 555
  of Weil 348
churches 147, 515
Church Fathers 422
Church of the East 83–84
circumambulation (of sanctuaries) 93
  ṭawāf (of pre-Islamic Meccan *kaʿba)* 89
circumcision 162
citadel *(qaṣaba)* 480

citizen, place of 695
civil, and democratic state 506
Civil Code of Egypt 461
civilization(s) 388
  Arabian, Mesopotamian, West Semitic 143
  Graeco-Byzantine 389
  Islamic 579, 813 n.13
  Persian 389
  Western 509
class distinction 584
classification
  and generalization 337
  of people, in Qur'an 336
  thematic 316
cleansing, pre-prayer ritual 447. *See also* ablutions
clear/unequivocal (verses) *(muḥkamāt)* 753. *See also muḥkam*
  vs. 'ambiguous' verses 773
cleric(s)/clerical
  elite *(ʿulamāʾ/fuqahāʾ)* 623–624
  in Russia, Muslim 260
clothing 578. *See also* garments
code-switching, between Arabic and Aramaic 120
codex/codices 134, 167–168, 198, 204, 218, 220. *See also* manuscript(s)
  Codex Amiatinus 220
  Codex Amrensis 1, 69, 208
  Codex Ṣanʿāʾ I 176–178
  of Companions 201, 204–205, 207
    maṣāḥif al-ṣaḥāba 197–198
  of Damascus 174–175
  formats/size 224, 233
  Imām Codex 286
  metropolitan *(maṣāḥif al-amṣār)* 204
  non-ʿUthmānic/pre-ʿUthmānic 201, 645
  Parisino-petropolitanus 170–173, 174–177, 206–207, 221–222
  Qur'an 284, 459, 833
  scripts of 58, 229
  small 233
  Umayyad (of Fusṭāṭ) 174–175, 224
  ʿUthmānic 200, 204, 289, 503, 623, 638, 645
    canonical validity of, and Ismāʿīlīs 728
    consonantal ductus of 641
    orthography/linguistic inconsistencies in 197–198
codicology 11, 170, 232
codification
  of *muṣḥaf* 45
  of Qur'an 101, 194, 221, 306, 458, 638
coefficient of variation (CV) (of sura) 351
cognates, female 450
coherence 321
  linear, symmetrical 366
  of Qur'an 12–13, 315, 495, 534, 546
    lack of 316–317
  of suras 318, 367, 494–495
    literary 346
    longer 364
    structure 368
  theory 320
cohesion 42
coin(s)/coinage 240, 247
  Fatimid 246–247
  Qur'anic quotations on 175
collation (process/procedure) 176–177
collection(s)
  museum, databases of 252
  of Qur'an 101, 177, 205, 620, 836
    during caliphate of ʿUthmān 457
    extant fragments of 638
    history of 543–544
    in written form 184
  Toledan Collection (alias the Cluniac Corpus) 541–542, 548
collectors (of Qur'an manuscripts) 224
collegium, of Muslim scholars 268
colloquial (varieties) 287. *See also* dialect(s); language
colonial(ism) 408–409, 502, 504, 506, 813 n.13
  of Catherine the Great 261
colonialist (agendas) 601
colonization 507
colophon(s) 168, 169, 230 (fig. 14.3)
colour 232, 739, 796
comedians 580
comic (books) 69, 580
command(s)/commandments 335
  of God 523, 738, 800
  from Qur'an 502
  re. aggression/fighting 516, 518

'command the good and forbid/prevent wrong,' 513, 529
commentary(ies) 4, 8, 20, 228, 258, 306, 545, 667, 669, 696, 702, 709, 819. *See also* Shīʿa/Shīʿī; Sufi(s)
  anthologies of 73
  early 306, 612, 637
  historical 74
  Ibāḍī, earliest extant 735
  of Ibn Kathīr 697
  of Ibn Wahb 637
  in margins 234, 260
  of al-Māturīdī 670
  medieval 698, 699
  modern Muslim 698
  mystical 711, 714, 756, 760, 763, 819
    of al-Anṣārī 753
  of Neuwirth 548
  of Nursi 40
  of Qushayrī 750
  and scripture, differentiating between 612
  on the *Shāṭibiyya* 211
  of al-Ṭabarī 493
  tafsīr 17, 250, 542, 553, 818 (*See also tafsīr*)
  traditional 4, 8, 16, 507, 698, 819
    Muslim 46–47
  vs. translations 557, 559
  types of 762
    composite 558
    deductive, on legal-doctrinal topics 658
    dogmatic 819
    encyclopedic 651, 769, 832
    grammatical 17
    historical 74
    institutional 702
    madrasa-style 821–822
    Muʿtazilī 670, 772, 824
    paraphrastic 556
    popularizing 702
    post-classical 829
    Salafi 854
    scientific 854–855
    sectarian 819
    thematically organized 651
    theological 766
    Urdu 370
    verse-by-verse 838
commentators 39, 303, 795
  classical 304–305
  Ibāḍī 744
  of special topics 638
commerce 29. *See also* trade
commercial
  contacts with Muslims [re. Italy], 258
  production, volume of 232
  workshops 233
commodification, globalized 585
communication 367, 659
  divine/from God 419–421, 423
    to Muḥammad 492
    to prophets 437
    -to-human 426
  between humans and animals 421
  of Qur'anic *waḥy* 422
  spoken 118
community(ies) 30, 35, 46, 478, 530, 576, 685. *See also umma*
  of Christians, Jews 102, 131
  early 420, 620, 644
    to post-Prophetic 627
  formation/establishment of 497, 528, 623
  idealized 508
  interpretive [re. S. Fish], 30
  of Islam/Islamic 685
    and social order (based on *īmān, taqwā, islām*) 467
  of Jews/Jewish 84, 102, 131, 145–146, 149, 496
  monotheistic 145–146
  of Muḥammad 495, 812
  Muslim 70, 607
  polis 420
  prophets sent to 420, 489
  religious 370–371, 447
  Syriac ascetic 424
  Syriac Christian 33–34
  umma 447, 461, 502
Companions (of Muḥammad) 620, 661, 774
  copies/codices of *(maṣāḥif al-ṣaḥāba)* 185–186, 197–198, 204–205, 207
  interpretation/explanations of 634, 844
  variants attributed to 199
  writing down the revelations 184

companions (of the imams), early texts
attributed to 710
Companions of the Cave 99, 129–130
comparative (approaches/method) 286, 652
compendia
Matériaux pour un Corpus Inscriptionum Arabicarum (MCIA) 240–241
Répertoire Chronologique d'Épigraphie Arabe (RCEA) 240–241
compensation 455, 470, 535
fidya 531
compilations 611
of *muṣḥaf* 833
process of 675
of Qur'an 46, 68, 167, 347, 503
dating of 220
Shīʿī view of 70
of variant Qur'anic recitations *(kutub al-qirāʾāt al-majmūʾāt)* 833
complementarities 319, 323
complementary (parts of sentence) 332–333
composite, redactional 351
composition 112, 381
concentric 364
methods of 617
of Qur'an 12, 32–33, 363, 365, 374, 375, 381, 804, 836
authorial 31
historical 71
of text of suras 316
rules of 700
of sacred texts 325
Semitic, *vs.* Qur'anic 365
theories of
general 372
literary 143
comprehension
naṣṣ (of text) 856
tafhīm (of scripture) 855
compulsion 742–743
none, in religion 518
concatenation 364
concentric
composition 324, 364
construction(s) 324, 496
conciseness, *vs.* expansiveness 567
concision
and brevity 771
in translations 559
concordance 297, 622
of/to Qur'an 545
by Flügel 266
concubines 451. *See also* slave(s); women
conduct 447, 470. *See also* behaviour
rules of 14, 445
sulūk, verses related to 466
confidence intervals 352
configurations *(hayʾāt)* 809
conflict
eschatological 154
global 602
i.e., in relation to translations of Quran 542–543
military 541
Palestinian/Israeli 504
resolution 437
conjunctions 322
conquest(s). *See also* expansion
of Mecca 52
of Middle East [re. Alexander the Great] 81
consensus 101, 403, 423, 468, 492, 660
among readers/readings 196, 202
koine 285
re. *iʿjāz* 376, 390
re. language of Qur'an 277, 283
re. revelations 153
re. specific interpretations 514
re. superiority of Fāṭima 499
conservatism, of Qur'anic tradition 226, 235
conservative (ideologically) 702
conservators 225
consistency
lack of 613–614
rule of 574
consonantal
outline/skeleton of Qur'an *(rasm)* 125, 205, 222, 456
text 186, 201
consonant(s). *See also* grammar
pointed/pointing 183, 187
roots 661
conspiracy [re. origins of Islam], 33
constellations 808. *See also* astronomy

constitution 507–510
  Islamic 508–509
  of Medina 100, 455
  new Ottoman 508
  Qur'an as 507–509
consultative (bodies) 461
consumer culture, global 585, 589–590
contemporaneity, and modernity (conflation of) 693. *See also* modernity
contemporary (issues/events) 320, 736. *See also* modern
content 349
  conceptual 616
  over form 541
contentual (features) 349
context(s) 16, 341, 342, 574, 656, 661, 801
  -based *tafsīr* 654
  -dependent meaning 657
  and effect on *tafsīr* and translation 576
  etymological arguments over 307
  Ḥijāzī 98–99
  historical 566, 827
    in Medina 737
    of Qur'an 8, 9–10, 33–34, 66, 97–98, 103–104, 106, 812, 839
  -independent, universal meanings 662
  Islamicate 562
  lack of [re. an 'empty Ḥijāz'], 98
  late antique 9, 15, 45, 67, 129, 137–138
  literary 347
  local conditions and 41
  maqām 366, 577
  Meccan and Medinan 658
  oral 611
  -oriented linguistics (hadith) 658
  polemical 159
  of Qur'an/revealed text 10, 46–47, 105, 609, 643, 653, 856
  role of 572
  of situation/situational 332, 567, 568
  siyāq 565, 571, 576
  theory of 566
  types of 565
    cultural 49
    geographical 100–101, 105
    oral 611
    social 715
    temporal 491, 851
    textual 567
  of warning 575–576
contextual
  approach 506
  effects 13, 367
  framework, of Qur'an 128
  -historical *vs. versus* rational-universal meanings 661
  Qur'anic scholarship 129
contextualization 246, 654, 662
  sources/materials for 105–106
  of text/Qur'an 433, 507, 611
contextualize, and demythologize 43
contingency 699
continuity 762
  vs. discontinuity 579
  of Qur'anic text, stylistic 838
  of sura 368
contracts 450
contradiction(s) 639, 669, 671, 794
  internal 623
  re. Todorov 613
contradictory (material) 55–56
contrast 341
  taḍādd 337
convention, and belief 549
converts/conversions
  and command of Arabic 639
  to Islam 374, 496–497, 518, 519, 520, 522, 523
    among translators and scholars 546
    of Jews and Christians 635, 683, 687
  from Judaism 683
  to Judaism 91, 144
  reports from 687
  and translations of Qur'an 228
conviction (high evidentiary bars for) 452
Coptic (language) 299
  al-lugha al-qubṭiyya 841
Coptic Orthodox Church 83
Copts 84
copy(ies)
  ceremonial or presentation 228
  costs of 220
  format/size [i.e., vertical or oblong], 173, 175

for popular and prophylactic functions 235
production and diffusion of 178
of Qur'an
contemporary with ʿUthmān's reign 168
early/earliest 168, 169–170, 176
huge, for Ilkhanids 231
Samarqand 265
copyists 170, 302, 304
chancery secretaries as 228
corrections by/diacritics 177
of Qur'anic text 168, 171–172
and style of writing 174
Corpus Coranicum (project) 35, 45, 67, 202–203, 219, 548
correlations
rawābiṭ 317
science of (*ʿilm al-munāsaba*) 317
between verses and suras 317–318, 319
correspondence(s) 369
or interrelationships *(munāsabāt)* between verses or suras 347
thematic 317
corrupt(ed)
and sinful natures 755
taḥrīf [re. ʿUthmānic recension], 711
corruption 35, 814
of early scriptures 686
and generation 784
cosmological (view, i.e., sacred elements) 85
cosmology 721
esoteric 755
of Ismāʿīlīs 723
medieval 408
mystical 747
Neoplatonic/Neoplatonist 406–407, 732
cosmopolitanism 111
cosmos 806, 814, 849
councils
of Constantinople (in 381 CE) 82, 152
ecumencial (of Chalcedon, Ephesus, Nicaea) 152
covariance 358
between MVL and lexical profile 357–358
phenomenon of 349
covenant(s) 34, 146–147, 425
ʿahd 437
divine/of God 146, 422–423
with Adam and Abraham 732
and human kind 412
with (Children of) Israel 152, 437
with Moses 492, 624
history of 455–456
imagery of 624
mīthāq 423, 437
as pre-eternal 747
or testament *(diathéké)* 147
craftsmen 268
createdness (of Qur'an) 43, 769
makhlūq 378
Muʿtazilī notion of 43, 245
creatio ex nihilo 434
creation 431, 477, 684, 685, 727
of Adam 528, 682
biblical story of 528
of Eve, from rib of Adam 528
i.e., emanation 725
of Jesus 682
of man/humankind 334, 528, 731, 807
narratives on 688
nature of, in Islam 434
of/by God 434–435, 806, 808–810, 815
out of nothing/*ex nihilo* 434, 781, 809
creationism 815
Creator 405, 800
knowledge of 468
creature(s) 800
distinction between God and 787
divine *(malak)* 438
out of the earth *(dābbat al-arḍ)* 475
substance/matter created from 438–439
creditors 449
creedal (matters) 712
creed(s) 149, 522. *See also* doctrine(s)
communal or individual 359
of Judaism 156
Muslim, Christian polemic against 425
of Nicaea (325 CE) 82 (*See also* councils)
Nicene-Constantinopolitan 10, 156
crimes 452
critical. *See also* edition(s)
approach 66, 67
meaning of, *vs.* academic 28

criticism 601, 686, 746, 827
biblical 30, 48, 300, 624
canonical 382
defined 28–30
form 382
formal 684
hadith 686
'high,' German school of 621
higher 45
literary 394–395
American and European 283
and *iʿjāz* studies 376–377
rules of modern 850
Saidean tradition of 601
and theory 383
social 852
textual 222, 301, 592
critics 329, 686
literary 391
of Qur'an 797
critique 128
of Islam, feminist 484
of Jews 370–371
of neo-fundamentalists 506
of pre-Islamic poetry 404
of Quraysh 517
cross-pollination 834–835
cross-references (in Qur'an) 567
Crusaders 521
cruxifixion 152–153
cult(s)
aniconic 92
polytheistic 90–91
practices 102
of Raḥmānān ('the Merciful One') 84
cultural
achievements/production, of Islamic world 256, 679
appropriation 666
contacts with Muslims [re. Italy], 258
context/background
of Arabian Peninsula 46
of Late Antiquity 498
and Qur'an 49
diffusion [re. Thesis of], 10, 142–143, 144
exchanges 88
memory 17, 627
notions and sensibilities 536
orientations 255
resources, Indonesian 583
studies 856
transformation/upheaval 409, 677–678
culture(s) 143, 375, 388, 509
Arabic, appreciation of in West 544
book, modern 558
Christian 57, 84
Greek 81
Hellenistic 81
influence of 365–366
Jewish 48, 57
low/mass/popular 585
vs. high/elite 579
material, in Qur'an 36
Near Eastern 129
oral 578
popular 579, 580–581
and Qur'an 16, 75, 578, 590
print 558
Cuneiform, texts in 115
curators 225
curses 123
customs
of Bedouins 644
pre-Islamic 502
customs, local 40, 578
cycles
of Adam 730
of nature 477
of prophets and imams 732
of recurrent events 86

D

daʿā (supplicate) 448
Dadanitic (ANA script) 115
dahr (time; fate) 394, 403
dance 580, 585
darkness, and/*vs.* light 405, 747
Darwinism 814, 855
datation, modern techniques of 169
dating
of Qur'anic texts 170, 348
of Rippin 654

da'wa, concept and hierarchy of 731, 732
day, and night 812
dead 483–484
  raising/reviving 435, 477
  things *(al-mayta)* 141
Dead Sea Scrolls 158
death 482, 755
  after, and before the Day of Resurrection 589
  definitions of 815
  and eternal life 64
  first and second 481, 790
  individual human 482–483
  of a non-believer *(kāfir)* 455
  Qur'an references to (and killing) 475
  and rebirth, symbolism of 408 n.5
  and sleep 785
debate(s) 99, 320, 363
  in Arabian Peninsula 45
  intellectual 825, 826
  religious 497, 826
  style of 735
  theological 245
debtors 449
Decalogue 451, 454, 456
decipherment 115, 244
decolonization 545
deconstructed *(tafkīk)* 701
decoration 220, 222. *See also* ornaments
  purposes for 218
  of Qur'an 36, 544
  between suras 173
decree(s)
  of Catherine II (in 1787) 262 (fig. 16.3)
  divine/of God 743, 782
  legal 116
deductive (methods) 662
deed(s) 478
  accountability for 472
  evil 479
  good 478, 479, 586
    and faith 741–742
  records of 576
defence 451
  of Muslims (permitted) 516
  of prophecy *(ithbāt al-nubū'āt)* 725
definitive (meaning) *vs. mutashābih* (indefinite) 567
deity(ies) 84–85, 87, 88, 800
  astral 84, 86
  of Dadān 115
  dedications to 116
  Dusares (Nabataean) 124
  Dushara 90
  mentioned in Qur'an 86, 124
  monotheistic 123
democracy 852
demonology 437. *See also* Satan
demonstration
  logical 654, 659
  standards of 810
demonstrative (method) 784
denial *(takdhīb)* 742
deontological (ethics) 468
derivation, idea of 685
dervishes, whirling 580, 585
descendants 304
  of ('Alī's) son al-Ḥusayn 730
design (proofs) 852
despotism, condemnation of 595
destiny, individual 406
destruction 82, 405
  divine/power of God 410, 435
  of people of Noah 406
determinism/determinists
  heresies of 710, 712
  and Islam 851
deviations (statistical) 186
devil(s) 47, 437–438. *See also* Satan
  shayāṭīn 431, 438
dhabīḥ (sacrifice) 492. *See also* sacrifice
dhakara (recollect) 448
dhikr (meditation; remembrance) 146, 589–590
Dhū l-Qarnayn 132–136, 475
diachronic (approaches to Qur'an) 13, 320, 347, 349, 358–359, 372
diacritics/diacritical 171, 206, 209, 270, 503
  dots/points 188, 270, 283
  errors involving 260
  marks 205, 206
  use of 177, 199, 221

dialect(s) 114, 115, 283, 640, 834, 840
ancient, knowledge of 278
of Arabic 121, 283, 285, 287, 578
modern/contemporary 286, 289
Ḥijāzī 288, 290
Meccan 199, 279
of Muḥammad 278
Old Arabic 277, 290
original Qur'anic 12
regional 279, 284, 287
seven 185–186, 712
studies 277, 289
tribal 284, 288
vs. regional dialects 287
dialogue
ḥiwār 337–338
interreligious 474
between man and God 853
diaspora 510
dichotomy
between exegesis based on tradition and exegesis based on reason 820–821, 822
between *tafsīr* and *taʾwīl* 760
tafsīr bi'l-raʾy, vs. tafsīr bi'l-maʾthūr 828
between those who believe, and those who do not believe 431
dictatorship 408
dictionary(ies)
of Arabic terms 296
of Qur'an 266, 309, 661
ḍidd (pl. *aḍdād*) 639
diet(ary) 447–448
laws/rules 92, 141, 448, 496
Jewish 141, 448, 454
differences/disputes 727. *See also* debate(s)
diglossia
of inter-tribal poetic koine and tribal varieties 279
of regional dialects and Modern Standard Arabic 279
of tribal and regional dialects 287
digression, by association of ideas 318
dihān (pigment of paint; colour) 796
dīn 842
defined/meaning of 446–447, 465
dirāya (knowing esoteric meaning of) 722
disbelief/unbelief 481, 578, 614
infidelity of *(kufr al-shirk)* 741–742
kufr 436, 517
disbelievers/unbelievers 34, 134, 338, 341–342, 478, 479, 489, 573, 576, 740–742, 800
and believers 804
on Day of Judgement 482
on Day of Resurrection 477
faces of 740
God sets a seal over 71
in hell/in Fire 481, 483
kāfirūn 451
killing of 612
of Mecca 571
mushrikūn, grave sinners as 741–742
re. do not obey 514
rejected the Prophet, demanded signs 575–576
re. references to Qur'anic inscriptions 241
war of religion against 518
disciples (of Jesus) 152
discipline (of men)
fi'l-adab 530
of husbands, toward wives 450
disclosure (*kashf*) 849. *See also* unveiling
discontinuity 316
re. Todorov 613
discord/trials 517. *See also* test(s)
discourse 31, 338, 567
Ashʿarī 673
common literary 284
formal, of Classical Arabic 278
funerary 249
Liedersprache (lyric) 278, 284
literary 383
markers 13
modern juristic 517
philology as dominant form of 672, 674
political 505
of reform 16
Shīʿī 673
traditional religious 853
discursive
formations, Muslim 464
section (apologetic, polemic, exhortation) 320

disengagement *(tajarrud)* (from created world) 761
disjointedness (in Qur'an) 372
dislocation (of Palestinian people) 410
disobedience 743
  humankind lured into 489
  instilling the desire to obey and the fear of disobedience *(targhīb wa-tarhīb)* 340–341
  toward God 146, 742
  of wife, to husband 532, 535
    nushūz 530–531
disparity *(tafāwut)* principle of 725
dispensation, religious 447
dispute(s) 743
  referred to God and Muḥammad 453
dissemination 716
  of Qur'anic text 458
dissociation *(barāʾa)* from (imams') enemies 710
distribution, of material *(tawzīʿ al-mādda)* 341
diversity 470, 695
  cultural 583
  linguistic 111
  religious 71
divination (seeking the will of heaven from mantic practices) 89, 92, 234, 580, 586–587, 770
  arrows 89, 103
  fālnāma (book of divination) 234
divine 762
  epithets/titles 91, 120
  qualities, of Qur'an 802
diviners *(kuhhān)* 288
division(s) 207, 319. *See also* sura(s); verse(s)
  at end of lines 226
  people of (*ahl al-firaq*, i.e. Khawārij) 742
  of time and space [re. Qur'an], 592
divorce 338–340, 346, 369, 449–450, 534, 612, 635
  by triple repudiation (on one occasion) 767
diyānat al-yahūd 144
doctrine(s) 640, 656–657
  criticizing Catholics 596
  eschatological (in Qur'an) 14–15, 472–473, 484
  legal 51, 205, 457–459
  Neoplatonic 723
  religious 824–825
  and rulings 651, 652–653
  Sufi 842
documentation, physical (lack of) 219. *See also* evidence
documents 120. *See also* materials
  religious 44
dogma 824–825
  as fluid 436
  in Qur'an 430–431, 432, 439
  religious 28, 829
Dome of the Rock 224, 242
  decoration of 174
  inscription on 155, 175, 244, 250
dominion (of God) 738–739
dots 229. *See also* diacritics/diacritical; pointing
doublet [re. literary devices], 364
doubt 726
  and detractors of the Prophet 375
  literary dialogue on American 602
dowry 449
doxologies 354
dramatis personae 15, 497
  defining 491
  in Qur'an 490, 495, 500
    shared with Bible 488
ḍ-r-b [root], 535
dream(s) 586, 755. *See also* vision(s)
  and engagement with Qur'an 756
  interpretation 580, 586
  visions 420
dualism 90, 434, 710
duality (of exoteric *(ẓāhir)* and esoteric *(bāṭin)*) 252
Dutch translations/retranslations (of Qur'an) 542–543
ʿ-d-w [root]: *al-ʿādiyāt* (to run, speed, gallop, dash, race) 572

E

earth 408, 725, 726, 807, 812
  bears witness on Last Day 478
  as temporal 434–435
  term *(arḍ)* 726–727

Easter 92
eastern
  lands 229
  taste 597, 600
eclipses 89, 810
ecology (defined) 287
economic
  life, reflection of 453
  situation, historical 103
  transaction [re. amulets], 588
ecstasies 756
ecstatic
  union (between God and chosen servants) 751
  utterances/visions 756–757
Eden, Garden of 408
  biblical 480
edict
  of 1785 (on religious tolerance) 260
  of Milan (313 CE) 82
edition(s) (of Qur'an/Qur'anic text). *See also* print(ed); translations
  critical 261, 266
  Egyptian (1924) 268–269
  European 261
  facsimiles 11, 255, 264
    of early manuscripts 219
    publication of 171
  first print of Arabic text and English translation 256
  by Flügel 264
  history of/historical 255, 270
  hybrid 544
  Kazan 260–261, 262 (fig. 16.3) 263–264
  by Marracci 258
editorial (intrusion) issues of 611
education 558, 561. *See also* madrasa(s)
  educated few *vs.* uneducated many 579
  role of 695
  of scholars (*ʿulamāʾ*) 697
egalitarian(ism)
  concept of marital rights 535
  gender (in Qur'an) 527–528
  and just moral/social order 506
Eid stamp 584
eirenic (agenda) 60
eisegesis 716
ekphrastic epigram 408
elect 707. *See also* elite(s)
elegy 391
elision 795
elite(s) 579, 624, 672, 785, 786. *See also khāṣṣa / khāṣṣ*
  and masses/non-elites 578–580
  vs. ordinary believers 753
  spiritual *(khāṣṣa,* pl. *khawāṣṣ)* 749, 753
ellipsis 658, 771
ellipted (phrases) 499
elocution *(faṣāḥa)* 395
  recitational *(tajwīd)* 834
eloquence 342, 694. *See also balāgha; bayān*
  balāgha 395
  bayān 770
  rhetorical 380
  secrets of 794–795
emanation 19
  of Soul from Intellect 731
  waḥy (from God) 723
embellishment (of Qur'an) 11, 342
emblems, Qur'anic 588. *See also* decoration
emendations 198
  to words in Qur'anic verses 301–302
empirical realm *(ʿālam al-shahāda)* 761
emulation (of Qur'an) 390
enamelled/enamelling 252
ʿĒn ʿAvdat (inscription) 119
encounters (direct) with God 757
encouragement 339, 342
encyclopedia(s) 317–318
  of dream interpretation 586
  Encyclopaedia of Islam 330, 331, 343, 494, 576
  Encyclopaedia of the Qurʾān 217, 283, 320, 330, 701, 806
  Encyclopedia of Arabic Language and Linguistics 283, 343
  on Islam 256
  Oxford Handbook of Arabic Linguistics 331, 343
end
  al-ʿāqiba 722
  of life 14, 472
  of this world 392, 473, 475
  of time 136, 420, 435, 453, 473, 475, 732

endowment(s)
  to funerary complexes 229
  notices *(waqfiyya)* 218, 224–225
  of Qur'an manuscripts 234–235
enemies 451
  of God, Jews described as 738
  of the imams 709–710, 713, 729
  of Islam, fighting 521
English (language)
  as an Islamic language 702
  poetry, and allusions to Qur'an 594
  translations (of Qur'an) 4, 543, 545, 547, 560
    of Irving 600
    of Muhammad Ali 559
    by Sale 543
  works of *tafsīr* 702
entertainment, modern (and Islamic belief) 583
entrust(ment) *(tafwīḍ)* 808
epigraphic (evidence) 9–10, 84–85, 111, 243–244
epigraphy 11, 167, 175, 239, 279, 295
  pre-Islamic 114, 125
  Qur'anic 245
epilogue (in suras) 368
epiphany [re. God becoming manifest and visible], 420
epistemological
  aspects 760
  claims/challenges 810–811
  perfection 790
epistemology(ies) 31, 708, 755, 761–762, 776
  Aristotelian and Platonic 661, 662
  Islamic scientific 813
  and legal theory 459
epistles 396
epistolography 626
epitaphs 249
  re. Rbbl bn Hfʿm 115
epithet(s) 800. *See also* name(s)
  of Allāh 799
  of Allāt 124
  divine 91, 120, 308
  'lord of the heavens and the earth,' 122
  of man 800
  'Merciful One,' 91
equality 536
  gender 852, 855
  of men and women 43, 533
  ontological 528–529
  in retribution and bequests 369
equivalence, approach to 615
equivocal *(mutashābihāt)* (words/expressions) 834. *See also mutashābih*
errors 35
  of scribes 301
eschatological (events) and angels 438
eschatology 70, 99, 249, 346, 350, 420, 440, 468, 600, 669, 780
  ākhira 403, 657
  and apocalyptic topics 14, 473–474
  Neoplatonic 732
  passages on 136, 320, 352–353, 363
  Shīʿī views of 473
  in Sunna 472–473
  symbolism of 103
eschaton (Gr. ἔσχατα, 'the final things') 474
esoteric 749. *See also bāṭin;* mystical; *ta'wīl*
  approach(es) 707, 709
  aspects/features 711, 712, 750–752
  bāṭin 252, 749
    and/*vs. ẓāhir* (exoteric) 252, 729
esotericism 708, 711
essence 53, 791
  divine names of 788
  and existence 783
Essene (probationary period) 162
eternal *(khālidīna fīha)* [re. hell], 481
eternity 743, 784
ethical
  actions 422
  directives 612–613
  practices/lifestyle 464–465, 467–468, 481
  thought 437
ethics 64, 404, 506, 658
  akhlāq 466, 468
  and/of Qur'an 14, 464, 466, 469–470
    as book on 852
    as egalitarian 15, 533–534
  of appreciating the Other 546
  Aristotelian 661
  deontological 468
  Islamic 405, 466–468
  Sharīʿa-derived political *(al-siyāsa al-sharʿiyya)* 468
  of war and peace 515

Ethiopic (language) 299, 548
  lisān al-ḥabasha 841
ethno-cultural (group), ʿArab and ʿAjam as 285
ethos 128
  of justice (Qur'anic) 534, 536
  khuluq; khulq (moral behaviour or character) 464–465
  of *muruwwa* 402, 404
  pre-Islamic 402, 404, 411
etymology/etymological 294–295, 306–309, 310, 640, 661, 826
  approach 301
  arguments 307–309
  context, *vs.* root 661
  ishtiqāq, works on 300
  of Islamic nomenclature 722
  of *nushūz* 531
  of the word 'paradise,' 480
eulogy(ies) 354
  prophetic 407
European
  centres of research and scholarship on Qur'an 544
  Jewish scholars 685
  language scholarship 837
evangelium, Muḥammadan 623–624, 628
evidence 336
  from early Qur'an manuscript tradition 302
  epigraphic 84–85, 111
  inner-Qur'anic 357
  material 68
  standards of, in modern Islamic law 815
evil 90, 466, 468, 753, 782, 790
  and lower soul 747
  origin of 438
  those who do/evildoers 135, 478, 481
evolution 807, 814–815, 855
  literary, unilinear 349
evolutionary (hypotheses/model) 349, 358–359
evolutionism 434
exaggeration
  ghuluww 395
  re. Qur'an translations 544
exception *(istithnāʾ)* 788
exclamations 334–335
exegesis/exegeses 16, 53, 73–74, 98, 298, 434, 542, 557, 636, 714, 717. *See also* commentary(ies); Sufi(s); Sunnī; *tafsīr*
  Akbarian [re. Ibn al-ʿArabī], 762
  Akhbārī 678, 713
  Ankara school of 42, 505
  approaches to 670
  in Arabic, for scholars by scholars 714
  and the Bible 678
  dogmatic 823, 824
  eschatological discourse in 473
  forms of 16, 203
  and grammar 608, 646
  and hadith/prophetic traditions 769, 820–821, 822
  and hermeneutics 727
  Ibāḍī 736
  of Ibn Kathīr 823
  of Ibn Wahb 657
  Ismāʿīlī 722, 732
  isrāʾīliyyāt materials in 689
  Jewish 653
  and law 826–827
  levels of 759
  and *maghāzī-sīra* accounts 624
  manuscripts of Qur'anic 610
  masoretic (textual/lexical) 203, 637, 768
  methodology of 736
  Muʿtazilī 772–773
  Nishapuri school of 835
  and other fields of knowledge 826
  philosophical 19, 781, 787, 788, 789
    of Ibn Sīnā 785–786, 789
  pre-Buyid/Buwayhid 721
  process of 827
  rational-theological *(tafsīr bi'l-raʾy)* 775
  of Sayyid Quṭb 508
  Shīʿī 676, 707–708, 709, 834
    female voice in 716
    traditional 712–713
    and *walāya* 710
  sources of 834
  of al-Ṭabarī 660, 768
  and *taʾwīl* 19, 722
  and theology 774

types of 17, 626, 637
allegorical 610, 768
analogical 759
androcentric 528
anthological 307
classical 17
conventional 562, 753
cosmological 759
dogmatic 823, 824
esoteric/mystical 19, 708, 748–749, 750, 756, 761–762
exoteric 854
experiential 756
haggadic 683, 768
halakhic 768
juristic 713
Masoretic 203
metaphorical 842
metaphysical 759
moderate 752
modern/contemporary 715–716, 855
narrative 57, 102, 611, 682, 711, 768
outward *(al-tafsīr al-ẓāhir)* 754–755
philological, and situational 753
political 508
pre-modern 818
rationalist 507
rational-theological *(tafsīr bi'l-raʾy)* 775
scientific 19, 775
topical *(tafsīr mawḍūʿī)* 716
traditional 156, 769, 772, 824
and women/female 533, 716
exegetes 305, 329, 528, 613, 687, 715, 752
approach of 820
classical 294, 298, 304–305, 307–309
Ibāḍī 738
medieval source on 667
modern 698
paraphrasing/referencing other exegetes 638, 656
post-traditional 824
pre-modern 536, 820, 828
on *ṣabr* 513
strategies of 294, 707
exegetical
activities 639, 683
approaches 303
methods 654, 656, 759, 760–761
task (filling in 'blanks' of scripture) 612
techniques, development of 607
texts/treatises 16, 197, 545, 610
topoi 761
exempla/exemplar
Muḥammad as excellent *(uswa ḥasana)* 468
of Qur'an 5, 10, 15, 128, 138, 294
exhibitions (of calligraphy/manuscripts) 217, 219
exhortations 105, 316, 335
exile 34
existence 760, 762, 786, 791
of God 782, 812, 852
time of (an *ajal*) 434
existent, and non-existent 788
existential (crisis) 409
exordium 315
exoteric/literal 750. *See also ẓāhir*
dimension 762
ẓāhir 252, 729
expansion
geographic (under Umayyads/ Abbasids) 457–458
and military conquests 518
experience
direct (between *tilāwa* and *matluw)* 381
of divine in Islam 384
tajriba 809
explanandum 349
explication (of Qur'an), procedures for 19
exploitation, political 601. *See also* oppression
expression *(tarjama)* 743. *See also tarjama, tarjamat*
expulsion (of Adam) from Garden 436
extra-canonical (reports and traditions) 682
extra-Qur'anic
information/data 357
narratives/traditions 348, 684
sources 97–98, 712
text/literature 494, 512
worldview 825, 826
extra-Shīʿī (sources of authority) 712
extrinsic (approaches, to Qur'an) 379–380, 382

F

fables (in Qur'an) 490. *See also* stories
façade(s)
of Aqmar Mosque (Cairo) 246 (fig. 15.2)
inscriptions on 242
Facebookers 580
face(s)
as radiant 739
of unbelievers/infidels 739–740
wajh (of God) 473, 786, 788
facsimile (editions of Qur'an) 11, 255, 264
of early manuscripts 219
publication of 171
faḍāʾil
books 684
genre 842–843
al-Qurʾān 842, 844
faith 467, 612, 614, 743, 744, 750
in God, certitude in 586
īmān 467
Nicene-Chalcedonian 153
profession of *(shahāda)* 245
proof of 694
pure *(ḥanīfan)* 806
and science 855
and works/good deeds 734, 741–742
faithfulness 747
faithful one *(muʾmin)* 762. *See also muʾmin*
faʾl (sign or omen) 586
fall (of humankind) 528
fallacy(ies)
etymological 490, 841
genetic 54
fālnāma (book of divination) 234
al-Fals (deity; idol) 86
falsafa 780, 787, 809, 834. *See also* philosophy
in Andalusia 785
and *kalām*, integration between 661
falsehood/falseness 726
bāṭil 849
falsification
re. variant readings 70
/tampering (with Qur'an) 503–504
family (life) 748
patriarchal (structure) of 535–536
of Prophet 730, 856
faqīh (jurist) 752
faṣāḥa (in Qur'an) 795
faṣl 795
wa'l-waṣl ('disjoining and joining' of parts of sentence) 333
fasting 147, 369, 447–448, 612, 731, 751
in Ramadan 340
ṣāʾim 448
fate 807
deification of 124
of individual 407
fātiḥa (opening [of collection of verse]) 584
al-Fātiḥa
and Hip-Hop scripts 582
importance/virtue of 587, 755
Fatimid(s) 246–247, 252, 722, 731
coins 246–247
mission *(daʿwa)* 247
and pre-Fatimid sources 728
fatwas, *vs.* interpretive discourse 696
females 124. *See also* women
as secondary to male 528
and subordination 856
feminist(s) 43, 716
Muslim scholars/exegetes 15, 527, 533, 535–536
readers of Qur'an 534
fighters 613
fighting 350, 448, 566. *See also* jihad; wars/warfare
cessation of 522
conduct of 451, 516–517
as defensive 519
ghazw, as obligatory 519
jihād 513
justifications for 451
and Muslims 371, 451, 515, 518, 522
in sacred months 88, 451, 625–626
verses on 521
figurative 772
expressions *(majāz)* 834
finispieces 224, 226
fiqh (law; jurisprudence) 42, 205, 628, 658, 661, 662, 666, 735, 780, 810, 812
beginnings of 655
and theology 737
tradition 468
fire/Fire 479, 742, 790. *See also* Hell

intense 481
firmaments 479. *See also* heaven(s)
fī sabīl allāh 512
fitna 516–517
polytheism *(shirk)* as 517
tribulation *(balāʾ)* as 517–518
fiṭra / *fiṭrī* 532, 806
folios
analysis of 220–221
of Samarqand Kūfic Qur'an 264 (fig. 16.4)
size of 173
folk
chosen *(awliyāʾ Allāh)* 762
(ahl) [i.e., the imams], 709
folkloric (themes/traditions) 660, 690
fonts 269–270
food 392, 458, 725. *See also* diet
fākiha (fruits) *rummān* (pomegranates) 796
forbidden 339
honey *(niʿam)* 800
foreign
aʿjamī (Qur'an) 841
origin (of terms) 304, 307–308
rūmī (paper) 232
vocabulary/words 12, 28, 298–299, 301, 307, 309, 640, 841
forgiveness 436–437, 451
form 363, 372, 624
and content 365, 375–376, 393
criticism 382
and history 32
literary 363, 402
sīra as 621
nawʿ and *jins* 377, 380
oral 282, 425, 636
poetic/of poetry 402, 410
of Qur'an 184, 541–542, 545
re. inscriptions 249
verbal 173
formal
analysis 363
arrangements (of Qur'an) 374
features/parameters 349, 356
format 228
to aid in visual memorization 233
horizontal 174, 228
squarish 229
vertical 226
formative (*tafsīr*) (one of seven classifications of, re. Goldziher) 609
formulaic
address 364
markers of caesurae 320, 362
formulations ([of Qur'an] written, ingested, buried, worn) 590
fortitude, patience *(ṣabr)* 396
foundation (of the House [re. Abraham]) 131–132
foundational
muḥkam 738
verse 739
fragmentary (nature of texts) 616
fragmentation, internal 408
fragment(s) 410
attributed to Ibn al-Muqaffaʿ, 393
attributed to Musaylima 389, 392
of Qur'an 175, 187, 265, 389 n.1
in Berlin 197
from Great Mosque in Sanaa 219
in Istanbul 176
Kūfī and Ḥijāzī 270
in libraries 267
from parchment manuscripts 220
of varying sizes 169–170
freedom 28
of religion 518
free will 430–431, 743, 854
Muslim belief in 694
French
Structuralism 624
translations (of Qur'an) 542, 544–546, 559
friends (of God/saintly *(awliyāʾ)*) 747, 749, 751
friezes (of Qur'anic texts) 248
frontispiece 226, 245
architectural, large manuscript with 220, 224
with geometric ornaments 224
function (of building/object) 243, 245, 247
functional (yield) 281–282
Fun^Da^Mental 581
fundamentalists 746
funerary (monuments) 249

furqān (redemption, salvation, and distinction) 146, 304–305
future *(maʾāl)* [i.e. hereafter], 465

G

gambling 341, 369
gamesmanship 235
Ganymede (and *wildān)* 132
Garden 392, 435
  sin of Adam in 436
garden(s) *(jannat naʿīm; jannāt al-maʾwā)* 480
garments *(libās)* 536
garrison towns 287
gender(ed) 15, 71, 527, 856
  approaches 850
  differences 534
  egalitarianism, in Qur'an 527–528
  equality 852, 855
  identities and relationships 533
  -inclusive language 528
  inequity 534
genealogy
  Aaronid, of Mary 131
  absence of, in Qur'an 491
  of Arabs 767
  prophetic 684
generalization *(taʿmīm)* 336–337
generation, and corruption 784
generosity 470
  of God 456
Genesis, Qur'anic rewriting of 456
genetic fallacy 54
Geniza (of Cairo) 144, 162
genre(s) 320, 359, 388–389, 391, 557, 651, 684, 826
  asbāb al-nuzūl 347, 838, 843
  encyclopedic 654, 656, 658
  exegetical 651
  gharīb al-Qurʾān 299, 840
  khaṭāba, rasāʾil and *shiʿr* 377
  literary 321, 365, 402, 683
    Islamic 684
    of *qiṣaṣ al-anbiyāʾ*, 396, 688
  mashāhid 627
  mukhtaṣar 658
  populist 693
  prose 626
  of Qur'an 381, 422, 559, 771
  and sub-genres
    of literature 833–834
    of Qur'anic lexicology 840
  of Sufi literature 750
Gentile(s) 161, 162
geographic(al)
  data, Caucasian 137
  location, of a verse's revelation 836
  parameters of context 491
geography (of seventh-century Arabia) 543
geometrical (methods) 811
German
  biblical criticism 624
  translations and retranslations (of Qur'an) 542–545, 547, 622
    of Neuwirth 548
ghafūr 336, 569
  raḥīm 800–801
gharīb 660–661
  al-Qurʾān (texts) 299, 840
  works 651, 660–661, 840
ghāshiya (overwhelming [hour of disaster and punishment]) 474
Ghassanids 83
ghazw (military campaign) 519
ghulāt (extremist [elements]) 729
  of Shīʿī 671, 721
gifts
  diplomatic 235
  of scripture and prophecy 624
glad tidings *(al-bushrā)* 586
glass 251–252
global
  crises 582
  movements 343
globalization 504
glorification 802–803
  of God 336
glosses 611, 679, 710
  exegetical 198
  Ibāḍī works of 737
  literature of *(ḥawāshī, ḥāshiyah)* 675
  of Qur'an *(tafsīr al-Qurʾān bi-l-Qurʾān)* 715
gnomic (verse) 391, 394

Gnostic (sources) 732
Gnosticism 434
gnostics (*ʿārifūn*) 749, 753–755, 758, 762
God 70, 102, 156, 248, 434, 438, 466–467, 468, 772, 790
  acts/actions of 336, 431, 754, 800
  anthropomorphic (features/descriptions) 734, 737–738, 753
    sitting on a throne (*ʿarsh*) 435
  attribute(s) of 338, 639, 740, 743, 754, 769, 786, 834
    eternal/eternity of 251, 784
    gentleness (*birr*) 751
    justice 380
    al-Māturīdī's teaching on 775
    mercy 440
    nature of 637
    physical 772
  authority of 435–436
  as the author of the text 857
  belief in 147, 365
  commands of 523, 800
  -consciousness 467
  and covenant with Children of Israel 437
  and creation 434–435, 477, 809–810, 815
    of man/humans 334, 434
    of supernatural beings (jinn, angels (*malāʾika*) and devils (*shayāṭīn*)) 431
  denuded of all content (*taʿṭīl al-khāliq*) 726
  described
    as Almighty (*ʿazīz*) 569
    as Creator 14, 330, 440
    as in heaven 739
    as Magisterial Speaker 158–159
    as not tiring 141
    as One/oneness (*tawḥīd*) of 489, 614, 724
    as only authentic lawgiver 855
    as the only necessary Being 786
    as the only Real One (*al-ḥaqq*) 758
    as perceptible 741
    as ruler/sovereign 431, 435, 855
    as *al-ṣamad* 156
  design of 814–815
  doctrines regarding 744
  dominion or power of 739
  essence/being of 743, 754, 784, 788
  existence of 430, 782, 812, 852
  Face/face (*wajh*) of 473, 786, 788
  as the First principle 790
  friends/protégés (*awliyāʾ*) of 747
  glorification of 336
  'High God' (theory of Watt) 432
  and humans/man 64
    dialogue 853
    distinction between 787
  inheres in all things 759
  judgement of 855
  knowledge of 575, 784
  Moses' request to see 740
  name(s) of 156, 255, 336 (*See also* name(s))
  and nature, (His) control over 815
  nature of 794
  omnipotence of 808
  power of 809
  presence of/encounters with 747, 757
  producing things from opposites 334–335
  proof (*ḥujja*) of 423
  providence of 815
  for the sake of (*fī sabīl allāh*) 514
  signs/*āyāt* of 437, 852
  sovereignty of 435, 855
  transcendence/immateriality of 19
  unity/uniqueness of 156, 724, 782, 812, 857
  wisdom of 726, 808, 810
  word/speech of 419, 772, 851–852
    essential (*al-kalām al-nafsī*) 743
    as inexhaustible 677
goddess(es) 434, 578
  S.ms. (Shams) 121
Godhead 90
god(s) 91, 92, 102, 570
  figural representations of 88
  Greek 81
  Jewish, Christian, Muslim 59
  of Olympus 132
  pre-Islamic 123
Gog and Magog 137, 475
gold 230–231
  leaf 226, 250
  letters, inscription in 243

good
  and/*vs.* evil 99, 409, 434, 466, 478, 753
  deeds 135, 478, 479, 514, 527
  enjoin good and forbid evil, as universal duty 461
  things *(al-ṭayyibāt)* 448
  universal 468
Gospels 52, 56, 153, 157, 160, 393, 420, 757
  abrogated 459
  authors of 45
  canonical 60
  of Marcion 160
  of Matthew 162
  of Thomas 156–157
governance (of society) 510
government 855. *See also* state
  and administration of *umma* 503
  form of 507
  Qur'anic 508
grace 470, 497
  minna 751
graffito/graffiti 115, 117, 123, 175
  art/artistic 584–585
  early Arabic 105, 245
  Nabataean, from the Sinai 119
grammar/grammatical 114, 115, 186, 269, 327, 328, 331, 338, 546, 548, 610, 613, 639–640, 641, 644–646, 653, 656, 659, 820
  adjectives, in intensive form *(ṣifa mushabbaha)* 336, 568
  adverbs of place 566
  analysis 203, 211
  approach 615
  Arabic 4, 6 n.12, 36, 40, 53, 119, 286, 297, 331, 338, 342, 696
  Aramaic 119
  bad 329, 333
  case and mood endings/markers 279, 286, 290, 640, 641
  case dimension of Arabic 282
  clause of purpose (with *li)* 575
  comparative, of Semitic languages 295
  conditional sentences 454
  conjunctions 333, 337, 796
  constructions 366
  definite article 113, 114, 278, 571
  definite *vs.* indefinite subject 332
  discipline 769
  discourses 210
  ellipsis *(iḍmār)* 643
  and exegesis 608, 646
  explanations 641, 768, 832
  features of ASA 113
  gemination 641
  inflection 12, 199
  interrogative 642
  jussive 645
  kāf of comparison 796
  Kufan 643
  laʿalla and *li-kay* 640
  lām al-taʿlīl 575
  mafʿūl (passive) 114
  mimation 113
  negation
    min (for *taʿmīm al-nafī)* 570
    with particle *mā* and *lam* 114
  nouns 639
    described by an active participle 572
    indefinite 337
    masculine and feminine plural 530
  nunation *(tanwīn; nūn)* 113, 172, 225
  parataxis [re. *iltifāt*], and binarity 322
  particles 337, 814
    conditional *(law)* 741
    introductory *(inna)* 320
    reopening *(waw)* 320
  plural, of majesty 330, 334
  predicate (of sentence) 332–333
  preposition *ilā* (at/to) 739
  pronouns 566, 738
    indefinite (*man,* 'whoever') 454
    shifts 320
  proof texts 210
  punctuation 738
  Qur'anic 754, 827
  relative pronoun 639
    feminine singular *(allatī)* 278
  singular and plural forms 834
  suffixation, prefixation, and conjunctions 196
  of Taymanitic 115
  verbs 278, 639
  vowels 256, 641

fatḥa and *kasra* 256
grammarians 17, 278, 286, 645–646, 754, 833
Arab/Arabic 111, 752
on particle *lan* 741
and syntax 626
graphic
distinctions/accuracy 176–177
novels 580
revolution 228
grave
life in 483
visitation 578
Great Game (1813–1907) 264
Greek Orthodox Church of Constantinople 83–84
Greek(s) 115, 121, 153, 299, 548, 579
apokalypsis 419
and Babylonian oracle texts 424
-Islamic philosophy 776
language/linguistics 81–82, 657
al-lugha al-rūmiyya, yūnāniyya 841
New Testament 152, 159
group *(majmūʿa)* 319
Guarded Tablet [re. Qur'an], 758
guardianship *(qiyāma)* (of men, over women) 528, 532
guidance 614, 726
hidāya 787
of prophets 99
guides 747
divinely ordained *(ḥujja)* 708
Gujarati (language) 562
Gunpowder Empires 235

H

ḥadhf (omission) 333
hadith 40, 55, 66, 364, 459, 530, 585, 626, 653, 654, 656, 658–659, 666, 712, 715, 735, 739, 829, 838, 844. *See also* reports
authenticity/veracity of 44, 51–52, 616, 823
-based approach 712, 713, 819
collections/compilations 153, 609, 634, 833
Ibāḍī 734, 738
criticism/critiques 682, 686, 712, 823
exegetical 656, 659, 662, 710, 752, 822–824, 832
importance of 853
isnād-cum-matn technique 52
legislative/juristic 460, 622
literature 44, 435
and eschatology 475
terminus technicus in 200
mode of transmission of 608, 610
and predestination and free will 430
and Qur'an 674
harmonized 656–657
scholarship 210, 750, 824
of seven *aḥruf* 191
Sunnī 660, 671, 674, 712
and *tafsīr* 634, 655, 669, 670, 674, 819
al-thaqalayn 708, 713
Ḥafṣ (redact) 261, 266, 269
apparatus criticus based on 201
Ḥafṣ ʿan ʿĀṣim (reading) 268
Hagarenes *(muhājirūn)* 154
haggadic 672, 838
approach (of Wansbrough) 611
exegesis 683, 768
narrative (mode of interpretation) 610, 637, 819
hagiographic (narratives) 672
ḥajj 240, 339. *See also* pilgrimage
ḥākimiyyah (sovereignty) 695
ḥakīm [re. God's wisdom (2:32)], 569
halakhic
category (of Wansbrough) 612
legal (mode of interpretation) 610, 637, 819, 838
as type of exegesis 768
hamartiology (study of sin) 436
Hamas (movement) 508–509
poetry of 411
Ḥanbalī(s) *(madhhab)* 660
handbooks 71
handwritten
books 268
manuscripts 218
production 178
ḥanīf, pl. *ḥunafāʾ* (pre-Islamic monotheist; true) 431, 496
Muslims as 91
Qur'anic usage of 308–309
re. heathen *(ḥanpā)* in Aramaic and Syriac 308

ḥaqīqa, pl. *ḥaqāʾiq* (inner, true reality)
 of being, philosophical system of 721
 of meaning, in Qur'an 749
 unveiled to mystics and imams 714
ḥaqq (law) 445–446
al-ḥāqqa (divine name) 786
 as 'First' or 'Highest Being,' 782
al-ḥāqqa (the indubitable or inevitable [reality of the hour]) 474
ḥaraj (something difficult; legal excuse) 446
ḥarām, and *ḥima* 105
 ḥarrama (God has made unlawful) 454
ḥarb (war) 512. *See also* wars/warfare
*ḥarf*s (lit. 'edge') seven 185–186
harmony 801
ḥasana (good deeds) 465
ḥāshiyyas (glosses) 676
Hausa 556, 558
 translations 557, 560–561
ḥawāmīm (chapters of Qur'an) 303
healing, Qur'anic 588, 589
hearing 762
heart 739–740, 751, 785–786, 790
 of Muḥammad 727, 852
 station of 761
 Sufi imagery of (polishing the mirror of) 754
 of 'universal servant,' 758
heaven(s) 394, 434, 483, 725, 739, 811 n.10. *See also* paradise
 admittance into 436
 and earth, connections between 807
 and hell, as part of created cosmos 434
 in Magian and Zoroastrian tradition 132
 Qur'anic depictions of 394
 seven 479, 483, 812
Hebrew
 prophets 423
 scriptures 365, 369
Hebrew (language) 1, 47, 82, 112, 115, 162, 299
 and divine theophany 493
 al-lugha al-ibrāniyya 841
 origins of words in Qur'an 33
 and Semitic rhetorical devices 496
 sources composed in 548
 translation of Qur'an 2 n.4
hegemony 695
 of West (cultural, economic, military) 507
heirs (of the Prophet) 747
 waṣāyā (imams as) 707
Hellenistic-Roman (period) 81
Hellenization 81
hell(fire)/Hell 135, 394, 472, 474, 477, 478, 711. *See also* fire
 descriptions of 338, 394, 483, 600
  seven gates of 479
  topography of 638
 designations for 481
 eternity of 434
 glimpses/visions of 483, 484
 jahannam 435
 people of 341
 temporary, for sinning Muslims 742
henotheism 84, 90, 434
hereafter/Hereafter 394, 473, 484. *See also* afterlife
 life in 789
 as physical world 481
 and poetry 391–392
 Qur'anic terms for [i.e., *al-ākhira*], 403
 salvation/rewards in 527, 747
heresy(ies) 542
 of anthropomorphists 712
 defining 153–154
 of determinists 712
 of Epiphanius 162
 growth/spread of 256
heretic(s) Christian 155
hermeneutical
 approaches 611, 820–821, 834
  to Qur'an 374, 382, 666
 framework 533
 principles 721, 820, 821, 843
 problems, in exegetical traditions 73
 propaedeutic 714
 strategies, for contemporary reading 75–76
 tools 825
hermeneutic(s) 19–20, 652, 708, 844, 856, 857–858
 applied 818
 and (concept of) *bayān* 654, 659
 discipline of, from Prophet 723
 Islamic 380–381
 Ismāʿīlī 652, 730
 of liberation 509, 855

Mālikī 658
and methods (of al-Ṭabarī, Ibn Sīnā, Ibn ʿArabī) 652
principles 45, 726
of Qur'an/Qur'anic 245, 388, 505, 509, 534, 727, 818, 828, 843
and science 813
Shīʿī 673, 676
and influence of Muʿtazilī theology 773
Sunnī 670, 673, 678
of *tafsīr* 822
of *tawḥīd* 533
of the temporal and eternal 384
types of
contemporary 848–849
female/feminist 536, 855
humanist 853
literary 848, 850
performative 842–843
philosophical 20, 379, 732, 848–849, 850–851, 857–858
radical 844
rational 712
spiritual/mystical 407, 848–849
thematic 852
traditional 850
hermeneuts, contemporary Muslim 851
heroism, pre-Islamic 412
heterodox (religion) 579
hidden/esoteric *(bāṭin)* 749. *See also bāṭin;* esoteric
and apparent *(ẓāhir)* 708
hierarchy(ies) 726
ʿālam al-waḍʿ (i.e., *ʿālam al-dīn)* 732
in the *daʿwa* 732
of divine names 760
of interpretations 715
between men and women 529, 532
ontological or sociological 536
of Qur'anic verses 754
of *tafsīr* texts 697
hierophanic (time) 627, 629
high, *vs.* low 579–580
higher, spiritual world 725, 790
Ḥijāzī
corpus 171, 173
origins of Islam 623
style 169–170, 171, 173, 174–175, 177, 220–222
al-Ḥijr, people of 642
hijra 52, 154, 347
re-enactment of the prophetic 411
ḥikma (wisdom) 469, 568
Himyarite (kingdom) 84
Himyaritic 113
Hindi (language) 729
translations 556
Hindu (elites) 579
Hindustani Press 559
hip-hop 583–585
artists 580
scripts and Qur'anic terminology 582
Hismaic 114
historians 67, 98–99, 100–103, 432, 668, 678
art 218, 225, 231–232
of Islam 309
revisionist 85, 154, 836
historical
approaches 31, 303, 850
-critical 183, 319–320
material *(akhbār)* 620
-philological methods 309
historicism 545
historicity 52, 851–852, 856
of materials/sources 628, 689
of Qur'an 56, 381
and tales *(qiṣaṣ)* about prophets 850
historiographical
paradigm, Salafī 668
questions 608
historiography 153, 239, 503
of *tafsīr* 819
historization (of the holy Book) 852
history(ies) 98–99, 543, 610, 653, 853
and/of Islam 11, 433, 464, 473, 851
early 53, 66, 153, 688
and sciences 608
and/of Qur'an 2, 32, 34–35, 68, 99–100, 167–168, 189, 201, 203, 255, 267, 492–493
as above 699
and place in 491
revelation and collection of 543–544
as source of 9, 55–56, 622
teleology of 410–411
translations into Western languages 541

history(ies) (*contd.*)
of the Covenant 455, 456
cyclical 100, 730
definition of, and political concerns in 684
human, theocratic understanding of 406
intellectual 234, 678, 823
literary, Western 592
and meaning 699
of origins of Islamic legal doctrine 458
preceding Muḥammad/pre-Islamic 644, 684, 685
prophetic/of Muḥammad 44, 669
redefining 695
revisionist 155, 432
vs. sacred history 44
social 11, 234
universal, collections of 684
Hizbullah 508
poetry of 411
ḥ-k-m [root], 446
homicide, accidental 450–451
homiletic
function 455, 838
indexation 842
Qur'an as 498
texts 393, 445
homographs 171–172
variants of (e.g., *ḥāʾ, rāʾ, sīn, ṣād)* 226
homonyms 834
ishtirāk, works on 300
wujūh 841
homophony 364
honesty 470, 696
hope 341, 584
hostility/hostile (tone/intent)
of Marracci 543
to Muslims 520
prohibition against initiating 516
of Qur'an translations 541
toward Muḥammad 517
Hour
advent of 100
portent of, Jesus as 475
al-sāʿa 474–475, 639
signs of 473, 475
ḥ-s-n [root: beauty; good; excellence], 465
Hubal (deity; idol) of Quraysh 86
hudā (guidance) 340, 657
Hudhayl (tribe) 86
ḥudūd 41, 191
ḥujja, pl. *ḥujaj* (proof) 423, 514, 559–660
al-bāligha (inimitably persuasive) 659
as rank in *daʿwa* hierarchy 727
ḥukamāʾ, 762
ḥukm 855
as decision/judgement 568
as rule, ruling, law, wisdom 446
humanity 857
realm of *(nāsūt)* 762
humankind 364, 571. *See also* masses
division of 479
fall of 528
in Qur'an 488–489
return to God of 484
human(s) 434, 438
action and divine ordinance 408
autonomy of 743
beings, *vs.* animals 753
body(ies) (*See also* body(ies))
recreated 477
as 'vehicle,' 754
counterpart (the microcosm) 761
Jesus as 152
responsibility (al-Māturīdī's teaching on) 775
rights 510
superiority over other created beings 438
utterance *(muwāḍaʿa)* 380
will 743 (*See also* free will)
humility 470
themes of 751
ḥunafāʾ (sing. *ḥanīf*) in north-west Arabia 91–92
hunting 448
ḥuqq (Heb.) 446
ḥūr ʿīn (wide-eyed [maidens]) 480
and Hera 132
ḥuriyyāt 803
ḥurūf. *See also* letters
pointing of 201–202
readings of Qur'an 196
seven modes 209
ḥusn (beauty) 465

('living') 123
hybrid (editions [of Qur'an translations]) 544
hybridity (in *tafsīr)* 693
hymns
  Christian 57, 154
  pre-Islamic Christian strophic 199
  South Arabian Hymn of Qāniya 121
hyperbaton (an inversion of the order for rhetorical effect) 499
  al-taqdīm wa'l-ta'khīr 658
hyperbole *(ighrāq)* 395
hypocrisy (*kufr nifāq)* infidelity of 741
hypocrites 489, 742
hypotheses 620
hysteron proteron 771

I

Ibāḍī(s) 18, 699, 737, 740, 741
  doctrines of 734, 743
ibāna 770
ʿibāra (literal [as level of meaning in Qur'an]) 749
Iblīs 438–439. *See also* Satan
  rebellious behaviour of 751
iconoclastic (attitudes) 381
iconography 218, 253
  Christian, in watermarks 232
identification (re. Wansbrough's procedure devices) 768, 832
identity 53, 364
  construction 150
  Persian communal 561
  politics of 579
ideological
  current *(al-tayyār al-aydūlūjī)* 699
  tools 669
ideology(ies)
  Islamist 412
  liberal 54
  political, of European origin 695
idiolect (of Muḥammad) 282, 290
idioms (Qur'anic) 388, 391, 579, 580, 583
  as archetype of Arabic 771
idolaters 149, 479, 574
idolatry 710, 759
  shirk, polemics against 433
idol(s) 86, 89, 91–92, 102–103
  worship of 102, 148, 529, 578
ignorance 739, 743
iḥsān (excellence; integrity) 465
ījāz (brevity) 333
iʿjāz 377, 382, 423, 659, 772, 795
  al-balāgha (inimitability of rhetorical understanding) 381
  al-bayānī (rhetorical/literary) discourses 376
  concept of 13, 378, 423
  debates/discussions on 374, 384
  al-ʿilmī 376
  and literary criticism 376–377
  question/nature of 375, 379–381, 384
  al-Qurʾān (miraculous nature; inimitability of Qur'an) 328, 375, 794, 802, 818, 842
  studies, classical 383–384
  al-tashrīʿī (legal/doctrinal) discourses 376
  treatises on 655
ijtihād 461, 737
ikhrāj al-kalām ʿalā khilāf muqtaḍā al-ẓāhir (departure from what is expected) 333
Ikhshidids 253
*ikhtilās / takhfīf (*pronouncing lightly*)* 286–287
ikhtiyār 194, 202
  period of 189–190
  use of, proscribed 209–210
ilhām (inspiration; revelation) 14
Ilkhanids 231
  manuscripts made for 229–230
illumination/Illumination
  God as true source of 405
  philosophy of 790
  of Qur'an 170–171, 174, 218, 222, 224–225, 228, 231, 245
illuminators 231
illustrations 218, 542
  Qur'anic 395
ʿilm al-badīʿ (science of embellishment) 329, 332
ʿilm al-bayān (science of eloquence) 328, 329, 332
ʿilm al-maʿānī (science of meanings) 317, 328, 329, 330–331, 332, 333, 342, 567, 576
  as semantics 315

ʿilm al-munāsaba (science of correlation [between verses or suras]) 315, 317–318
iltifāt (grammatical shift) 322, 329, 333, 338, 342
image(s)/imagery 14, 388, 389, 393, 435, 798, 802–804
  of covenant 624
  dynastic, projection of 224
  figural 218
  of Jews and biblical stories 688
  Mosaic 411
  of Muḥammad 622
  poetic 801, 802–803
  prohibition of 87
  Qur'anic 33, 392, 408, 581, 584, 757, 761, 796
    commercial 453
  of Saracens/of Turks 256
  Sufi ('polishing the mirror of the heart') 754
imaginary 789
  things *(umūr mawhūma)* 810
imagination 789
  language of 798
imamate
  of ʿAlī 246, 730
  Ismāʿīlī concepts of 732
Imāmī(s) 18, 724. *See also* Shīʿa
  religious and legal doctrines 767
  Shīʿī 206, 766, 773
  Twelvers 721
imam(s) 710, 716–717
  cycles of 732
  enemies of 709–710, 713, 729
  as heirs of the Prophet *(waṣāya)* 707
  inner teachings of 713
  of Ismāʿīlīs 723
  and knowledge of/from 708, 730
  legitimate 724
  and revelation/Qur'an 708, 709, 713
  as the speaking Qur'an *(al-kitāb al-nāṭiq huwa-l-walī)* 709
  as those rooted in knowledge *(al-rāsikhūna fī-l-ʿilm)* 708
  walāya of 707–708, 713, 716
Imam(s) (Twelver Shīʿī) 673
  glosses attributed to 18
  verses referring to 249
īmān (faith; belief) 467, 614. *See also* belief(s); faith
  vs. kufr (ingratitude and disbelief) 466
  ta'wīl of 730
imitation (of Qur'an) 389, 392
  attributed to Ibn al-Muqaffaʿ, al-Mutanabbī, al-Maʿarrī 393
immigration, large-scale (in twentieth century) 545
immorality (in the text) 614
immortality (of the soul) 472, 785
imperative(s) 453–454
  e.g., *iṣbirū/ṣābirū* 513
  mode, of speaking 403
imperialism 545. *See also* colonial(ism)
  Islamic response to 507
imperialist (agendas) 601
imperial scriptoria 224
implausibility [re. Todorov], 613
inappropriateness [re. Todorov], 613
incantations 255
incarnation/Incarnation
  Christian doctrine of 93, 433
  divine 435
incoherence, apparent (in Qur'an) 322
Indian (language) 299
  al-lugha al-hindiyya 841
indicators *(madlūlāt)* 743
indices, compositional 324–325
individuation 384
Indonesian
  language 702
  tafsīr works, modern 701–702
inductive (methods) 662
infallibility *(ʿiṣma)* of the prophets [re. Shīʿī theology], 711
infanticide 470
  of girls 91, 474
infidelity 743
  kufr 741–742, 800
infidels 593, 742, 751, 754
  faces of 739
  of Quraysh 812
inflection 285, 289
  grammatical 12, 199
  iʿrāb 286

ingratitude 742
inheritance 449–450, 457, 458
inheritors *(awṣiyāʾ)* (of the Prophet) 710
inimitability (perfection; beauty [of Qur'an]) 377, 593, 655, 694
  iʿjāz al-Qurʾān 13, 280, 290, 316, 389, 395, 548, 771, 834, 850
    doctrine of 654, 827, 842
    nature of 390, 655
  linguistic 300, 423, 659
injunction(s) 730, 748
  for legitimate armed combat 515
  moral 354, 730
injuries [re. torts], 451
injustice 857
  ẓulm 396
ink 176, 220
  carbon-based, *vs.* tannin-based 226
inner/innermost
  dimension *(bāṭin)* 729
  meaning of happenings *(taʾwīl al-aḥādīth)* 724
  secret *(al-sirr)* 751
ins (humans) and *jinn* 794
inscription(s) 11, 111, 117–119, 122–123, 233, 242, 245–246, 250
  ANA 113
  Aramaic 119
  architectural 246
    around the Taj Mahal in Agra 233
    at Biʾr al-Watawit (Cairo) 253
    on Dome of the Rock 155, 242 (fig. 15.1) 243, 244, 250
    from Ḥegrā 113, 124
    in Madaba, Arabic-language 118
    on mihrab of Great Mosque of Qayrawan 245
    on portal of Masjid-i ʿAli (Isfahan) 248–249, 249 (fig. 15.3)
  ASA 122
  bilingual Greek-Safaitic 121
  corpus/compendia of 240, 244
  Dadanitic 115
  at ʿĒn ʿAvdat 119
  funerary 249
  Hismaic 114
  historiography of 240
  Jewish 122
  layout of 11
  materials of 243, 250
  monumental 115
  mosaic 224, 242–243
  Nabataean 85, 87, 118, 119, 124
  in North Arabia 118, 125
  Palmyrene 85
  pre-Islamic 105, 121
  public 116, 118
  Qur'anic (texts) 11, 175, 233, 239, 244
    database of 240–241
    inscribed 241–242
    on solid supports 239
    used on objects 247, 251–252
  in South Arabia 117, 122
  style of 11, 117, 243, 250
    and funerary discourse 249
  technique of 11, 250, 252
  Thamudic 115
insertions, later 351, 357–358
inspiration 421, 603, 781
  divine 42, 757, 762
institutes/academies
  Academic Association of Chinese Islam 559
  Bavarian Academy of Sciences 200
  Berlin-Brandenburg Academy of Sciences 548
  Centre for Islamic Studies at SOAS 64
  Detroit Institute of Arts 232
  Institute of Sharīʿa Sciences in Muscat 736
  Istanbul-based Research Centre for Islamic History, Art and Culture (IRCICA) 554–555
  King Faisal Centre for Research and Islamic Studies 231
  Leningrad Institute of Oriental Studies 265
institutions
  Islamic 558
  of learning *(madāris)* 769, 775
  of meaning, in Qur'an 548
Intellect, and emanation of Soul from 731
intellection 783, 789
  theory of 787
intellect(s) 708, 737–738, 740–741, 750
  ʿaql 844
  human, function of 787
  universal 790

intellectual(s)/intelligentsia
  Egyptian 560
  Muslim 263, 484, 505, 509
  non-ulama 558, 562
  Ottoman 559
intelligent (design proofs) 852
Intelligent Design 855
intelligible, and non-intelligible 789
intent *(niyya)* 588, 590
intention *(qaṣd)* of the text 325
interactions
  kind and just (as mandated in Qur'an) 522
  between prophets, angels, common people, and communities in the Qur'an 496
intercalation 448
intercession 742, 769
  of angels, prophets, martyrs, scholars 742
  shafāʿa 711
  through the Qur'an 587
intercessors 747
interconnections/interconnectedness 690. *See also* correlations
inter-faith (concerns) 431
interlinear. *See also* translation(s)
  of groups of verses 797–798
interlinear (works/translations) 555–557, 558, 562
  Persian 228, 263, 555–556
interlocutors 433
international relations 513
internet 580, 589. *See also* online
  medium of 693
  role of 18
  and *tafsīr* 698, 702
interpretation(s) (of Qur'an) 72, 104, 608–609, 673–674, 848. *See also* commentary(ies); exegesis/exegeses; *tafsīr*
  Akhbārī traditions of 678
  and/*vs.* literal (meaning) 726, 744, 753
  anti-colonial 507
  Companions or Successors asked about 634
  of dreams *(taʿbīr)* 755
  of every verse and individual words 668
    of term *jaʿala* 640
    of 'virgins of paradise' *(ḥūr ʿīn)* 283
  evolution of 267
  experts in 635
  genre of scriptural 695
  hierarchy of 715
  human, and reasoning 654
  inner-Qur'anic 32
  literal 726
    of anthropomorphic descriptions of God 738
  modes of 43, 819
    masoretic (textual/lexical) 819
  previous/of earlier authorities 699, 821–822
  reformist 507
  sciences of 744, 806–807
  Shīʿī/Ismāʿīlī 729
  as social critique of Muslim societies 506
  Sufi 673, 746
  tafsīr 609, 774
  taʾwīl 708, 774, 854
  techniques of 613
  tools of 615
  types of
    aesthetically oriented 797
    esoteric 18, 721, 730, 761–762
    historical 65
    modern/contemporary 39, 64, 65
    philosophical 782
    scientific 700
    traditional 301
interpretive
  activity/process 856–857
  Andalusi/North African tradition 676
  method, *logical* necessity of 776
  technique *(tanāsub)* 678
  tools 669
interruption (and suspension of composition) 339–340
intertextual
  arguments 676
  comparisons 104
  parallels (between Qur'anic verses and Jewish and Christian scriptural and exegetical traditions) 97
  relationships 141
intertextuality 13, 366, 372, 688, 713
  negative 131 n.3, 402

Qur'anic, with Bible 143
interwar period/years 559–560
intimacy
expressions of (between God and mystical lover) 757
proximity (between God and human servants) 747
intimate conversation *(munājāt)* 740
intra-Qur'anic (references) 661
intratextuality 713
in oaths 573
as Qur'an glossing the Qur'an *(tafsīr al-Qurʾān bi-l-Qurʾān)* 715
introduction(s) 320–321, 322, 353
to Qur'an 65, 66
intuition *(ḥads)* 783
invasion
of Kuwait, Iraqi 547
of Medina 340
invective 391
inversion (of logical order [re. Arabic language]) 771
invisible (realm) 756
and visible world 755
invocation 175, 243
formula (i.e. *basmala*) 221, 302, 581
of Muḥammad 233
Qur'anic 588
inward. *See also* esoteric
baṭn 760 (*See also bāṭin*)
sciences of Qur'an, *vs.* outward 754
ipseity/Ipseity (divine/of God) 782, 790
iqraʾ (re. of Qur'an on Mount Ḥirāʾ) 51
iqtibās (citations of the Qur'an) 405
iʿrāb 279
Arabic, lowest-yield 290
significance, or irrelevance of 281–282
system of 285
at time of Muḥammad 283
Iran(ian) revolution 508
Iraqis, *vs.* Syrians 504
irjāʾ, 657
ishāra (allegorical; allusive [levels of meaning in Qur'an]) 749
Ishrāqī 789–790
philosophy 40, 789
school (in Iran) 785
islām (submission) 467
taʾwīl of 730
Islam(ic) 28, 42, 54, 58, 432, 464, 490, 541, 543, 560–561, 623, 807
as apocalyptic movement/and eschatology 472–473, 600
and Christianity 10, 33, 295
culture 60, 376, 584
early 56, 59, 634
formative period/environment of 53, 153, 685
as form of Judaism 257–258
hostility/negative attitude toward 49, 517, 685
lands, central 229
as messianic movement 154
movements, revolutionary 508
normative 623
origins of 51–52, 53–54, 55, 57, 59–60, 66–67, 111, 474, 607–608, 620, 621, 623
Arab 688
date of 464
narrative of 358
period of 34
and Qur'an as historical source for 55–56
Syro-Palestinian 154–155
traditional Muslim understanding of 58
outreach/promotion and spread of 514, 561
Persianate 561
practice 339, 552
vs. Qur'an 42
reception of (American) 601
reviving/revival of 39
rise/emergence of 65, 66, 154–155, 241, 543, 608
and milieu 9, 72
studies/Studies 64, 258, 608, 668
academic 15, 41, 76
and reference works 689
Swahili, development of 561
tradition 7–8, 11, 67
world 29, 42, 667
and Arab scholarship 701
role of the kingdom [re. Saudi Arabia], 269
worldview 851

Islamic Foundation of Nairobi 560
Islamic Republic [re. Iran], 508
Islamist(s) 851
movements/ideology 411–412
Islamization 280, 666
of the legal system 461
ism (nomen) and *musammā* (nominatum) 769–770
Ismāʿīlī(s) 248, 724, 726, 728
doctrine 721, 731
early sources 729
Ismāʿīlism 247, 732
isnād(s) 304, 635, 638, 658, 670
complete 734
-cum-matn 52, 57, 616, 628
institution 767
system 58
of al-Ṭabarī 659, 670
Israelites 134, 144, 148
banū Isrāʾīl 348
isrāʾīliyyāt (biblical stories and Jewish and Christian sacred history) 17, 492–494, 644, 682, 696, 735, 824, 829
Qur'anic and extra-Qur'anic narratives on 684
spread of 683–684
study of corpora of 689
and *tafsīr* 528, 687, 699
term/definition of 686–688
istaʾnafa (to indicate a caesura in a verse) 642
istiʿāra (metaphor) 394, 795, 801, 802–803
istidlāl (reasoning from evidence) 809
istifhām (questioning) 333, 642
istikhāra (seeking goodness and the best outcome) 586
iṣṭilāḥāt (work) 836
iʿtibār 645, 700, 757
iṭnāb (expansion) 333
ittibāʿ (emulation; affiliate) 469

J

Jacobites (Monophysites) 161
jahannam (Hell; Gr. *gehenna*, Heb. *gêhinnōm*) 481, 800. *See also* fire; Hell
jāhiliyya 100, 578, 695
heathendom 508
jallā (God makes something manifest) 423
jannāt firdaws (or *al-firdaws*) 480. *See also* heaven(s); paradise/Paradise
jest/joke 396
tafakkahūn 571
Jewish
biblical tradition 628
Christianity 309
Christians 104, 162
as confessional group 33
and religious texts 33–34
influence
on Islam 58, 689
on Muḥammad 621
on Qur'an 5 n.10, 101, 432, 621
re. cabbalistic ciphers 302
legends/mythology 59, 685
models 57
practices and traditions 10, 148, 162
scholarly reform (termed *Wissenschaft des Judentum*) 621
sources, and influences 294–295, 498, 685
thought, on nature of revelation 379
Jews 56, 85, 102, 141, 365, 521, 573, 579, 644, 741
of Alexandria 155
of Arabia 142, 156
Babylonian 59
and Christians 161, 162
and covenant with God 146
critique of 370–371
described as God's enemies 738
and dietary rules/eating practices 141, 448, 454
Hellenized and Romanized 82
on Last Day 477, 479
and Muḥammad 424, 489
information to 142, 144, 644
polemics against 686
and Muslims 683
as elected religious community 370–371
new converts from among 635
Palestinian 152
and prophecy 490
Qur'an on 144, 147
yahūd 145, 348
j-h-d [root], 512
jihad (*jihād*) 15, 451, 512, 523, 582, 612, 737, 742

as construct in later exegetical and juridical literature 15
defined
as fight and praxis 857
as holy war 515, 523
as struggle, exertion, striving 512, 523, 582
of two types: external and internal 513–514, 751
fī sabīl allāh (in the path of God) 512, 514
military/combative 510, 513–514
against non-Muslims *qua* non-Muslims 523
as primarily defensive 515
al-nafs 583
non-combative nature of 514
secondary literature on 519
jinās (homonymy) 330, 332
jinn 375, 431, 434, 437–439, 477, 590, 794, 803–804
division of 479
made of smokeless flame/fire 439, 489
in Qur'an 488
jinsiyya (generic) 571
jizya (poll-tax) 516, 521
payment of 520, 522
j-n-n [root], 480
journals
Journal of Qur'anic Studies 8 n.19, 64, 601
Journal of Research and Qur'ānic Studies 270
Journal of the International Qur'anic Studies Association 8 n.19
Muslim World 64
Judaeo-Christian
-Islamic 'God,' 59
sect, Muḥammad as member of 154
sectarian milieu 57, 59–60
Judaic (figures in Qur'an) 490
Judaism 58, 60, 84–85, 90–91, 92, 154, 378
in Arabia 143
Arabic terms for 144
and Islam 685
as a form of 257–258
origins of 33
late antique 807
and Qur'an 10, 144, 145, 295
judaization 90
Judaizing 144
Judgement Day/Day of 339, 446, 478–479, 484, 576, 586
judgement(s)
of the dead 102, 431
divine/of God 404, 446, 472, 473, 476, 479, 855
ethical 467
final 446, 473
prescriptive 612
jumla/jumal inshāʾiyya (affective sentences) 335, 566
jurisprudence 204, 378, 712, 737, 750. *See also* *fiqh;* law(s)
jurist(s) 304, 752
fuqahāʾ, 774
mujtahid 459
justice 422, 484, 530
concept of (*ʿadl* and *qisṭ*) 465, 857
divine/of God 383, 431, 439, 478
at end of time 476
primordial scale of 586
Qur'anic 534, 536
ʿadl-i Qurʾān 461
social 581
juxtapositions 337
of secular and religious 396
of variant traditions 366

K

Kaʿba 98, 432, 451, 516, 574, 575, 749
and Abraham 370–371
cube, and calligraphy 584
liberation of 319, 371
qibla changed to 370
rebuilding of 131
sacred temple, or sacred house (*al-masjid al-ḥarām, al-bayt al-ḥarām*) 88, 448
kaʿba(s) (in Arabia) 88–89
circumambulation (*ṭawāf*) of, in pre-Islamic times 89
kāfirūn (non-believers) 336. *See also* disbelievers
kāhin (priest; seer; revealer of divine will) 89
kalāla 456–457

kalām (theology; theological discourse) 377–378, 421, 666, 774, 780, 810–812, 826, 852
Allāh (God's word/speech) 375–376, 377, 419, 421, 423, 621
and anti-*kalām* 694
Ashʿarī 661, 785, 787
demise of 694–695
and *falsafa,* integration between 661, 787
ideas 786–787
leaders of 376
and mystical circles 791
as rational speculation into the nature of God 807
and *tafsīr* 673, 807, 814
Kalb (tribe) 86
Karrāmiyya 228, 250–251, 835
Kazan Qur'an (editions) 260–261, 262 (fig. 16.3) 263–264
Kemalist (governments) 40
kerygma, as aim of salvation history 624
kerygmatic (theologies) Christian 384
khabar, pl. *akhbār* (account) 628, 642
khalaqa [verb: created], 640
khalīfa (representative; vice-regent) of God 438. *See also* caliph(s)
khamr
grapes 640
wine 341
khānaqāh (hospice) 252
Khārijī, pl. Khawārij 504, 568, 741–742
theology 460
khāṣṣa / *khāṣṣ* 762, 828
khayr (good) 465. *See also* good
khuluq or *khulq* (moral behaviour; character; ethos) 464. *See also* character; ethics
khurūj (departing from what is expected) 338
khuṭba (sermon) 191, 394. *See also* preaching
kināya (metonymy) 332
wa-taʿrīḍ (and allusion) 395
kingdom(s) (of nature, i.e., animal, vegetable/plant, and mineral) 732, 809
kings 134, 419, 552
Jewish 91, 160
Kirghiz 260
kitāb, pl. *kutub* (book(s)) 146, 183, 185, 244–245, 305, 421, 423–424, 425, 426, 574, 578. *See also* book(s); *kitāb*
of God *(allāh)* 245
al-jihād/siyar 518
meaning of 305, 423, 426, 574
as discursive exposition *(logos)* 424–425
as Qur'an 576
as scripture 284, 424, 461
orthography of Qur'an *(al-rasm);* variant readings of scripture *(al-qirāʾāt)* 834
works of knowledge *(al-jāmiʿa)* 834
knowledge 29–30, 602, 726–727, 730, 743, 821, 849
conceptions of 773
divine 378, 783
early Islamic branches of 628
excellence of 708
exoteric and esoteric 727, 729
of human affairs 378
ʿilm 465, 628, 726, 740
of the imams 708
Islamic science of 695
of *isrāʾīliyyāt* 683
of Judaism 142
link between creation and 781
modes of 695, 781
mystical; gnosis *(maʿrifa)* 740, 749, 754
of the true state of affairs *(maʿrifat al-ḥaqāʾiq)* 722
power of 790
of prophets (what is possible and impossible for God) 740
religious 626, 628
revealed, levels of 729, 730
scientific 853
special, of successors of the Prophet 708
of *tafsīr,* historical 667
those firmly rooted/well-grounded in 642, 724, 738, 758 (*See also al-rāsikhūna fī-l-ʿilm*)
transmitted *(naql)* 844
universal 784
known, and unknown 789
koine 284
commercial or trade 289, 290
inter-tribal 285
inter-tribal poetic *vs.* tribal varieties of Arabic 279
literary 277–278, 290

formal 12, 290
Old Arabic 281
koineization 287
Kubrawī (school) 756, 757, 762
Kufan (system of verse division) 350
kuffār (those outside the *umma* of the Prophet) 741. *See also kāfirūn*
kufr (ingratitude; infidelity; disbelief) 466, 739
nifāq (of hypocrisy) 741
niʿma (for God's blessing) 741–742
shirk (unbelief) 741
Kunstprosa 280

L

Lakhmids 83
lament(s) 395, 572
lamp *(miṣbāḥ)* 252
language(s) 72, 334, 366, 379, 412, 546–547, 656, 701, 712, 795–796, 824, 826, 834. *See also* Arabic (language); dialect(s)
access/privilege 578
adapted to contemporary usage 639
of administration and culture 81–82
affinities among 296
ambiguities of 459, 612
of Ancient Yemen (Sabaic, Minaic, Qatabanic, Ḥaḍramitic) 112
and/of Quraysh 278, 375
approaches to 388
classification of 299
conceptions of 381
current in Ḥijāz 48
evolution/change of 613, 802
figurative 330, 332, 394
human 377, 379, 655
inflected 279, 281, 284
ʿarabiyya 283
Islamicate 64, 552, 554–555, 693, 702–703
literary 284
metaphorical 781, 797–798, 802
nature of 378, 794
of/in Qur'an 1, 8, 12, 42, 277–278, 294, 378, 390, 547, 581, 757, 770
artistic/high 285, 797
and dialects of old Arabia 278
lexicographical analysis of 71
original 277, 285–286, 288–289
profane and divine concepts of 653, 659
published 277
science of 754
statutory 452
style/qualities of 327, 374, 576
superiority of 796
oriental 5, 296
origin of 300
philosophy (of Saussure) 853
politics of 546
and prophecy 408–409
rationalist 809
regional 562
scholarly 555
sciences of *(ʿilm al-lugha)* 770
Semitic 295, 299
spirit of 546
status of 384
study of 645, 825
theory of 653–654, 659, 771
unwritten, of Arabian traders and shippers 284
vernacular/everyday 117, 552, 642, 715
of written documents *vs.* vernacular 117
langue (language) 421
last day/Last Day 136, 147, 477
belief in 365
description of 600
Qur'an(ic) 476, 599
Last Supper, sura as interpretation of 456
al-Lāt (deity; idol) 86
laṭāʾif (subtle [levels of meaning in Qur'an]) 749
late antique
Arabia 102, 105
context 129, 132
of Qur'an 9, 103, 106
intellectual trends 101
Near East, multicultural 111
theological terms 133
Late Antiquity 433, 488, 494–495, 498
area of 492
Hellenistic context of 403
Qur'an in 9, 15
lawful/lawfulness 754
aḥalla (God has made) 454
ḥalāl 141, 448

lawgiver
God as only authentic 855
Moses as prophetic 422
prophets 424, 426, 732
lawḥayn (between two boards) as description of *muṣḥaf* 170
law(s) 36, 53, 146, 316, 346, 445–447, 610, 635, 669, 767, 826–827. *See also* prescriptions; ruling(s); Sharīʿa
and burden on believers 454
classical works on 300
code/manual 420–421, 455, 518
customary, pre-Islamic Arabian 450
dietary 141
family 449, 453
modern Islamic, and standards of evidence 815
of Moses 419
of nature 726
personal, and ritual 505
as post-Qur'anic phenomenon 457
(derived from/grounded in) Qur'an, hadith, Sunna 445, 458, 460, 508, 651, 655, 666
Qur'an(ic) 447, 455, 458, 460, 661, 834
religious 446–447
Saudi Arabia(n) Basic Law *(al-niẓām al-asāsī li'l-ḥukm)* 461, 509
on war and peace 516
layout 250–251, 547
of inscriptions 11
leaf(s)/leaves
in bright colours 232
on glair 220
price of 222
lectionary, pre-Qur'anic 57
lectiones 202, 206, 210–211
Left, (those on, *vs.* Right) 479
Islamic 506
leftists 746
legal 611
activity 118
content, positive 456
discipline 769
discourses/arguments 14, 17, 637, 826
halakhic (type of interpretation) 610, 637, 819, 838
injunctions/regulations 99, 352
issues/topics 612, 656, 662
obligations/requirements 41, 453
principles 612, 656–657
stage of *tafsīr* [re. Wansbrough], 652
status (of a slave woman) 767
strategies 304
structures (of Islam) 612
subjugation (of Jews and Christians) 521
system(s) 446, 613
Islamization of 461
theory, Islamic 458–459, 467
legends/legendary 55, 99, 687
legislation 370–371, 447, 452
introduced gradually 341
Qur'anic 304–305, 458
secular 447
legislative
passages 14, 364, 445, 455–456
role of Qur'an, and incompleteness 458–459
legitimacy
of exegetical methods 822
and Qur'an 461, 746–747
letter(s) 728, 743
alif 187, 221–222, 229
bāʾ, 751
disconnected/broken/isolated *(al-ḥurūf al-muqaṭṭaʿā)* 302, 346, 354, 369, 586
hamza 172, 270
Medinan convention (of coloring dots) 225
ḥurūf 191, 302
mīm 225, 751
mysterious 302, 397, 424
precise number of (for specific suras) 835
shapes of/spaces between 221–222, 244
significance of 302–303
sīn 751
lex credendi 433
lexical
analysis 653
data in the Qur'an 298, 307
differences, infinitesimal 204
explanations 203, 636, 768, 782, 832
features 357, 711
item(s) 639

meaning(s) 712
parameters 358
stage of *tafsīr* [re. Wansbrough], 652
lexicographical
approaches/methodologies 661
meanings 744
lexicography 610, 662, 712, 713, 825, 834
lexicology
phraseological 842
Qur'anic 840
semantic 657
lexicons 307. *See also* dictionary(ies)
Arabic 296
of al-Rāghib 661
lexis 669
lex orandi 433
lex talionis (retaliation for homicide and wounding) 452
liability
for pagan or pre-Qur'anic acts 454
tort 449
liberal (ideology) 54
liberalism, political 854
liberalization (of translation activities) 560
liberation
Qur'an as means of 856
theology (Qur'an as work of) 43
women's 856
libraries 17, 267, 678
Bibliothèque nationale de France 170, 219, 220, 304
Chester Beatty Library (Dublin) 219
of al-Ḥākim (Cairo) 677
John Rylands University Library 556
of mosques 207, 697
Nag Hammadi Library 157
National Library of Iran 228
Public Library (St. Petersburg) 264
Libyan Daʿwa Society 561
Liedersprache (lyric discourse) 278, 284, 290
life
after death 482
and/*vs.* death 337, 409, 435
eternal 484
forms of *(Lebensformen)* 548
in the grave 483
in the hereafter 789
ḥayy 123
objective/purpose of 482, 731
of Prophet Muḥammad 297, 493, 620, 628, 644 (*See also* biography *(sīra)*)
extra-Qur'anic Arabic sources for 97–98
spiritual, and eschatology 473
ligatures, use of 118
light
and darkness, theme of 747
divine/of God 741, 790
primordial 729
Liḥyān (kingdom) 85
limit *(ḥadd)* 762
linear
-atomistic method 318
connectivity 367
relationship of sura (from beginning to end) 371
lingua franca, inter-tribal 284
linguistic(s) 210, 613, 651, 653–654, 744, 852–853, 856
ambiguity 440, 615
analyses 658, 809, 833
in later grammatical works 641
approach 366–367
to Qur'an, of al-Ṭabarī 770
Arabic 114, 653, 658 (*See also* Arabic (language))
comparative 285
departments, and study of Arabic 343
explanations 710
as main analytical framework 662
modern 568
pragmatic 657
profane 653
and Qur'an 10, 16, 125, 459, 544
rhetorical 654, 657
of Sībawahyi 653, 662
structure, synthetic 281
and *tafsīr* 17, 653–654, 656
theory(ies) 320, 641
linguists 308, 646, 795
lisān 421
aʿjamī 288
ʿarabī; ʿarabiyy (Arabic) 285
mubīn (understandable language) 282

literacy 111, 578. *See also* writing
  in pre-Islamic context 10
literal
  ʿibāra; iʿtibār message 749, 757
  meaning/reading of Qur'an 695, 744, 825, 829
    vs. hidden, true meaning 722
literality 853–854
  muḥkamāt 853
literary 382, 623, 798. *See also* genre(s)
  anthologies/prose 395–396
  approaches 378, 380–381, 384, 850
    modern [re. Qur'an], 374, 383
  aspects/character/attributes (of Qur'an) 32, 309, 376, 798
  assimilation 143
  character, cohesion, and unity of chapters 303
  classics 592
  constructions 500
  construct(s) 624
  criteria, applied to Qur'anic text 363
  development, process of 357, 358–359
  devices 364, 495
  diction of Arabs, formal 199
  discipline 769
  features/qualities 350, 390, 410
    of text/Qur'an 72, 357, 542, 544
    of translations 549
  influence, of Qur'an 8, 13
  issues 794
  level 851
  perspective/angle 64, 369
  register 549
  school (of Romanticism) 597
  strategies 629
  studies 142, 383, 395, 795, 797, 823
  theory 375, 593
  tradition
    early Islamic 204
    larger Near Eastern 365
    medieval Arabic 388
    Western 495–496, 602–603
  units 319
literate
  vs. non-literate (societies) 116–117
  and semi-literate/illiterate (populations) 578–579
literati 391
literature(s) 128, 306, 388, 546, 672
  advice 470
  biblical 48
  Christian and Jewish 48, 101, 685, 688, 689
  exegetical 105, 371
    tafsīr 528
  hermeneutical 833, 842
  Islamic/Muslim 261, 685
    influences on English literature/poetry 594
  juristic (on jihad) 513
  medieval, on meaning of Qur'an 695
  narrative 396, 689
  oral 118, 185
  Qur'an as 71–72
  secondary 434, 437, 439, 701–702, 843, 857
    on jihad 519
  secular, and sacred revelation 601
  Western
    impact of Qur'an on 16
    and Qur'an 592, 601–603
lithographs (of Qur'an) 268
lithography 11, 255, 268
liturgy 503, 541
  religious 118
  teshmeshtā 130
living, *vs.* dead 483
loan words 155, 160, 636, 640
  Arabic 118, 300
  Aramaic 295
  non-Arabic 305
  South Arabian 295
loci probantes 768, 832
logia 289
  exegetical 749–750, 752, 756
  prophetic 623–624
logic 364, 654
  of conversation 549
  Semitic, *vs.* Greek 324
logograms 302
looking (*naẓar* [at God]) 739–740
lord/Lord 782–783, 786

Lordship 569, 783
lore
  biblical 59, 683
    reports, narratives, and traditions on 686
  Jewish, and *isrā'īliyyāt* 688
  normative oral and literary 746
  Sufi 748
lots, drawing of *(maysir)* 452
love 747
  lyric 391, 395
lugha 640
  lughāt al-Qur'ān 299–300
lustre tiles 252
  short suras on 244

M

macrocosm
  and microcosm 408
  primeval *(al-ʿālam al-kabīr)* 760
madhhab, pl. *madhāhib* 654
  Ḥanbalī 660
  jarīrī (of al-Ṭabarī) 658–659
Madh'ij (tribe) 86
madman *(majnūn)* Qur'anic denial of Muḥammad as 375
madness, accusations of 133
madrasa(s) 240, 562
  curriculum, Ottoman 557, 679
  -style (commentary) 821–822
  system 675–677
Madyan, people of 490
maghāzī (military expeditions) 621, 623, 628, 644
  treatise on 636
maghāzī-sīra
  accounts/reports 620, 624–625, 628
  narratives/traditions 626–628
    and Qur'anic verse(s) 629
Magian (traditions) 132
magic 16, 578, 580–581, 590, 796
  (referenced) in Qur'an 133
  and Muḥammad 588
  role of 585–586
  white *vs.* black 590
magisteria, non-overlapping 807
mahdī (messianic figure; the Guided One) 475–476, 711
  advent of 729
Mahomet (as literary character) 594–595, 596, 598
majālis (sessions) 396
majāz (figurative, non-literal speech/language) 330, 382, 395, 615, 794–795, 801, 802
Malay 556
  tafsīr (modern) 701–702
male 124. *See also* man/men
  attitudes, authoritarian 532
  –female relations 527–528, 529
Mālikī (legal methodology) 658
Mamluk(s) 252, 265
  sultans of Egypt 230–231
maʿnā, pl. *maʿānī* 380, 653, 659, 712, 722, 771
  al-Qur'ān, genre of 204, 208
al-Manāt (deity; idol) 86, 124, 434
Mandaeans 85, 90
Manichaeans 85
Manichaeism 157
Manichees 160
Manifesto of 1775 (of Russia) 260
mankind. *See* humankind
manliness *(murū'a/muruwwa)* 465
man/men 70, 732
  actions of 800
  as created by God 334
  defense of 517
  and God's revelation 853
  hearts of [re. Qur'an], 184–185
  as messengers 437
  as microcosm 790
  perfect 760
  of understanding *(fuqahā')* 191
  and women [re. rights, guardianship], 529–531, 535
manna 571
manners, and customs (of Bedouins) 644
mansūkh (abrogated) 839–840. *See also* abrogation
mantic (speech) 426
mantis (seer) 420
manuals (of dream divining) 586

manumission, act of 305
manuscript(s) 35, 45, 177–178, 217, 218, 220–221, 234, 555, 617, 697. *See also* codex/codices; papyrus (pl. papyri)
  Arabic and Islamic 200
  Bibliothèque nationale de France
    Arabe (328a 328c 6140) 175–176, 220
    fragments in 170
  bilingual 228
  of Blue Qur'an 220, 225–226
  boxes, for storage of 218, 232, 234
  British Library (Or. 2165) 172, 174, 195 [fig. 13.1], 207, 220
  of caliph 168–169
  Codex Parisino-petropolitanus 175, 177, 207, 221–222
  critical editions of 212
  deluxe/luxury 229, 231–232
  Dublin (CBL Is 1615) 170
  editorial work (on text of Qur'an) 172
  end of line/line-end fillers 173, 174
  Ḥijāzī style/group 175, 221
  illuminated 235, 245
  Istanbul (TIEM ŞE 321) 174
  large, with architectural frontispiece 220, 224
  Nurse's Qur'an (given by nurse of Zirid prince) 235
  paper 226, 228
  as physical objects 220
  of Qur'an 68–69, 205, 218–219, 225, 234, 245, 610
    dating of 288
    early/earliest 11, 58, 68, 171, 173, 187, 202, 204, 212, 219, 220, 264, 283, 288, 302
    as historical document 235
    history of 255
    production of and market for 233
    research on/study of 198, 218, 267
    Umayyad 224
  in Saint Petersburg (NLR Marcel 13, NLR Marcel 18/2 or 9) 173, 174
  Ṣanʿāʾ I 68, 207, 220
  signed by ʿAlī ibn Hilāl (Ibn al-Bawwāb) 226, 227 (fig. 14.2) 228
  Tashkent 168–169, 220, 225
  tradition 8, 173, 302
maqālīd (keys) 640
maqām 567, 573, 576, 578
  in the citadel of Aleppo 248
  concept of 567–568
maqāma 396–397
Marathi (language) 562
marginalia 542, 557
margins 173, 174, 222
  commentaries in 234, 260
  qirāʾāt in 258
  of Qur'an manuscripts 171
marital. *See also* marriage
  relations/relationship 532–533, 536
  rights, reciprocal concept of 535
markers
  chronological, MVL as 357–358
  compositional 320
  minor *(wa iḏ, laqad, wa, yā)* 320
  of possession/ownership 302–303
  stylistic 352
market
  book 264
  for Qur'an manuscripts 233
  role of, in Qur'an production 228
mark(s) disambiguation 270
marriage 346, 369, 449, 612
  contract and dissolution of 450–451
  of and to slaves 305, 450
  temporary 767
martyrdom (of Christians) 84
martyrs, intercession of 742
maʿrūf (that which is good) 465
marvels (of the sea) 687
Marwanid(s) 222
  hypothesis [re. Casanova], 57
masaḥa (wipe; stroke; anoint) 160
Mashīaḥ (Heb.) 160
masīḥiyyūn (followers of Jesus as) 161
al-masīḥ/al-Masīḥ, 160
  Jesus as 161
masjid (place of worship) 130. *See also* mosque(s)
  al-aqṣā 243
  al-ḥaram (sacred house/place of worship) 100, 448
maskh or *masūkhiyya* (metamorphosis) 729
masons 116

masorah 840
Masoretes 155
masoretic (textual/lexical) 610, 614
  exegesis 203, 637, 768
  mode of interpretation 819
masses 785. *See also* humankind; man/men
  revelation as for 781
masters (Sufi *shaykh*s or *pīr*s) 747
materialism 710, 814
materialist (views) 812
material(s) 220, 226, 228, 235, 277, 366, 783
  biblical, from Jewish sources 295
  development (of Qur'an) 68–69
  in early seventh-century Ḥijāz 100–101
  in/of Qur'an 99, 103, 167–168, 176, 218, 280
    cultural 36
    historical 100
    re. on 'hearts of men,' 184–185
  literary (from Judaeo-Christian tradition) 10
  proto-Qur'anic 306
al-mathal wa'l-mamthūl (the metaphor, and the one represented by the metaphor) 726
mathematical (abstractions/methods) 810–811
matn 304
  approach (combined with *isnād)* 628
matrilineal (emphasis on the line of Jesus) 497
matter, struggle between spirit and 747
mausolea 246
mawadda, Qur'anic injunction of 730
maysir 103
Mazdaism/Mazdeans 579, 728
meaning(s) 566, 572, 609, 613–614, 853. *See also maʿnā;* word(s)
  change of [re. variant readings], 183
  esoteric 708
  excellence in, precision in expression *(ḥusn al-maʿnā wa jazālat al-lafẓ)* 377
  as a fixed entity 700
  as formal and substantial 653
  in/and context 568, 659
  levels/layers of 614, 821, 853
  not tied to history or contingency 699
Meccan 840. *See also* sura(s)
  -Medinan historical progression 34
  vs. Medinan suras 32, 42, 643, 836–837
  pagans 515, 516
  parts 347–348
  periods/phases 359
    First, Second, and Third 32, 837
    and jihad 513
media 40, 716
medicine 580–581, 590
  re. medical mediation, and Qur'an 588
Medinan 658. *See also* sura(s); verses
  vs. Meccan suras 32, 42, 643, 836–837
  parts 347–348
  period (1/622–11/632) 359, 502, 515, 621, 623
  revelations 161
meditation 747
  of Muḥammad, in the cave of Ḥirāʾ, 92
  voluntary *(dhikr)* 589–590
meeting (the Lord) *(liqāʾ Allah)* 478
Melkites (Chalcedonian Orthodox) 161
members 365
  re. syntagma 322–323
memorization 233–234 (fig. 14.4)
memory (of Companions and Successors) 635
mêmrā 129–130, 132
merchants 260, 263
  lingua franca of 284
merciful 91
  All-Merciful/the Merciful 569
  from *rḥm* 123
mercy 437
  divine/of God 436, 440, 482
  prescriptions of 587
  Qur'an as universal source of 578
merit-of-sura/-verse 827
merits (of Qur'an)
  faḍāʾil al-Qurʾān 833
  literary 798
Mesopotamian (civilization/environment) 143, 623
message
  divine/of God 143, 421, 547
    oneness of 378
  of the Prophet 405
  Qur'anic 335, 565, 854
  repeated *verbatim* 420–421

messenger(s) 47, 423, 437, 440, 474, 479, 488–489, 747
angels as 489
vs. human beings 571
as channel of communication 158
with counterparts in the Bible 489
of God *(rasūl Allāh)* 100, 489
between God and the prophet 421
preceding Muḥammad 683
referred to as 'prophet' *(nabiyy)* 350
sent to kings around the world 552
sin of rejecting 490
Messiah 497
status of Jesus as 497
messiah, final *(qāʾim* or *mahdī)* 732
messianic
figure (*mahdī* or Guided One) 475–476
movement 154
promise 420
messianism 154, 711
meta-language, *tafsīr* as intellectual 666
metalepsis 771
metaphor 332, 342, 394, 453, 737, 739
in Arabic 300
of garments (for mutual comfort and joy between men and women) 536
majāz 755
Qur'anic 252
metaphorical (exegesis/interpretation) 639, 842
metaphoricity *(majāz)* 383
metaphysical
aspects/issues 722, 760
challenges of science 811
metaphysics 714, 747, 762, 776
monistic (unitive [of Ibn ʿArabī]) 755, 758–759, 761
Qur'anically based 756
traditional scientific 813
meteorites/meteor showers 88, 89
methods/methodologies 651, 652–654, 819, 820
for analysing primary sources 458
of Ibn Kathīr 669
inductive and deductive 662
legal 651, 658
lexicographic 661
linguistic-based 819
literary, biblically informed 363
of al-Māturīdī 774
Muʿtazilī 772
pragmatic 367–368
of al-Rāzī 775–776
of al-Shāfiʿī 654
of al-Ṭabarī 654, 659, 766, 770–771
tafsīr/of Qur'anic exegesis 651, 654, 662, 736, 823
traditional, critiques of 533
metre(s) 411
poetic 422
Mevlevis 585
microcosm *(al-ʿālam al-ṣaghīr)* 760
micro-level (between verses) 321
Midrash 492–493
miḥna (strife) 381
mihrab/*miḥrāb* 131
inscriptions on 247–248
Great Mosque (Qayrawan) 245
Selimiye Mosque (Edirne) 248
military. *See also* fighting; jihad
activity 512, 514, 516, 520
defence 517, 530
expeditions 767
service (i.e., *jizya* in exchange for exemption from) 521
minarets
inscriptions on 242, 246–247
at Jām 250, 251 (fig. 15.4)
minbars 240
Kutubiyya (Cordoba) 248
minhāj 447
miniscule (hand/script) 117
for carving perishable materials 112
South Arabian 123
minorities 695
religious 85
miracle(s) 56, 76, 376, 595, 770. *See also* *iʿjāz*
divine 477
effected by reading Qur'an 672
of healing by Jesus 378
of Moses, parting of the sea 378
of Muḥammad 328, 376, 378, 397
physical 586

of Qur'an 39, 47, 378, 546, 813
characteristics of 694
nature of/inimitability of (*iʿjāz al-Qurʾān*) 743, 794
miʿrāj (Prophet's celestial ascent) 593
mirror
composition 324 (fig. 19.2)
constructions 323–324, 496
Mishnah 496
mission. *See also* message
of Muḥammad 304, 489
universal 489, 552
missionary(ies) 88, 405, 554, 559, 561
activities 16
Christian 3 n.6, 84, 553–554, 559
translations/renderings (of Qur'an) by 558–560
Euro-American 552–553
Muslim 554, 558
modern 29
crisis of uncertainty 602
life, and Qur'an 699
Muslim attitudes 687
setting, and place of 'medieval' in 694
modernism/Modernism 410, 601
modernist(s) 268, 702
current/movement 431
Salafism as 460
Muslim 746
and Qur'an 507, 700
tafsīr (one of seven classifications of, re. Goldziher) 609
modernity 29–30, 409, 411, 502, 505, 671, 696, 698, 852
challenges of 409, 851–852
cultural tribulations of 693
demise of *kalām* in the wake of 694
engaging with 715
and Islamic world 39
and Qur'an 41–43, 857–858
modernization, politics of 269
modernizers 41–43, 44, 46
modesty 696, 731
monastery(ies)
Muslims prevent destruction of 515
of St Pachomius 157
monasticism, Christian 748
Mongols 521
monistic/unitive (metaphysics [of Ibn ʿArabī]) 755, 758–761
monks 515
monotheism 59, 84–85, 92, 146–147, 149, 430, 432
in Arabia 431–432
conventional vision of 759
dualistic 85
Himyarite 90
inviting people to 529
and Islam 87, 92, 257
Jewish 84
spread, among pagans 256
tawḥīd ('Oneness') 431, 440
trend toward 90–92
monotheistic
context/environment 34, 60, 87, 105
movement/revolution 56, 66
period 122
sacred literature/holy books 67, 284
monotheists 145, 479
Arab [re. Hagarenes], 154
biblical 102–103, 104
Qur'anic 56
sectarian milieu of 66
sinning 741–742
month(s) 89
sacred 88, 520, 573, 575, 625–626
monumentalization, method of 232
monuments
funerary 249
at Ḥegrā 118
moon 86
sun and 808–809
morality 59–60, 506
engagement with prophetic 469
moral(s) 14, 99, 465, 468–469
archetype 469
codes 470, 507
/ethical/legal connotations (of verses) 749
injunctions 354, 730
morphemes, common Qur'anic 357
morphology 735, 737, 826
Aramaic 121
mortality 391

mosque(s) 147, 241, 247–248, 515
al-Azhar (Cairo) 232
Almoravid Mosque (Marrakesh) 248
ʿAmr ibn al-ʿĀṣ (al-Fusṭāṭ) 206, 208, 221, 224
Aqmar Mosque (Cairo) 246 (fig. 15.2)
Aqsa Mosque (Jerusalem) 243
of Bībī Khānum 265
congregational (in Samarqand) 231
Great Mosque of Basra 190
Great Mosque of Damascus 218–219, 224
Great Mosque of Qayrawan (Tunisia) 235, 245
Great Mosque of Sanaa 207, 219, 222
of al-Ḥākim (Cairo) 247
of Ibn Ṭūlūn (Cairo) 244
inscriptions on 239, 241, 247
Jamʿa Mosque (Delhi) 241
Khwāja Akhrār (Samarqand) 264
lamps 240, 251–252
large hypostyle 224–225
large parchment volumes made for 228
manuscripts donated to 218
Masjid-i ʿAlī (Isfahan) 248, 249 (fig. 15.3)
in Moscow 260
Ottoman, and inscriptions 241
of Prophet (Medina) 245
Selimiye Mosque (Edirne) 248
ʿUmariyya Mosque (Mosul) 245
mother(s)
of Jesus, Mary as 499
mentioned in Qur'an 489
motif(s) 134–136, 388
of caves 130, 136
indexes of [re. Islamic studies], 689
Judaeo-Christian 435
of Muslim literature 685
in Qur'an 685, 771
mountain(s) 474, 476, 725, 726, 727, 740
crumbling to dust 751
God's manifestation to 740–741
those who live in 136
movable type (printing) 11, 255, 268, 557
MTV, Islamic 580
mūʾadhdhin/muezzin 261, 598
muʿāraḍa 375
mubīn [re. of Qur'an], 133
mufassirūn (commentators; theologians) 46–47, 55, 568
early/pre-modern 807, 811, 814
muftis/*muftiyat* 260, 696
Mughal Empire 678
Mughals 677
muḥaddith 55, 752–753
muḥaqqaq/*rayḥān* 226
muḥkam, pl. *muḥkamāt* (clear, unambiguous [verses]) 736, 737, 820, 828, 842
muḥmila (characters to mark undotted variants of homographs, e.g., *ḥāʾ*, *rāʾ*, *sīn*, and *ṣād*) 226
muḥsinūn (those who strive to reach excellence) 465
Mujāhidīn-e Khalq (Iranian revolutionary group) 700
mujtahids (jurists qualified to make independent legal rulings) 660
mujūn (poetry of wine, love, indecent revelry) 407
mukhtaṣar (genre) 658
mullā 261
multiformity, *vs.* uniformity 185
multilingualism 111
multiplicity 798
multi-religious 502
multivalency 614
muʾmin, pl. *muʾminūn* (believer(s)) 336, 431. *See also* believers
munāfiqūn (hypocrites) 350, 354. *See also* hypocrites
munāsaba or *tanāsub* (suitability; harmony) 797–798, 799
muqaddam wa-muʾakhkhar 642–643
muqarnas (cornices) 250
muqaṭṭaʿāt (detached letters) 729. *See also* letter(s)
muruwwa (generosity; valour; manliness) 402, 405, 465
musammā (nominatum), and *ism* (nomen) 769–770
musāwā (equality) 333
muse(s) 421
museums
databases of collections 252
Evkaf Museum (Istanbul) 219

Turkish and Islamic Arts Museum 169
Türk ve Islam Eserleri Müzesi 219
muṣḥaf, pl. *maṣāḥif* 858. *See also* codex/codices; Qur'an(ic)
ʿ*Alī* 711
al-amṣār (metropolitan codices) 176, 198, 204
arrangement of suras in 495
as 'between two boards' *lawḥayn* 170
canonical form of 491
of Companions 186, 198
written copies of 185–186
destruction of non-conforming ones 188
literature 201, 204
Muṣḥāf al-Madina 270
project, of al-Ḥajjāj 58, 171, 177, 188–189, 627
ur-text of 500
ʿ*Uthmān* (primary codex) 198
mushrik, pl. *mushrikīn* (one who associates [something with God]) 102–103, 104, 431, 574
mushtabihāt (texts) 840
music 580–581, 585, 590
Maroc-hop 582
Muslim heavy metal 580
Muslim rapper response 581
popular 16
prohibited 585
musicians, Javanese 583
muslim 431
Muslim Brothers/Brotherhood 508, 854
Muslim League 507
Muslim(s) 342, 371, 405, 481, 507, 562, 581, 741, 851. *See also* converts/conversions; scholars
in al-Andalus 520
and/*vs.* non-Muslims 44, 510, 518, 542
entertainment/performers 583
and fighting 371, 451, 515, 518, 522
as half-Christian 258
as *ḥanīf*, pl. *ḥunafāʾ* (true) 91
intellectuals 263, 484, 505, 509
-Jewish exegetical relationship 689
and Jews 683
as elected religious community 370–371
muslim (lit., 'one who submits') 431, 849
on Qur'an/scripture 35, 507
modern approaches 46, 75–76
reformers 268, 687
resurrected and judged 479
rule/political domination
acceptance of/submission to 518, 519–520, 523
legitimate *versus* illegitimate 15
in Russia 260, 263, 265
sinning, and temporary punishment 742
as term (synonymous with 'Turk') 542
tradition 267, 609–610
toward Bible 686
women 588, 856
youth 580
mustaqarr (permanent) 729
mustawdaʿ (temporary; trustee) *vs.* *mustaqarr* (permanent) 729
muṭābaqat al-kalām li-muqtaḍāʾl-ḥāl (conformity of the utterance to the requirements of the situation) 567
mutakallim, pl. *mutakallimūn* (theologians) 377, 378, 808
pre-modern 814
scepticism of 810
mutashābih, pl. *mutashābihāt* (unclear; ambiguous; indefinite; allegorical) 567, 586, 820, 828
verses 725, 726, 842
mutawātir (transmitted by multiple authorities to the source, such that they could not have agreed on an error [readings]) 190
Muʿtazila/Muʿtazilī(s) 376, 383, 654, 672–673, 739, 741, 768, 776, 824. *See also* *tafsīr*; theology
approach (rationalist) 766, 797
doctrines/thought/views of 712, 743
on afterlife 482
on the createdness of Qur'an 43
on divine attributes 380
on *ḥudūth* or *khalq* (creation) 381
heresies 710
methods 772–773
milieu 780
scholars/theologians 378, 482, 721, 834
muttaqīn (God-conscious) 336, 341

muwāfaqāt (texts) 843
MVL [i.e., mean verse length], 350–356
  comparisons, and chronology 359
  divergences/variations in 352
  and formulaic density 355–356
  and literary, stylistic, lexical features 357
  of suras 351–352
  and types of introductions 354
mysterium tremendum (of the divine) 548
mystical
  moment *(wārid al-waqt)* 758
  path 754
  system 788
mysticism 669, 753
  eschatology in 473
  Maghribi and Andalusi 757
  philosophical 732
  taṣawwuf 780, 848
mystics (Muslims/Sufis) 747–748, 756, 854. *See also* Sufi(s)
mythology
  Mesopotamian 410
  Persian 556
myth(s) 99, 132
  and kerygma 624
  themes of 629

N

Naassenes (gnostic sect) 157
Nabataean(s) 117–118, 124, 299, 640
  Aramaic 118, 119
  language *(al-lugha al-nabaṭiyya)* 841
  Old Arabic 284
  religious beliefs/worship of 86, 87
  sources/evidence 85, 89
nafs wāḥida 528–529
named [i.e. God], 760
name(s) 82, 100, 725
  Babel 640
  divine/of God 123, 336, 782
    'Allāh,' 786
    al-asmāʾ al-ḥusnā (beautiful) 255, 590, 843
    al-awwal wa'l-ākhir wa'l-ẓāhir wa'l-bāṭin 788
    al-ʿaẓīm (the Supreme) 788
    hierarchies of 760
    ninety-nine 786
    al-raḥmān 306, 354
  of Jesus 159–160
  personal 82, 86, 113
  of prophets 248
naqdī (critical) *vs. naẓarī* (theoretical) *[tafsīr]*, 656, 659
naqlī (traditional [bodies of knowledge]) 776
Naqshbandiyya (brotherhood) 265
narratio 626
narration(s) 315
  in Qur'an, biblical 295
  re. Torah 420
narrative(s) 99–100, 128, 280, 316, 322, 346, 468, 611, 683, 689
  accounts *(qiṣaṣ)* 422
  Arabic 97–98
  -based opinion 712
  of biblical lore/stories 320, 682, 686, 690
  of the Companions of the Cave 129–130
  on creation and the prophets *(qiṣaṣ al-anbiyāʾ)* 688
  of Dhū'l-Qarnayn 132, 136
  haggadic (mode of interpretation, re. Wansbrough) 610, 637, 819
  of Ibn Isḥāq 98
  khabar 493
  of the life of Jesus 93
  linear 566
  material 97, 99
  of origins, Islamic 358, 620
  of Pharaoh 129
  principle (of *taṣrīf*) 495
  of Qur'an/Qur'anic 10, 12, 100, 137, 294, 306, 352, 498, 682, 684–685
  religious 92–93
  stage of *tafsīr* [re. Wansbrough], 652
  synoptic 491
  synthetic 702
narratology 382
al-nās (people; mankind) 571. *See also* humankind; people(s)
naṣārā 161, 309
nasīb 402
nāsikh (abrogating) 839
  al-Qurʾān 839–840

naskh (abrogation) 252–253, 838, 839–840, 844. *See also* abrogation
doctrine of 827
Nasr (god [mentioned in Qur'an]) 86
naṣr (God's help) 161
nastaʿlīq (hanging) 233
nationalism 558, 562
Arab 508
nationalist (Islamic sentiments, in Turkey) 561–562
National Mahommedan Association 507
nation(s) 478, 530. *See also* state
and Islam 506
state 558, 695
nāṭiq (lit., speaking prophet, lawgiver) 723, 724
first to sixth 730–731
synonymous with *samāʾ*, 727
nature 70, 92, 405, 465, 477, 585, 726, 813
and composition/order, design in 814
divine
i.e., of Jesus Christ 83, 141
lāhūt 754
as a divine book 813–814
God's signs in 809
universal 790
world of 732, 806–807, 812, 854
naẓāʾir (lexical item) 639
Nazarenes/Nazaret/Nazara 161–162
naẓarī (theoretical) *tafsīr* as (*vs. naqdī*, or critical) 656, 659
naẓm (coherence; organic unity; composition) 315–317, 381, 694, 795
Qur'anic 370, 378, 802
theory of 13, 370
Nazoreans 161–162
necessity 784
of existence 791
and possibility 790
negated/negation, and affirmation 783, 789
Negro (language) *(al-lugha al-zanjiyya)* 841
neo-fundamentalist (tendencies) 506
neo-Muʿtazilī (theologians) 694
Neoplatonic 790
doctrine 723
sources 732
Neoplatonism 406–407, 721
Neopythagoreanism 721
Nestorian(s) 161
Church 83
New Atheists 54, 60
New Testament 39, 152, 156, 158, 162, 365, 369, 384, 410, 419. *See also* Bible; Gospels
apocalypse 420
canonical writings of 53
Greek 152, 159
and Hebrew Bible 147
on name of Jesus/Christians 161
niʿam (beneficence) 800
Nicene-Constantinopolitan Creed 10, 156
niche *(mishkāt)* 252
night
and day 123, 812
or day [re. verses revealed in], 837
night (journey/ascension, of Muḥammad) 243, 586, 593, 756
Nilometer (in Cairo) 243
Nishapuri (school of exegesis/*tafsīr*) 671, 675–676, 835
nobility 469
dvorianstvo 260
karam 406
nomad(s)/nomadic 116–117, 499
inscriptions of 123
of North and Central Arabia 115
peoples, semi-nomadic 88
pre-Islamic 123
nomenclature (Islamic) etymology of 722
non-Arabic
languages 578, 701
in Yemen 113
words 660–661, 840
non-being 784, 788
non-believers 455. *See also* disbelievers
treaties with 643
non-combatants 516
non-existence
and God's essence 788
and light of existence 790
pure *(ʿadam maḥḍ)* 755
non-existent, and the existent 788, 789
non-Muslim(s) 31, 433, 824
aggressive war against 518
entering heaven 436

non-Muslim(s) (*contd.*)
of pre-Islamic and early Islamic period 91
qua non-Muslims 519, 523
sympathizers (with Qur'an) 545
urged to convert 481
normative 670
command 519
framework, Qur'an as 407
Islam 623
and popular religion 579
norms (acceptable to readers of Qur'an) 189
notes 542. *See also* commentary(ies)
tanbīh 738
with translation of Qur'an 546
novel *(badīᶜ)* traits 395. *See also badīᶜ*
numbering (system of Qur'an) 241
numerology (science of numbers) 586–587, 761
numismatics 11, 167
nursing, and weaning 450
nushūz 530–532, 534–535

O

oases (of Ḥijāz) 102
oaths 320, 335, 350, 353, 363, 389, 572–573
as aspect of political leadership 437
breaking 450
items sworn by *(al-muqsam bihi)* and object of *(al-muqsam ᶜalayhi)* 572
qasam 123
re. accusations and adultery 452
obedience 342, 743
desire to, and fear of disobedience *(targhīb wa-tarhīb)* 340–341
to God 350, 529
not due to a sovereign 508
to Qur'an 340, 505
of wives *(qānitāt)*, to husbands 530–532
objectivity 28, 319
of text, and interpreter's subjectivity 851
object(s) 247
bāzūband (armlet or armband) 247
inscriptions on 239–240, 242
invested with special power 588
material/physical 11, 578, 726
of ocular vision 739
obligations/duties 449
deontological ethics as system of 468
lists of (in Qur'an) 456
markers of [re. imperative verbs], 453
of Muḥammad 451
to pray/give alms 446
religious 513–514, 529, 741, 812
obscure/ambiguous (verses) *(mutashābihāt)* 753
obscuriantia (muskhil) 834
observation 809, 813
occasionalism 808
occasions. *See also* revelation
order of, in the Prophet's biography 625
of revelation *(asbāb al-nuzūl)* 834–835
Occident 599
odes 405. *See also qaṣīda*
on Muḥammad (of al-Būṣīrī) 391
offspring/progeny 536, 708
omens 89. *See also* divination
omissions 567, 614, 711
and additions 173
of words and verses 728
of *muḍāf* (first part of *iḍāfa* construct) 333
omnipotence
of God 472, 477, 481, 482, 808
realm of divine *(jabarūt)* 762
omniscience, divine 784
oneness (of God) 14, 56, 430, 614. *See also tawḥīd*
online 716. *See also* internet
medieval genre of *tafsīr* recreated 698
resources 590
onomastica (in Greek transcription) 118
ontological
differences between male and female 535–536
equality [re. fall of humankind], 528–529
superiority, of men over women 531–533
ontology 761
opinion(s)
heretical 829
personal *(raʾy)* 610, 713
public 850
opponents (of Muslim community) 102. *See also* enemies
oppressed *(mustaḍᶜafūn)* 857
oppression 146, 304, 515

oracle
communication 14
and prophecy (difference between) 424
Oracle (of Apollo at Delphi) 420
oral
context 611
form 282, 425, 636
-formulaic structure/theory 282, 455
shift to written (document) 185, 187, 228
speech, Qur'an as 424
transmission 289, 304–305, 620, 670
of Qur'an 176, 424, 503
orality 142, 455
role of, and written material 610
orator *(khaṭīb)* 493
oratory 88, 770
order 440, 465
conceptual (*tartīb*, of philosophy) 854
of consonantal skeleton *(rasm)* 456
of creation, natural 435
of final events 473
of Qur'anic revelation 347, 493, 545, 643, 716, 835, 837, 840, 854
of suras/chapters 187, 316, 346, 370, 494, 588, 621, 836–837
and *āyas* (verses) 198, 315, 625, 637, 661
orders *(ṭarīqa,* pl. *ṭuruq)* 746
Orenburg Mohammedan Religious Council 260
organization (of Qur'an) 346
as lacking 493
Orient 599
and Occident 790
orientalism 60
orientalists/Orientalists 144, 261, 269, 316, 558, 601, 858. *See also* translations (of Qur'an)
Scientific Association of Russian Orientalists 265
Western 144, 269
on order of Qur'an 316
oriental/Oriental (studies) 258, 553–554
ornaments/ornamentation 170, 173. *See also* decoration
geometric 224
between suras 171
verse counts, ten markers, chapter divisions, etc., 222
orphans 369, 449–450, 490
Orthodox Church 152, 263
orthodox(y)
Greek 82
moderate 702
religion 579
Sunnī 660, 769–770
orthoepic (marks/signs) 172, 206
orthographic
conventions 221
features/enhancement 172
of ʿUthmānic codices 197
peculiarities (in Qur'an) 170, 173
problems (in first printed text) 256
reforms 188
variants 198
orthography 173, 197, 208, 264, 535, 669
ambiguous 176
defective 174
early Arabic 186
of Qur'an 171, 187, 270
Other, ethics of appreciating 546
Ottoman Empire 506, 554, 558, 559, 678–679
vs. Christendom 255
Ottoman(s) 235
calligraphy/calligraphers 233, 584
military threat 542
patronage (of *tafsīr)* 679
and wars with Russia 258, 260
Ottoman Turkey 256, 268
outer/outward/exoteric
shell (*ṣadaf*) 755
ẓāhir, ẓahr 729, 749, 760
vs. inward (sciences) 754–755

P

pacts. *See also* covenant(s); treaty(ies)
ʿahd 520
mīthāq 423, 437, 747
with Muḥammad 517
paganism, pre-Islamic 432–433, 759
pagan(s) 87, 449, 454, 570
Arab/Arabian 518, 570
who abandon polytheism 517–518
ideologies 85

pagan(s) (*contd.*)
Meccan 515–516
mushrikūn 451
spreading monotheism among 256
Syriac word for *(ḥanpā)* 91
(idol) worship 102, 432
page(s)
number of lines per 221
setting (of codices) 174
painters (Indonesian) Qur'anic style of 583
pair *(zawj)* 724
palaeographic
analysis 219
differences in letter shapes 222
group [re. Qur'an MSS], 173
palaeography 11, 167
Palestinian
/Israeli conflict 504
Jesus movement 152, 162
Jews 152
literature 410
palimpsest 198, 207, 222. *See also* codex/codices; manuscript(s)
folios 223 (fig. 14.1)
Mingana (in Cambridge) 222
Ṣanʿāʾ, 173, 176, 267, 288
pan-Arabism 508
panegyric 391, 406
paper 217, 231–232
manuscripts 226, 228
new technology of 677
papyrology 11, 167
papyrus (pl. papyri) 170
Ahnas (dated 22/643) 171
chancery 280
fragments, publication of 267
of Petra 118, 120
parables *(mathal,* pl. *amthāl)* 101, 724, 843
Paraclete 158–159
promised by Jesus 157, 159
paradigm
Qur'anic 19, 409, 411, 666
rhetorical 655, 657
Salafī 700
historiographical 668
paradise/Paradise 132, 252, 393–394, 395, 472, 474, 477, 479, 711, 739
descriptions of 338, 408, 479–480, 755, 796
four rivers of 135
joys of 600
and hell 337, 481, 484
inhabitants/people of 341, 480, 738
levels/ranks of 482, 742
scenes of/in 483, 484, 803
and sinful 408, 742
virgins of *(ḥūr ʿīn)* interpretation of 283
paradox 334
paraenesis 346
paragraph(s) 319, 321
paraklētos (advocate, comforter) mission of 157
parallel(s)/parallelism 322–323, 364, 371, 726
constructions 323, 496
between courtly and religious spheres 408
between universe (macrocosm) and human (microcosm) counterpart 761
paraphrases 542, 555, 557
paraphrastic (commentaries) 556
parchment 170–171, 172, 176, 217, 221, 226, 229
large volumes for mosques 228
manuscripts 234
as aide-mémoires 228
vertical-format sheets of 221
pardon(ing) 470. *See also* forgiveness
parents 449–450
kindness to 469
parody, of Qur'an 389–390
parole (speech) 421
paronomasia 325
paronymy 364
particularities, stylistic and rhetorical 771
particular(s)
and general 658
God's knowledge of 783–784
khāṣṣa, pl. *khawāṣṣ* 534, 809
partner(s)
awliyāʾ, 529
sharik 573
partnership, of men and women 533
part(s) 365, 739
qism 319
and sub-parts 323, 365
passages
awrād 760

as level (of text) 323, 365
from physical world to world beyond death 589
Passover 92
patience/patient 584
as aspect of jihad 613
forbearance 513–514
patriarchal 502
and chauvinist society 856
family (structure) 535–536
Judaic line of Abraham 497–498
systems of power and privilege 43
patriarchalization (of society) 528
patriarchs 83, 684
patronage, official 175
patron(s) 242–243, 248
of Islam, Catherine as 261
name/identity of 228, 252
patronymics 120
patterns 802
of stress [re. words or verses], 801–802
structural (in Meccan suras) 363
pause (*waqf*) 645
peace 522, 523
abode of *(dār al-salām)* 480
penance 448, 449
penning 231. *See also* writing
Pentateuch 456. *See also* Bible
People of Justice and Unity *(ahl al-ʿadl wa-'l-tawḥīd)* 735
People of the Book 46–47, 70, 146–147, 148, 149, 161, 496, 515–516, 521
ahl al-kitāb 145, 244
fighting against 519
kufr, unbelief *(shirk)* 741
people(s)
of the book 85
common *(ʿāmma*, pl. *ʿawāmm)* 749
re. Sunnīs 722
indigenous 579
nomadic, semi-nomadic 88
qawm 287
of Moses *(mūsā)* 145
settled 116–117
perceptions 513
perceptive (faculty) 786
perdition 405
perfected one *(muḥsin)* 762
perfection
human/of man 760, 770
intellectual, goal of 787
of Mary 47
of Qur'an 828
performance 282
musical 583
public, of *tafsīr* 580
ways of *(adab* pl. *ādāb)* 469
pericope(s) 306, 489, 493–494
Pharaoh 129
in Qur'an 12, 129, 494
retribution 100
periodization, of manuscript production 174
periphrasis 768, 832
periphrastic (restoration) 840
permission 333
divine *(idhn)* 762
peroration 315
persecution 516–518, 523
/trials *(fitna)* 517
Persian(s) 299, 553, 555, 640, 671, 702, 753
language *(al-lugha al-fārisiyya)* 841
personality (of Muḥammad) 852. *See also* character
persuasion 128, 335–336
Petra Papyri 118, 120
petroleum, role of 504
Pharaonic (texts) 322, 365
phenomenology/phenomenological 426
approach 289
phenomenon(a)
celestial 811 n.10
of covariance 349
natural 87, 89, 123, 376, 405
philologists 754
Kufan and Basran 299–300
philology/philological 176, 307, 674, 676, 743–744, 820, 824, 825–826, 844
Arabic 2, 4, 672, 696
authority of 671
biblical 4–5, 294, 296, 301, 310
classical 266
criticism, rules of 300
dicta 305
as dominant form of discourse 672, 674

philology/philological (*contd.*)
method 383
perspective/angle 64
and Qur'an 3, 491, 752–753, 770
and religious dogma, dilemma between 829
Semitic 295, 301
studies/scholarship 1, 299, 308, 491, 696
and *tafsīr* 671, 672–674
philosopher(s)
/mystic 791
on paradise 482
philosophy/philosophical 19, 64, 90, 661, 712, 714, 784–785, 826, 851
approaches 304, 850
Aristotelian-Avicennian 776
Avicennan 712
ideas (ipseity, quiddity, existence) 782
interpretations/explanations 780, 782, 791
Ishrāqī (of Illumination) 40, 789–790
Islamic 434, 677, 732
language (of Saussure) 853
mistrust of 829
Platonic 661
problems/questions 725, 854
prophetic 849
and Qur'an 426, 781
and Sufism 785
Phoenician (script) 112
phonemes/sounds
ār 799
īm 800
phonetics 327
photograph(s) 219, 252
of oldest copies of Qur'an 266
phraseology 355
phrase(s) 248
juxtaposing 322
meaning of 638
Qur'anic 391–392, 411
physical
chastisement, symbolic 535
exertion (of religious obligations) 514
harm/torture 515, 531
realm 726
pidgin (varieties) 287
piece(s) 322–323, 365
maqṭaʿ, 319
pietism, Sunnī 672
pietistic, *vs.* political 673
piety 747, 750, 821, 857
Islamic, and death 435
and writing *tafsīr* 827
pigment (analysis) 225
pilgrimage 86, 93, 447–448, 451, 612, 731. *See also* hajj
of Dante, divine 593
prohibitions during 88
rituals of, by pre-Islamic Arabs 88
pillars (five) 612
pious, attributes of (the) 448, 449
place, and direction 739
placement [re. inscriptions], 243
plagiarism 676
Platonic
epistemologies 661–662
philosophy 661
pleasure (of God) (*riḍā*) 483
pledges 453, 747. *See also* oaths
breaking 520
fulfilling 339
pluralism 42
democratic 431
religious 54, 509
poetics 394
European 593
Islamist 412
poetry/poems 88, 228, 299, 303, 380, 391, 395, 584–585, 656, 658, 659, 661, 672, 759, 767, 795, 802
Abbasid 408
as act of encoding 407
Arabic 105, 122, 401, 615, 626
ancient 283, 295
Classical 279, 290
of modern age 408–409
and Qur'an 13–14, 544
secular and profane 388
dīwān (collected poems [of Ibn ʿArabī]) 397
of Hamas and Hizbullah 411
language of 277–278
narrative, Italy's tradition 593
oral 282–283

pre-Islamic 72, 105, 132–133, 284, 285, 394, 401–404, 615, 767
and *iʿrāb* 281–282
Jāhilī 113
of Thamūd 132
of al-Qaeda 411–412
and Qur'an/Qur'anic 13, 72, 121, 133, 391, 394, 401–405, 408, 409, 599, 802
and religion 390–391, 394
role/function of 407, 409
shiʿr 421–422
types/kinds of 397, 405
anti-colonial 409
ascetic and mystical 407
Bacchic, homoerotic, obscene 394
cosmological 392
English, and allusions to Qur'an 594
politico-religious 405
of revelry 407–408
Romantic/European 598–599
secular 388, 391
poet(s) 288, 390–391, 394, 422, 795
English 596
literary language of 284
modern, and use of Qur'anic citations 409
and Muḥammad 375, 403
Persian 598
-prophet, role of 409
Sufi/mystical 391, 594
pointing 222, 225
diacritical 283
qāf and *fāʾ*, 229
pole
celestial equator 810
of Qurʾān 708
spiritual *(quṭb)* 758
polemical
attitude/tone 296, 541, 687
passages (in Qur'an) 352–353
topoi 624
works/treatises 35, 730
anti-Islam 256
anti-Ismāʿīlī 728
polemicists 54
polemics 28, 128, 144, 150, 346, 455, 543, 561–562, 596, 620, 710, 714, 834
anti-Islamic/anti-Muslim 155, 256, 425, 437
anti-Shīʿī, modern 711
against 'association' of other beings with God 354
Catholic–Protestant 542
Christian and Jewish 35, 54, 622
against Muḥammad/Islam 425, 686
pre-modern 142
within Christianity 542
intra-Muslim 562
against Jews 350
against *munāfiqūn* (hypocrites) 350
nature of 558
Qur'anic
against 'associators' *(mushrikūn)* 154
against idolatry *(shirk)* 433
religious 541
between Sunnism and Shīʿism 673
political
movements/upheaval 255, 409
vs. pietistic 673
political science 505
politic(s) 18, 437, 502, 700
of identity 579
of language 546
of modernization 269
and Qur'an 15, 64, 505–506, 548, 583
text as 503
Turkization 268–269
poll-tax *(jizya ʿan yadin)* 301
polysemes, Qur'anic 840–841
polysemy, aspects of *(al-wujūh wa'l-naẓāʾir)* 300
polytheism 84, 91, 517–518, 614
Arab/of Arabia 86, 154
polytheistic
cults 90–91
idol worshippers 102
polytheists 34, 241, 515–516, 643, 742
Arab 154, 156, 157, 520
mushrikūn 514, 520, 573–574
polyvalence, of Qur'anic text 533
polyvalent (readings) 669, 822, 823, 827
poor/destitute 449, 470
oppression of 146
popularizers 39, 40, 41
popularizing (commentaries) 702
positivist (approach) 464

postcolonial
  dynamic 546
  ruptures 504
post-colonialism 502
Postmodernism 601
postmodernist
  approaches *(taʾwīl)* 701
  reading (or radical reading, *al-qirāʾa al-taʾwīliyya*) 699
poverty 504. *See also* poor/destitute
power 569–570, 700
  from angels, jinn, spirits 590
  divine 478, 790
  objects invested with 588
  patriarchal systems of 43
  skewed relationship of [re. marriage, gender issues], 535
  spiritual 603
  symbols of 265
  of words 586, 588
pragmatism 654
praise 323, 395, 397
praxis thought 849
prayer(s) 113, 191, 233–234, 243, 339, 342, 447–448, 513, 520, 523, 529, 573, 583, 598, 612, 731, 738
  ablutions/cleansing prior to 447, 456–457
  of adoration/petition 323–324
  attributed to Jesus 156
  call to 561, 583, 598
  communal or individual 359
  congregational, on Fridays *(al-jumʿa)* 448
  direction of 811–812
  fātiḥa, and Lord's Prayer 10, 156
  formulas, protective 589
  graffiti containing 115
  obligatory *(ṣalāt/namaz),* in Persian 556
  requirement of/obligation to 446, 447, 812
  ritual *(ṣalāt)* 248, 447–448, 465, 589
  rugs 240
preachers, popular 625
preaching 580
predestination 430–431, 694, 769, 772
  divine (al-Māturīdī on) 775
predestinationists 768
predetermination, divine 753
predictions, historical (in the Qur'an) 827
pre-existence (in the heavens) 709
prefaces 542
prelude *(muftataḥ)* 412
pre-modernity 502
prescriptions 454
  of mercy (from diviner/saints) 587
  quasi-legal 350, 354–355
  Qur'anic 505, 856
    aḥkām al-Qurʾān 834
presentation(s) 232, 494
  of Qur'an 182, 188, 189
    copies/manuscripts 224, 234
preservation
  of Qur'an 8, 11
    early copies 232, 234
  of *tafsīr* heritage 678–679
presses
  Asiatic Press (St. Petersburg) 260–262, 262 (fig. 16.3)
  Hindustani Press 559
  Kazan University Press 263
  King Fahd Holy Qur'an Printing Complex 269, 270
pride 534
priest (Heb. *kōhēn,* root k-h-n, 'predict, tell the future') 89
print(ed)
  culture 558
  editions of Qur'an 11, 208, 261, 263
    earliest 3 n.7, 263
    full Arabic text (in Russia) 260
  revolution 693–694, 697
  tafsīr works, availability of 697
  technology 16, 558
  translation of Qur'an, first 542
  uniformity of 233
printing (movable type) 11, 255, 268, 557
prisoners (of war) 451, 520
prklts / periklutos 157
proclamation(s)
  divine 437
  of Muḥammad 497
  in Qur'an 356, 378, 469
Procrustean (approach) 307
production
  of major *tafsīr* works, critical editions of 668

nature/method of 231, 232
of Qur'an manuscripts 222, 235
changes to 229
expense of 220
physical nature of 226
in pre-modern period 233
profane, and divine/sacred 615, 653, 659
profession
of faith, public 518
with the tongue 742
progress 470
prohibition(s) 335
of alcohol 341
of areas (i.e., *ḥaram*) 566
against fighting non-combatants 516
of music 585
during pilgrimages 88
re. marriage 449
promise (of God, *waʿd Allāh*) 412
pronominalization 643. *See also* grammar
pronunciation, rules of 843
proof 315
ḥujja 423, 559–660
of Muḥammad's message, Qur'an as 378
-texts
Qur'anic citations as 721
for Shīʿī tradition 708
propaganda 635
anti-Islamic 258
Christian 137
war 411
property, possession of 303, 305
prophecy(ies) 43, 406, 437, 467–469, 490, 624
after Muḥammad 857
doctrine of 14
and language 408–409
of Muḥammad 146, 365, 370
and oracles, differences between 424
Prophet 100, 741
as a charismatic leader, bearer of God's message 627
names of 248
successor of 504
prophetes 420
prophethood 34, 70, 376, 468, 759
Ismāʿīlī concepts of 732
as manifestation of divine mercy 436–437
of Muḥammad 375, 475
treatment of, in Qurʾān 624
prophetology 133, 490, 496
prophet(s) 375, 376, 419, 431, 474, 489–490, 494, 581, 707, 747
and abilities given by God 435
Arabian 490, 493
bear witness 478–479
biblical 684, 686, 690
as community 489, 492
killing of 146, 149
lawgivers 424, 426, 732
minor 475
missions of 489, 759
Muḥammad's status as 769
Musaylima, as false 389
nabī, nabiyy, anbiyāʾ, 350, 422, 749
preceding Muḥammad 622, 683
in Qur'an 70, 488, 494, 700
and dreams and visions 586
episodes of lives of 491
references to earlier prophets 622
rank of 800
role of/model 140, 409, 437, 495
stories of 99–100, 338, 342, 396, 644, 684
ancient 721
esoteric interpretation *(taʾwīl)* of 730–731
post-Qur'anic 687
studies of 423
as *ummī* 157
propitiatory 247
proscription(s) 315, 335, 404, 587. *See also* prohibition(s)
against initiating fighting 516
prose 389, 626, 795
rhymed 393, 770
proselytism, and translations of Qur'an 228. *See also* missionary(ies)
proselytization 558, 562
Christian 82
prosody, poetic 395
prostration (of angels to Adam) 438–439
Protestant(s) 256, 553
Churches 152
vs. Islam 258
on Qur'an 543–544

proto-Muslim(s) 59, 154
proto-Structuralist (approach) 797
provenance 228, 682
  of Blue Qur'an 226
  of Qur'an 100–101, 284, 383, 592
    and *iʿjāz* 377, 380, 382
    vocabulary 294, 307, 640
providence (of God) 489, 814–815
provision (of/from God) 572, 738
proximity (between God and human servants) 747
Psalms 146, 322
pseudepigraphal (writings) 496
pseudo-correction, absence of 285
psychology/psychological (aspects) 760–761, 852
public 40–41, 697–698, 702
  commodity 580
  reading/texts 155, 239
  rights of 470
  square/sphere 558, 585–586
publications
  British-Indian 263
  of *muṣḥaf* 561
  of Qur'an 255
    early manuscripts 267
    in Latin script 268
    with metal type 268
    in Russia 258, 260
  of al-Ṭabarī and Ibn Kathīr 697
publicists 256
punishment 146, 472–473, 484, 754
  in the afterlife/hellfire 14, 742
  earthly corporal or capital 452
  eternal 403, 481
  ḥadd 40–41, 42
  vs. kindness 134
  in Qur'an 42, 135, 403, 405, 407
  re. *Neṣḥānā* 136
  stories 424
purification (rituals) 85. *See also* ablutions
purity 447, 755
  ritual 184
  spiritual 750

Q

qaḍāʾ, precedence of (over *qadar*) 731
qadar (divine decree) 731, 782
Qadarīs 768
Qadiani Ahmadiyya Muslim Mission 560
qadīr 336
Qadiriyya (Sufi) order 561
al-Qaeda, poetry of 411–412
qāʾim ('one who will arise') 730, 732
  and cancellation of Sharīʿa 727
  Shīʿī beliefs on 475
al-Qalīs (temple) (Ṣanʿāʾ) 89
qānitāt (women obedient to God and husbands) 532
al-qāriʿa ([the hour of] the crashing blow) 474
qaṣīda (polythematic mono-rhymed ode) 401–402, 405, 406
al-qaṣr (restricting statements) 333
qawad (retaliation) 455
qawwali 585
qawwal [re. Nusrat Fateh Ali Khan], 585
qawwāmān 530
q-ḍ-y [root], 446
qibla 811–812
  change of/new 368, 370, 811
    to the Kaʿba 370–371
qirāʾāt (readings) 194, 196, 266, 278, 283, 286, 818, 820, 840
  canonical and non-canonical 199, 205, 289
  corpus of 197–199, 204, 212
  literature on 186, 189, 208, 210
  manuscripts 11, 200
  in margins 257
  medieval tradition of 202
  scholarship, classical 200
  science of 178
  specialist books of 191
  synthesis of 194, 206, 208
  of Umayyad period 206–207
  vowelling of 202
qiṣāṣ 580
qiṣaṣ al-anbiyāʾ (stories of the prophets) 683, 688
  authority for 644
  books/literature 684, 832
  genre 396, 688
qisṭ (equity) 465
qitāl (fighting) 512, 523
  as *jihād al-sayf* 513

in Qur'an 520
quarto volumes 174
quasi-divine status 406–407
quiddity(ies) 782–783, 790–791
Qumran Scrolls 161
quotations/citations 396
of authorities 669
biblical, and passages 686
poetic 299
quasi-quotation (*iqtibās*) (of Qur'anic material) 392
Qur'anic 57, 167, 249, 394, 407, 409, 565, 580, 626, 784
on coinage 175
by Ibn Sīnā 782
qurā ʿarabiyya (Arab villages) 288
qurʾān (reading, recitation, recited text) 183–184, 284, 306, 389, 421, 423
parallels Syriac *qeryāna* 426
Qur'an(ic) 5 n.10, 43, 54, 459, 503, 597, 620, 635, 654, 672, 709, 822. *See also* chronology(ies); codex/codices; manuscript(s); order; palimpsest
and/in Arabic 48, 57, 153, 553
and/on Jewish and Christian
antecedents 31
literature, as derivative from 104
practices 10, 140
and/on Jews/Judaism 10, 144, 145, 147, 295
and/on Muḥammad
as author of 43, 142, 205
life/biography (*sīra*) of 97–98, 621–622
as not a poet 402
approaches to 820 (*See also* diachronic)
atomistic 318, 566, 568, 569, 715, 852, 856
direct/straightforward 40
European and German 46
hermeneutical 499
historical 43
historio-critical 183
modern 35
new 510, 700
secular, *vs.* traditional Muslim 46
traditional 39
arguments in 334, 336
background of 34–35
and Bible/biblical 147, 456
antecedents, stories traced to 685
comparisons 142, 143–144, 490
differences and similarities 47, 491, 546
on equal footing 144, 488
literature/material 48, 59, 142, 143, 686
record, textual superiority over 35
scholars 491
as biblical homily 101
borrowing 142
as clear 39, 41
as a constitution 508–510
as created 378, 769
Muʿtazilī notion of 43, 245
critique of (*odium theologicum*) 490
as dialogic text 566
discourse 335–336, 338, 498, 853
approaches to 495
disjointed character of 346
with Jewish Christianity 309
as divine rhetoric 658
editions of
Cairo edition (1924) 196, 208–209, 241, 264, 268–269
facsimile 11
Golden 265
Renaissance 597
eloquence of 342, 770
equated with human language 655
equated with the Sunna 678
essentialist attitudes toward 7–8
etiquette
ādāb al-Qurʾān 842–843
handbooks (*ḥamalat al-Qurʾān*) 833
formulas 280
glossary of 841
as God's
bayān 659
book (*kitāb allāh*) 245
speech/word 375, 377, 419, 423, 621, 759
holistic method/approach/reading of 318, 522, 523, 533–534, 536, 581
and hostile accounts, in modern times 48–49
importance of 544, 547
in literary studies 395
inclusion in modern 'Canon,' 592
and Jesus 160, 461, 479

Qur'an(ic) (*contd.*)
as 'Law of Muḥammad' *vs.* 'Book' of Muslims 541
logia and *sīra* 628
meaning of 44, 191, 309, 552
levels of 749, 762
as literal/non-literal 744
and task of translators 548
as multivocal 715
mystification of 547–548
nature/status of 66, 245, 374, 694, 819
as (not) divine revelation 142
as eternal/eternity of 42, 298, 374, 378, 381, 699, 709
as exalted/noble 184, 821
as fixed text 16, 182, 203, 267, 305
as a living source of divine manifestation 426
as a living text 36
as in need of clarification 612
as non-linear 601
as non-spatial, non-temporal 183–184
as rooted in context 565
as sacred 580, 771
as *sālim min al-muʿāraḍa* (matchless or immune to emulation) 377
as sent down 'on seven edges' (*ʿalā sabʿat aḥruf*) 185
as silent (*sāmit*) imam 709
as speaking 711
as special, intertribal, fully inflected *ʿarabiyya* 283
as uncreated 245, 389 n.1, 699
as unique/unique style of 277, 375, 378, 389, 395
as universal 42, 578
as word/Word of God 42, 245, 425, 467
and the *Neṣḥānā* 136–137
Noah's Ark 855
original 281, 284
origins of 65, 111, 143
and pessimistic, anthropocentric world-view [re. Neuwirth], 402–403
phrases 391–392, 411
power/use of 589–590
references in 584
to contemporary events 103
to contemporary Jews and Christians 131
to earlier prophets 622
to nature/natural world 806, 814
references to, in literature 594, 596
as reformulation of Syro-Aramaic urtext 309
representations, art historical aspects of 69
revealed
gradually/in stages 338
in seven *ḥūrūf* or modes 209
sale of 260
salvific nature/powers of 672–673, 827
sanctification of, as above history 699
social logic of 101, 103
sources for/of 31, 492
contemplation and inspiration 746
data for Muslims 34
history of communities 104
its own context 99
standardized 194, 203
studies/Studies 7, 28–29, 33, 204, 327, 798
developments of/in 1, 500
in English 342–343, 576
foundational figures in 31
and German scholars 266
history of 35, 284
methodologies of 45
modern 319
as *sui generis* text 363, 388–389
teachings/beliefs of 341, 433
terms used for (*al-kitab, al-dhikr, al-furqān*) 146, 424
transliteration of 155, 168 (*See also* transcription(s))
trilingual 556
understandings of, through Qur'an 545
wording of 782–783
qurʾāniyyūn (Qur'anists) 460
Quraysh 86, 100, 517
infidels of 812
language/speech of 277, 278, 375
qurrāʾ, 289, 645
as reciters of Qur'an; as *ahl al-qurā* (people of villages) 288
quṣṣāṣ (professional storytellers) 623, 635

R

Rabbinic/rabbinic(al)
  elements in Qur'an 491
  literature/narratives 455, 689
  model 623
  texts/sources 496, 653
rabbis *(rabbāniyūn)* 145
radiocarbon (analysis) 171, 221
rāfiḍī (rejectionist, anti-Sunnī) 710–711
raḥīm 569, 799
Raḥmān ('The Merciful One') 92
al-Raḥmān (All-Merciful/the Merciful) 306, 354, 569
al-rajīm, meaning of 301, 305
Ramadan 448
ranks *(ḥudūd)* 732
al-raqīm 137
  interpretation of 129–130
rasāʾil (treatises) 729
al-rāsikhūna fī-l-ʿilm (those rooted/steeped in knowledge) 642, 722. *See also* knowledge
  imams as 708
rasm (skeletal form/outline) 182, 194, 222, 503
  letters 270
  of the *muṣḥaf* 188–189, 191
  orthographic enhancement of 170, 172
  ʿUthmānī 169, 267
  variants 176–177
rasūl (messenger) 438
rational
  contemplation 749
  Qur'anic message as 854
  -theological exegesis *(tafsīr bi'l-raʾy)* 775
rationalism 716
rationalist(s) 376
  investigation 809, 812
  Muʿtazilī approach 766, 797
rationality, role of 854
rayb al-manūn 133
readability 218, 226
readers/Readers 549, 645
  consensus among 196
  fourteen 190
  seven 190–191, 194
readings/Readings (of Qur'an) 105, 182, 185, 190–191, 194, 210, 586, 615, 701. *See also qirāʾāt;* recitation/reciting; variant
  of Abū ʿAmr ibn al-ʿAlāʾ, 286
  of Abū Jaʿfar 190
  alternative/different 188–189, 638, 710
    eight 190, 211
    eleven 190
    fourteen 190, 211
    seven 182–183, 186, 197, 202, 210–211, 221, 261, 266, 268, 286, 638
    ten 182, 190–191, 211
  of ʿĀṣim 190
  authentication of 69, 210
  choice *(ikhtiyār)* between 189
  development/formation of 69, 189, 199
  of Ḥafṣ ʿan ʿĀṣim 268
  Ḥimṣī 191
  with *iʿrāb* 279
  and law 205
  linear 324
  and meaning/*tafsīr* 186, 201, 673
  of Nāfiʿ, 190
  origin of 204
  qirāʾa, pl. *qirāʾāt* 286, 425, 656, 658, 701, 712
    or *ḥurūf* 196
    radical *(al-taʾwīliyya)* 699
    shādhdha 205
  quarrels of theologians over 503
  religious/ritualistic role of 123
  standardization/canonization of 11, 182, 638
    rules of 268
  and tales of miracles effected by 672
  types of
    androcentric 533
    figurative 497
    holistic 523, 534, 536
    intertextual 497
    modernist 700
    polyvalent 669, 822, 823, 827
    sectarian 206
    vocalic 638, 641, 645
  of Yaʿqūb 190
real *(ḥaqq)* 786
Real *(al-ḥaqq)* God as 758

realities (of God and the universe) 758
reality 789
 eternal 482
 ḥaqīqa, pl. *ḥaqāʾiq* 722, 723, 752, 755
  people of the true *(ahl al-ḥaqīqa)* 758
  realization of the true *(ḥaqīqat)* 754–755
 people of singular 714
realm
 of divine power *(al-jabarūt)* 761
 of divine sovereignty *(al-malakūt)* 761
 spiritual 726
Realpolitik 518
reason(ing) 336, 376, 506, 523
 dialectical 659
 human 438, 737, 773, 813
 independent 825
 legal 459
  ijtihād 461, 737
 and reflection 854
 and revelation 732, 855
 in *tafsīr* 659
rebuke *(mann)* 470
recension(s) 222, 459
 of ʿAbd al-Razzāq al-Ṣanʿānī 637
 of ʿAlī (i.e., *muṣḥaf ʿAlī*) 711
 of Ibn Masʿūd or Ubayy 176
 markers of 225
 non-ʿUthmānic 223 (fig. 14.1)
 of Warqāʾ, 637
reception(s) (of Qur'an) 65, 76, 504
 European, British, and American 601
 history of 374, 381, 384
 medieval Latin 76
 by Muḥammad 629
 twenty-first-century 602
 Western 76, 597
recitation/reciting 36, 73, 172, 194, 503, 561, 583, 585, 586, 625, 634–635. *See also* *qirāʾāt*
 art of 754
 canonical 711
  seven 712
  in Sunnī tradition 716
 dhikr 757–758
 differences in 710–711
 elocution *(tajwīd)* 834
 formal 196
 liturgical 424
 matlū (content of) 379
 physical act of 306
 rules of 843, 844
 Sunna of 206
 systems of 185, 198, 277, 278
  qirāʾāt 283
 talismanic uses of 73
 tilāwa (or annunciated word) 379, 760
 times of 589
reciters (of Qur'an) 197
 qurrāʾ, 191
reckoning 754
 ḥisāb 446, 478
recorded events *(akhbār)* 406 n.4
records
 of deeds 474, 479, 574, 576
 written, of revelations 167
redaction 44–45, 206, 372
 of Ḥafṣ 266, 269
 of *muṣḥaf* 45
 of suras 456
redemption 528
 al-furqān 146
reductionism 60
reductionist (approach) 492
redundancy 614
referents, of anaphors 643
reflexive thought *(al-fikra)* 790
reform 16
 agendas (Islamic) 562
 of Arabian customary law 450
 of Qur'anic text 174
 socio-political 426
Reformasi (Period of Reform) [re. Indonesia], 583
Reformation (age) 76
reformers
 Muslim 268, 687
 social 736
reformist (agenda) 558, 736
 of Salafī movement 699
refrain (as litany) 366
refutations 258, 315, 377, 380, 548, 659, 731
 of Marracci 4, 7, 543
 of Muslim doctrine 542
 of Qur'an 2–3

regionalization [re. recensions], 225
regulations 320. *See also* law(s)
rejection *(iʿrāḍ)* 534
relevance theory 320, 367
reliability. *See also* authenticity
  of hadith 44
  of *isrāʾīliyyāt* 682
relic(s)
  adoration 578
  Samarqand 265
religion 30, 44–45, 123, 466, 517–518, 522, 579, 588, 614, 800. *See also dīn;* Islam(ic)
  anthropology of 432
  and the contemporary world 716
  and female and male believers 529
  fighting for the sake of 517
  freedom of 518
  of Islam 45, 365, 376, 506, 510
  Mesopotamian and Greek 90
  monotheistic 149–150
  new 141, 146, 149
  origins of 58
  popular 578–580
  sacred history of 44
  and science 807, 809–810, 855
  South Arabian 86
  study/analysis of 28, 30, 45
    pre-Islamic 432, 433
    Western approaches toward 685
  and 'web of significance,' 92–93
religiosity, of Jews and Christians 147
religious
  movements 255
  studies 7, 30, 53, 823
  zeal 88, 412
Religious Administration of Muslims in Tashkent 265
remarriage 450
remembrance *(dhikr)*
  of death *(al-mawt)* 435
  of God 747
  People of *(ahl al-)* 145
  /reminder [re. name of Qur'an], 145, 146
Renaissance (thinkers) 256
renewal 405. *See also* reform
  and development of Islamic religious, political, and social thought 505
renunciation (of this world) 755
repent(ance) 520, 573, 742
  of Moses 740
  and punishment 452
repetition 321, 325, 341, 497, 498, 658
  effective *(takrār muʾaththir)* 338
  phrasal 364
  thematic 369
reports 684. *See also* hadith; tradition(s)
  about Ibn ʿAbbās' teachings 636
  ascribed to Muḥammad and Companions 767
  on biblical lore 686
  of foreign origins [re. *isrāʾīliyyāt],* 687
  Muslim 685
  prophetic *(gharīb al-ḥadīth)* 841
  from successors 609
  and traditions 682, 684
research
  institutions in the West 702
  new tools of 689
resolve *(ʿazm)* 406
responsibility, moral (*taklīf*) 439
resurrection/Resurrection 102, 334, 336, 431, 473, 477, 482, 754. *See also* afterlife; hereafter
  and afterlife 34
  argumentation oath to prove 573
  as beginning of second life 482
  of the body/bodily 394, 481
    belief in 472
  Day of 435, 476, 477, 589, 740
  of the dead 472, 572
  and judgement 14
    qiyāma 489
retaliation
  lex talionis 452
  qawad 455
  qiṣāṣ 451
retranslations (of Qur'an) 542–544. *See also* translation(s)
retribution 34
  divine 100
  violent 535
return *(maʿād)* (from annihilation to existence) 481–482

rhetoricians 329
 Arab 332, 422
Rḥmnn (lit., 'the merciful') 122
rhyme 47, 121–122, 172, 320, 325, 338, 346, 349, 362–363, 389, 411–412, 455, 581, 799–801
 clausula 321
 end- (of verses) 566
 īm 799
 īn, ūn 800
 īr 799
 on *-iyyā* 392
 patterns 350
 prose 380, 770
 in Qur'an 32, 121, 582
 rhyming parallel 408
 and rhythm (*fāṣila wa-īqā*ʿ) 337
 schemes 350, 582
 in translations 555
rhythm(ic) 320, 338
 *īqā*ʿ, 337
 structure (of Qur'an) 801
Riʾām in Ḥimyar 89
ribā (usury) 453
Right (those on, *vs.* Left) 479
righteous 134
 ṣāliḥīn 490
righteousness 790
 doing 147
 ṣalāḥ, 465
right(s) 470
 of ʿAlī 729
 of divorced women and widows 339
 of husband 532, 856
 of the imams 710
 of men, over women 530
 path 488
ring
 composition 324, 364, 369, 404
 structures 425
 theory of textual cultural anthropology 382
rituals 36, 59–60, 92, 115, 123, 447, 746
 ablution/purification 85, 123
  and wiping feet 205
 of circumambulation 89
 communal 561
 Islamic 730
 Qur'anic 59–60
riwāya (transmission of reports) 722
rococo 544
Roman Catholic (church) 152
Roman Church 596
Roman Empire 81–82, 105
Romans 82, 84, 579
romanticism/Romanticism 544, 597
Romantics 600
roundel (on façade of Aqmar Mosque, Cairo) 246 (fig. 15.2)
rūḥ al-qudus ('holy spirit') 439
rule(s) 447
 foreign, submission to 507
 juristic *(aḥkām)* 466
 of Muḥammad and his household 449
 Muslim, legitimate *vs.* illegitimate 502, 503–504
 normal *(istiṣḥāb al-aṣl)* [re. grammar], 342
 and principles 776
 from Torah 452
ruling(s) 656
 and doctrine 651, 652–653
 ḥukm as 446
 legal 210, 820, 826, 839
al-ruqūd 130
Russian (retranslations [of Qur'an]) 543
Russkiy gosudarstvenniy istoricheskiy arkhiv (Russian State Historical Archive; RGIA) 260
Rustamids 734

S

sabab, pl. *asbāb* (cause) 137, 423
 technical meaning of 838
Sabbath 640
 observances of 148–149, 162
sabbiḥ (extol) 448
Sabeans/Sabians (Ṣābiʾūn) 85, 147, 298, 365, 477, 479
ṣabr (patient forbearance) 512, 513, 523
 as *jihād al-nafs* 513
Sabra and Shatila (Massacre) 410
sabt (Sabbath, Saturday) 640

sacred 252, 408, 585, 599
calendar 448
history 44
and Shīʿī cause 711
houses 88
language of 546
months 88, 573, 575, 625–626
of Dhū'l-Qaʿda, Dhū'l-Ḥijja, and al-Muḥarram 520
fighting in 451, 625
and profane, comparison of texts 615
provenance (of Qur'an) 592
revelation, and secular literature 601
scriptures, as historical texts 383
sites 88, 578
spaces 105
texts 256, 365, 548
sacredness
baraka 218
of the Book, denial of 853
of earlier copies (of Qur'an) 232, 234
sacrifice 93
of Abraham 131–132
animal 89, 123
pagan 448
of son of Abraham, re. Ismail 492
sacrificial (offerings/animals, *hady* and *budn*) 447–448
ṣadaqāt 449
sādin (pl. *sadana*) (guardian of a sanctuary and its idols) 89
Safaitic corpus 114
Safavids 234, 678, 713
vs. Ottomans 714
safe-keeping *(ḥirz)* 458
sages 420, 715
ṣaḥifas 636
sāʾiʾ (travel) 448
saint *(walī)* 714
sajʿ, 266, 380, 393, 802
or rhyming prose 422
sakar (what produces intoxication) 341
salaf (predecessors; pious ancestors) 844, 851
al-salaf al-ṣāliḥ, 460
and Sunnī *tafsīr* tradition 669, 670
Salafī(s) 54, 60, 697, 823
commentaries 854
movement 660, 696
school *(al-madrasa al-turāthiyya* or *al-taṣawwur al-salafī)* 699
views/paradigm 560, 668, 700
Salafism 460
ṣalāḥ, 465
ṣalāh/ṣalāt (prayer) 122, 448
sale 452
of Qur'ans 260
ṣāliḥ (pious person) 465
Salsabīl 392
salvation 365, 404 n.3, 405, 408, 762
in the Hereafter 747
history 17, 623–624
design of 489
in Qur'an 494
as manifestation of divine mercy 436
path *(dīn)* 465
powers of 585
Qur'anic understandings of 436
salvific
nature of Qur'an 827
powers of Qur'an 672–673
samāʾ (sky, heavens) 727
al-ṣamad 303, 782–783, 841
meaning of 301, 305, 308
Samanids 556
Samaritans 59
sanad-cum-matn (study/analysis) 626, 629
Ṣanʿāʾ I (codex/palimpsest) 154, 169, 172–173, 176, 207–208, 222, 288
publication of 267
sanctification (of Qur'an) as above history 699
sanctuary (Abrahamic, proper location of) 496
Saracen, as term 542
ṣarfa (turning away) 379–380
ṣarḥ, 129, 137
Sasanian Empire 83–85, 105
Satan 338, 394
and evil 70
and fall of humankind 528
jihād against 751
Shayṭān 438
'satanic verses,' 434, 627
satisfaction (of God) *(riḍwān)* 483

saved *(saʿīd)* 742
sawād al-aʿẓam (the great multitude of the Muslims) 672
s-b-ʾ [root], 354
s-b-t *[*root*]*, 640
scepticism 44, 624, 808
  re. of sources 55
  of some *mutakallimūn* 810
schism and dissent *(fitna)* 854
scholars/scholarship 29, 60, 554
  -colleagues *(aḥbār)* 145
  European and American 553
  exegeses for and by (in Arabic) 714
  German 331
  intercession of 742
  legal 625, 752
  Muslim 279, 288, 505, 508
    collegium of 268–269
    feminist 527, 533
  of Oman 735
  of Qur'an 53
  Qur'anic 4–5, 8, 64
    contemporary 798
    contextual 129
  Shīʿī 503–504, 834, 854
  on *tafsīr* 698
  ʿulamāʾ, 46, 468, 697
  Western 559
School of Oriental and African Studies (SOAS) 329
school(s)
  of Ibn ʿArabī 714
  Islamic 652
  of legal thought (*madhhab*s) 460
  modern *(al-madrasa al-ḥaditha)* 699
  Peripatetic 789
  of readings 189–190, 266
  Salafī *(al-madrasa al-turāthiyya* or *al-taṣawwur al-salafī)* 699
  of thought 797
science(s) 716, 727, 787, 809, 814
  and/in *tafsīr* 19, 795, 806–807, 812–815
  and/of Qur'an 315, 317–318, 737, 854, 855
    approaches to 43–45
    classical 20
    interpretation 744, 806–807
    of the kernels of *(ʿulūm al-lubāb)* 755
    outward and inward 754
    truth of 813, 815
  associated with colonialism 813 n.13
  astral 807
  and faith, relation between 855
  and Islam 17, 807, 813, 815
    development of 608
  metaphysical and epistemological challenges of 811
  modern 76, 812, 855
    and Qur'an 434, 812
  process of acquiring 781
  and Qur'anic references 814
  rational *(ʿaqlī)* 776–777
  and religion 807, 809–810, 855
  religious (exoteric and esoteric) 722
  social 695
  Sufi 750
  terminology from 809
  Western natural 507
Scientific Association of Russian Orientalists 265
scientism 814–815
  challenges of 806
Scientology (Eighth Dynamic of) 59
scribal
  centres 117
  institution/profession 419–420
  practices, North Arabian and Syrian 119
scribe(s) 116, 222, 268, 301–302
  royal *(al-kātib al-malikī)* known as Golden Pen *(zarīn qalam)* 232
scriptio continua (of Late Antiquity) 171
scriptio defectiva 198, 221, 289
  rasm 283
  vs. scriptio plena 170
scriptio inferior 172–173, 176, 207–208
  dating of 208
scriptio plena 170, 172, 173, 222
scriptio superior (later text) 172–173
script(s) 173, 226, 228–229
  Ancient North Arabian (ANA) 113, 115, 117
  Arabic 118, 198, 270
  cryptic 729
  Hismaic 118
  for inscriptions 252 (*See also* inscription(s))

script(s) (*contd.*)
  kufic 222, 228, 235, 243–244
    floriated 252–253
  Latin 112
  of Mecca and Medina 169
  monumental 112, 117, 222
  of *muṣḥaf* 174
  Nabataean 114, 118
  Phoenician 112
  of Qur'an 169, 171
    as initially defective 57
  rounded, proportioned [re. Six Pens], 226
  south Arabian 729
  South Semitic 112
  style of 174–175
    B Ia 175
    bold, with colors, on objects 242
    cursive forms 119
    hanging *nastaʿlīq* 233
    Ḥijāzī 223 (fig. 14.1) 265
    O I 174
    round 228
    uniform 222
  Thamudic 113
  transitional 118, 119 n.4
scripturalism (Qur'anic) 844
scripturalization 503
scripture 140–141, 623–624
  Arabian monotheistic 280
  Baha'i 59
  Christian 140, 554
  deriving rulings and doctrine from 651
  devices to explicate 768
  esoteric reading of 708
  immune to criticism 827
  Islamic 601
  Jewish 140
  as *kitāb* 284, 424, 461
  pre-Qur'anic [re. Jews and Christians in possession of], 145
  reconciling science with 854
  reference to, in poetry 411
  revealed 365, 686
  unity of 613, 615
scrolls 218
sea(s) 474, 476
  fetid [re. Dhū'l-Qarnayn], 134–136
  parting of, miracle of Moses 378
season(s)
  and pilgrimage 88
  spring 92
  verses revealed in 837
secrecy, and openness 337
secret
  of secrets *(sirr al-sirr)* 751
  of secrets/innermost secret 707
sectarian
  allegiances 245
  aspects of the early tradition 707–708
  environment, and *tafsīr* 674
  milieu, Judaeo-Christian 624
  rivalry 235
sectarianism 228, 562
section(s) 365
  and subsections 321, 323, 365
  in suras/dividing suras 368, 369
sect(s) 594
  and Islamic schools (shaped *tafsīr* methods) 652
secular (settings [of Qur'an inscriptions]) 240
secularism 40, 411
sedentary 502
seeing (God, possibility of) 740
seers 419
segment(s) 322–323, 365
  bimember 323
self
  -causing agents 54
  -disclosures, divine 757 (*See also* unveiling)
  formation of *(tazkīya al-nufūs)* 469
  lower *(al-nafs al-ammāra)* 514
  -manifestation, divine 759
    epiphaneia 421
  -referential(ity) Qur'anic 72, 354
  -reflexivity 60
  understanding of *(fiqh al-nafs)* 468
sema (sign) 420
semazen/twirler 585
semeion (sign *enthymeme*) 422
seminary(ies)
  Christian and Jewish 27
  for Islamic Theology 27

Qur'anic (teaching seven canonical readings) 211
Shīʿī 677
Turkish theological schools 27
semiotics 852–853, 856
Semitic Civilization Thesis 10
sensation 789
sense(s)
five outer and five inner 786
and meaning, distinction between 853
wujūh 614
sensory 470
perception, world of 724
sentence(s)
conditional 337
meaning of 565
parts of 332
structure 338, 642
types: affective, declarative (*khabariyya*) 335
verbal 335
separators (between chapters) 222
Septuagint 155, 158
sequence 365
and sub-sequence 323, 365
Serbo-Croatian, translations (of Qur'an) 559
sermon(s) 394
English 596
sex/sexual 536
relations 531, 535
forbidding illicit 339
unlawful 452
shaʿāʾir (rites; ceremonies [of pilgrimage]) 448
shadda 172
shādhdh (irregular; non-standard; non-canonical) 199–200, 201
readings/variants 183, 189–191
Shāfiʿī (legal methodology; *madhhab*) 658, 835
fiqh 661
jurist (*faqīh*) 752–753
shahāda (creed), *taʾwīl* of 730
shaping (of Qur'an text, to fit space) 250
sharaʿa (promulgate; institute) 446
shares (of estate) fixed 450
sharʿī (objectives) 661
sharīʿa 446
level of (outward practice of faith) 714
Sharīʿa (external law of Islam) 318, 467, 505, 722, 731–732, 737, 752, 754
application of 855
cancellation, abrogation (by *qāʾim*) 727
classical demands of 699
in constitutions or civil codes 461
-derived political ethics (*al-siyāsa al-sharʿiyya*) 468
esoteric interpretation of 730–731
as immutable 42
Muslims receive 370–371
promulgated (by *nāṭiq*) 727
Qur'an-based (*al-sharīʿa al-qurʾāniyya*) 470
role of 510
shayāṭin 438–439. *See also* Satan
Shaybanids 265
sheets
full-*baghdādī* 230
loose 218, 232
Shīʿa/Shīʿī 673, 711, 713–714, 722, 824. *See also* Imāmī(s); Ismāʿīlī(s)
and alternative sacred history 711
defined 717
doctrines/tenets 728, 732
exegesis/commentaries 668, 707–708, 709
and emerging female voice in 716
first major Persian 712
traditional 676, 713
ghulāt (extremists) 671, 721
imams 752 (*See also* imam(s))
rāfiḍī (rejectionist, anti-Sunnī) 710–711
religious establishment 747
on revelation 377, 711
Sufis 660, 714–715
-Sunnī rivalries 684
themes/issues 710, 748
and view (of Qur'an) 43, 246, 503, 673
rejection of ʿUthmānic recension 711, 716
works/treatises 615, 651, 672, 699
Shīʿism 253, 714
and Sunnism 673
Twelver 249
shirʿa, and *minhāj* 446–447

shirk 808
shrine(s) 103, 218
  at Mashhad 219, 234
  at Qum 219
sh-r-k [root], 354
sh-r-ʿ [root], 446–447
shurūḥ (commentary) 674
sh-w-r [root], 461
ṣibgha 137, 791
  Allāh 133
Ṣiffīn, battle of 504
sign(s) 34, 421
  āya, pl. *āyāt* 183, 363, 405, 423, 758, 796, 849
    of God 149, 436, 806
    narrative examples of 422
    in Qur'anic sense 408
  and 'conditions of the Hour' *(ashrāṭ al-sāʿa)* 474–475
  divine/of God 146, 421, 482, 741, 852
    in nature 809
  Heb. *'othôt*, sing. *'ôth* 420
  in nature or history 320
  or omens 586
  pausal 266
  reflecting on 377
sijjīl (baked clay or stone) 306
Sikh (scriptures) 59
ṣila 643
silkscreens 219
simile(s) 332, 342, 573, 796
sinful *(fisq)* 452
singing *(ghanniya)* 583
sinners, grave (as unbelievers, *mushrikūn*) 741–742
sin(s) 89, 452, 614
  of Adam in the Garden 436
  azlām (major) 452
  hamartiology (study of) 436
  of rejecting messengers 490
sīra (biography of the Prophet) 51–52, 54, 66, 376, 621–622, 627–628, 644. *See also* biography
  accounts/literature 627, 838
  and historical accuracy 55
  on pagan traditions 84
  and Qur'an 52, 56–57, 349 n.1, 358, 621, 623
    exegesis *(tafsīr)* 17, 423, 611, 622, 627–628
ṣirāṭ jaḥīm 479
Six Pens (Ar. *al-aqlām al-sitta;* P. *shīsh qalam*) 226, 229
siyāq 567, 571, 573, 576, 578
  al-mawqif 567
  al-naṣṣ 567, 570, 574
size 175, 231
  of folios 173, 174
  of script [re. monumentalization], 174
  standardization, of paper 229
slander/back-biting, as forbidden 470
slaughter, ritual 448
slavery 449–450
slaves 449
  freeing of *(taḥrīr raqaba)* 450–451
  legal status of women 767
  marriage of 305
sleep 785
  and death 785
sleepers in the cave [re. *Sūrat al-Kahf*], 129, 489, 644. *See also* Companions of the Cave
social 700
  change/upheaval 409, 506
  equals 455
  order 695
  structures 458
  theory 54
  values 506
socializing 287
society 388, 468
  civil, Islam-oriented 484
  contemporary 431
  democratic, United States as 581
  as patriarchal and chauvinistic 856
  Western 573
Society for the Promotion of Christian Knowledge (SPCK) 543
sociological (perspective/angle) 64
sociology 505
  methods of 36
socio-political
  ideas 507
  interpretation 506
  prosperity 505
  realities (of Yathrib/Medina) 503

solar system *(al-niẓām al-shamsī)* 812
something *(al-shay')* 783
  discussion of 788
son/Son
  of Abraham, identity of 492
  of God, Jesus as the preexistent 152
  of God, ʿUzayr/al-Masīḥ as 148
soothsayer *(kāhin)* 375
soothsaying 133
sorcery 578
  proscribed 587
soul 474, 724, 789, 796, 849
  at death/death of 481, 482–483
  descriptive accounts of 470
  disembodied 747
  emanation of (from Intellect) 731
  human 747, 782, 787
  illumination of 790
  immortality of 785
  jihād against 751
  or spirits, of martyrs *(arwāḥ al-shuhadā')* 483
  at peace *(al-muṭma'inna)* 747
  of prophets 492, 725
  purification of 749
  reunited with bodies 481
  single *(nafs wāḥida)* 528–529
  sorted into classes 477
  as synonymous with heart 786
  universal 790
  World of 732
sound 743
  patterns 801
source(s) 667, 689, 834
  al-ʿayn 722
  biblical (traditional and apocryphal) 294
  Byzantine 85
  Christian 131, 498, 685
  -critical model 352
  Hermetic 732
  late antique 105, 131, 138
  literary 9, 294, 296
  Muslim, validity of 620
  Neoplatonic 732
  non-Muslim 433
  of/for Qur'an 33, 492, 616, 834
  pagan 85
  Patristic 131
  post-Qur'anic 348
  primary 64, 111
    Arabic 2–3, 296
    and methodologies for analysing 458
  of *sīra,* and its historicity 628
  Syriac 85, 304, 548
South Arabian studies 295
South Asian (translations) 553
sovereignty 570, 695
  divine/of God 435–436, 440
    absolute *(rubūbiyya)* 747
    ḥākimiyya 855
    realm of *(malakūt)* 762
spatial
  boundaries of Qur'an 16
  origin 359
speaker (and addressees) shifts of 320
specialists, need for 635
speculations *(wahm)* 645
speech 184, 332, 469, 657, 842
  act 653
  direct *(kalām mubashir)* 337–338
  divine/of God 377, 709, 741, 772
    essential *(al-kalām al-nafsī)* 743
    eternal 459
    kalām Allāh 376, 380–381 (*See also kalām*)
    Qur'an as 378
  initials (re. *bal, kallā*) 320
  mantic 426
  prophetic 422
  Qur'anic, formal aspects of 71
  of Quraysh 277
  virtuous 470
spirit
  animal 790
  divine/of God 439, 709
  intercession 578
  and matter 747
  nafs 481
  psychic 790
  rūḥ, pl. *arwāḥ*, 481, 751, 758, 787
    holy *(al-qudus)* 142
    world of *(ʿālam al-)* 756
spoils (of war) 613, 751
sponsors 242

stages (sing. *navbat*) 753
stand (for Qur'an)
giant stone *(lawḥ)* 265
for loose-leaf sheets 232
standard deviation (of sura) (SD) 350–351
standardization 182, 222
of large hypostyle mosque 224
method of (*āyat bar kinār;* 'with freestanding verses') 233
of practice 221–222
of seven sets of *variae lectiones* 209
of sizes, paper 229
of text of Qur'an 58, 187, 199, 201, 204
timeline of 305
and uniformity of printing 233
of the ʿUthmānic skeletal text 188
stars/planets 86, 474, 476, 809, 812
motion of fixed 808
state 247. *See also* government
Abbasid 406
democratic 506, 507
Islamic concept/notion of 505, 854–855
based on Sharīʿa 855
Muslim 508
secular 506
station (of the heart) 761
statistical analysis 837
status
of Jews 145
legal (of a slave woman) 767
of Muḥammad 375–376
steadfast *(al-ṣābirīn)* 490
stemmatics (families of manuscripts) 222
stones 87–88, 754
for sacrifice *(anṣāb)* 103
stoning, debate over 711
stopping places *(waqafāt)* acceptable *(ḥasana)* *vs.* full verse endings *(tāmma)* 187
stories 105, 735–736
of Abū Jahl and the rabbis 768–769
of Adam 364, 368
of the ancients *(asāṭīr al-awwalīn)* 99
biblical 17, 682, 688
of Israelites 145
Christian 130
completeness of 499
of Ibrahīm 784
illustrative 672
Jewish 48
Qur'an retellings of 33
and legends 687
of Mary, retelling of 498
of prophets 396, 683–684
of the Qur'an, artistic portrayal *(al-taṣwīr al-fannī)* 798
storytellers 628, 683
storytelling
Qur'anic 73
Sufi metaphysical 759
straight path/bridge *(ṣirāṭ)* 479
strife 518
structural
analysis approach 143
complexity, of Medinan suras 366
unity (of Qur'an) 494
within each sura 32
of longer multi-thematic suras 320–321
of suras of Meccan period 32
structuralism 34
French 624
structure 834
chiasmus 321
cyclical in nature 369
literary 47, 349
morphological 840
pairing 366
of (text of) Qur'an 8, 12, 65, 143, 319, 321, 322, 372, 381, 799
inner/internal 65, 500
of suras 321, 362, 363, 364, 366, 369
inner 13
synchronic approach to 13
syntactic 641, 643
thematic 346–347
style/stylistics 393, 394–395, 712, 715
development 358
Maghribi 229
of Qur'an 8, 12, 46, 122, 327, 330, 336, 343, 390, 600
copies [i.e., O I, O Ib, etc.] 174
habits of *(ʿādāt al-kitāb al-ʿazīz)* 338
as inimitable 566
of Meccan and Medinan parts 348
quality *(bayān)* of 771

sun/Sun (*contd.*)
  place of setting of [re. Dhū'l-Qarnayn], 134–136
supercommentary 45, 829
superfluity [re. Todorov], 613
superiority (ontological, of men, over woman) 531–533
supernatural
  elements, of Qur'anic/Muslim worldview 435
  in Qur'an 14, 437–438
supersession 839
superstitions 89, 92, 369, 578, 746
supplications 335, 447
support(s) (writing)
  material [e.g., parchment, paper], 217
  papyrus, flat stones, palm ribs, shoulder-blades 167–168
  solid 239
suppression 304, 839
sura(s) 323, 346, 389, 393, 424, 582, 583, 735. *See also* order
  allusive nature [re. of *al-Kahf]*, 134
  arrangement of 317, 493, 495
  beginnings and endings of (and correspondence) 317–318, 321
  building blocks of 363
  categorization of 643
  and Christian hymns 57, 154
  coefficient of variation (CV) of 351
  as complementary/conceptual pairs 319, 425
  content of 366, 491
  context of 366, 371
  dividers between 188, 222
  divisions into/of 318, 346, 359, 368
    into textual blocks 356
  dynamic of 370–371
  final two 588
  first thirty [re. reorganized by Welch], 316
  groups 315, 370
    thematic 319
  and Ibn ʿArabī, poems for each 407
  internal
    dynamics of 495
    organization of 491
  introductions of 353–354
  late additions to 456
  with legal material 355
  long/length of 372
    formulaic 425
    sections 13
    unity and coherence of 364
    verses in 349
  on luster tiles 244
  macro-level (between suras) 321
  as mantic speech 424
  Meccan 32, 121–122, 284, 320, 355, 359, 455–456, 474, 548, 656, 735, 801
    as formally/thematically defined verse groups 362–363
    as reworked Christian hymns 154
    as spiritual 42
  Meccan *vs.* Medinan 32, 42, 643, 836–837
  Medinan 160, 320, 355, 363, 455–456, 656, 735, 801
    on law and administration 42
    as thematically complex, longer 366, 372
  merit-of- (or merit-of-verse) traditions 827
  number of letters, words, etc., 835
  and oaths 353
    on pattern *wa'l-fāʿilāt* 572
  order/sequence of 168, 173, 222, 621, 836
    canonical 661
    longest to shortest 316
    textual 625
  pictures of 583
  and *qaṣīda,* structural parentage between 404
  rearrangement of 359
  redaction 351, 456
  re. inscriptions and citations of 240
  relationship between 315
  of Sharīʿa [i.e., *al-Baqara*], 370
  short, terse 425
  spirit *(rūḥ)* of individual 397
  structure of 316, 320, 362, 364, 494
    inner 13
  style/stylistics of 352, 362
    parameters of 356–357, 358
  by sura 659, 660, 801
  textual analysis of 352
  thematic links between 346

theme of
ʿ*amūd* 13, 318–319, 370–371
eschatological 473
titles 225, 247
named after prophets 489–491, 495
transposing letters of 728
as units 32, 72
as unity 318–319, 320, 358, 364, 367
and verses 317–318, 319, 829
surrealism 796
suspension (of composition) 338–340
sustenance, lawful means of 754
Suwāʿ (god mentioned in Qur'an) 86
Swahili (translations [of Qur'an]) 559–560
sword verse 573–574
syllable(s) (to measure verse length) 350 n.2
syllogism, Qur'anic 422
syllogistic demonstration *(enthymeme)* 422
symbiosis 688
symbolism 14, 761, 791, 800
of the *basmala* 751
of death and rebirth 408 n.5
of (mysterious) letters 303
symbols 265, 669, 755, 758
of paradise (green) 479
of unity 370
world of 849
symmetry(ies) 322
game of 322
indicators 364–365
vs. linearity 365–366
principle of 365
total: between members, segments, or whole pieces 324
synagogues 147
of Jews, Muslims defend 515
synchronic (study of Qur'an) 372
synecdoche 244
of the particular for the general 771
synergy 688
synonymous 542
parallelism 323
synonyms 173, 660, 834
naẓāʾir 841
tarāduf, works on 300
synonymy(ies) (similar to similar) 318, 323, 325, 364
syntactic (nature) 643
syntagmas 321, 322
syntax 669, 796, 834
defined 315
of Qur'anic text 321
synthesis
of al-Ghazālī 787
of reason and revelation 732
Sufi-Shīʿī exegetical 762–763
of variant readings 197–198, 212
synthetic approach, *vs.* diachronic view 320
Syriac 299, 308, 424, 640
canonical and/or proto-scriptural urtext 57
Christianity, texts of 128
church *qeryāna* (lecture) 424
influences on Qur'an 199, 295
language *(al-lugha al-suriyāniyya)* 841
New Testament translated into 159
theme 283
translated into Arabic 159
word *kallūtā* 457
Syrian Orthodox Church 83–84
Syrians, *vs.* Iraqis 504
Syro-Aramaic 154–155, 199
urtext 309
systematic (analytical method) 367
systematization (of readings and verse-numbering systems) 189

T

tablet(s)
alwāḥ [re. to Moses], 146
inscribed 130, 137
of lead 129
Preserved *(al-lawḥ al-maḥfūẓ)* 183–184, 709, 755
Tabūk, battle of 521
tafsīr (exegetical commentaries/interpretation [of Qur'an]) 258, 299, 315, 328, 393, 620, 621–622, 626, 658, 661, 669, 695, 795, 798, 810–811, 832, 858. *See also* commentary(ies); exegesis/exegeses; Sunnī; *taʾwīl*
availability of 693, 697
of Bayyūḍ 736

tafsīr (exegetical commentaries/interpretation [of Qur'an]) (*contd.*)
categorization of 819
re. Wansbrough 610–611
classical 376, 668, 669, 671–672, 675, 695
gendered 76
classifications of [re. Goldziher], 609
and context/context-based 566, 654
critical editions of 668, 678
cultural influences on 702
cumulative nature of 607, 676, 678
dating of 655
discipline/field of 16, 18, 666–668, 818, 823
early period of 608–609, 615–616, 672, 722
of al-Farrāʾ, 661
function of 651, 669, 670
genre of 553, 607–609, 611, 613, 662, 669, 671, 698, 819, 820, 821, 823, 832
and Ḥanbalīs 655
history of 35–36, 652, 667, 668, 674–675, 678–679, 696, 697, 698, 722, 823
Ibāḍī 18, 734–735, 737
complete 743–744
of Ibn ʿAbbās 767
of Ibn Sallām 18, 658, 661
in Islamicate languages 18
Ismāʿīlī 18, 721
and *isrāʾīliyyāt* 528, 687, 699
and *kalām* 673, 807, 814
and law 826, 834
literature/books on 16, 186, 191
manuscripts 667
medieval 17, 678, 696
recreated online 698
methodologies 651, 652, 662
of al-Ṭabarī 770–771
modern/contemporary 17–18, 652, 693–694, 696, 699, 701, 702
and internet 698, 702
of Muḥammad ibn al-Sāʾib al-Kalbī 637
of al-Muḥāsibī 656
Muslim 35–36, 303
Muʿtazilī 670, 673–674, 675, 743, 824
Nishapuri school of 671, 675–676
of non-Sufis 19, 752
and other genres/disciplines 652, 662, 668, 826
Ottoman contribution to/patronage of 17, 679
Persian 753
and philology 671, 676, 696
pre-modern 812, 814
professionalization of 672–673
and regional(ism) 675, 702
resurgent activities in 703
of al-Ṣanʿānī 655
of Sayyid Quṭb 383
and science 19, 795, 806–808, 812–815
sectarian (one of seven classifications, re. Goldziher) 609
Shīʿī 18, 671 (*See also* Shīʿa/Shīʿī)
stages of: narrative, legal, lexical, rhetorical, allegorical [re. Wansbrough], 652
Sufi 750, 752 (*See also* Sufi(s))
of al-Ṭabarī 652, 655, 660, 661, 673
texts/works of 36, 558, 609, 611, 672, 684, 697
early 608–609, 611, 672
modern Turkish 701–702
published 668, 698
and theologizing 695
in time of/ascribed to the Prophet 301, 634
tradition 45, 673, 696, 769, 822, 823, 829
and translations 553, 557, 679
types of
anthological 822
bi'l-maʾthūr (tradition-based) 674, 752, 822–823, 828
as collected comments 636
conventional 761
critical and theoretical (*naqdī* and *naẓarī*) 656, 659
encyclopedic 654, 677, 807
haggadic 672
ʿilmī (scientific) 434, 807–808
mawḍūʿī (topical) 696, 716
mystical/esoteric 671, 750, 753
al-nabī 634
outward (*ẓāhir*) 754–755, 760
Qur'an glosses the Qur'an (*tafsīr al-Qurʾān bi-l-Qurʾān*) 715
vernacular 557

writing 637
as an act of piety 827
of al-Zamakhsharī 263
of Zayd ibn ʿAlī 637
taḥaddī (challenge verses) 375, 377–378
tahajjada (pray or keep vigil) 448
taḥrīf (corrupted; warped) 206, 712, 716
biblical text as 494
Shīʿī definition of 711
tajnis (paronomasia) 799
tajwīd (rules of pronunciation, recitation) 843
takhfīf 641
taklīf (responsibility for actions) 430
tales *(qiṣaṣ)* of prophets 850. *See also qiṣāṣ;* stories
talisman(s) 247, 580
rolls 235
Talmud 492–493, 596, 685
references to Christians 159
Tamberlaine (character) against 'Mahomet,' 595
Tamil (language) 562
Tamīmīs 288
tamnun (give or show favour) 570–571
tamthīl 795, 802–803, 804
tanāsub (interpretive technique) 678
tanzīl, inzāl 184, 421, 437, 708, 709–710
vs. taʾwīl 723
taqdīm or *muqaddam wa-muʾakhkhar* 642
taqdīr (reconstruction) 615
taqwā (piety; awareness; fear of God) 465, 467, 857
targhīb ('awakening desire to obey') 340–341
Targum 48, 305
tarhīb (awakening fear of disobedience) 340–341
taʾrīkh 658
ṭarīq/ṭarīqa (way to God; spiritual path) 714, 749
tarjama, tarjamat (Qur'anic) 554–555
tartīb al-daʿwa (ranking of the entire universe in its proper sequence) 732
taṣawwuf (mysticism; Sufism) 780, 785
tashbīh 795, 802–803
Tashkent (manuscript) 168–169, 225
tasjīʿ (rhymed prose) 797, 799
taṣrīf (diversifying meaning) 657
Tatar(s) 263
and Islam 261
mūrzās 260
*tathbīt dalāʾil al-nubuwwa (*authenticating the signs of Muḥammad's prophethood) 375
tathqīl 641
tawahhum [re. Ibn ʿArabī], 798
tawfīq 800
tawḥīd (God's unity; oneness) 380, 472, 578, 782–783, 857
doctrine/worldview of 378, 430–431, 433
Ashʿarī 383
emergence of (in pre-Islamic Arabia) 431–432
taʿwīdh (small metal boxes containing Qur'anic verses in Arabic) 588
Shīʿī 585
taʾwīl (esoteric, allegorical interpretation [of Qur'an]) 699, 709–710, 714, 721–722, 726, 738–739, 755, 760, 776, 849, 853, 858
of Fatimids 730–731
and imams 713, 732
Ismāʿīlī 18, 721–722, 723, 724–728, 729, 731, 732
of al-Māturīdī 775
of al-Sijistānī 724–725, 728
of al-Ṭabarī 660
and *tafsīr* 722, 760, 774, 820, 850
tawqīf 800
tawqīʿ/riqāʿ, 226
tawrāt 146
tawwāb 336
taxation 303
taʾyīd (divine support/inspiration) 723
Taymanitic 115
technology
of fonts 270
of paper 677
print 16, 558
television
presence 40–41
programmes/shows 693, 716
Temple Mount (Jerusalem) 153, 478

temple(s) 90, 92, 131, 241
in Arabia 88–89
Atargatis, at Manbij 87
Bayt al-Lāt in Ṭā'if 89
hayklā 130
Ma'ram Bilqīs (of god Almaqah) 84
Mary (metaphorically) as 497
al-Qalīs in Ṣanʿā', 89
temporal
boundaries of Qur'an 16
sequence of Qur'anic proclamations 356
spread/origin (of Qur'an) 358–359
temporary respite *(barā'a)* 643
termination (of life, existence) *(fanā')* 473
terms/terminology 349, 350, 364, 419, 616, 641–642, 685, 828, 834
from Jewish exegetical tradition 610
for Jews, Christians, unbelievers 573
linguistic [re. Izutsu], 421
philosophical 809
and Sībawayhi 641
Sufi 761
and suras 354, 356
technical 616, 836
theological, late antique 133
terra nullius 491–492
terrorist (slogan) 582
tesserae 250
testaments 612
test(s) 747
ibtalā, and Abraham 132
tevâfuklu (style) 233, 234 (fig. 14.4)
text/textual 228, 239, 251, 382, 460, 611, 616, 625, 635, 639. *See also* codex/codices; quotations/citations; recension(s)
Akkadian 322, 365
analysis 505, 798
of suras 352, 367
archetypal, in heaven 302
arrangement/composition *(naẓm al-Qur'ān)* 316, 375
biblical 494, 686
canonical 58, 168, 268
category 613–615
classical grammatical 200
as coherent and unified 613–614
context 567–568, 736
as cultural phenomenon 701
hybrid 557
literary 6, 297, 850
early Islamic 203–204
liturgical (of Syriac Christianity) 128
Patristic 496
pre-Islamic Christian 280
profane/secular *vs.* sacred 365, 615
of Qur'an 31, 106, 266, 270, 277, 459, 492, 504, 548, 853 (*See also* transmission; ʿUthmānic)
coherence of 315
developed during lifetime of Muḥammad 31–32
by Flügel 209, 266
history of 189, 197–198, 303, 545
as literary 700
as multivocal 715
non-ʿUthmānic 201, 207
organization of 167, 614
original, unpointed and unvowelled 199
unified 261, 268
as without context 98
relations 366, 372, 684
secular 365
skeletal, standardized 182, 186–187, 188 (*See also rasm*)
specialists 225
types 642
Ugaritic 322, 365
textuality 367, 381–382
atomistic vision of Qur'anic 347
textus receptus (Qur'an as fixed text) 203
Thamūd 99, 410
people of 490
Qur'anic portrayal of 132
theft, amputation for 452, 458
thematization (of Qur'anic text) 858
theme(s) 296, 304, 320–321, 338, 372, 405
analysis of 363–364
-based reading 856
in/of Qur'an 65–66, 70, 294, 365, 436, 453, 580, 585, 771, 819
eschatological 474
theological 65, 453
in/of suras 13, 352, 367–368, 371, 405
narrative 468

of poetry/poetic 401–402, 404–405, 406
and verse length 350
theologians 379
Ashʿarī 378, 482, 752
neo-Muʿtazilī Muslim 694
Protestant 256
in Turkey (Ankara School) 41–42
theological 58–59, 579
approach 304, 374, 380
vs. critical approach 34
concerns/issues 53
iʿjāz 376, 382, 383 (*See also iʿjāz*)
discipline of 769
discourse/argument/debate 245, 376, 384, 637, 696, 712
ideas 453, 767
perspective/angle 64, 382
position 59, 771
quality *(contenu sapiential)* 771
speculative reflection/thought *(kalām)* 375, 382, 384 (*See also kalām*)
treatises 204
works (*ʿaqīda* literature) 694
theology 36, 54, 60, 245, 378, 434, 596, 669, 673, 735, 744, 824, 857. *See also kalām*
academic 28
Ashʿārī-Sunnī 776
Christian 82, 156, 379, 384
of Paul 153
Trinitarian 90, 154
and crypto-theology 54, 55
dialectical *(kalām)* 467
disputative 843
doctrines of 384, 544
dogmatic 439, 623
and exegesis 774
and *fiqh* 737
and Ḥanbalīs 655
of *iʿjāz* 380 (*See also iʿjāz*)
Islamic 378, 379, 694–696
schools of thought of 544
Khārijī, pl. Khawārij 460
liberation (Qur'an as work of) 43
of the literary 379, 380–381
Muʿtazilī 460, 673, 712, 769, 773
normative 426
and philosophy 379, 677, 783, 785
pluralist 60
and predestination and free will 430
of Qur'an/Qur'anic 467, 468, 494
rational 712
of religious pluralism 54
scholastic 829
scriptural 18, 693
Shīʿī 710, 762
Trinitarian 90, 154
theophany 493
theoros 420
thinkable 852
thirtieth *(juzʾ)* 233
throne 595, 812
of God 436, 480, 709, 738, 739, 772, 790
ʿarsh 248, 435, 738–739
kursī 248, 738
of Mercy 483
thuluth/naskh 226
ṭibāq (antonymy; contrast) 330
Timurids 265, 713
titles (for chapters of Qur'an) 303
tolerance 42
religious 256, 260
tomb(s)/tombstones 115, 252
of elite 89
inscriptions on 240
-sanctuaries 578
topical (treatises) 696
toponyms, Ḥijāzī 100
Torah 56, 157, 224, 393, 420
abrogated 459
and Jesus 152
Jewish 757
tradition of interpretation 637
quotes the Torah 731
Qur'anic rewriting of 456
rabbinical concept of oral and written 424
reference in Qur'an *(tawrāt)* 146
rules from 452
second Torah (Deuteronomy) 420
torment, lasting *(ʿadhāb muqīm)* 481
tort(s) 449, 451, 454
law, rules of Qur'anic 455
torture (in Fire) 483
Tower of Babel (narrative) 129

trade 232, 287
  dishonesty in 490
  fairs 86, 88
  koine 285, 289, 290
  lingua franca 284
  of Muslim merchants 260
  of Russia, with Central Asia 263
traders 102, 284
traditional *(tafsīr)* (one of seven classifications, re. Goldziher) 609
traditionalism 199, 776
  Sunnī 769, 829
traditionalists 824, 858
  strategy/agenda 769, 823
traditionists 766
  critique 654, 659
tradition(s) 19, 43, 620, 628, 767, 852. *See also* reports
  Andalusi 676
  -based *tafsīr (bi'l-maʾthūr)* 674, 752, 822–823, 828
  biblical 57, 494, 622
  cultural
    of Late Antiquity in the Ḥijāz 495
    local western Arabian 105
  exegetical 71, 133, 493, 498, 671
    ascetic-mystical (Sufi) 19
    attributed to Ibn ʿAbbās 653
    Jewish, terminology from 610
    Persian 671
    Shīʿī 676
  gharīb 661
  going back to non-Muslims 824 (*See also* *isrāʾīliyyāt*)
  Hermetic 422
  interpretive
    vs. philological approach 825
    Sufi 679
  Judaeo-Christian 10, 128, 132
  Judaic 493
  legal 41, 51, 452, 456, 458
  literary
    early Islamic 204
    larger Near Eastern 365
    medieval Arabic 388
    Western 495–496, 602–603
  maghāzī-sīra 628
  monotheistic 140, 144
  oral 133, 142, 185, 621, 629
  pagan 84
  Peripatetic 791
  philological 307
  prophetic 204, 475, 628, 661, 767, 768, 832 (*See also* hadith)
  rabbinical 688
  vs. reason dichotomy [re. exegesis], 820–821
  religious 92, 128
    of Babylon 81
    Near Eastern 102
  re. popularizers 41
  scholarly 258, 698
  vs. scientific approach 45
  Shīʿī 660, 749
    Twelver 712, 773
  Sufi 19, 660
  Sunnī 670
  supercommentary 829
  Syriac 497
  textual 176, 183, 282, 562, 669, 697
  turāth 851
trait
  negative 534
  sajīya 465
transcendence 381
  of God 431
transcribing (Qur'an), horizontal format of 224
transcription(s) 232, 839
  in Greek 114
  of Qur'an 11, 171, 217–218, 222, 224, 350 n.2
    muḥaqqāq/rayḥān 226
  of the Six Pens 229
transcultural
  approach 652
  theory of language 654
transitional (hinge) 364
transitions 321
translations (of Qur'an) 1–3, 8, 64, 65, 74, 77, 255, 541–543, 549, 552–553, 557, 558–559, 597
  into African and Asian languages 553–554
  Dutch 542–543
  English 4, 545, 547
    of Irving 600
    of Muhammad Ali 559
    by Sale 543

first 542, 552
French 545, 546, 559
of Savary 544
as a genre 554, 558
German 542, 544, 545, 547, 622
of Neuwirth 548
Hebrew 2 n.4
historicist-philological 545
interlinear 228, 263, 555–557, 562
in Islamicate languages 554–555, 562
Italian 542
Latin 2–3, 6, 258, 541
Malay 557, 559
modern/contemporary 270, 546–547, 556, 558–559, 560–561
by Muslims 559
Persian/Persianate 553, 557, 562, 753
interlinear 228, 263
publication/printing of 562
with Arabic (in Europe) 256
ban on 258
Serbo-Croatian 559
with suras in chronological order 545
taboo surrounding 555
tri-lingual (Arabic-Persian-Turkish) 556
Turkish 228, 555–556, 557, 559, 562
Urdu 559, 562
vernacular 553–554
European languages 542
into Western languages 15, 541, 545
translation(s) 543, 547–548, 555
of the Bible, early Arabic 686
vs. commentaries 557, 559
'freestanding,' 559
movement (of early Abbasid caliphs) 406
of primary Arabic sources 296
vs. retranslations 542–544
as a separate genre 557–558
and *tafsīr* 4 n.8, 576
of *tafsīr* works 679
'thick,' 548
translators 547–549, 600
and conversion to Islam 546
missionary 554
Muslim 545, 554
transliteration (of Zirker) [i.e., *Deutsche Morgenländische Gesellschaft*], 350
transmission 142–143, 191, 198, 210, 459, 614, 617, 627
cross-cultural 601
etiquette 638
form of *(riwāya,* pl. *riwāyāt)* 190
of hadith/traditions
chains/modes of 44, 608, 610, 833, 838
multiple *(tawātur)* 210
history of 678
line/chain back to Ibn ʿAbbās 636, 767
oral 289, 304, 620, 670
of Qur'an 5, 7, 8, 11, 32, 65, 140, 174, 177, 184, 194, 200, 207, 210, 269, 304–305, 307
handwritten 167, 169, 176
oral 176, 304–305, 424, 503, 639, 670
written 177, 184
of the Seven (readings) 190–191
and teaching of *qirāʾāt* 208
through translation 549
verbatim 421
transpositions 173
travel 29
travellers 449, 470
treatises
on obscure and difficult passages *(kutub al-gharāʾib wa'l-mushkilāt)* 833
or epistle *(risāla)* 394
on Qur'anic homonyms and synonyms *(kutub al-wujūh wa'l-naẓāʾir)* 833
syntactic *(kutub al-maʿānī)* 833
theological 204
treaty(ies) 88
Arab-Christian (scripts and texts of) 228
of al-Ḥudaybiya 52
with non-believers 643
violation of 523
tree(s) 725
godly *vs.* corrupt 727
of hell 727
Zaqqūm 481
tribe(s) 375
Arabian (ʿĀd and Thamūd) 99
al-asbāṭ 145
Jewish (Banū Thaʿlaba, Banū Qurayẓa, Banū Qaynuqāʿ) 84
Quraysh 100
tribulation *(al-balāʾ)* 517–518

tribute *(jizya)* 451
triglossial (context) 284–285
Trinity 90
  defence of 596
  Qur'anic attacks on 433
tropes 395, 601
Trumpet 477–478
  blasts of 483
    nāqūr; ṣūr 476
trust (in God) *(thiqa)* 749
truth(s)/Truth 30, 53, 446, 530, 614, 754
  absolute 28, 786
  arbiter of 811
  behind the 'Islamic event,' 624
  book as 245
  of certainty *(ʿilm ḥaqq al-yaqīn)* 849
  ḥaqq 849
  hidden *(ḥaqāʾiq)* 18
  religious 28
  visions of 797
ṭūr (mountain) 640
Turcophone (translations) 562
turjumān (figure of) 383
Turkic (translations) 556
Turkish 553, 559, 702
  Islam, nationally oriented 561
  language *(al-lugha al-turkiyya)* 841
  Old Anatolian 556
Turkization politics 268–269
Twelver Shīʿī 504. *See also* Shīʿa/Shīʿī
typeface (Arabic) 261, 269–270
typesetting, new Arabic 260
typography 268
  Arabic computer 269
typology(ies)
  Arabo-centric 698
  of exegesis *(tafsīr)* 701, 818–819

U

al-ʿudūl ʿan al-aṣl (departure from the original norm) 342
Ugaritic 496
  term *(ṣmd)* 308
ʿulamāʾ (Islam's religious hierarchy) 562, 580, 698, 722, 755
  Egyptian 560
  interpretations 43, 561
  on readings 191
  reformist 558, 562
ʿulūm (sciences)
  al-badīʿ; al-balāgha; al-bayān; al-maʿānī 795
  al-Qurʾān (of the Qur'an) 381, 836, 844
    field of 832, 833
    work/treatise 834–835
umam khāliya (communities destroyed by divine retribution) 402
Umayyad(s) 153, 222, 224, 728
  buildings 174, 224
  dynasty 504
  wars of expansion 519
umma (community) 561, 627, 725
  vs. aʾimma (imams) 711
  ideal of 508
  of the Prophet 741
  sinners as part of 742
unambiguous (*muḥkam* [verses]) *vs.* those in need of interpretation *(mutashābih)* 72, 820
unbelief. *See* disbelief
unbelievers 34, 489, 514, 573, 740–742, 800, 804. *See also* disbelievers
  on Day of Judgement 482
  fighting/killing of 518, 612
  God sets a seal over 71
  kāfirūn 451
  mushrikūn, grave sinners as 741–742
understanding, *vs.* glorification 802
unequivocal ambiguous, *vs.* unequivocal verses 754
ungrateful, as tendency of humans 436
unicity, divine 708
Unicode Consortium 270
unification (of Qur'anic text) 268
uniformity 185
  of printing 233
  of thickness [re. script], 229
unilinear (literary evolution) 349
union
  ecstatic, between God and chosen servant 751
  experiential (with Creator) 758
Unitarian movement 256
unity 615, 798

and coherence, of longer suras 364
of God, man, and universe 759
of Muslim world 268
of Qur'an 614
chapters 303
structure in 799
religious (lack of among Christians) 84
symbols of 370
thematic 12, 367
/uniqueness (of God) 782
universality (of the text) 856
universal(s) 789
ʿāmm 534
linguistic 661
order 725
servant *(al-ʿabd al-kullī), vs.* partial servant *(al-ʿabd al-juzʾī)* 758
Soul 482
universe/Universe 732
as construed out of two worlds 781
empirical 758
hierarchy of 439
as macrocosm, *vs.* human counterpart as microcosm 761
physical, and signs *(āyāt)* of scripture 758
principle of 783
Qur'anic view of (as cosmically dualist) 434
university(ies) 27, 29–30
and Arabic studies in West 333
al-Azhar University 560
Durham University 343
Euro-American 31
Leeds University 343
School of Oriental and African Studies (SOAS) 329
University of Aix-en-Provence 331
Western 343
unlawfulness, markers of 454
Unseen *(al-ghayb)* 407
unthinkable 852
untranslatability (of Qur'an) 384
unveiling
exegetical *(taʾvīl kashfī)* 753
kashf 740, 758
people of (supersensory) (*ahl al-kashf*) 761
urban centres 287, 803
Urdu 553, 556, 702
language 562
tracts/works 562
re. Mawdūdī 702
urtext 57
Syro-Aramaic 309
uṣūl al-dīn (roots of the faith) 430
categories in 657
uṣūl al-fiqh (bases of the law) 458, 654
works 839
usury 146, 149
prohibitions against 470
ʿUthmānic. *See also* codex/codices; recension(s)
collection/recension 199, 203, 207, 221, 625, 710–711
Shīʿa reject 711, 716
Qur'an 153–154, 168–169, 171, 264, 265
rasm 173, 178, 207
variations from 175–177
script, development of 652
textus receptus 627
vulgate 177–178
utilitarianism (labeled *maṣlaḥa)* 460
utopia (retrospective) 851
utopian (re. Sayyid Quṭb's exegesis) 508
utterances, nonsensical (*khuzaʿbilāt* [of Musaylima]) 390
Uyghur 555
al-ʿUzzā (deity; idol) 86, 124, 434

V

vain *(bāṭil)* 786
valid *(muḥkama)* 522
variae lectiones 199, 768, 832, 840
corpus/materials of 200–202, 204
formation of 206
standardization of seven sets of 209
study of 202, 203–204
variant (Qur'anic readings) 11, 206, 266, 503, 545, 615, 638, 659, 712, 735, 737. *See also* *qirāʾāt;* readings
canonical 196, 205
earliest Shīʿī views of 70
genesis/source of 198–199, 641
attributed to Companions 199
as scribal mistakes 176

variant (Qur'anic readings) (*contd.*)
non-canonical 178, 196, 199, 201
pre-ʿUthmānic 208, 303
qirā'āt 261, 268, 286, 645, 834
as *shādhdh* (irregular; non-standard; non-canonical) 183, 197
synthesizing of 202, 210
types of 711
textual 173, 614
vocalic and consonantal 198
variations 183, 185–186, 196
veracious ones *(ṣiddīqūn)* 758
verbal (echoes and correspondences) 13, 368
vernacular 555
Arabic 155
commentaries 16
Persianate Islam 561
Qur'an, changed to formal and literary language 279
reading culture 556
tafsīr 557
translations/renderings 77, 553–554
use of 119, 715
vernacularization (in African languages) 558
verse-by-verse
basis, of *tafsīr* 832
as exegetical method 659
scriptural commentaries 838
ta'wīl 728
verse(s) 32, 205, 240–241, 245, 322, 346, 492, 533, 638, 852. *See also* abrogation
abrogated *(mansūkh)* 516, 820, 840
challenge *(taḥaddī)* 375, 377–378
commentary on 546
correlations with/relationship to suras 315, 317–318, 319
counting 207, 221
division of/into 171–172, 178, 207
Kufan system of 350
endings/-ending markers 187, 346
into groups of five and ten 188
with *ūn* 799
of *(Sūrat al-) Fātiḥa* 317, 587
foundational *(muḥkam)* 738–739
as greatest antidote *(al-tiryāq al-akbar)* 754
groups 362, 797
and Jewish and Christian exegetical traditions 97
on jihad/fighting 513, 522–523
length 349–350, 351, 357
short 566
light 405, 747, 756, 781–782, 787, 842
āyat al-nūr 247–248
epistemic and ontological implications of 755
exegesis of 790
markers/marking 188, 222, 225
ten-verse 247
mean verse length (MVL) 350–351
Meccan or Medinan 643, 835, 836, 840
Medinan 835, 836–837, 840
muḥkam and *mutashābih* 725, 726, 842
mutashābihāt 753
with the name Ismāʿīl 248, 249 (fig. 15.3)
narrational *(āyāt al-akhbār)* 625
numbering 187, 189, 266, 737, 835
poetic 403, 408, 410, 599
in emulation of the Qur'an 406
preferred by Shīʿī 246
on punishment 42
re. inscriptions 175, 240, 246–248
revealed [i.e., when and where], 635, 836–837
sequence of 198, 728
with socio-political message 510
Sufi 761
of sword 520–521
themes of 405
of throne *(āyat al-kursī)* 241
types of 754, 837
used by the Prophet in sermons 634
versification (of Qur'anic phrases) 392
video-bloggers 580
vignettes 621
villagers *(ahl al-qurā)* 645
violence 71
physical 535, 856
virginity (of Mary) 47, 131
virgins (*ḥūr ʿīn* [of paradise]) 283
virtue(s) 30
ethical 406
khuluq pl. *akhlāq* 469

of *ṣabr* 513
visible (world) and invisible 755
visionary
and ecstatic elements/experiences 751, 757
experiences of Muḥammad 748
vision(s) 420–421, 423, 586, 741, 756, 796
ecstatic 757
of God/divinity 739–740, 852
monistic (unitive) 759
of Muḥammad (subsequent to ascension *(miʿrāj)*) 423
theocentric (of Islam) 403
of the Truth 797
visual
complexity 244
language 231
recognition 244
space 796
vocabulary 123, 309, 321, 393, 614, 641. *See also* foreign; word(s)
Arabic 118, 119
Aramaic 119–120
of Qur'an/Qur'anic 294–295, 297–300, 305–306, 309, 310, 366, 454, 467, 834, 840
chronological approach to 306
from earlier religions 33, 154
etymological approach to 301
everyday/commercial 103
foreign (of non-Arabic origin) 12, 297–299, 301, 307, 309, 841
lexical study of 125
vocalization(s) 155, 189, 196, 711, 735, 737
dots for 224–225, 229
of Qur'an 155, 543
of seven readers 194
of short vowels 209
vocatives 354
yā ayyuhā 320
voice 585
vowels 209, 286, 641. *See also* grammar
annotation of 198
dots to indicate 174, 188, 222
long 183, 187, 198
short 172, 174, 183, 198, 206, 209, 222, 286
signs 503

W

Wadd (tribe) 86
waḥdat al-wujūd 714
Wahhabi (movement) 694–695
wahm 645
waḥy, waḥī (inspiration; revelation) 14, 421–422, 800, 842
waiting period 450
walad (son; offspring) 570
walāya (authority of the imams) 707, 708, 710, 713, 716, 730
walls/barriers
of Alexander 136–137
inscriptions on 242
al-wāqiʿa (the occurring [hour of terror]) 474
wardatan (rose; red) 796
warning/threatening 339, 575
prophetic, of doom 404
of punishment story 494
wars/warfare 136, 371, 408, 411–412, 449, 451–452, 515
aggressive, against non-Muslims 518
with Byzantium 521
Christian–Muslim 255, 593
expansionist 514, 519
against God and Prophet 452
jihad, as not holy 523 (*See also* jihad)
re. United States, in Afghanistan and Iraq 581
Russia, against Ottomans 258, 260, 261
spoils of/booty 449, 613, 751
world 545
waṣāyā (rank of plenipotentiary)
of ʿAlī 728
of the imams, as heirs of the Prophet 707
waṣīy (deputy; successor of the Prophet; legatee; plenipotentiary) 723, 727
ʿAlī as 731
waṣl 795
water 134–135, 582
as gift from God 243
as symbol of life 480
watermarks 232, 235
wayfarer (mystical/Sufi) 407, 750
wealth 586, 614
websites 702

West 597
hegemony of 507
writing of, and Islamic scripture 601
Western 31
Canon, and Qur'an's addition to 592–593
scholarship/studies 66, 559, 682, 687
understanding of Islam 541
widows 369, 490
wilāya 530
will 790
of God 790
waṣiyya 458
wine 103, 369, 408 n.5
of grapes *(khamr)* 452
in paradise 480
winter solstice 92
wisdom 129, 727, 808
Avicennian 777
of God 726, 810
pursuit of *(ḥikma)* 469
received *(naql)* 749
Wissenschaft des Islams 45
Wissenschaft des Judentums 45
witness *(shāhid)* 453, 762
wives 531. *See also* women
and husbands, as garments 535–536
of Muḥammad 340, 856
womankind 528
women 339, 527, 532, 588, 856
and attacks on Islam 48
as being in hell 489
as calligraphers 235
and children 516–517
exegetes, in Persian 716
Jewish and Christian [re. marriage to], 449
liberation of 856
and men, equality of 43, 527, 529–530
moral agency of 527, 529
Muslim 588, 856
obedient to God and husbands 530–531
in paradise 395
Qur'anic verses on 15, 76, 489, 534–535
rights of 510
role/position of 76, 534, 695, 854
wordplay 128, 245, 248, 581
word(s) 294, 304, 350 n.2, 639, 643, 743, 751. *See also* foreign
ambiguous 661
difficult *(gharīb)* 393, 636
exceptional 660–661
of God 709, 851–852
kalām Allāh 384, 419 (*See also kalām*)
monumentalizing 231
Sufi attitude to 760
as temporal and eternal 379, 383
vs. word of Prophet 425
history of usage of 294, 296, 307, 310
in inscriptions 244, 248
link-, 364
meaning of, Qur'anic 33, 295, 299–300, 301, 306, 309, 565, 614, 638, 640, 655, 735
ashbāh 639
furqān 393
īmān 614
subverting 307
at time of revelation 570
wajh, wujūh 566, 572, 574–575, 639
median, or hook 321, 325
non-Arabic 660–661, 840
number of, for specific suras 835
order 377, 795
of consonantal skeleton *(rasm)* 456
'correcting,' 642
rearrangement of 711
power of 586, 588
'Qur'an,' 541
rare *(nawādir)* 645
and repetition 321
spaces between 221, 226
substitution 711
world 337, 781, 790
Graeco-Roman 60
higher 782
ideal 484
material 588, 790
next 337, 452
of religion *(ʿālam al-waḍʿ)* 732
renunciation of 755
of the spirits *(ʿālam al-arwāḥ)* 756
supra-lunar 781, 782
temporary, evils of 391
visible 755
worldview
extra-Qur'anic 825, 826

mystical 757
of Qur'an 306, 363, 437, 466
and modern science 76
as theocentric 766
Sunnī 776
worship
acts of 196
and angels 438
astral 808
of goddesses 578
house of *(bayt ṣlūtā)* 130
of idols/stones 87, 148, 529, 578
in the Levant 86
moderation in 748
of one God 469
places of 515
pre-Islamic, astral character of 86
regulation of (in pre-Islamic times) 89
spiritual centre of 370
at temple in Jerusalem 132
worshippers 103
writing 115, 184, 420, 492, 578, 636, 677, 803
apocryphal and pseudepigraphal 496
complexity of 244
historical 622
on legal doctrine 458
Maghribi style 229
role of 116, 123
scholarly *(ʿilm)* 635
supports [re. recording of Qur'an], 168, 217
written
aide-mémoire or hypomnēmata 620
material 167, 610
Qur'an 44, 167, 177–178, 217
by Jews 144
by Muḥammad 142
by others 184
on palm leaves, rocks, and 'hearts of men,' 32
scroll *(sefer)* 420
wrongdoers 521
/oppressors *(al-ẓālimīn)* 516
wrongdoing 450, 517
wujūh (aspects of meaning) 566, 568, 575, 639, 657
and conciseness of style 576–577
re. Muḥammad 570, 571
in translation 574
wa'l-naẓāʾir 840–841
works/material 651, 842

Y

Yaghūth (deity; idol) 86
al-yahūdiyya 144
yaqīn (certain; certitude) 404, 412
Yaʿūq (deity; idol) 86
yawm (day of) 476
al-dīn 446
Yezidis 90
yom ha-ddīn/yom dīnā (Heb., Aramaic: 'Day of Judgement') 446

Z

zabūr (Hebrew Bible) 146
ẓāhir (outward; exterior; exoteric) 710, 717, 724, 730, 828
Ismāʿīlīs on 722
Ẓāhirī (legal methodology) 658
zakāh (poor-tax) 122, 520, 731
zakā [root], 661
al-ẓālimūn (evildoers) 336, 516
al-zamān (Time) 394
Zaqqūm, tree of 481
Zaydī(s) 721
works 676
zeitgeist (of interwar period) 559
Zoroastrianism 85, 434
and physical or spiritual ascents to heaven 132
Zoroastrians 479, 516, 521
zuhd, books on 684
ẓulm 516